T0376735

THE ROUTLEDGE HANDBOOK OF ARCHAEOTHANATOLOGY

The Routledge Handbook of Archaeothanatology spans the gap between archaeology and biological anthropology, the field and laboratory, and between francophone and anglophone funerary archaeological approaches to the remains of the dead and the understanding of societies, past and present.

Interest in archaeothanatology has grown considerably in recent years in English-language scholarship. This timely publication moves away from anecdotal case studies to offer syntheses of archaeothanatological approaches with an eye to higher-level inferences about funerary behaviour and its meaning in the past. Written by francophone scholars who have contributed to the development of the field and anglophone scholars inspired by the approach, this volume offers detailed insight into the background and development of archaeothanatology, its theory, methods, applications, and its most recent advances, with a lexicon of related vocabulary.

This volume is a key source for archaeo-anthropologists and bioarchaeologists. It will benefit researchers, lecturers, practitioners and students in biological anthropology, archaeology, taphonomy and forensic science. Given the interdisciplinary nature of these disciplines, and the emphasis placed on analysis *in situ*, this book will also be of interest to specialists in entomology, (micro)biology and soil science.

Christopher J. Knüsel is Professor of Biological Anthropology, University of Bordeaux, France. His research centres on the use of biological anthropological data within its archaeological context to address social relations in the past, including specifically violence and warfare and morphological changes linked to specialisation. With Martin J. Smith, he co-edited and contributed to *The Routledge Handbook of the Bioarchaeology of Human Conflict* (2014).

Eline M.J. Schotsmans is a research fellow at the University of Bordeaux, France, and the University of Wollongong, Australia. Her research lies at the interface between archaeoanthropology and forensic sciences with a focus on mortuary sequences, preservation practices, taphonomy and method development through experimentation. Her positions in France, Belgium, the United Kingdom and Australia helped to broaden her perspective of francophone and anglophone funerary archaeological approaches.

THE ROUTLEDGE HANDBOOK OF ARCHAEOTHANATOLOGY

Bioarchaeology of Mortuary Behaviour

Edited by

Christopher J. Knüsel and Eline M.J. Schotsmans

Routledge
Taylor & Francis Group

LONDON AND NEW YORK

First published 2022
by Routledge
2 Park Square, Milton Park, Abingdon, Oxon OX14 4RN

and by Routledge
605 Third Avenue, New York, NY 10158

Routledge is an imprint of the Taylor & Francis Group, an informa business

British Library Cataloguing-in-Publication Data
A catalogue record for this book is available from the British Library

Library of Congress Cataloging-in-Publication Data
Names: Knüsel, Christopher, editor. | Schotsmans, Eline M., 1981- editor.
Title: The Routledge handbook of archaeothanatology /
edited by Christopher J. Knüsel, and Eline M.J. Schotsmans.
Description: Abingdon, Oxon ; New York, NY : Routledge, 2021. |
Includes bibliographical references and index.
Identifiers: LCCN 2021019619 (print) | LCCN 2021019620 (ebook) |
ISBN 9781138492424 (hardback) | ISBN 9781351030625 (ebook)
Subjects: LCSH: Archaeothanatology. | Funeral rites and ceremonies. |
Human remains (Archaeology) | Human skeleton--Analysis.
Classification: LCC CC77.B8 R68 2021 (print) |
LCC CC77.B8 (ebook) | DDC 930.1/0285--dc23
LC record available at https://lccn.loc.gov/2021019619
LC ebook record available at https://lccn.loc.gov/2021019620

ISBN: 978-1-138-49242-4 (hbk)
ISBN: 978-1-032-11436-1 (pbk)
ISBN: 978-1-351-03062-5 (ebk)

DOI: 10.4324/9781351030625

Typeset in Bembo
by KnowledgeWorks Global Ltd.

CONTENTS

Contents

FIGURES

TABLES

LIST OF CONTRIBUTORS

Edeltraud Aspöck is a researcher in the Austrian Centre for Digital Humanities and Cultural Heritage at the Austrian Academy of Sciences, where she carried out her project 'Microtaphonomy and interpretation of reopened graves' funded by the Austrian Science Fund. She obtained her Ph.D. at the University of Reading, UK, in 2009. Her research interests are mortuary archaeology, digital archaeology and the Early Medieval period.

Frédérique Blaizot is Professor of Roman Archaeology at the at the Unité Mixte de Recherche (UMR) 8164, Histoire, Archéologie et Littérature des Mondes Anciens (HALMA), at the University of Lille in France. She worked for 30 years as archaeo-anthropologist at the French National Institute for Preventive Archaeological Research (Inrap), Lyon. Her research focusses on the reconstruction of the original arrangement, organisation and architecture of burials and the socio-cultural interpretation of funerary practices. She has published *Pratiques et Espaces Funéraires dans le Centre et le Sud-Est de la Gaule au Haut-Empire* in *Gallia* (2009), and *Les Espaces Funéraires de l'Habitat Groupé des Ruelles, à Serris (Seine-et-Marne, Île-de-France) du VIIᵉ au XIᵉ siècles* (Ausonius Éditions, 2017).

Philippe Blanchard is a French archaeologist working in Tours, France, for the French National Institute for Preventive Archaeological Research (Inrap). He is a specialist in funerary archaeology of the medieval, modern and contemporary periods. He has been studying European Jewish cemeteries for more than 20 years and has carried out excavations of many medieval funerary sites of the Jewish community of Châteauroux, Indre region of the Middle Loire Valley of central France.

David Brönnimann is a post-doctoral researcher in the Integrative Prehistory and Archaeological Science (IPAS) research group in the Department of Environmental Science, University of Basel, Switzerland. His research focus is on the microscopic analysis of archaeological sediments and bones. He is particularly interested in the combination of different methods, such as micromorphology and histotaphonomy.

Fanny Bocquentin is an archaeo-anthropologist at the French National Centre for Scientific Research (CNRS). Her work is devoted to the reconstruction of evolutionary trends in socio-biological identities and burial practices of the Near Eastern Epipaleolithic and Neolithic periods. She served as Head Anthropologist for several major sites, including Eynan-Mallaha, Raqefet, Wadi-Hammeh 27, and Motza, and co-directed the excavation of the Pre-Pottery Neolithic site of Beisamoun.

Christine Bonnet is a ceramologist at the French National Institute for Preventive Archaeological Research (Inrap) Rhône-Alpes, Unité Mixte de Recherche (UMR) 5138, Archéologie et Archéométrie (ArAr), Lyon, France. Her research focusses on ceramic production in the Rhône-Alpes region during the Roman period. She developed a specific scientific approach focussed on the funerary treatment of vases, published as part of a volume of *Gallia*, edited by Frédérique Blaizot in 2009. Her specific methods makes it possible to identify ritual practices during funerary ceremonies.

Thomas J. Booth is a Senior Research Scientist at the Francis Crick Institute in London, UK. His 2014 Ph.D. thesis investigated variation of bacterial bio-erosion in archaeological human remains and its relationship with early post-mortem treatment. He has since continued to research the taphonomic significance of bacterial bio-erosion and general diagenesis of bone.

Bruno Boulestin is an anthropologist at the University of Bordeaux, France. His speciality is the study of bone modifications and corpse treatments. His research, based on the use of archaeological, bioarchaeological and socio-anthropological data, focusses on the study of practices surrounding death, violence and warfare, and social organisation in prehistoric and protohistoric societies.

Isabelle Cartron is Professor of Medieval Archaeology, Bordeaux Montaigne University, France. Her research centres on the social history of the Early Middle Ages, particularly on funerary practices and objects. She directs archaeological excavations in Aquitaine, southwest France, and acts as co-head of the research programme, *Mémoire Familiale et Patrimoine: Sociétés Antiques et Médiévales*, with Marcelo Cândido da Silva, University of Sao Paulo, Brazil. She is co-director with Dominique Castex of the Thanat'Os collection, published by Ausonius, Bordeaux, since 2012.

Dominique Castex is a French National Centre for Scientific Research (CNRS) First Class Senior Researcher at the University of Bordeaux, France. Her research focusses on the study of historical populations from a palaeoethnological perspective based on archaeo-anthropological observations and the analysis of biological characteristics of human remains and associated funerary practices, especially in the context of epidemic crises in Antiquity and the Early Middle Ages.

Paul N. Cheetham is Senior Lecturer in Archaeological Science at Bournemouth University, UK. Specialising in forensic archaeology and archaeological geophysical survey, as co-director of the Durotriges Project his current research focusses on the Iron Age to Roman transition in Britain. He has geophysically surveyed cemeteries and burial monuments in the UK, Germany, Greece, Cyprus, and, most recently, Vix in France.

Gaëlle Clavandier is Associate Professor of Sociology and Anthropology, University of Lyon, and the Jean Monnet University, Saint-Etienne, France. Her research focusses on contemporary funerary transitions in Western countries, especially involving the transformation of the body, topics including ash, the fetus, and human remains. She has led several projects focussed on an informed sense of on-going transformation within the funerary realm that help to appreciate potential discontinuities in past funerary practices. She published *Sociologie de la Mort* (2009).

Patrice Courtaud is a French National Centre for Scientific Research (CNRS) Research Engineer at the Unité Mixte de Recherche (UMR) 5199, De la Préhistoire à l'Actuel: Culture, Environnement, et Anthropologie (PACEA), University of Bordeaux, France. His research focusses on the funerary practices and health status of past people recovered from individual burials and cemetery excavations. He has particular interests in slave cemeteries in the French West Indies.

Boyd B. Dent initially trained as an engineering geologist in the early 1970s (B.Sc.). He re-focussed his experience and developed a research capability in hydrogeology (environmental aspects) from 1994 (M.Sc., Ph.D.). This led to the development of a specialised interest and practice in the geoscience of cemeteries, an expertise that has involved him in international cemetery and forensic science investigations and commentary.

Germaine Depierre is 'classe exceptionnelle' research technician for the French Ministry of Culture, seconded to the French National Centre for Scientific Research (CNRS) and the Unité Mixte de Recherche (UMR) 6298, Archéologie, Terre, Histoire et Sociétés (ARTEHIS), in Dijon, France. She teaches human osteology and funerary practices at the University of Bourgogne Franche-Comté, France. She has developed fundamental research on cremations addressing both current practices and those of the past which inspired her recent (2014) book, entitled *Crémation et Archéologie. Nouvelles Alternatives Méthodologiques en Ostéologie Humaine* (Dijon: Éditions Universitaires de Dijon, Collections Art, Archéologie et Patrimoine).

Henri Duday is Emeritus Director of Research at the French National Centre for Scientific Research (CNRS) at the University of Bordeaux, France. Through his teaching and the excavation of several Neolithic collective burials, he founded the Bordeaux School of Archaeothanatology, a term he created with Bruno Boulestin. He has published *The Archaeology of the Dead: Lectures in Archaeothanatology* (Oxbow, 2009). He is currently working on the study of cremation graves.

Patrice Georges-Zimmermann is an archaeologist at French National Institute for Preventive Archaeological Research (Inrap) and member of the Unité Mixte de Recherche (UMR) 5608, Travaux et Recherches Archéologiques sur les Cultures, les Espaces et les Sociétés (TRACES) of Toulouse Jean Jaurès University. He has excavated funerary sites in France and Africa. He is also an expert in forensic archaeology for the Justice Department and works for the French National Gendarmerie (National and Military Police force).

Karina Gerdau-Radonić is an independent biological anthropologist affiliated with the University of Strasbourg, Unité Mixte de Recherche (UMR) 7044, Archimède, and Visiting Fellow (and former Senior Lecturer) at Bournemouth University, UK. She specialises in archaeothanatology and has worked in Peru, Britain and France. Currently, she is working on a project on the Linienbandkeramik (LBK) populations from eastern France.

Yves Gleize is Associate Researcher at the French National Institute of Preventive Archaeological Research (Inrap) and the University of Bordeaux in France. His research focusses on funerary practices in marginal areas and inter-cultural contacts in the Mediterranean region and in Eastern Africa. He is currently participating in a research project at the world heritage site of Lalibela (Ethiopia) and leads the archaeological excavation of the crusader cemetery at 'Atlit (Israel).

Sarah Gluschitz is a fellow and Medical Illustrator at the Department of Anatomical Sciences, St. George's University, Grenada, West Indies. She creates interactive directed learning activities for medical students and teaches visual workshops to students and faculty alike. Since 2016, she has sought innovative ways of visualising the process of human decomposition in actualistic forensic taphonomic experiments.

Emma C. Green completed her doctoral research at the University of Sheffield in 2018. Her research focusses on applying an archaeothanatological approach to the identification of wooden containers in late Anglo-Saxon graves across England.

Mark Guillon is a physical anthropologist, archaeologist and researcher for the French National Institute for Preventive Archaeological Research (Inrap) and the University of Bordeaux, France. His main research links development-led archaeology with investigation of large medieval and modern cemeteries within and outside settlements. His recent work deals with a holistic systemic approach synthesising funerary practices with biological correlates of identity.

Mogens B. Henriksen (Ph.D., Prehistoric Archaeology) is curator at the Odense City Museums, Odense, Denmark. His research focusses on graves and mortuary practices from the Late Bronze Age to the Viking Period. A special area of interest is cremation graves and cremation practices, complemented with actualistic cremation experiments.

Jean-Bernard Huchet is an entomologist at the French National Centre for Scientific Research (CNRS), working at both the National Museum of Natural History in Paris, and the University of Bordeaux, France. In 1996, he initiated a new discipline, dubbed 'funerary archaeoentomology', which aims to interpret past funerary practices from the study of insect remains recovered from archaeological contexts.

Sacha Kacki is a researcher at the French National Centre for Scientific Research (CNRS), attached to Unité Mixte de Recherche (UMR) 5199, De la Préhistoire à l'Actuel: Culture, Environnement, et Anthropologie (PACEA), University of Bordeaux in France. His research centres on the health and disease of past populations, with particular focus on plague epidemics. He has contributed to the excavation and anthropological study of numerous European mass graves, which provide new insights into the palaeoepidemiology of plague and the burial treatment of its victims.

M. Victor Klinkenberg is a research fellow at the University of Cyprus and co-directs the excavations at the Chalcolithic settlement at Palloures, Cyprus, with Bleda S. Düring, Leiden University. His research focusses on reconstructing activities and archaeological formation processes using digital and geoarchaeological methods, especially micromorphology. After completing his Ph.D., published as *Reading Rubbish* in the *Publications de l'Institut Historique-Archéologique Néerlandais de Stamboul* (PIHANS) series of the Uitgaven van het Nederlands Instituut voor het Nabije Oosten te Leiden, he was appointed a research and teaching positions at Leiden University in the Netherlands.

Christopher J. Knüsel is Professor of Biological Anthropology, University of Bordeaux, France. His research centres on the use of biological anthropological data within its archaeological context to provide insights into past social organisation, social inequality, violence and warfare, élites and occupational specialists, and division of labour based on age and sex. He co-edited *The Routledge Handbook of the Bioarchaeology of Human Conflict* (2014) with Martin J. Smith.

Mélie Le Roy is Lecturer in Prehistory, Queen's University Belfast, UK. Her research centres on the social consideration of children in archaeological contexts to provide insights into past social organisation. She co-edited with Eileen Murphy *Children, Death and Burial* (2017) for Oxbow Books and is a guest co-editor with Caroline Polet of *Children at Work* (2019) for the Routledge journal *Childhood in the Past*.

Richard Madgwick is a Senior Lecturer in Archaeological Science at Cardiff University, UK. His research focusses on osteoarchaeology, and he uses macroscopic, microscopic and molecular methods to pursue particular interests in depositional practice, mobility and foodways. He has published widely on these themes, including research on the iconic sites of Stonehenge, Navan Fort, Llanmaes and Danebury in the UK.

Bruno Maureille is First Class Director of Research, French National Centre for Scientific Research (CNRS), Unité Mixte de Recherche (UMR) 5199, De la Préhistoire à l'Actuel: Culture, Environnement, et Anthropologie (PACEA), University of Bordeaux, France, where he is Head of the Department of Archaeological Sciences. His research focusses on Neandertal biological variability and on archaic *Homo* mortuary/funerary activities. He has written the initial descriptions of several European Neandertal fossils, including the recently re-discovered Le Moustier 2 Neandertal perinate burial (MIS 3). He directed the excavations at the Southwest French Mousterian sites of Les Pradelles (MIS 4) and Regourdou (MIS 5).

Patrice Méniel is a Director of Research at the French National Centre for Scientific Research (CNRS), Unité Mixte de Recherche (UMR) 6298, ARchéologie, TErre, HIstoire et Sociétés (ARTEHIS), University of Burgundy, Dijon, France, where he directs the archaeozoology laboratory. Based on the analysis of faunal remains from archaeological contexts, his research focusses on human-animal relations during the Protohistory and Roman period, with a particular interest in funerary and sacrificial practices in France and in neighbouring countries. He has written several syntheses and textbooks on archaeozoological research.

Hayley L. Mickleburgh is a forensic archaeologist with research interests in forensic taphonomy, the archaeology of death and burial, methods of detection and excavation of forensic (mass) graves, and the use of 3D visualisation methods as research and education tools. Since 2015 she has conducted a programme of human decomposition experiments to improve methods and interpretations in forensic archaeology and archaeothanatology.

Mike Parker Pearson is Professor of British Later Prehistory at University College London's Institute of Archaeology and a Fellow of the British Academy, UK. He is the author of *The Archaeology of Death and Burial* as well as many other books and articles on funerary archaeology. His current main project, running since 2003, is focussed on Stonehenge and its stones, burials and surrounding landscape.

Cordula Portmann obtained her B.A. and M.Sc. at University of Basel, Switzerland. Her research focusses on microstructural and histotaphonomical analyses of human remains, as well as multi-stage mortuary practices of the late La Tène settlement of Basel-Gasfabrik, Switzerland.

Liv Nilsson Stutz is a Senior Lecturer at Linnaeus University in Sweden. She specialises in the archaeology of death and burial, practice theory, and ritual studies and has published widely on burial archaeology and the intersections between archaeological methods and theory. Together with Sarah Tarlow, she edited the *Oxford Handbook of the Archaeology of Death and Burial*.

Astrid A. Noterman has been affiliated with Stockholm University, Sweden, as part of a project funded by the Swedish Research Council, entitled 'Interacting with the Dead. Belief and Conflict in Early Medieval Europe' and led by Alison Klevnäs. Her on-going research centres on early medieval grave reopening and in 2020 she co-edited *Rencontre autour des Réouvertures de Tombes* with Mathilde Cervel.

Thomas Romon is an archaeologist at the French National Institute for Preventive Archaeological Research (Inrap) in Guadeloupe, the French West Indies, and is attached to the Unité Mixte de Recherche (UMR) 5199, De la Préhistoire à l'Actuel: Culture, Environnement, et Anthropologie (PACEA), University of Bordeaux in France, where he has participated since the 1990s in research on funerary practices of the Colonial period in the Lesser Antilles.

Stéphane Rottier is a bio-anthropologist and archaeologist and, since 2007, has served as Maitre de Conférences at the Unité Mixte de Recherche (UMR) 5199, De la Préhistoire à l'Actuel: Culture, Environnement, et Anthropologie (PACEA) at the University of Bordeaux in France. His research focusses on funerary practices in Late European Prehistory (Neolithic, Bronze and Iron Ages) and on the methods and theory of archaeothanatology.

Miles Russell is Director of Archaeological Fieldwork at Bournemouth University, UK, and co-director of the Durotriges Project, investigating the Iron Age to Roman transition in Southern Britain. His most recent publications include *UnRoman Britain* (2011) with Stuart Laycock and *Hillforts and the Durotriges* (2017) with Dave Stewart.

Géraldine Sachau-Carcel is a research fellow at the Unité Mixte de Recherche (UMR) 5199, De la Préhistoire à l'Actuel: Culture, Environnement, et Anthropologie (PACEA), University of Bordeaux, France. Her research focusses on funerary practices in complex burials from antiquity through the use of innovative methodology based on 3D imaging. She is archaeothanatological field manager at the site of Kyme, ancient Cumae, in Italy and collaborator at the Centre Jean Bérard, French National Research Centre (CNRS) in Naples, Italy.

Aurore Schmitt is archaeo-anthropologist at the French National Centre for Scientific Research (CNRS), Paul Valéry University in Montpellier, France. Her research concerns mortuary practices in the Neolithic and the Bronze Age in the Mediterranean area, specifically exploring collective burials, non-funerary practices and cremation. She has conducted and has participated in many field projects in France and Crete and co-edited *Gathered in Death* (2018) with Sylviane Déderix (Belgian National Centre for Scientific Research FRS/FNRS, University of Louvain La Neuve UCL and Belgian and French School of Athens, Greece).

Eline M.J. Schotsmans is a research fellow at the University of Bordeaux in France and the University of Wollongong in Australia. Her research lies at the interface between archaeo-anthropology and forensic sciences with a focus on mortuary sequences, preservation practices, taphonomy and method development through experiments. She has held positions in Belgium, the United Kingdom, France and Australia, which helped to broaden her archaeothanatological perspective in both a theoretical and empirical way. Eline previously edited *Taphonomy of Human Remains* (Wiley, 2017) with Shari Forbes and Nicholas Márquez-Grant.

Martin Smith is Principal Academic in Forensic and Biological Anthropology, Bournemouth University, UK. His research integrates biological anthropology with the wider archaeological record to address questions regarding past lifeways, mortuary practices, violence and conflict, and social organisation. He has authored/edited over 50 publications, including the *Routledge Handbook of the Bioarchaeology of Human Conflict* (2014) with Christopher J. Knüsel.

Janne Sperrevik is a former Master's student from Bournemouth University planning to pursue a Ph.D. within archaeology and anthropology. Her research interests focus on burial practices in prehistory, and cognitive development and cultural innovations of early humans. She has recently been undertaking archaeological work with the University of Bergen at Mesolithic, Neolithic and Bronze Age sites in Western Norway.

Vera Tiesler, Ph.D., is Research Professor at the Universidad Autónoma de Yucatán, Mérida, Mexico. Coming from an interdisciplinary academic background surrounding archaeology, her academic interest lies in illuminating life and death among the ancient Maya and of past society in general. Her work focusses on the Maya burial record and includes active fieldwork at Palenque, Calakmul, and Chichén Itzá. By exploring skeletal information jointly with other material and discursive media, her research addresses ancient lifestyles and death practices, physical appearance and different forms of permanent body enhancement, violence, sacrifice, and ancestor veneration.

Anne-marie Tillier is Emeritus Research Director at the French National Centre for Scientific Research (CNRS), University of Bordeaux, France. Her research centres on the origins of *Homo sapiens* in Southwestern Asia, and she has excavated at the sites of Qafzeh, Kebara and Hayonim (Israel) providing new insights on palaeopathology, palaeoauxology (growth studies) and early funerary behaviour. She has edited/co-edited four thematic volumes on methodological aspects of the archaeology of death.

Maiken Ueland received her Ph.D. from the University of Technology Sydney (UTS) in 2016. She is an Australian Research Council (ARC) Discovery Early Career Research Fellow at UTS and the Deputy Director of the Australian Facility for Taphonomic Experimental Research (AFTER), the only facility in the Southern Hemisphere that permits the donation of human cadavers for the study of forensic taphonomy. She specialises in forensic taphonomy by using analytical, biochemical and spectroscopic techniques to conduct human post-mortem investigations.

Daniel J. Wescott is Professor of Anthropology at Texas State University, San Marco, Texas, USA, and the Director of the Forensic Anthropology Center at Texas State University. His research in skeletal biology focusses on bone biomechanics and skeletal variation applicable to forensic anthropology, bioarchaeology, and palaeoanthropology. His taphonomic research provides insight into methods for estimating the post-mortem interval, interpreting crime scenes, and detecting clandestine remains.

Eleanor Williams is Senior Lecturer in Archaeology at Canterbury Christ Church University, UK. One of her main research interests centres on medieval monastic funerary rites, with a focus on the relationship between historical texts and the osteoarchaeological record. She explores this relationship in a Cluniac context in her co-edited volume *Archaeologies of Rules and Regulation: Between Text and Practice* (2018).

Aurélie Zemour is a research associate at the Unité Mixte de Recherche (UMR) 5607 Ausonius, Bordeaux Montaigne University, in France, where she held a post-doctoral position as Junior Chair in the Archaeology of Death until 2019. Apart from methodological developments, her research focusses on the Mesolithic and early Neolithic of Southwestern Europe. She co-edited *Qu'est-ce Qu'une Sépulture? Humanités et Systèmes Funéraires de la Préhistoire à Nos Jours* (2016) with Michel Lauwers.

FOREWORD I

I whole-heartedly congratulate Christopher Knüsel and Eline Schotsmans for putting together this timely new handbook of body-anchored mortuary studies. Ensouled by the contributors' shared passion surrounding French-born 'archaeothanatology', this lavishly illustrated volume documents a myriad of old and new conceptual and procedural tools. Jointly, these come to illuminate the many faces of solid mortuary research on the dead, past and present. Harking back on many decades of evolving archaeothanatological experience, this book certainly sets a new global standard both in burial excavations and depositional reconstructions of human skeletal remains and their contexts.

Especially the sustained cross-fertilisation between actualistic studies and archaeology demonstrates the heuristic power of archaeothanatology in reconstructing depositional sequences, not solely for reconstructing ancient burial practices but also at the service of forensic investigation.

Archaeothanatology, which examines the precise interaction of biological and cultural components of death during and after detailed field recording, has been practiced and taught in France for over four decades now. Probably due to language barriers, it has been only quite recently, however, that the francophone way of conducting skeletal research has been made available to the broader international community. The year 2009 saw the first comprehensive compendium entitled *The Archaeology of the Dead. Lectures in Archaeothanatology* (Oxford: Oxbow). This volume contains lecture transcriptions on different burial contexts under the guiding aegis of *anthropologie de terrain*, now 'archaeothanatology'. Translated into English with the help of Anna Maria Cipriani and John Pearce, this work was compiled by its principal exponent, Henri Duday, who founded, shaped and led the School of Archaeothanatology from the time he joined the University of Bordeaux in France during the seventies of the last century.

Now a CNRS[1] emeritus researcher, Henri Duday holds a doctorate in human medicine and additional degrees in archaeology, anthropology and biological statistics. His interdisciplinary background and his keen scientific curiosity had an influence on his early field experience with Neolithic funerary assemblages in southern France. Duday concocted new schemes of detailed skeletal recording and recognised distinctive disarticulation patterns, laying the groundwork for

---

1 *Centre National de la Recherche Scientifique* or French National Centre for Scientific Research

today's archaeothanatological reconstructions. Embedded in French *paléo-ethnologie*, this finely grained, structured way of voyaging into ancient deathways soon came to add new layers to the agenda once set forth by André Leroi-Gourhan and Francophile post-war *préhistoire* in general.

By thinking about the roles of death and of the dead to the living, this line of research clearly goes beyond any methodological approach. Instead, archaeothanatology is best likened to a mortuary 'philosophy', which is sustained inductively by layered methodological approaches. Reflecting on the care of the body and its decomposition before, during and after interment. This approach enables elucidation of *gestes funéraires,* or 'funerary gestures', to which the dead body was once subjected. More generic thoughts on death and the afterlife offer viable meanings and motives to mortuary practices, including for those archaeological cultures that lack a written record.

A charismatic researcher and professor, Duday has offered five decades worth of intense course-work and workshops in osteology and archaeothanatology, not only in France but in different parts of continental Europe (Spain, Italy and Switzerland). Outside continental Europe, his dissemin-ation efforts would lead him also to the United States and to Mexico. In my country, Mexico, it has been thanks to Duday's former student, Grégory Pereira[2] that archaeothanatology has been assimilated and applied with growing success. Since the nineties of the last century, the continuous archaeothanatological dialogues have contributed in Mexico to a number of breakthroughs in Mesoamerican mortuary archaeology. In this area, archaeothanatology's most important contri-bution lies surely in the reconstruction of distinctive mortuary sequences and a dazzling com-plexity of past posthumous body treatments, including excarnation, cultural bone fragmentation, underwater depositions and mummy bundling. To fill gaps in the knowledge of the past, regional scholarship has adapted archaeothanatological recording to the needs and requirements of badly deteriorated skeletal assemblages and has incorporated archaeothanatological dialogues into the reconstruction of unique ritual practices, staged in a body-anchored indigenous universe.

My own encounter with French archaeothanatology came in 1995, while beginning my career in Maya bioarchaeology. Grégory Pereira, my historian colleague Elsa Malvido and I joined forces to organise the first international colloquium on Mesoamerican mortuary treatments in Mexico City. This event was to include an 'innovative' workshop on the French School of Archaeothanatology, offered by Henri Duday. A resounding success, it brought to the table a number of experts on ancient Mexican burial rites and Aztec sacrifice, along with an enthusi-astic crowd of students which would grow in the following years into an academic tradition of Mesoamerican archaeothanatologists.

Later that same year, Henri Duday invited me to join an excavation of a Neolithic cave site at Corconne in Southern France. Freshly arrived from Mexico, I was keen to join of what I thought would be a 'hands-on' excavation of human burials in a narrow, gridded cave. Once in place, however, I was assigned the task to excavate and hand-record strata of tiny stones and muddy pebbles in a sterile earthen layer, close to the cave entrance. As Henri explained to the group of excavators, we needed to understand how particles of different consistency, spher-icity and size would percolate and settle, and how these once could have interacted with the formation processes of the human assemblages still imbedded in the soil. As no bones surfaced that required recording, Henri recorded pebble fragments in the same way. Indeed, most of the others among the team seemed to pursue this slow recording task against the backdrop of refined conversations of French history and prehistory, discussions on bones and almost any-thing else cultural.

---

2 A well-known CNRS researcher at the University of Paris 1 Panthéon-Sorbonne, specialising in Mesoamerican Archaeology

I recall these anecdotes because they make clear two of archaeothanatology's core attributes: firstly, 'French School' of mortuary research, as we still call it in Mexico, was (and probably still is) quite francophone. Despite all its manifest academic blessings, it would not quickly conquer international archaeology and raise the global levels of mortuary excavations. Secondly, 'orthodox' archaeothanatology operates in and foremostly from the field with all its time-consuming steps, starting with itemised anatomical and contextual descriptions, numbering, lifting and packing. Although time-consuming, these tasks are never conceived among archaeothanatologists as mechanical registration chores, but as an heuristic tool to facilitate a comprehensive recognition of unique taphonomic processes, a better reconstruction of grave preparations and corpse placement, and a deeper understanding of ancient mortuary pathways in general.

From all of the above, I predict four major impacts of the timely *Routledge Handbook of Archaeothanatology*, brilliantly conceived and compiled by Christopher Knüsel and Eline Schotsmans. Apart from bringing actualistic (experimental) forensic research to the forefront of body-anchored mortuary research, this volume promotes global capacity-building and dissemination at a time when mortuary archaeology stands at a crossroads. The editors' invaluable efforts towards terminological standardisation will come to facilitate global dialogue and international scholarly communication. The fruitful combination of cutting-edge digital photogrammetry and carefully accrued field data are bound not only to operationalise mortuary recording but also to enhance their quality. It is the archaeothanatologist's choice to decide what can be done (and what is to be prioritised) to redress the interplay between quality recording and time constraints. Each of the contributions of this handbook appears to have engaged in such a challenging decision–making process during which the progression of decomposition sequences and cultural interactions is first laid out, then patterned archaeothanatologically and, finally, understood.

Different from the original *anthropologie de terrain* – *sensu* seventies and eighties of the last century, today's archaeothanatological inquiries can be informed directly and prominently by the results from the forensic sciences. This new amalgam is possible and accepted outside the francophone academic world and, as becomes patent among the chapters and the lexicon by Knüsel and colleagues, infuses not only past *gestes funéraires* with novel knowledge – almost by natural extension – makes them conversant with forensic crime-scenes, truly an invaluable legacy to the generations of both archaeo-anthropologists and forensic scientists to come.

Vera Tiesler
Research Professor in Anthropology
Coordinator, Laboratory of Bioarchaeology
Facultad de Ciencias Antropológicas
Universidad Autónoma de Yucatán
Mérida, Mexico

FOREWORD II

I first heard of 'archaeothanatology' about 15 years ago from Christopher Knüsel, one of the editors of this volume. He was in a state of high excitement because he had been translating a paper by Henri Duday which would introduce Anglophone researchers to an entirely novel approach to skeletal remains. This was a major advance in a field that the New Archaeology called middle-range theory or, as we now tend to call it, taphonomy.

Many years earlier, as a Ph.D. student researching the archaeology of death in 1979–1984, I'd encountered 'thanatology' as a rather different subject. For English-speaking sociologists it was already a well-developed sub-discipline exploring the social context of death, dying and bereavement, a research field which had developed since the 1950s through classic works such as *The Meaning of Death* (Feifel, 1959), *The Psychology of Death* (Kastenbaum and Aisenberg, 1972) and *On Death and Dying* (Kübler-Ross, 1969). Yet the two subjects – thanatology and archaeothanatology – had relatively little in common despite their shared ancient Greek etymology.

In the Classical world, Thanatos was variously a deity, *daimon* (spirit) and personification of death, so one might expect that archaeothanatology – literally 'the study of ancient death' – would serve as an encompassing term for the archaeology of death, already a substantial field of investigation within archaeology by the end of the 20th century.

Yet, that is not quite how things turned out. As Frédérique Blaizot explains in this collected volume, archaeothanatology started out as *anthropologie de terrain* (field anthropology), a primarily taphonomic study focussed on the remains of the dead themselves. Blaizot aptly sums it up as a 'reverse journey' through the taphonomic events that occur after death. It focusses on the dead themselves – its major difference, according to Bruno Boulestin, from the wider-ranging archaeology of death as developed by English-speaking New Archaeologists. It is worth adding that the Anglophone archaeology of death also included post-processualist as well as processualist approaches.

Archaeothanatology's focus on the dead themselves is followed by other contributors. For Aurore Schmitt, its remit of study is the funerary, post-funerary and non-funerary treatment of human remains. Fanny Bocquentin uses the term in her paper to indicate an excavation protocol for the contextual study of human remains, while Karina Gerdau-Radonić and colleagues sum up its defining features as attention to detail, focus on patterns of articulation, and spatial relationships of all items and individuals in a grave.

Yet, we should be careful not to define archaeothanatology as merely a methodology or set of techniques. Fanny Bocquentin notes that it has many meanings, and reminds us that Boulestin and Duday originally intended archaeothanatology to encompass the archaeology of death in all its dimensions. This comes through in many of the contributions to this volume. For Liv Nilsson Stutz, archaeothanatology is trans-disciplinary, combining archaeology, archaeo-anthropology/bioarchaeology, taphonomy, physiology and anatomy in an integrated framework. In his chapter on burials with accompanying dead, Bruno Boulestin demonstrates that archaeothanatology is just the starting point for reconstructing past societies and their social stratification.

The editors of this volume, Christopher Knüsel and Eline Schotsmans, have brought together researchers not just with different areas of expertise but also from different research traditions. For too long, language has divided French and English-speaking researchers over approaches to the archaeology of death. This very substantial volume brings them together for the first time in a major endeavour which reveals the range and potential of archaeothanatological approaches. Beginning with a section on methodological guidelines, this book takes the reader through a wide range of period-specific applications from earliest humans to the early modern period and also examines aspects beyond the corpse itself. The section on associated remains covers everything from grave goods and animal offerings to insect infestations, while the last section considers associated sciences, experiments and legal considerations.

I think this will be an important book, not just because it breaks down linguistic and national divides in archaeological research agendas but because it shows just how vibrant and exciting the archaeology of death has become, firmly integrating science and humanities in our quest to understand the human condition through the treatment of our mortality over the long term of history and human evolution.

Mike Parker Pearson
Professor of British Later Prehistory
Institute of Archaeology
University College London
United Kingdom

ACKNOWLEDGEMENTS

Our heartfelt gratitude goes in the first place to Dominique Castex who contributed much to the genesis of this book. We realise that without her help, the book would not have looked the same and would not have had the same contributors onboard.

We are much obliged to Henri Duday. Although archaeothanatology has different meanings to different people, not always as its founders intended, Henri and colleagues triggered many archaeo-anthropologists to observe and analyse the skeleton in its depositional environment from a different perspective.

Many thanks to all authors of this book. It was not always an easy ride because of language and cultural differences. We thank Matthew Gibbons, Kangan Gupta, Imran Mirza and the Routledge publishers team for their encouragement and patience with this process.

We offer our gratitude to Vera Tiesler and Mike Parker Pearson who provided the forewords to this volume. We are also very grateful to Lucy Martin for creating the cover image for this book and to our colleagues for their feedback during the making of it.

We are much obliged to our colleagues for their support, helpful comments and interesting discussions, in particular Fanny Bocquentin, Bruno Boulestin, Rhea Brettell, Dominique Castex, Karina Gerdau-Radonić, Bonnie Glencross, Sacha Kacki, Bruno Maureille, John Robb, Richard 'Bert' Roberts, Stéphane Rottier, Aurore Schmitt, Martin Smith, Anne-marie Tillier and Howard Williams.

We would like to thank our partners, Carol Palmer and Kris Vleeschouwer, for their patience, understanding and support throughout the process of the preparation of this book and over the course of our careers, as well as through a pandemic.

Finally, we are grateful to our institutions for supporting this project: the Université de Bordeaux (France) and the University of Wollongong (Australia). The work commenced when the editors were supported by the French State under the 'Investments for the future' IdEx Programme (Initiatives d'Excellence), Bordeaux, ANR-10-IDEX-03-02, and further completed with funding from the European Union's Horizon 2020 Research and Innovation Programme (Marie Skłodowska-Curie Actions Global Fellowship, grant agreement 794891).

INTRODUCTION

Archaeothanatology, funerary archaeology and bioarchaeology: perspectives on the long view of death and the dead

Christopher J. Knüsel

PACEA, De la Préhistoire à l'Actuel: Culture, Environnement et Anthropologie,
UMR 5199, CNRS-Université de Bordeaux, Pessac, France

Eline M.J. Schotsmans

PACEA, De la Préhistoire à l'Actuel: Culture, Environnement et Anthropologie,
UMR 5199, CNRS-Université de Bordeaux, Pessac, France

Centre for Archaeological Science (CAS), University of Wollongong, Wollongong,
Australia

The funerary archaeological record arguably represents the most planned and most heavily and consistently ritualised archaeological context, yet it is a general observation that chroniclers, legists and biographers detail little about the physical manifestations of funerary ceremonies in their writings. The grave is also one of the most common and repeatedly formed, but highly variable archaeological features, encountered. These features are constructed and maintained specifically to receive the corporeal remains of a deceased person as part of funerary practices. The dead are the central focus, and the treatment accorded to them reflects the intentions and tolerances of an unknown number of participants of equally unknown social identities. As part of orthopraxy transmitted orally in untold numbers of sermons, speeches, tributes, paeans, eulogies, invocations and codified actions, the chroniclers of the past considered perhaps that everyone knew and understood what transpired and thus did not require detailed description or explanation. Or, perhaps, sensitive information could not be accessed, as indeed is the case in some ethnographic cases (cf. Woodburn, 1982). The successful dissemination and homogenising effect of these spoken, sung and performative events can be perceived in the similarities among burials from the same time and place, forming the funerary record that is uncovered upon excavation. Even on a rare occasion when obsequies are described, they are often made in the context of stories of heroic proportions and following unusual events that do not resemble those performed more commonly. Unfortunately, the most basic aspects, such as items of personal adornment, preparatory and grave-side ritual, body preparation and those contributing to it, positioning and disposition of the body, specific location of burial within a burial ground, and burial markers and maintenance of burial spaces are rarely recorded in any detail in protohistoric and historic societies (although cf. Williams, Chapter 17, this volume, for a rare, though ideal exception of a medieval Cluniac *Customary*). Written sources are both limited and have limitations as to what information they convey.

DOI: 10.4324/9781351030625-1

The meaning and motivations behind the practices encountered in the funerary record are even less accessible, often completely lacking in written sources. And, if detailed in ethnographic sources, the physical patterns relating to human actions are not recorded and thus difficult to transpose to archaeological patterning. Of course, prehistory lacks texts altogether and burying the dead is rarely depicted. Even if depicted, the meaning behind the scenes portrayed is obscure. Like burials themselves, they require detailed comparative contextual and scientific analytical study to discern their significance for the living as well as for the dead. As with all archaeological contexts, the biological and material remains, their patterning and organisation, are affected by taphonomic decomposition and post-burial diagenesis, factors that alter the 'original picture' of the grave, its location and its contents.

Despite these deficiencies, the funerary record – in a baffling variety of contexts and depositions (organisation and layout) through time and space – provides a supremely important source of social information about the past. These funerary contexts and their remains are among the most abundant archaeological contexts encountered, having been relied upon – disproportionately – for defining archaeological cultures and traditions and for perceiving social change in the past. Although the result of one of the most orchestrated of archaeological contexts, in the absence of careful excavation, observation and recording, funerary contexts are difficult to interpret. Without precise recording and description, which is often the case for earlier excavations, the amount of social information gleaned is greatly reduced, and that which is preserved is less clearly interpretable and susceptible to increased equifinal uncertainty. Whatever the case, the ultimate goal of the study of these contexts remains to attain insight into the social processes that formed the archaeological record in order to reconstruct a particular society. In short, by documenting the meaning and significance of funerary remains, researchers provide an otherwise unwritten sociocultural history.

In order to reach an interpretation, detailed documentation and recording of all archaeological remains (i.e. the '*appareil funéraire*': the human remains, burial content, and the burial arrangement, organisation and architecture) is fundamental. The common division between archaeology and anthropology, both biological and sociocultural, complicates this endeavour, even if these disciplines are found in the same university and sometimes in the same department. Often – still too often – archaeologists excavate the burial and the skeleton is subsequently sent to the laboratory where it is analysed by 'a specialist', a biological anthropologist/osteologist. Ideally, field and laboratory personnel should be one and the same to ensure coordination between the field and the laboratory. Joint-working helps to foster the application of analytical protocols, recording, documentation and analysis. Ultimately, this integrated approach would aid more holistic and well-grounded interpretations (cf. Guillon, Chapter 32, this volume). Archaeothanatology, the core of this book, tries to bridge this gap between the field and the laboratory.

The genesis of this book

In 2013, Matthew Gibbons, commissioning publisher for archaeology for Routledge publishers, requested one of the editors (CJK) to edit the 'Routledge Handbook of Archaeothanatology'. Interest in the field of archaeothanatology had grown over the previous few years in English-language scholarship (see below), as was most evident in the numbers attending conference sessions and the demand for workshops on the subject in which the editors have participated. Several reasons, among them, doubts about the legitimacy of taking on the task and the size and complexity of the project, and in the process of moving from the British to the French university system made CJK initially decline the request. Matthew persisted after CJK moved to the

University of Bordeaux. Routledge was looking for an editor who had enough knowledge and contacts with the French-speaking world of archaeo-anthropology to bring what had been largely French-language research to the attention of English-speaking scholars. In 2016, CJK contacted the other editor, ES, about the possibility of producing such a book. After several more months of consideration and discussion CJK and ES decided to go ahead with the book, motivated mostly by the lack of English-language publications and, as a result, misunderstandings and only partial awareness – or complete unawareness – of the subject. The two editors have some legitimacy to undertake such a task. Both have been working at the University of Bordeaux, De la Préhistoire à l'Actuel: Culture, Environnement, et Anthropologie (PACEA) UMR 5199, considered the 'home' of archaeothanatology, and as part of the Human Remains Team at Çatalhöyük in Turkey, responsible for both the excavation as well as the laboratory analysis of human remains from complex collective burials at this 9 000-year-old Neolithic site. Both of them had also been conducting archaeo-anthropological research at the interface between the francophone and anglophone worlds, and both had attained proficiency in both English and French.

Great help and support came from PACEA colleague Dominique Castex, who brainstormed with the editors about the content and participants who might agree to be included in such a book. This required the contributors to express themselves in English rather than in French, no small undertaking owing to the vocabulary and concepts being developed in the latter. Like Dominique, each of the authors of this book recognised the utility of the archaeothanatological approach and the value of such a book to foster wider dissemination of its use, together with the need for better descriptions and well-developed standards. But the question was: how does one do this for a diverse and far-flung international community? This question is the motivation behind this volume, and its immediate objective is to take stock of what has been done in archaeothanatology, and to disseminate the concepts and methods to a wider community.

Archaeothanatology – what is it?

'Archaeothanatology' is a transliteration of the French '*archéothanatologie*', a discipline that grew out of biological anthropology and fundamentally altered the way many French archaeo-anthropologists approach mortuary contexts. It derives its name from the compound word formed by 'archaeo' ('ancient') and 'thanatology', which is the study of death, its practices, physical and societal effects, as well as the social and cosmological concepts surrounding death. For this reason, it is also referred to as the 'Archaeology of Death' in English (Duday, 2006b; Schmitt, 2017) ('*Archéologie de la Mort*' in French). Its most salient feature is that it places human remains at the centre of archaeological research (cf. Duday and Masset, 1987).

The origins of the archaeothanatological approach can be traced back to a publication by André Leroi-Gourhan, Gérard Bailloud and Michel Brézillon (1962) on the Neolithic collective grave at Mournouards (Mesnils-sur-Ogre, Marne, France) (see below) and were further formalised by Henri Duday (1978, 1987) in the 70s and 80s. As defined by Boulestin and Duday (2005, 2006), the main goal of archaeothanatology is to reconstruct the structure and organisation of past societies from the analysis of the treatment, handling and management of the deceased. Initially known as 'field anthropology' ('*anthropologie de terrain*'), archaeothanatological analysis commences – ideally – in the field with detailed observations and recording of the human remains and their burial arrangement, organisation and architecture. In other words, it does not consider the human remains alone but also associated items and their arrangement (cf. Part 3, this volume) and the entire funerary area in its broadest sense. Boulestin (Chapter 2, this volume) summarises the archaeothanatological approach in three phases: 'The first is field observations, the second is reconstructing the disposition of the remains at the time of their final deposition, and the way the assemblage was constituted, and the third is the interpretations in terms of mortuary behaviours and social information more generally'. Internationally, archaeothanatology is often perceived as a method, a 'different' type of mortuary analysis that integrates biological anthropology and detailed archaeological field observation as a means to bridge the divide between archaeology and anthropology, a sentiment illustrated by a comment from Fanny Bocquentin: 'Personally, I do not use it [the word "archaeothanatology"] very much in French, but in contrast, I find it very useful to use it in English [-language publications] in order to inform people that this specific protocol is quite unique and draws on an expertise of which not everyone is aware' (*'Personnellement je ne l'utilise pas beaucoup non plus en français par contre je le trouve très utile en anglais pour faire comprendre que notre démarche est spécifique et relève d'une vraie expertise que tout le monde n'a pas'*) (Bocquentin, pers. comm., September 2018) (cf. Bocquentin, Chapter 9, this volume). Moreover, as Bruno Boulestin has remarked: 'we [French archaeo-anthropologists] are more rigorous in the development of our interpretative thought processes. I think that, fundamentally, archaeothanatology is, above all else, a particular school of thought that represents a different approach' (*'On est bien plus rigoureux sur le cheminement interprétatif chez nous. Fondamentalement, l'archéothanatologie c'est avant tout une école de pensée particulière, je crois'*) (Boulestin, pers. comm., August 2019). Vera Tiesler (2011: 491) summarised archaeothanatology in a similar way: 'Archaeothanatology is a mindset in scholarship which is anchored in a pro-active approach to conducting and thinking about funerary archaeology'.

The adoption of archaeothanatology outside France

After a period of development and application lasting over 40 years from its introduction, the development of archaeothanatology went unnoticed in English-language publications until the 2000s, when francophone scholars started to cite and describe archaeothanatology in English-language publications (e.g. Murail *et al.,* 2004; Zeytoun *et al.,* 2004; Bocquentin, Kodas and Ortiz, 2016), which also included polyglot anglophone scholars (e.g. Roksandic, 2002; Nilsson Stutz, 2003) and Spanish-speaking scholars (e.g. Tiesler, Suzuki and Pereira 2021) who adopted and applied the method after participation in Duday's courses, adapting it to the circumstances of their research (e.g. Tiesler, Foreword I, this volume).

The first publication in English by Henri Duday appeared as a translation by one of the present editors for the co-edited volume with Rebecca Gowland, entitled *Social Archaeology of Funerary Remains,* in 2006. In 2009, John Pearce and Anna Maria Cipriani undertook a translation of the transcribed Italian version of Henri Duday's lectures, which had also appeared in 2006 as *Lezioni di Archeothanatologia: Archeologia Funeraria e Antropologia di Campo* (*Lectures in Archaeothanatology: Funerary Archaeology and Field Anthropology*) (Duday, 2006a). Like its Italian predecessor, this English translation (Duday, 2009), entitled *The Archaeology of the Dead: Lectures in Archaeothanatology,* is based on courses that Henri Duday has been delivering on analytical approaches to human remains in France and Italy over many years (cf. Tiesler, Foreword I, this volume; Depierre, Chapter 4, this volume, who both make allusion to the sustained influence of these courses that run to the present day). One measure of the success of these efforts is that biological anthropologists are now routinely employed in the excavation of burial sites as part of the development process in France, as detailed by Guillon (Chapter 32, this volume).

In the preface to the Italian volume and in its English translation, Paola Catalano, Soprintendenza Speciale per i Beni Archeologici di Roma, and Stéphane Verger of the École Pratique des Hautes Études note that the motivation for these lectures was to create a common procedure for the excavation, recording and study of Roman Imperial period burial grounds. At the same time, these lectures were intended to renew the dialogue between archaeologists, anthropologists, historians and those responsible for the care of archaeological cultural heritage. That dialogue fostered collaborative research and teaching of human remains analysis that extended from the field to the laboratory. Catalano and Verger nicely encapsulate the intent of this dialogue. As it has developed and continues to develop – for it is an unfinished journey, documented in successive publications – it forms an ever better-constructed and more elaborate bridge between these often separate and disparate pursuits, unifies them and makes them aware of joint interests, problems and solutions. That archaeothanatology is only now making its presence known more globally is a testament to the extent of restrictive divisions in academia and research and how fleeting, difficult and rare intra-disciplinary, inter-disciplinary and trans-disciplinary communication is. Despite more, and at face value anyway, easier communication, it seems that these barriers are as robust and intractable as ever. The editors and authors intend this volume to form a bridge between a group of ideas and a vast body of accumulated research to bring it to a larger and more varied academic audience.

Archaeothanatology and funerary archaeology

The relationship between archaeothanatology and funerary archaeology also requires discussion because these subject domains overlap but remain stubbornly independent, even when they are best employed in a mutually re-enforcing way. Consideration of these shared research interests reveals important insights into the disciplinary place of human remains found in archaeological contexts that clarify this relationship. Dominique Castex observes: 'In fact, archaeothanatology is almost a synonym of funerary archaeology but has a much broader remit because it investigates sociological aspects of death and because it is not exclusively limited to funerary practices, but includes the broader framework of so-called mortuary practices, such as trophy collecting and cannibalism, amongst others' ('*En fait archéothanatologie est bien quasi-synonyme d'archéologie funéraire mais avec une vision beaucoup plus vaste car elle fait aussi appel aux aspects sociologiques de la mort et qu'elle s'inscrit dans le cadre plus général des pratiques dites mortuaires qui ne se limitent donc pas exclusivement au funéraire. Intégration par exemple de l'étude des trophées, des témoignages d'anthropophagie, etc.*') (Castex, pers. comm., September 2018). Zemour (2016: 27) distinguishes funerary archaeology from archaeothanatology, writing: 'It [archaeothanatology] also stretches beyond the interests of funerary archaeology which, by definition, does not deal with mortuary practices and thus everything relating to the handling of corpses outside the funerary sphere, such as sacrifice, autopsy, etc.' ('*Il dépasse aussi celui de l'archéologie funéraire qui, par définition, n'aborde pas les pratiques mortuaires et ainsi tout ce qui touche aux manipulations de cadavre hors de la sphère funéraire, au sacrifice, à l'autopsie, etc.*)'. (cf. Chapter 34, this volume, for the meanings of 'funerary' and 'mortuary'). Both Castex and Zemour emphasise the difference between the individuals receiving funerary treatment from those found in an archaeological context but lacking such evidence. These non-funerary, mortuary treatments include the use made of human bodies for other non-funerary purposes that operate within humans groups, extending to those involving a desire to effect individual behaviour and, ultimately on a group level, social change. The continued separation of these two research traditions hinders the development of integrated studies required to address broader, more over-arching inter-disciplinary research questions. Ultimately, the integration of these studies would place them in a better position to address not only inter-disciplinary but also trans-disciplinary questions, which must return to the basic demographics of the dead in order to be incorporated into population and site comparisons through time and across geographic space. To summarise, archaeothanatology considers both funerary and mortuary practices, in addition to the social meaning of such contexts and the symbolic messages these entail.

Archaeothanatology and bioarchaeology

Other than linguistic differences that form a formidable impediment for many, another reason for the slow adoption of the term 'archaeothanatology' outside of France is that especially Jane Buikstra's (2006) definition of 'bioarchaeology', with its emphasis on social aspects of the funerary record, in addition to the biological information gleaned from skeletal remains with the incorporation of bioarchaeologists from the commencement of projects, occupies much of the disciplinary map of archaeothanatology. This form of bioarchaeology seems more in keeping with the original holistic intent of archaeothanatology as proposed by Henri Duday (Boulestin and Duday, 2005; Duday, pers. comm., February 2018). Many researchers may therefore be unaware of the term and, if aware of it, how it relates to bioarchaeology as defined by Buikstra, thus hindering the adoption of the methods as well. Moreover, Clark Spencer Larsen's (1997, 2006) definition of bioarchaeology, being similar in many respects to Buikstra's and equally influential, has been more strongly associated with a greater emphasis on the biological and cognate natural scientific approaches to the study of human remains, which fits some uses of the term bioarchaeology as employed in France – that is to say, with a reduced emphasis on the funerary context and social aspects of funerary behaviour. Buikstra's version with its use of social theory to frame questions distinguishes it from even the broadest definition of archaeothanatology as it is currently understood in France, although it accords with some current developments in France through an increasing interest in and consideration of gender, for example, from archaeological contexts (Knüsel, pers. obs.).

Despite variable descriptive terms, researchers have employed archaeothanatological concepts in studies of human remains in their archaeological context for a number of years, with francophone scholars occasionally publishing their results in English. Some examples are Murail *et al.* (2004) for distinguishing between primary and secondary infant burials based on the state of skeletal articulation; Zeytoun *et al.* (2004) for reconstructing funerary practices even when preservation of skeletal remains is poor, the method being referred to specifically as 'field physical anthropology' and the specifics of burial practices described under the rubric of 'funerary archaeology'. Other anglophone scholarship includes publications by Willis and Tayles (2009) on identifying voids in burials excavated into clay, Harris and Tayles (2012) on identifying the presence of coffins in a manner similar to that employed by Green (Chapter 23, this volume), as well as Crevecoeur, Schmitt and Schoep (2015) on documenting complex funerary practices in prehistoric Crete. The latter authors specifically comment on 'the absence of detailed information on the nature and taphonomy of human remains in Minoan cemeteries [that] limited the extent to which complexity and variation in Minoan funerary practices could be reconstructed and largely restricted discussion to architectural and artefactual data' (Crevecoeur, Schmitt and Schoep, 2015: 294). This comment chimes with the experiences of many who have worked with older excavation reports of funerary contexts that, even if published, often separate the treatment of human remains from their burial context and produce an insufficient synthesis as a result. These deficiencies provide opportunities for legacy studies performed after remains have been excavated, but they are poorer for the lack of integration possible after the passage of many years and as the original excavators and their memories perish. Although not within the original purview of archaeothanatology, these studies continue to provide many research opportunities as older excavations and their remains are re-visited, or indeed analysed for the first time, sometimes long after having been excavated (cf. Nilsson Stutz, Chapter 10, this volume).

As noted above and in the Lexicon, Chapter 34 of this volume, in contrast to the original definition of Henri Duday, some people view archaeothanatology as a method of recording and excavation of human remains, a different way of analysing a burial context and the human and material remains that it contains. Many other practitioners, however, advance the notion that the subject is an all-encompassing approach – a paradigm – applied to the remains of the deceased and their contexts. The definition of archaeothanatology presented in publications over the years has also varied. Some see archaeothanatology as a type of bioarchaeological approach to funerary remains (cf. Nilsson Stutz, 2016). Sometimes archaeothanatology is equated with funerary taphonomy as a consequence of Knüsel and Robb's (2016) paper – an equation that was not wholly anticipated but which is clearly linked since an archaeothanatological approach relies on distinguishing taphonomic effects from human manipulation of remains. In their review of new directions in bioarchaeology, Knudson and Stojanowski (2008: 407) discuss archaeothanatology as a methodological development. They associate *anthropologie de terrain* with taphonomy and a means by which to reconstruct funerary rites in the absence of material remains of them to study funerary symbolism. In addition to social theory, their review encapsulates the following topics, all part of bioarchaeology: osteological age and sex determination, palaeodemography, bio-distance analysis, biogeochemistry, taphonomy and topics including disability and impairment, gender identity, identities of age and the life course, social identity and body modification, embodiment and ethnic and community identities. For these researchers, bioarchaeology forms a link between the biological and social sciences that bridges evolutionary and social theory. While acknowledging archaeothanatology as a field method applied to excavation, they also see it as a means to establish mortuary identity (Knudson and Stojanowski, 2008: 408), but also note: 'financial and temporal constraints, a greater commitment to population-based research, and a lack of publications in English have precluded widespread adoption of *anthropologie de terrain* in the United States'. This comment reflects language barriers, with much work published solely in French and some work published in English hindered by translation problems that obscure archaeological contextual associations, blur concepts and hinder the transmission of reasoning processes. To date, there has also been a tendency to produce case-studies rather population-level treatments, but this is a necessary step when a new paradigm is introduced in order to showcase its utility (though see below for future directions to address broader research questions). The authors' comment about financial and temporal constraints is an example of how archaeothanatology is not always perceived accurately outside France. When trained 'archaeothanatologists' or 'field anthropologists' take part in an excavation, the excavation is not necessarily slowed down (cf. Guillon, Chapter 32, this volume).

Most importantly, though, Knudson and Stojanowski (2008: 415) envision that the methodological developments of archaeothanatology and those made through the application of biochemical approaches and biodistance analysis, among others, will lead to greater contributions to broader academia, specifically to research questions in the social and biological sciences. This type of trans-disciplinary synthesis should be a shared goal of both bioarchaeology and archaeothanatology. Being that archaeothanatology encompasses all dimensions – with a greater emphasis on the burial context of human remains – the closest cognate in English-language scholarship to accommodate the multiple and varied disciplinary definitions is 'human bioarchaeology', as adopted to distinguish the earlier definition of bioarchaeology in the United Kingdom from its use by Buikstra in 1977 to refer specifically to human remains in their burial context (cf. Knüsel, 2010).

Like archaeothanatology, bioarchaeology is also about 40 years old and developed in parallel with archaeothanatology at about the same time but without mutual recognition. In many places, including France and the United Kingdom, the term 'bioarchaeology' retains its original definition and thus refers to the study of all biota from archaeological contexts. Since the transliterated form of *archéothanatologie*, 'archaeothanatology', refers only to human remains and their contexts at present (although see below), this similarity, too, suggests the closest equivalent is 'human bioarchaeology', a term adopted in the UK where the lexical terrain was already occupied by the original definition of the term 'bioarchaeology', as it is in France. It seems, then, that archaeothanatology and human bioarchaeology or *archéo-anthropologie* (archaeo-anthropology), a term sometimes equated with *archéothanatologie* by some francophone researchers, share the same interests. Whatever the specifics of the case, archaeothanatology can be seen as a close equivalent to human bioarchaeology, and their differences are mutually beneficial and re-enforcing when encountered and synthesised.

Despite terminological conflicts, the motivation behind the use of these terms is the same: to advance a synthesis between the physical analysis of human remains and their funerary context – in a grave, at a site and in a regional framework. This synthesis permits greater insight and acuity when comparisons are made through time, thus diachronically from one period to another, and across geographic space for contemporary sites and their remains, both human and funerary. With regard to the victims of violence, Knüsel and Smith (2014: 15) envisioned a synthesis of bioarchaeology and archaeothanatology to aid investigation and interpretation of complex deposits of human remains, writing: 'The often non-normative nature of the casualties of conflict make their recovery more difficult than for normative burials of the same date and place. The importance of having what have become known as osteoarchaeologists and archaeothanatologists involved from the planning phase of excavation is an important prerequisite to recover individuals and to record the position and patterning of the remains. Archaeothanatological insights, when joined with a bioarchaeological orientation, provide considerable scope to improved recovery, interpretation, and a theoretically informed over-arching context for such studies'.

The long view of death and the dead

As the contributions to this volume and their references show, archaeothanatology has more often been applied to Holocene human remains and their contexts. However, its tenets are equally applicable – and even more crucial – for the study of earlier members of the human lineage, where the very existence of funerary behaviour has been questioned and much debated (cf. Maureille, Chapter 8, this volume; Tillier, Chapter 7, this volume). Here, the act of funerary deposition takes on exceptional interest as an indicator of behavioural modernity in groups whose physical appearance differed from that of more recent humans. In two articles, Gargett (1989, 1999) challenged the notion that some Eurasian Neandertals and Early Anatomically Modern Humans owed their presence in the archaeological record to intentional (i.e. ritualised) inhumation. Even with the subsequent demonstration that the Middle Palaeolithic Neandertals are genetically related to more recent Eurasian populations (Green *et al.*, 2010), the question of the origin of the behaviour remains a powerful inducement to research into the circumstances and meaning of these depositions (Pettitt, 2011). Although a number of interred remains from Palaeolithic contexts have been considered, often retrospectively, their rarity combined with many having been excavated decades ago means that the evidence, though suggestive of intentional interment, remains contentious and debated (cf. Rendu *et al.*, 2014, 2016; Dibble *et al.*, 2015; Pomeroy *et al.*, 2020; Maureille, Chapter 8, this volume; Tillier, Chapter 7, this volume).

Despite other mammals regularly occurring as complete skeletons in single as well as in multiple and sometimes mixed contexts with human remains and artefacts – and often considered to have been deposited due to their symbolic and ritual significance – similar methods have not been applied to non-human faunal remains as an aid to reveal the ritual intent implicit in their deposition. By the same token, zooarchaeologists with their knowledge of multi-species skeletal anatomy do not often have the opportunity to excavate such remains, even when found in funerary contexts with human remains. Thus while some biological anthropologists have become field-based as well as laboratory-based human bioarchaeologists, many archaeozoologists have not realised this parity to the same extent. However, as Méniel (Chapter 25, this volume) forthrightly observes: '… it is beneficial that the archaeozoologist is invited to the excavation and not only confined to laboratory study of bones after excavation'. This is sage advice, echoed for human remains for some years (see above) since the presence of faunal remains reflects human selection in addition to and sometimes beyond their dietary importance. Moreover, for synanthropic species, human presence alone is enough. This means that the presence of these species in human sites and in human burials may owe more to ecological and taphonomic factors as much as to ritual ones. Thus these remains found in burials require the same type of arguments to distinguish funerary from mortuary contexts for these animals (cf. Jenkins, 2012). It seems that there is ample scope to extend archaeothanatological principles throughout bioarchaeology to include non-human faunal remains, including those of insects, as demonstrated by Huchet and Castex (Chapter 26, this volume) and plant remains, a subject that is not addressed in this text, despite efforts to fill this gap.

Thanatology

As noted above, thanatology refers to the study of death and dying and the practices associated with them. This phenomenon has thus become of interest to both ethologists and psychologists interested in the extent of the awareness of death in non-human species. Among such species, there is increasing evidence for behavioural responses to conspecific deaths, even if there is debate about whether or not a thanatology of non-human species is justified (Anderson, 2011), but with increasing acceptance today (Anderson, 2020). The question has evolved from a desire to know if non-human animals are aware of their own mortality to determine 'to what extent they recognize death in others and how they "felt" in response', or at least how animals respond to dead conspecifics (Gonçalves and Biro, 2018: 2), which is a much more tractable question open to comparative observational testing among a variety of invertebrates as well as vertebrates. Clearly, answers to this question have implications for both the palaeontological and archaeological records as a means to explaining the presence and context of remains.

Albeit not universally so, some non-human animals, including chimpanzees (Goodall, 1986; Anderson, Gillies and Lock, 2010), who carry dead infants (Biro et al., 2010), and elephants, who show increased interest in the bones, especially the tusks, of deceased conspecifics (McComb, Baker and Moss, 2006), exhibit what has been termed compassion (Fashing and Nguyen, 2011). Although some species evince certain mortuary behaviours, they do not apparently perform funerary rites for the dead and appear to lack a developed capacity for symbolic representation, which distinguishes their behaviour from these defining human proclivities. In one of the most detailed cases, at the death of the matriarch Flo, Flint, her 'son' (i.e. male offspring), mourns his mother's loss and eventually dies after a three-week period of grief (Goodall, 1986: 66, 103), so there is an emotional response and apparent 'mourning' (acknowledgement of loss), but without funerary treatment and no inhumation of the dead.

The question of the origin and the number of species showing thanatological behaviour remains a question of great interest that applies to earlier hominins as well (Dirks et al., 2016). The scattered and fragmented nature of the majority of hominid species may suggest that early on in these lineages, the dead were left where they died, or to where they had been moved, but without inhuming them, even if post-mortem defleshing was performed (Trinkaus, 1985; White, 1986; Russell, 1987), a funerary practice documented in the European Mesolithic (Toussaint, 2011) and Neolithic of both Europe (Robb et al., 2015) and the Near East (Erdal, 2015).

Archaeothanatological methods and analysis remain promising for the greater clarity they bring to arguments and the potential resolution of such debates. In order to demonstrate early evidence of mortuary activity among earlier members of the genus *Homo* and paraphyletic kin, these arguments are linked as much to taphonomic contextual information relating to depositional processes as to skeletal element representation and appearance. For *Homo naledi* in Rising Star Cave, South Africa, the arguments focus on the evidence necessary to demonstrate whether or not complete bodies were deposited, even in the absence of other evidence of funerary behaviour (Dirks *et al.*, 2016; Val, 2016). In her critique of the mortuary origin of these remains, Val (2016: 146) makes specific reference to archaeothanatological studies of disarticulation and desiccation of bodies that would indicate if the remains were found in their primary (i.e. initial) location and thus had not been transported from elsewhere by natural processes. The burial context of these remains as much as the remains themselves, then, are central to these discussions, and in this example, the importance of archaeothanatology comes to the fore because it draws the evidence of detailed skeletal analysis and mortuary context together to identify potential funerary behaviour.

Initially, in his review of primate thanatology and mortuary/funerary archaeology, Pettitt (2018) did not reference archaeothanatology, but in a more recent article, Pettitt and Anderson (2020) do cite archaeothanatology, but without a clear definition and application of the concepts involved. Here, too, there appears to be a lack of mutual awareness that may have developed as a result of these treatments deriving from a collaboration between primatologists and archaeologists, while neglecting bioarchaeologists (those specialising in the analysis of human and non-human faunal remains and biological anthropologists, from which archaeothanatology developed). Much could be gained by joining forces and the resulting synthesis of shared interests. If this synthesis is to transpire, then some common descriptive terms and definitions will be required to facilitate trans-disciplinary communication.

Multi-lingual terminologies: the foundation on which to build

Archaeothanatological studies focus on observations of the layout and patterning, the disposition or placement of the skeletal remains and associated objects upon excavation, immediately upon exposure. Prior to their removal, this is the best time – and the last opportunity – to observe these remains *in situ*. Recording of observations is fundamental at this stage as once remains are removed from context, these relationships are lost and cannot be completely replicated. In their publication of 1962 on the Neolithic collective burial at Mournouards (Mesnils-sur-Ogre, Marne, France), Leroi-Gourhan and colleagues described the position of the remains in order to demonstrate the successive deposition of corpses and their state, whether complete cadavers when they disturbed remains or already completely skeletonised or partly so (partly articulated, fleshed). Over a decade later, Ambroise and Perlès (1975), while drawing inspiration from Leroi-Gourhan, Bailloud and Brézillon's (1962) published account, employed an *in situ* photograph (*'grâce à l'amabilité du Professeur Leroi-Gourhan'*; 'thanks to the kindness of Professor Leroi-Gourhan') (Ambroise and Perlès, 1975: 58) of the remains from the Grotte des Enfants, Grimaldi Caves in Liguria, Italy, to demonstrate that the reconstruction of the Upper Palaeolithic burials, discovered in 1901 and published in 1912 by Edouard Cartailhac and René Verneau from the Muséum national d'Histoire naturelle and others, had been altered and therefore were not in their original positions as displayed in the Musée d'Anthropologie préhistorique de Monaco. As noted by Formicola and Holt (2015: 13) more recently, this multiple interment was also simultaneous, so also fitting the use of the term 'multiple' by some researchers to mean deposited 'at the same time' (see the associated Lexicon entries for 'burial' and 'multiple deposition', Chapter 34, this volume).

Rather than the younger male and older female being in a side-by-side position, the female had actually been deposited in a rather ungainly and physiologically unconventional flexed or contracted and prone (ventral decubitus) position, face down (occipital bone upper-most in the grave), with the upper limbs flexed beneath the torso and the lower limbs laterally rotated and abducted with both knees and the hips flexed, such that the plantar surface of the medially rotated left foot and posterior aspect of the left tibia and fibula appear upper-most in the grave and beneath the left femur. These articulated segments were displayed in a position contrary to that seen in the photograph of the remains before their removal.

In their 1975 paper, Ambroise and Perlès made the important observation that: 'This experience showed us that the comparison of the homologous segments posed descriptive problems due to a lack of a precise and appropriate vocabulary'. ('*L'expérience nous a montré que la comparaison des segments homologues posait des problèmes de description, par manque de vocabulaire précis et approprié*'.) (Ambroise and Perlès, 1975: 57). The lack of vocabulary to describe this position meant that it had been 'normalised' to a physiologically conventional and more intimate appearance in the display. As deployed to describe the positions of these skeletal remains in the preceding paragraph, this vocabulary exists in standardised anatomical terms in use in medicine, surgery, medical imaging and dentistry. These terms apply as much to the bones and teeth and their parts as to the position of elements/fragments to one another. If employed more universally and consistently, this standard descriptive vocabulary would allay many of the communication problems experienced by human bioarchaeology/archaeothanatology researchers, with positive effects on clarity in archaeological research more generally.

Moreover, the standard references of the skeletonised body can be applied to standardise references to the grave, its internal constructions, grave goods (items of personal adornment) and grave inclusions (Knüsel, 2014). The position of material remains can lead to insights into their identification and significance. A case in point is Burial 43 at the Chalcolithic site of Varna, Bulgaria, with regard to a 'golden penis sheath' (Taylor, 1996: 175–182) placed in the mid-line and inferior to the pelvic region in the former museum display, a position that is not faithful to the position of this object as revealed immediately after archaeological excavation. In table 1 of the more recent publication on the dating of this iconic site, the authors note that this object was located: 'On the right side of pelvis …' (Higham *et al.*, 2007: 644, table 1; cf. Chapman *et al.*, 2006), but the effect and enduring legacy of this identification are present in the second phrase of this description: '… there was a gold penis sheath'. The shape and hollowed form of this object, with holes around the perimeter of the larger of its two openings, to accommodate attachment is more congruent with this object having been a decorative ferrule on a shafted object rather than a decorative embellishment of a phallus, although this does not deny the fundamental importance and presence of such imagery in the past and its potential to influence funerary practices.

This means that, if used appropriately and consistently, even in the absence of photographs, the position of all of these grave elements can be understood by reference to the remains which motivated their deposition and/or construction in the first place, permitting faithful comparisons from one feature, time period and location to another. The same system applies to 3D representations of these features and the remains contained within them (Mickleburgh *et al.*, Chapter 28; Sachau-Carcel, Chapter 31, this volume). Standard anatomical terms are the key here and require awareness and proficiency for their practical use.

This volume is as much about linguistic and disciplinary terminology as it is about the study of human remains in their archaeological context (cf. Boulestin, Chapter 2, this volume; Knüsel, Gerdau-Radonić and Schotsmans, Chapter 34, this volume). This statement should not be passed over lightly. Differences in language, even among researchers using the same language, sometimes disguise differences in practice that have fuelled the separation of research traditions which have subsequently developed largely in isolation in different parts of the world. This phenomenon has not gone unnoticed, and an increasing and bewildering variety of approaches have tried to overcome it – repeatedly – but without complete success in recent decades. Both archaeothanatology and bioarchaeology are milestones in these endeavours for inter-disciplinary approaches. The goal is to improve communication and to share practices so that spoken and written words unify, rather than isolate – or even alienate – scholars with similar and shared interests. One of the greatest impediments to this endeavour is non-standard terminology that draws on colloquial expressions and 'popular' culture. Their use does not aid communication and has the opposite effect – or worse – to disguise and confuse, such that similar phenomena go unrecognised owing to differences in tradition and language. As a consequence, non-standard uses impede synthetic treatments upon which inter-disciplinary and trans-disciplinary research programmes depend.

Many disciplines face and have faced the same situation, and various long-lasting standards have been produced, from the Linnaean Hierarchy to the periodic table in chemistry. In anatomy, a comparatively old subject with roots in the ancient and medieval worlds and in Greek, Latin and Arabic, this type of endeavour has resulted in division, discord and confusion with many terms used to describe anatomical structures and many attempts at consensus up until the present time frustrated by discord and disagreement (Warwick, 1978). Two standard works are the result of such endeavours: one of long descent from the 19th century, the *Nomina Anatomica* (1989) produced by the I.A.N.C. (International Anatomical Nomenclature Committee), which provides standard lists of anatomical descriptive terms in Latin, and its successor, the *Terminologia Anatomica: International Anatomical Terminology*, the first edition published in 1998, and the second edition in 2011, produced by the FIPAT (Federative International Programme on Anatomical Terminologies, 2011). The FIPAT provides lists of the Latin terms translated into English, and there is a Spanish version. The *Nomina Anatomica*, on the other hand, has been translated into a number of languages, including French. Fabry *et al.* (2006) reviewed the history of these volumes and compared the French *Nomina Anatomica* and *Terminologia Anatomica*, finding that 76.5% of the terms referred to the same Latin anatomical structure due to their common descent from the *Nomina Anatomica*. Since anatomical terms form the basis of both archaeothanatology and human bioarchaeology this shared common ground can lead the way for the use of standard terms as a whole for the funerary context because the remains of the deceased form the central focus of both.

Both of these texts contribute much to standard use in anatomy upon which many varied disciplines draw standard use and much-shared understanding, from medicine and anatomy to biological anthropology and biomechanics and medical imagery. These have been used in subsequent standard textbooks in musculoskeletal anatomy and biological anthropology/oste-ology, including those widely disseminated and translated into French, *Human Osteology* by Tim D. White, Michael T. Black and Pieter A. Folkens (2012), translated as *Traité d'ostéologie humaine: anatomie-anthropologie-paléontologie* by Jean-Pol Beauthier, Philippe Lefèvre and François Beauthier (2016) and classic anatomy publications, such as Abrahams *et al.* (1993) *McMinn's Clinical Atlas of Human Anatomy*, translated into French as *McMinn & Abrahams' Atlas Clinique d'Anatomie Humaine. Imagérie Clinique et de Dissection* by Abrahams *et al.* (2014).

Curiously, the names of muscles, ligaments, tendons and bones have been unhelpfully and unnecessarily transliterated into French when they have remained in unchanging Latin else-where. The problems introduced by this reluctance to use Latin are apparent. As an example, with the largest muscle group in the body, the gluteal muscles, which if left in their French form 'fessier', the members of the group divided into *grand*, *moyen* and *petit*, would translate as 'big, middle and little buttock muscle', for *M. gluteus maximus*, *medius* and *minimus*. Like their anglophone counterparts, francophone speakers do not employ these French transliterated terms in publications and professional oral presentations, where the Latin forms are employed. This situation appears to be changing since Warwick (1978: 223) lamented that: 'Only a minority of anatomists currently use *Nomina Anatomica*, either in teaching or writing'. It seems best to use Latin as a universal, 'dead' language and thus largely unchanging terminology for bones and muscles (cf. Stone and Stone, 1990, for the latter) and for the dentition (e.g. van Beek, 1983). Fortunately, terms of orientation have retained their Latinate forms in French and English, and thus terms of orientation remain standard, with minor orthographic differences, for example, 'flexion', 'extension', 'adduction' and 'abduction', among others, remain standard descriptive terms for movement, useful for the description of skeletal dispositions in archaeological contexts as well. As concerns language use and meaning, Fabry *et al.* (2006: 551) note that Latin, because of its neutrality and international character, as well as its role as a repository of anatomical knowledge, still plays an active role in the creation of multi-lingual terminologies. There is thus a basis for shared use in these anatomical descriptive terms.

Interpretations: from funerary actions/gestures to funerary rites

In their editorial introduction for the first issue of *Bioarchaeology International*, Baker and Agarwal (2017: 2) note: 'In France, different terminology is used for investigation of ritual surrounding death (*gestes funéraires*), the study of field anthropology (*anthropologie de terrain*) ….' Although a cogent observation, this assessment does not capture the full significance of archaeothanatology. It is not only a different terminology but also the meaning and application of terms have been more profoundly discussed and dissected in francophone academic circles. As mentioned above, one of the achievements of archaeothanatology is that it has very successfully opened a sustained debate about the meaning and material correlates of the descriptive terms used to describe human remains, their archaeological context, and patterning in order to make questions of interpretation more explicit, better defined, and to place researchers in a better position to address grander, inter-disciplinary and trans-disciplinary questions based on interpretations of the more detailed patterns revealed. Despite this, to date, archaeothanatology/human bioarchaeology has been under-represented in broader archaeological interpretive endeavours, defined as 'big questions' (cf. Kintigh *et al.*, 2014a, 2014b) despite many of the subjects being hallmarks of human bioarchaeological research and considerable in-roads having been made to address many of them (cf. Knudson and Stojanowski, 2008). Many of the questions posed about health and well-being, violence and warfare, movement, mobility and migration, population growth, reactions to climate change and identity, among others, cannot be satisfactorily addressed, let alone answered, without recourse to human remains and their funerary and mortuary contexts. In what promise to be seminal studies, archaeology and bioarchaeology seem to play themselves out in different and separate arenas to the detriment of both, but especially to (human) bioarchaeology because it is a newer subject than is archaeology. Synthesis of archaeological questions with human bioarchaeology/archaeothanatology depends on the following conceptual approach to human remains recovered from archaeological contexts. Funerary actions, gestures, or deeds (*gestes funéraires*) – the most basic element of this conceptualisation – are recognised through taphonomic observations and analyses of remains in their find context (Duday *et al.*, 1990). The identification of funerary gestures/actions/deeds is the most basic step in archaeothanatological enquiry. When these deeds are repeated in a series of depositions in a given time and place, and depending on contextual information, they comprise funerary practices (*pratiques funéraires*) for a specific time and place. As such, one can group chrono-cultural contexts based on these shared characteristics. Major research questions (*la problématique*) about social behaviour come into play at this level. Funerary rites (*rites funéraires*) are the ceremonies and principles that govern and structure practices. The identification of funerary rites – what Boulestin defines as the third phase in the deductive process in Chapter 2 in this volume – '… concerns the unseen, what has not been passed on, the immaterial, such as behaviours, social norms and ideas, as well as the material part that has not been preserved, in other words, all that calls for interpretations and hypotheses'. This further interpretive step draws on analogies from ethnohistory and social anthropology, further aided by actualistic research and ethnoarchaeology. The social interpretation of the funerary context continues to be both intriguing but also the most problematical part of this endeavour, with chronological and geographic synthetic treatments based on these social interpretations in the offing that will match those anticipated by other archaeological insights revealing aspects of social change, belief and cosmology, such as the importance of the observation of celestial events (cf. Parker Pearson *et al.*, 2021) and migration (Buikstra *et al.*, 2004).

Interdisciplinary research

An apt criticism of archaeothanatological reconstructions of the original layout and disposition of skeletal remains (called phase two by Boulestin, Chapter 2, this volume) is that they rely on unvalidated taphonomic hypotheses of skeletal disarticulation and movement (Mickleburgh *et al.*, Chapter 28, this volume; Schotsmans *et al.*, Chapter 27, this volume). These reconstructions have tended to depend on reasoned arguments that account for repeated patterns encountered in a series of graves, but without the backing of actualistic/field experimental data or modern cemetery research to demonstrate the processes underlying these repeated observations. They thus remain solely descriptive and reliant upon repeated observations that are in many cases consistent but ultimately do not resolve the possibility of equifinal patterning. Many of these scenarios are thus open to criticisms invoking affirmation of the consequent and circular reasoning. What matters is not a rigid one-cause-one-result interpretation, but a critical reflection that integrates all contextual evidence in order to move beyond these case studies to employ population-level comparisons to address higher-level interpretive questions relating to social structure (named social positions) and social organisation (relationships among the living that define social formations, such as polities, sodalities and other social groupings based on social identity and group membership) (cf. Le Roy and Rottier, Chapter 11, this volume; Rottier, Chapter 13, this volume).

Most recently, these higher-level questions have concentrated on mass migrations in the past, and these have taken centre-stage, leaving the patterning of the deceased as a largely secondary concern. Although many aDNA studies have been deployed to reveal population movements that reveal genetic patterning on a grand geographic scale through time (e.g. Haak *et al.*, 2008, 2015; Fernández *et al.*, 2014; Allentoft *et al.*, 2015; Kılınç *et al.*, 2016) or regional population movements and resulting admixture (e.g. Rivollat *et al.*, 2015; Beau *et al.*, 2017), a smaller number have concentrated on intra-site relationships among graves (e.g. Le Roy *et al.*, 2016). These have demonstrated, in some cases, that certain funerary patterns, grave location and grave-types relate to kin-based relations in the early medieval period (Deguilloux *et al.*, 2014), with co-burial of a suspected brother and sister in a collective grave in Mycenaean-period Greece (Bouwman *et al.*, 2008) and at earlier Neolithic Çatalhöyük (Yaka *et al.*, 2021) and kin relationships in mass graves of victims of violence (Haak *et al.*, 2008; Meyer *et al.*, 2009; Schroeder *et al.*, 2019).

What are the next steps?

This volume was conceived in a desire to integrate and synthesise traditions of research and scholarship that had developed in parallel with little interaction. The work of integration will continue in the future; if this book fosters integration and aids the speed with which integration advances, these will be measures of the legacy of this volume. As noted above, archaeothanatological enquiry is an unfinished journey. There is considerable opportunity for ground-truthing of previous archaeothanatological observations and further development of research questions addressing social organisation in the past. There is also a great opportunity and much more work required to integrate social theory that has had such an impact in human bioarchaeology with the archaeothanatologically uncovered and attested patterns to answer questions about the human social condition and modifications of it in the past.

Terminology and shared definitions form the platform for the whole of archaeothanatology, from field observations and recording to the analysis of contextual features that reveal longer-term histories of human intervention (e.g. Aspöck and Banerjea, 2016; Aspöck, 2018; Aspöck, Gerdau-Radonić and Noterman, Chapter 16, this volume). A repeated mantra in archaeothanatology, as in other observational sciences, is the separation of observation from interpretation (see above) (cf. Boulestin, Chapter 2; Schmitt, Chapter 6, this volume; Schotsmans *et al.*, Chapter 27, this volume). This separation is fundamental, as previously noted in palaeopathological research (cf. Ortner 1994; Appleby, Thomas and Buikstra, 2015), which is also dependent on pattern recognition. Mixing of observation with interpretation obscures patterning that thus becomes hidden behind abstractions that make phenomena seem equivalent when they may not be and obscures variation. Therefore, there is a very heavy emphasis on the descriptive terms used in the field and interpretive terms used after a full analysis of skeletal and funerary remains within their funerary context in archaeothanatology. A full interpretation cannot be attained without the full integration of the biological aspects of the remains, associated material remains with which they are found and of the archaeological feature(s) which accommodate both.

Human remains are controversial and ambiguous in law, as in life (cf. Clavandier, Chapter 33, this volume); they pose questions about the very meaning of life and are reminders of mortality, often persisting long after the completion of funerary ceremonies and beyond memory. The absence of autonomy and consciousness means that the living in their quest to understand and to come to terms with individual and collective mortality animate the dead. All of this goes to say that the synthesis that this book attempts between human remains and funerary contexts is both difficult and problematical from the outset, and the editors as messengers have courted controversy in assembling and producing it. Though continued controversy may be one enduring result, it is also hoped that this book fosters greater awareness, familiarity, better communication and greater consensus across linguistic and disciplinary terrain. As Parker Pearson comments in the Foreword to this volume: 'For too long, language has divided French and English-speaking researchers over approaches to the archaeology of death'. This starts with the title of this volume: archaeothanatology.

References

Abrahams, P.H., Boon, J., Spratt, J.D. and Hutchings, R.T. (1993). *McMinn's clinical atlas of human anatomy with DVD*. 6th ed. St. Louis: Mosby.

Abrahams, P.H., Spratt, J.D., Loukas, M. and Schoor, A.-N. (2014). *McMinn & Abrahams' atlas clinique d'anatomie humaine. Imagérie clinique et de dissection*. Issy-les-Moulineaux: Elsevier Masson.

Allentoft, M.E., Sikora, M., Sjögren, K.-G., Rasmussen, S. Rasmussen, S.M., Stenderup, J., Damgaard, P.B., Schroeder, H., Ahlström, T., Vinnet, L., Malaspinas, A.-S., Margarya, A., Higham, T., Chivall, D., Lynnerup, N., Harvig, L., Baron, J., Della Casa, P., Dabrowski, P., Duffy, P.R., Ebel, A.V., Epimakhov, A., Frei, K., Furmanek, M., Gralak, T., Gromov, A., Gronkiewicz, S., Grupe, G., Hajdu, T., Jarysz, R., Khartanovich, V., Khokhlov, A., Kiss, V., Kolář, J., Kriiska, A., Lasak, I., Longhi, C., McGlynn, G., Merkevicius, A., Merkyte, I., Metspalu, M., Mkrtchyan, R., Moiseyev, V., Paja, L., Pálfi, G., Pokutta,

D., Pospieszny, L., Price, T.D., Saag, L., Sablin, M., Shishlina, N., Smrčka, V., Soenov, V.I., Szeverényi, V., Tóth, G., Trifanova, S.V., Varul, L., Vicze, M., Yepiskoposyan, L., Zhitenev, V., Orlando, L., Sicheritz-Pontén, T., Brunak, S., Nielsen, R., Kristiansen, K. and Willerslev, E. (2015). Population Genomics of Bronze Age Eurasia. *Nature*, 522, pp. 167–172.

Ambroise, D. and Perlès, C. (1975). Note sur l'Analyse Archéologique des Squelettes Humains. *Revue Archéologique du Centre de la France*, 14(1–2), pp. 49–61.

Anderson, J.R. (2011). A Primatological Perspective on Death. *American Journal of Primatology*, 73, pp. 410–414.

Anderson, J.R. (2020). Responses to Death and Dying: Primates and Other Mammals. *Primates*, 61, pp. 1–7.

Anderson, J.R., Gillies, A. and Lock, L.C. (2010). Pan Thanatology. *Current Biology*, 20, pp. R349–R351.

Appleby, J., Thomas, R. and Buikstra, J. (2015). Increasing Confidence in Paleopathological Diagnosis – Application of the Istanbul Terminological Framework. *International Journal of Paleopathology*, 8, pp. 19–21.

Aspöck, E. (2018). A High-Resolution Approach to the Formation Processes of a Reopened Early Bronze Age Inhumation Grave in Austria: Taphonomy of Human Remains. *Quaternary International*, 474, pp. 131–145.

Aspöck, E. and Banerjea, R.Y. (2016). Formation Processes of a Reopened Early Bronze Age Inhumation Grave in Austria: The Soil Thin Section Analyses. *Journal of Archaeological. Science: Reports*, 10, pp. 791–809.

Baker, B.J. and Agarwal, S.C. (2017). Stronger Together: Advancing a Global Bioarchaeology. *Bioarchaeology International*, 1(1–2), pp. 1–18.

Beau, A., Rivollat, M., Réveillas, H., Pemonge, M.-H., Mendisco, F., Thomas, Y., Lefranc, P. and Deguilloux, M.F. (2017). Multi-scale Ancient DNA Analyses Confirm the Western Origin of Michelsberg Farmers and Document Probable Practices of Human Sacrifice. *PLoS ONE*, 12(7), e0179742.

Biro, D., Humle, T., Koops, K., Sousa, C., Hayashi, M. and Matsuzawa, T. (2010). Chimpanzee Mothers at Bossou, Guinea Carry the Mummified Remains of Their Dead Infants. *Current Biology*, 20, pp. R351–R352.

Bocquentin, F., Kodas, E. and Ortiz, A. (2016). Headless but Still Eloquent! Acephalous Skeletons as Witnesses of Pre-pottery Neolithic North-South Connections and Disconnections, *Paléorient*, 42(2), pp. 33–52.

Boulestin, B. and Duday, H. (2005). Ethnologie et archéologie de la mort : de l'illusion des références à l'emploi d'un vocabulaire. In: C. Mordant and G. Depierre, eds., *Les Pratiques Funéraires à l'Âge Du Bronze en France*. Actes de la table ronde de Sens-en-Bourgogne (10–12 juin 1998). Paris: Éditions du Comité des Travaux d'Histoiriques et Scientifiques (CTHS), pp. 17–30.

Boulestin, B. and Duday, H. (2006). Ethnology and Archaeology of Death: From the Illusion of References to the Use of a Terminology, *Archaeologia Polona*, 44, pp. 149–169.

Bouwman, A.S., Brown, K.A., Prag, A.J.N.W. and Brown, T.A. (2008). Kinship between Burials from Grave Circle B at Mycenae Revealed by Ancient DNA Typing. *Journal of Archaeological Science*, 35, pp. 2580–2584.

Buikstra, J.E. (1977). Biocultural dimensions of archaeological study: a regional perspective. In: R.L. Blakely, ed., *Biocultural Adaptation in Prehistoric America*. Athens: The University of Georgia Press, pp. 67–84.

Buikstra, J.E. (2006). On the 21st century. In: J.E. Buikstra and L.A. Beck, eds., *Bioarchaeology: The Contextual Analysis of Human Remains*. Amsterdam: Academic Press, pp. 347–357.

Buikstra, J.E., Price, T.D., Wright, L.E. and Burton, J.A. (2004). Tombs from the Copán acropolis: a life-history approach. In: E.E. Bell, M.A. Canuto and R.J. Sharer, eds., *Understanding Early Classic Copán*. Philadelphia: University of Pennsylvania Museum of Archaeology and Anthropology, pp. 191–212.

Chapman, J., Higham, T., Gaydarska, B., Slavchev, V. and Honch, N. (2006). The Social Context of the Emergence, Development and Abandonment of the Varna Cemetery, Bulgaria. *European Journal of Archaeology*, 9(2–3), pp. 159–183.

Crevecoeur, I., Schmitt, A. and Schoep, I. (2015). An Archaeothanatological Approach to the Study of Minoan Funerary Practices: Case-studies from the Early and Middle Minoan Cemetery at Sissi, Crete. *Journal of Field Archaeology*, 40, pp. 283–299.

Deguilloux, M.F., Pemonge, M.H., Mendisco, F., Thibon, D., Cartron, I. and Castex, D. (2014). Ancient DNA and Kinship Analysis of Human Remains Deposited in Merovingian Necropolis Sarcophagi (Jau-Dignac-et-Loirac, France, 7th–8th Century AD). *Journal of Archaeological Science*, 41, pp. 399–405.

Dibble, H.L., Aldeias, V., Goldberg, P., McPherron, S.P., Sandgathe, D. and Steele, T.E. (2015). A Critical Look at Evidence from La Chapelle-aux-Saints Supporting an Intentional Neandertal Burial. *Journal of Archaeological Science*, 53, pp. 649–657.

Dirks, P.H.G.M., Berger, L.R., Hawks, J., Randolph-Quinney, P.S., Backwell, L.R. and Roberts, E.M. (2016). Comment on 'Deliberate Body Disposal by Hominins in the Dinaledi Chamber, Cradle of Humankind, South Africa'. *Journal of Human Evolution*, 96, pp. 149–153.

Duday, H. (1978). Archéologie Funéraire et Anthropologie: Application des Relevés et de l'Etude Ostéologique à l'Interprétation de Quelques Sépultures Pré- et Protohistoriques du Midi de la France. *Cahiers d'Anthropologie*, 1, 55–101.

Duday, H. (1987). Contribution des observations ostéologiques a la chronologie interne des sépultures collectives. In: H. Duday and C. Masset, eds., *Anthropologie Physique et Archéologie. Méthodes d'Etude des Sépultures*. Paris: Editions du CNRS, pp. 51–59.

Duday, H. (2006a). *Lezioni di archeothanatologia: Archeologia funeraria e antropologia di campo*. Transcribed by Enrica Monzeglio, Translated and Edited by Rossella Pace, Stéphane Verger and Paola Catalano. Roma: Soprintendenza Archeologica.

Duday, H. (2006b). L'archéothanatologie ou l'archéologie de la mort (Archaeothanatology or the archae-ology of death). Translated by C.J. Knüsel. In: R.L. Gowland and C.J. Knüsel, eds., *Social Archaeology of Funerary Remains*, Oxford: Oxbow Books, pp. 30–56.

Duday, H. (2009). *Archaeology of the dead: Lectures in archaeothanatology*. Translated by A.M. Cipriani and J. Pearce. Oxford: Oxbow Books.

Duday, H., Courtaud, P., Crubézy, E., Sellier, P. and Tillier, A.-M. (1990). L'Anthropologie de 'Terrain': Reconnaissance et Interprétation des Gestes Funéraires. *Bulletins et Mémoires de la Société d'Anthropologie de Paris*, 2 (3–4), pp. 26–49.

Duday, H. and Masset, C. eds. (1987). *Anthropologie Physique et Archéologie. Methodes d'Etude des Sépultures*. Paris: Editions du CNRS.

Erdal, Y.S. (2015). Bone or flesh: Defleshing and post-depositional treatments at Körtik Tepe (Southeastern Anatolia, PPNA Period). *European Journal of Archaeology*, 18(1), pp. 4–32.

Fabry, P., Baud, R., Burgun, A. and Lovis, C. (2006). Amplification of Terminologia Anatomica by French Language Terms Using Latin Terms Matching Algorithm: A Prototype for Other Language. *International Journal of Medical Informatics*, 75(7), pp. 542–552.

Fashing, P.J. and Nguyen, N. (2011). Behavior toward the Dying, Diseased, or Disabled among Animals and Its Relevance to Paleopathology. *International Journal of Paleopathology*, 1, pp. 128–129.

Fernández, E., Pérez-Pérez, A., Gamba, C., Prats, E., Cuesta, P., Anfruns, J., Molist, M., Arroyo-Pardo, E. and Turbón, D. (2014). Ancient DNA Analysis of 8000 B.C. Near Eastern Farmers Supports an Early Neolithic Pioneer Maritime Colonization of Mainland Europe through Cyprus and the Aegean Islands. *PLoS Genetics*, 10(6), e1004401.

FIPAT (Federative International Programme on Anatomical Terminologies) (2011). *Terminologia Anatomica: International Anatomical Terminology*. 2nd ed. Stuttgart and New York: Thieme.

Formicola, V. and Holt, B.M. (2015). Tall Guys and Fat ladies: Grimaldi's Upper Paleolithic Burials and Figurines in an Historical Perspective. *Journal of Anthropological Sciences*, 93, pp. 1–18.

Gargett, R.H. (1989). Grave Shortcomings: The Evidence for Neanderthal Burial. *Current Anthropology*, 30(2), pp. 157–190.

Gargett, R.H. (1999). Middle Palaeolithic Burial Is Not a Dead Issue: The View from Qafzeh, Saint-Césaire, Kebara, Amud, and Dederiyeh. *Journal of Human Evolution*, 37(1), pp. 27–90.

Gonçalves, A. and Biro, D. (2018). Comparative Thanatology, an Integrative Approach: Exploring Sensory/Cognitive Aspects of Death Recognition in Vertebrates and Invertebrates. *Philosophical Transactions of the Royal Society B*, 373, pp. 1–12.

Goodall, J. (1986). *The chimpanzees of Gombe: patterns of behavior*. Cambridge, MA: The Belknap Press of Harvard University Press.

Gowland, R. and Knüsel, C.J., eds. (2006). *Social archaeology of funerary remains*. Oxford: Oxbow Books.

Green, R.E., Krause, J., Briggs, A.W., Maricic, T., Stenzel, U., Kircher, M., Patterson, N., Li, H., Zhai, W., Fritz, M. H-Y., Hansen, N.F., Durand, E.Y., Malaspinas, A.-S., Jensen, J.D., Marques-Bonet, T., Alkan, C., Prüfer, K., Meyer, M., Burbano, H.A., Good, J.M., Schultz, R., Aximu- Petri, A., Butthof, A., Höber, B., Höffner, B., Siegemund, M., Weihmann, A., Nusbaum, C., Lander, E.S., Russ, C., Novod, N., Affourtit, J., Egholm, M., Verna, C., Rudan, P., Brajkovic, D., Kucan, Ž., Gušic, I., Doronichev, V.B., Golovanova, L.V., Lalueza-Fox, C., de la Rasilla, M., Fortea, J., Rosas, A., Schmitz, R.F., Johnson, P.L.F., Eichler, E.E., Falush, D., Birney, E., Mullikin, J.C., Slatkin, M., Nielsen, R., Kelso, J., Lachmann, M., Reich, D. and Pääbo, S. (2010). A Draft Sequence of the Neandertal Genome. *Science*, 328, pp. 710–722.

Haak, W., Brandt, G., de Jong, H.N., Meyer, C., Ganslmeier, R., Heyd, V., Hawkesworth, C., Pike, A.W.G., Meller, H. and Alt, K.W. (2008). Ancient DNA, Strontium Isotopes, and Osteological Analyses Shed Light on Social and Kinship Organization of the Later Stone Age. *Proceedings of the National Academy of Sciences of the United States of America*, 105(47), pp. 18226–18231.

Haak, W., Lazaridis, I., Patterson, N., Rohland, N., Mallick, S., Llamas, B., Brandt, G., Nordenfelt, S., Harney, E., Stewardson, K., Fu, Q., Mittnik, A., Bánffy, E., Economou, C., Francken, M., Friederich, S., Pena, R.G., Hallgren, F., Khartanovich, V., Khokhlov, A., Kunst, M., Kuznetsov, P., Meller, H., Mochalov, O., Moiseyev, V., Nicklisch, N., Pichler, S.L., Risch, R., Rojo Guerra, M.A., Roth, C., Szécsényi-Nagy, A., Wahl J., Meyer, M., Krause, J., Brown, D., Anthony, D., Cooper, A., Alt, K.W. and Reich, D. (2015). Massive Migration from the Steppe Was a Source for Indo-European Languages in Europe. *Nature*, 552, pp. 207–211.

Harris, N.J. and Tayles, N. (2012). Burial Containers – A Hidden Aspect of Mortuary Practices: Archaeothanatology at Ban Non Wat, Thailand. *Journal of Anthropological Archaeology*, 31, pp. 227–239.

Higham, T., Chapman, J., Slavchev, V., Gaydarska, B., Honch, N., Yordanov, Y. and Dimitrova, B. (2007). New Perspectives on the Varna Cemetery (Bulgaria) – AMS Dates and Social Implications. *Antiquity*, 81(313), pp. 640–651.

Jenkins, E. (2012). Mice, Scats and Burials: Unusual Concentrations of Microfauna Found in Human Burials at the Neolithic site of Çatalhöyük, Central Anatolia. *Journal of Social Archaeology*, 12, pp. 380–403.

Kintigh, K.W., Altschul, J.H., Beaudry, M.C., Drennan, R.D., Kinzig, A.P., Kohler, T.A., Limp, W.F., Maschner, H.D.G., Michener, W.K., Pauketat, T.R., Peregrine, P., Sabloff, J.A., Wilkinson, T.J., Wright, H.T. and Zeder, M.A. (2014a). Grand Challenges for Archaeology. *American Antiquity*, 79(1), pp. 5–24.

Kintigh, K.W., Altschul, J.H., Beaudry, M.C., Drennan, R.D., Kinzig, A.P., Kohler, T.A., Limp, W.F., Maschner, H.D.G., Michener, W.K., Pauketat, T.R., Peregrine, P., Sabloff, J.A., Wilkinson, T.J., Wright, H.T. and Zeder, M.A. (2014b). Grand Challenges for Archaeology, *Proceedings of the National Academy of Sciences of the United States of America*, 111(3), pp. 879–880.

Kılınç, G. M., Omrak, A., Özer, F., Günther, T., Büyükkarakaya, A.M., Bıçakçı, E., Baird, D., Dönertaş, H.M., Ghalichi, A., Yaka, R., Koptekin, D., Açan, S.C., Parvizi, P., Krzewińska, M., Daskalaki, E.A., Yüncü, E., Dağtaş, N.D., Fairbairn, A., Pearson, J., Mustafağolu, G., Erdal, Y.S., Çakan, Y.G., Togan, İ., Somel, M., Storå, J., Jakobsson, M. and Götherström, A. (2016). The Demographic Development of the First Farmers in Anatolia. *Current Biology*, 26(19), pp. 2659–2666.

Knudson, K.J. and Stojanowski, C.M. (2008). New Directions in Bioarchaeology: Recent Contributions to the Study of Human Social Identities. *Journal of Archaeological Research*, 16, pp. 397–432.

Knüsel, C.J. (2010). Bioarchaeology: A Synthetic Approach/Bio-archéologie: Une Approche Synthétique. *Bulletins et Mémoires de la Société d'Anthropologie de Paris*, 22, pp. 62–73.

Knüsel, C.J. (2014). Crouching in Fear: Terms of Engagement for Funerary Remains. *Journal of Social Archaeology*, 14(1), pp. 26–58.

Knüsel, C.J. and Robb, J.E. (2016). Funerary Taphonomy: An Overview of Goals and Methods. *Journal of Archaeological Science: Reports*. In: C.J. Knüsel and J.E. Robb, eds., Special Issue on Funerary Taphonomy, 10, pp. 655–673.

Knüsel, C.J. and Smith, M.J. (2014). Context is everything. In: C.J. Knüsel and M.J. Smith, eds., *The Routledge Handbook of the Bioarchaeology of Human Conflict*. London: Routledge, pp. 1–24.

Larsen, C.S. (1997). *Bioarchaeology: interpreting behavior from the human skeleton*. Cambridge: Cambridge University Press.

Larsen, C.S. (2006). The changing face of bioarchaeology: an inter-disciplinary science. In: J.E. Buikstra and L.A. Beck, eds., *Bioarchaeology: The Contextual Analysis of Human Remains*. Amsterdam: Academic Press, pp. 375–415.

Le Roy, M., Rivollat, M., Mendisco, F., Pemonge, M.-H., Coutelier, C., Couture, C., Tillier, A.-M., Rottier, S. and Deguilloux, M.-F. (2016). Distinct Ancestries for Similar Funerary Practices? A GIS Analysis Comparing Funerary, Osteological and a DNA Data from the Middle Neolithic. *Journal of Archaeological Science*, 73, pp. 45–54.

Leroi-Gourhan, A., Bailloud, G. and Brézillon, M. (1962). L'Hypogée II des Mournouards (Mesnil-sur-Oger, Marne). *Gallia Préhistoire*, 1, pp. 23–133.

McComb, K., Baker, L. and Moss, C. (2006). African Elephants Show High Levels of Interest in the Skulls and Ivory of Their Own Species. *Biology Letters*, 2, pp. 26–28.

Meyer, C., Brandt, G., Haak, W., Ganslmeier, R.A., Meller, H. and Alt, K.W. (2009). The Eulau Eulogy: Bioarchaeological Interpretation of Lethal Violence in Corded Ware Multiple Burials from Saxony-Anhalt, Germany. *Journal of Anthropological Archaeology*, 28(4), pp. 412–423.

Murail, P., Maureille, B., Peressinotto, D. and Geus, F. (2004). An Infant Cemetery of the Classic Kerma Period (1750–1500 B.C., Island of Saï, Sudan). *Antiquity*, 78, pp. 267–277.

Nilsson Stutz, L. (2003). Embodied rituals and ritualized bodies tracing ritual practices in Late Mesolithic burials. Lund: Almqvist & Wiksell International.

Nilsson Stutz, L. (2016). Building Bridges between Burial Archaeology and the Archaeology of Death: Where Is the Archaeological Study of the Dead Going? *Current Swedish Archaeology*, 24, pp. 13–35.

Nomina Anatomica (1989). 6th ed. Edinburgh: Churchill Livingstone.

Ortner, D.J. (1994). Descriptive methodology in paleopathology. In: D. Owsley and R. Jantz, eds., *Skeletal Biology in the Great Plains: Migration, Warfare, Health, and Subsistence.* Washington, DC: Smithsonian Institution Press, pp. 73–80.

Parker Pearson, M., Pollard, J., Richards, C., Welham, K., Kinnaird, T., Shaw, D., Simmons, E., Stanford, A., Bevins, R., Ixer, R., Ruggles, C., Rylatt, J. and Edinborough, K. (2021). The Original Stonehenge? A Dismantled Stone Circle in the Preseli Hills of West Wales. *Antiquity*, 95(379), pp. 85–103.

Pettitt, P.B. (2011). *The Paleolithic origins of human burial.* London: Routledge.

Pettitt, P. (2018). Hominin Evolutionary Thanatology from the Mortuary to Funerary Realm: The Palaeoanthropological Bridge between Chemistry and Culture. *Philosophical Transactions of the Royal Society B*, 373, pp. 1–16.

Pettitt, P. and Anderson, J.R. (2020). Primate Thanatology and Hominoid Mortuary Archaeology. *Primates*, 61, pp. 9–19.

Pomeroy, E., Bennett, P., Hunt, C., Reynolds, T., Farr, L., Frouin, M., Holman, J., Lane, R., French, C. and Barker. G. (2020). New Neanderthal Remains Associated with the 'Flower Burial' at Shanidar Cave. *Antiquity*, 94(373), pp. 11–26.

Rendu, W., Beauval, C., Crevecoeur, I., Bayle, P., Balzeau, A., Bismuth, T., Bourguignon, L., Delfour, G., Faivre, J.P., Lacrampe-Cuyaubère, F., Muth, X., Pasty, S., Semal, P., Tavormina, C., Todisco, D., Turq, A. and Maureille, B. (2016). Let the Dead Speak. Comments on Dibble et al.'s Reply to 'Evidence Supporting an Intentional Burial at La Chapelle-aux-Saints'. *Journal of Archaeological Science*, 69, pp. 12–20.

Rendu, W., Beauval, C., Crevecoeur, I., Bayle, P., Balzeau, A., Bismuth, T., Bourguignon, L., Delfour, G., Faivre, J.-P., Lacrampe-Cuyaubère, F., Tavormina, C., Todisco, D., Turq, A. and Maureille, B. (2014). Evidence Supporting an Intentional Neandertal Burial at La Chapelle-aux-Saints (Corrèze, France). *Proceedings of the National Academy of Sciences of the United States of America*, 111, pp. 81–86.

Rivollat, M., Mendisco, F., Pemonge, M.-H., Safi, A., Saint-Marc, D., Brémond, A., Couture-Veschambre, C., Rottier, S. and Deguilloux, M.-F. (2015). When the Waves of European Neolithization Met: First Paleogenetic Evidence from Early Farmers in the Southern Paris Basin. *PLOS ONE*, 10, e0125521.

Robb, J.E., Elster, E., Isetti, E., Knüsel, C.J., Tafuri, M.A. and Traverso. A. (2015). Cleaning the Dead: Neolithic Ritual Processing of Human Bone at Scaloria Cave, Italy. *Antiquity*, 89(343), pp. 39–54.

Roksandic, M. (2002). Position of skeletal remains as a key to understanding mortuary behavior. In: W.D. Haglund and M.H. Sorg, eds., *Advances in Forensic Taphonomy: Method, Theory, and Archaeological Perspectives.* Boca Raton: CRC Press, pp. 99–117.

Russell, M.D. (1987). Mortuary Practices at the Krapina Neanderthal Site. *American Journal of Physical Anthropology*, 72, pp. 381–397.

Schmitt, A. (2017). Middle Neolithic Burials in Mediterranean France: Honouring or Rejecting the Dead? *West & East* II, pp. 63–82.

Schroeder, H., Margaryan, A., Szmyt, M., Theulot, B., Włodarczak, P., Rasmussen, S., Gopalakrishnan, S., Szczepanek, A., Konopka, T., Jensen, T.Z.T., Witkowska, B., Wilk, S., Przybyła, M.M., Pospieszny, Ł., Sjögren, K.-G., Belka, Z., Olsen, J., Kristiansen, K., Willerslev, E., Frei, K.M., Sikora, M., Johannsen, N. N. and Allentoft, M.E. (2019). Unraveling Ancestry, Kinship, and Violence in a Late Neolithic Mass Grave. *Proceedings of the National Academy of Sciences of the United States of America*, 116(22), pp. 10705–10710.

Stone, R.J. and Stone, J.A. (1990). *Atlas of the skeletal muscles.* Dubuque: Wm. C. Brown Publishers.

Taylor, T. (1996). *The prehistory of sex.* New York and Toronto: Bantam Books.

Tiesler, V. (2011). Book Review of 'The Archaeology of Dead: Lectures in Archaeothanatology'. *European Journal of Archaeology*, 14(3), pp. 491–494.

Tiesler, V., Suzuki, S. and Pereira, G., eds. (2021). *Tratamientos mortuorios del cuerpo humano. Perspectivas tafonómicas y arqueotanatológicas.* Mexico City: Centro de Estudios Mexicanos y Centroamericanos, University of Okayawa, and Universidad Autónoma de Yucatán.

Toussaint, M. (2011). Intentional Cutmarks on an Early Mesolithic Human Calvaria from Margaux Cave (Dinant, Belgium). *American Journal of Physical Anthropology*, 144(1), pp. 100–107.

Trinkaus, E. (1985). Cannibalism and Burial at Krapina. *Journal of Human Evolution*, 14, pp. 203–216.

Val, A. (2016). Deliberate Body Disposal by Hominins in the Dinaledi Chamber, Cradle of Humankind, South Africa? *Journal of Human Evolution*, 96, pp. 145–148.

van Beek, G.C. (1983). *Dental morphology: an illustrated guide.* 2nd ed. Oxford: Wright publishers.

Warwick, R. (1978). The Future of *Nomina Anatomica* – A Personal View. *Journal of Anatomy*, 126(1), pp. 221–223.

White, T.D. (1986). Cut Marks on the Bodo Cranium: A Case of Prehistoric Defleshing. *American Journal of Physical Anthropology*, 69, pp. 503–509.

White, T.D., Black, M.T. and Folkens, P.A. (2012). *Human osteology*. Amsterdam: Elsevier/Academic Press.

White, T.D., Black, M.T. and Folkens, P.A. (2016). *Traité d'ostéologie humaine: anatomie-anthropologie-paléontologie*. Translated by Jean-Pol Beauthier, Philippe Lefèvre, François Beauthier. Louvain-la-Neuve: Deboek Supérieur.

Willis, A. and Tayles, N. (2009). Field Anthropology: Application to Burial Contexts in Prehistoric Southeast Asia. *Journal of Archaeological Science*, 36(2), pp. 547–554.

Woodburn, J. (1982). Social dimensions of death in four hunting and gathering societies. In: M. Bloch and J. Parry, eds., *Death and the Regeneration of Life*. Cambridge: Cambridge University Press, pp. 187–210.

Yaka, R., Mapelli, I., Kaptan, D., Doğu, A., Chyleński, M., Erdal, O.D., Koptekin, D., Vural, K.B., Bayliss, A., Mazzucato, C., Fer, E., Çokoğlu, S.S., Kempe Lagerholm, V., Krzewińska, M., Karamurat, C., Gemici, H.C., Sevkar, A., Dağtaş, N.D., Kılınç, G.M., Adams, D., Munters, A.R., Sağlıcan, E., Milella, M., Schotsmans, E.M.J., Yurtman, E., Çetin, M., Yorulmaz, S., Altınışık, E., Ghalichi, A., Juras, A., Bilgin, C.C., Günther, T., Storå, J., Jakobsson, M., de Kleijn, M., Mustafaoğlu, G., Fairbairn, A., Pearson, J., Togan, İ, Kayacan, N., Marciniak, A., Larsen C.S., Hodder, I., Atakuman, C., Pilloud, M., Sürer, E., Gerritsen, F., Özbal, R., Baird, D., Erdal, Y.S., Duru, G., Özbaşaran, M., Haddow, S.D., Knüsel, C.J., Götherström, A., Özer, F. and Somel, M. (2021). Variable Kinship Patterns in Neolithic Anatolia Revealed by Ancient Genomes. *Current Biology*, 31, pp. 1–14.

Zemour, A. (2016). De l'anthropologie de terrain à l'archéologie de la mort: histoire, concepts et développements. In: M. Lauwers and A. Zemour, eds., *Qu'est-ce Qu'une Sépulture? Humanités et Systèmes Funéraires de la Préhistoire à Nos Jours*, Antibes: Éditions de l'Association pour la Promotion et la Diffusion des Connaissances Archéologiques (APDCA), pp. 23–34.

Zeytoun, V., Gatto, E., Rougier, H. and Sidibe, S. (2004). Dia Shoma (Mali), a Medieval Cemetery in the Inner Niger Delta. *International Journal of Osteoarchaeology*, 14, pp. 112–25.

PART I

Archaeothanatology – methodological guidelines

1

METHODOLOGICAL GUIDELINES FOR ARCHAEOTHANATOLOGICAL PRACTICE

Frédérique Blaizot

HALMA, Histoire, Archéologie et Littérature des Mondes Anciens, UMR 8164, Université de Lille, Lille, France

Introduction

By restoring the invisible, archaeothanatology contributes to the reconstruction of more complete funerary contexts (Duday, 1978, 2005, 2009) and offers additional tools for addressing social relations and cultural identities among past populations (Blaizot, 2017). The interpretation of the original arrangement, organisation and architecture[1] of burials represents the fundamental primary information on which to construct a typo-chronology of burials, to define funerary practices from a cultural (identity of human groups) and social (mechanisms of differentiation within groups) perspective in order to exploit what is known or partly known of funerary practices from other sources, such as texts for historic periods, as well as to reveal diachronic changes in these practices.

The aim of this chapter is not to repeat the methodological procedures related to the identification of the conditions in which bodies decompose (in a void or in a filled space), nor to the demonstration of vanished furnishings, nor to the understanding of actions behind funerary behaviour through time, as in secondary deposit analysis. These analytical principles have previously been published (Duday, 2006, 2009; Duday, Le Mort and Tillier, 2014), in addition to several case studies (Blaizot, 2014; Castex and Blaizot, 2017). Rather, this contribution reviews the conditions necessary for the application of archaeothanatology and emphasises that the method is based upon a detailed analysis of taphonomic anomalies. Interpretation of anomalies is not based on a simple established fact, or even on the analysis of isolated facts where one observation would be equal to a particular event, but on latent data which must be identified and synthesised, and the relevance of which must be examined in each case.

---

1 The original French terms are '*appareil funéraire*' and '*dispositif funéraire*', words that cannot be translated as a strict, single-word English equivalent. These have been translated as 'burial arrangement, organisation and architecture', which are close conceptual equivalents.

DOI: 10.4324/9781351030625-3

Principles and conditions of application

When the cadaver becomes a skeleton, modifications produced by the disarticulation of the joints of the body occur. The extent of such modifications varies according to the conditions of decomposition. Archaeothanatology consists of a reverse journey through the taphonomic events observed in the field and the correlation of these events with one another. With the archaeological evidence from the burial, for example, the form of the pit in plan and cross-section, the nature of the sediment, preserved items such as stones or nails, the collapse of grave pit walls, among others, aid to establish a hypothetical interpretation of the method and manner of deposition that fits the set of observations revealed by such an analysis.

To implement this method solid training is required – not only in the interpretation and recording of archaeological evidence but also in a thorough knowledge of human anatomy and the various articulations that determine movements of skeletal elements. It is therefore essential to understand the manner in which bones are displaced during different movement events, as well as the conditions under which disarticulation of the various joints occurs and their relative timing. A 'taphonomic anomaly' arises when the position, orientation, or placement of a bone or set of bones does not correspond to that expected in a given situation (as determined by the overall position of the remains of the skeleton). Taphonomic anomalies are defined by reference to theoretical knowledge concerning the decomposition stages of cadavers and are founded on two premises: the first is when certain events, which should occur, do not occur, and the second is when certain events, which should not have occurred, do indeed occur.

It is these anomalies that are recorded in the field and subsequently analysed in their archaeological context. The excavation must be meticulous, the articulations well-exposed, all pieces of bone left in place, with the exact position of the bones and the state of the articulations recorded in detail (Duday, 1978). The analysis of these anomalies will not only be used to define the initial or original position of the body, but also to identify the depositional environment in which decomposition took place (Duday, 1990), followed by determining the constraints exerted on the cadaver by the burial environment – both natural and humanly conceived – during decomposition in order to reconstruct them. The simplest example is that of the rotation of the head: anatomically, when the head pivots only the first cervical vertebra follows its movement. If a skeleton is found on its back (supine) with the cranium in lateral view and the atlas in frontal view, or with the atlas and the axis, or even the lower cervical vertebrae, in lateral view, the bones have rotated secondarily – after deposition. When the skeleton lies on a flat-bottomed surface away from the walls of the grave pit, this movement, which is produced by the effect of gravity and determined by the shape of the cranium, is normal; on the other hand, if the cranium has remained in an unstable (unsupported) position resting on its occipital bone, or if it is just inclined to the side, then this movement will have been prevented or halted by an object that has disappeared through decomposition. Interpreting these constraints represents the beginning of the analysis, which consists of correlations of taphonomic events with one another and with the tangible elements of the grave structure.

The need to correlate archaeological and anatomical evidence and taphonomic events with one another

The first question addressed is that of the depositional environment in which decomposition took place, whether the burial occurred in a void or a filled space (Duday, 1990, 2009: 32–40). This determination will guide the analysis, the aim of which is to restore the original burial arrangement. As explained by Duday (1990, 2009), the evidence for decomposition in a void is based on 'positive' evidence: movements and displacements produced outside the initial space occupied by the body, whereas evidence for decomposition in a filled space is based on 'negative' evidence: the lack of movement or displacement outside of the initial space occupied by the body. In fact, decomposition in a filled space may be difficult to demonstrate as it depends on the nature of the sediment: for example, very gravelly sediment of fluvio-glacial origin does not produce the same effect as looser, fine-grained sediment. In the first case, the sediment will cover small bone elements and articulations as and when the soft tissue decomposes, producing an effect of delayed infilling of the initial space occupied by the body contingent upon the (variable) length of time the body takes to decompose (Duday, 1990), a process to which it is very difficult to attribute a taphonomic signature.

Although decomposition in a filled space is produced when the body is covered with earth during decomposition, it is important to resist convenient interpretations. Indeed, certain factors may contribute to the modification of the decompositional environment, such as intentional mummification prior to burial (Maureille and Sellier, 1996), low permeability of a coffin lid combined with very loose sediment, or the direct deposition of a body in a narrow grave pit with a concave floor (Castex and Blaizot, 2017: 278–281). Figures 1.1A and 1.1B illustrate these phenomena; in both cases the articulations are well-maintained, the initial space occupied by the body is preserved, notably the torso as indicated by the positions and appearance of the ribs, and the hands remain in anatomical connection in an unsupported and unstable position on the ribs. The two skeletons demonstrate a progressive infilling of the initial space occupied by the cadaver, but this cannot be attributed to the immediate covering of the body in the grave by sediment because traces of a lid, or of its presence exist. The narrowness of the grave pit, the grain size of the sediment and the permeable lid made from juxtaposed planks and branches (Blaizot, 1999) explain the rapidity of the infilling of the grave of skeleton A (Figure 1.1). In the second case, individual B, the grooved profile of the pit floor has allowed the initial space occupied by the body to be preserved and has also prevented small bones from rolling outside of that initial space (for further information, cf. Duday, 2009; Castex and Blaizot, 2017).

On the other hand, burials C and D in Figure 1.1 present characteristics which suggest immediate infilling of the grave pit. Skeleton C shows no signs of decomposition as reflected in the disarticulation of the skeleton in a void. The disarticulation of the cervical vertebrae is not significant because this has occurred beneath the cranium, which, due to its leaning against the wall of the pit, provided an underlying void. The position of the upper limbs, although leaning against the walls of the grave pit, are anomalous: for the right upper limb, even the bones of the hand are in an unsupported position, and for the left side, the distal end of the forearm is raised. Also, although the floor of the pit is flat, the three-dimensional space (the 'volume') occupied by the pelvis is preserved. As for skeleton D, the bones which abut the walls of the pit argue against the presence of a container, whereas all the movements recorded seem to have taken place within the initial space occupied by the body, but the sections made in the field reveal the collapse of the walls of the grave. The position of the cranium, the foot phalanges, the shoulders and the raised left hand may not, therefore, be signs of an immediate covering of the body but result from the presence of eroded soil from the edges of the pit that supported these structures in these positions. These examples demonstrate that analysis of taphonomic anomalies must never fail to consider field records, as 'field anthropology', the original name used for archaeothanatology, would suggest.

Some anomalies caused by an irregular pit floor may be misleading. For example, skeleton A in Figure 1.2 is characterised by a general 'stretching' in length produced by gaps between anatomical regions; these displacements were likely produced in a 'crescendo' (gradually increasing in extent) manner and relate to the effects of decomposition of a plank floor raised on sleepers

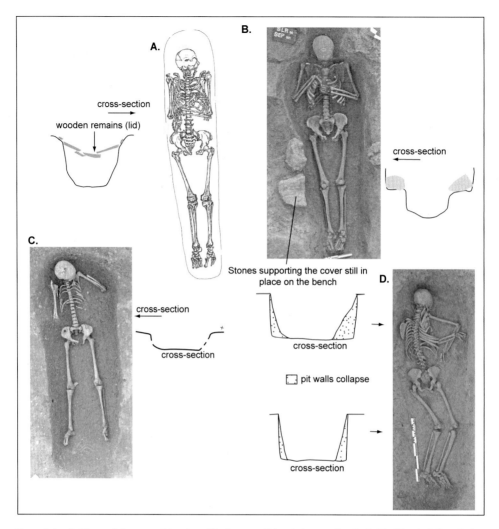

Figure 1.1 A. Signs of decomposition in a filled space of the skeleton of an individual buried directly in a pit dug in powdery wind-borne soil and closed with a lid (Porsuk, Uluktsla, Turkey, 11th–12th centuries AD); B. The same signs of decomposition in a filled space in a narrow pit with a concave floor, closed with a lid held in place with blocks on a 'bench' (Les Ruelles, Serris, France, 10th century AD); C and D. Immediate infilling of the pit after burial (C: Grange-Rouge, near Louhans, France, 16th century AD) and (D) with pit wall collapse (Quincieux, Rhône, Les Forgettes, 8th–9th centuries AD) (Images: F. Blaizot).

placed on a sloping pit floor (Blaizot, 2014, 2017). However, in this case, the ruptures and displacements of pieces of the plank floor were not caused by sleepers but by large stones of the sediment into which the pit was dug. Here, the instability produced by the plank floor reflects the presence of this wooden structure, which would not be the case with a flat pit floor (see below).

Variation in the size of grave pits has a considerable effect on the skeletal remains found within them, as shown by the skeletons illustrated in Figure 1.2B. In both cases the pit is the sole repository of the body, which had been covered with a lid, but the cross-sections are different. The flattened floor beneath the upper half of skeleton 904 has allowed the pelvis to open out and the V-shaped profile located beneath the knees has drawn the long bones of the lower limbs and feet toward the median longitudinal axis of the body. The sternal ends of the ribs are upright

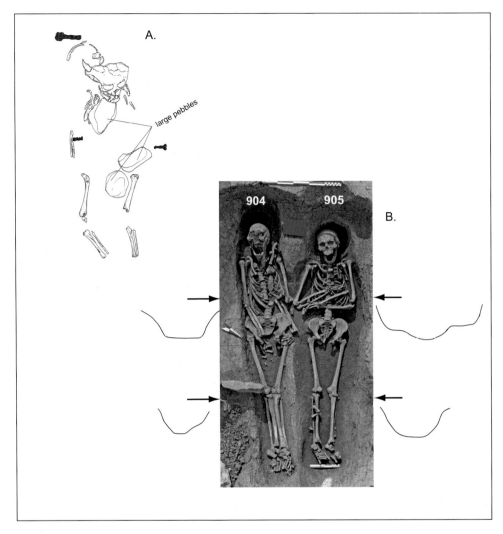

Figure 1.2 A. Displacement and breakup of a plank floor caused by the presence of large pebbles in the sediment (Clinique Saint-Charles, Lyon, 4th century AD); B. Example of two graves in which the cross-sections differ but in which each body was buried directly in a pit (Les Ruelles, Serris, France, 10th century AD) (Images: F. Blaizot).

because of the narrowness of the pit. Beneath the upper half of skeleton 905, the pit has the profile of a ledged gutter which explains the preservation of the initial volume for the pelvis and ribs through the presence of the gutter and the position of the elbows slightly away from the trunk on the ledge, whereas the lower limbs have remained largely in place owing to the trough-like profile beneath them.

Unexpected events that generate re-arrangements should not be mistaken for phenomena due to the decomposition of burial furnishings. For example, the settling of an underlying pit or an animal burrow may produce displacements which could be confused with the collapse of a lid or wall, or the instability of a plank floor (Figures 1.3 and 1.4). The collapse of a wall or a lid produces disarticulations and displacements in the same direction (as in Figure 1.3, skeleton A and in Figure 1.4, skeletons A and C), while the passage of a burrowing animal, if it occurs while

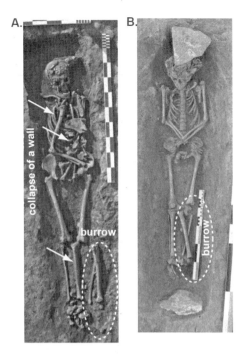

Figure 1.3 Examples of taphonomic anomalies caused by burrowing animals. A. Example from the second third of 8th to early 11th centuries AD from Les Ruelles, Serris, France; B. Les Forgettes, Quincieux, Rhône, France 8th–9th centuries AD (Images: F. Blaizot).

the pit is unfilled, will push the bones to either side of this 'corridor' (as in skeleton B, Figure 1.4), stacking of the bones (as in the skeletons from Figures 1.3A and 1.4B), or even lifting them (as in Figure1.3B and the right radius of skeleton C in figure 1.4C).

The collapse of a lid can also cause segments in anatomical connection to pivot, as is the case in Figure 1.5A. The re-arrangements recorded here do not result from the displacement due to a plank floor as no sign of collapse is observed; there are no strongly tilted or inverted bone elements, none have slid behind others, and there is no plate effect[2] (Duday, 2009; Blaizot, 2014). The re-arrangements observed for groups of bone elements, the right ribs and the middle thoracic vertebrae, the last two thoracic vertebrae, and the first four lumbar vertebrae, must relate to the displacement of the manubrium, but that of the left twelfth rib and the tenth thoracic vertebra, and the lifting and displacement of the sacrum into a position anterior to the left ilium suggest that a violent collapse from above the right-hand side of the skeleton (the humerus has not been displaced) had occurred. These re-arrangements can be compared to those affecting the skeleton in Figure 1.5B; although the movement of the right shoulder and upper limb may follow from a collapse of the wall on this side, and the re-arrangements affecting the median part of the thoracic and abdominal areas can be attributed to the displacement of parts of a plank floor. In fact, the inversion, tilting and alignment of some ribs to the median longitudinal axis of the skeleton, as well as the displacement and inversion of the thoracic vertebrae illustrate the effects

---

2 'Plate effect' refers to overlying bones from one anatomical region by bones of another anatomical region when maintained in a position of contact with one another (cf. Chapter 34, this volume, '*Effet de plaque*').

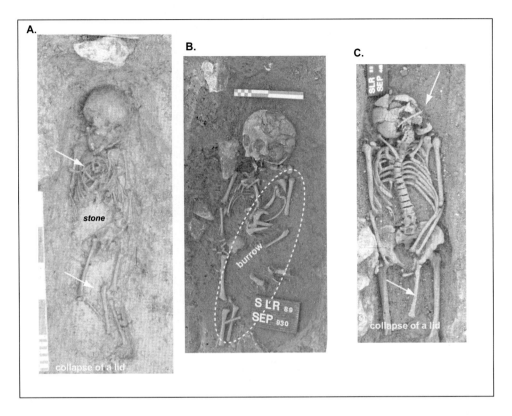

Figure 1.4 Examples of taphonomic anomalies caused by burrowing animals and collapse of walls and/or a lid. A, B and C. Examples from the second third of the 8th to early 11th centuries AD from Les Ruelles, Serris, France (Images: F. Blaizot).

of a marked collapse of the vertebral column which has tumbled towards the bottom of the grave pit (Figure 1.5B). The hypothesis of a collapsed plank floor can be argued due to the 'plate effect' observed beneath the knees, with the distal ends of the femora overlapping with the proximal ends of the tibiae. Displacements generated by water can produce at first impression similar anomalies. However, they are characterised by movements which are very often independent of the morphological characteristics of the pit (for example, the direction of floor tilt), and by the frequent overlying of cancellous-filled elements, or by the position of such elements a few centimetres above the pit floor; the *ossa coxae* often pivot on their axis. In skeleton 1.5C the left *os coxae* has pivoted through 45° and has been displaced downwards with the left patella lying on it, the sacrum has migrated in front of the left upper ribs, a lumbar vertebra can be seen in front of the left elbow, another in the pelvis and a third between the femora (Figure 1.5, skeleton C).

Displacements by water are not always a stumbling block to interpretation; they may also permit burial arrangements to be clarified through revision of earlier interpretations. In the example of a burial in a stone sarcophagus (Figure 1.6A) displacements caused by variations in the water table are illustrated by downward displacement of the cranium, the right *os coxae*, and the thoracic and lumbar vertebrae, the right clavicle, the right tibia and the left fibula, and upward displacement of the left tibia, the left radius, and the thoracic and lumbar vertebrae. Spongy (i.e. cancellous-filled) bones, such as vertebrae, had floated because they lie a few centimetres above the floor of the stone sarcophagus. It can be seen, however, that the displaced bones do not touch

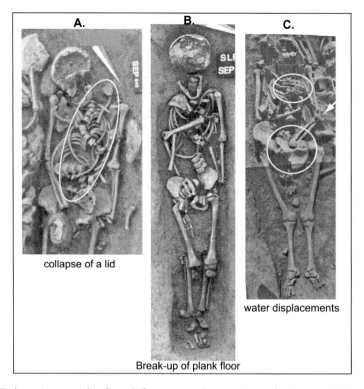

Figure 1.5 Taphonomic anomalies from different causes that may be confused, examples from Les Ruelles, Serris, France. A. Lid collapse, late 8th–10th centuries AD; B. Breakup of plank floor, 9th century AD; C. Water displacements, second third of 8th to late 9th centuries AD (Images: F. Blaizot).

the walls of the sarcophagus but are found in a small rectangular area; the body had been placed in a wooden container within the stone sarcophagus. The once presence of a wooden container can also be supported by the lateral orientation of the inferior parts of the scapulae; this position indicates that the upper limbs were in abduction at the time of deposition, and thus the elbows were leaning against a wall that has not preserved. The second example concerns a series of well-preserved Neolithic skeletons excavated at Clermont-Ferrand (Puy-de-Dôme, France) which have no, or very few, hand and foot bones. During the 1980s this phenomenon was interpreted as evidence for mutilation of the body but was explained differently after a further excavation of the site. As the burial pits were not visible on the surface, a large surface area was excavated level by level, revealing small bones scattered at a distance from the skeleton and lying at various depths, up to 15 cm. These variations can be explained by fluctuations of the water table, which has since been confirmed by geoarchaeological analysis showing that during the Middle Neolithic the area had been marshland (Figure 1.6B)

Finally, it should be recalled that preserved parts of the funerary architecture, such as nails, stones and tiles, must be subject to the same recording requirements as the bones and are essential in order to understand movements of remains during the process of decomposition. For example, stones may be used to prevent a single-log coffin from rolling, to wedge plank walls, or even to keep a lid in place (as illustrated in Figure 1.1B). Only meticulous analysis of the position of these objects, their location, depth, tilt, and their relationships to taphonomic anomalies can define their role (see below). Similarly, the presence of nails does not necessarily signify a coffin in which all the parts (the floor, sides and lid) are nailed together. A precise three-dimensional record,

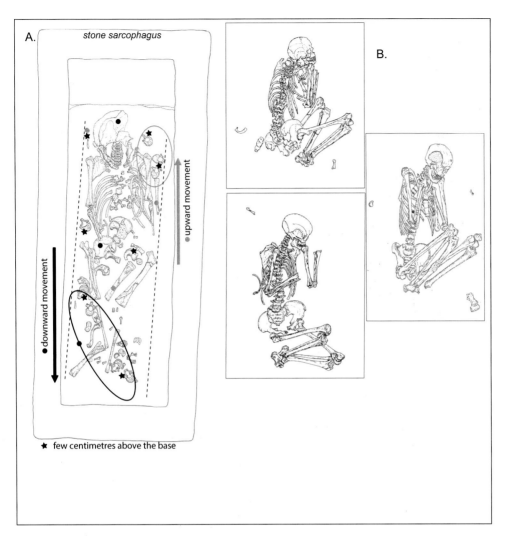

Figure 1.6 A. Water displacements attesting to the presence of a wooden container inside a sarcophagus (Mairie, Saint-Paul-Trois-Châteaux, Drôme, Late Antique); B. Fluctuation of the water table producing displacement of smaller bones (Le Brézet, Clermont-Ferrand, Puy-de-Dôme, second half of the 5th millennium BC) (Images: F. Blaizot).

showing their orientations, and the analysis of their position relative to the archaeothanatological evidence from the skeleton can reveal much more varied constructions.

Containers exist where only the lid is joined to the sides; some nails may not belong to the container but rather to a lid that had sealed the grave pit, whereas other isolated nails may come from salvaged planks that were used occasionally to repair a container. At least six nails from burial A in Figure 1.7 can be linked to the presence of a lid because they are in contact with the bones of the superior half of the skeleton. Four of them have one end turned down over what appears to be the width of a wooden piece, which could suggest the longitudinal planks of a lid put together by means of cleats. The ten nails located on either side of and very close to the skeleton probably relate to the attachment of the lid to the long sides of the container, as all but three lie between 3 and 8 cm above the floor of the grave pit. In example B in Figure 1.7, where all the

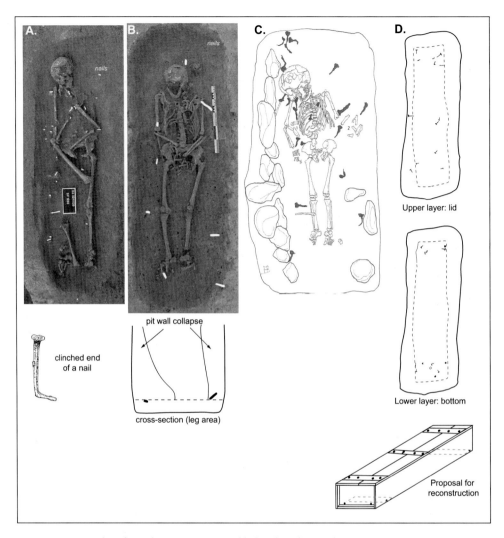

Figure 1.7 Examples of wooden structures assembled with nails. A and B. Les Forgettes at Quincieux, Rhône (mid-4th to mid-5th centuries AD and mid-5th to 7th centuries AD, respectively); C. 25 rue de Flesselle, Lyon (mid-3rd to 4th centuries AD); D. La Grande Borne at Clermont-Ferrand, Puy-de-Dôme (last quarter of the 3rd–4th centuries AD) (Images: F. Blaizot).

nails lie between 5 and 12 cm above the floor of the pit, three were found far from the skeleton in various orientations. Two hypotheses can be proposed in this case. The first is that the nails belonged to the lid of the container, which- from the taphonomic anomalies- can be interpreted as a coffin made from a single log of wood, and the rotting of this container had caused the nails to fall to the base of the coffin. The distance of the nails would signify that the pit was unfilled but sealed by a cover. The second hypothesis is that the nails do not belong to the coffin at all but to this cover that sealed the pit. One of the nails is very large, of the type used by carpenters, and thus suggests the once presence of a sizeable cover. The depth and disorderly orientation of the nails in burial C in Figure 1.7 indicate that they had fallen into the grave pit from above. Lying above and to the right of the cranium and beyond the line of stones, the cluster of nails lying between 6 and 10 cm above the pit floor indicates the size of the cover that sealed the pit.

The nails correspond to those that define a transverse line and extend into the space occupied by a food deposit located to the side of the left elbow of the skeleton. They illustrate a construction whereby the planks of the cover had been fixed by a perpendicular piece of wood, and the differences in their construction are reflected in the different ways the cover had collapsed. The examples described above also demonstrate that tailored recording permits the methods of plank assembly to be clarified. In burial D in Figure 1.7, where the planks had been fixed by transverse cleats, two had been used for the floor and three for the lid.

Reconstructing the burial arrangement, organisation and architecture: a difficult exercise

Although archaeothanatological observations and recording permit insight into the arrangement, shape and architecture of grave furnishings made from perishable materials, it is very important to fully understand that the identification, classification, and interpretation of taphonomic anomalies does not provide a direct reading of the original object. The analysis produces variables that can explain the internal mechanism of an event, such as constraints, collapse, plate effects, and gutter effects, which can provide the explanatory background for a series of events, but the reconstruction of the relevant burial arrangements is an interpretation of these events. The preceding examples have shown that imponderable factors may obscure or modify the course of events due to the effects of water, varying types and timings of collapse, grave wall erosion, irregular pit floors, and burrowing animals. In fact, all events deriving from the same phenomenon may not be expressed in the same way, nor will others occur systematically: the patterns needed for the interpretation of specific events as revealed through the analysis of anomalies may not be found together in the grave. In short, the different stages of decomposition linking the anomalies that define an event, and the correlation of events with one another, provide potential explanations but must also accommodate missing and irrelevant information that is the result of random interactions between variables, intrinsic to the initial type of burial and extrinsic circumstantial variables from the grave context. These processes can be illustrated through the use of several examples addressed below.

The initial indicator for the deposition of a container in an unfilled pit (a 'chamber grave') is wall collapse (Figure 1.8A); such collapses are more likely to be seen in cross-section than in plan, and their identification requires the infilling of the excavated pit incrementally. Walls built of stone or tile which fall or tilt towards the exterior also represent evidence that the pit was furnished (see below with discussion of Figure 1.11A). This can also be deduced from the extent of displacement of bones or anatomical segments beyond the limits of the initial space occupied by the burial container. This is the case when a wooden floor, originally raised on sleepers, breaks into several separate parts (as in Figure 1.2, skeleton A) (cf. Blaizot, 2014: figs. 8, 9, 10, 11), as a result of a burrowing animal (as in Figure 1.4, skeleton B) or when a wall collapses, as in a burial under a wooden, saddleback cover (as in Figure 1.8, skeleton B) – the left humerus lies beyond the limit of the container, itself recognised by the constraint of the left foot maintained in an unstable position.

Finally, other, sometimes indirect, observations may support the presence of a hypothetical chamber grave. For example, Merovingian stone slab graves that were once sealed by a wooden cover permitted re-use for multiple burials as revealed by the analysis of the disarticulated bones of successively interred individuals. Because re-use of graves requires access to the deposits inside and re-organisation of their contents is required. Archaeothanatological analysis of the piles of bones (Duday, 1987; Blaizot, 1996) shows that they were re-organised with each successive deposit, as the example in Figure 1.8, burial C, illustrates. Analysis of second-order anatomical

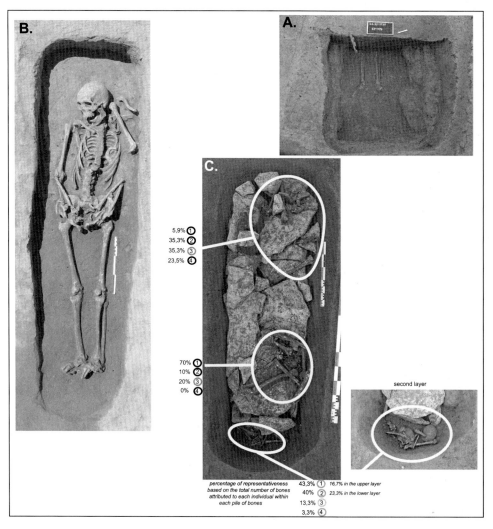

Figure 1.8 Indicators of fitted pits: A. Les Forgettes, Quincieux, Rhône (mid-4th to mid-5th centuries AD); B. Burial from Lalabre at Châteauneuf-du-Rhône, Drôme (Late Antiquity); C. Les Forgettes, Quincieux, Rhône (mid-6th to 7th centuries AD) (Images: F. Blaizot).

connections[3] reveals the remains of four unequally represented skeletons, the bones of which are mixed together in three areas of the grave: the east and west quarters of the cover and the east end of the pit floor. Nevertheless, the bones from skeletons 1 and 2 in Figure 1.8C were mainly found at the east end (65% and 64%), while the bones from skeletons 3 and 4 in the same figure, although less well-represented, were mainly found on the lid of the slab construction (Figure 1.8C). Although the bones of skeleton 2 were found dispersed more or less similarly throughout the east end heap, those from skeleton 1 are principally found in the upper part of the heap (62%), while those from skeletons 3 and 4 lie at the bottom. It could be that this pile at the east

---

3 Matching of elements from the same individual based on articular contiguity, robustness, bone size and appearance (Duday, 1987) (cf. Chapter 34, this volume).

end had been formed during the primary inhumation of skeleton 1, whose degree of representativeness may indicate that it was the penultimate burial. Another scenario is just as likely, though; this space was chosen for secondary deposits at the time of the second burial, and the heap was re-organised at each subsequent deposit by a reduction in the number of bones preserved, as would seem to be indicated by the relative under-representation of skeletons 3 and 4. Finally, the fact that the bones from the different skeletons present are not separated by soil is evidence that at least one cover sealed the cavity formed by the slab construction.

Nevertheless, in numerous cases, burials do not provide sufficient evidence enabling a chamber grave to be identified: the container may not have been placed in an unsupported position, the sides of the container were neither displaced, nor had they collapsed, phenomena which would draw the bones in their wake, and the pit may not have been preserved in sufficient depth to observe the possible collapse of the edges. The presence of walls determined by the constraints recorded on the skeleton does not necessarily imply that the body had been deposited in a complete, transportable container: panels may have simply been erected around the body placed directly on the pit floor. Generally, arguments in favour of a plank floor can only be sustained when the base becomes unstable during the decomposition of the body, or when its own decomposition produces disruptions or collapse in a U-shape, its former presence indicated by the position of the skeleton (Duday, 2009: 48; Blaizot, 2014: 265–269).

On the other hand, absence of evidence is not evidence of absence, as skeleton A from Figure 1.9 demonstrates: although the skeleton shows no specific anomaly indicating a plank floor, with only limited pelvic opening, ribs pointing downwards and not horizontally, and with skeletal integrity retained, woody traces found on the pit floor beneath the skeleton indicate the presence of a container with a plank base. The difficulties in determining the form of plank containers, rectangular, trapezoidal or hexagonal, will not be addressed here any further (see Blaizot, 2014: 265–269), but suffice it to recall that collapse of a plank base can modify the interpretation of the original form of a container. This is the case in burial B in Figure 1.9, where the position of the feet, maintained in medial view, and medial to the elements of the lower limb above, does not indicate the trapezoidal plan of the container but results from the collapse of the U-form coffin base; the knees of the skeleton are turned inwards, medially, while the tibiae remain in anterior view, which is anatomically incompatible. The knees and, to a lesser degree, the feet have slipped into the newly formed concavity in the direction of the longitudinal median axis of the body (Figure 1.9B).

The collapse of plank floors into a trough-like depression may lead to the formation of an inaccurate impression, for example, leading to the reconstruction of a monoxylous (i.e. formed from a single wooden log) coffin whose concavity may vary not only from one example to another but also among containers of a similar type (Blaizot, 2014: 269–273). The constraints recorded on skeleton C in Figure 1.9 indicate a narrow container, whereas the displacement toward the median plane of the right lower limb and foot, as well as that of the left foot, demonstrates either the presence of a soft lining at the bottom of the container, or a U-shaped section of the base at this level. The raised distal end of the left humerus with its proximal end seen in lateral view is compatible with oblique walls, as is, though to a lesser extent, its complete medial rotation, even though the shaft is not found in front of the ribs. This anatomical region, however, does not show signs of attraction towards the longitudinal median axis of the body. In support of the once presence of a hypothetical monoxylous container, it would seem that the floor was carved deeply, in the form of a gutter in the area of the legs (tibiae and fibulae) and feet, the left being less inclined than that of the right side. However, analysis of wood remains shows that fibres from the base are oriented west/east, while elements from the sides are oriented north/south, which is

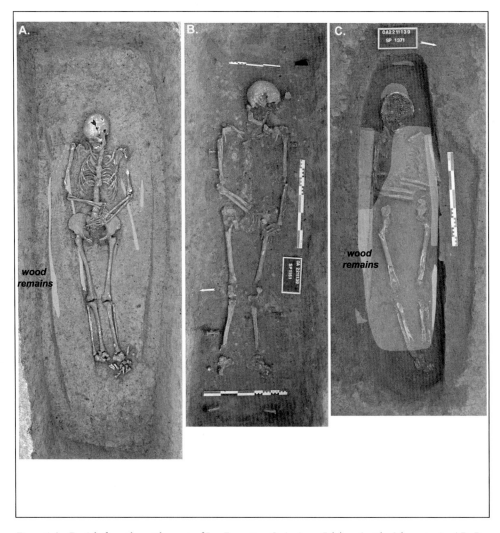

Figure 1.9 Burials from the settlement of Les Forgettes, Quincieux, Rhône. A. 6th–8th centuries AD; B. mid-4th to mid-5th centuries AD; C. mid-5th to 6th centuries AD (Images: F. Blaizot).

an argument in favour of assembled wooden pieces and refutes the hypothesis of a monoxylous coffin. The anomalies observed involving the lower half of the skeleton could then instead be attributed to a longitudinal collapse attested by the position of the left foot placed partly behind the right foot.

This last example highlights two major difficulties encountered in this exercise, the first being to reconstruct the architecture of the container (e.g. nailed coffin, un-nailed plank coffin, monoxylous coffin), and the second to reconstruct the original form of the burial. The plan of the container indicated by the skeletal anomalies recorded suggests that a hollowed-out tree trunk rather than a plank container was involved, but taking into account the median displacement of the left lower limb and the observed constraints of the skeletal remains, including the unstable contact between the cranium, the right shoulder and upper limb, and the raised left elbow, a hexagonal plan is suggested. As analysis of the wood fibres has demonstrated that the container is formed of planks, this hexagonal plan may be explained by the use of warped panels, but the symmetry evident in the distribution of the skeletal remains renders this hypothesis doubtful; in this case, the use of laterally convex planks attached to a boat-shaped base may be imagined, similar to vessels constructed of pegged or tied planks or to barrels bound by vegetal strapping. Such a construction reminiscent of boat-shaped stone sarcophagi of the same period but this time in wood, unless it is simply a container made from a hexagonal wooden plank construction held together without nails.

In archaeological contexts where the edges of burial pits are not clearly defined, it may be difficult to differentiate a single-log bier with a widened trough-like floor from an anthropomorphic pit grave from burial under a wooden saddleback construction. The wooden saddleback construction is largely absent from regional typologies, probably because it is difficult to identify. In order to resolve this question analysis of taphonomic anomalies found in skeletons buried under tile saddleback constructions was undertaken to record recurrent features linked to their use. It can be clearly seen that the upright walls of this type of construction exert constraints on the cranium, the upper limbs according to their relative positions, on the *ossa coxae* and on the feet in a body lying on its back (as in Figure 1.10A). But these constraints are also found in pit graves due to their gutter-like floor and where the slanting walls of the grave pit widen, sometimes to form a ledge, and thus can exert the same type of constraints on the skeleton (Figure 1.10B).

When the walls are very slanted, their bases are placed at a distance from the upper members of the body (Figure 1.10C), and force is exerted on the most prominent parts of the skeleton, namely the cranium, which is found in an unstable position, and the feet which are in a plantarflexed position, as well as, to a lesser degree, the *ossa coxae*, which show very limited flattening (Figure 1.10D); the elbows may be a little apart from the body and slightly raised recalling the situation seen in pit graves. On the other hand, when the walls of the construction are only slightly slanted, the force exerted on the upper limbs is comparable to that generally found in single-log containers: the scapulae are in a protracted position, and the humeri are parallel to the vertebral column and in an elevated position (Figure 1.10E). Recording of the pit in both plan and cross-section, if the contours are clearly defined, as well as taking depth measures to beneath the bones (Duday, 1978), is therefore essential for understanding the cause of the anomalies observed in the skeleton.

The inhumation presented in Figure 1.10F, placed under a tile framework with a built floor, aids to illustrate this scenario. The incomplete rotation of the cranium and eversion of the feet and the slight opening of the pelvis are due to the slanting walls of the pit; the same applies to the left patella, which has fallen medially with respect to the femur when it fell to the side of the element. The close articulation of the pubic symphysis and the righting of the ribs is reminiscent of what is produced in a pit grave where the body lies directly on the floor of the grave: it sinks progressively into the sediment as it is softened by decomposition fluids. Certainly, the presence of tiles beneath the body indicates that this is not a pit grave; however, if the framework had not been built of tiles, the depth measures recorded beneath the skeleton, which determine a 'ground effect'[4] would support the rejection of a hypothetical pit grave based on the disposition of the skeletal remains: the elbows being distant from the torso, a fallen right patella, and a cervical vertebra, which are displaced above the left shoulder, lying at the same depth as the cranium, the vertebral column, and the calcanei. The relative maintenance of the ribs in anatomical position can thus be attributed, not to the pit profile, but to the permeability of the construction, with sediment entering gradually from above, which is probably also the case above for the pelvis, in addition to the force exerted by the slanting walls of the container.

---

4 '*Effet de terre*' in French is the effect exerted on the skeleton from the shape of the grave floor (cf. Chapter 34, this volume).

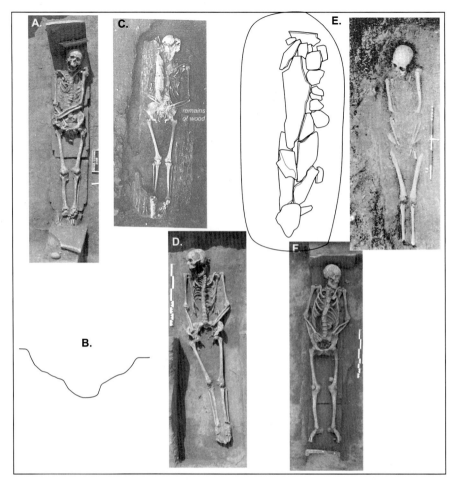

Figure 1.10   Similar taphonomic anomalies caused by different burial arrangements and architecture. A, D and F. Burials beneath a tile saddleback construction from Lalabre at Châteauneuf-du-Rhône, Drôme (4th–5th centuries AD); B. Cross-section of an anthropomorphic pit burial (9th century AD); C. Burial under a wooden saddleback construction from Saint-Georges at Vienne, Isère (6th–7th centuries AD); E. Burial under a stone slab saddleback construction from L'Esperelle at Roquemaure, Gard (6th–7th centuries AD) (Images: F. Blaizot).

In Europe archaeothanatological reconstructions may rely on only a few published assemblages in which perishable material has been preserved (as in water-logged conditions), or based on architectural arrangements of durable material, such as stone or tile constructions that, some-times, have been imitated in wood. The results of archaeothanatological analysis can then only be compared to these preserved examples that serve as references for those instances lacking such preservation. The exercise of reconstruction is a very complex undertaking, first of all due to the unusual nature of the arrangements themselves, with some of the constructions being hardly imaginable. At Landévennec (Finistère, Brittany, France), planks formed of small transverse beams were found, as well as constructions in which several poles covered the body and held in place above the bottom of the pit by long branches (Bardel and Perennec, 2012); at Quimper (Finistère, Brittany, France), containers excavated at Place Laënnec had slanting inner walls and flat lids, held together by mortise and tenon joints or cords (Dietrich *et al.*, 1999). Although the skeletons associated with these different contraptions indicate an unstable floor construction and collapse and constraints compatible with saddleback construction walls, respectively, neither archaeological nor archaeothanatological analyses facilitate a precise interpretation of the burial arrangements.

This complexity also arises due to the impact that several occurrences – combined – may exert on the skeleton, which is responsible for the uncertainty mentioned previously. A good example is provided by the cephalic niches found in various types of burial, including pit graves, sarcophagi, and stone constructions, as well as wooden containers such as single-log coffins that appear at the beginning of the Carolingian period (8th–9th centuries AD). A cephalic niche, when relatively closely fitting to the size of the head, maintains the cranium in frontal view along the vertebral axis. However, a great majority of single-log (i.e. monoxylous) containers have a gutter-shaped transverse cross-section internally, which contributes to maintenance of the cranium in this position as well; the presence of a cephalic niche may thus go unnoticed. Conversely, the rotation of the cranium within a monoxylous container may not indicate the absence of a cephalic niche but rather a flattening of the floor of the container and a greater width at the head-end of the container, providing an empty space that permits movement.

The difficulty of achieving accurate reconstructions is even more acute for periods lacking documentation, which is the case for most of the burials found in circular or shaft-type pits frequently encountered during the Neolithic period. In the example presented in Figure 1.11, the body had been placed in a niche in the wall at the bottom of a deep circular pit, with the *ossa coxae*, the right ribs, and feet abutting the pit walls. The modifications recorded for the left shoulder, with the left humerus and clavicle displaced upwards with respect to the scapula, indicate that the forearm provided a prop on the grave floor, which conforms to the incline recorded beneath the bones. When the position of the skeleton pressed against the rounded wall of the pit is taken into account, the nature of the empty space formed by the modification of the shoulder and the collapse of the knees cannot be equated with the presence of a wooden box. Similarly, the fact that the bones follow the shape and slope of the pit floor and its irregularities is incompatible with the hypothesis of a plank floor. Several arrangements may be envisaged to explain these phenomena, such as a container with non-rigid walls, one made of skin or basketwork, for example, or a series of inclined planks where one end rested on the pit floor at a distance from the body with the other end against the pit wall. One could also imagine a flat cover having been placed higher up at the entrance to the shaft. The archaeological evidence, combined with the lack of pictorial representations and stone fittings, does not facilitate more precise interpretations.

Conclusion

The reconstruction of the original arrangement, organisation and architecture of burials does not depend only on observations of the skeleton or immediately visible phenomena, but on an analysis conducted on the whole assemblage of the remains *in situ* and their reciprocal relations, which lie behind the causal mechanisms responsible for the anomalies linked to an event, but do not provide a direct explanation of the original arrangements. It must be remembered that in order to reconstruct plausible scenarios and hypothetical forms of burial, which are only a reflection of a more varied reality, the relationships between elements of the burial not in direct contact with the body are lost, for example, forms of containers and lids, but also details of construction methods, which often provide insights that permit differentiation of burials by period. Finally, it must be accepted that in a funerary assemblage, the arrangements of some burials cannot be interpreted because the circumstances of decomposition are not systematically reflected in the disposition of the skeleton or by the form of the burial pit, some burials being more informative than others.

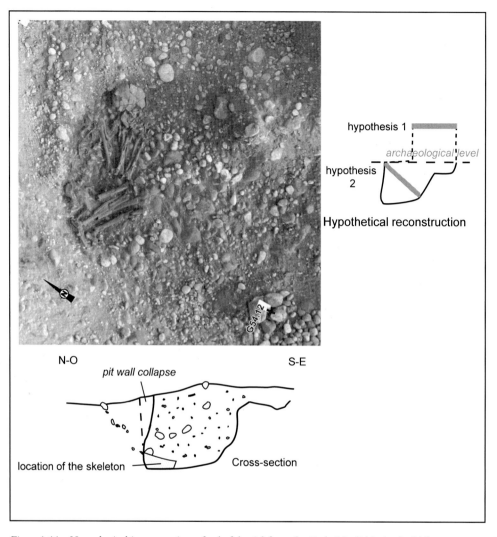

Figure 1.11 Hypothetical interpretation of a shaft burial from the Early Neolithic (end of 6th millennium BC or first half of the 5th millennium BC) at Meximieux, Ain, France. (Images: F. Blaizot).

This is why the question of 'methodological tools' is a delicate one: to become involved in archaeothanatology means being faced with many clues and riddles as well as countless solutions. The need to record the burial rigorously, in plan, cross-section and type of infill in the grave pit, the local environment of the grave, and anatomical anomalies of the skeleton is fundamental. Furthermore, archaeothanatological interpretations require access to references; just as it is not possible to practice philosophy without reading philosophers, it is difficult to practice archaeothanatology without full knowledge of the principles and examples upon which the method has been founded and of those which continue to enrich it. As Duday frequently states, archaeothanatology constructs its references as and when it is applied.

References

Bardel, A. and Perennec, R. (2012). Landévennec (Finistère): quelques aménagements funéraires en bois du VIIe au XIe s. In: *Le bois dans l'architecture et l'aménagement de la tombe: quelles approches?* Saint-Germain-en-Laye: Association française d'archéologie mérovingienne. Actes de la table-ronde d'Auxerre, 15–17 octobre 2009, Centre d'études médiévales d'Auxerre et DRAC de Haute-Normandie (Service régional de l'archéologie), Mémoires publiés par l'Association française d'Archéologie mérovingienne, XXIII, pp. 193–208.

Blaizot, F. (1996). L'apport des méthodes de la paléo-anthropologie funéraire à l'interprétation des os en situation secondaire dans les nécropoles historiques. *Archéologie Médiévale*, XXVI, pp. 1–22.

Blaizot, F. (1999). L'ensemble funéraire tardo-antique de Porsuk: approche archéo-anthropologique (Ulukisla, Cappadoce méridionale, Turquie). Résultats préliminaires. *Anatolia Antiqua Eski Anadolu*, VII, revue de l'Institut Français d'Études Anatoliennes, pp. 179–218.

Blaizot, F. (2014). From the skeleton to the funerary architecture: a logic of the plausible. In: A.-M. Tiller and M. Galetova, eds., *Methodological Approaches in Funerary Archaeology and Corpse Taphonomy, Anthropologie: International Journal of the Science of Man* (Brno), 52(3), pp. 263–284.

Blaizot, F. (2017). *Les espaces funéraires de l'habitat groupé des Ruelles, à Serris (Seine-et-Marne, Île-de-France) du VIIe au XIe s. De la restitution des dispositifs d'inhumation à l'organisation, la dynamique et l'expression des systèmes funéraires*. Bordeaux: Ausonius, Maison des Sciences de l'Homme d'Aquitaine, Travaux d'Archéologie Funéraire, Thanat'Os 4.

Castex, D. and Blaizot, F. (2017). Reconstructing the original arrangement, organisation and architecture of burials in archaeology. In: E.M.J. Schotsmans, N. Márquez-Grant and S.T. Forbes, eds., *Taphonomy of Human Remains: Forensic Analysis of the Dead and Depositional Environment*. Chichester: Wiley-Blackwell Publishers, pp. 277–295.

Dietrich, A., Gallien, V., Langlois, J.-Y., and Guillon, F. (1999). *Quimper (Finistère), Place Laënnec, rapport d'études de deux sépultures d'enfants*. Rennes: Association pour les Fouilles Archéologiques Nationales (Afan), Service régional de l'archéologie.

Duday, H. (1978). Archéologie funéraire et anthropologie. Application des relevés et de l'étude ostéologiques à l'interprétation de quelques sépultures pré- et protohistoriques du Midi de la France. *Cahiers d'Anthropologie*, 1, pp. 55–101.

Duday, H. (1987). Contribution des observations ostéologiques à la chronologie interne des sépultures collectives. In: H. Duday and C. Masset, eds., *Anthropologie Physique et Archéologie, Méthodes d'Étude des Sépultures*, Actes du colloque de Toulouse, 4–6 novembre 1982. Paris: Centre National de la Recherche Scientifique (CNRS), pp. 51–59.

Duday, H. (1990). Observations Ostéologiques et Décomposition du Cadavre: Sépultures en Espace Colmaté ou en Espace Vide? *Revue du Centre Archéologique de la France*, 19(2), pp. 193–196.

Duday, H. (2005). L'archéothanatologie ou l'archéologie de la mort. In: O. Dutour, J.-J. Hublin and B. Vandermeersch, eds., *Objets et Méthodes en Paléoanthropologie*. Paris: Comité des Travaux Historiques et Scientifiques (CTHS), pp. 153–217.

Duday, H. (2006). Archaeothanatology or the archaeology of death. In: R. Gowland and C.J. Knüsel, eds., *Social Archaeology of Funerary Remains*, translated by C.J. Knüsel. Oxford: Oxbow Books, pp. 30–56.

Duday, H. (2009). *The archaeology of the dead: lectures in archeothanatology*. Oxford: Oxbow Books.

Duday, H., Le Mort, F. and Tillier, A.-M. (2014). Archaeothanatology and funeral archaeology, application to the study of primary single burials. In: A.-M. Tiller and M. Galetova, eds., *Methodological Approaches in Funerary Archaeology and Corpse Taphonomy, Anthropologie: International Journal of the Science of Man* (Brno), 52(3), pp. 235–246.

Maureille, B. and Sellier, P. (1996). Dislocations en ordre paradoxal, momification et décomposition: observations et hypothèses, *Bulletins et Mémoires de la Société d'Anthropologie de Paris*, 8(3–4), pp. 313–328.

2

A TALE OF TWO WORLDS

Terminologies in archaeothanatology

Bruno Boulestin

PACEA, De la Préhistoire à l'Actuel: Culture, Environnement et Anthropologie,
UMR 5199, CNRS-Université de Bordeaux, Pessac, France

Introduction

Issues about terminology are often deemed futile ones, and surprisingly enough even famous archaeologists sometimes write that they do not truly matter. It must be said straightaway that, on the contrary, they are fundamental, and under no circumstances whatsoever should one consider making good science without the appropriate terminologies. That will, therefore, be the very first point to be discussed here. The quest for a terminology for the archaeology of death is a very long story, in English, as noted by Sprague (2005: 13ff.), and in French alike, and still the time when a simple and clear vocabulary that would allow researchers to communicate unequivocally with each other has not yet come. It is true for each language taken separately, and even more so when it comes to translating from one language to another. Some people do not seem to care, whereas others, on the contrary, are well aware of the need for change. In the English language, after several decades during which 'it appears that the accurate description of burials was sacrificed for "science" ' (Sprague, 2005: 7) owing to the pre-eminence of the New Archaeology at that point and to the predominance of models over observation, attempts have been made of late to sort out burial terminology (Sprague, 2005; Knüsel, 2014). In the advantageously more precise French language, the necessity to dust off the terminology became more and more urgent as archaeothanatology was developing. During the past 40 years, several researchers endeavoured to do so, and within this framework they conducted a thorough reflection on several concepts, among which that of burial is pivotal (see below). Some of the propositions produced by these works are quite interesting and testify to a change in the right direction, but there is still much to do to achieve a comprehensive and consistent vocabulary everyone can understand, even internationally. Is it necessary in the first place to re-examine words that have been used out of habit for decades and which, because their meaning is vague, ambiguous and sometimes even contradictory, still carry long-established errors. This implies the necessity to reflect on each and every concept requiring translation into words. The present chapter does not intend to resolve every difficulty that might be encountered; it only endeavours to emphasise the main ones and explain in what way they can be a problem. Above all, though, it aims at setting out the overall principles on which future work on terminology may rely.

DOI: 10.4324/9781351030625-4

Terminology: How, and for what?

In its primary meaning, a terminology is a group of specialised words belonging to a science or to a field of activities or knowledge which forms a system of concepts: these words are called terms. In this case, 'vocabulary' is sometimes used with the same sense. In this definition, it is necessary to clarify at once two important points related to one another.

To begin with, in what way are these words specialised? At first, they may be so because they are technical terms belonging exclusively to the specified field and are used only by specialists in this very field. This is, for instance, the case for most of the anatomical terminology. However, terms belonging to a specific terminology may also be used in the common language, the one used in everyday life – what Gallay (2011: 254) calls a natural language, as opposed to a scientific language. What makes these words specialised, then, is their linguistic use, which is specific to the field. To be more precise about it, whereas the specialised meaning more or less usually meets the common meaning, the scientific use is (or should be) more strictly controlled than the natural use.

The latter point leads to the second one, as indicated in the definition given earlier, namely the 'system of concepts'. In order to fully understand this idea, it is necessary to grasp the difference between notion and concept first. Both are abstract constructions and often mixed up, but in reality, they are opposites. A notion is intuitive knowledge which synthesises the main traits of an object (either abstract or concrete), yet without either precision or any scientific meaning. It usually covers a rather vague, yet implicit and widely accepted overall idea. The notion of 'skull', for instance, is so very commonly shared that everyone agrees on it and understands its meaning. On the contrary, the concept is a specified idea, created with more accuracy and precision by scientists or scholars for whom the meaning has been set once and for all. For an anthropologist, for instance, a skull without its face is not a skull anymore: the term refers only to a specific and precisely defined state of preservation of the skeleton of the head (when whole); other states of preservation are described using other terms, such as neurocranium for the faceless skull (Boulestin, 2015). In sum, the difference between notion and concept lies in the degree of precision. The notion is merely perceived, whereas the concept is built and conceived through scientific analysis that defines its characteristics and discriminates what belongs precisely to the underlying idea: hence, the production of concepts is the task of researchers. Back to the issue of specialised words, the notion characterises the natural, common language, and is accepted everywhere. The concept characterises the specialised, scientific language; it is more accurate and better controlled, but in return it is, in principle, limited to a specific field, outside which it is not effective. Lastly, concept and specialisation are the basis for the difference between an ordinary word and a term (Khan, 2016).

Concepts are thus the key to a terminology or at least a good terminology. Why is terminology necessary? To describe, of course, but above all to communicate unambiguously using a specialised language in a specific field, to permit researchers to understand each other and to be sure that the idea behind a word is the same for every researcher. That is why notions are not enough: most of the time, they are far too imprecise to be used in a technical or scientific discourse that everyone must understand similarly. Imprecision has another consequence, though, beyond the mere descriptive issue: it hinders the interpretation of the facts considerably. Lacking enough precision means running the risk of placing facts of different orders on the same level and at once preventing any further more general analysis. Misusing a word, or giving it an incorrect meaning, means not only to wrongly qualify the facts but also, of course, to misconceive the ideas it represents. Finally, it is important to stress that the problems of imprecision are crucial when it comes to translations where bilingual or multilingual terminology is considered. It is indeed not only just the question of translating a word, which any dictionary can do, but of transposing an idea. Here, again, this is why concepts have to be defined very accurately in order to use terms which describe the same objects with confidence when translated from one language to another.

The production of concepts necessary to establish a terminology is the task of researchers, above all things because it means undertaking some genuine, often long-lasting research. It requires managing, sorting out, and processing all the intuitive and imprecise notions, so that a consistent vocabulary will eventually come out, along with clearer synonyms and definitions. It took over a century, for instance, from the first *Basiliensia Nomina Anatomica* in 1895 (Jamieson, 1916) to the current applicable issue of the *Terminologia Anatomica* (FIPAT, 2011) to thoroughly sort out the international anatomical classification, which relies, however, on simple concepts. It can take many years, though, for a single complex concept to be characterised satisfactorily. Take the example of the concept of burial. It does not belong to any particular terminology, yet the burial is the main object of study in archaeothanatology and in the archaeology of death; it is pivotal, whatever the approach. Paradoxically, though, for most researchers this topic remains a mere notion. English-speaking researchers, in particular, never took the trouble to address the issue until recently. Things turned out differently in France owing to the development of archaeothanatology. The first archaeological definition of *sépulture* (French for 'burial') was proposed in 1988 by Leclerc and Tarrête. Many discussions followed, though, to achieve a more refined concept (Leclerc, 1990; Boulestin and Duday, 2005, 2006; Baray and Boulestin, 2010: 13–27, 139–165) which led, more than a quarter of a century later, to the following formulation: '*Lieu où sont déposés les restes d'un ou de plusieurs défunts, ce dépôt étant conçu comme définitif et intervenant dans le cadre d'une cérémonie dont la finalité est d'honorer au moins un des défunts au travers de sa dépouille*' ('a place in which the remains of one or several dead individuals are deposited, this deposition being considered as permanent and taking place within the framework of a ceremony which aims at honouring at least one of the dead through their remains') (Boulestin, 2012: 37). This in-depth work enabled archaeologists, at least French ones, to realise that each and every deposit of human remains cannot be generously termed a burial: the choice between burial and non-burial is often obvious, yet sometimes it demands a real discussion and, at times, the distinction is impossible to make. As Leclerc (1990: 13) put it: '*Reconnaître une sépulture, ce n'est jamais une simple constatation; ce ne peut être qu'une interprétation des vestiges*' ('acknowledging a burial is never a simple factual observation; it can only be an interpretation of the archaeological remains').

Burial was chosen as an example because it is a fundamental research topic, and also because it perfectly demonstrates that one cannot jump automatically from a notion to a concept. To make this transition requires systematic reflection on the ideas behind the words, though this reflection may not always be equally complicated. This choice also made it clear that even though a concept has been defined satisfactorily, its application sometimes requires an interpretation. In this way, the concept of burial is an interpretative concept. As such, it is different from the concept of skull, and more generally speaking from those of the anatomical terminology mentioned above, which refer to terms used for description only, requiring no interpretation whatsoever. These are thus descriptive concepts. The difference between the two forms of concept is fundamental, in particular when it comes to terminological issues. To delve further into this point, it is necessary to return to some aspects of reasoning in archaeology, in general, and in archaeothanatology, in particular.

Some major points with regard to reasoning in archaeology and their impact on terminologies

There is no use giving a detailed account on reasoning in archaeology here since several excellent works have theorised the interpretative mechanisms in this discipline; it suffices to take a closer look at those proposed by Gardin (1979 in particular, 1980 for the English translation) and Gallay (1986, 2011). As a reminder, put most simply, archaeologists generally use two reasoning processes. The first is built based on the observation of material remains and leads to conclusions pertaining to social behaviours: this is the empirical inductive approach. The transition from observations to conclusions is built through a sequence of inferences or interpretative suggestions. The second process follows the opposite direction: relying on a theoretical framework, the archaeologist develops some hypotheses, tries to deduce from them observable material consequences, then does fieldwork to try and find elements that can validate them: this is the hypothetico-deductive approach. The chapter on accompanying dead provides an example of this approach in archaeothanatology (cf. Boulestin, Chapter 5, this volume). Both approaches, inductive and deductive, are ideals, though in practice, they co-exist and intertwine frequently.

Whether priority is given to observations in order to build a more general theory, or, on the other hand, to the theoretical framework in order to provide validation experimentally through the examination of empirical data, one thing does not change: there are two clearly different worlds, that of facts, observations, and data on the one hand, and that of theories, models and hypotheses on the other; in other words, a descriptive and (in principle) objective world, versus an interpretative and subjective one. Of course, both worlds are interconnected – the very goal being to connect them – but they are, nevertheless, separated by a frontier, or at least a threshold. According to Gallay (2011: fig. 6.6), this threshold marks the limit between what pertains to science (typological and compiling constructions based on material facts) and what pertains to plausible logic (explanatory constructions based on interpretative options). Whatever the scientific work carried out, this threshold should be respected and marked because facts are usually unchangeable: once an observation has been acknowledged and validated, there is no reason why it should be modified. On the contrary, interpretations are free; they may vary according to the authors and change over time. It cannot be otherwise: a single archaeological vestige cannot but suggest several competing interpretations since an unequivocal relationship between a given observation and a specific explanation hardly ever exists. The descriptive basis of reasoning has thus to be fixed and only the interpretative component must be allowed to vary. It becomes clear, then, that if the threshold between them is not respected, and if interpretative elements are incorporated in the descriptions, there is a high risk of fixing them as well. As a consequence, the meaning attached to the facts will be very difficult to remove later. This is often how premises that are at first considered hypothetical turn progressively into supposed knowledge.

This major issue has obvious consequences for archaeological terminologies. Terminologies that claim to be simply descriptive have nevertheless often a tendency to mingle interpretations and descriptions almost systematically. This is true in the first place for material vestiges and features since the terms used to describe them have, in most cases, a functional meaning, referring more often to uses than to forms (they are defined by analogy with objects whose function is known, or even, when there is no possible comparison, with the idea of what their function could be). Considering tools, for example, it has long been pointed out that their real function could be very different from that implied by their name (e.g. Péquart, 1938; Cauvin, 1983). Many scrapers were certainly never used to scrape or scratch anything, and neither were most of the burins used to cut or carve. The same remark applies to features: many of those termed 'hearth' certainly never saw any fire, and 'silos' are aplenty which never contained any grain. Archaeologists have long been wont to make do, yet all these words do not respect the threshold between description and interpretation, and consequently, they should be used only when it comes to interpretation. For objects and features, though, there are a number of technical constraints which nevertheless imply a certain degree of functional convergence. But when descriptions refer to behaviours, integrating a functional dimension into the observational vocabulary raises many more problems. Terms are then defined at best by analogy with behaviours documented in ethnohistory, at worst based on ethnocentric interpretations. Different practices can obviously result in the same material consequence, and a single practice can lead to different results: there is never any strict and univocal correspondence between a given observation and a practice (let alone a social fact).

From all these remarks, the following basic principles can be established, which ideally, all archaeological terminologies should respect.

1. Whether descriptive or interpretative, the vocabulary must be defined on the basis of clear concepts, and not on more or less approximate notions, in order to avoid any ambiguity among researchers and to make the translation from one language to another easier.
2. The language which is used must respect the threshold between the interpretative and descriptive worlds, or, as Gallay (2011: 256) puts it, if the scientific speech and the literary speech are both legitimate, both must be accepted as such and clearly dissociated. In practice, this implies that the same terms cannot be used on both sides of the threshold: descriptive and interpretative terminologies cannot share any terms.
3. Interpretative terminologies must obviously be built on the basis of concepts developed from data coming from ethnohistory or social anthropology since the ideas covered by the terms have to reflect the intentions of the agent's actions. These terminologies are used in reasoning in order to define a field of possibilities, but one must remain aware that even though social concepts are precisely defined, applying them to archaeological data requires further interpretation (see the example of burial above).
4. It is essential to endeavour to find the lexical resources to describe the facts accurately without any *a priori* interpretation, which in practice means the use of only descriptive terms in descriptive terminologies. For years this position was defended by Leroi-Gourhan, who introduced the notion of *vocabulaire d'attente*; its translation into English by Darcque and Van de Moortel (2009) as 'non-committal vocabulary' is probably the best way to account for the concept. Leroi-Gourhan indeed wanted to develop a vocabulary made up of generic descriptive terms, in order to avoid engaging the meaning too early, and consequently to leave the door open for further reflection: '*un vocabulaire qui ne laisse pas une partie des faits inaperçue ou qui n'emprisonne pas les observations dans une architecture préétablie et arbitraire*' ('a vocabulary that does not leave a part of the facts unnoticed, nor imprisons the observations in a pre-established and arbitrary architecture') (Leroi-Gourhan, 1975: 1). The quest for this vocabulary was mostly pursued within seminars held at the *Collège de France* – one of which dealt with the vocabulary of burials (Leroi-Gourhan, 1975) – but, unfortunately, the reports remain in the form of grey literature and far too restricted in their dissemination. And yet, this way is precisely the one to follow.

The particular case of reasoning in archaeothanatology

In principle, reasoning in archaeothanatology is not different from that applied more generally in archaeology: it is no more than an application to the specific field of mortuary practices. The details are addressed in other chapters of the present book, nevertheless, the general principle of the archaeothanatological approach ought to be recalled.

In archaeothanatology as it has been conceptualised and defined originally by Boulestin and Duday (2005, 2006) on the basis of the latter's previous works, the analysis of mortuary practices is no longer focused on the features or on the goods found with the dead, but on the dead themselves, which is the major difference with the archaeology of death, as it was initially conceived by English-speaking researchers (Brown, 1971; Chapman, Kinnes and Randsborg, 1981). Archaeothanatological research is based, to begin with, on a precise analysis of how the human remains are organised, and how they relate to each other at the moment they are uncovered in order to reconstruct, in the first instance their post-depositional taphonomic history, and then, from there, their arrangement at the time of the final deposition, as well as the way the assemblage was constituted.[1] This initial approach is supposed to begin in the field through observations and meticulous recording, which is why in France, it used to be called *anthropologie de terrain* (field anthropology) and led to the creation of a true professional body of archaeologists of death, trained both in archaeology and human osteology. Nevertheless, an analysis can sometimes be carried out at least partially *a posteriori* on documents such as plans or photographs (Boulestin, 2016). Yet, archaeothanatology should not be reduced to field anthropology: even though the dead are placed centre-stage, it does not neglect grave goods and the features that contain them in any way; it tries to define at best mortuary behaviours and place them in their chrono-cultural context by taking into account all their dimensions. Lastly, like the standard archaeology of death, the ultimate goal of archaeothanatology is to derive information on the structure and organisation of the early societies from the analysis of mortuary practices. At this level, the interpretations put forward are based in particular on models constructed upon data taken from social anthropology and ethnohistory.

To sum up, the archaeothanatological approach thus involves three phases. The first is field observations, the second is reconstructing the disposition of the remains at the time of their final deposition, and the way the assemblage was constituted, and the third is the interpretations in terms of mortuary behaviours and social information more generally. The threshold between descriptive and interpretative worlds can be placed immediately between phases 2 and 3. This implies already that different vocabularies must be used for phases 1 and 2 on the one hand, and for phase 3 on the other, and also that the terminologies used for the former two must be composed only of descriptive terms and noncommittal vocabulary. Phase 3 will not be developed here. It concerns the unseen, what has not been passed on, the immaterial, such as behaviours, social facts, and ideas, as well as the material part that has not been preserved, in other words, all that calls for interpretations and hypotheses. For this phase, concepts and terminologies must be based on data from ethnohistory or from social anthropology, as, for instance, the concept of burial previously addressed (theoretically, only in this phase can a burial be qualified as such). At this level, there is very often a lesser or greater degree of uncertainty, and many times it is impossible to decide between various interpretations. Phases 1 and 2 have been developed in detail in other publications (Boulestin and Duday, 2005, 2006, for the theory; Duday 2006, 2009, for the practical approach in English), so only a few reminders will be needed prior to concentrating on the issue of the associated terminologies.

Theoretically, the purpose of the field observations phase (phase 1) is to get a precise account of the number, nature and organisation of the bones, and how they relate to each other, in particular the presence or absence of any anatomical articulations. If need be, the description of the human remains may be complemented by the description of the artefacts or the animal remains found along with the human bones. It is better to use a noncommittal vocabulary for the former unless a clear function can be identified without any doubt from their positions or

---

1 In this instance, final deposition means the ultimate intentional anthropic action. It marks the transition to the post-depositional phase, which includes all the accidental or unintended actions and the natural processes that may afterwards disturb the organisation of the remains. It is important to note that this deposition does not necessarily involve burying (for instance when it takes place in the chamber of a dolmen) and, above all, that it does not always portend a funerary meaning (when emptying, arranging or transferring the remains).

characteristics. The feature containing the deposit may be described according to the same principle as well. Reconstructing the disposition of the bones at the time of the final deposition, and the way the assemblage was constituted (phase 2) relies on the analysis of the post-depositional changes. This is what standard taphonomic analysis deals with. The point is to reconstruct what happened between the final deposition and the time of discovery. To do so, the taphonomic analysis considers not only the human bones but also all the elements forming the archaeological assemblage, taking into account the processes of decomposition of the corpse (bones moving after the soft tissues have disappeared), as well as the natural or anthropic disturbances that might have occurred.

In practice, according to the case in question, the importance of each phase may vary, and the transition between them be marked to a lesser or greater extent. For instance, when the anatomical articulations of the skeleton are completely or almost completely preserved, and it is obvious that the body remained in the position in which it was deposited originally, phase one can simply read 'a fully articulated skeleton', adding only the specifics necessary to establish the way the assemblage was constituted. Moreover, there is no use at this stage to provide a detailed systematic description of each and every bone when describing the original disposition of the body. Things are different if, even when the anatomical articulations are not entirely preserved, the bones are still sufficiently organised to show that the body was deposited when fully articulated. It becomes necessary, then, to thoroughly split the two phases, first by describing precisely what is observed, and then by carrying out the taphonomic analysis. Comparing a meticulously recorded final organisation with an already known initial organisation – that of the human skeleton – will permit an assessment of the post-depositional processes in order to support a suspected original disposition, and to establish the way the assemblage was constituted. Contrary to these two examples, it may happen that the bones do not reflect any anatomical organisation any longer. Then it becomes impossible to reconstruct whole bodies. At best, it is possible to observe a certain form of obviously intentional organisation (for instance, the bones of an individual gathered in a heap or a bundle of long bones), and only presume this is how it actually looked at the time the bones were finally deposited. At worst, the bones may have been completely disturbed, and it is often very difficult to reconstruct a completely unknown initial organisation. In both examples, phase 1 largely prevails and is fundamental. In the first example, phase 2 is limited most of the time to repeating the observations. In the second one, the challenge is to try and determine whether the disorganisation existed prior to the burying of the remains, or took place after deposition. It is then necessary to make use of spatial analyses, osteological quantification, and to search for bone modifications, in addition to field records. Yet, the hypotheses that can be made with regard to assemblage formation already pertain to phase 3.

Terminologies in archaeothanatology: uses and misuses

The previous developments provide the necessary bases to address the core issue: terminologies in archaeothanatology. As was already pointed out, the intention in this contribution is not to give exhaustive and definitive solutions, but to appraise what is satisfying at present, or on the contrary, what must be improved and how. To begin with, a reminder of the three great principles which must guide this evaluation: (1) the terms of phases 1 and 2 of archaeothanatological reasoning, the only one dealt with in this paper, must be different from those used for phase 3; (2) they must be only descriptive and noncommittal; (3) their definition has to be based on precise concepts everyone must be able to understand in the same way, and not on more or less vague notions. Next, three types of procedures must be distinguished.

Describing the facts

When it comes to describing facts pertaining to bones, such as their identification, organisation and relationships (a procedure which characterises the entire phase of field observations but which can also partly concern the next phase), there is no room left for interpretation. It requires only precision and rigour. The international anatomical terminology (FIPAT, 2011) provides all the necessary vocabulary for the proper descriptions of the bones, though it can be complemented by details specific to anthropology (Boulestin, 2015), and it meets all the requirements for a good terminology. Sometimes, though, it is not possible to decide (for instance, on the identification, side or exposed surface of a bone), due to the extent of degradation of the bone remains, or to a lack of documentation when reviewing earlier data. In any case, the word 'indeterminate' is enough to indicate the undecidability. With regard to anatomical articulations, there are theoretically only two potential states: two bones are either articulated or they are not, hence it should be easy to decide between them. In practice, though, distinction is often made between a strict articulation, with no bone displacement at all (as is the case *in vivo*), and a loose one, when the anatomical articulation is preserved but the bones are slightly displaced. This does not change the dichotomy articulated/disarticulated. To describe articulations for the whole skeleton, Sprague suggests the category 'articulation', meaning 'the degree to which the skeleton is still in anatomical order' (Sprague, 2005: 29), and this refers, of course, to the observed state and not to the state of the corpse at the time of the final deposition. Among the terms used in his terminology, it is worth noting that 'semi-articulated' and 'partial articulation' lack precision, that 're-articulated' does not make any sense, and that 'disturbed' is logically inconsistent with the rest of the classification and is at the same time interpretative – 'a disturbed burial is best described when accompanied with speculation concerning how and when the disturbance occurred' (Sprague, 2005: 83). It would then be good practice to limit this terminological category to the two extreme configurations, that is '(fully) articulated' when the anatomical links of the skeleton are completely or almost completely preserved, and '(fully) disarticulated' when there are no more articulations, and to describe meticulously all the intermediate states. These terms may also apply to portions of the skeleton, not necessarily to whole skeletons. Lastly, it is important to point out that mastering the use of the anatomical terminology and being able to identify articulations are prerequisites for meticulous data recording, and ideally, this is why, as in France, only someone trained in human osteology should carry out the excavation of human bone assemblages.

Reconstructing the disposition of remains

Now, when it comes to reconstructing the position of the human remains at the time of their final deposition, the feasibility of doing so ranges from the obvious to the impossible. When there is no longer any anatomical organisation (as in a fully disarticulated deposit), only the position of the bones can be described, which harkens back to the previous procedure and the use of the anatomical terminology. It is not very different when body parts are involved: their position and orientation can be described using the same terms as for individual bones (for example, proximal, distal, medial or lateral). Specific terms to describe the position or orientation exist only for whole or almost whole bodies. First, for these two parameters, there can be no interpretation, only sometimes the impossibility to decide. Either one can describe a position or orientation, or one cannot, for the same reasons as stated above, in addition to possible uncertainties that persist after taphonomic analysis (when post-depositional disturbances are so great that the original position or orientation remains uncertain). Second, there are so many words accumulated over decades of research that one ends up not knowing what their precise meaning may be. Sprague

(2005: 10–11, 83–115) and Knüsel (2014: 38–42) pointed out the issues about position and orientation in the existing terminologies, and it can be summed up as follows: lack of coherence, rigour and precision. In other words, all that must be rejected. So, this mishmash of words must be swept away in order to get back to more precise and unequivocal terms.

With regard to the position, Sprague (2005: 29–31) chooses to distinguish the 'position' proper ('the relationship of the body parts to each other') from the 'deposition' ('how the body is deposited'). Even if it does not seem justified to use different terms, distinguishing between both aspects in the description is a good principle. The overall position (Sprague's 'deposition') can be described simply since the possibilities are limited: if one leaves aside the extremely rare cases where the dead have been deposited with the weight supported only on the feet (i.e. standing or squatting), either the upper part of their body is supported vertically mostly on the buttocks (i.e. on the ischia), in which case they are seated, or, in all the other cases, the dead are lying down. When they are lying down, the way the trunk is in contact with the ground enables to specify 'on the back', 'on the stomach' or 'on right or left side'.[2] To decide between seated and on the back, a 45° oblique angle between the trunk and the ground can be considered a logical limit. Nothing else is required. To describe the position of each body part (Sprague's 'position'), there is no terminological answer that would be both simple and precise, and that would exhaust all the possibilities (which Sprague's terminology does not do). In order to be rigorous, a literal description is necessary, as it is recommended also by Knüsel (2014: 41–42), and works any time. To achieve this, one can combine:

- indications of the relationship between two parts (e.g. right hand on pelvis, left foot under the right thigh, left upper limb alongside the trunk …),
- indications of the overall positions of the limbs (e.g. lower limbs together and extended …),
- and, to be more precise, indications of the position of the anatomical parts in reference to the joint movements by noting the joint, movement and range (e.g. right knee flexed at 90°, neck turned right 45° and inclined to the right at 20°, left elbow fully extended, etc.).[3]

Once more, the anatomical terminology provides all the general and specific terms required for these descriptions. The prefix 'hyper' (extended, flexed …) can be used to describe ranges that are larger than the maximum physiological ones. Lastly, when in a group the positions are stereotyped, or when it is necessary to categorise deposits for overall analyses, it can be termed in a concise way. One must then describe the overall shared characteristics, still according to the previous principles, though, or using words immediately comprehensible (e.g. haphazard) and avoiding those too vague (crouched, flexed, contracted, and so on).

With regard to orientation, Sprague (2005: 160–115) describes anarchical and unnecessarily complicated uses. It is both simple and unambiguous, indeed, to define the head-pelvis (and not head-foot) axis and to say in which direction the head is pointing in reference to one of the eight or sixteen major directions of the compass, depending on the desired accuracy. Likewise, the term 'facing' indicates the direction of the face (facing zenith or nadir when looking upwards). For instance, head to the North, facing East (or facing zenith) should not give rise to any confusion.

---

2 In French, the expression *decubitus dorsal, ventral* or *latéral*, which has the same meaning, is rather commonly used, more rarely though in English.

3 Movements are those of the joints. Logically, it is best to use 'flexed knee' and not of a 'leg flexed on the thigh'. Likewise, the head proper is not flexed, the neck is. Yet, all these choices of words are understandable and precise enough.

Reconstructing the way the assemblage was constituted

When reaching the third type of procedure and dealing with the reconstruction of the way the assemblage was constituted, the issue becomes trickier and the problems of terminologies are much more important than those encountered thus far. This procedure refers to Sprague's (2005) first three categories, 'form of disposal', 'body preparation' and 'individuality', to which a fourth, quite particular to French archaeothanatology, can be added, namely the space in which decomposition occurred (meaning to determine whether the body was deposited in a space left empty or immediately filled). So far, there has been room for undecidability, but not for interpretation. Now, this is very different. Indeed, these four characteristics cannot be directly observed, and they can be established only by going through a process of factual transformation; in other words, facts have to be interpreted. Contrary to phase 3 of the reasoning, though, this interpretation remains (or should remain) only material: theoretically, the question is not to determine the meaning of the acts, let alone to define mortuary or, more broadly, social behaviours. However, since there is interpretation, then over-interpretation or even complete misinterpretation is possible, and publications are aplenty in which there are moot conclusions about the way the assemblage was constituted. It is better to acknowledge that a characteristic is sometimes undecidable.

Each of the four characteristics mentioned above would call for a (sometimes very long) development, but it is impossible to do it here. Only the essential ones are treated here and at once two of these characteristics put aside. Body preparation, defined as the 'activity that prepares the body for placement in a container or grave' (Sprague, 2005: 29) is actually a rather imprecise notion of overlapping activities included in 'form of disposal', and the limits between the two categories are quite blurred. Anyway, from an archaeological point of view, these preparations are either impossible or very difficult to identify (for clothing and wrapping, see Boulestin, 2016: 15). Moreover, no specific terminology is required here. The space of decomposition does not raise any terminological issue either, since there are only two possibilities, empty or filled, to which indeterminate can be added. The difficulties lie elsewhere (Boulestin, 2016: 14ff.).

For Sprague (2005: 73), individuality 'is concerned with the number of human individuals involved in a specific container or pit'. His table 2 though is utterly inconsistent since contradictory criteria, such as the number of individuals, their completeness, the presence or not of articulated bones, and the simultaneity or not of the depositions are all mixed up. It is impossible to use such a terminology. More generally, the vocabulary used in English regarding the number of individuals and the relative chronology of their deposition is very ill-defined and lacks any form of consensus. The French terminology is much more thorough. It is extensively discussed in another chapter (cf. Boulestin and Courtaud, Chapter 3, this volume), but in summary, individual burials (*sépultures individuelles*), which contain only one dead person, are opposed to plural burials (*sépultures plurielles*), which contain at least two people. Among the latter, following the suggestion by Leclerc and Tarrête (1988) and provided field data and the taphonomic analysis allow it, distinction can be made between multiple burials (*sépultures multiples*) and collective burials (*sépultures collectives*) according to the chronology of the depositions. The term multiple burials is used when it can be demonstrated that the dead were all deposited at the same time; collective burials refer to graves for which it can be demonstrated, on the contrary, that the dead were not deposited on a single occasion. If nothing can be demonstrated, the term 'plural' must be kept as a noncommittal one. The French terminology has obviously no international reach, but it is simple, precise, easy to implement and has proved to work for three decades; it would thus be a good thing if it were more widely used. In any event, the English terminology should at least be clarified.

Sprague's (2005: 28) form of disposal 'depends on how many processes are utilised, simple using only one and compound using two or more'. This is a typical example of the kind of terminology that is impossible to apply since it intermingles factual and functional. In principle, archaeology is at best able to make hypotheses on what happened before the final deposition on the grounds of observed facts, and at worst is unable to say anything about it. Hence, the opposition simple/compound may be useful to categorise practices documented by ethnology, but certainly not archaeological facts. This opposition echoes the traditional one made between primary and secondary burial, two words that are surely the most criticisable, the worst defined and the least consensual (including primary, *contra* Knüsel, 2014: 46) of all the terminologies used in the archaeology of death (Sprague, 2005: 66ff.) (cf. Schotsmans *et al.*, Chapter 27, this volume). This situation can be attributed to the long history of these two notions – fathered by Magnus Bruzelius at the beginning of the 19th century (Bruzelius, 1822) – which over time have amalgamated aspects based both on observations (preservation or loss of articular connections) and interpretations (nature of the process leading to the final deposition, in particular when it comes to knowing whether it is an immediate burial or a delayed one, with or without transfer of the remains). Mixing these two notions is now so deeply rooted in archaeological practice that it can even be found in the most recent terminological developments (e.g. Knüsel, 2014: 46–50). This is the perfect example of the use of imprecise notions which has endured in the absence of thorough reflection regarding the actual concepts behind these words. And yet, attention had already been drawn to the problems raised from using them (Boulestin and Duday, 2005, 2006). In practice, if one wishes to describe the state of the remains at the time of their final deposition using some noncommittal vocabulary, a radical change of habits is imperative. An initial solution would be to reject systematically any reference to behaviours when using the terms primary or secondary, that is to say, to use exclusively definitions referring only to the state directly observed or inferred from observations (Boulestin and Duday, 2006: 166):

- 'primary: deposition of a corpse, or part of a corpse, made when the skeletal elements are still in complete anatomical articulation;
- secondary: deposition of remains made when the skeletal elements are partially or completely disarticulated'.

It would certainly be wiser, though, to totally stop using these ambivalent words. On the one hand, this would lead to simply speak of bodies or body parts deposited 'fully articulated', 'partially disarticulated', 'fully disarticulated' or 'in an indeterminate state' to describe the state of the remains at the time of the final deposition, and on the other hand to use 'simple' and 'compound' (or 'single-stage' and 'multi-stage') disposal in order to refer to practices documented in ethnohistory.[4] Today, this is certainly the best way to stop blending these observations and interpretations into single terms.

Conclusion

Terminologies in archaeothanatology tell a tale of two worlds, a descriptive world in which one does one's best to reconstruct the modalities of the final deposition of human remains and what happened afterwards, and an interpretative world in which the mortuary behaviours and social

---

4 In French the exact equivalents are '*pratique en un seul temps*' et '*pratique en plusieurs temps*', even though they are not much used.

facts that led to the deposition are discussed. Crossing the threshold between these two worlds is often difficult, sometimes impossible, but never obvious. This is why the vocabulary must be different on each side of the threshold. It must accurately express the intellectual path by which one tries to travel from one world to the other. Above all, it must forbid any interpretative pre-supposition in the descriptive world. The principles put forward in this paper should aid to avoid this situation and to use only terminologies based on clear and precise concepts. Some of these terminologies provide satisfaction already, but others still need further work. This is the only way to get people working on death in ancient societies to finally understand each other perfectly.

Acknowledgement

The original text was translated from French by E. Boulestin.

References

Baray, L. and Boulestin, B., eds, (2010). *Morts anormaux et sépultures bizarres. Les dépôts humains en fosses circulaires et en silos du Néolithique à l'âge du Fer.* Dijon: Éditions Universitaires de Dijon.

Boulestin, B. (2012). Champ de la discipline: concepts et mise en œuvre. In: L. Bonnabel, ed., *Archéologie de la Mort en France.* Paris: La Découverte, pp. 24–39.

Boulestin, B. (2015). Conservation du Crâne et Terminologie: Pour en Finir avec Quelques Mots de Tête! *Bulletins et Mémoires de la Société d'Anthropologie de Paris*, 27(1–2), pp. 16–25.

Boulestin, B. (2016). *Les sépultures mésolithiques de Téviec et Hoedic: révisions bioarchéologiques.* Oxford: Archaeopress.

Boulestin, B. and Duday, H. (2005). Ethnologie et archéologie de la mort: de l'illusion des références à l'emploi d'un vocabulaire. In: C. Mordant and G. Depierre, eds., *Les Pratiques Funéraires à l'Âge du Bronze en France.* Paris and Sens: Éditions du Comité des Travaux Historiques et Scientifiques (CTHS) and Société Archéologique de Sens, pp. 17–35.

Boulestin, B. and Duday, H. (2006). Ethnology and Archaeology of Death: From the Illusion of References to the Use of a Terminology. *Archaeologia Polona*, 44, pp. 149–169.

Brown, J.A., ed. (1971). Approaches to the Social Dimensions of Mortuary Practices. *Memoirs of the Society for American Archaeology*, 25, pp. 1–112.

Bruzelius, M. (1822). Nordiska fornlemningar från Skåne. *Iduna*, IX, pp. 285–333.

Cauvin, J. (1983). Typologie et fonctions des outils préhistoriques: apports de la tracéologie à un vieux débat. In: M.-C. Cauvin, ed., *Traces d'Utilisation sur les Outils Néolithiques du Proche-Orient.* Lyon: Maison de l'Orient et de la Méditerranée.

Chapman, R., Kinnes, I. and Randsborg, K., eds. (1981). *The archaeology of death.* Cambridge: Cambridge University Press.

Darcque, P. and Van de Moortel, A. (2009). Special, ritual, or cultic: a case study from Malia. In: A. L. D'Agata and A. Van de Moortel, eds., *Archaeologies of Cult: Essays on Ritual and Cult in Crete in Honor of Geraldine C. Gesell.* Princeton: American School of Classical Studies at Athens, pp. 31–41.

Duday, H. (2006). Archaeothanatology or the archaeology of death. Translated from the French by C.J. Knüsel. In: R. Gowland and C.J. Knüsel, eds., *Social Archaeology of Funerary Remains.* Oxford: Oxbow Books, pp. 30–56.

Duday, H. (2009). *The archaeology of the dead. Lectures in archaeothanatology.* Oxford: Oxbow Books.

FIPAT (Federative International Programme on Anatomical Terminologies). (2011). *Terminologia anatomica. International anatomical terminology.* 2nd ed. Stuttgart: Georg Thieme Verlag.

Gallay, A. (1986). *L'archéologie demain.* Paris: Pierre Belfond.

Gallay, A. (2011). *Pour une ethnoarchéologie théorique.* Paris: Éditions Errance.

Gardin, J.-C. (1979). *Une archéologie théorique.* Paris: Hachette.

Gardin, J.-C. (1980). *Archaeological constructs: an aspect of theoretical archaeology.* Cambridge and Paris: Cambridge University Press and Éditions de la Maison des Sciences de l'Homme.

Jamieson, E.B. (1916). *The Basle Anatomical Nomenclature (BNA) being an alphabetical list of terms showing the old terminology, the B.N.A. terminology, and the suggested English equivalent.* London and Edinburgh: W. Green & Son.

Khan, S.H. (2016). The Distinction between Term and Word: A Translator and Interpreter Problem and the Role of Teaching Terminology. *Procedia – Social and Behavioral Sciences*, 232, pp. 696–704.

Knüsel, C.J. (2014). Crouching in Fear: Terms of Engagement for Funerary Remains. *Journal of Social Archaeology*, 14(1), pp. 26–58.

Leclerc, J. (1990). La Notion de Sépulture. *Bulletins et Mémoires de la Société d'Anthropologie de Paris*, 2(3–4), pp. 13–18.

Leclerc, J. and Tarrête, J. (1988). Sépulture. In: A. Leroi-Gourhan, ed., *Dictionnaire de la Préhistoire*. Paris: Presses Universitaires de France, pp. 963–964.

Leroi-Gourhan, A., ed. (1975). *Séminaire sur les structures d'habitat. Sépultures*. Paris: Collège de France – Ethnologie Préhistorique.

Péquart, S.-J. (1938). Difficulté de présumer la destination d'un outil préhistorique ou moderne d'après sa morphologie. *Bulletin Mensuel de la Société des Sciences de Nancy*, III(1), pp. 7–19.

Sprague, R. (2005). *Burial terminology: a guide for researchers*. Lanham, MD: Altamira Press.

3

WORDS BETWEEN TWO WORLDS

Collective graves and related issues in burial terminology

Bruno Boulestin and Patrice Courtaud

PACEA, De la Préhistoire à l'Actuel: Culture, Environnement et Anthropologie, UMR 5199, CNRS-Université de Bordeaux, Pessac, France

Introduction[1]

As far as terminology in archaeothanatology is concerned, problems waiting for a solution are aplenty. Some of them, though, are trickier to address than others, notably those regarding the analytical procedure for reconstructing the way assemblages were constituted. The reason is that, at this stage, what needs to be known cannot be observed directly and can only be established by interpreting observations, but also that, at the same time, this interpretation must remain only material, without determining the meaning of the acts, let alone defining mortuary or more broadly social behaviours (this will take place in the next phase of the reasoning only). One stands on the boundary between the descriptive world and the interpretative world, which makes it particularly challenging to follow the desirable rule according to which the vocabulary must be different on both sides of this boundary (cf. Boulestin, Chapter 2, this volume).

Vocabulary with regard to the number of individuals and the relative chronology of their deposition is especially affected by this difficulty. Indeed, some of the terms used, notably (but not only) that of collective burial, are typically words between two worlds because they are used to refer to archaeological features and also to address those documented ethnographically, which seems to contradict the rule mentioned in the first paragraph. Obviously, there are consequences, but above all, it begs the question of whether this situation is sustainable, keeping in mind that if the answer is 'no', the use of 'collective burial' may have to be restricted to either archaeology or ethnology, and another term to replace it in one or the other discipline will be required.

---

1 This chapter can be read on its own, but some of the points addressed here refer to the chapter about terminology in archaeothanatology in general (cf. Boulestin, Chapter 2, this volume), which it complements. Moreover, the questions dealt with in this contribution have been developed concurrently in a more detailed version in French (Boulestin, 2019).

DOI: 10.4324/9781351030625-5

Nevertheless, as it will be seen later, the use of 'collective burial' can be maintained in both archaeological and ethnological disciplines while remaining perfectly consistent, to be employed only under specific conditions.

The same vocabulary raises another issue, which is partly independent from the previous one: it is based on notions that are sometimes ill-defined and not always identical, in particular from one language to another. From this perspective, it is very difficult for researchers to have a shared terminology they can use to understand each other without ambiguity (Boulestin, Chapter 2, this volume), and this is a concern that must of necessity be settled. This subject being the easiest to deal with, it will be addressed first.

Some ill-defined notions and a non-consensual terminology

This section focuses on the comparison of terminological uses between the French and English languages. The French terminology, the first to be dealt with, will serve as a reference, not because it is preponderant, but because it is both relatively simple to apply and accurate, and above all because it has been set for three decades.

During the 1980s, French researchers working on mortuary practices, from the Neolithic in particular, have felt the necessity to clearly distinguish between two main ways of '*fonctionnement*' for burials containing several dead, based on the relative chronology of the depositions of bodies.[2] This is why Leclerc and Tarrête (1988) suggested that the term *sépulture collective* (collective burial) should be used for features containing several bodies deposited successively, as opposed to the term *sépulture multiple* (multiple burial), which refers to a grave that received several individuals during a single event.[3] Since it is not always possible to decide between the two cases in archaeological contexts, the term *sépulture plurielle* has been secondarily introduced to designate a feature containing several individuals, but for which the relative chronology of the depositions cannot be determined. This term has no equivalent in the English language, but there are several good reasons to translate it as 'plural burial'. First, one of the definitions of the adjective 'plural' is 'containing, involving, or composed of more than one person, thing, item, etc.' (*Collins Dictionary*[4]), making it a suitable one. Next, 'plural burial' is not used otherwise, so there is no risk of confusion or mixing with another concept. Finally, *sépulture plurielle* is already translated 'plural burial' not only by French researchers but also by non-French ones who use the French terminology (e.g. Kharobi and Buccellati, 2017). For all these reasons, this translation will be used hereinafter.

Since then, this terminology has not changed and has oftentimes proved to be effective, being systematically used in archaeothanatology by French researchers for various periods and situations. It has also been used since the 2000s by Spanish researchers, who borrowed and directly transposed it (except for *sépulture plurielle*), and hence speak of *sepultura múltiple* or *colectiva* with the exact same meaning as in French (Alfonso Quintana and Alesan Alias, 2003: 16). The only improvement that can be made today is to rephrase the definitions slightly so that they are more precise (Boulestin, 2019).

---

2 We have chosen to keep the French term '*fonctionnement*', which has no exact equivalent in English. It refers to the way in which the grave fulfils its function (containing the dead), meaning in practice how it was constituted and used (cf. Knüsel, Gerdau-Radonić and Schotsmans, Chapter 34, this volume).

3 Throughout this chapter, the terms 'grave' and 'burial' will be used interchangeably. This is a long-established usage in archaeology, and that doesn't raise any particular problem.

4 https://www.collinsdictionary.com/dictionary/english/plural.

Hence, the French terminology can be formalised as such:

- At a first level, there is an opposition between burials that contain only one dead person (*individuelles*) and those containing at least two people (*plurielles*).
- At a second level, among the latter, provided field data and taphonomic analysis permits it, a distinction is made between *sépulture multiple*, when it can be demonstrated that the dead were all deposited at the same time, and *sépulture collective*, when it can be demonstrated, on the contrary, that the dead were not deposited on a single occasion.
- If nothing can be demonstrated, the term *plurielle* is kept as a non-committal one.

For the sake of completeness, mass burials should be mentioned at this point. The term 'mass grave' is hardly ever used in archaeothanatology for three reasons.[5] First, it is nothing more than a specific type of multiple burial, the identification of which requires an interpretation, as Schmitt and Déderix (2018: 197) emphasise. Secondly, and contrary to what Knüsel (2014: 43) asserts, mass graves are not 'well defined', and the accepted definition of 'mass grave' varies, whether in archaeology or in forensic sciences (Haglund, Connor and Scott, 2001: 57; Rosenblatt, 2015: 13–14; Barker *et al.*, 2017: 256–257; see also below).[6] Lastly, this term is too strongly associated with contemporary genocides and ethnic cleansings, and many French researchers think it should not be used outside a forensic context.

Contrary to the French use, the English one is somewhat confused, as seen by simply taking a look at three main studies on terminology published in the last 15 years. In Sprague's (2005: 29, 73–79) synthetic work, a distinction is made between the burials containing a part of a body (fragmentary), a whole body (single), two bodies (double) and any number of bodies arranged in order (multiple, implying articulation) or mixed without order (mass, implying disarticulation). Among the multiple burials, the author distinguishes between those containing two or more individuals interred at one time (contemporary), and those containing two or more individuals buried at different times (consecutive). Moreover, he considers the term 'collective' as 'unacceptable' (Sprague, 2005: 74) but does not provide any reason. This classification is inconsistent since contradictory criteria such as the number of individuals, their completeness, the presence or not of articulated bones, and the simultaneity or not of the depositions are all mixed up.

For his own part, Knüsel (2014: 43–46) favours the expression 'collective burial', which 'refers to the successive deposition of burials in the same feature over time' (thus corresponding to Sprague's 'multiple consecutive'). On the other hand, for Knüsel 'multiple' retains a generic meaning since he writes that 'the term multiple burial relates only to features with more than a single individual in the most general sense with collective, reduction of the corpse and mass burials differentiated on their extent of disarticulation'. As a consequence, a collective burial is always seen as a specific form of multiple burial, as is the mass burial (defined on the basis of a series of criteria partially contradicting Sprague's own). Nevertheless, Knüsel seems to liken North American ossuaries to collective burials, whereas these features actually result from the single and simultaneous deposition of the remains of several individuals.

---

5 A French equivalent, *sépulture de catastrophe* (catastrophic burial), existed but has now fallen into disuse.
6 Some archaeologists or forensic experts define mass graves as based purely on the number of bodies (the number itself varies), others think mass grave implies not only a certain number of bodies, but also specifics about how they are placed together, still others take in consideration the dynamics which brought the grave about, adding for example the criterion of manner of death.

Two years later, Knüsel undertakes a paradigm shift, since if collective deposition is still defined as 'human remains deposited successively over time rather than in a single episode', multiple deposition becomes a 'simultaneous deposition of several bodies in the same place' (Knüsel and Robb, 2016: 658 and table 1). This time, the French opposition is used since the collective burial does not appear as a form of multiple burial any longer. At the same time, a mass grave is defined as 'a deposition of multiple individuals in a single episode (for instance, following a disaster, a massacre or epidemic)', which makes it strictly equivalent to the multiple burial.

It is of no use to dwell on these contradictions in terminology. It is clear that the vocabulary concerning the number of individuals and the relative chronology of their deposition is not at all consensual. This is true on an international level, and true also within the English language itself, with sometimes authors providing different definitions two years apart. Not to mention the German language, where *Mehrfachbestattung* means roughly multiple burial, while *Nachbestattung* or *Kollektivbestattung* refer rather to the collective burial, but in truth uses vary tremendously (Weiss-Krejci, 2018: 107). For all researchers to be able to at least speak about the same thing when using the same terms, the same conventions should be adopted, and adhered to. For the reasons mentioned above, French terminology will be used in this chapter.

Words between two worlds

The vocabulary that has just been discussed was created by archaeologists in an attempt to describe the '*fonctionnement*' of burials containing several people on the basis of archaeological observations. Still, it is used as well, in particular the term 'collective burial', to characterise graves or practices observed in ethnological contexts. There are two reasons why this is the case. The main reason is that since there are no direct sources available, researchers are forced to rely on ethnographic documents and observations to try and understand the way prehistoric burials were constituted and used. This is true for Neolithic collective burials, in particular, and understandably archaeologists have looked for seemingly comparable ethnographic models, with similarities with regard to the architecture of the graves and their '*fonctionnement*' (the most widely used model is that from Madagascar, e.g. Parker Pearson and Regnier, 2018). The formal reason is that ethnologists, for their part, never attempted to classify the burials and establish a coherent vocabulary to identify the various categories precisely. In particular, they have no generic term to describe the grave referred to as collective by archaeologists; this is a word they hardly ever use, and never with the meaning given in archaeothanatology (in ethnology, this term always means 'which involves or concerns a group of individuals'). For instance, with regard to Madagascar, Bloch (1971) never uses the term 'collective'. In truth, this is because ethnologists do not require it since they speak of family, lineage, or ancestral burials, which means that they do what archaeologists cannot do, they refer directly to the group using the tombs. By force of circumstance, archaeologists cannot use ethnographic terminology that does not exist to refer to ethnographic examples, and thus the archaeological vocabulary is projected onto ethnographic situations.

Hence, there is a series of terms, in particular that of 'collective burial', belonging to two different worlds, which leads researchers to oscillate between two frames of reference: one based on archaeological observations and the other based on interpretations of them using ethnographic analogies. In practice, this results in a persistent temptation to transform definitions intended to simply describe a '*fonctionnement*', into new ones embedding social meanings, in other words to mix up observational criteria with interpretations. After all, this is a rather classic mechanism: at the beginning, a purely archaeological vocabulary is projected (by archaeologists) onto ethnographic situations, thus loading it with a functional dimension which, in return, they attempt to re-introduce into archaeology. This is a long-established temptation, but until now there has been at least a consensus to maintain the essentially descriptive nature of the definition of the collective burial. Very recently, though, Schmitt and Déderix (2018) have suggested that this type of burial should be characterised rather by its social function, said function being considered as a politico-economic one, based on kinship. As a consequence, the meaning of the terms changes since the collective grave is no longer defined by the succession of depositions but by that of the deaths of individuals. For Schmitt and Déderix (2018), a burial is referred to as 'collective' whenever it gathers together individuals who died at different times, be they buried at the same time or not. This notably counter-current suggestion, particularly in France, raises two major issues. On the one hand, it implies relinquishing the term 'collective burial' in archaeology, and, more broadly, the whole vocabulary since it shifts that vocabulary entirely to the ethnological side. Moreover, the writers explain that the terms 'collective' and 'multiple' must be moved from the descriptive phase of the archaeological analysis to the interpretative one. Since the current uses have been deeply rooted for several decades, in particular with regard to 'collective burial', this is likely impractical and, in any case, definitely a potential source of confusion. On the other hand, it does not resolve the issues arising when one crosses the threshold between the descriptive and the interpretative worlds. It relocates and even exacerbates the difficulties. Thus, this solution does not seem to be relevant.

For identical reasons, turning the collective burial into an exclusively archaeological entity, and thus renouncing to use the term in ethnology after forty-odd years of regular use, is also undesirable, and probably not any easier either. This means that the best option is to carry on using the terminology in both frames of reference. At first glance, it could seem in total contradiction with the principles stated in other works (Boulestin and Duday, 2005, 2006; Boulestin, Chapter 2, this volume), as reiterated above. In truth, this is not contradictory at all. It is strongly discouraged to resort to identical terminologies for descriptive and interpretative phases of the analytical reasoning, but it is not forbidden at all to use the same vocabulary in archaeology and in ethnology, under two imperative conditions. The first is that this vocabulary must not refer to ideas or social behaviours. Said in a different way, whereas interpretative terminologies should be restricted to ethnology, on the contrary it is perfectly possible to use archaeological descriptive terms in ethnology. In this case, the first condition is met since 'multiple', 'collective' and 'plural' describe a '*fonctionnement*'. The second condition is that the same words must describe exactly the same concepts in both disciplines, with an utterly unequivocal relationship. A counter-example to this is given by the terms 'primary' and 'secondary', which describe a state of remains in archaeology and a practice in ethnology, whereas various practices can correspond to a same state, and reciprocally. The following section will demonstrate that, on the contrary, the second condition is met here as well.

The referential analytical unit, and the two main ways to gather the dead together

Theoretical framework

Gathering the dead is not something every social group practices. The deceased are sometimes scattered in various places, put in an isolated pit (this is often the case among nomadic peoples, hunter-gatherers or pastoral herders; e.g. Walthall, 1999; Fukui, 2001), abandoned, or buried at sea. Sometimes, though, the bodies themselves become scattered, as for instance in 'sky burial', cannibalism, or dispersed cremated remains. These scattering practices certainly affected a very large proportion of the dead in the past, and most of them escape archaeological recognition today.

Groups which, on the contrary, wish to gather their dead together have various possibilities to do so. Nevertheless, only two ways are fundamentally different, to such extent that they are usually considered as distinct phenomena (Castex *et al.*, 2011: 9): gathering burials, on the one hand,

and gathering the dead in the same burial, on the other hand. As a consequence, the reference space that is used to distinguish between these two possibilities is obviously the burial, and for that matter, the terms 'individual', 'multiple' or 'collective' refer to, and only to, the burial. Still, this point seems to be problematic (Weiss-Krejci, 2018: 110), and exploring it in further detail is useful.

Whatever the chosen definition (cf. Boulestin, Chapter 2, this volume), the burial is above all a place: there is no burial without an identified place. This is even more precise than that since, in order to contain one or several deceased individuals, this place must be a three-dimensional space, i.e. a volume (a pit, a monument, a natural or artificial cavity, for example). There is little difference if this volume is filled or remains a void after the bodies have been deposited: even full, a volume is still a volume. This volume belongs to the dead it contains: this is *such* a person's, or *such* a group's burial. Quite often, though, a body may be contained in practice within several volumes of increasing size, successively nested into each other, and the question arises about what characterises the volume that defines the burial. In the first instance, there is often what is commonly called 'soft wrapping material' (*enveloppes souples* in French) around the dead body: clothes or shrouds, for example. These wrappings, whatever their nature, simply cover the corpse, but they do not contain it. As such, they cannot be considered as an additional volume and thus can be ignored. In the second instance, one can find a movable disposal container, usually a coffin. Contrary to soft wrappings, this container is an actual volume, which moreover belongs to the person it contains. But nobody, anywhere, will ever consider the coffin as a burial, simply because, even though this is a volume, this is not a place (that is a defined and, thus, a fixed portion of space), precisely because of its movable nature. In other words, the coffin is a movable object, whereas a burial is an immovable asset. Following the same principle, a funerary urn is not a burial, whereas a stone sarcophagus, which is fixed to the ground or to the monument containing it, is. Above the coffin is the burial, which sometimes may itself be contained in a larger volume such as a burial vault, a crypt, a mausoleum or any other monument; these monuments usually group several burials. In sum, the referential analytical unit, the burial, is the smallest possible non-movable (or immovable) volume (three-dimensional space) containing one or several bodies.

With these specifications having been provided, two possible social choices are left for gathering the dead together: either give each of them an individual burial, then group the burials inside a bigger volume (built or natural) or within the same communal space (a cemetery or a plot within a cemetery); or group the dead within a single burial, in which case the burial itself is the communal place. These two ways of burying the dead refer to the same general idea, which is grouping the deceased, as opposed to separating them. What defines the cemetery is the wish to gather burials together in a same place (Boulestin, 2016: 251ff.). What defines the communal burial is the wish to group the dead within a same burial. The distinction is not less fundamental, though, and it expresses two different social choices. The descriptor 'communal burial' could be used, since the qualifying adjective perfectly conveys its distinguishing feature: it is shared by several people. As can be noted, however, there is a strict similarity between this concept and the definition in French of 'plural burial' (*sépulture plurielle*) since it is a burial that contains at least two people, as opposed to the individual burial, which contains only one person. It is thus legitimate to open up the archaeological term to ethnology straightaway, and this is the choice recommended in this chapter.

Identifying a plural burial in archaeology

At first glance, it seems easy to identify a plural burial in archaeology: at least two bodies in the same place may be enough. In reality, three characteristics should be demonstrated, or at least strongly presumed: 1. that it is a single burial, 2. that the grouping of the bodies in the same place did not happen by chance, 3. that it really is a burial (meaning a feature resulting from funerary practices).

The first point relies on an ability to demonstrate that the dead are in the same burial, in other words that the volume in which they are contained was intended as a single one, corresponding to a single grave. This is not an issue when the bodies are commingled or in close contact with each other. However, this is different when they are lying apart, all the more so when they are in places that can be disassociated from one another. Two specific examples can illustrate this. Some Neolithic monuments have several chambers or are subdivided into distinct cells. Were these monuments intended as single burials, or as structures housing separate burials? The same ambiguity exists with regard to natural cavities, when the bodies were placed in different chambers or galleries: in this case, it is difficult to know whether the cave was regarded as a burial as a whole, or whether, instead, it functioned as a cemetery, the different parts of the cavities being seen as distinct graves. In both examples, it is usually almost impossible to decide, and often researchers conclude that this is a single burial. At least the question must be raised, and when doubt is high, then the term 'plural burial' should not be used. Undecidability can then be marked by the use of 'a set of individuals' (*ensemble d'individus* in French), the term 'set' being neutral enough to simply describe that the dead are present in the same location, without further interpretation.

The second point conveys the idea that, even in a single volume, the presence of several bodies does not automatically make it a plural burial. The following example illustrates this idea: if a dolmen contained successively one dead individual from the Neolithic, and another from the Bronze Age, it is obviously not a plural burial but a monument that was used twice as an individual burial. In passing, it is important to note that had several individuals been buried during the Neolithic, then the monument would be both a Neolithic plural burial and a Bronze Age individual burial. This stresses an often-unnoticed aspect: it is only the specific use made of a place that permits it to be defined as burial. Said in a different way, a place is a burial only within the framework of a given use (hosting one or several bodies at the end of their last funerals) and at a given time, and the characteristics of the burial can be defined only with reference to those of that use. This aspect is obvious for natural cavities in particular, the major difference being that they are obviously not 'built' to become burials.

Back to the central issue, if several dead individuals have been placed in a single volume, one can speak of a plural burial only if this has taken place during the same phase of use, and not on the occasion of distinct, separate funerary uses. This refers, of course, to the will to gather the dead together, and it is no wonder this problem occurs here exactly in the same terms as for the groupings of burials, where some groupings result from a succession of opportunistic behaviours, and others from deliberate intention. Only the latter can be described as cemeteries (Boulestin, 2016: 251ff).

In practice, most of the time it is possible to distinguish different uses of a same space, based on stratigraphic relationships, accompanying goods, osteological studies (lack of any relationship between bone elements), and radiocarbon dating. Nevertheless, sometimes these elements are not conclusive and make it impossible to decide, for instance in the case of graves used many times during the Middle Ages, and for which it is difficult to know whether they are burials where several bodies were deposited successively, or whether they are spaces used several times as individual burials. As previously discussed, when it is impossible to decide, one should speak of a 'set of individuals' and not of a plural burial.

Lastly, the third point is that speaking of a 'burial' implies that the demonstration has been made, or at least that there are enough arguments to strongly presume that an archaeologically observed gathering of dead persons is really the consequence of funerary practices, which pertains to the interpretative phase of analytical reasoning (Boulestin and Duday, 2005, 2006; Courtaud and Duday, 2008; Boulestin, Chapter 2, this volume). There are two types of situations that require discussion. The first case is a grouping carried out beyond the funerary time, in other words after the funeral. The second situation refers to the case when the dead are gathered together without any funerary rite whatsoever. Most of the time, the context can help to identify these situations, but it is not always the case, and as soon as one suspects a non-funerary rite or is in doubt, the term 'burial' should be avoided. Here, the uncertain nature of the use of the place forbids its characterisation as a grave. In this case, the term 'gathering' (*rassemblement* in French) can be used, indicating that uncertainties on the first two points have been resolved, and that the intention of gathering the dead is considered likely, but without any presupposition with regard to the reasons that motivated this gathering. On the other hand, one should reject the terms 'deposit' and 'deposition', which cause problems in English and in French alike, and which should be used only when referring to a single action, in order to avoid confusion between action and result (for example, a collective *deposition* – the result – arises from a succession of individual or multiple *depositions* – the actions –; on this point, see Boulestin, 2019: 717–718).

The two main types of plural burials

Theoretical framework

There are several possible ways to subdivide the plural burials encountered in ethnology into different types, even without introducing any social function. However, on the one hand, not all the options permit predictions to be made to best characterise the variants observed in archaeology because the material consequences that can be deduced from them are not easily observable. And on the other hand, the variants must refer to markedly different practices. Moreover, it is necessary to be simple and to avoid overly complex classifications. That being said, it seems that the most pertinent way to proceed is to divide the burials into two major exclusive categories, those that are used only once and those that are used several times (implying over a same phase of use). This division meets all the previous criteria and, above all, it seems to be the most fundamental one, socially speaking, at this level of analysis. In a plural burial used only once, all the dead are gathered at one time, and no individual will ever be added later. This is a limited use over time, and no further use is ever planned. Plural burials used only once imply also that all the deposited persons are either already dead (at the same time or not) at the time the place is established as a burial, or killed at that point. On the contrary, plural burials used repeatedly are intended to gather dead persons deposited on several occasions. At the time they are established, they are planned to receive more dead people later, those being in principle not all dead yet.

Once again, these two main types of '*fonctionnement*' strictly match the definitions in French of 'multiple burial' (*sépulture multiple*) and 'collective burial' (*sépulture collective*), respectively. Saying that a burial was used only once amounts to saying that the dead were all deposited at the same time, whereas a repeated use means that the dead have not been deposited on a single occasion (both cases require demonstration in archaeology). This is no wonder since from the beginning the definitions in French have been conceived to embed what seemed to be the most relevant distinction from an ethnological point of view. Again, this means that archaeological terms can be safely used to describe an ethnological '*fonctionnement*'.

There are many reasons with which to explain multiple burials (Boulestin, 2018). The main ones pertain to the practice of the accompanying dead (cf. Boulestin, Chapter 5, this volume) and to mortality crises resulting from massacres, epidemics or famines, but there are also less frequently encountered reasons. Moreover, one should add to this burial category the pits constituted on the occasion of ceremonies for the 'Feast of the Dead' carried out by the western Iroquoians, the Huron-Wendat in particular, and some Algonquians (for the former, among many publications, one can refer to the synthetic studies by Tooker, 1964: 134–140 and Trigger, 1987: 85–90; for the latter, see Hickerson, 1960). Although these pits gather bodies of individuals who died at different times and were transported from different locations, they are used only once and all the individuals are buried at the same time.

Collective burials can display extremely variable characteristics and manners of use, and this tends to hide what makes their unity: the core idea that, at the time they are created, one knows that other people will be added later, or that at least this possibility remains open. In practice, this idea translates into the fact that when people stop using the burial, the dead it contains at that point were not deposited at one time. This is just a consequence, though, and what is really at the heart of the concept is the possibility to gather the dead later (above all) and at different times (possibly).

Without trying to explain the underlying reasons why collective burials are chosen, two observations can be made. The first is that although these burials are often considered, in both archaeology and ethnology, as belonging to a group, a collectivity, or a community, it is not always the case (for instance, in Sumba, Indonesia; Jeunesse and Denaire, 2018). On the other hand, and this forms the second observation, all those documented in ethnohistory have one essential property in common: they refer to kinship, in that they gather people being related by consanguinity, affinity or adoption. This is not true at all for multiple burials, which gather people who can have family links, but also social links of various kinds, or who are simply linked by the way they died (Boulestin, 2008, 2018). And this is, in particular, not the case for the Huron-Wendat pits, which the new definition provided by Schmitt and Déderix (2018) would categorise as a collective burial. With the classic division adopted in this contribution, the familial attribute of the collective burials is not subject to any ethnologically known exception, and this is one of the main reasons why this division is socially fundamental.

It is also important to insist on another aspect of the '*fonctionnement*' of collective burials: an obligatory consequence of the necessity to be able to deposit the dead several times over is the ability to have repeated access to the burial. This is an essential characteristic, stressed mostly in archaeology, which necessitates that the volume of the burial must remain unfilled over the period of its use, on the one hand, and that the burial can be reopened if it has been closed, on the other hand.

Lastly, a few additional remarks:

- In a collective burial, several deceased individuals can be deposited at the same time, as long as not *all* the dead are deposited at the same time;
- The succession of depositions of individuals in a collective burial does not necessarily follow the chronological order of their deaths: wherever these burials exist, transporting the remains from one burial to another is a common practice, and a dead person can very well be deposited in a burial after another who died long after them;
- Even if it is often thought that collective burials are used over a long period of time, ethnology shows that, in truth, the duration of their use (meaning the period during which the dead are deposited) varies tremendously, ranging from a few years to several generations, and the concept of collective burial does not require setting a minimum length of time;
- Ethnology demonstrates also that there are collective burials with only two individual depositions and, as a consequence, a burial containing only two individuals buried at two different moments, even close in time, meets this concept perfectly.

The distinction between 'multiple' and 'collective' in archaeology

To begin with, it is important to emphasise a specific point again: in archaeology, the subdivision of plural burials implies that all factors of ambiguity with regard to this qualification have been clarified. If not, the subdivision does not make sense and one should keep to the neutral designation 'set of individuals'. Moreover, using the term 'burial' implies presumption of a funerary context, but in a non-funerary or dubious context, the term 'gathering' should be used.

In practice, it is more or less difficult to demonstrate simultaneity or succession – sometimes it is even impossible – but it always requires an interpretation of field observation that makes mistakes possible. These issues have been addressed in other contributions (Boulestin, 2016: 14–19; 2018), but a quick reminder might be useful. There are several sources of difficulty, and they may result in a variety of uncertainties. The archaeological demonstration of simultaneity or succession is indeed based chiefly on osteological criteria. If the deposition of a body in close contact with another did not cause a disturbance of the skeletal articulations, simultaneity will be deduced; otherwise, succession will be inferred. There are already two obvious situations for which it is impossible to decide between these two possibilities: whenever the dead are not in contact (whether there are disturbances or not) and whenever the bones no longer display any anatomical organisation. In the other cases, limitations of interpretation are two-fold.

The first limitation comes from the fact that depositions that were made at different times are not always archaeologically discernible. First, this can be due to the time lapse between them being shorter than the time necessary for the most labile joints to become disarticulated; this period can be substantially increased on some occasions should the decomposition process be slowed or stopped. Secondly, soft wrappings may compress the body to the point of hindering bone displacements, even after decomposition. In these cases, one will conclude that the depositions were made simultaneously, even if in reality there were made successively. This limitation is inherent to the methods and irresolvable at present, and there are no means to assess it. Although one must come to terms with this limitation, it should not result in undecidability, which otherwise would be systematic.

The other limitation concerns the relationship established between bone disturbances and a possible time gap between inhumations. Generally speaking, before being able to conclude that disturbances of skeletal articulations result from depositions of bodies made at different times – a relationship that is made automatically much too often – in principle all other possible causes must have been ruled out, including simultaneous depositions of corpses already partially or fully disarticulated, disarticulation of joints due to post-funeral movements of people within the burial and manipulations, or disturbances occurring after the burial is no longer in use. Contrary to the previous limitation, this one leads to over-interpretation to the benefit of succession at the expense of simultaneity. In any case, when in doubt or when faced with a situation in which it is impossible to decide, the qualifying term 'plural' should be used. The reader will also find in this volume some chapters on excavation and study methods, as well as case studies concerning multiple burials (cf. Castex and Kacki, Chapter 18, this volume) and collective burials (cf. Schmitt, Chapter 12, this volume).

Synthesis and perspectives

What must be kept in mind above all is that there is a real possibility to use the same vocabulary for the number of individuals and the relative chronology of their deposition in both archaeology and ethnology, as long as a few precautions are taken: (1) the referential analytical space must be clearly defined; (2) the concepts behind each term and what they imply in practice must be clearly defined; (3) under no circumstances should a social function be embedded in the definitions. This latter condition is particularly important: this is because the definitions describe a *'fonctionnement'*, and not a social function, that one can maintain the equivalence between the two frames of reference. In the first instance, the terminology cannot be asked to do more: knowing which 'collectivity' used a collective burial, and what this means socially, pertains to another level of interpretation, the very one, besides, in which one has to decide whether or not a particular deposit is actually a burial. These precautions being taken, the terms 'multiple burial' and 'collective burial' permit description of each case perfectly coherently (*contra* Weiss-Krejci, 2018: 121).

Obviously, this coherence also requires that the same terms cover the same concepts everywhere and that researchers adopt the same conventions in order to be able to understand each other, even on an international level, if possible. In this contribution, French terminology has been used as the basis for discussion. The intention is not to impose this terminology internationally, but again it is important to underline that it is simple, precise, easy to implement and has proved to work for three decades; these are reasons why it would be a good thing if it were more widely used. In this terminology, the following definitions are essential:

- The referential analytical unit (which corresponds to the burial in a funerary context) is the smallest possible identified volume (i.e. a materially delimited three-dimensional space) containing the body or bodies, that volume being immovable.
- If only one dead person has been deposited in this volume, one uses 'individual deposit' (*dépôt individuel*).
- If at least two people have been deposited in this volume over a same phase of use, one uses 'gathering' (*rassemblement*).
- A gathering is termed 'multiple' (*multiple*) whenever it is possible to demonstrate that all the individuals have been gathered at the same time.
- A gathering is termed 'collective' (*collectif*) whenever it is possible to demonstrate that all the individuals have not been gathered at one time.
- A gathering is termed 'plural' (*pluriel*) whenever it is not possible to demonstrate its multiple or collective nature, in other words if it gathers at least two people without further precision.
- In a funerary context, that is when the volume is intended to receive the deceased at the completion of their ultimate funeral, then one can speak of a 'burial'. This burial is termed 'individual' if it contains only one dead person, and 'plural' if it gathers several dead individuals together. In the latter case, it can be either multiple, or collective.

These definitions apply in the first instance to archaeology within the framework of an empirical-deductive approach, with reasoning progressing in the shape of a decision tree (Figure 3.1). At the bottom is a set of individuals found in the same place, and more precisely in a same volume considered to be the referential analytical unit. If there are enough arguments to presume that this volume was originally conceived as single and that the individuals were deposited within the same phase of use, then one can speak of 'gathering'. Next, one tries to demonstrate that the gathering is either multiple or collective, and if it is not possible to decide, then it must be termed 'plural'. Lastly, at a higher level of interpretation, the question of the funerary context is raised, and if this context is presumed, then this volume can be termed a 'burial'. At each stage, there is a non-committal term available to mark possible uncertainty, be it temporary or definitive: 'set of individuals' if it concerns spatio-temporal singleness, 'plural' if it is not possible to decide between multiple and collective, and 'gathering' when indetermination relates to the funerary nature of the deposit.

The same terminology can be applied in a similar way within the framework of a hypothetical-deductive approach, for instance in a theoretical model constructed on ethnographic information.

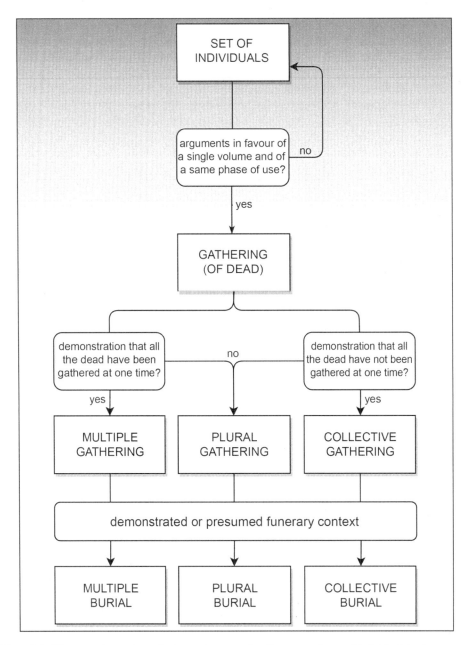

Figure 3.1 The reasoning and terminology relevant to the discovery of a set of individuals in the same archaeological volume.

In a funerary context, on the first level there can be two possible ways to gather the dead together: either each of them gets an individual burial, and the burials are grouped in a bigger volume, such as a vault, or in the same space, as in a cemetery; or all the dead are gathered in a plural burial. On the second level, some plural burials are used only once and will never be used again (multiple), whereas others are used several times (collective). In a non-funerary context, when the volumes cannot be referred to as burials, one speaks of gatherings of the dead, either collective (like the so-called ossuary of the 'Gibbet of Montfaucon' which was in Paris) or multiple (common pits that contain the victims of a massacre, for instance).

The division thus established between 'multiple' and 'collective' is fundamental in that in a funerary context it permits identification of some specific mortuary behaviours. Whereas multiple burials are created to gather together people who can be linked in various ways and who necessarily are already dead or are killed on this occasion, all the collective burials documented in ethnography are established to group kin, even though for some of them death has yet to come. Since this very reason has no known exception in ethnography, it seems possible to conjecture that all archaeological collective burials were created to gather kinship-related people. Besides, it is important to underline that if multiple burials are likely to exist in each and every social group, in particular when mortality crises occur, collective burials exist in only some of them. This could explain why, in Europe, there is no clear evidence of collective burials before the Neolithic, whereas multiple burials are attested as early as the Gravettian period (Henry-Gambier, 2008).

This terminology provides a sturdy foundation upon which to build further reflection since, of course, this is just the beginning and many other questions remain unanswered. The first, and probably the most paramount, is what led some people to choose to gather together kinship-related people in a cemetery and others to opt for the collective burial. This difference of social choice seems very difficult to explain at present. Even within collective burials, there are many variants. This fact has been acknowledged in archaeology and ethnology alike, and it would be of the highest interest to try and match the forms observed in both disciplines. In order to be able to establish reliable relationships, the ethnological model will have to be extended by subdividing what is currently a single category. But this will have to be done in a relevant way, by attempting to respect three principles: first, to sort out what pertains to matters of detail, and what reflects the structures of social groups and how these groups function; next, to select criteria that can be actually translated into terms of social organisation or social functioning; and last, among these criteria, to select those that can also be translated into archaeologically observable facts. This will not be an easy task, and it represents a serious challenge for the coming years, but at least an adapted conceptual and terminological basis from which to begin is already available.

Acknowledgements

The reflections presented in this contribution have benefited over the past years from the outcomes achieved by the ethnological research program carried out on Sumba Island (Indonesia) under the supervision of Christian Jeunesse (University of Strasbourg, France), in which one of us (BB) takes part. The original text was translated from the French by E. Boulestin.

References

Alfonso Quintana, J. and Alesan Alias, A. (2003). Métodos de recuperación, tratamiento y preparación de los restos humanos. In: A. Isidro and A. Malgosa, eds., *Paleopatología: la Enfermedad no Escrita*. Barcelona: Masson, pp. 15–24.

Barker, C., Alicehajic, E. and Naranjo Santana, J. (2017). Post-mortem differential preservation and its utility in interpreting forensic and archaeological mass burials. In: E.M. J. Schotsmans, N. Márquez-Grant and S.L. Forbes, eds., *Taphonomy of human remains. Forensic analysis of the dead and the depositional environment*. Oxford: John Wiley & Sons, pp. 251–276.

Bloch, M. (1971). *Placing the dead. Tombs, ancestral villages, and kinship organization in Madagascar*. London and New York: Seminar Press.

Boulestin, B. (2008). Pourquoi Mourir Ensemble? À Propos des Tombes Multiples dans le Néolithique Français. *Bulletin de la Société Préhistorique Française*, 105(1), pp. 103–130.

Boulestin, B. (2016). *Les sépultures mésolithiques de Téviec et Hoedic: révisions bioarchéologiques*. Oxford: Archaeopress.

Boulestin, B. (2018). "Pourquoi donc Tous ces Chasseurs-Cueilleurs Font-Ils des Tombes Doubles?" *Bulletin de la Société Préhistorique Française*, 115(1), pp. 43–52.

Boulestin, B. (2019). Faut-Il en Finir avec la Sépulture Collective (et Sinon Qu'en Faire)? *Bulletin de la Société Préhistorique Française*, 116(4), pp. 705–723.

Boulestin, B. and Duday, H. (2005). Ethnologie et archéologie de la mort: de l'illusion des références à l'emploi d'un vocabulaire. In: C. Mordant and G. Depierre, eds., *Les Pratiques Funéraires à l'Âge du Bronze en France*. Paris and Sens: Éditions du Comité des Travaux Historiques et Scientifiques (CTHS) and Société Archéologique de Sens, pp. 17–35.

Boulestin, B. and Duday, H. (2006). Ethnology and Archaeology of Death: From the Illusion of References to the Use of a Terminology. *Archaeologia Polona*, 44, pp. 149–169.

Castex, D., Courtaud, P., Duday, H., Le Mort, F. and Tillier, A.-M., eds. (2011). *Le regroupement des morts. Genèse et diversité archéologique*. Bordeaux: Maison des sciences de l'Homme d'Aquitaine et Ausonius (Travaux d'Archéologie Funéraire – Thanat'Os 1).

Courtaud, P. and Duday, H. (2008). Qu'est-ce qu'une sépulture? Comment la reconnaître. In: B. Vandermeersch, J.J. Cleyet-Merle, J. Jaubert, B. Maureille, and A. Truq, eds., *Première Humanité. Gestes Funéraires des Néandertaliens*. Paris: Éditions de la Réunion des Musées Nationaux, pp. 15–24.

Fukui, K. (2001). Socio-Political Characteristics of Pastoral Nomadism: Flexibility among the Bodi (Mela-Me'en) in Southwest Ethiopia. *Nilo-Ethiopian Studies*, 7, pp. 1–21.

Haglund, W.D., Connor, M. and Scott, D.D. (2001). The Archaeology of Contemporary Mass Graves. *Historical Archaeology*, 35(1), pp. 57–69.

Henry-Gambier, D. (2008). Comportement des Populations d'Europe au Gravettien: Pratiques Funéraires et Interprétations. *Paleo*, 20, pp. 399–438.

Hickerson, H. (1960). The Feast of the Dead Among the Seventeenth Century Algonkians of the Upper Great Lakes. *American Anthropologist*, 62, pp. 81–107.

Jeunesse, C. and Denaire, A. (2018). Current collective graves in the Austronesian world. A few remarks about Sumba and Sulawesi (Indonesia). In: A. Schmitt, S. Déderix and I. Crevecoeur, eds., *Gathered in death. archaeological and ethnological perspectives on collective burial and social organisation*. Louvain: Presses Universitaires de Louvain, pp. 85–105.

Kharobi, A. and Buccellati, G. (2017). The Dignity of the Dead. The Case of Ancient Urkesh and Modern Tell Mozan, Syria (2000–1600 BC). *Paléorient*, 43(2), pp. 165–175.

Knüsel, C.J. (2014). Crouching in Fear: Terms of Engagement for Funerary Remains. *Journal of Social Archaeology*, 14(1), pp. 26–58.

Knüsel, C.J. and Robb, J. (2016). Funerary Taphonomy: An Overview of Goals and Methods. *Journal of Archaeological Science: Reports*, 10, pp. 655–673.

Leclerc, J. and Tarrête, J. (1988). Sépulture. In: A. Leroi-Gourhan, ed., *Dictionnaire de la Préhistoire*. Paris: Presses Universitaires de France, pp. 963–964.

Parker Pearson, M. and Regnier, D. (2018). Collective and single burial in Madagascar. In: A. Schmitt, S. Déderix and I. Crevecoeur, eds., *Gathered in death. Archaeological and ethnological perspectives on collective burial and social organisation*. Louvain: Presses Universitaires de Louvain, pp. 41–62.

Rosenblatt, A. (2015). *Digging for the disappeared: Forensic science after atrocity*. Stanford: Stanford University Press.

Schmitt, A. and Déderix, S. (2018). What defines a collective grave? Archaeological and ethnological perspectives on collective burial practices. In: A. Schmitt, S. Déderix and I. Crevecoeur, eds., *Gathered in death. Archaeological and ethnological perspectives on collective burial and social organisation*. Louvain: Presses Universitaires de Louvain, pp. 195–214.

Sprague, R. (2005). *Burial terminology. A guide for researchers*. Lanham: Altamira Press.

Tooker, E. (1964). *An ethnography of the Huron Indians, 1615–1649*. Washington, D.C.: U.S. Government Printing Office (Smithsonian Institution, Bureau of American Ethnology Bulletin 190).

Trigger, B.G. (1987). *The children of Aataentsic. A history of the Huron people to 1660*. Montréal: McGill-Queen's University Press.

Walthall, J.A. (1999). Mortuary Behavior and Early Holocene Land Use in the North American Midcontinent. *North American Archaeologist*, 20(1), pp. 1–30.

Weiss-Krejci, E. (2018). Who is who in the grave? A cross-cultural approach. In: A. Schmitt, S. Déderix and I. Crevecoeur, eds., *Gathered in death. Archaeological and ethnological perspectives on collective burial and social organisation*. Louvain: Presses Universitaires de Louvain, pp. 107–123.

4

SECONDARY CREMATION BURIALS OF PAST POPULATIONS

Some methodological procedures for excavation, bone fragment identification and sex determination

Germaine Depierre

ARTEHIS, Archéologie, Terre, Histoire et Sociétés, UMR 6298, CNRS-Université de Bourgogne-Ministère de la Culture, Dijon, France
Translated from the original French by Christopher J. Knüsel, and Eline M.J. Schotsmans

Introduction: initial developments

French archaeology has fully integrated the study of cremated human remains, as well as systematically including specialists in the field phase of research, thanks to the commitment of Henri Duday to the training of archaeological fieldworkers, regardless of their institutional affiliation, including members of the French research council *Centre National de la Recherche Scientifique* (CNRS), from the Ministry of Culture, museums, local authorities and public or private agencies, through a series of short courses. The first such course in mainland France took place at the Musée de l'Ephébe in Cap d'Agde (Hérault, South of France) in 1992 and continued for nine years. For two weeks, it brought together an average of eight participants (Duday, Depierre and Janin, 2000; Depierre, 2014: 142ff.). The author of this contribution continued this type of training while teaching at the University of Burgundy Franche-Comté, in particular for masters and doctoral candidates in archaeology.

It is important to highlight that the Cap d'Agde courses marked a turning point in consideration of burnt human remains in archaeology, but they were not the first to take an interest in the subject. The sorting of bone fragments during the study of burnt human remains was already recommended by Gejvall in the late 1940s (Gejvall, 1947; 1981) and then, again, by Brothwell (1981), before Duday took up the subject (Duday, Depierre and Janin, 2000), who initiated, among other practices, spreadsheets for recording cremated remains.

This contribution does not aim to present all of the methods related to the study of cremations. They are too numerous and include a very diverse range of subjects, among them the following: separation of burnt animal remains from those of human origin, calculation of the minimum number of individuals, determination of sex and age-at-death, recognition of pathological abnormalities, types of fragmentation, intensity of combustion, creation of comparative weight

DOI: 10.4324/9781351030625-6

reference samples, post-cremation treatments of remains, including their placement in containers and the recognition of organic matter used in their manufacture, the construction of grave structures and the excavation and layout of them. This contribution focuses on the excavation of cinerary urns and the human remains assemblages they contain, cremated remains without containers and those in perishable containers, and the determination of sex from such remains, which is closely linked to the weight of the bones.

The excavation of urns: the fundamental importance of the recognition of burnt human remains

The excavation of urns, or rather of bone assemblages that include ceramic vessels containing the bones which often become fragmented during their excavation and lifting, formed the basis of part of the activities of the Cap d'Agde short courses (Figure 4.1). At that time, the urn contents were completely explored with the aim of losing as little information as possible. For a container of 0.15 m to 0.25 m in maximum diameter, with 0.10 m to 0.30 m layer of bone, the excavation as well as the cleaning of the bones and their identification, took about five days, or one working week. The results of this type of short course – the methods used, their merits, but also, and above all, the critical review of the former, exhaustive method has been published (Duday, Depierre and Janin, 2000). Indeed, a week of work for a single urn when a site may have hundreds of them can rarely be justified financially without prejudicing other studies, including recording of the site, study and drawing of grave goods, and study of animal remains, in addition to the drafting and editing of reports which must be systematically returned to the regional archaeological service within a defined period of time. During these courses, it was already anticipated that the length of time necessary for such studies could be reduced to two or three days, which is still a substantial investment. Due to the dissemination of the results of these courses, the excavation of only the urns can now be carried out much more rapidly and accomplished in a day to a day-and-a-half, on

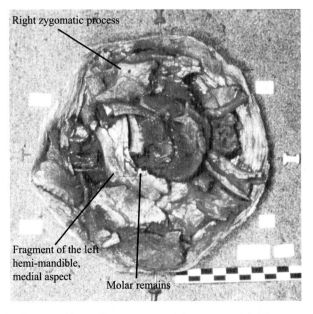

Right zygomatic process

Fragment of the left hemi-mandible, medial aspect

Molar remains

Figure 4.1 Example of an assemblage of bones excavated during one of the short course sessions in Agde, Hérault, France (Photograph: G. Depierre).

average, perhaps 4–8 hours. This means that the complete analysis would take, on average, half a day, which is still not trivial financially, but which remains achievable with previous experience, even for large sites. For those sites with only a few cremated secondary burials, urn excavations can be anticipated to take longer. In this context, it is essential to emphasise that the excavation of the urn should be carried out by a specialist in the study of cremations and burnt bone remains, preferably the same person who carried out the field recovery.

Experience shows that immediately recording bone assemblages in order to identify particular fragments is most effective and avoids artificially increasing fragmentation during excavation and recording. During the excavation of the urn, the bones are put out to dry after each fragment is recovered in order to easily remove the soil matrix, or, if necessary, perhaps by passing them under running water and lightly brushing them to ensure that they are in the best condition for analysis. The loose sediment from the excavation is sieved in order to recover isolated bone fragments. The residue from sieving should be retained. This procedure means that time is not lost between the excavation of the bone assemblage and the study of the remains. Moreover, the residue retrieved from the sieve may provide important insights for the later interpretation of the site.

This procedure was followed during the study of the site of 'Petit Moulin', a Bronze Age necropolis in Migennes (Yonne, France), which is in the course of publication. Once the excavation had been completed, it appeared that two areas of the site could be differentiated, one containing the majority of secondary cremation burials and the other area contained the majority of inhumations, which were particularly well accompanied with grave goods when compared to the cremation burials. The initial thought was that this reflected a social duality: the poor (cremation) on one side, the rich (burial) on the other. However, the study of sieve residues by L. Staniaszek (Institut National de Recherches Archéologiques Préventives, Inrap, Grand Est) permitted the identification of a piece from the beam of a balance and a gold thread with a thickness on the order of a micron. For all periods, individuals interred with balances are considered to have a special status, and the presence of gold thread seems only to confirm this association. Based on this evidence, the suspected social duality initially envisaged could no longer be maintained. It was therefore necessary to entertain the possibility of a unique treatment of the corpse associated with this particular site, if not being exclusive to it.

The actual excavation of the urn, whether made from perishable material or not, does not require a long period of training if the excavator already has a good knowledge of burnt bone remains. Two to three days can be enough to obtain a requisite degree of autonomy, with confidence and speed obtained through repeated practice. This is greatly aided by a specialist who can act in the role of a tutor to whom the newly trained excavator can refer if in doubt. The identification of bone fragments from the intentional cremation of a corpse, however, requires longer training and preferably a good knowledge of human bones (see below).

In recent years, an approach to the study of the fill of the urns has been developed using computed tomography combined with photogrammetry that permits 3D reconstruction (e.g. Anderson and Fell, 1995; Harvig, Lynnerup, and Amsgaard Ebsen, 2012; Višnjić *et al.*, 2013; De Larminat *et al.*, 2017; Cavalli *et al.*, 2015; Nicolas *et al.*, 2016; Vidal, 2017; Le Goff *et al.*, 2019). This also requires very good knowledge of burnt human bones. Even though the results are impressive, they relate only to studies of very small samples at a still experimental stage. The discussion here will not focus on this type of study because the time required, the added familiarity necessary for virtual bone identifications, and the cost of the instrument means they may not be applicable for use with large assemblages – whether the equipment employed is of medical or industrial specifications, the cautions of Nicolas and colleagues (2016: 6): 'access to technology, the required skills, and analytical limits of instrumentation' ('*l'accès à la technologie, des compétences requises et des limitations de l'appareillage*') merit consideration.

The financial constraints inherent to salvage archaeology may make it necessary to sample bone assemblages and to move them from the site to a storage and/or study area. The use of radiography, especially since the advent of digital systems, can greatly help to recognise clusters of artefacts in order to ascertain their usefulness for relative dating. This process can also help to prioritise samples based on a preliminary survey of those recovered from a site. X-rays can also help to show the sediment thickness covering the urn contents to remove them more quickly in order to reach the human remains, as well as indicating if the urn was filled with sediment before or after having been tilted on its side, which helps to reconstruct the layout of burial features. Becker and colleagues (2003) demonstrated the capacity of classical radiography of urns to identify artefacts, their location before excavation, and to aid exploration and emptying of the assemblage of human remains from the urn. Obviously, when using medical or even industrial equipment, the size of the sample must be easy to manipulate by hand. This can prove difficult for protohistoric remains and particularly those from the Bronze Age, a period often characterised by the use of large urns, more than 30 cm up to nearly 50 cm, and more so if archaeologists retain thick sediment that surrounds vases in block-lifting in the field, even before applying plaster or polyurethane foam around them. Although these lifting methods are less used today, advantageously replaced by excavation following the original layers of the contents as closely as possible, which are often maintained in place with cling film. Archaeological storage facilities, however, still contain these older voluminous samples that are too large to study using conventional radiography, computed tomography or other means of imaging. Although it is prudent not to deny the advent of 'virtual archaeology', at this time it still seems premature to recommend that these new approaches replace the manual excavation of bone deposits in the short or medium term.

Bone identification

While conventional excavation techniques can easily be acquired in a few days, the same is not applicable for the identification of burnt bone fragments. This training can be obtained through specialised short courses or university courses. One of the most obvious consequences of cremation is the ways in which the process transforms remains. Remains shrink, deform, break (Figures 4.1–4.3), and curl to a variable extent depending on their anatomical location, their size, and their structure (the phalanges and smaller long bones are rarely deformed, for example), and depending on their location in the pyre. Shrinkage may be between 5% and more than 25%, according to various authors (e.g. Anderson, 1957; Van Vark, 1970; Strzałko, Piontek and Malinowski, 1974; Eckert, James and Katchis, 1988; Mayne Correia, 1997; Dokládál, 1999).

Shrinkage of more than 27% was observed for two fragments of the same humerus (Figure 4.4) in burial 132 from the protohistoric necropolis of Gourjade in the Tarn region of Southern France (Giraud, Pons and Janin, 2003; Depierre, 2014: 45, fig. 12). This example demonstrates the fact that colour alone does not correspond to the extent of heat exposure of the bones but also that the extent of deformation must be taken into account. Similarly, during the study of burial 109 of the Ordaschi Major site (Hungary), two clavicles, a right and a left, were excavated by archaeologists and attributed to two different individuals, a robust adult and a slender adult, based solely on their size and thickness. After re-examination, it was possible to show that they had not experienced the same thermal exposure in the fire, the left being less burnt than the right. The soft tissue attachment areas, however, remained symmetrical (Depierre 2014: 46, fig. 13). They were, in fact, two clavicles from the same individual, the left clavicle having been protected from the high-temperature zone of the fire by having fallen into the ash, which acted as a thermal shield of the remains from the heat of the fire.

The fragmentation and the deformation of cremated bones mean that notions of normal bone shape and proportions must be adjusted to permit identification. Bones can no longer be thought

Deformed left femur

Acetabulo-femoral
articulation

Figure 4.2 A corpse in the process of cremation in a modern French crematorium: detail of the left femur (Photograph: G. Depierre).

Cover of the coffin

Right radius

Right ulna

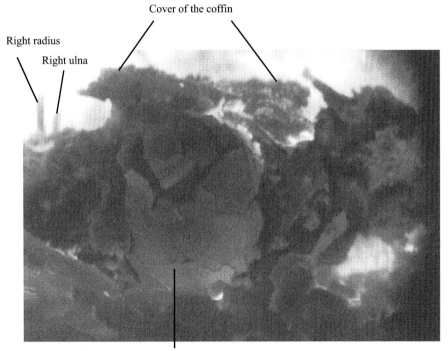

Cranium in the process of fragmentation

Figure 4.3 A corpse in the process of cremation in a modern French crematorium: detail of the superior part of the corpse (Photograph: G. Depierre; cf. Depierre, 2014: 285, fig. 215b).

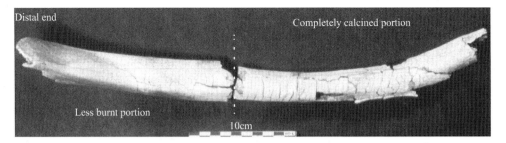

Figure 4.4 The right humerus from Grave 312 from Gourjade, Tarn, France (Photograph: J. Roger).

of only as a whole element or based solely on their external shape. The soft tissue attachments on the surface of bones and the organisation of the trabeculae within bones are fundamental aids to identification of fragments (Figure 4.5). These are characterised by lacunae in the cancellous bone architecture of vertebral bodies, in longitudinal alveoli in the body of the ribs, and which give a bubbly appearance to the diploë of the cranial vault, an appearance that is close to that of certain faunal bones at the distal end of the humerus; and in the irregularities in the thickness of the cortex at the attachment of the *pronator teres* muscle on the diaphysis of the radius (Figure 4.5). To aid in the identification of burnt bones, a reference collection of sectioned dry bones of specific regions (Figures 4.5 and 4.6) has been developed. These reference samples help comparison between burnt bone fragments and these reference specimens. Long bone cross-sections from both slender and robust adults, as well as immature individuals, have also been rendered photographically to support identification (Figures 4.6 and 4.7).

In the intermediate-term students can acquire truly independent research skills during doctoral studies. Training offered during the completion of a Master's degree is, however, too short. Archaeological training with a human osteology option is often provided in the second year of a two-year Master (Bologna Agreement Master's degree offering), like that at the University of Burgundy Franche Compte. It is therefore necessary that students possessing a Master's degree within this speciality have the support of a specialist, so that bone identifications and interpretations and conclusions are not in doubt. This type of training has so far posed no problems for work in professional archaeological enterprises, whether public or private. It seems essential in the context of training to attain the capacity to identify as precisely as possible fragments in order to facilitate conjoining of them. This requires recording during study that is more developed and flexible than that those of the tables of numbers and weights developed by Duday during the Cap d'Agde courses (Duday, Depierre and Janin, 2000) to accommodate novel observations made as the research progresses (see below). Information collected during recording varies depending on the bone sample studied. It is most often entered in a notebook specific to the excavator of the bone assemblage at a given site. The phrase 'fragment from axis', for example, is not enough. What is the anatomical location of the fragment? Is it the apex of the axis? Does it include the superior and/or inferior articular surfaces or not? Are degenerative bone changes present? If yes, where do these occur? Above all, it is important to be clear about the reasoning process followed for the identification in order to highlight relevant morphological features present on the fragment. This type of procedure is fundamental to developing best research practices to aid calculation of the Minimum Number of Individuals (MNI). This approach to identification will also permit making informed strategic choices at a later stage – for example, by being able to choose the type and quantity of information that will be lost if it is necessary to carry out a more rapid study than required. Salvage archaeology often requires this type of adjustment due to time constraints.

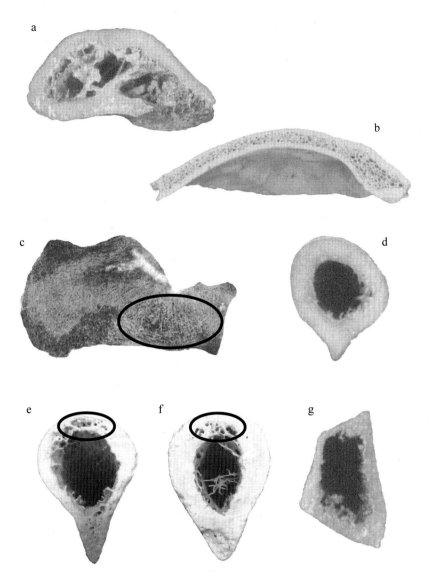

Figure 4.5 Specific features of bone cross-sections: (a). Trabecular organisation at the distal end of humeral diaphysis; (b). Spongy cancellous bone ('air cells') of the mastoid process of the cranium; (c). Orientation of the trabecular struts in the right calcaneus; (d). Tear-drop-shaped cross-section of the mid-diaphysis of the right radius; (e). Pores in the cortical bone at the attachment site of *M. pronator teres* (the pronator tubercle) of the left radial diaphysis in a gracile individual; (f). pores in the cortical bone at the attachment site of *M. pronator teres* (the pronator tubercle) of the right radial diaphysis in a robust individual; (g). angles and thicknesses of the right fibular diaphysis (Photographs: G. Depierre).

With the initial stages of bone sorting accomplished, the most frequent subsequent question asked about the remains is the most difficult to provide, namely what is the sex and age of the deceased? This corresponds to what more 'forensically-minded' English-speaking researchers call 'the biological profile' (Nugent, 2010). The similarity between English-speaking and French research traditions stops at the determination of sex and the estimation of the age-at-death of

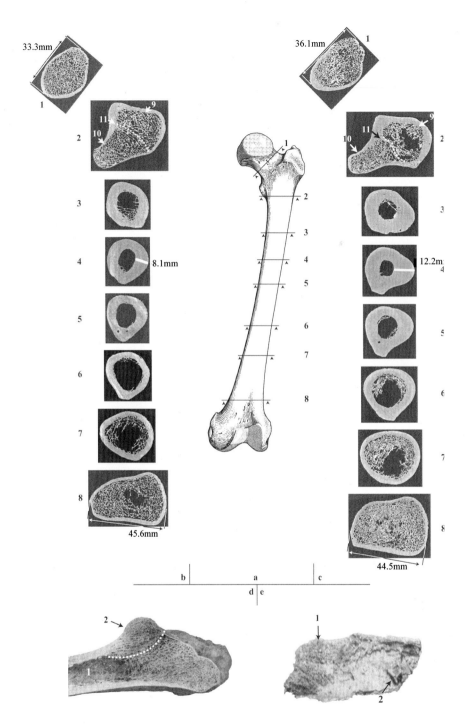

Figure 4.6 Adult left femur. (a). Anterior aspect showing transverse cross-sections in (b). a gracile adult, and (c). a robust adult; (d). Proximal end of the femur (1: medullary cavity and 2: lesser trochanter, with a dotted line separating the two); (e). a fragment from the posterior portion of the distal end, (1: spongy cancellous tissue of the distal end; 2: thick, cylindrical trabeculae, from bottom to top and from right to left) (after Depierre, 2014: 491, fig. 419).

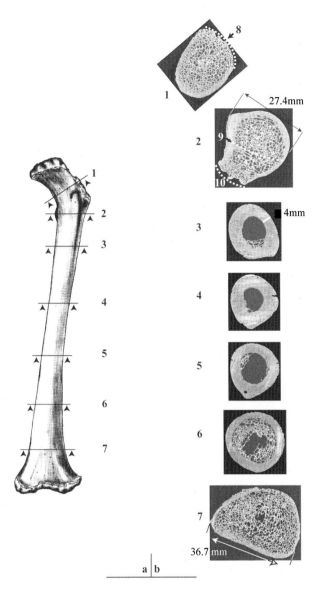

Figure 4.7 The left femur of a nine-year-old child: (a). anterior aspect and location of transverse cross-sections (Reproduced with kind permission of S. Wheeler; cf. Baker *et al.*, 2005: 168, fig. 10.8); (b). images of the cross-sections (CAD after Depierre, 2014: 513, fig. 441).

the deceased, since the latter, French researchers, do not address the population origin of the individuals under study. This type of question is more often than not of medico-legal interest for contemporary populations, but this type of determination remains difficult to answer even for contemporary populations in a forensic context. In the 1970s, however, Eastern European researchers tried to restore the morphological features of cremated individuals in an attempt to judge morphological variability among past populations to address migrations, a study regularly carried out for un-cremated individuals (e.g. Chochol, 1953, 1955; Schaefer, 1960, 1961, 1964; Gladykowska-Rzeczycka, 1974).

Sex determination: a question of weight?

The entire archaeological community in the broadest sense agrees that the bone that provides the most reliable sex determination is the *os coxae*, morphologically (e.g. Bruzek, 1991, 2002; Bruzek and Ferembach, 1992; Bruzek, Castex and Majo, 1996) and osteometrically (Murail, Bruzek and Braga, 1999, 2000). The *ossa coxae* permit a primary sex determination meaning that they can be used on all humans without chronological or geographical limits. For skeletons of uncremated individuals, provided that these bones are sufficiently complete, this poses few problems. If some of these skeletons do not have complete *os coxae*, it may be possible to make a secondary diagnosis with the better-preserved bone elements of all individuals in the assemblage (e.g. Bruzek, Castex and Majo, 1996). The validity of this type of determination, based on sexually dimorphic bone size, must be confirmed on those individuals from whom sex could be determined based on the *ossa coxae* of the specific population concerned. Despite these possibilities, the number of individuals of indeterminate sex may be quite high depending on the extent of the preservation of the remains.

Research on burnt human remains has two essential features. The first, already mentioned above, relates to deformation, fragmentation, and shrinkage of bones, alterations that are not favourable to the preservation of *ossa coxae*. If the cremation is tended or managed ('*crémation conduite*' in French) by manipulations of the corpse or parts of it during cremation, as is done in contemporary India (Grévin, 2004), or if the bones are manipulated while they are hot, they will fragment at the slightest touch. In Figure 4.8, the left *os coxae* was extracted from a modern

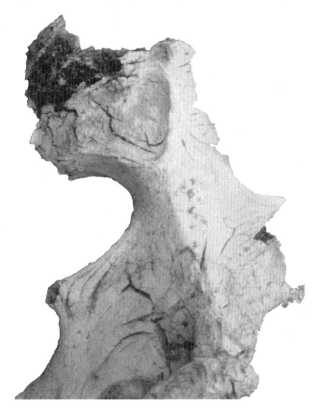

Figure 4.8 The left *os coxae* of a male retrieved from the cremation oven with fireplace tongs (Photograph: G. Depierre).

cremation oven in which the cremation of the deceased had been carried out with extreme care. The relevant elements for the determination of sex (in this case, a male) were retained. However, in archaeology this type of preservation is rare, if not extremely rare, with the exception, perhaps, of pyre excavations, because the bones had been handled only after being cooled. Several authors (e.g. Kurila, 2015) attest to the *ossa coxae* being too extensively damaged to be used in sex determination of secondary cremation burials (i.e. those transported and deposited at a distance from the pyre).

The second essential feature concerns funerary practices and which remains are placed in the cinerary urn. Most of the urns in secondary cremation burials excavated in mainland France contain only a part of the skeleton, i.e. a few hundred grams, while the average weight of a skeleton usually greatly exceeds a kilogram. During research carried out in crematoria on modern individuals, the average weight of the skeleton after cremation differed according to age and the experimental facility employed. Average weights range from 1766.7 g (Herrmann, 1976) to 3105.1 g (McKinley, 1993) regardless of sex. Bass and Jantz (2004) suggested an average value of 2858.2 g. The author carried out this type of experiment in France, in a single crematorium (Depierre, 2014). The sample included 103 cremations, 48 females and 55 males. The average total weight of the females was 2374.3 g, while that of the males was 3113.8 g. Having used the protocol developed by McKinley (1993), the weight was also calculated after excluding fragments less than 2 mm in size, which provided the following values: 2021.9 g and 2747.6 g for females and males, respectively. Without dividing the sample by sex, these results were close to those reported by Bass and Jantz (2004): 2765.8 g and 2406.1 g, after removing the smallest fragments. The lowest total weight was that of an 84-year-old female (1456.3 g), the highest (4009.6 g) was that of a 67-year-old male. After removing the weight of fragments less than 2 mm in size, the lowest weight still came from the 84-year-old female (1166.2 g) and the heaviest fragments (3640.5 g) came from a 45-year-old male. In these studies, it should be noted that regardless of the place or country in which weight information was obtained, the bulk of the samples comprised deceased persons over 50 years of age at death, and many over 60 years of age at death. The lower weight of older females is largely due to the thinness of the bones, most certainly linked to the effects of the menopause and decalcification of bones. The trabecular organisation of the spongy bone tissue of smaller bone fragments, such as those from vertebrae and the proximal end of the femur, are often very porous and thus not very dense, and the walls of the long bones are not very thick. They are all very fragile.

Structures linked to the cremation of individuals from past populations and, in particular, individual secondary burials of adults discovered in mainland France produce values that are much lower than those from modern crematoria. To take a few examples of individual graves of adults, from 52 graves that provided the sample for the short course at Cap d'Agde (Hérault, France), 48 were selected for analysis. The average bone weight of these was 714.2 g, with a standard deviation of 418.3 g (Duday, Depierre and Janin, 2000: 19ff.). The overall study of the three major cemeteries of the Castrais (Tarn, France) provided an average weight of 603.5 g (Roger *et al.*, 2003). The data from 10 protohistoric cemeteries located in the Lot, the Tarn, the Tarn-et-Garonne, the Aude and the Hérault regions (Lenorzer, 2006) are presented in Table 4.1. The individual average weights are less than 500 g, and the maximum weight exceeds a kilogram in only three cases. The Late Bronze Age necropolis at Ensisheim/Reguisheimerfeld (Haut-Rhin, France) produced 14 individual burials, the median weight of which was 527.2 g (first quartile: 92.2 g; third quartile: 774.4 g) (Prouin, 2007: 176ff.). Of the 92 individual secondary burials from the Reims necropolis at 84–86 Avenue André Malraux in Lorraine, France, the average weight of the bone samples was 449 g, with a standard deviation of 320.7 g (Barrand Emam, 2012: 273ff.). Only four cremations, or 4.3% of the total, provided more than one kilogram of bone. For the

Table 4.1 Summary table of the average weight data in grams from various sites in France (after Lenorzer, 2006)

Sites	Number of individuals	Mean	Standard deviation	Min.	Max.	References
Camp de l'Église-sud, Flojac-Pouzols (Lot)	14	237.3	131.7	82.3	514.4	Pons *et al.* (2001); Lenorzer (2006)
Camp d'Alba, Réalville (Tarn et Garonne)	31	428.5	261.6	163.3	665.9	Janin *et al.* (1997); Lenorzer (2006)
La Ferme du Frau, Cazals (Tarne et Garonne)	72	248.8	170.6			Lenorzer (2006)
Place de Vigan, Albi (Tarn)	8	59.2	39.1	10.6	140.6	Lenorzer (2006)
Castres, Le Causse (Tarn)	283	445.2	272.1	32.3	1439.9	Roger *et al.* (2003); Lenorzer (2006)
Castres, Gourjade (Tarn)	233	689.7	43.7	27.3	2210.9	Roger *et al.* (2003); Lenorzer (2006)
Castres, Le Martinet (Tarn)	87	245.7	186.5	25.7	885.7	Roger *et al.* (2003); Lenorzer (2006)
Mailhac: Le Moulin, Cimetière du Grand Bassin, Le Grand Bassin II (Aude)	126	484.7	359.8	2.3	1587	Taffanel *et al.* (1998); Janin *et al.* (2002); Lenorzer (2006)
Couffoulens, Las Peyros (Aude)	32	355.3	218.3	8.1	740.4	Passelac *et al.* (1981); Duday (1981); Lenorzer (2006)
Agde, Le Peyrou (Hérault)	87	620.8	278.4	92.4	1252.1	Duday (1989); Lenorzer (2006)

67 individual burials in the necropolis at Bavay (La Fâche des Près Aulnoys, Nord, France), the average bone weight was 482.4 g, with a standard deviation of 309.1 g, six of them, or 8.9% of the total, contained one kilogram or more of bone, (Barrand Emam, 2012: 365ff.). Finally, for the Thérouanne necropolis (Arras Road, Pas-de-Calais, France), the 13 individual burials, including a pyre-burial, produced an average weight of 369.5 g, with a standard deviation of 470.6 g. Two, including the pyre-grave, produced more than a kilogram of bone (Barrand Emam, 2012: 424ff.). These three necropolises date to the Roman period. The 150 deposits of the necropolis at Vatteville-la-Rue, Landes (Seine-Maritime, France), also dated to the Roman period, produced an average weight of 291.9 g, with a range between 2.4 g and 1097.1 g (Gadacz, 2019: 197ff.). The author also calculated the average weight by excluding the smallest assemblages, those of less than 100 g of bone, and the value remained low: 351.2 g (minimum of 102 g and maximum of 1097.1 g).

These examples from mainland France are representative of the average bone weight produced by most individual secondary cremation burials in most of the protohistoric and Roman period necropolises uncovered to date. This implies that the entirety of the remains of the deceased were not placed in the grave, or that not all of the remains had been removed after the completion of the cremation due to fragmentation, especially in the case of tended cremations (see above, cf. Grévin, 2004), or perhaps due to the compromised state of health of the individual and low bone mass. Note that it is rare to be able to make the link between the cremation material taken from the pyre and the material placed in the grave because it is uncommon to have individual cremation areas that correspond to a specific secondary burial. In certain cases, the remains coming from the cleaning of the pyre can be deposited (thrown?) into the grave.

The weight of the urn contents can be added to the amount of bone found in the grave-pit, and this figure approaches the average weight of a complete skeleton after cremation. Depending on the case in question, perhaps it is best to consider that a portion of the remains was not placed in the grave and may have been deposited elsewhere, in an individual or collective family grave, thus in a grave defined by the social group to which the deceased belonged. Alternatively, it could have been deposited in several places, distributed and associated with other deceased individuals in other funerary structures.

When studying the burials from the Roman necropolis of Porta Nocera in Pompeii (Italy) (cf. Duday, Chapter 15, this volume), the amount of burnt bone from funerary structures linked to the cremation of corpses was such that Duday classified them into seven categories (Van Andringa *et al.*, 2013: 12). These range from 'extremely high weight' (≥ 2000 g) to 'extremely low weight' (≤ 749 g) (Table 4.2). By comparing this classification with the average weights of the sites presented in Table 4.1, their total weights would systematically place them in the lowest class. It thus seems that in this very specific case, from a total of 47 receptacles containing the remains of a single individual, there were 16 males (34%), 21 females (44.7%), and only ten individuals of undetermined sex (21.3%), a result that is remarkable. The fact that the weights of the remains of males are heavier than those of females has been demonstrated statistically (Van Andringa *et al.*, 2013: 870, note 6). If the weight data of females is considered (Table 4.2), a third of them provide values that place them in the last two categories, that is to say, 'very low, between 750 g and 999 g and extremely low, below 749 g' (Duday, 2013: 12). For only three of these eight females, the determination of sex is based on classic osteological features observable on the bones of the pelvis. These come from graves 8, 42 and 205, and for the last, only one osteological observation was relevant, 'a broad and deep pre-auricular sulcus on the left ilium' ('*un sillon préauriculaire large et profond sur l'ilium gauche*') (Van Andringa *et al.*, 2013: 661). One of the authors (Duday) recognised that this single characteristic could be insufficient if it was not associated with the extreme thinness of the bones due to their demineralisation. This individual is therefore considered to be a 'probable female' (Van Andringa *et al.*, 2013: 666). The remains from three other graves (numbers 25, 28, 43) were also attributed to probable females because of their extremely gracile bones associated with them also being elderly; they would therefore be post-menopausal females. The certainty of this determination only seems assured for individual 43, whose frontal bone bears evidence of *hyperostosis frontalis interna* (Van Andringa *et al.*, 2013: 149). The sex determination of the last two individuals is based on the epitaph linked to the grave (burial 2) and the specific shape of the funerary stele (burial 101). For the latter, the study of the bone remains produced only a single sex-related characteristic 'the greater sciatic notch seems rather open' ('*la grande incisure ischiatique semble plutôt ouverte*') (Van Andringa *et al.*, 2013: 753), which one of the authors (Duday) considers to be insufficient for positive sex determination. For the five males tabulated in the last three categories (Table 4.2), the determination of sex is based in only one case (for burial 18) on classic osteological characteristics; for the other four (burials 1, 11, 15B et 21B), it is the morphology of the stelae or the epitaphs which make it possible to specify the sex of the deceased.

Burials containing the remains of individuals of undetermined sex are found in the third, fourth, fifth and sixth classes of bone weight, but not the last. In all cases, the fragment identification rate is considered to be medium (between 80% and 84.9%) or poor (between 70% and 74.9%) due to heavy bone fragmentation. The same problematical situation is found in the graves for which sex determination was possible. What contributes to the difference in results is whether or not several classic osteological characteristics of the *os coxae* are available for assessment, if pathological conditions related to sex (osteoporosis) are present, and the extent of the detail of archaeological information relating to the sex of the deceased indicated on stelae or associated

Table 4.2 Summary table of the weight data of the individual graves from the Porta Nocera necropolis, Pompeii, Italy (after Van Andringa *et al.*, 2013) (ind. = indeterminate)

Grave number	Sex	Class 1	Class 2	Class 3	Class 4	Class 5	Class 6	Class 7
		≤ 2000 g	1750 to 1999 g	1500 to 1749 g	1250 to 1499 g	1000 to 1249 g	750 to 999 g	≥749 g
1	M						930.4	
3	M				1332.2			
6	M		1803.5					
7	M		1789.2					
11	M					1241.5		
12	M			1560				
15B	M					1041.9		
16	M		1835.8					
17	M	2005						
18	M							740.3
21B	M					1114.2		
31	M		1757.2					
32	M		1901.8					
34	M				1392.2			
40	M				1453.6			
45	M				1377			
	N=16	1	5	1	4	3	1	1
2	F							621.7
8	F						753.8	
19	F			1563				
21A	F			1552.9				
25	F						983.3	
26	F				1305.5			
28	F						810.3	
30	F				1478.8			
33	F			1518.3				
42	F						845.9	
43	F							546.8
44	F					1034		
101	F						823.4	
102–107	F			1566.6				
202	F					1071.8		
203	F					1230.6		
205	F						780.6	
206	F					1033.8		
207	F			1527.4				
212	F					1119		
213	F		1967.4					
	N=21	0	1	5	2	5	6	2
9	Ind.					1092.1		
13	Ind.					1007.1		
15A	Ind.			1520.1				
22	Ind.				1236.8			
36	Ind.						915.3	
41	Ind.						974.2	
46	Ind.				1488.5			
47	Ind.						922	
208	Ind.			1564.4				
211	Ind.				1409.7			
	N=10	0	0	2	3	2	3	0

epigraphy. However, necropolises like that from Pompeii are rare in Italy and even more so in mainland France, where it should be recalled that the quantity of bone weights is generally low.

More recently, the opportunity to study the cremation burials of the Roman necropolis of 'À la Montagne', in Avenches (Switzerland), revealed an average weight of 483.6 g for individual adult burials (Depierre and Supryk, 2017: 158). The only available distinctive sexual characteristic was skeletal robustness; some extremely robust individuals were very likely to have been males. Conversely, while extremely gracile individuals could be associated with post-menopausal females, only a certain number of males could be confirmed, which does not contribute any real clarity to the overall results from this site.

As has already been emphasised above, in the necropolis of Porta Nocera cremation burials produced higher human bone weights for males than for females, but without being able to determine a value above which would indicate a male or below which a female.

Weight as a criterion for determining the sex of cremated individuals was regularly relied upon in the late 60s and early 70s (e.g. Malinowski, 1969; Malinowski and Porawski, 1969; Rösing, 1977a, 1977b) based on the principle that females have lighter skeletons than males. The results, though, have the same limitations: only extreme weights can be taken into account, the very heavy in a given population will be attributable to males and the lowest in the same population to females. But what does this entail for average values that include both males and females? Van Deest and colleagues (2011) explored this type of research fairly recently in a sample of North American individuals. This study on contemporary cremations was conducted in the same crematorium used in medico-legal research. The goal was to provide the best possible methods to identify the deceased from house or car fires involving several individuals. The weight results were compared with individual data from three other samples of the same type, which showed a large number of overlaps in weight. Using statistical tools, the authors tried to overcome this pitfall by calculating a border value or 'sectioning point' obtaining a weight of 2697.3 g for this value. For these four samples of the North American population, weights higher than this value were accepted as being the cut-off for male weights and, below it, for female weights. These data made it possible to correctly classify 80.2% of the males and 82.1% of the females, which nevertheless means that in each group there was an error of almost 20%; in other words, one individual in five would be misclassified.

Even if the validity of this sectioning point between males and females is accepted, it must be emphasised that these authors note that this is only valid for the population concerned; the current North American population. It cannot be used for, among others, South American or Asian populations, for example, modern or not. Therefore, in no case can it be directly applicable to the study of populations from the past.

Other methods use metric data from modern experimental cremations (e.g. Nugent, 2010; Gonçalves, 2011a, 2011b, 2014; Gonçalves, Thompson and Cunha, 2013; Cavazutti *et al.*, 2019). The identified remains or portions of them are variable but derive in the main from the skull, the proximal and distal ends of the humerus, the *ossa coxae*, the proximal parts of the femora, the talus and calcaneus. Most osteometric observations are based on the measurements developed by Steele (1976). In all these studies, many bone measurements are necessary to carry out sex determination. However, in archaeological reality, as has already been stressed, it is rare to have more than four of these elements, the most relevant being the *ossa coxae*. The error rate in the classifications carried out as a result of this experimental research work, overall, was around 30%, although, in these modern cremations, the researchers benefited from being able to study the entire skeleton. It is therefore obvious that for the study of past populations, when a more or less greater portion of the skeleton is placed in a grave but had become heavily fragmented during the cremation process, these methods contribute little in the way of resolution.

Being aware of these difficulties, a good number of researchers have targeted their methodological approaches on the temporal bone and, in particular, on the petrous pyramid, which is considered to preserve well during the process of cremation. Initiated in the early 1980s by Wahl (1981) and Schutkowski (1983), this research has been mainly followed up by Graw and Wahl in a series of publications (e.g. Graw, 1999; Wahl and Graw, 2001; Graw and Haffner, 2000; Graw, Schulz, and Wahl, 2003, Graw, Wahl and Ahlbrecht, 2005; Todd, Graw and Dietzel, 2010) on burnt as well as unburnt bones and always for forensic purposes, even if they envisage a use for 'archaeologically-oriented anthropologists'. Quite recently, Masotti and colleagues (2013) took up this theme in a study of bone remains from modern cremations. They focused on the lateral angle of the internal acoustic meatus and showed that an angle of 45° could be a borderline value between males and females in unburnt skeletal remains, but it was not the same for remains from modern cremations. The value that would separate male from female remains was 37° due to the effect of cremation on the remains. However, their conclusion draws attention to many overlapping values, and these researchers state that this method can help confirm the sex determination when other osteological characteristics can also be assessed.

One could continue to present other methods from the literature, but all of them remain difficult to use for cremated remains from past populations. The assessment presented here is not intended to be pessimistic but rather intended to be realistic. As McKinley (1994: 19) noted, it seems that sex determination from archaeological contexts depends more on 'the presence of certain bones within a cremation' than on the continued search for specific methods applicable to burnt bones.

Conclusion

Studying secondary cremation burials is challenging. This chapter discussed excavation techniques, bone identification and sex determination. Basic research on the determination of sex from deliberately cremated corpses provides results that are systematically described as encouraging, but they are more likely to be used for forensic purposes rather than funerary cremations. At the beginning of the 1960s, Wells (1960) did not envisage that it would be possible to determine the sex of more than 30% of cremated individuals based on osteological observations for any given deposit. The success of determination can now be significantly higher, as shown by the example of the study of the necropolis of Porta Nocéra (Italy), where the form of stelae and epigraphs associated with graves attest to the sex of the deceased. This example remains a remarkable exception, however. Indeed, the difficulty in using artefacts associated with the deceased to aid sex assessment is often only used to demonstrate their relevance to sex determination. Objects of a given geographical and chronological affiliation cannot be transferred to another region or period. Therefore, the elements on which the determination of sex is based must always be specified, burial-by-burial. Of course, this unavoidable problem of the sex of the cremated dead can be considered only if determinations based on the analysis of human remains pose no doubt about their reliability.

Acknowledgement

The author would like to thank L. Staniaszek from the Institut National de Recherches Archéologiques Préventives (Inrap) Grand Est.

References

Anderson, H.J. (1957). *Experimetelle unterschungen über das verhalten von knochen beim verbrennen*. Ungedruckte Semestralarbeit, Keil: Anthropologische Institut der Universität Kiel.
Anderson, T. and Fell, C. (1995). Analysis of Roman Cremation Vessels by Computerized Tomography. *Journal of Archaeological Science*, 22, pp. 609–617.

Baker, B., Dupras, T. and Tocheri, M. (2005). *The osteology of infants and children*. College Station: Texas A&M University Press.

Barrand Emam, H. (2012). Les pratiques funéraires liées à la crémation dans les ensembles funéraires des capitales de cités du Haut Empire en Gaule Belgique: Metz-Divodurum, Bavay-Bagacum, Thérouanne-Tervanna. Unpublished doctoral thesis, Université de Lyon II Lumière, Lyon.

Bass, W.M. and Jantz, R.L. (2004). Cremation Weights in East Tennessee. *Journal of Forensic Sciences*, 49, 5, pp. 901–904.

Becker, M.H., Breuer, H. and Schafberg, R. (2003). Diagnostik an Brandgräbern der Römischen Kaiserzeit. *Jahresschrift für Mitteldeutsche Vorgeschichte*, 86, pp. 133–65.

Brothwell, D.R. (1981). *Digging up bones: the excavation, treatment and study of human skeletal remains*. 3rd ed. London: British Museum and Oxford University Press.

Bruzek, J. (1991). Fiabilité des procédés de détermination du sexe à partir de l'os coxal: implications à l'étude du dimorphisme sexuel de l'homme fossile. Unpublished doctoral thesis, Museum National d'Histoire Naturelle, Institut de Paléontologie Humaine, Paris.

Bruzek, J. (2002). A Method for Visual Determination of Sex, Using the Human Hip Bone. *American Journal of Physical Anthropology*, 117(2), pp. 157–168.

Bruzek, J., Castex, D. and Majo, T (1996). Évaluation des caractères morphologiques de la face sacro-pelvienne de l'os coxal. Proposition d'une nouvelle méthode de diagnose sexuelle. *Bulletins et Mémoires de la Société d'Anthropologie de Paris*, 3(3–4), pp. 491–502.

Bruzek, J. and Ferembach, D. (1992). Fiabilité de la Méthode Visuelle de Détermination du Sexe à Partir du Basin, Proposée par le 'Groupe de Travail d'Anthropologues Européens'. Application à l'Os Coxal. *Estratto dall'Archivio per l'Anthropologia e la Etnologia*, 22, pp. 145–161.

Cavalli, F., Innocenti, D., Črešnar, M. and Vinazza, M. (2015). Multidetector computed tomography and micro-excavation of prehistoric urn from Novine/Hoarachkogel (Slovenia/Austria). In: M. Črešnar, M. Mele, K. Peitler and M. Vinazza, eds., *Archäologische Biographie einer Landschaft an der Steirisch-Slowenischen Grenze / Arheološka Biografija Krajine ob Meji Med Avstrijsko Štajersko in Slovenijo*. Ljubljana: Schild von Steier, 6, pp. 238–244.

Cavazzuti, C., Bresadola, B., D'Innocenzo, C., Interlando, S. and Sperduti, A. (2019). Towards a New Osteometric Method for Sexing Ancient Cremated Human Remains. Analysis of Late Bronze Age and Iron Age samples from Italy with gendered grave goods. *PLOS ONE*, 14(1), pp. 1–21.

Chochol, J. (1953). Anthropologicky Rozbor Luzickych Zarovych Hrobu z Hrusova (Anthropological analysis of graves from Luzice and Hrusov). *Archeologicke Rozhledy*, 5, pp. 597–601.

Chochol, J. (1955). Anthropologicky rozbor lidskych pozustatku ze zarovych hrobu (Anthropological analysis of human remains from cremation burials). In: *Referaty o pracovnich vysledcich Ceskoslovenskych archeologu za rock*. Liblice: Ceskoslovenska Akademie ved Archeologicky ustav, Cast I, pp. 16–25.

De Larminat, S., Corbineau, R., Corrochano, A., Gleize, Y. and Soulat, J., eds. (2017). *Rencontre autour de nouvelles approches de l'archéologie funéraire: actes de la 6e Rencontre du Gaaf, L'Institut national d'histoire de l'art (INHA), Paris, 4-5 avril 2014*. Reugny: Le Groupe d'Anthropologie et d'Archéologie Funéraire (GAAF).

Depierre, G. (2014). *Crémation et archéologie. Nouvelles alternatives méthodologiques en ostéologie humaine*. Dijon: Éditions Universitaires de Dijon, Collections Art, Archéologie et Patrimoine.

Depierre, G. and Supryk, A. (2017). Etude anthropologique des structures liées au rite de crémation. In: S. Sauteur, ed., *A la Montagne. Une Nécropole du Ier Siècle après J.-C. à Avenches, Aventicum XXI*, pp. 149–161.

Dokládál, M. (1999). *Morfologie spálených kostí, význam pro identifikaci osob (Morphology of burnt bones, importance for personal identification)*. Brno: Masaryk University.

Duday, H. (1981). Étude des restes osseux provenant de la nécropole de 'Las Peyros' à Couffoulens (Aude). In: M. Passelac, G. Rancoule, and Y. Solier, eds., *La Nécropole de 'Las Peyros' VIe siècle avant Jesus-Christ, à Couffoulens, Aude, (Découverte d'un Second Groupe de Tombes). Revue Archéologique de Narbonnaise*, 14, pp. 54–70.

Duday, H. (1989). Étude anthropologique de la Nécropole du Peyrou à Agde. In: A. Nickels, G. Marchand, and M. Schwaller, eds., *Agde, la Nécropole du Premier Âge du Fer*. Paris: Centre National de la Recherche Scientifique (CNRS), *Revue Archéologique de Narbonnaise*, Supplement 19, pp. 459–472.

Duday, H. (2013). L'étude anthropologique des sépultures à crémation. In: W. Van Andringa H. Duday, S. Lepetz, D. Joly, and T. Lind, eds., *Mourir à Pompéi: Fouille d'un Quartier Funéraire de la Nécropole Romaine de Porta Nocera (2003–2007)*. Collection de l'École Française de Rome, 468, pp. 5–16.

Duday, H., Depierre, G. and Janin, T. (2000). Validation des paramètres de quantification, protocoles et stratégies dans l'étude anthropologique des sépultures secondaires à incinération. L'exemple des nécropoles protohistoriques du Midi de la France. In: B. Dedet, P. Gruat, G. Marchand, M. Py and M.

Schwaller, eds., *Archéologie de la Mort, Archéologie de la Tombe au Premier Âge du Fer*. Lattes, UMR 154 ARALO, 2000, Actes du XXIe Colloque International de l'Association pour l'Étude de l'Âge du Fer Conques-Montrozier 8–11 mai 1997 (Monographies d'Archéologie Méditerranéenne), 5, pp. 7–29.

Eckert, W.G., James, S. and Katchis, S. (1988). Investigation of Cremations and Severely Burned Bodies. *The American Journal of Forensic Medicine and Pathology*, 9(3), pp. 188–200.

Gadacz, M. (2019). *Le cimetière gallo-romain des 'Landes' à Vatteville-la-Rue (Seine-Maritime, Normandie, France). Approche archéothanatologique des sépultures secondaires à crémation et des structures associées.* Unpublished doctoral thesis, Université de Bourgogne.

Gejvall, N.-G. (1947). Bestamming av Braiida ben Fran Forntida Gravar. *Fornvannen*, 1, pp. 39–47.

Gejvall, N.-G. (1981). Determination of Burned Bones from Prehistoric Graves. *Ossa Letter*, 2, pp. 7–12 (translation of the 1947 article).

Giraud, J.-P., Pons, F. and Janin, T., eds. (2003). *Nécropole protohistoriques de la région de Castres (Tarn. Le Causse, Gourjade, Le Martinet)*, Documents d'Archéologie Française, Série Archéologie Préventive 94.

Gladykowska-Rzeczycka, J. (1974) Anthropological Investigations on the Bone Remains from Crematory Cemeteries in Poland. *Homo*, 25(2), pp. 96–116.

Gonçalves, D. (2011a). The Reliability of Osteometric Techniques for the Sex Determination of Burned Human Skeletal Remains. *Homo*, 62(5), pp. 351–358.

Gonçalves, D. (2011b). *Cremains. The value of quantitative analysis for the bioanthropogical research of burned human skeletal remains.* Unpublished doctoral thesis, Universidade de Coimbra, Portugal.

Gonçalves, D. (2014). Evaluation of the Effect of Secular Changes in the Reliability of Osteometric Methods for the Sex Estimation of Portuguese Individuals. *Cadernos do GEEvH (Group of Studies in Human Evolution)*, 3(1), pp. 53–65.

Gonçalves D., Thompson T.J.U., Cunha E. (2013). Osteometric Sex Determination of Burned Human Skeletal Remains. *Journal of Forensic and Legal Medicine*, 20, pp. 906–911.

Graw, M. (1999). Metric Sex Determination of the Skull Base. *Homo*, 50(199), pp. 101–106.

Graw, M. and Haffner, H.T. (2000). Morphognostically accessible sex dimorphism of the *Pars petrosa ossis temporalis*. In: L. Ventre, C. Moreschi and P.R. Bergamini, eds., *La Prognosi in Medicina Legale -Prognosis in Forensic Medicine*. Il Tetragono, Udine 2000, II(1), pp. 61–64.

Graw, M., Schulz, M. and Wahl, J. (2003). A Simple Morphological Method for Gender Determination at the Petrous Portion of the *Os temporalis*. *Forensic Science International*, 136, pp. 165–166.

Graw, M., Wahl, J. and Ahlbrecht, M. (2005). Course of the *Meatus Acusticus internus* as Criterion for Sex Differentiation. *Forensic Science International*, 147, pp. 113–117.

Grévin, G. (2004). L'Ethnologie au Secours des Archéologues. L'Étude des Crémations sur Bûchers, *Archéologia*, 408, pp. 44–51.

Harvig, L.L., Lynnerup, N. and Amsgaard Ebsen, J. (2012). Computed Tomography and Computed Radiography of Late Bronze Age Cremation Urns from Denmark: An Interdisciplinary Attempt to Develop Methods Applied in Bioarchaeological Cremation Research. *Archaeometry*, 54(2), pp. 369–387.

Herrmann, B. (1976). Neuere Ergebnise zur Beurteilung Menschlicher Brandknochen. *Zeitschrift für Rechtsmedizin*, 77, pp. 191–200.

Janin, T., Burens, A. and Carozza, L. (1997). *La nécropole protohistorique du Camp d'Alba à Réalville (Tarn-et-Garonne), Archives d'Écologie Préhistorique.* Lattes et Toulouse: Association pour la Recherche Archéologique en Languedoc Oriental (ARALO).

Janin, T., Taffanel, O., Taffanel, J., Boisson, H., Char-Denon, N., Gardeisen, A., Hérubel, F., Marchand, G., Montecinos, A. and Rouquet, J. (2002). La Nécropole Protohistorique de Grand Bassin II à Mailhac, Aude (VIè – Vè siècle avant notre Ère). *Documents d'Archéologie Méridionale*, 25, pp. 65–122.

Kurila, L. (2015). The Accuracy of the Osteological Sexing of Cremated Human Remains: A Test Based on Grave Goods from East Lithuanian Barrows. *Collegium Antropologicum*, 39(4), pp. 821–828.

Le Goff, I., Culot, S., Bigot, J.-J., Huart, P. and Poisson, A. (2019). Nouvelles technologies numériques, nouveau regard porté sur les crémations. In: S. Eusèbe, T. Nicolas, V. Gouranton and R. Gaugne, eds., *Archéologie: Imagerie Numériques et 3D: Actes du 3e Séminaire Scientifique et Technique de l'Institut National de Recherches Archéologiques Préventives (INRAP), 26-27 Juin 2018, Rennes.* 10.34692/74qm-s229.hal-02437147v2

Lenorzer, S. (2006). *Pratiques funéraires du Bronze Final IIIb au premier Âge du Fer en Languedoc occidental et Midi-Pyrénées: approche archéo-anthropologique des nécropoles à incinération.* Unpublished doctoral thesis, Université de Bordeaux I.

Malinowski, A. (1969). Synthèse des Recherches Polonaises Effectuées jusqu'à Présent sur les Os des Tombes à Incinération. *Przeglad Antropologiczny*, 35, pp. 127–147.

Malinowski, A. and Porawski, R. (1969). Identifikationsmöglichkeiten Menschlicher Brandknochen mit Besonderer Berücksichtigung ihres Gewichts. *Zacchia di Medicina Legale, Sociale, e Criminologica*, 5(3), pp. 392–410.

Masotti, S., Succi-Leonelli, E. and Gualdi-Russo, E. (2013). Cremated Human Remains: Is Measurement of the Lateral Angle of the *Meatus acusticus internus* a Reliable Method of Sex Determination? *International Journal of Legal Medicine*, 127(5), pp. 1039–1044.

Mayne Correia, P. (1997). Fire modification of bone: a review of the literature. In: W.D. Haglund and M.H. Sorg, eds., *Forensic taphonomy: the fate of human remains*. Boca Raton, FL, CRC Press, pp. 275–293.

McKinley, J.I. (1993). Bone Fragment Size and Weights of Bone from Modern British Cremations and the Implications for the Interpretation of Archaeological Cremations. *International Journal of Osteoarchaeology*, 3, pp. 283–287.

McKinley, J.I. (1994). *The Anglo-Saxon cemetery at Spong Hill, North Elmham, part VIII: the cremations. East Anglian Archaeology*, 69. Norfolk: Field Archaeology Division, Norfolk Museums Service.

Murail, P., Bruzek, J. and Braga, J. (1999). A New Approach to Sexual Diagnosis in Past Populations. Practical Adjustments from van Vark's Procedure. *International Journal of Osteoarchaeology*, 9, 1999, pp. 39–53.

Murail, P., Bruzek, J. and Houët, F. (2000). Stability of the human pelvic sexual dimorphism pattern allows probabilistic sex diagnosis among *Homo sapiens sapiens*. In: *Abstracts of the 12th congress of the European anthropological association*. Cambridge, England, 8–11 September, pp. 55–56.

Nicolas, T., Gaugne, R., Tavernier, C., Gouranton, V. and Arnaldi, B. (2016). La Tomographie, l'Impression 3D et la Réalité Virtuelle au Service de l'Archéologie. *Les Nouvelles de l'Archéologie*, 146, pp.16–22.

Nugent, T.G. (2010). *The estimation of biological profile from unprocessed human cremated remains*. Unpublished Master's thesis, Texas State University, San Marcos.

Passelac, M., Rancoule, G. and Solier, Y. (1981). La Nécropole de 'Las Peyros', VIe siècle avant Jesus-Christ à Couffoulens, Aude, (Découverte d'un Second Groupe de Tombes). *Revue Archéologique de Narbonnaise*, 14, pp. 1–70.

Pons, F., Janin, T., Lagarrigue, A. and Poignant, S. (2001). La Nécropole Protohistorique du Camp de l'Église-Sud (Flaujac-Poujols, Lot). *Documents d'Archéologie Méridionale*, 24, pp. 7–81.

Prouin, Y. (2007). *La nécropole d'Ensisheim/Reguisheimerfeld (Haut-Rhin): illustrations des pratiques funéraires en Alsace*. Unpublished doctoral thesis, Université de Bourgogne.

Roger, J., Duday, H., Pons, F. and Janin, T. (2003). Étude anthropologique. In: J.-P. Giraud, F. Pons, and T. Janin, eds., *Nécropole Protohistoriques de la Région de Castres (Tarn. Le Causse, Gourjade, Le Martinet)*, Documents d'Archéologie Française, Série Archéologie Préventive, 94. Paris: Maison des Sciences de l'Homme, pp. 181–232.

Rösing, F.W. (1977a). Methoden und Aussgemöglichkeiten der Anthropologischen Leichenbrandbearbeitung. *Archäologie und Naturwissenschaften*, 1, pp. 53–80.

Rösing, F.W. (1977b). Die Leichenbrände der eisenzeitlichen Gräberfelder von Bargstedt I, Harsefeld und Issendorf III. In: H.J. Hässler, ed., *Zur inneren Gliederung und Verbreitung der vorrömischen Eisenzeit im südlichen Niederelbe-Gebiet*. Hildesheim: A. Lax, pp. 117–129.

Schaefer, U. (1960). Anthropologische Untersuchungen einiger Leichenbrände des Gräberfeldes. In: J. Brandt, ed., *Das Urnengräberfeld von Preetz in Holstein*. Keil: Offa-Bücher 16, pp. 93–111.

Schaefer, U. (1961). Grenzen und Möglichkeiten der anthropologischen Untersuchung von Leichenbränden, *Bericht über den V. Internationalen Kongreß für Vor- und Frühgeschichte in Hamburg*. Berlin, pp. 717–724.

Schaefer, U. (1964). Beiträge zum Problem der Leichenbrände. *Zeitschrift für Morphologie und Anthropologie*, 55, pp. 277–282.

Schutkowski, H. (1983). Über den Diagnostischen Wert der *Pars petrosa ossis temporalis* für die Geschlechtbestimmung. *Zeitschrift für Morphologie und Anthropologie*, 74, pp. 129–144.

Steele, D.G. (1976). The Estimation of Sex on the Basis of the Talus and Calcaneus. *American Journal of Physical Anthropology*, 45, pp. 581–588.

Strzałko, J., Piontek, J. and Malinowski, A. (1974). Mozliwosci identyfikacji szczatkow ludzkich z grobow cialopalnych w swietle wynikow badan eksperymentalnych (Possibilities for Identifying Human Remains from Cialopoeia Graves in Light of Experimental Research Results). In: M. Ćwirko-Godycki, ed., *Metody, Wyniki i Konsekwencje Badan Kosci z Grobow Cialopalnych (Methods, Results and Consequences of Investigations of Bones from Cremation Burials)*. Uniwersytet imienia Adama Mickiewicza w Poznaniu, Wydzial Biologii i Nauk o Ziemi, Seria Antropologia, 2, pp. 31–42.

Taffanel, O., Taffanel, J. and Janin, T. (1998). *La nécropole du Moulin à Mailhac (Aude)*. Lattes, Association pour la Recherche Archéologique en Languedoc Oriental (ARALO). Monographies d'Archéologie Méditerranéenne 2.

Todd, N.W., Graw, M. and Dietzel, M. (2010). 'Lateral Angle' of the Internal Auditory Canal: Non-Association with Temporal Bone Pneumatization. *Journal of Forensic Science*, 55, pp. 141–144.

Van Andringa, W., Duday, H., Lepetz, S., Joly, D. and Lind, T. (2013). *Mourir à Pompéi: fouille d'un quartier funéraire de la nécropole romaine de Porta Nocera (2003–2007)*. Collection de l'École Française de Rome, 468.

Van Deest, T.L., Murad, T.A. and Bartelink, E.J. (2011). A Re-examination of Cremains Weight: Sex and Age Variation in a Northern California Sample. *Journal of Forensic Sciences*, 56(2), pp. 344–349.

Van Vark, G.N. (1970). *Some statistical procedures for the investigation of prehistoric skeletal material*. Unpublished doctoral thesis, Rijkuniversiteit te Groningen, Groningen.

Vidal, P. (2017). L'apport de la tomodensitométrie à la fouille des crémations. In: F. Hanut, ed., *Du Bûcher à la Tombe. Diversité et Évolution des Pratiques Funéraires dans les Nécropoles à Crémation de la Période Gallo-Romaine en Gaule Septentrionale*, Namur: Institut du Patrimoine Wallon, pp. 336–339.

Višnjić, J., Cavalli, F., Percan, T. and Innocenti, D. (2013). Žarni Ranoželjeznodobni Grob iz Berma. Rezultati Arheoloških i Medical Diagnostic Computer Tomography (MDCT) Istraživanja (The Early Iron Age Urn Grave from Beram. The Results of Archaeological and Medical Diagnostic Computer Tomography (MDCT) Research). *Historia Archaeologica*, 44, pp. 67–154.

Wahl, J. (1981). Ein Beitrag zur Metrischen Geschlechtsdiagnose Verbrannter und Unverbrannter Menschlicher Knochenreste- Ausgearbeitet an der *pars petrosa ossis temporalis*. *Zeitschrift Rechtsmedizin* 86, pp. 79–101.

Wahl, J. and Graw, M. (2001). Metric Sex Differentiation of the *Pars Petrosa Ossis Temporalis*. *International Journal of Legal Medicine*, 114, pp. 215–223.

Wells, C. (1960). A Study of Cremation. *Antiquity*, 34(133), pp. 29–37.

5

THE ACCOMPANYING DEAD

Bruno Boulestin

PACEA, De la Préhistoire à l'Actuel: Culture, Environnement et Anthropologie,
UMR 5199, CNRS-Université de Bordeaux, Pessac, France

Introduction

One of the trickiest problems encountered in prehistoric archaeology is the ability to make reliable inferences regarding the social structure of ancient societies for which no written sources are available. One question, in particular, is raised on a regular basis: when and how did hierarchy and social inequalities appear? Yet, the ever-growing number of publications dealing with the subject proves how difficult it is to find elements that would permit, if not to decide, at least to reason on the basis of strong arguments. Owing to the lack of written accounts describing the organisation of societies, the difficulty lies in finding models that must not only be general enough to be extrapolated to prehistoric populations but that can also result in criteria useable in archaeology. This difficulty increases all the more in the deeper past, becoming a major one when addressing the hunter-gatherer populations of the Mesolithic or the Upper Palaeolithic (e.g. Price and Feinman, 1995, 2010; Flannery and Marcus, 2012; Kelly, 2013: 241ff.).

For 50-odd years and since the seminal works of Saxe (1970) and Binford (1971), the analysis of mortuary practices has remained one of the most important lines of evidence used by archaeologists to reflect on social organisation and try to demonstrate the existence of status differences. The idea underlying this approach – one of the pivotal concepts in the New Archaeology – is that the way a person is treated in their grave reflects their social position, and that the 'complexity' of the system of mortuary differentiation increases along with the 'complexity' of the society (O'Shea, 1984: 21). Even though this approach has been criticised, or at least warily regarded by many authors ever since its very beginning (Ucko, 1969; Brown, 1981 were among the first to do so), it has been and still is nonetheless largely in use to detect inequalities and social stratification. In practice, the studies focus, in general, on two aspects. On the one hand, one assesses the energy expended to create the grave: what amount of work, of time, and what degree of planning did it require? On the other hand, one tries to quantify the wealth of the ornaments and grave goods found in each grave, and from there to bring out contrasts. A few simple – shall we say simplistic? – interpretive rules are added to this: for instance, if a subset of graves is wealthier, it is interpreted as that of an elite. If the wealthy graves are mostly those of aged adults, it is likely that wealth may have been acquired during the lifetime. If there are wealthy children's graves, an ascribed social position is postulated (Ames, 2007). This approach works more or less adequately when contrasts are significant, but when they are not, it meets its limits, the main one touching on a long-discussed issue (see Ucko, 1969): how does one evaluate the 'wealth' of a grave?

Paradoxically, whereas features and grave goods have always been at the core of the analyses, the dead themselves have long been almost completely overlooked, even though they are both

DOI: 10.4324/9781351030625-7

at the heart of the funerary practices and the reason for them. It is probably because it was hard to see *a priori* how they could provide direct insights on social structure. Sometimes, though, it has been suggested that the elites are likely to be better nourished than the common people, to live longer, and possess specific activity markers (Ames, 2007), but this model is as weak as the differences are difficult to demonstrate.

The new approach to the archaeology of death developed in France over the last 30 years and christened 'archaeothanatology' by Boulestin and Duday (2005, 2006) has been trying to fill this void: it now focusses the analysis on mortuary practices, not on the features and goods accompanying the dead but on the dead themselves. This approach begins by meticulously analysing how the human remains are organised, and how they relate to one another at the time of their discovery, which permits reconstruction of their positions when they were definitively disposed of and the characteristics of that deposition. Relying on the analysis carried out in the field, along with those of the features in which the dead were deposited, of the grave goods and on the biological data, archaeothanatology attempts, in a second step, to describe the mortuary behaviours in the best possible way and to place them in their chrono-cultural context. Lastly, its final objective is to draw, from these analyses, information on the structure and organisation of ancient societies, relying, in particular, on models established from social anthropology and ethnohistory.

The issue of the accompanying dead is the perfect example of the analytical approach employed in archaeothanatology. It shows how the meticulous study of mortuary practices, in particular the post-death treatment of some individuals, backed up with an appropriate theoretical framework, can help to reconstruct some aspects of the social structure of past populations. Rather than going from fieldwork to social interpretation, this issue will be addressed here through a hypothetico-deductive reasoning process. In other words, this means starting with the theoretical framework, which will make it possible to express a number of general sociological rules, then trying to deduce archaeologically observable consequences, and finally demonstrating, with an example, that there are cases where these consequences are congruent with the recurring characteristics of some empirically identified mortuary practices.

Theoretical framework: ethnohistory and sociology of the practice of accompanying dead

Definition and scope of the concept

The practice of accompanying dead has been known and documented for a very long time. As early as the 5th century BC, Herodotus (*Histories*, IV) reported that among the Scythians, on the death of a king, some of his followers and servants were strangled and buried with him. Credit goes to Testart, though, not only for having introduced the expression '*morts d'accompagnement*' (accompanying dead) but also for having shown that this was a significant and universally spread practice, as well as having analysed its social meaning (Testart, 2004a, 2004b).

What are accompanying dead, then? These are people who kill themselves or are killed on the occasion of the death of a 'figure' (meaning a person having a major and public social role). This general definition encompasses all the cases inventoried by Testart, as well as others he did not consider. Going into further detail, it will become clear, below, that different forms of accompaniment must be distinguished.[1] Nevertheless, it must be highlighted at this stage that if, in most

---

1 For the sake of simplification, the word 'accompaniment', when used alone, is meant as the metonymical equivalent of 'practice of accompanying dead'.

cases, the accompanying dead are buried with the main figure, it can sometimes be otherwise: on some occasions, they can be buried in another place, or sometimes simply discarded. The first option is the most accessible to archaeological analysis; the second is difficult to discuss, although it can be suggested, and the third remains beyond reach.

What Testart's work showed in the first place was how frequent this practice was: the first historical testimonies date back as early as the earliest written sources, and ethnography has reported its occurrence almost everywhere in the world at some point or other. It would be both fastidious and useless to list all the documented cases here, and the reader can refer to the first three chapters of the first volume of Testart's 2004 publication, *Les morts d'accompagnement. La servitude volontaire I*, for numerous examples, keeping in mind that his listing is far from exhaustive, given the huge number of existing testimonies. In summary, the two main traits of the ethno-historical enquiries of this practice are:

1. Accompaniment in death encompasses the five continents. Even in Europe this tradition has been acknowledged at various points in the past, depending on the area: Caesar (*The Gallic Wars*, III, 22 and VI, 19) leaves little doubt that it existed among the Gauls, and Homer's narrative of Patroclus' funeral implies that it could have been the case as well in protohistoric Greece (*Iliad*, XXIII, 1. 171ff.). To the North and the East, apart from the above-mentioned Scythians, historical testimonies exist also for Scandinavia and the Kievan Rus (Boyer, 1994: 181ff.).
2. Accompaniment exists in societies that display a great variety of forms of social organisation. It is present in States, of course, in particular monarchies (the Shang and Zhou dynasties in China, Natchez in North America, Vanuatu in Oceania, Ashanti, Buganda and Kongo in Africa, among others). Nevertheless, it seems absent in larger States, vanishing progressively as they become more highly developed and more bureaucratic. This practice can be encountered also in non-state societies, which neo-evolutionist American classifications would describe as chiefdoms, for instance African lineage societies such as Balla, and Beti, among others. Lastly, and rather more astonishingly at first glance, the practice of accompanying dead also exists in some hunter-gatherer societies; the most typical example is provided by societies from the North American Northwest Coast culture area (Tlingit, Nootka, and Chinook, among others). Hunter-gatherers will be addressed again later.

To conclude on the range of this concept, it is obvious that the tradition of accompanying dead is neither anecdotal, nor limited to a handful of societies. Moreover, its wide geographical distribution, long time-depth and the lack of relationship with a specific political organisation lead to conclusions that are general enough to be confidently extrapolated to past populations. This is all the more true since there is no reason to think that accompaniment does not pre-date the earliest written sources. It is therefore time to explore the related social implications.

Various forms and social implications of accompaniment

Defining the social implications of accompaniment begins by characterising the social relationships between the accompanying dead and the accompanied social figure; it will help determine what information accompaniment can provide about the society in which it is performed. According to the ethnohistoric enquiry carried out by Testart, and to some other cases he did not mention, there can be several forms of social relationships, hence several forms of accompaniment. Nevertheless, these forms can be classified into a limited number of main categories. A possible classification was recently suggested (Boulestin, 2018) but that classificatory system can be slightly modified to make the different social implications stand out more clearly.

To begin with, one situation can be removed: suicide for love, which Testart (2004a: 185) named 'the Tristan and Iseult (Isolda) type of accompaniment'. This behaviour is a mental disorder that pertains to psychiatry, and even though it is not confined to legends only, it remains altogether anecdotal. Regarding the other situations, the accompanying persons can be categorised into three groups.

Group 1 comprises:
- Children, mostly younger ones, who are killed at the death of a parent since they could not survive without them. This is an extremely widespread practice for which Testart gave a few ethnographic examples, but for which evidence is provided throughout the world.
- Children from the Guayaki of Amazonia, who are killed within the framework of the very specific *jepy* custom, described by P. Clastres (1972: chap. VI) but oddly overlooked by Testart. According to this tradition, at the death of a mature hunter and warrior, a child – usually one of the deceased's daughters – is killed to both accompany him and make up for the injustice he suffered upon his death.
- Wives who are killed or kill themselves at the death of their husbands; this practice is widespread as well, the latter option illustrating the well-known Indian *sati* custom.

Group 2 includes:
- Captives executed at the death of the person who captured them. This is a very common practice.
- Slaves purchased in order to be killed during funerals (e.g. Borneo, some African lineage societies).

The following two remain anecdotal:
- Workers killed to protect the secret of a place of inhumation and thus avoid plundering (Huns).
- People who happened to come across the funeral convoy and were killed for the same reasons (Mongols).

Group 3 is composed of:
- Royal servants who follow their king in death (e.g. Shang and Zhou dynasties in China).
- Personal slaves killed at the death of their master, an extremely common custom (e.g. Northwest Coast culture area, Sub-Saharan Africa).
- Friends, companions, or followers who vowed not to outlive their chief should the latter be killed in (e.g. the Gauls).

And more rarely:
- Free subjects who commit suicide at the death of their king (Natchez).

What conclusions can be drawn from all this? First, all accompanying dead share a common characteristic, whatever the above-mentioned category they belong to: they all have a *dependent social relationship* with the figures they accompany. Either they are in a state of dependency owing to their situation (slaves or prisoners of war, for example), or they are free men, though subordinate, or even subjected to the accompanied person. There can also be an affective dependency to some extent, in particular with regard to the accompanying individuals from group 3. Beyond this common characteristic, there are differences between the three groups, so that the deriving social implications vary.

For group 1, accompaniment simply shows how children are subjected to adults (they cannot outlive them, or they must keep them company as in the Guayaki example), or women to men. This double subjection is so common (it exists in almost all the societies, except in some modern ones) that it does not provide much additional social information. Furthermore, here the limit of the definition is reached, since the accompanied person is not necessarily an important or public figure. This form of accompaniment testifies only to the authority (or the domination) exercised among the members of the nuclear family, and as a consequence is termed 'non-hierarchical accompaniment' to distinguish it from the other forms.

It is different in the two other groups, which include forms of accompaniment that have in common a demonstration of the effect of direct power on people on a scale larger than that of the family, be they dependent by status or free subordinate men (in which case political power is involved). This is why the words 'hierarchical accompaniment' (Testart, 2004a: 182) are used for these two groups. This form of accompaniment necessarily implies that the society practising it was *stratified and hence hierarchical*. The difference between the two groups lies in the specific nature and the duration of the social link between accompanying and accompanied that existed before death. In group 2, this link is non-personal or limited (to the relationship between victor and vanquished, as so often happens, or between paymaster and workers). The accompanying persons never participate willingly. It is different in group 3 where the relationships between the accompanied person and the accompanying people had been firmly established before death, and usually for a very long time. Moreover, these relationships are not limited to a situation of dependency: most of the time, loyalty is involved. This dependency and this fidelity have a fundamental dimension in the sense that they are personal. The accompanying dead in this group have a personal relationship with the person they accompany. These characteristics explain why some of them are willing to die: they commit suicide because their personal attachment, in every sense of the word, to the dead figure is so strong that they cannot contemplate outliving him or her.[2] It is important to point out that, astonishingly enough, personal loyalty affects the slaves as well; Testart's argumentation on this topic (2004a: 213–219) is very convincing.

In summary, the practice of accompanying dead testifies each time to a social relationship of subordination between the accompanying and the accompanied. When not limited to the nuclear family, this relationship implies the existence of a stratified and hierarchical society. In this case, little or no connection may have existed between the accompanied and the accompanying before death. In many cases, though, there was often a personal relationship, not only of dependency but also of loyalty between them during their lifetimes. Testart focussed his study on this latter form, which he regarded as the fullest definition of accompaniment, inasmuch as it perpetuated in death a specific social relationship that existed among the living. He suggested that these relationships of personal loyalty might have played a role in the origin of the State (or at least of despotic States, or those fostering strong personal power), a hypothesis he developed in the second volume of his work (Testart, 2004b). This issue will not be further developed here, but as a conclusion it seems important to point out that at a time when social anthropology and biological anthropology (through palaeogenomics) concentrate on kinship and gender studies, the major role played by the social relationships beyond kin-based ones underlying accompaniment in past societies should not be overlooked.

---

2 This aspect of personal loyalty is present in the *sati* as well.

Differences between accompaniment and sacrifice

Historians of religion, ethnologists, and archaeologists do not ignore the practice of accompanying dead. But commonly, it is almost systematically termed 'sacrifice'. Not only is this incorrect, but it also conveys a very serious misinterpretation of what accompaniment truly means. Testart (2004a: 29–34, 2005) provides a detailed argumentation on this statement, but the main reason is that the accompanying dead are not destined to a supernatural power and, moreover, they are not even considered an offering. They were the 'property' of the main deceased person in life and simply remained so in death. There is no transfer. The possession is maintained throughout the transition from life to death, contrary to the renunciation of ownership implicit in sacrifice. Generally speaking, accompaniment is absolutely not a fundamentally religious practice, whereas sacrifice is one by nature; it pertains essentially to sociology. Add to this that on one hand, the forms of killing in accompaniment are usually different from those used by the same population for a sacrifice and, on the other hand, above all that the word 'sacrifice' is never used in ancient witness accounts, which is a sign that accompaniment was not considered as such by the populations who performed it.

Observable archaeological consequences

Principles of archaeological identification of accompaniment

Only cases of accompanying people present in the grave will be addressed here, since it is difficult, even impossible, to identify examples of the other cases. Discussing a practice of accompaniment in an archaeological assemblage is part of the wider debate involving graves that contain several dead persons buried simultaneously, in France what is called a 'multiple burial' (cf. Boulestin and Courtaud, Chapter 3, this volume). Since this general discussion is beyond the scope of this review, readers are invited to refer to works where it has been more thoroughly detailed (Boulestin, 2008, 2018). In a few words, relying on the principle that simultaneity of burials has been established, in particular from osteological observations made during field excavation, there are three main possibilities: (1) the dead were buried simultaneously, but did not die at the same time; (2) they were the victims of mortality crises triggered by epidemics, famine, or an episode of armed violence; or (3) they form evidence for the practice of accompaniment, that can, in turn, be either hierarchical or non-hierarchical. The point, then, becomes how to differentiate between these possibilities.

The outcome of Testart's ethnohistoric enquiry (2004a: 176ff.*)* showed that in all cases of hierarchical accompaniment the grave displayed elements of asymmetry pertaining to three aspects:

- spatial arrangement, with the important deceased person in a privileged position;
- position of the bodies, the accompanied person and the accompanying dead having been treated differently;
- grave goods, quantitatively and/or qualitatively more significant for the main figure.

These aspects are more or less pronounced, and they can be combined in different ways, sometimes consistent and sometimes diverging, but they can always be observed to some degree. The following two examples have been chosen because they are documented in both ethnohistory and archaeology.

The first example is provided by the Tolstaya Mogila Scythian kurgan, in Ukraine, dated to the 4th century BC. It thus slightly post-dates Herodotus's narrative and shows that his description and the archaeological discoveries match perfectly (Schiltz, 1994: 417ff.). The kurgan contained two burials. The main one, which had been looted and heavily disturbed, was difficult to decipher, but the lateral burial (Figure 5.1) was much better preserved. It belonged to a female and a child, both richly attired and deposited on a litter or in a sarcophagus in the centre of the funerary chamber (numbers 1 and 2 in Figure 5.1). Two additional corpses were discovered next to the female and the child, one on each side; one was that of a male with a quiver and arrows, the other was that of a female, and both seem to have been deposited without much ceremony (numbers 4 and 5 in Figure 5.1). Another man was placed in the antechamber in a haphazard position, next to the wheels of a chariot (number 6 in Figure 5.1). Lastly, a meagrely attired young girl had been placed in a recess (number 3 in Figure 5.1). These four accompanying persons are interpreted, respectively, as a bodyguard, a cook, a coachman, and a young servant, in other words people at the service of the young female. Whatever the reality of these suggested roles may have been, the asymmetry of the spatial organisation of the dead, positions of the bodies and ornaments is plainly obvious between the female and the child on the one hand, and the four other dead individuals on the other hand.

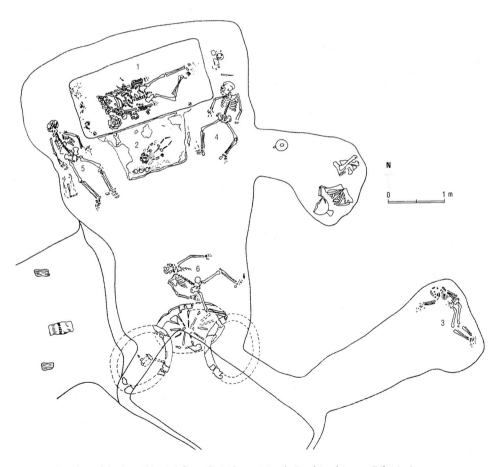

Figure 5.1   Plan of the lateral burial from the Tolstaya Mogila Scythian kurgan (Ukraine).

1: Female, 2: child, 3: young servant, 4: 'cook', 5: 'bodyguard', 6: 'coachman' (Schiltz, 1994: fig. 361; Reproduced with kind permission of V. Schiltz).

The second example is provided by the grave of *Mwasoe Nua*, a chief documented by oral tradition and said to have lived during the 15th century AD on Tongoa, the northernmost island of the Shepherd archipelago (Vanuatu). Collective memory recalled the location of the grave, which was excavated by Garanger (1972: 91–92). The grave contained five people (Figure 5.2). *Mwasoe Nua* was in a central position, lying on his back. He was surrounded by three women lying on their sides and arranged around him, one to his right, one to his left and the third at his head. A male lying on his back, slightly to the right side of the central figure, would have been the chief's *atavi*, that is to say his servant responsible for maintaining peace. Tradition has it that all the accompanying dead would have been buried alive, the man having been drugged beforehand. In this example, asymmetry of grave goods is not obvious, whereas asymmetry of spatial organisation and of posture places the chief occupant of the grave in a clearly privileged situation.

Asymmetry in death makes sense and can be perfectly explained: it reflects the hierarchy that existed among the deceased persons during their lifetimes. In other words, it means that the

Figure 5.2 Burial said to be that of Mwasoe Nua (set TO-29-1 of Mangarisu, Tongoa, Vanuatu) (Garanger, 1972: fig. 257).

organisation of the dead people in the grave is in accordance with this hierarchy. Observations show also that the degree of asymmetry is on the whole proportional to the social gap between the accompanied and the accompanying. The archaeological consequence is that a multiple grave displaying significant asymmetry leads to a discussion of hierarchical accompaniment, whereas this hypothesis is likely to be excluded with a lesser marked or a lack of asymmetry. The first case pertains to groups 2 and 3 as described earlier; the second case could relate to group 1, or may not be any form of accompaniment whatsoever.

So, a set of archaeologically observable criteria with regard to the way the individuals were treated after death can provide information on the structure of the studied society, on whether a hierarchy existed, and potentially on how important it was. The archaeological analysis of burials is to date certainly the best basis for the identification of hierarchical accompaniment. Nevertheless, other factors may be of some use in the argumentation: manner or possible causes of death, provided they can be determined; age and sex composition of the human assemblage in the grave; and biological differences between the central dead figure and the accompanying dead revealed by palaeogenomics or stable isotope analysis.

Limits of the interpretation

It is coherent to interpret asymmetry in a multiple grave in terms of hierarchical accompaniment and, conversely, hierarchical accompaniment implies asymmetry. Nevertheless, discussions have to take into account some interpretative limits. On the one hand, a lack of asymmetry does not imply a non-hierarchical society, but simply a society in which accompaniment is not in use (this custom does not exist in all hierarchical societies). On the other hand, there are three difficulties. The first is that asymmetrical human deposits do not necessarily reflect a form of accompaniment. Some examples from epidemic cemeteries show that it is necessary, in case of a mortality crisis, to deal urgently with a large number of corpses, which can sometimes lead to asymmetrical burials (Boulestin, 2008: 115). Bodies that have been disposed of can also sometimes display various positions with a certain degree of asymmetry. The second difficulty lies in the fact that it is not always easy to state that an asymmetry is significant when it is not clearly marked, when there are only two individuals (a double grave), or when there are burials of very young children. The third difficulty lies in the interpretation of these borderline cases, which theoretically could reflect just as much a lesser-marked hierarchical accompaniment, a non-hierarchical accompaniment, or the absence of accompaniment.

The theoretical principle of archaeological identification of hierarchical accompaniment may be quite robust, but in practice a systematic discussion of the three aspects of asymmetry (spatial arrangement, position of the body and grave goods) should always be carried out. Not only these three aspects must be examined, but also the overall organisation of the deposit, as well as its context, must be taken into account. The interpretation is all the easier if the degree of asymmetry is great, and the empirical enquiry shows recurrent archaeological patterns. Isolated cases, though, are always tricky issues. These situations will be illustrated with two examples.

Archaeological applications

A conclusive case: human deposits in Neolithic circular pits

The empirical enquiry

Over the millennium spanning between 4500 and 3500 BC, a new way of disposing of the dead developed in Europe, with bodies deposited in circular pits often considered to be disused silos (i.e. grain stores). They may contain a single individual, or the deposit may be of several individuals; grave goods and, occasionally, animal remains were sometimes deposited with the human bodies. In addition to entire articulated skeletons, these pits also yield anatomical parts or isolated bones as well.

These deposits in circular pits have been known since the end of the nineteenth century and were for a long time considered by researchers as mere marginal phenomena, never receiving systematic review, and thus raising little interest (Jeunesse, 2010; Chenal *et al.*, 2015 for a more detailed historical account). During the final decade of the past millennium, the research conducted by Beeching and colleagues in the Rhône Valley began to stimulate a change of perspective. They demonstrated that in the pits containing several individuals a recurring opposition actually existed between a person in an 'exceptional' or a 'central' position, and other people described as secondary, or termed '*corps-rejets*' ('reject bodies'; Beeching, 1991; Crubézy, 1991; Beeching and Crubézy, 1998). It took a few more years and the organisation of a round-table discussion in 2006 on the issue of human deposits in circular pits to acknowledge that this pattern was not limited to the Rhône Valley, but was part of a consistent system stretching over a wider area within Europe (Baray and Boulestin, 2010; Jeunesse, 2010). Later, a review of the area of the Upper Rhine (Lefranc *et al.*, 2010) and an examination of the phenomenon on a European scale carried out by Jeunesse and colleagues within the framework of an unpublished research project have reasserted the unity and consistency of the practice.

Twenty-five years of French research on human deposits in circular pits from 4500 to 3500 horizon have helped set an empirical model of practice, the characteristics of which are the following:

1. There is a large group of burials that display two main traits: (a) they are scattered among settlements, and (b) the pits in which the dead were deposited are cylindrical in shape;
2. This group includes a majority of pits with only a single individual deposited in them, and a much smaller sub-sample with several individuals;
3. Most often the archaeothanatological analysis conducted in the field makes it possible to establish that, for the pits containing several individuals, the bodies were deposited simultaneously;
4. The privileged nature of a single body in relation to the others is repeatedly found because it is the only one laid out in a so-called 'conventional' or 'regular' position, as observed in the great majority of the confirmed burials in the study area (placed on the back or on the side, with the upper and lower limbs together and flexed, the latter resting on the ground). All the other dead are in haphazard positions and seem to have been disposed of disrespectfully and with no apparent rule. The privileged nature of one particular body can sometimes be reinforced by its central position in the middle of the pit, and by the grave goods found beside him or her.

Two major reasons testify that this kind of disposal of the dead reflects a consistent and unitary phenomenon, a regular funerary practice, and is not just anecdotal. To start with, from a geographical point of view, it exists in all the cultures in an area stretching at least from the Rhône Valley (Chasséen Culture) to Central Europe (Slovakia and Hungary; Baalberge Culture). Secondly, chronologically speaking, not only it is quite homogeneous, but a close examination of the various dates also shows a wave of cultural advance, starting in Alsace or Bavaria, and spreading to the east and southwards. The earliest deposits possibly date back to the Bischheim culture, surely to the BORS (Upper Rhine western Bischheim) Epi-Roessen group. The model could extend, with variants, to Mediterranean France (Schmitt, 2017) and to Catalonia (Gibaja *et al., 2016)*, though these areas call for further research.

Compliance of the empirical model with the theoretical model

The privileged nature of a specific body in relation to others in circular pits with multiple deposits completely mirrors the asymmetry that exists in hierarchical accompaniment, as depicted by the following two examples from France. The first one is pit 69 from 'Les Moulins' at Saint-Paul-Trois-Châteaux, in the Rhône Valley (Drôme department); this is one of the cases coming from the Chasséen Culture upon which Beeching based his demonstration (Figure 5.3). This pit yielded the bodies of three adults deposited simultaneously (Beeching, 1991; Crubézy, 1991; Beeching and Crubézy, 1998). There is clearly a primary individual, a female, and two secondary ones (a male and a female). In this case asymmetry exists on three levels: the primary subject has been placed in the centre of the pit (the only part of the pit visible from the edge without leaning over it), the others being against the wall of the feature (thus spatial asymmetry); she is

Figure 5.3   Chasséen burial in pit 69 of 'Les Moulins', Saint-Paul-Trois-Châteaux (Drôme, France) (Photograph: Beeching-Cordier/CAPRA Valence; Reproduced with kind permission of A. Beeching).

the only one in a conventional position, the others being in haphazard positions (thus postural asymmetry); a vessel was found next to her head, the other individuals having no associated grave goods (thus asymmetry in grave goods). The second example is provided by feature 28 from Didenheim, in Alsace (Haut-Rhin, France), belonging to the Munzingen Culture and excavated in 2002 by the French company *Antea Archéologie* (Figure 5.4). The feature contained four bodies

Figure 5.4 Photograph and plan of grave 28 from Didenheim (Haut-Rhin, France), Munzingen Culture. A: individual no. 1, B: individual no. 2, C: individual no. 3, D: individual no. 4; 1: antler cup, 2: pottery bowl (Photograph and plan: Antea Archéologie; Reproduced with kind permission of M. Roth-Zehner).

buried simultaneously: an adult of undetermined sex in a conventional position (individual 3), and three immature individuals (a teenager, an older child and a very young child) in haphazard positions. In this example there is no spatial asymmetry, but the postural asymmetry is obvious. There is also a possible asymmetry in grave goods, since a pottery bowl and an antler cup were found near the head of individual 3 and are likely associated with him or her.

For the geographical area and time period under discussion, many other multiple human deposits in circular pits can be analysed, likewise in terms of more or less pronounced asymmetry, and there is a consensus to interpret them as evidence for practices of hierarchical accompaniment. These recurring observations show that the organisation of the graves is the result of human will and did not just happen by accident, as could be the case for other types of multiple deposits, in particular those related to mortality crises. Nevertheless, attention must be drawn to the fact that if the model of accompaniment remains the most relevant to explain the human deposits in circular pits with one individual in a conventional position and one or several others in haphazard positions in a same feature at the present time, it does not account for the deposits which contain only one or several dead belonging to the second category. This model is hence doubtlessly incomplete.

Social deductions

Since asymmetrical multiple deposits in circular pits relate to hierarchical accompaniment, it can be deduced that only the figure in a conventional position underwent a regular funerary rite, whereas the rest were killed to accompany him or her. Noticeably though, accompaniment has not been observed in Neolithic cultures prior to 4500 BC. It seems that around that date, society went through fundamental changes that have yet to be precisely characterised. Secondly, it must be pointed out that in all the cultures where this practice has been acknowledged, grave goods are especially poor, no single artefact standing out as an obvious sign of wealth. It is as though the accompanying dead were themselves the major source of wealth transferred into the Afterlife.

Who were these accompanying people, then? By a process of elimination, it had initially been suggested that they may have been slaves killed at the death of their owner, in particular since circular pits are a far cry from royal graves, and since the presence of sometimes very young children leaves out the hypothesis of companions or friends (Testart *et al.*, 2010). Later discoveries, notably in Alsace, such as Bergheim pit 157 (Chenal *et al.*, 2015) or Achenheim feature 124 (Chenal and Lefranc, 2017), suggest more and more that the phenomenon of human deposits in circular pits from the 5th and 4th millennia BC are generally indicative of a warlike atmosphere, in this area at least. If so, most of the accompanying dead could be prisoners of war. Both hypotheses are not mutually exclusive, and accompaniment by slaves and by captives may have co-existed. For that matter, in all ethnohistoric examples the execution of enemies or strangers goes every time with accompaniment by members of the society itself (Testart, 2004a: 200). A war context explains almost all the facts, and in particular the cases that cannot be explained by the sole accompaniment. The presence of children is no counter-argument: ethnography has demonstrated that feuds and wars do not spare children or women, who can be killed and tortured as well (Knowles, 1940). In both eventualities, either captives or slaves, the individuals found in haphazard positions in circular pits are dependent. Their accompanying an important figure in death demonstrates the existence of highly stratified and hierarchical societies, likely to be also subjected to endemic armed violence. Archaeothanatological analysis is able to provide this type of social information.

Uncertainty: what about hierarchical accompaniment before the Neolithic?

As demonstrated by ethnographic examples, hierarchical accompaniment exists among some hunter-gatherer societies; the key question remains whether it existed in European prehistory. Indeed, giving a positive answer would explicitly imply that during the Palaeolithic or Mesolithic there were groups of hunter-gatherers, probably sedentary – those that some call 'complex' – marked by wealth inequality, which would shed light on a major social hypothesis sometimes put forward (see above references) but yet to be demonstrated. Nevertheless, this issue faces difficulties that equal its potential implications. Two of these difficulties regarding the limits of interpretation have been mentioned earlier. On the one hand, possible hierarchies may be expected not to have been strongly marked, and as such asymmetries in accompaniment may be hard to identify. On the other hand, the very small number of multiple burials known for each period and each region prevents construction of empirical models and demands consideration of each case individually. Henry-Gambier (2008) raised a third difficulty: no one can affirm that asymmetry in multiple burials has maintained the same meaning from the Palaeolithic through the historical periods. In other words, one cannot formally exclude the possibility that asymmetry conveyed a message altogether different from that of hierarchical accompaniment among hunter-gatherers from the ancient past.

Even though these difficulties preclude definitive answers, a few examples, in particular some Gravettian multiple burials, provide the possibility of hierarchical accompaniment being present among some prehistoric hunter-gatherers, contrary to what Testart (2004a: 186) argued: that there was no evidence of it. Attention must be drawn in particular to two examples upon which his conclusion was based: the two triple Gravettian graves from Barma Grande (Italy) and Dolní Věstonice (Czech Republic). Testart (2004a: 183) counted them as symmetrical, but Henry-Gambier (2008: 414–416) is more dubious and rightly underlines that this symmetry is relative. At Barma Grande, the adult is laid on his back, whereas the two teenagers placed on his right are on their sides, facing him. Asymmetry is not prominent, but the comparison with Roy Mata's grave in Retoka, Vanuatu (Garanger, 1972), which is a documented example of accompaniment, shows that in both cases the configurations are disconcertingly similar (Boulestin, 2018). At Dolní Věstonice, the layout of the bodies and the position of the upper limbs of the left individual (DV 13) make the centrally positioned body (DV 15), the first to have been deposited in the grave, the stand-out figure (Figure 5.5). The latter is also distinguished by the presence of ochre on his pelvis. The individual on the right (DV 14) was inhumed lying face-down.

A close examination of the archaeological evidence makes it possible to reject, at least for these two Gravettian examples, the complete absence of asymmetry in Upper Palaeolithic graves. Interpreting the documents from this period is no easy task, and there are several possible explanations for simultaneous burials or deaths (Boulestin, 2008, 2018), so one cannot state out-of-hand that these graves testify to hierarchical accompaniment. This is a hypothesis that cannot be put aside either, and the analysis opens the door to a new interpretative way to understand the multiple burials of prehistoric hunter-gatherers.

Conclusion

Archaeothanatology is far from limited solely to reconstructing how dead people were buried and to the analysis of field observations. This analysis is just the starting point of a more general interpretative approach, the highest objectives of which are to reconstruct the ways in which ancient societies functioned. Because the way the dead, or at least some of them, are treated depends closely on the way societies are structured. Nevertheless, further interpretation requires

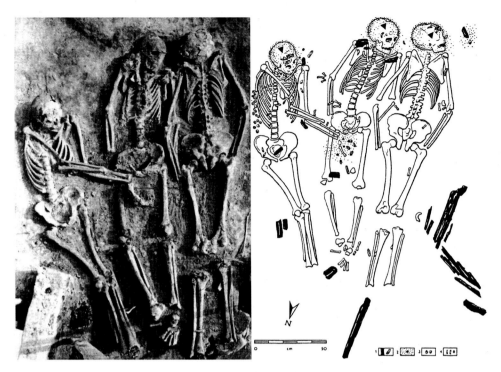

Figure 5.5   Photograph and plan of the triple burial from Dolní Věstonice 13–15.

1: Wood (compact charcoal fragments) and selected artefacts, 2: ochre, 3: molluscs, 4: human teeth, pierced animal teeth and pierced ivory pendants (Svoboda, 2006: figs. 4.4 and 4.5; Reproduced with kind permission of J. Svoboda).

construction of theoretical frameworks robust enough to back up the reflections, parallel to the analysis of field data. On this basis, the model of accompanying dead is certainly one of the most interesting and most stimulating models social anthropology has produced over the past few years. What it showed here is that through the archaeothanatological analysis, under favourable circumstances, the dead themselves, and not only their graves, ornaments and grave goods, can convey information about aspects as difficult to tackle as the social stratification of societies.

Acknowledgement

The original text was translated from the French by E. Boulestin.

References

Ames, K.M. (2007). The archaeology of rank. In: R. A. Bentley, H. D. G. Maschner and C. Chippindale, eds., *Handbook of Archaeological Theories*. Lanham: Altamira Press, pp. 487–513.

Baray, L. and Boulestin, B., eds, (2010). *Morts anormaux et sépultures bizarres. Les dépôts humains en fosses circulaires et en silos du Néolithique à l'Âge du Fer*. Dijon: Éditions universitaires de Dijon.

Beeching, A. (1991). Sépultures, territoires et société dans le Chasséen méridional. L'exemple du Bassin rhodanien. In: A. Beeching, D. Binder, J.-C. Blanchet, C. Constantin, J. Dubouloz, R. Martinez, D. Mordant, J.-P. Thévenot and J. Vaquer, eds., *Identité du Chasséen*. Nemours: éditions de l'Association pour la Promotion de la Recherche Archéologique en Île-de-France (APRAIF), pp. 327–341.

Beeching, A. and Crubézy, É. (1998). Les sépultures chasséennes de la vallée du Rhône. In: J. Guilaine, ed., *Sépultures d'Occident et Genèses des Mégalithismes*. Paris: Éditions errance, pp. 147–164.

Binford, L.R. (1971). Mortuary Practices: Their Study and Their Potential. *Memoirs of the Society for American Archaeology*, 25, pp. 6–29.

Boulestin, B. (2008). Pourquoi Mourir Ensemble? À Propos Des Tombes Multiples Dans Le Néolithique Français. *Bulletin de la Société Préhistorique Française*, 105(1), pp. 103–130.

Boulestin, B. (2018). « Pourquoi Donc Tous Ces Chasseurs-Cueilleurs Font-Ils des Tombes Doubles? ». *Bulletin de la Société Préhistorique Française*, 115(1), pp. 43–52.

Boulestin, B. and Duday, H. (2005). Ethnologie et archéologie de la mort: de l'illusion des références à l'emploi d'un vocabulaire. In: C. Mordant and G. Depierre, eds., *Les Pratiques Funéraires à l'Age du Bronze en France*. Paris and Sens: Éditions du Comité des Travaux Historiques et Scientifiques (CTHS) and Société archéologique de Sens, pp. 17–35.

Boulestin, B. and Duday, H. (2006). Ethnology and Archaeology of Death: From the Illusion of References to the Use of a Terminology. *Archaeologia Polona*, 44, pp. 149–169.

Boyer, R. (1994). *La mort chez les anciens Scandinaves*. Paris: Les Belles Lettres.

Brown, J.A. (1981). The search for rank in prehistoric burials. In: R. Chapman, I. Kinnes and K. Randsborg, eds., *The archaeology of death*. Cambridge: Cambridge University Press, pp. 25–37.

Chenal, F. and Lefranc, P. (2017). Violence préhistorique à Achenheim. *Archéologia*, 550, pp. 12–13.

Chenal, F., Perrin, B., Barrand-Emam, H. and Boulestin, B. (2015). A Farewell to Arms: A Deposit of Human Limbs and Bodies at Bergheim, France, c. 4000 BC. *Antiquity*, 89(348), pp. 1313–1330.

Clastres, P. (1972). *Chronique des Indiens Guayaki*. Paris: Plon.

Crubézy, É. (1991). Les pratiques funéraires dans le Chasséen de la moyenne vallée du Rhône. In: A. Beeching, D. Binder, J.-C. Blanchet, C. Constantin, J. Dubouloz, R. Martinez, D. Mordant, J.-P. Thévenot and J. Vaquer, eds., *Identité du Chasséen*. Nemours: Éditions de l'Association pour la Promotion de la Recherche Archéologique en Île-de-France (APRAIF), pp. 393–398.

Flannery, K. and Marcus, J. (2012). *The creation of inequality: how our prehistoric ancestors set the stage for monarchy, slavery, and empire*. Cambridge: Harvard University Press.

Garanger, J. (1972). *Archéologie des Nouvelles-Hébrides. contribution à la connaissance des îles du centre*. Paris: Office de la Recherche Scientifique et Technique Outre-Mer (ORSTOM).

Gibaja, J. F., Duboscq, S., Esteve, X., Coll, J. M., Marti, M., Martin, A., Mestres, J. Oms, X., Pou, R., Roig, J. and Subira, M. E. (2016). Restes humains dans les structures néolithiques du nord-est de la péninsule Ibérique: dépôts ou sépultures? In: M. Lauwers and A. Zemour, eds., *Qu'est-ce qu'une Sépulture? Humanités et Systèmes Funéraires de la Préhistoire à nos Jours*. Antibes: Éditions de l'Association pour la Promotion et la Diffusion des Connaissances Archéologiques (APDCA), pp. 193–209.

Henry-Gambier, D. (2008). Comportement des Populations d'Europe au Gravettien: Pratiques Funéraires et Interprétations. *Paleo*, 20, pp. 399–438.

Jeunesse, C. (2010). Les sépultures en fosses circulaires de l'horizon 4500–3500: contribution à l'étude comparée des systèmes funéraires du Néolithique européen. In L. Baray and B. Boulestin, eds., *Morts Anormaux et Sépultures Bizarres. Les Dépôts Humains en Fosses Circulaires et en Silos du Néolithique à l'âge du Fer*. Dijon: Éditions universitaires de Dijon, pp. 28–48.

Kelly, R. L. (2013). *The lifeways of hunter-gatherers: the foraging spectrum*, 2nd ed. Cambridge: Cambridge University Press.

Knowles, N. (1940). The Torture of Captives by the Indians of Eastern North America. *Proceedings of the American Philosophical Society*, 82, pp. 151–225.

Lefranc, P., Denaire, A., Chenal, F. and Arbogast, R.M. (2010). Les Inhumations et les Dépôts d'Animaux en Fosses Circulaires du Néolithique Récent du Sud de la Plaine du Rhin Supérieur. *Gallia Préhistoire*, 52, pp. 61–116.

O'Shea, J.M. (1984). *Mortuary variability: an archaeological investigation*. London: Academic Press.

Price, T.D. and Feinman, G.M., eds. (1995). *Foundations of social inequality*. New York: Plenum Press.

Price, T.D. and Feinman, G.M., eds. (2010). *Pathways to power: new perspectives on the emergence of social inequality*. New York: Springer.

Saxe, A.A. (1970). *Social dimensions of mortuary practices*. Unpublished Ph.D. thesis, University of Michigan, Ann Arbor.

Schiltz, V. (1994). *Les Scythes et les nomades des steppes, 8ᵉ siècle avant J.-C. – 1ᵉʳ siècle après J.-C.* Paris: Gallimard.

Svoboda, J.A. (2006). The burials: ritual and taphonomy. In: E. Trinkaus and J. Svoboda, eds., *Early Modern Human Evolution in Central Europe. The People of Dolni Věstonice and Pavlov*. Oxford: Oxford University Press, pp. 15–26.

Schmitt, A. (2017). Middle Neolithic Burials in Mediterranean France: Honouring or Rejecting the Dead? *West & East*, II, pp. 63–82.

Testart, A. (2004a). *Les morts d'accompagnement. La servitude volontaire I*. Paris: Éditions Errance.
Testart, A. (2004b). *L'origine de l'État. La servitude volontaire II*. Paris: Éditions Errance.
Testart, A. (2005). Doit-on parler de « sacrifice » à propos des morts d'accompagnement? In: J.-P. Albert and B. Midant-Reynes, eds., *Le Sacrifice Humain en Égypte Ancienne et Ailleurs*. Paris: Éditions Soleb, pp. 34–57.
Testart, A., Jeunesse, C., Baray, L. and Boulestin, B. (2010). Les Esclaves des Tombes Néolithiques. *Pour la Science*, 396, pp. 74–80.
Ucko, P. J. (1969). Ethnography and Archaeological Interpretation of Funerary Remains. *World Archaeology*, 1(2), pp. 262–280.

6

DENIED FUNERAL RITES

The contribution of the archaeothanatological approach

Aurore Schmitt

ARCHÉOLOGIE DES SOCIÉTÉS MÉDITERRANÉENNES, UMR 5140, CNRS-UNIVERSITÉ PAUL VALÉRY-MINISTÈRE DE LA CULTURE, MONTPELLIER, FRANCE

Introduction

Since the 1980s, mortuary archaeology has benefited from the development of a series of new approaches focussing on human remains: bioarchaeology (Buikstra, 1977) and funerary taphonomy, especially in English-language scholarship (Haglund and Sorg, 2001; Knüsel and Robb, 2016). In France, 'field anthropology' (Duday, 1981), also called 'archaeothanatology' (Boulestin and Duday, 2006) as well as 'funerary archaeology' or 'funerary anthropology' (Duday *et al.,* 1990) has travelled a completely parallel path. From 2000, the followers of this approach realised that intentional actions involving the manipulation of human remains do not, necessarily, form part of funerary cycles (Boulestin and Baray, 2010). The word 'funerary' was too restrictive since the discipline does not study only the funerary practices but also the treatment of the dead that does not form part of the funeral. Archaeothanatology thus investigates funerary, post-funerary, and non-funerary treatment of human remains. All of these treatments of dead bodies are therefore qualified as 'mortuary' (Boulestin, 2012).

The purpose of this chapter is to discuss how to identify the denial of funerary rituals and practices. This particular issue is considered a difficult task in archaeothanatology because a positive attitude towards a dead person is easier to demonstrate than the contrary (Duday, 2010). However, several archaeologists have recently argued that the heuristic potential of cross-cultural comparisons is under-estimated in French scholarship, and have recommended the use of ethnographic and historical data to help define and interpret the mortuary record (Baray, Brun and Testart, 2007; Gambier and Boulestin, 2012). This approach, adopted in the present chapter, enables the definition of clear research aims, makes it possible to distance oneself from one's own cultural standards, and widens the sphere of possible hypotheses.

Theoretical framework and concept

A brief note on vocabulary

In English, the generic term 'burial' is used to refer to human remains deposited (buried) in the ground but also to a stage in the funerary process, which leads to confusion between those accorded funerary rites and those lacking them. In this chapter, 'deposit' is preferred to burial at

DOI: 10.4324/9781351030625-8

a descriptive level. It is a neutral descriptive term since deposits may or may not be 'funerary'. When burial is used in this chapter, it refers to a grave or a tomb. Inhumation corresponds to the action of covering a body with sediment.

Funerary, post-funerary, non-funerary treatments of the body and the skeletal remains

It is very important to distinguish these three categories from one another – funerary, post-funerary, and non-funerary (Figure 6.1). At the death of an individual, two scenarios are possible: either the deceased is deemed worthy of a funeral – in which case the corpse may be deposited in a grave – or not. In the first case, the funerary treatment of the corpse and the underlying religious and social ideologies may take a wide variety of forms (Frazer, 1934; Guiart, 1979). Moreover, different forms of funerary treatment usually co-exist even within a single given society (Ucko, 1969). Death is a period of transition that defines the funerary cycle, in the course of which the deceased dies socially, the corpse disintegrates, those left behind mourn their loss, and society undergoes re-organisation (Hertz, 1907; van Gennep, 1909). The end of the funerary cycle marks the end of the mourning period as well as the departure of the 'soul' to the 'world of the dead'.

Once the funerary cycle has been completed (Duday *et al.*, 1990; Weiss-Krejci, 2011), skeletal remains may continue to be manipulated. Post-funerary treatments include a wide range of rituals, the best known are ancestor cults, commemorations, and cults of relics. The bones may also be retrieved from funerary spaces to be re-deposited in ossuaries (medieval charnel houses, for example), with or without ceremonies, to make room for new graves. Such a practice is conducted for practical reasons but the bones are preserved in a sacred area and are still respected. For example, open-air areas of discarded burnt bones and ritual objects from the cleaning of

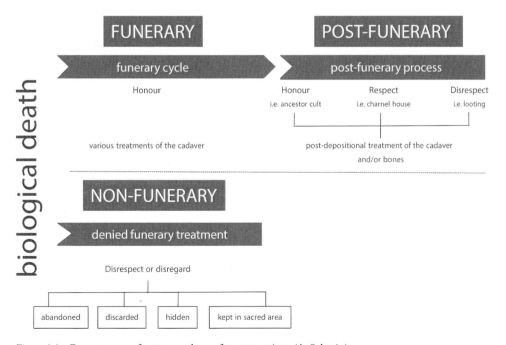

Figure 6.1 Funerary, post-funerary and non-funerary actions (A. Schmitt).

pyres are documented in Thailand (Pautreau and Mornais, 2005). Re-opened graves due to grave robberies (Aspöck, 2011) or profanation are a completely different category of post-funerary treatment. These actions are particularly disrespectful towards the deceased. The post-funerary treatments listed above are applied to the remains of the deceased who had funerals and a final funerary deposition in a grave. Non-funerary treatments are discussed in the next section.

Who is denied funerals and why?

The fate of being denied a funeral befalls particular categories of people determined by the circumstances of their demise and/or the role and status of the individual in society. Ranking by manner of death is the starting point of this classification.

Killing

Murder victims

Victims of murder hidden or abandoned by the killer are deprived of funerals. Corpses may be concealed, mutilated, dismembered, burned, among others, to prevent their discovery, identification and to destroy evidence. If the corpses are later discovered and exhumed, these will be re-buried according to the funerary rituals of the community to which the victim belongs.

The accompanying dead (funerary retainers)

Some individuals are killed to accompany the deceased in the afterlife (Testart, 2004) (cf. Boulestin, Chapter 5, this volume). Relations in life are perpetuated in death. Accompanying deaths are a consequence of the personal bonds of loyalty established between leaders and their followers who have different social statuses. Among those concerned by the scope of this classification are those who would be denied funerals if they died before the person s/he was supposed to accompany in death, such as servants or slaves.[1]

Sacrificial victims

A sacrifice is an offering to a divinity (Testart, 2009). Sacrificial victims could be slaves, captives imprisoned during warfare, or criminals (Law, 1985).

Transgressors

Those who misconduct themselves, or do wrong during their lifetimes (Weiss-Krejci, 2013) are socially de-classified by their own community: criminals, murderers, suicides, heretics and political opponents, for example. Many of them would have had standard funerary treatments if their social status had remained unchanged during their life span. Improper or disrespectful treatments serve as a means to punish the person, demonstrating religious and/or political power.

---

1 The slave, as defined by Law (1985), is excluded from the society in which s/he lives (Testart, 2004). Denial of funerary treatment of slaves depends on the society in question.

Enemies during warfare[2] and genocide victims (victims)

This category implies a conflict between two populations. In some cases, corpses are kept away from their community of origin by an opposing group whose aim, among others, is to demonstrate its religious and/or political power, as with the category of transgressors, above.

No killing

Outcasts

Individuals classified as outcasts belong to a social rank that does not have the right to funeral rites, such as slaves or strangers in certain communities (Hertz, 1907).

Circumstances of death

Persons whose circumstances of death modify their mortuary status such as women who died during child-birth, very young people, or those who died by accident, or of a particular disease (Moréchand, 1975).

Inaccessible bodies

People who died by accident but are missing, or corpses abandoned because the number of victims and the circumstances prevent the performance of funeral rites. In the case of warfare, the treatment of the enemy is not involved in this category; it is the incapacity to manage extraordinary mass mortality by the community.

The notion of deprivation of burial

Deprivation of burial is a legal sanction for some individuals such as from the above categories of enemies in warfare or transgressors. In Roman Law, depriving someone of burial was a measure reserved for the most serious cases of high treason, though some public enemies might have had discrete funerals (Ferries, 2011). Burial deprivation in ancient Greece consisted of the abandonment of the body without funerals outside territorial borders (Helmis, 2007). Repatriation was possible if the individual had been rehabilitated. In contrast, if one was recognised as guilty after death, it was possible to exhume the individual and have him/her removed from the city. Burial deprivation also affected bad Christians, such as those excommunicated in Late Antiquity and during the Early Middle Ages. When the ecclesiastical community controlled funerals and burials at the end of the 9th century in Europe excommunication was an ordinary penal sanction (Lauwers, 2016). In the 12th century, references to deprivation of burial are numerous. Jews, pagans, heretics, excommunicants, suicides, adulterers, thieves and those sentenced to death were among the groups denied burial. No ceremonies were organised, and the location of disposal of the corpse was located outside the funerary space reserved for Christians. Topographical exclusion was a way to display punishment and/or exclusion (Vivas, 2015). This process is a means to banish or exile undesirable social elements from the community in life as well as death. Since the individuals were excluded, they were deprived of the funerary customs performed for the members of the community (Boulestin and Baray, 2010). The deprivation of burial is thus a punishment. Transgressors were

---

2 Whatever the scale of warfare.

also treated in this manner. A slave was not deprived of a funeral, however, since, regardless of social status, s/he would not have lost the right to these rituals. As a consequence, burial deprivation does not concern all of the dead who were not granted funeral rights, only some of them.

What treatment(s) for the bodies of individuals without funerals?

After death, the corpse (completely or partly) is either intentionally transformed, or it remains complete. The range of modifications is great. The treatment of the corpse of a person sentenced to death is often violent (torture or mutilation before dying or to cause death). After killing, the corpse can also be desecrated: mutilated,[3] dismembered, and/or exposed. This event takes place in a specific location or at the place in which the killing occurred. In the Middle Ages, the gibbet or gallows was used as a place of exhibition; corpses were left hanging until in an advanced stage of decay (Vivas, 2015). Such treatment aimed to impress the living. This action was thus staging intended for the survivors. The dead body or a part of it may also have been displayed to neutralise the reaction of an opponent in a political conflict: a corpse placed on the gallows or at the side of the road was thus instrumentalised (Anstett, 2016).

The way a person is killed and/or the treatment of the cadaver may be related to beliefs in an afterlife and certain treatments provide a means to prevent the salvation of the soul of the deceased. For various reasons, the fate of the soul was often related to the state of the body. For example, the purpose of Roman decapitation was to prevent individuals from having status in the world of the dead (Hinard, 1984). The fate of heretics burned at the stake is an example of a treatment that was intended to inhibit resurrection (Davies, 2005). Desecrated bodies were also supposed to have an effect on both the living and the deceased, as did normative funerary rituals but the intended effect was the opposite.

Corpses may also be destroyed such as through burning in a crematorium during the Holocaust (van Pelt, 2014). Political opponents hidden shortly after their deaths were sometimes exhumed in order to destroy their remains and to discard them where they could not be found, in the ocean for instance (Lopez-Mazz, 2015). Trophies are a different category of transformation. Human body parts, many times from an enemy killed during warfare, could be transformed to play a role in particular rituals (Mendoza, 2007). Trophies, such as severed heads, could be exposed. The consumption of human flesh in exocannibalism[4] mainly relates to warfare (Boulestin *et al.*, 2009), or could be a judicial procedure that also transforms the body.

The final treatment of the body

Whether the body is transformed or not, or the person sentenced to death or not, the final treatment of the remains is particularly difficult to track in the literature. The means of killing are rather well-documented, whereas what happens to the corpses afterwards is rarely described. The same applies to the victims of sacrifice, and particularly to persons who are denied a funeral and/or burial because of their outcast status. Victims of political massacres and genocides who are buried (or not) without funerals have recently started to be analysed in order to question the social legacy of mass violence (Anstett and Dreyfus, 2014) and to provide rare comparative studies to investigate violence in the past.

---

3 Throughout history, corpses of individuals (sentenced to death for instance) have been dissected and examined in detail for medical investigations. This action also led to mutilation, but, in this case, the motive is different.

4 Endocannibalism, consumption by one's own group, is a funerary treatment.

Abandoned corpses or body parts left at the place of death

Two cases can be distinguished. Owing to an extraordinary event, the normative funerary rites fail to be performed, as after an accident or a battle. Abandonment of human remains occurs also when they are considered to be refused. For instance, on the Esquiline Hill in Rome, slaves or low social status individuals sentenced to death rotted on the spot after their execution (Hinard, 1987).

Discarded corpses or body parts

In this category, dead bodies considered as waste are removed from their place of death and thrown away. The locations of deposits vary: refuse areas, open areas, forests, oceans, rivers, etc. These people are denied funerary treatment because of their social status as outcasts or criminals, for example, or due to the circumstances of their death, and are often discarded (Moréchand, 1975; Magalhães, Matos Fernandes and Santos, 2015; Wasterlain, Costa and Ferreira, 2018; Wouassi, 2020). Judicial procedures often stipulate that corpses of hanged criminals be interred close to the gibbet or gallows. This particular area is fenced or ditched but displayed for all to see. Inhumation without ritual and far from the cemetery is intended to dishonour the dead. The aim of such treatment is to perpetuate the punishment (the death sentence) on the cadaver (Vivas, 2016). Remains of exocannibalism are discarded after consumption. When a trophy is no longer powerful, it may be destroyed and/or discarded (Allard and Taylor, 2016).

Hidden corpses or body parts

The purpose of the deposition is to make them disappear and to hide them from their community but also from future victims and survivors in the case of genocide (Anstett, 2016). This concealment denies the identity of the person.

Inhumation of corpses in a sacred area

The accompanying dead may be placed in the grave of a deceased person that they thus join in death, as a consequence, are often found in sacred places. Victims of sacrifices may also be buried in the court temple where the sacrifice took place (Vail and Hernández, 2007). As cadavers have a particular symbolic function they are integrated into ritualised areas.

The dead who are denied funerals are, in most cases, considered waste, though not systematically so (trophies are often discarded after a time and the accompanying dead are not considered detritus). Actions that lead to the reification of the human remains do not constitute a homogeneous group. Denial of proper funerary treatment is also not necessarily associated with the desecration of the corpse. Furthermore, the different treatments listed above will leave no uniform archaeological signatures, on the one hand and, on the other hand, inhumation or natural covering is far from frequent. It is, however, the *sine qua non* condition that permits archaeologists to find the remains and reconstruct their history.

How to highlight the denial of funerary treatment through archaeoanthropological evidence?

First, it is important to recall that funerals do not necessarily imply a burial space (a grave). If human remains are absent or few in certain archaeologically defined cultures, this does not mean that individuals were denied funerals, whether or not it is possible for archaeologists to find evidence for burials or whether or not the funerary ritual included a final place of burial. On the contrary, denial of funerary treatment means that no burial occurred. However, an inhumation (the action of covering a complete body or a portion of it with sediment) is possible. A conjunction of both phenomena in past societies may occur: no burial when funeral rites are performed and also a denial of funerary rites for a part of the society.

Appropriate terminology for the non-funerary record

The definition of precise terms is one of the specific strengths of the archaeothanatological approach. Several terms to describe non-funerary actions and depositions should be avoided.

In the archaeological literature, non-funerary practices may be deduced from deviant or unusual deposits that can only be identified if there are enough burials to identify a 'norm' in funerary practices. An individual is buried a certain way relative to the norm for the period/or the population under examination (Murphy, 2008). The term 'deviant' has been discussed in German and English literature, but Aspöck (2008) challenges the usefulness of such a concept. Furthermore, deviant or unusual does not mean that the deceased was denied a funerary rite. At present, knowledge of the full variability of the funerary record in past populations is not extensive enough to pursue such a goal. Deviant or unusual treatment of the corpse can sometimes signal high and even very special status (Weiss-Krejci, 2008). Terms such as 'deviant', 'unusual', and 'non-normative' should be avoided to describe a deposit because it is an over-simplification in an attempt to classify every human assemblage outside the scope of existing burial classifications. For this reason, these terms are not used in archaeothanatology. The words atypical ('*atypique*') (i.e. Oudry-Braillon and Billard, 2009), and enigmatic ('*enigmatique*') (Duday, 2010) have been suggested. Moreover, the notion of norm and its utility in archaeothanatology is debated today (Boulestin, 2016). This term has also been criticised by historians specialising in the funerary record (Treffort, 2004).

Recently, a new term was introduced by French scholars: the 'non-burial' ('*non-sépulture*') (Rodet-Belarbi and Séguy, 2013, 2016). The term refers to corpses treated like waste because they retain no social identity. They are denied humanity and remembrance, a condition that is often associated with outcasts. For these scholars, the 'non-burial' excludes individuals denied burial as excommunicants or those sentenced to death, for the displayed bodies of enemies, and for victims of crime. Since all these cases lead to the absence of evidence for funerary rites, it is hard to understand why they are not included. If the 'non-burial' is not the exact opposite of 'burial', despite containing the negation ('*non*') of a burial ('*sépulture*'), it demonstrates itself to be an inadequate term. Moreover, these excluded individuals may also be denied humanity and remembrance. How does one refer to them then? The term 'non-funerary treatment' seems best – which is the opposite of funerary treatment. It means that the archaeological record indicates disrespect for the dead body.

The term 'cemetery' is also problematic. In archaeothanatology, it refers to a precise historical context (Lauwers, 2016) that is exclusively funerary in nature and related to the rise of Christianity. The term 'funerary space' is preferred when the context falls outside this definition. The use of 'execution cemeteries' (Reynolds, 2009) is thus composed of two contradictory terms. The cemetery is a special funerary space dedicated to a Christian community. Executed individuals are not included in this communal area. Transgressors and criminals are indeed excluded from the 'cemetery'.

Step 1: evidence of an intentional act of disrespect

As this book is dedicated to archaeothanatology, its approach and its methods will not be described here. The aim is to discuss how to identify individuals who had no access to funerary rites. As a consequence, it is necessary to identify the evidence for funerary treatment in the archaeological record. As burials are the most frequent evidence in archaeology for funerary sites, this discussion is based on the final deposition of a dead body. The definition of burial in archaeothanatology has been discussed in Boulestin and Baray (2010). The definition proposed by Boulestin (2012: 37) is adopted here: 'a burial is a context that contains the bones of one or several deceased individuals deposited during a ceremony honouring at least one of these deceased individuals through the treatment of his/her bodily remains' (*'une sépulture est un lieu où sont déposés les restes d'un ou de plusieurs défunts, ce dépôt étant conçu comme définitif et intervenant dans le cadre d'une cérémonie dont la finalité est d'honorer au moins un des défunts au travers de sa dépouille'*). Demonstrating that a deposit results from the performance of funerary rites necessitates looking for material or contextual evidence suggesting that the aim of the deposit was to honour the deceased. Funerary gestures refer to actions that are reverential by nature. As a consequence, denial of funerary treatment connotes a negative reaction towards the dead. In these circumstances, the dead body is treated as waste, and when this is not the case, the cadavers of such individuals are not provided with the necessary honours (as in the case of the accompanying dead). The following criteria provide a means to identify a non-funerary treatment. They follow from the first part of this chapter. No single criterion alone is decisive. They have to be looked at in combination with each other in order to obtain the whole picture.

The human remains

This step involves examination of several types of evidence. 'Disposition' refers to the mode of disposing of the dead once the original position of the body has been identified through taphonomic analysis. As far as a primary deposit is concerned, an arranged body is likely to be related to the performance of funerary rites, even if, in rare cases, they are not (see contradictory evidence section, below). The position resulting from the action of throwing a body in a pit with or without the hands tied behind the back provides valuable evidence of such a negative action. However, it is important to note that not all irregularly placed bodies are reflective of disrespect for the dead. Pragmatic solutions in the case of multiple simultaneous deposits during extraordinary mortality situations often lead to a lack of body arrangement. The meaning of many dispositions is problematic. A corpse introduced through the narrow opening of a storage pit that is not followed by any other manipulation is, however, neither thrown nor disposed of. The resulting position of such action varies but still remains identifiable (Schmitt, 2017). Ethnographic analogy documents instances of such bodies being placed in large pits (Sewane, 2003). Only the 'founder' of the grave, the first one in the feature, is placed by the officiants, the other individuals sharing the same grave will be placed successively, but they, too, receive funerary rites. Actions that lead to the initial positioning of a dead body are very important but they only commence the investigation, rather than provide a clear interpretation of it, alone.

Element representation of the skeleton, anthropogenic bone modification, traces of burning, evidence of peri-mortem trauma are relevant for determining whether or not a body had been mutilated, cannibalised or exposed to gnawing of scavenging animals, dismembered, or burnt, for example. The challenge is to distinguish these anthropogenic actions from events related to natural processes (a dead body may have lain in an open space before being covered by sediment) but also the effect of decay and the post-depositional process itself. Skeletal information is meaningful when evaluated jointly with evidence from contextual material.

The feature, the stratum and their contents

The size, shape and the fill of a feature can help define if it had an exclusive funerary function, or whether it was secondarily re-used after serving its original function (such as storage pit transformed into a refuse pit). If this secondary status does not guarantee a non-funerary practice, it can facilitate the identification of a context that deserves closer investigation. The general disposition (internal arrangement) of the remains of material cultural items discovered in a feature in relation to the dead body also help to determine the status of the deceased (Boulestin and Baray, 2010). The analysis of the fill, whether anthropogenic or natural, provides evidence to identify the actions that led to the archaeological as well as the anthropological assemblage. Apart from the human remains, the content of the feature provides crucial information. For instance, detritus in contact with human remains suggests a non-funerary treatment. The discovery in many geographical areas of babies, children and adults thrown into a refuse area during antiquity, and not carefully disposed of, clearly indicates a lack of regard for these corpses (Rodet-Belarbi and Séguy, 2013, 2016). Meanwhile, cannibalised remains disposed of in a refuse area are not necessarily related to a non-funerary treatment. This is true only in exocannibalism. In the case of endocannibalism, even if the consumption is a funerary treatment, the remaining bones and body parts not eaten may be considered to be waste. Their relation to the refuse area is then ambiguous. Complete corpses or disarticulated remains discovered in refuse pits from prehistory to modern times pose many questions (Schmitt and Anstett, 2020).

Another important issue is the distinction between post-funerary and non-funerary treatments. The absence of objects associated with the body in a burial is found in many archaeological circumstances, but this criterion is not evidence for non-funerary treatment. In addition, the killing of individuals to accompany precious goods is documented. For instance, at the site of the 'Aérodrome' in Colmar (Haut-Rhin, France) (Lefranc et al., 2012), 56 copper beads (prestige items for this period) were found near a body in a very unconventional position (on its stomach, decubitus ventral). This association was interpreted as a human offering. The presence of an object may also result from superstition related to fear of the dead person (Reynolds, 2009). In this case, the person is not honoured but both the disposition of the deceased and the internal arrangement of the funerary space help to put things in perspective. The presence of objects associated with human remains likely excludes a non-funerary gesture in many cases but the reverse is not true.

The location of the features or the stratum containing human remains is relevant if the funerary spaces of the society under study have previously been identified. For instance, from the 10th century AD in Europe, the community of a village is buried in a cemetery close to a religious building. Isolated human remains clearly excluded from this sacred area, which are contemporaneous with such an organisation, suggest differential treatment that may be rather negative in nature. The criteria need to be looked at in combination to be informative. The exercise will be easier to apply when the funerary customs of a society are well documented, either through the historical record or through a high number of previously excavated burials. Space dedicated to executed individuals in England during the Early Middle Ages has been identified through several shared criteria: among them, the geographical remoteness of such areas and the body treatment, such as evidence for amputation, decapitation, a body having been thrown into, rather than deposited in a context (Reynolds, 2009).

In Late Neolithic Southern France, collective burial was the most frequent funerary treatment. However, single inhumations in domestic pits have also been discovered in settlements. In these features, some individuals were deposited in a pit with no associated objects. At the sites of Fabrys (Roussillon, Vaucluse, France) and 'Les Martins' (Bonnieux, Vaucluse, France), these individuals were probably excluded from collective burial, and they might have even been denied funerary rites (Schmitt, Remicourt and D'Anna, 2017), but it is not always necessarily the case. When knowledge about a society is limited, the task is more difficult. Even when putting all the evidence together, several hypotheses are likely to fit the evidence, and it will not be possible to favour one over the others (Oudry-Braillon and Billard, 2009). One case from the 'Châtelliers du Vieil-Auzay' site in Vendée, western France, is very eloquent in this regard (Duday, 2010). Three burial chambers were inserted in an earthen mound. Each chamber contained two individuals buried simultaneously. Five carefully deposited individuals had a vase placed in the vicinity of their heads. All skeletons provided evidence of violent deaths. If some aspects, such as the earthen mound, position of the corpse, and grave goods, reflect funerary treatments, the manner of death also suggests ritualised killing.

Contradictory evidence

Inhumations in settlements from the Middle Neolithic in Southern France are a relevant example for contradictory evidence. Features containing human remains are always located in lowland domestic contexts (or close to their limits). The most frequent pattern is the primary inhumation in a domestic pit (referred to as 'circular pits') whose initial function prior to the deposition of bodies or human bones was different, for instance as silos for storing grain. Human remains from this geographical and chronological region are not representative of the entire deceased community but more varied funerary customs are often completely unattested. As a consequence, the presence of the dead in the space inhabited by the living might have stemmed from a special social status rather than from a systematic rule (Perlès, 2009). If the regular practice consisted of burying the deceased close to their residence, these settlements would provide evidence in the form of many individual sets of human remains, which is far from being the case. The non-funerary nature of deposits in circular pits has been proposed recently in a large geographical scale study focussing on the 5th and 4th millennia BC (Jeunesse, 2010). Discarded bodies after killing, use of mutilated corpses as war trophies, burials containing accompanying dead are plausible hypotheses explaining the available anthropological and archaeological evidence (Chenal *et al.*, 2015; Lefranc, Denaire and Jeunesse, 2017). In contrast, primary deposits in circular pits in southern France are frequent, making their interpretation more difficult. The lack of direct indication for violent injuries has made some scholars sceptical of non-funerary hypotheses. However, even if direct evidence for violence is rarely found, it has been attested upon occasion (Michel and Sendra, 2014). The analysis is based on the contrast observed between deposits that are clearly related to funerary deposits and those which have different characteristics (discarded bodies, absence of objects, presence of refuse on or beneath the deceased). It has been proposed that this pattern is in accordance with non-funerary gestures (Schmitt, 2017). Some cases are more enigmatic. Individuals are deposited on their left sides (this is the conventional position for the period) associated with few objects in domestic pits that have been transformed into refuse pits. Recent work on more recent periods shows that some individuals placed in these refuse areas may have been treated with respect (Zagaria, 2019). A refuse area may not be the chosen ideal; it may be the only available or acceptable space to bury the deceased. Waste areas are consequently the only resting place for people who do not possess rights of access to the regular funerary space. However, for some of them, the family or social group wanted to treat them with respect, even if a more normative burial was forbidden. This might explain why some individuals are discarded in the same kind of pits (domestic pits transformed into refuse pits) and some are not. Though the evidence appears contradictory, historical and contemporaneous data may help clarify the situation.

Step 2: interpreting non-funerary treatments

Once disrespect towards the deceased has been demonstrated, the cause for this treatment may be interpreted. As there is no necessary correlation between the treatment of the dead body and the cause of the denial of funerary rites (Table 6.1), this second step is as complex as the first one.

Table 6.1 Relation between non-funerary treatment and causes of denial of funerals

	Treatment of (complete or partial) human remains			
Cause of denied funerals	Abandoned	Discarded	Hidden	Kept in sacred area
Killing — Murder victims				
Accompanying dead				
Sacrificed individuals				
Transgressors				
No killing — Enemies and genocide victims				
Outcasts				
Individual status changed by manner of death				
Inaccessible individuals				

Evidence of violent injuries on skeletal remains will provide evidence to elucidate the manner of death and may help to explain the mortuary treatment. However, according to the context, the status of the deceased (enemy, transgressor) should be assessed. The range of explanations will, in most cases, remain wide.

In addition to the analysis of the body treatment, the biological identity of the individual (sex, age-at-death, pathology, geographical origin available from biochemical analysis, such as strontium and aDNA) will provide relevant supplementary supporting evidence (Pokutta, 2014; Beau *et al.*, 2017). In many cases, this evidence may sometimes enable, first, to sustain an argument for a non-funerary treatment and, second, to provide an explanation for such an action.

Discoveries of individuals in refuse disposal areas, especially in wells from Antiquity (Rodet-Belarbi and Séguy, 2013) indicate limited regard towards the person during his/her lifetime. As far as neonates found in thee contexts are concerned, two main hypotheses explain the reasons for such treatment. First, they were victims of infanticide and their corpses were hidden in refuse areas. Second, infant mortality was very high in past populations and funerals were not performed for this group by the community (Rodet-Belarbi and Séguy, 2016). In both cases, individuals treated in this manner were considered waste and discarded. In this case, there is no doubt that funerary rites were denied; but many other contexts are challenging.

To propose that a non-funerary treatment corresponds to depriving an individual of burial, it is necessary to have identified what is (are) the funerary treatment(s) in the group under study. For pre-literate archaeological societies, the record is often insufficient to identify the complete scope of the funerary treatment available. This type of variety is attested by ethnographic reports, however. It is also observed in historical contexts for which relevant sources are can be found. The discovery of *juxta cimiterium* ('near cemetery') inhumations is difficult to interpret. Corpses are deposited and covered with earth but are found outside the communal funerary sacred space dedicated to Christian burial. This sign of exclusion is not sufficient to assert that the individual was deprived of burial (Vivas, 2015). This anomalous location may rather be a temporary space since the deceased may be re-integrated in the cemetery once the period of banishment has passed (Vivas, 2015). Historical texts for the Christian religion are normative.

They are not, unfortunately, a reflection of reality. Only a small part of the funerary practices and rituals performed for the dead are mentioned (Treffort, 2004). Deprivation of burial is difficult to identify, even for historic periods.

The notion of abandonment deposits, which is one possible interpretation of non-funerary treatment, needs to be considered as well. The '*sépulture de relégation*' (abandonment contexts) (Villes, 1987) has been much debated in archaeothanatology. First considered as a temporary term, since it is composed of the word burial, it implies that it is a funerary practice but also an exclusion from the funerary space of the community. It is related to the ostracisation of socially undesirable individuals. According to Villes (1987), the identification criteria of this are: absence of funerary objects, presence of debris and detritus in the grave fill, unusual position of the body, faunal remains found in the same type of features, and several individuals in a single feature. The victims of this abandonment deposit might be slaves, war captives, heretics, outcasts or convicts. The problem with this concept is that it associates two contradictory terms. Therefore, the definition has been discussed and re-defined (Boulestin and Baray, 2010). An abandonment burial is a burial reserved for marginal individuals who may have had funerary treatments but are found away from the funerary space of the community. This term should thus be avoided when non-funerary treatment is suspected.

Conclusion

In accordance with the archaeothanatological approach, the identification of non-funerary actions and practices commences with detailed field observations of all the mortuary evidence, including the interment location, the local environmental context, the type of feature, the funerary objects, as well as the human remains. After the original form of the deposit has been reconstructed, the challenge is to identify evidence for disrespectful treatment. The difficulty of the task depends on the cases studied and affects the process of interpretative reasoning, since in archaeology, the aim is to deduce 'why' and 'who' from the 'how'. Archaeothanatology is an appropriate approach since it is based on a clear distinction between terms used during analysis and those employed at the interpretative level. For the particular issue of denied funerals and burials, it proves particularly relevant. This point is crucial as it highlights a major difference with other academic traditions.[5] In addition, archaeothanatological analysis and interpretation remain crucial complements to written sources that provide, in fact, little information on non-funerary treatments, or might not always give accurate information.

Finally, even if the discipline is considered to be objective,[6] it is influenced by the current geo-political and/or cultural context in which it is developing. The contemporaneous context in which scholars live has a deep impact on the way actions from the past are considered. Far from the 'peace and love' social movement that characterised the way Neolithic society was perceived until recently, it is not surprising that for several decades, evidence of violence between communities and discrimination against individuals within groups is only now being scrutinised by archaeologists and biological anthropologists. For this reason, non-funerary actions are likely being over-estimated in the archaeological record. It is probably the price to pay for realising that they are part of past mortuary behaviours, and that they are relevant to the history of past societies.

---

5 In the 'Terminology in Funerary Archaeology' session, organised by Christopher Knüsel, Pascal Sellier, and Martin Smith at the 21st annual meeting of the European Association of Archaeologists (2015, Glasgow), Liv Nillson Stutz stressed that the question addressed by the development of archaeothanatology outside of France is how the archaeothanatological approach can be implemented by archaeologists driven by different theoretical traditions.

6 Archaeology is not an objective discipline, even in the deductive Cartesian tradition of French scholars who consider that things are knowable and explicable by rationality, by pure deduction.

References

Allard, O. and Taylor, A.C. (2016). Traitement des cadavres et mémoire des personnes en Amazonie. In: M. Lauwers and A. Zemour, eds., *Qu'est-ce Qu'une Sépulture? Humanités et Systèmes Funéraires de la Préhistoire à Nos Jours*. Antibes: Éditions de l'Association pour la Promotion et la Diffusion des Connaissances Archéologiques (APDCA), pp. 141–154.

Anstett, E. (2016). Qu'est-ce qu'un charnier? Traitement des dépouilles et dépôts multiples dans les contextes contemporains de violence de masse. In: M. Lauwers and A. Zemour, eds., *Qu'est-ce Qu'une Sépulture? Humanités et Systèmes Funéraires de la Préhistoire à Nos Jours*. Antibes: Éditions de l'Association pour la Promotion et la Diffusion des Connaissances Archéologiques (APDCA), pp. 279–292.

Anstett, E. and Dreyfus, J.M. (2014). *Destruction and human remains. Disposal and concealment in genocide and mass violence*. Manchester: Manchester University Press.

Aspöck, E. (2008). What actually is a deviant burial? Comparing German-language and anglophone research on deviant burials. In: E.M. Murphy, ed., *Deviant Burial in the Archaeological Record*. Oxford: Oxbow book, pp. 17–34.

Aspöck, E. (2011). Past 'Disturbances' of Graves as a Source: Taphonomy and Interpretation of Reopened Early Medieval Inhumation Graves at Brunn am Gebirge (Austria) and Winnall II (England). *Oxford Journal of Archaeology*, 30(3), pp. 299–324.

Boulestin, B. and Baray, L. (2010). Problématique des dépôts humains dans les structures d'habitat désaffectées: introduction à la table ronde. In: L. Baray and B. Boulestin, eds., *Morts Anormaux et Sépultures Bizarres. Les Dépôts Humains en Fosses Circulaires et en Silos du Néolithique à l'Age du Fer*. Dijon: Éditions Universitaires de Dijon, pp. 13–27.

Baray, L., Brun, P. and Testart, A. (2007). *Pratiques funéraires et sociétés. Nouvelles approches en archéologie et en anthropologie sociale*. Dijon: Éditions Universitaires de Dijon.

Beau, A., Rivollat, M., Réveillas, H., Pemonge, M-H., Mendisco, F., Thomas, Y., Lefranc P. and Deguilloux, M.-F. (2017). Multi-Scale Ancient DNA Analyses Confirm the Western Origin of Michelsberg Farmers and Document Probable Practices of Human Sacrifice. *PLoS ONE*, 12(7), e0179742, doi.org/10.1371/journal.pone.0179742.

Buikstra, J.E. (1977). Biocultural dimensions of archeological study: A regional perspective. In: R.L. Blakely, ed., *Biocultural Adaptation in Prehistoric America*. Athens: University of Georgia Press, pp. 67–84.

Boulestin, B. (2012). Champ de la discipline: concepts et mise en œuvre. In: L. Bonnabel, ed., *Archéologie de la Mort en France*. Paris: La Découverte, pp. 25–41.

Boulestin, B. (2016). Normes funéraires. Illusions et vérités. In: M. Lauwers and A. Zemour, eds., *Qu'est-ce Qu'une Sépulture? Humanités et Systèmes Funéraires de la Préhistoire à Nos Jours*. Antibes: Éditions de l'Association pour la Promotion et la Diffusion des Connaissances Archéologiques (APDCA), pp. 363–378.

Boulestin, B. and Duday, H. (2006). Ethnology and Archaeology of Death: From the Illusion of References to the Use of Terminology, *Archaeologia Polona*, 44, pp. 149–169.

Boulestin, B. and Baray, L. (2010). Problématique des dépôts humains dans les structures d'habitat désaffectées: introduction à la table ronde. In: L. Baray and B. Boulestin, eds., *Morts Anormaux et Sépultures Bizarres. Les Dépôts Humains en Fosses Circulaires et en Silos du Néolithique à l'Age du Fer*. Dijon: Éditions Universitaires de Dijon, pp. 13–27.

Boulestin, B., Zeeb-Lanz, A., Jeunesse, C., Haack, F., Arbogast, R.M. and Denaire, A. (2009). Mass Cannibalism in the Linear Pottery Culture at Herxheim (Palatinate, Germany). *Antiquity*, 83, pp. 968–982.

Chenal, F., Perrin, B., Barrand-Emam, H. and Boulestin, B. (2015). A Farewell to Arms: A Deposit of Human Limbs and Bodies at Bergheim, France, c. 4000 BC. *Antiquity*, 89(348), pp. 1313–1330.

Davies, D.J. (2005). Fire. In: D.J. Davies and L.H. Mates, eds., *Encyclopedia of Cremation*. Aldershot: Ashgate Publishing, pp. 186–195.

Duday, H. (1981). La Place de l'Anthropologie dans l'Étude des Sépultures Anciennes. *Cahiers d'Anthropologie Paris*, 1, pp. 27–42.

Duday, H. (2010). Les dépôts énigmatiques de restes humains, ou les limites de la réflexion archéothanatologique. In: M.G. Belcastro and G. Ortalli, eds., *Sepolture Anomale. Indagini Archeologiche e Antropologiche dall'Epoca Classica al Medioevo in Emilia Romagna*. Borgo San Lorenzo: All'Insegna del Giglio (Quaderni di Archeologia dell'Emilia Romagna 28), pp. 39–42.

Duday, H., Courtaud, P., Crubezy, E., Sellier, P. and Tillier, A.M. (1990). L'Anthropologie 'de Terrain': Reconnaissance et Interprétation des Gestes Funéraires. *Bulletins et Mémoires de la Société d'Anthropologie de Paris*, 2(3-4), pp. 29–50.

Ferries, M.C. (2011). Outrages à Magistrats: les dommages infligés au corps des magistrats à Rome à la fin de la République. In: L. Bodiou, V. Mehl and M. Soria, eds., *Corps Outragés, Corps Ravagés de l'Antiquité au Moyen Âge*. Turnhout: Brepols, pp. 317–334.

Frazer, J. (1934). *La crainte des morts dans les sociétés primitives*. Paris: Éditions Nourry.

Gambier, D. and Boulestin, B. (2012). *Crânes trophées, crânes d'ancêtres et autres pratiques autour de la tête: problèmes d'interprétation en archéologie*. Oxford: Archaeopress (British Archaeological Reports (International Series)) 2415.

Guiart, J. (1979). *Les Hommes et la mort: rituels funéraires à travers le monde*. Paris: Le Sycomore.

Haglund, W.D. and Sorg, M.H., eds. (2001). *Advances in forensic taphonomy: method, theory, and archaeological perspectives*. Boca Raton: CRC Press.

Helmis, A. (2007). La privation de sépulture dans l'Antiquité grecque. In: E. Cantarella, ed., *Vorträge zur Griechischen und Hellenistischen Rechtsgeschichte*. Vienna: Verlag der Österreichishen Akademie der Wissenschaften, pp. 259–268.

Hertz, R. (1907). Contribution à une Étude sur la Représentation Collective de la Mort. *Année Sociologique*, 10, pp. 48–137.

Hinard, F. (1984). La male mort. Exécutions et statut du corps au moment de la première proscription. In: *Du Châtiment dans la Cité: Supplices Corporels et Peine de Mort dans le Monde Antique*. Rome: École Française de Rome, pp. 295–311.

Hinard, F. (1987). Spectacle des exécutions et espace urbain. In: *L'Urbs: Espace Urbain et Histoire (Ier siècle av. J.-C. – IIIe siècle ap. J.-C.)*. Rome: École Française de Rome, pp. 111–125.

Jeunesse, C. (2010). Les sépultures en fosses circulaires à l'horizon 4500-3500: contribution à l'étude comparée des systèmes funéraires du Néolithique européen. In: L. Baray and B. Boulestin, eds., *Morts Anormaux et Sépultures Bizarres: Les Dépôts Humains en Fosses Circulaires et en Silos du Néolithique à l'Âge du Fer*. Dijon: Éditions Universitaires de Dijon, pp. 29–54.

Knüsel, C. and Robb, J. (2016). Funerary Taphonomy: An Overview of Goals and Methods. *Journal of Archaeological Science: Reports*, 10, pp. 655–673.

Lauwers, P. (2016). Sépulcre, sépulture, cimetière. Lexique, idéologie et pratiques sociales dans l'Occident médiéval. In: M. Lauwers and A. Zemour, eds., *Qu'est-ce Qu'une Sépulture? Humanités et Systèmes Funéraires de la Préhistoire à Nos Jours*. Antibes: Éditions de l'Association pour la Promotion et la Diffusion des Connaissances Archéologiques (APDCA), pp. 95–111.

Law, R. (1985). Human Sacrifice in pre-Colonial West Africa. *African Affaires*, 84, pp. 53–87.

Lefranc, P., Arbogast, R.M., Chenal, F., Hilbrand E., Merkl M., Strahm, C., van Willigen, S. and Wörle, M. (2012). Inhumations, Dépôts d'Animaux et Perles en Cuivre du IVe Millénaire sur le Site Néolithique Récent de Colmar 'Aérodrome' (Haut-Rhin). *Bulletin de la Société Préhistorique Française*, 109(4), pp. 689–730.

Lefranc, P., Denaire, A. and Jeunesse, C. (2017). Human remains of the 4th millennium BC in the south of the Upper-Rhine valley. In: H. Meller and S. Friederich, eds., *Salzmunde- Regel oder Ausnahme? Internationale Tagung, Halle. Tagungen des Landesmuseums für Vorgeschichte Halle*, pp. 521–531.

Lopez-Mazz, J. (2015). The concealment of bodies during the military dictatorship in Uruguay (1973–84). In: E. Anstett and J.M. Dreyfus, eds., *Destruction and Human Remains. Disposal and Concealment in Genocide and Mass Violence*. Manchester: Manchester University, pp. 83–97.

Magalhães, B.M., Matos Fernandes, T. and Santos, A.L. (2015). The Unburied Prisoners from the Jail of the Inquisition of Évora, Portugal. *Journal of Anthropological Archaeology*, 39, pp. 36–41.

Mendoza, M. (2007). Human trophy taking in the South American Gran Chaco. In: R.J. Chacon and D.H. Dye, eds., *The Taking and Displaying of Human Body Parts as Trophies by Amerindians*. Boston: Springer, pp. 575–590.

Michel, J. and Sendra, B. (2014). Les sépultures chasséennes en contexte d'habitat de plein air du site de Saint-Antoine II à Saint-Aunès (Hérault). In: I. Sénépart, F. Leandri, J. Cauliez, T. Perrin and E. Thirault, eds., *Chronologie de la Préhistoire Récente dans le Sud de la France, Actualités de la Recherche*. Toulouse: Archives d'Ecologie Préhistorique, pp. 549–568.

Moréchand, G., (1975). Contribution à l'Étude des rites Funéraires Indiens. *Bulletin de l'Ecole Française d'Extrême-Orient*, 62, pp. 55–124.

Murphy, E.M. (2008). *Deviant burial in the archaeological record*. Oxford: Oxbow Books.

Oudry-Braillon, S. and Billard, C. (2009). Trois Sépultures Atypiques du Second Âge du Fer à Reviers (Calvados). *Revue Archéologique de l'Ouest*, 26, pp. 105–115.

Pautreau, J. P. and Mornais, P. (2005). Structures de combustion traditionnelles en Thaïlande du Nord. In: C. Mordant and G. Depierre, eds., *Les Pratiques Funéraires à l'Âge du Bronze en France*. Paris: Éditions du Comité des Travaux Historiques et Scientifiques (CTHS), pp. 47–60.

Perlès, C. (2009). Interacting with the dead: from the disposal of the body to funerary rituals, In: C. Perlès, ed., *The Early Neolithic in Greece*. Cambridge: University Press, pp. 273–282.

Reynolds, A. (2009). *Anglo-Saxon deviant burial customs*. New York: Oxford University Press.

Rodet-Belarbi, I. and Séguy, I. (2013). Des humains traités comme des chiens. In: H. Guy, A. Jeanjean and A. Richier, eds., *Le Cadavre en Procès. Techniques et Culture*, 60, pp. 60–73.

Rodet-Belarbi, I. and Séguy, I. (2016). Qu'est-ce qu'une non-sépulture en période historique (Antiquité, Moyen-âge, Époque moderne)? In: M. Lauwers and A. Zemour, eds., *Qu'est-ce Qu'une Sépulture? Humanités et Systèmes Funéraires de la Préhistoire à Nos Jours*. Antibes: Éditions de l'Association pour la Promotion et la Diffusion des Connaissances Archéologiques (APDCA), pp. 211–224.

Pokutta, D.A. (2014). Journey to Murder: Atypical Graves of the Long Distance Immigrants in the Early Bronze Age Europe. *Sprawozdania Archeologiczne*, 66, pp. 91–100.

Schmitt, A. (2017). Middle Neolithic Burials in Mediterranean France: Honoring or Rejecting the Dead? *West and East*, II, pp. 63–82.

Schmitt, A. and Anstett, E. (2020). *Des cadavres dans nos poubelles: Des restes humains en contextes détritiques de la préhistoire à nos jours*. Paris: Petra.

Schmitt, A., Remicourt, M. and D'Anna, A. (2017). Inhumations Individuelles en Contexte Domestique au Néolithique Final en France Méridionale. Une Alternative à la Sépulture Collective? *Bulletin de la Société Préhistorique Française*, 114(3), pp. 469–496.

Sewane, D. (2003). *Le souffle du mort: la tragédie de la mort chez le Batammariba du Togo et du Bénin*. Paris: Plon.

Testart, A. (2004). *Les morts d'accompagnement: la servitude volontaire I*. Paris: Éditions Errance.

Testart, A. (2009). Partir dans l'au-delà accompagné ou le rôle des fidélités personnelles dans la genèse du pouvoir. In: J. Guilaine, ed., *Sépultures et Sociétés. Du Néolithique à l'Histoire*. Paris: Éditions Errance, pp. 71–80.

Treffort, C. (2004). L'interprétation historique des sépultures atypiques: le cas du haut Moyen Âge. In: L. Baray, ed., *Archéologie des Pratiques Funéraires. Approches Critiques*. Bibracte: Centre Archéologique Européen, pp. 131–140.

Ucko, P.J. (1969). Ethnography and archaeological interpretation of funerary remains. *World Archaeology*, 1, pp. 262–281.

Vail, G. and Hernández, C. (2007). Human sacrifice in Late Postclassic Maya iconography and texts. In: V. Tiesler and A. Cucina, eds., *New Perspectives on Human Sacrifice and Ritual Body Treatments in Ancient Maya Society*. New York: Springer, pp. 120–164.

van Gennep, A. (1909). *Les rites de passage*. Paris: Picard.

van Pelt, R.J. (2014). Sinnreich erdacht: machines of mass incineration in fact, fiction, and forensics. In: E. Anstett and J.M. Dreyfus, eds., *Destruction and Human Remains*. Manchester: Manchester University Press, pp. 117–143.

Villes, A. (1987). Une hypothèse: les sépultures de relégation dans les fosses d'habitat protohistoriques en France septentrionale. In: H. Duday and C. Masset, eds., *Anthropologie Physique et Archéologie: Méthodes d'Études des Sépultures*. Paris: Centre National de la Recherche Scientifique (CNRS), pp. 167–174.

Vivas, M. (2015). *Prope aut juxta cimeterium*: un espace d'inhumation pour les « mauvais morts » (XIE–XVe siècle). In: C. Treffort, ed., *Le Cimetière au Village dans l'Europe Médiévale et Moderne*. Toulouse: Presses Universitaires du Midi, pp. 193–206.

Vivas, M. (2016). L'inhumation des condamnés à mort aux fourches patibulaires (Moyen âge-Époque moderne. In: M. Lauwers and A. Zemour, eds., *Qu'est-ce Qu'une Sépulture? Humanités et Systèmes Funéraires de la Préhistoire à Nos Jours*. Antibes: Éditions de l'Association pour la Promotion et la Diffusion des Connaissances Archéologiques (APDCA), pp. 241–259.

Wasterlain, S.N., Costa, A. and Ferreira, M.T. (2018). Growth Faltering in a Skeletal Sample of Enslaved Nonadult Africans Found at Lagos, Portugal (15th–17th Centuries). *International Journal of Osteoarchaeology*, 28, pp. 162–169.

Wouassi, R. (2020). Des kwopo'oh aux tombes: les mutations dans les formes d'inhumation chez les Bamileke (Ouest-Cameroun). In: A. Schmitt and E. Anstett, eds., *Des Cadavres dans nos Poubelles. Des Restes Humains en Contextes Détritiques de la Préhistoire à Nos Jours*. Paris: Petra.

Weiss-Krejci, E. (2008). Unusual life, unusual death and the fate of the corpse: a case study from dynastic Europe. In: E.M. Murphy, ed., *Deviant Burial in the Archaeological Record*. Oxford: Oxbow Books, pp. 169–190.

Weiss-Krejci, E. (2011). The formation of mortuary deposits. In: S.C. Agarwal and B.A. Glencross, eds., *Social Bioarchaeology*. Chichester: Wiley-Blackwell, pp. 68–106.

Weiss-Krejci, E. (2013). The unburied dead. In: S. Tarlow and L. Nilsson Stutz, eds., *The Oxford Handbook of the Archaeology of Death and Burial*. Oxford: Oxford University Press, pp. 281–301.

Zagaria, V. (2019). The clandestine cemetery: burying the victims of Europe's border in a Tunisian coastal town. In: A. Schmitt and E. Anstett, eds., *Corpses in rubbish dumps. Human remains and violence*, 5(1), Special Issue, pp. 18–37.

PART II

Period-specific applications

7

EARLY PRIMARY BURIALS

Evidence from Southwestern Asia

Anne-marie Tillier

PACEA, De la Préhistoire à l'Actuel: Culture, Environnement et Anthropologie,
UMR 5199, CNRS-Université de Bordeaux, Pessac, France

Introduction

Southwestern Asia attracted the attention of the scientific community at the beginning of 20th century with excavations conducted at sites located in Palestine (Skhul, Tabun and Qafzeh) that contained Middle Palaeolithic layers below historical deposits. Interestingly, the Skhul site on Mount Carmel was seen as 'one of the most remarkable of prehistoric sites by virtue of the cemetery it contained' (McCown, in Garrod and Bate, 1937: 106). Indeed, ten individuals were uncovered from layer B in front of the entrance of the cave and originally thought to represent single inhumation burials. Later, additional discoveries were added through long-term projects in Northern Israel (Qafzeh, Wadi Amud, Kebara, Hayonim, and, more recently, Manot and Misliya) and Northern Syria (Dederiyeh and El Kowm).

Today, six sites in Syria and Israel (Figure 7.1) provide evidence of hominin deposits associated with Mousterian assemblages that were not simply depositional accidents but represent deliberate burials. Yet, a re-examination of the Skhul documentation leads to questions concerning the number of burials commonly accepted at the site (Tillier *et al.*, 1988; supprimer le surlignement Tillier, 1995, 2009). Today, a minimum number of 11 primary burials (i.e. deposition of the deceased soon after death in exactly the same location where the skeletonised remains were found) in the Mediterranean Levant (Tillier, 2009), 1 in Syria (Dederiyeh) and 10 in Israel (Tabun, Skhul, Qafzeh, Amud and Kebara) are accepted. In reality, all the sites mentioned have revealed a higher representation of skeletal elements (Table 7.1) and the possibility that some of them represent remains of post-depositionally dispersed burials (e.g. Dederiyeh, Skhul) is unresolved.

The purpose of this chapter is not to go through all the cases identified, but to illustrate the diversity in the patterns of body decomposition, location and types of funerary deposits based on a few examples (Table 7.1).

To present, biostratigraphic data combined with chronometric investigations using thermoluminescence (TL) and Electron Spin Resonance/Linear Uptake (ASR/LU) analyses of the stratified deposits established the antiquity of burials in Southwestern Asia at Skhul and Qafzeh. This human tradition of funerary behaviour occurred over a long period of time as documented notably at Kebara and Amud.

DOI: 10.4324/9781351030625-10

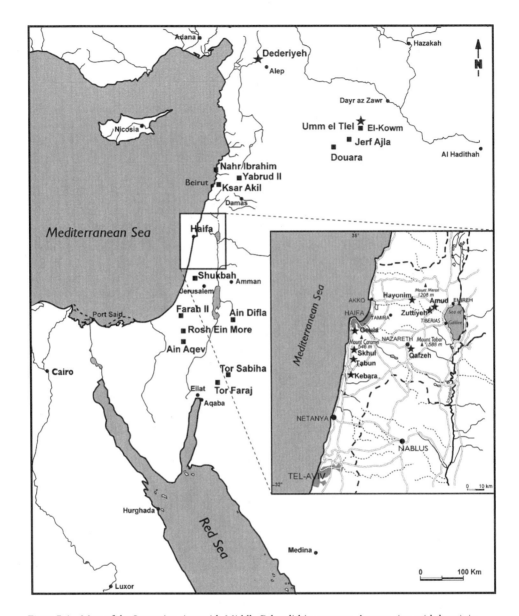

Figure 7.1 Map of the Levantine sites with Middle Palaeolithic contexts. Among sites with hominin remains (black stars), six (Skhul, Tabun, Qafzeh, Kebara, Amud and Dederiyeh) provide evidence of individuals deliberately buried.

The decay of the corpse in an empty space

Most of the Levantine burials (10/11) contained remains of one individual; the majority of them come from old discoveries, so documentation and field observations are often incomplete. Yet, the relations between various elements of the skeleton permit characterisation of the environment in which the body decay occurred and to understand the natural taphonomic processes that took place in the deposit.

Table 7.1 Selected Levantine burials mentioned in the text. MNI = number of individuals documented in the site

Levantine sites	MNI*	Primary burials	Individuals buried
Amud	14	2 single	1 infant, 1 adult
Dederiyeh	15(?)	1 single	1 child
Kebara	23	1 single	1 adult
Skhul	10	3 single	1 child, 2 adults
Qafzeh	28	1 double, 3 single	3 non-adults, 2 adults

Note: * Yet, it should be noted that some individuals are represented by partial skeletons or fragmentary bones, while others consist only of teeth.

Sources: McCown and Keith (1939), Vandermeersch (1969a, 1970), Bar Yosef and Vandermeersch (1981), Akazawa *et al.* (1995) and Akazawa and Muhesen (2002), Hovers *et al.* (1995), Tillier (1999, 2009) and Tillier *et al.* (2003).

Use of a natural niche

An infant burial was uncovered from Unit B2-8 at Amud Cave, located along the Wadi Amud, where it flows into the Jordan Valley (Rak, Kimbel and Hovers, 1994). The Amud 7 skeleton was lying on its right side in a small niche. Hovers *et al.* (1995: 52) noted, 'A natural niche in the rock face of the cave wall served as burial structure, the body laid down directly on the bedrock …'. From the published photograph, it is clear that the cranium had been compressed, several bones in disequilibrium did not maintain their original position (as illustrated by the mandible for instance) and the rib cage appears flattened. It seems that its filling with sediment inside the original volume once occupied by the corpse did not immediately follow the disappearance of the soft tissues; thus the decay of the corpse occurred in a natural empty void. Radiometric dates for Unit B2-8 place the Amud 7 burial at 57.6 ± 3.7 ka B.P. (Valladas *et al.*, 1999; Rink *et al.*, 2001).

The use of a natural niche for hominin deposits was not restricted to infants (less than one year old at death) or very young children, as illustrated by one of the interments from the Qafzeh site located about 3km east of Nazareth in Lower Galilee (Figure 7.1). The skeleton of the Qafzeh 8 adult found during excavations carried out from 1965 to 1979 by Vandermeersch (1966) was resting on its right side in a natural niche in layer XVII. Qafzeh 8 was oriented East-West, facing East, with upper limbs lying along the body and the lower limbs flexed to fit in the niche (around 1 m long × 0.8 m wide). Tchernov (1981) assumed that the Qafzeh Mousterian layers documented a 'northward expansion of the African and Saharo-Arabian biotic zone', suggesting an age around 100 ka BP that corresponds to a warm phase of OIS 5 (Bar Yosef and Vandermeersch, 1981). Application of radiometric techniques (TL, ESR, Schwarcz *et al.*, 1988; Valladas *et al.*, 1988) has confirmed the antiquity of the hominin occupation and indicated that the Mousterian sequence covered a short time span, around 92 ± 5 ka BP (Valladas *et al.*, 1988). The archaeological assemblage associated with the hominin remains was described later as a 'Tabun C-type' Mousterian industry, in which centripetal and/or bi-directional lithic reduction preparations prevailed with typical products being side scrapers and large oval and quadrangular Levallois flakes (Hovers, 2009).

The Dederiyeh 1 burial

The Dederiyeh cave from the Afrin valley in northern Syria (Figure 7.1) revealed a small sample of fossil hominins in the Mousterian layers, i.e. mainly two incomplete child skeletons (Akazawa *et al.*, 1995; Akazawa and Muhesen, 2002). Dederiyeh 1 (*circa* 2 years old at death) was uncovered in 1990, 1.5 m below the surface in layer 11 (Akazawa *et al.*, 2002). The skeleton of this child was lying on the back and oriented North-South, the upper limbs extended along the body and lower limbs partly flexed (Figure 7.2). A large part of the skeleton was still in anatomical connection. The head originally rested on a stone, which that was probably located at a higher position than the rest of the body, was not in its original position in the deposit during its decomposition. Bones of the skull have clearly moved after the collapse due to soft tissue decomposition, and have fallen outside of the space originally occupied by the head (Tillier,

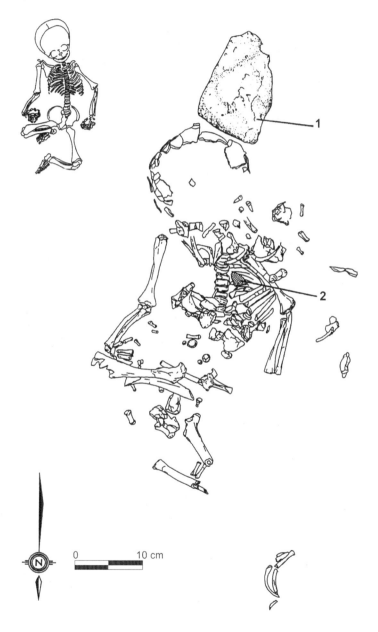

Figure 7.2 The Dederiyeh 1 child burial (Reproduced from published reports with permission of T. Akazawa and S. Muhesen).

2008). The mandible and the hand and foot bones moved from their original positions, some of them spreading outside of the space originally occupied by the corpse. All these observations lead to the suggestion that the Dederiyeh 1 deposit was a primary burial and that decomposition probably occurred in a void. No chronometric data are available for layer 11 that might enable us to place the Dederiyeh 1 burial chronologically within the known sample from the Levant. Yet, Akazawa and colleagues noted that the Mousterian lithic assemblage from Dederiyeh shares similarities with that identified in Amud and Kebara caves, and they suggested a possible similar chronological age for the Syrian layers.

Earth graves and body decomposition in 'filled-in graves'

In the case of earth graves, the presence of mobile and dry sediment surrounding the corpse permits the filling of the interior volume of the corpse that is slowly freed by decay of soft tissue, with the bones maintaining their original positions. Yet, it appears that sometimes, geochemical processes can alter the sediments surrounding the skeletonised body, and this can easily explain the lack of information with regard to the original burial environment and/or limits of a pit (or grave) dug to contain the corpse. In such cases, the observation of anatomical connections and bone orientations helps in identifying the primary state of deposit, the appreciation of the type of burial environment, and the recognition of constraint effects.

Child burials and variation in body position

The Skhul 1 child deposit was unearthed in 1931 in a hard limestone breccia, some 1.75 m deep in front of the mouth of the cave. According to McCown (1934), 'The skeleton [...] showed by the position of its parts that the child has been buried in a squatting posture with body flexed forwards'. This contracted position means that the corpse probably was in a narrow space, and that sediment replaced the perishable elements of the cadaver as they disappeared. This child was about 3 years of age at death. The antiquity of the Skhul Mousterian layers, first suggested by McCown, was later confirmed by radiometric techniques. Results from TL on burnt flints provide an average date of 119 ± 18 ka BP (Mercier *et al.*, 1993) for layer B, which is in agreement with those of ESR analysis (ESR/LU: 101 ± 12 ka, Stringer *et al.*, 1989).

The non-adult Qafzeh 11 burial discovered in 1970 was unearthed in layer XXIII at the bottom of the Mousterian archaeological sequence on the terrace. The deceased, about 13 years of age at death, was lying on the bedrock, in front of the mouth of the cave, in a pit, with the upper limbs flexed, and the hands positioned near the face, facing west. The pelvic region and the lower limbs extended to the south from the location of the remains of the skull, which were post-depositionally damaged by a large stone.

Adult burials, funerary space size and location

Within the Mousterian Skhul hominin sample, at least two primary adult burials can be authenticated. Like the child deposit, they were located in front of the cave, and unearthed in the same hard limestone breccia. The Skhul IV skeleton (Figure 7.3) was lying on its right side, in a pit, with upper and lower limbs tightly flexed. The head was oriented towards the east. The position of the foot bones resting below the pelvic area against the western wall of the pit illustrates a constraint effect, resulting from the small size of the funerary space. Foot bones and hand bones had kept their anatomical connections. Unlike Skhul IV, Skhul V was lying on its back, the head flexed upon the chest and oriented to the west, with upper and lower limbs tightly flexed.

Figure 7.3 The Skhul IV adult burial *in situ*. The foot bones are resting against the pit wall (Source: A.M. Tillier, after Garrod and Bate, 1937).

McCown (in Garrod and Bate, 1937: 100) noted: 'it would seem that the deceased had been crowded into a grave of inadequate size'.

In 1961 and 1964, a Japanese team working in the Wadi Amud site found some hominin remains. The most complete specimen was an adult skeleton, Amud 1, buried close to the wall, an unusual location (Suzuki and Takai, 1970). This skeletonised adult was lying on its left side, with his lower limbs tightly flexed, the feet under the pelvis. The size of the pit itself (around 1 m long) probably influenced the contracted position of the body. While the skeleton appeared in an anatomically natural arrangement, most of the bones showed post-mortem alteration resulting from the peripheral pressure of the sediment. Amud 1, according to Hovers *et al.* (1995), is stratigraphically more recent than Amud 7, but no chronometric dates are available to provide an estimate of the time span between the two layers in the stratigraphic sequence.

The Qafzeh 25 adult was buried in a depression in layer XVII, and only the upper part of the skeleton was preserved at the time of its discovery in 1979. A sounding made in 1934 during the first excavations conducted by Neuville and Stekelis had truncated the deposit. The skeletonised body was lying on its back in natural articulation, oriented northeast-southwest, with the head to the north. The upper limbs were flexed with the right one crossing the chest. Both hands were near the face, as also found in the Qafzeh 11 burial. In general, the position of Qafzeh 25 body was quite similar to that of Skhul V.

The earliest multiple burial at Qafzeh

A special burial containing the remains of two individuals associated with a Mousterian context in Southwestern Asia, unique in Eurasia, originates from the Qafzeh site (Vandermeersch, 1966).

Due to the diagenetic alterations of the sediment (resulting in a hard limestone breccia), the exact limits of the grave were impossible to identify in the field, but they can be deduced from the relative position of the bones. The two individuals have been deposited simultaneously or within a very short period of each other in a narrow pit (*circa* 50 cm wide by 1.5 m long). The oldest individual, Qafzeh 9 (15–19 years of age at death), oriented north-south, was lying on the left side, the right hand on the left forearm, and lower limbs slightly flexed (Figure 7.4). The position of the right upper limb and pelvis (still in natural articular arrangement) indicates the presence

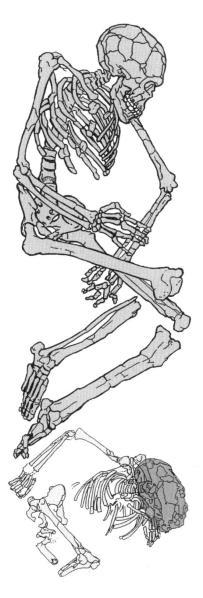

Figure 7.4 The double burial from Qafzeh: Qafzeh 9 is oriented north-south and the child Qafzeh 10, oriented east-west, appears in a contracted position as shown by the left upper limb found beneath the skull (after Tillier, 1995).

of the pit wall. A few centimetres separated the left toes of this individual from the right upper limb of the second deceased individual in this grave, the Qafzeh 10 child, about 6 years of age at death. This child, oriented east–west, was lying on the left side with the left upper limb tightly flexed under the cranium, while the right upper limb was extended along the body. The lower limbs were also flexed with the right knee joint being at the level of the pelvis. The buried bodies decomposed in an earth-filled grave.

The uniqueness of this burial leads, of course, to questions of its significance: indeed, even if the actions can be identified, the motivation and the thought processes remain unknown. In the analysis of such deposits, questions arise related to the circumstances of death and to possible family links between the deceased, being among the most alluring. A pathological investigation conducted on two skeletons reveals only minor bone lesions on Qafzeh 9 (Tillier *et al.*, 2004; Coutinho Nogueira, Coqueugniot and Tiller, 2018; Coutinho Nogueira *et al.*, 2019), while the Qafzeh 10 child exhibited pathological lesions that indicated episodes of trauma during childhood (Tillier, 1999; Tillier *et al.*, 2004; Dutour and Tillier, 2018). The most serious was a premature craniosynostosis of the right side of the coronal suture that has affected the cranial development and was probably fatal in the absence of proper medical treatment.

The question of commingled primary deposits

The Skhul hominin sample

At Skhul, a majority of the individuals (7/10) show poor bone preservation and lack of ana-tomical connections. McCown suggested that they represented relics of interments secondarily destroyed. Two immature individuals, Skhul VIII and X, consist of a few fragments of bone, and it seems rather difficult to establish that they represent either parts of commingled primary burials or remains of a post-mortem arrangement. A few bones of the remains of the adult Skhul IX were found mixed with animal bones but they showed no traces of cut marks or gnawing.

Secondary human action to explain the disturbance of several primary interments at Skhul, as suggested by McCown (in Garrod and Bate, 1937: 92–107), remains a working hypothesis: indeed, the idea that such an action might reflect a funerary or ritual practice could not be deduced at the site. Yet, the marked occurrence of associated (i.e. gathered in one place) skeletons of hominins is impressive and represents a unique case among the Mount Carmel sites. Direct dating (ESR) on hominin remains or animal bone fragments associated with the burials (Grün *et al.*, 2005) indicates that the Mousterian sequence covers a longer time period than previously thought, lasting from *circa* 131 ka to 93 ± 12 ka BP, if the dates are correct; some hominin deposits (e.g. Skhul IX) predated others at the site (e.g. Skhul I, V, II).

The Dederiyeh 2 mixed assemblage

The remains of the Dederiyeh 2 child were found in a pit (70 cm long × 50 cm wide × 25 cm deep) in layer 3. A large part of the skeletal elements of this child, who died at about 2 years of age, was preserved; yet the bones show no natural articulation and are in the pit together with fragments of tortoise shell. Following Akazawa *et al.* (2002: 76), 'the isolated bones found in the pit might be the remains of an intentional burial that has been disturbed'. Layer 3 which contained Dederiyeh 2 was dated by radiocarbon measurements between 48.1 ± 1.2 ka and 53.6 ± 1.8 ka BP (Akazawa *et al.*, 2002), but such measurements are close to the quantification limit. Therefore, the authors suggested that, based on similarities in the lithic assemblages, the Dederiyeh Mousterian layers could be closer in age to those from the Amud and Kebara sites, a chronological assignment that requires a confirmation through direct application of radiometric techniques.

From archaeological remains and animal items to grave goods

In addition to deliberate burials, two of the Levantine sites mentioned provide other evidence of symbolic behaviour: at Skhul, Garrod and Bate (1937) reported the presence of marine shells that were recently described as shell beads (Vanhaeren *et al.*, 2006), but no indication of their stratigraphic provenance is available. At Qafzeh, ochre fragments were used as well as marine shells with natural perforations, and both were found on the terrace in the same area where the burials were discovered but with no direct associations (Vandermeersch, 1969b; Hovers *et al.*, 2003; Taborin, 2003; Bar-Yosef Mayer, Vandermersch and Bar-Yosef, 2009).

Thus, the occurrence of animal-derived items in funerary contexts involves a small portion of the dead in the available sample (less than 30%), and questions arise about their selection and meaning. Part of a cervid maxilla was lying on the Amud 7 infant pelvis, and its location within the space once occupied by the body, in contact with the bones, led Hovers and colleagues (1995) to suggest that it had been of a funerary offering. Found in 1992, the Amud 7 infant skeleton has been only partially described (Rak, Kimbel and Hovers, 1994; Been and Rak, 2012) and the preliminary description of the skeletal remains does not provide evidence to undertake an interpretation of the circumstances of death for this young individual (about 10 months of age at death).

In the case of the Skhul V male, a large boar mandible was lying beneath his left forearm and close to the tightly flexed right upper limb, attesting to a non-accidental incorporation. The Skhul V burial with this associated item represents a unique case documented from the site. Meanwhile, no traces of serious bone lesions or injuries were found on the skeletal elements that would indicate disabling conditions during lifetime for this adult male; there is only non-trauma-related degenerative disease of the right temporo-mandibular joint (McCown and Keith 1939: 374). The animal bone element was introduced intentionally, however, as mentioned by McCown, 'its presence is a subject for speculation rather than explanation' (in Garrod and Bate 1937: 100–101).

Finally, on the upper part of the chest of Qafzeh 11 (Figure 7.5), near his/her face, part of two fallow deer antlers were lying in close contact with the palmar side of the hand bones and near to the face of the individual. Such a location, within the original spatial arrangement of the remains, attests to an intentional funerary action. Like Skhul V, the Qafzeh 11 burial documents a special funerary treatment of the deceased that is unique at this site (Vandermeersch, 1970; Tillier, 1995). The non-adult Qafzeh 11 individual appears to have been unhealthy during his/her short life, and one can reasonably speculate about the disabling conditions that this young individual had to face and the circumstances of death (Tillier, 1999; Coqueugniot *et al.*, 2014). Qafzeh 11 suffered severe cranial trauma that produced brain growth retardation and neurological and psychological disorders with personality effects. This injured non-adult individual had been well cared by other members of the social group and clearly subjected to ritual treatment at death. In the three burials reviewed here, the animal remains consist of cephalic elements (maxilla, mandible and antlers), the selection of which appears to indicate repeated funerary behaviour.

A non-normative funerary deposit: the Kebara 2 'headless' burial

Kebara Cave, located in southern part of Mount Carmel, at about 13 km south of Wadi el Mughara, and 60 to 65 m above sea level demonstrates a long period of Mousterian occupation from unit VI to unit XII, *circa* 64 to 48 ka BP (Valladas *et al.*, 1987; Schwarcz *et al.*, 1989). The excavations were first conducted by Stekelis (1951–1965) and later under a multi-disciplinary Israeli-French project that lasted from 1982 to 1990 (Bar Yosef and Vandermeersch, 1991; Bar Yosef *et al.*, 1992). A majority of the hominin remains were found in Units IX to XII containing

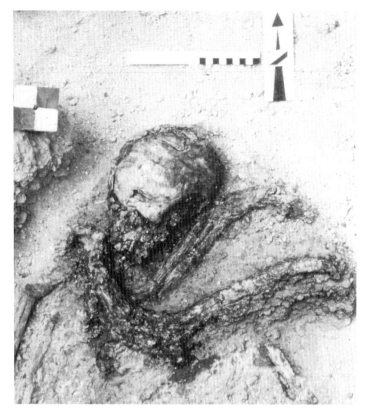

Figure 7.5 Upper part of the Qafzeh 11 non-adult burial showing fragments of fallow deer antlers placed near the face, in contact with the hands (Source: A.M. Tillier; after Vandermeersch, 1970).

a 'Tabun B-type' Mousterian industry (Bar Yosef and Meignen, 1991), between *circa* 6.2 and 8.0 m below datum. The Kebara hominin sample (MNI = 23) includes a large amount of fragmentary skeletal and dental remains that were found in isolation (e.g. Smith and Tillier, 1989; Tillier *et al.,* 2003). Within the sample, two individuals are more complete, the Kebara 1 infant and the Kebara 2 adult male (Arensburg and Smith, 1977; Arensburg *et al.*, 1985; Bar Yosef and Vandermeersch, 1991; Tillier *et al.*, 2003).

Kebara 2 originated from Unit XII in the central area of the cave dated to ca. 60 ka BP (Valladas *et al.*, 1987). The body was in a pit (around 60 cm wide and less than 25 cm deep) of anthropogenic origin as documented by the underlying truncated hearths (Figure 7.6). The Kebara 2 male was lying on his back, oriented east-west; the cranium was missing, but the well-preserved mandible was present, resting on its base. The once head, as documented by the anatomical position of the cervical vertebrae, mandible and hyoid bone, was originally at a slightly higher level than the rest of the body against the northern pit wall. The upper limbs were crossed on the chest, while only the proximal half of the left lower limb was preserved (the deposit has been damaged by an old sounding made by Turville Petre in the 1930s). The skeleton appeared lying against the steep northeastern side of the pit, as shown by the persistent connections of right humerus and right *os coxae*, which were in correct anatomical position (Figures 7.7A and 7.7B). All skeletal elements were in anatomical position, especially importantly the looser ligamentous connections that disarticulate earlier during body decomposition (e.g. hyoid and hand bones). There is no

Figure 7.6 The Kebara 2 burial in square M20. Black arrows indicate the truncation of the underlying hearths at the time the pit had been dug.

evidence for the collapse of the thoracic cavity after decomposition of the soft tissues. Such field observations suggest that there had been a progressive filling of the space with sediment: the Kebara 2 adult body had decomposed in a filled grave.

Analysis of the skeletonised remains enabled postulation of the occurrence of later hominin manipulation rather than an animal-scavenging signature for the absence of the cranium. No traces of bone fragmentation or disturbance by external agents, or animal gnawing were noted. The removal of the cranium followed the complete decay of the cranio-cervical ligaments (prone to disarticulate later in decomposition), including those between the atlas and the cranium. The complete preservation of the cervical vertebrae in anatomical connection, the position of the mandible resting on its base, that of the hyoid *in situ*, and the presence of the isolated right upper third molar next to the right lower one are noteworthy.

As already noted, numerous discoveries of Mousterian funerary deposits were made long ago, resulting in incomplete records with regard to the spatio-temporal context in which skeletal elements were found. Furthermore, preservation of the skeletons was sometimes poor and frequently more attention was given to the skull during the excavation, as illustrated for instance by the adult Qafzeh 6 individual (Vallois and Vandermeerch, 1972). Isolation of the whole skull, or solely the cranium in Levantine Mousterian archaeological contexts remains an unusual circumstance (e.g. Manot 1; Hershkovitz *et al.*, 2015), while there is sometimes an over-representation of isolated infracranial and dental remains, as well documented by the Kebara hominin fossil record itself (Tillier *et al.*, 2003).

In the Southern Levant, it is noteworthy that the practice of skull and cranial removal from primary burials appeared with the Natufian culture, possibly around 12 000–11 000 BP

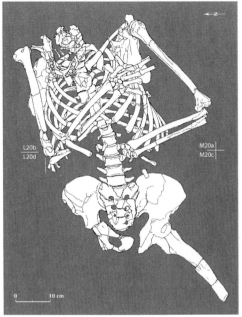

Figure 7.7   The Kebara 2 adult male skeleton (Left) *in situ* and (Right) drawing after cleaning (B) (D. Ladiray, Centre Français de Recherche de Jérusalem).

(Belfer-Cohen, 1988; Weinstein-Evron, 2009). This funerary practice became more common in the Levant during the Pre-Pottery Neolithic (e.g. Le Mort, 1994; Chamel, 2014; Bocquentin, Kodas and Ortiz, 2016) and was sometimes associated with secondary treatment of the retrieved elements, such as plastering. With regard to the Kebara 2 adult male, it cannot be demonstrated that the cranial removal preceded a secondary funerary gesture in the form of archaeological evidence for an intervention facilitating retrieval because there is an absence of direct evidence for the latter.

Concluding remarks

To conclude, sites from the Northern and Southern Levant provide substantial documentation of funerary behaviour of nomadic hunter-gatherers during the Middle Palaeolithic. Firstly, the spatial location of burials varies, either inside (Kebara, Amud and Dederiyeh) or outside (Skhul and Qafzeh) of the cave. Yet, variation in burial location cannot serve as an argument to suggest differences in funerary behaviour between the hominin groups represented: at Qafzeh, for instance, the absence of both hominin and animal bones inside the cave was explained by diagenetic alterations of the layers, while lithic artefacts were abundant there. Secondly, the burials show no standardisation in body position or body orientation to the four cardinal points. Thirdly, most of the burials (10/11) are single primary deposits, with no evidence of selection based on age-at-death. A unique case of a multiple burial is known from Qafzeh, but a relationship between the two deceased individuals can only be postulated on the basis of the non-metric traits identified on their skeletal elements (Tillier, 1999), due to absence of successful DNA analysis. Finally, among the accepted deliberate burials are the earliest known in Eurasia, around 130–100 ka BP, at Skhul and Qafzeh. A large chronological gap separates these initial burials from those identified at Kebara, Amud and, perhaps, Dederiyeh.

Mediterranean Levantine sites attest to the early emergence in Southwestern Eurasia of rich and diverse deliberate burials. Another important observation to stress is that this expression of symbolic behaviour is present in distinct hominin groups, either anatomically modern humans as at Qafzeh and Skhul, or other local hominins in Kebara, Amud, and Dederiyeh, whose phylogenetic status represents a continuing matter of debate (Tillier *et al.*, 2003). To the present day, European sites have revealed only late Mousterian burials that were solely associated with Neandertals.

In summary, the Levantine deliberate burials dated to the Middle Palaeolithic, though limited in number, furnish a wealth of information about human behaviour of Mousterian nomadic hunter-gatherers. Two burials analysed in detail – those of Qafzeh 11 and of Qafzeh 9 and 10 – bear evidence of severe pathological conditions, which shed light on the care taken over deposition of the dead, no matter their physical status. The relative abundance of anthropological finds in Qafzeh and Skhul and the sequential concentration of burials are meaningful and lead to the suggestion that they may document early evidence of gatherings of burials in the same location in the Near East (Tillier, 2009). Interestingly, as mentioned before, the radiometric dates favour a relatively short Mousterian occupation span at Qafzeh, while the Mousterian sequence at Skhul seems to a cover longer period of time.

References

Akazawa, T. and Muhesen, S., eds. (2002). *Neanderthal burials. Excavations of the Dederiyeh Cave, Afrin, Syria.* Kyoto: International Research Center for Japanese Studies.

Akazawa, T., Muhesen S., Dodo, Y., Kondo, O., Mizoguchi, Y., Abe, Y., Nishiaki, Y., Ohta, S., Oguchi, T. and Haydal, J. (1995). Neanderthal Infant Burial from the Dederiyeh Cave in Syria. *Paléorient*, 21(2), pp. 77–86.

Akazawa, T., Muhesen, S., Kondo, O., Dodo, Y., Yoneda, M., Griggo, C. and Ishida, H. (2002). Neanderthal burials of the Dederiyeh Cave. In: Akazawa T., Muhesen S., eds., *Neanderthal burials. excavations of the Dederiyeh Cave, Afrin, Syria.* Kyoto, International Research Center for Japanese Studies, pp. 75–90.

Arensburg, B., Bar Yosef, O., Chech, M., Goldberg, P., Laville, H., Meignen, L., Rak, Y., Tchernov, E., Tillier, A-m. and Vandermeersch, B. (1985). Une Sépulture Néanderthalienne dans la Grotte de Kébara (Israël). *Comptes rendus de l'Académie des Sciences de Paris*, 300(II), pp. 227–233.

Arensburg, B. and Smith, P. (1977). A mousterian skeleton from Kebara Cave. In: B. Arensburg and O. Bar Yosef, eds., *Moshe Stekelis memorial volume.* Jerusalem: The Israel Exploration Society, pp. 164–176.

Bar Yosef, O. and Meignen, L. (1991). Les outillages lithiques moustériens de Kebara (fouilles 1982-1985). Premiers résultats. In: *Le Squelette Moustérien de Kébara 2.* Paris: Editions du Centre National de la Recherche Scientifique (CNRS) (Cahiers de Paléoanthropologie), pp. 49–85.

Bar Yosef, O. and Vandermeersch, B. (1981). Note concerning the possible age of the Mousterian layers in Qafzeh Cave. In: J. Cauvin and P. Sanlaville, eds., *Préhistoire du Levant.* Paris: Centre National de la Recherche Scientifique (CNRS), pp. 281–285.

Bar Yosef, O., Vandermeersch, B., Arensburg, B., Belfer-Cohen, A., Goldberg, P., Laville, H., Meignen, L., Rak, Y., Speth, J. D., Tchernov, E., Tillier, A-m. and Weiner, S. (1992). The Excavations in Kebara Cave, Mount Carmel. *Current Anthropology*, 33(5), pp. 497–550.

Bar-Yosef Mayer, D., Vandermeersch, B. and Bar-Yosef, O. (2009). Shells and Ochre in Middle Paleolithic Qafzeh Cave, Israel: Indications for Modern Behaviour. *Journal of Human Evolution*, 56, pp. 307–314.

Been E. and Rak Y. (2012). Amud 7, a Neandertal Infant from Amud Cave, Israel. *American Journal of Physical Anthropology*, 147(S 54), p. 94.

Belfer-Cohen, A. (1988). The Natufian Graveyard in Hayonim Cave. *Paléorient*, 14(2), pp. 297–308.

Bocquentin, F., Kodas, E. and Ortiz, A. (2016). Headless but Still Eloquent! Acephalous Skeletons as Witnesses of Pre-pottery Neolithic North-South Connections and Disconnections. *Paléorient*, 42(2), pp. 33–52.

Chamel, B. (2014). *Bioanthropologie et pratiques funéraires des populations du Proche-Orient: l'impact de la néolithisation. étude de sept sites Syriens 9820–6000 cal. BC.* Unpublished Ph.D. thesis, Université Lumière Lyon 2.

Coqueugniot, H., Dutour, O., Arensburg, B., Duday, H., Vandermeersch, B. and Tillier, A-m. (2014). Earliest Cranio-encephalic Trauma from the Levantine Middle Palaeolithic: 3D Reappraisal of the Qafzeh 11 Skull, Consequences of Pediatric Brain Damage on Individual Life Condition and Social Care. *PLoS One*, 9(7), pp. 1–10.

Coutinho Nogueira, D., Coqueugniot, H., and Tillier, A.-m. (2018). La microtomodensitométrie, nouvel outil d'analyse de fossiles humains anciens: l'exemple de Qafzeh 9. *Supplément des Bulletins et Mémoires de la Société d'Anthropologie de Paris*, 30, p. S14.

Coutinho Nogueira, D., Dutour, O., Coqueugniot, H., Tillier, A.-m. (2019). Qafzeh 9 Mandible (ca. 90–100 kyrs BP, Israel) Revisited: μ-CT and 3D Reveal New Pathological Conditions. *International Journal of Paleopathology*, 26, pp. 104–110,

Dutour, O. and Tillier, A-m. (2018). L'enfant Qafzeh 10 (Israël) daté du Paléolithique moyen et le diagnostic d'un chondroblastome de l'épiphyse fémorale distale. *PALEO*, 29, pp. 99–105.

Garrod, D.A.E. and Bate, D. (1937). *The stone age of Mount Carmel, volume I*. Oxford: Clarendon University Press.

Grün, R., Stringer, C., McDermott, F., Nathan, R., Porat, N., Robertson, S., Taylor, L., Mortimer, G., Eggins, S. and McCulloch, M. (2005). U-series and ESR Analyses of Bones and Teeth Relating to the Human Burials from Skhul. *Journal of Human Evolution*, 49, pp. 316–334.

Hershkovitz, I., Marder, O., Ayalon, A., Bar-Matthews, M., Yasur, G., Boaretto, E., Caracuta, V., Alex, B., Frumkin, A., Goder-Goldberger, M., Gunz, P., Holloway, R.L., Latimer, B., Lavi, R., Matthews, A., Slon, V., Bar-Yosef Mayer, D., Berna, F., Bar-Oz, G., Yeshurun, R., May, H., Hans, M.G., Weber, G.W. and Barzilai, O. (2015). Levantine Cranium from Manot Cave (Israel) Foreshadows the First European Modern Humans. *Nature*, 520, pp. 216–219.

Hovers, E., (2009). *The lithic assemblages of Qafzeh Cave*. Oxford: Oxford University Press.

Hovers, E., Ilani, S., Bar Yosef, O. and Vandermeersch, B. (2003). An Early Case of Color Symbolism. *Current Anthropology*, 44(4), pp. 491–522.

Hovers, E., Rak, Y., Lavi, R. and Kimbel, W. H. (1995). Hominid Remains from Amud Cave in the Context of the Levantine Middle Palaeolithic. *Paléorient*, 21(2), pp. 47–62.

Le Mort, F. (1994). Les sépultures. In: M. Lechevallier and A. Ronen, eds., *Le Gisement de Hatoula en Judée Occidentale, Israël. Mémoires et Travaux du Centre de recherche français à Jérusalem 8*. Paris: Association Paléorient, pp. 39–57.

McCown, T.D. (1934). The oldest complete skeleton of Man. *Bulletin of the American School of Prehistoric Research*, 10, pp. 13–19.

McCown, T.D. and Keith, A. (1939). *The stone age of Mount Carmel volume II: the fossil human remains from the Levalloiso-Mousterian*. Oxford: Clarendon Press.

Mercier, N., Valladas, H., Bar Yosef, O., Vandermeersch, B. and Joron, J.L. (1993). Thermoluminescence Date for the Mousterian Burial Site of Es-Skhul, Mt Carmel. *Journal of Archaeological Science*, 20, pp. 169–174.

Rak, Y., Kimbel, B. and Hovers, E. (1994). A Neandertal Infant from Amud Cave Israel. *Journal of Human Evolution*, 26, pp. 313–324.

Rink, W. J., Schwarcz, H., Lee, H.K., Rees-Jones, J., Rabinovitch, R. and Hovers, E. (2001). Electron Spin Resonance (ESR) and Thermal Ionization Mass Spectrometric (TIMS) 230Th/234U Dating of Teeth in Middle Paleolithic Layers at Amud Cave Israel. *Geoarchaeology*, 16, pp. 701–717.

Schwarcz, H.P., Grün, R., Vandermeersch, B., Bar-Yosef, O., Valladas, H. and Tchernov, E., (1988). ESR Dates for the Hominid Burial site of Qafzeh in Israel. *Journal of Human Evolution*, 17, pp. 733–737.

Smith, P. and Tillier, A-m. (1989). Additional infant remains from the Mousterian strata, Kebara Cave (Israel). In: O. Bar Yosef and B. Vandermeersch, eds., *Investigations in South Levantine prehistory*. BAR International Series 497, pp. 323–336.

Stringer, C.B., Grün, R., Schwarcz, H. and Goldberg, P. (1989). ESR Dates for the Hominid Burial Site of Es-Skhul in Israel. *Nature*, 338, pp. 756–758.

Suzuki, H. and Takai, F., eds. (1970). *The Amud Man and his cave site*. Tokyo: Academic Press of Japan.

Taborin, Y. (2003). La mer et les premiers hommes modernes. In: *Echanges et Diffusion dans la Préhistoire Méditerranéenne, Colloque de Nice 1996 du Comité des Travaux Historiques et Scientifiques (CTHS)*. Paris: Éditions de CTHS, pp. 113–122.

Tchernov, E. (1981). The biostratigraphy of the Middle East. In: O. Aurenche, M.-C. Cauvin, and P. Sanlaville, eds., *Préhistoire du Levant: Processus des Changements Culturels. Hommage à Francis Hours, Colloques Internationaux du Centre National de la Recherche Scientifique (CNRS) 598*. Paris: Éditions du CNRS, pp. 67–97.

Tillier, A-m. (1995). Paléoanthropologie et Pratiques Funéraires au Levant Méditerranéen durant le Paléolithique Moyen: Le Cas des Sujets Non Adultes. *Paléorient*, 21(2), pp. 63–76.

Tillier, A-m. (1999). *Les enfants moustériens de Qafzeh: interprétations phylogénétique et paléoauxologique*. Paris: Éditions du Centre National de la Recherche Scientifique (CNRS) (Cahiers de Paléoanthropologie).

Tillier, A-m. (2008). Early child deliberate burials. Bioarchaeological insights from the Near Eastern Mediterranean. In: K. Bacvarov, ed., *Babies reborn: infant/children burials in pre- and protohistory*, Workshop 26, XVth UISPP Congress, British Archaeological Reports (International Series). Oxford: Archaeopress, pp. 3–14.

Tillier, A-m. (2009). *L'homme et la mort: l'émergence du geste funéraire en préhistoire*. Paris: Éditions du Centre National de la Recherche Scientifique (CNRS),

Tillier, A-m., Arensburg, B., Duday, H. and Vandermeersch, B. (2004). Dental pathology, stressful events and disease in Levantine early anatomically modern humans: evidence from Qafzeh. In: N. Goren-Inbar and J.D. Speth, eds., *Human Paleoecology in the Levantine Corridor*. Oxford: Oxbow Books, pp. 135–148.

Tillier, A-m., Arensburg, B., Rak, Y. and Vandermeersch, B. (1988). Les sépultures néanderthaliennes au Proche-Orient Etat de la question. *Paléorient*, 14 (2), pp. 130 – 134.

Tillier, A-m., Arensburg, B., Vandermeersch, B. and Chech, M. (2003). New Human Remains from Kebara Cave (Mount Carmel): The Place of the Kebara Hominids in the Levantine Mousterian Fossil Record. *Paléorient*, 29(2), pp. 35–62.

Valladas, H., Joron, J.L., Valladas, G., Arensburg, B., Bar Yosef, O., Belfer-Cohen, A., Goldberg, P., Laville, H., Meignen, L., Rak, Y., Tchernov, E., Tillier, A-m. and Vandermeersch, B. (1987). Thermoluminescence Dates for the Neanderthal Burial Site at Kebara in Israel. *Nature*, 330, pp. 159–160.

Valladas, H., Mercier, N., Hovers, E., Frojet, L., Joron, J.L., Kimbel, W. and Rak, Y. (1999). TL Dates for the Neandertal Site of Amud Cave Israel. *Journal of Archaeological Science*, 26, pp. 182–193.

Valladas, H., Reyss, J.L., Joron, J.L., Valladas, G., Bar Yosef, O. and Vandermeersch, B. (1988). Thermoluminescence Dating of Mousterian 'Proto-Cro-Magnon' Remains from Israel and the Origin of Modern Man. *Nature*, 331, pp. 614–616.

Vallois, H.V. and Vandermeersch, B. (1972). Le Crâne Moustérien de Qafzeh (Homo VI): Étude Anthropologique. *L'Anthropologie*, 76(1-2), pp. 71–96.

Vandermeersch, B. (1966). Nouvelles Découvertes de Restes Humains dans les Couches Levalloisio-Moustérienne du Gisement de Qafzeh (Israël). *Comptes Rendus de l'Académie des Sciences de Paris*, 262, pp. 1434–1436.

Vandermeersch, B. (1969a). Les Nouveaux Squelettes Moustériens Découverts à Qafzeh (Israël) et Leur Signification. *Comptes Rendus de l'Académie des Sciences de Paris*, 268, pp. 2562–2565.

Vandermeersch, B. (1969b). Découverte d'un Objet en Ocre avec Traces d'Utilisation dans le Moustérien de Qafzeh (Israël). *Bulletin de la Société Préhistorique Française*, 66, pp. 157–158.

Vandermeersch, B. (1970). Une Sépulture Moustérienne avec Offrandes découverte dans la Grotte de Qafzeh. *Comptes Rendus de l'Académie des Sciences de Paris*, 270, pp. 298–301.

Vanhaeren, M., D'Errico, F., Stringer, C., James, S.L., Todd, J.A. and Mienis, H.K. (2006). Middle Paleolithic Shell Beads in Israel and Algeria. *Science*, 312, pp. 1785–1788.

Weinstein-Evron, M. (2009). *Archaeology in the archives: unveiling the Natufian Culture of Mount Carmel*. Boston and Leiden: Brill.

8

THE EARLIEST EUROPEAN BURIALS

Bruno Maureille

Translated from the original French by Christopher J. Knüsel

PACEA, De la Préhistoire à l'Actuel: Culture, Environnement et Anthropologie,
UMR 5199, CNRS-Université de Bordeaux, Pessac, France

Introduction

A pre-occupation with the dead, whether individually or collectively, is one of the most symbolic of human behaviours. Implicit in evidence for these behaviours are cognitive capacities that permit the expression of sentiments transmitting particular values through the actions made on behalf of the dead. These also reflect important social structuring principles of the group. Europe – from the Atlantic coast and the Iberian peninsula to the Ural Mountains, or from North to South from the North European Plain, North of the 50th parallel, to the northern borders of the Black and Caspian Seas – was home to members of the Neandertal lineage who, for the first time in the history of humanity, attributed special attention to certain dead group members. During the last third of the Middle Palaeolithic or Mousterian period, they invented the grave (Leclerc and Tarrète, 1988) for the deposition of individuals as primary earthen burials.

In Europe, the Mousterian (*circa* 350 000 to 45 000 years ago) is characterised by the appearance of a novel lithic blade manufacturing technique called the 'Levallois technique' (Jaubert, 1999; Delagnes, Jaubert and Meignen, 2007). The first evidence of the mastery of this technique is found at Ambrona (Spain) about 350 000 years ago (e.g. Santoja and Pérez-González, 2010), or perhaps a little earlier at Cagny-la-Garenne in France (Tuffreau and Antoine, 1995). The Eurasian Mousterian sees the development of different human lineages (Neandertal and Denisovan), both of which had their origins in the Lower Palaeolithic, and at the beginning of the Upper Palaeolithic (*circa* −45 000 years; Higham *et al.*, 2014; cf. Banks *et al.*, 2019), their disappearance. At the present time, there are no anatomically modern humans (AMH) associated with the Mousterian period in Western Eurasia, as the taxonomic status of the recent Apidima 1 specimen is inconclusive (*contra* Harvati *et al.*, 2019).

After reviewing the principal sites of primary Neandertal burials in Europe based on an acceptable definition of their contexts (see below) (Figure 8.1 and Table 8.1; cf. Defleur, 1993; Vandermeersch *et al.*, 2008; Pettitt, 2011), this chapter considers a synthesis of interpretive hypotheses on a regional scale, without considering the whole of the Eurasian landmass occupied by Neandertals. The author is aware that this leads to an intentional 'overlooking' of geographic distances and a 'flattening' of chronological differences. However, this approach also avoids a case-by-case study in order to propose more general hypotheses about treatments of, for example, buried individuals, variations in funerary gestures/deeds, questions of potential burial goods, and

DOI: 10.4324/9781351030625-11

140

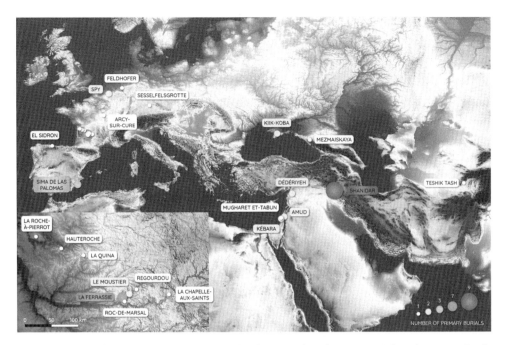

Figure 8.1 Map of the generally accepted Neandertal primary burials in Eurasia. The colours are related to landscape altimetry (dark green/blue: sea level, teal/white: low altitudes, beige to ochre to dark brown: high altitudes) (CAD image: F. Lacrampe-Cuyaubère (Archéosphère, Quirbajou); Archaeological data: B. Maureille; Cartographic data: Jarvis *et al.*, 2008).

the burial types and their funerary taphonomic signatures. These hypotheses are, therefore, very debatable, but at least they serve to provide reflections for future research. This chapter is based on the distribution and geographic extent of the Mousterian lithic techno-complexes as defined by prehistorians and the established chronology of them, which are not the subject of this chapter.

It must be emphasised that this chapter will not address the question of whether or not secondary funerary treatments were performed in the Lower and Middle Palaeolithic. Even if the author is an adherent of the existence of such treatments (Mussini and Maureille, 2012), such questions are more complex than those addressing the existence of primary burials at this time, and thus outside the scope of this contribution. Additionally, it does not consider the mortuary behaviours that led to the accumulation of Pre-Neandertals at La Sima de los Huesos in Spain (Bocquet-Appel and Arsuaga, 1999; Carbonell *et al.*, 2003) or, the various sites for which cannibalism has been suggested as the most likely explanatory hypothesis for the taphonomic signatures identified on the human remains, for example from Gorjanovic-Kramberger (1906) at Krapina to Mussini (2011) at Les Pradelles.

How many sites and fossil specimens are there in Eurasia?

Between 600 000 and 40 000 years ago over the entire study region, activities associated with the Neandertal lineage are known from dozen of thousands of sites that mainly produced lithics. Sites with hominin remains are much rarer, perhaps fewer than 300. These hominin remains are almost always isolated finds, most often found scattered among faunal remains or other archaeological material. The remains are incomplete, with isolated teeth often amongst the most well-preserved of them. Sometimes the presence of human remains is explained by no other hypotheses than

Table 8.1 List of the European Neandertal primary burials discussed in this contribution

	Specimen / fossil designation	Year of discovery	Country	Running number of countries	Running number of sites	Site types	Site function	Running number of sites by country	Running number of primary burial by country	Running number of primary burials by site	Skeletal preservation	Skull and/or infra-cranium from the same individual	Sex	Age-at-death	Presence of physically impairing pathological condition (yes/no)
1	Feldhofer 1	1856	Germany	1	1	Cave	Residential	1	1	1	Partial	Sk + infracr.	M	Adult	Yes
2	Spy 1	1886	Belgium	2	2	Probable cave	Residential	1	1	1	Partial	Sk + infracr.	F	Adult	No
3	Spy 2	1886	Belgium						2	2	Partial	Sk + infracr.	M	Adult	No
4	Le Moustier 1	1908	France	3	3	Rock-shelter	Residential	1	1	1	Sub-complete	Sk + infracr.	I	Juvenile	Yes
5	La Chapelle-aux-Saints 1	1908	France		4	Cave	Residential	2	2	1	Complete	Sk + infracr.	M	Adult	Yes
6	La Ferrassie 1	1909	France		5	Probable cave	Residential	3	3	1	Complete	Sk + infracr.	M	Adult	Yes
7	La Ferrassie 2	1910	France						4	2	Sub-complete	Sk + infracr.	F	Adult	No
8	La Quina H5	1911	France		6	Cliff foot	Residential	4	5	1	Sub-complete	Sk + infracr.	F	Adult	Yes
9	La Ferrassie 3	1912	France						6	3	Less than partial	Sk + infracr.	I	Juvenile	No
10	La Ferrassie 4	1912	France						7	4	Sub-complete	Sk + infracr.	I	Neonate	No
11	Le Moustier 2	1914/1996	France						8	2	Complete	Sk + infracr.	I	Neonate	No
12	La Ferrassie 5	1920	France						9	5	Partial	Sk + infracr.	I	Fœtus	No
13	La Ferrassie 6	1921	France						10	6	Partial	Sk + infracr.	I	Juvenile	No
14	Kiik-Koba 1	1924 à 26	Ukraine	4	7	Cave?		1	1	1	Less than partial	Infracr.	M	Adult	No
15	Kiik-Koba 2	1924 à 26	Ukraine						2	2	Less than partial	Infracr.	I	Juvenile	No
16	Regourdou 1	1957	France		8	Cave	No human occupation	5	11	1	Sub-Complete	Sk + infracr.	I	Adult	Yes
17	Roc-de-Marsal 1	1961	France		9	Cave	Residential	6	12	1	Complete	Sk + infracr.	I	Juvenile	No
18	Arcy-sur-Cure Grotte du Renne child 3764	1963	France		10	Cave	Residential	7	13	1	Probably partial	Sk + infracr.	I	Juvenile	Not documented

(Continued)

Table 8.1 List of the European Neandertal primary burials discussed in this contribution (*Continued*)

	Specimen / fossil designation	Year of discovery	Country	Running number of countries	Running number of sites	Site types	Site function	Running number of sites by country	Running number of primary burial by country	Running number of primary burials by site	Skeletal preservation	Skull and/or infra-cranium from the same individual	Sex	Age-at-death	Presence of physically impairing pathological condition (yes/no)
19	Châteauneuf sur Charente 1	Not published	France		11	Probable cave	?	8	14	1	Less than partial	Sk + infracr.	I	Juvenile	Not documented
20	La Ferrassie 8	1973	France						15	7	Sub-complete	Sk + infracr.	I	Juvenile	No
21	La Roche-à-Pierrot 1	1979	France		12	Rock-shelter	Residential	9	16	1	Partial	Sk + infracr.	F	Adult	Yes
22	Mezmaiskaya burial 1	1993	Russia (Caucasus)	5	13	Cave	Residential	1	1	1	Complete	Sk + infracr.	I	Neonate	No
23	Sesselfelsgrotte	1968/69/70	Germany		14	Cave	?	2	2	1	Less than partial	Sk + infracr.	I	Neonate	No
24	Las Palomas 92	Not published	Spain	6	15	Probable cave	?	1	1	1	Partial	Sk + infracr.	I	Adult	Not documented
25	Las Palomas 96	Not published	Spain						2	2	Sub-complete	Sk + infracr.	F	Adult	Not documented
26	Las Palomas 97	Not published	Spain						3	3	Partial	Sk + infracr.	I	Juvenile	Not documented
27	El Sidron J1	Not published	Spain		16	Cave	?	2	4	1	Sub-complete	Sk + infracr.	M	Juvenile	Not documented

Note: Sk = skull (cranium and mandible); M = male; F = female; I = Indeterminate; ? = unknown.

those invoking cannibalism (Defleur *et al.*, 1999; Maureille *et al.*, 2010; Mussini, 2011; Defleur and Desclaux, 2019) or carnivore activity (e.g. Giacobini and Piperno, 1991; Beauval *et al.*, 2005). There are thus somewhat more than 400 more or less complete hominin fossil skeletons and isolated remains from this period. One of the most important questions posed of these discoveries concerns how to distinguish those resulting from funerary treatments in primary burials from those buried by natural taphonomic processes and, moreover, from those disturbed during their initial discovery and subsequent excavation some time ago.

How does one recognise a Neandertal primary burial?

The recognition of an earthen primary grave must be demonstrated by means of scientific interpretation that best explains the presence and distribution of human remains in their sedimentological and archaeological context. The working hypothesis employed here is that proposed by Vandermeersch (1995: 17), which stipulates that in the Mousterian 'there are no graves without skeletons and, conversely, it is unusual for there to be a skeleton without a burial…' (*'Il n'y a pas de sépultures sans squelette et inversement, il est exceptionnel qu'il y ait squelette sans sepulture ….'*). Indeed, the intentional deposition of a fresh cadaver into its final place of deposition and its 'protection' following interment out of respect for the dead favours good preservation of the bones, their anatomical integrity and, in the best of cases, their anatomical connections. From the hundreds of European hominin remains, there are only about 30 for which one can be certain that cranial and infra-cranial elements derive from the same individual, and roughly another 15 that can be considered to be complete skeletons. Of course, it is clear that a buried skeleton in anatomical connection or in partial connection is not synonymous with earthen primary grave. Remains from more ancient lineages, for example, the Australopithecines found at Sterkfontein and Malapa (South Africa) (Clarke, 1998; Val, 2013), were found as partially complete skeletons with skeletal elements in connection but there is no suspicion that funerary treatments had been performed. The same argument for burial is levelled for the more recent remains of *Homo naledi* on the basis of the nature of the bone assemblage, the presence of preserved anatomical connections, the absence of macrofaunal remains, the presence of few taphonomic signatures (excluding those related to snails and beetles), and due to the deep karstic context of their discovery (Dirks *et al.*, 2015). But there is no consensus on whether this was part of funerary practices or not (Thackeray, 2016; Val, 2016). The question of the existence of potential funerary treatments in our prehistoric predecessors is therefore always going to be difficult to confirm.

Recent critiques

This difficulty may partly explain why in the 2010s there was a revival of criticism for the existence of some Neandertal primary burials. Researchers challenged the discoveries from Roc-de-Marsal 1 (Sandgathe *et al.*, 2011) and La Chapelle-aux-Saints 1 (Figure 8.2) (Dibble *et al.*, 2015). In the latter article the authors developed observations necessary to define the 'operational sequence' (*'chaine opératoire'*) that would characterise primary intentional Neandertal burials. For example, it is necessary for the burial pit to be of anthropogenic origin, and there must be funerary goods. Without these features, it is not possible to be certain of the existence of funerary treatment.

It is true that for the consideration of the existence of a primary burial, other than the study of the human remains, their taphonomic stigmata and their anatomical connections, it is necessary to consider the sedimentological, archaeological and depositional contexts, such as the presence of an artificial anthropogenic feature, for example a pit (Rendu *et al.*, 2014, 2016). In addition

Figure 8.2 One of the famous plans showing the pit and position of the La Chapelle-aux-Saints Neandertal published by the Bouyssonie brothers (By B. Maureille, based on Bouyssonie, Bouyssonie and Bardon, 1908). Note that the cave opens to the left, while in the original drawing it opens to the right. This error on the plan had escaped the notice of archaeologists for 100 years.

to the rediscovery of the burial pit during recent excavations at La Chapelle-aux-Saints (at the Bouffia Bonneval) (Figure 8.3) and the demonstration of its anthropogenic origin, these researchers produced the first comparative taphonomic study of the human remains of a Neandertal and the faunal remains coming from the same archaeological context. Thus,

Figure 8.3 The burial pit of La Chapelle-aux-Saints 1 as it appeared in 2012 (cf. Rendu *et al.*, 2014). This is the oldest preserved funerary structure in the world at present. (Photograph: B. Maureille).

the taphonomic history of this Neandertal confirmed the primary nature of its burial due to its protection from taphonomic effects. On the contrary, in re-visiting another discovery, Maureille *et al.* (2015a) showed that Regourdou 1 (Montignac, France), first discovered in 1957 (Bonifay and Vandermeersch, 1962; Bonifay *et al.,* 2007), lacked clear evidence of a funerary deposit. The study of the taphonomic damage on human remains and on brown bear bones from this site does not make it possible to distinguish separate taphonomic histories for the hominin and the ursid remains. If this had been a human burial, then one would expect to find evidence of a more protected burial history for the human when compared to ursid remains. But, according to the faunal and hominin evidence at Regourdou, the Regourdou 1 skeleton is the only medium-sized mammal for which the entire skeleton (except the cranium) has been found in a position respecting the anatomical logic of the body. Despite the destructive circumstances of this discovery and a rescue excavation occupying less than two days and performed by prehistorians with little experience of human anatomy, the original position of the remains of the deceased has been recently identified (Maureille *et al.,* 2015b). Moreover, subsequent taphonomic processes that had disturbed the human deposit, and which explain the dispersion of the human remains, have also been demonstrated (Pelletier *et al.,* 2017). Thus, and until new investigations are carried out, the simplest hypothesis to explain the presence of Regourdou 1 Neandertal skeleton in this deposit is that of an intentional burial in a karstic context.

Unfortunately, such pioneering research such as that at La Chapelle-aux-Saints and Regourdou has not yet been undertaken on other discoveries, or are not yet published. For example, the taphonomic study of the Saint-Césaire 1 adult Neandertal (Figure 8.4), discovered in 1979 (Lévêque, Backer and Guilbaud, 1993), is anticipated in the near future. If considered as a potential primary burial (Table 8.1), it could also be the result of secondary funerary treatments (Vandermeersch, 1993). Moreover, it should be noted that, after skeletonisation, at least some parts of the skeleton were disturbed – and/or partially destroyed – by underground water – as demonstrated by the dissolution of almost entire left half of the cranium (excepted thirteen left teeth) and the position of some hand remains (phalanges) in another part of the excavation, in square F4, other than the one where a concentration of hominin remains were found in a 70 cm diameter circular area at the intersection of squares F3 and F4.

Outline of potential primary European Neandertal burials

In 2019, counting generously – that is to say, considering the presence of cranial and infra-cranial remains from a single individual uncovered in a limited area of a site that had been inhabited by groups of Neandertals and that had also been protected from carnivore scavenging – there are 27 cases that argue for the existence of funerary treatments related to primary Neandertal burials. This figure does not take into account remains from Altamura (Italy) that appear to be the result of what may have been an accidental death (Pesce Delfino and Vacca, 1993).

These burials were discovered in only six countries: Germany, Belgium, France, Russia and Ukraine, of which 61% (N=16) come from France. In total, they represent 17 sites, of which 50% (N=8) are in France, including Le Moustier, La Chapelle-aux-Saints, La Ferrassie, La Quina, Arcy-sur-Cure/Grotte du Renne, Regourdou, Hauteroche (also known as Châteauneuf-sur-Charente), and Roc-de-Marsal. Only a single site comprises more than two burials: La Ferrassie in the Dordogne (France).

Some 55% (N=15) of the 26 discoveries were made in the 19th or first half of the 20th centuries. This number explains the unsatisfactory detail of the data associated with all of these

Figure 8.4 The excavation area and the '*en bloc*' lifting of the human remains from Saint-Césaire, France (Photograph: F. Lévêque).

discoveries with regard to the application of the principles and methods of archaeothanatology (cf. Duday, 2009). This situation has hardly improved with most recent discoveries. Indeed, apart from the remains of three separate individuals from brecciated blocks of the Las Palomas site from Spain, which corresponds probably to the first Neandertal burials found in the Iberian Peninsula (Walker *et al.*, 2011), there have been no further discoveries of Neandertal suspected primary burials in Europe since 1993.

Four of the most recently excavated sites produced the remains of neonates or very young children but very little published information is available for them. One is a perinate from Mezmaiskaya 1 (Russian Caucasus Mountains) (Golovanova *et al.*, 1999). It is only documented by a single published picture of the human bones, but the image of the burial is at least in part a reconstruction of the position of the lower limb bones and probably those of the cranial vault as well. Indeed, the three lower limb bones recorded, two femora and a tibia, are supposed to reflect the position of the lower limbs in flexion, but these are, instead, a femur, a tibia, and a humerus. Moreover, the proximal end of the tibia is placed near the proximal end of the

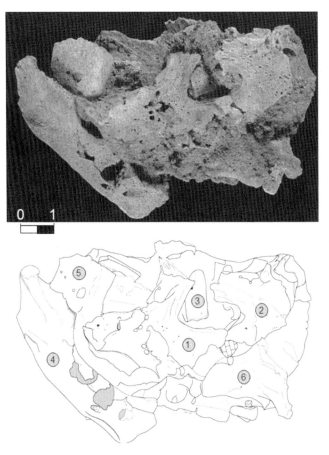

Figure 8.5 The block of sediment in which the skull remains of the Le Moustier 2 newborn infant were found (Photograph: P. Jugie, from the collections of the Musée National de Préhistoire; CAD image: B. Leprètre). 1: right maxilla, 2: left maxilla, 3: right nasal bone, 4: right hemi-mandible, 5: right sphenoid greater wing, 6: left occipital *pars basilaris*.

femur. The second discovery is that of another newborn, Le Moustier 2. Several disarticulated elements were collected from the site in 1914 by Denis Peyrony, and were identified in 1996 in the collections of the Musée National de Préhistoire (National Museum of Prehistory) in Les Eyzies-de-Tayac, Dordogne, and studied between 1997 and 2001 (Maureille, 2002a, 2002b) (Figure 8.5). Their very precisely documented taphonomic study will be published soon. The third case corresponds to the partial skeleton of a newborn found among the faunal remains from Sesselfelsgrotte (Germany) excavated between 1968 and 1970 and published much more recently (Rathgeber, 2006). The fourth discovery included in this treatment is that of the remains – some of them in anatomical connection – of a child from El Sidrón J1 (Spain) found in square G6 of the site (Rosas *et al.*, 2017). This is the only well-preserved partially complete skeleton from the site, which has also produced the thousands of scattered bone remains of at least 12 other individuals for which cannibalism has been levelled to explain their anthropogenic stigmata (Rosas *et al.*, 2006). Although this individual is included among the 26 cases here, the interpretation of the mechanism that contributed to the creation of this assemblage remains intriguing.

A non-random chronological and geographical distribution

Thus these 27 European cases derive from 15 sites that are not equally distributed geographically (Table 8.1 and Figure 8.1), which indicates that if a single Neandertal burial is found at a site, there is, in theory, a good chance of finding a second one. This also means that the many archaeological assemblages in the entire region occupied by the Neandertals – some of them having produced isolated human remains – have not (yet) produced primary burials, including from sites in Italy, Croatia, Greece, Portugal, and the Czech Republic. This could be the result of different funerary treatments being practiced in these regions based on culturally specific traditions, or due to chronological differences. This distributional pattern could also be the result of the historical development of the discipline, and the speed (and the quality) of the excavation process, and unequal opportunities for discoveries from certain sites. These two possibilities are not mutually exclusive.

On a smaller geographical scale – for example, that of Southwest France – there are two geographical areas that are very close to one another, a 450 km² part of the Vézère Valley in Périgord Noir and a 3000 km² area close to the Tardoire Valley in Angoumois, where the history of excavation is quite similar. These two areas border one another without an apparent geographical or palaeoenvironmental barrier and are characterised by the same limestone formations containing caves and rock shelters. For the first area, however, there are nine sites where human remains have been discovered, including 11 potential burials, and no site with evidence of carnivore-related activity. In the second area, there are 15 sites with human remains, of which only two have a potential burial and four (Rochelot, Castaigne Cave, Les Pradelles, La Chaise Cave (*Grotte de la Chaise*)) have human remains with evidence of large carnivore activity. It is important to note that in the Charente region, relative to the Périgord Noir, there may be a higher proportion of older sites, those dating prior to oxygen isotope stage 4 (so earlier than 60 000 to 70 000 years ago). This suggests that in Southwest France, the presence of these primary burials could be linked to their similar date, unique cultural practices and/or to specific geomorphological conditions (again without being mutually exclusive).

It is instructive to recall that on a Eurasian scale, however, two sites (Figure 8.1) contribute almost half of the known discoveries. These are La Ferrassie in the Dordogne (France) with seven cases (Figure 8.6) and Shanidar in Iraqi Kurdistan (nine to ten cases). Without these sites, the extent of the diversity of Neandertal funerary treatments would be very different. How can one explain this particular site 'density' of these primary burials? For the moment, there does not appear to be a scientific answer. These two sites are considered to be long-occupied habitations of Neandertal groups. There could therefore be a number of reasons, such as topography that facilitates the relative ease of finding the sites, for example, at Shanidar cave, in a mountainous environment. Or based on geography, such as the site of La Ferrassie being located halfway along the Vézère Valley – a particularly active area during the Middle Palaeolithic, perhaps due to its beneficial palaeoenvironmental conditions, rich in food resources – and the Bergerac region, where there are sources of exceptional quality flint lithic materials. Common to both cases are water sources that were present during the Mousterian (at Shanidar it flows into the cave). These localities were probably attractive meeting places for exchange and burials. The site of Shanidar is the subject of renewed scientific interest through a project led by G. Barker, C. Hunt and E. Pomeroy, which will provide new and very important results for elucidating Neandertal funerary behaviour (cf. Pomeroy *et al.*, 2017).

Present-day research progresses much more slowly and much more precisely than that of preceding generations. It is estimated that with the techniques available today, it would take almost 200 years (excavating all year round) to extract the volume of sediment removed from the site

Figure 8.6 One of the rare photographs of the excavation of the grave of the adult La Ferrassie 1 (Peyrony, 1934). Note the footprints around the border of the excavated area.

of La Ferrassie by D. Peyrony and J.-L. Capitan in 20 years. Perhaps, this could explain why the resumption of excavations at the sites of Roc-de-Marsal (2003–2010), La Ferrassie (2010–2015) and, more recently, Le Moustier (2014–present) has not yet resulted in the discovery of new evidence for burial.

The chronology of European burials

The oldest attested burial relates to the activity of members of the Neandertal lineage but it is not European. It was discovered in the Middle East in 1931/32 in the Mugharet-Tabun site (Garrod and Bate, 1937; Bar-Yosef and Callander, 1999) (Figure 8.7) and is represented by the remains of Tabun C1, a skeleton with slender bones, supposedly of a female Neandertal, which is nearly 120 000 years old if it was found, as reported, in level B at the site, or from 130 000 to 170 000 years old, if instead, it was contemporary with layer C.

Figure 8.7 Exposed layers of the excavation and preparation for the '*en bloc*' lifting of the grave of the Neandertal Tabun C1 (Israel) (*Source*: O. Bar-Yosef).

All European burials are more recent than that of Tabun C1 and are related to Marine Isotope Stage 3 (60 000 to 35 000 years ago). They have been dated in a variety of ways. The most recent, Spy 1 and 2 and Feldhofer 1, dating to about 40 000 years ago, were discovered in northwestern Europe, the first two of which are associated with transitional Middle to Upper Palaeolithic techno-complexes. Others are older, such as Roc-de-Marsal 1 and Regourdou 1. They are essentially associated with Levallois debitage. The oldest could be that of Regourdou 1 (Bonifay, 1964) and related to MIS 5b (95 000 to 84 000 years ago). Neandertal burials in Europe are not contemporary and are associated with different lithic techno-complexes that perhaps relate to different cultural traditions. Contrary to what has often been written, the Mousterian of La Quina-type is very poor in documented primary burials, which is interesting from the perspective that this techno-complex is associated with highly mobile groups and often evidence of cannibalism (for example at Combe-Grenal, Les Pradelles).

The nature of the European sites and their function

Most of European Neandertal primary burials are located inside caves or what were caves during Middle Palaeolithic times (Table 8.1). The others are found in rock shelters (N=2 sites) or at the foot of cliff (N=1 site). At the present time, no Neandertal burials have been found in open-air sites.

In addition, with the exception of the Regourdou site, which was a karstic cave that served as a hibernation cave for brown bears (*Ursus arctos*), Neandertals buried their dead in long-term residential sites (Delagnes and Rendu, 2011). This could indicate a symbolic association, a way of appropriating space. Or, it could also have had practical reasons, simply due to ease of access and the physical conditions, the health status and/or age at death of the Neandertals who were living and dying in the area. The third of these hypotheses seems most likely since there is a specific distribution of Neandertals buried according to their age class or health status. Of course, these three possibilities are not mutually exclusive. Moreover, none of the sites were exclusively used for burial.

Who was inhumed?

Neandertal burials comprise adults as well as children and infants (Table 8.1). A considerable number of adult and immature individuals present pathological bone disorders (Table 8.1). In more than 50% (N=6) of adults there is evidence for a congenital or a traumatic pathological condition, such as in La Chapelle-aux-Saints 1 (Boule, 1911–13; Trinkaus, 1985) and La Quina H5 (Martin, 1923; Straus and Cave, 1957), which would have limited or impaired their mobility as active hunter-gatherers. Moreover, there are also a high number of newborns (N=5). These young individuals are the most often documented among Neandertals for the whole of the Palaeolithic. As a reminder, only two burials of newborns are known for the whole of the Upper Palaeoltihic Gravettian period, though there are nearly 120 primary burials of individuals stretching from the Atlantic coast to the Urals (Henry-Gambier, pers. com.; Pettitt, 2011). In addition, in Neandertal sites, there is a lack of 'older teenagers', 'young adults' or individuals in the prime of life and in good physical condition while some of them, seem to have died during hunting activities or due to conflict (Churchill *et al.*, 2009) (cf. Sala *et al.*, 2015). The suggestion is that these buried Neandertals are found near where they had lived, or near those find locations where they had performed activities. Then, most studied Neandertal skeletons probably represent a biased sample of the population with a lack of those individuals that were least dependent on the rest of the community, likely having received other funerary treatments, perhaps in open-air sites which may have completely disappeared due to more recent land-use.

With respect to sex – assuming that Neandertal remains from primary burial contexts have been accurately assessed for sex – there are slightly more adult males (58%, N=7) than females (42%, N=5). This proportion is very uncertain in view of the small number of individuals considered and merits further investigation using ancient DNA in the future.

What funerary treatments?

Although only individual inhumations have been considered, it seems that the deceased may have been deposited in anthropogenic pits (i.e. La Chapelle-aux-Saints 1 and Le Moustier 2), or in natural depressions (i.e. Roc-de-Marsal 1), or sometimes slightly modified natural depressions (i.e. La Ferrassie 1). They do not seem to have been the subject of standardised funerary treatments. Thus, the bodies had not been oriented in the same way; there is no specific burial disposition relating to the topographic location of the sites or to cardinal points of orientation. Certainly, there is topographical proximity, as with La Ferrassie 1 and 2, La Ferrassie 3 and 4, and Kiik-Koba 1 and 2 and, moreover, at La Ferrassie, there are no intercutting deposits. For the European Mousterian, however, it is not possible to discern if there were specific burial locations (but this, on the other hand, can be considered a possibility for the Levant and for the Shanidar and Kebara sites). The position of the body is also variable: on the back (supine) with the upper limbs splayed to either side of the mid-line of the body (La Ferrassie 1), in a more flexed position (La Chapelle-aux-Saints 1), or in a supine position with the right upper limb flexed and the hand brought back towards the trunk while the left upper limb was probably in extension and perpendicular to the axis of the body and lower limbs extended (Regourdou 1), or ventrally (Roc-de Marsal 1).

Relative to the more standardised discoveries of the Upper Palaeolithic Gravettian period, it seems that the position of certain individuals is peculiar (e.g. La Ferrassie 1 or Roc-de-Marsal 1). Finally, in the sites that have yielded more than one interment, there is no area where children would have been buried separately from adults, or potential females separately from potential males.

Concerning the material accompanying the deceased

There are no definitive associations between a deceased individual and artefactual or faunal remains. While this had been assumed in some cases (La Chapelle-aux-Saints 1, La Ferrassie 1, 5 or 6 and Regourdou 1), the information is too weak to be admissible according to current criteria. To date, therefore, there is no evidence for funerary offerings in the European Mousterian. If this criterion were a necessary requisite to define a primary Neandertal burial, none would qualify as such. Moreover, recall that in the common use of the term, an offering is a gift to a deity, or one that is deposited with a religious intention. For the Middle Palaeolithic, one tends to consider that the offering is identified by its uniqueness. According to Vandermeersch (1976: 727) they are: '… objects which are exceptional in their size, in relation to the archaeological content of the layer, or by their arrangement in the burial' ('… *objets qui présentent un caractère exceptionnel, par leurs dimensions, par rapport au contenu archéologique de la couche, ou par leur arrangement dans la sépulture*'). For more recent periods, such as Neolithic, protohistory and history, scholars consider it better to identify offerings only if certain objects of the same type are repeatedly found in burials. Otherwise, it is impossible to distinguish between 'emotional, unusual, or accidental' inclusions and funerary inclusions that imply that the (funerary) offering is part of practices that are codified by a rite. The definition of what constitutes a funerary offering as defined by the community of recent prehistorians, protohistorians, and historians is the one that should be retained for the Palaeolithic period as well.

Can one speak of religious behaviour in the Mousterian?

In Testot and Dortier's (2005) edited book, entitled *La Religion, Unité et Diversité* (Religion, Unity and Diversity), the question of the origins of religion is quickly addressed by recalling the great antiquity and diversity of burials, the possibility that Upper Palaeolithic decorated caves may have been religious sanctuaries, and by observations of the religious practices of supposedly primitive historical societies.

Various scholars of prehistoric archaeology have written on prehistoric religion, including Leroi-Gourhan (1964) and Otte (1993). Leroi-Gourhan (1964) states '… to tackle the problem of prehistoric religion without immediately warning the reader that s/he is engaging on slippery and uneven terrain would be lacking in charity towards him' ('… *aborder le problème de la religion préhistorique sans avertir d'emblée le lecteur qu'il s'engage sur un terrain glissant et semé de ravins serait manquer de charité à son égard*'). He adds that '… it may be useful to also define what will be understood (…) by the word "religion", and first of all to say that no distinction will be made between religion and magic, for lack of a means to establish a separate definition. The very meaning of the word "religion" will be very restricted in its use; it is simply based on manifestations of concerns that seem to go beyond material remains' ('…*il est peut-être utile de définir également ce qui sera entendu (…) par religion, et tout d'abord de dire qu'aucune distinction ne sera faite entre religion et magie, faute de matériaux réellement fondés pour établir une séparation. Le sens même du mot "religion" sera très restreint dans son usage; il est simplement fondé sur les manifestations de préoccupations paraissant dépasser l'ordre matériel*'). Otte (1993) writes '… since religious behaviour is universal, apparently present at all times and in all places, it is therefore one of the fundamental components of human experience' ('... *le comportement religieux étant universel, présent apparemment en tout temps et en tous lieux, il constitue donc une des composantes fondamentales du phénomène humain*'). He adds that religion is 'a collective, instituted behaviour, with rules and codifications (....) Religion also implies practices and leads to notions of morality (....) These practices are therefore determined by tradition; they imply prescriptions and dogmas; they are regulated by a socially integrated power' ('*un comportement collectif, institué, avec ses règles et ses codifications (...) La religion implique aussi des pratiques et aboutit à la notion de morale (...) Ces pratiques sont par conséquent déterminées par la tradition; elles impliquent des prescriptions et des dogmes; elles sont réglementées par un pouvoir socialement intégré*'). On the question of religious behaviour in the Palaeolithic there are clearly opposed opinions. In the Middle Palaeolithic, discussions of possible religious behaviour should be based on archaeological evidence, but for many, the same data will never produce a single explanation and will always remain too fragmented to provide a complete assessment.

Conclusion

For the Middle Palaeolithic, it should no longer be possible to propose the existence of a Mousterian burial without scientific demonstration that stretches beyond that of ordered arrangements of inhumed remains. Unfortunately, even in the case of very recent discoveries, primary data are still too often absent or unpublished. Even if a complete critical and impartial review of primary European Neandertal burials based on a synthesis of archaeological and palaeoanthropological evidence has yet to be produced, it is possible to argue for the existence of these burials not being simply incidental deposits. European Mousterian people intentionally buried some of their dead.

In Europe, burials are individual and inhumed in full earthen graves. These burials were not standardised, the bodies having been deposited in different positions, sometimes taking advantage of natural sedimentary features. The sites that produced these burials were, in the main, residential places, most of them also being caves. They are characterised by the presence of very young individuals (infants and small children) and physically impaired adults. There are almost no older teenagers or young adults. Supposed males seem to be more numerous than females.

The factors that favoured the expression of these behaviours towards the Mousterian dead remain unknown. A prophylactic concern does not seem to be able to be retained as an explanation since it probably would have been easier to get rid of a corpse by abandoning it to scavengers or throwing it in a river, rather than burying it. Moreover, certain regions have more burials than others, which is the same for the levels in which lithic technological traditions have been found. The existence of Neandertal primary burials could therefore have a stronger cultural component than what has been supposed to date. Moreover, in the case of the Eurasian Mousterian, the observation that these burials are found at the extremes of their geographical range and their existence for nearly 80 000 years (from 120 000 years ago with Tabun C1 to 40 000 years ago for the burials at Spy) supports the notion of a behaviour rooted in cultural traditions. If intentional burial is considered to be the oldest and longest-lasting symbolic practice, it is – for the moment – impossible to go beyond the documenting the diversity of practices and funerary gestures, and especially whether or not they were supported by beliefs. Fortunately, in France and the Levant new discoveries are in the process of being excavated and described. The discovery of the Ein Qashish human remains (Been *et al.*, 2017) ensures that new and newly focussed attention is being paid to the context of the discovery of Neandertal human remains. The Shanidar site will certainly be the place for important new discoveries (Pomeroy *et al.*, 2020). It seems assured that the 2020s will see the sample discussed in this contribution clearly increase in size, which should likewise improve the appreciation of the diversity of Neandertal funerary treatments in Eurasia, perhaps by incorporating results of other disciplinary fields in order to begin to break down barriers hindering the development of new ideas.

References

Banks, W.E., Bertran, P., Ducasse, S., Klaric, L., Lanos, P., Renard, C. and Mesa, M. (2019). An Application of Hierarchical Bayesian Modelling to Better Constrain the Chronologies of Upper Paleolithic Archaeological Cultures in France between ca. 32,000–21,000 Calibrated Years Before Present. *Quaternary Science Reviews*, 200, pp. 188–214.

Bar-Yosef, O. and Callander, J. (1999). The Woman from Tabun: Garrod's Doubts in Historical Perspective. *Journal of Human Evolution*, 37(6), pp. 879–885.

Beauval, C., Maureille, B., Lacrampe-Cuyaubère, F., Serre, D., Peressinotto, D., Bordes, J.-G., Cochard, D., Couchoud, I., Dubrasquet, D., Laroulandie, V., Meignen, L., Lenoble, A., Mallye, J.-B., Pasty, S., Primault, J., Rohland, N., Hofreiter, M., Pääbo, S. and Trinkaus, E. (2005). A Neandertal femur from a hyena den at Les Rochers-de-Villeneuve (Lussac-les-Châteaux, Vienne, France). *Proceedings of the National Academy of Sciences of the USA*, 102(20), pp. 7085–7090.

Been E., Hovers, E., Ekshtain, R., Malinski-Buller, A., Agha, N., Barash A., Bar-Yosef Mayer, D.E, Benazzi, S., Hublin, J.-J., Levin, L., Greenbaum, N., Mitki, N., Oxilia, G., Porat, N., Roskin, J., Soudack, M., Yeshurun, R., Shahack-Gross, R., Nir, N., Stahlschmidt, M.C., Rak, Y., and Barzilai O. (2017). The First Neanderthal Remains from an Open-Air Middle Palaeolithic Site in the Levant. *Scientific Reports*, 7, 2958.

Bocquet-Appel, J.-P. and Arsuaga, J. L. (1999). Age Distributions of Hominid Samples at Atapuerca (SH) and Krapina Could Indicate Accumulation by Catastrophe. *Journal of Archaeological Science*, 26(3), pp. 327–338.

Bonifay, E. (1964) La Grotte de Régourdou (Montignac, Dordogne). Stratigraphie et Industrie Lithique Moustérienne. *L'Anthropologie*, 68(1-2), pp. 49–64.

Bonifay, E. and Vandermeersch, B. (1962). Dépôts Rituels d'Ossements d'Ours dans le Gisement Moustérien du Régourdou (Montignac, Dordogne). *Compte Rendus des Séances de l'Académie des Sciences*, 255(1ᵉʳ octobre 1962), pp. 635–636.

Bonifay, E., Vandermeersch, B., Couture C. and Panattoni, R. (2007). *La sépulture néandertalienne du Regourdou (Montignac-sur-Vézère, Dordogne)*. Documents du Centre d'Études et de Recherche sur les Lacs, Anciens Lacs et Tourbières (C.E.R.L.A.T.), Mémoire numéro 4.

Boule, M. (1911–13). *L'Homme fossile de La Chapelle-aux-Saints*. Paris: Masson & Cie.

Bouyssonie, A., Bouyssonie, J. and Bardon, L. (1908). Découverte d'un Squelette Humain Moustérien à La Chapelle-aux-Saints (Corrèze). *Comptes Rendus de l'Académie des Sciences*, 21, pp. 1414–1415.

Carbonell, E., Mosquera, M., Ollé, A., Rodríguez, J.P., Sala, R., Vergès, J.M., Arsuaga, J.L. and Bermúdez de Castro, J.M. (2003). Did the Earliest Mortuary Practices Take Place More than 350 000 Years Ago at Atapuerca? *L'Anthropologie (Paris)*, 107(1), pp. 1–14.

Churchill, S.E., Franciscus, R.G., McKean-Peraza, H.A., Daniel, J.A. and Warren, B.A. (2009). Shanidar 3 Neandertal Rib Puncture Wound and Paleolithic Weaponry. *Journal of Human Evolution*, 57(2), pp. 163–178.

Clarke, R.J. (1998). First Ever Discovery of a Skull and Well Preserved Skeleton of *Australopithecus*. *South African Journal of Sciences*, 94(10), pp. 460–463.

Delagnes, A. and Rendu, W. (2011). Shifts in Neandertal Mobility, Technology and Subsistence Strategies in Western France. *Journal of Archaeological Science*, 38(8), pp. 1771–1783.

Delagnes, A., Jaubert, J. and Meignen, L. (2007). Les technocomplexes du Paléolithique Moyen en Europe occidentale dans leur cadre diachronique et géographique. In: B. Vandermeersch and B. Maureille, eds., *Les Néandertaliens, Biologie et Cultures, documents préhistoriques 23*. Paris: Comité des Travaux Historiques et Scientifiques (C.T.H.S.), pp. 213–230.

Defleur, A. (1993). *Les sépultures néandertaliennes*. Paris: Centre de la Recherche Scientifique (CNRS) Éditions.

Defleur, A., White, T.D., Valensi, P., Slimak, L. and Cregut-Bonnoure, E. (1999). Neandertal Cannibalism at Moula-Guercy, Ardèche, France. *Science*, 286(5437), pp. 128–131.

Defleur, A. and Desclaux, E. (2019). Impact of the Last Interglacial Climate Change on Ecosystems and Neanderthals Behavior at Baume Moula-Guercy, Ardèche, France. *Journal of Archaeological Science*, 104, pp. 114–124.

Dibble, H.L., Aldeias, V., Goldberg, P., McPherron, S.P., Sandgathe, D. and Steele, T.E. (2015). A Critical Look at Evidence from La Chapelle-Aux-Saints Supporting an Intentional Neandertal Burial. *Journal of Archaeological Science*, 53, pp. 629–657.

Dirks, P.H.G.M., Berger, L.R., Roberts, E.M., Kramers, J.D., Hawks, J., Randolph-Quinney, P.S., Elliott, M., Musiba, C.M., Churchill, S.E., de Ruiter, D.J., Schmid, P., Backwell, L.R., Belyanin, G.A., Boshoff, P. Hunter, K.L., Feuerriege, E.M., Gurtov, A., Harrison J. du G, Hunter, R., Kruger, A., Morris, A, Makhubela, T.V., Peixotto, B. and Tucker, S. (2015). Geological and Taphonomic Context for the New Hominin Species *Homo naledi* from the Dinaledi Chamber, South Africa. *eLife*, 4, pp. 1–37, e09561.

Duday, H. (2009). *The archaeology of the dead. Lectures in archaeothanatology*. Oxford: Oxford University Press.

Garrod, D.A.E. and Bate, D.M. (1937). *The stone age of Mount Carmel*. Oxford: Clarendon Press.

Giacobini, G. and Piperno, M. (1991). Taphonomic considerations on the Circeo 1 Neandertal cranium. Comparison of surface characteristics of the human cranium with faunal remains from the paleosurface. In: M. Piperno and G. Scichilone, eds., *The Circeo 1 Neandertal skull, studies and documentation*. Roma: Libreria dello stato, pp. 457–486.

Golovanova, L.V., Hoffecker, J.F., Kharitonov, V.M. and Romanova, G.P. (1999). Mezmaiskaya Cave: A Neanderthal Occupation in the Northern Caucasus. *Current Anthropology*, 40(1), pp. 77–86.

Gorjanovic-Kramberger, D. (1906). *Der Diluviale Mensch von Krapina in Kroatien*. Wiesbaden: C.W. Kreidel's Verlag.

Harvati, K., Röding, C., Bosman, A.M., Karakostis, F.A., Grün, R., Stringer, C., Karkanas, P., Thompson, N.C., Koutoulidis, V., Moulopoulos, L.A., Gorgoulis, V.G. and Kouloukoussa, M. (2019). Apidima Cave Fossils Provide Earliest Evidence of *Homo sapiens* in Eurasia. *Nature*, 571, pp. 500–504.

Jarvis, A., Reuter, H.I., Nelson, A. and Guevara, E. (2008). *Hole-filled seamless SRTM data V4*. International Centre for Tropical Agriculture (CIAT); http://srtm.csi.cgiar.org/.

Jaubert, J. (1999). *Chasseurs et artisans du Moustérien*. Paris: La Maison des Roches.

Higham, T., Douka, K., Wood, R., Bronk Ramsey, C., Brock, F., Basell, L., Camps, M., Arrizabalaga, A., Baena, J., Barroso-Ruíz, C., Bergman, C., Boitard, C., Boscato, P., Miguel Caparrós, M., Conard, N.J., Draily, C., Alain Froment, A., Galván, B., Gambassini, P., Garcia-Moreno, A., Grimaldi, S., Haesaerts, P., Holt, B., Iriarte-Chiapusso, M.-J., Jelinek, A., Jordá Pardo, J.-F., Maílo-Fernández, J.M., Marom, A., Maroto, J., Menéndez, M., Metz, L ., Morin, E., Moroni, A., Negrino, F., Panagopoulou, E., Peresani, M., Pirson, S., de la Rasilla, M., Riel-Salvatore, J., Ronchitelli, A., Santamaria, D., Semal, P., Slimak, L., Soler, J., Soler, N., Villaluenga, A., Pinhasi, R. and Jacobi, R. (2014). The Timing and Spatiotemporal Patterning of Neanderthal Disappearance. *Nature*, 512, pp. 306–309.

Leclerc, J. and Tarrète, J. (1988). Sépulture. In: A. Leroi-Gourhan., ed., *Dictionnaire de la Préhistoire*. Paris: Presses Universitaires de France (PUF), pp. 963–964.

Leroi-Gourhan, A. (1964). *Les religions de la Préhistoire*. Paris: Presses Universitaires Françaises (PUF).

Lévêque, F., Backer, A.M. and Guilbaud, M. (1993). *Context of a late Neandertal*. Madison, WI: Prehistory Press.

Martin, L. (1923). *Recherches sur l'Évolution du Moustérien dans le Gisement de La Quina. Tome 3. L'Homme fossile de La Quina. Archives de Morphologie générale et expériementale*, vol. 15. Paris: Doin.

Maureille, B. (2002a). A Lost Neanderthal Neonate Found. *Nature*, 419(6902), pp. 33–34.

Maureille, B. (2002b). La Redécouverte du Nouveau-Né Néandertalien Le Moustier 2. *Paleo*, 14, pp. 221–238.

Maureille, B., Mann, A., Beauval, C., Bordes, J.-G., Bourguignon, L., Costamagno, S., Couchoud, I., Fauquignon, J., Garralda, M.D., Geigl, E.-M., Grün, R., Guibert, P., Lacrampe-Cuyaubère, Fr., Laroulandie, V., Marquet, J.-Cl., Meignen, L., Mussini, C., Rendu, W., Royer, A., Seguin, G. and Texier, J.-P. (2010). Les Pradelles à Marillac-le-Franc (Charente). Fouilles 2001–2007: nouveaux résultats et synthèse. In: J. Buisson-Catil and J. Primault, eds., *Préhistoire entre Vienne et Charente. Hommes et Sociétés du Paléolithique, Association des publications chauvinoises, mémoire XXXVIII*. Chauvigny: L'Association des Publications Chauvinoises (APC), pp. 145–162.

Maureille, B., Gomez-Olivencia, A., Madelaine, S. and Holliday, T. (2015a). Nouveaux Restes Humains Provenant du Gisement de Regourdou (Montignac-sur-Vézère, Dordogne, France). *Paleo*, 26, pp. 117–138.

Maureille, B., Holliday, T., Royer, A., Pelletier, M., Madelaine, S., Lacrampe-Cuyaubère, F., Muth, X., Le Gueut, E., Couture-Veschambre, C., Gomez-Olivencia, A., Discamps, E., Texier, J.-P., Turq, A. and Lahaye, C. (2015b). Importance des Données de Terrain pour la Compréhension d'un Potentiel Dépôt Funéraire Moustérien: Le Cas du Squelette de Regourdou 1 (Montignac-sur-Vézère, Dordogne, France). *Paleo*, 26, pp. 139–159.

Mussini, C. (2011). *Les restes humains moustériens des Pradelles (Marillac-le-Franc, Charente, France): étude morphométrique et réflexions sur un aspect comportemental des Néandertaliens.* Unpublished Ph.D. thesis, Université de Bordeaux 1.

Mussini, C. and Maureille, B. (2012). Têtes coupées: données archéo-anthropologiques et lignée néandertalienne. In: B. Boulestin and D. Henry-Gambier, eds., *Crânes Trophées, Crânes d'Ancêtres et Autres Pratiques Autour de la Tête: Problèmes d'Interprétation en Archéologie.* Actes de la table ronde pluridisciplinaire, Musée national de Préhistoire, Les Eyzies-de-Tayac (Dordogne, France), 14–16 October 2010. Oxford: British Archaeological Reports (International Series) 2145, pp. 47–52.

Otte, M. (1993). *Préhistoire des religions.* Paris: Masson.

Pelletier, M., Royer, A., Holliday, T.W., Discamps, E., Madelaine, S. and Maureille, B. (2017). Rabbits in the Grave! Consequences of Bioturbation on the Neandertal 'Burial' at Regourdou (Montignac-sur-Vézère, Dordogne). *Journal of Human Evolution*, 110, pp. 1–17.

Pesce Delfino, V. and Vacca, E. (1993). An Archaic Human Skeleton Discovered at Altamura (Bari, Italy). *Rivista di Antropologia*, 71, pp. 249–257.

Pettitt, P. (2011). *The Palaeolithic origins of human burial.* New York: Routledge.

Peyrony, D. (1934). *La Ferrassie, Moustérien, Périgordien, Aurignacien.* Préhistoire, tome III, Paris: Librairie E. Leroux.

Pomeroy, E., Hunt, C.O., Reynolds, T., Asouti, E., Bennett, P., Bosch, M., Burke, A., Farr, L., Foley, R., French, C., Frumkin, A., Goldberg P., Hill, E., Kabukcu, C., Lahr, M.M., Lane, R., Marean, C., Maureille, B., Mutri, G., Miller, C.E., Mustafa, K.A., Nymark, A., Pettitt, P., Sala, N., Sandhathe, D., Stringer, C., Tilby, E. and Barker, G. (2020). Issues of Theory and Method in the Analysis of Paleolithic Mortuary Behaviour: A View from Shanidar Cave. *Evolutionary Anthropology*, 29, pp. 263–279.

Pomeroy, E., Lahr, M.M., Crivellaro, F., Farr, L., Reynolds, T., Hunt, C. and Barker, G. (2017). Newly Discovered Neanderthal Remains from Shanidar Cave, Iraqi Kurdistan, and Their Attribution to Shanidar 5. *Journal of Human Evolution*, 111, pp. 102–118.

Rathgeber, T. (2006). Fossile Menschenreste aus der Sesselfelsgrotte im unteren Altmühltal (Bayern, Bundesrepublik Deutschland). *Quartär*, 53/54, pp. 33–59.

Rendu, W., Beauval, C., Crèvecoeur, I., Bayle, P., Balzeau, A., Bismuth, T., Bourguignon, L., Delfour, G., Faivre, J.-P., Lacrampe-Cuyaubère, F., Muth, X., Pasty, S., Semal, P., Tavormina, C., Todisco, D., Turq, A. and Maureille, B. (2016). Let the Dead Speak… Comments on Dibble et al.'s Reply to 'Evidence Supporting an Intentional Neandertal Burial at La Chapelle aux Saints'. *Journal of Archaeological Science*, 69, pp. 12–20.

Rendu, W., Beauval, C., Crevecoeur, I., Bayle, P., Balzeau, A., Bismuth, T., Bourguignon, L., Delfour, G., Faivre, J.-P., Lavcrampe-Cuyaubère, F., Tavormica, C., Todisco, D., Turq, A. and Maureille, B. (2014). Evidence Supporting an Intentional Neandertal Burial at La Chapelle-aux-Saints. *Proceedings of the National Academy of Sciences of the USA*, 111(1), pp. 81–86.

Rosas, A., Martínez-Maza, C., Bastir M., García-Tabernero A., Lalueza-Fox, C., Huguet, R., Ortiz, J.E., Julia, R., Soler, V., de Torres, T., Martínez, E., Cañaveras, J.C., Sánchez-Moral, S., Cuezvak, S., Lariol, J., Santamaría, D., de la Rasilla, M. and Javier Fortea, J. (2006). Paleobiology and Comparative Morphology of a Late Neandertal Sample from El Sidrón, Asturias, Spain. *Proceedings of the National Academy of Sciences of the USA*, 103(51), pp. 19266–19271.

Rosas, A., Ríos, L., Estalrrich, A., Liversidge, H., García-Tabernero, A., Huguet, R., Cardoso, H., Bastir, M., Lalueza-Fox, C., de la Rasilla, M. and Dean, C. (2017). The Growth Pattern of Neandertals, Reconstructed from a Juvenile Skeleton from El Sidrón (Spain). *Science*, 367(5367), pp. 1282–1287.

Sala, N., Arsuaga, J.L., Pantoja-Pérez, A., Pablos, A., Martínez, I., Quam, R.M., Gómez-Olivencia, A., Bermúdez de Castro, J.M. and Carbonell, E. (2015). Lethal Interpersonal Violence in the Middle Pleistocene. *PLoS ONE* 10(5), e0126589.

Sandgathe, D.M., Dibble, H.L., Goldberg, P. and McPherron, S.P. (2011). The Roc de Marsal Neandertal Child: A Reassessment of its Status as a Deliberate Burial. *Journal of Human Evolution*, 61(3), pp. 243–253.

Santoja, M and Pérez-González, A. (2010). Mid-Pleistocene Acheulean Industrial Complex in the Iberian Peninsula. *Quaternary International*, 223, pp. 154–161.

Straus, W.L. Jr. and Cave, A.J.E. (1957). III. Pathology and Posture of Neandertal Man. *The Quarterly Review of Biology*, 32(4), pp. 348–363.

Testot, L. and Dortier, J.-F. (2005). *La religion, unité et diversité.* Auxerre: Sciences humaines éditions.

Thackeray, J.F. (2016). The Possibility of Lichen Growth on Bones of *Homo naledi*: Were They Exposed to Light? *South African Journal of Sciences*, 112(7/8), Art.a0167.

Trinkaus, E. (1985). Pathology and Posture of the La Chapelle-Aux-Saints Neandertal. *American Journal of Physical Anthropology*, 67, pp. 19–41.

Tuffreau, A. and Antoine P. (1995). The earliest occupation of Europe: Continental Northwestern Europe. In: W. Roebroeks and T. van Kolfschoten, eds., *The earliest occupation of Europe*. Leiden: University of Leiden, Publications of the Institute of Prehistory, pp. 147–163.

Val, A. (2013). *A 3D approach to understand the taphonomy of the early hominins from the Plio-Pleistocene cave site of Malapa*. Unpublished PhD Thesis, University of the Witwatersrand, Johannesburg.

Val, A. (2016). Deliberate Body Disposal by Hominins in the Dinaledi Chamber, Cradle of Humankind, South Africa? *Journal of Human Evolution*, 96, pp. 145–148.

Vandermeersch, B. (1976). Les sépultures néandertaliennes. In: H. de Lumley, ed., *La Préhistoire française, t. 1.* Paris: Éditions du Centre National de al Recherche Scientifique (CNRS), pp. 725–727.

Vandermeersch, B. (1993). Was the Saint-Césaire discovery a burial? In: F. Lévêque, A.M. Backer and M. Guilbaud, eds., *Context of a late Neandertal*. Madison: Prehistory Press (Monographs in World Archaeology), pp. 129–131.

Vandermeersch, B. (1995). Le problème des premières sépultures. In: J.-P. Cros and J.-M. Large, eds., *La mort, passé, présent, conditionnel*, Groupe Vendéen d'Etudes Préhistoriques (GVEP). La Roche-sur-Yonne, pp. 17–23.

Vandermeersch, B., Cleyet-Merle, J.-J., Jaubert, J., Maureille, B. and Turq, A., eds. (2008). *Première humanité, gestes funéraires des Néandertaliens*. Paris: Réunion des Musées Nationaux.

Walker, M.J., Ortega, J., Parmová, K., López, M.V. and Trinkaus, E. (2011). Morphology, Body Proportions, and Postcranial Hypertrophy of a Female Neandertal from the Sima de las Palomas, Southeastern Spain. *Proceedings of the National Academy of Sciences of the USA*, 108(25), pp. 10087–10091.

9

BEYOND THE FORMAL ANALYSIS OF FUNERARY PRACTICES?

Archaeothanatology as a reflexive tool for considering the role of the dead amongst the living. A Natufian case study

Fanny Bocquentin

Translated from the orginal French by Christopher J. Knüsel

ArScAn, Archéologies et Sciences de l'Antiquité, Équipe Ethnologie Préhistorique, Laboratoire Cogitamus, Paris, France UMR 7041, CNRS-Université Paris Nanterre. Nanterre, France

Introduction

The term 'archaeothanatology' has many accepted meanings (cf. Knüsel and Schotsmans, Introduction, this volume; Knüsel, Gerdau-Radonić and Schotsmans, Chapter 34, this volume). In this chapter, the word is employed in a restrictive manner with respect to that proposed by the originators of the term (Boulestin and Duday, 2005), who intended it to mean the archaeology of death in all its dimensions, similar to Thomas (1975) who considered 'anthropothanatology' as the disciplinary study of death in all its dimensions. Here, it is used to indicate an excavation protocol for the contextualised study of unearthed human remains. The reading of tapho-nomic processes acts as an intellectual time machine that reveals the archaeological remains in their initial state, just after deposition. The reconstruction of the funerary space, of the original space occupied by the corpse, and of ephemeral elements that did not preserve, permits insight into appearance of the original deposit, including disposition of the inhumed individual, the potential wrappings of the corpse and of burial containers. A typology of funerary treatments that aids in the identification of archaeological cultures can thus be defined. The synthesis of these treatments with biological data from the skeletal remains permits insights into the structuring principles of past societies.

Through consideration of the spatial relationships between the different constituents of the grave, the cadaver, the structure of the grave, and the grave inclusions and, by extension, the limits of the grave with respect to the rest of the site, archaeothanatology provides the means to address even bigger research questions. Beyond the reconstruction of the decomposition

DOI: 10.4324/9781351030625-12

environment, the spatial relationships within the grave facilitate the reconstruction of the gestural dynamics at the time of the deposition of the corpse-or of skeletal remains-and for a period of time afterwards in the form of disturbances of the remains, retrieval and/or gathering of elements, for example. These observations lead, in addition, to addressing questions of the extent of the preparations of the corpse prior to its final deposition. Thus, a technical reading of the funerary remains reveals the steps taken to process the remains and establishes their sequence as a succession of interactions (Thevenet *et al.*, 2014). The identification and analysis of this funerary *chaîne opératoire* permits not only the reconstruction of the temporal dynamics of the funerary practices but also serves as a means to unlock the technical, social and ritual aspects that characterise them (e.g. Pereira, 2013; Valentin *et al.*, 2014). The term *chaîne opératoire*, borrowed from the writings of André Leroi-Gourhan (1964) with regard to technical systems, returns to the notion of a materially transformative process – here of the cadaver – which is subjected to an inevitable biological transformation (decomposition) that the society asserts mastery over though ritual and a re-affirmation of its collective sustainability (Hertz, 1907).

A re-distribution of social roles through the performance of funerary rites

A rite is defined as the enactment of coded actions embedded in a collective ritual context where each actor has a more or less clearly defined role. Rituals arouse collective emotions and most often result in a change of status for one or more protagonists, an individual or a group of individuals (e.g. Le Roux, 2018). On the occasion of a death, neither the survivors, nor the dead can escape this rule. Funerary ritual is defined as a rite of passage, presenting a universal tertiary structure: separation from the group ('*séparation*'), a liminal period ('*marge*'), and re-integration ('*intégration*') into another group (Hertz, 1907; van Gennep, 1909; Thomas, 1996). In addition to the material management of the corpse and the care of the bereaved, it is also a question of attributing a new status to the deceased within the community of the dead. If death breaks social bonds, then ritual restores them. The liminal period can be of variable duration, sometimes relating to the time necessary for the decomposition of the corpse of the dead (Hertz, 1907; Thomas 1980, 1996), but it also acknowledges a mental and emotional necessity: the progressive acceptance by the living of the separation from the dead individual (Hertz, 1907). This is also a period of danger during which the corpse disintegrates, with the soul of the deceased wandering and the survivors in disarray.

Once this period of instability has passed, the deceased joins the community of the dead and a new status is assigned to them (the deceased) according to their social value – based on lineage, age, sex, attributes and skills – to collective beliefs and circumstances of death. This status may depend in some societies on the extent of active participation of the deceased person among the survivors, and their eventual transformation into an 'ancestor'. 'The deceased is reclaimed as a protective ancestor or simply as a model or symbol of the cohesion of the group, completing the victory of life over death' ('*La récupération du défunt comme ancêtre protecteur ou simplement comme modèle ou symbole de la cohésion du groupe, parachève la victoire de la vie sur la mort*') (Thomas, 1996: 127, translated by CJK). Funerals are therefore one of the most important social events for the individual as well as for the group (Hertz, 1907). 'The group requires activities that hold the attention of its members, who direct their imaginations in a definite manner that recalls to all involved the beliefs of the group. But the central figure upon which collective activity will be focused is the body of the deceased that acts as a focus for the funerary rites after death' ('*Il faut au groupe des actes qui fixent l'attention de ses membres, qui orientent leur imagination dans un sens défini, qui suggèrent à tous les croyances. Or la matière sur laquelle s'exercera après la mort l'activité collective, qui servira l'objet aux rites, c'est naturellement le corps même du défunt*' (Hertz, 1928 [1907]: 75, translated by CJK). In a small community where each individual has multiple responsibilities, the death of a member makes them particularly vulnerable and the redistribution of roles can be complex. This is why funerary rituals are particularly elaborate and significant (Thomas, 1996).

Although the theatricality may escape the archaeologist in great measure, two essential elements of the rites remain accessible: the surviving material remains, of which the human remains form a part, and their spatial positions relative to one another. Within the space of the grave but also within the occupied settlement, and even more broadly, within the anthropised landscape, the place and the position of the deceased are not random. The location of the corpse in the grave and the position of the grave in the landscape makes it possible to address the place of the dead (Testart, 2004) but also the part played by the dead in society (Bloch, 1971) in the same way that dynamic studies of spatial relationships make it possible to address social inferences generally (Leroi-Gourhan, 1964). The often fundamental part played by the dead in a society is a relatively familiar subject to historians, notably medievalists (references in Gordon and Marshall 2000), and to anthropologists (e.g. Berthod, 2005; Baudry, 2006; Delaplace, 2008). However, archaeologists rarely address the role of the dead in past societies. It must be recognised that not all sites lend themselves equally well to this question. The absence of remains (the rarity of burials in the Palaeolithic, for example), and the physical separation of the world of the dead from that of the living (use of cemeteries, chamber tombs and caves away from settlements) in many chronocultural contexts do not lend themselves easily to archaeological investigations of such questions. Yet the life force, the power of protection or disturbances attributed to the dead by survivors are ubiquitous in all societies and permit interrogation of the moving border that separates the worlds of the living and the dead. 'Underpinning such beliefs and practices were anxieties about negotiating and even identifying the boundary between life and death itself, reminding us that the categories of "the living" and "the dead" are themselves less fixed and more fluid than we are accustomed to expect' (Gordon and Marshall, 2000: 7).

The Near East: fertile ground for consideration

Especially in Near Eastern prehistoric research, upon which this contribution draws, the question of the relationship between the living and the dead is a salient research question. In the past, scientific discourse concentrated – as it still does today – on the retrieval, treatment and embellishment of crania (and sometimes whole skulls) that were over-modelled with plaster, painted, and modified in the prehistoric past. These practices appear for the first time at the end of the Epipalaeolithic Natufian period (13 000–9600 cal BC), and continue throughout the pre-ceramic Neolithic (9600–6400 cal BC). Plastered crania, which appear in the middle and late PPNB in the southern Levant (8200–7200 cal BC) and then re-appear in Anatolia in Late Neolithic or Pottery Neolithic contexts (6300–5000 cal BC), are remarkable pieces that have not failed to focus the attention of researchers. Although reformulated, nuanced and still debated (e.g. Wright, 1988; Schmandt-Besserat, 2002; Verhoeven, 2002; Bonogofsky, 2006; Testart, 2008), the existence of ancestor worship in the Neolithic based on these transformed crania (Kenyon, 1957) has been broadly supported more recently (e.g. Stordeur and Khawam, 2007; Fletcher, Pearson and Ambers, 2008; Benz, 2010a; Bocquentin, 2013; Khawam, 2014; Slon *et al.*, 2014).

Among the most cited articles on this particular kind of treatment of crania, Kuijt (2008) highlights two phases of this ritual practice. First, the removal of the cranium, which affects the integrity of the deceased, whose body and head are therefore dissociated. The final act of re-burial, then, often associates several crania in a collective deposit. Thus, final collection and deposition would be part of the same symbolic system: breaking up the individual to build collective identity in an ever-regenerated life cycle. A large number of researchers place emphasis on the ceremonial power of this ritual for maintaining, or even strengthening, community cohesion from the end of the Epi-palaeolithic, a period that experienced a series of environmental, economic and social upheavals (e.g. Kuijt, 1996; Goring-Morris and Kuijt, 2000; Benz, 2010a, 2010b; Goring-Morris and Belfer-Cohen, 2013). Thus, the majority of deposits of crania would come from burials of community members after decomposition of the body. This multi-stage treatment, confirmed by the numerous acephalic skeletons found (Cornwall, 1956a; Bocquentin, Molist and Milevski, 2016), echoes the process of accession to ancestor status frequently described by sociologists, primarily by Hertz (1907). This does not exclude other more unusual cranial acquisition and treatment *chaînes opératoires*, previously suggested (Schmandt-Besserat, 2002; Testart, 2008), or clearly identified (Santana *et al.*, 2012; Bocquentin, 2013; Boz and Hager, 2013; Bocquentin, Molist and Milevski, 2016; Haddow and Knüsel, 2017). These, although a minority according to research to date, testify to the existence of other paths to ancestralisation, other than through crania collected from burials, in addition to other purposes for such practices and other potential eschatological destinies for the dead.

The removal of skulls and their subsequent treatment are not the only testaments to the profound changes that took place in the relationship between the living and the dead. It is also important to consider the great number of individuals in primary burials that had been left intact, a group which represents about 67% of the total Near Eastern burial sample (Bocquentin, Molist and Milevski, 2016). The observation of contextual, funerary and biological evidence suggests that the dead were not as passive as they may appear. From the beginning of the Natufian, when a fully sedentary lifestyle is clearly attested for some communities, the living and dead coexisted in the same space. From a few dozen burials known at the beginning of the Epi-palaeolithic, several hundred individuals were buried in these settlements in the Natufian. It is commonly accepted that the dead bear witness to a new attachment to territory (e.g. Henry, 1985; Belfer-Cohen, 1988; Perrot *et al.*, 1988; Bar-Yosef and Belfer-Cohen, 2002), and reflect a new relationship to space and to the natural world, now split between the sedentary village and the world outside it (Valla, 1999). Perhaps above all, though, these more numerous burials provide evidence of a profoundly changed relationship with the dead and the remains of the dead. Although there is early evidence of funerary rituals for both anatomically modern humans and Neandertals that dates to over 100 000 years ago (e.g. Belfer-Cohen and Hovers, 1992; Rendu *et al.*, 2014), prior to the Natufian period, burials are extremely rare throughout the world. Burial was likely an exceptional event and other funerary treatments would have predominated, for example immersion in water or surface deposition that leaves no trace. In many respects, a burial provides a symbolic and material place for the dead that makes them stand out: integrity *versus* fragmentation of the body; grouping together in one place *versus* dispersal of the dead; permanence *versus* transience of the remains. Thus, as the treatment of the corpse changes, there are strong indications that the status of the dead within society was also changing. A perfectly contextualised archaeology of death, aided by a detailed archaeothanatological approach makes it possible to better appreciate this status and the social place occupied by the deceased in past societies.

The sedentarisation of the dead

The reason for the increased number of burials in the Natufian may seem obvious – occupation of sites being longer, deaths in the same place were more numerous and burials were thus more frequent. But this is not only about that: a palpable planning of the space where the living and the dead would cohabit for the longer term was established. Thus, a typical plan of a

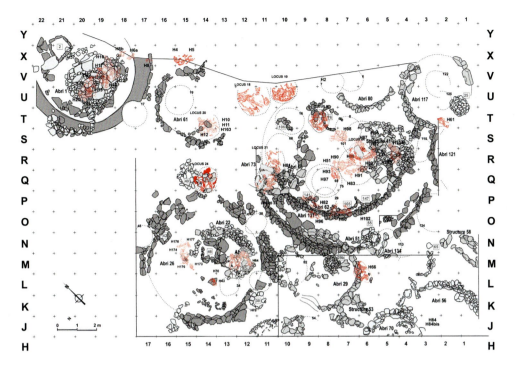

Figure 9.1   Plan of the Early and Late period phases of the Natufian site of 'Ain Mallaha/Eynan, Israel. Note the palimpsest of burials (in red) and shelters ('abri' on the plan) that can give an impression of a 'cemetery' but which in fact is the result of various interactions and stratigraphic relations between the living and the dead over a long period of time (modified after Bocquentin, 2003).

Natufian settlement, like that of 'Ain Mallaha/Eynan (Israel), which was occupied over three phases (Figure 9.1), shows a palimpsest of burials and domestic structures. Cases of strict contemporaneity are rare and, when it does occur, it concerns mainly the burial of very young children (Perrot *et al.*, 1988; Valla *et al.*, 2007). In the Early Natufian (13 000–11 600 cal BC), burials sometimes follow the establishment of habitations, dug into their abandoned floors but more frequently they precede them (Valla and Bocquentin, 2008). Thus, on several sites, the graves are the earliest evidence of habitation (Bar-Yosef and Goren, 1973; Goring-Morris and Kuijt, 2000; Bocquentin, 2003, 2018; Valla and Bocquentin, 2008; Edwards *et al.*, 2018), which suggests that they were a pre-requisite for the establishment of a group camp on virgin soil. In addition, the establishment of houses above burials is not random; they are oriented in the same cardinal directions, with the deceased placed in the centre of the future inhabited space and, in the case of semi-circular structures, near the entrance (Valla and Bocquentin, 2008). Nothing, therefore, appears to be left to chance and, more than demonstrating a simple attachment to territory, the burials serve as to anchor the village in a specific spatio-symbolic system. This inter-stratification of floors and burials gives the strong impression that living and dead participated together in the structuring of the inhabited space and in the continuity of occupation. All of them are actors in an incipient sedentarisation that is continuously re-enforced.

Over time, this close connection between the living and the dead changes. During the Late Natufian (11 600–9600 cal BC), dedicated funerary spaces appear, sometimes lasting long enough to be considered the earliest cemeteries (cf. discussion in Bocquentin 2003: 345–346).

The burials are placed outside the house at a short distance from it (Perrot *et al.*, 1988; Noy, 1989). Some caves also seem to have been used solely for funerary activities (Belfer-Cohen, 1988; Grosman, Munro and Belfer-Cohen, 2008; Nadel *et al.*, 2013; Yeshurun, Bar-Oz and Nadel, 2013). As a consequence, this relative isolation of the dead completely alters the landscape; graves once integral to, and sequestered within the inhabited space, became visible to the living and also to neighbouring communities. Erected stones and deeply engraved grinding stones (or mortars) mark the funerary space, a place that will never be re-investigated by the living. The relationship to the corpse also changes; on some sites planned cranial retrieval practices seem to have become the norm (Belfer-Cohen, 1988; Bocquentin, Molist and Milevski, 2016); elsewhere, successive burial depositions in the same structure are followed by subsequent manipulation and re-organisation of remains (Bocquentin, 2003). Groupings of individuals in graves changed as well, many of which were family-related in the Early Natufian according to discrete trait frequency and distribution based on a pioneering study on a single trait (Smith, 1973) and firmly confirmed by a more comprehensive study of 147 traits (Bocquentin, 2003: 378–407). For the Late Natufian, such family clusters could not be identified but age-at-death, on the contrary, seems to have been, in some sites, a criterion for grouping (Bocquentin, 2003: 263–265). The graves of the Late Natufian are therefore characterised by their visibility, their accessibility over a lengthy period of time, as well as by their grouping. The dead are spatially distanced from the living but are re-visited, manipulated, and moved to form a collective body. It is as if the physical distancing of the deceased was compensated for by the emergence of the treatment of skeletonised remains for a certain period of time. It is interesting to note that this disruption of the relationship with the dead occurs in a context of climatic deterioration (the Younger Dryas) during which a re-organisation of the settlement pattern takes place, and a return to greater mobility for some groups cannot be excluded (e.g. Perrot *et al.*, 1988; Bar-Yosef and Belfer-Cohen, 1992; Weissbrod *et al.*, 2017). This configuration marks a break in a rather linear process since, at the end of the Late Natufian (sometimes called the Final Natufian), houses and burials are again superimposed (Valla *et al.*, 2010; Grosman *et al.*, 2016), alternating at a more and more rapid pace (Bocquentin, 2007, 2012; Bocquentin, Cabellos and Samuelian, 2013).

Archaeothanatology: from micro-history to a belief system

Because of its precise and detailed recording methods, its capacity to reconstruct the appearance of the original funerary space and identify post-depositional processes, archaeothanatology offers an unprecedented research avenue to address precisely the physical place occupied by the corpse and through it, the social role the dead played in the eyes of survivors after the completion of the funerary rituals. In the Natufian context, the majority of burials were excavated before the 1980s and thus did not benefit from a recording method specifically adapted to the recognition of funerary practices. Even today, the Near East, and more particularly the southern Levant, remains a place where archaeothanatology is not applied, despite the occasional efforts of some archaeo-anthropologists trained in this discipline. This resistance, which is still very much alive today, can be explained in part by the fact that biological anthropology and funerary archaeology have remained areas treated completely independently of one another in this region. Archaeothanatology, a discipline that places the skeleton back at the heart of the bio-cultural entanglement, thus finds little resonance. It is quite surprising when one recalls excavations directed by Kathleen Kenyon at the site of Tell-el-Sultan (1952–1958), ancient Jericho, where Ian W. Cornwall undertook exceptionally detailed recording of skeletons *in situ* well ahead of his time, successively uncovering and recording each bone layer, with notes on the orientation of bones upon exposure, their anatomical relationships, and joint disarticulations (Cornwall, 1956a; Bocquentin and Wagemakers, 2014). He justified use of these excavation techniques not only for the proper understanding of funerary practices but also to facilitate more effective biological analysis (Cornwall, 1956b). Even if his pioneering work was not applied afterwards, the development of 'field anthropology' (*anthropologie de terrain*) in France from the 1970s, in parallel with the emergence of anthropologically contextualised approaches in the United States, showed how cultural as well as biological aspects but, above all, the interactions between them, benefited from such an approach.

In a Natufian context, archaeothanatology has an additional advantage – it aids to unravel the complex stratigraphy in which semi-buried houses, burials, pits and soil disturbances of all kinds become intermingled on sites where the cuts of pits are often not visible (Valla and Bocquentin, 2008). Chrono-stratigraphic reading and the reconstruction of the sequence of events, however, are crucial for understanding the relationship between burials and settlements and, by extension, between the dead and the living. The combination of archaeothanatology with the appropriate excavation techniques of occupation floors permitted a closer look at these relationships at the site of 'Ain Mallaha/Eynan (Valla *et al.*, 1999, 2001, 2004, 2007; Valla and Bocquentin, 2008). For instance, the site provides an edifying case of funerary deposition between two floors of superimposed occupations (Bocquentin, Cabellos and Samuelian, 2013) which can now be better understood. Building 203 contains the burial of a mature or elderly female buried on her back with her flexed knees above her chest (H156: Figure 9.2). The careful removal of the upper (L203a) and lower (L203c) levels of the floor, revealed the following observations: the corpse was placed on the lower-most surface of the floor, without digging a pit, but directly lying on a fireplace (L234), part of juxtaposed fire installations bearing witness to a large open area of pyrotechnic activity (Figure 9.3). The upper floor (L203a) located just 10 cm above the first floor (L203c) does not show evidence of either disturbance, but it is clearly indicated by numerous flint debris scatters and large faunal remains strewn across the level following the slope of the structure (Samuelian, 2019). The intermediate level (L203b), which contains the grave, is a fill comprised of pebbles brought to the site and into which two post-holes (L205 and L213) had been dug into the floor beneath (L203c). At the same time the semi-circular wall that circumscribes the structure was also enhanced by a second course of stones. Lastly, the burial pit of a young child (H167) had been excavated into this fill before the upper floor had been added (Valla *et al.*, 2001; Samuelian, 2019). For this part, the archaeothanatological analysis of the adult burial H156 reveals other elements of the sequence (Valla *et al.*, 2001: 85–88; Bocquentin, Cabellos and Samuelian, 2013). Based on observations of preserved and disarticulated joints, and owing to a 'wall effect' ('*effet de paroi*') and 'constraint effect' ('*effet de contrainte*') it was concluded that this individual was deposited as a corpse as a primary burial within a rigid rectangular container. The container had been re-opened after decomposition had occurred. On this occasion, the right tibia and fibula, the upper-most elements in the deposit, were removed. The right femur had been displaced to the left upper corner of the grave and the cranium had been rotated onto its lateral side. These actions must have been performed while the container was still unfilled with sediment; all of these manipulations seem to have been performed to reduce the space occupied by the remains in order to level off the fill and prepare the new occupation floor (Bocquentin, Cabellos and Samuelian, 2013). It is possible that the cranial vault was crushed at the same time, unless the crushing of the cranium resulted from trampling related to the occupation above it. In addition, the analysis of the spatial distribution of all the material above the grave, lying on the upper floor, provides one last insight. The density of material comprised of tools and waste were not random and indicate a preserved occupation floor, which had been rapidly buried after the abandonment of the structure. Sleeping areas devoid of material and

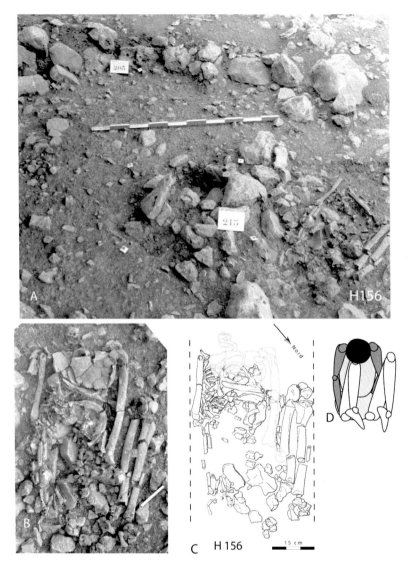

Figure 9.2 Plan and photographs of skeleton H156, Final Natufian, 'Ain Mallaha/Eynan, Israel.
A: skeleton H156 (adult female) being excavated lying next to posthole 213, background: wall 203;
B: exposure of the skeleton; C: Drawing of the skeleton: the bones in light grey (cranium and right femur) are those which had been displaced after the decay process; D: schematic initial position of the corpse (modified after Bocquentin, Cabellos and Samuelian, 2013; Photograph: F. Valla).

under the sheltered part of the structure on one side, and several activity areas with coherent accumulations of material on the other side could be identified. The most obvious activity, flint-knapping, was carried out from two sitting places across from one another that are located just above the burial (Figure 9.3) (Samuelian, 2019).

Why is this information of interest to funerary archaeology? It is the sequence of events that is remarkable: the complete restructuring of the space that is contemporary with the funerary deposition. The death of this adult female is immediately followed by the abandonment of the

Floor 203a

Phase 203b

Floor 203c

Figure 9.3 Superimposed plans of structure 203 at 'Ain Mallaha/Eynan, Israel, representing the three sequences of occupation levels in the same place (redrawing: M. Ballinger after Samuelian, 2019). The lower-most level (203c) is characterised by juxtaposed fire installations bearing witness to a large open area of pyrotechnic activity. Right above one of the hearths (L234), H156 was placed within a coffin. A complete restructuring of the space occurred during phase 203b contemporary with the funerary deposition that resulted from the building of a shelter (postholes 205 and 213). The shelter would have been inhabited by the living (floor 203a) only after decay of the corpse had occurred, as demonstrated by archaeothanatological evidence. Flint-knapping was then performed directly above the grave (data from Samuelian, 2019).

pyrotechnic activity open area and the erection of an awning typical of Natufian shelters with their post-holes and semi-circular walls. The funerary container was placed against one of the post-holes, at what would become the threshold of the future house. Then, a few weeks or months later, after the corpse had decomposed but the funerary container was still sealed, the skeleton was purposely partly disarticulated to reduce the height of the grave. Whether or not this space reduction was also related to a specific funerary rite cannot be confirmed based on this evidence. Levelling of this area was immediately[1] followed by the occupation of the structure with major domestic activities taking place just above the skeleton. This micro-chronological sequence makes it possible to refute any potential coincidence or *ad hoc* behaviours. Her death and the funerary ritual that followed, gave this female a new status but it also caused a change in function of this part of the village. The duration of the time necessary for decomposition of the corpse provided an intermediate period when the configuration of the new space had already occurred but had not yet been re-occupied by the living. Interestingly, it echoes the liminal period described by sociologists (e.g. Hertz, 1907; van Gennep, 1909; Thomas, 1996). The positioning of the burial at the threshold between the covered and open parts of the shelter is not insignificant; it materialises an area of passage perhaps symbolising the passing from one world to another, involving instability and danger. Thus, the burial served as a benchmark. This seems to be a testament to a system of thought in which the living and dead are indissociable and heavily entangled. It is interesting to note that it is the burial of a female that determines the location of an activity, flint-knapping, considered a male activity for symbolic reasons among many sub-contemporary groups (e.g. Testart, 2014). This hypothetical opposition is one that other cases may support or refute in the future. The fact remains, however, that this evidence provides the impression that the deceased dictated the re-organisation of daily activities, at the moment of her death but also after her decomposition.

Status and the agency of the dead: formulation of an untapped discourse

The involvement of the dead in the world of the living among the Natufians is not only confined to the structuring and re-structuring of settlements; their role is multiple (Bocquentin, 2018). Just as the place of burial is not random, the deposition of the corpse and the form of the burial is carefully thought out. The arrangement of the body, the limbs, the head, the wearing of adornments, the objects included (i.e. in the sense of placed, not worn) in the funerary space form a set of indicators of the identity and the social role that the deceased occupied (e.g. Belfer-Cohen, 1995; Byrd and Monahan, 1995; Bocquentin, 2003; Grosman, Munro and Belfer-Cohen, 2008; Byrd and Rosenthal, 2016). But it is not only this. The deceased, at the centre of the ceremony, also partakes in the identity of the group, whether this identity is common to all Natufians or whether it is specific to a single community only (e.g. Bocquentin, 2003; Bocquentin *et al.*, 2010; Goring-Morris and Belfer-Cohen 2013; Grosman and Munro, 2016).

It also supports a much more complex discourse which seems to have been narrated by the funerary rites and which is materialised through a complex staging of the various elements of the burial. In a convincing way, Valla (1999, 2012) invokes the narration of a myth of the relations between humans and nature, specifically applied to an exceptionally complex burial that he excavated on the terrace of Hayonim Cave (Israel). The meticulous examination of the arrangement of the various actors (humans, dogs, remains of gazelles and turtles, and blocks of stone), their symmetrical or oppositional arrangement, and the symbolism of the numbers in which they partook led Valla to conclude that this narrative was about the dichotomy between the wild world and the world of humanity and the specific place of the dog, which had only recently become part of the latter. The rigorous description of the remains, accompanied by detailed iconography, is based – not coincidently – on fieldwork conducted by an anthropologist trained in archaeothanatology (Valla, Le Mort and Plisson, 1991).

---

1 On an archaeological time-scale, it could have been a few days or a few weeks, but in any case too little time for the structures to be eroded or buried. The various stratigraphic units are in direct contact. The superior surface of cranium H156 is flush with the base of the floor L203a.

Figure 9.4 Four of the individuals discovered in grave H28-32 at the Early Natufian site of El Wad, Mount Carmel, Israel. Note the perpendicular orientation of the juvenile skeleton on the lower right-hand side of the photograph associated with bone pendants (Image courtesy: D.A.E. Garrod archival collection (2018001/53), Musée d'Archéologie National (MAN), Saint-Germain-en-Laye, France).

Such descriptive detail is rare, yet complex burials of this type are not, especially in the Early phase of the Natufian. For example, two multiple burials at El Wad (Israel) excavated in the 1930s under the direction of Garrod provide a glimpse of extraordinary collective narratives. The study of the osteological collection in parallel with the examination of the field record archives – and an archaeothanatological reading of the photographs of the site (Bocquentin, 2003) – permits the interpretation to go beyond a succinct description of 'fragmentary skeletons, packed together in some confusion' (Garrod and Bate, 1937: 18). In the first grave, the MNI consists of eight individuals (six adults, a teenager and a child). The only photograph (Figure 9.4) permits recognition of four individuals, of which three are placed side-by-side in various positions (*procubitus*, *decubitus* lateral) and the fourth perpendicular to the first three. The latter is the child, the only individual who wears an item of personal adornment. Was this individual more valued than the others? The location of this child on the edge of the burial seems to cast doubt on this hypothesis. The full articulation of the joints of these four individuals make the hypothesis of a simultaneous deposition more likely. Four (or eight) simultaneous deaths (due to catastrophic or accidental circumstances) in a small Natufian community must have represented an unusual crisis. Perhaps it is the narrative of this event that is staged? Whatever the case, elements of a discourse observed elsewhere in Natufian contexts (a single bejewelled individual buried among several other unadorned individuals (cf. Belfer-Cohen, 1995) and the perpendicular arrangement of bodies (Bocquentin, 2003; Valla, 2012) suggest that the practice transcends this particular event and has a still wider meaning.

The osteological remains of the second burial have not been identified in the collection today (Bocquentin, 2003). According to Garrod, there were seven individuals superimposed on two levels, those of the higher level being arranged in a circle (Garrod and Bate, 1937). One of them had an elaborate headdress. The photograph makes it possible to identify at least four articulated skeletons carefully arranged around a vertically broken half-mortar. In this particular case, the mortar does not seem to have been a simple accompaniment. Placed in the centre of the grave, it gives the impression of being the focus (Bocquentin, 2014). The associated dead are not centrally placed, and their place in the burial is shared and peripheral. What was their role? Did they serve a purpose or, rather, represent a quest for new landmarks that sedentarisation imposes on the living? These last two examples do not permit further interpretation due to the lack of an excavation adapted to recording of even the most tenuous material clues of these prehistoric discourses. However, they do help to highlight the complexity of Natufian funerary ritual, and the already crucial place occupied by the dead in these hunter-gatherer societies before the advent of the Neolithic. In fact, as long as the excavation has been properly carried out, a closer look at each individual burial or several grouped Natufian burials indicates a unique story of the deceased, of a ceremony, of a society, and of a destiny to come.

Another case study, the so called burial of *the shaman* is one of the most spectacular examples from the Natufian period, based on the amount of material associated with the burial (Grosman *et al.*, 2008). Articulated elements of wild animals and one human foot were deposited in the grave in close proximity to the dead disabled female. Due to adequate recording, the authors propose a reconstruction of the sequence of preparation, filling and covering of the burial and, through it, a reconstruction of the funerary ceremony and the feast that characterised it (Grosman and Munro, 2016). This effort to reconstruct the *chaîne opératoire* of an exceptional event is remarkable. It highlights the preparations made for the funeral, the particulars of the funerary banquet, the number of guests, while emphasising the major social role played by the funerary ceremony (cf. Hayden, 2009; Yeshurun, Bar-Oz and Nadel, 2013). Yet, this discourse centred on archaeological material culture detracts somewhat from the central place occupied by the deceased at the ceremony. The spatial arrangement of the grave, likely codified in its smallest details, may also be an unexpected source by which to address the social role (potential and plausible) of a shaman and its significance as represented through the burial rite. Investigating the initial position of the corpse and its exact spatial and temporal relationship with all the other elements could provide a chain of deductions, reconstructing the narrative evoked by the burial and celebrated at the ritual feast.

Putting everything together: verticalisation of the Natufian world?

As in the Neolithic, not all of the dead could have had the same significance in the Natufian period. Those who have been exhumed so far can in no way represent the entire population; they have been selected. This selection is evident through age and sex composition of the sample collected thus far, which in no way reflects a natural population profile (see detailed discussion in Bocquentin, 2003: 284–305). The age-specific mortality and the sex ratios show a substantial deficit of females and children who died before the age of five years of age. They are not represented in the expected proportions in relation to the number of adult men (who themselves might also have been selected). The numbers of those selected is not constant through time. Each place and time period corresponds to selection for which sex and age-at-death are not the only determinants (Bocquentin, 2003, 2007). Could they have been linked to a privileged birth status, a specific position in a lineage, a special function in society, to the circumstances of death? It would be necessary to get access to the whole population to better identify the reasons a deceased person was buried in the settlement or, on the contrary, to have been excluded from it. Because discoveries of isolated or grouped Natufian burials not directly related to a settlement have not been made to date (excluding the cemeteries of the Late Natufian mentioned above), it must be assumed that this missing portion of the population may not have been buried. A more traditional mode of funerary treatment, which leaves no trace, such as surface deposition of bodies, may have been practiced.

The present Natufian sample is therefore the result of a palimpsest of individuals selected to be buried in settlements based on criteria that are largely elusive. They testify to only a fraction, perhaps a minority, from a funerary programme where the care of the body and the eschatological destiny of the deceased varied. Moreover, the funerary treatments received by that part of the community selected to be buried near the living are also diverse and elicit complex bio-socio-cultural inferences. Was ancestor worship already in place in the Natufian period? If ancestors are defined in the anthropological sense as those who had authority and can affect the living (e.g. Krauskopff, 2007), it is on a case-by-case basis that the issue must be debated. The deceased found in a circle around the mortar at El Wad may well have had only a passive role. On the other hand, the female buried in structure 203 in Mallaha might have had authority. At least it seems that her death served as a 'lever for action' (Papadaniel, 2018: 372) through the condemnation of an activity area and the development of a dwelling in which part of production took place exactly above the burial location.' Other Natufian burials, described elsewhere, placed above similarly abandoned structures, often related to fires (Bocquentin, 2003: 181; Valla *et al.*, 2001, 2004). Thus, the sedentary dead occupy space in a non-random way. The village is not a simple resting place for a selected category of the deceased; it is a space in which they hold a very specific post-mortem function. The deceased serves as a means to facilitate discourse, a guarantor of social order, and a bearer of cultural identity – founding, transforming and perpetuating the inhabited space. The deceased forms an essential reference point in a key historical period in which human societies were re-positioning themselves in relation to their environment and belief systems.

The beginnings of the repeated practice of burial first appears in a Geometric Kebaran context (*circa* 15–13 000 cal BC) but, at a very late stage, nearly contemporaneous with the emergence of the Natufian (Maher *et al.*, 2011). Today, only speculation on the reasons for this new appropriation of the dead through their sedentarisation can be offered. The complexity of the funerary practices testifies to the importance and the diversity of the roles of the dead from the earliest Natufian. They provide insight into the funerary treatments and through them, more broadly, into the cognitive and social construction of Natufian identities and societies. Funerary ritual plays a key role in the rooting of communities not only to a particular geographic place but even more so in the context of a new materiality, duration, and stability. The Natufians consciously or not, and not unlike the nomadic peoples who preceded them, put in place an economy of accumulation by settling down. Their houses were perennial, regularly renovated and were occupied by several successive generations, sometimes maintaining a remarkably identical structuring of the inner space (Valla 1988, 1991). Some heavy tools, such as deeply ground mortars, passed from one generation to another. Could the dead be participating in this same sort of dynamism: collect, preserve, accumulate, protect, and transmit? Even more than a question of territoriality, it is the rooting in a new materiality that is palpable: that of the *Mantrace* (Galinon-Mélénec, 2011), a humanly driven process which does not cease to perpetuate their habitat and their production, to anthropise their immediate environment, to control and accumulate their resources and assets. In this context, the development of the phenomenon of burial may appear to be a desire not to conceal but to preserve the dead through their enduring remains. Faced with the inescapable process of decomposition, the burial of bodies ensures the integrity of the skeleton. The Natufians inscribed themselves through their own bodily durability, stability by inhumation, unlike some sub-modern nomadic peoples who see the burying of the body as a barrier to the liberation of spirit and reincarnation (cf. Hamayon and Garanger, 1997).

The question of transmission finds a strong echo in what Hamayon (1990) described in a different context but which lends itself to comparison. Hamayon is interested in the evolution of shamanism during the transition from hunting to a livestock-raising economy among the Buryat pastoralists of central Siberia (early to mid-20th century). She describes the tilting of the world order from horizontal to vertical. Hunting societies cooperate with nature in a relationship of exchange for a life negotiated on a level playing field. Herders, on the other hand, survive and thrive on the strength of the effort and knowledge of the previous generation that has been successful in herding cattle and finding pasturage. A relationship of alliance with nature gives way to a relation of filiation, from one based on reciprocity to one founded on subordination. Thus, while relations with nature become hierarchical, the relationship with the souls of the dead, of secondary importance among hunter-gatherers, becomes dominant among pastoralists (Hamayon, 1990: 634, 736–737).

If the Natufians are definitely not pastoralists, sedentarisation led them on a comparable path of dependence on the previous generation. Material and territorial transmissions but also demographic growth could cause a rupture in the relations which maintain a strict balance with nature, as described in all the hunter-gatherers societies through a system of beliefs that encourages egalitarian relationships, whether shamanic or otherwise (e.g. Lambert, 2014). Yet, in Natufian societies the rupture is already in progress, environmental over-exploitation is attested (e.g. Munro, 2004; Stutz *et al.*, 2009; Yeshurun, Bar-Oz and Weinstein-Evron, 2014; Grosman *et al.*, 2016). The search for increased productivity is accompanied by technical innovations is a well-attested evolutionary process (Testart, 2012), likely leading to surplus production (e.g. Testart, 1982, 2012; Hayden, 2009). Relationships with nature and beliefs are likely to be profoundly affected by this disruption of the economic equilibrium. This is why it is legitimate to wonder if the new relationships that the Natufians wove with their dead, were not the stuttering beginnings of a change in mentality and perspective. A slow change to a vertical world where nature was relegated to secondary importance, and where the deceased were assigned a major role in the structuring of daily life by their omnipresence and their powers of action. Thus, human feelings of dominance over their environment, which is essential for triggering an economy based on the domestication of plants and animals according to Cauvin (1994), could be linked to a break in the balance between humanity and nature generated by sedentarisation among the Natufians. This idea is not new, although the causes invoked are different (e.g. Binford, 1968; Bar-Yosef and Belfer-Cohen, 1989; Hayden, 2009; Goring-Morris and Belfer-Cohen, 2011, 2012), but the place of the dead in this cognitive, economic and technical process has been little discussed. This chapter shows that funerary rites are one of the most visible and early materialisations of this irreversible social phenomenon.

Epilogue

To shed light on the different meanings of past funerary rituals, and to address the place occupied by the dead in a given society, there is no better choice than the detailed study of (1) the physical place reserved for graves in the landscape and the settlement, (2) the physical place reserved for the dead in the grave itself. Treatment of the corpse reveals not only the place that the deceased occupied in the society of the living but also the place reserved for it as a new actor in the world of the dead. Detailed contextualisation of each skeleton unearthed is an indispensable prerequisite for the construction of scientific discourse on this subject. Archaeothanatology is an extremely valuable tool for archaeo-anthropologists/bioarchaeologists; it is indispensable and should form part of a continuing dialogue about the relationship between archaeological and bio-anthropological evidence. It is this type of synthesis that permits gathering of essential primary data that will support interpretations built on robust and sustainable foundations.

Acknowledgements

I would like to thank Eline Schotsmans, Christopher Knüsel and Dominique Castex for their invitation to contribute to this book. They showed a lot of patience and accepted an article that was slightly different from the initial idea. I am particularly grateful to Christopher Knüsel for the great translation work he has done from the French version. I would also like to thank Michèle Ballinger who gave me precious help with Figure 9.3. This article is also the result of many rich discussions with my colleagues, archaeologists and archaeo-anthropologists. The working group led by Jean Leclerc, Philippe Chambon and later Pascal Sellier (CNRS, UMR 7206) focussed on methodological aspects, was always an important source of inspiration for trying to go one step further. My warm thanks also go to François Valla for his encouragement and advice in the field when digging grave H156 in 1998; its full significance was revealed after Nicolas Samuelian did a meticulous analysis of the different phases of occupation of the shelter where the grave was found.

References

Baudry, P. (2006). *La place des morts: enjeux et rites, Nouvelles études anthropologiques*, Second Edition. Paris: L'Harmattan.

Berthod, M.A. (2005). La Vie des Morts dans le Regard des Anthropologues. *Anthropos*, 100, pp. 521–536.

Bar-Yosef, O. and Belfer-Cohen, A. (1989). The Origins of Sedentism and Farming Communities in the Levant. *Journal of World Prehistory*, 3(4), pp. 447–498.

Bar-Yosef, O. and Belfer-Cohen, A. (1992). From foraging to farming in the Mediterranean Levant. In: A.B. Gebauer and A.B. Price, eds., *Transitions to agriculture in prehistory*, Prehistory Press: Madison, pp. 21–48.

Bar-Yosef, O. and Belfer-Cohen, A. (2002). Facing environmental crisis. Societal and cultural changes at the transition from the Younger Dryas to the Holocene in the Levant. In: R.T.J. Cappers and S. Bottema, eds., *The dawn of farming in the Near East: studies in early near eastern production, subsistence, and environment*. Berlin: Ex-Oriente, pp. 55–66.

Bar-Yosef, O. and Goren, N. (1973). Natufian Remains in Hayonim Cave. *Paléorient*, 1, pp. 49–68.

Belfer-Cohen, A. (1988). The Natufian Graveyard in Hayonim Cave. *Paléorient*, 14, pp. 297–308.

Belfer-Cohen, A. (1995). Rethinking social stratification in the Natufian culture: the evidence from Burials. In: S. Campbell and A. Green, eds., *The archaeology of death in the ancient near east*. Exeter (UK): The Short Run Press, pp. 9–16.

Belfer-Cohen, A. and Hovers, E. (1992). In the Eye of the Beholder: Mousterian and Natufian Burials in the Levant. *Current Anthropology*, 33, pp. 463–471.

Benz, M. (2010a). 'Little poor babies' – creation of history through death at the transition from foraging to farming. In: T. L. Kienlin and A. Zimmermann, eds., *Beyond elites*. Universitätsforschungen zur Prähistorischen Archäologie, 215, pp. 169–182.

Benz, M. (2010b). Beyond death – the construction of social identities at the transition from foraging to farming. In: M. Benz, ed., *The principle of sharing. segregation and construction of social identities at the transition from foraging to farming*, Studies in Early Near Eastern Production, Subsistence, and Environment. Berlin: Ex-Oriente, pp. 249–276.

Binford, S.R. (1968). A Structural Comparison of Disposal of The Dead in The Mousterian and Upper Paleolithic. *Southwestern Journal of Anthropology*, 24, pp. 139–151.

Bloch, M. (1971). *Placing the dead. Tombs, ancestral villages and kinship organisation in Madagascar*. London and New York: Seminar Press.

Bocquentin, F. (2003). *Pratiques funéraires, paramètres biologiques et identités culturelles au Natoufien: une analyse archéo-anthropologique*. Unpublished Ph.D. thesis, Talence: Université Bordeaux 1.

Bocquentin, F. (2007). A final Natufian population: health and burial status at Eynan-Mallaha. In: U. Zilberman Uri, M. Faerman Marina, L.K. Horwitz and T. Kahana, eds., *Faces from the past: diachronic patterns in the biology of human populations from the Eastern Mediterranean: papers in honour of Patricia Smith*. Oxford: Archaeopress, pp. 66–81.

Bocquentin, F. (2012). Des hameaux partagés par les vivants et les morts. Pratiques funéraires des premières sociétés sédentaires au Proche-Orient. In: N. Schlanger and A.C. Taylor, eds., *La Préhistoire des Autres. Perspectives Archéologiques et Anthropologiques*. Paris: La Découverte, pp. 291–304.

Bocquentin, F. (2013). Après la mort, avant l'oubli. Les crânes surmodelés du Levant sud. *Les Nouvelles de l'Archéologie*, pp. 54–59.

Bocquentin, F. (2014). Frail Echoes from Natufian Mortar Sounds of Ritual Food Processing. Comment on Rosenberg and Nadel 'The Sounds of Pounding: Boulder Mortars and their Significance to Natufian Burial Customs'. *Current Anthropology*, 55, pp. 799–800.

Bocquentin, F. (2018). Sédentarisation. In: A. Piette and J.-M. Salanskis, eds., *Dictionnaire de l'Humain*. Nanterre: Presses Universitaires de Paris Nanterre, pp. 503–510.

Bocquentin, F., Cabellos, T. and Samuelian, N. (2013). Graves in context: field anthropology and the investigation of interstratified floors and burials. In: O. Bar-Yosef, and F. Valla, eds., *Natufian foragers in the levant: terminal pleistocene social Changes in Western Asia [papers from a symposium held in 2009], Archaeological Series*. Ann Arbor, MI.: International Monographs in Prehistory, pp. 185–192.

Bocquentin, F., Chambon, P., Goff, I.L., Leclerc, J., Pariat, J.-G., Pereira, G., Thevenet, C. and Valentin, F. (2010). De la Récurrence à la Norme: Interpréter les Pratiques Funéraires en Préhistoire. *Bulletins et Mémoires de la Société d'anthropologie de Paris*, 22, pp. 157–171.

Bocquentin, F., Molist, M. and Milevski, I. (2016). Connections and Disconnections in the Late Prehistory and Protohistory of the Levant: Discussion and Perspectives. *Paléorient*, 42, pp. 203–208.

Bocquentin, F. and Wagemakers, B. (2014). I. W. Cornwall at Tell es-Sultan: pioneer in archaeothanatology. In: B Wagemakers, ed., *Archaeology in the land of 'tells and ruins': a history of excavations in the holy land inspired by the photographs and accounts of Leo Boer*. Oxford: Oxbow Books, pp. 131–145.

Bonogofsky, M. (2006). Complexity in context: plain, painted and modeled skulls from the Neolithic Middle East. In: M. Bonogofsky, ed., *Skull collection, modification and decoration*. Oxford: Archaeopress, pp. 15–28.

Boulestin, B. and Duday, H. (2005). Ethnologie et archéologie de la mort : de l'illusion des références à l'emploi d'un vocabulaire, In: C. Mordant and G. Depierre, eds., *Les Pratiques Funéraires à l'Âge Du Bronze en France, Actes de la table ronde de Sens-en-Bourgogne (10–12 juin 1998)*. Paris: Éditions du Comité des Travaux d'Histoiriques et Scientifiques (CTHS), pp. 17–30.

Boz, B. and Hager, L.D. (2013). Living above the dead: intramural burial practices at Çatalhöyük. In: I. Hodder, ed., *Humans and landscapes of Çatalhöyük: reports from the 2000-2008 seasons*. Los Angeles: Cotsen Institute, pp. 413–440.

Byrd, B.F. and Monahan, C.M. (1995). Death, Mortuary Ritual, and Natufian Social Structure. *Journal of Anthropological Archaeology*, 14, pp. 251–287.

Byrd, B.F. and Rosenthal, J. (2016). Celebrating the dead: placing prehistoric mortuary practices in broader social context. In: A.P. Sullivan III and D.I. Olszewski, eds., *Archaeological Variability and Interpretation in Global Perspective*. Louisville: University Press of Colorado, pp. 233–265.

Cauvin, J. (1994). *Naissance des divinités, naissance de l'agriculture: la révolution des symboles au Néolithique*. Paris: Centre National de la Recherche Scientifique (CNRS) Éditions.

Cornwall, I.W. (1956a). *Bones for the Archaeologist*. London: Phoenix House Ltd.

Cornwall, I.W. (1956b). The Pre-Pottery Neolithic Burials, Jericho. *Palestine Exploration Quarterly*, 88, pp. 110–124.

Delaplace, G. (2008). *L'invention des morts. sépultures, fantômes et photographie en Mongolie contemporaine, Nord-Asie 1*. École Pratiques des Haute Études (EPHE): Centre d'Études Mongoles & Sibériennes.

Edwards, P.C., Anton, M., Bocquentin, F., McNamara, K.J., Prossor, L., Shewan, L., Valdiosera, C. and Valka, A.M. (2018). La Trobe University's 2016 season of field sampling and archaeological excavation at the site of Wadi Hammeh 27. *Annual of the Department of Antiquities of Jordan*, 59, pp. 273–290.

Fletcher, A., Pearson, J. and Ambers, J. (2008). The Manipulation of Social and Physical Identity in the Pre-Pottery Neolithic. *Cambridge Archaeological Journal*, 18, pp. 309–325.

Galinon-Mélénec, B., ed. (2011). *L'Homme trace. Perspectives anthropologiques des traces contemporaines*. Paris: CNRS Éditions.

Garrod, D.A.E., Bate, D.M.A. (1937). *Mugharet el Wad description and excavations*. In: D.A.E. Garrod and D.M.A. Bate, eds., *The stone age of Mount Carmel*. Oxford: Clarendon Press.

Gordon, B. and Marshall, P., (2000). Introduction: placing the dead in late medieval and early modern Europe. In: B. Gordon and P. Marshall, eds., *The place of the dead. death and remembrance in late medieval and early modern Europe*. Cambridge: Cambridge University Press, pp. 1–16.

Goring-Morris, A.N. and Belfer-Cohen, A. (2011). Neolithization processes in the Levant: the outer envelope. *Current Anthropology*, 52(S4), pp. S195–S208.

Goring-Morris, N. and Belfer-Cohen, A. (2013). Different strokes for different folks: Near Eastern Neolithic mortuary practices in perspective. In: I. Hodder, ed., *Religion at Work in a Neolithic Society*. Cambridge: Cambridge University Press, pp. 35–57.

Goring-Morris, N. and Kuijt, I. (2000). The quick and the dead. The social context of aceramic Neolithic mortuary practices as seen from Kfar HaHoresh. In: I. Kuijt, ed., *Life in Neolithic farming communities: social organization, identity, and differentiation*. New York, Kluwer Academic/Plenum Publishers, pp. 103–136.

Grosman, L. and Munro, N.D. (2016). A Natufian Ritual Event. *Current Anthropology*, 57, pp. 311–331.

Grosman, L., Munro, N.D., Abadi, I., Boaretto, E., Shaham, D., Belfer-Cohen, A. and Bar-Yosef, O. (2016). Nahal Ein Gev II, a Late Natufian Community at the Sea of Galilee. *PLoS ONE*, 11(1), pp. e0146647.

Grosman, L., Munro, N.D. and Belfer-Cohen, A. (2008). A 12,000-year-old Shaman Burial from the Southern Levant (Israel). *Proceedings of the National Academy of Sciences of the United States of America*, 105, pp. 17665–17669.

Haddow, S.D. and Knüsel, C.J. (2017). Skull Retrieval and Secondary Burial Practices in the Neolithic Near East: Recent Insights from Çatalhöyük, Turkey, *Bioarchaeology International*, 1, pp. 52–71.

Hamayon, R. (1990). *La chasse à l'âme: esquisse d'une théorie du chamanisme sibérien. Mémoires de la Société d'ethnologie*. Nanterre: Société d'Ethnologie.

Hamayon, R.N. and Garanger, M. (1997). *Taïga, terre de chamans*. Paris: Imprimerie Nationale.

Hayden, B. (2009). The Proof Is in the Pudding: Feasting and the Origins of Domestication. *Current Anthropology*, 50, pp. 597–601.

Henry, D.O. (1985). Preargricultural sedentism: the Natufian example. In: T.D. Price and J.A. Brown, eds., *Prehistoric hunter-gatherers: the emergence of cultural complexity*. Academic Press, New York, pp. 365–381.

Hertz, R. (1907). Contribution à une étude sur la représentation collective de la mort. In: R. Hertz, ed., *Sociologie Religieuse et Folklore, Bibliothèque de Sociologie Contemporaine*. Paris: Presses Universitaires de France.

Kenyon, K. (1957). *Digging up Jericho*. London: Ernest Benn.

Khawam, R. (2014). *L'Homme et la mort au néolithique précéramique B: l'exemple de Tell Aswad*. Unpublished Ph.D. thesis, Université de Lyon 2.

Krauskopff, G. (2007). Ancêtres. In: P. Bonte and M. Izard, eds., *Dictionnaire de l'ethnologie et de l'anthropologie*. Paris: Presses Universitaires de France (PUF), pp. 65–66.

Kuijt, I. (1996). Negotiating Equality through Ritual: A Consideration of Late Natufian and Prepottery Neolithic a Period Mortuary Practices. *Journal of Anthropological Archaeology*, 15, 313–336.

Kuijt, I. (2008). Place, Death, and the Transmission of Social Memory in Early Agricultural Communities of the Near Eastern Pre-Pottery Neolithic. *Archeological Papers of the American Anthropological Association*, 10, pp. 80–99.

Lambert, Y. (2014). *La naissance des religions: de la préhistoire aux religions universalistes*. Paris: Fayard/Pluriel.

Le Roux, D. (2018). Rituel. In: A. Piette and J.-M. Salanskis, eds., *Dictionnaire de l'humain*. Nanterre: Presses Universitaires de Paris Nanterre, pp. 493–501.

Leroi-Gourhan, A. (1964). Le Geste et la parole. *Technique et Langage. Sciences d'Aujourd'hui*, Vol. I. Paris: Albin Michel.

Maher, L.A., Stock, J.T., Finney, S., Heywood, J.J.N., Miracle, P.T. and Banning, E.B. (2011). A Unique Human-Fox Burial from a Pre-Natufian Cemetery in the Levant (Jordan). *PLoS ONE*, 6, pp. e15815.

Munro, N.D. (2004). Zooarchaeological Measures of Hunting Pressure and Occupation Intensity in the Natufian: Implications for Agricultural Origins. *Current Anthropology*, 45, pp. S5–S34.

Nadel, D., Danin, A., Power, R., Rosen, A., Bocquentin, F., Tsatskin, A., Rosenberg, D., Yeshurun, R., Weissbrod, L., Rebollo, N.R., Barzilai, O. and Boaretto, E. (2013). Earliest Floral Grave Lining from 13,700–11,700-year-old Natufian Burials at Raqefet Cave, Mt. Carmel, Israel. *Proceedings of the National Academy of Sciences of the United States of America*, 110, pp. 11774–11778.

Noy, T. (1989). Some aspects of Natufian mortuary behavior at Nahal Oren. In: I. Hershkovitz, ed., *People and culture in change: proceedings of the second symposium on upper palaeolithic, mesolithic and neolithic populations of Europe and the Mediterranean Basin part 1, British Archaeological Reports (BAR)* (International Series) Oxford: Archaeopress, pp. 53–57.

Papadaniel, Y. (2018). Mort. In: A. Piette, J.-M. Salanskis, A. Raulin and I. Rivoal, eds., *Dictionnaire de l'humain*. Nanterre: Presses Universitaires de Paris Ouest, pp. 369–374.

Pereira, G. (2013). Une archéologie des temps funéraires? Introduction. *Les Nouvelles de l'Archéologie*, 132, pp. 3–7.

Perrot, J., Ladiray, D., Solivérès-Masséi, O. and Ferembach, D. (1988). *Les hommes de Mallaha (Eynan), Israel, mémoires et travaux du Centre de Recherche Française de Jérusalem*. Paris: Association Paléorient.

Rendu, W., Beauval, C., Crevecoeur, I., Bayle, P., Balzeau, A., Bismuth, T., Bourguignon, L., Delfour, G., Faivre, J.-P., Lavcrampe-Cuyaubère, F., Tavormica, C., Todisco, D., Turq, A. and Maureille, B. (2014). Evidence Supporting an Intentional Neandertal Burial at La Chapelle-aux-Saints. *Proceedings of the National Academy of Sciences of the USA*, 111(1), pp. 81–86.

Samuelian, N. (2019). Les abris du Natoufien final de Eynan-Mallaha, Israël. *Organisation spatiale et interprétation fonctionnelle, Mémoires et Travaux du Centre de Recherche Français de Jérusalem*. Paris: De Boccard.

Santana, J., Velasco, J., Ibáñez, J.J. and Braemer, F. (2012). Crania with Mutilated Facial Skeletons: A New Ritual Treatment in an Early Pre-Pottery Neolithic B Cranial Cache at Tell Qarassa North (South Syria). *American Journal of Physical Anthropology*, 149, pp. 205–216.

Schmandt-Besserat, D. (2002). From Behind the Mask: Plastered Skulls from 'Ain Ghazal. *Origini*, 24, pp. 95–140.

Slon, V., Sarig, R., Hershkovitz, I., Khalaily, H. and Milevski, I. (2014). The Plastered Skulls from the Pre-Pottery Neolithic B Site of Yiftahel (Israel) – A Computed Tomography-Based Analysis. *PLoS ONE*, 9, pp. e89242.

Smith, P. (1973). Family Burials at Hayonim. *Paléorient*, 1, pp. 69–71.

Stordeur, D. and Khawam, R. (2007). Les Crânes Surmodelés de Tell Aswad (PPNB, Syrie). Premier Regard sur l'Ensemble, Premières Réflexions. Syria. *Archéologie, Art et Histoire*, 84, pp. 5–32.

Stutz, A.J., Munro, N.D. and Bar-Oz, G. (2009). Increasing the Resolution of the Broad Spectrum Revolution in the Southern Levantine Epipaleolithic (19–12 ka). *Journal of Human Evolution*, 56, pp. 294–306.

Testart, A. (1982). *Les chasseurs-cueilleurs, ou l'origine des inégalités*. Université Paris X Nanterre: Société d'Ethnologie.

Testart, A. (2004). *Les morts d'accompagnement. La servitude volontaire I*. Paris: Errance.

Testart, A. (2008). Des crânes et des vautours ou la guerre oubliée. *Paleorient*, 34, pp. 33–58.

Testart, A. (2012). *Avant l'histoire: L'évolution des sociétés, de Lascaux à Carnac*. Paris: Gallimard.

Testart, A. (2014). *L'amazone et la cuisinière. Anthropologie de la division sexuelle du travail*. Paris: Gallimard.

Thevenet, C., Rivoal, I., Sellier, P. and Valentin, F. (2014). Introduction. In: F. Valentin, I. Rivoal, C. Thevenet, and P. Sellier, eds., *La Chaîne Opératoire Funéraire. Ethnologie et Archéologie de La Mort, Travaux de La Maison de l'Archéologie & l'Ethnologie, René-Ginouvès*. Paris: De Boccard, pp. 7–9.

Thomas, L.-V. (1975). *Anthropologie de la mort*. Paris: Payot.

Thomas, L.-V. (1980). *Le cadavre: de la biologie à l'anthropologie*. Éditions Complexe, Bruxelles.

Thomas, L.-V. (1996). *Rites de mort*. Paris: Fayard.

Valentin, F., Rivoal, I., Thevenet, C. and Sellier, P., eds. (2014). *La chaîne opératoire funéraire. Ethnologie et archéologie de la mort. Travaux de la Maison de l'Archéologie & l'Ethnologie, René-Ginouvès*. Paris: De Boccard.

Valla, F.R. (1988). Aspects du sol de l'abri 131 de Mallaha (Eynan), Israël. *Paléorient, Préhistoire du Levant II. Processus des Changements Culturels* 14, pp. 283–296.

Valla, F.F. (2012). *Les Fouilles de la terrasse d'Hayonim (Israël), 1980–1981 et 1985–1989, Mémoires et travaux du centre de recherche français à Jérusalem 10*. Paris.

Valla, F. (1991). Les Natoufiens de Mallaha et l'espace, In: O. Bar-Yosef and F. Valla, eds., *The Natufian culture in the Levant*, International Monographs in Prehistory. Ann Arbor, MI, 1, pp. 111–122.

Valla, F. (1999). The Natufian: a coherent thought? In: W. Davies and R. Charles, eds., *Dorothy Garrod and the Progress of the Palaeolithic: Studies in the Prehistoric Archaeology of the Near East and Europe*. Oxford: Oxbow Books, pp. 224–241.

Valla, F. and Bocquentin, F. (2008). Les maisons, les vivants, les morts: le cas de Mallaha (Eynan), Israël. In: J.M. Cordoba, M. Molist, M.C Perez, I. Rubio, S. Martinez, eds., *Proceedings of the 5th International Congress on the Archaeology of the Ancient Near East*, Vol. III. Madrid: Centro Superior de Estudios sobre el Oriente Próximo y Egipto, pp. 521–546.

Valla, F., Bocquentin, F., Plisson, H., Khalaily, H., Delage, C., Rabinovich, R., Samuelian, N., Valentin, B. and Belfer-Cohen, A. (1999). Le Natoufien final et les nouvelles fouilles a Mallaha (Eynan), Israel 1996–1997. *Journal of the Israel Prehistoric Society*, 28, pp. 105–176.

Valla, F.R., Khalaily, H., Samuelian, N. and Bocquentin, F. (2010). What Happened in the Final Natufian? *Mitekufat Haeven: Journal of the Israel Prehistoric Society*, 40, 131–148.

Valla, F., Khalaily, H., Samuelian, N., Bocquentin, F., Valentin, B., Marder, O., Rabinovich, R., Le Dosseur, G., Dubreuil, L. and Belfer-Cohen, A. (2001). Le Natoufien final de Mallaha (Eynan), deuxième rapport préliminaire: les fouilles de 1998 et 1999. *Journal of the Israel Prehistoric Society*, 31, pp. 83–184.

Valla, F., Khalaily, H., Valladas, H., Tisnerat-Laborde, N., Samuelian, N., Bocquentin, F., Rabinovich, R., Bridault, A., Simmons, T., Le Dosseur, G., Rosen, A., Dubreuil, L., Bar-Yosef Mayer, D. and Belfer-Cohen, A. (2004). Les fouilles de Mallaha en 2000 et 2001: 3ème rapport préliminaire. *Journal of the Israel Prehistoric Society*, 34, pp. 49–244.

Valla, F., Khalaily, H., Valladas, H., Kaltnecker, E., Bocquentin, F., Cabellos, T., Bar-Yosef Mayer, D., Le Dosseur, G., Regev, L., Chu, V., Weiner, S., Boaretto, E., Samuelian, N., Valentin, B., Delerue, S., Poupeau, G., Bridault, A., Rabinovich, R., Simmons, T., Zohar, I., Ashkenazi, S., Delgado Huertas, A., Spiro, B., Mienis, H., Rosen, A.M., Porat, N. and Belfer-Cohen, A. (2007). Les Fouilles de Ain Mallaha (Eynan) de 2003 à 2005: Quatrième Rapport Préliminaire. *Journal of the Israel Prehistoric Society*, 37, pp. 135–383.

Valla, F.R., Le Mort, F. and Plisson, H. (1991). Les fouilles en cours sur la terrasse d'Hayonim. In: O. Bar-Yosef F. R. Valla, eds., *The Natufian culture in the Levant*, International Monographs in Prehistory, Archaeological Series 1. Ann Arbor, Michigan, pp. 93–110.

van Gennep, A. (1909). *Les rites de passage*. Paris: Emile Nourry.

Verhoeven, M. (2002). Transformations of Society: The Changing Role of Ritual and Symbolism in the PPNB and the PN in the Levant, Syria and South-East Anatolia. *Paléorient*, 28, 5–14.

Weissbrod, L., Marshall, F.B., Valla, F.R., Khalaily, H., Bar-Oz, G., Auffray, J.-C., Vigne, J.-D. and Cucchi, T. (2017). Origins of House Mice in Ecological Niches created by Settled Hunter-gatherers in the Levant 15,000 Years Ago. *Proceedings of the National Academy of Sciences of the United States of America*, 114, pp. 4099–4104.

Wright, G.R.H. (1988). The Severed Head in Earliest Neolithic Times. *Journal of Prehistoric Religion (Göteborg)*, 2, pp. 51–56.

Yeshurun, R., Bar-Oz, G. and Nadel, D. (2013). The Social Role of Food in the Natufian Cemetery of Raqefet Cave, Mount Carmel, Israel. *Journal of Anthropological Archaeology*, 32, pp. 511–526.

Yeshurun, R., Bar-Oz, G. and Weinstein-Evron, M. (2014). Intensification and Sedentism in the Terminal Pleistocene Natufian Sequence of el-Wad Terrace (Israel). *Journal of Human Evolution*, 70, pp. 16–35.

10

WHAT CAN ARCHAEOTHANATOLOGY ADD?

A case study of new knowledge and theoretical implications in the re-study of Mesolithic burials in Sweden and Denmark

Liv Nilsson Stutz

DEPARTMENT OF CULTURAL SCIENCES, LINNAEUS UNIVERSITY, KALMAR, SWEDEN

Introduction

The comparative study of the Mesolithic hunter-gatherer burials at Skateholm (Southern Sweden) and Vedbæk-Bøgebakken (Eastern Denmark) underscores that archaeothanatology can bring both more information and deeper insight, even when applied to previously studied materials. Not all information gleaned from archaeothanatological approaches must necessarily be the product of applying the approach in the field, but analyses can be highly valuable in studying older excavation documentation. Archaeothanatology was conceived as a field approach, hence its original name '*anthropologie de terrain*' (i.e. Duday *et al.*, 1990), and there is no doubt that the approach can be most fully realised when the excavation and documentation of the human remains is carried out in the field and under the supervision of anthropologists with the appropriate training. Yet, as the activity of excavation itself is destructive (e.g. Bonnie, 2011; Demoule, 2011), it seems appropriate to explore the potential of transferring the approach to archival materials. This may be especially valuable when researching archaeological periods for which burials are relatively unusual, the record is extremely partial, and for which there is a need to extract as much information as possible from all available sources. This is certainly the case for the Mesolithic in Europe. Archives are rich with documentation from older excavations that were not carried out with an archaeothanatological approach. Today, several projects, from the Baltic and Scandinavia to the Iberian Peninsula, illustrate that the archival approach can be very productive (Nilsson Stutz, 2003; Peyroteo Stjerna 2016; Torv, 2016).

This chapter presents the study of two late Mesolithic burial sites from Southern Scandinavia, sometimes referred to as 'cemeteries', referring to the fact that they contain a large number of inhumations that appear to relate to one another and have a connection to nearby occupation sites. The method used in this study is an application of archaeothanatological principles to archival documents. Several questions present themselves when taking on this kind of project. The first relates to the quality of the excavation records. Is the documentation appropriate

DOI: 10.4324/9781351030625-13

and does it have enough detail to allow for the archaeothanatological analysis to be reliable? A second question relates to the degree to which archaeothanatology can really add anything. Will archaeothanatology really lead to new inferences that the original analysis did not? In cases of what appears to be very straightforward, homogenous data, perhaps archaeothanatology will only confirm what previous researchers observed. This chapter will show that document-based archaeothanatological study of Mesolithic sites has provided significant new knowledge.

The sites discussed here were excavated in the 1970s (Vedbæk-Bøgebakken) and the early 1980s (Skateholm). They were documented in a similar manner (burial features were drawn at a scale of 1:5 or 1:10), with detailed descriptions of the features and a great number of 'z-values' for associated skeletal elements, permitting analysis of detailed differences in depth between different parts of the skeleton. This turned out to be a crucial resource and permitted consideration of the impact on the processes of decomposition and disarticulation of, for example, minor rotations of the entire body. The burials were photographed in high resolution; thus identification of individual bones and their three-dimensional position could be observed in detail. Among the weaknesses in the documentation was that the drawings and some photographs focussed on the overall rendition of the position of the skeleton and did not document specific bones in detail. Moreover, with a few exceptions, the visual documentation was not made for several layers of the deposit. Instead, they were limited to maximum exposure of the burial. This limited the possibility of, for example, determining the exact position of cervical vertebrae to assess the possible rotation of the cranium during the decomposition process. This shows that the documentation, in drawings and photographs, set certain limits to how detailed the archaeothanatological analysis could be. Still, it was detailed enough to make the archaeothanatological analysis not only possible but also productive in that it added new data and information about the mortuary practices that had not been noted by traditional archaeological approaches. In addition to the new data, the analysis, which ultimately aims at reconstructing past practices, also facilitated a more interpretative form of archaeology, one that relies on a deeper understanding of the practice and lived experience from the study of mortuary rituals.

Archaeothanatology can, in many ways, be viewed as a trans-disciplinary approach. At face value, it provides an approach to recovery, documentation, and analysis that combines disciplinary perspectives from archaeology, archaeo-anthropology/bioarchaeology, taphonomy, physiology and anatomy in an integrated framework, connecting the archaeological fieldwork to the osteological analysis. The applied method in and of itself highlights the interpretative dimension of fieldwork and documentation and constitutes a form of reflexive archaeology. But the potential for trans-disciplinarity can be pushed even further by making connections with more interpretative traditions in contemporary archaeology. As will also be demonstrated in this chapter, the potential for such interpretative work is great for archaeothanatology – even for archival analyses – helping to strengthen connections between the method and specific theoretical concepts and models.

Overview of the sites

Skateholm

Skateholm, located on the southern-most coast of Sweden, is an area with several sites dating to the Mesolithic, including two – potentially three – burial areas. Two of them, Skateholm I and II, were excavated in the 1980s, and the third, Skateholm III, is inferred from a note about human remains and red ochre uncovered during gravel extraction in the 1930s. The two excavated burial areas were located in low-lying islands in what, at the time, was a shallow lagoon of brackish water. As the sea level rose, the islands were submerged. Skateholm II, which is the older of the two, was eventually submerged, and the human occupation was moved to Skateholm I, an island at a slightly higher elevation, which, in turn, also was covered by rising waters. There is thus a chronological relationship between the two. For Skateholm II, there are no reliable C14 dates from the human remains, but charcoal dates from the settlement layers place it at 5700–4700 cal. BC (Lidén and Eriksson, 2002). At Skateholm I, bone samples from the burials have been dated to 5300–5000 cal. BC and additional dates obtained from charcoal in the graves extend the use to 4700 cal. BC, with even younger dates (4300 cal. BC) from the adjacent settlement site (Lidén and Eriksson, 2002). On each island, the burial area was located in close proximity to a contemporaneous occupation site, which was situated closer to the shore. The burial area was higher up on each of the islands.

The older site, Skateholm II, contained 22 distinct burial features and one empty burial pit. Twenty-two individuals were buried here, including 18 adults and older sub-adults and four children. The burials predominantly consisted of primary interments in oval pit-grave features without a clear pattern of orientation. One case of cremation was documented, and one pit included only deposited deer antlers. In most of the burials, the dead were placed supinely on the back, with the limbs in extension; alternatively, some of the bodies were placed in a sitting position (which occurs in five of the burials). The majority of the burials were individual ones, but two double graves also occurred. The bodies were accompanied by rich and varied depositions, including deer antlers, red ochre, beads and other artefacts and fish bones that have been interpreted as food remains. The area also included the remains of a house structure with very thick red ochre deposits, interpreted as some form of ritual structure relating to the preparation of the bodies for burial (Larsson, 1993).

At Skateholm I, the excavation documented 64 distinct burial features and 63 individuals, including 56 adults/older subadults and seven children. Here, the basic programme of primary inhumation in oval pit-grave features was repeated, but the position of the body was more varied when compared with those of the older site. In addition to the positions documented in Skateholm II, this area also included bodies placed on the side with the limbs flexed. Other variations occur: for example, a body placed ventrally (i.e. prone) and another placed with the lower limbs crossed. Two cases of cremation were recorded at Skateholm 1, and in one case, a partial individual was buried. The majority of the interments were single inhumations, but six double graves were found, with four of them consisting of an adult together with a child. While there are still depositions of artefacts, food and ochre, the number and variation in grave goods is decreased compared to those found at Skateholm II. Dogs had been buried at both sites, both in separate burial features and with humans.

The burials were excavated under the supervision of Lars Larsson in the early 1980s (Larsson, 1988a). The graves were carefully documented with drawings at a scale of 1:10 (including detailed depth measurements throughout the features and of the human remains). The drawings, field notes, and photographs in both colour and black and white constituted the basis for the archaeothanatological analysis. Due to the detailed drawings and photographs, the exact position of the bones could typically be determined. When this was not possible, it was due to poor preservation rather than insufficient documentation. Despite the superficial appearance of well-preserved bone, the skeletal material was most often in very poor condition. Many of the osteological measurements were taken in the field before lifting the remains that often resulted in their fragmentation.

Vedbæk-Bøgebakken

The burial area at Vedbæk-Bøgebakken was also part of a larger context of several sites clustered around a prehistoric fjord landscape on the eastern coast of Denmark. The site was excavated in 1975 as a rescue effort, in conjunction with the construction of a new school (Albrethsen and Brinch Petersen, 1977; Brinch Petersen, 2015). The excavation yielded an occupation site and adjacent graves. Similar to the situation at Skateholm, the burials were located on the slope just above the occupation site.

The site contained 18 graves with 22 individuals, including 17 adults and 5 children (of which 3 were newborns). The site also included what has been interpreted as a single empty grave feature. The burials predominantly consisted of primary single inhumations in filled-in grave-pit features. The pits were oriented east-west and were sometimes lined up in a parallel pattern close together. With a single exception of a body buried on the right side with the limbs flexed, the individuals were buried on their backs with their limbs in extension. Three graves contained more than one individual; two of these are double graves and the other is a triple grave. Red ochre and rich grave goods consisting of artefacts in flint, tooth and shell beads, and deer antler accompanied the bodies. The graves were carefully documented with drawings at a scale of 1:5 or 1:10 (including detailed depth measurements throughout the features and of the human remains) and photographs in both colour and black and white, which together constituted the basis for the archaeothanatological analysis. Due to the detailed drawings and photography, the exact position of the bones could be determined.

For all three sites, the burials were numbered by grave feature and not by individual. Some burials included several individuals, including dogs, and some graves included only dogs, and this can create some confusion in the numbering of the graves. This study only concerns the human burials. When excluding burials not containing humans, the study includes in total 95 burials and 107 individuals. To avoid confusion, the study will be based on the numbering of grave features.

Mesolithic mortuary practices revisited

The results of the archaeothanatological analysis have been published in extensive detail (Nilsson Stutz, 2003). This account includes only the main patterns and a discussion of a few selected examples to demonstrate to what extent the use of an archaeothanatological approach contributed new knowledge about the mortuary practices at these sites. Given that these two sites were already published, well known, and continuously discussed within Mesolithic archaeological circles, and the fact that the burials were mainly primary in nature, it might appear that an archaeothanatological analysis would have little to add to what has already been said about them. This, however, is not the case. The results of the analysis show that an archaeothanatological approach added information that can be divided into four categories:

1. New, robust taphonomic evidence to confirm previous interpretations;
2. Increased detail and understanding of previously inferred processes;
3. Challenges to old interpretations;
4. New discoveries.

Confirmation of previous interpretations with taphonomic evidence

Given the character of the sites, with predominantly primary burials, one obvious contribution of the archaeothanatological analysis was to confirm interpretations that had been proposed based on traditional archaeological observations. In light of the archaeothanatological re-analysis, a more source-critical methodology often strengthens claims that could not really warrant such strong support previously.

This is the case for the nature of the burials, where careful evaluation of the evidence pertaining to the state of the labile articulations demonstrated that the majority of the burials (60/95 are *clearly primary* and an additional 13 were considered *probably primary* (a category assigned to cases where the state of preservation was too poor to allow for a clear determination, but where the presence of diagnostic bones, such as metacarpals or phalanges, in an anatomically correct position were considered as indicative of a primary deposition) (cf. Boulestin, Chapter 2, this volume; Schotsmans *et al.,* Chapter 27, this volume). It is significant to underline that the evidence was not contradictory, only lacking, and there was no indication that would contradict the interpretation of a primary burial. A few cases challenge the established norm of primary burial at these sites. Three cases of cremation at Skateholm can be confirmed as strictly non-primary in character. In addition, grave 13 at Skateholm I presents an interesting case that does not fit into any clear category for the nature of the burial. A feature measuring 1.1 by 0.5 m contained the incomplete skeletal remains of an adult male (Figure 10.1). The skeleton was disarticulated, with the exception of the left radius and ulna, the left carpal bones, and the bones of the right foot. The osteological report further indicates that the right hand and left foot were missing. The maintenance of the labile articulations of the bones of the right foot and the left carpals indicates that the cadaver was buried in a relatively fresh state. However, the disarticulation of the rest of the skeleton indicates some sort of processing before burial, and when weighed together, this does not indicate a natural process of decomposition and disarticulation. It has been suggested that the body was cut up or mutilated before burial (Persson and Persson, 1984), and this seems plausible, even if it has not been confirmed, since the bone itself was in such poor condition that there has not been any analysis of the surfaces for evidence of cutmarks. For grave 13, the documentation was not quite detailed enough to draw a firm conclusion, but the positions of the skeletal elements suggest that the remains were most likely placed inside a container at the time of burial. This would indicate that the body was not immediately visible to onlookers at the time of burial.

Previous publications suggested the existence of traditional 'secondary burials' (i.e. a form of final deposition of the human remains after one or several previous depositions or treatments resulting in the partial or complete disarticulation of the skeleton; cf. Boulestin, Chapter 2, this volume; Schotsmans *et al.,* Chapter 27, this volume) at Skateholm (Larsson, 1984). The archaeothanatological analysis did not support these interpretations, and this will be discussed in more detail below. In 18 cases, the preservation was too poor to permit interpretation. This was due exclusively to poor preservation of the bone or significant disturbance of the burial. Similarly, while it had not been a focus for previous interpretations, archaeothanatology could demonstrate that the majority of the bodies had decomposed in filled spaces, indicating that they had been buried in pits that were immediately filled with sediment. From an archaeothanatological perspective, it is owing to taphonomic evidence for 'primary burial in filled spaces' that the initial position of the body was rather easy to infer correctly. Further nuances could then be added regarding minor movements affecting skeletal remains.

Increased detail and understanding of processes previously inferred

The archaeothanatological analysis could partially confirm – and significantly nuance – what can now be seen as over-confident assertions put forward in the older publications. An example of this is the archaeothanatological evidence of wrapping of the body, a practice that has been assumed to have been widely practiced in the Mesolithic. It is rarely discussed in detail, but

Figure 10.1 Skateholm I, grave 13. The burial contains a partially well-articulated but incomplete skeleton, indicating that the body was buried in parts, probably inside some form of container (Photograph: L. Larsson).

wrapping is often depicted in reconstructions. Yet, the evidence is often only impressionistic. The archaeothanatological indicators for wrapping, at least when the individual was placed on the back, will be clearest when the mortuary practices significantly constricted the body, to the point of elevating the shoulders upward and rotating them forward (i.e. anteriorly), bringing the clavicle into a vertical position, and maintaining a considerable *effet de paroi* ('wall effect') along the sides of the body, sometimes even with bilateral pressure along the entire area of the upper limbs, thoracic cage, pelvis and lower limbs. Such wrapping should be positively identifiable with the sufficiently detailed documentation from Skateholm and Vedbæk-Bøgebakken. Yet, archaeothanatological study might not be able to rule out instances where the body has been loosely wrapped – especially if the materials used were not resistant enough to prevent the penetration of the surrounding sediment during decomposition.

The re-analysis of the documentation did confirm some isolated instances of wrapping, but there was no evidence that it was common practice. Wrapping of the body can be suggested for three individuals lying on their backs. The best example of a clear wrapping of the body can be seen in grave 22 in Vedbæk-Bøgebakken, which exhibits all the indicators of a tight wrapping of the body described above and with a clear indication that the pressure did not originate from the sides of a small burial pit since it was large enough to accommodate large deer antlers positioned behind the cranium. Two additional cases in Skateholm (graves 22 and XVI) also exhibit several of the diagnostic traits: the projection upward and forward of the shoulders, a rotation upward (superiorly) and inward (medially) of the upper limbs, a clear *effet de paroi* of the upper limbs, and strong bi-lateral pressure on the upper part of the body (Skateholm grave XVI, Figure 10.2). Other cases, where an *effet de paroi* could be observed to affect some parts of the body – often forming a curvature along the body and sometimes occurring in combination with secondary empty spaces - but where the

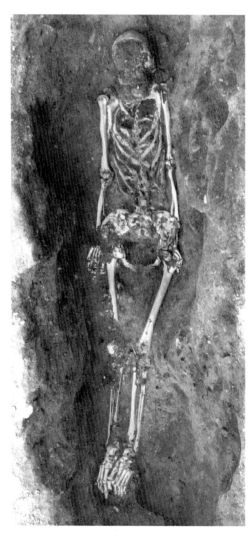

Figure 10.2   Skateholm II, grave XVI. The skeleton exhibits several diagnostic traits for wrapping of the body (Photograph: L. Larsson).

184

diagnostic indicators for bilateral pressure and projection of the shoulders were missing – another category, that of 'soft container', was tentatively proposed for a total of four burials. Altogether, this brings the number of cases for wrapping to at least three, and possibly up to seven across the two sites. It may be stated that wrapping was an occasional practice, but it was probably quite rare. Therefore, there is only limited undisputable positive evidence for wrapping of the body.

It is interesting to note that archaeothanatological analysis of two burials at Skateholm I illustrates how, sometimes, wrapping and burial in a constricted space appear to be plausible alternatives, with neither being strongly favoured over the other as a hypothesis. In these two cases, the body was constricted, having been placed in the grave lying on one side, with the limbs flexed tightly in front of the body. Grave 58 contained a body placed on its right side. Not only were the limbs tightly flexed in front of the body, but also an *effet de paroi* can be traced along the anterior side of the body, from the hyperextended distal phalanges of the left foot to the cranium, which is also hyperextended. The limits of the pit itself were difficult to determine (Figure 10.3).

Figure 10.3 Skateholm I, grave 58. The body was placed on the right side with the limbs tightly flexed in front of the body. An *effet de paroi* can be seen along the anterior side of the body, from the hyperextended distal phalanges of the left foot to the cranium, which is also hyperextended (Photograph: L. Larsson).

It is possible that the pressure could originate from the body being placed in a very constricted space, but a tight wrapping of it cannot be excluded either. Grave 60, also in Skateholm I, contained a body deposited in a very small pit (0.7 by 0.5 m). It has been interpreted as a bundle burial, but the presence and anatomically correct position of several of the hand bones indicate a primary deposit in a very constricted space, one that could have been possible if the body was wrapped tightly at the time of burial.

The detailed information generated by an archaeothanatological analysis thus provides a deeper understanding of the taphonomic processes, including those that may have previously been proposed. A further example of this is grave 28 in Skateholm I, a primary burial of an adult male placed on his back with the limbs in extension (Figure 10.4). In the initial publications, it was suggested that the missing left radius and ulna, the left ilium, and the left femur could be explained by intentional removal. The evidence supporting this interpretation was the lack of evidence of disturbance noted during the excavation of this grave. The archaeothanatological analysis came to the same conclusion but added several important insights into what had transpired. The analysis concluded that it was a primary burial and that the body had decomposed in a filled space (the other bones had barely moved, including the right patella as well as balancing on its lateral side, and the bones of the right foot, still perfectly articulated). The bones appear to have been removed at a fairly late stage in the process of decomposition, at a stage when the left patella (which was found *in situ*) would have already been disarticulated from the distal end of the femur. This observation makes it harder to explain how so many bones could have been removed without causing more disturbance to the bones in the immediate vicinity. Note, for example, how the bones of the left hand are almost completely undisturbed. Given these observations, the analysis led to a hypothesis that this burial would have been prepared in advance for the intervention. The body would have been placed in the filled pit, but perhaps covered by a lid of some sort – made of wood, or perhaps hide – that could be lifted up to expose the decomposed body without having to search through sediment for it and cause a wider disturbance. This, in turn, poses questions about why this individual was selected for this particular treatment at the time of burial. Perhaps this individual held a powerful position in the society, or perhaps his death in some way stood out and thus motivated people to come back and retrieve bones that later might have served as powerful signs or metonymies of the individual or the story he came to represent within myths, storytelling and rituals performed by the group. It is also possible that the bones were less associated with a specific individual and might have come to refer more broadly to the collective of the dead within a broader cosmology.

Challenging older interpretations

Archaeothanatological analysis not only confirms or nuances previous hypotheses. It can also call into question previous interpretations. While the hypothesis of a common practice of wrapping the body has already been addressed above, a more thorough-going challenge may be posed for the existence of coffins and the use of boats as coffins in these sites (e.g. Larsson 1988b: 112; Kannegaard Nielsen and Brinch Petersen, 1993: 76–77). Archaeologists typically identify a coffin based on primary evidence of decomposed wood (or for other periods, sometimes the presence of nails). This has been observed for burials IV and XX in Skateholm II and graves 10 and 11 in Vedbæk-Bøgebakken, where a dark trace of wood could be followed around the body or parts of it. From an archaeothanatological point of view, a coffin is identified as an empty space in which the body decomposes, and it is identified through the secondary evidence of how it affects the spatial distribution of the bones. This means that archaeothanatology can be helpful

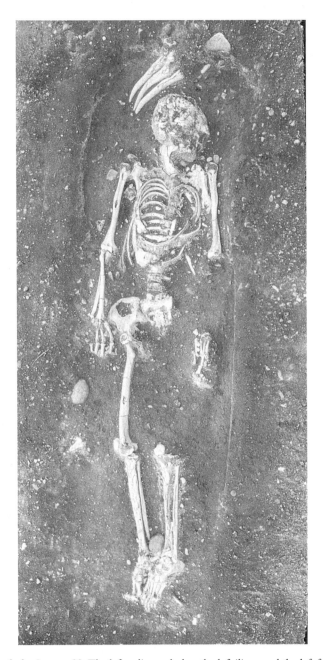

Figure 10.4 Skateholm I, grave 28. The left radius and ulna, the left ilium, and the left femur could have been removed from the burial at an advanced stage in the process of decomposition. The minimal disturbance indicates that the intervention was carefully planned (Photograph: L. Larsson).

to further the analysis of what kind of structure the preserved decomposed wood might have had. For the Skateholm cases, the archaeothanatological analysis clearly indicated that the body decomposed in a filled space. There is no movement outside of the initial volume occupied by the cadaver. Grave 11 in Vedbæk-Bøgebakken does not contain any human remains, and one interpretation put forward by the excavators is that the body was removed from the grave. If that were the case, its initial placement within a coffin of some kind would have been helpful in this process. Unfortunately, since there are no human remains left, an archaeothanatological analysis cannot test this hypothesis. For grave 10 in Vedbæk-Bøgebakken, the situation is more complex. Here, the body was placed on top of deer antlers, slightly elevating the body from the pit floor. But even in this case, there were only very slight movements outside of the initial volume of the cadaver, and there are no clear indications of a coffin creating an empty volume for the decomposition. The presence of wood in these cases, however, is undeniable. It is more likely that the wood remnants originate from some other arrangement, such as less durable construction, for example, an envelope made of bark, like the one preserved in the Mesolithic burial in Korsør Nor (Norling-Christiansen and Bröste, 1945). It would leave remnants of decomposed wood, but it would not necessarily have created a longer-lasting barrier preventing the surrounding sediment to penetrate the volume once occupied by the body as the soft tissues decomposed.

Other examples of previous interpretations that can be rejected through archaeothanatological analysis concern the practice of simultaneous versus successive deposition of bodies within the same grave. For most burials with more than one individual, the original interpretation of simultaneous deposition can be confirmed by archaeothanatological analysis. In grave 41 in Skateholm I (Figure 10.5), however, archaeothanatological analysis refuted the previous interpretation of a successive deposition. In this grave, a male is buried on his right side with his limbs flexed. A child was held facing him. The child was placed on its left side with the upper limbs along the body and the lower limbs flexed at 90° at the hip and the feet placed against the pelvis of the adult. The hyperflexion of the right wrist of the male, which is placed immediately in front of the face of this child, was initially viewed as unnatural and interpreted as the result of a disturbance caused by a secondary deposition of the child in the burial. The archaeothanatological analysis does not support this interpretation. There is no indication that this grave had been re-opened. There is no disturbance of the skeletal articulations that would be the result of successive burial in the same grave. In fact, the burial is remarkably undisturbed. The hyperflexion of the wrist can be explained as the result of the weight of the head of this child being displaced into secondarily formed voids, which would have put pressure on the hand and the wrist during the process of decomposition, thus creating an exaggerated spreading in the distribution of the bones.

New discoveries

The final and perhaps most rewarding result of archaeothanatological analysis of archival documentation involves new discoveries, as the taphonomic study can make visible burial structures that were not previously seen.

In Vedbæk-Bøgebakken, the most exciting new discovery was generated by what is probably the most well-known burial from either site, the iconic grave 8 in Vedbæk-Bøgebakken, where a woman was buried with a newborn by her right side, laid on its back (Figure 10.6). The neonate was placed on top of the wing of a swan. The archaeothanatological analysis of this burial revealed interesting and contradictory indicators for the space of decomposition. The woman was lying on her back, with the lower limbs in extension. The cranium presents the anterior and superior surfaces upper-most and the cervical vertebrae are slightly flexed. The vertebral column is almost completely intact but presents a sinusoidal pattern with a couple of abrupt dislocations at the level of L3-L4, T9-T10, and T8-T9. These kinds of dislocations occur naturally but can also be exaggerated under certain circumstances. The thoracic cage exhibits a relevant, highly unusual pattern of decomposition. The first four ribs show a normal pattern for a supine

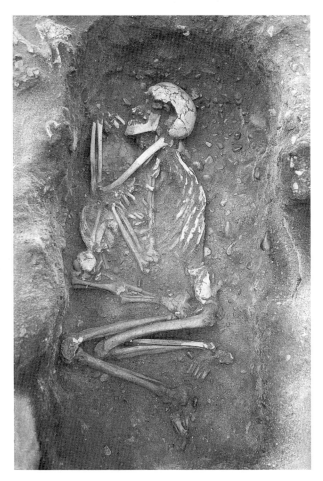

Figure 10.5 Skateholm I, grave 41. A double burial containing a male arranged to hold a child at the time of burial. The archaeothanatological analysis supports a simultaneous deposition and calls into question previous interpretations suggesting the re-opening of the grave (Photograph: L. Larsson).

body decomposing in a filled-in space, with (anatomically) anterior parts of the ribs projecting downward (caudally) and forward (anteriorly). For the rest of the ribs, the pattern is dramatically different and can be described as a 'lateral expansion' of the rib cage, with the posterior extremities of the ribs dislocated from the vertebrae and projecting anteriorly, with the bodies of the ribs distributed horizontally in the rib cage with the anterior parts of the ribs in front of the humeri on both sides, thus occupying spaces outside of the initial volume occupied by the cadaver. These movements indicate an empty space of decomposition. Yet, it does not map onto previously recognised patterns of decomposition, indicating a more unusual burial structure that would have influenced the post-decomposition arrangement of the skeleton of this female. The pelvis is well preserved and the sacro-iliac joints and the pubic symphysis are disarticulated, with the lateral collapse of the ilia. This is a common indicator for an empty space of decomposition, but normally a lateral rotation of the femora and a lateral movement of the patellae would be expected. This is not the case here. The femora remain in their original position, slightly rotated medially. The right patella has slid medially during decomposition and is resting against the anterior and lateral sides of the medial condyle of the femur. The left patella has slid laterally and is resting

Figure 10.6 Vedbæk-Bøgebakken, grave 8. The double burial contains a woman buried with a newborn placed on the wing of a swan to her left. The archaeothanatological analysis suggests that the body of the woman was placed on organic material that during decomposition left a void beneath the body, which would explain the unusual pattern of distribution of the bones of the thoracic cage (Photograph: L. Larsen; Source: The National Museum, Copenhagen; Reproduced with a CC-BY-SA license).

against the lateral side of the medial condyle of the femur. In contrast to the impression of an empty space, the bones of the hands and feet are remarkably well articulated, indicating progressive infilling of the original volume of the body during decomposition, a hypothesis strengthened by the fact that the extremities are placed in unstable positions on small stones, which would have contributed to their destabilisation due to the lack of support from the surrounding soil.

When considered together, there are indicators for both open and filled spaces of decomposition around different areas of the body. The pattern observed for the thoracic cage indicates that there must have been an empty space behind and around the thorax of the individual at the time of decomposition, a void into which the ribs could collapse into posteriorly. This would explain the lateral expansion of the ribs and the verticalisation of their posterior extremities. The movement of the ribs superiorly and laterally also indicates that the thorax was pressed superiorly since the normal movement of the ribs would be the opposite: caudally and anteriorly. The suggestion is that the body was placed initially on top of some organic material, which decomposed and created an empty space into which the bones could collapse posteriorly. The force with which the body was projected superiorly suggests that there might have been beam supports that did not evenly support the area around the thorax. A wooden beam structure behind the body that separated it from the immediate bottom of the pit structure may be the most straightforward explanation. This model would also account for why other parts of the body are unaffected since it would allow for hands, lower limbs, and feet to decompose surrounded by sediment that would progressively fill the voids in the initial volume of the decomposing body, thus hindering significant movement. While the interpretation is only supported by the spatial pattern of the bones, there are similar – if only occasional – practices of placing organic materials under the interred body. In fact, the child in the same grave is also placed on top of an organic object (the wing of a swan). Other burials at Vedbæk-Bøgebakken contain deer antlers placed beneath the head (grave 22) and body (grave 10) of the dead. Similar patterns of partial empty spaces behind the body, although not nearly as clear and convincing, can be observed in several other graves, including grave 6 in Vedbæk-Bøgebakken (however, this burial is severely disturbed), and grave IX in Skateholm II (where the pattern affects only the right hemi-thorax).

Deeper insights into practice and experience

In addition to yielding new data and more robust arguments to back up, nuance or refute previous interpretations of the mortuary practices at the sites, the application of archaeothanatology also changes the understanding of mortuary ritual at a deeper level. Archaeothanatology is very focussed on both the physical handling of the body and the changing state of the human cadaver. This allows for a strong connection to theories of embodiment and ritual practice. In fact, archaeothanatology provides a unique synergy between archaeological material, methods and theory, all focussed on the reconstruction of ritual *practice*. The theoretical work has been developed in more detail elsewhere (Nilsson Stutz, 2003, 2008), but here, only a brief account of the theoretical connections to the material sources and the methods used is presented in order to discuss the kinds of results this approach yielded in the study of Skateholm and Vedbæk-Bøgebakken.

Approaching topics such as ritual from the perspective of archaeological remains is challenging. There is no access to informants to explain the meaning of the practices and, most of the time, there is not even access to texts describing what was going on. Only the preserved material vestiges of what people in the past *were doing* remains (i.e. the practices). While this is often viewed as a shortcoming, ritual theory grounded in practice theory (Bell, 1992, 1997) suggests that embodied practice may be the most fundamental aspect of ritual. Practice – or the way of doing things – is often shared throughout a culture through learning, habit, discourse, and judgment. Practices may be highly structured and faithfully reproduced, even if they are ascribed different or, as the opposite case may be, very generic *meanings*. It is through physical engagement, embodied knowledge and practice that ritual generates its effects of 'creating a world' – a structure (*sensu* Bourdieu, 1977) or ontological reality. When it comes to mortuary rituals, they can be approached as a specific rite of passage (van Gennep, 1909; Turner, 1969), one that effects the transition from life to death. These rituals tend to handle two co-existing dilemmas: the loss of a social being and the emergence of a cadaver – a dead body in a state of transformation. The dead body can be likened to an *abject* (Kristeva, 1980), a liminal category that challenges the social and cultural order. It is no longer alive – no longer a subject – and the effects of this can be readily perceived through the transformations that immediately follow death (and that archaeothanatology has reconstructed for consideration in mortuary archaeology). At the same time, it is not yet any object, it still maintains part of that subjectivity, partially embodying the character of a person. All mortuary rituals include practices that engage the dead body by transforming it, controlling it and ultimately re-defining it from life to death, from person to cadaver. Through these ritual practices of handling the body, a death that is acceptable, controlled and perhaps even desirable and good, is produced. Moreover, the most fundamental structures are often reproduced without being negotiated, and repetition can thus be viewed as particularly significant in this process. From an archaeological perspective, this means that, while access to thoughts or words of people in the past is lacking, the application of proper methodologies permits access to these crucial practices relating to the cultural production of death. The questions can then be posed: what do the practices indicate with regard to the relationship between the body and the person? In addition, the focus on practice and the cultural production of death and dying permits a better appreciation for the lived experience of these rituals, with a further theoretical connection to the kind of insights provided by an archaeology of the senses (e.g. Day, 2013; Hamilakis, 2015; Nilsson Stutz, 2019).

When looking at the mortuary practices at Skateholm and Vedbæk-Bøgebakken from this perspective, the focus shifts to what people there were doing with their dead and what these embodied ritualised practices might reveal about their understanding of life and death, the body, the self, and so on. When applied to the case study of Skateholm and Vedbæk-Bøgebakken, it was possible to discern a pattern for a normative burial, a production of death which was almost non-negotiable and which reflects very deep structures and beliefs about life, death and the body. In almost all the cases, the body was buried in a fresh state, often arranged in a life-like position – an impression that is emphasised in cases where more than one body is buried in the same grave, and the bodies are arranged to relate to each other, having been turned towards each other, sometimes with one holding the other (as in the case of grave 43 in Skateholm, described above). The body is most often treated in death as if it still maintains a degree of its humanity. This impression is further strengthened in cases where the body was shielded from contact with the covering soil or lifted up, placed on a platform of some kind, including placement on the wing of a swan (as in the case of grave 8 in Vedbæk-Bøgebakken). This ritually staged last image of the dead – as very life-like – would have been a salient feature in the Southern Scandinavian Mesolithic understanding of death. Maintaining the integrity of the dead body was central. This may also explain why so few of the burials were disturbed at these sites. Disturbances do occur in a few instances, and in those cases, there is little evidence of attempts to rectify the event. In those instances, it is almost as if the individuality of the body would have been gradually stripped away from the bones over time and underground. However, there are also tensions within this system. The careful extraction of bones from the burial described above (grave 28 from Skateholm I) indicates a keen knowledge and awareness of the decomposition of the body and an attention to the process. Perhaps this burial indicates the beginning of a transition towards an emerging emphasis on the essence of bone as symbol and representation – as part of a cosmology that would become increasingly more central after the transition to the Neolithic, but that already may have had its roots in increasingly sedentary hunter-gatherer communities in Southern Scandinavia. There are a few burials that appear almost anathema to the burial programme, as is the case with the incomplete body concealed by a sack (grave 13). There are various possible scenarios that might explain this situation. Perhaps the body was treated in an explicitly different way to underscore a message to the community, or alternatively, the manner of death was perceived as so destructive that the burial was an attempt to shield the onlookers from the state of the cadaver, ones which had broken away from the norm to the point of challenging the potential for the ritual to produce a good death.

Conclusion

The study of the Mesolithic burials at Skateholm and Vedbæk-Bøgebakken shows both the potential for applying an archaeothanatological analysis to older excavation materials, producing completely new results but also providing evidence to support, nuance and even refute older interpretations. In addition to the added information, the study also reveals the potential that comes from combining archaeothanatology with practice-centred archaeological and social theory to gain a deeper understanding of the mortuary rituals in the past.

References

Albrethsen, S.E. and Brinch Petersen, E. (1977). Excavation of a Mesolithic Cemetery at Vedbæk, Denmark. *Acta Archaeologica*, 47, pp. 1–28.

Bell, C. (1992). *Ritual theory, ritual practice*. Oxford: Oxford University Press.

Bell, C. (1997). *Ritual; perspectives and dimensions*. Oxford: Oxford University Press.

Bonnie, R. (2011). 'Haven't We Dug enough Now?' Excavation in the Light of Intergenerational Equity, *Archaeological Dialogues*, 18(1), pp. 48–58.

Bourdieu, P. (1977). *An outline of a theory of practice*. Cambridge: Cambridge University Press.

Brinch Petersen, E. (2015). Diversity of Mesolithic Vedbæk. *Acta Archaeologica*, 86(1), pp: 7–13.

Day, J. (2013). Introduction: making senses of the past. In: J. Day, ed., *Making Senses of the Past: Toward a Sensory Archaeology*. Carbondale: Southern Illinois University Press, pp. 1–31.

Demoule, J.-P. (2011). We still have to excavate – but not at any price. *Archaeological Dialogues*, 18(1), pp. 5–10.

Duday, H., Courtaud, P., Crubézy, E., Sellier, P. and Tillier, A.-M. (1990). L'Anthropologie 'de terrain': reconnaissance et interprétation des gestes funéraires. *Bulletins et Mémoires de la Société d'Anthropologie de Paris*, 2 (3–4), pp. 29–50.

Hamilakis, Y. (2015). *Archaeology and the senses: human experience, memory, and affect*. Cambridge: Cambridge University Press.

Kannegaard Nielsen, E. and Brinch Petersen, E. (1993). Grave, mennesker og hunde. In: S. Hvass and B. Storgaard. *Da Klinger i Muld: 25 Års Arkæologi i Danmark*. København: Aarhus Universitetsforlag, pp. 76–80.

Kristeva, J. (1980). *Pouvoirs de l'horreur*. Paris: Editions du Seuil.

Larsson, L. (1984). Skateholmsprojektet. På spåren efter gravsedsförändringar, ceremoniplatser och tama rävar. *Limhamniana*, pp. 49-84.

Larsson, L. (1988a). *The Skateholm Project I. Man and environment*. Lund: Regiae Societatis Humaniorum Litterarum Lundensis LXXIX.

Larsson, L. (1988b). *Ett fångstsamhälle för 7000 år sedan, boplatser och gravar i Skateholm*. Kristianstad: Signum.

Larsson, L. (1993). The Skateholm Project: Late Mesolithic coastal settlement in Southern Sweden. In: P. Bogucki, ed., *Case Studies in European Prehistory*. Ann Arbor: University of Michigan Press, pp. 31–62.

Lidén, K. and Eriksson, G. (2002). Mammalian stable isotope ecology in a Mesolithic lagoon at Skateholm. *Journal of Nordic Archaeological Science*, 13, pp. 5–10.

Nilsson Stutz, L. (2003). *Embodied rituals and ritualized bodies: tracing ritual practices in late Mesolithic burials*. Acta Archaeologica Lundensia Series 8, (46). Stockholm: Almqvist & Wiksell International.

Nilsson Stutz, L. (2008). Capturing ritual practice: an attempt to harmonize archaeological method and theory. In: L. Fogelin, ed., *Religion, Archaeology and the Material World*. Carbondale: Southern Illinois University Press, pp. 159–178.

Nilsson Stutz, L. (2019). Sensing death and experiencing mortuary ritual. In: R. Skeates and J. Day, eds., *The Routledge Handbook of Sensory Archaeology*. London: Routledge, pp. 149–163.

Norling-Christiansen, H. and Bröste, K. (1945). Skeletgraven fra Korsør Nor. Et menneskefund fra ældre stenalder. *Nationalmuseets Arbejdsmark*, pp. 5–17.

Persson, O. and Persson, E. (1984). *Anthropological report on the Mesolithic graves from Skateholm, Southern Sweden: excavation seasons 1980–82*. Lund: Lunds Universitets Historiska Museum.

Peyroteo Stjerna, R. (2016). *On death in the Mesolithic: or the mortuary practices of the last hunter-gatherers of the South-Western Iberian Peninsula, 7th–6th millennium BCE. Occasional papers in Archaeology*. Uppsala: Uppsala University.

Torv, M. (2016). Persistent Practices: a Multi-Disciplinary Study of Hunter-Gatherer Mortuary Remains from *circa* 6500–2600 cal. BC. Unpublished Ph.D. thesis. Tartu University, Estonia.

Turner, V. (1969). *The ritual process: structure and anti-structure*. Brunswick and London: Aldine Transaction Publishers.

van Gennep, A. (1909). *Les rites de passage: étude systématique des rites*. Paris: Émile Nourry.

11

NEOLITHIC BURIALS OF INFANTS AND CHILDREN

Mélie Le Roy

LAMPEA, Laboratoire méditerranéen de préhistoire Europe Afrique, UMR 7269, CNRS-Aix Marseille University, Aix-en-Provence, France

School of Natural and Built Environment, Archaeology-Palaeocology, Queen's University Belfast, Belfast, Northern Ireland, United Kingdom

Stéphane Rottier

PACEA, De la Préhistoire à l'Actuel: Culture, Environnement et Anthropologie, UMR 5199, CNRS-Université de Bordeaux, Pessac, France

Introduction

In archaeology much of the data used to understand past behaviours derives from the funerary world. More specifically, studies focus on the status of each individual and the place occupied by death in society (Thomas, 1975). Indeed, the relationship to death and its inclusion in everyday life is expressed in the funerary practices and in the space dedicated to the deceased. The way the deceased is deposited may suggest a symbolic consideration between the dead and those left behind. The differences identified through the study of funerary practices and biological data potentially reflect variations in social status within the population. As such, funerary practices could be related to social status, sex and age-at-death (Thomas, 1975; Suzuki, 2000).

During the Neolithic in France, which dates from 5700–2100 BC (Tarrête and Le Roux, 2008), funerary practices changed from a single burial tradition (one person deposited in one burial structure) to collective burial sites, in which several individuals accumulated over time with the regular or sequential addition of corpses in a single burial structure, which became almost exclusively found. This change gradually occurred over the course of the period, but it did not necessarily occur at the same time in the different regions of interest. For the purposes of this study and in order to avoid the influence of phenomena too dependent on a given period or a geographical area, the Neolithic was divided into three broad time spans: the Early Neolithic (5700–4900 BC), the Middle Neolithic (4900–3500 BC), and the Late Neolithic (3500–2100 BC). To date, results within this chronological period in France demonstrate that funerary practices (e.g. position of the body, grave good associations and location of burials) varied and changed considerably. In this highly complex context, one may wonder what place young individuals had within these Neolithic societies. Children are rarely, if at all, mentioned in studies and their details are often embedded within descriptions of the rest of the population.

DOI: 10.4324/9781351030625-14

This chapter aims to undertake a social consideration of Neolithic immature individuals through the study of funerary practices, funerary selection and through comparisons with ethnographic examples related to age–at–death.

Materials and methods

Data collection

To provide a reliable sample of archaeological sites for analysis, an inventory of burial sites dated to the Neolithic was constructed for France. This work was based on an exhaustive review of the archaeological literature regarding these funerary sites (monographs, books and articles), as well as data from original research results of the authors (Bec Drelon, Le Roy and Recchia Quiniou, 2014; Le Roy *et al.*, 2014; Le Roy, 2015, 2018; Le Roy and Bec-Drelon, 2016; Bouffiès *et al.*, 2017; Jean *et al.*, 2019; Le Roy, Brunel and Lateur, 2019). A total of 1301 burial sites (Figure 11.1) were identified and organised by the nearest town in order to provide an idea of the

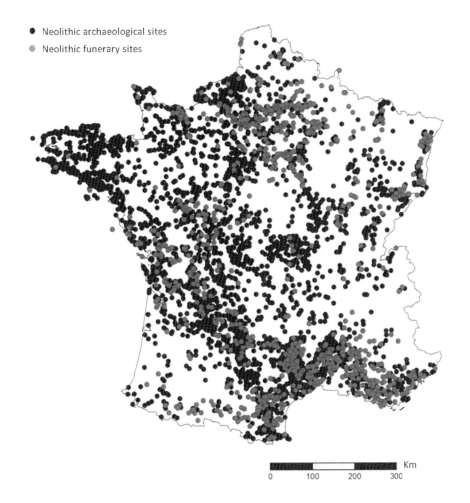

Figure 11.1 Distribution of Neolithic archaeological sites and funerary archaeological sites in France.

distribution of available sites. The archaeological and anthropological data were gathered into a database. Archaeological information included the different types of structures uncovered (e.g. pits, megalithic tombs), site location (e.g. burial in open air or cave sites) and anthropological data (e.g. minimum number of individuals, number of immature individuals, age-at-death, etc.). To avoid methodological bias in comparing archaeological sites, only sites for which methods to assess individual age-at-death were reported in publications and considered reliable (Moorrees, Fanning and Hunt, 1963a, 1963b; Fazekas and Kósa, 1978; Ubelaker, 1989; Scheuer and Black, 2000) were selected. The skeletal remains of immature individuals (0–19 years, N=2790 over the 3 periods) is the focus of this study.

Description of funerary practices

The archaeothanatological approach requires a consideration of taphonomy; this is a common term used in archaeological studies that refers to all processes related to the preservation or alteration of organic remains following burial (Efremov, 1940; Lyman, 2010). In the field of funerary archaeology, the term applies to the corpse and the various processes that affect the body after its deposition (Sorg and Haglund, 2002; Duday, 2009; Nawrocki, 2009; Schotsmans, Márquez-Grant and Forbes, 2017). The ultimate goal of the archaeothanatological approach is to reconstruct social behaviour from the treatment of the dead, reconstructing the grave as it would have been in its original form and the interactions between people based on evidence from their graves.

For each immature individual recorded in the database and for whom data were available, the general position of the body, mainly based on observations of the disposition of the torso, were recorded. There are several positions: on the left side, on the right side, on the back (supine) or on the front (prone). The four limbs (right and left upper limbs and lower right and left limbs) examined separately may present in four states each: in extension (the limb has no degree of flexion), in slight flexion (the angle of flexion of the limb is less than 20°), in flexion (the angle of flexion of the limb is between 20° and 90°) or in hyperflexion (the angle of flexion of the limb is greater than 90°). Finally, the orientation of the cephalic extremity with respect to the feet of the dead according to the different cardinal points was used to establish the initial position of the body.

Most of the samples employed in this study derive from the archaeological literature and the most homogeneous data with regard to funerary practices were selected. The funerary practices included the position of the body and limbs, the associated grave goods (flint, ceramic, ochre, faunal remains and shell fragments) and the location of the burial (within a domestic settlement or in a strictly funerary area). Only differences in funerary treatment were used to identify distinctive patterns. Indeed, when each individual was buried the same way, it is difficult, if not impossible, to discern distinctive behaviours, even if it does not necessarily mean that no differentiation was made during their lifetimes (Thomas, 1975). Furthermore, the different elements considered were not all treated with equal importance. Interpretations derived from observations of funerary practices, such as grave good associations and position of the bodies, are strongly dependent on the number of individuals involved in the study. On the contrary, the location of burials, within settlements or in strictly funerary sites, is much more discriminating, and this location was used to identify social differences based on age-at-death (Le Roy, 2017; Le Roy *et al.*, 2018; Le Roy, Rottier and Tillier, 2018).

Study of funerary selection based on age-at-death

Although exact mortality rates in ancient societies (Sellier, 1996; Séguy and Buchet, 2011) are unknown, observations of 'pre-jennerian' and 'pre-industrial' populations (Ledermann, 1969) are the most like those of Neolithic populations, following the same pattern of archaic mortality as far as it is known (Masset, 1987; Sellier, 1996). Note that this would only provide an 'average picture' of reality (Buchet and Séguy, 2002). The main purpose of such an approach is to demonstrate any over-or under-representation of age classes[1] in relation to a so-called 'natural' mortality rate. It is in no case aimed at establishing an accurate mortality profile for Neolithic populations (Buchet and Séguy, 2002; Le Roy *et al.*, 2018).

Four major types of funerary selection based on the age-at-death of immature individuals were observed within the Neolithic funerary sites (Figure 11.2). The first type of funerary selection (Type 1) corresponds to a 'normal' mortality curve. No age class differs significantly from the expected theoretical values (Figure 11.2). This type of curve may indicate that the entire population was buried in the same place without exception based on age-at-death. Type 2 funerary selection is characterised by a significant under-representation of one or two age groups below 5 years of age (Figure 11.2). Such a deficit within the sample would lead to the conclusion that

Shape of the mortality profile for each type of funerary selection

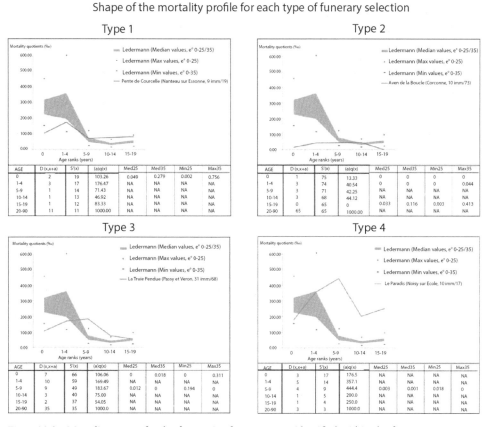

Figure 11.2 Mortality curves for the four major funerary types identified within the funerary archaeological sites from Neolithic France (imm = immature; e° = life expectancy; D = number of deaths; S = number of survivors; q = mortality quotient).

---

1 Immature individuals are normally classified into age classes, which are generally used in demographic studies of archaeological series (five-year age classes, with the exception of the first two, which are one to four years and five to nine years (e.g. Masset, 1987; Sellier, 1996; Séguy and Buchet, 2011).

individuals in age class [0] years and/or [1–4] years received different funerary treatments and were not included in the burial site with the older members of the population. Funerary selection Type 3 includes both an under-representation of younger children (less than 5 years of age) and an over-representation of older immature individuals (greater than 5 years of age) (Figure 11.2). Socio-cultural selection can be considered in these instances, and these funerary complexes appear to have been used for the burial of older immature individuals with the youngest having been excluded. The possibility that a mortality crisis due to an epidemic or a violent episode was responsible for a mortality curve such as this is also possible, as has already been demonstrated for more recent periods (Castex and Drancourt, 2005). Funerary selection Type 4 shows a significant over-representation of one or more age groups (Figure 11.2). In this type, only children aged greater than 5 years of age-at-death are represented. These age groups have the lowest expected mortality rates according to natural mortality models (e.g. Ledermann, 1969). The anomaly could be due to the under-representation of adults.

Ethnographic comparisons

The interpretation of the role or place of individuals within societies is based essentially on an understanding of the relationship between material culture and materialisation of social identity or, more precisely, the way in which material culture is used in the staging or the production of an identity. In 1968, Binford proposed a new definition of social identity by establishing the social *persona*, a composite of the statuses occupied by an individual up until the time of death as represented in the funerary context of the deceased (Binford, 1968). The status of the individual within a particular social group can thus be established from funerary assemblages, although the fact that a society may express its social organisation in other ways cannot be entirely ruled out (Thomas, 1975). In 1985, Hodder defined 'post-processual archaeology', which attempts to understand the structure of a society in a more subjective way by interpreting archaeological remains (Hodder, 1985). For some years now, this movement has focussed on the specific issue of the place of children within the past social organisation (Lucy, 2005) because children are producers and consumers of material culture and also convey a social identity (Derevenski, 1994). Furthermore, there are changes in production and consumption linked to the changing status of a child as s/he passes through childhood. Each of these changes could be at the stage at which a particular 'rite de passage', as theorised by van Gennep (1909), is initiated. One can expect these acts to have left their mark on the material attributes correlated to each status. Therefore, the identity of the deceased can be approached via ethnographic studies and applied to answer questions inherent in the definition of gender, ethnicity, belief/religion and especially, with respect to this study, questions of age and status. In this study, examples drawn from the ethnographic literature were used to determine how the different stages of childhood might have influenced funerary practices.

Results and discussion

The consideration of funerary practices in relation to the exclusion or inclusion of certain age classes highlights changes in funerary behaviour concerning social age groups related to age-at-death, body position and location of the burial. It is then possible to propose age classes of a social nature for each Neolithic period and for the large regional areas distinguished within France (Le Roy, Rottier and Tillier 2018; Figure 11.3). A certain consistency can be observed between the three main divisions identified: Children [0–11], Adolescents [8–15] and

Adults [>15].[2] Note that more numerous and reliable data was available for the Middle Neolithic, which permitted the definition of an additional age class of Little Children [0–1] (Figure 11.3). One must bear in mind, however, that these transitional ages are not always accurate due to the imprecision in estimating the age-at-death of individuals but also due to the small sample sizes available. The proposed age classes are dependent upon the availability of individual data. For example, published Early Neolithic burial sites are extremely rare, few sites are thus available to be included in this analysis. Also, the Late Neolithic with its more frequent collective burial sites makes it difficult to describe individual funerary practices related to age-at-death. In the latter case, the situation may be improved through very specific analyses for which individual information from collective burials then becomes available (e.g. Le Roy *et al.*, 2014, 2020), but these case studies are still very rare.

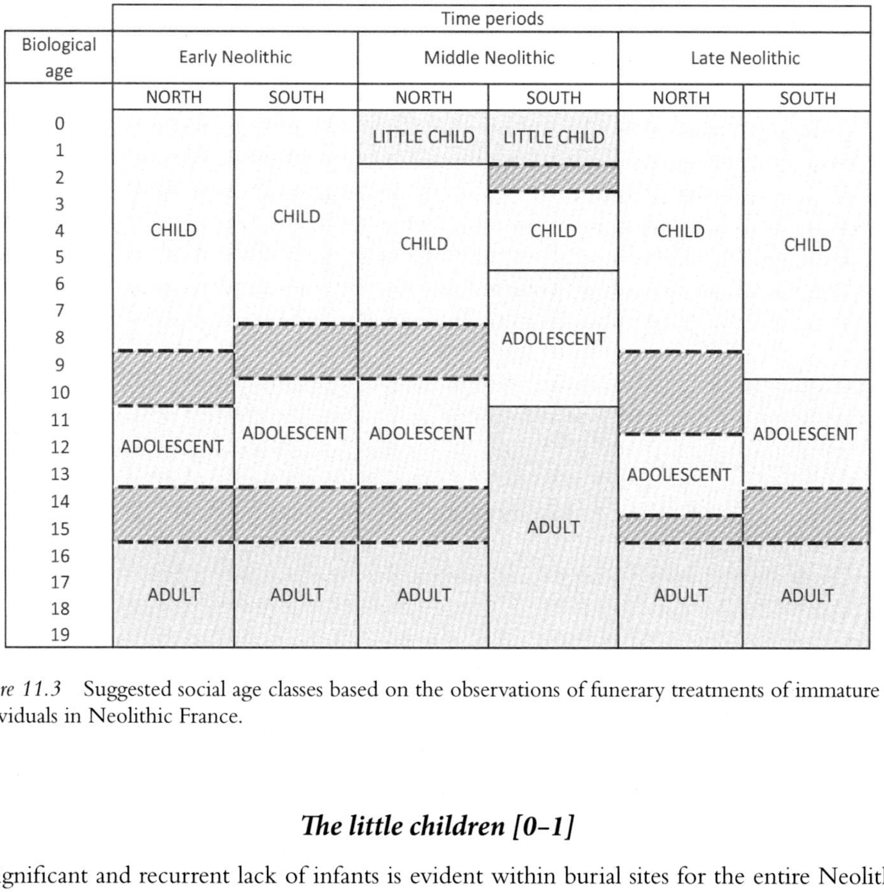

Biological age	Time periods					
	Early Neolithic		Middle Neolithic		Late Neolithic	
	NORTH	SOUTH	NORTH	SOUTH	NORTH	SOUTH
0	CHILD	CHILD	LITTLE CHILD	LITTLE CHILD	CHILD	CHILD
1						
2			CHILD			
3				CHILD		
4						
5						
6						
7						
8	ADOLESCENT	ADOLESCENT	ADOLESCENT	ADOLESCENT	ADOLESCENT	ADOLESCENT
9						
10						
11						
12				ADULT		
13					ADOLESCENT	
14						
15						
16	ADULT	ADULT	ADULT		ADULT	ADULT
17						
18						
19						

Figure 11.3 Suggested social age classes based on the observations of funerary treatments of immature individuals in Neolithic France.

The little children [0–1]

A significant and recurrent lack of infants is evident within burial sites for the entire Neolithic period (Le Roy, 2017; Le Roy *et al.*, 2018); therefore, this age class is only significantly visible in the archaeological record for the Middle Neolithic period. Indeed, the second and third types of funerary selection are frequently observed throughout the Neolithic period, indicating

---

2 The terms 'children', 'adolescents' and 'adults' were arbitrarily chosen by the authors.

a lack of younger individuals in the funerary assemblages where the other age groups are well represented (Figure 11.2). Numerous cases are observed within the sample for the entirety of the Neolithic, showing a wide diversity in types of burial structure and burial tradition (from burial grounds of single burials to collective burial sites). For example, the burial ground of 'Les Octrois' (Ensisheim, Haut-Rhin, eastern France), dating from the Early Neolithic shows a significant under-representation of infants (along with children younger than 5 years of age-at-death) (Jeunesse, 1995, 1998). This observation partly explains the difficulty of identifying a more precise social age class for the youngest individuals and the lack of a clear difference with the following age class.

During the Middle Neolithic, numerous sites also present a significant lack of young individuals across the whole variety of contexts represented: open-air burial grounds (e.g. 'La Goumoizière' in Saint Martin-la-Rivière (Vienne, southeastern France) (Patte, 1971; Verjux, Simonin and Richard, 1998; Chambon, 2003) and collective burials in megalithic structures (e.g. 'La Pierre Virante' in Xanton Chassenon (Vendée, western France) (Joussaume, 1976; Chambon, 2003). Nevertheless, for those individuals recovered from burial sites, specific funerary treatment can be identified. In northern France, for example, infants are completely excluded from settlements and are only found within strictly funerary sites, whereas in the South of France, they are preferentially buried next to domestic structures. In both cases, the body positions, the nature of the grave goods and the location of the burial differ significantly from the following age classes, potentially marking a change of social status. For example, young children in northern France are more likely to be buried on the left side or on the back (i.e. supinely), whereas older children show more often a predilection for the right side and positions on the back (Le Roy, 2015).

Finally, the Late Neolithic includes a large number of funerary sites where younger children are significantly missing. Most of the burials are collective, either in megalithic structures (e.g. 'Dolmen la Caumette' in Notre Dame de Londres (Hérault, western France) (Bec Drelon, Le Roy and Recchia Quiniou, 2014), pits (e.g. 'Les Réaudins' in Balloy (Seine-et-Marne, Île-de-France, northern France (Chambon and Mordant, 1996), in hypogea (e.g. Essomes-sur-Marne (Masset, 1995, 1997) or in caves (e.g. 'Clos d'Ayan' in Vesc, Drôme, southern France); Beeching *et al.,* 1987). No funerary patterning permits differentiation for any particular treatments between younger and older children.

The recurrent under-representation for these young people suggests a special status for them. Indeed, this has been frequently observed in ethnographic studies; for example, among the Sea Dayak (Iban) (of Southeast Asia) and Papuans (people of the Indonesian Peninsula and New Guinea), the youngest individuals benefit from a unique funerary ritual wherein they are deposited in a dead tree trunk or suspended from its branches (Hertz, 1970). From an archaeological point of view, such practices are difficult, if not impossible, to identify. These acts are considered to represent a direct return to their origins. The death of a young child generates a strong and almost immediate social reaction. Since these children have not yet been integrated socially into the community, it is not necessary to exclude them slowly over an extended funerary period. They can therefore return directly to the spirit world: 'The death of a newborn is an infra-social phenomenon; the society has not yet put anything of itself into the child and one does not feel afflicted by the disappearance of the child and remains indifferent' (Hertz, 1970: 77, first author's translation). This attitude does not necessarily call into question the social consideration of these young children but expresses a different meaning of their death compared to those of the rest of the group (cf. Veit, 1993). This age class also provides other insights. First, the intentionality of burying infants is sometimes not so evident (Le Roy and Murphy, 2020). For example, the case of the collective burial of 'La Hoguette' at Fontenay-le-Marmion (Calvados, northern

France) (Chambon, 2003) demonstrates the presence of a foetus among the remains. One may wonder if its presence is not accidental rather than intentional and, in fact, it was a pregnant woman that had been buried within this burial structure. Another case study revealed the presence of three infants in a ditch, interpreted as an abandonment of corpses for which no funerary rites were performed ('des sépultures de relégation') on the site of 'La Croix Magret' at Berry-au-Bac (Aisne, eastern France) (Dubouloz *et al.*, 2005). Also, this age class is the most frequently uncovered in multiple burials (e.g. 'Genevray' at Thonon-les-Bains, Auvergne-Rhône-Alpes, eastern France) (Baudais *et al.*, 2006; Gatto and Gisclon, 2007), 'Porte aux Bergers' at Vignely (Seine-et-Marne, northern France) (Chambon and Lanchon, 2003) 'Les Patureaux' at Chichery (Bourgogne-Franche-Comté in north-central France), (Chambon *et al.*, 2010; Thomas, Chambon and Murail, 2011). One may wonder whether these were opportunistic depositions since they did not apparently receive a proper burial. On the contrary, other cases do not leave any doubt of the willingness to bury very young children. For example, the case of 'Terrasse Lavimona' at Villeneuve-les-Tolosane (Haute Garonne, southwestern France (Brossier *et al.*, 2000) presents an infant buried in a seated position where the inclusion of ceramic vessels helped to maintain the body in this position. Finally, examples of associations with exceptional grave goods raise the question of specific status; in the necropolis of 'Porte aux Bergers' at Vignely (Seine-et-Marne, Île de France, north-central France), one infant was buried with a wolf axis vertebra transformed into a pendant (Thomas, Chambon and Murail, 2011), and also in the site of 'Montbeyre La Cadoule' at Teyran (Seine-et-Marne, Île de France, north-central France) a ceramic spoon was found associated with a very young child (Tchérémissinoff, 2003).

The children [0/1–8]

This age group is visible in the archaeological record for each period studied for this contribution. Nevertheless, a few differences in funerary treatments with respect to age-at-death occur, depending on the period and geographical area (Figure 11.3). During the Early Neolithic, no distinction in terms of funerary ritual can be found for individuals between 0 and 10 years old. In both the northern and southern regions, a wide variety of body positions and grave good associations are present. The only difference between the two geographical areas concerns the location of burials: children are only buried within strictly funerary burial sites in the northern area, whereas in the south, they are present in settlements only (Figure 11.4).

As mentioned above, during the Middle Neolithic, an age class representing the younger children is visible in the archaeological record, implying that this social category of children concerns slightly older individuals from 1.5 to 9 years of age. There are only a few cases showing great care in the funerary treatment of these children, as at the site of 'Coste Rouge', Beaufort (Soumont, Hérault, southern France) (Vaquer *et al.*, 2007) where a child of [5–7] years of age-at-death is buried alone within a stone chest (Figure 11.4A).

This age class does not present a unique form of treatment in terms of funerary practices compared to the rest of the population. Indeed, they show no specific position, grave good associations or burial locations. In short, they are buried like anybody else in both the north and south regions. This particular shared characteristic is observed at a regional scale but is also visible at only single sites as illustrated by the thorough study of the site of 'Les Noisats' (Gurgy, Yonne, Bourgogne-Franche-Comté, north-central France) (Le Roy, 2015). A high proportion of children aged under nine years of age-at-death were associated with adult male burials (Le Roy *et al.*, 2016). In addition, funerary practices were also very similar between adult males and

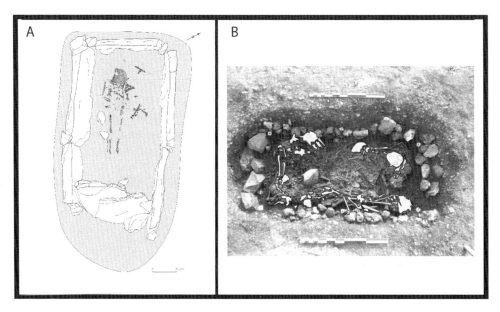

Figure 11.4 Examples of Neolithic child burials in France. 4A. 'Coste Rouge' in Beaufort, Middle Neolithic, the remains of an immature individual of 5–7 years of age-at-death, positioned supinely and buried within a megalithic chest, (Vaquer *et al.,* 2007: 137, fig. 3); 4B. 'La Truie Pendue' in Passy-Véron, late Neolithic, position of the immature remains of an individual under nine years of age-at-death (in white) on the edge of a collective burial (from Le Roy *et al.,* 2014; Photograph: S. Thiol).

children; both were often buried within a pit, associated with ochre, flint and faunal remains (Le Roy, 2015).

On the contrary, during the Late Neolithic, children under nine years of age show a very wide variety of body positions. No consistency seems to appear among the large sample of collective burial sites included in the sample. Firstly, it is worth remembering that it is not possible to identify individuals among these collective burials. However, as shown with the study of the collective burial site of 'La Truie Pendue' (Passy/Véron, Yonne, Bourgogne-Franche-Comté, north-central France) (Le Roy *et al.,* 2014), it is also possible that this lack of consistency reflects a specific funerary treatment to optimise the use of space. Children under nine years of age-at-death seem not to form a major portion of buried individuals and were added to the burial in a way to fill the voids left within the structure, which resulted in a very wide variety of burial positions (Figure 11.4; Le Roy *et al.,* 2020). This age class, however, does show some peculiarities that differ from the succeeding age classes, especially with regard to the grave goods associated with the individuals on a regional scale. Indeed, during the different periods, the individuals with an age-at-death between 0 and 1–8 years old are mostly buried like the rest of the population; on the back or the left side during the Early Neolithic, on the back with mostly ceramic pots in the northern part during the Middle Neolithic, and finally during Late Neolithic most are buried within collective graves.

Nevertheless, there are some particular differences. For example, during the Early Neolithic, some children were buried with bone figurines (Allard, Dubouloz and Hachem 1997), and the use of ochre in funerary practices for this specific age class occurs frequently in the Paris Basin during the Middle Neolithic. In addition, the presence of complete necklaces made of faunal bone or shell in association with individuals from this age group is quite often found during the Late Neolithic.

The adolescents [7–15]

The age class comprised of those individuals with an age-at-death of [7–15] years of age shows a wide variety of body positions and grave good associations throughout the Neolithic period. Nevertheless, some recurrent observations occur in different periods and regions. Individuals in northern France are more likely to be buried on their right sides during the Early Neolithic. At the same time, people from the south are mostly found with necklaces made of shells. During the following period, individuals continue to show the same wide variability. It is difficult to dissociate them from the rest of the population because they do not possess any specific burial position, grave good associations or burial locations. Nevertheless, some repeated patterns occur during the Middle Neolithic for southern adolescents, who were only buried within settlements, similar to the adult cohort. Finally, at the end of the Neolithic period, northern individuals usually have ochre within their burials. Except for this inclusion, once again, heterogeneity in burial rituals is the most obvious pattern. The inability to identify a specific treatment for this age class is even more important since it is the one most often represented among the funerary remains at the sites reviewed here. Therefore, this absence of pattern could possibly reflect a specific treatment that did not leave traces in the archaeological record and that is thus not yet possible to define.

The 'adults'

Finally, this last social age class still shows the same north/south dichotomy. During the Early Neolithic, the individuals from northern sites are mostly found within strictly funerary sites, whereas the ones from southern sites are more likely to be buried within settlements. Nevertheless, the most significant observation is a clear shift in funerary treatments between the younger individuals and those over 14 years of age-at-death. Beyond this age, there are no differences that can be identified in adults with regard to body position and associated grave goods. During the following period, the Middle Neolithic, this relationship is more visible for the northern sites, where individuals over 15 years of age-at-death are buried like the older members of the group. Concerning sites from the South of France, the shift seems to happen a bit earlier in the life course, around 13 years of age-at-death. Later on, during the Late Neolithic, this tendency is reversed, and a clear shift is visible in the South of France from the age of 14 years of age-at-death, whereas northern individuals are less visible.

Conclusion

The initial objective of this study was, first, to synthesise information on Neolithic subadults in France in order to define their funerary treatment. A geographic and diachronic analysis on the scale of France for the entirety of the Neolithic was carried out to highlight differences in funerary treatments, taking into account the different ages at the time of death. The purpose of this synthesis was to identify changes in the treatment of the different age groups to develop a perspective based on a social consideration of non-adults in Neolithic societies based on archaeothanatological evidence. As noted during this study, the funerary treatment of immature individuals varies during the Neolithic and regionally within France. There are differences between sites found in the northern, southern, eastern and western regions of France. Differences in treatment are also evident when compared to those of adults. However, the most notable disparities in this synthesis are certainly those observed according to the different ages at death of immature individuals. Indeed, there are differences in the associations of burial furnishings, body position, place of burial and distribution within funerary sites. This permitted identification of age categories with changes in funerary practices, which suggests the existence of age thresholds during which potential changes in social status of immature individuals within society would have occurred. Differences in the treatment of individuals by age classes are fundamental to this type of study. Indeed, when the treatment in death is similar in every respect, it is impossible to discern distinct behaviors, and it appears that there were no age distinctions made during the life course (Thomas, 1975).

Changes definitely occur at different stages of childhood, quite homogeneously depending on the period and the location. For example, a shift seems to occur around 7 years of age for all Neolithic children and also again around 14/15 years of age. This could reflect physical changes, for example, the loss of the deciduous dentition or the onset of puberty, each life course event giving rise to a new status. These then may reflect changes in the social structure of the group, based on new roles and attendant responsibilities that are reflected in funerary practices. The results presented here represent a new departure in the analysis of Neolithic funerary remains that could lead to further studies in order to be confirmed more generally.

References

Allard, P., Dubouloz, J. and Hachem, L. (1997). Premiers éléments sur cinq tombes rubanées à Berry-au-Bac (Aisne, France): principaux apports à l'étude du rituel funéraire danubien occidental. In: C. Jeunesse, ed., *Le Néolithique Danubien et ses Marges entre Rhin et Seine: XXIIe Colloque interrégional sur le néolithique, 27-29 octobre 1995,* Association pour la Promotion de la Recherche Archéologique en Alsac (APRAA), Strasbourg, pp. 31–43.

Baudais, D., Gatto, E., Gisclon, J. L. and Saintot, S. (2006). Coffres en pierre-coffres en bois: la nécropole néolithique moyen de Genevray (Thonon-les-Bains, Haute-Savoie, France). In: P. Moinat et P. Chambon, eds., *Les Cistes du Chamblandes et la Place des Coffres dans les Pratiques Funéraires du Néolithique Moyen Occidental: Actes du Colloque de Lausanne, 12 et 13 mai 2006.* Cahiers d'Archéologie Romande 110; Société Préhistorique Française, Mémoire XLIII, Lausanne pp. 155–176.

Bec Drelon N., Le Roy M. and Recchia Quiniou J. (2014). Autour de la chambre: nouveaux éléments de réflexion sur les structures tumulaires. Apport des fouilles récentes de cinq dolmens de l'Hérault In: I. Sénépart, F. Léandri, J. Cauliez, T. Perrin and E. Thirault, eds., *Chronologie de la Préhistoire Récente dans le Sud de la France: Acquis 1992–2012/Actualité de la Recherche.* Toulouse: Archives d'Ecologie Préhistorique, pp. 569–582.

Beeching, A., Brochier, J., Matteucci, S., Pahin, A. and Thiercelin, F. (1987). Les Sépultures et les Dépôts d'Ossements Humains dans le Chasséen de la Moyenne Vallée du Rhône. *Actes des Rencontres Néolithiques de Rhône-Alpes,* 3, pp. 75–82.

Binford, L.R. (1968). Archeological perspectives. In: S.R. and L.R. Binford, eds., *New Perspectives in Archeology.* Chicago: Aldine, pp. 5–32.

Bouffiès, C., Le Roy, M., Tchérémissinoff, Y., Gros, O. and Gros, A-C. (2017). Étude Anthropologique et Spatiale du Dolmen des Abrits n°2 (Beaulieu, Ardèche): Recrutement Funéraire et Modalités de Gestion d'une Sépulture Collective du Néolithique Final, *Ardèche Archéologie,* pp. 31–39.

Brossier, S., Marlière, P., Lelovier, L. A., Marty, P., Vidaillet, F., Bouby, L., Carrere, I., Cayn, P., Gaudin, E. and Servelle, C. (2000). Le site chasséen de Villeneuve-Tolosane. In: J. Vaquer, M. Gandelin, M. Remicourt, Y. Tchérémissinoff, eds., *Défunts Néolithiques en Toulousain,* Toulouse: Archives d'Ecologie Préhistorique, pp. 313–318.

Buchet, L. and Séguy, I. (2002). La Paléodémographie: Bilan et Perspectives. *Annales de Démographie Historique,* 1, pp. 161–212.

Castex, D. and Drancourt, M. (2005). D'un site funéraire à la détection d'une crise épidémique. Identités biologiques et patrimoine génétique. Actes du colloque Épidémies et Société dans le Monde Occidental XIe-XXIe, *Revue Sociologie Santé Collection 'Les Etudes Hospitalières',* 22, pp. 190–209.

Chambon, P. (2003). *Les morts dans les sépultures collectives néolithiques en France: du cadavre aux restes ultimes,* Vol. 35. Paris: Centre National de la Recherche Scientifique (CNRS).

Chambon, P., Delor, J. P., Augereau, A., Gibaja Bao, J. F., Meunier, K., Thomas, A., Murail, P. and Molez, D. (2010). La Nécropole du Néolithique Moyen de Sur les Pâtureaux à Chichery (Yonne). *Gallia Préhistoire,* 52(1), pp. 117–192.

Chambon, P. and Lanchon, Y. (2003). Les Structures Sépulcrales de la Nécropole de Vignely (Seine-et-Marne). *Mémoires de la Société Préhistorique Française*, 33, pp. 159–173.

Chambon, P. and Mordant, D. (1996). Monumentalisme et Sépultures Collectives à Balloy (Seine-et-Marne). *Bulletin de la Société Préhistorique Française*, 93(3), pp. 396–402.

Derevenski, J.S. (1994). Where are the Children? Accessing Children in the Past. *Archaeological Review from Cambridge*, 13(2), pp. 7–20.

Dubouloz, J., Bostyn, F., Chartier, M., Cottiaux, R. and Le Bolloch, M. (2005). La Recherche Archéologique sur le Néolithique en Picardie. *Revue Archéologique de Picardie*, 3(3), pp. 63–98.

Duday, H. (2009). *The Archaeology of the dead: lectures in archaeothanatology*. Oxford: Oxbow Books.

Efremov, I.A. (1940). Taphonomy: A New Branch of Paleontology. *Pan-American Geologist*, 74, pp. 81–93.

Fazekas, I. G. and Kósa, F. (1978). *Forensic fetal osteology*. Budapest: Akadémiai Kiadó.

Gatto, E. and Gisclon, J.L. (2007). La gestion de l'espace sépulcral dans les coffres de Genevray (Thonon-les-Bains, Haute-Savoie, France). In: P. Moinat et P. Chambon, eds., *Les Cistes du Chamblandes et la Place des Coffres dans les Pratiques Funéraires du Néolithique Moyen Occidental: Actes du Colloque de Lausanne, 12 et 13 mai 2006.* Cahiers d'Archéologie Romande 110; Société Préhistorique Française, Mémoire XLIII, Lausanne pp. 177–194.

Hertz, R. (1970). Étude sur la Représentation de la Mort. In: R. Hertz, G. Balandier, M. Mauss, eds., *Sociologie Religieuse et Folklore*. Paris: Presse Universitaire de France, pp. 1–83.

Hodder, I. (1985). Postprocessual archaeology. *Advances in Archaeological Method and Theory*, 8, pp. 1–26.

Jean, N., Le Roy, M., Durand, V., Gély, B. and Lemercier, O. (2019). Étude Anthropologique du Dolmen du Bronze Ancien du Pala 2, *Archaeologische Korrespondantzblats*, 49(2), pp. 183–195.

Jeunesse, C. (1995). Les groupes régionaux occidentaux du Rubané (Rhin et Bassin parisien) à travers les pratiques funéraires. *Gallia préhistoire*, 37(1), pp. 115–154.

Jeunesse, C. (1998). La Synchronisation des Séquences Culturelles des Bassins du Rhin, de la Meuse et de la Seine et la Chronologie du Bassin Parisien au Néolithique Ancien et Moyen (5200–4500 av. J.-C.). *Bulletin de la Société Préhistorique Luxembourgeoise*, 20–21, pp. 337–392.

Joussaume, R. (1976). Dolmen de Pierre-Levée à Nieul-sur-l'Autize (Vendée). *Bulletin de la Société Préhistorique Française*, 73(1), pp. 398–421.

Le Roy, M. (2015). *Les enfants au Néolithique: du contexte funéraire à l'interprétation socioculturelle en France de 5700 à 2100 ans av. J.-C.* Unpublished doctoral thesis, Université de Bordeaux.

Le Roy, M. (2017). How were infants considered at death during the Neolithic period in France? In: E. Murphy and M. Le Roy, eds., *Children, Death and Burial: Archaeological Discourses*, 5. London: Oxbow Books, pp. 19–34.

Le Roy, M. (2018). Reprise de la fouille du dolmen des Abrits 2 (Beaulieu): Résultats anciens et préliminaires, *Nouveaux cahiers du Grospierrois – Grou Peïro*, pp. 25–31.

Le Roy, M. and Bec-Drelon, N. (2016). Le dolmen des Isserts (Saint-Jean-de-la-Blaquière, Hérault): étude anthropologique d'une collection ancienne. In: J. Cauliez, I. Sénépart, L. Jallot, P.A. De Labriffe, C. Gilabert and X. Gutherz, eds., *De la Tombe au Territoire et Actualité de la Recherche: Actes des 11e Rencontres Méridionales de la Préhistoire Récente*. Toulouse: Archives d'Écologie Préhistorique, pp. 467–475.

Le Roy, M., Brunel, E. and Lateur, N. (2019). 'Archaïque Toi-Même!' Découverte Anthropologique à la Grotte de l'Archaïque (Saint-Remèze). *Ardèche Archéologie*, 36, pp. 30–35.

Le Roy, M. and Murphy, E. (2020). Archaeothanatology as a tool for interpreting death during pregnancy: examples from Medieval Ireland, In: R. Gowland and S. Halcrow, eds., *The Mother-Infant Nexus in Anthropology: Small Beginnings, Significant Outcomes*. Cham: Springer, pp. 211–233.

Le Roy, M., Rivollat, M., Mendisco, F., Pemonge, M.H., Coutelier, C., Couture, C., Tillier, A.-m., Rottier, S. and Deguilloux, M.F. (2016). Distinct Ancestries for Similar Funerary Practices? A GIS Analysis Comparing Funerary, Osteological and aDNA Data from the Middle Neolithic Necropolis Gurgy 'Les Noisats' (Yonne, France). *Journal of Archaeological Science*, 73, pp. 45–54.

Le Roy, M., Rottier S., De Becdelièvre, C. and Thiol, S. (2020) Attente ou catastrophe? Analyse d'une sépulture collective de la fin du Néolithique. In Noterman A. and M. Cervel, eds., *Ritualiser, Gérer, Piller*. Poitiers: Actes de Rencontres du Groupe d'Anthropologie et d'Archéologie Funéraire (GAAF), pp. 202–209.

Le Roy, M., Rottier, S., De Becdelièvre, C., Thiol, S., Coutelier, C. and Tillier, A.-M. (2014). Funerary Behaviour of Neolithic Necropolises and Collective Graves in France. Evidence from Gurgy 'Les Noisats' (Middle Neolithic) and Passy/Véron 'La Truie Pendue' (Late Neolithic). *Archäologisches Korrespondenzblatt*, 3, pp. 337–351.

Le Roy, M., Rottier, S., Santos, F. and Tillier, A-m. (2018). Funerary treatment of immature deceased in Neolithic collective burial sites in France. Were the children buried with adults? In: G. Lillehammer, and E. Murphy, eds., *Across the Generations: The Old and Young in Past Societies*. Childhood in the Past Monograph Series 8, 2018, AmS-Skrifter 26. Museum of Archaeology, University of Stavanger, pp. 21–34.

Le Roy, M., Rottier, S. and Tillier, A.-m. (2018). Who Was a 'Child' during the Neolithic in France? *Childhood in the Past*, 11(2), pp. 69–84.

Ledermann, S. (1969). *Nouvelles tables-type de mortalité*. Paris: Presses Universitaires de France.

Lucy, S. (2005). Ethnic and cultural identities, In: M. Díaz-Andreu, M.D.A. García, S. Lucy, S. Babic and N.D. Edwards, eds., *The Archaeology of Identity: Approaches to Gender, Age, Status, Ethnicity and Religion*. London: Taylor & Francis, pp. 86–109.

Lyman, R.L. (2010). Taphonomy, Pathology, and Paleoecology of the Terminal Pleistocene Marmes Rockshelter (45FR50) 'Big Elk' (*Cervus elaphus*), Southeastern Washington State, USA. *Canadian Journal of Earth Sciences*, 47, pp. 1367–1382.

Masset, C. (1987). Le 'recrutement' d'un ensemble funéraire. In: H. Duday and C. Masset, eds., *Anthropologie Physique et Archéologie: Méthodes d'Étude des Sépultures*, Paris: Centre National de la Recherche Scientifique (CNRS), pp. 111–134.

Masset, C. (1995). Sur la Stratigraphie de la Chaussée Tirancourt (Somme). *Revue Archéologique de Picardie*, 9(1), pp. 135–139.

Masset, C. (1997). La Sépulture Collective Néolithique d'Essômes-sur-Marne (Aisne). *Revue Archéologique de Picardie*, 1(1), pp. 5–17.

Moorrees, C., Fanning, E. and Hunt, E. (1963a). Age Variation of Formation Stages for Ten Permanent Teeth. *Journal of Dental Research*, 42, pp. 1490–1502.

Moorrees, C., Fanning, E. and Hunt, E. (1963b). Formation and Resorption of Three Deciduous Teeth in Children. *American Journal of Physical Anthropology*, 21, pp. 205–213.

Nawrocki, S.P. (2009). Forensic taphonomy, In: S. Blau and D. Ubelaker, eds., *Handbook of Forensic Anthropology and Archaeology*. New York: Routledge, pp. 284–294.

Patte, E. (1971). Quelques Sépultures du Poitou du Mésolithique au Bronze Moyen. *Gallia Préhistoire*, 14(1), pp. 139–244.

Scheuer, L. and Black, S. (2000). *Developmental juvenile osteology*. London: Academic Press.

Schotsmans E.M.J., Márquez-Grant N. and Forbes S.L. (2017). *Taphonomy of human remains: forensic analysis of the dead and the depositional environment*. Chichester: Wiley.

Séguy, I. and Buchet, L. (2011). *Manuel de paléodémographie*. Nice: Institut National d'Etudes Démographiques.

Sellier, P. (1996). La mise en évidence d'anomalies démographiques et leur interprétation: population, recrutement et pratiques funéraires du tumulus de Courtesoult. In: J.F. Piningre, ed., *Nécropoles et Société au Premier Âge du Fer. Le Tumulus de Courtesoult (Haute Saône)*. Paris: Éditions de le Maison des Sciences de l'Homme, pp. 118–202.

Sorg, M. and Haglund, W. (2002). Advancing forensic taphonomy: purpose, theory, and process, In: Haglund, W. and Sorg, M., eds., *Advances in Forensic Taphonomy: Method, Theory, and Archaeological Perspectives*. New York: CRC Press, pp. 3–30.

Suzuki, H. (2000). *The price of death: the funeral industry in contemporary Japan*. Stanford: Stanford University Press.

Tarrête, J. and Le Roux, C.T. (2008). *Archéologie de la France. Le Néolithique*. Paris: Éditions Picard.

Tchérémissinoff, Y. (2003). Les Sépultures Chasséennes de Narbons (Haute-Garonne): Description, Comparaisons et Fonctionnement. *Mémoires de la Société Préhistorique Française*, 33, pp. 81–90.

Thomas, L.V. (1975). *Anthropologie de la mort*. Paris: Payot.

Thomas, A., Chambon, P. and Murail, P. (2011). Unpacking Burial and Rank: The Role of Children in the First Monumental Cemeteries of Western Europe (4600–4300 BC). *Antiquity*, 85, pp. 772–786.

Ubelaker, D.H. (1989). *Human skeletal remains, excavation, analysis, interpretation*, 2nd ed. Washington, DC: Taraxacum.

Van Gennep, A. (1909). *Les rites de passage: étude systématique des rites*. Paris: Éditions A. & J. Picard.

Vaquer, J., Duday, H., Gandelin, M., Hérouin, S. and Tresset, A. (2007). La Tombe de Coste Rouge à Beaufort (Hérault) et la Question des Tombes à Dalles Néolithiques dans le Nord-Est des Pyrénées. *Gallia Préhistoire*, 49(1), pp. 127–159.

Veit, U. (1993). Burials within Settlements of the Linienbandkeramik and Stichbandkeramik Cultures of Central Europe. On the Social Construction of Death in Early-Neolithic Society. *Journal of European Archaeology*, 1(1), pp. 107–140.

Verjux, C., Simonin, D. and Richard, G. (1998). Des sépultures mésolithiques aux tombes sous dalles du Néolithique moyen I en région Centre et sur ses marges. In: J. Guilaine, ed., *Sépultures d'Occident et Genèses des Mégalithes (9000–3500 Avant Notre Ère)*. Paris: Errance, pp. 61–70.

12

DEFINING COLLECTIVE BURIALS

Three case studies

Aurore Schmitt

ARCHÉOLOGIE DES SOCIÉTÉS MÉDITERRANÉENNES, UMR 5140, CNRS-UNIVERSITÉ PAUL
VALÉRY-MINISTÈRE DE LA CULTURE, MONTPELLIER, FRANCE

Introduction

The aim of the study of collective burials[1] is to reconstruct the history of tombs from the time of their construction to abandonment. This chapter sets out to answer questions such as whether or not complete bodies or already skeletonised remains were deposited and if there was any patterning related to their deposition. In addition, such studies consider if inclusions or items of personal adornment were associated with the individuals and whether or not the internal space of the tomb was used completely or only in part. These studies also seek to reconstruct the sample population profile of those who were selected for inclusion in them (the proportions of males and females, adults, children, and infants) and to document if the architecture of the monument changed during the period of its use. This integrated archaeothanatological approach includes both biological aspects of the dead and archaeological contextual information (Duday, 1981).

The history of archaeothanatology is directly related to the study of collective burials since some of the earliest excavations of osteological remains were carried out on Neolithic collective burials. Leroi-Gourhan, Bailloud and Brézillon (1962) were the first to apply the excavation technique that they later developed for settlements at the Mournouards hypogeum (Marne, France, 3300–3000 BC), including horizontal hand-stripping of layers of sediment, photographic coverage and systematic 3D recording of all elements. This site provided new insights into the funerary world and marked a dramatic turning point in the archaeology of death, for both excavation and study, becoming a reference for all other such sites since. As a consequence, collective tombs were finally considered as global systems. The methods were further enriched and developed by Henri Duday, notably during the research excavations of two collective burials, the karst shaft of La Boucle at Corconne (Gard, France, 3500–3000 cal. BC) and the dolmen of Les

---

1 For the meaning of the term 'collective burial', the author is referring to the French meaning of *'sépulture collective'* (collective burial) used for features containing several bodies deposited successively, as opposed to the term *'sépulture multiple'* (multiple burial), which refers to a grave that received several individuals during a single event (cf. Boulestin and Courtaud, Chapter 3, this volume; Knüsel, Gerdau-Radonić and Schotsmans, Chapter 34, this volume). The term 'plural' burial, from French *'sépulture plurielle'*, refers to graves containing more than a single individual without respect to the timing of depositions.

DOI: 10.4324/9781351030625-15

Peirières at Villedubert (Aude, France, 2500–2200 cal. BC) (Duday, 1987a, 1987b, 2005, 2009), both sites becoming places to experiment with new methods as well as for field schools. From this point in time, particular attention was also drawn to the way in which bodies decomposed and the effects the depositional context had on the decomposition of bodies.

From one funerary context to another, the approach during fieldwork is generally the same. Yet, laboratory (or post-excavation) analysis of the collective burial has its unique characteristics. The reconstruction of the way the assemblage was constituted relies mainly on the analysis of the spatial organisation of the remains combined with the quantification of skeletal part representation. Each bone fragment has to be identified, fragments of the same element conjoined and homologous elements belonging to the same individual have to be matched. These steps are part of the quantitative analysis; the quantification of the numbers of various bones and teeth and their fragments that form the basis of an estimation of the Minimum Number of Individuals (MNI) (Boulestin, 1999; Adams and Byrd, 2014; Knüsel and Robb, 2016). These data also have to be integrated with the spatial analysis of the context in order to observe and quantify the distances between conjoined and paired bones and the distribution of the still articulated elements, as well as isolated and disarticulated bones that both contribute to interpretation of the assemblage. The first task is to link the disarticulated fragments with the complete elements since some bones will have been moved during successive disturbances.

One of the crucial characteristics of these burial contexts is the long-lasting period of use and the repeated returns to the tomb. Combined with the effects of variable funerary practices, these characteristics result in increasing complexity in the organisation of the human remains. The more individuals in the grave and the longer the time of use, the longer and more complex the analysis becomes. The lengthy analysis required partly explains the discrepancy between the number of excavated collective burials and the paucity of published papers (Chambon, 2003; Déderix, Schmitt and Crevecoeur, 2018). This lack is due to the difficulty of dealing with a huge amount of data. Fortunately, for the last decade, new investigative tools, Geographic Information Systems (GIS) and photogrammetry, have become available. The aim of this chapter is to present three case studies in order to illustrate the methods used to record the data in the field and to analyse them in the laboratory, and to highlight the difficulties encountered when reconstructing the funerary practices and processes leading to the formation of archaeo-anthropological assemblages. It also brings to light the complexity of the interpretation of tombs containing the remains of several individuals.

The Villard dolmen (Lauzet-Ubaye, France)

The use of collective burials to inhume people spread throughout the South of France in the last third of the 4th millennium BC. Collective tombs gradually became more widespread as well as more heterogeneous as the architecture of the tombs, their locations and grave inclusions became increasingly diversified. Among the 300 collective graves inventoried in Provence (South of France), few have benefited from a level of recording permitting a thorough analysis and reconstruction of their use. This was the case of the Villard dolmen, which belongs to the group of Alpine dolmens. It was excavated during the summers from 1980 to 1983. It is a passage grave (the passage being as wide as the chamber itself) with a small chamber. The dolmen is partly covered by a tumulus (Sauzade, 2011). Most human remains (N=1762) were recorded in three dimensions and drawn. Each recorded bone was associated with a file indicating its identification. After the excavation, all fragments of the same bones were glued together and marked. Photographs were also taken (Figures 12.1 and 12.2). These documents enabled detailed analysis. Unfortunately, the drawings and photographs provided only a 2D-plan and are not

Figure 12.1 The Villard dolmen (Lauzet–Ubaye, Provence, France), photograph of the upper level of the funerary layer (Photograph: G. Sauzade).

good substitutes for direct observations of *in situ* remains that enable more detailed taphonomic analysis.

A study based on field documentation proposed a reconstruction of the funerary actions leading to the creation of funerary layers in this tomb (Chambon, 2003): level 0 consisted of several successive deposits of adults and children, who were partially removed to deposit at least seven deceased individuals, found in partial articulation by the excavators, forming level 1. The third and last event was the introduction of remains removed from the first level, forming level 2.

The entire series of human remains was studied in 2014 for a monograph publication of the entire monument (Sauzade and Schmitt, 2020). The chamber contents consisted of 2608 human remains (2197 bone fragments and 411 teeth). One hundred and forty pieces were articulated (5%). The MNI amounts to 25 individuals, 16 adolescents and adults and 9 children. From the osteological study, only males were attested, but a recent DNA analysis showed that there were at least four females and five males buried in the tomb (Olalde *et al.*, 2018 and unpublished results). Using GIS, a complete map of this material aided a study of the spatial distribution of the remains. Based on the distribution of 28 pairs and 58 matching bones, movement of remains was for the most part horizontal and concerned mainly the upper and lower funerary layers (Figure 12.3). The spatial analysis revealed that several bones, some from the same individuals from the lower layer, moved both horizontally and vertically, very far from their original place of deposition, including long bones and compact bones such as tarsals.

The percentage of representation (PR) (Boulestin, 1999) was chosen in preference to the bone frequency MNI since it enables accounting for the comparison of each part to the others based on the MNI and to include bones such as phalanges, carpals and vertebrae in the analysis. The PR indicates a lack of the smallest and/or most fragile elements, the carpals, sacrum, vertebrae,

Figure 12.2 The Villard dolmen (Lauzet–Ubaye, Provence, France), photograph of the lower level of the funerary layer (Photograph: G. Sauzade).

Figure 12.3 The Villard dolmen (Lauzet–Ubaye, Provence, France), west–east projection of the large pair-matched bones (A. Schmitt).

metacarpals and foot phalanges. It was difficult to determine the extent of the preservation of the bodies at the time of deposition. The lack of the smallest and most fragile bones would suggest that they were secondary depositions disturbed and moved when other remains were placed in the small chamber. As also noted by Chambon (2003), the lack of preserved labile joints among the articulated elements, such as those of the hands and feet, raises questions. It may be that the bodies were already partially decomposed when they were introduced into the tomb, which would explain why persistent joints remained in articulation and that the elements from labile articulations were missing. This question remains open.

As the upper layer (Figure 12.1), characterised by more heavily fragmented remains and by the absence of articulated bones, seemed different from the lower layer (Figure 12.2), a comparison of the osteological profiles of both layers thus seemed relevant. Both layers showed similar tendencies. Fragmentation is more often observed in the upper part of the funerary layer of collective burials in dolmens since empty spaces remain for a longer period before being completely filled by sediment (Sauzade and Schmitt, 2020). In addition, in the Villard dolmen, there is clear stratigraphic evidence that the spaces between the upper part of the slabs composing the chamber were not fully sealed beneath the tumulus when the filling of the chamber commenced. The subsequent collapse of the southern-most slab outward from the chamber wall when the tumulus was dismantled for agricultural purposes in the 18th century also enabled manipulation of the bones. As a consequence, in accordance with Chambon (2003), it seems that much of the oldest funerary material (level 0) had been disturbed and some remains removed. However, there is no clear evidence that level 2 represents the remains of this disturbance. The lack of articulations and fragmentation could be related to the changes within the dolmen through time before and after its abandonment, as well as to modifications that occurred during its funerary use.

In tombs where both skeletons and isolated bones are represented, mechanical alterations preferentially affect isolated bones more often when compared to elements in articulation. This can distort comparisons and interpretations. Moreover, the repeated movements of certain bones and their ever-growing fragmentation introduce background noise in the osteological profiles that bias the interpretation of long-used contexts.

Four radiocarbon dates from the base and the top of the funerary layers are in accordance with stratigraphic relationships revealed by the mapping of human remains and the relative dates of the grave inclusions, respectively, both dating to the end of the Late Neolithic and the beginning of the Bronze Age (Sauzade and Schmitt, 2020). As there was only evidence of Bell Beaker cultural objects, supported by radiocarbon dates, this tomb was considered by Sauzade to be a Bell Beaker dolmen. However, Chambon (2003) argues that pottery evidence and human bones relating to a subsequent use could have been removed with the removal of bones from level 0. This question, too, remains unresolved.

The collective burial at Collet-Redon (Martigues, France)

The site of Collet-Redon (Bouches du Rhône region) was excavated between 1960 and 1982 and yielded evidence of domestic occupations dating from the late Neolithic and the Bronze Age. In 2006, a grave was discovered 200 m to the north of the site. It was excavated completely over two seasons in 2014 and 2015 (Schmitt *et al.*, 2018). The standard recording system of field anthropology was applied for human remains: each layer was photographed and a full inventory was made of all the bones within it. The photographs were printed on-site in order to have a document on which the inventory numbers of the bones could be transferred as they were removed from context. The inventory sheet contained the anatomical fragment identification, their preservation state, their orientation and which aspect of the bones was upper-most. This record was complemented with photogrammetry, which is a precious tool that permitted the creation of stratigraphic sections from the horizontal excavation layers. In addition, this technique enabled the production of 3D images that are fundamental when studying the relationships between human remains and other types of archaeological data. However, it is important to emphasise that this tool is absolutely not a substitute for the other types of records. GIS was not used since the amount of data did not require such a technique. In this instance, a database and drawings in Illustrator™ were sufficient.

The orientation of the monument was northeast-southwest, and it was constructed in a rectangular pit 2.4 m long by 2.2 m wide, with the walls preserved to a depth of 25 cm. About 0.6 m² was removed to the east during the excavation of a geomorphological trench that led to the discovery of the tomb. Two parallel walls were built against the northwestern and southeastern walls of the pit, each of them comprised of two large foundation blocks. Part of the internal surface area was covered by a paved surface made up of 10 cm-sized stones and constructed after the walls and the first funerary deposit had been made. The stones come from unmodified local limestone available near the site. The infilling consisted of two layers. Stratigraphic Unit (SU) 11, the lower level of the infilling (layer 1), extends over the whole surface. It covered both articulated and disarticulated bones (Figure 12.4).

SU 7 (layer 2) consisted of a brown silty series of soils intermixed with fine gravel. It covered the paving and the dissociated bones (Figure 12.5) as well as an incomplete individual found in articulation. The tomb and its infilling were covered by SU 9, a stony-clayey sediment that extended slightly beyond the monument area, in particular to the west, where the density of stones decreased progressively.

Layer 1 contained the remains of primary depositions, portions of which had likely been partially removed. The MNI indicated three adults and three immature individuals. The most represented bones were carpals and phalanges. Layer 2 contained an incomplete articulated individual placed on the surface of the paving and a pile of disarticulated bones along the northeastern wall. The best-represented bones were long bones with an MNI of eight (six adults and two children). The formation and the internal chronology of this secondary deposit[2] could correspond to several scenarios. (1) There could have been the repeated 'reductions' of individuals (i.e. displacements to one side when additional individuals were added) deposited on the paving, but nothing demonstrates that these individuals were not already partially decomposed when they were placed in the tomb. Among the missing elements are those that are the most fragile and may have undergone differential preservation as a result. However, these bones could also have been those that may not have been collected if dry bones had been transferred from the place where the corpses were initially deposited and the process of decomposition had already commenced. (2) They could also be those remains from the first layer that had been moved in order to install the paving but were kept in the tomb afterwards. In view of this hypothesis, the overall MNI is limited to seven adults and four immature individuals. In addition, the refits and matches observed among the bone and dental remains show no links between the two funerary layers.

Despite the use of a very precise recording system for a relatively small amount of human remains, the reconstruction of the funerary actions – and especially those of the secondary deposit from layer 2 – remains difficult. Several scenarios may explain the patterning of the archaeological and anthropological evidence. The major question concerned whether or not

---

2 The deposit of these remains comprised skeletal elements that were partially or completely disarticulated.

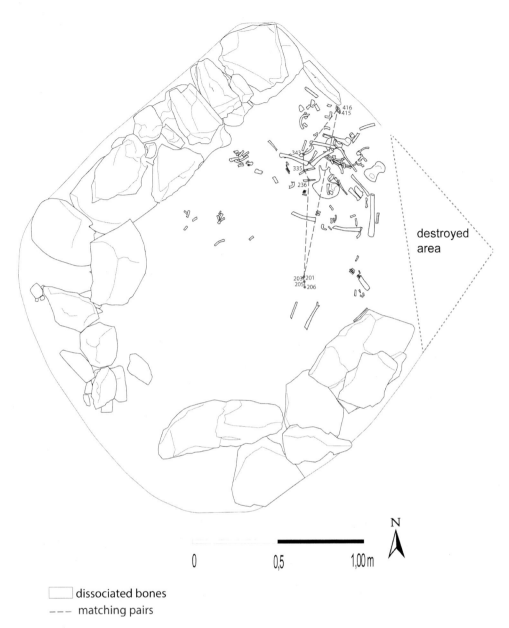

destroyed area

N

0   0,5   1,00 m

☐ dissociated bones
--- matching pairs

Figure 12.4 The Collet-Redon tomb (Martigues, Bouches du Rhône, France), drawing of the compartment and bones in Unit 11 (A. Schmitt).

the remains in this tomb could be referred to as a 'collective burial'. The succession of primary deposits in the first layer is rather assumed than demonstrated. For layer 2, the partially articulated individual and the secondary deposit may have been placed at the same time. Even if successive 'reductions' of the skeletal remains may be suspected, there is no evidence that this was the case. The burial would be collective only if it is assumed that the whole of the material found within the tomb was the result of, at least, two successive events. If the two layers were considered as two different phases of use (cf. Boulestin and Courtaud, Chapter 3, this volume), the burial

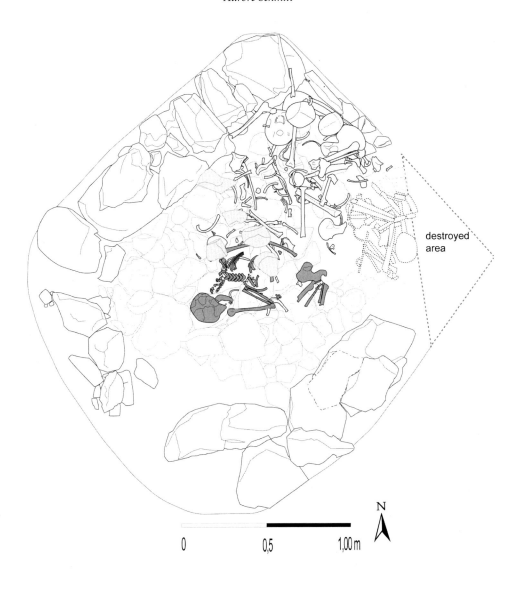

destroyed
area

N

0   0,5   1,00 m

☐ dissociated human bones

▨ individual in partial connection

⬚ dissociated human bones from the 2006 survey

Figure 12.5 The Collet-Redon tomb (Martigues, Bouches du Rhône, France), drawing of the compartment, the pavement and the remains in Unit 7 (A. Schmitt).

would instead simply be a 'plural' (the remains of several individuals being present but without being able to indicate the timing of these depositional events; cf. Knüsel, Gerdau-Radonić and Schotsmans, Chapter 34, this volume) rather than a collective burial comprised of repeated successive depositions.

Four radiocarbon dates on human bones place the beginning of funerary activity in this tomb between 3710 and 3360 cal BC and the end between 3490 and 3030 cal BC. With such an early date, this tomb could be one of the oldest collective burials in southeastern France, but this would be true only if collective gathering of human remains is related to ideological changes that occurred at the end of the Neolithic, as proposed by Chambon (2003). The site of Bréguières (Alpes-Maritimes, France) used at the end of the 6th and the beginning of the 5th millennium BC is currently considered to be the oldest collective tomb found in southern France (Provost *et al.*, 2017). In this case, it is likely that a hypothetical ideological underpinning relating specifically to collective tombs (cf. Boulestin and Courtaud, Chapter 3, this volume; Schmitt and Déderix, 2018) existed before the 4th millennium BC. A future challenge is to test this hypothesis.

The Minoan cemetery of Sissi (Crete)

The site of Sissi occupies a coastal hill in northern Crete, about 4 km to the east of the palace site of Malia. It has been excavated under the direction of Jan Driessen (Université Catholique de Louvain (UCL), Louvain-la-Neuve, Belgium) since 2007. Settlement remains dating to the Early, Middle and Late Bronze Age (third to first millennium BC) have been discovered, in addition to an extensive cemetery of rectangular tombs of Prepalatial and Protopalatial date (*circa* 2400–1700 BC) in Zones 1 and 9 situated on the northern and eastern sides, respectively, of the Kephali tou Agios Antoniou Hill (locally known as 'Bouffo'). Sissi was the first site where field anthropology was applied on a large scale (Crevecoeur and Schmitt, 2009; Schoep *et al.*, 2012). Minoan funerary practices were informed (and still are) by the study of architecture, objects and ethnographic models. As human remains were often discovered mixed together, it was assumed that the mortuary practices followed a two-stage process characterised by the use of a temporary place where the body decomposed followed by the deposition of the skeletal remains in a different and final resting place (Branigan, 1987; Soles, 2001). However, this model was never validated taking into account the actual assemblages of human remains. Crevecoeur, Schmitt and Schoep (2015) showed that the archaeothanatological approach provided a different perspective of Minoan mortuary practices, not only because the human remains were excavated and recorded by trained anthropologists but also because their interpretations relied on an epistemological process composed of a three-step interpretive reasoning process (Boulestin and Duday, 2006). The first step involves field observations and recording. The second step comprises the analysis of the observations recorded in the field, aiming to reconstruct the original appearance of the deposit and the actions that led to its appearance. Funerary practices, based on demonstrated repetitions of actions, are next interpreted in the third and final step within a social framework. Biological data, material inclusions deposited with the bodies, characteristics of the burial structure and specific characteristics of the site are all considered and cross-analysed in order to, firstly, reconstruct the practices and, secondly, interpret their meanings. In this section, the aim is to present different mortuary practices for which the application of the term 'collective gathering' (as defined by Boulestin and Courtaud, Chapter 3, this volume) is challenging.

In zone 1, compartments 1.9 and 1.10 are associated by their close topographical proximity and the sharing of a common wall, which suggest that they were constructed at the same time (Figure 12.6). In compartment 1.10, measuring 1.70 by 1.20 m, two handmade, straight-sided cups were found, suggesting a date in the Early Minoan III-Middle Minoan IA periods (*circa* 2650–1720 BC) (Schoep *et al.*, 2012). The compartment was constructed of four walls forming a rectangular shape. The bedrock on which it was built was levelled internally with a pebble floor. A second layer covered several articulated elements commingled with disarticulated remains, both types of remains being poorly preserved. The room contained at least 20 individuals, both children and adults. Adults and adolescents shared the same orientation in the eastern part of the compartment, with their cephalic extremities placed towards the southeast corner and the lower limbs in a flexed position beneath the thorax in a prone position (decubitus ventral).

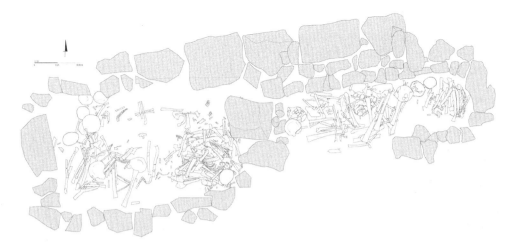

Figure 12.6   Sissi, Crete, bone assemblages in compartment 1.9 (right) and 1.10 (left) (A. Schmitt).

Several crania were gathered in the northwest corner. There was a complete absence of carpals and tarsals and an almost complete absence of metacarpals, metatarsals and vertebrae, as well as phalanges. The state of the corpse when introduced into the compartment was difficult to reconstruct. The under-representation of smaller bones and larger cancellous-filled bones may relate to poor preservation. In this case, it seems that the bodies had been introduced in a complete state and manipulated to achieve the spatial pattern identified. Compartment 1.10 can be considered, minimally, a plural gathering. There is also evidence of successive deposits (manipulation of bones after decay when the remains of another individual were deposited), so its collective character and its funerary nature attest to it having been a collective burial.

Compartment 1.9 is rectangular (1.8 m by 0.75 m). Only one layer was identified. It covered bones that were directly deposited on a south to north strongly sloping bedrock surface. Most of the crania were found in this lower bedrock layer. Long bones were oriented east to west, following the topography of the bedrock. No articulations or anatomical joint congruities were observed. The MNI amounts to at least 13 individuals (9 adults/adolescents and 4 children). By comparison with the compartment beside it, the remains in compartment 1.9 were interpreted as a plural gathering of individuals after skeletonisation had occurred in another location. It was not possible, however, to determine if the assemblage had been the result of only one or several events, and thus 'plural' because no greater resolution can be accorded. As these depositions are associated with compartment 1.10, it seems that 1.9 was used as an ossuary comprised of already defleshed bones and not a burial *per se*. The age-at-death profile of this assemblage is similar to that of compartment 1.10, but no matching pairs were found between the two compartments. If the model of a two-stage process were applied to these two features, compartment 1.10 would have been a temporary space for decomposition and compartment 1.9 would have received the remains of individuals from secondary funerary ceremonies, thus being the grave. However, based on the evidence, the adopted archaeothanatological approach suggests that 1.10 was the grave and 1.9 related to a post-funerary treatment.

A second example from Sissi, in Zone 9, corresponds to the southwest sector of the cemetery. Excavation of Tomb A (Figure 12.7) has been completed, and study of the material is on-going, but sufficient data has already been collected to address mortuary practices. Tomb A consists of at least seven compartments. Preliminary pottery studies date the tomb to the Middle Minoan I and Middle Minoan II periods (*circa* 2100-1700 BC). Compartments 9.3 and 9.9 contained

Figure 12.7 Sissi, Crete, aerial photograph of zone 9 with the location of the chambers of tomb A (Image courtesy: EBSA (Belgische School te Athene); Photograph: N. Kress, A. Schmitt and S. Déderix).

no human bones. Compartment 9.5 is a square space that opens to the south of compartment 9.4 (Figure 12.7). It was built during the spatial re-organisation of the tomb. The internal space comprised several floor levels. A deposit including complete cups, some ceramic sherds and two human long bones was found on one of the floor surfaces (Schmitt and Sperandio, 2018). Compartment 9.1 was partly described in another paper (Crevecoeur, Schmitt and Schoep, 2015). The present chapter focusses on compartments 9.2 and 9.8.

Compartment 9.2 measures 4.5 m by 2.5 m (Schoep *et al.*, 2013). Three different burial layers were identified within it (Figure 12.8). In order to construct compartment 9.2, the bedrock was levelled with pebbles, stones and ceramic sherds (layer 1) upon which a *larnax* (a small sealed coffin) had been deposited. A secondary deposit comprised of incomplete remains of at least three individuals was found in the southeast corner of the compartment. Is this initial funerary sequence better designated as a collective (deposited one after another) or a multiple (deposited all at once) gathering of remains? The individuals had already skeletonised when manipulated, but their remains could have been gathered at one time or several times. The hypothesis of successive 'reductions' (remains disturbed and moved when others were deposited) within the *larnax* remains to be verified. It could also be the remains of several primary deposits in the compartment that were, in part, removed and deposited beside the *larnax*.

A floor of beaten earth sealed the entire room, covering the secondary deposit and the lower part of the *larnax* (layer 2).

A large broken fragment of the larnax had been placed horizontally on top of this layer 2, on which individual 2 had been deposited supinely with the upper limbs flexed across the thorax and the lower limbs flexed and drawn up to the thorax, a position which can only be explained by hypothesising that the lower limbs were bound together or constrained by a restrictive perishable material, such as for example, a piece of textile or a basket (Figure 12.8). This second funerary sequence clearly occurred after the decay of the soft tissue of individual 7, after which the corpse was deposited in the *larnax* lying supinely, with the lower limbs flexed and drawn up towards the cephalic extremity (head-end of the grave) and the flexed knees probably resting

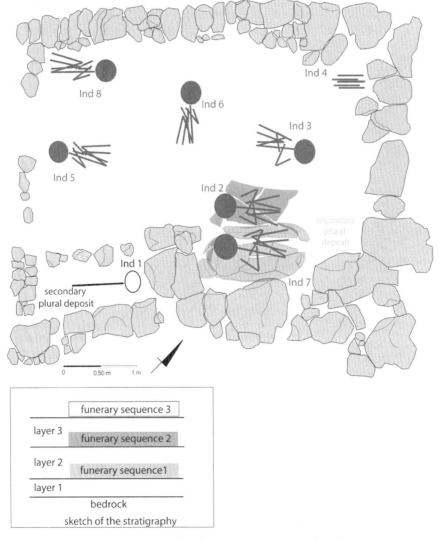

Figure 12.8   Sissi, Crete, room 9.2 and its three funerary sequences (A. Schmitt).

218

against the sides of the container. S/he was attributed to this funerary sequence. There seems to have been a clear desire to gather individuals 2 and 7 in the same place, so it is likely that both individuals are part of the same sequence. The primary burials of four additional adults (3, 5, 6 and 8), lying on their sides (right or left) in very contracted positions complete this funerary sequence, as well as a group of several long bones attributed to a single individual but for which the nature of the deposit (primary or secondary) is not clear. This funerary sequence contained more than a single individual. There is no evidence for succession among burials 3, 5, 6 and 8 since the deposit is in each case formed by undisturbed primary burials, the integrity of the deceased being maintained. The exact chronological relationship between these four burials and the set of remains composed of individuals 2 and 7, respectively, cannot be established because of the lack of stratigraphic relationships. As a consequence, it is possible to establish that it is a collective gathering only of individuals 2 and 7.

The second funerary sequence was sealed by sediment (layer 3). A final primary burial was placed in a small area delimited by several stones aligned in parallel with the south wall of compartment 9.2 (funerary sequence 3). Under individual 1, a male, were the incomplete remains of four other individuals (one adult and three perinates) (Figure 12.8). It is a gathering of more than a single individual, forming a succession of deposits comprised of individual 1 and the underlying set of partial individuals. On this basis, this can be considered a 'collective gathering'.

Compartment 9.2 is composed of three different plural gatherings separated by sediment. The collective nature of only two of them (individuals 7 and 2 and individuals 1 and the secondary deposit below) is clear. The reconstruction of the initial actions leading to the formation of both secondary assemblages is limited, but they could have been primary depositions disturbed by removal of remains. Moreover, the relative timing of the deposits cannot be reconstructed; the individuals could have been buried at the same time or one after another.

Compartment 9.8 had been built afterwards, or at the same time as compartment 9.5 (Figure 12.7). Because compartments 9.4 and 9.5 share common walls, they are considered to be part of tomb A (Schmitt and Déderix, in press). The initial funerary sequence of human remains was placed on a pebble floor (FE 143). Most of the human remains appear to have been removed afterwards, with only residual remains left in place. After being disturbed, the layer was sealed by an earthen floor (FE 153). Four pits were dug into this floor in order to deposit individual primary burials (second funerary sequence). Three of them were in *pithoi* (ceramic vessels). The pit in which *pithos* FE127 was placed was larger than the others and was filled with human bones (Figure 12.9). This secondary bone deposit (Bone Deposit 2) comprised around 150 bones belonging to at least three incompletely represented individuals (Figure 12.9). Another secondary deposit (Bone Deposit 1) was found in the southwest corner of the compartment (Figure 12.9). It is stratigraphically at the same level as the primary burials. This compartment could have been used for successive primary burials. What was uncovered, then, was the state of the remains at abandonment, with the bodies remaining in their primary place of deposition because the tomb was no longer in use. The on-going study of human remains will partly shed light on this issue but will not resolve all the difficulties of reconstructing the funerary actions leading to its creation.

The second funerary sequence of this compartment shows evidence of plural gathering, as a same phase of use is presumed. Three pottery containers had possibly been installed in one episode or one after another. Whatever the scenario, the chronology of the individual primary deposits in each *pithos* remains unclear. The secondary deposit (Bone Deposit 2) could have originated from the disturbed remains of the individuals that were primary depositions in FE 127 (Figure 12.9), as observed in zone 1 (Schoep *et al.*, 2012). In this case, the entire pit, FE 128, could be considered as a collective gathering. As far as secondary deposit 1 is concerned, it could

Figure 12.9 Sissi, Crete, room 9.8 and the location of Bone Deposit 1, Bone Deposit 2, pit FE128 and *pithos* FE127 (Image courtesy: EBSA (Belgische School te Athene); Photograph: A. Schmitt).

be either the remains of the first funerary sequence in FE 143 (a single event) or the manipulated remains of burials originally in a *pithos* (successive events). The collective nature of the assemblage is evident for only a portion of the set of individuals.

The two compartments from zone 9 provide evidence of different practices when compared with those observed in 1.9 and 1.10 (from zone 1). In 1.10, there does not seem to have been a desire to preserve the integrity of the individuals deposited there, and there was only a single funerary phase of use which is considered to be collective in nature for 1.10 and a deposit of several individuals in compartment 1.9. In zone 9, Tomb A consisted of several compartments, including 9.1, 9.2 and 9.8, comprised of several layers of floors that sealed previous funerary sequences, each one being considered a single phase of use. Preservation of skeletal integrity seemed to be the rule in some of them, while other individuals were manipulated and remains were partly moved when another deceased individual had been deposited.

The compartments received a succession of plural gatherings, but only some seem to have been collective in nature. The final issues to be addressed are, on the one hand, the significance attaching to the installation of a new floor and, on the other hand, the reasons for burying an individual in one room rather than in another since, architecturally, all of the compartments constitute a single tomb.

Conclusion

The aim of this chapter was to present three cases of 'plural' burials. Today, powerful tools permit the management of large amounts of field data and the analysis of the spatial organisation of burials and reconstruction of funerary treatments of the body. However, reconstruction of the funerary actions responsible for the patterning of the archaeo-anthropological assemblage is still sometimes limited. To identify collective gatherings, it is necessary to demonstrate that the set of individuals was produced by a succession of deposits. The task is particularly challenging for secondary deposits comprised of several individuals. In this case, the reconstruction of the chronology of events leading to such gatherings is difficult. The identification of the number of events (were the disarticulated individuals gathered at one or several times?), contributing to an assemblage is not always possible.

Plural burials (those containing the remains of several individuals) should be examined rigorously and remain in this category if the succession of deposits is not clear. Many Late Neolithic burials in dolmens or caves are considered collective because this particular funerary mode was frequently employed during this period. Yet, for many of them, their collective nature has not been adequately demonstrated (Schmitt *et al.*, 2018). This issue forms a major challenge for the future. A second one will be to propose social hypotheses to explain the occurrence of collective burials as a whole (Schmitt and Déderix, 2018; Boulestin and Courtaud, Chapter 3, this volume).

References

Adams, B.J. and Byrd, J.E., eds. (2014). *Commingled human remains, methods in recovery, analysis and identification*. San Diego: Academic Press.

Boulestin, B. (1999). *Approche taphonomique des restes humains. Le cas des mésolithiques de la grotte des Perrats et le problème de cannibalisme en préhistoire récente européenne*, British Archaeological Reports International Series 776, Oxford: Archaeopress.

Boulestin, B. and Duday, H. (2006). Ethnology and Archaeology of Death: From the Illusion of References to the Use of Terminology. *Archaeologia Polona*, 44, pp. 149–169.

Branigan, K. (1987). Ritual interference with the human bones in the Mesara *Tholoi*. In: R. Laffineur, ed., *Thanatos. Les Coutumes Funéraires en Egée à l'Âge du Bronze*. Liège: Université de Liège (Aegaeum 1), pp. 43–50.

Chambon, P. (2003). *Les morts dans les sépultures collectives néolithiques en France: du cadavre aux restes ultimes*. Paris: Centre National de la Recherche Scientifique (CNRS).

Crevecoeur, I. and Schmitt, A. (2009). Etude archéo-anthropologique de la nécropole (Zone 1). In: J. Driessen, M. Anastasiadou, I. Caloi, T. Claeyes, S. Déderix, M. Devolder, S. Jusserat, C. Langorh, Q. Letesson, I. Mathiodaki, O. Mouthuy and A. Schmitt, eds., *Excavations at Sissi. Preliminary Report on the 2007–2008 Campaigns*, Louvain: Presses Universitaires de Louvain, pp. 57–93.

Crevecoeur, I., Schmitt, A. and Schoep I. (2015). An Archaeothanatological Approach to the Study of Minoan Funerary Practices. Case-studies from the Early and Middle Minoan Cemetery at Sissi, Crete. *Journal of Field Archaeology*, 40, pp. 283–299.

Déderix, S., Schmitt, A. and Crevecoeur, I. (2018). Introduction: towards a theoretical and methodological framework for the study of collective burial practices. In: A. Schmitt, S. Déderix and I. Crevecoeur, eds., *Gathered in Death. Archaeological and Ethnological Perspectives on Collective Burial and Social Organisation*. Louvain-la-Neuve: Presses Universitaires de Louvain, pp. 21–39.

Duday, H. (1981). La Place de l'Anthropologie dans l'Étude des Sépultures Anciennes. *Cahiers d'Anthropologie*, 1, pp. 27–42.

Duday, H. (1987a). Contribution des observations ostéologiques à la chronologie interne des sépultures collectives. In: H. Duday and C. Masset, eds., *Anthropologie Physique et Archéologie: Méthodes d'Étude des Sépultures*. Paris: Centre National de la Recherche Scientifique (CNRS), pp. 51–60.

Duday, H. (1987b). Organisation et fonctionnement d'une sépulture collective néolithique. L'aven de la Boucle à Corconne (Gard). In: H. Duday and C. Masset, eds., *Anthropologie Physique et Archéologie: Méthodes d'Étude des Sépultures*. Paris: Centre National de la Recherche Scientifique (CNRS), pp. 89–104.

Duday, H. (2005). L'archéothanatologie ou l'archéologie de la mort. In: O. Dutour, J.J. Hublin and B. Vandermeersch, eds., *Objets et Méthodes en Paléoanthropologie*. Paris: Éditions du Comité des Travaux Historiques et Scientifiques (CTHS), pp. 153–207.

Duday, H. (2009). *The archaeology of the dead: lectures in archaeothanatology*. Oxford: Oxford University Press.

Knüsel, C.J. and Robb, J. (2016). Funerary Taphonomy: An Overview of Goals and Methods, *Journal of Archaeological Science: Reports*, 10, pp. 655–673.

Leroi-Gourhan, A., Bailloud, G. and Brézillon, M. (1962). L'Hypogée 2 des Mournouards (Mesnil-sur-Oger). *Gallia Préhistoire*, 5, pp. 23–133.

Olalde, I., Brace, S., Allentoft, M.E., Armit, I., Kristiansen, K., Rohland, N., Mallick, S., Booth, T. Rohland, N., Mallick, S., Szécsényi-Nagy, A. and Mittnik, A. (2018). The Beaker Phenomenon and the Genomic Transformation of Northwest Europe. *Nature*, 555 (7695), pp. 190–196.

Provost, S., Binder, D., Duday, H., Durrenmath, G., Goude, G., Gourichon, L., Delhon, C., Gentile, I., Vuillien M. and Zemour, A. (2017). Une Sépulture Collective à la Transition des VIe et Ve Millénaires BCE: Mougins – Les Bréguières (Alpes-Maritimes, France). *Gallia Préhistoire*, 57, pp. 289–336.

Sauzade, G. (2011). Caractérisation Chronoculturelle du Mobilier Funéraire en Provence au Néolithique Final et au Bronze Ancien: Evolution des Rites Funéraires Liés à l'Inhumation Individuelle ou Collective et Distribution Chronologique des Sépultures, *Préhistoires Méditerranéennes*, 2, pp. 71–104.

Sauzade, G. and Schmitt, A. (2020). *Le dolmen du Villard au Lauzet-Ubaye (Alpes-de-Haute-Provence) et le contexte funéraire alpin au Néolithique final: réflexions sur le mobilier et les pratiques funéraires au campaniforme en Provence*. Aix-en-Provence: Presses Universitaires de Provence.

Schmitt, A., Bizot, B., Ollivier, V., Canut, V., Guendon, J.-L., Viel, L., Vella C. and Borschneck, D. (2018). Un Exemple Inédit en Provence de Sépulture Collective du Néolithique Récent/Final, le Site de Collet-Redon (Martigues). *Gallia Préhistoire*, 58, pp. 5–45.

Schmitt, A. and Déderix, S. (2018). What defines a collective grave? In: A. Schmitt, S. Déderix and I. Crevecoeur, eds., *Gathered in Death. Archaeological and Ethnological Perspectives on Collective Burial and Social Organisation*, Louvain: Presses Universitaires de Louvain, pp. 195–214.

Schmitt, A. and Déderix, S. (in press). The Prepalatial and Protopalatial cemetery: zone 9. In: J. Driessen M. Anastasiadou, I. Caloi, T. Claeyes, S. Déderix, M. Devolder, S. Jusserat, C. Langorh, Q. Letesson, I. Mathiodaki, O. Mouthuy and A. Schmitt, eds., *Excavations at Sissi VV. Preliminary Report on the 2017–2019 Campaigns*. Louvain-la-Neuve: Presses Universitaires de Louvain.

Schmitt, A. and Sperandio, E. (2018). The cemetery (zone 9): report on the 2016 campaign. In: J. Driessen M. Anastasiadou, I. Caloi, T. Claeyes, S. Déderix, M. Devolder, S. Jusserat, C. Langorh, Q. Letesson, I. Mathiodaki, O. Mouthuy and A. Schmitt, eds., *Excavations at Sissi IV. Preliminary Report on the 2015–2016 Campaigns*. Louvain-la-Neuve: Presses Universitaires de Louvain, pp. 59–76.

Schoep, I., Schmitt, A., Crevecoeur, I. and Déderix, S. (2012). The cemetery at Sissi: report of the 2011 Campaign. In: J. Driessen M. Anastasiadou, I. Caloi, T. Claeyes, S. Déderix, M. Devolder, S. Jusserat, C. Langorh, Q. Letesson, I. Mathiodaki, O. Mouthuy and A. Schmitt, eds., *Excavations at Sissi. Preliminary Report on the 2011 Campaigns*. Louvain-la-Neuve: Presses Universitaires de Louvain, pp. 27–50.

Schoep, I., Schmitt, A., Crevecoeur, I. and Déderix, S. (2013). The cemetery at Sissi: report on the 2011 campaign, In: J. Driessen, M. Anastasiadou, I. Caloi, T. Claeyes, S. Déderix, M. Devolder, S. Jusserat, C. Langorh, Q. Letesson, I. Mathiodaki, O. Mouthuy and A. Schmitt eds., *Excavations at Sissi III. Preliminary Report on the 2011 Campaign (Aegis 6)*, Louvain-la-Neuve: Presses Universitaires de Louvain, pp. 27–51.

Soles, J. (2001). Reverence for dead ancestors in prehistoric Crete. In: R. Laffineur, ed., *Potnia. Deities and Religion in the Aegean Bronze Age*, (Aegaeum 22). Liège: Université de Liège and Austin: University of Texas Press, pp. 229–236.

13

DIFFERENT BURIAL TYPES BUT COMMON PRACTICE

The case of the funerary complex at Barbuise and La Saulsotte (France) at the beginning of the Late Bronze Age

Stéphane Rottier

PACEA, De la Préhistoire à l'Actuel: Culture, Environnement et Anthropologie, UMR 5199, CNRS-Université de Bordeaux, Pessac, France

Introduction

At the beginning of the Late Bronze Age (14th to the 12th centuries BC), the riverine confluences of the southeast Paris Basin hosted a necropolis containing two apparently very different types of burials. The grave types were divided into two main groups based on their shapes on the surface of the site: 'short-pit' graves with the deceased sitting or squatting, and 'elongated-pit' graves with the deceased lying supinely. The latter are also distinguished by the number of individuals they include: one or more, and usually two. However, a detailed analysis of these grave types shows that they are not necessarily fundamentally different. In particular, they both reflect a common practice aimed at the recovery of human remains after deposition. Examples of burials from Frécul at Barbuise and La Saulsotte show the importance and relevance of a functional approach to the study of funerary treatments to form a more general perspective of the behaviours surrounding death within this early Late Bronze Age society.

The funerary complex at Barbuise and La Saulsotte (Aube, France)

At the sites of 'Le Bois Pot du Vin' (BPV), near the neighbouring communes (townships) of La Saulsotte and Barbuise-Courtavant (Aube, France) (Figure 13.1), a sitting or squatting position characterises just over a third of the burials, while the rest of the burials containing one or more individuals are supine.

Elongated pit-graves, containing one or more deceased individual(s)

At Barbuise and La Saulsotte, the extended position of the deceased was found in almost two-thirds of the burials (Rottier, 2003) (Figure 13.2). In most cases, the individual was lying supinely,

DOI: 10.4324/9781351030625-16

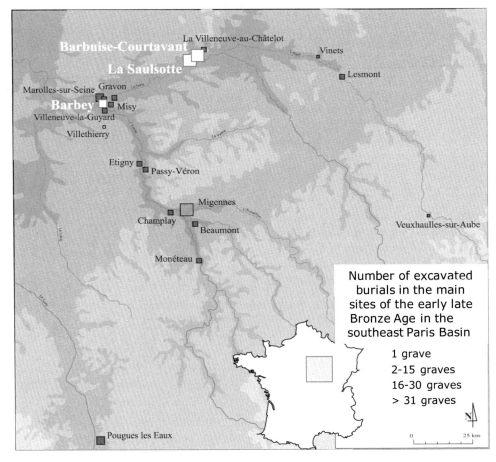

Figure 13.1 The location of the main sites from the southeastern Paris Basin with inhumations dating to the early Late Bronze Age (14th–12th centuries BC).

with the lower limbs extended parallel to one another. In the interests of consistency and comparison, the descriptions of the disposition of human remains from the feet to the head applied to burials in a sitting position were also applied to these extended positions here. Despite the poor state of preservation, the bones of the feet and lower limbs demonstrate either a close or slightly separated position of the feet. Some individuals are slightly flexed at the knee. The original position of the forearms was not always easy to define due to poor preservation of the bones of the hands. The upper limbs were either extended along the trunk or lying in front of the abdomen (BPV.93.82, Figure 13.2). In several graves, there were indications that the head was flexed anteriorly with respect to the torso.

In most cases where two individuals occupied the same pit, they were placed side-by-side in the same orientation. In some pits, there were only tibiae/fibulae and the bones of the feet and, in others, sometimes only elements of the cranium. Both individuals in grave BPV.93.91 (Figure 13.3) were also placed in the same orientation and lay on their right sides, not on their backs. In some burials, the two individuals were placed in opposite directions (Figure 13.3).

One grave contained three individuals (BPV.93.38) and another at least four individuals (BPV.93.52). In the first, the three individuals were lying on their backs, limbs extended,

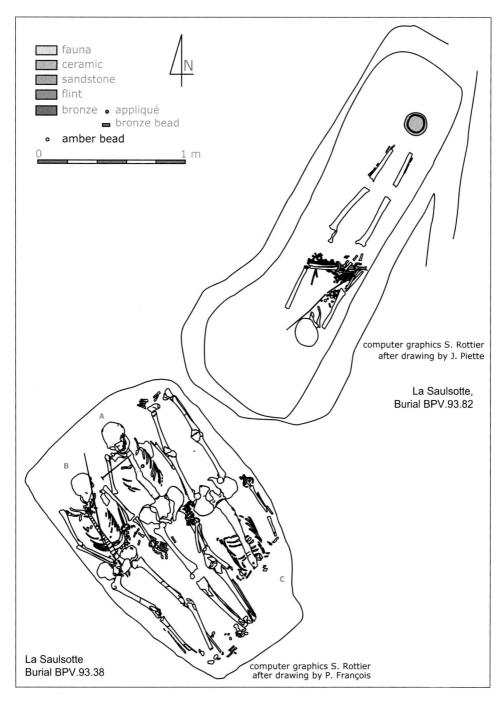

Figure 13.2 Two examples of undisturbed elongated-pit graves, including those with one and several inhumed individuals.

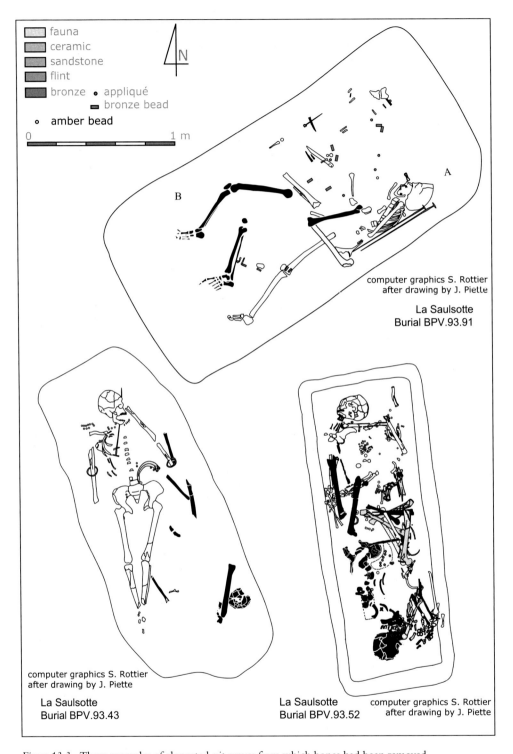

Figure 13.3 Three examples of elongated-pit graves from which bones had been removed.

side-by-side, two in the same direction and the third in the opposite direction. Here, both variants of double graves were therefore present in a single grave. In BPV.93.52, even with re-arrangements of the remains, the position of crania at both ends of the pit and the mainten-ance of a few anatomical connections demonstrate the opposed orientation of the two inhumed individuals (Figure 13.3).

Short pit-graves with individuals in a sitting or squatting position

The sites at 'Ferme de Frécul' at Barbuise – La Saulsotte produced nearly 50 examples of short-pit graves (Figure 13.4, and Rottier, 2003, 2005). Displaced bones within these graves provide some evidence for decomposition having taken place in an open space (Figure 13.5). The bones of the lower limbs were less often displaced in relation to the rest of the skeleton because of their more stable position at a lower level in the pit. Flexed knees were found uppermost in the grave or anterior to the torso. The position of tibiae indicates that the knees were flexed and placed anterior to the torso in a seated burial. If the lower limbs were placed to one side, the patella was located in front and at half the length of the tibia, and the knees were drawn up through hip flexion (Rottier, 2003, 2016). The *ossa coxae* disarticulated laterally or fell anteri-orly. The vertebral column showed a greater extent of disarticulation of the cervical vertebrae and the first three or four thoracic vertebrae. The lumbar vertebrae were most often articulated. The trunk was more or less vertical. When the body was leaning forward and when shoulders were near the anterior walls of the grave, the cranium fell anteriorly to the left side (Figure 13.5E). The container may have provided a space located to the left of the corpse in the grave, which permitted displacement of the cranium to the left side and posteriorly. Thus, evidence of horizontal compartmentalisation was recognised and, above all, vertical compartmentalisation because movements of elements occurred in an empty space before falling to the base of the grave (Rottier, 2016).

Due to the presence of this empty space, the upper limbs were more prone to movement. The hands were sometimes close to the bottom of the grave on each side of the lower limbs. In grave GDF.00.1315, where the feet and tibiae were not affected by these movements (see below), hands and forearms, especially those of the right side, showed no evidence of major dis-turbance (Figure 13.4). The hands could have been placed one beside the other, situated on the lower limb at the knee or close to the pelvis. In many cases, it is possible to envisage binding of the wrists, knees, or wrists with the ipsilateral knee (Rottier, 2003). Indeed, the position of the hands anterior to the femora at the knees is not in a stable position. The use of binding should therefore be considered a way to obtain this hand/knee combination. In all cases, at the moment of binding, the body was likely no longer in *rigor mortis*, that is to say, more than 48 hours after death when the body is flexible and can be manipulated (Thomas, 1975). After or before this period, the position of the body can be maintained by binding, even before placing the deceased in a burial container. Another possibility would be to place the body directly into the container. In this case, flexion may have been maintained by the shape and narrow structure of the container. The position of the forearm and hand could also have been due to the size of the receptacle. The position at 'Ferme de Frécul' in short-pit graves appears to be standard (Rottier, 2004, 2005).

Summary

Two different types of graves are markedly distinguished based on their shapes: one comprises a short-pit and the other an elongated-pit. In addition, elongated-pit graves may contain several

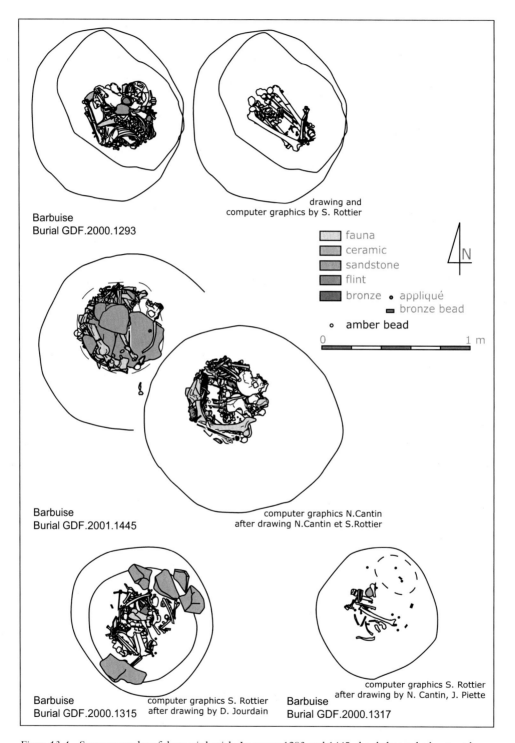

Figure 13.4 Some examples of short-pit burials. In graves 1293 and 1445, the skeletons had not yet been removed. In the lower two drawings, several bones are missing.

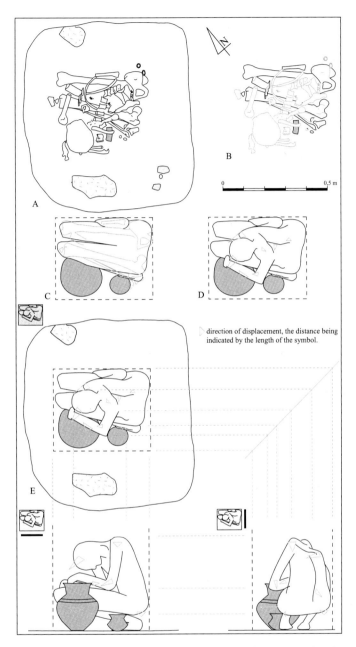

Figure 13.5 The method by which reconstructions of the position of the deceased at the time of deposition is obtained, applied here to burial 12 at Barbey – 'Les Cent Arpents' (Seine-et-Marne, France). The first step is to record the remains to identify the bones that have not been moved from those that have been moved only a small amount after the deposition of the corpse. A. Plan of burial 12 (modified from the original drawing of C. and D. Mordant); B. The bones that had been moved are drawn more clearly here; C. The original space occupied by the corpse is reconstructed, starting with the bones that showed no movement; D. Skeletal elements in unstable positions are then reconstructed with regard to the extent of displacement by archaeothanatological analysis of the burial. Profiles are then reconstructed through taphonomic analysis; E. The reconstructed height of the corpse taking into account anatomical proportions of the body.

individuals, which further differentiates them from short-pit graves. Therefore, the initial interpretation of these two different types of pit might be the result of completely different practices or rites. Nevertheless, a very detailed taphonomic approach shows a similar funerary process despite different shapes, positions and contents.

Funerary processing of the dead

As mentioned above, many graves did not contain a complete skeleton (Figures 13.3 and 13.5). The bone may have been absent due to mechanical stripping, natural disturbances, or anthropogenic re-arrangements. Among these, disturbances due to looting or older 'excavations' must be distinguished from intentional manipulations of these deceased individuals by contemporary people. These intentional actions can be interpreted as part of the funerary processing of the dead. The challenge is to recognise these various aspects in burials during excavation and taphonomic analysis. At Barbuise and La Saulsotte, less than 20% of the deceased lacked evidence of disturbance. Interventions by people in the past (that is to say, without graves having been disturbed by machines or other indeterminable interventions) could be demonstrated for almost half of the dead. The vast majority of them had been subjected to bone removals, at least in part. Others were represented by a few bones at most having been found in a secondary position, while other intact burials also had bones removed. These interventions are considered to have occurred post-burial (Figure 13.6). This difference can be demonstrated through taphonomic analysis (Rottier, 2003, 2005, 2009). It is, therefore, possible to distinguish the graves which did not undergo re-working from those which had undergone different degrees of re-working, including through re-use of the same grave for another burial. The rarer secondary deposits observed in graves already hosting a deceased individual could also be identified as post-burial interventions.

The removal of bones may be event-related. They affect both burial types; those with the deceased in a supine position as well as those in an upright seated or squatting position (Figures 13.2 to 13.5), apparently regardless of sex or age. In contrast, supplementary ('extra') human bones were found only in graves in which the deceased was in a squatting or sitting position, including those of both males and females. These deposits appear very codified and could be bones taken from other graves. In some cases, they are placed on a layer of faunal bones, which are likely symbolic in nature.

Bone removal and deposition in other graves have already been proposed in relation to Bronze Age sites, especially in the large necropolis of Gemeinlebarn F (northern Austria) (Neugebauer, 1991), dated to the 18th and 17th centuries BC. Neugebauer sees this as a consequence of successive lootings of this site. The description of looted and/or disturbed graves was defined, moreover, by 'degrees of looting', corresponding to what is considered here as 'bone-gathering'. Several graves from Gemeinlebarn F still contained metal objects, sometimes quite large ones, such as dagger blades. This evidence militates against the hypotheses of looting. At Gemeinlebarn F, an *os coxae* is the most frequently missing element, with the cranium and one or both femora being next most commonly absent. This absence could be due to an initial phase of collection of the same bones as observed at Barbuise and La Saulsotte (Rottier, 2009). The following episodes of collecting appeared to target the humerus and pectoral girdle or one or both tibiae. Finally, the last stages of this process reflect the collection of all major long bones, crania and pelvic girdle.

The 'disturbed' appearances of graves in many European Bronze Age sites have apparently always been interpreted as resulting from looting. In the light of observations made at Barbuise and La Saulsotte, the possibility of post-burial practices to collect bones from graves,

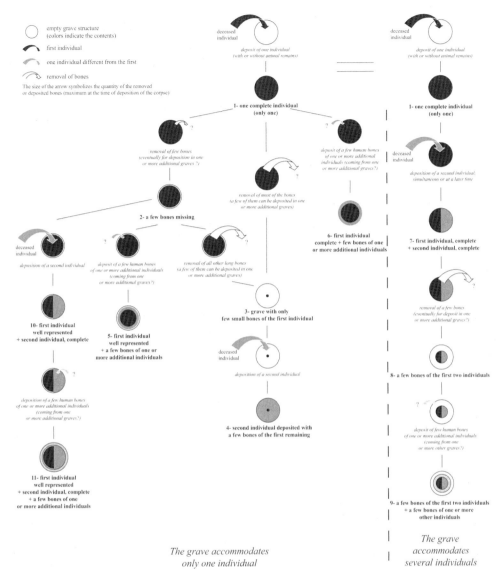

Figure 13.6 The funerary process characterising burials at Barbuise and La Saulsotte (Aube) at the beginning of the Late Bronze Age (14th–12th centuries BC).

presumably in a highly regulated manner, must now be taken into account. It is quite likely that these practices may be found in other burial sites that are believed to have suffered systematic looting.

Through taphonomic analysis, the criteria required to re-interpret those graves previously regarded as looted graves can be considered anew. With regard to the funerary processing proposed here (Figure 13.6 and Rottier, 2009), these so-called 'disturbed graves' and the many published Bronze Age sites yielding looted or disturbed graves should be re-visited. For many of them, it is possible to try to re-interpret the data, even if it is impossible to do the same for older excavations with as much confidence.

Information from sites such as the 'Gours aux Lions' necropolis in Marolles-sur-Seine (Mordant and Mordant, 1970), less than two kilometres from Barbey 'Cent Arpents' (Seine-et-Marne), implies a similar scenario. Indeed, most of the burials at this site would match with this pattern of cases 2 and 3 (Figure 13.6) according to the number of 'missing bones'. The absence of the cranium and mandible and long bones is reported, and several graves contain only a few of the smaller bones of the skeleton, confirming the similarity with neighbouring graves at Barbey 'Les Cent Arpents' (Rottier, 2004, 2005).

In previous publications collecting of grave goods or other materials is well known but often interpreted as looting and thus having nothing to do with funerary practices. For the site of 'Gours aux Lions' at Marolles-sur-Seine (Seine-et-Marne) the 'disturbed graves' have already been published as being of anthropogenic and intentional in origin (Mordant and Mordant, 1970). Thus, the recovery of grave goods but also bones, including the cranium, was foreshadowed at the beginning of the Late Bronze Age. Evidence for manipulation for the same period has also been identified in the same region at the 'Prés Pendus' Passy-Verron (Yonne) (Depierre *et al.*, 1997, 2000). These affect the supine burials in which removal was observed, but cremations were very likely also manipulated. This parallel is interesting, especially if burial is considered as a transitional stage followed by the gathering of a few bones, as well as cremation was undertaken before collecting bones prior to the final deposition in the grave. This could be seen as an intermediate stage between death and the aggregation/incorporation of the deceased into the world of the dead, following the concepts of Arnold van Gennep (1909).

This indicates that during the Bronze Age, the grave was not always a closed context because subsequent removals or depositions occurred. In addition, many graves were reported as having been looted because the skeleton was not complete or was apparently in anatomical disorder. The sitting or squatting position of the deceased presented here shows particularly well that the absence of anatomical order correlates with the original position of the deceased at the time of burial and not necessarily due to disturbance. This analysis shows that the interpretation of looting has often been stated without further description of the remains. The observation and recording of the relative position of each bone are essential during excavation to permit fundamental taphonomic analysis, which will ultimately influence the interpretation.

The early-Late Bronze Age (14th–12th centuries BC) funerary complex in the basins of the Yonne, Haute-Seine, and Aube rivers

The fact that these burials occur for an extended period of time and that removal and secondary deposits of bones were performed over the course of this period provides a completely different perspective of death-related behaviour as opposed to burials viewed as a single point in time. The presence at the same site of a variety of practices and grave types contradicts the notion that a standard type of necropolis existed during that period. The concept of a funerary complex encompasses this type of manipulation of the dead, and at the same time, also suggests a variable conception of death (Leclerc, 1990; Depierre *et al.*, 1997). In the funerary complex, burial patterning constitutes evidence for the intervention of the living in the world of the dead. The burial complex represents a privileged place for the conduct of the many rituals related to the passage from a state of 'living' to a 'dead' state. This is the period during which regular interventions in the grave may take place before the deceased has really entered the world of the dead. The concept of a funerary complex also implies an organisation, not only of the ceremonies but also of the physical management of the body, the structure of the grave, and the available funerary space. It seems that the relationship between the deceased and his/her contemporaries is the source of modifications since there is a common pattern of treatment in this case.

Spatial organisation

At Barbuise and La Saulsotte, the graves were located on gravel domes that formed slight topo-graphic positive reliefs with respect to areas that are considered to be palaeochannels. It seems that these hollows became small ponds during the Bronze Age before being filled in during the Gallo-Roman period (Rottier, 2003). The graves are located on either side of these ponds. At 'Grèves de Frécul', the dead – in a sitting position- are oriented differently, depending on whether they are north or south of the palaeochannels: in the north, burials are oriented towards the southeast, and in the south, they are oriented to the northwest (Figure 13.7). This peculiarity can in no way be generalised to other sites since it has not been observed elsewhere. However, it is interesting to consider that these areas of water acted as borders between two funerary traditions. Even if the graves have similar shape, structure and features on both sides, the dead are nevertheless distinguished by their differing orientations and also by their grave goods. The suggestion that males come from the outside of the region due to the existence of an uxorilocal

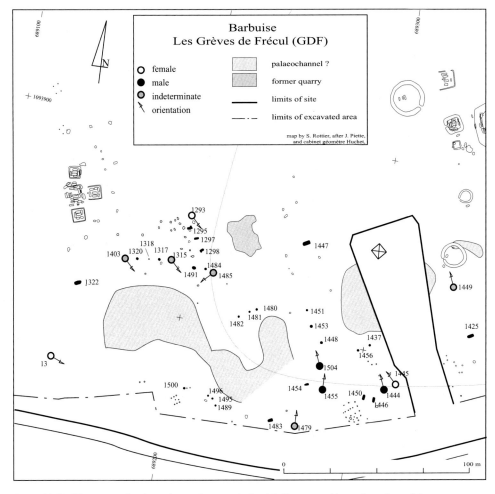

Figure 13.7 The opposed orientations of corpses in burials from one side to the other of the palaeochannel at Barbuise (Aube).

233

social system (Rottier, 2003) may support this hypothesis since all males are located to the south of this boundary.

It seems that these wetlands heavily influenced the spatial organisation of the site. Some alignments at the 'Grèves de Frécul' are located parallel to the edges of these palaeochannels. The structuring role of the hydrography in the implementation of funerary complexes of the early Late Bronze Age is also found in Passy-Véron (Burgundy-Franche-Comté, France), where enclosures and burials appear to be located between two palaeochannels that join to the south (Depierre *et al.*, 1997).

The structuring of space at Barbey does not show the same use of the surrounding topography but is probably organised according to precise geometric rules. The similarity to the arrangement of graves in the northwestern group of graves at 'Bois Pot de Vin' seems to attest to a model form of spatial organisation that is at play (Figure 13.8). The meaning of this spatial organisation, however, remains to be explained. In contrast, it becomes increasingly clear that this arrangement forms a pattern when the distribution of burials is considered; these occur at regular intervals over an arc of 33m in diameter at Barbey and at Barbuise and La Saulsotte, a phenomenon that is also found in Marolles, where Graves 1, 12, 7, 8, 6 and 11 are all located on the same arc of a circle whose diameter is also 33 m. However, at Marolles, no similar grid system organisation as identified as at the other two sites has been found, even if the alignments are similar.

Alignments have also been observed at a different scale for graves within a restricted area (Rottier, 2003). Alignments have been noted, for example, at 'Grèves de Frécul'. In the valleys of the Yonne and Haute-Seine, this can also be seen on the majority of sites with enclosures, which corresponds, again, to areas reserved for burial. Two similar patterns are superimposed in the funerary complex of the 14th to the 12th centuries BC in the southeastern Paris Basin. On the one hand, the broad outlines of the funerary complex were imposed by topographic features, mainly hydrological ones. On the other hand, burial groupings seem to be established

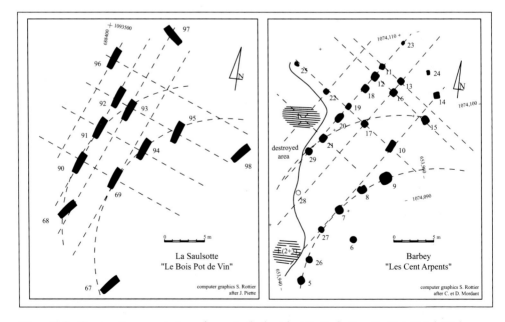

Figure 13.8 Comparative organisation of space in the burials at La Saulsotte – 'Le Bois Pot de Vin' (Aube) and in Barbey – 'Les Cent Arpents' (Seine-et-Marne), located 30 kilometres from each other.

according to a standardised organisation, with dimensions and geometric shape rules. Moreover, these funerary complexes often extend over several tens of hectares. Vast portions of the territory, often bordering floodplains, would thus have been employed for this purpose.

The burial programme

The identification of organising principles of some burials in Barbuise and La Saulsotte 'Frécul' and Barbey 'Cent Arpents' provides the basis for consideration of the entire burial complex to determine if specific organisational rules and management existed.

The demonstration of patterning in graves reveals a process punctuated by anthropogenic interventions that provides a dynamic image of funerary behaviour at the beginning of the Late Bronze Age. Within this funerary complex, graves contain evidence resulting from different stages of funerary processing. If this hypothesis of regular interventions through time is correct, it may be possible that the higher proportion of graves displaying an advanced stage in this process indicate that this processing occurred over a longer period of time. In this context, it is possible to order the steps from the beginning of the funerary process to the end. The order of the steps may be inferred from standard actions linked to the differing patterns observed (Figure 13.6). Stages 1 and 7 are initial ones, followed by stages 2, 3, 8 or 10 and/or finishes with stages 4, 5, 6, 9 or 11. The frequency of each of these stages among graves permits interpretations in terms of general processing of the corpse as part of the funerary programme. Table 13.1 shows the cremations, which take on an increasingly important role over time in the southeast Paris Basin. A high percentage of burials with the initial stage of the funerary process (1 or 7) could mean that the site had not been used over a long enough period for post-burial interventions to occur. On the contrary, the burials could have been made over a relatively short period of time. The site at Barbey represents an example of this pattern.

Table 13.1 The percentage of graves with evidence for the various stages of the funerary programme at Barbuise and La Saulsotte 'Frécul' (Aube, France) and Barbey 'Les Cent Arpents' (Seine-et-Marne, France). The unpublished data relating to the older discoveries by Lamarre are in italics because of their imprecise descriptions. In grey: the percentages of the two groups from 'Bois Pot de Vin' (BVP), Barbuise and La Saulsotte (Aube, France) (first column, 1 to 11: stages of the funerary process, see Figure 13.6)

Stage of the funerary programme	Frécul, phase 1 45.7% of 105 of which:	Frécul, phase 1 BPV Nord-Ouest 92.3% of 13 of which:	Frécul, phase 1 BPV Sud-Est 60.9% of 23 of which:	Frécul, phase 2 46.7% of 15 of which:	Frécul, Lamarre 51.1% of 47 of which:	Barbey 54.2% of 24 of which:
1	25.0	8.3	21.4	14.3	58.3	46.2
7	2.1	0.0	7.1	0.0	0.0	0.0
2	18.8	33.3	14.3	28.6	37.5	0.0
3	29.2	33.3	28.6	0.0	0.0	30.8
8	12.5	25.0	14.3	14.3	0.0	0.0
6	0.0	0.0	0.0	28.6	0.0	7.7
5	4.2	0.0	0.0	0.0	0.0	0.0
9	2.1	0.0	7.1	0.0	0.0	0.0
4	0.0	0.0	0.0	0.0	0.0	7.7
10	2.1	0.0	7.1	0.0	0.0	0.0
11	0.0	0.0	0.0	0.0	0.0	7.7
cremation	4.2	0.0	0.0	14.3	4.2	0.0

A large percentage of burials displaying stages 2, 3 and 8 can be interpreted as synchronous graves, so these indicate the deposition of greater number of the deceased over a shorter period of time. The north grouping at 'Bois Pot de Vin' may then have been established relatively quickly and represents a generally synchronous grouping. This assessment assumes a rhythmic process, with graves being prepared to permit two to three 'seasons of removal'. The periodicity of these post-burial interventions is still unknown.

Considering the same periodicity of these cycles at both sites, and based on the two preceding interpretations, the grouping of burials at Barbey 'Cent Arpents' may well have had a shorter duration than the two groups at 'Bois Pot de Vin'. Thus, a greater number of graves located in the same group indicating a standard pattern appear to relate to a synchronous period of processing of the remains. Assuming that this relationship can be transposed onto several groups of the funerary complex, it becomes possible to determine their sequence of implementation. Based on these hypotheses, it appears that the northwest grouping at 'Bois Pot de Vin' was established before the southeast grouping. In this regard, it is important to note as well that the number of cremations increases at 'Frécul' in the latest phase of use. It is perhaps also possible to use this rate as a chronological marker since cremation replaces burial early in the Late Bronze in the southeastern Paris Basin, eventually becoming the predominant type of burial.

Another way to interpret the frequency of these burials may be that these are variants of the behaviour of groups with slightly different practices. This interpretation partly overlaps with the first, as the practices and behaviours can vary from one group to another but also change over time within the same group. The difficulty in distinguishing between these two possibilities decreases as the relative chronology of them becomes better appreciated. Cyclical recovery does not appear to be a regionally or chronologically specific behaviour. A detailed reading of grave taphonomy can address their relative dating, complementing those indicated by the goods they contain and their architecture. This funerary programme, common to all the graves whatever their size or the burial position of the deceased, seems to be due to common practice. Differences can be interpreted as the expression of individual social differentiation, probably related to a more broadly defined funerary rite.

Beyond the differences: specific and general behaviours

Within this funerary programme, there are some elements that may reflect social structural elements underpinned by beliefs. These structuring elements are recognised as fundamental in so-called ranked societies (Hertz, 1907; van Gennep, 1909; Radcliffe-Brown, 1969; Godelier, 1984; Kristiansen and Rowlands, 1998), among which proto-European societies would form a part (Kristiansen and Rowlands, 1998; Harding, 2000). Here, two main aspects can be identified: the funerary process that is the same for all of the deceased and specific features observed in several graves. These may be explained as a form of spiritual behaviour aimed at a specific part of the population. The 'social skin' (as defined elsewhere for these sites by Rottier, 2003, 2010) may have also played a role in this spiritual or 'magico-religious' field. To decipher it, the objects or costumes that carry symbolic content are of utmost importance, but this is currently possible only very partially (Rottier, 2010).

General behaviour and funerary processes

Symbolic signalling unrelated to social hierarchy seems best-suited to describe societal reactions to death. Many authors have accepted that funerary rites depend on sex, age and social position of the deceased (van Gennep, 1909; Binford, 1971). While this may be partly true, especially for children, who do not seem to be treated like the rest of the population in the context studied here, it would be more accurate to say that it is the materialisation that varies from one individual to another, while the ritual aspects remain similar for the entire population. These variations can be seen as adaptations of the rite to the social position of the deceased.

For the sites of Barbuise and La Saulsotte, the funerary programme seems to be applied to all of the burials. The manipulative behaviour is regulated so that all individuals in the group are involved, regardless of their social position in terms of kinship, sex, or other social status. There is a single ritual sequence, following the 'rites de passage' of van Gennep (1909), with succession from separation to liminal and aggregation/incorporation rites, for each individual. The resulting expression of funerary gestures/actions can then differ with regard to material associations on the basis of social relationships that the deceased had with contemporaries. At the beginning of the Late Bronze Age, children were apparently peripheral and did not receive the same treatment. Access to the funerary programme is permitted only for individuals who are actually active parts of the social organisation in a socially functional sense. Activities begin with a specified learning phase, including age of accessibility that is not necessarily fixed. The presence of children in some of the sites from the early Late Bronze Age in the southeast Paris Basin could then be explained by their early entry into the society as recognised adults. This access may also be conditioned by kinship. The fact that only children of certain lineages were entitled to receive burial similar to that of adults may explain the very low proportion of younger immature individuals included in burial sites in the initial stage of the Late Bronze Age.

The different steps of the funerary process highlighted above are probably the most tangible evidence of ritual regulation for the dead included in this study. This phenomenon seems to involve all of the dead, whether their graves were monumental or not, male or female, elderly or young adult. This spiritual social aspect (part of a 'magico-religious society' as van Gennep (1909) called it) thus covers the funerary practices for the entire population. The funerary process described here is probably only one aspect of these practices that can be placed in the 'conventional' ritual sequence of a 'rite de passage', as defined by Arnold van Gennep (1909). This sequence is characterised by a succession of stages to separate the dead from the living world and integrate them into the 'world of the dead'. For archaeological remains considered here, the beginning of the separation step can be seen as the time of burial. This primary burial then undergoes processing at the end of which the deceased is integrated in the 'world of the dead', whatever that may be. The duration of this process can be spread more or less over time and can occur in one or more episodes. This is Hertz's (1907) period of transition, or the liminal period of van Gennep (1909), in which the deceased is no longer entirely in the world of the living but not yet in the domain of the dead. This phase can also correspond to the period of mourning among the living. This period of mourning would be punctuated by post-burial interventions and could be considered completed by the end of the funerary process. The change in status or condition of the individual is thus gradual. The aggregation/incorporation of the deceased into the world of the dead would only be complete at the end of the funerary process aimed at the recovery of the bones of the deceased, a process that would reach its final conclusion when bones removed from the grave had been deposited in their final destination (Hertz, 1907; Thomas, 1975). At this stage of reflection, several hypotheses can be proposed with regard to this funerary process.

The first is to consider a location for the 'secondary burial', where the bones are definitively placed. This place may be for collective or individual deposition. A second possibility would be to consider that, at the end of the funerary process, the remains of the dead no longer possess a social identity, which allows them to be treated as material objects. A third possibility would be the use of these bones to represent the deceased or the spirit of the deceased in a subsequent spiritual life, at the group or small group level, such as the family, for example. Bones can then be re-used in a funerary context to represent aggregation/incorporation of another deceased individual or their respective spirits. Within this hypothesis, the use of relics in a cult of ancestors may also be a possibility. Moreover, in this case, the symbolic value of the cranium and long bones may be important (Thomas, 1975; Dumas-Champion, 1995; Guilmain-Gauthier and Gauthier, 1995; Le Fur, 1999).

Of these hypotheses, the second seems least likely. The first and third are both defensible. The acceptance of one or the other depends on the system of thought accorded to the population in question. If the thought mode is 'linear', in which everything has a beginning and an end, the hypothesis of a final, secondary location may be more accurate. If the thought mode is 'cyclical', in which everything is continually re-instated in a 'cycle of life', then a spiritual life hypothesis can be entertained based on the re-integration of 'bones and what they represent' in the form of a secondary burial place located, for example, within the village, in homes, or in the graves of other individuals. Sioui (1994: 224) described 'the first social principle' [of the Wendat, ancestors of the Huron-Wendat, an Iroquois-speaking First Nations people] … is 'the recognition of the Great Sacred Circle of life or relationships'. Sioui (1989, 1994: 294) noted that the social organisation of most Amerindian peoples was based on a system of concentric circles, from the individual ('self') to the universe, through the Family, the Lineage, the Clan, the Village, the Nation, the Confederation, the Continent and the World. Membership of all things in a circle is evident in this conception. Thus, during the *Great Feast of Souls* bodies and bones were recovered from cemeteries and put in an ossuary or collective burial in the centre of the village in order to aggregate/incorporate the dead within the world of the living and build and maintain 'family' relationships (in a social, not a biological sense) during ceremonies of soul amalgamation. The spirit of the dead was then re-integrated into inner circles (Sioui, 1994: 294), mainly at the (social) family, lineage, clan and village levels. Many community members then become brothers through the aggregation of their ancestors to each other. This celebration was undertaken approximately every 12 years. It is possible that the funerary process outlined for the early Late Bronze Age of the southeast Paris Basin was one such cyclical ceremony of recurring behaviours. The physical evidence from the graves seems to accord with a concept of periodicity in post-burial interventions.

Particular behaviours

In addition to the funerary processes that seem to apply to all of the graves, some behaviours are specific to only certain deceased individuals. These include an unusual burial position and animal bone deposits.

The seated position does not characterise all individuals. No criteria, such as grave goods or burial structures or osteological data related to activity or a special status of these individuals in the social structure, seems to be implicated. In the archaeological literature, the interpretations proposed to explain the seated position are not very numerous. The most current interpretation suggests that the disposition of the deceased reflects the flexed position of the foetus and attributes it to a symbol of rebirth (Binford, 1971; Baroin, Barreteau and von Graffenried, 1995). The fact that the flexed position of the body prevents the spirit of the deceased from straying or returning to the living is often mentioned (Wilder and Whipple, 1917; Tyler, 1921, cited in Binford, 1971). Herodotus (1959) explained the use of a seated position of the dead among Libyans as a means to ensure that their souls did not remain prisoners of the body. Hertz (1907: 75) also reported that in 'some Caribe peoples of French Guiana' the dead person is deposited in a pit, 'sitting on a seat, with all his ornaments and weapons: [one] brings him food and drink until the bones are completely stripped'. This indicates a position adopted during a transitional period before the soul is finally admitted to the land of the dead. It, therefore, suggests that, in many cases, the sitting position is associated with a temporary period to permit the separation of the soul and body of the deceased. This kind of belief would fit nicely with the funerary process highlighted here. However, this process is not specific to the sitting position. It could be a transitional period, a liminal period between death and the end of the bone recovery funerary process. In the graves studied here, the difference cannot be demonstrated from the evidence for bone removals. In contrast, the addition of some human bones of one or more individuals is more common in short-pit graves than in elongated ones.

The interpretation of the seated position as being related to human sacrifice, as at the Iron Age site of Acy Romance (Ardennes, France), seems questionable (Lambot, Méniel and Metzler, 1996; Lambot and Méniel, 2000). In the absence of a convincing argument, this is still a hypothetical possibility, but the foundations of which seem fragile. In Central and Eastern Europe, many Middle and Late Bronze Age sites, where the presence of human bones in positions not in accordance with what seems expected in a burial, have been interpreted in terms of sacrifice (Jelinek, 1990a and b), without providing a more convincing demonstration. However, several sites have yielded many disarticulated human remains, mostly long bones, some of which show signs of intentional breakage. These bones are spread over large areas, in residential areas or in the ruins of older habitations (Tihelka, 1969; Hrala, Sedlacek and Vavra, 1990; Salas, 1990; Jelinek, 1990b). Close to one of these sites, some graves have been described as missing bones (Hrala, Sedlacek and Vavra, 1990; Outram *et al.*, 2005; Harding *et al.*, 2007). Interpretation of bone breakage invariably makes reference to cannibalism (Jelinek, 1990b) while spreads of bones are considered as cultic, without further detail, as is often the case in the absence of hypothesis-testing (Hrala, Sedlacek and Vavra, 1990). Although the sacrificial explanation remains highly speculative, the existence of areas of secondary deposition could have existed at the beginning of the Late Bronze Age in the southeast Paris Basin. This perspective corresponds to a collective burial structure that could house the bones taken from the graves. Intentional fracturing could then have been undertaken to increase the number of remains from an individual to eventually add fragments in a number of different places: in homes, in this collective area or in the graves of other individuals. It is an example of the latter case that can then be seen at Barbuise and La Saulsotte.

Community or ethnic affiliation of the deceased can also sometimes be viewed as the cause of specific positioning of the body in the grave (Baroin, Barreteau and von Graffenried, 1995; more particularly Gauthier, 1995). This hypothesis does not seem to hold at Barbuise and La Saulsotte. It is only possible to propose a distinction between people who may have had a social impact on one or another of the social groups constituting the community.

Besides the position of the deceased, the main difference observed between supine and seated individuals in graves is the creation of animal bone deposits above the seated individuals. This was not observed in the burials of supine individuals. In addition, these deposits appear to have a symbolic value due to the amount of bone and the number and type of species present (Rottier, 2003). Horses and dogs appear to have had a particular importance in these burials. In many instances, these two animals are used, alone or in combination, to represent a guide for the soul of the deceased, to lead it to its destination, or, alternatively, as a means to appease the soul of the deceased (e.g. Gnoli and Vernant, 1982; Bodson, 2000). Thus, the creation of such deposits could be a way to interact with the spirits of the dead. The most numerous deposits that also include horse and dog remains are those for the dead whose bones have not (not yet?) been removed. Considering removal of bones as a step in the integration of the dead or their spirits in the world of the dead, or the community of ancestors, it is also possible, as in many other beliefs, that such integration can begin only if it is certain that the soul of the dead person is willing to join this world of the dead (Hertz, 1907; van Gennep 1909; Thomas 1975; Gnoli and Vernant, 1982).

The presence of horses, dogs and even human bones in combination with bone removal in some graves may thus be linked in such practices of integration over the course of time.

Conclusion

The direction taken by archaeothanatology in recent years is to provide the most objective reading of the data possible. The development of field methods has made considerable progress in terms of gathering information through observation, description and understanding of taphonomic phenomena. The study of the burial sites of Barbuise and La Saulsotte 'Frécul' at the beginning of the Late Bronze age is not only based on a basic biological study of sex and age-at-death of the population but also involves a detailed taphonomic approach to the study of the grave as a whole. The extraordinary complexity of the burial positions observed could be addressed only through a long and necessarily highly descriptive recording of the human remains and the grave context. From this, the first level of interpretation followed, which resulted in recognition of post-burial practices and defined the funerary programme. Following on this, a second level of interpretation centred around the concept of 'social skin' was discussed (Rottier, 2003, 2010), emphasising the social organisation of the population.

The taphonomic study of the remains of the dead and the grave as a whole enables the reconstruction of the transformative process of the deceased, but also to understand the layout of the grave structure and the distribution of space within the grave. In this way, the interpretive value of the differences of the two positions, supine and seated, could be assessed. The appearance of what appeared to be small chests of perishable material in which the dead are placed in a sitting position also brought new insights. The interior of these boxes is often compartmentalised horizontally and, above all, vertically. This structure appears to be designed to permit post-burial bone recovery from the graves. Re-opening of graves was not only confined to the dead in a sitting or squatting position but also affected individuals buried supinely. The position of the accompanying objects appears to be variable from one site to another but relatively constant within a single funerary location, regardless of the social status of the deceased. The approach adopted here also made it possible to consider site-specific practices, perhaps including the existence of an officiant(s) who organised the burial and implemented the transmission of the protocols to follow.

Similarly, taphonomic analyses helped to highlight the existence of funerary processes common to all individuals, whether seated or supine. This process is based on the intervention of the living in the graves in order to collect the bones of the deceased. No specific order of removal has been established, although the *ossa coxae* and the cranium seem most often to be the target, followed by the femora and humeri. The amount of bone removed each time is not consistent. In addition, a variant of this funerary process involves depositing a few human bones, mostly *os coxae* and femora in the grave. This practice is more common in burials in which the deceased is seated. It coincides in most cases with the presence of abundant faunal bone deposits made over time and not all at once.

All these post-burial practices have been interpreted as part of rites of passage, in the classic sequence proposed by van Gennep (1909), where a period of separation is followed by a liminal period ending with integration or aggregation/incorporation of the deceased. The establishment of the grave marks the period of separation and from which the liminal period begins. This could correspond to the period of mourning among the living and the time required for the soul or essence of the dead person to be separated from the body of the deceased. The end of this period would then be symbolised by the bone recoveries that permit the integration of the soul, or spirit, of the dead person to a place that has not left any trace among the archaeological sites presented here. The demonstration of the existence of this ritual sequence is particularly important at the beginning of the Late Bronze Age in the southeastern part of the Paris Basin. In this context, the widespread transition to cremation practices is not surprising. It is made possible by the similarity of the funerary processing of the deceased, the cremation of the body accelerating the decomposition of the corpse before the interventions permitting the recovery of bones. The liminal period is then reduced, but the ritual sequence is the same. This similarity of practices is an essential condition to explain the rapid adoption of a different method of processing the body at the transition between the initial and middle stages of the Late Bronze Age.

References

Baroin, C., Barreteau, D. and von Graffenried, C. (1995). *Mort et rites funéraires dans le bassin du lac Tchad*. Séminaire du Réseau Méga-Tchad, 12–14 septembre 1990, Paris: Office de la recherche scientifique et technique outre-mer (ORSTOM) éditions, collection Colloques et Séminaires.

Binford, L.R. (1971). Mortuary Practices: Their Study and Their Potential. *Memoirs of the Society for American Archaeology*, 25, pp. 6–29.

Bodson, L., ed. (2000). *Ces animaux que l'homme choisit d'inhumer. Contribution à l'étude de la place et du rôle de l'animal dans les rites funéraires*, journée d'étude, Université de Liège, 20 mars 1999, Colloques d'histoire des connaissances zoologiques.

Depierre, G., Jacquemin, M., Mordant, C. and Muller, F. (2000). Propositions pour une Nouvelle Lecture des Pratiques Funéraires au Bronze Final. La Nécropole de Passy-Véron, « Les Prés Pendus » (Yonne). In: B. Dedet, P. Gruat, G. Marchand, M. Py and M. Schwaller, eds., *Archéologie de la Mort, Archéologie de la Tombe au Premier Age du Fer*. Lattes: Actes du XXIème colloque international de l'Association Française pour l'Étude de l'Âge du Fer (A.F.E.A.F.), Conques – Montrozier, 8–11 mai 1997, Monographies d'Archéologie Méditerranéenne (M.A.M.) 5, pp. 179–193.

Depierre, G., Jacquemin, M., Muller, F., Collet, S. and Mordant, C. (1997). La Nécropole des « Prés Pendus » sur les Communes de Passy et de Véron (Yonne): Un Complexe Funéraire du Bronze Final I-IIa. *Revue Archéologique de l'Est*, 48, pp. 3–50.

Dumas-Champion, F. (1995). Le Destin de la Tête, Le Culte des Crânes chez les Koma du Cameroun. In: C. Baroin, D. Barreteau and C. von Graffenried, eds., *Mort et Rites Funéraires dans le Bassin du lac Tchad*, Séminaire du Réseau Méga-Tchad, 12–14 septembre 1990, Paris: Office de la recherche scientifique et technique outre-mer (ORSTOM) éditions, Collection Colloques et Séminaires, pp. 153–162.

Gauthier, J.-G. (1995). Tombes et rites funéraires en pays Fali (Nord-Cameroun). In: C. Baroin, D. Barreteau, and C. von Graffenried, eds., *Mort et Rites Funéraires dans le Bassin du Lac Tchad*, Paris: Séminaire ORSTOM, 12–14 septembre 1990, pp. 47–62.

Gnoli, G. and Vernant, J.-P., eds. (1982). *La mort, les morts dans les sociétés anciennes*, Cambridge and Paris: Cambridge University Press and Maison des Sciences de l'Homme.

Godelier, M. (1984). *L'idéel et le matériel. Pensée, économies, sociétés* Paris: Fayard.

Guilmain-Gauthier, C. and Gauthier, J.-G. (1995). Evolution des rituels funéraires au Cameroun: exemples Fali et Bassa. In J.M. Large, ed., *La Mort Passé, Présent, Conditionnel*, actes du colloque de la Roche-sur-Yon, juin 1994, La Roche-sur-Yon: Groupe Vendéen d'Etudes Préhistoriques, pp. 87–93.

Harding, A.-F. (2000). *European societies in the Bronze Age*. Cambridge: Cambridge University Press.

Harding, A.F., Šumberová, R., Knüsel, C.J. and Outram, A.K. (2007). *Velim: violence and death in Bronze Age Bohemia: the results of fieldwork 1992–95, with a consideration of peri-mortem trauma and deposition in the Bronze Age*. Prague: Institute of Archaeology of the Czech Academy of Sciences.

Herodotus (1959). *Histoires*, Livre IV, chapitre 190, Paris: Les Belles Lettres.

Hertz, R. (1907). Contribution à une Étude sur la Représentation Collective de la Mort. *L'Année Sociologique 1905–1906*, pp. 48–137.

Hrala, J., Sedlacek, Z. and Vavra, M. (1990). The Research of Bronze Age Hill Settlement in Velim, near Kolin. *Anthropologie (Brno)*, 28(2–3), pp. 189–195.

Jelinek, J. (1990a). Human Sacrifice and Rituals in Bronze and Iron Ages: The State of Art. *Anthropologie (Brno)*, 28(2–3), pp. 121–128.

Jelinek, J. (1990b). A Late Unetice Pit with Human Remains in Cézavy, near Blucina. *Anthropologie (Brno)*, 28(2–3), pp. 149–158.

Kristiansen, K. and Rowlands, M., eds. (1998). *Social transformations in archaeology, global and local perspectives*. London and New York: Routledge.

Lambot, B. and Méniel, P. (2000). Le Centre Communautaire et Cultuel du Village Gaulois d'Acy Romance dans son Contexte Régional. In S. Verger, ed., *Rites et Espaces en Pays Celte et Méditerranéen, Étude Comparée à Partir du Sanctuaire d'Acy-Romance (Ardennes, France)*. Rome: Collection Ecole Française de Rome, pp. 7–139.

Lambot, B., Méniel, P. and Metzler, J. (1996). Á Propos des Rites Funéraires à la Fin de l'Age du Fer dans le Nord-Est de la Gaule. In: D. Castex, P. Courtaud, P. Sellier, H. Duday and J. Bruzek, eds., Les Ensembles Funéraires du Terrain à l'Interprétation. *Bulletin et Mémoires de la Socété d'Anthropologie de Paris, n.s.*, 8(3–4), pp. 329–343.

Le Fur, Y., ed., (1999). *La mort n'en saura rien, reliques d'Europe et d'Océanie*. Paris: Réunion des Musées Nationaux.

Leclerc, J. (1990). La Notion de Sépulture. In: E. Crubezy, H. Duday, P. Sellier and A.-M. Tillier, eds., *Anthropologie et Archéologie: Dialogue sur les Ensembles Funéraires, Bulletin et Mémoire de la Société d'Anthropologie de Paris, n.s.*. 2(3–4), pp. 13–18.

Mordant, C. and Mordant, D. (1970). *Le site protohistorique des Gours-aux-Lions à Marolles-sur-seine (Seine-et-Marne)*. Mémoire de la Société préhistorique française, 8.

Neugebauer, J.-W. (1991). *Die Nekropole F von Gemeinlebarn, Niederösterreich*, Römisch-Germanische Forschungen, 49.

Outram, A.K., Knüsel, C.J., Knight, S. and Harding, A.F. (2005). Understanding Complex Fragmented Assemblages of Human and Animal Remains: A Fully Integrated Approach. *Journal of Archaeological Science*, 32 (12), pp. 1699–1710.

Radcliffe-Brown, A.R. (1969). *Structure et fonction dans la société primitive*, Paris: Éditions de Minuit.

Rottier, S. (2003). *Pratiques funéraires de l'étape initiale du Bronze final dans les bassins de l'Yonne et de la Haute-Seine: L'exemple des sites funéraires de Barbuise – Courtavant – La Saulsotte et Barbey aux XIVème, XIIIème et XIIème siècles avant J.-C.*, Thèse de Doctorat, Université de Bourgogne.

Rottier, S. (2004). Des Pratiques Funéraires Originales de la Phase Initiale du Bronze Final à Barbey « Les Cent Arpents » (Seine-et-Marne). In: C. Mordant and G. Depierre, eds., *Les Pratiques Funéraires à l'Âge du Bronze en France*, Actes de la table ronde de Sens-en-Bourgogne, 10–12 juin 1998, Éditions Documents Préhistoriques 19, Paris: Éditions Comité des Travaux Historiques et Scientifiques, pp. 459–474.

Rottier, S. (2005). Les Sépultures en Position Assise ou Accroupie de la Phase Initiale du Bronze Final des Confluences Seine/Aube et Seine/Yonne (France). *The Bronze Age in Europe and the Mediterranean, Le Secrétariat du Congrès, ed., Actes du XIVe congrès international de l'UISPP*, BAR International Series S1337, Oxford: Archaeopress, pp. 33–41.

Rottier, S. (2009). Fonctionnement des Tombes du Début du Bronze Final (XIV-XIIème s. av. J.-C.) dans le Sud-Est du Bassin Parisien (France). *Bulletins et Mémoires de la Société d'Anthropologie de Paris*, 21(1–2), pp. 19–46.

Rottier, S. (2010). Eléments de la « Peau Sociale » au Début du Bronze Final (XIVe-XIIe s. av. J.-C.) dans le Sud-Est du Bassin Parisien. *Bulletin de la Société préhistorique française*, 107(1), pp. 121–135.

Rottier, S. (2016). The Seated Dead: Evidence of Funerary Complexity from the Early Late Bronze Age, 14th–12th centuries BCE in France. *Journal of Archaeological Science: Reports*, C.J. Knüsel and J.E. Robb, eds., Special Issue on Funerary Taphonomy 10, pp. 810–818.

Salas, M. (1990). To the Problem of Human Skeletal Remains from the Late Bronze Age in Cézavy, near Blucina. *Anthropologie Brno*, 28(2–3), pp. 221–229.

Sioui, G.E. (1989). *Pour une autohistoire amérindienne: essai sur les fondements d'une morale sociale*. Québec: Presses de l'Université de Laval.

Sioui, G.E. (1994). *Les Wendats: une civilisation méconnue*. Québec: Presses de l'Université de Laval.

Tihelka, K. (1969). *Velatice Culture Burials at Blučina*. Prague: National Museum.

Thomas, L.-V. (1975). *Anthropologie de la Mort*. Paris: Bibliothèque scientifique Payot.

van Gennep, A. (1909) (1981). *Les Rites de Passage*. Paris: Picard.

Tyler, J.M. (1921). *The New Stone Age of Northern Europe*. New York: Charles Scribner's Sons.

14

DEATHWAYS OF THE DUROTRIGES

Reconstructing identity through archaeothanatology in later Iron Age southern Britain

Karina Gerdau-Radonić

ARCHIMÈDE, MAISON INTERUNIVERSITAIRE DES SCIENCES DE L'HOMME, UMR 7044, UNIVERSITÉ DE STRASBOURG, FRANCE

CENTRE FOR ARCHAEOLOGY AND ANTHROPOLOGY, BOURNEMOUTH UNIVERSITY, POOLE, UNITED KINGDOM

Janne Sperrevik, Martin Smith, Paul N. Cheetham, and Miles Russell

CENTRE FOR ARCHAEOLOGY AND ANTHROPOLOGY, BOURNEMOUTH UNIVERSITY, POOLE, UNITED KINGDOM

Introduction

Through its careful and systematic observations of funerary deposits and their content, archaeothanatology lends itself well to the reconstruction of funerary practices and rituals, and, in the process, to establishing normative patterns of the funerary ritual through which a community expresses its identity. Despite debate on whether or not it is possible to accurately reconstruct such intangible aspects of life as behaviour and identity using archaeological evidence (Hodder, 1982, 1994; Metcalf and Huntington, 1991; Jones, 2002), ethnographic, sociological and even forensic studies demonstrate that the conduct of peoples and the identities it reflects leave material traces in patterns that are at least broadly consistent. It is, therefore, possible through such observations to reconstruct, albeit partially, past actions and consequently the identities they express.

The current chapter presents an exceptional assemblage from the modern county of Dorset (United Kingdom), where local geology, mainly chalk, offers excellent conditions for bone preservation, while the Iron Age communities of the region, in the late pre-Roman Iron Age known as the Durotriges, practised a more formal tradition of burying their dead than was common to much of Britain at the time. The discovery at Winterborne Kingston (Dorset; Figure 14.1) of human burials dating from the later Iron Age to the late Roman period

DOI: 10.4324/9781351030625-17

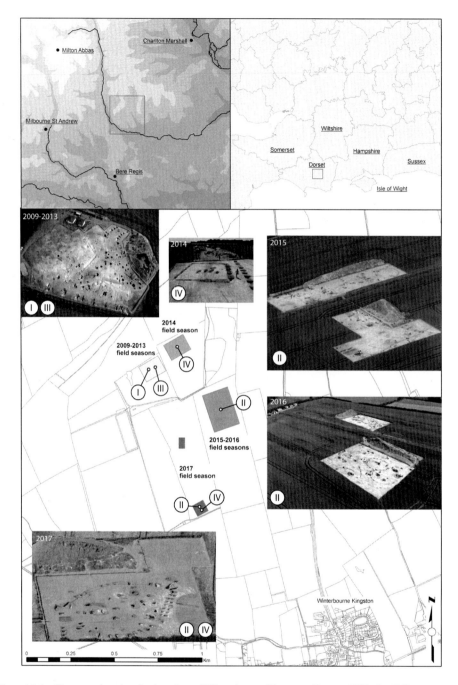

Figure 14.1 Site map showing the location of Winterborne Kingston (Dorset, UK), the different excavation areas and the types of burials by phase within each area.

enabled the application of an archaeothanatological approach not previously brought to bear on British burials of this date. This series of inhumations also permits comparisons through time, revealing a range of nuances and variations in treatment that would otherwise have remained undetected.

The British Iron Age

The British Iron Age is a rather paradoxical time from the viewpoint of biological anthropology. Archaeological remains from this period (conventionally regarded in southern Britain to date from *circa* 750 BC to the Claudian invasion by Rome in AD 43) present the most rich and comprehensive picture of life available for any specified time in British prehistory. The data presented by earthwork structures, domestic dwellings, landscape divisions, artefacts of all kinds, faunal remains and environmental deposits combine to reveal a rich and complex society occupying a landscape that was both densely settled and, with many regions providing evidence for landscape divisions, consistent with a large and thriving population. The rich nature of the overall archaeological record for the time is equalled only by the relative paucity of human remains from Iron Age Britain. Human burials are all but unknown for many regions, despite geological conditions that are conducive to bone survival in areas where the burial record for other periods is comprehensive. The most commonly accepted explanation for this absence of evidence assumes that people must have disposed of their dead by means that are not obvious archaeologically, such as cremation (without subsequent collection and burial of the burned bone) or excarnation (Carr and Knüsel, 1997). Some support is given for the latter by the phenomenon of 'stray' human bones and bone fragments that often occur in anthropogenic contexts on Iron Age sites in the absence of any signs of formal burial. In consequence of this general dearth of skeletal remains, the overall contribution of biological anthropology towards understanding Iron Age life has been less comprehensive than for other periods that have a more abundant burial record.

Moreover, as is often the case in Britain, a large proportion of the sample of skeletal material from Iron Age contexts that exists in museum collections was excavated during the earlier and middle twentieth century and recorded to varying standards during recovery (for examples cf.: Wheeler, 1943; Cornwall and Bennett-Clark, 1954; Brewster, 1971; Keepax, 1979; Cunliffe, 1984; Dent, 1984; Aitken and Aitken, 1990). Opportunities to apply modern standards and approaches to the recording and interpretation of Iron Age burials *in situ* are relatively infrequent and often comprise only single examples when they occur.

The Durotriges: a people apart?

Ptolemy's (2011) *Geographia* Book II, Chapter 2 (second century AD) cites a people referred to as the Durotriges living in an area that would place them broadly within the modern English counties of Dorset and southern Wiltshire. The notion that groups named by Ptolemy as occupying parts of Britain at the time of the Roman conquest might be distinguishable through archaeological investigation on the basis of differences in material culture has proved difficult for much of Britain, leading some authors to conclude that such 'tribal' identities may be a Roman invention aimed at dividing the population for administrative purposes, rather than reflecting the lived reality of first century AD Britons (Wigley, 2001; Mattingly, 2004; Moore, 2011). However, such post-modern re-appraisals of classical sources can, in turn, be challenged, at least in the above-named counties where, among the named tribes in southern Britain, the Durotriges are probably the most archaeologically distinctive. Across an area roughly equal to modern Dorset, the coinage, pottery, settlement-forms and burial practices of the Durotriges distinguish them from their immediate neighbours (Gale, 2003: 125–126; Papworth, 2011: 9; Stewart and Russell, 2017: 1–5). Arguably, however, it is their distinctive burial rite which is most commonly deployed to define and categorise Durotrigian identity.

Unlike the majority of other later Iron Age societies, the Durotriges appear to have preferred inhumation, rather than less archaeologically detectable forms of body disposal such as cremation or excarnation (Whimster, 1981: 37; Papworth, 2008: 82–86; Sharples, 2010: 277–280). Although there is variation in orientation and associations, the 'typical' Durotrigian burial is set in a flexed position, usually on the right side with lower limbs drawn up towards the chest and cardinal orientation of the head towards the north (Whimster, 1981; Papworth, 2008: 83; Sharples, 2010: 227–228; Russell *et al.*, 2014: 220–221; Harding, 2016: 85). Grave goods are comparatively rare but, where found, principally comprise locally manufactured handled tankards and bead-rim bowls (Papworth, 2008: 83–84; Harding, 2016: 84), perhaps originally containing food or drink for the deceased, as well as imported Gallo-Belgic and Samian wares of the early and mid-first century AD (Whimster, 1981: 50; Aitken and Aitken, 1990: 79; Russell *et al.*, 2017: 108–109). Dress accessories, where encountered, include simple copper–alloy brooches at the head or chest, bangles and finger or toe rings and, occasionally, glass beads (Wheeler, 1943: 351–360; Bailey, 1967: 147–159; Aitken and Aitken, 1990: 76–79; Russell *et al.*, 2014, 2017). In exceptional cases more unusual forms of metalwork, such as decorated bronze mirrors, toiletry sets, swords or other weapons such as spearheads, have been noted (Bailey, 1967; Aitken and Aitken, 1990; Fitzpatrick, 1997; Russell *et al.*, 2019).

Inclusions of joints of meat, when included, may have been subject to a degree of selection based on sex. At Whitcombe (Dorset, UK), for example, it has been suggested that sheep/goat was associated exclusively with male interments while pig was more common with females (Aitken and Aitken, 1990; Harding, 2016: 85, 181). In Maiden Castle (Dorset, UK), only male graves appear to have included cattle bone, whereas joints of lamb were found with males and females (Harding, 2016: 181). Notwithstanding, this gender distinction around food offerings does not appear to be the case for other burials identified elsewhere (Aitken and Aitken, 1990; Davies *et al.*, 2002: 122; Murden, 2014; Harding, 2016: 181).

Durotrigian inhumations, in both shallow, oval-shaped grave-cuts and stone-lined cists (Papworth, 2008: 83; Harding, 2016: 84) can be found as apparently isolated single burials or clustered together in small cemeteries (e.g. Bailey, 1967; Aitken and Aitken, 1990; Davies *et al.*, 2002; Valentin, 2003). Sometimes these burials appear to have deliberately targeted earlier features, cemeteries being placed within the partially backfilled remains of long-abandoned monuments, such as at Winterborne Kingston (Dorset, UK) (Russell *et al.*, 2014: 220–221; Russell *et al.*, 2017: 106–108), at Maiden Castle (Dorset, UK) (Wheeler, 1943: 357–358) and probably also at Spettisbury Rings (Dorset, UK) (Akerman, 1859: 188; Gresham, 1939). Perhaps the appropriation of disused monuments for burial was an effective way of re-writing the meaning of earlier monuments and laying claim to them as their own.

Dating the so-called 'Durotrigian cultural package' has proved particularly difficult for the archaeological indicators comprising distinctive artefacts, settlement-types and burial practices, which vary in both quality and quantity across the region, making it difficult to consider the Durotriges as a wholly unified tribal group (Papworth, 2008: 374). The development of a distinctive identity on coins, from the mid-first century BC, however (Cottam *et al.*, 2010: 110–113), may indicate the late evolution of a common economic and political structure, possibly due to a strengthening of social relationships and alliances (Papworth, 2008: 375).

Quite how long the cultural traits of the Durotriges were maintained following the Roman invasion is unclear, although the distinctive burial practice seems to have continued at least until the later second century AD (Papworth, 2008: 376). Some evidence suggests that Durotrigian coins were still being minted into the second century AD (de Jersey, 2000; Papworth, 2008: 377), while regionally distinctive black-burnished ware pottery continued at least into the fourth century AD (Allen and Fulford, 1996: 223–281).

Tracing transitions: the Durotriges project 2009–2017

The Durotriges Project (Bournemouth University 2009–2017) was designed to investigate native and Roman settlements in central southwestern Britain. The project examined the transition from 'Durotrigian' (native) occupation to a more securely 'Roman' settlement footprint, the possible survival of native culture patterns into the Roman period, and the extent of both native and Roman influences into the fifth and sixth centuries AD.

Fieldwork was conducted in four stages. Stage 1, on land near Winterborne Kingston in Dorset, focussed upon an Early Iron Age 'banjo' enclosure (these are small ditched enclosures, broadly circular with a single elongated entrance) and Durotrigian cemetery (Russell *et al.*, 2014), while stage 2 investigated a small, stone-built Roman villa and a sub-Roman (i.e. Post-Roman) longhouse with associated agricultural features and cemetery (Russell *et al.*, 2015). Stage 3 commenced in 2015, concentrating upon an extensive area of Iron Age roundhouse settlement and associated burials (Russell *et al.*, 2016), and stage 4, with a final season in 2017, focussed on an enclosed Durotrigian farmstead and associated prehistoric features (Russell *et al.*, 2017). Formal human burials were found throughout the project, facilitating a diachronic analysis of both burial treatment and the individuals represented in a specific area of landscape over a period of centuries, as well as permitting a comparison with other examples recorded from the region of southern Britain that appears to represent Durotrigian territory.

The form of inhumation burials encountered divide into four phases that equate roughly with successive phases of occupation across the excavated areas. The first of these (phase I) comprised the re-use of five storage pits cut into the chalk in and around the banjo enclosure as funerary contexts, into which human bodies were placed (Russell *et al.*, 2014: 200). These inhumations date from around 250–100 BC and are more correctly characterised simply as 'later Iron Age' or proto-Durotrigian, rather than Durotrigian burials *per se* as they lack the aspects of material culture that unambiguously identify the latter. Phase II is represented by eight human burials close to Later Bronze Age ditch systems and Middle Iron Age roundhouses. These appear to be early examples, perhaps the earliest yet discovered, of Durotrigian style burials placed in formally dug, shallow graves. Later, at a time when the Middle Iron Age banjo enclosure was no longer in use and the ditch bounding this feature had largely filled in, the now defunct site came to be re-used as a burial ground into which a further 17 inhumations were placed in formal grave cuts rather than pits (Phase III). The boundary of this new 'cemetery' appears to have been defined by the course of the old enclosure ditch with all but two of the 17 burials recovered being found within (Russell *et al.*, 2014: 220). The phase IV burials encountered during the project were six formal, supine inhumations wearing Roman-style hobnailed footwear and buried in coffins. This latter group, five of whom were buried in a small square enclosure close to the villa, appear to date from the mid-fourth century AD (Russell *et al.*, 2015: 158–161). While a variety of comparisons between this group and those of the earlier phases are warranted, these Romano–British-style burials have not been included in the current consideration of funerary taphonomy. Two further Early Bronze Age burials and a disturbed burial containing only two forearms with hands and no other contextual information have also been excluded from this study.

Methods

Archaeothanatology

The reader should refer to the first part of the book for details on archaeothanatology and its methods. The archaeothanatological approach was applied both in the field (2015–2017) and to archival material from the excavations. Individuals were considered flexed if both lower limbs were flexed at an angle equal or inferior to 90° at the hip and the knee joint or semi-flexed if at least one lower limb was flexed at an angle superior to 90° at either the hip or the knee joint.

Osteological data collection methods

To assess the morphological variations of the pelvis, Klales, Ousley and Vollner's (2012) revised version of the Phenice (1969) method was employed, alongside an assessment of the expression of the greater sciatic notch (Walker, 2005). The morphological variations of the cranium and mandible were assessed using Buikstra and Ubelaker's (1994) descriptions and comparative illustrations, as modified by Walrath, Turner and Bruzek (2004).

Age assessment was based upon skeletal and dental development and degeneration, applying multiple methods where possible, but with the greatest emphasis placed on the public symphysis, auricular surface and sternal rib ends (Loth and İşcan, 1989; Brooks and Suchey, 1990; Scheuer and Black, 2000; Yoder, Ubelaker and Powell, 2001; Buckberry and Chamberlain, 2002). For the purposes of the current study, individuals assessed to have been less than 15 years old at death were excluded, with those aged 15 or above considered 'adults' on the basis that pre-modern societies are likely to have placed more emphasis on reproductive status than chronological age in defining such socially constructed categories (Laz, 1998; Clark-Kazak, 2009).

The proto-Durotrigian and Durotrigian burials

Phase I (Middle Iron Age): individuals in pits

These comprised five reused storage pits, each containing the remains of one individual: one female, three males and one juvenile of unknown sex. All adults were assessed as being over 25 years old. The disposition of the individuals varied (Table 14.1). One male (413) (Figure 14.2A) and the female (5059) (Figure 14.3A) were laid on a north (head) – south (feet) axis, with their bodies facing west. The two other males and the juvenile were oriented on an east (head) – west (feet) axis, their lower limbs and cranio-facial skeleton turned towards the north, except for 741, whose cranio-facial skeleton was turned toward his abdomen, while his lower limbs were turned north (Figure 14.2A). Four individuals were flexed (Figures 14.2A–D). Female 5059 had one lower limb flexed and the other semi-flexed (Figure 14.3A). One male (413) was lying on his right side (Figure 14.2A). Three individuals were supine, but slightly tilted towards their right sides, two of whom had their heads and lower limbs turned towards the same side, the third, as already mentioned, had his face turned towards his chest and abdomen (741; Figure 14.2B). The female (5059) (Figure 14.3) was prone, with her head and flexed lower limbs towards the left. Upper limbs presented a wider range of degrees of flexion (Table 14.1; Figures 14.2 and 14.3), with four individuals presenting flexed or semi-flexed upper limbs and one individual having one extended upper limb and the other flexed (413) (Figure 14.2A).

The female in deposit 5059 lay prone at the bottom of the pit on a bed of refuse of animal bones which showed signs of weathering (Figure 14.3A). Her head was tilted towards her left shoulder. Her upper limbs were flexed at the elbows, with her hands resting anterior to her

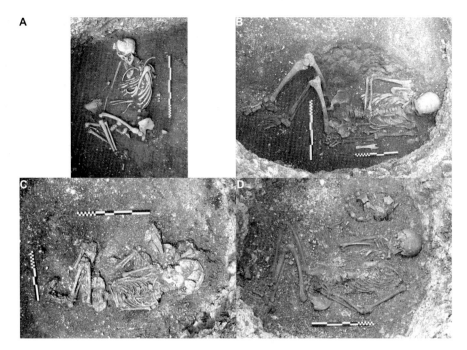

Figure 14.2   Four pit burials. A. 413; B. 741; C. 1076; D. 11017. North is up.

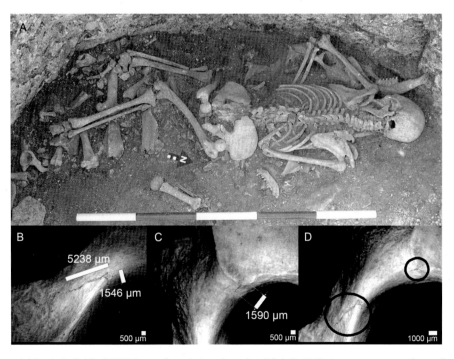

Figure 14.3   A. Individual 5059 in a refuse pit (north to the right); B–D. Peri–mortem cut marks on the superior left aspect of her axis, superior views (B. Anterior is towards upper right corner; C. Anterior is up; D. Anterior is towards upper right corner).

Table 14.1 Deposits by phase, listing sex, age category, orientation, position and degree of flexion of each

Burial number	Sex	Age	Orientation*	Position**	Degree of flexion	Comments
Phase I (Middle Iron Age)						
741	M	Ad	E-W/N/W	S-R	Elbows 90°; hips 90°; knees 45°	
1076	?	Juv	E-W/N/N	S-R	R elbow 90°, L elbow 45°; hips 90°; knees < 45°	
5059	F	Ad	N-S/W/W	P-L	Elbows < 90°; R hip and knee ≥ 90°; L hip and knee < 90°	
11017	M	Ad	E-W/N/N	S-R	R elbow > 90°; L elbow < 45°; hips 90°; knee 45°	
413	M	Ad	N-S/W/W	OR	R elbow extended; L elbow > 90°; hips 90°; knees 45°	
Phase II (Late Iron Age)						
348	F	Ad	SE-/NE/NW	OR	R elbow extended; L elbow > 90°; R hip 90°; L hip 45°; knees < 45°	
699	F?	Ad	E-W/N/N	OR	Elbows, hips, knees < 45°	Over 782
721	?	Ad	SW-NE/S/?	S-R	R elbow <45°; L elbow 90°; hips 45°; knees < 45°	Disturbed; cranium, mandible and upper torso missing
782	M	Ad	E-W/S/S	OL	Elbows extended; hips 90°; knees < 45°	Under 699
787	F	Ad	E-W/N/N	S-R	Elbows 90°; hips 90°; knees ≤ 45°	Over 803
803	F?	Ad	E-W/N/W	S-R	R elbow <45°; L elbow 45°; hips <45°; knees < 45°	Under 787
966	M	Ad	E-W/N/W	S-R	R elbow 90°; L elbow 45°; hips < 45°; knees < 45°	
1005	?	Juv				Not included in analysis
Phase III (Latest Iron Age)						
5251	M?	Ad	SE-/NE/NE	S-R	R elbow 45°; L elbow 90°; hips 90°; knees 45°	
5333	M?	16–18yrs	S-N/NW/ NW	S-R	Elbows 45°; hips 90°; knees < 45°	
6136	M?	Ad	S-N/NW/ NW	P-L	Elbows 45°; hips 45°; knee < 45°	
7089	M?	15–18yrs	N-S/NE/NE	S-R	R elbow < 45°; L elbow 90°; hips 45°; knee < 45°	
10007	F?	Ad	N-S/W/W	P-L	Elbows?; hips < 45°; knee < 45°	
10053	M	Ad	E-W/N/N	S-R	Elbows < 90°; hips 45°; knees < 45°	
10060	F	Ad	NE-W/ NW/W	S-R	R elbow < 45°; L elbow 90°; hips 90°; knee 45°	
10148	M?	Ad	N-S/W/W	OR	Elbows 45°; hips < 45°; knee < 45°	
11048	F	Ad	N-S/W/W	P-L	R elbow 90°; L elbow 45°; hips < 45°; knees < 45°	

(Continued)

Table *14.1* Deposits by phase, listing sex, age category, orientation, position and degree of flexion of each (*Continued*)

Burial number	Sex	Age	Orientation*	Position**	Degree of flexion	Comments
11069	F	Ad	E-W/N/N	P-L	Elbows < 45°; hips 45°, knee < 45°	
13002	F?	Ad	E-W/N/N?	S-R	R elbow < 45°; L elbow?; hips 45°; knees < 45°	Cranium, mandible and upper torso missing
066	?	Ad	E-W/N/N	S-R	R elbow < 45°; L elbow 90°; hips 90°; knees 45°	
503	?	?				Disturbed; information missing
540	?	Ad	N-S/W/W	P-L	Elbows 45°; hips < 45°; knees < 45°	
1005	?	Adol./YAd	N-S/W/W	OR	R elbow extended; L elbow 45°; hips > 90°; knees 45°	
1007	?	Ad	N-S/E/E	P-R	R elbow < 45°; L elbow 45°; hips 45°; knees < 45°	
1070	?	Ad	SE-NW/NE/NE	OR	R elbow < 90°; L elbow 90°; hips 90°; R knee < 45°; L knee 45°	

Notes: *Head-feet/torso and limbs/face; **S-R = supine to right; P-L = prone to left; OR = on right side; OL = on left side; M = male; F = female; Ad = adult; Juv = juvenile; YAd = young adult; Adol = adolescent.

abdomen. Her right lower limb was flexed (angle inferior to 90°) and left lower limb was semi-flexed (angle superior to 90° at the hip). The flexed right elbow touched the inferior right ribs.

With one notable exception, none of the skeletal elements of any of the individuals were located outside of the original volume occupied by the body, indicating decomposition occurred in a filled space (Figure 14.2). The exception was one rib of individual 413 (Figure 14.2A), which had been displaced superiorly and posteriorly to the left shoulder of the individual, outside of the original volume occupied by the corpse. This skeletal element was found displaced and its position, as recorded by the image, is therefore not a consequence of excavation but of some previous taphonomic process. Furthermore, other upper torso bones (two additional ribs, the hyoid, the sternum, the left clavicle) were also displaced but within the original volume occupied by the body, in a space delimited superiorly by the neck, to one side by the left ribcage and hip, to the other side by the right upper limb and both knees, and inferiorly by the right leg (tibia and fibula). The left clavicle, for example, was in the area of the abdominal cavity and the sternum in the angle between the left thigh and the left leg. The most plausible explanation is that the displacement is a consequence of animal burrowing.

It is also possible the bodies were wrapped or fully clothed but buried in an empty space, as a lid could have covered the pit, and the shroud or clothing would have limited the displacement of the skeletal elements. Two individuals had a brooch each (11017 and 413). The brooch of 11017 was within 2 to 4 cm of the facial skeleton of that individual, anterior to the nose (Figure 14.4D). The brooch for 413 was found lateral to the right arm (humerus) (Figure 14.2A[1]). Given these unusual positions, it is unlikely the items were worn on clothing but may have been used to fasten a shroud around the body. All individuals but one (5059 F) were buried with grave goods

---

1 The brooch was lifted before any photographs were taken. There are no visual records of its placement in the field.

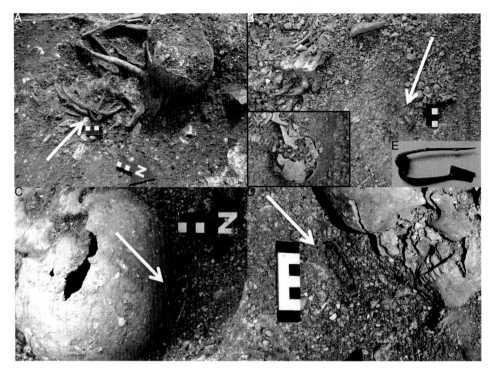

Figure 14.4 The placement of four of the recovered brooches (white arrows). A. DBD12 1005; B. 10007; C. 10060; D. 11017; E. Brooch.

in the form of a joint of meat (pork) and/or later Iron Age vessels. One also had a decorated 'weaving comb' carved from animal bone (741) and two, as previously mentioned, had a brooch each (11017 and 413).

The female in deposit (5059) had no grave goods but lay on a 'bed' of refuse which included pottery, shale, pebbles and cattle, horse and dog bones showing signs of weathering. Additionally, this individual displayed signs of peri–mortem sharp force trauma to her first and second cervical vertebrae (Figures 14.3B–D).

Phase II (Late Iron Age)

This phase comprised seven adults (four females, two males and one undetermined individual) and one juvenile buried in purposefully dug-out individual graves. An archaeothanatological analysis was not conducted in the field on the juvenile burial (1005), and it was not possible to carry out the analysis from the archival material pertaining to this burial. This individual is therefore excluded from the subsequent analysis and discussion. One burial had been partially cut by subsequent developments and the complete skull (cranium and mandible) and part of the torso were missing (721). The adult deposits broadly conform to the distinctive style of Durotrigian burial (Papworth, 2008: 82–86): flexed bodies lying on their right sides or supine with limbs to the right, with one exception, a male with the limbs to the left (782; Figure 14.5B). All are flexed, five have their heads to the east and feet to the west, one is aligned southeast to northwest (348), and one is aligned southwest to northeast (721; Table 14.1). All but two (721 and 782) have their torsos facing north, with the heads turned to face north or west. Individual 782, turned towards his left, was facing south, as is what remains of 721 (Table 14.1). Female 803 (Figure 14.5C),

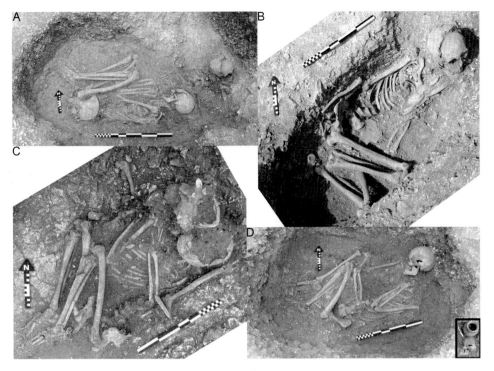

Figure 14.5 Four phase II burials. A. 699 and the cranium of 782 to the east; B. 782; C 803; D. 966.
North is up.

whose head had tilted posteriorly and appeared in an inferior view, was looking west towards her
feet, but the rest of her body is turned northwards. As for the individuals in phase I, there is variation in the degree of flexion of the upper limbs (extended to flexed; Table 14.1), but the lower
limbs are systematically flexed at the hips at an angle equal or inferior to 90° and at the knees at
an angle inferior or equal to 45°.

Unusually, in two cases, pairs of burials were set directly above one another (699 over 782;
and 787 over 803; Figure 14.5A). The uppermost interment of each of these pairs appears to
have been intentionally placed over the previous occupant, not disturbing in any way the burials
beneath. Stratigraphically, in both cases, the pit for the upper burials cuts into the fill of the lower
burials. So the burials are sequential. Yet, at this time, nothing about the disposition of these
burials can help determine more precisely the relative timing between each inhumation. Clearly,
the people burying the later individuals knew about the earlier burials and respected them. There
may have been some sort of grave marking indicating the location, but they must have also
known more or less how deep the earlier bodies were, as these were not disturbed, the sediment
protecting the earlier burial from any disturbance the second burial may have caused. The length
of time between the burials – days, weeks, months, years – is as of yet undetermined.

What few grave goods were identified comprised a black-burnished-ware pot, placed at the
feet of one burial (721) and a locally produced Gallo-Belgic type butt beaker, a large drinking
vessel more commonly manufactured in the early half of the first century AD (Russell *et al.*,
2016: 108–109), placed in the vicinity of the head of another (966). A single fibula copper brooch
was found with burial 878, appearing on the lateral side of the left cheek of this individual. He
was also buried with a joint of pork placed anterior to his face.

As with the individuals in the pit burials, except individual 803, none of the skeletal elements of the individuals were located outside of the original volume occupied by the body. This is indicative of burial in a filled space. Furthermore, the location of the brooch found on the cheek of 878 is again suggestive of a brooch fastening a shroud or garment used to wrap the body rather than a piece of clothing worn by the deceased. The shroud would provide a 'wall effect' to contain the skeletal elements within the original volume occupied by the body. In the case of burial 803, the cranium had tilted posteriorly and slipped inferiorly towards the upper chest. This movement, however, as discussed below, is not necessarily contrary to the notion of use of a shroud or of a body in a filled space.

Phase III (Latest Iron Age)

This phase comprised the largest number of burials, 17. The individuals were placed in formal dug-out graves in and around the banjo enclosure and consisted of 5 adult females and 4 adult males, 6 undetermined adults, and 2 male teenagers (over 15 years old). One of the burials (503) was disturbed and only a partial set of remains was recovered, representing mainly the torso; it has therefore been left out of the subsequent analysis. The upper and lower limbs of the remaining 16 individuals were flexed. Seven individuals were placed in a north-south axis (head to feet), two were south to north, four were laid east to west, two southeast to northwest and one was northeast to southwest (Table 14.1). The head was always turned towards the same side as the limbs, with two exceptions: individual 066 who was supine with his upper and lower limbs turned right, but his head turned to face towards his abdomen and his hips, and individual 13002, whose upper torso and cranium and mandible were missing, and for whom it was thus not possible to ascertain the orientation of the head. All individuals but one (15/16) were facing (torso and cranio-facial skeleton) a point between the northeast and the west, with only one individual facing towards the east (torso and cranio-facial skeleton), the individual in burial 1007. Six individuals were prone with their limbs to their left (5/6) or to their right sides (1/6), two were lying on their right sides, and the remainder were supine with their limbs to their right sides (8/16).

Associated finds consisted mainly of complete or fragmented ceramics, lithic and metal items, and a range of non-human bones. Black-burnished-ware pots accompanied four burials, while a further two had been deposited with a joint of pork and one with a joint of beef. In all but one case (5333), the vessels were placed anteriorly to the body, with the individual facing the item (Figure 14.6). In burial 5333, however, the pot was placed posterior to the head of the individual and superior to his left shoulder (Figure 14.6B). The same applies to the joints of meat that were placed as grave inclusions (Figure 14.6). These tend to lie anterior to the body of the individual, except in the case of burial 1070, where the non-human remains had been placed lateral to the left shoulder joint of the individual and appear on the shoulder (Figure 14.6A).

Four individuals (two females, one male and one individual of undetermined sex) were buried with a single bronze fibula brooch, usually worn to fasten a clothing item. Two brooches were found around the head, lateral to the right temporal region (10007 F) and superior to bregma (10060 F) (Figures 14.4B and 14.4C, respectively). One brooch was found dorso-lateral to the left ribcage (1005; Figure 14.4A.) and the other one lateral to the right elbow (5333 M).

As with the burials from the previous phases, the skeletal elements of all individuals were located within the original volume occupied by the body (Figure 14.6). This is particularly striking of the individuals who have been buried on their right sides (1005, 1070 and 10148). Their vertebrae had maintained anatomical connections and had not been displaced posteriorly, nor have the scapulae (Figure 14.6A). This is suggestive of burial in a filled space. Furthermore,

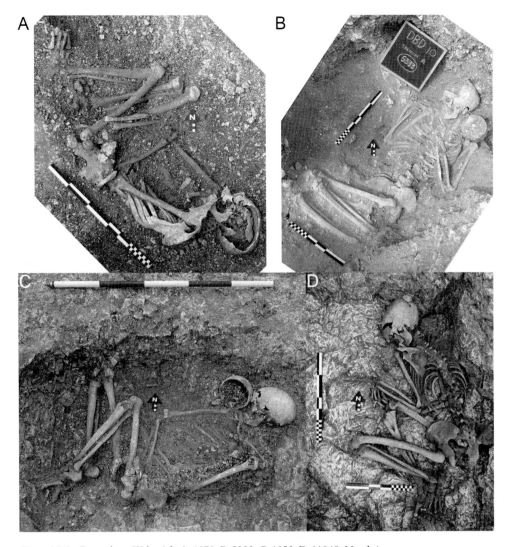

Figure 14.6 Four phase III burials. A. 1070; B. 5333; C. 1053; D. 11048. North is up.

the position of the brooches (Figure 14.4) around the head (10007 and 10060), against the back of an individual (1005), or beside the elbow (5333) is suggestive of a brooch used to fasten a shroud wrapping the body, rather than a decorative item on clothing or used to secure clothing (see discussion below).

Discussion

Durotrigian funerary rites and identity

The phase II and III burials consolidate the notion of a Durotrigian identity which pre-dated the Claudian invasion of Britain, as also attested by the evidence from the coinage, ceramics and settlement patterns found in Durotrigian sites. Funerary rites are a means to maintain and augment cohesion within a community and to assert its identity as well as that of its dead. The Durotriges also used their formal burial rite as a way to appropriate pre-existing abandoned settlements by depositing their dead in and around these sites, particularly at entrances. At Winterborne Kingston, seven burials (phase II) were added to the backfill of a boundary ditch dating to the Late Bronze Age, while the interior of an Early Iron Age banjo enclosure gave way to organised forms of burial (phase III) at some point in the late pre-Roman Iron Age. Such depositions, with burials set down inside and across defunct monuments, also occurred at Maiden Castle (Wheeler, 1943: 357–358) and probably also at Spettisbury Rings (Dorset, UK) (Akerman, 1859: 188; Gresham, 1939), hillforts largely abandoned by the start of the first century BC (Sharples, 1991: 116; Stewart and Russell, 2017: 155–170). Perhaps the appropriation of disused hillforts, banjo enclosures, and Bronze Age ditches for burial was a defining element of Durotrigian inhumation, social groups effectively rewriting the meaning of earlier monuments and claiming them as their own.

The Durotriges had a standard burial practice which consisted of depositing the corpse of an adult in a formal dug-out grave only big enough to fit the body in a flexed position, usually with only a few grave goods such as a pot or a single joint of meat. It is likely individuals were wrapped in a shroud, or perhaps a garment they had worn in life, such as a cloak. The placement of brooches around the head or towards the back of the individuals (Figure 14.4) is suggestive of fastenings for a shroud held in place around the body, rather than an item used to adorn or fasten clothing. The brooch would have been placed where needed to secure the garment, at the top of the head in one case, for example. Once a body was wrapped, it would have been easier to transport and the flexed position better maintained.

In the case of burial 803 (Figure 14.5C), whose head had tilted posteriorly and slipped inferiorly towards the upper chest, this movement may have been due to an empty space beneath and behind the cranium and anterior to the upper torso. If individuals were buried in a shroud and then covered with earth, the shroud could have filled the space behind and beneath the head of individual 803, even cushioning it, as well as filling in the space in front of the head, anterior to the upper torso. Once the cloth decomposed after skeletonisation of the individual, the cranium was free to tilt backwards and slip inferiorly towards the chest. Additionally, there is no evidence for cutmarks to indicate that the head may have been placed in that position on the chest after it was intentional severed from the body.

The use of a shroud also explains certain variations in the disposition of the dead and their accoutrements. Bodies were meant to be supine with the head turned towards the same side as the lower limbs (preferably right) and the grave goods placed anterior to the body. However, once wrapped it may have been difficult to ascertain which was the front or the back of the corpse and even the top and the bottom. Hence, some individuals came to be prone, on the side or turned left. Nothing in the position of the accoutrements suggests that these would have been placed within the shroud. Furthermore, the position of one of the pots, wedged between the shoulder and cranium of an individual (5333; Figure 14.6B) but posterior to the cranium, is again suggestive of the use of a shroud. Except for three exceptions, including individual 5333, accoutrements are found anterior to the bodies with the cranio-facial skeleton directed more or less towards these objects.

Orientation was only important in a general sense. Whereas in phase II, all burials but one (721) were clearly aligned according to an east (head) – west (feet) axis[2] and, but for one exception, the ventral aspect of the torso was turned to the north (Table 14.1), the phase III burials displayed much more variation. The ventral surface of the bodies faced a point between north

---

2 Though burial 348 was aligned along a southeast–northwest axis, it can still be construed as broadly conforming to an east–west lay-out.

and west, which meant most corpses were placed in a somewhat north–south axis, yet a third are east–west (Table 14.1). Arguably, these variations could be a product of body treatment and not something more ritualistic. Additionally, these variations do not appear linked to sex-based differences. Finally, if individuals were shrouded, the burials could have occurred in an empty space, with only a lid covering the grave, as the shroud would limit the displacement of the skeletal elements once decomposition started. However, for the dug-out graves, the most likely explanation is that the shrouded bodies were covered in sediment at the time of burial, as no evidence for a cover has been found.

The size of the graves may be further linked to the choice of burying individuals in a flexed position. Though most of the grave walls do not hug the body tightly, they provide only space enough to place a corpse and a few accompanying items. Originally, the choice may have been purely practical, possibly acquiring ritual meaning only later. It is easier and faster to dig a small grave for a flexed body than a larger grave for an extended one. It is also worth noting that the compacted chalk subsoil of south Dorset remains challenging to dig through using modern tools and excavating a grave of any proportions would involve substantial effort. The burials are similar to those from other Durotrigian sites, such as recorded from Alington Avenue, Dorchester (Davies *et al.*, 2002), Litton Cheney (Bailey, 1967), Maiden Castle (Wheeler, 1943) and Tolpuddle Ball (Hearne and Birbeck, 1999) (all in Dorset, UK), and emphasise that the Durotriges were much more than an administrative division from the perspective of the Roman occupiers. They seemed to have retained their distinctive identity, at least in the early phases of Roman hegemony.

Pit-burials – proto-Durotrigian?

Despite the similarities in body treatment and accoutrements, the pit burials stand out as different from those of phase II and III due to the choice of burial space: re-used storage pits. Again, while all aspects of funerary treatment may acquire symbolic meaning over time, it is important to remember that any specific practice may have initially been rooted in practicality. The position of the bodies in the pits may, in fact, have been a product of the size of the 'container'. It is not possible to inhume an extended adult corpse in these pits, and hence the body needed to be flexed to some degree. Orientation is also variable with two being placed along a north (head) – south (feet) axis, with the ventral surfaces of the bodies, turned westward, and three placed along an east–west axis, like the phase III burials.

The pit-burials also stand out for what is known about the treatment of the dead at the time. As previously mentioned, there is a dearth of human remains for the Iron Age, in particular, and British prehistory, in general, as opposed to later periods, which seemingly has more to do with the treatment of the dead (cremation with no collection of the remains or excarnation with no defined disposal) than with preservation of the remains. As such, finding a select few individuals (five) buried within re-used storage pits makes these burials non-normative for the time period. Moreover, it is unclear whether the selection is a positive one, outstanding members of the community entitled to special treatment, or, on the contrary, negative selection consisting of individuals denied community funerary treatment and access to the funerary space, but whose relatives and friends had sought to somehow honour them after their death, had therefore performed a ritual (possibly private) and buried them in a dis-used storage pit.

Deposits in pits occur at other sites in Dorset and Hampshire for the same time period, for example, Gussage-All-Saints (Wainwright, 1979), Maiden Castle (Wheeler, 1943), and

Danebury (Cunliffe, 1984; Cunliffe and Poole, 1991; Cunliffe 1992). The deposits have the appearance of formal burials and are usually found supine, in flexed or semi-flexed positions, invariably associated with items that can be interpreted as grave goods such as pottery vessels. At these sites, the pit burials also stand out as non-normative, raising the question once more of whether these are the product of a positive or a negative selection. Similar arguments have been proposed for certain French prehistoric burials identified as non-normative, where the individuals may have been denied funerary treatment and access to a formal burial space but not denied a burial *per se* (Boulestin and Baray, 2010) as well as Iron Age burials in other parts of Britain, where King (2013) suggests that violent deaths might have selected individuals for exceptional forms of mortuary practice. Cunliffe (1992) suggested the human remains found in the pits in Danebury (Hampshire, UK) were offerings to the chthonic deities as they were found in former grain storage silos and because deposits of animal meat and other items had been found in other disused storage pits, seemingly as votive offerings to these deities. With the currently available data, any of these proposed interpretations are possible (exceptional burials, sacrifices, non-normative). Notwithstanding, because the differences in Winterborne Kingston between the pits with human remains (excepting 5059) and the phase II and III burials are limited to the use of a pre-existing pit, these appear as burials, and it is, therefore, tempting to see a continuum from these pit burials to the later more commonly encountered Durotrigian funerary practice. The pit burials may have inspired the Durotrigian burials, regardless of whether the former were normative or not. However, just as with the adoption of previously occupied sites as burial grounds, the appropriation and elaboration of such a burial practice need not imply any continuity of population. The Durotriges may, in fact, in this respect be an immigrant group seeking to legitimise their rights of occupation. Their mode of settlement, small individual farmsteads in polygonal enclosures often set within earlier settlement types, for example, at Gussage All Saints (Wainwright, 1979), could also support the possibility for an incoming cultural group.

Furthermore, the individuals in pits might, on the one hand, appear to have been buried in a filled space because the skeletal elements have not moved outside of the original volume once occupied by the body. However, if the bodies were also in a shroud, it is possible they could have been buried in an empty space, with the pit being covered by a lid. The shroud would have thus limited the movement of the skeletal elements, and the lid would have permitted delayed or gradual infilling of the burial space.

Finally, deposit 5059 at Winterborne Kingston stands out, even among the pit burials (Figure 14.3). This female was placed in a disused storage pit which contained a sheet deposit of waste beneath the body. She was not provided with any accoutrements, and her position does not show the same treatment as do the other interments. Whereas the other four individuals have been buried with pots or joints of meat and have been carefully positioned in a flexed pose, supine, to ensure they comfortably fit in a pit previously emptied of its content, individual 5059 was placed prone in a pit containing the weathered bones of horse or cow, her lower limbs appearing flexed (left) and semi-flexed (right) because she did not fit extended in the pit (Figure 14.3A), her left knee and both her feet sinking into the refuse beneath her body. Additionally, the unhealed cut marks on the lateral left surface of her axis (superior) and atlas (inferior Figures 14.3B–D) indicate she had been subjected to violence shortly before or at the time of her death. She may have been executed, murdered within her own community, or attacked and killed in an episode of conflict with another group. Whatever the cause, the woman was disposed of in a refuse pit. As a consequence, it is difficult to view this evidence as funerary treatment, and it is instead suggestive of an example of 'non-funerary treatment' (cf. Schmitt, Chapter 6, this volume, for a discussion on denied funeral rites). Certainly, this individual presents a significant exception with regard to the absence of grave goods and the general lack of evidence for signs of care and respect. It is hard to reconcile such treatment with 'positive' selection. If this woman had been subjected to judicial killing for some perceived crime or ritual killing for sacrificial reasons, as Cunliffe (1992) suggested for the deposits in pits at Danebury (Hampshire, UK), she might represent a local version of the sort of treatments apparent for various European bog bodies dating from the later Iron Age (Brothwell and Gill-Robinson, 2002; Lynnerup, 2009). In discussing non-normative burials from Iron Age Britain, King (2013) notes the potential parallels with Native American practices where slaves were ritually killed for a variety of reasons in order to serve wider community concerns. Knüsel and Glencross (2017) cite an interesting example from an earlier period at the Neolithic site of Çatalhöyük (Turkey) where an individual suffering from debilitating pathology (fibrous dysplasia) and bearing multiple healed cranial injuries was deposited in a midden after death rather than afforded the normative funerary treatment observed in other burials at the site. A possible interpretation suggested for the latter is that this man was treated as a scapegoat, with his death providing social catharsis that restored or affirmed group cohesion at a time of perceived crisis. Returning to burial 5059 at Winterborne Kingston, an alternative possibility is that her violent death might have conferred a distinctive status as one of the 'dangerous dead' who having met her demise through unnatural circumstances, then required special funerary measures to protect the living against supernatural repercussions that her body might otherwise present.

Conclusion

The archaeothanatological approach, with its attention to detail, its focus on articulation patterns and on the spatial relationship of all items and individuals in a grave, has added detail to the Durotrigian burial style previously identified in other sites from southern England. The practice was broadly construed as that of adults buried in small purposefully dug-out individual graves big enough to fit one flexed body and a few accoutrements such as joints of meat and ceramic vessels. Individuals were flexed, placed on their right sides and facing north (i.e. cranio-facial skeletons) (Whimster, 1981; Papworth, 2008, 83; Sharples, 2010: 227–228; Harding, 2016: 85). The current study has demonstrated individuals were buried wrapped in a shroud, which in some cases was fastened with a single bronze fibula brooch. Orientation was only vaguely important, most individuals were placed in a somewhat north–south axis, facing somewhere between the north and the west, but this was not a fixed parameter. Individuals were apparently intended to be flexed and supine slightly turned to their right.

The study has also highlighted the non-funerary treatment of a female (5059) who possibly suffered a violent death. Though the individual was also found in a pit like other proto-Durotrigian burials identified (phase I), she had been buried prone on refuse, a position not recorded for the other Phase I deposits, nor for those from Phase II. Furthermore, the disposition of her body did not display the same repetitive pattern as reflected in the other burials.

Future research will endeavour to ascertain whether the proto-Durotrigian burials identified here are examples of non-normative Iron Age funerary treatment, representing either a positive or negative selection of the individuals inhumed, as, for example, suggested by King (2013). The project also seeks to identify whether or not the Durotriges were a local group adopting a distinctive form of burial or incomers settling in the area and bringing their culture and habits from elsewhere in the British Isles or from mainland Europe, using their dead to claim possession of the lands for their descendants.

References

Aitken, G. and Aitken, N. (1990). Excavations at Whitcombe, 1965–1967. *Proceedings of the Dorset Natural History and Archaeological Society*, 112, pp. 57–94.

Akerman, J. (1859). Some Antiquities Discovered at Spettisbury, near Blandford, Dorset. *Proceedings of the Society of Antiquaries London*, 4, pp. 188–191.

Allen, J. and Fulford, M. (1996). The Distribution of South-East Dorset Black Burnished Ware Category I Pottery in South-West Britain. *Britannia*, 27, pp. 223–281.

Bailey, J. (1967). An Early Iron Age/Romano British Site at Pins Knoll, Litton Cheney. *Proceedings of the Dorset Natural History and Archaeological Society*, 89, pp. 147–159.

Boulestin, B. and Baray, L. (2010). Problématique des dépôts humains dans les structures d'habitat désaffectées. In: L. Baray and B. Boulestin, eds., *Morts Anormaux et Sépultures Bizarres. Les Dépôts Humains en Fosses Circulaires et en Silos du Néolithique à l'Âge du Fer.* Dijon: Éditions Universitaire de Dijon, pp. 13–27.

Brewster, T.C.M. (1971). The Garton Slack Chariot Burial, East Yorkshire. *Antiquity* 45, pp. 289–292.

Brooks, S., and Suchey, J.M. (1990). Skeletal Age Determination Based on the *Os pubis*: A Comparison of the Ascadi-Nemeskeri and Suchey-Brooks Methods. *Human Evolution*, 5, pp. 227–238.

Brothwell, D. and Gill-Robinson, H. (2002). Taphonomic and forensic aspects of bog bodies. In: W. Haglund and M. Sorg, eds., *Advances in Forensic Taphonomy: Method, Theory and Archaeological Perspectives.* London: CRC Press, pp. 119–132.

Buckberry, J. and Chamberlain, A. (2002). Age Estimation from the Auricular Surface of the Ilium: A Revised Method. *American Journal of Physical Anthropology*, 119, pp. 231–239.

Buikstra, J.E. and Ubelaker, D.H. (1994). *Standards for data collection from human skeletal remains.* Fayetteville, Arkansas: Arkansas Archaeological Survey Report Number 44.

Carr, C. and Knüsel, C.J. (1997). The ritual framework of excarnation by exposure as mortuary practice of the early and middle Iron Ages of central southern Britain. In: A. Gwilt, and C. Haselgrove, eds., *Reconstructing Iron Age Societies: New Approaches to the British Iron Age*, Oxford: Oxbow, pp. 167–173.

Clark-Kazak, C.R. (2009). Towards a Working Definition and Application of Social Age in International Development Studies. *Journal of Development Studies*, 45, 1307–1324.

Cornwall, I. and Bennett-Clark, M. (1954). The Human Remains from Sutton Walls. In: K. M. Kenyon, ed., *Excavations at Sutton Walls, Herefordshire. Archaeological Journal*, 110, pp. 1–87.

Cottam, E., de Jersey, P., Rudd, C. and Sills, J. (2010). *Ancient British coins.* Aylsham, UK: Chris Rudd.

Cunliffe, B. (1984). *Danebury: an Iron Age hillfort in Hampshire, volume 2: the excavations 1969–1978: the finds.* London: Council for British Archaeology Report 52b.

Cunliffe, B. (1992). Pits, Preconceptions and Propitiation in the British Iron Age. *Oxford Journal of Archaeology*, 11, pp. 69–83.

Cunliffe, B. and Poole, C., eds. (1991). *Danebury: an Iron Age hillfort in Hampshire, volume 5: the excavations 1979–1988: the finds.* London: Council for British Archaeology Report 73b.

Davies, S., Bellamy, P., Heaton, M. and Woodward, P. (2002). *Excavations at Alington Avenue, Fordington, Dorchester, Dorset, 1984–87.* Dorchester: Dorset Natural History and Archaeological Society Monograph 15.

De Jersey, P. (2000). *Durotrigian cast bronze.* Oxford: Chris Rudd Celtic Coin List 49.

Dent, J.S. (1984). *Wetwang Slack: an Iron Age cemetery on the Yorkshire Wolds.* Unpublished M.Phil. Thesis, University of Sheffield, UK.

Fitzpatrick, A. (1997). A 1st-century AD 'Durotrigian' Inhumation Burial with a Decorated Iron Age Mirror from Portesham, Dorset. *Proceedings of the Dorset Natural History and Archaeological Society*, 118, pp. 51–70.

Gale, J. (2003). *Prehistoric Dorset.* Stroud: Tempus.

Gresham, C. (1939). Spettisbury Rings, Dorset. *Archaeological Journal*, 96, pp. 115–131.

Harding, D. (2016). *Death and burial in Iron Age Britain.* Oxford: Oxford University Press.

Hearne, C. and Birbeck, V. (1999). *A35 Tolpuddle to Puddletown Bypass, Dorset, 1996–8.* Salisbury: Wessex Archaeology Report 15.

Hodder, I. (1982). *Symbols in action: ethnoarchaeological studies of material culture.* Cambridge: Cambridge University Press.

Hodder, I. (1994). The interpretation of documents and material culture. In: N.K. Denzin and Y.S. Lincoln, eds., *Handbook of Qualitative Research.* Thousand Oaks: Sage, pp. 393–402.

Jones, S. (2002). *The archaeology of ethnicity: constructing identities in the past and present.* Abingdon (UK): Routledge.

Keepax, C. (1979) The human bones. In: G. Wainright, ed., *Gussage All Saints: An Iron Age Settlement*. London: Her Majesty's Stationary Office (HMSO), pp.161–170.

King, S. (2013) Socialized violence: contextualizing violence through mortuary behaviour in Iron Age Britain, In: C.J. Knüsel and M.J. Smith, eds., *The Routledge Handbook of the Bioarchaeology of Human Conflict*. London: Routledge, pp. 185–200.

Klales, A.R., Ousley, S.D. and Vollner, J.M. (2012). A Revised Method of Sexing the Human Innominate Using Phenice's Nonmetric Traits and Statistical Methods. *American Journal of Physical Anthropology*, 149, pp. 104–114.

Knüsel, C.J. and Glencross, B. (2017). Çatalhöyük, archaeology, violence. In J. Allison and W. Palaver, eds., pp. 69–75. *Handbook of Mimetic Theory and Religion*. New York: Palgrave Macmillan.

Laz, C. (1998). Act your age. *Sociological Forum*, 13, 85–113.

Loth, S.R. and İşcan, M.Y. (1989). Morphological assessment of age in the adult: the thoracic region. In M.Y. İşcan, ed., *Age Markers in the Human Skeleton*. Springfield, Illinois: Charles C. Thomas, pp. 105–135.

Lynnerup, N. (2009). Computed tomography scanning and three-dimensional visualization of mummies and bog bodies. In: R. Pinhasi and S. Mays, eds., *Advances in Human Paleopathology*, Chichester: Wiley, pp. 101–119.

Mattingly, D. (2004). Being Roman: Expressing Identity in a Provincial Setting. *Journal of Roman Archaeology*, 17, pp. 5–25.

Metcalf, P. and Huntington, R. (1991). *Celebrations of death: the anthropology of mortuary ritual*. 2nd ed. Cambridge: Cambridge University Press.

Moore, T. (2011). Detribalizing the Later Prehistoric Past: Concepts of Tribes in Iron Age and Roman Studies. *Journal of Social Archaeology*, 11, pp. 334–360.

Murden, J. (2014). The Langton Herring Mirror and Grave Goods. *Proceedings of the Dorset Natural History and Archaeological Society*, 135, pp. 205–208.

Papworth, M. (2008). *Deconstructing the Durotriges: a definition of Iron Age communities within the Dorset environs*. British Archaeological Reports (British Series) 462. Oxford: John and Erica Hedges Ltd.

Papworth, M. (2011). *The search for the Durotriges: Dorset and the West Country in the Late Iron Age*. Stroud: History Press.

Phenice, T.W. (1969) A Newly Developed Visual Method of Sexing the *Os Pubis*. *American Journal of Physical Anthropology*, 30(2), pp. 297–301.

Ptolemy, C.. (2011). *Geographia* (translated by E.L. Stevenson). New York: Cosimo Classics.

Russell, M., Cheetham, P., Evans, D., Gale, J., Hambleton, E., Hewitt, I., Manley, H., Pitman, D. and Stewart, D. (2016). The Durotriges Project, Phase Three: An Interim Statement. *Proceedings of the Dorset Natural History and Archaeological Society*, 137, pp. 173–177.

Russell, M., Cheetham, P., Evans, D., Gerdau-Radonić, K., Hambleton, E., Hewitt, I., Manley, H., Smith, M. and Speith, N. (2015). The Durotriges Project, Phase Two: An Interim Statement. *Proceedings of the Dorset Natural History and Archaeological Society*, 136, pp. 215–222.

Russell, M., Cheetham, P., Evans, D., Hambleton, E., Hewitt, I., Manley, H. and Smith, M. (2014). The Durotriges Project, Phase One: An Interim Statement. *Proceedings of the Dorset Natural History and Archaeological Society*, 135, pp. 217–221.

Russell, M., Cheetham, P., Hewitt, I., Hambleton, E., Manley H. and Stewart, D. (2017). The Durotriges Project, 2016: An Interim Statement. *Proceedings of the Dorset Natural History and Archaeological Society*, 138, pp. 106–111.

Russell, M., Smith, M., Cheetham, P., Evans, D., Foulds, E., Joy, J., Hoogmoed, A. and Manley, H. (2019). The Girl with the Chariot Medallion: A Well-Furnished, Late Iron Age Durotrigan Burial from Langton Herring, Dorset. *Archaeological Journal*, 176, pp. 196–230.

Scheuer, L. and Black, S. (2000). *Developmental juvenile osteology*. London: Academic Press.

Sharples, N. (1991) *Maiden Castle: excavations and field survey 1985–6*. London: English Heritage.

Sharples, N. (2010). *Social relations in later prehistory: Wessex in the first millennium BC*. Oxford: Oxford University Press.

Stewart, D. and Russell, M. (2017). *Hillforts and the Durotriges: a geophysical survey of Iron Age Dorset*. Oxford: Archaeopress.

Valentin, J. (2003). Manor Farm, Portesham: Excavations on a Multi-Phase Religious and Settlement Site. *Proceedings of the Dorset Natural History and Archaeological Society*, 125, pp. 23–70.

Wainwright, G. (1979). *Gussage All Saints: an Iron Age settlement in Dorset*. London: Her Majesty's Stationary Office (HMSO).

Walker, P.L. (2005). Greater Sciatic Notch Morphology: Sex, Age, and Population Differences. *American Journal of Physical Anthropology*, 127, pp. 385–391.

Walrath, D.E., Turner, P. and Bruzek, J. (2004). Reliability Test of the Visual Assessment of Cranial Traits for Sex Determination. *American Journal of Physical Anthropology*, 125, pp. 132–137.

Wheeler, M. (1943). *Maiden Castle. Society of Antiquaries Report 12*. Oxford: Oxford University Press.

Whimster, R. (1981). *Burial practices in Iron Age Britain*. Oxford: British Archaeological Reports (British Series) 90.

Wigley, A. (2001). Searching for the Cornovii in the Iron Age: A Critical Consideration of the Evidence. *West Midlands Archaeology*, 44, pp. 6–9.

Yoder, C., Ubelaker, D.H. and Powell, J.F. (2001). Examination of Variation in the Sternal Rib End Morphology Relevant to Age Assessment. *Journal of Forensic Sciences*, 46, pp. 223–227.

15

THE ROMAN CEMETERY
OF PORTA NOCERA
AT POMPEII

The contribution of osteological re-associations to the study of secondary cremation burials

Henri Duday

Translated from the original French by Christopher J. Knüsel and Eline M.J. Schotsmans

PACEA, De la Préhistoire à l'Actuel: Culture, Environnement et Anthropologie, UMR 5199, CNRS-Université de Bordeaux, Pessac, France

Introduction

Twenty years ago, Duday, Depierre and Janin (2000) presented a methodological review of new approaches to the study of cremation burials to highlight the need to excavate cremated human remains deposits in successive layers, an idea which had already been put forward by Grévin (1990), and to establish a quantitative approach based on the weight of remains, consisting of the total weight of burned bones and the relative weight of the remains of the head, trunk and upper and lower limbs, rather than of bone fragment counts (Depierre, 2014: 257ff.).

The excavation of the necropolis of Porta Nocera in Pompeii[1] (40 BC–79 AD) (Figure 15.1) led to the implementation of a research protocol still little explored in cremation contexts: the systematic study of anatomical connections through re-fitting of fragmented pieces. This method aims to identify remains of the same individual, animal or human, in an archaeological cremation assemblage, as well as fragments of the same object, such as sherds of the same vase and flint flakes from the same core. Osteological re-associations[2] (*liaisons ostéologiques*) are one of the most effective means of understanding the 'functioning' (i.e. the assemblage formation processes) of large Neolithic collective burials (Duday, 1987). In addition to conjoining exercises by anatomical connections, these re-association exercises are based on the principle of exclusion due to incompatibility between different parts of the skeleton employed to estimate the minimum number of

---

1 Research Programme of the École française de Rome and the Soprintendenza archeologiche di Pompei, directed by William Van Andringa and Sebastien Lepetz, from 2003 to2007. The graves discussed in this chapter are the subject of a monograph (Van Andringa, Duday and Lepetz (2013)).

2 The original French term is '*liaisons ostéologiques*', here translated as 're-associations', but in other publications translated as 'osteological linkages' (cf. Duday, 2009).

DOI: 10.4324/9781351030625-18

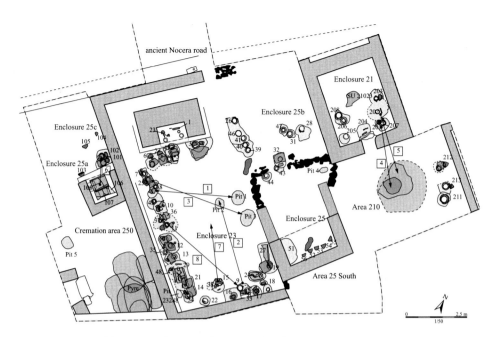

Figure 15.1 Map of the excavated areas in the necropolis of Porta Nocera in Pompeii. The arrows indicate distant re-associations, as described in the text. SU = Stratigraphic Unit (Plan courtesy of T. Lind, and computer-assisted design (CAD) courtesy of C. Chevalier.).

individuals represented in the bone assemblage. First-order associations are identified during excavation and correspond to the sometimes numerous anatomical connections in primary cremation burials or 'pyre-graves', a term that is preferred to that of the *bustum*[3] (cf. Bel *et al.*, 2008).

Second-order re-associations are established during laboratory study. They relate to bones that are no longer in anatomical order. For cremations, re-fits between fragments, the symmetry between pairs of bones from the opposite sides of the body, those at the same developmental maturation stage, and those possessing lesions of the same pathological process are also potentially informative. Contrary to these, the connections made through articular congruity or by similarity in the degree of robustness are not very reliable because thermal alterations from exposure to fire produces substantial deformation and warping. In addition, the destruction of molecules by exposure to heat destroys the palaeobiochemical relationships that once existed.

In secondary cremation burials, the analysis of the treatment of the body involves not only the modifications effected on the pyre but also those that relate to the collection of all or part of the burnt bone remains and the means by which they were transported to the grave, followed by their final deposition, as well as evidence for post-depositional interventions and, of course, commemorative funerary treatments. It is thus a whole succession of funerary actions that requires deciphering. Associated remains that connect different areas of the site or different stratigraphic units permit dynamic reading of the funerary sequence, which can also shed light on characteristics of the treatment of bodies.

---

3 In Latin, the term *bustum* covers a number of very different entities, including the pyre, but could also refer to a grave or a burial. However, it more specifically designates a pyre built inside the family funerary enclosure, as opposed to the *ustrinum,* which is a 'public' location, independent of the family enclosure (Rich, 1883). A *bustum* is therefore not a primary cremation burial, in the sense in which it is wrongly used by many archaeo-anthropologists.

The remains of the dead distributed in different areas of the same grave

Collecting burnt bones and cleaning the cremation area

The first case to consider is that of secondary burials that reveal burnt human bones deriving from the same individual in two separate topographic or stratigraphic units within the same grave, for example, in a funerary receptacle, such as a ceramic vase, a glass or lead vessel, or within an enveloping perishable material container, or as part of ash deposits dumped into the pit, either before or after the placement of a cremation urn. First of all, in the case of a funerary receptacle, there is material that derives from the manual collection of bone fragments from the cremation area and, in the case of cremation material in the grave fill, the ashes derived from cleaning of the area after the cremation, which is often only a partial and thus incomplete cleaning. In both cases, the bone remains should logically belong to the same individual. At the Porta Nocera site in Pompeii there are many cases where this hypothesis can be verified owing to re-fits between remains (burnt human bones but also from fragments of lamps or worked bones, for example) coming either from the urn, or from the fill of the grave and re-assembled from contiguous fragments. These were identified in graves 11, 13, 25, 31, 32, 44, 46, 102, 203, 205 and 208, based on the maturational stage of the remains, in graves 10, 37, 201, 15B, 21A and 21B by the symmetry between elements, and, in grave 28, through analysis of remains affected by pathological lesions.

If the urn contained the remains of several individuals, interest shifts to determining to which individual(s) the accumulated cremated remains belong. In enclosure 23 of the *Vesonii* family (grave 15) contained a receptacle, an amphora of Betic-type that had been cut beneath its shoulder and inserted in an inverted position in the grave-pit (Van Andringa, Duday and Lepetz, 2013: 553ff.). It contained the cremated remains of two individuals: uppermost, an elderly probable adult male (individual 15A, comprised of 1520.1 g of burned bone) and, below, a rather gracile adolescent whose epitaph indicates that he was a young man, Eliodorus, who died at the age of 18 (individual 15B, comprised of 1041.9 g of burnt bone). In the pit, apart from the amphora, charcoal-rich ash (Stratigraphic Unit [SU] 23123) comprising 134.1 g of burnt bone fragments, related exclusively to adolescent 15B. It is clear that this grave was conceived as having to accommodate the remains of two individuals from its inception: the receptacle is much larger than those of most of the other graves, and the burnt bones were introduced through the bottom of the cut amphora, which was sealed by a removable cap. A relatively long time had elapsed, however, between the two deposits, time necessary for the settling and consolidation of the sediment of the lower individual.

These observations make it possible to reconstruct the history of this grave: a teenager dies, he is burned on a pyre; a cut amphora is inserted upside down in a pit dug for this purpose, and afterwards the burned bones are collected and then introduced through the bottom of the cut amphora. The cremation area was then cleared, with the residue deposited outside the amphora in the pit. The pit was subsequently filled completely, the stele bearing the name of Eliodorus was placed and the bottom of the amphora was sealed with a cap, in this case, made of the bottom cut from another amphora. Several years likely passed, and the elderly adult, who had probably expected to have been placed in the same grave, died. His body was burned on the pyre. The cap closing the cut bottom was temporarily removed so as to permit the introduction of the cremated bones of the second individual collected from the cremation area and these deposited in the amphora. Afterwards, it was re-sealed again.

In grave 21 within the same enclosure 23 of the *Vesonii* family, an amphora had received the burnt remains of three individuals successively (Van Andringa, Duday and Lepetz, 2013: 489ff.). A child 6 to 9 months of age at death (individual 21C) is represented by only 21.9 g of burnt bone.

Later, the remains of an adolescent, individual 21B, comprised of 1114.2 g of burnt bones, was placed in the amphora, while another portion comprising 390.8 g had been poured with ashes into a pit dug to the south and east of the amphora. Finally, the remains of a young woman, individual 21A comprised of 1552.9 g, was, in turn, placed in the amphora, with the residues from her cremation area (141.7 g of burnt bones) being deposited in a chest made of flat tiles in the bottom of the grave, where the uncremated and articulated skeleton of a child of about 18 months of age-at-death had been placed (as indicated by internal stratigraphic relationships). Two vertebral bodies of this young woman, 21A, were embedded in the mortar used to repair the libation tube inserted in the neck of the amphora. The osteological re-associations were decisive in deciphering these funerary sequences, which were also confirmed by re-fits between the fragments of an oil lamp and a worked bone pin.

In other cases, the ashes from the pyre-site were not placed in the pit but rather in a vase placed in the grave, next to the funerary urn. The excavations at Porta Nocera did not provide an example of this type of arrangement, but in the neighbouring site of Cumes, a Roman cemetery located about 50 km northwest of Pompeii, the small chamber of mausoleum 34010 contained an urn (34219) and a large *unguentarium* (34218), which comprised 744.5 g and 122.4 g of burnt bones, respectively, both of which had been placed on the masonry floor. Re-fits between two contiguous fragments of the cranium (34219.R03 and 34218.R05) and two contiguous fragments of the left humerus (34219.R08 and 34218.R11) show that the two containers contained the remains of the same deceased elderly adult female.

The characteristics of residues from the cleaning of a cremation area

The study of the graves from Porta Nocera made it possible to characterise ashy residues from the cleaning of a cremation area: the total weight of burnt bones is generally lower than the weight of the urn contents, an average weight without small fragments, that is very low (hence a rather low or very low identification rate) (Figure 15.2). The ponderal index[4] for the remains of the hands is close to or even higher than the reference value (2.5% of the total weight of the skeleton for an adult individual, according to Lowrance and Latimer (1957)) while the ponderal index of the feet is lower, like those of other anatomical regions, in addition, of course, to ash and charcoal. These differences are quite clear for graves 15B, 21A and 21B (Table 15.1). Further discussion can be found in the monograph devoted to this funerary area (Van Andringa, Duday and Lepetz, 2013: 880–883), but it will suffice here to recall the essential arguments. Since collection preferentially comprises the most bulky bones or fragments (therefore the heaviest), it seems logical that the residual remains would be a very small amount (hence a very low average weight)[5] and represent

---

4 The 'ponderal index' or 'weight index' ('*l'indice pondéral*') of an anatomical region is equal to the weight of burned bones corresponding to a particular region of the body compared as a percentage to the total weight of cremated human bones. In other words, it is the relative weight distribution per anatomical region, which enables the researcher to assess if all parts of the skeleton are represented, or if certain anatomical regions are favoured or excluded (cf., for example, Lowrance and Latimer, 1957; Duday, Depierre and Janin (2000).

5 The 'average weight without small fragments', as mentioned in the text and tables, is calculated by the sum of (1) the weight (g) of all of identifiable fragments of known anatomical origin, (2) the weight (g) of flat bone fragments, (3) the weight (g) of spongy (trabecular) bone fragments (short bones or epiphyses) and (4) the weight (g) of unidentified diaphysial fragments, then divided by the number of fragments of the above-mentioned bones, in other words, divided by (1) the number of identifiable fragments of known anatomical origin (2) the number of flat bone fragments, (3) the number of spongy bone fragments and (4) the number of unidentified diaphysial fragments (cf. Duday, Depierre and Janin, 2000)

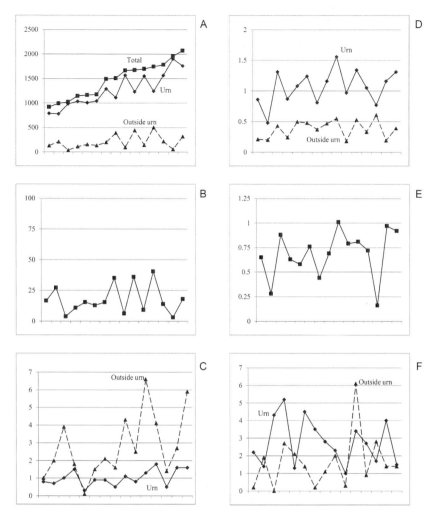

Figure 15.2 The results of the main analytical procedures applied to the comparison between bones contained in urns, i.e. bones collected from the cremation area ('Urn' is denoted by the continuous line) and the remains found in the grave-pit, i.e. bone deriving from the cleaning of the cremation area ('Outside Urn', denoted by the dotted line) from the Porta Nocera necropolis in Pompeii. Only the graves for which the remains from cleaning of the cremation area were deposited in the pit are displayed. From upper left down to right down: A. The total weight of cremated bones; B. The percentage ratio of the total weight of the bones found in the pit to the total weight of the bones found in the urn; C. The ponderal index of the hands; D. The average weight of the fragments, excluding small fragments; E. The difference between the average weight in urns and pits, excluding small fragments; F. The ponderal index of the feet.

only a fairly low total weight. The hands are relatively poor in soft tissue, their dehydration in the heat of the pyre is therefore rapid, and they self-combust much faster than the parts containing more water, such as the trunk and portions of the limbs. The phalanges therefore tend to disarticulate fairly quickly, and they fall into the deep part of the pyre where they are covered by ashes, the ashes behaving like a 'heat shield' which stops combustion. After the fire goes out, when the collection of burnt remains occurs, the bones of the hands are for the most part not visible because they are deeply buried in the ash layer. The funerary receptacle therefore contains only

Table 15.1 A comparison of the characteristics of the remains from the manual collection of the cremation area (the contents of the funerary receptacle) and the residues from the cleaning of the cremation area. Grave 15, individual B (Eliodorus) and grave 21, individuals A (Vesonia Urbana) and B. The symbol '+' is an indication of great quantity

	Pompeii Porta Nocera, grave 15B		Pompeii Porta Nocera, grave 21A		Pompeii Porta Nocera, grave 21B	
	Amphora	Pit	Amphora	Chest 29	Amphora	Pit
Total weight	1041.9 g	134.1 g	1552.9 g	141 g	1114.2 g	390.8 g
Average weight without small fragments[5]	1.24 g	0.48 g	1.34 g	0.53 g	1.16 g	0.47 g
% identified	77.3	52.9	83.7	68.0	69.5	40.1
Ponderal index of the hands	0.8	1.5	0.8	6.6	0.1	1.6
Ash	0	+++	0	+++	+	+++

a very small number of hand remains, but a thorough cleaning of the cremation residues reveals more of them. The fact that the bones of the feet do not follow the same pattern is due, on the one hand, to the fact that the tarsus contains bulky bones which are generally picked up during manual collection and, on the other hand, to the fact that, in some cases at least, the deceased may have been cremated wearing shoes. The presence of shoe nails is not uncommon occurrence from material collected during the cleaning of cremation areas.

A final observation that is important to mention is the following: when the deposits contain burnt worked bones (decorations from the funerary bier or from a chest deposited on the pyre), these are more abundant in the residues from the cleaning of the cremation area than they are in the deposits resulting from the manual collection. This shows that the manual collection is specifically intended to carefully recover the remains of the deceased.

Manually collected remains placed in two funerary vases

When the amount of manually collected remains is particularly abundant – even from only a single individual grave – remains are sometimes distributed between two cremation vessels. The site of Cumes provides a particularly relevant example. Mausoleum 34009 contained four containers just within the entrance, including an urn (34226), on the cover of which a bowl had been placed (34221). The weight of burnt bones contained in urn 34226 is considerable, some 3519.1 g. The amount in the bowl is lower: 1047.6 g. There is no doubt that most of these two sets of cremated remains relate to a single individual, an extremely robust adult with many characteristic pathological lesions.

Several osteological re-associations were indeed established with certainty between the two batches of burnt bones: a relationship based on symmetry between the right (34226.R06) and left (34221.R02) mandibular condyles, re-fitting between two fragments of an axis vertebra, 34226.R06 and 34221.R04, and between two fragments of a distal phalanx of the hallux, 34226, R07 and 34221.R04, and, lastly, numerous associated fragments due to the presence of the same pathological lesions (porotic hyperostosis with an increased bone weight of the ribs and vertebrae, in particular). With a total weight of 4566.7 g, there are certainly some remains that relate to a second, much less robust individual, but they represent only a rather small weight, less than 200 g. The 'principal' subject is therefore represented by more than 4300 g of burnt bone. Several graves from the same necropolis have produced assemblages of burnt human bones with weights much greater than 3000 g, with percentage representativeness greater than 90%, and even 95%,

Table 15.2 The main characteristics of the contents of the two super-positioned vessels (urn 34226 and bowl 34221) at the entrance to mausoleum 34009 from the Roman necropolis of Cumes. The comparison of the ponderal indices shows that the bowl received fragments in the main from the head and trunk, while the urn contained elements mainly from the limbs and trunk

	Urn 34226	*Bowl 34221*
Total weight	3519.1 g	1047.6 g
Average weight without small fragments[5]	2.89 g	2.78 g
% identified	88.1	95.0
Ponderal index – hands	1.4	2.6
Ashes	0	0
Ponderal index – skull (cranium and mandible)	2.2	63.1
Ponderal index – trunk	24.5	26.8
Ponderal index – upper limbs	16.5	4.9
Ponderal index – lower limbs	44.9	0.1

which leaves little doubt about the fact that they relate to the remains of single individuals. The explanation for this apparent anomaly is, in fact, due to a pathological process called osteopetrosis, a bone disease that makes bones abnormally dense and appears to be linked to endemic fluorosis (high levels of fluorine content from telluric waters). This demonstrates that urn 34226 and bowl 34221 contained the remains of a very robust adult suffering from osteopetrosis. The contents of the two containers represent remains from manual collection from the cremation area and not from its cleaning up. For the two containers, the ponderal indices without fragments are comparable; there is no increase in the ponderal index of the hands, or in the carbonised remains and ash (Table 15.2).

The comparison of the ponderal indices for each of the major anatomical regions shows that the bowl contents comprise mainly elements of the head, neck and thorax, while the urn contains mainly the remains of the upper and lower limbs, abdomen and thorax. This opposition becomes clearer through comparison with the distribution of the vertebrae between the bowl and the urn. They contain, respectively, 62.2 g and 2.7 g of fragments relating to the cervical vertebrae, 62.1 g and 196.9 g to the thoracic vertebrae, 3.2 g and 196.4 g to the lumbar vertebrae and 0 g and 147.6 g to the sacrum. Whether the collection was carried out by two different people or by the same person in two consecutive burnings, it is certain that it resulted in a very clear separation following a strict anatomical logic. The cremation had therefore not been 'tended', meaning that the *ustor*, the cremation attendant, did not place the different body parts into the central area of the pyre.

The remains of a deceased individual deposited in the grave of another individual in several groups

In addition to remains found within the same grave, the excavation sometimes furnishes the opportunity to study structures incontestably linked to the same funerary assemblage but which are not true interments, or not in every case 'final' interments.

Enigmatic interment pits

Three small similarly sized pits, pit 1, pit 2 and pit 3, were uncovered in the central portion of enclosure 23 (Figure 15.1). They are all between 40 cm and 55 cm in diameter and 20 cm to 22 cm deep. The actual depth of the pits was confirmed by the sealing of the levels with deposits

Table 15.3 Necropolis of Porta Nocera in Pompeii, enclosure 23. The content of the pits 1, 2 and 3 compared to the contents of graves 8, 9 and 25, with which they could have been associated. For grave 25, note the abundance of burnt worked bone fragments; the total weight of worked bones in relation to the total weight of burnt human bones (as a percentage) is significantly higher in the residues from the cleaning of the cremation area, whether at the bottom of double grave 25, or in the isolated pit F3. The symbol '+' is an indication of great quantity

| | | | | | Grave 25 | | |
	Grave 8	Pit F1	Grave 9	Pit F2	Urn	Pit	Pit F3
Total weight	753.8 g	57.0 g	1092.1 g	71.1 g	983.3 g	38.3 g	48.9 g
Average weight without small fragments[5]	1.05 g	0.30 g	1.84 g	0.33 g	1.31 g	0.43 g	0.44 g
% identified	82.6	63.0	91.8	61.3	76.6	45.7	37.4
Ponderal index – hands	0.3	1.6	0.7	3.7	0.9	3.9	0.8
Ash	0	+++	0	+++	0	+++	+++
Worked bones (number)	0	0	0	1	72	180	22
Worked bones/human bones (%)	0	0	0	2.1	10.8	54.3	66.5

linked to the eruption of Mount Vesuvius in 79 AD. They were indicated by ashy sediment, and all three produced small quantities of burnt bone fragments. This type of deposit is characteristic of the cleaning of a cremation area (Table 15.3). Each of these pits could be linked to one of the graves in enclosure 23:

- A link between pit 1 and grave 8 (Figure 15.1, number 1) was established based on re-association relating to joint contiguity between a maxillary second right molar (F1.233120) and a right maxilla (T8. 232515) and re-fitting of contiguous fragments between a fragment of the right articular mass (F1.233120) and the body (T8.232516) of the same cervical vertebra.
- A link between pit 2 and grave 9 (Figure 15.1, number 2) was established based on a symmetrical pairing between left (F2.233078) and right (T9.23415) mandibular condyles.
- It was not possible to establish a definitive osteological connection among the burnt human fragments found in pit 3, but there is a very high probability that they relate to the burnt worked bones found in this pit that are similar to remains found in grave 25 (Figure 15.1, number 3).

In graves 8 and 9, there was no ash deposited in the pit where the urn containing the burnt remains was placed. The situation is different when compared with grave 25, which contained a double burial with a similar internal arrangement indicated by two stelae (Van Andringa, Duday and Lepetz, 2013: 339ff.). Grave 25 contained urn T7, which contained the remains of an elderly adult, probable male comprised of 1789.2 g of burnt bone, and urn T25, which contained the remains of an elderly adult woman comprising 983.3 g of burnt bone. A bed of ashes and charcoal (stratigraphic units 232626, 232723 and 232724) found beneath the two vases at the bottom of the pit also contained burnt bones. Osteological analysis showed re-fitting of contiguous fragments with the content of urn T25: the frontal process of a left zygomatic bone (bottom of pit, stratigraphic unit 232723) conjoined with a fragment of the body of the zygoma from the same side (T25.232621) and the right mandibular condyle (stratigraphic unit 232724 from the bottom of the pit) with a fragment of mandibular ascending ramus (T25.232623). Many connections were also found between fragments of worked bones. However, no relationships were found with urn T7.

The analysis leads to the following interpretation. The area in which the T25 female had been cremated had been manually collected and the remains were then placed in a ceramic urn.

The material from the subsequent cleaning of the cremation area was deposited at the bottom of the pit of the double grave (grave 25) containing urns T7 and T25, but of which another portion was deposited in small pit 3, which was more than 4 m from the grave. From a structural point of view, the distance that separates them from the graves to which they are connected and the osteological quantitative data from pits F1 and F2 have many similarities with pit F3, but in these two cases, they are the only remains that relate to the cleaning of the cremation area.

In situ cremation areas

In Pompeii, the eruption of Mount Vesuvius in 79 AD 'froze' the thoroughfares within the city and its surroundings in place, which makes it possible to observe the necropolises in their state of use. Several cremation areas were excavated in area 250, west of enclosure 23 (Van Andringa, Duday and Lepetz, 2013: 763ff.); De Larminat and Leptetz in (Van Andringa, Duday and Lepetz, 2013: 763ff.). Farther east, behind enclosure 21 that borders the road, an equipped platform (area 210) was also used to build pyres.

The pyre and the grave of the child, 'Bebryx'

In enclosure 21 (Figure 15.1), a white marble stele marked the grave of a child, a boy named 'Bebryx' (grave 201). The urn located at the foot of the stele contained the burnt remains of a child whose age at death was estimated to have been between 5 and 6 years. Ashes (stratigraphic unit 21108) were dumped into the pit before the stele was put in place; there is no doubt that they came from the cleaning of the pyre on which Bebryx was cremated: the crowns of the lower left (stratigraphic unit (SU) 21108) and right (urn, R05) premolars were symmetrical and at the same stage of maturation. This complementarity is straightforward between, on the one hand, the remains resulting from collection and deposited in the urn and, on the other hand, those that came from the cleaning of the cremation area and were deposited in the grave pit.

In this case, however, excavation of area 210, outside enclosure 21, revealed an area 35 cm by 35 cm (stratigraphic units 21035, 21036 and 21038) in which the burnt bones of an immature individual had been intentionally gathered together showing numerous links with those of Bebryx (Figure 15.1, number 4) based on maturation stage, bone symmetries, such as between distal portions of the right (T201.R02) and left (210036) humeri and first metacarpals T201.R03 and 21035) and dental germs of the first permanent right (T201.R01) and left (210038) mandibular molars and the maxillary permanent second right (T201.R04) and left (210038) molars, as well as perfect articulation between the sternal parts, the first (T201.R02), second (210038), third (T201.R04) and fourth (210038) sternebrae; further evidence is provided by two contiguous fragments of a thoracic vertebra (T201.R02 and stratigraphic unit 210038).

This quite exceptional case offers the opportunity to observe both the result of manual collection, the residues from the partial cleaning of the cremation area, and what remained within it after the completion of the two previous steps. Among these three subsets, the last two share many similarities (Table 15.4). The fragments remaining in the cremation area further support the indices previously described as being specific to residues from cleaning, with an average weight without small fragments,[5] and a higher hand ponderal index. Even if they are significantly higher than the value found for the urn 201 (0.3 g), the values of this index for the residues deposited in the pit (0.9 g) and for the cremation area proper (1.6 g) may seem quite low compared to the classical reference value, which is 2.5 g. It is not known, however, if the ponderal index of the head is much higher in children (it amounts to 45.8 g for the whole of grave 201), while the reference value in adults is only 20.4 g. As a consequence, the ponderal indices of the other

Table 15.4 The comparative composition of the contents of the different stratigraphic units from the burial of Bebryx, a child who died at the age of 6 years from the Porta Nocera necropolis at Pompeii: the contents of the urn, ashes deposited in the pit and residues remaining within cremation area 210 (study by E. Portat and H. Duday). For comparison, the right column shows the composition of the residues remaining at pyre 5 in area 250 (study by S. de Larminat). The symbol '+' is an indication of great quantity

	Bebryx			Cremation area 250
	Grave 201		Cremation area 250	
	Urn	Pit		Pyre 5
Total weight	268.2 g	22.0 g	31.7 g	530.0 g
Average weight without small fragments[5]	0.42 g	0.16 g	0.08 g	0.14 g
% identified	98.4	94.1	96.5	66.5
Ponderal index – hands	0.3	0.9	1.6	4.7
Ash	0	++	++++	++++

regions of the skeleton of a child are therefore greatly reduced. The data relating to pyre 5 of the cremation areas excavated in zone 250, trends in the same direction (Table 15.4, right column).

A long-use cremation area

Area 210 also produced the very partial remains of at least two other individuals, an adult-sized individual (an adult or adolescent) and an adult. The adult (Figure 15.1, number 5) was identified based on a left temporal fragment (210036) from the roof of the external auditory meatus that could be joined to another fragment of the same temporal, found in the urn of grave 202 (T202. R05) located immediately north of the grave of Bebryx (grave 201). The epitaph indicates that it was the grave of Stallia Haphe, probable founder of enclosure 21 (Van Andringa, Duday and Lepetz, 2013: 610ff.). Osteological analysis confirmed that the remains were those of a female who died at over 30 years of age. However, if the burial of Bebryx dates from the last decade of the occupation of Pompeii (phase 3 of enclosure 21, 70–79 AD), then the grave of Stallia Haphe is clearly older (phase 2, 0–40 AD). The time between the two deposits was therefore more than 30 years. With Bebryx having died at the age of 6, it is impossible that he could have been the son of Stallia Haphe. Their deaths were at least two or maybe three generations apart. This shows that the same location, immediately behind enclosure 21, opposite the ancient road, was therefore used to build pyres several decades apart.

The unexpected death of Castricia Prisca and the creation of a probable delayed burial

A small funerary monument, 25a, was built to house the burnt remains of a freed woman, Castricia Prisca, who died at the age of 25 years. The bones placed in a masonry chest (grave 107, stratigraphic unit 250213) at the foot of the stele which bears her name, are actually those of a young female whose age-at-death can be estimated between 25 and 30 years. The appearance of the deposit, with an approximately circular outline at a distance from the sides of the chest, suggests that they must have been placed in a perishable container, perhaps a folded cloth or cloth

Table 15.5 A comparison of the contents of the chest from grave 107 (mausoleum 25a) and the deposit of ashes at the bottom of grave 102 from the Porta Nocera necropolis in Pompeii. The two sets relate to Castricia Prisca, a young woman who died at the age of 25

	Castricia Prisca,	*Grave 102, Pit,*
	grave 107, context 250213	*context 250172*
Total weight	1566.6 g	96.9 g
Average weight without small fragments[5]	1.56 g	0.55 g
% identified	89.6	72.5
Ponderal index – hands	0.9	4.3
Ash	0	+++

bag. Graves 101 and 102 are located immediately to the northeast of this funerary niche. Their appearance is like most of the graves in the necropolis of Porta Nocera, with a stele at the foot of the grave-pit that contains the cremation urn sealed with a lava stone plate. The urn from grave 101 contained the burnt remains (823.4 g in total) of an adult, most likely female. In contrast, the urn from grave 102 was completely empty, but at the bottom of the pit was a small ashy deposit rich in charcoal (stratigraphic unit 250172) with burnt bone fragments.

The systematic search for re-associations showed that this assemblage 250172 relates to the individual from grave 107 – that is to say, to Castricia Prisca (Figure 15.1, number 6): a fragment of the occipital squama joins perfectly to the internal occipital protuberance (T107.R03), a fragment of a maxilla with the frontal process of the right maxilla (T107.R03), the left coronoid process of the mandible with the left mandibular ascending ramus (T107.R02), and a fragment of the right pubis with the right ilio-pubic ramus (T107.R02); in addition, a medial fragment of the left petrous temporal is perfectly symmetrical with the right petrous (T107.R01) and the base of the second left metacarpal is symmetrical with that of the right (T107.R03).

Assemblage 250172 has all the characteristics of residue from the cleaning of a cremation area (Table 15.5), including a reduced bone weight, a very low average fragment weight, an over-representation of the bones of the hands and, of course, the presence of ashes and charcoal. Van Andringa, Duday and Lepetz (2013: 737) proposed the following plausible interpretation of this context. When Castricia Prisca died, the funerary monument for this still very young woman was not yet built. A relatively simple grave, grave 102, was therefore prepared for her, her body was cremated, the bones were collected from the cremation area and placed in a flexible container which was then, in turn, placed in the urn in the grave. Previous to this, the area on which her pyre had been erected was cleared and the residue was dumped in the bottom of the pit. Then, the funerary niche was built, grave 102 was re-opened, and the 'bag' containing the bones was transferred to the masonry chest located under the niche at the foot of the stele bearing the name of Castricia Prisca. Grave 102 was therefore only a place of transient deposition, a 'delayed burial' ('*sépulture d'attente*') at the bottom of which only the little heap of ashes from the cleaning of the cremation area remained in place.

Paths for the dead … or 'the metaphor of Little Thumb' ('Le Poucet')

The deceased were therefore burned on pyres built in areas reserved for this use. Their remains were then picked up, wrapped in cloth (a bag or folded cloth) and transported to the grave where they were usually placed within a ceramic or lead urn, and sometimes in a perishable container. The use of cloth or tissue has been found within several graves studied at Pompeii (Moulherat, 2013) and at Cumes (Cavassa *et al.*, 2014), where tissue fibres were found adhering to the inner wall of the urn or on the surface of burnt bones, preserved as a result of contact with coins and the abiotic effect of copper salts.

It is hypothesised that the graves of enclosure 23 were regularly visited because the repeated trampling of the clay-silt sediment led to the creation of hollowed pathway. One pathway seemed to go from the entrance to the centre of the enclosure and the other developed parallel to it. It is not impossible that it connected the graves of enclosure 23 and 25 to the corresponding cremation zone, the exact location of which is not known, but which is probably east or south-east of enclosure 23 (south of area 210?). It is indeed on this pathway and around it that most of the burned human bone fragments found were distributed in frequented areas, independent of the graves and pits F1, F2 and F3 (Van Andringa, Duday and Lepetz, 2013: 911, fig. 462). They are most probably burnt fragments 'lost' during the transfer of the bones from the cremation area to the final burial (hence the 'Little Thumb' metaphor, so small that they were overlooked after dropping to the ground). This scenario seems to be confirmed by the connection between two contiguous fragments of a tibia (Figure 15.1, number 7). One was found on the surface in the centre of enclosure 23 (stratigraphic unit 23648.5), and another inside the amphora that constitutes the funerary receptacle of grave 15 (upper-most subject, an elderly adult, stratigraphic unit 23113.R04).

The remains of several deceased individuals in the same grave

'Collection errors', evidence for the existence of an 'ustrinum'

Secondary cremation burials are, for the most part, found in individual graves, but it is not uncommon for a grave to contain burnt bones of two individuals, and sometimes even more – hence the need for a precise identification of the bone fragments and, in particular, their lateralisation. This observation is based on relationships of exclusion: incompatibility of the maturation stage or the age-related senescent changes between fragments or, more rarely, the presence of double or triple burials, when the total weight of burned bones is much higher than the expected value for a single individual.[6]

The question then arises as to whether or not the remains in the grave represent a true double burial, or even if several individuals had been deposited in the same grave at different times, or whether the presence of a second individual resulted from a 'mistake' made during collection from the cremation area. When there are spaces in the necropolis reserved for the building of pyres, some residual fragments of an earlier cremation may indeed have been picked up with the remains of the 'principal' deceased individual. The distinction depends on the relative quantification of human remains: in a burial that intentionally contains several individuals, each individual must be represented by a fairly large quantity of burnt bones, in number and in weight, with variation based on the age-at-death of the individual(s). On the contrary, during a 'collection error', only a few fragments attest to the presence of the additional individual, their numbers always being very small compared to those of the principal individual. If the supernumerary fragment(s) was (were) found in the urn or amongst the cremated remains in the pit, the interpretation is the same: they represent an individual burial and, furthermore, this evidence demonstrates the existence of a place reserved for the successive construction of several pyres, which is usually referred to as an *ustrinum*.

---

6 Taking into account the reservations mentioned above, it is necessary to ascertain that the deceased did not suffer from a pathological condition accompanied by hyperostotic or new bone formation processes.

Osteological re-associations that reveal the relative chronology of cremations

When a grave is part of a coherent funerary complex and, furthermore, if the whole has been completely investigated, it is sometimes possible to identify the individual to whom the residual fragment derived which, in turn, may provide insight into the order in which the two deceased individuals had been cremated. Thus, in enclosure 23, the urn from grave 37 contained 297.5 g of burned bones of a 4- to 6-year-old child, but also a single fragment of an adult-sized tibial shaft weighing 3.3 g (stratigraphic unit 232332-R01), which could be conjoined (Figure 15.1, number 8) to a tibial fragment of the adult from grave 9 (stratigraphic unit 23414-R04): the two individuals therefore had been burned at the same location, but the adult from grave 9 before the child from grave 37.

Conclusions and future research

This journey through a Pompeian necropolis illustrates research avenues to be pursued through the use of osteological (re-)associations for the study of secondary cremation burials. They can offer unexpected perspectives on the way graves were designed and the way human bodies and their remains were manipulated and managed. They can provide information on the funerary sequence, the relative chronology of burials, and of the funerary structures that were previously thought to be inaccessible to archaeological enquiry. The complexity of the highlighted evidence contrasts starkly with a falsely normative image entertained prior to analysis, namely that the dead were treated in a single uniform manner in each case.

The analysis and interpretation of cremations require the application of rigorous investigation methods, including going as far as one can to identify bone fragments. In each deposit, in each exposed layer, each fragment must be identified to its anatomical origin in such a way that it is easy to return to them to seek possible links with a fragment from another stratigraphic unit in the same grave, from another area within the necropolis, or from another grave from the same or another enclosure. The research protocol must be rigorous and, above all, systematic. Admittedly, this type of research requires a great deal of time: in the Porta Nocera necropolis (enclosure 21, 23, 25 and 25a), 98 425 burned bone fragments (excluding the smallest fragments) were analysed. Such an investment in time is therefore not possible for all excavated sites, but when the opportunity presents itself to study a coherent and complete set of burials and funerary structures related to the treatment of the bodies of the deceased, osteological re-associations are the most effective anthropological analytical procedure to apply to this aspect of the archaeology of death.

References

Bel, V., Blaizot, F. and Duday, H. (2008). Bûcher en fosse et tombe-bûcher: problématiques et méthodes de fouille. In: J. Scheid, ed., *Pour une Archéologie du Rite: Nouvelles Perspectives de l'Archéologie Funéraire*. Rome: École française de Rome (Collection de l'École française de Rome), pp. 125–142.

Cavassa, L., Duday, H., Médard, F. and Munzi, P. (2014). Cumes, la nécropole romaine de la 'Porta Mediana' (Campanie, Italie). Restes de tissus dans un tombeau d'époque augustéenne. In: J. Ortiz, C. Alfaro, L. Turell and M.J. Martínez, eds., *Textiles and Dyes in the Mediterranean World, Vth Purpureae Vestes International Symposium*. Valencia: Publicacions de la Universitat de València, pp. 87–101.

Depierre, G. (2014). *Crémation et archéologie: nouvelles alternatives méthodologiques en ostéologie humaine*. Dijon: Éditions universitaires de Dijon (Collection Art, Archéologie et Patrimoine).

Duday, H. (1987). Contribution des observations ostéologiques à la chronologie interne des sépultures. In: H. Duday and C. Masset, eds., *Anthropologie Physique et Archéologie. Méthodes d'Étude des Sépultures*. Actes du colloque de Toulouse (4–6 novembre 1982). Paris: Centre National de la Recherche Scientifique (CNRS), pp. 51–60.

Duday, H. (2009). *Archaeology of the dead: Lectures in archaeothanatology.* Translated by A.M. Cipriani, and J. Pearce, Oxford: Oxbow Books.

Duday, H., Depierre, G. and Janin, T. (2000). Validation des paramètres de quantification, protocoles et stratégies dans l'étude anthropologique des sépultures secondaires à incinération. L'exemple des nécropoles protohistoriques du Midi de la France. In: B. Dedet, P. Gruat, G. Marchand, M. Py and M. Schwaller, eds., *Archéologie de la Mort, Archéologie de la Tombe au Premier Âge du Fer.* Lattes: Monographies d'Archéologie Méditerranéenne, pp. 7–29.

Grévin, G. (1990). La Fouille en Laboratoire des Sépultures à Incinération. Son Apport à l'Archéologie. *Bulletins et Mémoires de la Société d'Anthropologie de Paris*, 2, pp. 67–74.

Lowrance, E.W. and Latimer, H.B. (1957). Weights and Linear Measurements of 105 Human Skeletons from Asia. *American Journal of Anatomy*, 101, pp. 445–459.

Moulherat, C. (2013). Des linges et des sacs pour les restes osseux: les vestiges de tissus. In: W. Van Andringa, H. Duday and S. Lepetz, eds., *Mourir à Pompéi: Fouille d'un Quartier Funéraire de la Nécropole Romaine de Porta Nocera (2003-2007).* Rome: Collection de l'école française de Rome number 468, 2, pp. 1105–1118.

Rich, A. (1883). *Dictionnaire des antiquités grecques et romaines.* Paris: Firmin Didot.

Van Andringa, W., Duday, H. and Lepetz, S. (2013). *Mourir à Pompéi: fouille d'un quartier funéraire de la nécropole romaine de Porta Nocera (2003-2007).* Rome: Collection de l'école française de Rome.

16

REOPENING GRAVES FOR THE REMOVAL OF OBJECTS AND BONES

Cultural practices and looting

Edeltraud Aspöck

AUSTRIAN CENTRE FOR DIGITAL HUMANITIES AND CULTURAL HERITAGE, AUSTRIAN ARCHAEOLOGICAL INSTITUTE, AUSTRIAN ACADEMY OF SCIENCES, VIENNA, AUSTRIA

Karina Gerdau-Radonić

ARCHIMÈDE, MAISON INTERUNIVERSITAIRE DES SCIENCES DE L'HOMME, UMR 7044, UNIVERSITÉ DE STRASBOURG, FRANCE

CENTRE FOR ARCHAEOLOGY AND ANTHROPOLOGY, BOURNEMOUTH UNIVERSITY, POOLE, UNITED KINGDOM

Astrid A. Noterman

DEPARTMENT OF ARCHAEOLOGY AND CLASSICAL STUDIES, STOCKHOLM UNIVERSITY, STOCKHOLM, SWEDEN

CESCM, CENTRE D'ÉTUDES SUPÉRIEURES DE CIVILISATION MÉDIÉVALE, UMR 7302, POITIERS, FRANCE

Introduction

Human remains buried in graves do not always 'rest in peace' eternally. Throughout the world, graves are often reopened[1] as part of funerary or post-funerary rituals (Hertz, 1960; Danforth, 1982; Verdery, 1999; Aspöck, 2005; Kümmel, 2009; Weiss-Krejci, 2011; Aspöck et al. 2020). Possible motivations for reopening graves are manifold. In many instances, the reopening may not be sacrilege but actually form part of ritual practices. These could include the removal of grave goods or body parts for symbolic reasons, such as for use as relics (Geary, 1986), the manipulation of the body in the context of beliefs in *revenants* (Barber, 1988), or when mortuary practices are thought

---

1 The word 'reopened' is preferred to 'disturbed' as this includes graves which have been disturbed, desecrated, or reopened for ritual or other reasons.

DOI: 10.4324/9781351030625-19

to have failed (Goody, 1962: 151; Aspöck, 2011). Other causes of post-funeral 'disturbances' of graves may include ancestral rites and ancestral appropriation, veneration and commemoration of important individuals, political disputes, looting, desecration, as well as curiosity and scientific research.

In Early Medieval Europe, the dead were usually interred individually soon after death. Recent research of reopened graves from that period indicates that the frequent removal of objects from them were not simple cases of looting, at least as it is understood today and as interpreted for a long time by archaeologists. It seems to have been a far more complex phenomenon incorporating elements of more than one of the above-mentioned motivations for grave reopening (Aspöck, 2005, 2011, 2015; Van Haperen 2010, 2013, 2016, 2017; Zintl, 2012a, 2012b2019; Klevnäs, 2013, 2015, 2016; Klevnäs et al. 2021; Noterman, 2016; Noterman *et al.* 2020). Hence, what at first sight seems to be a straightforward case of 'grave robbery' for materialistic reasons may be part of a specific cultural mindset. Nevertheless, it is rarely easy to distinguish the many reasons for reopening graves in the archaeological record as the removal of objects for looting or for symbolical purposes may leave similar evidence.

Similarly, within collective graves, it may be difficult to ascertain ritual practices such as the removal of objects and body parts because of the commingling and manipulation of the remains with continued additions to the grave. Research in Andean collective and individual pre-Columbian graves, for example, indicates that individuals may be incomplete within both types of graves for ritual reasons, or because the grave was partially emptied for practical reasons (Carmichael, 1995; Millaire, 2004; Gerdau-Radonić, 2008; Gerdau-Radonić and Makowski, 2011).

Archaeothanatological analyses of graves reopened for object and body part removal are rare and recent. Although 'disturbed' graves are frequently excavated and studied, analysis usually focuses on the intact structures of the grave, the looted structures being considered too 'damaged' to contain any useful data. In the Andes, grave reopening, whether due to looting or for ritual reasons (e.g. Carmichael, 1995; Millaire, 2004; Gerdau-Radonić and Makowski, 2011), is well-known and documented, but there are only six published archaeothanatology papers on four sites: one of a looted grave (Gerdau-Radonić and Herrera, 2010) and five that focus on funerary treatment that included grave reopening and the addition or removal of goods and body parts as part of the funerary practices (Gerdau-Radonić, 2008; Gerdau-Radonić and Makowski, 2011; Klaus and Tam, 2015; Toyne, 2015; Klaus, 2016). In Europe, the reopening of Merovingian graves soon after burial is a practice well known to archaeologists and scholars. Nevertheless, for a long time, these were seen as 'disturbances' of the archaeological record, making such graves unattractive for full analysis. As a consequence, the recording of information pertaining to the reopening was limited. Most of the few applications of archaeothanatological analysis of reopening practices have been carried out in France (Chenal and Barrand-Emam, 2014; Roth-Zehner and Cartier, 2007). Only recently, Noterman (2016b) completed a more extensive study of reopened early medieval graves in the French administrative regions of Normandie, Hauts-de-France, Île-de-France, and Grand Est.

This chapter will first introduce the taphonomic characteristics of reopened individual inhumations typically found in two archaeological periods with large-scale grave reopening for object removal: the central European Early Bronze Age and the European Early Medieval periods. It will then discuss some characteristics of reopened collective graves. This will be followed by three case studies showcasing the contribution of archaeothanatology to the study of reopened graves with evidence for the removal of grave goods and human remains. In a micro-archaeological study of a reopened Early Bronze Age inhumation grave from Austria, the archaeothanatological approach was extended to the disturbed parts of the skeletons to achieve a detailed perspective of the treatment of the human remains when the grave was reopened

(Aspöck, 2018). The second case study presents examples from the archaeothanatological analysis of graves from two early medieval cemeteries from the Grand Est region of France (Noterman, 2016). Finally, the analysis of a disturbed deposit from Central Perú (Pachacamac, Lima) highlights the differences between a destructive looting episode and ritualistic grave reopenings.

Graves reopened for the removal of grave goods and body parts

Taphonomy of reopened individual inhumation graves

Grave reopening for object removal soon after burial has been identified globally and across all archaeological periods (Aspöck et al. 2020). 'Soon' refers to the reopening of graves within some generations after deposition, i.e. at a time when funerary customs were still understood, the identity of the dead person may still have been known and those who attended the funeral may still have been alive. Such activities are different to the re-use of burial monuments hundreds or thousands of years after deposition (e.g. Bradley and Williams, 1998). Archaeological analysis and interpretation of reopened individual inhumation graves typically considers six main questions (Table 16.1).

Reopening soon after burial was endemic in the cemeteries of the central European Early Bronze Age as well as in those of the Early Medieval period across Europe. Both periods are characterised by the interment of the dressed body in individual graves as primary deposits, usually in containers, and frequently with a high number of grave goods. Cemeteries could consist of small groups or several hundred graves. In both periods, grave goods were for long the focus of research, and their quantity and quality were, for example, seen as an indicator of social status (e.g. Sprenger, 1999; Effros, 2006; Alduc-Le Bagousse, 2009). Grave disturbance was seen as a hindrance to this type of research, and the value of evidence from grave reopening for research into funerary practices and to approach the meaning of grave goods and human remains, as well as other topics, was not recognised for a long time.

In the Early Bronze Age and Early Medieval periods, bodies were predominantly buried in some form of container. Grey-lilac soil staining, the position of the skeletal remains and the filling of the empty space with darker sediment are evidence for the use of containers during the central European Early Bronze Age (Neugebauer, 1994; Krenn-Leeb, 2011). More specifically, there is evidence for tree-trunk coffins (trees cut in half and hollowed out), often with stone settings and coverings, or wooden cists in rectangular or trapezoidal form. For the Medieval period, Merovingian graves present a great variety of containers and 'constructed pits' (Crubézy *et al.,* 2000; Galinié and Zadora-Rio, 1996; Henrion, 2012). Bodies could be buried, for example, in a wooden coffin with pegged or nailed walls, a wooden framework built directly in the pit, a chamber grave, a sarcophagus or a stone container. The deposition of a body directly into a simple pit, without container, was less common before the 7th century, especially north of the Loire (Schnitzler, 2008; Annaert and Verslype, 2010). The containers of the Early Bronze Age and Early Medieval periods share one essential element: an empty space into which the body was deposited.

Table 16.1 Questions to ask regarding reopened individual graves

---

What was the original appearance of the grave before the reopening?
When and how did the reopening of the grave take place?
What kind of grave manipulations took place upon reopening?
Which grave goods and body parts were taken and which ones were left behind?
When and how did the re-filling of the grave take place?
How did natural formation processes affect the final archaeological evidence of the reopened grave?

Anthropogenic disturbance of these inhumations is often identified through anomalies in the position of the skeleton. However, such anomalies can also be the result of natural processes which the archaeothanatological approach helps to distinguish from human interference. Such natural processes may be due to the original layout of the grave and the decay of architectural elements and grave goods. The decay and subsequent voids may lead to the taphonomic movements of bone influenced by the original shape of the container and position of the body within it (Fiocchi, Chevalier and Lapie, 2012). Furthermore, the progressive decay of constituent parts of containers, especially if the body was laid on a wooden platform above the grave floor may lead to the displacement of the remains (Blaizot, 2008) as would water coming into the grave (Duday, 2009).

Another type of archaeological evidence for human interference can be one or more additional pits found in the area of the grave-pit. Such intrusive pits may be visible during excavation if the fill is different. However, as these intrusive pits were usually re-filled with the original sediment removed when the pit was dug, they can at times be difficult to distinguish or not visible at all. Consequently, the disturbance of the burial may come as a surprise to the excavator. Other types of evidence for grave reopening include displaced, missing and fragmented grave goods, as well as the destruction of grave furniture (e.g. Aspöck, 2005, 2011; Noterman, 2015; Châtelet, 2017).

If the archaeological evidence is well preserved, it is possible to determine the stage of decomposition of the body at the time of the reopening, permitting an estimate of the amount of time that elapsed between the moment of burial and the reopening event (Sági, 1964; Neugebauer, 1991; Aspöck, 2005, 2011; Noterman, 2016). Knowledge of the length of the interval between burial and the reopening enables the exclusion of certain interpretations and provides support for others (Aspöck, 2005; Kümmel, 2009). Ethnographic records document that the relationship between the living and the dead changes over time and according to the different stages of the rite of passage that the funerary process represents (Kümmel, 2009; van Gennep, 1960).

Based on research by Neugebauer (1991) and Sági (1964), Aspöck (2005, 2011) distinguished four categories of reopened graves based on the state of decomposition at the time of the intrusion (categories A to D). These categories have been applied to regional studies of early medieval grave reopening, permitting quantification of evidence so as to retrace the temporal development of these post-funerary practices (e.g. Klevnäs, 2013; Van Haperen, 2017)[2].

Category A: It is rare and controversial to establish evidence for graves that were reopened when the body as well as all the grave furniture were still un-decayed and intact. It is usually a matter of interpretation whether the bodies were moved inside the grave or even completely removed from a grave as part of the grave reopening. Archaeologically, such graves would have clear signs of reopening and possibly contain an intact skeleton in a very unusual position, or no human remains at all, yet still contain grave goods or remaining fragments of objects (cf. Brunn am Gebirge, grave 27; Winnall II, grave 11) (Aspöck, 2005, 2011, 2015; Aspöck and Stadler 2005).

Category B: Graves with the human body in the process of decomposition when the grave was reopened are also rather rare. Early grave reopening, before the complete decomposition of the organic tissues of the body, can be identified through the presence of labile and persistent joints still in anatomical articulation, or as two contiguous bones in anatomical proximity retrieved as a set despite being displaced within the grave (cf. Vitry-la-Ville) (Noterman, 2016) (Figure 16.1). Nevertheless, it is also necessary to consider whether or not the presence of clothes or a shroud

---

2 Klevnäs (2013) has further subdivided these categories, with separate schemes for the decay of the body and the coffin.

Figure 16.1 The reopening of grave 224 from Vitry-la-Ville (Marne, France) occurred before the complete decomposition of the body. Despite the disturbance of the right upper limb, anatomical connections between the humerus and scapula – in proximity – and the humerus and ulna – in articulation – are preserved (Tixier, 2019; Photograph: G. Grange; reproduced with permission of Études et valorisations archéologiques (Éveha, Limoges, France)).

may have kept the joints connected after the decomposition of soft tissue (cf. Weiden am See) (Aspöck, 2018) (Figure 16.7).

Category C: If the grave was reopened before the collapse of the funerary container, and there was still an empty space in the grave, the disturbed skeletal remains may spread horizontally across parts or most of the area of the former container (cf. Brunn am Gebirge, Austria) (Aspöck, 2005, 2011) (Figure 16.2). In such cases, bones may be considerably intermingled, resulting from the skeletonised remains being 'searched through'. One characteristic is that there is little bone damage because the empty space permitted the bone to be moved easily. Additionally, there may be little or no bone loss and no bones will be in the infill of the pit. Another characteristic may be that the bones appear to abut against obstacles that have disappeared (a 'wall effect' or an 'alignment effect' ('*délimitation linéaire*') (cf. Blaizot 2008; as in Figure 16.3). In many instances, this type of bone displacement can attest to the former presence of a wooden container that decomposed without leaving visible traces and hence was not recorded at excavation (Aspöck, 2005, 2011; Noterman, 2016). This type of evidence is found frequently.

Category D: Bone displacement can be vertical when the reopening occurred after the collapse of the container and the complete infilling of the structure. Skeletal remains can be found a few centimetres above the bottom of the funerary structure or distributed through the full depth of the grave infill (e.g. Brunn am Gebirge, Austria) (Figure 16.2). In this particular case of grave disturbance, bones are often fragmented and their preservation is not optimal. Indeed, the presence of sediment may have rendered difficult the displacement of some bones and increased their fragility. Thus, when this category of reopened grave is excavated, it is usual to find poorly preserved and highly fragmented bones.

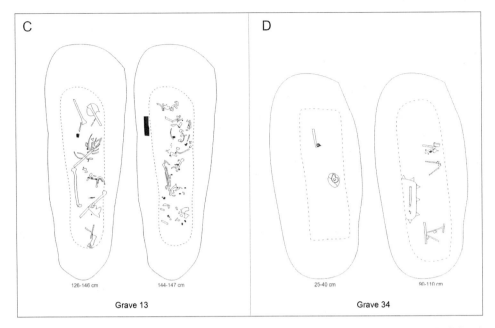

Figure 16.2 Early Medieval cemetery at Brunn am Gebirge, Austria: grave 13, where the body had already decomposed, but there was still an intact coffin providing a hollow space where human remains and objects could move (category C); and grave 34, where the coffin had already broken down (category D) (Images: E. Aspöck).

However, some cases of reopening are difficult to understand. For example, bones in the infill of a burial do not necessarily mean that the reopening took place in a filled space. A deposit of displaced bones distributed horizontally and on the same level, yet above the bottom of the grave, may indicate the presence of a cover system at the time of the reopening, where the bone that was removed from the skeleton had been placed. In this situation, the height of the displaced bones will indicate the depth of the container cover (Figure 16.4). Sometimes displaced bone may be found higher up in the grave fill. Accumulations of finds and human remains higher up in the infill of a reopened grave, may indicate partial re-filling after the reopening (Aspöck, 2005, 2011). In such cases, pits remained apparent on the surface of the cemetery and human remains and finds accumulated at the bottom of these pits. Such accumulation may be intentional or accidental. In Brunn am Gebirge, Austria, there was a high frequency of crania in such pits. However, they were found with surface finds such as snails and objects from previous periods, indicating that they may have ended up in the pit accidentally during the gradual re-filling (Aspöck, 2005, 2011).

Fragmentation of human bone and objects in a grave can occur accidentally during the reopening of a grave, but some damage may have also been intentional. This information is important for interpreting the reopening. Notwithstanding, it is usually difficult to distinguish whether damage was intentional or accidental (Châtelet, 2017; Van Haperen, 2017). Bone damage has been shown to reveal information about the tools used to access the graves, for example, bone damage to an early medieval skeleton may result from a pointed and angular iron probe or a sharp-edged tool (Thiedemann and Schleifring, 1992; Chenal and Barrand-Emam, 2014) and indicate which areas of the skeleton were targeted (Thiedemann and Schleifring, 1992; Beilner and Grupe, 1996; Keller, 2013; Keller and Teschler-Nicola, 2013).

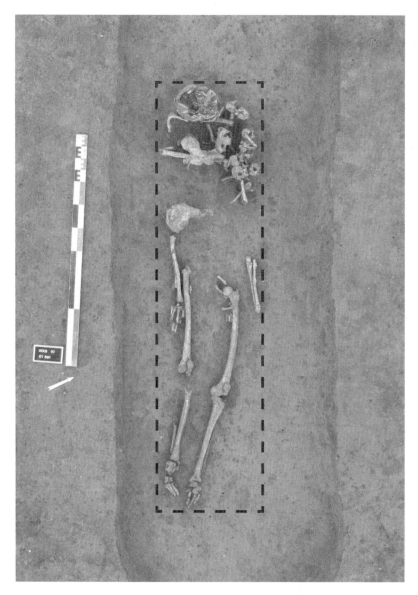

Figure 16.3 Disturbed bones were pushed westward and abutted against the wall of the wooden container of grave 561, Kolbsheim (Bas-Rhin, Alsace, France) (Denaire and Barrand-Emam, 2013; reproduced with permission of Antea Archéologie, Habsheim, France).

Many reopened graves show a significant absence of bone. For example, in Merovingian graves across Europe, large parts of the skeleton are often missing (Aspöck, 2005; Zintl, 2019; Klevnäs, 2013; Noterman, 2016; Van Haperen, 2017). Differential bone preservation of the displaced bone, in particular, may be the cause. However, in some graves, the preservation of the remaining skeleton is good while significant parts of the skeleton are missing from the grave (Noterman, 2016). Similarly, with respect to bone damage, it is difficult to ascertain whether or not the human remains were removed from graves intentionally or accidentally. In the Netherlands, a deposition of human femora was found in a settlement context, giving weight to Van Haperen's

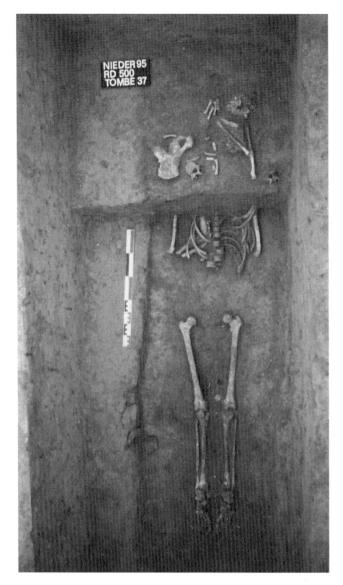

Figure 16.4 Individual 37 from the Niedernai site (Bas-Rhin, Alsace, France) in which the left hemi-
thorax and pelvic area had been disturbed. Several bones, including the ribs, both radii, vertebrae and right
os coxae, were discovered in the infill of the grave. They all appeared at the same level, suggesting they
had probably been placed on the lid of the wooden container prior to the reopening (Zehnacker, 1996;
reproduced with permission of Association pour les Fouilles Archéologiques Nationales (AFAN), France).

argument that not only grave goods but also human bones were removed intentionally from
some graves for further socio-cultural practices (Van Haperen, 2017). Human remains, and in
particular stray finds of human bone, found at occupation sites have in the past often been
ignored by archaeologists because they were 'not supposed to be there'. Hopefully, with modern
standards of excavation, further evidence about what happened to the bones removed will come
to light from analysis of cemetery as well as non-cemetery sites.

Careful stratigraphic observation is required to reconstruct the infilling of the grave. Layers of fine sediment in some contexts indicate that, after the reopening, the grave was left open for some time before it was re-filled (Neugebauer, 1991). Recently, micromorphology has successfully characterised the process of re-filling (Aspöck and Banerjea, 2016). The information on when the grave was re-filled, and how much, is important for the reconstruction of the practices that were carried out and to discuss the background of the reopening. For example, at Brunn am Gebirge in Austria, only graves that had been reopened when the body was already decomposed had evidence that they had been partially re-filled (see above), while those where the body was still in the process of decay when the grave was reopened showed evidence for complete re-filling (Aspöck, 2005, 2011).

Other information recorded to analyse larger datasets tackling the question of grave reopening include: position and extent of the reopening pit, area of disturbance of the skeleton (to discuss whether certain areas of the body were targeted), quantity of human remains or areas of the body remaining in the grave, objects still in the grave, objects removed from the grave and fragmentation of grave goods and bone (Neugebauer, 1991; Neugebauer-Maresch and Neugebauer, 1997; Aspöck, 2005; Kümmel, 2009; Zintl, 2012, 2019; Klevnäs, 2013; Noterman, 2015, 2016; Van Haperen, 2017) (Table 16.1).

Taphonomy of reopened collective graves

Collective graves must, by their very nature, be reopened.[3] In some of these, the reopening is only linked to the funerary practices undertaken for the body or bodies being deposited, even though the new arrival may lead to manipulation and reorganisation of the previously deposited remains. In other instances, the reopening and the manipulation of these pre-existing remains within the grave are also part of funerary practices (Déderix, Schmitt and Crevecoeur, 2018). How can archaeologists proceed to distinguish between these different situations: (1) a reopening and manipulations which are purely intended to accommodate a new corpse; (2) those which are part of a complex funerary ritual requiring the ceremonial manipulation of the preceding dead, regardless of whether or not a new deceased individual needs to be accommodated, and (3) those parts of other rituals, such as necromancy, the religious worship of certain dead individuals or beliefs that place the living under the protection of the dead, which require the reopening of graves and the manipulation and/or retrieval of the remains of certain individuals?

Ethnographic accounts indicate that distinguishing between the situations described above on the basis of material evidence within funerary contexts is difficult. Similar behaviours among different groups may relate to different beliefs, just as different behaviours may express similar beliefs (e.g. Goody, 1962; Metcalf and Huntington, 1991; Déderix, Schmitt and Crevecoeur, 2018). Additional contextual information is necessary to attempt to interpret the rite, funerary or not (Déderix, Schmitt and Crevecoeur, 2018). However, internal comparisons can be valid if contextual information is available (Goody, 1962: 38–39).

In a collective grave, while the structure is in use, the bodies are placed within an empty space that remains accessible throughout the use of the structure. If the structure is purposefully in-filled, this will occur at the end of its period of use. Displaced artefacts and remains

---

3 Despite several definitions in English for collective deposits, here, we opt for Knüsel and Robb's (2016: table 1) definition. Please note, that, to date, in French, a '*dépôt collectif*' is defined as containing only sequential deposits (Leclerc and Tarrête, 2004), though that definition is currently being revisited by some scholars (Schmitt and Déderix, 2018, 2019).

Table 16.2 Questions about collective graves to help establish if the remains contained within have been manipulated in order to arrange the contents of the grave, as part of the funerary ritual or for some other sort of rite

---

Has the burial been reopened since it was sealed? More than once?
Is a specific type of body part systematically missing from all or some individuals?
Has a particular individual been more or less affected by the manipulations than the others?
Were votive offerings to one or all the deceased added over time?
Can the extent of fragmentation and displacement be solely explained by the long-term use of the structure?
Are human remains or certain items usually found only within funerary contexts or are they also found in other types of contexts and sites?
Is there evidence at other types of sites for funerary and/or non-funerary rituals that may help explain some, if not all, of the manipulations within a collective grave?

---

within a collective grave may be a by-product of the long-term use of a structure necessitating the displacement of the remains to make room for new entries, or they may be the product of a complex ritual requiring the displacement of the remains and artefacts. In such a context, an archaeothanatological approach will help collect relevant information to aid interpretation of the sequence of events within the grave (Gerdau-Radonić, 2007, 2008; Gerdau-Radonić and Makowski, 2011; Schmitt and Déderix, 2018) (Table 16.2).

Just as for the individual graves previously discussed, in order to untangle the non-funerary from the funerary behaviour within a collective grave anomalies must be identified. The types of anomalies will vary with the nature of the archaeological evidence. For example, for graves that have been filled after use, is there a reopening pit apparent post-dating the definitive closure of the grave? Evidence for a reopening pit of this nature may be similar to that described above for reopening pits of individual graves (cf. Carmichael, 1995; Millaire, 2004; Haddow and Knüsel, 2017). For graves that were sealed, was the seal broken, or was a secondary entry point created?

It is important to stress that displaced and missing human remains and other finds may be part and parcel of the funerary ritual (Gerdau-Radonić, 2007, 2008; Gerdau-Radonić and Makowski, 2011; Déderix, Schmitt and Crevecoeur, 2018; Schmitt and Déderix, 2018). The key is, therefore, to establish if there is a pattern and whether or not the pattern can be best explained by differential preservation of skeletal remains, funerary behaviour or other activity. Are remains missing because the collective grave contains secondary deposits, because they did not preserve well, or because they have been removed as part of a ritual? Comparisons with nearby sites with a similar environment may help address the effects of differential preservation. Similarly, human remains found in non-funerary contexts, as well as items usually only associated with burials, may also help clarify whether certain goods or bone elements or parts of elements were removed. In the Andes, where ancestor worship was well-established by the time of the Spanish conquest and is well-documented through ethnohistoric accounts (Cieza de León, 1945; Guamán Poma de Ayala, 1987; Salomon, 1995; Taylor, 2001), non-funerary ritual behaviour has been identified and linked to ancestor worship practices in collective graves by identifying post-mortem manipulations out of the ordinary. The addition of selected body parts to the entrance of a tomb and the removal of lower limb bones after complete skeletonisation from an otherwise undisturbed individual in a tomb, where the remains of other individuals had been 'reduced' to make room for all the deceased, stood out as unusual, not only within the grave but also by comparison with other collective graves at the site (Gerdau-Radonić, 2007, 2008; Gerdau-Radonić and Makowski, 2011). These practices can be better explained when viewed in light of other discoveries both within- and outside of funerary contexts (Millaire 2004; Gerdau-Radonić, 2007, 2008; Gerdau-Radonić and Makowski, 2011; Haddow and Knüsel, 2017).

Case studies of reopened individual graves from the European Bronze Age and Early Medieval period

In central European cemeteries of the Early Bronze Age, many graves were reopened in the past and, in most cases, grave goods removed (Rittershofer, 1987; Neugebauer, 1991; Neugebauer-Maresch and Neugebauer, 1997; Sprenger, 1998, 1999; Kümmel, 2009: 170–172). The position of the finds and skeletal remains show that the reopening usually took place not long after burial, sometimes when bodies were not fully decomposed and empty spaces permitted movement of bones and grave goods within graves. The traditional interpretation of this activity was in the past 'grave robbery', i.e. looting driven purely by materialistic motives (e.g. Neugebauer, 1994). An alternative explanation was that valuable grave goods were recovered after a certain period and returned to the families and heirs (Hänsel and Kalicz, 1986: 52).

While a large-scale analysis of grave reopening from Early Bronze Age central Europe is still lacking, a range of research projects focussing on early medieval grave reopening across Europe has shown that this is a complex phenomenon (Aspöck, 2005, 2011, 2015; Klevnäs, 2013, 2015, 2016; Klevnäs *et al.,* 2021; Noterman, 2015, 2016; Noterman *et al.*, 2019; Van Haperen, 2010, 2013, 2016, 2017; Zintl, 2012, 2019).

From England to Transylvania, many early Medieval graves were reopened, leaving grave-goods and bones in a fragmented condition or missing altogether. The phenomenon, traditionally labelled 'grave-robbing', was often seen only as a hindrance to research. In France, for a long time, grave reopening for object removal was seen to exemplify the avarice of the Merovingians (Cochet, 1857 [1970]). As in other research traditions, such as the German-language one, this interpretation of post-depositional intervention was not based on any qualitative or quantitative analysis but was an unquestioned premise.

The very first studies on grave reopening appeared during the second half of the 20th century (Salin, 1952). In 1978, Helmut Roth published the first documented synthesis on the practice in Western Europe (Roth, 1978). Recent regional studies carried out in England (Klevnäs, 2013, 2015, 2016), the Netherlands (Van Haperen, 2010, 2013, 2016, 2017), Germany (Zintl, 2019), Austria (Aspöck, 2005, 2011), France (Noterman, 2016) and Transylvania (Dobos, 2014) are based on new methods and have shown that grave reopening is a rich source of information on European Early Medieval society. New questions have appeared following these studies and researchers now agree that personal enrichment does not seem to be the sole purpose of these acts because all case studies showed a deliberate, consistent selection of certain grave-good types (Klevnäs *et al.*, 2021; Zintl, 2019; Klevnäs, 2013; Noterman, 2016; Van Haperen, 2017).

A micro-archaeological study of a reopened Early Bronze Age grave in Austria

Background to research

As outlined above, evidence for reopening can be difficult to interpret, in particular, if the taphonomic processes of a grave are not adequately recorded. Kümmel (2009: 77) pointed out that similar types of evidence have been presented as supporting evidence for opposing interpretations. Hence, to improve the understanding of the archaeological evidence of reopened inhumation graves and to create a reference for future analyses, microstratigraphic excavations of a reopened inhumation grave (object 229, MNR 32026.13.03, Gst. 1023/439-444) at the Early Bronze Age cemetery of Weiden am See, eastern Austria, were carried out (Aspöck and Banerjea, 2016; Franz *et al.*, 2017; Aspöck, 2018). The cemetery belongs to the so-called Wieselburg/Gáta Culture (2000–1600 BCE, Bronze Age A2). The Wieselburg/Gáta Culture cemeteries are characterised by up to a few hundred individual graves. The deceased were buried in a flexed or hyperflexed position, furnished with jewellery, copper alloy objects (e.g. daggers) and sometimes large sets of pottery (Hicke, 1987; Leeb, 1987; Krenn-Leeb, 2011; Nagy, 2013). A reconstruction of the excavation process was created based on the 3D model of the excavated surfaces (Aspöck and Banerjea, 2016:Video 1, which can be viewed at https://doi.org/10.1016/j.jasrep.2016.07.003).

In this high-resolution case study, archaeothanatology was extended to the analysis of the disturbed skeletal elements – the position of each of the disturbed remains was recorded as an aid to identifying the actions carried out on the skeleton when the grave was reopened. A model of a complete skeleton was positioned on the grave plan to indicate the estimated position of the corpse as a reference (see below regarding Figure 16.7). The disturbed bone was found intermingled, but it also showed some layering, i.e. bone elements appeared above or below each other, which enabled analysis of the sequence of the actions – which bones were moved first, which ones later (Aspöck, 2018: Appendix B).

Results: anthropogenic and natural post-depositional processes

At excavation of grave feature 229 (MNR 32026.13.03, Gst. 1023/439-444), individual 1 (an adult probable male) was found immediately below the surface in a prone position surrounded by a setting of large stones (Figure 16.5). Individual 1 was a primary deposition, and the body moved from a position on the left side to a prone position in the early stages of decomposition. No evidence for anthropogenic post-depositional manipulation was found.

The formation processes of reopened grave feature 229 include slow-acting, natural, long-term processes and human activity (rapid, short-term processes (cf. Aspöck, 2018: figure 16.8). The uneven position of individual 1 was at least partly caused through taphonomic processes related to individual 2 underneath (Figure 16.6). The slumping vertebral column of individual 1 may have resulted from the decomposition of the large volume of soft tissue in that area, as well as the perishing of organic material, such as coffin boards (Blaizot, 1998) and the compaction of the fill of the reopening pit underneath. The descending of the lower limbs is very likely related to the collapse of the coffin of individual 2 below. This causal connection between the formation processes of individual 1 (deposit 1) and individual 2 (deposit 2) supports the inference of a short time interval between the two depositions – at variance with the statistical results of the C14 measurements which provided a 95% probability of 1970–1850 BCE calendar years for individual 2 and 1780–1660 BCE for individual 1, hence that 150 to 250 years had passed between deposition of individual 2 at the bottom of the grave and the burial of the upper individual 1 (Aspöck and Banerjea, 2016).

Beneath deposit 1, evidence for a reopening pit was found in the form of a funnel-like structure in the western half of the grave pit. At the bottom of the grave, the outline of a coffin with 'handles', typical of Wieselburg-Gáta culture (Krenn-Leeb, 2011), appeared, and a dark fill defined the outline of the area of disturbance (Figure 16.5). Inside the coffin, the human remains of individual 2 (male, aged 25 to 35 years at death) beneath the dark fill were disturbed, while the lower part of the vertebral column, the pelvic girdle and the lower limbs (in flexed position) were not affected by the disturbance. The positioning of these undisturbed bones shows a pattern typical for a body decomposing in an empty space and indicates that the upper body of

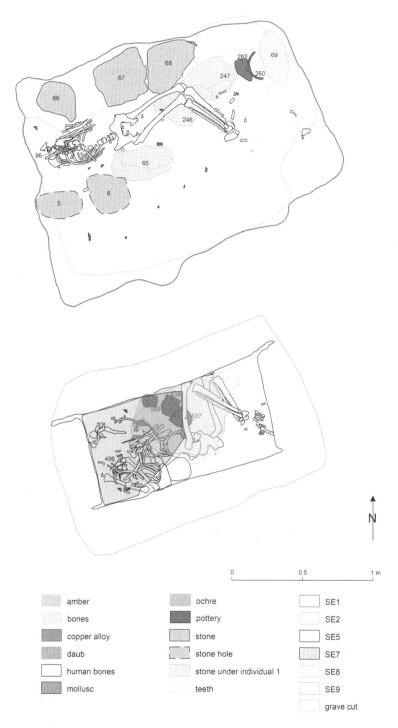

Figure 16.5 Individual 1 (top) and individual 2 (bottom) from grave feature 229 at Weiden am See 2013 (SE refers to stratigraphic units) (Austrian Federal Monuments Authority Identifier: MNR 32026.13.03, Gst. 1023/439-444) (Images: I. Petschko and M. Börner; Concept: E. Aspöck; Reproduced from Aspöck, 2018; with permission of Elsevier Publishing Company).

Figure 16.6 The lower limbs of the uppermost individual 1 were positioned above part of the coffin of individual 2, at the bottom of the grave, which remained intact after the reopening – and decomposed at a later stage. The slumping vertebral column of individual 1 was above the re-fill of the reopening pit (Images: S. Štuhec; Concept: E. Aspöck; Reproduced from Aspöck, 2018; with permission of Elsevier Publishing Company).

individual 2 had also moved into a semi-prone position post-depositionally. Individual 2 was a primary deposit found with three pots and the shaft of a copper alloy pin.

Despite the disturbance, the skeleton of individual 2 was well preserved (Keller, 2014; Aspöck, 2018: Appendix B). No breakages related to the reopening of the grave were found, i.e. all bone breakages were post-mortem, not peri-mortem and may have been related to soil pressure (Wahl and König 1987: 122; Keller, 2013; Keller and Teschler-Nicola, 2013). There was little bone loss, and all the disturbed bone was found intermingled within a defined area of disturbance at the bottom of the coffin – without any vertical displacement. This evidence indicates that the coffin was still intact when the grave was reopened, which means that there was still an empty space which permitted bone movement without leading to bone damage.

The possible sequence of actions that were carried out with the human remains of individual 2 during the reopening was reconstructed based on the analysis of the positioning of the bones and the direction of their movements (Figure 16.7) (Aspöck, 2018). The coffin was broken into in the area where the skull would have been positioned, and the cranium and mandible were the first bones to have been moved. This may have been done to create a space to stand or to crouch. Additionally, such a procedure would have caused minimal damage to the human remains. An area to the west of the primary position of the head was devoid of bone and may be where

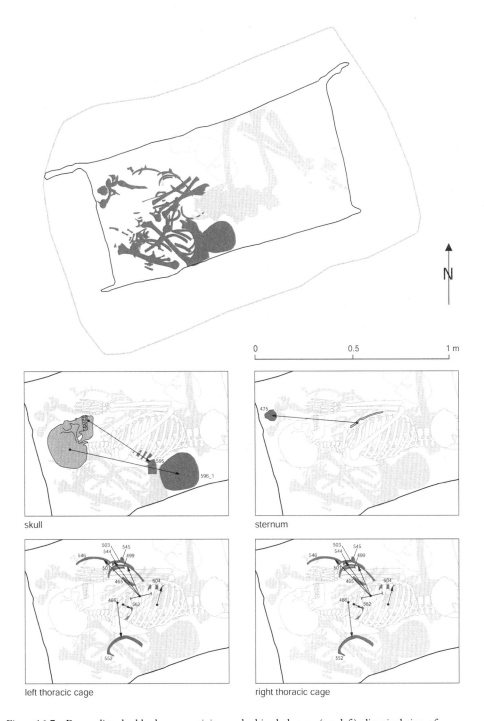

Figure 16.7   Bones disturbed by human activity marked in dark grey (top left); disarticulation of bones using the estimated position of the corpse as a reference (Images: S. Fragner; Concept: E. Aspöck; Reproduced from Aspöck, 2018 with permission of Elsevier Publishing Company). *(Continued on next page)*

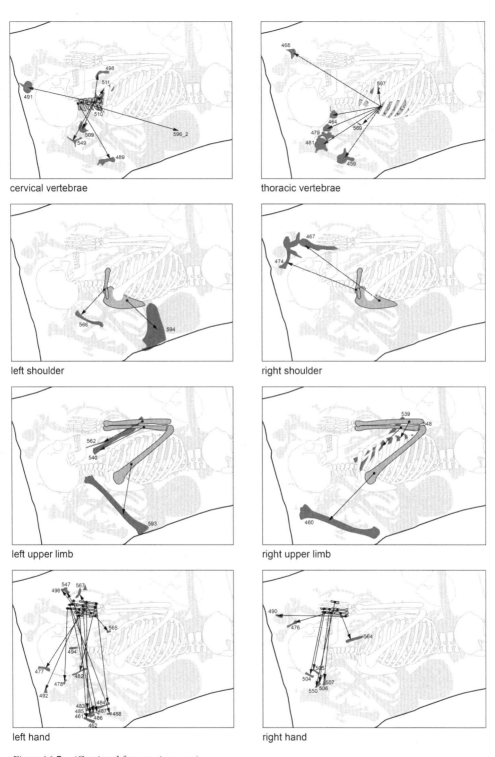

cervical vertebrae

thoracic vertebrae

left shoulder

right shoulder

left upper limb

right upper limb

left hand

right hand

Figure 16.7   (Continued from previous page)

the person was positioned. There was very little space and little bone damage, which makes it unlikely that two people entered the coffin at the same time. The person then continued moving the cervical vertebrae and hand bones in several directions. Then the bones further away were shifted starting with the right humerus, sternum and right shoulder. The superior three right ribs were moved last. Often more than one bone was grabbed at once (e.g. several ribs seem to have been shifted together). Some bones were moved while still in articulation, which may be due to differential preservation within the coffin or skeletal elements had been held together by organic material. Many of the remains were displaced to the south of the primary position of the thoracic cage and cranium of the buried male. Assuming that the person was crouching in order to access the grave, he or she would have been facing the dead body in order to see what they were doing, and thus it is likely that most of the action would have been carried out with the right hand. It seems no tools were used because all the displaced bones would have been within reach of the hands, and the lower part of the body remained undisturbed.

Thirteen hand bones and two ribs of individual 2 showed green coloration (Keller, 2014), but only the shaft of a copper alloy pin was found. Green marks on bones from reopened graves may result from coppery alloy objects in their original position, from objects that have been moved upon reopening (secondary position) or objects that were removed from a grave, if they were in the grave long enough to cause green marks on bone (Sprenger, 1998, 1999). In this case, the shaft of the copper alloy pin was likely to have been found in a secondary position, but it had left green marks on other bones before it was moved during the reopening. Nevertheless, there are still too many green-coloured bones to result from only one pin and no fragments of other copper alloy objects were present in the grave (it is unlikely that any fragments would have been missed, as all the sediment was wet-sieved). Copper alloy objects found in comparable graves that may have caused green colorations of the hand bones and ribs – and which may have been removed upon reopening – include jewellery such as necklaces with copper alloy beads and rings, torcs and small daggers (Sauer, 2009; Krenn-Leeb, 2011; Nagy, 2013).

The results show that those who entered the grave removed copper alloy objects. It seems that the people who took the grave goods avoided damaging the bone and that searching the skeleton was done very systematically and without tools by a single person only at a time. Hence, the evidence points to there not being any hostile attitude towards the dead person or the burying community, and it questions the long-established picture that strangers or enemies of the burying community looted the graves to gain access to copper-alloy objects, without any respect for the dead. An analysis of a larger number of reopened Early Bronze Age graves will show if this interpretation is supported by more cases.

Case studies from France: early medieval grave reopenings

Recent regional studies of grave reopening in Early Medieval Europe

Recent regional syntheses on post-depositional disturbances have totalled more than 7000 early medieval graves from almost 80 sites (Zintl, 2019; Klevnäs, 2013; Klevnäs *et al.*, 2021; Noterman 2016b; Van Haperen, 2017; Noterman *et al.*, 2020). About 50% of these graves had been reopened, showing that this was not a rare practice, but that post-burial intervention has been present in Western Europe for several centuries. Differences exist between the regions studied, or even within the regions themselves, due to the complexity of the early medieval practices. Nevertheless, these regional analyses produce common results. Grave reopening occurred between the 6th and 7th centuries AD in cemeteries that were still in use. Graves of juveniles were not spared from disturbances and represent, for example, 13% of cases in France (Noterman, 2016) and

56% of those in a German case study (Zintl, 2019). The selection of distinct types of grave goods is common to all regions studied. Objects with an economic and symbolic meaning, such as swords, seaxes and fibulae, were targeted for removal. The rate of disturbance between female and male graves does not differ much, except in the Netherlands, where those responsible for the reopenings seem to have prioritised male burials with grave goods (Van Haperen, 2017).

Archaeothanatological applications to grave reopenings in the Grand Est region, France

The application of the tenets of archaeothanatology to early medieval reopened graves in France (Chenal and Barrand-Emam, 2014; Noterman 2016) is fundamental to the study of reopening practices and contributes to the dating of reopenings, the identification of the objects taken, and many other elements. The following examples are from a recent study of 332 graves from the French Grand Est region (Noterman 2016). Of these graves, 46% were reopened.

To understand the background of grave reopening, it is necessary to determine how much time passed between burial and the reopening (see above, categories A–D). In most of the early medieval cases, the practice took place when grave furnishings such as wooden containers were still well or partially preserved and therefore when the empty space within graves had not been completely filled. In most cases, the bodies were completely – or almost completely – decomposed.

These elements suggest that grave reopening occurred while the funerary space was still actively used, as attested in Vitry-sur-Orne (Lorraine, France). At this early medieval site, several graves were used for successive inhumations (Guillotin and Mauduit, 2012). In the undisturbed graves, the bodies appeared to touch each other; there was no soil between them. Graves were covered by a lid that maintained an empty space during decomposition of the bodies. It also suggests that these particular structures were built in order to be opened multiple times and not only for a single burial.

Grave 108 presents at least four successive phases of deposition (Figure 16.8). The first two adult males (Individuals 1 and 2) were deposited and their remains were collected and set aside (*réduction*) before the burial of the third individual (Individual 3). Their bones were mostly located in the eastern part of the grave. It is interesting to note that individual 1 was not completely decomposed during the movement of the remains: the cranium was still articulated with the atlas, and the sacrum with the last lumbar vertebra. Individual 3, an adult male, was supine, head to the west, with the upper limbs in extension. Very few bones were disturbed: the left *os coxae*, a fragment of the sacrum, the right tibia and fragments of the right fibula were moved beyond the original space occupied by the body. The nature of this disturbance is difficult to specify and may be the result of an anthropogenic intervention or the consequence of the burial of individuals 4 and 5. The last two deposits (Individuals 4 and 5) appeared to have been partially disturbed. Initially, individual 4, an adult male, was placed supinely in the centre of the burial structure before being 'pulled' towards the western end of the pit. Displaced bones are located to the east of the structure, in contact with the bone from the reductions of individuals 1 and 2. The same can be observed in the case of individual 5, an adult female, who is in close proximity to the previous human deposit. Despite the disturbances, several anatomical connections were maintained during the manipulation of the two individuals (Individuals 4 and 5), which means that decomposition was not yet fully completed and/or textile elements preserved the anatomical coherence of the bodies.

The disturbance took place in an empty space, in which bones were displaced towards the bottom of the grave and were found in direct contact with each other, as well as between

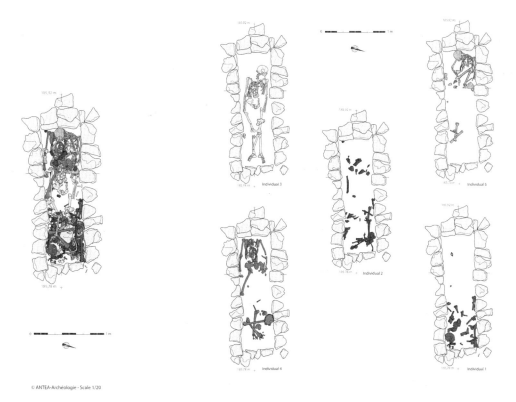

© ANTEA-Archéologie - Scale 1/20

Figure 16.8 At least four successive phases of deposition in grave 108 at Vitry-sur-Orne (Moselle, Lorraine, France) (Guillotin and Mauduit, 2012; reproduced with permission of Antea Archéologie; Habsheim, France).

successive deposits. It is therefore very likely that the reopenings occurred during the continued use of the site. Similar examples in Vitry-sur-Orne suggest that the burying community had knowledge of and perhaps even a certain tolerance for the practice. Some 50% of the burials of the site were reopened and most of them in a similar way to that of grave 108. (Guillotin and Mauduit, 2012; Noterman, 2016).

The selection of grave goods can be examined in various ways: a comparison of the number and types of grave goods between undisturbed graves and reopened graves, the discovery of fragments from a missing artefact, as well as from the taphonomic study of the skeletal remains (Noterman, 2016). In the latter case, displacement of one or a small number of bones in a limited area may indicate the removal of a particular type of object. At the site of Illfurth (Alsace, France), weapons were present in 84% of male graves (Roth-Zehner and Cartier, 2007; Noterman, 2016). All of the seaxes recovered came from intact graves. The large majority were placed on the left side of the body (13 cases) and at or near the area of the pelvis (23 cases). Only two seaxes were found on the right side of skeletons, on or under the right upper limb. When analysing the reopened graves and comparing them with undisturbed graves, it is in some cases possible to determine whether or not a weapon, either a sword or seax, had been taken. From 19 reopened graves containing weapon elements, nine individuals had sustained disturbances of the pelvic region of the skeleton. The disturbance of the entire skeleton was rare, with only four cases observed.

Figure 16.9 Grave 186 (Illfurth, Haut-Rhin, Alsace, France) shows a very precise disturbance in the pelvic area. Small bronze rivets from a weapon scabbard were discovered near the left elbow (number 4). The iron belt had not been removed (numbers 1 to 3), attesting to selective removal from this grave (Roth-Zehner and Cartier, 2007; Reproduced with permission of Antea Archéologie, Habsheim, France).

The study of the disturbance of the *ossa coxae* and adjoining bones (femora, lumbar vertebrae) or elements that were spatially close (forearm and hand) may provide evidence for the removal of a seax. In grave 186, the left forearm, left *os coxae* and left femur were moved (Figure 16.9). No other skeletal disturbance related to a post-depositional intervention is visible in this funerary structure. Fourteen small bronze rivets from the remains of a weapon scabbard were discovered near the left forearm. All these observations lead to the conclusion that a weapon, presumably a seax, had been collected at Illfurth. Those responsible for the reopening of the grave were probably mainly interested in this particular artefact and left behind elements from an iron belt, an iron knife and a bronze coin – all were still in place on or near the body at the time of the excavation.

Observation of bone displacement, sometimes associated with the presence of residual metallic elements in the grave, may also attest to the removal of dress accessories such as brooches or buckle-plates. As in any study of grave reopenings, it is necessary to compare intact graves with disturbed graves to determine what may or may not have been taken based on the pattern of the deposition of objects. Knowledge of the burial customs of a region is necessary to identify an incomplete pair of fibulae or fragmentary belt, for example.

The removal of the elements of a belt is attested at the site of Illfurth (Alsace, France). Individual 30, a male, presents a disturbance targeted at the pelvic region (Roth-Zehner and Cartier, 2007): lumbar vertebrae, sacrum and the left *os coxae* had been disturbed and fragmented (Figure 16.10). Several fragments of objects, including the remains of a belt were discovered scattered from the lower part of the thorax to the femora. It seems, therefore, that a dress accessory was taken when the grave was reopened, and that the latter must have been in a poor state of preservation. The upper limbs and femora were undisturbed, which rules out the possibility of the removal of a weapon (seax or sword). Individual 206, a female, has been disturbed in two specific areas: the neck and pelvic regions (Roth-Zehner and Cartier, 2007) (Figure 16.11). The cranium and mandible, the cervical vertebrae, left scapula and left clavicle had been moved. The lower thoracic and lumbar vertebrae, the *ossa coxae* and the left forearm and hand were also disturbed. The only grave goods found were necklace beads and an iron knife. The location of the disturbances and the sex of the deceased suggest the removal of a belt and perhaps jewellery placed at the neck and on the left hemi-thorax (perhaps a fibula?).

Conclusions of French early medieval case studies

In the early Middle Ages, the practice of grave reopening covers a large part of France, but it is undoubtedly in the east that it is the most common. The different examples presented in this chapter attest that a disturbed grave can provide considerable information about the type of objects deposited with the deceased, the type of burial structure, such as a coffin or chamber, and other funerary practices. If focussing only on the Grand Est region of France, several points should be noted: weapons seem to be removed more frequently in the cemeteries in this region than in the other parts of France; female graves are slightly more targeted by reopenings in the eastern regions; in most cases, the disturbances are limited and affect only a small part of the skeleton (Noterman, 2016). The sites of Illfurth and Vitry-sur-Orne demonstrate that a thorough study of disturbed graves is possible, provided that all elements constituting the grave are taken into account, including the skeletal remains, grave goods, the type of burial container and the possible filling anomalies, which in certain circumstances represent the main argument to identify a reopening (Gubellini, Cense-Bacquet and Wilusz, 2013).

Recent studies (Aspöck, 2005, 2011; Klenäs *et al.*, 2021) have shown that the large majority of reopenings occurred during the on-going use of the cemeteries, on skeletonised bodies, and before the collapse of the container and the filling of the funerary structure. The comparison between regional studies of early medieval grave reopening attests to similarities in its manifestation across western and central Europe. The regularity of the reopening during the same historical period, its frequency in cemeteries, and the selection of objects without regard for the value of their metal constituents are arguments against the *ad hoc* classification of the phenomenon as materialistic 'grave-robbing'.

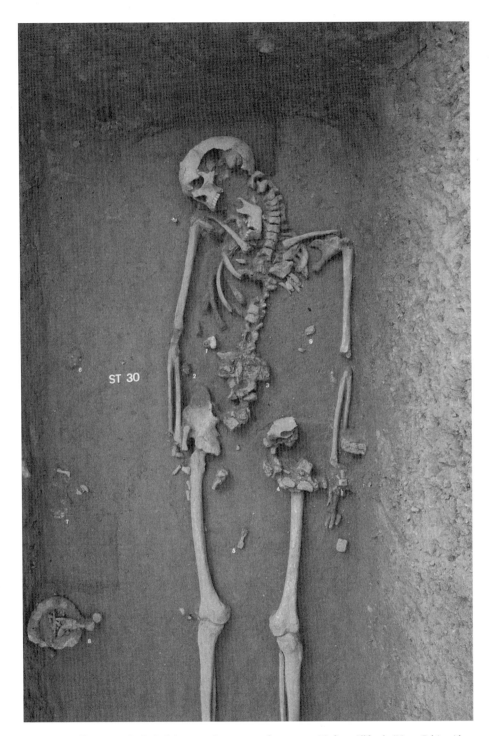

Figure 16.10 The removal of a belt but not the weapon from grave 30 from Illfurth (Haut-Rhin, Alsace, France) caused very little disturbance to the skeleton: only the lumbar vertebrae, the sacrum and the left *os coxae* were moved. The various iron components of a belt (numbers 2 and 3) are still in place (Roth-Zehner and Cartier, 2007; Reproduced with permission of Antea Archéologie, Habsheim, France).

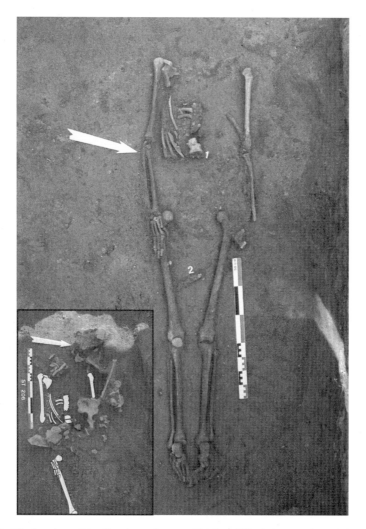

Figure 16.11 The location of the disturbance in grave 206 from Illfurth (Haut-Rhin, Alsace, France) suggests that a belt and a piece of jewellery had been removed during the reopening. The displaced bones appear just above the skeleton (in white) in a very limited area, probably corresponding to the limits of the reopening pit (Roth-Zehner and Cartier, 2007; Reproduced with permission of Antea Archéologie, Habsheim, France).

Case study of a displaced funerary deposit from the Andes

Funerary treatment in the Andes

Before the 16th century, funerary treatment in the Andes varied through time and across geographic space from individual to collective graves, from purposefully dug-out pit graves to tombs built under natural rock outcrops, from extended to flexed bodies, sometimes including mummification. By the time of the Spanish Conquest (1532), in the majority of the Inca Empire, individuals were buried as funerary bundles (Figure 16.12). Their upper and lower limbs were flexed, and the individual was placed upright, as if squatting, on a woven basket and wrapped in textiles, which were held together

Figure 16.12 A. CF1, ranging rod 1m; B. CF2 funerary bundle, scale 10 cm. The individual is on his back and not in an upright position as is usual in the region. This may be due to the fact he has been displaced from his original burial context (see text); C. Individual 0, CF1, represented by the cranium and articulated mandible, the cervical and superior lumbar vertebrae, the sternum, right upper ribs, clavicle and scapula, scale 10 cm (Images courtesy of Professor K. Makowski, Programa arqueológico Escuela de Campo Valle de Pachacamac–Pontificia Universidad Católica del Perú (PATL–PUCP)).

by rope. Accoutrements, when present, were placed within the wrappings. Differences in status were displayed through selective mummification and the accoutrements and textiles, quantity and quality, used to wrap the body, as well as through rituals. Once the body was bundled it could be buried in an individual dug-out grave within a cemetery or in long-term collective tombs purposefully built above ground or under natural rock shelters. High-status males and community leaders were the focus of an elaborate ancestor worship cult, which involved the funerary bundle, containing all or parts of the remains, participating in regular rituals, for divination or for worship, and regularly receiving renewed offerings (Salomon, 1995; Isbell, 1997; Taylor, 2001).

Reopened graves in the Andes

Reopened graves are a long-standing component of the Andean archaeological landscape, whether reopened for ritual reasons, to desecrate or for monetary gain (looting). Historic and modern looting associated with the illicit trade in the antiquities has contributed greatly to the large numbers of reopened, disturbed and emptied graves that are found across the region, as did the 17th-century policy of the Catholic Church of converting the indigenous population to Christianity and 'extirpating idolatries' ('*Extirpación de Idolatrías*'; Arriaga, 1920; Duviols, 1971) by calling for the destruction of non-Christian graves. In the case of looting, though looted sites are often identified and studied, only the intact structures within those sites are excavated, the looted

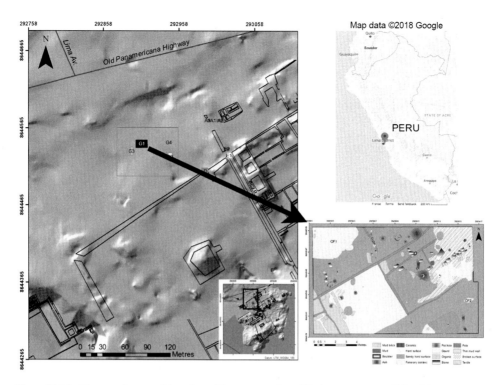

Figure 16.13 Excavated area and location of human remains of Pachacamac, a pre-Columbian sanctuary (Pachacamac plans courtesy of Professor K. Makowski, Programa arqueológico Escuela de Campo Valle de Pachacamac–Pontificia Universidad Católica del Perú (PATL–PUCP)).

structures are considered too 'damaged' or 'contaminated' to yield any useful information. At best, what is left is hastily recovered with little effort made to provide any further contextual information. This is unfortunate because some seemingly recently looted graves (within the last 100 to 150 years) may have been reopened in the past as part of prehistoric looting, for ritual desecration to dishonour the dead, or to extirpate idolatries during the colonial period (Arriaga, 1920; Duviols, 1971). By ignoring reopened graves considered too damaged or to have been looted in modern times, archaeologists may be missing important information on cultural practices from prehistory and historic times. Yet, it is the systematic approach of archaeothanatology that enables researchers to move past the 'disturbance' generated by the subsequent manipulation of the remains and retrieve evidence pertaining to the original deposit (cf. Gerdau-Radonić and Herrera, 2010).

Pachacamac

Pachacamac is a pre-Columbian sanctuary (Figure 16.13), today at the boundary of the southern suburbs of Lima, Peru. The site has a long history of continuous occupation dating as far back as the 2nd century and up to the 16th century AD, culminating in an important Inca oracle (*circa* AD 1470–1533; Eeckhout, 2013; Makowski and Vallenas, 2015). Since 2005, a team led by Professor K. Makowski has undertaken research in the northern and southern sections of the site in order to understand the role of the architecture, the entry and transit routes to the site, and where the construction workers and pilgrims resided (Makowski, 2016).

In 2011, human remains were found in two deposits, CF1 and CF2 (Figures 16.12 and 16.13), dating to the Late Horizon (LH) Inca occupation (*circa* 1470–1533 AD), but nothing on the surface or the surrounding layers indicated their presence. CF2 appeared as a shallow grave, 40 cm under the surface, with three *adobe* bricks located 15cm above the body. Additionally, the team was unable to determine the north and west limits of the hollow identified as CF1 or the opening and limits of the hollow containing CF2. Furthermore, both deposits were in an area destined for temporary LH encampments and workshops (Makowski, 2016) and appear as the last anthropogenic events in the area. The hollow containing CF1 disrupted the pre-existing LH structures (Makowski, 2011).

None of the authors participated in the excavation, but KGR was asked to analyse the remains and to provide an archaeothanatological assessment of the deposit based on photographs, drawings and other field records. Archaeothanatology was not originally meant to be applied to images but was intended for the field. Notwithstanding, an assessment can be made through visual field records, though the situation is not ideal and helps to highlight in some instances the information that is missing.

The finds

The hollow identified as funerary deposit CF1 was not excavated entirely, as it partially fell outside the excavation area. The minimum number of individuals in CF1 was estimated as 10. Notwithstanding, most skeletal elements represented only three or four individuals. The remains of CF1 consisted of juveniles and adult males and females. CF2 consisted of an adult male (based on the use of the analytical methods in Webb and Suchey, 1985; Albert and Maples, 1995; Scheuer and Black, 2000; Murail *et al.*, 2005).

The complete individuals were found in a flexed position, both upper and lower limbs flexed and placed anterior to the torso. This position is associated with a funerary bundle as described above and like the one found in CF2 (Figure 16.12B). It is likely that the incomplete individuals from CF1 had also been in that flexed position originally as this is the standard burial position for the region and time period. Though the remains were buried when found and were excavated, two of the crania and a few isolated skeletal remains from CF1 showed evidence of weathering (discolouration).

There were no associated accoutrements in either context, except for two ceramic vessels found in CF1 under two individuals. The remains of a dog, fully articulated and with its fur preserved, were also found in CF1. The human remains nearer the surface in CF1 were few, incomplete and disarticulated – although the partial remains of individual 0 were fully articulated (Figure 16.12C). Further below the surface and towards the northwest corner of the excavated area in CF1, the remains were more numerous and individuals were complete and articulated.

Discussion

The disposition of the remains in CF1 and CF2 appears as the result of an intentional disturbance of at least one funerary context, most probably in search of valuable objects. The hollows identified as CF1 and CF2 are not graves but the place in which the remains from one or several funerary deposits ended up after an episode of looting. The lack of well-delimited edges for CF1, the location of CF2 and its shallow depth (40 cm), the lack of funerary architecture, the sediment covering the remains, which is indistinguishable from the surface sediment, and the fact that the deposits represent the last anthropogenic events in the sector provide further support for the argument that CF1 and CF2 represent the contents of disturbed funerary deposits but are not the actual graves. Arguably, the pattern is such that the remains in CF1 appear to have been dragged towards the surface and the southeast. As they were displaced and searched for goods (the accoutrements were traditionally placed within the funerary bundles), skeletal elements fell from the bundles and were disassociated. Moreover, in the Andes, burials at a shallow depth are unknown.

The disturbance is unlikely to date to modern or colonial times though, by all accounts, it has the hallmarks of looting: disregard for the human remains and few grave goods remaining. From experience, modern disturbances leave evidence of their own time: cigarette butts, plastic bags, *etc.* The Spanish also leave evidence of their presence early on (Murphy *et al.*, 2010; Klaus and Tam, 2015; Klaus, 2016), but the contexts provide no evidence other than that from the Late Horizon. Moreover, the Spanish destruction of non-Christian graves during colonial times consisted of both desecration and looting. The bodies were removed and disposed of as required by law (Arriaga, 1920; Duviols, 1971). Some grave goods and accoutrements, especially metal ones, were considered valuable, but the remainder needed to be destroyed. Consequently, graves targeted during the campaign would be emptied of all their contents and everything would be taken or destroyed (including the bodies). In this particular instance, the bodies and some grave goods (probably missed by the intruders) remain. It is therefore likely the disturbance occurred during pre-Columbian times or very early in the colonial period but was not linked to the Extirpation of Idolatries campaign (Arriaga, 1920).

Moreover, in Andean reopening rituals, an effort was made to preserve the original burial deposit, including any funerary architecture, even if that only amounted to a dug-out pit. Where individual pits were reopened to remove or add items or remains, the original configuration of the deposit remained evident, and only those parts that needed to be disturbed for access or to re-arrange and re-organise items hold clues to the reopening by way of anomalies (Carmichael, 1995: 177; Millaire, 2004). In collective graves, the architecture was maintained intact, and though remains may be commingled, these are maintained within the structure. Destruction of graves, including the architecture, and withdrawal of the remains where these are not taken elsewhere for curation does occur in Andean prehistory. An example of such an occurrence has been accounted for by the re-use of the funerary space (and surviving funerary goods) by a later popu-lation (Gerdau-Radonić, 2007; Makowski *et al.*, 2012). As such, the disturbance at Pachacamac may be pre-colonial despite no subsequent occupation to attest to this.

Considering the degree of preservation of the individual in CF2 (including hair, soft tissue and fly pupae) and that of the well-articulated individuals and the dog in CF1, the individuals were either mummified or not fully decomposed when the disturbance occurred. Individual 0 (CF1), for example, closest to the surface, consisted of a well-articulated skeleton of the cephalic extremity and upper thorax (Figure 16.12C). The soft tissue holding the cervical and thoracic joints in articulation had not decomposed when the bundle was displaced. When displaced, the head was separated from the torso. Moreover, towards the northwest corner of the excavated area in CF1 there are scattered bones that appear as if thrown towards that area, rather than carefully placed or pushed aside (Figure 16.12A).

Because the remains have been disturbed, it is not possible to conclude when exactly during the use-life of the associated structures the burials had been made and subsequently destroyed. Although the reasons remain unknown, taking valuable objects was at least one of them, since the bundles appear to have been searched for accoutrements. Signs of weathering on some of the bones indicate that these were left at least partially uncovered and exposed to the elements but were progressively re-buried over time by the surrounding surface sand. Though Pachacamac is located near the mouth of the river Lurin, the site is in the desert that runs along the Peruvian coast and, before massive urbanisation started in the latter half of the 20th century, it was surrounded by sand dunes. Consequently, the dunes progressively covered the remains, which were once again uncovered in the 21st century by archaeologists.

The categories applied to the Bronze Age and early medieval Merovingian graves to determine the time elapsed between burials and reopening cannot be applied here because of different environmental conditions. Hair, fur and desiccated tendons and ligaments are still preserved, which would place these burials into category B above, not only at the time of the original disturbance but also at the excavation. Sand is highly permeable, permitting the decomposition fluids to flow. The muscular mass of soft tissue and the organs decompose but the ligaments and tendons desiccate and can be preserved for several hundred years. It is not unusual in the Peruvian central coast to find 1000-year-old remains with desiccated ligaments and tendons. Consequently, in this case, category B (still in the process of decay) can cover several hundred years.

It may be possible, though it appears unlikely in the cultural context, that the integrity of the skeletal remains and their tidy disposition was of no concern, particularly if enough time had elapsed between death and the ritual reopening, as for the European examples above. The pattern here does not fit other examples encountered in the area for the same or preceding periods showcasing examples of ritual grave reopening (Menzel 1976: 223-229; Carmichael, 1995; Millaire, 2004; Gerdau-Radonić, 2008; Gerdau-Radonić and Makowski, 2011) or colonial grave desecration (Arriaga, 1920; Duviols, 1971). In the Andes, disregard for the remains is a hallmark of looting, colonial desecration, and for reclaiming the funerary space. On the contrary, ritual activities showcased respect for the remains in the form of careful curation of skeletal elements (Menzel 1976: 223–229; Carmichael, 1995; Millaire, 2004; Gerdau-Radonić, 2008; Gerdau-Radonić and Makowski, 2011).

Conclusion

The careful and detailed analysis of the skeletal evidence under the guiding aegis of the archaeothanatological approach contributes to all the questions traditionally asked regarding reopened graves (Tables 16.1 and 16.2). However, areas which have been little covered by the traditionally-applied archaeological methods and where archaeothanatology contributes substantially are the analysis and identification of the original layout of the grave before reopening, the understanding of the state of decomposition of the remains upon reopening and the distinction between natural and human processes in the formation of a reopened grave.

Archaeothanatology is essential for the analysis of the original layout of the grave because it helps to identify the initial position of the deposited bodies and their burial environment. This helps to answer some questions surrounding the reasons for the reopening of graves, such as if specific types of graves and individuals had been targeted. What was the original layout of the grave? What was the original body position and furnishing of the body?

Furthermore, archaeothanatology contributes greatly to answer the question of the timing of the reopening. Detailed observations of the articulations of the human remains can be used to determine whether the body was already fully skeletonised or still partly in articulation (Duday et al., 1990; Duday, 2006). The case studies in this chapter highlight the importance of taking environmental factors into account and show that the criteria for the timing of reopening has to be defined for different types of funerary evidence and natural environments.

The most important observations relating to the questions posed by reopened graves are made during excavation. However, standard excavation protocols tend to ignore information pertaining to the intrusive cuts (location and size) or the exact position of the finds (grave goods, bones) in relation to the extent of the reopening pit, the funerary architecture and the skeletal remains, as these are not always considered relevant.

Consequently, the improvement of protocols for data collection during the excavation of reopened graves is imperative to facilitate the work of osteoarchaeologists and post-excavation analyses. One of the authors (AN) is reviewing the anthropological recording form devised by Meiklejohn and Constandse-Westermann in 1978 and reviewed by Courtaud in 1996 so as to make it applicable to reopened graves (Meiklejohn and Constandse-Westermann, 1978; Courtaud, 1996). In order to gather and record data in the most complete, clear and fastest way possible, the new protocol will take into account all the elements related to the disturbance, such as the location of artefacts and bones in the grave, consequences of the reopening on the integrity of the remains, and extent and shape of the reopening pit. Standardised recording of information collected in the field will permit understanding of these practices regionally, and enable cross-regional comparisons and quantification.

Acknowledgements

The authors would like to thank the editors for inviting them to contribute to this volume.

EA thanks the following people for their contributions to the figures: Irene Petschko and Mario Börner (Figure 16.5), Seta Štuhec (Figure 16.6) and Stefanie Fragner (Figure 16.7). The analysis of the case study of Weiden am See was supported by a Hertha Firnberg post-doctoral fellowship from the Austrian Science Fund (FWF): T595-G19.

KGR would like to thank Prof K. Makowski and his team from the Pontificia Universidad Católica del Perú for letting her study the material from Pachacamac and for the Pachacamac figures (Figures 16.12 and 16.13). Analysis of the Pachacamac remains was carried out thanks to a Santander Travel Grant through Bournemouth University and funding from Asociación Atocongo granted to Prof Makowski's team.

AN would like to thank Hélène Barrand-Emam (Antea Archéologie, France) and Benjamin Tixier (Éveha, France) for allowing her to access and use their data in this chapter.

References

Albert, A.M. and Maples, W.R. (1995). Stages of Epiphyseal Union for Thoracic and Lumbar Vertebral Centra as a Method of Age Determination for Teenage and Young Adult Skeletons. *Journal of Forensic Sciences*, 40(4), pp. 623–633.

Alduc-Le Bagousse, A., ed. (2009). *Inhumations de prestige ou prestige de l'inhumation? Expressions du pouvoir dans l'au-delà (IVe-XVe siècle)*. Caen: Publications du Centre de recherches archéologiques et historiques anciennes et médiévales (Craham).

Annaert, R. and Verslype L. (2010). Les dispositifs et les rites funéraires durant le haut Moyen Âge (fin du Ve-Xe siècle). In: S. Balace and A. De Poorter, eds., *Entre Paradis et Enfer. Mourir au Moyen Âge, 600-1600. Exposition du 2 décembre 2010 au 24 avril 2011 aux Musées Royaux d'Art et d'Histoire, Bruxelles*. Bruxelles: Fonds Mercator, Musées royaux d'art et d'histoire, pp. 99–113.

Arriaga, P.J. de (1920 [1621]). *La extirpación de la idolatría en el Perú*. Cuzco: Centro de Estudios Regionales Andinos 'Bartolomé de las Casas'.

Aspöck, E. (2005). Graböffnungen im Frühmittelalter und das Fallbeispiel der langobardenzeitlichen Gräber von Brunn am Gebirge, Flur Wolfholz, Niederösterreich. *Archaeologia Austriaca*, 87, pp. 225–264.

Aspöck, E. (2011). Past 'Disturbances' of Graves as a Source: Taphonomy and Interpretation of Reopened Early Medieval Inhumation Graves at Brunn am Gebirge (Austria) and Winnall II (England). *Oxford Journal of Archaeology*, 30(3), pp. 299–324.

Aspöck, E. (2015). Funerary and Post-Depositional Body Treatments at the Middle Anglo-Saxon Cemetery Winnall II: Norm, Variety and Forms of Deviance? In: Z. L. Devlin and E.-J. Graham, ed., *Death Embodied. Archaeological Approaches to the Treatment of the Corpse*. Oxford: Oxbow Books, pp. 86–108.

Aspöck, E. (2018). A High-Resolution Approach to the Formation Processes of a Reopened Early Bronze Age Inhumation Grave in Austria: Taphonomy of Human Remains. *Quaternary International*, 474(B), pp. 31–145.

Aspöck, E. and Banerjea, R.Y. (2016). Formation Processes of a Reopened Early Bronze Age Inhumation Grave in Austria: the Soil Thin Section Analyses. *Journal of Archaeological Science: Reports*, 10, pp. 791–809.

Aspöck, E. and Stadler, P. (2005). Die langobardenzeitlichen Gräber von Brunn am Gebirge, Flur Wolfholz, Niederösterreich. *Archaeologia Austriaca*, 87, pp. 169–224. http://www.jstor.org/stable/23782226

Aspöck, E., Klevnäs, A. and Müller-Scheessel, N., eds. (2020). *Grave disturbances: The archaeology of post-depositional interactions with the dead*. Oxford: Oxbow Books.

Barber, P. (1988). *Vampires, burial and death: folklore and reality*. New Haven, CT: Yale University Press.

Beilner, T. and Grupe, G. (1996). Beraubungsspuren auf Menschlichen Skelettfunden des Merowingerzeitlichen Reihengräberfeldes von Wenigumstadt (Ldkr. Aschaffenburg). *Archäologisches Korrespondenzblatt*, 26, pp. 213–217.

Blaizot, F. (1998). La Reconnaissance des Dispositifs en Matière Périssable et leur Interprétation: Exemples Tardo-Antique dans la Drôme et Proto-Médiéval en Seine-et-Marne. *Rencontre autour du cercueil. Journée du 28 janvier 1997, Groupe d'anthropologie et d'archéologie funéraire en Île-de-France (Gaafif). Bulletin de liaison*, n.s. 2(2), pp. 79–84.

Blaizot, F. (2008). Réflexions sur la Typologie des Tombes à Inhumation: Restitution des Dispositifs et Interprétations Chrono-Culturelle. *Archéologie Médiévale*, 38, pp. 1–30.

Bradley, R. and Williams, H. (1998). The Past in the Past: the Re-Use of Ancient Monuments. *World Archaeology. Abingdon: Routledge*

Carmichael, P.H. (1995). Nasca burial patterns: social structure and mortuary ideology. In: T. Dillehay, ed., *Tombs for the Living: Andean Mortuary Practices*. Symposium at Dumbarton Oaks, 12th and 13th October 1991. Washington, D.C.: Dumbarton Oaks Research Library and Collection, pp. 161–187.

Châtelet, M. (2017). La réouverture des tombes à l'époque mérovingienne: un acte rituel? À propos du bris des objets dans les sépultures des nécropoles de Matzenheim, d'Osthouse et d'Eckwersheim (Alsace, Bas-Rhin). In: I. Leroy and L. Verslype, eds., *Communauté des Vivants, Compagnie des Morts. Actes des 35e Journées de l'Association française d'archéologie mérovingienne*. Saint-Germain-en-Laye: Association française d'archéologie mérovingienne, pp. 171–182.

Chenal, F. and Barrand-Emam, H. (2014). Nouvelles Données Concernant le Pillage des Sépultures Mérovingiennes en Alsace: Mise en Évidence de Stries et d'Entailles sur les Restes Osseux Provenant des Sépultures Pillées de l'Ensemble Funéraire de Vendenheim (Alsace, Bas-Rhin). *Revue Archéologique de l'Est*, 62, pp. 489–500.

Cieza de León, P. (1945). *La Crónica del Perú*. Buenos Aires: Colección Austral. Espasa Calpe Argentina, S.A.

Cochet, J.B. (1857 [1970]). *Sépultures gauloises, romaines, franques et normandes (faisant suite à La Normandie souterraine)*. Brionne: Le Portulan.

Courtaud P. (1996). 'Anthropologie de Sauvetage': vers une optimisation des méthodes d'enregistrement. Présentation d'une fiche anthropologique. *Bulletins et Mémoires de la Société d'Anthropologie de Paris*, 8(3), pp. 157–167.

Crubézy, E., Lorans, E. and Masset, C., eds. (2000). *L'archéologie funéraire*. Paris: Éditions Errance.

Danforth, L.M. (1982). *The death rituals of rural Greece*. Princeton: Princeton University Press.

Déderix, S., Schmitt, A. and Crevecoeur, I. (2018). Towards a theoretical and methodological framework for the study of collective burial practices. In: A. Schmitt, S. Déderix, and I. Crevecoeur, eds., *Gathered in Death. Archaeological and Ethnological Perspectives on Collective Burial and Social Organisation*. Louvain: Presses universitaires de Louvain.

Denaire, A., Barrand-Emam, H. *et al.* (2013). *Kolbsheim « Vogeseblick », du village Néolithique ancien à la position de la Bruche de 1914*. Rapport final d'opération d'archéologie préventive. Antea archéologie, Service Régional de l'Archéologie (SRA) Alsace.

Dobos, A. (2014). Plunder or ritual? The phenomenon of grave reopening in the row-grave cemeteries from Transylvania (6th–7th centuries). In: M. Gligor, ed., *Archaeothanatology: An Interdisciplinary Approach on Death from Prehistory to the Middle Ages*, Annales Universitatis Apulensis, Series Historica, 18(II). Cluj-Napoca: Editura Mega, pp. 135–162.

Duday, H. (2006). L'Archéothanatologie ou l'Archéologie de la Mort. In: R.L. Gowland and C.J. Knüsel, eds., *The Social Archaeology of Funerary Remains*. Oxford: Oxbow Books, pp. 30–56.

Duday, H. (2009). *The archaeology of the dead. Lectures in archaeothanatology*. Oxford: Oxbow Books.

Duday, H., Courtaud, P., Crubezy, E., Sellier, P. and Tillier, A.-M. (1990). L'Anthropologie 'de Terrain': Reconnaissance et Interprétation des Gestes Funéraires. *Bulletins et Mémoires de la Société d'Anthropologie de Paris*, 2, pp. 29–49.

Duviols, P. (1971). *La lutte contre les religions autochtones dans le Pérou colonial: «l'extirpation de l'idolâtrie», entre 1532 et 1660*. Lima: Institut Français d'Études Andines; Paris: Éditions Ophrys.

Eeckhout, P. (2013). Change and Permanency on the Coast of Ancient Peru: the Religious Site of Pachacamac. *World Archaeology*, 45(1), pp. 137–160.

Effros, B. (2006). Grave goods and the ritual expression of identity. In: T. F. X. Noble, ed., *Roman Provinces to Medieval Kingdoms*. New York: Routledge, pp. 189–232.

Fiocchi, L, Chevalier, P. and Lapie, O. (2012). Les cercueils monoxyles du milieu du Xe s. à Souvigny (Allier). In: F. Carré and F. Henrion, eds., *Le bois dans l'architecture et l'aménagement de la tombe: quelles approches? Actes de la table ronde d'Auxerre, 15–17 octobre 2009*. Saint-Germain-en-Laye: Association française d'Archéologie mérovingienne, pp. 143–150.

Franz, N., Schwarzäugl, J. and Tögel, A. (2017). *Steinsichel und Bronzedolch. Urgeschichte in Weiden am See*. Horn: Ferdinand Berger & Söhne.

Galinié, H. and Zadora-Rio, E., eds. (1996). *Archéologie du cimetière chrétien. Actes du 2e colloque ARCHEA (Association en Région Centre pour l'Histoire et l'Archéologie)*, Orléans 29 septembre–1er octobre 1994. Tours: FÉRACF.

Geary, P.J. (1986). Sacred commodities: the circulation of medieval relics. In: A. Appadurai, ed., *The Social Life of Things: Commodities in Cultural Perspective*. Cambridge: Cambridge University Press, pp. 169–192.

Gerdau-Radonić, K. (2007). *Les tombes collectives de Tablada de Lurin (Vallée de Lurin, Pérou; Ier-IIIe s. ap. JC)*. Unpublished Ph.D. thesis, Université de Bordeaux 1.

Gerdau-Radonić, K. (2008). The Collective Burials of Tablada de Lurín, Lurín valley, Peru (AD 1-300). *Bulletins et Mémoires de la Société d'Anthropologie de Paris*, 20(3–4), pp. 275–279.

Gerdau-Radonić, K. and Herrera, A. (2010). Why Dig Looted Tombs? Two Examples and Some Answers from Keushu (Ancash Highlands, Peru). *Bulletins et Mémoires de la Société d'Anthropologie de Paris*, 22(3–4), pp. 145–156.

Gerdau-Radonić, K. and Makowski, K. (2011). Las sepulturas colectivas de Tablada de Lurín: una perspectiva desde la antropología biológica. In: L. Vetter, S. Téllez and R. Vega-Centeno, eds., *Arqueología Peruana: Homenaje a Mercedes Cárdenas*. Lima: Instituto Riva-Agüero, Pontificia Universidad Católica del Perú, pp. 145–176.

Goody, J. (1962). *Death, property and the ancestors: a study of the mortuary customs of the Lodagaa of West Africa*. London: Tavistock.

Guamán Poma de Ayala, F. (1987). *Nueva crónica y buen gobierno*. Colección Crónicas de América Number 29. Madrid: Historia 16.

Gubellini, L., Cense-Bacquet, D. and Wilusz, A. (2013). *Marquette-lez-Lille (Nord). Z.A.C. du Haut-Touquet, tranche 1*. Rapport final d'opération d'archéologie préventive. Archéopole: Service Régional de l'Archéologie (SRA) du Nord-Pas-de-Calais.

Guillotin, S., Mauduit, A., eds., (2012). *Vitry-sur-Orne, Vallange (Lorraine, Moselle)*. Rapport final d'opération d'archéologie préventive. Antea archéologie, Service Régional de l'Archéologie (SRA) Lorraine.

Haddow, S.D. and Knüsel, C.J. (2017). Skull Retrieval and Secondary Burial Practices in the Neolithic Near East: Recent Insights from Çatalhöyük, Turkey. *Bioarchaeology International*, 1(1–2), pp. 52–71.

Hänsel, B. and Kalicz, N. (1986). Das bronzezeitliche Gräberfeld von Mezöcsát, Kom. Borsod, Nordostungarn. *Bericht der Römisch-Germanischen Kommission*, 67, pp. 6–88.

Henrion F. (2012). Des mots pour en parler. In: F. Carré and F. Henrion, eds., *Le Bois dans l'Architecture et l'Aménagement de la Tombe: Quelles Approches? Actes de la table ronde d'Auxerre, 15-17 octobre 2009*. Saint-Germain-en-Laye: Association française d'archéologie mérovingienne, pp. 27–28.

Hertz, R. (1960). A contribution to the study of the collective representation of death. In: R. Hertz, ed., *Death and the Right Hand*. Translated by Rodney and Claudia Needham. London: Cohen and West, pp. 29–88.

Hicke, W. (1987). *Hügel- und Flachgräber der Frühbronzezeit aus Jois und Oggau*. Eisenstadt: Burgenländisches Landesmuseum.

Isbell, W. (1997). *Mummies and mortuary monuments: a postprocessual prehistory of central Andean social organization*. Austin: University of Texas Press.

Keller, C. (2013). *Differentialdiagnose von Frakturen am Beispiel des frühbronzezeitlichen Gräberfeldes Franzhausen I: Überlegungen zum Phänomen 'Grabraub'*. Unpublished Diploma thesis, University of Vienna.

Keller, C. (2014). *Anthropologische Untersuchung zweier Skelette aus Weiden am See*. Unpublished Report.

Keller, C. and Teschler-Nicola, M. (2013). Frakturen als Indikatoren für Gewalt und Grabstörungen – Möglichkeiten und Grenzen. *Mitteilungen der Anthropologischen Gesellschaft in Wien*, 143(18), pp. 113–130.

Klaus, H.D. (2016). Vida y Muerte en el Perú Colonial: Inicios de la Bioarqueología en Lambayeque Histórico (1536-1750 dC). *Boletín de Arqueología PUCP* (20), pp. 103–128.

Klaus, H.D. and Tam, M.E. (2015). *Requiem aeternam?* Archaeothanatology of mortuary ritual in colonial Mórrope, north coast of Peru. In: I. Shimada and J. Fitzsimmons, ed., *Living with the Dead in the Andes*. Tucson: University of Arizona Press, pp. 267–303.

Klevnäs, A. (2013). *Whodunnit? Grave robbery in Anglo-Saxon England and the Merovingian kingdoms*. British Archaeological Reports (International Series) 2582. Oxford: Archaeopress.

Klevnäs, A. (2015). Give and take: grave-goods and grave robbery in the early middle ages. In: A. Klevnäs and C. Hedenstierna-Jonson, eds., *Own and Be Owned: Archaeological Approaches to the Concept of Possession*. Stockholm: Department of Archaeological and Classical Studies, Studies in Archaeology 62, pp. 157–188.

Klevnäs, A. (2016). Overkill: reopening graves to maim the dead in Anglo-Saxon England. In: L. Gardela and K. Kajkowski, eds., *Limbs, Bones and Reopened Graves in Past Societies*. Bytow: Muzeum Zachodniokaszubskie w Bytowie, pp. 177–213.

Klevnäs, A., Aspöck, E., Noterman, A.A., Van Haperen, M.C. and Zintl, S. (2021). Reopening Graves in the Early Middle Ages: From Local Practice to European Phenomenon. *Antiquity*, 95, pp. 1005–1026.

Knüsel, C.J. and Robb, J. (2016). Funerary Taphonomy: An Overview of Goals and Methods. *Journal of Archaeological Science: Reports*, 10, pp. 655–673.

Krenn-Leeb, A. (2011). Zwischen Buckliger Welt und Kleinen Karpaten: Die Lebenswelt der Wieselburg-Kultur. *Archäologie Österreichs*, 22, pp. 11–26.

Kümmel, C. (2009). *Ur- und frühgeschichtlicher Grabraub. Archäologische Interpretation und kulturanthropologische Erklärung*. Münster: Waxmann Verlag.

Leclerc, J. and Tarrête, J. (2004). Sépulture. In: Leroi-Gourhan A., ed., *Dictionnaire de la préhistoire*, 2nd ed. Paris: Presses Universitaires de France, pp. 1002–1003.

Leeb, A. (1987). Überblick über die Chorologie, Typologie und Chronologie der Wieselburgkultur. In: W. Hicke, ed., *Hügel- und Flachgräber der Frühbronzezeit aus Jois und Oggau*. Eisenstadt: Burgenländisches Landesmuseum, pp. 231–283.

Makowski, K. (2011). *Informe Final Proyecto de Investigación y Conservación Arqueológica 2010–2011 Programa Arqueológico – Escuela de Campo – 'Valle de Pachacamac' (Antecedentes: Lomas de Lurín 1999–2007, Tablada de Lurín 1991–1998). Convenio Asociación Atocongo S.A. – PUCP* (Pontificia Universidad Católica del Perú). Unpublished site report. Ministerio de Cultura, Peru. Available from: http://www.valledepachacamac. com/sites/patl.pucp.edu.pe/files/Informe_PATL_2010-2011.pdf (Last accessed: 13/09/18).

Makowski, K. (2016). Pachacamac y la política imperial Inca. In: M. Curatola and J. Szeminski, eds., *El Inca y la Huaca. La religión del poder y el poder de la religión en el mundo andino antiguo*. Lima: Fondo Editorial PUCP (Pontificia Universidad Católica del Perú), Universidad Hebrea de Jerusalen, pp. 153–208.

Makowski, K.C., Castro de la Mata, P.A., Escajadillo, G., Jiménez, M.D.R. and Tomasto, E.L. (2012). *Corpus antiquitatum americanensium Polonia-Perú: ajuares funerarios de los cementerios prehispánicos de Tablada de Lurín (Periodo Formativo Tardío, Lima, Perú)*. Krakow: Polish Academy of Arts and Science.

Makowski, K. and Vallenas, A. (2015). La Ocupación Lima en el Valle de Lurín: en los Orígenes de Pachacámac Monumental. *Boletín de Arqueología PUCP*, 19, pp. 97–143.

Meiklejohn, C. and Constandse-Westermann, T.S. (1978). The Human Skeletal Material from Swifterbant, Earlier Neolithic of the Northern Netherlands. I. Inventory and Demography. *Palaeohistoria*, 20, pp. 39–89.

Menzel, D. (1976). *Pottery style and society in Ancient Peru: art as a mirror of history in the Ica Valley, 1350-1570*. Berkeley: University of California Press.

Metcalf, P. and Huntington, R. (1991). *Celebrations of death: the anthropology of mortuary ritual*, 2nd ed. Cambridge: Cambridge University Press.

Millaire, J.F. (2004). The Manipulation of Human Remains in Moche Society: Delayed Burials, Grave Reopening, and Secondary Offerings of Human Bones on the Peruvian North Coast. *Latin American Antiquity*, 15(4), pp. 371–388.

Murail, P., Bruzek, J., Houet, F. and Cunha, E. (2005). DSP: A Tool for Probabilistic Sex Diagnosis Using Worldwide Variability in Hip-Bone Measurements. *Bulletins et Mémoires de la Société d'Anthropologie de Paris*, n.s. 17(3–4), pp. 167–176.

Murphy, M.S., Gaither, C., Goycochea, E., Verano, J.W. and Cock, G. (2010). Violence and Weapon-Related Trauma at Puruchuco-Huaquerones, Peru. *American Journal of Physical Anthropology*, 142(4), pp. 636–649.

Nagy, M. (2013). Der südlichste Fundort der Gáta-Wieselburg-Kultur in Zsennye-Kavicsbánya/ Schottergrube, Komitat Vas, Westungarn. *Savaria a Vas Megyei Múzeumok Értesítője*, 36, pp. 75–173.

Neugebauer-Maresch, C. and Neugebauer, J.-W. (1997). *Franzhausen: Das frühbronzezeitliche Gräberfeld I.* Horn: Ferdinand Berger & Söhne.

Neugebauer, J.-W. (1991). *Die Nekropole F von Gemeinlebarn, Niederösterreich. Untersuchungen zu den Bestattungssitten und zum Grabraub in der ausgehenden Frühbronzezeit in Niederösterreich südlich der Donau zwischen Enns und Wienerwald.* Mainz: Philipp von Zabern.

Neugebauer, J.-W. (1994). Zum Grabraub in der Frühbronzezeit Niederösterreichs. *Vorträge des Niederbayerischen Archäologentages*, 12, pp. 109–148.

Noterman, A.A. (2015). Early medieval grave robbery: the French case. In: L. Gardela and K. Kajkowski, ed., *Limbs, Bones and Reopened Graves in Past Societies.* Bytow: Muzeum Zachodniokaszubskie w Bytowie, pp. 149–176.

Noterman, A.A. (2016). *Violation, pillage, profanation: la perturbation des sépultures mérovingiennes au haut Moyen Âge (VIe-VIIIe siècle) dans la moitié nord de la France.* Unpublished Ph.D. thesis, University of Poitiers.

Noterman, A.A., Aspöck, E., Klevnäs, A., Van Haperen, M.C. and Zintl, S. (2020). La perturbation des sépultures au haut Moyen Âge: discussion et collaboration européenne. In: A. A. Noterman and M. Cervel, eds., *Ritualiser, Gérer, Piller: Rencontre autour des Réouvertures de Tombes et de la Manipulation des Ossements. Actes de la 9ème Rencontre du Gaaf (Groupe d'Anthropologie et d'Archéologie Funéraire), UFR SHA, CESCM, Poitiers (10–12 mai 2017)*, Chauvigny: Édition Association des Publications Chauvinoises.

Rittershofer, K.-F. (1987). Grabraub in der Bronzezeit. *Bericht der Römisch Germanischen Kommission Band*, 68, pp. 5–23.

Roth, H. (1978). Archäologische Beobachtungen zum Grabfrevel im Merowingerreich. In: H. Jankuhn, H. Nehlsen and H. Roth, eds., *Zum Grabfrevel in vor-und frühgeschichtlicher Zeit: Untersuchungen zu Grabraub und 'haugbrot' in Mittel- und Nordeuropa.* Göttingen: Vandenhoeck und Ruprecht, pp. 53–84.

Roth-Zehner, M. and Cartier E. (2007). *Illfurth, lieu-dit Buergelen*, Rapport final d'opération, Antea Archéologie, Service régional de l'archéologie (SRA), Alsace.

Sági, K. (1964). Das langobardische Gräberfeld von Vörs. *Acta archaeologica Academiae Scientiarum Hungaricae*, 16, pp. 359–408.

Salin, É. (1952). *La civilisation mérovingienne d'après les sépultures, les textes et le laboratoire. Deuxième partie: les sépultures.* Paris: A. et J. Picard.

Salomon, F. (1995). 'The beautiful grandparents': Andean ancestor shrines and mortuary ritual as seen through the colonial records. In: T.D. Dillehay, ed., *Tombs for the Living: Andean Mortuary Practices. A Symposium at Dumbarton Oaks, 12th and 13th October, 1991.* Washington, D.C.: Dumbarton Oaks Research Library and Collection, pp. 315–353.

Sauer, F. (2009). *Fundstelle Prellenkirchen – Die archäologischen Grabungen auf der Trasse der A6.* Wien: Bundesdenkmalamt.

Scheuer, L. and Black, S. (2000). *Developmental juvenile osteology.* San Diego: Academic Press.

Schmitt, A. and Déderix, S. (2018). What defines a collective grave? Archaeological and ethnological perspectives on collective burial practices. In: A. Schmitt, S. Déderix, and I. Crevecoeur, eds., *Gathered in Death. Archaeological and Ethnological Perspectives on Collective Burial and Social Organisation.* Louvain: Presses universitaires de Louvain, pp. 195–214.

Schmitt, A. and Déderix, S. (2019). Qu'est-ce qu'une sépulture collective? Vers un changement de paradigme. *Bulletins et Mémoires de la Société d'Anthropologie de Paris*, 31(3–4), pp. 103–112.

Schnitzler, B. (2008). *Rites de la mort en Alsace: de la Préhistoire à la fin du XIXe siècle.* Strasbourg: Musées de la Ville de Strasbourg.

Sprenger, S. (1998). Zur Rekonstruktion von entnommenen Bronzebeigaben anhand von Grünfärbungen am Skelettmaterial: Untersuchungen am frühbronzezeitlichen Gräberfeld Franzhausen 1, Niederösterreich. In: B. Fritsch, C. Strahm, I. Matuschik and M. Maute, eds., *Tradition und Innovation: Prähistorische Archäologie als historische Wissenschaft: Festschrift für Christian Strahm.* Leidorf: Rahden, pp. 417–427.

Sprenger, S. (1999). *Zur Bedeutung des Grabraubes für sozioarchäologische Gräberfeldanalysen. Eine Untersuchung am frühbronzezeitlichen Gräberfeld Franzhausen I, Niederösterreich.* Wien: Berger.

Taylor, G. (2001). *Huarochirí. manuscrito quechua del siglo XVII. ritos y tradiciones 1.* Lima: Institut Français d'Études Andines – Lluvia Editores.

Thiedemann, A. and Schleifring, J.H. (1992). Bemerkungen zur Praxis frühmittelalterlichen Grabraubs. *Archäologisches Korrespondenzblatt*, 22, pp. 435–439.

Tixier, B., ed. (2019). *Vitry-la-Ville (51), Le Cray. Une vaste nécropole du haut Moyen Âge.* Rapport final d'opération archéologique, Éveha, Service régional de l'archéologie (SRA) du Grand Est.

Toyne, J. M. (2015). The Body Sacrificed: A Bioarchaeological Analysis of Ritual Violence in Ancient Tucume, Peru. *Journal of Religion and Violence*, 3(1), pp. 137–171.

van Gennep, A. (1960). *The rites of passage*. London: Routledge and Kegan Paul.

Van Haperen, M.C. (2010). Rest in Pieces: An Interpretive Model of Early Medieval 'Grave Robbery'. *Medieval and Modern Matters, Archaeology and Material Culture in the Low Countries*, 1, pp. 1–36.

Van Haperen, M.C. (2013). The distributed dead: personhood from the perspective of reopened graves. In: B. Ludowici, ed., *Individual or Individuality? Approaches towards an Archaeology of Personhood in the First Millenium AD*. Stuttgart: Kommission bei Konrad Theiss Verlag, pp. 89–94.

Van Haperen, M.C. (2016). Merovingian reopened graves: a scenario-based approach to interpretation. In: L. Gardela and K. Kajkowski, eds., *Limbs, Bones and Reopened Graves in Past Societies*. Bytow: Muzeum Zachodniokaszubskie w Bytowie, pp. 123–147.

Van Haperen, M.C. (2017). *In touch with the dead: Early Medieval grave reopenings in the Low Countries*. Unpublished Ph.D. thesis, University of Leiden.

Verdery, K. (1999). *The political lives of dead bodies: reburial and post-socialist change*. New York: Columbia University Press.

Wahl, J. and König, H.-G. (1987). Anthropologisch-Traumatologische Untersuchung der Menschlichen Skelettreste aus dem Bandkeramischen Massengrab bei Talheim, Kreis Heilbronn. *Fundberichte aus Baden-Württemberg*, 12, pp. 65–193.

Webb, P.A. and Suchey, J. (1985). Epiphyseal Union of the Anterior Iliac Crest and Medial Clavicle in a Modern Multiracial Sample of American Males and Females. *American Journal of Physical Anthropology*, 68(4), pp. 457–466.

Weiss-Krejci, E. (2011). The formation of mortuary deposits: implications for understanding mortuary behavior of past populations. In: S. Agarwal and B. Glencross, eds., *Social Bioarchaeology*. Chichester: Wiley-Blackwell, pp. 68–106.

Zehnacker, M. (1996). *Une nécropole mérovingienne en plaine d'Alsace, Niedernai, « Kirchbuehl » (Bas-Rhin)*. Document final de synthèse (DFS) de sauvetage urgent, Afan, Service régional de l'archéologie (SRA), Alsace.

Zintl, S. (2012). Wiedergeöffnete Gräber der Merowingerzeit im Umland von Regensburg. In: M. Chytráček, H. Gruber, J. Michálek, R. Sandner and K. Schmotz, eds., *Fines Transire. 21. Treffen der Archäologischen Arbeitsgemeinschaft Ostbayern/West- und Südbhömen/Oberösterreich (Treffen vom 22. bis 25. Juni 2011 in Stříbro)*. Rahden-Westf: VML, pp. 189–197.

Zintl, S. (2019). *Frühmittelalterliche Grabräuber? Wiedergeöffnete Gräber der Merowingerzeit* (Regensburger Studien 24). Regensburg: Stadtarchiv Regensburg.

17

CLUNIAC FUNERARY PRACTICES

Eleanor Williams

ARCHAEOLOGY, SCHOOL OF HUMANITIES, CANTERBURY CHRIST CHURCH UNIVERSITY, CANTERBURY, UNITED KINGDOM

Introduction

A corpse, you will rot, crying out as you do. You who laugh with your beautiful mouth will moulder in the grave. Once a living being, you will become a worm. What more? You will putrefy (12th-century Cluniac poem, trans. Bruce, 2006: 105).

The rituals surrounding death and burial were integral to the Cluniac monastic world. Revealed in this extract from a Cluniac poem and 'meditative tool' (Bruce, 2006: 102) is the extent to which the monks were to immerse themselves in the world of the dead. Far from being shielded from the biological and emotional realities of death, they were encouraged to confront them. The funerary rites recorded in the later 11th-century *Customaries* of Cluny Abbey also reflect this. These texts describe how the dying and deceased monks were to be physically and spiritually treated (Paxton, 1993, 2013). They are sources of inestimable value for exploring both the materiality of the medieval monastic funeral, and attitudes to the dead and to the dead body, at different stages throughout the process. From the monk's approaching death to long after interment, they describe a protracted sequence of human actions that could variously leave their mark within the archaeological record. However, the *Customaries* outline only the formal, structured actions of the community, detailing 'everything considered worthy of admiration in Cluny's activities' (Cochelin, 2000: 22); in this respect, they present the ideal death and burial. The full complexity – and potential variability – of the Cluniac funerary process is, therefore, obscured not only in the documentary but also in the archaeological record. Excavated burials, which often appear as static entities of dry bones and earth, bear little resemblance to the initial or original funerary deposit. Taphonomic agents have transformed them, masking the elaborate sequences of events that went into their creation. With two such partial records, how can a fuller reconstruction of the individual actions performed to and for the Cluniac dead in different stages of the funerary process be conceived? Can variation in practice from the Cluny ideal be identified at other Cluniac houses? What types of 'less formal' practices took place that were omitted from the *Customaries*, and what can they also reveal about attitudes to death, burial, and the body?

Drawing on select examples of excavated burial contexts from two prominent Cluniac houses – La Charité-sur-Loire (Burgundy, France) and Bermondsey Abbey (London, England), this chapter considers how detailed taphonomic, archaeothanatological approaches can enhance the reconstruction of the Cluniac – and, more generally, the medieval

DOI: 10.4324/9781351030625-20

monastic – funeral. In so doing, it aims to demonstrate how this approach, even when applied post-excavation with the use of burial documentation, can offer more nuanced insights into the individual actions that shaped its performance than can the written sources alone.

Cluny Abbey and its funerary customs

Cluny Abbey, founded *circa* AD 909 in Burgundy, France, was one of the most significant monasteries of its time, establishing an extensive network of houses across Europe. Among its many influences on western monasticism, Cluny is recognised for its role in the ritualisation of death; venerating the dead became a quotidian part of life for the Cluniac Order. The written record left by Cluny is unparalleled for its insights into daily life (Cochelin, 2000) – and death; indeed, the later 11th-century Customary of Bernard outlines in considerable detail the ante- and post-mortem rites for the passing of a brother. It specifies a highly structured and ceremonial involvement of the whole monastic community from deathbed to graveside, with clearly defined roles. Brothers of the same rank as the deceased, for example, were to wash and prepare the body. This, Paxton (1993: 25) argues, encouraged the monks to meditate on their own deaths. As well as offering insights into Cluniac attitudes to the dead, the Customary describes the actions, and accompanying materials, for performing the rites. Important for archaeothanatological enquiries, this includes the procedures for preparing the body for burial and interment in the cemetery. Summarised below are select elements from the post-mortem rites presented in Paxton's (2013: 111–113, 145) translations of the text of the Customary: Once washed, the body was to be dressed in a shirt, cowl, night shoes and a *sudary* (a headcloth). The shoes were not open at the toes but stitched together.[1] The hood of the cowl was to be sewn down over the *sudary* and face on both sides. The hands were folded together on the breast outside the cowl, and the cowl, which was sewn in a number of places, was to be pulled together so that no part was loose. The night shoes (slippers) were then sewn together, and the body was placed on a bier.[2] In the cemetery, the body was lowered into the ground, and a wooden cover was placed over it.

Important to highlight is that, except in excellent preservation conditions, the specified elements of dress, their manner of fixing, and the grave cover are unlikely to survive. On the whole, direct archaeological indicators for funerary structures and body/preparation (e.g. remains of coffin wood, coffin nails, and dress items) can be scarce when excavated hundreds of years later.[3]

---

1 The roughly contemporaneous Customary of Ulrich, also based on practice at Cluny, describes these 'shoes' as being made of the same material as the *sudary* and wool shirt (Paxton, 1993: 104).

2 The Customary does not specify why the night shoes were to be sewn together, but as discussed in Knowles and Brooke (2002: 184) in relation to the 11th-century *Monastic Constitutions of Lanfranc*, as no coffin was used, sewing prevented disarray before and during burial. However, these procedures for preparing the dead should not be considered in purely practical terms. An ancient custom at Cluny was that those transporting the body for burial were to add one stitch to the wrapping (de Valous, 1970: 296); the act of sewing itself was imbued with symbolic meaning, connecting the dead, his memory, and the living community.

3 A rare example of burial dress preserved in a funerary context from Cluniac Lewes Priory is discussed by Woolley (1997: 143–146). A dark brown wool material described as a shroud or outer garment was identified in association with the left and right knees, upper right femur, and skull area. The remains of a lighter-coloured undergarment were also preserved in certain areas. A pair of leather soles survived, one of which contained pieces of the same wool material as the undergarment. Arguably this same garment was wrapped around the feet and the rest of the body (Woolley, 1997: 146).

Examples of well-preserved organic structures do exist for the medieval period (e.g. Gallien and Langlois, 1998; Bardel and Perennec, 2004; Blaizot, 2008); referents such as these are invaluable for refining knowledge of the impact of various types of funerary architecture on body decomposition and resulting skeletal patterning. More typically, however, organic materials in temperate climates do not preserve. Clothing generally decays with the corpse (Duday, Le Mort and Tillier, 2014), and it is problematic equating wood fragments or staining – or indeed a few nails or fittings – with specific modes of burial. Contemporary and modern burial disturbance in later medieval cemeteries adds a further layer of complexity; funerary elements could have been removed or are potentially intrusive. Reliance on direct archaeological indicators for reconstructing practice therefore conceals – or misrepresents – subtleties, and significant complexity, surrounding the treatment of the dead body. This issue is compounded when skeletal recording in the field is confined to the more readily observable overall body orientation, placement (e.g. supine or prone), and limb positioning; the full potential of the osteoarchaeological record is therefore lost.

The Customary concludes its attention on the physical body of the deceased the moment it is concealed below the cover. However, this is not the end, merely the start of an ongoing inter-related cultural and biological process; even when reduced to bones, the medieval dead were not inert. The soul continued to be 'managed' by the living, whilst the body was transforming through natural processes of decomposition and decay. A range of exogenous factors (e.g. the impact of human activity, animals, water, temperature, soil type and micro-organisms) also influences the body. Within medieval funerary landscapes, human activity played a significant role in the afterlife of the body. Here, the archaeological remains can shed light on the more 'informal' practices omitted from the Cluniac written record. Digging a grave often resulted in the discovery, handling, and re-deposition of previous interments, for which a range of management strategies have been identified from the medieval period (e.g. Blaizot, 1997; Gilchrist and Sloane, 2005; Gleize, 2007, 2010); Cluniac houses were no exception. Unsurprisingly, the *Customaries* make no mention of this practice, despite its commonality; it was certainly not 'worthy of admiration'. However, as discussed below, these interactions with the former dead could be a significant – albeit less structured – part of the funeral. As the overarching aim of archaeothanatology is understanding societies via funerary practices by reconstructing the initial burial deposits (Duday, Le Mort and Tillier, 2014), the inclusion, and spatial associations, of all elements should be observed and recorded. Re-deposited skeletal remains in discrete graves should not be considered merely 'intrusive' material. Various aspects of funerary practices can be discerned from different accumulations of bones, including evidence for re-arranging and the space assigned (or used) for later movements of remains (Roksandic, 2002: 111). With a focussed taphonomic approach, where the burial is considered as a 'dynamic whole' (Nilsson, 1998: 6), both short-term (e.g. body preparation and interment) and longer-term (e.g. treatment of disturbed remains) responses to the dead can be more fully understood.

The Cluniac funerary record

Excavations of funerary contexts have been conducted at Cluniac houses of varying size and status. In France and England, notable examples include Cluny Abbey (Baud, 2000), La Charité-sur-Loire (Billoin, 2005) and Saint-Nicolas-d'Acy (Bourry *et al.*, 1991) (France), and Bermondsey Abbey (Dyson *et al.*, 2011), and Lewes Priory (Lyne, 1997) (England). Two of the more important and extensively excavated dependencies of the Cluny motherhouse are the focus of this study: La Charité-sur-Loire (Burgundy) and its direct daughter house, Bermondsey Abbey (London) (founded *c.* 1059 and *c.* 1089, respectively).

La Charité-sur-Loire and Bermondsey Abbey: the burials

The Department of Greater London Archaeology/Museum of London conducted excavations at Bermondsey Abbey (Bermondsey) from 1984 to 1988. Some 202 individuals from discrete graves were recorded in a cemetery zone south of the church. Dating from around 1100 to 1430, 137 males/possible males, eight females/possible females and only one individual aged 15 or under were identified (Connell and White, 2011). Based on the demographic profile, it was proposed that the cemetery zone could have catered predominantly for the Bermondsey adult male monastic community (Dyson *et al.*, 2011: 131).

In 2003, David Billoin of Inrap (Institut National de Recherches Archéologiques Préventives) directed the excavation of 46 Cluniac-period burials from La Charité-sur-Loire (La Charité). Some 37 were from a cemetery area to the east of the church (dated mid-11th to the early-13th century) and nine were from within a later gallery built over this zone in the early-13th century. This gallery, which connected the main church of Notre Dame with an annexed church, was undoubtedly a highly prestigious burial zone; it could have helped facilitate the processions associated with the commemorations for the dead (Billoin, 2005). Biological anthropologist Luc Staniaszek identified 24 males and possible males from discrete graves. Including all re-deposited skeletal remains, over 100 individuals were represented; no females, and only two individuals under the age of 16, were recorded. This predominately adult male composition fits with the monastic nature of the site (Billoin, 2005).

Recording at La Charité followed archaeothanatological protocols in the field. For each burial, observation of the skeletal elements, their relative positions, and spatial relationship to the grave and associated structures/objects was undertaken; this permitted detailed taphonomic histories to be documented (Billoin and Staniaszek, 2005; Staniaszek, 2005). Informed arguments could then be made for the original position of the body, space of decomposition, mode of burial, the presence of further perishable inclusions (e.g. pillows), and strategies for managing disturbed skeletal remains. This chapter draws and builds on Staniaszek's observations. Conversely, the earlier excavations at Bermondsey did not follow archaeothanatological approaches. Although this type of study should begin in the field when all necessary observations can be made (Knüsel, 2014), research on prehistoric burial contexts (e.g. Nilsson Stutz, 2003, 2006; Willis and Tayles, 2009) has demonstrated how post-excavation analysis using photographs, drawings/plans, and field notes can also greatly enhance the reconstruction of funerary rites, even with a complete absence of direct archaeological indicators. A photographic record was available for Bermondsey – together with field notes and drawings – but the main limitations of the study must be acknowledged. Photographs were of variable quality and sometimes captured the burial from a shallow angle; this was not ideal for examining positioning of certain skeletal elements and their spatial relationship to the grave structure. Necessary detail was either absent or ambiguous for some burials. For example, the limits of grave cuts were not always clear; this is crucial information in isolating the influence of particular modes of burial or dress on the body from that of the feature itself (see below). Despite this, the excavation documentation was sufficiently detailed for a number of burials to permit different aspects of Cluniac funerary treatment to be reconstructed. Questions surrounding the complex relationship between Cluniac written sources and practice, and the adaptability of practice with respect to the Cluny 'ideal', could be addressed.

Archaeothanatology and Cluniac funerary rites

The Customary describes a bodily treatment that, in theory, if rigidly adhered to, could produce distinct skeletal patterning, with a high degree of uniformity across Cluniac contexts. Integral to this is the ability to isolate the results of deliberate human (funerary) actions on the body – and the way it decomposes and disarticulates – from the influence of natural processes. As the body decomposes, there will always be some degree of movement of skeletal elements within the initial volume of the cadaver; this is dictated primarily by gravity (Duday, 2006). However, the extent and nature of movement will vary depending on the surrounding burial environment. Understanding the ways in which the skeleton disarticulates and the creation and subsequent infilling of empty spaces as the soft tissue decomposes is fundamental to archaeothanatology (Nilsson Stutz, 2005; Duday, 2009). Where an individual is buried in plain earth, for example, there is a more rapid infilling of these spaces. In this instance, even labile articulations (those that lose their connection the quickest, such as the hand and distal foot bones) (Knüsel, 2014) are more easily maintained. These bones become 'fixed', and can even rest in unstable, precarious positions above the grave floor. Where an individual body decomposed in a void, as the Cluniac *Customaries* imply (e.g. under a cover or in a coffin), movements of bones can be more extensive and even take place outside of the initial volume occupied by the once cadaver (Duday, 2006). Various methods of body preparation (e.g. elements of dress), modes of burial, and the inclusion of grave furnishings – both perishable or not – can all influence this process. Carefully observing the spatial relationships between bones and all other elements of the grave is therefore fundamental, and opens up possibilities to reconstruct both the original position of the body, as well as various aspects of the burial context itself. The following discusses the methodological process, along with some of the difficulties encountered with respect to three elements of the Cluniac funerary practices: pre-burial preparation of the body, the burial, and post-burial skeletal manipulations.

Pre-burial preparation of the body

The original presence and nature of soft envelopes (e.g. loose and tight wrappings, clothing, and footwear) can be inferred from the spatial distribution of skeletal elements. This has been demonstrated for prehistoric- (e.g. Nilsson 1998; Nilsson Stutz 2006; Willis and Tayles, 2009) and historic-period (e.g. Bonnabel and Carré, 1996; Bizot and Signoli, 2009) contexts. The process documented by the Customary for body preparation could conceivably have produced distinct skeletal patterns. For instance, the forearms or hands would appear in close proximity over the trunk (possibly exhibiting a strong degree of symmetry), the feet would be positioned together (a sewing together of slippers), and the skeletal profile could exhibit constrictions along the body consistent with a wrapping (tightly sewn robes). However, observations must take into account the whole burial context. A narrow feature, for example, could also produce some comparable skeletal constrictions (Nilsson Stutz, 2006), as discussed below. Intra- and inter-site patterns in forearm positioning have been examined for medieval contexts. Schematics have been produced (e.g. Durand, 1988), and gendered patterns proposed for monastic sites (Gilchrist and Sloane, 2005). However, in exploring the deliberate arrangement of the deceased within the grave, it should be remembered that a body undergoes significant movement during decay and decomposition. For instance, for forearms placed over the thorax or abdomen, the bloat of the abdomen during the early stages of decay, and possibly its expansion and collapse, and the flattening of the ribcage later in decay, can have a substantial impact (Duday and Guillon, 2006). For example, intense bloat of the abdomen can move the upper limbs laterally to the sides of the body if there is a void that allows movement. In assessing the original position of the body, there are thus many important factors to consider; the space of decomposition, and whether infilling of the spaces left by the decomposition of soft tissues was sufficiently progressive enough to 'fix' the skeletal elements in their original place, is fundamental here.

An assessment of the individuals from discrete graves at La Charité and Bermondsey revealed, overall, some distinct inter-site differences in the spatial arrangement of skeletal elements, where a greater degree of uniformity was evident in the former (cf. Williams, 2018). Variation in methods of body preparation can be proposed. On the whole, individuals from La Charité corresponded more closely to the expected skeletal patterning for those prepared in accordance with the Customary. Individuals 158 and 186 demonstrate this (Figures 17.1 and 17.2).

Figure 17.1 La Charité grave 157, individual 158, demonstrating possible skeletal patterning of the upper limbs for body preparation in accordance with the Customary. The forearms are positioned together and at right angles over the torso, and there is a lateral constriction at the shoulders; the humeri are elevated and positioned anteriorly with respect to the longitudinal axis of the skeleton, there is verticalisation of the clavicles, and the scapulae are rotated so that the glenoid cavities are positioned more obliquely and directed superiorly. This could have resulted from tight wrapping/tightly sewn robes (Image courtesy: D. Billoin, Institut National de Recherches Archéologiques Préventives).

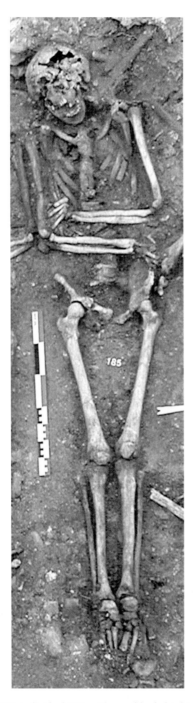

Figure 17.2 La Charité grave 185, individual 186, with possible skeletal indicators for tight wrapping/ tightly sewn robes. There is a strong convergence at the knees and ankles, and the feet are close together; the latter does not rule out a joining together of the night shoes. There is a lateral constriction at the shoulders that could suggest the former presence of a constrictive wrapping/tightly sewn robes. However, the close proximity of adjacent skeletal elements should be considered (Image courtesy: D. Billoin, Institut National de Recherches Archéologiques Préventives).

Both exhibit flexion at the elbows, with the forearms in close proximity to one another at roughly right angles across the torso. Indeed, for all 24 individuals assessed from La Charité, arrangements of the upper limbs were over the body (predominantly chest or abdominal region); only in four cases was a distinct asymmetry recorded. Arguably, for 158 and 186, this corresponds closely to their original positioning at the time of burial. Decomposition in a filled space can be proposed. There are no movements of bones outside of the initial volume of the cadaver and, in both cases, there are hand bones in close association with their corresponding forearms; these are possibly resting in positions of instability/disequilibrium with respect to the internal volume of the body.

Individual 186 exhibits a strong convergence at the knees and ankles (taken as ≤5 cm apart following Buquet-Marcon, Pecqueur and Detante, 2009), and the feet, which follow the axes of the tibiae, are close together. Night shoes (slippers) joined together and possibly made out of a woollen fabric that permitted a fairly rapid infiltration of soil could conceivably have produced this skeletal patterning. Positioning of the lower limbs could be assessed in 32 individuals from La Charité. For 21 (66%) of these, there was a clear convergence at the knees, and the feet were in close contact, often maintaining their articulations. Overall, these examples are less suggestive of a clothed burial, for which Buquet-Marcon, Pecqueur and Detante (2009) argue the knees, ankles and feet are more likely to be distinctly apart, with the bones of the latter having moved in opposing ways laterally (Figure 17.3).

Nineteen individuals (61% of the examinable sample) from La Charité exhibit skeletal constrictions, possibly deriving from tight-wrapping or sewn robes. For individual 158 (Figure 17.1), lateral constriction is evident at the shoulders. The humeri are rotated medially (the expected positioning for upper limbs arranged over the body in this manner), but they are positioned distinctly in an elevated and anterior position with respect to the longitudinal axis of the skeleton; some invisible element or 'wall effect' (Duday, 2006) could have maintained them in this position. There is also verticalisation of the clavicles, and the scapulae are rotated so that the glenoid cavities are positioned more obliquely and directed superiorly. This apparent constriction cannot be attributed to the sides of the grave feature; Staniaszek (2005) assessed these as indicating that the left shoulder, in particular, was at a distance from the grave wall. As decomposition took place in a 'filled space', a durable, tight burial container, for instance, could not have resulted in this spatial patterning. A constrictive wrapping (or tightly sewn robes) can instead be proposed. Caution is necessary, however, given that the lower limbs offer no clear supporting indicators; no general wall effect can be identified along the lower body (cf. Nilsson Stutz, 2006).

A comparable skeletal patterning can be observed for individual 186; possible lateral constrictions are also evident at the level of the shoulders. Although some form of tight wrapping cannot be discounted, for which the lower limbs offer supporting evidence, there are confounding factors. The upper limb of another individual is in close proximity to the right humerus of 186, and Staniaszek (2005) notes how the disturbed bones of the previous interment have impacted upon the positioning of the left scapula; it is showing its lateral border/aspect due to pressure from the surrounding material.

There was a much greater degree of variation in skeletal patterning for those examined from Bermondsey. In 20% (N=21) of the sample, at least one of the upper limbs was positioned alongside the body, and 23% (N=25) exhibited an asymmetrical arrangement of the upper limbs. In 31% (N=26), the lower limbs were distinctly apart, and the feet had clearly decomposed independently. Skeleton 168 demonstrates this (Figure 17.3). The lower limbs exhibit lateral rotation and are resting apart (around 10 cm at the ankles). The spatial patterning for the left and right foot bones is strongly comparable to an example from the Protestant cemetery of St Maurice, France (Buquet-Marcon, Pecqueur and Detante, 2009); here, their manner of lateral movement in opposite directions was argued to be more in line with a clothed burial. The former presence

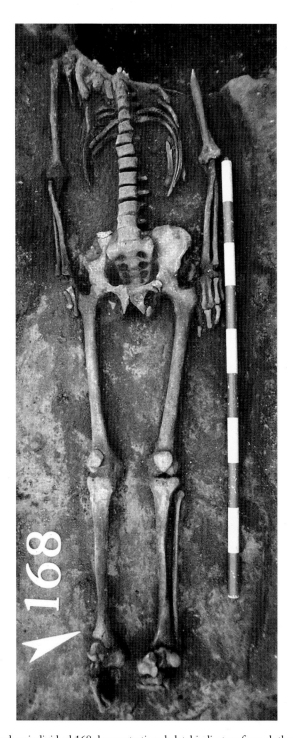

Figure 17.3 Bermondsey individual 168 demonstrating skeletal indicators for a clothed burial that is not in accordance with the Customary. The upper limbs are positioned alongside the body, the knees and ankles are distinctly apart, and the feet are laterally deviated ('out-turned'); tightly sewn robes and night shoes that have been joined together cannot be convincingly supported (Image courtesy: Museum of London).

of shoes could be proposed in the case of individual 168; there is a significant movement of left foot bones within a closely delimited space. As with the 14 individuals from Bermondsey exhibiting articulated laterally deviated ('out-turned') feet (where the bones showed their medial aspects), sewing together of the night shoes cannot be convincingly supported.

A constrictive wrapping could only be proposed for 17% (N=17) of the examinable skeletons. Individual 49 from Bermondsey exemplifies how markedly different the spatial patterning of skeletal elements in certain cases was compared to those examined at La Charité (Figure 17.4).

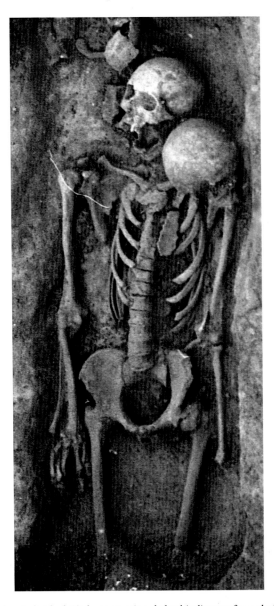

Figure 17.4 Bermondsey individual 49 demonstrating skeletal indicators for a clothed burial that is not in accordance with the Customary. The upper limbs are positioned alongside the body and distinctly apart from the thoracic cage; the latter exhibits a constricted 'rectangular' outline possibly indicative of the former presence of a sleeved garment with a separate bust (Image courtesy: Museum of London).

In Figure 17.4, a 'clothed burial' can be suggested. The upper limbs are positioned alongside the body, distinctly apart from the thoracic cage. The latter, which has maintained its original volume, appears constricted and exhibits a 'rectangular' outline (Buquet-Marcon, Pecqueur and Detante, 2009: 68). Fossurier (2009: 22–23) and Paresys (2009: 34) have described comparable examples for medieval sites in France; some form of sleeved garment with a separate bust has been proposed. The burial was truncated by a later interment; although the lower limbs cannot contribute further evidence, the skeletal patterning from the upper body clearly demonstrates a departure from Cluniac practice – clothed burial – as recorded in the Customary.

The burial

The Customary of Bernard describes a process where the deceased is possibly removed from the bier, placed supine in the grave, with the addition of a wooden cover over the body. From the examinable samples across both sites, decomposition in a 'filled space' was most prevalent, with 85% (N=28) and 80% (N=88) from La Charité and Bermondsey, respectively (e.g. Figures 17.1–17.4). However, there is an important distinction between 'mode of burial' and 'space of decomposition' (Tranoy, 2007). It is possible that non-durable wooden covers were placed over the graves (burial in a void), but either the wood decomposed relatively early, or they did not produce a tight seal, permitting a rapid infiltration of soil (decomposition in a filled space). Examples of loose-fitting wooden planks incorporated over graves at Cistercian Bordesley Abbey, England, demonstrate this complexity (Gilchrist and Sloane, 2005: 182). Where perishable covers could be attested at both sites, these were generally associated with more elaborate burial architecture such as stone cists, possibly suggesting that they were often reserved for those of certain status. In these cases, decomposition in a void was apparent due to movements of skeletal elements outside of the initial volume occupied by the cadaver. However, there was no evidence to support the former presence of a coffin; indicators such as 'linear delimitations' (Duday, 2009: 45) from coffin boards were not present (see below), and the presence of narrow head-niches would sometimes not permit an additional container.

For both sites, archaeothanatological approaches revealed modes of burial more clearly at odds with recorded customary procedures. Together with six other possible cases at Bermondsey, individual 130 exhibits skeletal evidence for interment within a coffin (Figure 17.5).

Figure 17.5 shows significant skeletal element movements within the initial volume occupied by the cadaver. There is a flattening of the ribs, and the hands (which were originally positioned over the thigh region) have disarticulated; the bones have stabilised on the base of the grave. There is some movement at the sacro-iliac joint; the *ossa coxae* have flattened to some degree, but the left ilium has maintained a raised position due to the underlying left forearm. The movements, including those at the more persistent joints, such as the sacro-iliac joint (Knüsel, 2014), indicate that these soft tissues were not progressively replaced by sediment. Unfortunately, this burial had been disturbed. This has particularly impacted the right side of the skeleton, possibly including the humerus and ulna, which show their lateral and posterior faces, respectively, uppermost. However, there is an overall body profile that could suggest burial within a closely fitted straight-edged container that tapered at the foot-end; delineation is apparent along the left side of the body from the proximal humerus to the distal fibula. The foot bones – although there is some possible disturbance within this region – have remained in a closely delimited space (cf. Blaizot, 2014). There is a possible lateral constriction evident at the shoulders, where the scapulae are angled more obliquely. The left humerus is rotated slightly medially. Although this could be the result of a coffin board, the cut edge could not be confidently determined within this region.

Figure 17.5 Bermondsey individual 130 demonstrating skeletal indicators for burial within a coffin. There are significant movements of skeletal elements within the initial volume occupied by the cadaver, with movements at the more persistent joints (e.g. the sacro-iliac joint) indicating delayed replacement of soft tissues by sediment. The overall body profile suggests burial within a straight-edged container that tapered at the foot end; delineation is apparent along the left side of the body from the proximal humerus to the distal fibula, and the foot bones have remained in a closely delimited space (Image courtesy: Museum of London).

Archaeological contextual evidence supports the osteological findings; wood fragments were recorded along the south edge of the burial, and frequent iron nails were recovered from the fill.

La Charité individual 315 illustrates the scenario where the body was interred supinely on a perishable structure and decomposed in a void that was most likely provided by a wooden covering (Figure 17.6). The archaeological evidence supports the latter; Staniaszek, (2005: 166–167) notes the presence of notches cut into the upper part of the pit walls that could have maintained an overlying structure. Decomposition in a long-lasting void is attested through the significant movements of skeletal elements both within and outside of the initial volume occupied by the cadaver. For example, there are displacements in the thoracic region, including a complete collapse of the ribcage. The cranium, which is detached from the mandible, has rotated to the left. The *ossa coxae* have flattened, and there is a lateral rotation of the femora, permitted by the disarticulation of the tibio-femoral joints (Knüsel, 2014). They show their posterior surfaces uppermost, as does the sacrum. These rotations can only have occurred due to the original presence of a structure, which following its disintegration created a secondary empty space. Staniaszek (2005) proposes a localised collapse of perishable support (probably planks) under the skeleton, which was placed along its long axis. There is no evidence in the form of constraints or linear delimitations to suggest deposition within a box-like structure, such as a coffin or bier (cf. Blaizot, 2014).

A unique find from these two sites was a deposit of charcoal adjacent to the feet of 315 (Staniaszek, 2005) (Figure 17.6). Similar examples have been recorded at Cluniac St-Nicolas-d'Acy (Bourry *et al.*, 1991). It could represent the remains of incense burning for symbolic or practical purposes. Schweitz (1981) cites a 12th-century text recommending that a fire should be lit near to the tomb to disguise bad odours. As with the coffin burial, if these two individuals were indeed monks, adaptations to Cluny customary practice may have been necessary measures. Decomposition begins almost instantaneously after death, and odours can start to be emitted from around 12–18 hours (Bardale, 2011: 154); a delayed burial may have required these steps to disguise putrefactive odours. Alternatively, they could represent individuals who died from an infectious disease, where deposition within a coffin or under a cover, together with charcoal burning, were thought to reduce the propensity to pollute. La Charité burial 205 included a thick layer of lime and charcoal over the body (Billoin, 2005); its position within the heavily used 13th-century gallery could have prompted such drastic measures to disguise the smell. Some of the individuals not wrapped according to the Customary could also represent those for whom minimal bodily contact was required. The ideal Cluniac funeral required an ideal death, but often this would not have been the case. A dead body is a complex entity around which the cultural necessities, but also the biological realities, of death must be negotiated, possibly promoting diverse responses from the living.

Post-burial skeletal manipulations

Evidence for the re-deposition of skeletal remains disturbed during grave digging was recorded at both La Charité and Bermondsey. Whilst some bones were incorporated into varying sized charnel pits, as evident at Bermondsey, a number of graves also included re-interred bones in the backfill, or in direct association with the body (i.e. in physical contact or purposefully arranged with regard to the new interment). Following Naji (2005: 181), it could be, however, that once body individuality was no longer evident, the remains (usually the bones) were considered material objects and thus treated pragmatically. Archaeothanatological enquiries suggest a more complex picture, indicating varied individual responses to the preceding dead. Two examples from La Charité and Bermondsey demonstrate this.

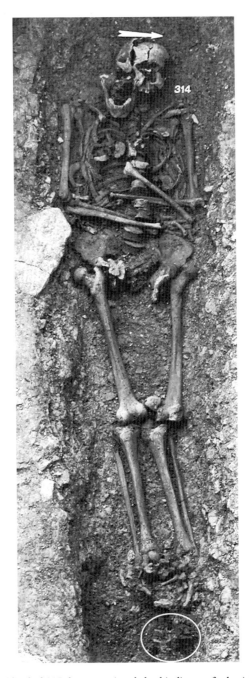

Figure 17.6 La Charité individual 315 demonstrating skeletal indicators for burial on a perishable structure and within a void provided by a perishable cover. There are significant movements of skeletal elements both within and outside of the initial volume of the cadaver. The complete lateral rotation of the femora to show their posterior surfaces uppermost attests to the original presence of a structure below the body, which following its disintegration created a secondary empty space. There is no evidence in the form of constraints or linear delimitations to suggest deposition within a box-like structure, such as a coffin. Circled is a charcoal deposit adjacent to the feet (Image courtesy: D. Billoin, Institut National de Recherches Archéologiques Préventives).

Burial 177 from the 13th-century gallery at La Charité included the skeletal remains of at least six re-deposited individuals (Staniaszek, 2005) positioned directly over and to the side of, skeleton 178, as well as in the backfill (Figure 17.7). This new interment was laid directly in the ground and decomposed in a filled space; there are no movements of bones outside of the initial volume of the cadaver, and even the more labile elements have been maintained in positions of instability. At the east end of the grave, the disordered assemblage of bones includes an articulated partial vertebral column and ribs; this individual was still in a state of decomposition at the time of disturbance, handling, and re-deposition.

Accumulations of bones such as these are often neglected, but they are no less important to consider for historic, than for prehistoric periods (Blaizot, 1997). They can reveal information on specific management strategies of funerary landscapes; here, the demands for burial within this prestigious gallery zone are clearly demonstrated. At the west end of the grave, a cranium and *os coxae* have been selected and deliberately positioned on either side of the head of 178. Arguably, this would have served to either protect (Staniaszek, 2005) or frame the head or to maintain it facing upward; this was a symbolically important position in medieval Christian thinking (Daniell, 1997: 178).

At both sites, there were numerous examples where burials included re-deposited crania and long bones that had been afforded prominent, highly visible, and carefully arranged positions with respect to the new interment (Figures 17.4 and 17.8). Figure 17.8 demonstrates this. Unfortunately, Bermondsey individual 187 was poorly preserved, but the re-deposited cranium, arguably deliberately placed over the abdominal region and facing east, has maintained its original position. However, it cannot be completely ruled out that the cranium was originally placed on the lid of a burial container, with its position on excavation representing a subsequent disintegration of the structure. Ideally, recording in the field should consider possible damage to skeletal elements – including re-deposited remains – that could have derived from such taphonomic events.

If the position of the cranium does indeed represent a deliberate placement, its preservation offers insight into some of the less formal and individual acts taking place in the course of a Cluniac funeral. It also contributes some complementary evidence of the manner of burial; decomposition in a filled space can be proposed. Burial in a void, where there is not rapid infilling of the internal spaces of the cadaver, the cranium would likely have been displaced with the significant taphonomic changes that occur in the abdominal region (Duday and Guillon, 2006) during the course of decomposition. As with the majority of examples discussed herein, this individual was interred directly in the ground and not within a closed container. The body and the remains of the former dead in direct physical contact would thus have been a very visible and emotive spectacle to those encircling the grave.

Following Gleize (2010), the evidence could suggest that certain bones were selected to possibly retain the deceased, or part of their body, in memory. Indeed, the hierarchical view of the body afforded the head particular significance; to represent the body, normally, the 'head' determined the place of burial (Binski, 1996: 55). In this respect, concern was not always solely for the newly deceased at the time of burial. Although the arranged *os coxae* and cranium in burial 177 could be seen as merely objects serving a functional purpose, they were still afforded a role in the funerary process. The Customary of Bernard describes how all the monks – including the boys and novices – were present at the graveside (Paxton, 2013); this was a community occasion. If indeed the examined burial zones were primarily reserved for the monastic dead, the living were brought face-to-face with deceased members of their own community. For an Order that actively encouraged regular meditation on the biological realities of death, the remains of the former dead (fully skeletonised or not) served as ideal tools for reflection at the grave edge; they

Figure 17.7 Examples of post-burial skeletal manipulations from La Charité burial 177. An *os coxae* and cranium are positioned flanking the cephalic extremity of individual 178, and at the east end of the grave, a still articulated partial vertebral column and ribs are situated amongst the re-deposited bones (Image courtesy: D. Billoin, Institut National de Recherches Archéologiques Préventives).

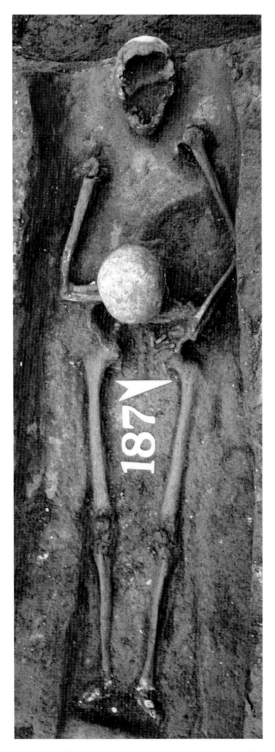

Figure 17.8 An example of a carefully re-positioned disturbed cranium placed over the abdominal region of Bermondsey individual 187 (Image courtesy: Museum of London).

too became part of this 'performative event' (Paxton, 2006). Through their handling and visible arrangement with respect to the new cadaver, the body was staged as one phase in a long process of decomposition and decay, and the individual as one within a wider community of the dead.

Conclusion

This chapter has aimed to demonstrate how archaeothanatological approaches – even where applied post-excavation – can reveal varied practical and symbolic actions surrounding the treatment of the Cluniac dead. Cluny Abbey strove to promulgate an image of perfection; the *Customaries* thus describe the ideal funeral, obscuring some of the individual responses and attitudes to death, burial, and the body, which can be revealed through detailed taphonomic study. Where excavation documentation permits, further medieval monastic sites could be re-visited using this approach to offer more nuanced insights into funerary treatment across contexts.

The *Customaries* were 'living texts' (Kerr, 2007: 14), and practice could be adapted. This high-resolution approach to reconstructing burials has offered new perspectives on the extent and nature of these adaptations, demonstrating a complex combination of practical and symbolic concerns on the part of the living monastic community. Certain practices seemingly followed the text more faithfully, such as the desired method of body preparation at La Charité. However, reconstructing aspects of practice for both the formal (pre-burial body preparation and interment) and informal (the treatment of disturbed remains) elements of the funeral revealed significant variability at both sites. The Cluniac ideal death required a protracted and intimate approach to the body, but on a fundamental level, the individual circumstances, and biological realities, of death could not always be so consistently managed, even by a reform-inspired Order.

References

Bardel, A. and Perennec, R. (2004). Abbaye de Landévennec: évolution du contexte funéraire depuis le haut Moyen Âge. In: A. Alduc-Le Bagousse, ed., *Inhumations et Édifices Religieux au Moyen Âge entre Loire et Seine*. Caen: Centre de Recherches Archéologiques et Historiques Médiévales (CRAHM), pp. 121–158.

Bardale, R. (2011). *Principles of forensic medicine and toxicology*. New Delhi: Jaypee.

Baud, A. (2000). La Place des Morts dans L'Abbaye de Cluny, État de la Question. *Archéologie Mediévale*, 29, pp. 99–114.

Billoin, D., ed. (2005). *La Charité-sur-Loire (58) 'Square des Bénédictins': Rapport de fouille*. Dijon: Institut National de Recherches Archéologiques Préventives (Inrap).

Billoin, D. and Staniaszek, L. (2005). Les sépultures. In: D. Billoin, ed., *La Charité-sur-Loire (58) 'Square des Bénédictins': Rapport de Fouille*. Dijon: Inrap, pp. 41–78.

Binski, P. (1996). *Medieval death: ritual and representation*. London: The British Museum Press.

Bizot, B. and Signoli, M., eds. (2009). *Rencontre autour des sépultures habillées. Actes du Colloque GAAF (Groupment d'anthropologie et d'archéologie funéraire) de Carry-le-Rouet (Bouches-du-Rhône)*. Gap: Éditions des Hautes-Alpes.

Blaizot, F. (1997). L'Apport des Méthodes de la Paléo-anthropologie Funéraire a l'Interprétation des Os en Situation Secondaire dans les Nécropoles Historiques – Problèmes Relatifs au Traitement et à l'Interprétation des Amas d'Ossements. *Archéologie Médiévale*, 26, pp. 1–22.

Blaizot, F. (2008). Réflexions sur la Typologie des Tombes à Inhumation: Restitution des Dispositifs et Implications Chrono-culturelles. *Archéologie Médiévale*, 38, pp. 1–30.

Blaizot, F. (2014). From the Skeleton to the Funerary Architecture: A Logic of the Plausible. *Anthropologie*, 52(3), pp. 263–284.

Bonnabel, L. and Carré, F., eds. (1996). *Rencontre autour d'un linceul. Actes de la journée d'étude organisée par le Groupment d'anthropologie et d'archéologie funéraire en Île-de-France (GAAFIF) et le Service régional de l'archéologie (SRA) de Haute-Normandie, Paris le 5 avril 1996*. Reims: CNRS Éditions.

Bourry, M., La Phung Xuan, F., Pereira da Silva, M., Cussenot, O. and Racinet, P. (1991). 'Vie' et Mort dans le Prieuré Clunisien de Saint-Nicolas d'Acy: Archéologie Funéraire et Anthropologie. *Revue Archéologique de Picardie*, 1(1–2), pp. 103–144.

Bruce, S. (2006). Nunc Homo, Cras Humus: A Twelfth-Century Cluniac Poem on the Certainty of Death (Troyes, Médiathèque de l'Agglomération troyenne 918, fols. 78v–79v). *The Journal of Medieval Latin*, 16, pp. 95–110.

Buquet-Marcon, C., Pecqueur, L. and M. Detante, M. (2009). Parés d'habits invisibles. In: B. Bizot and M. Signoli, eds., *Rencontre Autour des Sépultures Habillées. Actes du Colloque GAAF (Groupment d'anthropologie et d'archéologie funéraire) de Carry-le-Rouet (Bouches-du-Rhône)*. Gap: Editions des Hautes-Alpes, pp. 65–75.

Cochelin, I. (2000). Besides the book: using the body to mould the mind – Cluny in the tenth and eleventh centuries. In: G. Ferzoco and C. Muessig, eds., *Medieval Monastic Education*. Leicester: Leicester University Press, pp. 21–34.

Connell, B. and White, W. (2011). Human remains. In: T. Dyson, M. Samuel, A. Steele and S.M. Wright, eds., *The Cluniac Priory and Abbey of St Saviour Bermondsey, Surrey: Excavations 1984–95*. London: Museum of London Archaeology, pp. 263–274.

Daniell, C. (1997). *Death and burial in medieval England, 1066–1550*. London: Routledge.

de Valous, G. (1970). *Le monachisme clunisien des origines au XVe siècle: vie intérieure des monastères et organisation de l'Ordre*. 2nd ed. Paris: A. et J. Picard.

Duday, H. (2006). L'archéothanatologie ou l'archéologie de la mort. Translated by C.J. Knüsel. In: R.L. Gowland and C.J. Knüsel, eds., *Social Archaeology of Funerary Remains*. Oxford: Oxbow Books, pp. 30–56.

Duday, H. (2009). *The archaeology of the dead. Lectures in archaeothanatology*. Oxford: Oxbow Books.

Duday, H. and Guillon, M. (2006). Understanding the circumstances of decomposition when the body is skeletonized. In: A. Schmitt, E. Cunha and J. Pinheiro, eds., *Forensic Anthropology and Medicine: Complementary Sciences from Recovery to Cause of Death*. Totowa: Humana Press Inc., pp. 117–157.

Duday, H., Le Mort, F. and Tillier, A-M. (2014). Archaeothanatology and Funeral Archaeology. Application to the Study of Primary Burials. *Anthropologie*, 52(3), pp. 235–246.

Durand, M. (1988). Seconde Partie: Archéologie du Cimetière Médiéval. *Revue Archéologique de Picardie*, 6, pp. 27–206.

Dyson, T., Samuel, M., Steele, A. and Wright, S.M., eds. (2011). *The Cluniac Priory and Abbey of St Saviour Bermondsey, Surrey: excavations 1984–95*. London: Museum of London Archaeology.

Fossurier, C. (2009). Le site de Chanteloup-en-Brie (Ile de France): Études de cas et difficultés d'analyse taphonomique. In: B. Bizot and M. Signoli, eds., *Rencontre autour des sépultures habillées. Actes du colloque GAAF de Carry-le-Rouet (Bouches-du-Rhône)*. Gap: Éditions des Hautes-Alpes, pp. 21–27.

Gallien, V. and Langlois, J-Y. (1998). Typologie du cercueil à Saint-Denis. In: A. Dietrich and S. Vertogen, eds., *Rencontre Autour du Cercueil*. Paris: Groupment d'anthropologie et d'archeologie funéraire en Île-de-France (GAAFIF), pp. 23–25.

Gilchrist, R. and Sloane, B. (2005). *Requiem: the medieval monastic cemetery in Britain*. London: The Museum of London Archaeology Service.

Gleize, Y. (2007). Réutilisations de Tombes et Manipulations d'Ossements: Éléments sur les Modifications de Pratiques Funéraires au Sein de Nécropoles du Haut Moyen Age. *Aquitania*, 23, pp. 185–205.

Gleize, Y. (2010). Réutilisation de Tombes au Moyen Âge. Choix et Opportunités dans la Gestion des Espaces Funéraires. *Archéopages*, 29, pp. 48–57.

Kerr, J. (2007). *Monastic hospitality: the Benedictines in England c.1070–c.1050*. Woodbridge, Suffolk: The Boydell Press.

Knowles, D. and Brooke, C.N.L., eds/trans. (2002). *The monastic constitutions of Lanfranc*. New York: Oxford University Press.

Knüsel, C.J. (2014). Crouching in Fear: Terms of Engagement for Funerary Remains. *Journal of Social Archaeology*, 14, pp. 26–58.

Lyne, M. (1997). *Lewes Priory: excavations by Richard Lewis 1969–82*. Lewes: Lewes Priory Trust.

Naji, S. (2005). Death and remembrance in medieval France: A case study from the Augustinian monastery of Saint-Jean-des-Vignes, Soissons. In: G. Rakita, J. Buikstra, L. Beck, and S. Williams, eds., *Interacting with the Dead. Perspectives on Mortuary Archaeology for the New Millennium*. Gainesville: University Press of Florida, pp. 173–189.

Nilsson, L. (1998), Dynamic Cadavers. A 'Field Anthropological' Analysis of the Skateholm II Burials. *Lund Archaeological Review*, 4, pp. 5–17.

Nilsson Stutz, L. (2003). *Embodied rituals and ritualized bodies. Tracing ritual practices in late Mesolithic burials*. Stockholm: Almqvist and Wiksell International.

Nilsson Stutz, L. (2005). Setting it Straight. A Re-Analysis of the Mesolithic Barum Burial According to the Principles of Anthropologie 'de Terrain'. *Lund Archaeological Review*, 11–12, pp. 37–46.

Nilsson Stutz, L. (2006). Unwrapping the dead. Searching for evidence of mortuary practices at Zvenjnieke. In: L. Larsson and I. Zagorska, eds., *Back to the Origin. New Research in the Mesolithic-Neolithic Zvejnieki Cemetery and Environment, Northern Latvia*. Stockholm: Almqvist & Wiksell, pp. 217–233.

Paresys, C. (2009). Exemples de contraintes sur le squelette sans élément textile visible. In: B. Bizot and M. Signoli, eds., *Rencontre autour des sépultures habillées. Actes du colloque GAAF (Groupment d'anthropologie et d'archéologie funéraire) de Carry-le-Rouet (Bouches-du-Rhône)*. Gap: Éditions des Hautes-Alpes, 32–35.

Paxton, F.S. (1993). *A Medieval Latin death ritual: the monastic customaries of Bernard and Ulrich of Cluny*. Missoula, MT: St Dunstan's Press.

Paxton, F.S. (2006). Performing death and dying at Cluny in the High Middle Ages. In B. Morrill, J. Ziegler, and S. Rodgers, eds., *Practicing Catholic: Ritual, Body, and Contestation in Catholic Faith*. New York: Palgrave Macmillan, pp. 43–52.

Paxton, F.S. (2013). *The death ritual at Cluny in the Central Middle Ages / Le rituel de la mort à Cluny au Moyen Âge central*. Turnhout, Belgium: Brepols.

Roksandic, M. (2002). Position of skeletal remains as a key to understanding mortuary behaviour. In: W. Haglund and M. Sorg, eds., *Advances in Forensic Taphonomy: Method, Theory and Archaeological Perspectives*. New York: CRC Press, pp. 99–113.

Schweitz, D. (1981). Dépôts funéraires médiévaux en Vendômois et dans le Centre. *Revue Archéologique du Centre de la France*, 20, pp. 27–40.

Staniaszek, L. (2005). V. Catalogue des sépultures. In: D. Billoin, ed., *La Charité-sur-Loire (58) 'Square des Bénédictins': Rapport de Fouille*. Dijon: Inrap, pp. 81–180.

Tranoy, L. (2007). La mort en Gaule Romane. In: A. Ferdière., ed., *Archéologie Funéraire*. Paris: Errance, pp. 115–176.

Williams, E. (2018). Medieval monastic text and the treatment of the dead: an archaeothanatological perspective on adherence to the Cluniac customaries. In: B. Hausmair, B. Jervis, R. Nugent and E. Williams, eds., *Archaeologies of Rules and Regulation: Between Text and Practice*. Oxford: Berghahn, pp. 291–310.

Willis, A. and Tayles, N. (2009). Field Anthropology: Application to Burial Contexts in Prehistoric Southeast Asia. *Journal of Archaeological Science*, 36, pp. 547–554.

Woolley, L. (1997). Analysis of textiles and fibres. In: M. Lyne, ed., *Lewes Priory: Excavations by Richard Lewis 1969–82*. Lewes: Lewes Priory Trust, pp. 143–146.

18

'BRING OUT YOUR DEAD'

Funerary and public health practices in times of epidemic disease

Dominique Castex[1] and Sacha Kacki[1,2]

[1]PACEA, De la Préhistoire à l'Actuel: Culture, Environnement et Anthropologie, UMR 5199, CNRS-Université de Bordeaux, Pessac, France

[2]Department of Archaeology, Durham University, Durham, United Kingdom

Introduction

'Plague' has always stimulated human fears and anxieties: the simple evocation of this word awakens images of medieval drama, *Danse Macabre* and burial pits piled high with corpses. Written and iconographic sources relating to past epidemic episodes constitute strong evidence of these disastrous events. Their aim, however, was not necessarily to present the 'historic truth' and the subjectivity of authors often distorted the reflection of social reality. Due to the brutal and massive mortality produced by epidemics, it is commonly assumed that standard funerary practices were abandoned in favour of hasty, more pragmatic burials of the dead. Without denying the impact that epidemics could sometimes have on the burial of the dead, the idea of a pure and simple abandonment of funerary rituals in such a context appears too simplistic and requires investigation in view of the mounting archaeological evidence now available.

To date, there are very few papers devoted to this topic in the English-language literature; most that do exist are either focussed on graves that contain a large number of individuals (Knüsel, 1989) or limited to short case studies (Beauchamp, 2012). Many of the investigations performed to date on past epidemic diseases focus on the palaeobiology of the victims of epidemics, including studies on palaeodemography, palaeopathology and biomolecular diagnosis, as attested by an extensive bibliography on these topics. The effect of mass mortality on funerary practices, however, has been left almost completely unexplored, yet the subject remains a field of investigation of a great potential, owing to its promise for providing insight into the social dimension of past epidemics.

The purpose of this chapter is to illustrate the diversity of burial practices present in times of epidemics rather than to discuss the criteria used in archaeothanatology to identify

DOI: 10.4324/9781351030625-21

the simultaneous deposition of several bodies in the same burial pit (i.e. multiple burials).[1] The study of multiple burials is based on the same principles as for individual burials (cf. Blaizot, Chapter 1, this volume), with an additional approach that consists of assessing the relative chronology of the deposition of bodies that makes it possible to reconstruct the dynamics of the graves (Duday, 2008, 2009). Whatever the manner of death (massacres, wars, epidemics, etc.), each multiple grave has its own characteristics in terms of organisation and complexity, sometimes requiring the development of a methodological approach that differs from that most commonly used in archaeothanatology (Castex *et al.*, 2014; Kacki *et al.*, 2014; Castex and Blaizot, 2016).

Past epidemics: questions and study methods

For some time, two principal obstacles have delayed archaeological identification of epidemics. The first was linked to the lack of reliable methods to identify graves reflecting mortality crises, i.e. graves containing several individuals buried at the same time. The second concerned the difficulty of establishing a diagnosis of epidemics on the basis of a skeletal examination because acute diseases (e.g. plague, cholera, salmonellosis) cause no specific lesions on the skeleton.[2]

Only since the late 1980s, when preventive or rescue archaeology started its rapid expansion have burial sites linked to epidemic crises come to the fore. Archaeothanatological methods that have been introduced since that time have permitted the recognition of the simultaneous nature of specific deposits (Duday, 2008, 2009), thus making it possible to identify burial pits where several bodies were deposited in a relatively brief period of time. This, in turn, has allowed the identification of episodes of abnormal mortality (Castex *et al.*, 2014; Castex and Blaizot, 2016). In parallel, analytical techniques of human remains have improved progressively and led to the development of a number of tools that help to clarify the population effects of mortality crises. Initially, fundamental biological criteria can be exploited to reveal the demographic characteristics of the exhumed skeletal sample. Mortality crises do not affect the same sections of the population, and some epidemics are characterised by a specific demographic signature (Castex and Kacki, 2016). In addition, palaeopathological study of the skeletal remains is also informative, as it can reveal traumatic lesions pointing to accident or inter-personal violence as the cause of death (e.g. Colet *et al.*, 2014). Finally, biomolecular analysis is now essential because methods of extraction and

---

1 According to Leclerc and Tarrête (1988: 1002), the term 'multiple burials' refers to graves that contain several individuals who were buried simultaneously (e.g. Castex *et al.*, 2014: 299–300), as opposed to 'collective burials', which refer to burials formed by successive depositions of bodies over time (cf. Boulestin and Courtaud, Chapter 3, this volume; Knüsel, Gerdau-Radonić and Schotsmans, Chapter 34, this volume; Schmitt, Chapter 12, this volume). The simplest forms of multiple burials, i.e. those containing two, three or four individuals, are referred to herein as double, triple and quadruple burials, respectively, while the term 'multiple' is used to designate graves that contain more than four individuals. It is noteworthy that the term 'multiple', like that of 'collective', is still subject to debates (Boulestin, 2019). Although it is widely employed by French archaeologists, this term is still uncommon in the English-language literature, and is not always differentiated from the term 'collective' (cf. Knüsel and Robb, 2016). Moreover, the term appears ambiguous in the field of sociology, where mass deaths are frequently described as 'collective deaths' (Clavandier, 2004: 1).

2 These diseases lead to rapid death (or recovery), which occurs too rapidly for the body to develop identifiable skeletal lesions. They differ in this respect from other infectious diseases, such as leprosy, tuberculosis, and syphilis, which are non-fatal in the short term, and can be diagnosed through a macroscopic assessment of bone lesions.

amplification of ancient DNA fragments contained in skeletal remains permit the identification of various pathogens responsible for epidemics (e.g. Vågene *et al.,* 2018; Keller *et al.,* 2019). Thanks to archaeo-anthropological investigations, new sources of information on past epidemics have been revealed that now challenge some stereotypical interpretations. The proponents of the thus renewed investigation of epidemics, mainly archaeologists and anthropologists, provide a subtler picture of the impact of infectious disease outbreaks on the behaviour of past societies. Funerary behaviours adopted during mortality crises contribute to documenting the relationship of past populations to death as a result of epidemic disease.

The present contribution aims, firstly, to provide a comparative study of burial sites related to the Black Death (1347–1352 AD), i.e. the first outbreak of the second plague pandemic (Kacki and Castex, 2012). This synthesis will place the results previously obtained into a broader perspective with new data collected during the excavation of other burial sites completely or partly formed in epidemic periods, including sites that pre-date or post-date the Black Death, as well as sites related to other pathogens. Secondly, this contribution will review the medical theories that prevailed during the second plague pandemic (14th–18th centuries), the best-documented period from a historical point of view, in order to finally assess their potential influence on the variation in the burial treatments of plague victims across these centuries.

Rapid funerals and the persistence of customary funerary practices

Over the past few decades, several dozen epidemic-related burial sites have been excavated in Europe.[3] Not all of them, however, are of equal importance to the study funerary practices during epidemics. Some sites were studied only through palaeogenetic or palaeo-immunological analyses aimed at assessing the causative pathogen. The present study is limited to those sites for which information on details of how burials were deposited were available, thus allowing for a thorough examination of their variability across time and space (Table 18.1).

Multiple inhumations

Inhumations, and in particular multiple inhumations, can be considered as the only archaeological evidence permitting reliable identification of ancient mortality crises.[4] In fact, faced with uncustomary high numbers of deaths, it is generally easier to resort to the simultaneous inhumation of several individuals within the same grave (Figure 18.1). However, deaths due to epidemic disease can be handled variously according to the virulence of the epidemic, the number of deaths (which can vary from the start to the end of an epidemic outbreak), and the reaction of the population to the situation. Archaeological sites related to epidemic crises present in various forms, from cemeteries composed solely of individual graves to burial grounds consisting of numerous multiple burials. The oldest sites in the sample, which date from the 5th and 6th centuries AD, illustrate this diversity well: at Sens (Yonne, France), several juxtaposed multiple

---

3 It is noteworthy that many of these sites are located in France (more than 30), probably due, in great part, to a national heritage legislative framework that is particularly favourable to their discovery.

4 It is possible that cremation was practised during some epidemics, which would almost certainly escape archaeological identification. The grouping of burnt bones from several individuals within the same funerary structure can be demonstrated through archaeo-anthropological studies, but it is generally impossible to confirm that the cremation of several different bodies was simultaneous.

Table 18.1 Inventory of the sites taken into account in the analysis of burial treatment during epidemics; only sites with appropriate archaeological information have been included

Sites	Chronology	Epidemic nature	References
Clos des Cordeliers, **Sens** (France)	5th–6th century	Plague	Castex (2008)
Espace Pierre Mendès-France, **Poitiers** (France)	5th–6th century	Plague?	Godo (2010)
Grand cimetière, **Bourges** (France)	11th–16th century	Plague?	Georges and Blanchard (2007)
East Smithfield, **London** (Great Britain)	14th century	Plague?	Grainger et al. (2008)
Saint Pierre, **Dreux** (France)	14th century	Plague	Castex (2008)
St Laurent-de-la-Cabrerisse (France)	14th century	Plague	Kacki et al. (2011)
Vilarnau (France)	14th century	Plague	Passarrius et al. (2008)
Saints Just et Pastor, **Barcelona** (Spain)	14th century	Plague	Kacki and Castex (2014)
16 rue des 36 Ponts, **Toulouse** (France)	14th century	Plague	Gourvennec (2018
Lazzaretto Vecchio, **Venice** (Italy)	Mid 14th–late 16th century	Plague	Rigeade (2009)
Santa Clara, **Palma de Majorque** (Spain)	16th century	Plague?	Castex (2008)
Les Fédons, **Lambesc** (France)	16th century	Plague	Bizot et al. (2005)
San Michele, **Alghero** (Italy)	16th century	Plague	Milanese (2010)
Maria Troon, **Dendermonde** (Belgium)	16th–17th century	Plague?	Kacki (2016)
Lariey, **Puy-Saint-Pierre** (France)	17th century	Plague	Signoli et al. (2007)
Saint-Benoît, **Prague** (Czech Republic)	Late 17th century	Typhus?	Castex et al. (2011)
Hospitaliers de St Jean de Jérusalem, **Epinal** (France)	17th–18th century	Plague?	Réveillas (2010)
Hospice Sainte-Catherine, **Verdun** (France)	17th–18th century	Plague?	Réveillas (2010)
Issoudun (France)	Late 17th–early 18th century	Measles?	Souquet-Leroy et al. (2011)
Ilôt St Louis, **Boulogne-sur-Mer** (France)	18th century	Smallpox?	Castex and Réveillas (2007)
L'observance/Leca, **Marseille** (France)	1720–1722	Plague	Tzortzis and Signoli (2016)
Les Capucins de Ferrières, **Martigues** (France)	1720–1722	Plague	Tzortzis and Signoli (2016)
Le Délos, **Martigues** (France)	1720–1722	Plague	Tzortzis and Signoli (2016)
Rue Nicolas Roland, **Reims** (France)	Late18th–early 19th century	Cholera?	Paresys et al. (2019)

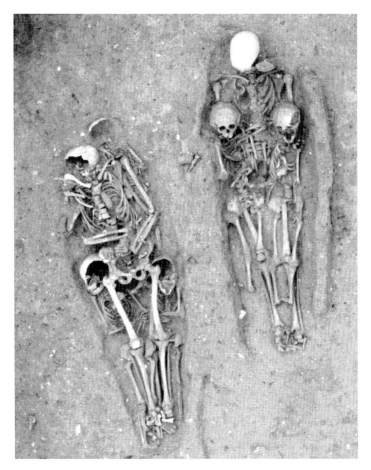

Figure 18.1 Two multiple graves from the site of L'Ilot Saint-Louis in Boulogne-sur-Mer (Pas-de-Calais, France) (Image courtesy: Archaeological Service of Boulogne-sur-Mer).

graves have been identified; on the contrary, at Poitiers (Vienne, France), individual and multiple graves are found together. A variety of types of burial are also found during the Black Death. The sites of Dreux (Eure-et-Loir, France) and Saint Mary Graces, East Smithfield, London (UK) are characterised by the presence of numerous multiple graves, whereas many plague victims at Saint-Laurent-de-la-Cabrerisse (Aude, France) received individual treatment. Similarly, at the beginning of the early modern period, the Les Fédons cemetery in Lambesc (Bouches-du-Rhône, France) furnishes ample evidence of the controlled management of the dead, with the majority of the victims buried in individual graves. The same controlled management is found at the chronologically contemporary sites of Dendermonde (East Flanders, Belgium) and Lariey de-Puy-Saint-Pierre (Hautes-Alpes, France). In more recent periods, this co-existence of individual and multiple graves seems to give way progressively to the preferential use of multiple burials. Apart from the Prague (Czech Republic) cemetery, all the burial sites included in this treatment dating to the early modern period contain only multiple graves.

From the juxtaposition of individual graves to the creation of veritable mass graves[5]

It is essential to take into account the number of bodies placed in graves in order to understand the accumulation of deaths in an epidemic context. In large towns, burial pits can contain several hundred bodies, as is the case in London, where the East Smithfield Black Death cemetery revealed several long trenches containing rows of skeletonised individuals. Similarly, the partial excavation of a contemporary multiple grave at Barcelona (Catalonia, Spain) has produced 120 plague victims from an estimated total of several hundred. A similar case was recognised in Toulouse, where three very large multiple graves each contained over 100 individuals. In smaller urban centres, the number of individuals is generally lower, although a few dozen individuals are sometimes found in the same pit. For example, at Dreux (Eure-et-Loir, France), some graves contain more than 20 skeletons. At the other extreme, rural sites generally reveal small funerary deposits. Simultaneous burial depositions often concern only two or three individuals, as at Vilarnau (Pyrénées-Orientales, France) and at Saint-Laurent-de-la-Cabrerisse (Aude, France). This observation suggests a hypothetical relationship between the size of burial pits and population size of the communities affected by epidemics.

Similar observations can be made for burial grounds dating to both before and after the Black Death. In the Early Middle Ages, the burial site of Sens (Yonne, France) confirms the presence of graves containing a large number of victims in an urban context. On the contrary, the site at Poitiers is characterised by the co-occurrence of different grave types (individual, double, triple and one quadruple). The joint use of individual and multiple graves, the latter containing more than a single individual, remains a frequent occurrence in more recent epidemics, as illustrated by the cemeteries of Dendermonde (East Flanders, Belgium), Lariey (Hautes-Alpes, France) and Lambesc (Bouches-du-Rhône, France) (Figure 18.2). Sites dating to the early modern period, however, reveal a different mode of body treatment. At this time, the juxtaposition of multiple burials containing a high number of individuals is observed (e.g. in Prague, Czech Republic; Issoudun, Indre, France; and Reims, Marne, France), but also veritable mass graves, such as those formed in Marseille and Martigues (Bouches-du-Rhône, France) during the 1720–1722 AD plague. This changing treatment of epidemic victims particularly concerns inhumation areas found in urban contexts.

These observations demonstrate that in periods of epidemic burials can take different forms, from the individual grave to veritable mass graves. Some tendencies are indicated according to the historical period and the demographic characteristics of the affected populations. This result is fundamental to achieving a better understanding of the history of epidemics, archaeological evidence permitting perception of certain subtleties that historical texts do not render so faithfully. Furthermore, these results underline the difficulty of identifying burial features linked to mortality crises. Individual graves may co-exist with multiple graves and may even be more numerous, if not unique, in some cases. In such conditions, it is fundamental to complement the

---

5 There is no real consensus on the definition of the terms 'mass grave' (see, for example, Boulestin and Courtaud, Chapter 3, this volume). According to Knüsel and Robb (2016: 657), a mass grave represents 'A deposition of multiple individuals in a single episode [...]; a mass grave is indicated by large numbers of articulated individuals placed tightly together and often in layers, in a single feature, and sometimes in a disordered state (i.e. in various orientations), which departs from the norm in a given time and place'. Based on this definition, the terms 'mass grave' is used herein to specifically refer to those multiple burials that are made of dozens of bodies lying in various positions and orientations.

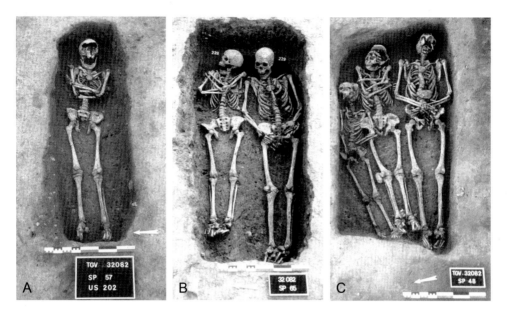

Figure 18.2   Examples of (A) individual, (B) double and (C) triple graves uncovered at the site of Les Fédons in Lambesc (Bouches-du-Rhône, France) (Image courtesy: Institut National de Recherches Archéologiques Préventives).

archaeological evidence with bioarchaeological analysis of the remains, permitting the identification of characteristics of the assemblage based on the age-at-death and sex of the deceased (Castex and Kacki, 2016).

Funerary treatments

Burial methods

The demands of burying great numbers of cadavers can lead to modifications in the funerary treatment of the dead. The use of individual containers, such as coffins, becomes unsustainable during an epidemic when the number of deaths rapidly overtakes the capacity to produce such containers. Similarly, the use of a single container to bury several individuals requires a larger than normal construction design that proves equally difficult to produce. It is thus logical to anticipate the preferential use of plain-earth burial pits filled with soil immediately after deposition of bodies.

Burial directly in earth is a characteristic common to the great majority of the sample of the victims of epidemics studied here, independent of the chronological context and/or the pathogen involved. In the Early Middle Ages, this characteristic can sometimes help to distinguish between graves from epidemics and those resulting from natural mortality. Indeed, in the Early Middle Ages, burials traditionally took place in containers of wood or other durable material (stone chests or *sarcophagi*). During later periods, on the contrary, burial directly in the ground is not limited to the victims of epidemics; some cemeteries containing graves linked to the Black Death also provide numerous simple earth-pits in periods preceding the outbreak of the epidemic. As an example, this type of grave was commonplace as early as the 11th and 12th centuries in the cemeteries of Saint-Laurent-de-la-Cabrerisse (Aude, France) and Vilarnau (Pyrénées-Orientales, France).

Although these earth-pit burials appear to be the majority in times of epidemics, they are in no way the only method of the treatment of the dead. In some graves linked to epidemics, the presence of metallic pins and archaeothanatological evidence suggests that the bodies were shrouded (e.g. in Lambesc, Bouches-du-Rhône, France; Issoudun; Indre, France; Prague, Czech Republic). Moreover, the use of containers was sometimes maintained, as in the Belgian site of Dendermonde, which produced a number of multiple graves where several deceased individuals were lying within one wooden container (Figure 18.3). At East Smithfield, at least 230 out of the 750 plague victims that have been excavated were interred in individual coffins. These examples show variation in the funerary equipment used in times of epidemic disease outbreaks. The deposition of bodies directly in earth-pits cannot alone indicate an epidemic context, no more than the adoption of more elaborate burial methods can exclude it.

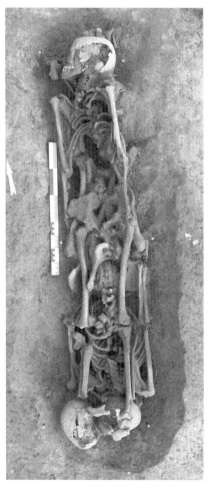

Figure 18.3 A multiple grave discovered at the site of Dendermonde (East Flanders, Belgium). The skeletons lie in various positions and orientations. The displacement of some bones suggests that decomposition took place in an empty space. Some compression effects are visible, such as the restricted alignment of the bones of the left upper limbs of the two individuals on the right-hand side of the photograph. These characteristics suggest that the bodies were buried in a wooden coffin. (Image courtesy: Antea Group Belgium).

Position of the bodies

In the two early medieval sites in the sample, individuals demonstrate standardised positions. In each case, they were buried supinely. In Poitiers, their cephalic extremities were oriented consistently to the west. In Sens, the orientations were more variable, depending on the grave examined.

Graves dating to the beginning of the second plague pandemic in the 14th century are also characterised by controlled management of the cadavers and a relative respect for the funerary practices that were in use before the epidemic. Individuals have the same orientation, being oriented on a roughly east-west axis, with the cephalic extremity generally to the west. Similarly, they lie, with rare exceptions, supinely,[6] more or less similar to those of bodies buried in non-epidemic times. Conversely, in some later contexts, the need to rationalise the space within multiple graves supplanted Christian norms. A 'head-to-tail' disposition is observed at several post-medieval sites related to epidemics (Figure 18.4). This positioning is, however, similar in most

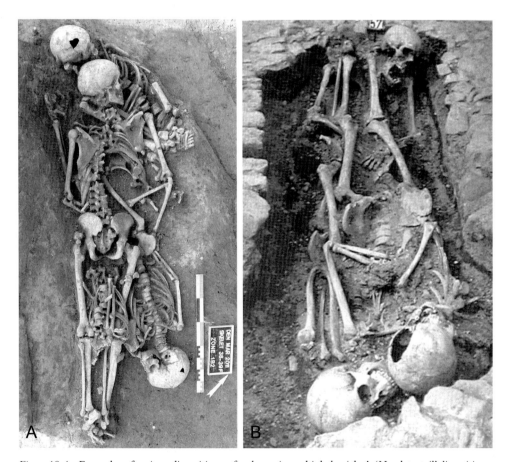

Figure 18.4 Examples of various dispositions of cadavers in multiple burials: A. 'Head-to-tail' disposition in Prague (Czech Republic); B. Prone disposition in Dendermonde (East Flanders, Belgium) (Image courtesy: Archaeological Service of Prague and Antea Group Belgium, respectively).

---

6 A few individuals were placed on their sides (two at Saint-Laurent-de-la-Cabrerisse and one at Vilarnau) and others in a prone position (one at Vilarnau, one at Barcelona).

of the sites (e.g. Lambesc, Bouches-du-Rhône, France; Dendermonde, East Flanders, Belgium; Prague, Czech Republic). More rarely, the 'head-to-tail' disposition is a recurrent finding in some sites, such as in Issoudun (Indre, France), a site that is also noteworthy for its high proportion, some 7%, of individuals placed in a prone (*procubitus*) position.

Until the beginning of the modern period, most victims of epidemic diseases underwent similar funerary treatment to that given those who died of natural causes. Although deposits on the side and face down could occur in some instances, they remain rare occurrences, even in the case of large burial pits containing several dozen bodies. Moreover, divergences in orientation seem to have been dictated by limitations of space for burying numerous individuals over a very short lapse of time. There is evidence for the strict and respectful handling of the dead at burial sites employed for the interment of the victims of epidemics in the early modern period (e.g. in Boulogne-sur-Mer, Pas-de-Calais, France and Reims, Marne, France). On the contrary, in other sites, the positions of skeletons reveal the abandonment of customary funerary practices and an anarchic treatment of the dead. An emblematic example of this shift is the mass grave of l'Observance in Marseille. This mass grave contained the skeletons of more than 200 victims of the 1722 AD plague epidemic lying in various positions and orientations with no apparent organisation, suggesting that some of them may have been thrown from the top of the pit. As with other aspects of burial treatment, the 18th century seems to mark a turning point in the treatment of the bodies of victims, the necessity of a rapid interment seemingly superseding all other considerations.

Grave goods and prophylactic treatments

Grave goods buried with the dead are relatively rare in graves related to epidemic crises. This information must, however, be treated differently according to the chronological context of the graves. It is interesting to underline their absence from the multiple graves of the Early Middle Ages at Sens and Poitiers in France. During this period, the presence of personal items of adornment, such as belt buckles, pins, and weapons) was frequent in France in non-epidemic contexts (e.g. Effros, 2003), and the hypothesis of a less elaborate funerary ceremonies during epidemic crises can be entertained to explain this absence. This difference could indicate either that the number of deaths had forced the survivors to modify traditional customs or that their condition as victims of an epidemic conferred an altered status on them, communicated through the aegis of the funeral. The absence of grave goods in the medieval period is not particularly informative, their deposition being infrequent at that time. Conversely, some epidemic graves of the modern period contained various personal effects such as coins (e.g. Lambesc, Bouches-du-Rhône, France; Prague, Czech Republic; and Boulogne-sur-Mer, Marne, France). In these cases, it is difficult to know, however, whether such objects were deliberately placed due to their symbolic value or, on the other hand, if they reveal an absence of preparation of the body (undressing, washing, etc.) before burial, with the aim of limiting physical contact with the corpses.

For some sites, such as those of Marseille, Martigues and Lambesc (all three located in the Bouches-du-Rhône, France), the absence of archaeological artefacts associated with the skeletons could indicate that the dead were admitted to hospitals or infirmaries prior to their deaths. It is also conceivable that the absence of personal belongings in the graves was a consequence of cultural prescriptions disseminated in *Ars moriendi* ('The Art of Dying') Latin texts; indeed, according to Christian conceptions at the end of the Middle Ages, the 'art of dying well' was to get rid of things that were superfluous (Ariès, 1949). Also, some references to contemporary multiple deaths show that such deprivation in death could testify to the wish of a population not to differentiate among victims linked by a common death (Clavandier, 2004).

The use of material with prophylactic properties during past epidemics is attested by some contemporary written sources, although rarely cited in publications on the subject (Harding, 1993; Gilchrist, 2019: 10). Archaeological evidence has confirmed this practice through the discovery of numerous graves containing lime, such as those from Martigues and Marseille (Bouches-du-Rhône, France) and those from Prague (Czech Republic). It is interesting to note that most of these examples date from the modern period. For the Middle Ages, only one grave containing lime has been discovered to date in the city of Barcelona.

Funerary spaces dedicated to the burial of victims of epidemics

The sudden and rapid increase in mortality may have influenced the choice of place of burial for the victims of epidemics. It might be expected that the victims of fatal and highly transmissible infectious diseases would be systematically excluded from traditional burial grounds, but, once again, archaeological examples testify to a great variability in the sites chosen for examination here. In the Early Middle Ages, it is difficult to generalise about this variation because of the limited number of sites from this period discovered to this day. However, these rare examples indicate that the graves of victims of epidemics were established in various places. The multiple graves found at Sens (Yonne, France) were integrated within an existing cemetery, which continued in use until the 10th century. On the other hand, the multiple graves discovered at Poitiers (Vienne, France) are situated in a disused neighbourhood of the ancient town and, in this case, the creation of a burial area dedicated solely to epidemic victims is suspected.

At the beginning of the second plague pandemic, burials of victims of epidemics were largely integrated within pre-existing parish cemeteries. In London, two cemeteries were created specifically to receive plague victims. One of them, at East Smithfield, has undergone a large, though partial excavation. It is one of the rare European examples of a new foundation of a cemetery reserved for victims of the Black Death. In France, such sites seem to have appeared later, towards the end of the 16th century.

At the end of the Middle Ages, victims of epidemics were, it seems, not generally excluded from consecrated ground. However, the location of the multiple graves within the cemeteries suggests that certain areas may have been reserved for them. At Dreux (Eure-et-Loir, France), graves containing multiple individuals are found on the margins of the burial site, in an area occupied previously by a limited number of graves. At the sites of Vilarnau (Pyrénées-Orientales, France) and Saint-Laurent-de-la-Cabrerisse (Aude, France), the plague pits were located in areas used for numerous burials before the epidemic. At Vilarnau, most of the multiple graves were situated in the eastern half of the burial ground, clustered in a limited area. At Saint-Laurent-de-la-Cabrerisse, the three multiple graves identified were located in the immediate proximity of the south lateral wall of the church. Whereas graves containing multiple individuals were sometimes grouped together, the variety of the areas occupied shows little in the way of common practice. In other words, it appears premature to conclude that such topographic characteristics reflect the will of the living to place the victims of epidemics in a selected area. It cannot be excluded that this re-grouping simply signals the only area of inhumation in use when the epidemic occurred. Furthermore, nothing refutes the possibility that individual graves containing victims of epidemics were located in other areas of the cemetery. Such a possibility is attested for the cemetery of Saint-Laurent-de-la-Cabrerisse (Aude, France), where two individual graves linked to the plague epidemic by the results of palaeo-immunological analysis are located on the eastern and southern edges of the burial area, some 20 m away from the group of graves containing multiple individuals.

During the centuries that followed the Black Death, new locations were adopted for the burial of victims of epidemics. When integrated within a pre-existing cemetery, graves containing multiple individuals were clearly grouped in a specific area (Figure 18.5). Moreover, sites dedicated

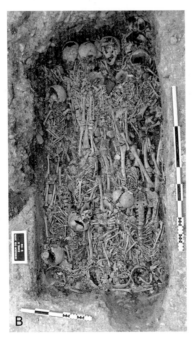

Figure 18.5 A. Examples of grouping of simultaneous burials; B. and detail of the skeletal assemblage in one of the burials from Issoudun (Indre, France) (Image courtesy: Institut National de Recherches Archéologiques Préventives).

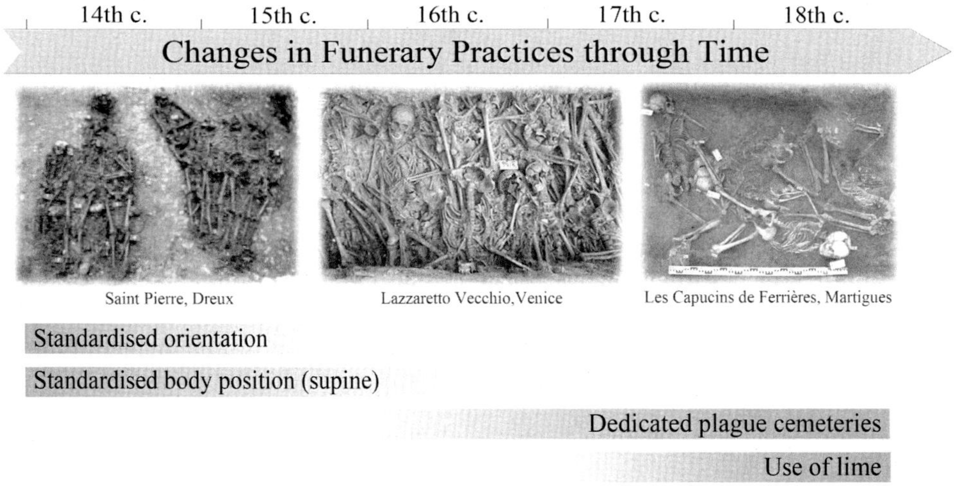

Figure 18.6 Changing funerary practices during the second plague pandemic (Source: the authors).

solely to the burial of victims of epidemics were commonly created. In France, the oldest known example of such a dedicated burial ground is the cemetery of Les Fédons in Lambesc (Bouches-du-Rhône, France), which was associated with a plague infirmary in use during the epidemic outbreak of 1590 AD. In succeeding centuries, other examples of similar cemeteries are documented, such as the cemetery of Lariey (Hautes Alpes, France) and the mass graves dug in the towns of Marseille and Martigues (Bouches-du-Rhône, France) in the early 18th century. In parallel, the hospitals of some towns also received people suffering from epidemic diseases. Multiple graves are found in their cemeteries (e.g. Bourges, Verdun, Épinal in France). Similarly, some religious establishments buried victims of mass mortality on their lands (e.g. in Dendermonde, East Flanders, Belgium; Palma de Mallorca, Mallorca, Spain).

In the light of archaeological discoveries made in the past 20 years, a clear change in the choice of burial sites for the victims of epidemics occurred. The parish cemetery was slowly abandoned, while burial sites destined to receive victims of epidemics progressively developed. The archaeological examples cited above reveal great variation in the burial treatment of victims of epidemics, far from the generally accepted stereotypes. But it is, above all, during the second plague pandemic, a period providing abundant archaeological evidence, that progressive modification of the treatment afforded to the plague-stricken is apparent (Figure 18.6). The reasons for this change in behaviour and its possible link to reactions of populations to infected individuals and concepts of disease transmission deserve further scrutiny. An initial review of the scientific and more commonly held perceptions of and explanations for the occurrence of contagion during the 14th–18th century is relevant in this regard.

The concept of plague in the late middle ages and modern period

Six centuries after the end of the first plague pandemic, plague re-appeared in Europe during the mid-14th century. The first five years of this second pandemic (1347–1352 AD), today known as the 'Black Death', produced enormous mortality, between 25% and 50% of the European population (Biraben, 1975). Numerous outbreaks recurred regularly in Europe during the 14th and 15th centuries and then occurred less frequently until the 18th century.

Divine punishment and the doctrine of miasma (14th–early 15th century)

The study of various medieval sources – medical, literary, philosophical texts and poetry – shows that three principal causes were proposed to explain the appearance and wide dissemination of plague within the population during the Late Middle Ages.

An expression of divine punishment

Contemporaries of the Black Death considered the disease to be an expression of God's anger, spread over the earth to punish humans for their sins (Flambard-Héricher, 2005). The only hope of survival was to turn to God with contrition and to do penance. Religious processions were organised regularly in places affected by plague and survivors were ordered to pray regularly in thanks to God. Other devotional practices included religious donations, pilgrimages, and, in some Italian towns, participation in brotherhoods dedicated to care of the sick and burial of the victims of the epidemic (Horrox, 1994: 96). The piety engendered by plague epidemics provoked a resurgence of movements such as 'Flagellants', a secular, essentially male, association of common people, whose members organised processions during which they flogged themselves in public as a sign of atonement for their sins (Calmet, 1738: 585–587).

Natural causes

A number of explanations were simultaneously developed by 14th-century scholarly medicine. It was declared that, although possibly the result of consuming bad food or water, the disease was principally caused by corruption of the air linked to the circulation of miasmas or toxic vapours (Arrizabalaga, 1994). Their inhalation was harmful, as the poison went directly to the heart producing corruption of the essence of the soul and destruction of the life force. One of the principal causes of the corruption may have been a conjunction of planets that led to the liberation of pestilential vapours on earth. This hypothesis conforms to Hippocratic medical doctrine, where a strong relationship exists between the microcosm (i.e. humans) and the macrocosm (i.e. heavenly elements). In addition to this astrological cause, abnormal climatic variations or even the south wind were held responsible. Foul air may have spread from stagnant water (lakes, marshes) or confined spaces (cellars, attics); it may have come from excrement or from decaying matter, particularly decomposing bodies. Illnesses could, according to some authors, fly from the eyes of a dying victim to those of the healthy person at their side watching over them (Santer, 2014: 61–62).

The struggle against plague was initially a combat against malodorous emanations through the use of certain spices, aromatic herbs and odoriferous woods. The rich could acquire sachets of ambergris.[7] Forms of magic appear and some writings about the plague tell of prescriptions using precious stones applied either internally or externally (Weill-Parot, 2004: 5–7). It was said that the corrupted air could enter the body not only by breathing but also through the pores of the skin, and it was advised to avoid activities that dilated the pores, such as baths, intense physical activity, sexual relations and excessive consumption of food and alcoholic drinks. These recommendations were accompanied by traditional medical treatments such as bloodletting, supposed to help expel corrupt humours. Various 14th-century medical writings report these

---

7 'Ambergris', or 'grey amber', is a strongly scented intestinal concretion of the sperm whale (*Physeter macrocephalus*).

instructions, amongst them the *Compendium de Epidemia*, a collective work compiled by members of the Paris Faculty as early as October 1348 (Rébouis, 1888) or the *Grande Chirurgie*, written in 1363 by Guy de Chauliac, physician to Pope Clement VI (Chauliac, 1363; Jacquart, 1997, 1998).

Human causes

Some people, unable to accept the unrelenting nature of the disease, sought a rational cause and human responsibility. Accusations were thus levelled against anybody outside the affected communities, such as strangers, travellers, paupers or even lepers. However, Jews were the most frequently incriminated. Accused of spreading the disease by poisoning well water, they were chased away, persecuted and often massacred, as was the case in Strasbourg, where 900 Jews were burned alive in a pit in their cemetery. Despite condemnations by the Catholic Church, numerous pogroms took place during the first years of the second pandemic.[8]

This brief panorama of medieval concepts about the causes of plague clearly shows a divine nature ascribed to the disease as well as the predominance of the theory of miasma[9] in medical thinking. It is undeniable, however, that the contagious nature of the disease was very quickly recognised by contemporaries of the epidemic.[10] Although a minority, some physicians, such as Guy de Chauliac, defended the idea of disease contagiousness from the start of the second pandemic. Furthermore, this hypothesis was supported by most of the contemporary chroniclers who considered that the disease could be contracted by simple contact with the victim or their possessions. This notion of contamination is also found in certain literary works (e.g. in *The Decameron* by Boccaccio, 1353).

Contagion theses began to take shape, but theological and medical quarrels did not seem to affect the attitudes of the general population as only the upper classes were conscious of the debates taking place. It is much later that medical guidelines became more widely available (Flambard-Héricher, 2005; Nicoud, 2005). The idea of contagion remained associated with moral fault, and consequently, good behaviour and morals continued as the best method of prevention. Royal and local authorities acted primarily to combat the corruption of the air by means of sanitary regulation (Horrox, 1994: 100), by street cleaning and by perfuming houses. Some medical practices were more pragmatic; without questioning the miasmatic theory, they very rapidly recommended isolation of the victims, initially timid suggestions becoming general and more efficient by the end 15th or early 16th centuries (Jacquart, 1980: 35–86).

Changing medical concepts and control measures (late 15th–16th century)

From the late 15th century, although mainly during the 16th century, the scholarly philosophy that formed the basis of medical study was criticised ever more frequently. New theories about nature and route of disease spread were formed. The most well-known remains that proposed by the Italian physician Jerome Fracastor, generally recognised by historians as having expressed

---

8 Archaeological evidence for genocide at Tárrega (Spain) can be cited; the excavation of part of the medieval Jewish cemetery has revealed the existence of several multiple burials from the mid-14th century related to a pogrom (Colet *et al.*, 2014).

9 The 'miasmatic doctrine' of Hippocratic theory of the 4th century BC does not deny contagion but rejects the attribution of contamination due to direct contact alone.

10 The word *contagium* was already employed by late medieval authors, such as Isidore de Seville (6th–7th century AD), concerning illnesses affecting a great number of people simultaneously (Huard and Grmek, 1977).

the first coherent theory of contagion (Fabre, 1998: 118–119). As of 1546, he asserted that specific plague germs, which he named *seminaria contagionum,*[11] existed. In parallel with these novel contagion theories, new methods of epidemic control were put into place. These measures, formally regulated during the first half of the 16th century, consisted principally of isolation of the infected or of suspected cases of infection (Biraben, 1976: 105). The use of quarantine, the first rational institutional response (Fabre, 1998: 113), was at first limited to the most urgent situations and adopted only occasionally[12] but became progressively widespread during the Renaissance. The creation and use of plague infirmaries intended to ensure care of the victims also became widespread in the late 16th century (Biraben, 1976:171). At the same time, large towns acquired specialised hospitals built for the purpose or by taking over former *leprosaria.*[13] Houses affected by the disease were marked with a cross and objects that had been in contact with the sick were disinfected by the use of fire. Restrictions on the burial of cadavers within towns increased, and municipal authorities acquired land outside their walls to bury plague victims. Therapies and prophylactic measures remained essentially unchanged, based upon the use of odoriferous substances to combat the pestilential air.

Opposing opinions and reinforcement of control measures (17th–18th century)

In the wake of Fracastor, some 17th-century physicians, such as the Jesuit Father Athanase Kircher in 1658, supported the idea of plague contagion, transmitted by a living agent carried in the air (Kircher, 1658). However, most physicians of the time remained fiercely opposed to this theory and continued to convey concepts inherited from the Middle Ages. The climax of this ideological quarrel was reached in 1720–1722 during the Great Plague of Marseille. Doctors Goiffon and Bertrand, both spirited defenders of the contagion theory (Bertrand, 1721; Goiffon, 1722), clashed with the opinions of almost all of the members of the Montpellier Faculty of Medicine. In their denial of contagion, these latter physicians did not hesitate to approach the plague-stricken and to undertake the autopsy of victims of the epidemic.

Contagion remained a matter of debate within the medical profession, but the measures undertaken to control the disease continued to be reinforced throughout the 17th century. Until that time, measures to combat plague had been decided locally or regionally but were now progressively codified at the government level. All insisted on the necessity for isolation of the sick and the importance of quarantine. In addition, recommendations were given concerning the sanitary conditions and burial methods of victims of the epidemic. In England, for example, it was recommended 'That none dying of the Plague be buried in Churches, or Church-yards [...] but in some other convenient places, and that a good quantity of *unslackt Lime* be put into the Graves with such bodies, and that such Graves be not after opened within the space of a year or more, less they infect others'.[14]

---

11 The medical treatise *De Contagione et Contagiosis Morbis* (Fracastor, 1546) recognises three types of contagion: by direct touch, indirect by clothing and goods, and at distance through the air.

12 The use of quarantine for the first time would seem to have been in 1377 at Ragusa (modern Dubrovnik) in Croatia (Grmek, 1980), although the first regulations concerning plague were established by Vicount Bernano at Reggio in 1374 (Nohl, 1986: 121–122).

13 Due to the decline in leprosy, *leprosaria* were transformed into hospitals or 'lazarettos' for the plague-stricken. Use of these 'lazarettos' became systematic as of the 16th century.

14 *Rules and orders to be observed by all justices of peace, mayors, bayliffs, and other officers, for prevention of the spreading of the infection of the plague* (1666).

In France, the State intervened directly by organising the isolation of affected districts by establishing *cordons sanitaires*. Moreover, in 1666, the creation of health centres responsible for applying the sanitary legislation defined by the political authorities of both province and state was made compulsory (Biraben, 1976: 143). However, the significant decline of plague during the second half of the 17th and in the 18th century was clearly the result of an international network of sanitary information, based on a system of bills of health for ships and sanitary passports for travellers (Buti, 1998). The preventive measures implemented became much more efficient than those adopted during previous centuries and finally drove plague out of Western Europe. Plague physicians, fitted with the notorious costumes invented by Charles de Lormes in the early 17th century, were, as always, powerless against the disease, the customary treatments being to administer theriac (i.e. ointments) and other mixtures of aromatic plants, as well as excision and cauterisation of infected ganglia.

The discovery of plague contagion mechanisms (end of the 19th century)

Finally, only at the start of the third plague pandemic did medical research have the means to elucidate disease contagion mechanisms after fundamental conceptual and technical advances made during the 19th century. In 1894, only a few months after a plague outbreak started to rage in Hong Kong, the French microbiologist Alexandre Yersin isolated the plague bacillus.[15] Yersin (1894) also highlighted the role played by rats in the propagation of the disease. Several years later, Paul-Louis Simond (1898) demonstrated that fleas feeding on the blood of these rodents were the vectors of transmission of the disease from rat to human. Henceforth, the knowledge of the vectors of contagion permitted the implementation of efficient measures to combat the spread of the disease, including extermination of rodent populations living in contact with human populations, as well as the use of insecticides to control vector ectoparasites.

Comparison of archaeological data and historical information

The understanding of plague and its modes of transmission developed slowly, conditioned in part by contemporary medical concepts but also by observations made by contemporaries concerning efficient measures to combat the propagation of disease. Archaeological evidence from the graves of plague victims reveals progressive changes in burial methods. Recognised changes in both plague epidemic management and burial practices do not strictly reflect each other, but the contextualisation of written sources and archaeological observations permits some parallels to be drawn that contribute to a better understanding of the diversity of burial practices observed.

At the start of the second pandemic, the measures adopted to combat the disease were rare, isolated and had no real efficacy. In the 14th century, it was generally thought that disease was caused by miasmas carried on the air and various objects and methods were used to try to ward off foul air. Most contemporary texts identify decaying bodies as an important source of corrupt air. It was, therefore, of utmost importance to bury the bodies of victims as quickly as possible, and it is this desire for rapid interment that provided the stimulus to place several bodies in the same pit. Quarantine measures, which later became generally applied in outbreaks, had not yet begun and contact with the bodies of victims was not, at first, considered a source of contagion. This is certainly, in part, the reason why burials, although carried out rapidly, respected most Christian funerary customs. The first evidence of continuity of practice comes with burial in consecrated

---

15 First named *Pasteurella pestis*, the bacillus was renamed *Yersinia pestis* in 1974 after its discoverer.

land; to do otherwise was hardly conceivable, notably because of popular belief concerning the divine origin of the epidemic. Most plague burials from the sample of 14th-century archaeological sites reflect this concern. In these funerary assemblages, the disposition and standard orientation of the dead indicate careful handling of the bodies that can hardly be distinguished from those who died from natural causes.

Other than assertions concerning contagion by a few physicians, medical concepts changed little during the 15th and 16th centuries, but the accumulation of empirical observations on the most efficient measures to protect against plague gradually led the authorities to increase epidemic control measures. By the mid-16th century, more and more importance was given to the isolation of the sick and the bodies of the victims. Archaeological discoveries echo this change. Although most 14th-century plague victim burials occupied parish cemeteries already in use, two known late 16th-century burial sites represent new foundations. At the Lambesc site (Bouches-du-Rhône, France), the cemetery was attached to a plague infirmary and remote from the town itself, while the cemetery at Dendermonde (East Flanders, Belgium) was attached to the Maria Troon convent and occupied a plot of land previously unused for burial. Two exceptions may, however, be noted: the Lazaretto Vecchio in Venice, where plague victims were received as early as the late 14th century, and the site of Alghero on Sardinia, where the victims of a late 16th-century plague epidemic were buried in a cemetery previously used for the attritional dead of the community. At the archaeological sites studied, heterogeneity can be observed in the placing and orientation of the bodies. The rationalisation of the burial space seems to have gradually taken precedence over respect for Christian norms at the same time as the sick were displaced from their homes and their interment thus conducted far from their surviving family and friends.

From the 17th century and more so during the 18th century, the active participation of the political authorities in the control measures against epidemic disease imposed a strict framework on the care and handling of the sick and dead. Communal salvation being considered more important than the fate of the individual, flight was no longer possible, and religious considerations took second place. Quarantine became the absolute rule, as illustrated at the sites of Marseille and Martigues (Bouches-du-Rhône, France). The plague-stricken victims, placed in the care of the plague infirmaries and hospitals of the town, were buried hurriedly at sites distant from the town. Archaeological evidence from the burials of victims reveals the sometimes chaotic handling of the cadavers. The need for a rapid burial and limited contact with the bodies consequently took precedence over any consideration of respect for the victims.

Conclusion

The current synthesis measures the contribution of some archaeological sources to interpretations of epidemic mortality crises. The examples developed herein provide a detailed and subtle vision of the handling of the dead in these contexts. This treatment appears at a far remove from the stereotypes generally assumed. Such observation must invite the greatest prudence when interpreting written and iconographic sources, which frequently provide a biased description of the events. Most of the sites on which this study is based reveal adaptations made and skills employed that past societies developed when confronted with epidemic crises. These observations demonstrate similarities and a chronological coherence between the development of the notion of contagion and the treatment of cadavers. The manifest care given to the burials of bodies at the beginning of the second pandemic, rarely documented previously, had gradually been abandoned during the following centuries in favour of less well-controlled, hasty burials owing to the increasing fear of contagion.

There is growing potential for archaeological research on epidemics as new burial sites are now regularly discovered. It is fundamental that the documented changes in funerary customs during epidemics made recently inform the examination of sites currently under study. Future work should endeavour, as much as possible, to study well-dated sites for which the pathogens that caused the deaths have been identified. This would permit study of the subtleties of burial treatment during periods of epidemic mortality, as well as their geographical and temporal variations. In parallel, this work should compare these burial sites with cemeteries representing natural mortality so as to define the customary local funerary characteristics before and after epidemics. In time, this approach has the potential to reveal evidence in burials hinting at mortality crises, notably in the absence of written sources and lacking clear archaeological evidence.

Acknowledgements

We wish to thank all the archaeologists and anthropologists who have contributed to the acquisition of data used in this synthesis. This research was funded by a ministerial grant from the French National Research Agency as part of a programme of investments for the future (Grant ANR-10-LABX-52) and by the Maison des Sciences de l'Homme d'Aquitaine (Projet Région Aquitaine, France). A special thanks to Frances Holden for translating this contribution from the original French.

References

Ariès, P. (1949). Attitudes devant la Vie et devant la Mort du XVIIe au XIXe Siècle: Quelques Aspects de leurs Variations. *Population*, 4(3), pp. 463–470.

Arrizabalaga, J. (1994). Facing the Black Death: perceptions and reactions of university medical practitioners. In: L. García-Ballester, R. French, J. Arrizabalaga and A. Cunningham, eds., *Practical Medicine from Salerno to the Black Death*. Cambridge: Cambridge University Press, pp. 237–288.

Beauchamp, A. (2012). The Black Death, Plague, and Mass Mortality. *University of Manitoba Anthropology Student's Association*, 30, pp. 1–16.

Bertrand, J.B. (1721). *Observations faites sur la peste qui règne à présent à Marseille et dans la Provence*. Lyon: A. Laurens.

Biraben, J.-N. (1975). *Les hommes et la peste en France et dans les pays européens et méditerranéens. Vol. I – La peste dans l'histoire*. Paris: Mouton.

Biraben, J.-N. (1976). *Les hommes et la peste en France et dans les pays européens et méditerranéens. Vol. II – Les Hommes face à la peste*. Paris: Mouton.

Bizot, B., Castex, D., Reynaud, P. and Signoli, M. (2005). *La saison d'une peste (avril-septembre 1590). Le cimetière des Fédons à Lambesc*. Paris: Centre National de la Recherche Scientifique (CNRS) Editions.

Boccaccio, G. (1353). *Le Decameron*. Edited and translated by G. Clerico (2006), *Boccace. Le Décaméron*. Paris: Gallimard.

Boulestin, B. (2019). Faut-il en finir avec la sépulture collective (et sinon qu'en faire?), *Bulletin de la Société Préhistorique Française*, 116(4), pp. 705–723.

Buti, G. (1998). Structures Sanitaires et Protections d'une Communauté Provençale Face à la Peste: La Valette (1720/1721). *Bulletins et Mémoires de la Société d'Anthropologie de Paris*, 10(1–2), pp. 67–80.

Calmet, A. (1738). *Histoire universelle sacrée et profane depuis le commencement du monde jusqu'à nos jours*. Strasbourg: chez Jean Renauld Doulssecker.

Castex, D. (2008). Identification and interpretation of historical cemeteries linked to epidemics. In: D. Raoult and M. Drancourt, eds., *Paleomicrobiology: Past Human Infections*. Berlin/Heidelberg: Springer, pp. 23–48.

Castex, D. and Blaizot, F. (2016). Reconstruction of original burial fittings in archaeology. In: E.M.J. Schotsmans, N. Márquez-Grant and S. Forbes, eds., *Taphonomy of Human Remains: Forensic Analysis of the Dead and the Depositional Environment*. New York: Wiley, pp. 277–294.

Castex, D., Brůžek, J., Sellier, P.,Veleminský, P., Kuchařová, H., Bessou, M., Sève, S., Lourenço, J.-M., Jůn, L. and Dobisíková, M. (2011). Bioarchaeological Study of a Mortality Crisis. Cemetery of St. Benedict in Prague, Czech Republic (17th–18th century AD): Methodological Approach. *Anthropologie (Brno)*, 49(1), pp. 79–88.

Castex, D. and Kacki, S. (2016). Demographic Patterns Distinctive of Epidemic Cemeteries in Archaeological Samples. *Microbiology Spectrum*, 4(4), pp. 1–11.

Castex, D., Kacki, S., Réveillas, H., Souquet-Leroy, I., Sachau-Carcel, G., Blaizot, F., Blanchard, P. and Duday, H. (2014). Revealing archaeological features linked to mortality increases. *Anthropologie (Brno)*, 52(3), pp. 299–318.

Castex, D. and Réveillas, H. (2007). Investigation sur une crise de mortalité à Boulogne-sur-Mer (Pas-de-Calais, XVIIIe s.). Hypothèse d'interprétation. *Bulletins et Mémoires de la Société d'Anthropologie de Paris*, 19(1–2), pp. 21–37.

Chauliac (de), G. (1363). *Chirurgia magna*. Edited by E. Nicaise (1890), *La grande chirurgie de Guy de Chauliac, chirurgien, maistre en médecine de l'université de Montpellier, composée en 1363*. Paris: Félix Alcan.

Clavandier, G. (2004). *La mort collective – pour une sociologie des catastrophes*. Paris: Centre National de la Recherche Scientifique (CNRS) Editions.

Colet, A., Muntané i Santiveri, J.X., Ruíz Ventura, J., Saula, O., Subirà de Galdàcano, M.E. and Jáuregui, C. (2014). The Black Death and its Consequences for the Jewish Community in Tàrrega: Lessons from History and Archaeology. *The Medieval Globe*, 1, pp. 63–96.

Duday, H. (2008). Archaeological proof of an abrupt mortality crisis: simultaneous deposit of cadavers, simultaneous deaths? In: D. Raoult and M. Drancourt, eds., *Paleomicrobiology: Past Human Infections*. Berlin/Heidelberg: Springer, pp. 49–54.

Duday, H. (2009). *The archaeology of the dead: lectures in archeothanatology*. Oxford: Oxbow Books.

Effros, B. (2003). Memories of the early medieval past. In: H. Williams, ed., *Archaeologies of Remembrance*. Boston: Springer, pp. 255–280.

Fabre, G. (1998). *Epidémies et contagions. L'imaginaire du mal en occident*. Paris: Presses Universitaires de France.

Flambard-Héricher, A.M. (2005). *Médecine et société de l'Antiquité à nos jours*. Rouen: Cahiers du Groupe de Recherche d'Histoire (GRHIS), Presses Universitaires de Rouen et du Havre.

Fracastor, J. (1546). *De sympathia et antipathie rerum liber unus, de contagione et contagiosis morbis et curativ, libri III*. Venice : Heirs of Lucantonio Giunta.

Georges, P. and Blanchard, P. (2007). Les sépultures multiples du '35, rue de Sarrebourg' à Bourges (18): discussion du contexte et interprétations envisagées. In: D. Castex and I. Cartron, eds., *Épidémies et Crises de Mortalité du Passé, Actes des Séminaires de la Maison des Sciences de l'Homme*. Pessac: Ausonius Éditions, Études 15, pp. 147–168.

Gilchrist, R. (2019). Magic and archaeology: ritual residues and 'odd' deposits, In: S. Page and C. Rider, eds., *The Routledge History of Medieval Magic*. Abingdon (UK): Routledge, pp 383–401.

Godo, C. (2010). *Les inhumations intra-muros de Poitiers entre le IVe et le VIIe siècles. Biologie, gestes funéraires et essai d'interprétation*. Unpublished MSc. thesis, Université de Paris Nanterre.

Goiffon, J.-B. (1722). *Relations et dissertation sur la Peste du Gévaudan*. Lyon: P. Valray.

Gourvennec, M. (2018). *Toulouse. 16, rue des Trente-Six Ponts*. Unpublished archaeological Report.

Grainger, I., Hawkins, D., Cowal, L. and Mikulski, R. (2008). *The Black Death Cemetery, East Smithfield, London*. London: Museum of London.

Grmek, M.D. (1980). *Le concept d'infection dans l'Antiquité et au Moyen Age, les anciennes mesures sociales contre les maladies contagieuses et la fondation de la 1ère quarantaine à Dubrovnik (1377)*. Zagreb: Rad Jugoslavenske Akademije.

Harding, V. (1993). Burial of the plague dead in early modern London. In: J.A.I. Champion, ed., *Epidemic Disease in London*. London: Centre for Metropolitan History, Working Papers Series 1, pp. 53–64.

Horrox, R. (1994). *The Black Death* (Vol. 1). Manchester: Manchester University Press.

Huard, P. and Grmek, M.D. (1977). Histoire de la médecine et des sciences biologiques. *École Pratique des Hautes Études. 4e Section, Sciences Historiques et Philologiques*, 109, pp. 863–879.

Jacquart, D. (1980). *Le regard d'un médecin sur son temps: Jacques Despars (1380?–1458)*. Paris: Bibliothèque de l'École des Chartes.

Jacquart, D. (1997). *La science médicale occidentale entre deux renaissances (XIIe–XVe s.)*. London: Variorum Collected Studies.

Jacquart, D. (1998). *La médecine médiévale dans le cadre parisien*. Paris: Fayard.

Kacki, S. (2016). *Influence de l'état sanitaire des populations anciennes sur la mortalité en temps de peste. Contribution à la paléoépidémiologie*. Unpublished Ph.D. thesis, Bordeaux: Université de Bordeaux.

Kacki, S. and Castex, D. (2012). Réflexions sur la variété des modalités funéraires en temps d'épidémie. L'exemple de la Peste noire en contextes urbain et rural. *Archéologie Médiévale*, 35, pp. 1–21.

Kacki, S., Rahalison, L., Rajerison, M., Ferroglio, E. and Bianucci, R. (2011). Black Death in the Rural Cemetery of Saint-Laurent-de-la-Cabrerisse, Aude-Languedoc, Southern France, 14th Century: Immunological Evidence. *Journal of Archaeological Science*, 38, pp. 581–587.

Kacki, S., Réveillas, H., Sachau-Carcel, G., Giuliani, R., Blanchard, P. and Castex, D. (2014). Réévaluation des arguments de simultanéité des dépôts de cadavres: l'exemple des sépultures plurielles de la catacombe des Saints Pierre-et-Marcellin (Rome). *Bulletins et Mémoires de la Société d'Anthropologie de Paris*, 26(1–2), pp. 88–97.

Keller, M., Spyrou, M.A., Scheib, C.L., Neumann, G.U., Kröpelin, A., Haas-Gebhard, B., Päffgen, B., Haberstroh, J., Ribera i Lacomba, A., Raynaud, C., Cessford, C., Durand, R., Stadler, P., Nägele, K., Bates J.S., Trautmann B., Inskip S.A., Peters, J., Robb, J. Kivisild, T., Castex, D., McCormick, M., Bos, K.I., Harbeck, M., Herbig, A. and Krause, J. (2019). Ancient *Yersinia pestis* Genomes from across Western Europe Reveal Early Diversification during the First Pandemic (541–750). *Proceedings of the National Academy of Sciences of the United States of America*, 116(25), pp. 12363–1237.

Kircher, A. (1658). *Scrutinium physico-medicum contagiosae luis quae pestis dicitur*. Leipzig: Bauerianis.

Knüsel, C.J. (1989). Community response to pestilence: the identification of epidemic disease in the archaeological record. In: S. MacEachern, D. Archer and R. Garvin, eds., *Households and Communities, Proceedings of the 21st Annual Chacmool Conference*, Calgary: University of Calgary, pp. 534–541.

Knüsel, C.J. and Robb, J. (2016). Funerary Taphonomy: an Overview of Goals and Methods. *Journal of Archaeological Science: Reports*, 10, pp. 655–673.

Leclerc, J. and Tarrête, J. (1988). Sépulture. In: A. Leroi-Gourhan, ed. *Dictionnaire de la Préhistoire*, Paris: Presses Universitaires de France, pp.1002–1003.

Milanese, M. (2010). *Lo scavo del Cimitero di San Michele ad Alghero (fine XIII-inizi XVII secolo): campagna di scavo, giugno 2008-settembre 2009*. Pisa: Felici Editore.

Nicoud, M. (2005). Les médecins et l'office de santé: Milan face à la peste au XVe siècle. In: A.-M. Flambard-Héricher, ed. *Médecine et Société de l'Antiquité à nos Jours*. Rouen: Cahiers du Groupe de Recherche d'Histoire (GRHIS), Presses Universitaires de Rouen et du Havre, pp. 49–74.

Nohl, J. (1986). *La Mort noire. Chronique de la peste d'après les sources contemporaines*. Paris: Payot.

Paresys, C., Roms, C., Richard, I. and Bonnabel, L. (2019). Saint-Remi de Reims, un cimetière de création post-révolutionnaire. In: N. Weydert, S. Tzortzis, A. Richier, L. Lanteri and H. Guy, eds., *Rencontre Autour de Nos Aïeux. La Mort de Plus en Plus Proche. Actes de la 8e Rencontre du Groupe d'Anthropologie et d'Archéologie Funéraire (Gaaf)*. Reugny: Groupe d'Anthropologie et d'Archéologie Funéraire,, pp. 111–120.

Passarrius, O., Donat, R. and Catafau, A. (2008). *Vilarnau. Un village du Moyen Age en Roussillon*. Canet-en-Roussillon: Éditions Trabucaire.

Rébouis, E. (1888), *Étude historique et critique sur la Peste*. Paris: Picard.

Réveillas, H. (2010). *Les hôpitaux et leurs morts dans le nord-est de la France du Moyen Âge à l'époque moderne. Approche archéo-anthropologique des établissements hospitaliers*. Unpublished Ph.D. thesis, Université de Bordeaux 3.

Rigeade, C. (2009). *Les sépultures de catastrophe: approche anthropologique des sites d'inhumations en relation avec des épidémies de peste, des massacres de population et des charniers militaires*. Oxford: British Archaeological Reports (International Series) 1695.

Rules and orders to be observed by all justices of peace, mayors, bayliffs, and other officers, for prevention of the spreading of the infection of the plague (1966). Published by His Majesties special command. London: The National Archives, SP29/155 f102.

Santer, M. (2014). *Confronting contagion: our evolving understanding of disease*. Oxford: Oxford University Press.

Signoli, M., Tzortzis, S., Bizot, B., Ardagna, Y., Rigeade, C. and Séguy, I. (2007). Découverte d'un cimetière de pestiférés du XVIIe siècle (Puy-Saint-Pierre, Hautes-Alpes, France). In: M. Signoli, D. Chevé, P. Adalian, G. Boëtsch and O. Dutour, eds., *Peste: entre Épidémies et Sociétés*. Florence: Firenze University Press, pp. 131–135.

Simond, P.L. (1898). La Propagation de la Peste. *Annales de l'Institut Pasteur*, 12, pp. 625–687.

Souquet-Leroy, I., Castex, D. and Blanchard, P. (2011). Le traitement des cadavres en temps d'épidémie: l'exemple d'Issoudun (XVIIIe siècle, Indre). In: H. Guy, A. Jeanjean, A. Richier, A. Schmitt, I. Sémépart and N. Weydert, eds., *Rencontre Autour du Cadavre. Actes de la 3e Rencontre du Groupe d'Anthropologie et d'Archéologie Funéraire (Gaaf)*. Reugny: Groupe d'Anthropologie et d'Archéologie Funéraire, pp. 131–137.

Tzortzis, S. and Signoli, M. (2016). Characterization of the funeral groups associated with plague epidemics. In: M. Drancourt and D. Raoult, eds., *Paleomicrobiology of Humans*. Washington, DC: American Society for Microbiology (ASM) Press, pp. 13–20.

Vågene, Å.J., Campana, M.G., García, N.M.R., Warinner, C., Spyrou, M.A., Valtueña, A.A., Huson, D., Tuross, N., Bos, K.I. and Krause, J. (2018). *Salmonella enterica* Genomes from Victims of a Major Sixteenth-century Epidemic in Mexico. *Nature Ecology & Evolution*, 2(3), pp. 520–528.

Weill-Parot, N. (2004). *La rationalité médicale à l'épreuve de la peste: médecine, astrologie et magie (1348–1500)*, Paris: Presses Universitaires de Vincennes.

Yersin, A.E.J. (1894). La Peste Bubonique à Hong-Kong. *Annales de l'Institut Pasteur*, 8, pp. 662–668.

19

JEWISH FUNERARY PRACTICES IN MEDIEVAL EUROPE

Philippe Blanchard

Institut National de Recherches Archéologiques Préventives (Inrap), Tours, France

PACEA, De la Préhistoire à l'Actuel: Culture, Environnement et Anthropologie, UMR 5199, CNRS-Université de Bordeaux, Pessac, France

Introduction

The archaeological study of the cemeteries of Jewish communities in the medieval period is a difficult subject to address in France as it is in many other European countries. The main reason is related to the rarity of this type of site because Jews represented only a small part of the population in the Middle Ages. For example, in France, historians and demographers estimate that they represented less than 1% of the total population in the 13th and 14th centuries (Schwarzfuchs, 1975: 89; Dupaquier, 1988: 261; Benbassa, 1997: 53). Another difficulty relates to a problem of location and access. Indeed, since the Jewish communities were definitively expelled from the Kingdom of France in 1394, the cemeteries, located on the immediate outskirts of cities, have been abandoned and forgotten over the centuries. In addition, the expansion of urban centres since the 19th century has often led to the re-use and sometimes destruction of burial remains by buildings that now seal access and prevent further investigation.

Another point that has not favoured research/investigation of Jewish cemeteries (and even more broadly of the archaeology of Judaism) is the lack of knowledge of this minority group in the history of medieval societies. In France, for example, with the exception of a few summary articles on the subject (Nahon, 1975: 139–159; 1980: 73–94), most historical and archaeological work on the Middle Ages do not mention Jewish communities at all or only very little. As a result, archaeologists have had little experience with these remains and may not have been able to locate, identify or interpret them, particularly in the absence of Hebrew inscriptions.

Finally, because of Jewish laws prohibiting disturbance of ancient graves, some of today's Jewish communities are campaigning for a ban on excavations in defiance of national legislation (Polonovski, 2011: 24). These groups exert religious, political or administrative pressure to stop archaeological research – or even to prevent it from the beginning. As a result, there is almost no osteological reference collection available from medieval Jewish cemeteries. As the very rare remains excavated are systematically re-interred, it is difficult to carry out anthropological studies, as well as radiocarbon dating and DNA analyses. For these reasons and despite the number of excavations since the 1980s and the development of preventive/salvage archaeology, discoveries, excavations and studies of Jewish cemeteries and their remains remain very unusual.

 DOI: 10.4324/9781351030625-22

To date, the history of Jewish communities has often only been understood solely from written sources. With many archaeological interventions related to recent development in urban areas, the sources from the soil are now beginning to speak, however. It is, therefore, time to initiate an archaeological review based on the inhumed remains of these communities. It will be interesting in the longer term to compare textual, iconographic and museographic sources with a perspective based upon archaeological remains.

This study is limited to the current geographical limits of Europe. With regard to chronology, the Middle Ages (6th–15th centuries) and, more rarely, the beginning of the Modern (16th–18th centuries) period were targeted. The sites selected are those with evidence of Jewish cemeteries from archaeological interventions, including survey, excavation and chance discovery, indicated by the discovery of human remains. Because of the variable nature of site information, coverage was uneven. Some instances refer to excavations with several hundred individuals excavated relatively recently using rigorous archaeological and anthropological methods, while others provide only summary observations of a few burials in the first half of the 20th century.

Results

Archaeological sites

Number

The number of archaeological sites with burials from Jewish communities is steadily increasing in Europe. The precise number of sites, though, largely depends on bibliographic references. Indeed, each piece of new literature provides an indication of potential new sites that cannot be confirmed until after a review of the published literature and translations of some of the sources. Nevertheless, some 75 sites are known at the present time (as of 2018) (Figure 19.1).

Distribution

Site distribution is very uneven. Spain has the most discoveries with 35 references. Afterwards comes Germany with 20 sites. In France, England and the Czech Republic, there were only between four and five. In addition, in Switzerland, Austria and Italy, only one to three (Figure 19.1). Apart from Prague (Czech Republic) and Cordoba (Spain), where archaeological excavations were carried out in two separate cemeteries each, in all other cities, only a single funerary site was investigated. The distribution of sites covers different Jewish communities, including those of the Sephardic[1] tradition around the Mediterranean basin (mainly Spanish sites) and those with Ashkenazi[2] influence.

---

1 In the Middle Ages, Sephardim corresponded to members of the historical Jewish communities residing or coming from the Iberian Peninsula. Today, by an extension of meaning, and because of cultural contacts and shared community practices, non-Ashkenazi Jews are called Sephardic, especially Jews from the Maghreb and the East (Attias and BenBassa 1997: 250–251).

2 The name Ashkenazi refers to the Jews of Central and Eastern Europe. They would find their origin at the beginning of the Middle Ages and are referred to as such from around the 11th century in the northeast of France and the eastern part of Germany. The Ashkenazis are characterised by particular customs, cultural heritage and traditions as well as the use of Yiddish (a mixture of German, Hebrew, Polish and Russian).

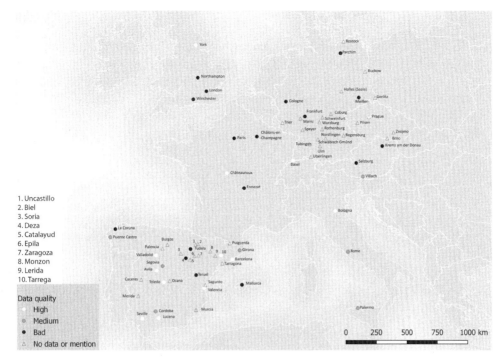

1. Uncastillo
2. Biel
3. Soria
4. Deza
5. Catalayud
6. Epila
7. Zaragoza
8. Monzon
9. Lerida
10. Tarrega

Figure 19.1 Map of archaeological interventions of medieval Jewish cemeteries in Europe with an assessment of the detail of available information, as of 2018 (P. Blanchard, Institut National de Recherches Archéologiques Préventives).

Chronology

Sites from the early Middle Ages (6th–11th centuries) remain virtually unknown, with the only example coming from Lucena in Spain, dating to the late 10th century. The origin is perhaps earlier, though, because the style of a stele fragment from the 8th or 9th centuries was re-used in a later structure dated to the 11th century. The sites of Puente Castro and Barcelona in Spain were in use in the 11th century, at the end of the Early Middle Ages but continued their use into the High Middle Ages. In fact, most examples date to the High and Late Middle Ages (12th–15th centuries). Only three of the cemeteries, those in Prague, Rome and Bologna (Italy), seem to have been in use until the 16th century (Curina and Di Stefano, 2019; De Cristofaro and Di Mento and Rossi, 2017). This also seems to have been the case for the cemetery at Seville (Spain), but at this site, the burial practices appear to be those of *conversos* (converts). Other cemeteries have been the subject of archaeological investigation in Poland and Lithuania, and these seem to date to the Modern period, but the question remains whether or not their origins could date back at least to the end of the Middle Ages.

Cemeteries

Location

All studied cemeteries were located outside cities, beyond the city walls (Figure 19.2). However, because of urban growth and development at the end of the Medieval period and the beginning of the Modern period, some funerary spaces with the passage of time have become located

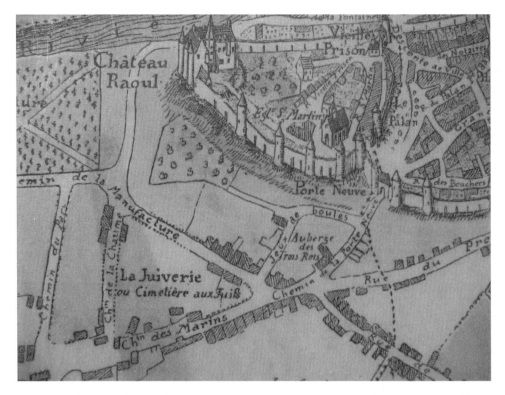

Figure 19.2 Location of the Jewish cemetery outside the city of Châteauroux, France (Source: Archives Départementales de l'Indre cote 500.276).

within the city limits. In these cases, the cemeteries were no longer in use. Old references are mentioned in the Bible (Luke 7, 12): "*As he approached the town gate, a deceased person was being carried out*". Similarly, the Mishnah (2.10 Bava Batra) states: "*Exclusion of human and animal cadavers and tanning industry materials from the city with a minimum distance of 50 cubits* [25 m]". Jewish cemeteries were never placed within cities and were never close to synagogues as is the case among Christians and their churches. The distance between the city walls and the cemeteries was variable. For example, in Barcelona, the path to reach the cemetery was long and difficult, but in Murcia, Cordoba, Valencia (Spain), York (England), Châteauroux (France) and Tárrega (Spain), where the cemetery was 900 m from the city gate, (Colet *et al.*, 2010: 240) Jewish funerary spaces were close to the city limits (Lilley *et al.*, 1994: 305; Casanovas Miró, 2002: 209; Blanchard and Georges, 2011: 304).

Topography

When topography permitted it, Jewish cemeteries were located in well-placed locations such as high on hills, slopes and bluffs. This responded to an aesthetic requirement from a Talmudic exclamation in *Sanhedrin* 96b: '*Their tombs are more lavish than your palaces*' (Nahon, 1980: 77–78). The sites in Barcelona, Segovia, Biel (Zaragoza) and Lucena (all in Spain) are good examples of this phenomenon (Casanovas Miró, 2002: 211, 212; Riquelme Cantal and Botella Ortega, 2011: 262).

Toponymy

The study of the original place names provides useful information and should not be overlooked. Several archaeological sites seem to have retained the memory of a relationship with a Jewish community. This is the case in Châteauroux with the word '*Jewry or Jewish cemetery/Juiverie ou cimetière aux juifs*' still present on an 18th-century map (Figure 19.2). In other cases, the place name evokes the high position of the location. This is a constant that is found in Barcelona and Girona (Spain) with '*Montjuic*', in Clermont-Ferrand (France) '*Montjuzet*', Bordeaux (France) '*Mont Judaic*', Marseille (France) '*Mont-Jusiou*', Macon (France) '*Montjuyf*' and '*Judenberg*' in Hagueneau (France) in the biggest cities (Nahon, 1980: 77). On the other hand, in Lucena, despite the archaeologically attested presence of a cemetery, there is no textual reference that indicates the presence of a Jewish cemetery, nor is there any indication in place names to suspect the existence of one (Riquelme Cantal and Botella Ortega, 2011).

Size

The overall size of the cemeteries as measured by surface area was difficult to determine because none of the sites were excavated in their entirety. Surface areas, however, could often be estimated in relation to the locations of individuals found in the excavated portion (see below). In Lucena, the site occupied a surface area of at least 3742 m^2 (Riquelme Cantal and Botella Ortega, 2011: 261–262). At Basel (Switzerland), a surface area of 3200 to 4500 m^2 is mentioned in a study based on the morphology of the plot (Alder and Matt, 2010: 25). In Girona, various excavations and geophysical surveys suggest an estimated area of 10,000–12,000 m^2 (Casanovas Miró, 2002: 210). An area of one hectare was estimated for Segovia (Spain) (Casanovas Miró, 2002: 211). The cemetery of Léon, in the suburbs of Puente Castro, estimated about 4000 m^2 (Casanovas Miró, 2002: 213). In Tárrega, painstaking work was carried out to achieve the calculation of the surface area, which was estimated at a minimum of 6648 m^2 (Colet *et al.*, 2010: 244). In York, the total estimated surface area for the cemetery was about 1500 m^2 (Lilley *et al.*, 1994: 529–533). Finally, in Châteauroux, burials were recognised over at least 3226 m^2 and, at a maximum, could extend over the entire surface available for this parcel of land, i.e. approximately 10,700 m^2.

Number of Jewish cemeteries in each city

Each Jewish community did not have its own cemetery. Consequently, there were fewer Jewish cemeteries than communities. A cemetery could therefore be used by several groups, sometimes coming from very far away, as was highlighted in Nordlingen (Germany), where 17 communities shared the same funerary space, some of which are 45 km distant (Harck, 2014: 344–345). Amongst cities where a cemetery is known (Figure 19.1), there seems to be only a single place of Jewish burial dating from the medieval period. Every rule has its exceptions, it appears that a few large cities had several Jewish cemeteries, which were often the result of successive expulsions suffered by the community. For France, this was the case in Paris, where there were three Jewish cemeteries, known mainly from texts. Two of these cemeteries seem to have been used at the same time (around the 13th century) (Robin, 1952), and the last was established when the two preceding ones were no longer in use. One of them, the first cemetery to be established, was accidentally discovered in 1857 during the construction of a building located near *Boulevard Saint-Germain,* indicated by many tombstones (Polonovski, 2011: 39–40). There is no archaeological information with regard to the second. However, one tombstone of the third cemetery is preserved at the Museum of Judaism in Paris. In Spain, Toledo may have had two distinct places, but only one of them has been partially excavated (Ruiz Taboada, 2009, 2013). In Switzerland, in Basel, two cemeteries are mentioned, but they are not contemporary (Alder and Matt, 2010: 19). In some cases, the textual sources suggest two Jewish cemeteries, but the second could be an extension of the first, as was certainly the case in Barcelona (Casanovas Miró, 2003: 504).

The surrounding areas

There is little information about the immediate environment of Jewish cemeteries in the medieval period. It seems that cemeteries were not far from the entrance to the city, as for example in Châteauroux. In Tárrega (Colet *et al.*, 2009: 105) and Ennezat (France) (Parent, 2011: 241), a road ran along both sides of the cemetery. In Seville, to the north, there was a path and a brook located on the eastern side, with an Islamic-period fortification wall to the west (Romo Salas *et al.*, 2001: 373).

Cemetery plots and architectural elements

The boundaries of the cemetery consisted sometimes of paths. In other cases, the boundaries of the cemetery were marked by ditches. This was the case in York (Lilley *et al.*, 1994: 322–323), where three trenches marked the northern, western and southern limits of the cemetery. The eastern boundary was bordered by a waterway. Medieval iconography demonstrates the presence of walls forming the boundaries of the funerary spaces. French texts also indicate their presence in Sens, Macon, Dijon and Brie-Comte-Robert in the first half of the 11th century (Nahon, 1980: 78). Similarly, later depictions from the 17th to 18th centuries portray mostly walled cemeteries (Jacobs, 2008: 43, 60, 67, 84). These structures have also been recognised in Seville (Santana Falcon, 2006: 325) in the form of a north–south wall of adobe (earth and lime mortar).

Access to the cemetery via doors, gates and stairs has never been identified from archaeological remains. Buildings within the cemetery were sometimes mentioned in medieval texts (Nahon, 1980: 78) and depicted in more recent sources (Jacobs, 2008: 85). Jewish cemeteries seem to have had a building used as a caretaker's house or a house used for purification. The latter type of facilities, such as wells and ponds, were sometimes illustrated in modern-period depictions, but none of these have been discovered during archaeological excavations of a medieval cemetery. However, it should be noted that in Châteauroux, a well, still in service today, is located in a space that could have corresponded to a reception courtyard and could therefore be contemporary with the cemetery. A project to dig the well is being considered to confirm this hypothesis. Another architectural element, vegetation, is also mentioned in texts. In 13th-century Tours (France), a vineyard was planted, and the cemetery in Carpentras (France) had an orchard (Nahon, 1980: 78). Iconography attests to the presence of trees in cemeteries (Metzger and Metzger, 1982: 80, 82, 84). This type of evidence has never been confirmed by archaeological remains, however.

Organisation of Jewish burial spaces

The organisation of the graves in the cemetery was, in most cases, very rigorous. Most often, the graves appeared in roughly aligned rows, as attested in Basel (Alder and Matt, 2010: 26), Barcelona, York (Lilley *et al.*, 1994) (Figure 19.3), Châteauroux (Blanchard and Georges, 2011: 306), Ennezat (Puy-de-Dôme, France) (Parent, 2011), Girona (Casanovas Miró and Maese Fidalgo, 2012: 11), Prague (Selmi Wallisova, 2011: 276), Seville (Santana Falcon, 2006: 324), Tárrega (Colet *et al.* 2010: 247, 254) and Toledo (Ruiz Taboada, 2009: 30), but sometimes there were groups or

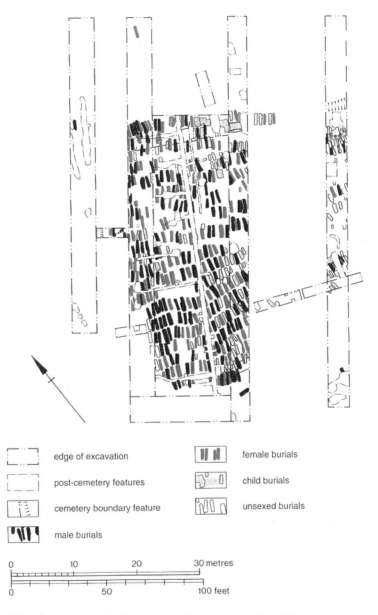

Figure 19.3 Map of excavation of the Jewbury Jewish cemetery in York, UK (Image courtesy: York Archaeological Trust in Lilley *et al.*, 1994: 322).

clusters of burials with minimal organisation (Tárrega, Seville) (Romo Salas *et al.*, 2001: 375), no specific organisation at all, as at Lucena (Botella Ortega and Casanovas Miró, 2009; Riquelme Cantal and Botella Ortega, 2011), or groupings within a quadrangular masonry structure (Ruiz Taboada, 2009: 30, 35). A high level of organisation was observed through the lack of overlapping or intercutting graves. Indeed, in almost all of the archaeological sites reviewed, the overlapping with or intercutting older graves was extremely rare. For example, in York, only 25 out of 482 excavated graves showed overlapping, and in only eight cases were the bones of the deceased disturbed (Figure 19.3) (Lilley *et al.*, 1994: 332). The same holds true in Prague, where only 2 out of 200 graves were recorded as intercutting (Selmi Wallisova, 2011: 280). In Lucena, no burial overlapping was found (Riquelme Cantal and Botella Ortega, 2011: 263). The burial pits were often juxtaposed with little space between each pit. In addition, it is interesting to note that at the site in Valladolid (Spain), some intersections of pits were found, but only the graves accommodating immature individuals intersected those of an adult (or *vice versa*), and one can therefore wonder if this indicates a desire to maintain family plots (Moreda Blanco and Serrano Noriega, 2009).

When a Jewish cemetery was over-populated and extension was not possible, the super-imposition of graves was allowed (Nahon, 1980: 86). The Jewish cemetery in Basel showed super-imposition of graves, with a bottom level being adults and the layer above, children and adolescents (Alder and Matt, 2010: 69). An excavation in 1983 in a cemetery in Puente Castro, Léon, revealed a similar phenomenon. The proposed interpretation of this type of organisation was that of a mortality crisis, but no argument to support this proposal was stated in the excavation report (Casanovas Miró, 2002: 214). Similarly, the last phase of the cemetery in Seville revealed some cases of super-imposed graves (Romo Salas *et al.*, 2001: 378–379). In many cases, the rigorous management of corpses and graves was the result of the maintenance of available space in order to respect the doctrine of Jewish law that prohibits disturbing ancient burials. Spaces between burials within the cemeteries were quite rare from an archaeological point of view, except in Seville (Romo Salas *et al.*, 2001: 377), where spaces were observed between graves (Santana Falcon, 2006: 324). In Châteauroux, a recent intervention revealed the presence of an internal passage, at least 1 to 2 m wide, between two rows of graves.

The use of ossuaries, as known from Christian cemeteries, is almost non-existent in Jewish burial places. Some grouping of bones or pushing aside of remains ('reductions' of the remains from the re-use of a grave) occurred sometimes but only very exceptionally when grave inter-cutting occurred. This may be the explanation for the four secondary burials excavated in Tárrega (Colet *et al.*, 2009: 108), two in Toledo (Ruiz Taboada, 2009: 38) and two more each in Lucena (Riquelme Cantal and Botella Ortega, 2011: 268), where there are two secondary graves from a total of 346 graves, and at Basel (Alder and Matt, 2010: 30–31). Treatment of the body according to specific criteria was observed in many places. In Châteauroux, York, Ennezat and Tárrega (Colet *et al.*, 2010: 253), burials of younger individuals were mostly placed in the eastern part of the cemetery (Blanchard and Georges-Zimmermann, 2015: 36). In the cemetery in Seville, individuals of only a few months old were arranged in specific rows and were from the fourth phase of cemetery use from the last third of the 15th century (Santana Falcon, 2006: 327) and, in Léon (Puente Castro), an area dedicated solely to children was discovered (Casanovas Miró, 2002: 215).

In Basel, the maintenance of graves was done in accordance with the characteristics of the social identity of the deceased. Adults were buried at the greatest depth, followed by pre-adolescents and adolescents and, closer to the surface, infants. This very particular method, according to age-at-death, does not appear to have been incidental but a response to limited space and the narrowness of the cemetery. It seems that some spaces were sometimes reserved for young people in Jewish cemeteries if one takes into account the location and concentration of the graves containing the bones of the youngest individuals (Lilley *et al.*, 1994: 522; Blanchard and Georges, 2011: 311; Selmi Wallisova, 2011: 282).

Conversely, there is no indication of distinctions based on the sex of the deceased, although this seems to have existed based on an 18th-century engraving (Engraving 1768 Ulrich, in the *Jewish Encyclopedia*, no date, III: 639). The concentration of male graves highlighted in York in the southwest corner of the cemetery probably does not reflect a distinction based on sex but is perhaps rather a sign of a specific social status – rabbis,[3] for example. Such groupings seemed to have occurred in the modern cemetery in Frankfurt am Main in Germany (Brocke, 1996), but it is not clear that this practice existed in the medieval period. Family plots are suspected in Toledo (Ruiz Taboada, 2009: 35) in quite large quadrangular constructions, measuring approximately 8 m × 5 m. Similarly, groupings of mother and child were recognised on the same site (Ruiz Taboada, 2009: 39). The exclusion of 'atypical' dead, sometimes referred to as an example of a 'bad death' ('*malemort*' in French) was practiced among Christians. The engraving of the eighteenth century mentioned above implies that it was also the case among those of the Jewish faith. To date, no evidence of this practice has been identified by archaeologists. However, there were cases where some female burials were reversed (feet westward), as in Tárrega. It was difficult to draw conclusions from such observations, but it is necessary to mention them in the hope of identifying similar cases in the future.

Funerary structures

Regulations for the treatment of bodies

Jewish law prohibits the use of cremation. Inhumation is the only permissible funerary treatment. Similarly, mass burials were prohibited but sometimes, in exceptional circumstances, such as in times of epidemics or massacres, they were employed. The rest of the time, the placing of the bodies was made in a single grave dug into virgin soil. In Seville, some of the burials seem to have been excavated into levels corresponding to an older Islamic occupation, but this is quite rare (Romo Salas *et al.*, 2001: 377; Santana Falcon, 2006: 324).

From an archaeological point of view, no cremations were identified, except perhaps in very rare cases, such as in Toledo, where charred remains of an individual were discovered (Ruiz Taboada, 2009: 38) in combination with nails and pieces of burnt wood. It appears to be the cremation of a small coffin (0.60 m maximum length) containing human remains, but the interpretation of these remains, as well as other cremations remains open to discussion. In a cemetery in Prague (Selmi Wallisova, 2011: 277), the charred remains of four people were discovered in a buried wooden chest. However, identification of animal bones with the human remains may suggest that these relate to accidental death as if the remains had been recovered from the rubble of a burned house.

Although cremation is rarely observed in archaeological investigations of Jewish cemeteries, this absence contrasts with the evidence for multiple and mass burials. Several sites had double and sometimes triple burials (Alder and Matt, 2010: 15). These were probably women who died during childbirth or relatives who died on the same day (Alder and Matt, 2010: 50). In these cases, a hypothetical mortality crisis is difficult to support.

Mortality crises have been confirmed or strongly suspected at some Jewish cemeteries, however. At Tárrega, 6 trenches contained 69 individuals, of which 50% showed traumatic injuries, indicating the manner of death through inter-personal violence (Colet *et al.*, 2011a). All deaths appeared to have been related to a pogrom dating to 1348, the plague year. Jews were sometimes targeted and massacred by Christians because they were suspected of spreading the epidemic by contaminating wells. In Valencia (Spain), 40 individuals were buried in a common grave

---

3 A rabbi is a person whose scholarship in the study of Torah enables him to make decisions or judgments in matters of Jewish law. He also supervises institutions designed to ensure Jewish life such as the slaughter of animals and ritual bathing. In the Middle Ages he emerged as the dominant communal figure in Judaism.

also dated to 1348 (Calvo Galvez, 2003). However, only ten individuals demonstrated violence-related injuries, while others might have died from the plague. Mass graves were also identified on the perimeter of the Jewish cemetery in York (Lilley *et al.*, 1994: 338, 348, 380–381), but in the absence of traumatic injuries, these individuals could have perished as a result of a probable childhood epidemic given the young ages at death of the deceased. The epidemic hypothesis is briefly mentioned among other hypotheses in order to explain the multiple graves in cemetery rows 39 and 40 at the Jewbury site in York (Lilley *et al.*, 1994, Fig. 187). In Seville, no multiple burials have been identified, but archaeologists have suggested some deaths were related to natural disasters (violent floods) (Romo Salas *et al.*, 2001: 379).

Types of burial and transportation of the deceased

The space in which bodies decomposed, such as in the empty space of a coffin or in earth-filled space (cf. Duday, 2009), is rarely mentioned in the studies reviewed. This is rather unfortunate because such insights would provide important details on burial methods. However, the numerous excavations carried out in recent years, Spain included, have made it possible to identify several types of burial elaboration.

Prior to discussing burial types in depth it is of interest to address the transport of bodies and how transportation affects the decomposition process. A few illustrations from the medieval period demonstrate the use of a coffin (Metzger and Metzger, 1982: 82–84, 235–239) or a stretcher to transport the corpse (Metzger and Metzger, 1982: 82–84; Jacob, 2008: 17–18). In Toledo, coffin rings were found along the side of the grave, demonstrating that coffins were transported in a manner similar to that represented in medieval depictions (Metzger and Metzger, 1982: 239). Coffins were used at the Jewbury site in York (Lilley *et al.*, 1994: 343–349.), at all of the French sites (Verbrugghe, 1994: 15; Blanchard and Georges, 2011: 306, Parent, 2011: 242), in the Czech Republic (Selmi Wallisova, 2011: 276) and at many sites in Spain (Casanovas Miró, 2002). In Basel, all adults were buried in coffins but infants were not (Alder and Matt, 2010: 34). The use of pine for the construction of the coffins was attested in Tárrega (Colet *et al.*, 2010: 255) and Basel (Alder and Matt, 2010: 36). The use of coffins in burials was found more predominantly outside of Spain, in what relates to the area of Ashkenazi cultural influence, and one may then wonder if this is part of a funerary tradition of this group. The different types of grave architecture observed on archaeological sites was not particularly diverse. Recent summaries of this subject exist for Spain (Casanovas Miró, 2002, 2003; Casanovas Miró and Maese Fidalgo, 2012), but none exist on the same scale for other countries in Europe.

To summarise, the six most common burial types in Spain (some of which may be found elsewhere in Europe) are:

1. A simple burial pit dug into the ground in which the deceased was placed, either coffined or uncoffined (Casanovas Miró, 2003: 515) (Figure 19.4). This type of burial was found on many sites in Spain, including in Barcelona, Lucena (Riquelme Cantal and Botella Ortega, 2011: 264), Tárrega and Toledo (Ruiz Taboada, 2011: 294–296), for example. The burial could have been accompanied by a wooden cover or a cover might have been lacking, despite the presence of a coffin (Colet *et al.* 2010: 247). The coffin was sometimes covered by stone slabs, as was observed in Barcelona in 1947 (Duran Sanpere and Millas Vallicrosa, 1947: 244–245). In cases where the coffin had a wooden or stone slab cover, the architecture of the burial pit should probably not be called 'simple', in the sense of unelaborated. In fact, such constructions were much more complicated and essential to support and maintain the constituent parts, such as benches, for example, in order to accommodate the individual inside.

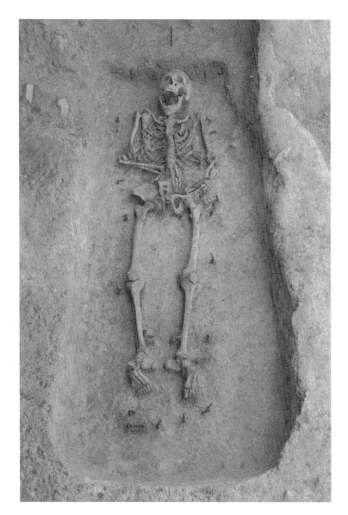

Figure 19.4 The burial pit of a primary inhumation with a nailed wooden coffin from the site at Tárrega, Spain (Image courtesy: Local Museum of Urgell-Tárrega).

2. An anthropomorphic burial pit, requiring a more elaborate excavation procedure, had side benches that formed an anthropomorphic space for the deceased. In France, these constructions are referred to as 'burial pits with side benches and covers', a type that is found between the eighth and thirteenth centuries but especially prevalent around the tenth and eleventh centuries (Blanchard and Poitevin, 2012). Examples of this type come from Barcelona (Duran Sanpere and Millas Vallicrosa, 1947: 241–244; Casanovas Miró and Maese Fidalgo, 2012: 89–93), Girona (Casanovas Miró, 2002: 210; Casanovas Miró and Maese Fidalgo, 2012: 93–95), Lucena (Riquelme Cantal and Botella Ortega, 2011: 266), Segovia (Casanovas Miró, 2002: 211) and Tárrega (Casanovas Miró and Maese Fidalgo, 2012: 95–98, Colet *et al.*, 2010: 251–252) (Figure 19.5). In most cases, no coffin was employed. The benches permitted the creation of an empty space that could be sealed using a cover in wood, stone or tiles.

3. A lateral chamber burial pit which consisted of a simple burial pit where the lower part of one of the sides was dug out to form a cavity or chamber in which to deposit a corpse

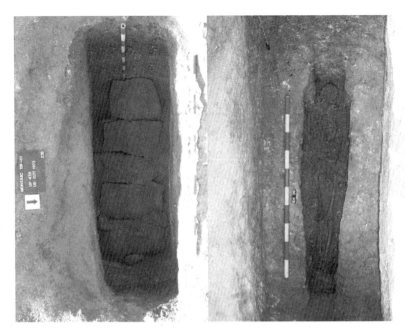

Figure 19.5 An anthropomorphic burial with a stone cover from the site of Montjuic excavated in 2001 in Barcelona, Spain (Image courtesy: X. Maese Fidalgo, Servei d'Arqueologia de Barcelona).

(Casanovas Miró, 2003: 516–517 (Figure 19.6). This structure looked like the *loculi* observed in Jewish catacombs in Rome (Vismara, 2011: 52). The cavity was sealed using tiles or stone slabs or perhaps wood in some cases where neither tile nor stone slabs have been discovered. Especially in the latter case, it is important to define the area in which the body decomposed in order to account for perishable parts of this construction that provided an empty space in which the decomposition of the body occurred. The use of a coffin was never observed in

Figure 19.6 View of a lateral chamber closed with stone slabs at the site of Montjuic excavated in 2001 in Barcelona, Spain (Image courtesy: X. Maese Fidalgo, Servei d'Arqueologia de Barcelona).

Figure 19.7　The cemetery at Toledo, Spain. Internal view of a '*lucillo*' (Image courtesy: A. Ruiz Taboada).

this type of interment. This third type was recognised in Barcelona (Duran Sanpere and Millas Vallicrosa, 1947: 239–241), Girona (Palahí *et al.*, 2000: 244) and Lucena (Riquelme Cantal and Botella Ortega, 2011: 264). This type of construction may have been borrowed from the Muslim populations of the Iberian Peninsula from the 7th century because this type of tomb would have resembled that of the Prophet Mohammed (cf. Gleize, Chapter 20, this volume).

4. A pit with vaulted masonry, usually of brick, called a '*lucillo*' in Spain (Figure 19.7). This vault, built after placing the body of the deceased, provided an empty space in which decay could take place. The vaults were built upon brick walls or directly on banks cut into the substratum. The outer face of the masonry vault could be seen on the surface of the cemetery or could have been covered if found within a pit. This type of burial accommodated a coffin in some cases. It has been attested in Cordoba (Casanovas Miró, 2003: 517–518) Seville (Casanovas Miró, 2002: 212) and Toledo (Ruiz Taboada, 2011: 295–299). In Toledo, a coffin was always associated with a *lucillo*.

5. A hypogeum or rock-cut tomb was observed in Segovia, but it appeared very poorly documented (Burdiel de las Heras, 1962; Fernández Esteban, 1997, 2003). Re-use of the sites as dwellings and refuse sites complicates the archaeological interpretation of this type of burial (Casanovas Miró, 2002: 211).

6. Cases of mass graves were rarely observed, as already mentioned above. The few examples observed to date do not permit interpretation of the circumstances for the use of such features. The number of bodies varied from 2 to 40. In York, a pit contained the remains of three children (Lilley *et al.*, 1994: 348), but near the northern boundary of the site, a series of small mass graves (see above) and deposits of coffins in small trenches, mostly containing immature individuals, were found.

Each type of burial identified also varied somewhat. Some anthropomorphic burial pit benches were replaced by holes in the side walls of the grave, facilitating the installation of a wooden cross-piece, which was then used to hold up planks that acted as a grave cover, as found in Barcelona and Tárrega (Colet *et al.*, 2010: 249). Similarly, the Jewish cemetery in Prague revealed one grave without benches but, instead, with stones on either side of the cranium and feet, which supported a wooden cross piece that, in turn, supported a cover comprised of several wood planks (Selmi Wallisova, 2011). Finally, pits existed in various forms (oval, rectangular, anthropomorphic and trapezoidal) either at the surface or at the bottom of the pit. In Spain, some reports mention a type of pit referred to as a 'bathtub', a rounded or oval feature located in the bottom of the pit, rather like a bowl (Casanovas Miró, 2002: 211; Colet *et al.*, 2010: 249). This seems to be only a variant of the simple pit, and it is thus unclear if this distinction can be sustained.

The different burial architectural features were quite interesting from a geographical point of view. Indeed, lateral chamber pits and *lucillo* were never found in Jewish cemeteries outside of Spain. However, the anthropomorphic pits with benches and wooden covers (and their variants) have been found throughout Europe in Christian cemeteries (Blanchard and Poitevin, 2012). Similarly, it seems that the exclusive use of coffins in a simple pit prevailed in some sites, which are in the era of the cultural influence of the Ashkenazi. Is it to be inferred from this that the use of coffins is a practice of these communities? Thus, different burial modes seem fairly well documented in Jewish cemeteries, but it is quite difficult to establish a typochronology of them. Furthermore, because Jewish law prohibited the intercutting of graves and because of the scarcity of grave inclusions, it is very difficult to date and establish a chronology of the architectural features. A few recent studies in Spain (Casanovas Miró, 2002) revealed that, in Girona, the oldest graves were anthropomorphic and 'bathtub' types, which were followed by a phase with lateral chamber pits. In Girona, as in Segovia, simple pit graves appeared to be more recent (Casanovas Miró, 2002: 211).

In Seville, phasing revealed that *lucillos* co-existed initially (Phase I–III) with simple pits. Later in time, only simple pits remained (Romo Salas *et al.*, 2001: 377; Casanovas Miró, 2002: 212). Finally, in Tárrega, anthropomorphic graves with benches and stone coverings were the oldest types (Colet *et al.*, 2010: 259). From all the above-mentioned types, evidence of patterns seems to emerge. Even when several grave types were identified, the body was almost never placed directly in contact with the earth; an empty space was always arranged around the body through the use of a coffin, *lucillo*, stone or wood covers and lateral chambers were sealed by slabs or tiles.

Grave markers

In order to respect the tenets of Jewish law that forbade the intercutting of graves, it was imperative to mark the presence of older burial pits in a sustainable manner. Various methods were adopted to mark the location of burials as a result. The most common was the placement of a stone on the surface. Most of the time, these stones were epigraphic. Commonly, horizontal slab stones were used in the Sephardic areas, while a funerary stele (vertical tombstone) was preferred in the Ashkenazi tradition (Nahon, 1980: 84).

In a small number of cases, archaeologists identified funerary steles and slab stones. These grave markers were absent in York and at sites in France, with the exception of Paris, where a series of beautiful steles was found. In Basel and in Prague, only fragments of such grave markers have been discovered. Some fragmented slabs were discovered on Spanish sites, as for example, at Léon (Puente Castro) (Casanovas Miró, 2002: 214). A complete slab was uncovered in Barcelona (Figure 19.8).

Grave markers can take other forms. In York, perishable materials may have been employed (Lilley *et al.*, 1994: 341). In Barcelona (Duran Sanpere and Millas Vallicrosa, 1947: 248–249) and

Figure 19.8 Funerary slab unearthed in 2001 during excavations in the Jewish cemetery in Barcelona (Image courtesy: X. Maese Fidalgo/Servei d'Arqueologia de Barcelona).

in Lucena (Riquelme Cantal and Botella Ortega, 2011: 267), blocks of stone, with or without epigraphic characters, were arranged after the filling of the pit (i.e. not visible on the surface of the site) or was placed flush with the ground level. They acted to alert the gravedigger when digging a new grave. A perimeter boundary around the pit at ground level comprised of stone or tiles was sometimes mentioned (Palahí *et al.*, 2000: 244; Ruiz Tabaoda, 2011: 292). In addition, the Toledo site showed a different marker indicated by the discovery of purified earth – without stones – in the fill of the pit (Ruiz Tabaoda, 2011: 292).

The architecture of the grave could also add to burial marking. Indeed, when the outer part of the *lucillo* was visible at the soil surface, it helped in the process of identification. But if it was covered by the fill of the burial pit, it would be encountered during renewed digging, indicating the need to change locations to the grave digger. The sample here also attests to stone slabs used as coverings. The markings of the pits, therefore, took many forms, whether external on the soil surface or internal.

Unique practices related to burial

A specific type of action related to the placement of the body is sometimes mentioned in written sources. Indeed, two sites, Toledo (Ruiz Tabaoda, 2009: 33) and Basel (Alder and Matt, 2010: 14, 70), revealed the presence of sediment under the cranium of the deceased (Figure 19.9).

Figure 19.9 The Jewish cemetery at Basel. Burials 16.1 and 16.2, a double burial of two women with a cushion of the earth under the cranium (Image courtesy: C. Glaser, Archäologische Bodenforschung Basel-Stadt).

This sediment appears to have once been part of cushions or sacks filled with earth and placed under the head. In Basel, a large amount of earth was placed in the coffin, under the cranium of adults only. Archaeologists considered that the soil may have come from the Holy Land, but analysis showed that it was taken from no more than a few kilometres away (Alder and Matt, 2010: 70). It was probably a symbolic deposit of pure soil in the graves of the Diaspora (Amiel, 1990: 403) as stipulated in by-laws of mid-fifteenth century documents from Spain and Portugal (Amiel, 1990: 395).

The archaeological population

Counting and estimation

The number of individuals found during archaeological excavations was highly variable. They range from only a few individuals at Châlons-en-Champagne (France) (Verbrugghe, 1994) to almost 500 at Jewbury in York (Lilley *et al.*, 1994). Despite having burials present, it was not always possible to draw generalisations, but sites with only a few burials were still of use for estimation of the number of individuals. Sites with at least 50 skeletons, such as at Basel and Deza (Spain) (Casanovas Miró and Ripoll, 1983) and especially those with several hundred, such as in Lucena, Prague, Seville, Tárrega and York, or those that resulted from several archaeological excavations, as at Barcelona and Seville, which were most informative, especially when they had been the subject of both excavation and a complete archaeo-anthropological study. The total number of individuals in a cemetery is rather difficult to estimate, however, because none of them had been the subject of exhaustive excavation. However, important work was carried out on the Tárrega site, where an estimated 785 individuals were buried over 214 years (about 3.66 deaths per year). In York, archaeologists believed they excavated half of the cemetery, which would have brought the total number of burials to about 1000, of which approximately 550 to 650 were adults (Lilley *et al.*, 1994: 533).

Age groups

Some sites offered results on age-at-death of interred individuals, including Basel (Alder and Matt 2010: 49), Tárrega (Colet *et al.*, 2010: 265) and York (Lilley *et al.*, 1994: 430). Generally, all age groups were found, but sometimes there was a much lower percentage in the younger age groups (Lilley *et al.*, 1994: 539; Colet *et al.*, 2010: 265). This phenomenon is not unique to Jewish cemeteries. Identical findings are often highlighted for Christian cemeteries. The discrepancies are probably related to areas of burial that had not been excavated, as seems to have been the case for York (Lilley, *et al.*, 1994: 539). In Basel (Alder and Matt, 2010: 49), 24 adults and 33 subadults were found. In York, 301 adults and 154 subadults were discovered.

Sex distribution

Sex was determined for the inhumed at some sites. In Basel, 9 females, 12 males and 3 indeterminate individuals were counted (Alder and Matt, 2010: 49). In Tárrega, 42% of the deceased adults were females, while only 29% were males. This large difference is likely related to the proportion of indeterminate individuals, which represented 29% of the total (Colet *et al.*, 2010: 266). In York, of the 314 adults examined, 151 were females, while 163 were males, producing a sex ratio of 1.08 males to 1 female (Lilley *et al.*, 1994: 431–433).

Health status of the population samples

It was possible to analyse the health status of the population samples for some sites with a greater number of burials. In Basel and Tárrega, there were no particular anomalies compared to other sites from the same period (Alder and Matt, 2010: 70; Colet *et al.*, 2010: 267–270). In York, the results of palaeopathological analysis of the buried population sample were compared with those from two non-Jewish contemporary sites in York. There was no significant difference in the sex ratio, for example, but other differences stood out slightly, such as individual stature (slightly shorter when compared with those of Christian sites, especially for males (Lilley *et al.*, 1994: 435–436) and the presence of lesions suspected to be associated with anemia, such as *cribra orbitalia*.

Burial practices

Orientation of the body

Orientations of bodies were mostly west to east, feet positioned eastward. This is no different from Christian burials. Some variants were observed in York (Lilley *et al.*, 1994: 337), where the dead were placed with the cephalic extremity oriented to the southwest. In Valencia, the cephalic extremity was oriented towards the south (feet to the north) and, in Deza (Spain), it was the reverse, cephalic extremity to the north and feet to the south (Casanovas Miró, 2003: 513).

Disposition of the body

In almost all cases, the bodies were buried supinely, i.e. lying on their backs. Ventral positioning (on the stomach) was not attested. However, in the sites of Lucena (Riquelme Cantal and Botella Ortega 2011: 268), Valencia, Teruel (Aragon, Spain) and Prague, one to two individuals were placed in a lateral, *decubitus* left or right position (Casanovas Miró, 2003: 520; Selmi Wallisova, 2011: 276). The example from Prague was perhaps in this position due to the presence of a hip injury rather than due to a particular funerary practice.

Position of the upper limbs and hands

In the vast majority of sites, the upper limbs were extended with the hands placed mostly along-side the body. Some variants were observed with one or two hands on the pubis or possibly on the abdomen (Figures 19.4 and 19.5). A crossed position of the hands on the chest or at the shoulders was extremely rare.

In York, the larger number of excavated graves permitted a more detailed and complete study of this aspect of funerary disposition (Lilley *et al.*, 1994: 391). Some 72.5% of the upper limbs were arranged alongside the body, and in 19.1%, at least one hand was placed on the pubis. In 5.1% of cases, both hands were resting on the pubis. In total, 96.7% of skeletons had their hands positioned inferiorly in the vicinity of the *ossa coxae* and femora. These positions were compared with two other York sites from the same period. It was observed that 40 to 60% of the upper limbs were in an inferiorly placed position (Lilley *et al.*, 1994: 390). This criterion, therefore, appeared to be particularly discriminating, and it is certainly one of the best indications of a Jewish burial.

Position of the lower limbs

The lower limbs were mostly extended. The crossed position of one or both limbs was anec-dotally observed, except perhaps in Lucena, where 38 cases were mentioned (about 10%). The feet were often adducted in close proximity but rarely crossed. In York, only one skeleton had crossed lower limbs (Lilley *et al.*, 1994: 352–353).

Preparation of the body

Specific practices related to the preparation of the body were observed in some cases. Occasionally, a small flat pebble or a ceramic fragment covered the orbital cavity (Figure 19.10), a practice seen in Prague (Selmi Wallisova, 2011: 277), Prostejov (Czech Republic) (Cizmar and Smid, 2000) and at sites from the modern period such as in Vilnius (Lithuania) (Gendrenas and Ozalas, 2003) and two other sites in Poland (Lublin and Wyszogród) (Fijalkowski, 2000: 338–342). Pebble or cer-amic fragments were also noted in the mouth of the deceased in both Prague and the Polish sites, and near the ankles or toes in Prague (Selmi Wallisova, 2011: 277) Similarly, three sites in Poland (Fijalkowski, 2000: 338–342) and the site in Prostejov in the Czech Republic revealed padlocks at the mouth of the deceased or in the immediate vicinity of the cranium. Most of these sites,

Figure 19.10 An example of sealing the orbits of the deceased, one of the funerary practices observed during the excavation of the Jewish cemetery in Prague, Czech Republic (Image courtesy: M. Selmi Wallisova, The Czech Society of Archaeology).

with the exception of those in Prague, dated to the modern period (17th–18th centuries), and therefore this practice could have been quite recent. No practice of this sort was found in the Iberian Peninsula. Covering of the orbital cavities was mentioned in the textual sources related to the Jewish cemetery in Koblenz during the 17th–18th centuries (Alder and Matt, 2010: 35). Regarding the meaning of these practices, ethnographic research suggested that these gestures were made so that 'the dead cannot report on what has happened down here in the Hereafter' (*'le mort ne puisse pas raconter dans l'Au-delà ce qui se passe ici bas'*) (Fijalkowski, 2000: 343).

Archaeologists also observed other actions related to the preparation of the body. Indeed, residues from textile, which were more or less well preserved, were found on or near the cranium of the deceased on sites in Barcelona (Duran Sanpere and Millas Vallicrosa, 1947: 252), Girona (Palahí *et al.*, 2000: 244; Casanovas Miró, 2002: 210), Basel (Alder and Matt, 2010: 31), Prague (Selmi Wallisova, 2011: 279–280), Tárrega (Colet *et al.*, 2010: 255) Valencia (Casanovas Miró, 2003: 522) and Seville (Romo Salas *et al.*, 2001: 376). When conservation was good, these remains were thought to be wearing a headdress (in the case of Barcelona) or a headband (in the case of Prague and Basel). Perhaps some ancient textile remains come close to the current practice of placing the prayer shawl (*Tallit*) on the head of the deceased.

The use of the shroud was difficult to define from an archaeological point of view in the absence of good preservation. However, the presence of copper alloy pins on the sites in Tárrega, Deza (Casanovas and Ripoll, 1983: 135–148) and Seville (Casanovas Miró, 2002: 212) suggested the presence of a shroud in the burial that was usually fastened by these types of copper alloy pins. The same interpretation was suggested for animal horn pins also used to fasten the shroud; these were identified in very limited numbers in the burials in York (Lilley *et al.*, 1994: 387). The same question could be asked about metal artifacts found at the shoulder of a skeleton from Barcelona with no apparent link to the coffin (Duran Sanpere and Millas Vallicrosa, 1947: 231–259). The Jewbury site in York provides archaeothanatological evidence related to funerary practices. Seven skeletons were described as 'tightly bound' (Lilley *et al.*, 1994: 387). On the contrary, the position of the hands and feet at the Lucena site indicated the absence of a shroud when the body was placed in the pit (Riquelme Cantal and Botella Ortega, 2011: 263).

Grave inclusions

In general, grave inclusions were not very common in Jewish burials. However, archaeological excavations in Spain reported them more frequently in Ashkenazi graves. Grave inclusions can be divided into three distinct categories: those worn by the deceased, those deposited in the grave, and those that appear to have accidentally found their way into the burial. Among the category of items worn by the deceased were personal adornments. Discoveries of this kind of item were often mentioned, including necklaces (Casanovas Miró, 2002: 214; Colet *et al.*, 2011b: 1021–1022), rings or signet rings (seals) (Duran Sanpere and Millas Vallicrosa, 1947: 242, 251; Casanovas Miró, 2002: 211, 215; Casanovas Miró, 2014: 262), earrings (Duran Sanpere and Millas Vallicrosa 1947: 243, 251; Amenos Martinez, 2014: 265), belt buckles and pendants (Casanovas Miró, 2002: 21) and bracelets (Colet *et al.*, 2011b: 1021–1022) in direct contact with the skeleton (Casanovas Miró, 2003: 522). Belt buckles were also found on other sites, such as at Prague and Châteauroux, and could have been parts of pieces of clothing or a type of fastening for a shroud (Casanovas Miró, 2002: 211; Alder and Matt, 2010: 29; Blanchard and George, 2011: 308; Selmi Wallisova, 2011: 275;).

Furthermore, it is important to highlight the presence of grave inclusions found in Tárrega because of the particular circumstances surrounding the death of the deceased in these cases, of which 50% showed traumatic injuries (see above). Two keys, buttons, a thimble and a series of ten amulets were found, which indicates that the usual funerary practices were not respected in these instances (Colet *et al.*, 2009: 119). The second category of inclusions includes tools that could have been worn by the deceased or had been deposited in the grave. A small knife was found in the hand of a deceased individual in the Jewish cemetery in Basel (Alder and Matt, 2010: 33), which could indicate that the deceased was a *Mohel* (circumciser). Several types of coins were discovered in 1937 in burials from Basel. These are, however, hard to interpret, as it was difficult to determine if they had been placed in a purse with the deceased at the time of burial or deposited in the grave later in time (Alder and Matt, 2010: 29–31).

The third category of inclusion relates to residual items, which include items not deliberately placed in the grave. For example, ceramic fragments and animal bones associated with colluvial and the mixing of sediments were observed in Basel (Alder and Matt, 2010: 35). A thimble was found in Girona that may have been lost during the deposition of the body in the grave (Palahí *et al.*, 2000: 244). Finally, a few isolated coins were mentioned in reports. Casanovas Miró (2002: 211) mentions these for the site at Segovia, Spain. It was unclear if they were intentionally deposited in the grave if they were worn by the deceased within a garment, if the coins fell into the grave for various reasons as a result of random loss, or if they had been deposited during the digging or the filling of the burial pit.

Phasing and dating

Due to the scarcity of intercutting among graves and rarity of funerary inclusions in the burials, it is difficult to phase burials. Thus, dating is largely based on textual sources, which were complemented by archaeological data, objects and epigraphy, and sometimes by a few radio-carbon determinations (Blanchard and Georges, 2011: 308).

Conclusion

This initial treatment of the subject of medieval Jewish cemeteries is still very much a work in progress, as many new sites appear regularly and much data remains to be analysed. However, it is possible to take stock now. If the number of cemeteries that have been the subject of an intervention appears, at present, to be relatively large, this observation must be strongly quali-fied. Indeed, many of these data (number of burials observed, excavated, type of burial) are unusable because of the early date of the discovery or observation and/or lacking or absent information reported. Similarly, many sites related to a limited number of graves. While these provide some information, it is often difficult to generalise from a sample limited to only a few burials. Moreover, very few sites have been excavated and analysed using modern archaeological and anthropological methods, respectively. Out of a total of 75 sites, less than a dozen in Europe are highly informative based on the number of burials (above 30), recent data and use of more rigorous methods (Figure 19.1).

An initial reflection is possible in order to assess the means of recognising a funerary space connected to a medieval Jewish community. Defining this relationship from an isolated grave is too suggestive. On the other hand, from the synthesis of a significant number of burials, it seems that certain types of evidence are trustworthy. First of all, the location of the site is important. It will never be in the immediate vicinity of a synagogue and must be located outside the city. This location, far from built-up urban occupation, should not be seen as a result of isolation and segre-gation of Jews from Christians. This choice seems to be based on the desires of the communities and meets the requirements for ritual purity (Blanchard, Georges and De Mecquenem, 2009: 17).

The second criterion for the identification of a Jewish cemetery is related to the extreme rigour with which graves were maintained to avoid intercutting of older graves. Contemporary Christian sites all have much higher occurrences of intercutting.[4] Finally, a third criterion relates to the position of the hands. Indeed, on these sites, almost all the deceased had their hands in an inferior position, alongside the body or on the pubis. The same positions can be found in Christian burials but, again, never in such high proportions (Lilley *et al.*, 1994: 390).

Some other features can also be taken into account, such as a slightly earlier use of the coffin among Jewish as opposed to among near contemporary Christian communities. Similarly, the presence of specific practices such as the use of a cushion of soil under the cranium, the covering of the orbital cavities, or particular burial methods (the *lucillo* or lateral cavities) also provide sound indications of Jewish practices. Taken in isolation, one of these criteria is probably not relevant, but the combination of them could be quite indicative.

It is therefore important to continue this type of study with the integration of new sites to continue testing the hypothetical patterns identified. It is also of interest to verify whether or not the practices identified in the medieval period are found in the same proportions in the modern period and in what ways they may have changed. Finally, the results of this work should be systematically compared with those relating to Christian and Islamic communities where possible (in Spain, in particular). In addition, comparative studies remain to be under-taken, for example, between Ashkenazi and Sephardic sites to observe potential differences while synthesising textual and iconographic sources with field data, which, for the moment, appear to provide very similar perspectives.

Acknowledgements

The author would like to thank Cari Leroux for her help with the translation from French to English.

---

4 By way of example, an excavation in Orléans, France, carried out on a burial area used between the 10th and 13th centuries revealed overlapping areas that vary between 29% and 38% depending on the area excavated (Blanchard *et al.*, 2010).

References

Alder, C. and Matt, C.P. (2010). Der mittelalterliche Friedhof der ersten judischen Gemeinde in Basel. In: C. Alder and C.P. Matt, eds., *Materialhefte zur Archäologie in Basel*. Basel: Hefte, 21, pp. 2–69.

Amenos Martinez, L. (2014). Parella d'arracades. In: J. Ramos Ruiz, I. Moreno Expósito, and M. Esqué Ballesta, eds., *Tragèdia al call, Tàrrega 1348, cataleg de l'exposicio. Tàrrega: Museu Comarcal de l'Urgell-Tàrrega*, p. 265.

Amiel, C. (1990). La « mort juive » au regard des Inquisitions ibériques. *Revue de l'Histoire des Religions*, 207(4), pp. 389–411.

Attias, J.-C. and Benbassa, E. (1997) *Dictionnaire de la civilisation juive*. Paris: Larousse, pp. 250–251.

Benbassa, E. (1997). *Histoire des Juifs de France*. Paris: Éditions du Seuil.

Blanchard, P., Cunault M., Kacki S., Poitevin G., Rouquet J., Yvernault F., Orléans, La Madeleine (2010). Hospitalité et recueillement à travers différentes occupations (IX–XVIIIe siècle), Volume 2, catalogue des sépultures. Rapport de fouille archéologique, Inrap Centre-Ile-de-France.

Blanchard, P. and Georges, P. (2011). Le Cimetière juif de Châteauroux redécouvert: apports de l'archéologie et confrontation des sources. In: P. Salmona and L. Sigal, eds., *L'Archéologie du judaïsme en France et en Europe*. Paris: La Découverte, pp. 301–313.

Blanchard, P., Georges, P. and De Mecquenem, C. (2009). Le cimetière juif au Moyen-Age, un lieu d'exclusion? *Archéopages*, 25, pp. 14–23.

Blanchard, P. and Georges-Zimmermann, P. (2015). Diagnostiquer un cimetière juif médiéval: l'expérience de Châteauroux (Indre, France). In: Courtaud, P., Kacki, S., and Romon, T., eds., *Cimetières et Identité*. Talence: Ausonius/Maison des Sciences de l'Homme d'Aquitaine Tanat'Os, 3, pp. 25–40.

Blanchard, P. and Poitevin, G. (2012). Restitution d'une architecture en bois dans les tombes à banquettes (X–XIe s.): l'exemple du site de la Madeleine à Orléans (Loiret). In: Carré, F. and Henrion, F., eds., *Le Bois dans l'Architecture et l'Aménagement de la Tombe: Quelles Approches? Actes de la table ronde d'Auxerre*, 15–17 octobre 2009. Paris: AFAM (Mémoires de l'Association française d'archéologie mérovingienne), pp. 389–396.

Botella Ortega, D. and Casanovas Miró J. (2009). El cementerio judio de Lucena (Cordoba). *MEAH (Miscelánea de Estudios Árabes Y Hebraicos) Sección Hebreo*, 58, pp. 3–25.

Brocke, M. (1996). *Der Alte judische friedhof zu Frankfurt am main: Unbekannte denkmäler und Inschriften*. Stuttgart: Jan Thorbecke Verlag.

Burdiel de las Heras I. (1964). Excavaciones en el antiguo fonsario u osario de los judios (Segovia). *Noticiario Arqueologico Hispano (Madrid)*, VI, pp. 216–226.

Calvo Galvez, M. (2003). Necropolis Judia de Valencia: Nuevos Datos. In: A.M. López Alvarez and R. Izquierdo Benito, eds., *Juderias y Sinagogas de la Sefarad Medieval*. Cuenca: Ediciones de la Universidad de Castilla-La Mancha, pp. 583–610.

Casanovas Miró, J. (2002). Las necropolis Judias Hispanas. Nuevas aportaciones In: Sociedad Estatal para la Acción Cultural Exterior ed., *Memoria de Sefarad*. Toledo: Centro Cultural San Marcos, pp. 209–219.

Casanovas Miró J. (2003). Las necropolis Judias Hispanas. Las fuentes y la documentacion frente a la realidad arqueologica. In: A.M. López Alvarezand R. Izquierdo Benito, eds., *Juderias y Sinagogas de la Sefarad Medieval*. Cuenca: Ediciones de la Universidad de Castilla-La Mancha, pp. 493–531.

Casanovas Miró, J. (2014). Anell Amb el nom Boneta. In: J. Ramos Ruiz, I. Moreno Expósito, and M. Esqué Ballesta, eds., *Tragèdia al call, Tàrrega 1348, cataleg de l'exposicio*, Tàrrega: Museu Comarcal de l'Urgell, pp. 262–263.

Casanovas Miró, J. and Maese Fidalgo, X. (2012). La pervivencia de les sepultures antropomorfes a les necropolis jueves medievals catalanes (segles IX–XV), In: Molist i Capella, N. and Ripoll López, G. eds., *Arqueologia Funeraria al Nord-Est Peninsular entre els Segles VI i XII*. Olèrdola: Muséu d'Arqueologia de Catalunya, 3(1), pp. 87–99.

Casanovas Miró, J. and Ripoll, O. (1983). Catalogo de los materieles aparecidos en la necropolis judaica de Deza (Soria). *Celtiberia*, 33(65), pp. 135–138.

Cizmar, M. and Smid, M. (2000). Vyvoj Prostejova v archeologicky a historickych pramenech v obdobi 10–16. stoleti [Le développement de Prostejov d'après les sources archéologiques et les documents historiques de première main datant du Xe au XVIe siècle], *Archaeologia Historica*, 25, pp. 77–102.

Colet, A., Muntané, J.X., Saula, O., Ruiz, J., Subirà, M.E. (2010). La necropolis medieval jueva de les Roquetes (Tàrrega, Urgell), Tribuna d'Arqueologia 2008–2009. *Generalitat de Catalunya: Servei d'Arqueologia i Paleontologia*, 13, pp. 239–273.

Colet, A., Muntané Santiveri, J.X., Saula Briansó, O., Ruiz Ventura, J., and Subirà de Galdàcano, E. (2009). Les fosses comunes de la Necropolis Medieval Jueva de les Roquetes I el pogrom de 1348 a Tàrrega. *Urtx, Revista Cultural de l'Urgell*, 23, pp. 104–179.

Colet, A. Muntané, J.X., Ruiz, J., Saula, O. and Subirà de Galdàcano. E. (2011a). Les fosses communes des Roqietes à Tàrrega. In: P. Salmona and L.Sigal, eds., *L'Archéologie du Judaïsme en France et en Europe*. Paris: La Découverte, pp. 247–260.

Colet, A., Ruiz, J., Saula, O., Subirà, M.E., Piera, M. (2011b). Els amulets de la necropolis medieval jueva de les Roquetes (Tárrega)., In: A. Colet, C. Navarro, and O. Saula, eds., *Actes del IV Congres d'Arqueologia Medieval i Moderna a Catalunya.Tarragona del 10 al 13 juny de 2010*.Tarragona: Associacio Catalana per a la Recerca en Arqyeologia Medieval, pp. 1021–1024.

Curina R. et Di Stefano V. (2019) – *Il Cimitero ebraico medievale di Bologna: un percorso tra memoria e valorizzazione*, Documenti ed Evidenze di Archeologia n° 13, Firenze, Cooperativa Archeologia.

De Cristofaro, A., Di Mento, M. and Rossi, D. (2017). Coraria Septimiana e Campus Iudeorum : Novita dai recenti Scavi fuori Porta Portese. *Thiasos, Revista di Archeologia e Architettura Antica*, 6, pp. 3–39.

Duday, H. (2009). *The archaeology of the dead. Lectures in archaeothanatology*. Oxford: Oxbow Books.

Dupaquier, J. (1988). *Histoire de la population française*. Paris: Presses Universitaires de France (P.U.F.).

Duran Sanpere, A. and Millas Vallicrosa, J.-M. (1947). Una necropolis judaica en el Montjuich de Barcelona. *Sefarad*, VII, pp. 231–259.

Fernández Esteban S. (1997). Analisis de las estructuras funerarias de la Cuesta de los Hoyos, Segovia. Un ejemplo de necropolis medieval judaica', *XXIV Congreso Nacional de Arqueologia, Murcia*, V, pp. 225–232.

Fernández Esteban S. (2003). El cementerio judio de la ciudad de Segovia en el medievo. In: A. M. Lopez Alvarez and B.R. Izquierrdo, eds., *Juderias y Sinagogas de la Sefarad Medieval*, pp. 557–582.

Fijalkowski, P. (2000). Les cérémonies d'enterrement des juifs de Pologne à la lumière des recherches archéologiques. In: D. Tollete, ed., *La Mort et ses Représentations dans le Judaïsme*. Paris: Honoré Champion, pp. 338–342.

Gendrenas, G. and Ozalas, E. (2003). Vilnius 2002, Karaliaus Mindaugo tilto Priegos. Zvalgomieji archeologiniai Tyrimai, Ataskaita. IV dalis. Desinysis Neries Krantas. Rinktines ir Olimpieciu gatviu rekonstrukcija ties zydu senosiomis kapinemis. Available at: http://www.lietuvospilys.lt/data/zydai. htm.

Harck, O. (2014). *Archäologische Studien zum Judentum in der europäischen Antike und dem zentraleuropäischen Mittelalter*. Petersberg: Michael Imhof Verlag (Schriften der Bet Tfila – Forschungsstelle für jüdische Architektur in Europa).

Jacobs, J. (2008). *Houses of life. Jewish cemeteries of Europe*. London: Frances Lincoln.

Lilley, J., Stroud, G., Brothwell, D.R. and Williamson, M.H. (1994). *The Jewish burial ground at Jewbury*. The Archaeology of York: The Medieval Cemeteries, 12(3). York: Council for British Archaeology.

Metzger, M. and Metzger, T. (1982). *La vie juive au Moyen-Age illustrée par des manuscrits hébraïques enluminés du XIIIe au XVIe siècle*. Fribourg/Paris: Office du Livre/Editions Vilo.

Moreda Blanco, J. and Serrano Noriega, R. (2009). *La necrópolis judía del Paseo de la Acera de Recoletos, Valladolid*. Valladolid, Espagne: Junta de Castilla y León, Consejería de Cultura y Turismo.

Nahon, G. (1975). L'archéologie juive médiévale en France, *Archéologie Médiévale*, 5, pp. 139–159.

Nahon, G. (1980). Les cimetières. In B. Blumenkranz, ed., *Art et Archéologie des Juifs en France Médiévale*. Paris: Les Belles Lettres (Franco-Judaïca), pp. 73–94.

Palahí, L., Jiménez, M.F., Prados, A., Freixas, P. (2000). Excavacions al cementiri jueu de Girona. In: Q. Esteba and M. Bodro, eds., *Cinquenes Jornades d'Arqueologia de les Comarques de Girona (Olot, 12-13 de maig de 2000)*. Girona: Universitat di Girona, pp. 243–246.

Parent, D. (2011). Le 'champ des juif' à Ennezat. In: P. Salmona, P. and L. Sigal, eds., *L'Archéologie du Judaïsme en France et en Europe*. Paris: La Découverte, pp. 235–246.

Polonovski, M. (2011). L'archéologie juive en France et en Europe : enjeux et perspectives, In: P. Salmona and L. Sigal, eds., *L'Archéologie du Judaïsme en France et en Europe*. Paris: La Découverte, pp. 31–42.

Riquelme Cantal, J.A. and Botella Ortega, D. (2011). La necropole médiévale de Lucena : contributions à l'archéologie juive en Séfarad. In: P. Salmona and L. Sigal, eds., *L'Archéologie du Judaïsme en France et en Europe*. Paris: La Découverte, pp. 261–271.

Robin, M. (1952). Les Cimetières Juifs de Paris au Moyen-Age. *Mémoires de la Fédération des sSociétés Historiques et Archéologiques d'Ile-de-France*, 4, pp. 7–19.

Romo Salas, A., García Vargas, E., Vargas Jiménez, J.M. and Guijo Mauri, J.M. (2001). Inhumaciones de grupos marginales en Sevilla. I. La minoria hebrea, *Archeologia Medievale*, XXVIII, pp. 373–381.

Ruiz Taboada, A. (2009). La necropolis medieval del Cerro de La Horca en Toledo. *Sefarad*, 69, pp. 25–41.

Ruiz Taboada, A. (2011). La nécropole juive de Tolède : type, construction et distribution des tombes. In: P. Salmona and L. Sigal, eds., *L'Archéologie du Judaïsme en France et en Europe*. Paris: La Découverte, pp. 287–300.

Ruiz Taboada, A. (2013). *La vida futura es para los devotos. La muerte en el Toledo medieval.* Madrid: La Ergastula.

Santana Falcon, I. (2006). Excavaciones Arqueologicas en el cementerio de la aljama judia de Sevilla (1992–2006). *Anales de Arqueologia Cordobesa*, II(17), pp. 317–330.

Schwarzfuchs, S. (1975). *Les Juifs de France.* Paris: Albin Michel.

Selmi Wallisova, M. (2011). Le cimetière juif médiéval du quartier de Nové Mesto à Prague. In: P. Salmona and L. Sigal, eds., *L'Archéologie du Judaïsme en France et en Europe.* Paris: La Découverte, pp. 273–285.

Verbrugghe, G. (1994). *Un cimetière juif médiéval, rue Saint-Joseph à Châlons-sur-Marne (Marne) (site number 51 108 031).* Unpublished report. Châlons-sur-Marne: Service Régional d'Archéologie (SRA) Champagne-Ardennes, p. 33.

Vismara, C. (2011). Les catacombes juives de Rome. In: P. Salmona and L. Sigal, eds., *L'Archéologie du Judaïsme en France et en Europe.* Paris: La Découverte, pp. 51–62.

20

ISLAMIC BURIALS

Muslim graves and graves of Muslims

Yves Gleize

Institut National de Recherches Archéologiques Préventives (Inrap),
Auvergne-Rhône-Alpes, Bron, France

PACEA, De la Préhistoire à l'Actuel: Culture, Environnement et Anthropologie,
UMR 5199, CNRS-Université de Bordeaux, Pessac, France

Introduction

The rise of Islam resulted in the rapid dissemination and development of new funerary practices during the Middle Ages in Arabia (Halevi, 2007), in the Middle East (Imbert, 1992), in Africa (Insoll, 1996), in the Mediterranean area (Chávet Lozoya, Sánchez Gallego and Padial Pérez, 2006; Faro Carballa *et al.,* 2007; Buturovic, 2016; Gleize *et al.,* 2016), then in the Far East (Ambary, 1985; Lambourn, 2008; Rosmawati, 2018), and finally more recently in America (Austin, 1984; M'bow and Kettani, 2001) and Oceania (Svanberg and Westerlund, 1999). The importance of resurrection and final judgment in Islam implies special care be taken in the performance of funerary rituals and specific practices (Tritton, 1938; Smith and Haddad, 1981; Ragib, 1992; Halevi, 2007). From the beginning of Islam (1st century AH[1]/7th century AD), Muslims have been attentive to recognising members of the Muslim community (*Umma*) and to distinguish themselves from other religious groups through their funerary practices (Halevi, 2007). However, funeral rituals are not specified in the *Quran* (Tritton, 1938; Welch, 1978; Smith and Haddad, 1981; Bowker, 1991; Halevi, 2007). The manner of burying the body and the construction of the Muslim tomb were established based on the interpretation of texts (*Hadīth* traditions[2] and law texts) and discussions between Muslim jurists and traditionists as for the other funerary rituals, such as the washing of the body and the funeral procession, for example. These normative rituals are based on the notion of the equality of all Muslims in the face of death. The practices were adapted from the events of the death of the Prophet Muhammad, in opposition to other existing customs but also by integrating and adapting other cultural practices (Halevi, 2007; King, 2009). Muslim funerary practices were instituted progressively during the first centuries after the Hegira (i.e. the 'Exile'), but it seems that some rules were already in place during the first century of Islam.

---

1 *Anno Hegirae*, denoted as AH, means 'in the year of the *Hijrah*' and indicates the year in the Islamic calendar.
2 Words and acts attributed to Muhammad and gathered into large collections during the 2nd and the 3rd centuries AH (8th–9th centuries AD).

DOI: 10.4324/9781351030625-23

Thus funerary practices are a very important element for analysing the process of Islamisation,[3] Muslim identity, but also possible cultural adaptations. Research has been limited for a long time to epigraphy (e.g. Schneider, 1983; Imbert, 1992; Grassi, 2002, 2004; Diem and Schöller, 2004; Halevi, 2007; Lambourn, 2008), but this approach focusses only on certain tombs and only a part of the funerary practices. In addition, burial excavations can provide other material elements of Muslim funerary rituals. However, attention to ancient Muslim funerary remains is variable according to region. In countries with significant influence of political Islam and with large Muslim communities, the excavations of Muslim burials are rare and even less publicly visible (Maynard and Museyibli, 2011; Petersen, 2013). But in Muslim and non-Muslim countries, Islamic funerary remains are increasingly threatened by urban development and building intensification which lead to adventitious discoveries and destruction of ancient cemeteries (Pradines *et al.*, 2009). These situations lead to the excavation of graves in current as well as past Islamised regions and to question whether the discovered dead are Muslim or not. The archaeology of Muslim burials has been limited by religious regulations but also by the fact that Islamic practices are *a priori* considered as very homogeneous such that they were thought to offer meagre insights into ancient Islamic societies. Overviews of archaeological remains, however, showed a variety of Muslim funerary practices (Simpson, 1995; Insoll, 1999; Halevi, 2007; Petersen, 2013; Bradbury, 2016). The present chapter highlights the importance of analysing Muslim funerary practices using archaeothanatological methods, but also the necessity to contextualise these findings. It is only in this way that changes in Muslim funerary practices and cultural differences in Muslim contexts can be studied fully.

Islamic funerary practices and the treatment of the deceased

In Islamic tradition, after being washed, the body of the deceased is wrapped in a shroud (Tritton, 1938; Ragib, 1992), which can be attested through the study of archaeological remains. Muslim graves discovered in arid contexts provided some examples of cloth remains (Lombard, 1978; Gayraud *et al.*, 1995; Sokoly, 1997). Without such vestiges, the presence of a shroud or other burial clothes is difficult to demonstrate through the application of archaeothanatological methods (Blaizot, 1996; Duday, 2009). In a Muslim grave discovered in Nîmes (France), the wrapping of the body was attested by the *in situ* position of a patella that should have disarticulated because the body had decayed in an empty space, and this bone was not held in place by the wall of the burial pit (Gleize *et al.*, 2016) (Figure 20.1). Furthermore, the use of the shroud is not a specific Muslim practice, and, finally, the presence of these funerary accoutrements cannot always be used to distinguish Muslim graves (Feliciano, 2005; Halevi, 2007: 88–90).

Traditionally, the deceased, once wrapped, is then carried in procession, often on a burial stretcher or bier (*jana'iz*) to the burial place. The bier or coffin may be used only to move the body, and neither may be placed in the grave. The wrapped body is thus directly buried in contact with the soil, without the presence of a wooden floor, as archaeothanatological analysis can attest due to the absence of displaced bones from the decay and collapse of such funerary furnishings (Gleize *et al.*, 2016). Even if archaeothanatological studies of Muslim graves are not common, the narrowness of the burial pit and the bottom of the pit rising at both ends, observed in several publications of Muslim cemeteries (Murillo Fragero, 2009), argue against the burial of a coffin and help to demonstrate the observation that bodies were directly deposited in the grave.

---

3 'Historical process at work during the formative era of Islam, by which persons and objects were made Islamic in character and became imbued with Islamic principles or forms' (Halevi, 2004: 124).

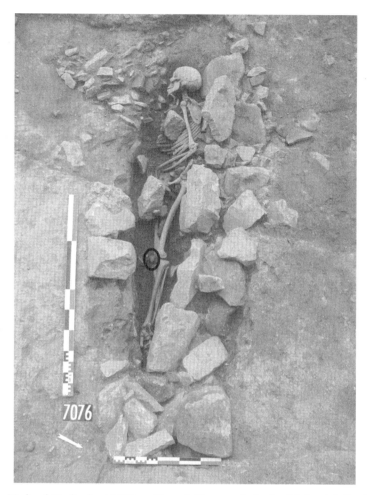

Figure 20.1 Medieval Muslim burial (Nîmes, France) (Photograph: Institut National de Recherches Archéologiques Preventives, modified by Y. Gleize).

However, ethnographic studies attest to rare examples of coffins in Muslim graves (Pierotti, 1864; Simpson, 1995). Remains of wood or iron nails are also are very rarely recorded in excavated Muslim burials (Gayraud *et al.*, 1995; Zych, 2003; Genequand, 2004; Arbel, 2017). The use of a coffin instead of a bier may be explained as a function of the exceptionally long distance to the place of burial (Majcherek and Kolataj, 2003) and by a body in an advanced state of decay. Closed coffins limit manipulations of the body during funerals, but it is unclear if the wooden structures discovered in graves are always coffins. Ethnographic surveys also attest to the use of open coffins (Pierotti, 1864). If wood remains and/or nails are not present, an archaeothanatological analysis is necessary to attest to the presence or not of a wooden floor or a bier under the body. Recently, the disarticulation of segments of anatomical areas observed in a skeleton excavated in the medieval Muslim cemetery of Bilet in Ethiopia (Loiseau *et al.*, 2021) attests to the collapse of the bones due to the decay of wooden boards or flooring originally under the body in the grave (pers. obs. author). Lastly, during the late Ottoman period, infants could be buried in a jar (Canaan, 1927; Stern *et al.*, 1978; Toombs, 1985), which was originally used in water wheel construction (Ayalon, 2000: 225).

In the Muslim grave, the positioning of the body is one of the most important rituals. Several *hadiths* indicate that the face of the dead must face the sacred *Kaaba* in Mecca (Tritton, 1938). The dead are buried in order to rise on the day of the resurrection facing this direction, called the *Qibla* (King, 1979). This practice of interment is archaeologically well-attested in many Muslim cemeteries and graves dated to the first two centuries of the Hegira (Canaan, 1927; Granqvist, 1965; Halevi, 2007: 188–189; Kressel, Bar-Zvi and Abu-Rabi'a, 2014) but also in the poetry of the Umayyad period (Gorzalczany, 2007). However, the orientation of the *Qibla* varied greatly in different regions and it was chosen and sought in different ways (King, 1979, 1985, 1995). Before the late 8th century, no mathematical solution existed for identifying this direction. Certain ancient Muslim traditions chose first Jerusalem and not Mecca for the direction of prayer and so for the orientation of the face of the dead (Halevi, 2007). In Nîmes (8th century AD/2nd century AH), the direction of the face in three Muslim graves varied between 150° and 180° (Gleize *et al.,* 2016), while the correct orientation should be 115°. These directions appear to be similar to those of several *mihrabs*[4] of early mosques in the Maghreb and al-Andalus (King, 1995) and not unintentional. Recently, Gibson (2017) explained this variation as due to the fact that there were different Qiblas, and the oldest was oriented on Petra (southern Jordan) or, in some cases, on a parallel line drawn between Petra and Mecca was used for the *Qibla*, but his hypothesis has been seriously criticised (King, 2018). In any case, the important thing for the believer is the desire to point to the *Qibla* even if it is not, in the end, correct.

Some texts specify the burial of the body on the right side with the aim of facilitating the orientation of the face towards Mecca (Halevi, 2007). This position forms the large majority in excavated Muslim cemeteries (e.g. Simpson, 1995; Chávet Lozoya, Sánchez Gallego and Padial Pérez, 2006; Faro Carballa *et al.,* 2007). The head could sometimes be elevated with mud bricks (Tritton, 1938; el Aswad, 1987). If there are religious explanations for the importance of placing the wrapped body in contact with the soil (Halevi, 2007), then not burying the body in a coffin also facilitates the manipulation of the head and of the cadaver towards Mecca and also the orientation of the body to permit this. Other archaeological examples attest to burials being placed on their backs in an Islamic context. In certain cases, this position could be linked with the use of a coffin (Genequand, 2004). Other peculiar positions have been observed, such as in a seated position (Insoll, 1999: 173).

In Muslim graves, the archaeological determination of the general body position is generally not problematic, except when the body has been deposited on a bier or as a secondary deposit. This means that the position of the face is not always obvious. If the body is placed on its side, the movement of the elements of the skull in response to gravity after decomposition is quite limited. On the other hand, if the deceased is buried on the back in an empty space, the disarticulation of cervical joints means that the skull may roll to the side and change the orientation of the face (Duday, 2009). In this case, the position of the skull can lead to misinterpretation of its original position (Lacam, 1965; Shingiray, 2018) if the position and orientation of the cervical vertebrae has not been recorded during excavation in order to determine the original position of the head and the direction of the face (i.e. the facial skeleton).

A Muslim burial usually consists of a single individual, as is the case for many archaeological examples. Texts do note the possibility of multiple burials in cases of epidemics. The traditionists advise distinguishing the dead by sex in the pit (Halevi, 2007: 181), but archaeological examples provide evidence of the presence of both females and males in the same burial (Petersen, 2013). In the literature, the distinction between collective deposits, re-uses of the burial

---

4 The niche in the mosque which indicates the *Qibla*.

pit and overlapping of skeletal remains from different graves is not always clear and analysis of the position of the bones is often missing. The intensive use of cemeteries in highly urbanised contexts, as in Cairo and Jerusalem, for example, during the Mameluke and Ottoman periods (13th–19th centuries AD/7th–14th centuries AH), produces overlapping burials, the destruction of older graves and the presence of many bones in secondary positions around the primary skeletal deposition (Pradines *et al.,* 2009). Graves may also be re-opened to bury a new body and the bones of previous individuals removed (Jettmar, 1967; Gayraud *et al.,* 1995: 9; Kulicka, 2008). Secondary deposits of bones in graves are often disarticulated and commingled, which is problematic in Muslim tradition and which is also why cremation of the body is not often practiced (Lavoie, 2011). Even if Muslim interments are intended to be rapid, ethnological (Titaÿna, 1930) and historical examples (Gayraud *et al.,* 1995) of displacement of bodies or skeletons over several thousand kilometres explains the presence of secondary deposits. Some scholars may have suggested that coffin burials seem to have been linked with secondary interments without demonstrating this through an analysis of the position of bones, however (Zych, 2003). Whatever the case may be, these long distance movements are part of memory and identity practices of the Islamic world (Sauvaget, 1950).

Based on egalitarian religious principles, Muslims are supposed to be buried without accompanying material (Halevi, 2007: 188), as is more often the case for Jewish (cf. Blanchard, Chapter 19, this volume) and Christian burials. Deposits of venerated objects exist, however, such as prayer stones in the graves of pilgrims (Simpson, 1995) or as footprints of the Prophet (imprints left by the Prophet Muhammad) in the burial chamber of an important person (Abdulfattah, 2014). Apart from these exceptional cases, ethnographic surveys and archaeological discoveries reflect that the ban on grave goods and funerary artefacts were only partly obeyed (Mustafa and Tayeh, 2014). Ceramics (e.g. water jugs) are occasionally placed close to the body (Pierotti, 1864; Toombs, 1985; Simpson, 1995: 245; Kulicka, 2008; Gorzalczany, 2009: 89–90). Simple jewellery (bracelets, necklaces, and earrings) are also reported in Muslim female burials from the Near East (Stern *et al.,* 1978; Ben-Tor and Portugali, 1987; Walker, 2001) and Western Mediterranean area (Chávet Lozoya, Sánchez Gallego and Padial Pérez, 2006). The presence of ring with an Arabic inscription does not, however, always provide evidence of an Islamic grave (Wärmländer *et al.,* 2015). In the case of wrapped bodies, it is not certain that these ornaments were visible during funerals. It is also possible that some beads came from rosaries (*misbaḥah* or *tasbīḥ*) added to the burial and that were not inside the body wrapping. Coins are frequently found in Ottoman Muslim burials (Guz-Zilberstein and Raveh, 1988–1989: 51). Some may have been used in jewellery buried with the dead or deliberately deposited in or on top of the graves (Pierotti, 1864). Other uncommon deposits have also been discovered, such as eggs (Agius, 2005). Finally, ceramics found in the vicinity of burials may testify to rites of commemoration (Verin, 1986; Dewar and Wright, 1993). Generally, the precise position of this material was often not recorded during excavation, and thus it is not possible to associate these remains with their specific funerary use (cf. Bonnet, Chapter 24, this volume).

The orientation and the shape of the burial pit

In normative Muslim practices, the importance of the position of the body influences the orientation and the morphology of the burial pit. The traditional orientation of the pit varies from region to region: for example, it is North-South in Spain and West Africa. In regions north and south of Mecca, East-West orientation may be problematic in distinguishing Muslim burials from those of other monotheistic religions (Canaan, 1927; Granqvist, 1965; Gorzalczany 2007; Halevi, 2007: 188–189; Kressel, Bar-Zvi and Abu-Rabi'a, 2014: 2). Within a Muslim cemetery, however, it is possible to observe small differences in the orientation of the pits. Gorzalczany (2007) suggested that minor variations in the orientation of graves are related to the annual variations in the direction of sunrise used to calculate the *Qibla*. Other scholars state that variations testify to different Muslim traditions, but, as seen above, these changes are not necessarily evidence of cultural variability or of different religious schools (King, 1995).

The shape of the pit can be an important indicator of Muslim graves (Casal, 2003; Gleize *et al.*, 2016). The body is placed in a narrow space (sometimes no more than 60 cm wide), which can be the bottom of a vertical pit (*Shaqq*) or a lateral niche (*Lahd*) (Figure 20.2). These two major types are thought to come from Mecca for the first and from Medina for the second. The *Lahd* type is supposed to have been used for the grave of Mohammed (Halevi 2007). In most cases, the niche was sealed with flagstones. Flat stone slabs and, less frequently, tiles generally seal the *shaqq*

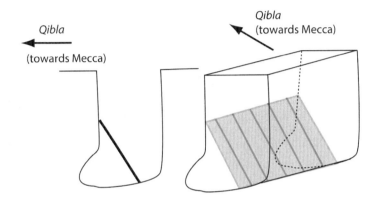

Reconstructed Section and View of *Lahd* Type

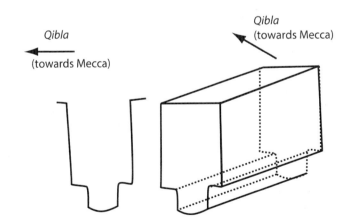

Reconstructed Section and View of *Shaqq* Type

Figure 20.2 *Lahd* (lateral) and *shaqq* (vertical) pits. The arrows indicate the direction of the Qibla (i.e. towards Mecca) (Drawing: Y. Gleize).

South-East   North-West

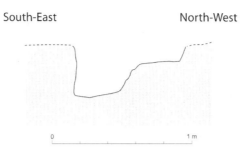

0   1 m

Figure 20.3   Section of a Muslim burial pit (Nîmes, France) (Drawing: Y. Gleize).

type (Castillo Armenteros, Navarro Pérez and Serrano Peña, 2011) or whole jars (Gorzalczany, 2009). The identification of unfilled space around the body – in the absence of stone slabs – also attests the existence of the use of planks for closure in some graves (Gleize *et al.*, 2016). Finally, when the soil is unstable, tradition advises that the side niche be constructed from stones or mud bricks (Ragib, 1992). Sometimes, the identification of the shape of the pit profile is difficult due to the levelling of the archaeological features (Faro Carballa *et al.*, 2007). The presence of a step or a side pit (Figure 20.3) (Gleize *et al.*, 2016), or staggered slabs covering the pit, or their inclination, may reflect the presence of a lateral niche (Gutiérrez Lloret, 2007; Gleize *et al.*, 2016) (Figure 20.4).

Grave-markers and surface features

Grave-markers are the most documented aspect of Muslim graves and here, again, great variation is observed. It is generally known that normative Islamic funerary rites did not indicate the construction of an ideal type of grave, nor any specific grave structures, embellishments, or even markers. But grave-markers could prevent the destruction of ancient burials by visibly highlighting their presence and also identify graves as Muslim (Ragib, 1970; Halevi, 2007).

Simple cist graves are common in Muslim cemeteries (Stern *et al.*, 1978). Muslim graves were often marked by simple arrangements of fieldstones (Figure 20.5) or rectangular box-like stone structures (Fauvelle, Hirsch and Chekroun, 2017), stepped superstructures (Rice, 1959) or platforms. The forms of the markers could be of very diverse construction, including those made of rubble (cairns), and square-shaped, round (Figure 20.6) or hexagonal (e.g. central Asian) enclosures. Graves could be decorated and covered with white plaster (Rice, 1959; Granqvist, 1965; Sion and Rapuano, 2017). In the same cemetery, the variety of types could sometimes be considerable (Horton, 1996; Fauvelle, Hirsch and Chekroun, 2017). Vertical markers are often erected at both ends (Insoll, 1999) (Figure 20.7). These stelae can be sometimes uninscribed (Leisten, 1990). Their Muslim nature is often identified by inscriptions in Arabic with basic biographical details, date of death, the text of the *Shahada*[5] or excerpts from the *Quran* (Figure 20.8). Some traditionists from the initial periods of Islam opposed inscriptions on graves based on the principle that Muslims must be equal in death (Halevi, 2007: 32–38). However, from the 1st century AH (7th century AD), some examples are known (Imbert, 1992) and from that time onwards, the numbers increase (Leisten, 1990; Halevi, 2007). Islamic archaeologists often study the process of Islamisation from isolated epigraphy on stelae, but this evidence must be analysed

---

5 The Islamic creed, one of the five pillars of Islam.

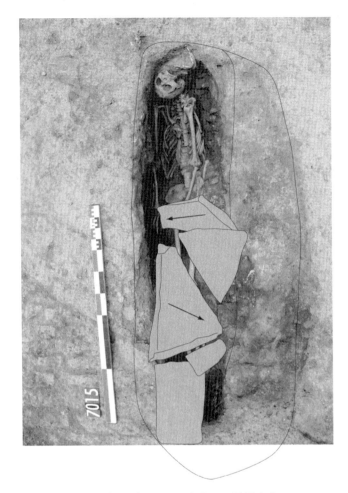

Figure 20.4 Slabs sealing a lateral niche (Nîmes, France) (Image:Y. Gleize).

Figure 20.5 Muslim grave markers (Wadi Rum, Jordan) (Photograph:Y. Gleize).

Figure 20.6 Muslim grave markers (Tigray, Ethiopia) (Photographs: Y. Gleize).

carefully because some stelae could have been moved over long distances for identity or for political reasons, such as demonstrated in stelae discovered in Goa (Mali) (Sauvaget, 1950); or for practical uses as stone ballast or for use as an anchor (Juvin and Massy, 2014). It is, therefore, difficult to discuss ambiguous cases, in particular stelae that had been re-used as building stones, as in France (Jomier, 1954, 1972, 1983; *contra* Bresc, 1984).

Some architectural elements could be added to the graves. In Alexandria, one extremity of the grave could be shaped like a *mihrab* niche and additional vertical poles placed at the other end in order to facilitate additional burials (Kulicka, 2008). Some Muslim tombs can be highly complex and monumental structures. The diversity of these monuments is also great

Figure 20.7 Muslim grave markers (Cyprus) (Photograph: Y. Gleize).

Figure 20.8 Inscription on Muslim tombstone (Cyprus) (Photograph: Y. Gleize).

(Grabar, 1966; Dickie, 1978; Leisten, 1999), as in traditional Muslim graves beneath *qubba* (domed mausolea) (Grabar, 1966; Gayraud, 1999; Petersen, 2018), mounds, towers, or pillars in East Africa (Sanseverino, 1983). The mausoleum of the Taj Mahal complex is one of the most spectacular cases (Koch, 2006). These tombs can be integrated into architectural complexes as in the Abbasid funerary complex at Fostat, with baths, gardens and resting places (Gayraud, 1999) and the Mamlūk Tomb-Chambers with a Koranic school and caravanserai in Jerusalem

(Ollendorff, 1982). These monumental tombs were erected in various Muslim cities (Insoll, 1999) and are clearly linked to the high social status of the individual despite traditional Islamic disapproval of ostentatious funerary investment (Halevi, 2007: 146–148).

Location of the graves

There is also great diversity in the location of Muslim graves. They can be isolated in the desert (Figure 20.9) or scattered in the countryside, as in Nîmes (Gleize *et al.*, 2016), but they are usually grouped in cemeteries (*maqbara*). Cemeteries could be placed on pre-existing ancient cemeteries and are thus located outside of cities, near city gates and main roads (Simpson, 1995; Casal, 2003), which were then later surrounded by new quarters (Figure 20.10). The epigraphic evidence confirms the once existence of an ancient Muslim cemetery within the city walls of Alexandria (Majcherek, 2007). Graves are not always placed near mosques. In a rural context, Muslim burial grounds could be placed near sources of water and associated with the shrine of a holy man or martyrs (Toombs, 1985; Simpson, 1995; Petersen, 2018).

The organisation of Muslim burial grounds has not been studied extensively. Some cases of areas reserved for the burials of children are known from Islamic cemeteries (Simpson, 1995). Burial grounds can be organised according to tribal or ethnic origins, as in Kufa or Timbuktu (Miner, 1953; Djaït, 1986; Halevi, 2007), but ethnoarchaeological research indicates that cemeteries are not always structured as family burial grounds, nor do they reflect social organisation. In these cases, the individuals buried close to one another are not necessarily of related persons (Lancaster and Lancaster, 1993).

Figure 20.9   Cairn re-used for a Muslim burial (Wadi Rum, Jordan) (Photograph: Y. Gleize).

Figure 20.10 Mamilla Cemetery (Jerusalem) (Photograph: Y. Gleize).

If Muslim cemeteries are intended for use only for the members of the *Umma* (Muslim community), historical and archaeological data provide evidence of some deviations. For example, in the Hajji Mansur cemetery (Ethiopia), a Christian grave is located in a Muslim burial ground (Fauvelle-Aymar *et al.,* 2006). In Senegal (Sall, 2017) and in South Africa (Apollonio, 1998), Christian-Muslim cemeteries can be found. The distinction between Muslim cemeteries and those of other religious groups could change based on the chronological, social and political contexts of them.

Funerary context between normative and syncretic practices

An overview of the archaeological evidence highlights the existence of common characteristics of many Muslim graves based on a number of requirements concerning the position of the body, the shape of the pit and the exterior appearance of the tomb (Halevi, 2013). Islamic burials cannot be 'categorised as something clinical' (Insoll, 1999: 199–200); the treatments of the dead differ as well, depending on the ideas and practices embodied within 'multiple forms of Islam' (Petersen, 2013: 241). Many authors have emphasised the relative diversity of funerary practices in the Muslim world and the difficulties of distinguishing between Muslims and non-Muslims (Simpson, 1995). It is, of course, important to date the ambiguous practices because individuals buried on the right side and facing towards the southeast are found in France in the Roman period, for example (Gleize, 2013), and Muslim burials may have been interred in much older cemeteries, as in Sicily at Rocca di Entella (Duday, 2009). In certain Muslim contexts, a great range of practices has been noted (e.g. Insoll, 1999; Petersen, 2013), including the presence of anomalies in a number of cases of Muslim graves (Canaan, 1927; Halevi, 2007: 189–190). Even if some texts and funeral manuals specify distinctive practices according to certain very special circumstances of death, such as martyrs or suicides (Petersen, 2013), the observed variability should be considered to go beyond and not be restricted to these particular cases. As discussed in this chapter, the evidence shows ambiguity between Muslim graves following Islamic funerary precepts and burials of Muslim people. It is clear that some Muslims were not buried following Islamic rules and the great variability in funerary practices ranges from normative practices to class-linked ones. It is necessary to contextualise the material remains in order to study Islamic cultures (Insoll, 1999). Changes in funerary practices could be due to political changes and the influence of a more or less pietistic elite and their respect for the pre-supposed normative practices of Islam. Historians and archaeologists must also be mindful of the ideological reconstructions of the Muslim world from the middle of the 8th century, which idealised early Islamic practices as opposed to the idea of a progressive Islamisation (Halevi, 2007). The same process exists for the writing of the Koranic verses (Deroche, 2019). Moreover, in *Dar-al-Islam* (the Islamic world), not everyone is Muslim. The *dhimmī* communities – originally People of the Book – are accepted and conversions are not obligatory. It is thus important to question the characterisation of funerary practices in areas of Islamisation or in contact situations between different cultural groups. From the beginning of the rise of Islam, it is necessary to consider a closer association of religious communities than customarily believed and, moreover, to deny that there are visible traces of these associations over the centuries. For example, pre-Islamic practices of grave marking continued and became incorporated into the Islamic burial rite (Halevi, 2013; Livne-Kafri, 2017). The issue of syncretism is an interesting but difficult one (Insoll, 2004; Clack, 2011). Such questions have already been raised when funerary practices seem to combine features of different rites with the arrival of Muslims (Manzano, 2006; Pauly, 2014). Distinction through archaeological data can be important in these cases. Spatial continuity phenomena – for example, the re-use of Visigothic funerary spaces for Muslim graves – may be evidence of legislation that had not yet been imposed or of a slow adaptation of the population to the norm or of appropriation of previous cemeteries (Manzano, 2006: 268–273). If Muslim burials can be distinguished from Christian or Jewish ones by the position of the body, it is more problematical with Pagan groups that have highly varied practices or used uncodified body positions. For example, in different cultures, the body could also be buried on the side, and niche burials were often used in Africa but also in Asia (Inskeep, 1986; Morris, 1992, Gleize *et al.*, 2015). From this perspective, it is necessary to re-analyse some archaeological evidence (Paris, Roset and Saliege, 1986).

The identification of Muslim funerary practices makes it possible to identify only the bodies buried according to normative practices. In Ruscino in southern France, where many lead seals inscribed in early Arabic Kufic script have been discovered, early medieval graves do not evince Muslim or Christian funerary customs (Rébé, Sénac and Raynaud, 2014). Were they Christians or Muslims? On the other hand, is it possible to consider a grave with a significant number of non-normative practices as Muslim? A recently published case of a so-called Islamicate[6] grave in the Republic of Kalmykia could share a number of different Muslim characteristics as in 'a niche burial slightly oriented to the south', 'the isolation of the face of the dead in the niche from the earth with wooden planks', 'feet pointing to *Qibla*', and 'an elevated head with the face turned to the right' (Shingiray, 2018). As noted above, these characteristics are ambiguous and the observation of published photographs attests to the possibility that the skull may have moved during the process of decomposition. Because this example was found at the margins of the Muslim world, this occurrence could attest to the presence of Islamic cultural influences. But, these funerary practices must not be interpreted necessarily as Muslim ones or even as indigenised Islamic. Research on Muslim funerary practices, especially in marginal regions, requires cross-analysis of archaeological, anthropological and biological information in their historical context (Gleize *et al.*, 2016). In the future, with these precautions in mind, it seems fundamental to analyse these marginal practices that could relate to changes in Muslim practices over time and in different geographic contexts.

---

6 Associated with regions in which Muslims are culturally dominant, but not specifically with the religion of Islam.

Conclusion

This incomplete overview highlights that the burial of a body in shroud, on the right side, facing Mecca in a simple grave and often in a side pit is the most common practice in the Muslim world, or at least represent the best evidence to identify a grave as Muslim, in the absence of inscriptions. It is important to mention that the identification of Muslim burials cannot be limited solely to the general position of the buried body, and the contribution of archaeothanatology is fundamental in order to record the position of the face and perishable funerary architecture.

The diversity of Muslim burials demonstrates that funerary practices in the Islamic world are not always homogeneous and the use of archaeothanatological methods is necessary to avoid misinterpretations. Changing practices, processes of Islamisation and the existence of many variable contexts thus require a precise analysis of the rites that appear to depart from normalised practices. It is necessary to contextualise this type of research to demonstrate whether or not such changes are social due to an elite social identity, chronological or cultural. Archaeological evidence demonstrates that Islam is not a monolithic culture, as also observed in other religions. Despite 'religious' difficulties and the lack of excavations, it is imperative to establish a funerary archaeology of Muslim practices or, more broadly, of the Muslim world using combined archaeological, biological and historical information. Muslim burials are an endangered archaeological heritage that could be at risk of being destroyed without detailed study, whereas there is great archaeological potential in several high-growth developing countries.

References

Abdulfattah, I.R. (2014). Relics of the Prophet and Practices of His Veneration in Medieval Cairo. *Journal of Islamic Archaeology*, 1(1), pp. 75–104.

Agius, D.A. (2005). Leave your homeland in search of prosperity. The ostrich egg in a burial site at Quseir al-Qadim in the Mamlūk period. In: U. Vermeulen and J. van Steenbergen, eds., *Egypt and Syria in the Fatimid, Ayyubid and Mamlūk Eras, IV*. Leuven: Uitgeverij Peeters, pp. 355–379.

Ambary, H.M. (1985). De l'Animisme à l'Islam: Le Témoignage de Quelques Monuments Funéraires de la Région de Bone. *Archipel*, 29(1), pp. 165–173.

Apollonio, H. (1998). *Identifying the dead: eighteenth-century mortuary practices at Cobern Street*, Cape Town. Cape Town: University of Cape Town.

Arbel, Y. (2017). Post-Medieval Muslim Burials in Jaffa: Archaeological Evidence and Historical Perspective. *Journal of Islamic Archaeology*, 4, pp. 87–112.

Austin, A.D. (1984). *African Muslims in Antebellum America: a sourcebook*. New York: Garland Publishing.

Ayalon, E. (2000). Typology and Chronology of Water Wheel (Saqiya) Pottery Pots from Israel. *Israel Exploration Journal*, 50, pp. 216–226.

Ben-Tor, A. and Portugali, Y. (1987). *Tell Qiri: a village in the Jezreel valley*. Jerusalem: Institute of Archaeology, the Hebrew University of Jerusalem.

Blaizot, F. (1996). Quatre études de cas. In: G. Hervé, F. Carré and L. Bonnabel, eds., *Rencontre autour du Linceul*, Bulletin de Liaison du GAAFIF (Groupe d'Anthropologie et Archéologie Funéraire en Île de France), Reims : GAAFIF, pp. 63–71.

Bowker, J.W. (1991). *The meanings of death*. Cambridge and New York: Cambridge University Press.

Bradbury, J. (2016). Presencing the past: a case Study of Islamic rural burial practices from the Homs Region of Syria. In: S. McPhillips and P. Wordsworth, eds., *Landscapes of the Islamic World: Archaeology History and Ethnography*. Philadelphia: University of Pennsylvania Press, pp. 210–218.

Bresc, H. (1984). Compte-rendu de Islam et Chrétiens du Midi (XIIe–XIVe s.). *Archives des Sciences Sociales des Religions*, 57(2), pp. 237–238.

Buturovic, A. (2016). *Carved in stone, etched in memory: death, tombstones and commemoration in Bosnian Islam*. London: Routledge.

Canaan, T. (1927). *Mohammedan saints and sanctuaries in Palestine*. Jerusalem: The Syrian Orphanage Press.

Casal, M.T. (2003). *Los cementerios musulmanes de Qurluba*. Arqueología Cordobesa 9. Córdoba: Universidad de Córdoba.

Castillo Armenteros, J.C., Navarro Pérez, M. and Serrano Peña, J.L. (2011). Las Maqbaras de marroquíes bajos (Jaén) en torno al 711. In: L.A. García Moreno and A. Vigil-Escalera, eds., *711, Arqueologia e Historia entre dos Mundos, volumen 1.*Alcalá de Henares: Comunidad de Madrid, pp. 275–292.

Chávet Lozoya, M., Sánchez Gallego, R. and Padial Pérez, J. (2006). Ensayo de Rituales de Enterramiento Islámicos en Al-Andalus. *Anales de Prehistoria y Arqueologia*, 22, pp. 149–161.

Clack, T.A.R. (2011). Syncretism and religious fusion. In: T. Insoll ed., *The Oxford Handbook of the Archaeology of Ritual and Religion*. Oxford: Oxford University, pp. 227–242.

Deroche, F. (2019). *Le Coran, une histoire plurielle. Essai sur la formation du texte coranique*. Paris: Seuil.

Dewar, R.E. and Wright H.T. (1993). The Culture History of Madagascar. *Journal of World Prehistory*, 7(4), pp. 417–466.

Dickie, J. (1978). Allah and eternity: mosques, madrasas, and tombs. In: G. Mitchell ed., *Architecture of the Islamic World*. London: Thames and Hudson, pp. 14–47.

Diem, W. and Schöller, M. (2004). *The living and the dead in Islam: studies in Arabic epitaphs*. Wiesbaden: Harrassowitz Verlag.

Djaït, H. (1986). *Al-Kufa. Naissance de la ville Islamique*. Paris: Maisonneuve et Larose.

Duday, H. (2009). *Archaeology of the dead: lectures in archaeothanatology*. Oxford: Oxbow.

el Aswad, E. (1987). Death Rituals in Rural Egyptian Society. *Urban Anthropology and Studies of Cultural Systems and World Economic Development*, 16(2), pp. 205–241.

Faro Carballa, J.A., Garcia Barberena Unzu, M., Unzu Urmeneta, M. and De Miguel Ibanez, M.P. (2007). El cementerio islámico de Plaza del Castillo (Pamplona). In: M.Á. Hurtado Alfaro, ed., *La Tierra te Sea Leve: Arqueología de la Muerte en Navarra*. Pamplona: Gobierno de Navarra, pp. 249–252.

Fauvelle, F.-X., Hirsch, B. and Chekroun, A. (2017). Le Sultanat de l'Awfât, sa Capitale et la Nécropole des Walasma'. *Annales Islamologiques*, 51, pp. 239–295.

Fauvelle-Aymar, F.-X., Hirsch, B., Bruxelles, L., Mesfin, C., Chekroun, A. and Ayenatchew, D. (2006). Reconnaissance de Trois Villes Musulmanes de l'Époque Médiévale dans l'Ifat. *Annales d'Ethiopie*, 22, pp. 133–175.

Feliciano, M.J. (2005). Muslim shrouds for Christian kings? In: C. Robinson and L. Rouhi eds., *Under the Influence: Questioning the Comparative in Medieval Castile*. Leiden: Brill Academic Publisher, pp 101–131.

Gayraud, R.-P. (1999). Le Qarafa al-Kubra, dernière demeure des Fatimides. In: M. Barrucand, ed., *L'Égypte Fatimide, Son Art et Son Histoire*. Paris: PUPS (Presses de l'Université Paris-Sorbonne), pp. 443–464.

Gayraud, R.-P., Björnesjö S., Gallo P., Mouton J.-M. and Paris F. (1995). Istabl ʿAntar (Fostat) 1994. *Annales Islamologiques*, 29, pp. 1–24.

Genequand, D. (2004). Nouvelles Recherches à Qasr al-Hayr al-Sharqi: La Mosquée Ayyoubide et la Nécropole. *Annales Archéologiques Arabes Syriennes*, 47–48, pp. 271–293.

Gibson, D. (2017). *Early Islamic Qiblas*. Vancouver: Independent Scholar's Press.

Gleize, Y. (2013). *Lyon. Clinique Lyon Champvert – 71 rue Benoist Mary*. Bron: Inrap (Institut National de Recherches Archéologiques Préventives) Rhône-Alpes Auvergne.

Gleize, Y., Bosc-Tiessé, C., Derat, M.-L., Rouzic, M., Sève, S., Ziegler, L., Goujon, A.-L., Mensan, R. and Bernard, R. (2015). Le Cimetière de Qedemt (Lalibela): Données Préliminaires Issues des Campagnes 2010 et 2012. *Annales d'Ethiopie*, 30, pp. 225–260.

Gleize, Y., Mendisco, F., Pemonge, M.-H., Hubert, C., Groppi, A., Houix, B., Deguilloux, M.-F. and Breuil, J.-Y. (2016). Early Medieval Muslim Graves in France: First Archaeological, Anthropological and Palaeogenomic Evidence. *PlosOne*: e0148583.

Gorzalczany, A. (2007). The Kefar Saba Cemetery and Differences in Orientation of Late Islamic Burials from Israel/Palestine. *Levant*, 39, pp. 71–79.

Gorzalczany, A. (2009). A New Type of Cemetery from the Late Mamluk and Early Ottoman Periods from Central Israel, *Levant*, 41, pp. 223–237.

Grabar, O. (1966). The Earliest Islamic Commemorative Structures. *Ars Orientalis*, 6, pp. 7–46.

Granqvist, H. (1965). *Muslim death and burial. Arab customs and traditions studied in a village in Jordan*. Helsinki-Helsingfors: Societas Scientiarum Fennica.

Grassi, V. (2002). A survey of the Arabic monumental and funerary inscriptions still present in Italy. In: S. Leder, H. Kilpatrick, B. Martel-Thoumian and H. Schönig, eds., *Studies in Arabic and Islam.*. Leuven: Uitgeverij Peeters, pp. 59–70.

Grassi, V. (2004). Le Stele Funerarie Islamiche di Sicilia: Provenienze e Problemi Aperti. *Mélanges de l'École Française de Rome*, 116(1), pp. 351–365.

Gutiérrez Lloret, S. (2007). La Islamización de Tudmir: balance y perspectivas. In: P. Sénac, ed., *Villes et campagnes de Tarraconaise et d'al-Andalus (VIe–XIe siècle)*. Toulouse: CNRS (Centre National de la Recherche Scientifique) - Université de Toulouse-Le Mirail, pp. 275–318.

Guz-Zilberstein, B. and Raveh, K. (1988–1989). Dor: Site K-60. *Hadashot Arkheologiyot*, 7–8, pp. 50–51.

Halevi, L. (2004). The Paradox of Islamization: Tombstone Inscriptions, Qur'anic Recitations, and the Problem of Religious Change. *History of Religions*, 44 (2), pp. 120–152.

Halevi, L. (2007). *Muhammad's grave: death rites and the making of Islamic society*. New York: Columbia University Press.

Halevi, L. (2013). Funerary practices. In: K. Fleet, G. Krämer, D. Matringe, J. Nawas and E. Rowson, eds., *Encyclopaedia of Islam*, 3rd ed. Leiden: Brill, pp. 116–126.

Horton, M. (1996). *Shanga: the archaeology of a Muslim trading community on the coast of East Africa*. London: British Institute in Eastern Africa.

Imbert, F. (1992). La Nécropole Islamique de Qastal al-Balqâ' en Jordanie. *Archéologie Islamique*, 3, pp. 17–59.

Inskeep, R. (1986). A preliminary survey of burial practices in the Later Stone Age, from the Orange River to the Cape coast. In: R. Singer and J.K. Lundy, eds., *Variation, Culture and Evolution in African Populations*. Johannesburg: Witwatersrand University Press, pp. 221–239.

Insoll, T. (1996). The Archaeology of Islam in Sub-Saharan Africa: A Review. *Journal of World Prehistory*, 10, pp. 439–504.

Insoll, T. (1999). *The archaeology of Islam*. Oxford: Blackwell.

Insoll, T. (2004). Syncretism, time, and identity: Islamic archaeology in West Africa. In: D. Whitcomb, ed., *Changing Social Identity with the Spread of Islam. Archaeological Perspectives*. Chicago: Oriental Institute, pp. 89–101.

Jomier, J. (1954). Deux Fragments de Stèles Prismatiques Conservés à Montpellier. *Arabica*, 1(2), pp. 212–213.

Jomier, J. (1972). Deux Nouveaux Fragments de Stèles Prismatiques Conservés à Montpellier. *Arabica*, 19(3), pp. 316 317.

Jomier, J. (1983). Note sur les stèles funéraires arabes de Montpellier. In: *Islam et Chrétiens du Midi.*, Toulouse: E. Privat, pp.62–63.

Juvin, C. and Massy J.-L. (2014). Une Stèle Prismatique du vᵉ/xiᵉ s. découverte en Corse. *Arabica*, 61, pp. 163–169.

Jettmar, K. (1967). The Middle Asiatic Heritage of Dardistan. (Islamic Collective Tombs in Punyal and Their Background). *East and West*, 17 (1/2), pp. 59–82.

King, D.A. (1979). Kibla (sacred direction). In: C.E. Bosworth, E. van Donzel, B. Lewis and C. Pellat, eds., *Encyclopaedia of Islam*, 2nd ed. Leiden: Brill, pp. 83–88.

King, D.A. (1985). The Sacred Direction in Islam. A Study of the Interaction of Religion and Science in the Middle Ages. *Interdisciplinary Science Reviews*, 10 (4), pp. 315–328.

King, D.A. (1995). The Orientation of Medieval Islamic Religious Architecture and Cities. *Journal for the History of Astronomy*, 26(3), pp. 253–274.

King, G. (2009). Camels and Arabian Balîya and Other Forms of Sacrifice: A Review of Archaeological and Literary Evidence. *Arabian Archaeology and Epigraphy*, 20(1), pp. 81–93.

King, D.A. (2018–2019). Review: Dan Gibson, Early Islamic Qiblas: A Survey of Mosques Built between 1AH/622 C.E. and 263 AH/876 C.E. *Suhayl*, 18, pp. 347–366.

Koch, E. (2006). *The complete Taj Mahal and the riverfront gardens of Agra*. London: Thames & Hudson.

Kressel, G.M., Bar-Zvi, S. and Abu-Rabi'a, A. (2014). *Charm of graves: perceptions of death and after-death among the Negev Bedouin*. Brighton: Sussex Academic Press.

Kulicka, A. (2008). Remarks on the Typology of Islamic graves from the Cemeteries on Kom el-Dikka in Alexandria. *Polish Archaeology in the Mediterranean*, 20, pp. 483–498.

Lacam, J. (1965). *Les Sarrasins dans le haut Moyen Age français*. Paris: G.-P. Maisonneuve et Larose.

Lambourn, E. (2008). Tombstones, Texts and Typologies – Seeing Sources for the Early History of Islam in Southeast Asia. *Journal of the Economic and Social History of the Orient*, 51(2), pp. 252–286.

Lancaster, W. and Lancaster, F. (1993). Graves and Funerary Monuments of Ahl al-Jabal, Jordan. *Arabian Archaeology and Epigraphy*, 4, pp. 151–169.

Lavoie, J.-J. (2011). La Légitimation religieuse du rite d'inhumation dans le Coran et la littérature du Proche-Orient ancien. Analyse historico-comparative. In: K. Fall and M. Dimé eds., *La Mort Musulmane en Contexte d'Immigration et d'Islam Minoritaire*. Laval: Presses Université Laval, pp. 91–114.

Leisten, T. (1990). Between Orthodoxy and Exegesis: Some Aspects of Attitudes in the Shari Æa Toward Funerary Architecture. *Muqarnas*, 7, pp. 12–22.

Leisten, T. (1999). Dynastic tomb or private mausolea: observations on the concept of funerary structures of the Fâtimid and Abbasid Caliphs. In: M. Barrucando, ed., *L'Egypte Fatimide: son art et son histoire*. Paris: PUPS (Presses de l'Université Paris-Sorbonne), pp. 465–479.

Livne-Kafri, O. (2017). Burial in the Holy Land and Jerusalem According to Muslim Tradition. *Liber Annuus*, 53, pp. 417–425.

Loiseau, J., Dorso, S., Gleize, Y., Ollivier, D., Ayenachew, D., Berhe, H., Chekroun, A. and Hirsch, B. (2021). Bilet and the wider world. New insights into the archaeology of Islam in Tigray. *Antiquity*, 95(380): 508–529.

Lombard, M. (1978). *Les textiles dans le monde musulman du VIIe au XIIe siècle*. Paris: Mouton.

Majcherek, G. (2007). Kom El-Dikka Excavation and Preservation Work. Preliminary Report, 2004/2005. *Polish Archaeology in the Mediterranean*, 17, pp. 21–34.

Majcherek, G. and Kolataj, W. (2003). Alexandria Excavations and Preservation Work 2001/2002. *Polish Archaeology in the Mediterranean*, 14, pp. 19–31.

Manzano, E. (2006). *Conquistadores, emires y califas. los Omeyas y la formación de al-Andalus*. Barcelona: Crítica.

Maynard, D. and Museyibli, N. (2011). Azerbaijan. In: N. Márquez-Grant and L. Fibiger, eds., *The Routledge Handbook of Archaeological Human Remains and Legislation*. London and New York: Routledge, pp. 35–40.

M'Bow, A.M. and Kettani A. (2001). *Islam and Muslims in the American continent*. Beirut: Center of Historical, Economical and Social Studies.

Miner, H. (1953). *The primitive city of Timbuktu*. Princeton: Princeton University Press.

Morris, A.G. (1992). *The skeletons of contact: a study of protohistoric burials from the Lower Orange River Valley, South Africa*. Johannesburg: Witwatersrand University Press.

Murillo Fragero, J.I. (2009). Registro estratigráfico de una necrópolis musulmana en la calle Toledo, 68 (Madrid). In: N. Benet, ed., *Actas de las Terceras Jornadas de Patrimonio Arqueológico en la Comunidad de Madrid*. Madrid: Comunidad de Madrid, pp. 89–98.

Mustafa, M.H. and Tayeh, S.N.A. (2014). Comments on Bedouin Funeral Rites in the Writings of Western Travelers and Explorers from the Late 19th and Early 20th Centuries. *Mediterranean Archaeology and Archaeometry*, 14(1), pp. 51–63.

Paris, F., Roset, J.-P. and Saliege J.F. (1986). Une Sépulture Musulmane Ancienne dans l'Aïr Septentrional (Niger). *Comptes Rendus de l'Académie des Sciences: Sciences de la Vie*, 303(12), pp. 513–518.

Pauly, M. (2014). La Diffusion de l'Islam à Mayotte à l'Époque Médiévale, *Taarifa*, 4, pp. 69–113.

Petersen, A. (2013). The archaeology of death and burial in the Islamic world. In: L. Nilsson Stutz and S. Tarlow, eds., *The Oxford Handbook of the Archaeology of Death and Burial*. Oxford: Oxford University Press, pp. 241–258.

Petersen, A. (2018). *Bones of contention: Muslim shrines in Palestine*. Singapore: Palgrave Macmillan.

Pierotti, E. (1864). *Customs and traditions of Palestine*. Cambridge: Deighton, Bell and Co.

Pradines, S., Laville, D., Matkowski, M., Monchamp, J., OHora, N., Sulayman, M. and Zurrud, T. (2009). Excavations of the Archaeological Triangle: 10 years of Archaeological Excavations in Fatimid Cairo (2000 to 2009). *Mishkah*, 4, pp. 177–219.

Ollendorff, F. (1982). Two Mamlūk Tomb-Chambers in Western Jerusalem. *Israel Exploration Journal*, 32(4), pp. 245–250.

Ragib, Y. (1970). Les Premiers Monuments Funéraires de l'Islam. *Annales Islamologiques*, 9, pp. 21–36.

Ragib, Y. (1992). Structure de la tombe d'après le droit musulman. *Arabica*; 39, pp. 393–403.

Rébé, I., Sénac, P. and Raynaud, C. (2014). *Le premier Moyen Âge à Ruscino entre Septimanie et Al-Andalus (VIIe–IXe s.)*. Lattes: Publications UMR 5140.

Rice, D.S. (1959). The Oldest Illustrated Arabic Manuscript. *Bulletin of the School of Oriental and African Studies*, 22, pp. 207–220.

Rosmawati (2018). Typology and efflorescence of early Islamic tomb and gravestone forms in South Sulawesi and Majene, West Sulawesi. In: S. O'Connor, D. Bulbeck and J. Meyer, eds., *The Archaeology of Sulawesi: Current Research on the Pleistocene to the Historic Period*. Canberra: ANU (Australian National University) Press, pp. 327–344.

Sall, M. (2017). Recherches académiques en Afrique de l'Ouest: le cas du Sénégal. In: A. Livingstone Smith, E. Cornelissen, O.P. Gosselain and S. MacEachern, eds., *Manuel de Terrain en Archéologie Africaine*. Tervuren: Musée Royal de l'Afrique Centrale, pp. 18–23.

Sanseverino, H.C. (1983). Archaeological Remains on the Southern Somali Coast. *Azania*, 18(1), pp. 151–164.

Sauvaget, J. (1950). Les Épitaphes Royales de Gao. *Bulletin de l'Institut Fondamental d'Afrique Noire (IFAN), Series B*, 12, pp. 418–440.

Schneider, M. (1983). *Stèles funéraires Musulmanes des Îles Dahlak (Mer Rouge)*. Le Caire: Institut Français d'Archéologie Orientale du Caire.

Shingiray, I. (2018). An Islamicate Body: A Case Study of a Nomadic Burial from the Core Territory of the Golden Horde. *Revue des Mondes Musulmans et de la Méditerranée (REMMM)*, 143, pp. 83–106.

Simpson, S.J. (1995). Death and burial in the late Near East. In: S. Campbell and A. Green, eds., *The Archaeology of Death in the Ancient Near East*. Oxford: Oxbow, pp. 240–251.

Sion, O. and Rapuano, Y. (2017). Yafo, Razi'el and Ratosh Streets. *Hadashot Arkheologiyot*, p. 129.

Smith, J.I. and Haddad Y. (1981). *The Islamic understanding of death and resurrection.* Albany: State University of New York Press.

Sokoly, J. (1997). Between Life and Death: the Funerary Context of Tiraz Textiles. *Riggisberger Berichte*, 5, pp. 71–78.

Stern, E., Barag, D., Arensburg, B., Rosenthal, R., Meshorer, Y., Johnson, B.L., Yellin, J. and Perlman I. (1978). *Excavations at Tel Mevorakh (1973–1976). Part I.* Jerusalem: Institute of Archaeology, the Hebrew University of Jerusalem.

Svanberg, I. and Westerlund, D. (1999). *Islam outside the Arab world.* Richmond: Curzon Press.

Titaÿna, (1930). *La caravane des morts.* Paris: Éditions des Portiques.

Toombs, L. (1985). *Tell el-Hesi: modern military trenching and Muslim cemetery in field I (strata I-II).* Waterloo, Ontario: Wilfrid Laurier University Press.

Tritton, A.S. (1938). Muslim Funeral Customs. *Bulletin of the School of Oriental and African Studies*, 9(3), pp. 653–661.

Verin, P. (1986). *The history of civilization in North Madagascar.* Rotterdam and Boston: A.A. Balkema.

Walker, B.J. (2001). The Late Ottoman Cemetery in Field L, Tall Hisban. *Bulletin of the American Schools of Oriental Research*, 322, pp. 47–65.

Wärmländer, S. K.T.S., Wåhlander, L., Saage, R., Rezakhani, K., Hamid Hassan, S.A. and Neiß, M. (2015). Analysis and Interpretation of a Unique Arabic Finger Ring from the Viking Age Town of Birka. *Scanning*, 37(2), pp. 131–137.

Welch, A.T. (1978). Death and dying in the Qurān. In: F.E. Reynolds and E.H. Waugh, eds., *Religious Encounters with Death.* College Park: Pennsylvania State University Press, pp. 183–199.

Zych, I. (2003). Wooden Coffins from the Moslem Cemetery at Kom el-Dikka. *Polish Archaeology in the Mediterranean*, 14, pp. 32–37.

21

RECOGNISING A SLAVE CEMETERY

An example from colonial-period Guadeloupe, Lesser Antilles

Patrice Courtaud

PACEA, De la Préhistoire à l'Actuel: Culture, Environnement et Anthropologie, UMR 5199, CNRS-Université de Bordeaux, Pessac, France

Thomas Romon

PACEA, De la Préhistoire à l'Actuel: Culture, Environnement et Anthropologie, UMR 5199, CNRS-Université de Bordeaux, Pessac, France

Institut National de Recherches Archéologiques Préventives (Inrap), Guadeloupe, France

Introduction

Since the beginning of the 2000s, the number of colonial funerary sites excavated in the French Overseas Territories has been on the order of 15. Their size varies from a few to several hundred burials, mainly from Guadeloupe (Figure 21.1), the island on which this contribution will focus. Due to the varied origins of French colonial society in the Lesser Antilles, each group theoretically has its own unique attributes, including after death, with its separate cemetery, its own characteristic funerary practices and biological composition (Romon *et al.*, 2009).

Conversely, in Martinique, another French island territory in the Lesser Antilles, archaeological research has been less intensive and human remains less well preserved or completely decomposed. This situation is also the same in French Guiana, for example, after the excavation of the Loyola Jesuit convent (Croteau and Auger, 1998; Le Roux, Auger and Cazelles, 2009), where a complete disappearance of the human skeletons was observed. The funerary archaeology of the colonial period of the other islands of the Lesser Antilles is quite varied. While burial sites were excavated earlier in some cases, as in Barabados and Montserrat (Handler and Lange, 1978; Watters, 1987; Orser, 1998; Haviser, 1999; Vergès, 2008; Courtaud, 2010), excavation was never undertaken in others. This contribution focusses on the cemetery of Anse Sainte Marguerite (Guadeloupe) (Figure 21.1), not only because of the large number of burials excavated there, but also because it was the first site for which the question of the archaeological recognition of a slave cemetery was raised.

DOI: 10.4324/9781351030625-24

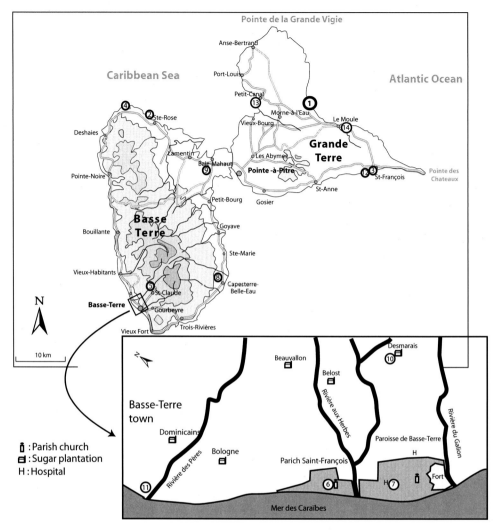

Figure 21.1 Map of Guadeloupe with locations of the places mentioned in the text. 1. Slave cemetery of Anse Sainte-Marguerite (Le Moule); 2. Cemetery of the colonial period of the Anse Nogent (Sainte-Rose); 3. Cemetery of the colonial period of Pointe des Pies (Saint François); 4. Probable slave cemetery of Cluny Beach in Sainte-Rose; 5. Probable slave cemetery from Morne Dauphine (Saint-Claude); 6. Saint-François parish cemetery (Basse-Terre); 7. Cemetery of the hospital of La Charité (Basse-Terre); 8. Probable slave cemetery from Doyon (Capesterre-Belle-Eau); 9. Probable slave cemetery from Jabrun (Baie-Mahault); 10. Cemetery of the Desmarais plantation; 11. Second cemetery of the military hospital of Basse-Terre at the Pointe des Pères (Baillif); 12. Slave cemetery of the Plage des Raisins Clairs (Saint-François); 13. Anse-des-Corps (Petit-Canal); 14. Autre Bord (Le Moule) (Image: T. Romon).

Populations and burial sites in the French West Indies during the colonial period

In the West Indies, the colonial period began with the discovery of the New World by Christopher Columbus in 1492. However, the colonisation of Guadeloupe was not effected until 1635, when French settlers took possession of the island. Before its discovery and colonisation, Guadeloupe was occupied by Amerindians, called 'Caribs' by the Europeans who frequented the region consisting of, first, Spanish and then French, British and Dutch, to collect wood, water and to trade with the indigenes of the region.

From 1635 onwards, French colonisation and the incessant conflicts with the British and Dutch brought about many upheavals, including the elimination of the Amerindian population mainly during the 17th century. After the annihilation of the indigenous population, the massive influx of people deported from West Africa occurred leading to the establishment of a hierarchical, segregated, and racialist society, dominated by a few white individuals with a religious framework for cultural practices, including the imposition of burial according to Roman Catholic funerary traditions in cemeteries. These constituted a colonial society comprised of mainly European, Caribbean (Creole[1]) and African peoples and social groups, with very distinct characteristics, each buried in their own cemeteries:

- Planters: were mainly of European descent. They marked their social position by erecting often monumental tombs in their family cemeteries. These cemeteries were called masters' cemeteries (*cimetière de maîtres*) located on the property of the plantation. Planters could also be buried in the parish church cemetery, as well as in privileged areas of the parish cemetery (Bégot, 1998).
- Craftsmen and merchants: Europeans or freed slaves who lived mainly in the city were most often interred in the parish cemetery (Pérotin-Dumon, 2000; Verrand, 2001). Throughout the Old Regime (before the French Revolution of 1789), this cemetery was closest to the church. After the French Revolution and the institution of new hygienic measures, these cemeteries became communal and moved in many instances outside the city.
- Cloistered ecclesiastics: of European origin and often assimilated into the society of the planters. They were buried in their own cemeteries on their plantations or in their monastic cemeteries. They could also have sought burial in the parish church.
- Foreigners and seafarers: if they died in Guadeloupe, they were buried in the cemetery of the hospital that very often received them before their death (Verrand, 1999; Paya and Romon, 2001). Until the 19th century, these cemeteries were located in the hospital grounds, then, as in the case of the communal cemeteries, moved outside the walls and ceased to be used at the end of the 19th century. The dead from the hospital were then interred in the district cemetery.
- The military: they were largely metropolitan. Members of the military were placed in the cemetery of the military hospital (Verrand, 1999; Kacki and Romon, 2013, 2015). The remains of officers were often repatriated to Europe. Otherwise, they may have been buried in the cemetery of the military fort or parish cemetery.
- Slaves: the most numerous and of African origin, they could be of Creole or native African origin. According to the 'Code Noir', they could be baptised, and this was often the case, and they were buried in the 'Negro Cemetery', which could have been specific to a single plantation or used in common by the inhabitants of several plantations. In the city, the slave cemetery was either completely isolated or adjacent to the parish cemetery, being separated from it by a wall. In all cases, the slave cemetery was always separate from the other burial sites. It was often located in marginal areas unsuitable for agriculture or economic development.

---

1 The term 'Creole' refers to any person born in the West Indies, regardless of their origin and status.

History of archaeological research on colonial cemeteries

This chapter focusses, in particular, on Guadeloupe, where the archaeological potential of colonial burial sites was not well known until recently. The first publication on this subject is that of Barbotin (1978): 'about human bones discovered at Anse Nogent in Sainte-Rose'. These bones are interpreted as coming from the cemetery of the first French settlers who settled at Pointe Allègre in 1635. However, information about these remains is very incomplete and the location of this discovery is no longer extant. Between 1982 and 1983, Bodu mentioned several rescue operations to recover colonial graves at Anse-des-corps (Petit-Canal), Anse Sainte-Marguerite (Le Moule), and Plage des Raisins-Clairs (Saint-François) (Figure 21.1) (Bodu, 1984). Ten years later, colonial graves were excavated on the Pointe-des-Pies site (Saint-François), being the first true archaeological funerary excavation in Guadeloupe (Richard, 1994). However, the real objective of this excavation concerned the Early Pre-Colombian levels but not the burials of the colonial period. In 1994, an archaeological evaluation was carried out on the Pre-Columbian site of Anse Sainte-Marguerite (Brokke and Knippenberg, 1994), where the presence of burials from the colonial period was recognised.

In 1995, hurricanes Luis and Marilyn marked a turning point in the history of the archaeology of colonial period cemeteries in Guadeloupe. Human bones were exposed by high tides on the Plage du Vieux Fort in Clugny (Sainte-Rose), as well as on the Pre-Columbian site of Morel au Moule. A landslide revealed more graves on the Morne Dauphine in Matouba (Saint-Claude). The status of these funerary sites was previously unknown from historical sources. Therefore a colonial-period funerary research project was initiated in 1997 on Anse Sainte-Marguerite which was suspected to have been the burial place of slaves (Courtaud, Delpuech and Romon, 1999; Courtaud and Romon, 2004).

The cemeteries of Basse-Terre

In the early 2000s, excavations in Basse-Terre revealed cemeteries which accorded perfectly with those known from archival documentation: the parish cemetery of the Saint-François district and the cemetery associated with the Hôpital de la Charité (Figure 21.1), both of which provided new insights into parish cemeteries and hospitals in Guadeloupe at the end of the Old Regime. These results provided a basis for comparison when studying funerary sites not documented by historical sources.

The parish cemetery in the Saint-François district

Until the beginning of the 19th century, the parish cemetery, which became 'communal' in 1795, was located near the parish church. Metropolitan hygienic laws were then applied in the French colonies, with in particular the *extra muros* (outside the walls) displacement of cemeteries. However, these rules were not applied in the same way in all the municipalities of Guadeloupe. Today, some municipalities such as Anse Bertrand or Vieux-Habitant still have their cemeteries in their original locations alongside the church. Others, such as Les Abymes or Pointe-à-Pitre, were located on the peripheries of cities, where they have been overtaken by urban expansion. Finally, some, such as Port-Louis or Sainte-Anne, still have their cemeteries in peripheral areas.

The current city of Basse-Terre is the result of the merger of two parishes, Basse-Terre and Saint-François, during the French Revolution in 1789. Until the second third of the 18th century, each of these two parishes had its own cemetery, adjacent to the church. In the first half of the 18th century, the cemetery of the parish of Basse-Terre was moved *extra muros* and then, with the fusion of the two parishes, abandoned in favour of that of Saint-François, which remained in its original location. The parish church of Saint-François was re-dedicated as a cathedral in 1850, and its cemetery was moved *extra muros* in the first quarter of the 19th century (Figure 21.1).

Salvage archaeological excavations carried out around the Cathedral of Basse-Terre (Bonnissent and Romon, 2004; Romon *et al.*, 2009) made it possible to study the cemetery of the Parish of Saint-François, which was the location of the religious order of the Capuchins and its cemetery, in use from the last quarter of the 17th century to the beginning of the 19th century. The study of parish registers (Verrand, 2001) indicates that it was intended for the burials of members of the white population of the district, but freedmen and those of colour were registered as being buried in the parish cemetery as well. The registry states that burials were also made inside the church. The cemetery reserved for slaves was separated from the parish cemetery by a wall.

The salvage excavation, which consisted of a 3 m × 4 m excavation in an area close to the cathedral, provided access to this cemetery population (Figure 21.2). A total of 45 graves in three levels were excavated, including those of seven men, 12 women, three children and three adolescents. Two burial phases were identified. The first phase did not contain any immature individuals but consisted of adults of both sexes. They were buried supinely, head oriented to the southwest. A trapezoidal coffin was used for half of the burials, while the other half was deposited directly in the ground ('full-earth' burials). Unlike the first phase, the most recent phase contained immature individuals. During this phase, the use of the hexagonal-shaped coffins became more systematic. The orientation of the deceased with the head to the southwest, however, was no longer systematic, some having the head in a northeast orientation. Re-use and intercutting of graves appeared to be common in both phases. An ossuary belongs to this second phase.

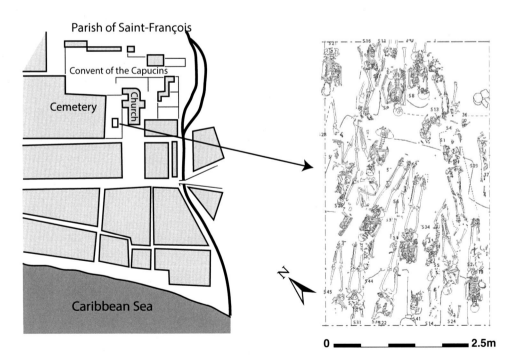

Figure 21.2 Left: The location of the parish church of Saint-François district of Basse-Terre and its cemetery from the map of Basse-Terre Town (1787-Saint-Méry Collection, ANOM F3 288-62); Right: Plan of the excavated area (Image: D. Bonnissent and T. Romon).

The study of health status shows many signs of bone degeneration (mainly cervical and lumbar degenerative disease), which seems to be related to age-at-death. Tooth-wear from the use of the clay tobacco pipes was frequent. An adult has a well-healed fracture of the right humerus. Another has mediolateral bowing of the tibiae and fibulae that may represent features of rickets (cf. Brickley and Ives, 2008). This childhood disease, linked to a vitamin D deficiency, is relatively rare in Guadeloupe, so it is possible that this individual was a first-generation migrant from Europe.

The graves were organised in successive rows with deliberate groupings. The shift in the orientation of the deceased with respect to cardinal directions is interpreted as a technical constraint related to the orientation of the church, which follows the urban plan parallel to the shoreline, itself oriented south-east to north-west. The associated grave goods consisted mainly of metal pins and bone buttons, indicators of dressed burials. No religious items, such as rosaries or medals were found.

The 18th-century parish cemetery adjoined the church and was characterised by individual graves in coffins or placed directly in the ground, with the heads for the most part to the west. It was reserved for people of European descent and freedmen in an apparently healthy condition. According to the registers, children were buried in a particular reserved area. The cemetery was neatly maintained. Apart from the remains of clothing, there were no associated grave goods.

The cemetery of the hospital of La Charité

The cemetery is located near the hospital and was managed by the religious authorities (Figure 21.1). It is located south of the chapel of the 'Frères de la Charité' ('Brothers of Charity'). The study of historical sources indicates that, in addition to the most disadvantaged and, in particular, the most religiously committed Europeans, it received sailors and foreigners. Until the construction of the Basse-Terre military hospital in 1766, it welcomed soldiers as well. Its cemetery accepted the burial of the dead between 1664 and 1788 (Verrand, 1999).

A portion of this cemetery was excavated over an area of 59 m² (Figure 21.3) as part of a salvage excavation (Paya and Romon, 2001). It comprised the skeletal remains of 109 individuals in primary deposits, including 48 men, 3 women, 5 adolescents, and 3 children, showing a clear predominance of adult males. The plan of the graves shows a completely different organisation to that of the cemetery of the Cathedral of Basse-Terre. Three burial phases were identified, each characterised by a change in the orientation of the graves along an east-west or north-south axis. When the cemetery had become saturated with burials, the surface was cleared and levelled and disturbed bones collected together and deposited in pits before a new burial phase began in an orientation perpendicular to the previous one.

The most frequent type of grave encountered were pits covered with nailed wooden planks. This type of construction permitted re-use of the grave and possibly to control decomposition of the bodies. Multiple individuals, placed supinely, could be placed in these graves, one after the other. Graves that were immediately filled with soil ('full earth' burials) are rare. When they do occur, they contain individuals placed ventrally or on one side and are interpreted as irregular burials, perhaps indicating a desire not to handle the body. Graves in a coffin are also rare; only two have been identified by the presence of nails. These employ trapezoid-shaped coffins. Finally, six rectangular pits contain bones deposited secondarily. They are interpreted as ossuaries intended to receive the elements disturbed over the course of cemetery use.

As with the parish cemetery, the main type of burial is the individual grave, with the majority of individuals being placed supinely. However, two types of burials not found in the parish cemetery have been identified. These are, on the one hand, double burials, including a simultaneous

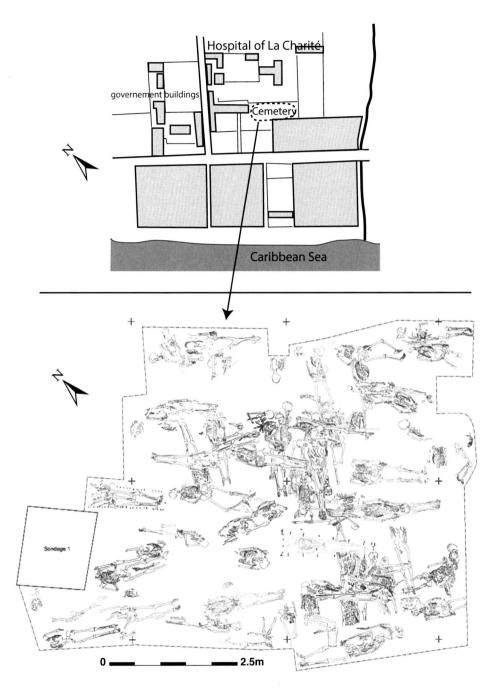

Figure 21.3 Top: location of the hospital of La Charité and its cemetery from the map of the town of Basse-Terre (1787-Saint-Méry Collection, ANOM F3 288-62); Bottom: Plan of the excavated burials (Image: D. Paya and T. Romon).

deposit of two deceased individuals in the same grave (Duday, 2009), which most probably reflects a desire to save the effort required to dig two pits for two deceased individuals close in time. On the other hand, several burials contain individuals placed on their sides or ventrally. This position may reflect the rapid burial of individuals who died due to contagious disease (Duday, 2019). Finally, most primary burials had been disturbed by the digging of subsequent graves. The displaced skeletal elements were placed either in a newly prepared grave as gathered, disarticulated remains (*réductions*) or collected and placed in ossuary pits. Within the latter, there was a tendency to collect and include crania specifically.

The excavated area contained mainly young adult males. Skeletal and dental health was apparently satisfactory. Most of the individuals died from diseases that did not leave any trace on the skeleton. Four individuals have consolidated fractures of the leg segment of the lower limb, and one has vertebral lesions similar to those found in a diffuse skeletal form of tuberculosis (cf. Baker, 1999). No grave goods were directly associated with burials, and there were no religious objects and no material indications of clothing.

The Anse Sainte-Marguerite cemetery

The funerary site is situated on the northeast coast of Grande-Terre (Figure 21.1), to the north of Le Moule, near the village of Gros Cap. It was established on a beach, where it occupies the slope of a coastal dune (Figure 21.4). The geographical location of this cemetery, far from any place of worship, in a rural area largely devoted to sugar cane crops, designated it *a priori* as a funerary site of a slave population (Courtaud, 2002, 2010).

Figure 21.4 View from the plateau of the beach at Anse Sainte-Marguerite (Anse Sainte-Marguerite), where the cemetery was established on the coastal slope of the dune (Photograph: P. Courtaud).

Aims and objectives of the excavation

Burials provide both sociocultural information relating to early populations, namely concerning their relationship with death and the dead, as well as biological data of past people. Therefore, the two main aims of this study focussed on understanding funerary practices and biological data in order to provide and compare it with supplementary information from the written sources.

Funerary practices

The 'Code Noir' was a decree originally created in 1685 under the reign of Louis XIV (Sala-Molins, 2006). It defined the conditions of slavery in the French colonial empire. Seven articles of the Code Noir state that Catholicism was the only religion for all slaves, who must have been baptised as soon as possible after arrival in the colonies (Articles 1 to 7). As for burials, owners were required by Article 14 to bury their baptised slaves in holy ground, in cemeteries designated for this purpose. As for unbaptised others, a simple burial in a field was sufficient. Unbaptised slaves, of whom there were many in the Old Regime (before the French Revolution of 1789), were thus deprived of cemetery burials. Secondly, baptised slaves who were to be deposited in the holy ground were not to be buried in the same places as free men.

Archaeological observations were carried out for individual graves and for the cemetery as a whole in order to address questions relating to the organisation and use of the burial area, including:

- In the case of baptised slaves, were Christian burial practices respected and which funerary treatments provide answers to this question?
- Conversely, is it possible to identify unbaptised individuals?
- Do certain elements indicate the persistence of African practices? These latter involve symbolism and complex situations that are beyond the scope of this chapter, given the great extent of the continent and the multitude of different populations that came to inhabit it. *A priori*, specific practices were not expected but rather practices different from Christian ones, such as, for example, the association of decorative elements or objects of African origin. In order to discern the organisation and use of burial areas, it is imperative to investigate by use of area excavations in order to uncover a sufficient number of skeletal remains.

Biological anthropology of the buried population

The first aspect to consider is the study of the selection of individuals for burial, which involves an estimate of age-at-death and identifying the sex of the deceased. The exploitation of these essential biological data permits a demographic profile of the burial population to be established. However, in this case, it should be mentioned that this population sample is not a natural one, but a sample partly made up of deported people, which substantially modifies the demographic characteristics anticipated for a 'natural' population. New arrivals regularly replaced those who succumbed to premature death, mainly due to deplorable living conditions. This introduces another aspect, namely health conditions, revealed by palaeopathological lesions of traumatic injuries, mechanical stress, dietary deficiencies and infections. However, palaeopathology will not be developed in this chapter. Studies in this area of interest are on-going, notably related to infectious diseases (Dutour *et al.*, 2005). Some examples of studies concerning the health condition of slaves, however, have been conducted in the past (Owsley *et al.*, 1987; Rathbun, 1987; Khudabux, 1999).

Results

The first objective was to identify a cemetery from colonial times and to determine its extent, its state of preservation and to establish the typology of the graves.

From east to west, the coastal area is divided into four parts (Figure 21.5):

- The current beach, about 30 m wide, is made up of partly consolidated coral sand (beach-rock) and did not contain any archaeological remains any longer. The development of a coastal path led to the disappearance of this part of the coastal dune and the graves which were located there:
- Behind the beach, a ridge of coastal dunes with a width of 40 m by 60 m and a height ranging from 0.50 m to 2 m. This part of the site is only partially preserved as sand retrieval damaged the northern extremity and the western slope. The total length of the dune is over 200 m, but it has been fragmented into five unequal parts by sand quarrying, each covered by some vegetation. The preserved part of the funerary site is located in this sector:
- A zone covered by shrub vegetation. The limestone bedrock, at a depth of a metre, underlies a clayey layer overlain by vegetation.
- A cliff leads up to the plateau, which lies at an altitude of 60 m above the coast

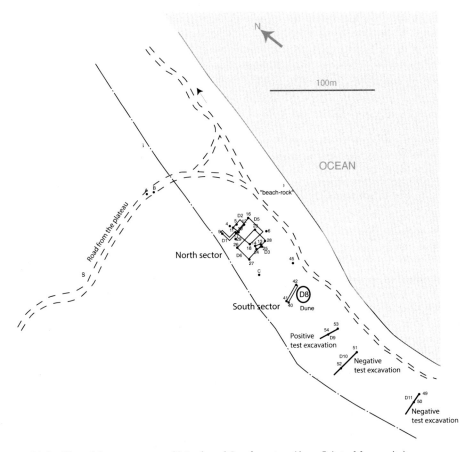

Figure 21.5 Plan of the two excavated North and South sectors (Anse Sainte-Marguerite) (Image: P. Courtaud).

The existence of water-rolled, fragmented human remains on the current beach is the only material evidence of washed-out graves. Previously, they were considered to date to the Pre-Columbian period due to the presence of an underlying Amerindian site disturbed by colonial-period graves and subsequently by the partial destruction of the dune. The identification of large areas disturbed by the massive recovery of sand in the 1970s and the threat of the progressive disappearance of the dune were decisive factors in the decision to conduct archaeological excavations at this site.

Several test trenches showed that the original extent of the cemetery extended over a length of at least 200 m. It must initially have included several hundred buried individuals, probably close to a thousand, which does not accord with the hypothesis that the dead derived from a single plantation. As this part of the island had only been colonised in the first half of the 18th century, the cemetery would have been used over the course of a century, or slightly more. This cemetery would thus have accommodated the dead from several plantations. At the end of the 18th century, in the neighbouring town of Petit-Canal, some 88% of the population were slaves (Schnakenbourg, 1977). Historical sources relating to the cemeteries from the colonial period (Boutin, 1998) mention small clusters of slave cemeteries established in inhabited areas and urban cemeteries such as that in Basse Terre and Pointe-à-Pitre, but there is no mention of funerary sites providing burial for slaves from several plantations. Within the cemetery, two zones were identified, the North and South sectors.

The North sector

The first three excavation seasons focussed on the North sector, where burials were numerous and well preserved. The excavated sector yielded close to 200 graves (Figure 21.6). Bone preservation was excellent, which was unexpected in this tropical context (Figure 21.7).

Figure 21.6 View of the North sector of the excavation. The graves were only identified by the outline of the grave pit on the surface. No architectural elements were preserved, except some coffin nails (Anse Sainte-Marguerite) (Photograph: P. Courtaud).

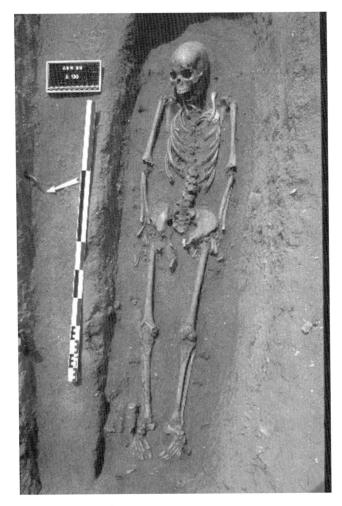

Figure 21.7 View of a simple grave of an adult lying supinely, with the head towards the east (S.130). Nails distributed around the skeleton indicate the remains of a hexagonal coffin (Anse Sainte-Marguerite) (Photograph: P. Courtaud).

However, not all skeletal remains were so well preserved. Firstly, the graves of children are smaller and not as deeply dug. These were thus more often exposed to disturbances. Children are, as a consequence, not as well-represented as adults. Secondly, many graves were re-used (Figure 21.8). These consisted of gathered, disarticulated skeletonised remains (*réductions*) that had been disturbed in the course of subsequent burials. The graves were organised in rows and were oriented east to west with the head oriented to the west in the majority of cases (Figure 21.9).

Inverted orientations were observed for about 5% of the remains, generally for children. Corpses were buried supinely in coffins, even the youngest individuals. Well-preserved nails attest to the presence of coffins. For adult coffins, 40 nails were used, whereas about 20 were employed for coffins of children. Two individuals had been deposited without coffins, directly in the ground. One of these is a 'conventional' grave of a child, with a 3-4- year-old child in a primary deposition. Sometimes, osteological indicators such as the maintenance of all bones within the space once occupied by the corpse clearly show that decomposition occurred in a

Figure 21.8 Anse Sainte-Marguerite – View of a re-used grave following the deposition of a new occupant. The bones of the first individual are scattered around the grave (S.165) (Photograph: P. Courtaud).

confined space, which excludes the hypothesis of an original empty space of decomposition such as a sealed coffin. The corpses were deposited in an extended position. Many graves were re-used and very frequently gathered, disarticulated remains (*réductions*) occurred within the grave. In this way, the same grave could contain the remains of several individuals and the remains of the same individual could also be distributed in two different graves. Re-use and gathered, disarticulated remains (*réductions*) are frequent in medieval European cemeteries as a result of over-crowding. Here, the existence of unused space near successive burials appears to demonstrate the desire to regroup the deceased in the afterlife. Although there is no supporting evidence, the criterion for successive burials of these individuals appears to be linked to kinship or ethnic ties.

Two graves (Figure 21.10) provide a good illustration of this phenomenon, where an earlier adult grave was partially intersected by that of a child. The adult cranium was secondarily deposited above the cranium of the child. These funerary practices suggest that particular care was taken and that the endearing image of the adult cranium 'protecting' the child's grave could have had symbolic value. This is close to the limits of archaeological inference, so it remains a

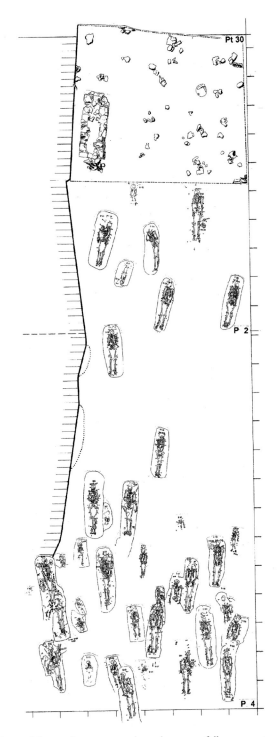

Figure 21.9 Plan of part of the northern sector where the graves follow an east-west axis (Anse Sainte-Marguerite) (Image: P. Courtaud).

Figure 21.10 This example illustrates the re-use of a grave and re-distribution of human remains. The cranium of the adult was moved and placed above the cranium of the child. This appears to have been premeditated rather than accidental (S.178–S.185) (Anse Sainte-Marguerite) (Photograph: P. Courtaud).

hypothetical explanation for this type of disposition of remains at present. The numerous groups, the quasi-systematic use of coffins, and the repeated orientation of the graves portray a very 'Christian' appearance for this funerary site. No African practices were discerned. Several rare graves contained objects, such as a kaolinite pipe, rosary beads (Figure 21.11), or a medal of Saint Mary dating to 1850. The medal provides a *terminus-post-quem*; the cemetery was used after the definitive abolition of slavery in 1848 in the French colonies, which raises questions as to the fate of slave cemeteries. Some were abandoned, while others were used for a few more years.

It appears that at Sainte-Marguerite, some of the newly freed population continued to use the former slave cemetery for a period of time. However, it is unclear whether this continued

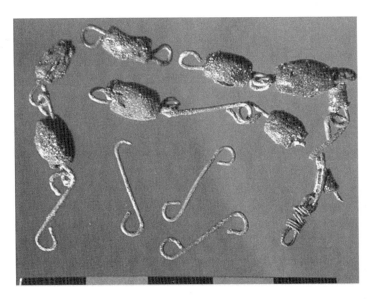

Figure 21.11 Detail of rosary beads covered by the hand of a deceased individual in the North sector (Anse Sainte-Marguerite) (Photograph: P. Courtaud).

use was due to deliberate choice to be near the graves of their relatives and ancestors or if due to prohibited access to holy ground. This is one of the main questions raised by this excavation.

Adults were buried dressed, as shown by the presence of bone and sometimes mother-of-pearl buttons, made from the inner layer of pearl oysters, near the pelvic area (Figure 21.12), indicating

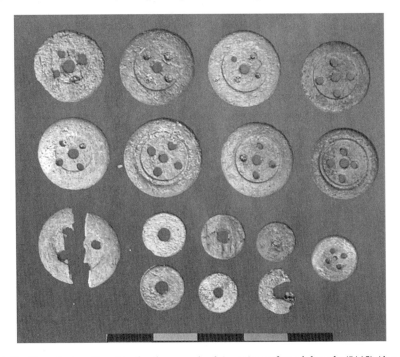

Figure 21.12 Bone buttons found in the thorax and pelvic regions of an adult male (S115) (Anse Sainte-Marguerite) (Photograph: P. Courtaud).

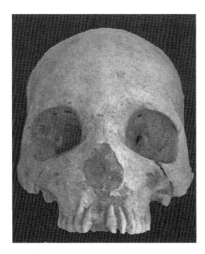

Figure 21.13   Facial view of cranium with filed and pointed upper incisors. This modification was carried out in adolescence or young adulthood. The cranial morphology is consistent with an African origin (Anse Sainte-Marguerite) (Image: P. Courtaud).

underpants, or in the area of the thorax, indicating a shirt. The only known examples of these garments come from archaeological finds. Similar objects were found in a grave at the Anse Bertrand chapel during a salvage excavation in the north of the island (Pichon, 1996).

Another element may confirm the use of the cemetery after 1848. This is the discovery of two partially destroyed brick-built tombs, where the exposed part of the structure has gone missing. The foundation is made up of crude or roughly square limestone blocks, with small coral bricks assembled with mortar surrounding the coffin. One of them contains the skeleton of an adult with Pott's disease, as defined by Ortner and Putschar (1985), a case of suspected vertebral tuberculosis, which may have contributed to the death of this individual. Cranial morphology suggests an African origin. The architecture of this tomb is not like that of other settler tombs (Bégot, 1998) but looks similar to those from the Delanoé cemetery (Boutin, 1998), a small funerary site on the plateau. Although no specific funerary practices point to an African origin, there is evidence of dental modification consisting of filing of anterior teeth in three individuals (Figure 21.13). As mentioned above, the good preservation, particularly of crania permits observation and quantification of certain morphological characteristics that also point to an African origin. The African characteristics, mainly of the facial skeleton (maxillary prognathism, large interorbital space, morphology of the nasal aperture) are particularly evident (Howells, 1989, 1995) (Figure 21.13).

In total, 215 individuals were exhumed in the North sector, consisting of 126 adults and 89 children and adolescents. The latter are under-represented, as are newborns. However, these hiatuses must be interpreted with caution, given the possibility for renewal of this population through in-coming slaves from elsewhere. The 82 individuals for whom an *os coxae* was well preserved were made up of 39 females and 33 males (in addition to 10 of indeterminate sex). This population sample appears to have been particularly disadvantaged; adult death occurred frequently before the age of 30 and certain significant pathological signs, such as numerous enthesopathies, infectious diseases point to frequent biological stress (Romon and Courtaud, 2002; Dutour *et al.*, 2005). On the basis of the archaeological material from the graves nearby, the North sector was used during the first half of the 19th century and a part after the abolition of slavery. A specific date for the end of the funerary use of this area remains unknown and could not be confirmed after the excavation.

The South sector

Once the initial aim to uncover large surfaces and gather a sufficiently large sample of exhumed skeletons in the North sector had been accomplished, a further season of excavation focussed on an area further to the south. The aim was to compare the spatial organisation, funerary practices and the population profile of this area with that of the North sector.

A test excavation was carried out via a trench perpendicular to the dune about 50 m along its southern extension, where disturbance did not appear to be too marked (Figure 21.5). This revealed a more chaotic organisation with regard to both the use of space and funerary architecture. This area was clearly different from the North sector (Figure 21.14). The area could be dated to the second half of the 18th century by surface ceramic finds. None of the graves contained material clearly associated with the deceased, apart from an intact bone crucifix found in a single grave, but as a secondary deposit, lying between the lower limb bones but probably originally decorating the coffin lid. Fifty-three graves were identified that contained the remains of 63 individuals, mainly from

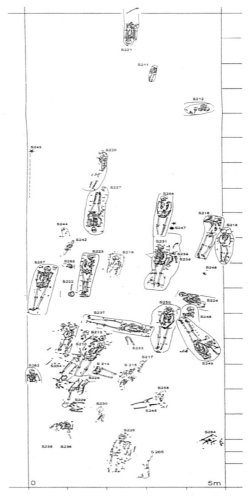

Figure 21.14 Plan of part of the South sector, which appears to be less well-organised than the North sector (Anse Sainte-Marguerite) (Image: P. Courtaud).

412

primary burials, but with 16% of the individuals having been removed as groups of disarticulated elements. This sector yielded a majority of full-earth graves (their occupants having been placed directly in the ground) (55%), with their heads to the west in half of the cases. This area of the cemetery thus appears to be less homogeneously organised. Moreover, no bone or mother-of-pearl buttons indicate the once presence of clothes; the only dress accessory uncovered was an iron belt buckle. Four more individuals with dental modifications were uncovered.

Discussion

Since the end of the 1990s, the number and variety of cemeteries explored in Guadeloupe and the quality of the documentation have provided quite an exceptional sample. Because of the partitioning of colonial society, which imposed separate cemeteries on each population group, the work carried out on funerary sites constitutes a rich field of investigation for questions relating to the status of cemeteries, funerary practices, and the biological composition and characteristics of the population samples they contain. In cemetery terms, the transmission of metropolitan French practices to the colonies is unequivocal. It testifies to the dominance of those of European descent. However, other groups adapted to colonial society, which resulted in the creation of their own funerary spaces. These 'Negro' cemeteries are in many ways identical to parish cemeteries in their organisation, use of space, and sacredness.

Almost all the cemeteries discovered in Guadeloupe over the past 20 years had been forgotten in the collective memory of the living society, especially those intended for the burials of enslaved people. Such graveyards, which were also far from religious, military or civilian buildings, have since then been interpreted as slave cemeteries. Determining the status of the buried populations, and therefore the identity of these cemeteries is one of the major challenges for archaeologists and historians. Several types of information must be taken into account:

- Historical sources: Archives and parish registers are very informative documents. However, they may be deficient due to often-insufficient preservation caused by accidents, such as fires, and natural disasters such as cyclones. Moreover, they contain very limited information, whether on the burial practices or about the enslaved people, in general. Moreover, it is important to remember that these written documents were produced by the free population and not by the enslaved.
- Funerary archaeology: The archaeothanatological approach made it possible to study the spatio-temporal organisation of the cemetery, to understand the decomposition processes of the burials and thus to reconstruct the skeletons that had been displaced by the numerous re-uses of the graves. The method has also proven very useful for assessing the presence of clothes and coffins, and for the reconstruction of the original burial position of the deceased.
- The biology of the deceased: Data on age-at-death, sex and general health status are extremely valuable in order to learn more about the buried population. An African origin was attested, especially for some adults.

The information collected about the Anse Sainte-Marguerite site can be extended to those obtained for other burials and cemeteries suspected to contain enslaved people, including La Plage des Raisins Clairs (Parish of Saint-François) (Rouquet, 2015) located on a beach, and two others inland, Jabrun, Baie-Mahaut (Martias, 2006), Doyon, Capesterre-Belle-Eau (Martias, 2005) and Morne Dauphine, Saint-Claude (Rousseau, Pichon and Vragar, 1997) (Figure 21.1). These salvage archaeological interventions have not been detailed here because they have been far less well-documented to date.

Conclusion

There is no evidence of any funerary practices of African origin. On the contrary, funerary rites seem to conform to Christian practice with the use of coffins and an east-west orientation of the graves with the head to the west. However, in the 18th century, in part of Anse Sainte-Marguerite, these two tendencies appear to have been less respected, which suggests that at that time, fewer individuals were baptised and which results in a more chaotic organisation of the funerary space. It is these features, however, which led to the identification of a cemetery containing the remains of the enslaved dating to the colonial period. The geographical location away from towns and religious places, in marginal areas such as a beach, are decisive factors for their identification. While these observations indicate the servile status of the buried population, there are also biological characteristics reflecting poor health and the presence of the practice of dental modification as found in some African populations (Handler, 1994).

Is it possible to irrefutably characterise the status of the people buried at these sites? The servile condition of an individual cannot be deduced from any single observation alone, whether archaeological or anthropological. It is the combination of a set of observations that provides a hypothetical identification of these cemeteries and for the identity of the buried population. It is, therefore, not the individuals identified as enslaved, but the overall funerary site that identifies it to be a slave cemetery (Courtaud, 2015).

This research is part of a larger, trans-disciplinary project about past Caribbean societies based on collaborations involving archaeologists, anthropologists and historians. This research theme, which is still in its beginning stages in French-speaking territories, requires the study of colonial society as a whole in order to restore the links that existed between each of its components.

References

Baker, B.M. (1999). Early manifestation of tuberculosis in the skeleton. In: G. Pálfi, O. Dutour, J. Deak and I. Hutas, eds., *Tuberculosis: Past and Present*. Budapest-Szeged: Golden Book and Tuberculosis Foundation, pp. 301–311.

Barbotin, M. (1978). Découverte de Crânes, Fémurs et autres Os … *Bulletin de la Société de l' Histoire de la Guadeloupe*, 38, pp. 3–37.

Bégot, D. (1998). Les tombes de colons: un art colonial. In: R. Boutin, J. Pézeron and D. Bégot, eds., *Patrimoine de Guadeloupe: Les Cimetières*. Special Issue, Basse-Terre: Société de l'Histoire de la Guadeloupe, 1, pp. 21–36.

Bodu, P. (1984). *Rapport sur une prospection au site de l'Anse Sainte-Marguerite, Commune du Moule (Grande-Terre)*, Basse-Terre: Service Régional de l'Archéologie de la Guadeloupe.

Bonnissent, D. and Romon, T. (2004). *Fouilles de la Cathédrale de Basse-Terre*. Document final de synthèse, Basse-Terre: Service Régional de l'Archéologie de la Guadeloupe.

Boutin, R. (1998). Le champ de repos. In: R. Boutin, J. Pézeron and D. Bégot, eds., *Patrimoine de Guadeloupe: Les Cimetières*. Special Issue, Basse-Terre: Société de l'Histoire de la Guadeloupe, 1, pp. 5–12.

Brickley, M. and Ives, R. (2008). *The bioarchaeology of metabolic bone disease*. Amsterdam: Academic Press.

Brokke, A.J. and Knippenberg, S. (1994). *Évaluation archéologique du site de l'Anse Sainte-Marguerite*, Basse-Terre: Service Régional de l'Archéologie de la Guadeloupe.

Courtaud, P. (2002). Le site de l'Anse Sainte-Marguerite (Guadeloupe, Grande Terre): présentation d'un cimetière d'époque coloniale. In: A. Delpuech, J.-P. Giraud and A. Hesse, eds., *Archéologie Précolombienne et Coloniale des Caraïbes*. Fort-de-France: Actes du Comité des travaux historiques et scientifiques (CTHS), pp. 283–294.

Courtaud, P. (2010). Approche archéologique des populations serviles. L'archéologie funéraire aux Antilles. In: M. Cottias, E. Cunin and A. de Almeida Mendes, eds., *Les Traites et les Esclavages. Perspectives Historiques et Contemporaines*, Paris: Éditions Karthala, pp. 301–308.

Courtaud, P. (2015). Le cimetière, miroir de l'esclavage. In: P. Courtaud, S. Kachi, and T. Romon, eds., *Cimetières et Identités*. Pessac: Thanat'Os, Éditions Ausonius, pp. 103–114.

Courtaud, P., Delpuech, A. and Romon, T. (1999). Archaeological investigations at colonial cemeteries on Guadeloupe: African slave burial sites or not? In: J.B. Haviser, ed., *African Sites: Archaeology in the Caribbean*. Princeton: Markus Wiener Publishers, pp. 277–290.

Courtaud, P. and Romon, T. (2004). Le Site de l'Anse Sainte-Marguerite (Guadeloupe, Grande-Terre): Présentation d'un Cimetière d'Époque Coloniale. *Journal of Caribbean Archaeology* (Special Issue), 1, pp. 58–67.

Croteau, N. and Auger, R. (1998). La mise en valeur du site de Loyola à Rémire, Guyane: communique l'archéologie coloniale. In: A. Delpuech, J.-P. Giraud and A. Hesse, eds., *Archéologie Précolombienne et Coloniale des Caraïbes*. Fort-de-France: Actes du CTHS (Comité des travaux historiques et scientifiques), pp. 315–321.

Duday, H. (2009). *The archaeology of the dead: lectures in archaeothanatology*. Oxford: Oxbow Books.

Duday, H. (2019): Les preuves archéologiques d'une crise brutale de mortalité: simultanéité du dépôt de cadavres, simultanéité des décès. In: D. Castex, ed., *Épidémies et Crises de Mortalité du Passé*. Pessac: Ausonius Éditions, pp. 15–21.

Dutour, O., Romon, T., Ardagna, Y., Tatillon, C. and Courtaud, P. (2005). Paléoépidémiologie de la tuberculose en Guadeloupe: Le cimetière d'esclaves de l'Anse Sainte-Marguerite. In: Ardagna, Y., ed., *L'Homme et ses Images, Mesures, Représentations, Constructions*, Actes du XXVe colloque du Groupement des Anthropologues de Langue Française. Marseille: C. Tatilon Service programmation assistée par ordinateur (PAO) et dessin assisté par ordinateur (DAO), pp. 355–362.

Handler, J.S. (1994). Determining African Birth from Skeletal Remains: A Note on Tooth Mutilation. *Historical Archaeology*, 28(3), pp. 113–119.

Handler, J.S. and Lange, F.W. (1978). *Plantation slavery in Barbados: an archaeological and historical investigation*. Cambridge, MA: Harvard University Press.

Haviser, J.B. (1999). *African sites: archaeology in the Caribbean*. Princeton: Markus Wiener Publishers.

Howells, W.W. (1989). *Skull shapes and the map: craniometric analyses in the dispersion of modern Homo*. Harvard: Peabody Museum of Anthropology and Ethnology.

Howells, W.W. (1995). *Who's who in skulls, ethnic identification of crania from measurements*. Harvard: Peabody Museum of Archaeology and Ethnology.

Kacki, S. and Romon, T. (2013). From Burials to Population Identity: Archaeological Appraisal of the Status of a Lesser Antilles Colonial Cemetery (Baillif, Guadeloupe), *Antiquity*, 87, pp. 829–839.

Kacki, S. and Romon, T. (2015). Le cimetière de la Rivières des Pères (Baillif, Guadeloupe): Identification du statut des défunts par l'approche archéo-anthropologique. In: P. Courtaud, S. Kachi and T. Romon, eds., *Cimetières et Identités*. Pessac: Thanat'Os, Éditions Ausonius, pp. 117–132.

Khudabux, M.R. (1999). Effects of life conditions on the health of a Negro slave community in Suriname. In: J.B. Haviser, ed., *African Sites: Archaeology in the Caribbean*. Princeton, NJ: Markus Wiener, pp. 291–312.

Le Roux, Y., Auger, R. and Cazelles N. (2009). *Les Jésuites et l'esclavage Loyola: l'habitation des Jésuites de Rémire en Guyane Française*. Québec: Presses de l'Université du Québec.

Martias, R. (2005). *Doyon, Capesterre-Belle-Eau, Guadeloupe: rapport de diagnostic archéologique*. Basse-Terre: Service Régional de l'Archéologie de la Guadeloupe.

Martias, R. (2006). *Jabrun, Baie-Mahault, Guadeloupe: rapport de diagnostic archéologique*. Basse-Terre: Service Régional de l'Archéologie de la Guadeloupe.

Orser, C.E. (1998). The Archaeology of the African Diaspora. *Annual Review of Anthropology*, 27, pp. 63–82.

Ortner, D.J. and Putschar, W.G.J. (1985). *Identification of pathological conditions in human skeletal remains*. Washington, DC: Smithsonian Institution Press.

Owsley, D.W., Orser, C.E., Mann, R.W., Moore-Jansen, P.H. and Montgomery R.L. (1987). Demography and Pathology of an Urban Slave Population from New Orleans. *American Journal of Physical Anthropology*, 74(2), pp. 185–197.

Paya, D. and Romon, T. (2001). *Le Cimetière de l'Hôpital de la Charité, Palais de Justice (Basse-Terre, Guadeloupe): document final de synthèse*. Basse-Terre: Service Régional de l'Archéologie de la Guadeloupe.

Pérotin-Dumon, A. (2000). *La ville aux îles, la ville dans l'île. Basse-Terre et Pointe-à-Pitre, Guadeloupe, 1650–1820*. Paris: Éditions Karthala.

Pichon, M. (1996). *Rapport de fouille archéologique à la chapelle d'Anse Bertrand*. Basse-Terre: Service Régional de l'Archéologie de la Guadeloupe.

Rathbun, T.A. (1987). Health and Disease at a South Carolina Plantation: 1840–1870. *American Journal of Physical Anthropology*, 74(2), pp. 239–253.

Richard, G. (1994). Premier Indice d'une Occupation Précéramique en Guadeloupe Continentale. *Journal de la Société des Américanistes*, 80(1), pp. 241–242.

Romon, T. and Courtaud, P. (2002). Etude biologique des squelettes du cimetière d'époque coloniale de l'Anse Sainte-Marguerite (Le Moule, Guadeloupe). In: A. Delpuech, J.-P. Giraud and A. Hesse, eds., *Archéologie Précolombienne et Coloniale des Caraibes*. Fort-de-France: Actes du Comité des travaux historiques et scientifiques (CTHS), pp. 295–299.

Romon, T., Courtaud, P., Paya, D., Bonnissent, D. and Verrand, L. (2009). La Place des Esclaves dans les Cimetières Coloniaux: Trois Exemples Guadeloupéens. *Archéopages*, 25, pp. 46–51.

Rouquet, J. (2015). *Plage des Raisins Clairs*, Rapport Final d'opération, Fouille de sauvetage archéologique urgent. Service Régional de l'Archéologie de la Guadeloupe, Basse-Terre.

Rousseau X., Pichon M. and Vragar Y. (1997). *Le cimetière du morne Dauphine (Saint-Claude)*. Rapport d'opération, SRA Guadeloupe.

Sala-Molins, L. 2006. *Le Code Noir ou le calvaire de Canaan*. Paris: Éditions de Presses Universitaires de France (PUF).

Schnakenbourg, C. (1977). Statistiques pour l'Histoire de Plantation en Guadeloupe et Martinique (1635–1835). *Bulletin de la Société d'Histoire de la Guadeloupe*, 31, pp. 3–121.

Vergès, F. (2008). Archéologie de l'esclavage, archéologie de l'absence. In: J.-P. Demoule and B. Stieger, eds., *L'Avenir du Passé. Modernité de l'Archéologie*. Paris: La Découverte, pp. 105–113.

Verrand, L. (1999). *Etude du cimetière de l'hôpital Saint Jean-Baptiste de la Charité, Basse-Terre, Guadeloupe – Volet de recherche CAOM (Centre des Archives d'Outre-Mer)*. Basse-Terre: Service Régional de l'Archéologie de la Guadeloupe.

Verrand, L. (2001). *Le cimetière de la cathédrale de Basse-Terre: rapport d'étude d'archives au centre des archives d'outre-mer*. Basse-Terre: Service Régional de l'Archéologie de la Guadeloupe.

Watters, D.R. (1987). Excavations at the Harney Site Slave Cemetery, Montserrat, West Indies. *Annals of Carnegie Museum*, 56(18), pp. 289–318.

PART III

Archaeothanatology of associated remains

22

ARCHAEOTHANATOLOGICAL APPROACHES TO ASSOCIATED REMAINS IN EUROPEAN FUNERARY CONTEXTS

An overview

Isabelle Cartron and Aurélie Zemour

Ausonius, Institut de Recherche Antiquité et Moyen Âge, UMR 5607, CNRS – Université Bordeaux Montaigne, Pessac, France

Introduction

The material found in graves invariably raises questions for archaeologists, whatever the period. Such material is often referred to as 'grave goods', but the term is very imprecise. It seems too restrictive nowadays, given the diverse nature and status of the remains that can be found in graves. The term is overly interpretative, as well. Not all of the items unearthed with skeletons are 'grave goods'. In the initial stages of analysis, it is better to employ 'associated remains'. This term (1) encompasses all of the remains found whether deposited deliberately or not, (2) covers their diverse natures by including both artefacts and ecofacts – i.e. tangible remains whether manufactured or otherwise (ceramic, lithic or bone, adornments and faunal remains) and more fleeting remains such as mineral, ash and plant macro-remains, (3) qualifies the degree of their association with the deceased, whether worn or deposited in the grave, and (4) does not pre-judge the role they might have played in the funerary ceremony (Zemour, 2013). The notion of 'grave goods' has changed with the way graves are understood. The archaeological approach to burial contexts has gone through several stages. Initially, the focus was on the architecture and 'grave goods' before shifting to the human remains. It was not until the late 20th century that burials came to be analysed and interpreted more holistically. What is referred today as the 'archaeology of death', or 'archaeothanatology', covers all periods and all types of deposits of human remains. This approach seeks, among other things, to reconstruct and interpret mortuary actions in conjunction with all of the other archaeological data. As graves are understood as *systems* and no longer as juxtaposed elements, they become a diversified and multi-disciplinary field of investigation. This affects the understanding of 'grave goods' quite fundamentally. New questions and study protocols have emerged, which progressively provide an increasingly refined understanding of the ways in which remains are associated with the deceased. After outlining

DOI: 10.4324/9781351030625-26

the changes in the approach to remains associated with the dead, this chapter illustrates specific examples and the main contributions of the current approach using cases drawn mostly from chrono-cultural contexts investigated by the authors, thereby contrasting the state of practice for prehistoric and historic periods.

Historiography

From the 17th to the mid-20th centuries, scholars focussed solely on the architecture of the grave and the objects found with the skeleton, but they largely ignored the skeleton itself. And yet, until the 19th century, the objects themselves were not specifically analysed and only those that were thought to be rare or of aesthetic or even market value were deemed of interest. 'Beautiful things' were treated as museum pieces and benefitted from an 'antiquarian' approach (Schnapp, 2012), so much so that people spoke of 'funerary treasures'. The discovery of the 'rich' grave of Childéric I at Tournai in the 17th century and the enthusiasm it prompted until the 20th century is emblematic of this type of approach (Kazanski and Périn, 1988; Knüsel, 2006; Brulet, 2016). That discovery also reflects the keen interest in the search for human origins, which intensified in the late 19th century with the construction of nationhood in Europe and particularly in France and Germany. These approaches enabled the transmission of numerous inventories of items now lost and the development of typologies.

As from the 1960s, associated remains were studied essentially as a basis for cultural typo-chronologies and to determine the sex of buried individuals. Special focus fell on the nature and quantity of 'grave goods'. The idea was to determine the status of the deceased in order to infer the structure of society (Binford, 1971: 21). This work led to the development of schemes for classifying the social categories of the deceased (the quality groups or 'Qualitätsgruppen' of the German school) based primarily on the valuation of wealth (Böhner, 1978). These approaches saw funerary spaces as an accurate reflection of the social organisation of the living. When funerary practices were then re-situated in their cultural context, with the idea that they were representative of a funerary ideology of that society and not of the way the society itself was structured, objects were no longer just symbols but became cultural evidence in their own right. Objects were then associated with 'archaeological cultures' related to the 'peoples' mentioned in ancient texts (Legendre *et al.*, 2007). The way associated remains were seen became radically changed by the idea of interaction between funerary actions/gestures and the geographical and cultural context in which they were performed.

In the early 1980s and above all in the 1990s, the objective was to identify the connection between remains and the deceased (O'Shea, 1984). In France, 'field anthropology' ('*l'anthropologie de terrain*') and, more particularly, taphonomic analysis contributed widely to identifying such connections. This 'dynamic approach to burials' ('*approche dynamique des sépultures*'), sought to reconstruct the original position and layout of the body, garments, the adornments and objects' ('*l'attitude originelle du corps, l'agencement des pièces d'habillement, des éléments de parure et du mobilier*') and the grave architecture was based on the examination of the position of the bones and non-human remains (Duday *et al.*, 1990: 29–30). The taphonomic analysis made it possible, in particular, to reconstruct longer enduring as well as perishable funerary items that proved to be highly diverse, multiplying the possibilities for the placement of objects around the deceased. The idea is to consider all remains in the immediate environment of the deceased, without presupposing how they might have been involved in funerary practices as is implicit, on the contrary, in the usual understanding of 'grave goods'. This is a difficult stage because the association of remains with the deceased is not always unequivocal and must be substantiated by argument.

In the early 2000s, the transition from field anthropology to the archaeology of death or archaeothanatology marked the development of deeper thinking about associated remains and the search for an appropriate methodology. For prehistoric periods, for example, Chambon and Augereau (2009: 196, fig. 3) identify six connections based essentially on the topography of remains. They posit that the connection between objects and the deceased varies and that remains in burial contexts are of variable status. The protocol they suggest identifies six statuses for objects in a funerary context: the clothing of the deceased, personal belongings, gifts made as a result of funerary rites, objects used during the funerary rites and then buried, objects associated with commemorative ceremonies and, finally, things that should not be present (Chambon and Augereau 2009: 196, fig. 4). Supporting the idea that objects in graves may be of different statuses, Clop (2008: 2, fig.1) contemplates their different levels of meaning as social products in their own right. Bailly and Plisson (2008: 3) take a similar view, suggesting that objects should be interpreted by describing three circles of varying radiuses around the body. The objects closest to the remains, thought to be the possessions of the deceased, supposedly provide information about the individual (sex, age, activities, status); the items deposited nearby are allegedly related to funerary practices, while others pertain to the commemoration of the deceased, collective practices of mourning and remembrance. For historic periods, this type of approach remains rare and little synthetic work has been produced (Bizot and Signoli, 2009).

These different approaches highlight the importance of recording the position and nature of every item in the grave at the time of discovery. This stage, which determines the relationship between the skeleton and the remains associated with it, is essential for documenting both funerary practices and the role of remains in those practices. On the strength of these methodological developments, a multi-proxy approach is recommended for an optimal interpretation of mortuary phenomena.

A multi-disciplinary approach

To conduct integrated research, the idea is to mobilise all of the archaeological sciences that aid the interpretation of burial actions/gestures (Corbineau, 2017). Therefore, it is essential to bring together a team and establish a specific protocol for the excavation stage. At present, this type of investigation is mainly reserved for remains that are exceptionally well-preserved. This is the case, for example, for the mausoleum at Jaunay-Clan (Vienne, France) excavated by Ségard in 2011 (Ségard, 2017). This monument, dating to late Antiquity (3rd–4th centuries AD), contained two limestone sarcophagi which contained lead containers with preserved organic and textile remains.

The excavation conditions must also be favourable in order to implement such an approach, especially in terms of time. This was the case for the grave of La Balance-Ilot P, (Avignon, Vaucluse, France), which was removed '*en bloc*' in 1974 by Courtin and Gagnières and excavated in the laboratory in 2009 (Zemour *et al.*, 2017). A multi-disciplinary approach (Figure 22.1) made it possible: (1) to reliably attribute this grave to the end of the Early Neolithic, (2) to reveal the presence of clothing (probably a jacket) with sophisticated embroidery work made up of 160 columbella shells and 16 stag teeth, all selectively chosen and (3) to determine the use of two types of pigment at two different points in time (one applied to the adornments and the other sprinkled over the body during the funerary ceremony). To date, this is the first reliable evidence of a garment in a grave dated to the early fifth millennium BC in the western Mediterranean. It has been possible to reconstruct this now vanished garment by combining taphonomic analysis with technological (manufacture) and use-wear analysis of the adornments and archaeozoological analysis of the deer teeth. This study also shows the role archaeometry can play in the analysis

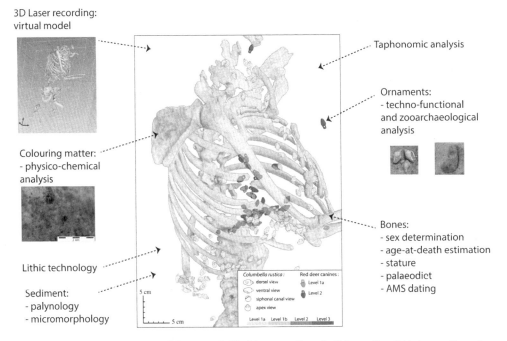

Figure 22.1 3D reconstruction of the upper half of the grave from La Balance-Ilot P (Avignon, France) with the ornamental elements and archaeological scientific approaches employed as part of a multi-disciplinary approach (S. Bonnardin, S. Sorin and A. Zemour).

of burial actions/gestures. Without physico-chemical analyses, it would have been impossible to identify the use of two different pigments at two different times in the burial process. Apart from the contribution of different specialties of archaeometry, this type of approach is also enhanced by new technologies such as the 3D reconstruction of graves (cf. Sachau-Carcel, Chapter 31, this volume). 3D modelling proves an essential medium for multi-disciplinary analysis. It is clear that the 3D model has greatly contributed to the identification of garments, in particular by enabling the detection of multi-directional pressure effects, which are difficult to detect from plans or photographs.

Thus, 3D modelling is a major medium for taphonomic analysis and can be very useful for identifying funerary garments or other perishable remains such as shrouds or coffins, which have proved hard to identify in the archaeology of death over the last 20 years (Bonnabel and Carré, 1996; Bizot and Signoli, 2009; Chambon and Thévenet, 2016).

The complementary contributions of archaeological sciences and taphonomic analysis

The role of archaeological sciences in identifying burial gestures/actions has been demonstrated in recent years. These analyses make it possible not only to specify certain burial gestures/actions but also to reveal others by complementary taphonomic analysis. They are now conducted in close connection with specific questions raised about the remains associated with the deceased. This development has also highlighted the existence of numerous grave furnishings made of perishable materials, for example, coffins, stretchers and couches.

Reconstruction of perishable items

Many previously unsuspected remains can now be reconstructed in or around graves. Such remains, whether organic (plant or animal) or inorganic (mineral or metal), often identified by taphonomic analyses, enhance the understanding of mortuary practices. The extent of taphonomic analyses increasingly reveals the initial presence of wooden caskets or funerary couches within containers such as early medieval sarcophagi (Gleize, 2012). The study of a grave at Saint-Martin de Bruch (Lot-et-Garonne, France) suggests the presence of this type of funerary couch (Cartron and Castex, 2016). The deceased, a female aged between 20 and 49 years, was buried in a large limestone sarcophagus with preserved lid. Although the bones were somewhat fragile, the taphonomic analysis concluded that decomposition had occurred in an unsealed environment. The disarticulation of bones suggests that the body was laid out on some sort of flooring or a stretcher set on cross beams (Figure 22.2). This might have been one of the funerary couches mentioned in medieval writings for transporting or laying out of the deceased (Santinelli, 2014).

Botanical analyses of the micro and macro-remains of plants, pioneered in the funerary context, especially for prehistoric periods, by Leroi-Gourhan (1968) and Bui and Girard (2003). They reveal evidence of plant deposits in various forms, used as bedding, cushions, bouquets or wreaths, changing the perception of some graves that were at first sight devoid of any associated remains. For example, initial findings of the study of the Italian parish graveyard at the 'Pieve di Pava' in San Giovanni d'Asso, Tuscany (Ricci *et al.*, 2012), reveal that several bunches of flowers had probably been laid out with the deceased in this medieval rural community. Similarly, botanical analysis by Corbineau (2014) led to the identification of abundant and diverse pollen in a lead-lined wooden coffin burial that dated to the second half of the third century AD at Bezannes (Champagne-Ardenne, France). The pollen showed high values for taxa that are not compatible with the local environmental record. This indicated that they originated from a wooded savannah area, for example, as found in Yemen, Sudan or Ethiopia (Corbineau, 2014; Schotsmans *et al.*, 2019).

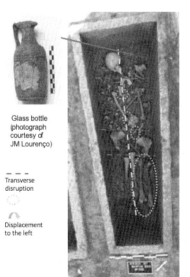

Glass bottle (photograph courtesy of JM Lourenço)

– – –
Transverse disruption

Displacement to the left

Bruch, Saint Martin, Grave SP 002

The disorder of the bones reflects decomposition of the body on a perishable wooden floor (a stretcher?) consisting of two raised, justaposed planks supported by logs at each end.

Associated remains

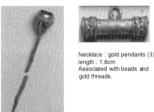

Necklace : gold pendants (3) length : 1.8cm Associated with beads and gold threads.

'Pin, gold, bronze and garnet' length = 7cm (photographs courtesy of Materia Viva 2013)

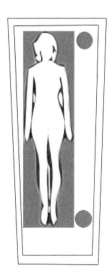

Figure 22.2 A reconstruction of the wooden structure of Bruch SP002 (I. Cartron and D. Castex).

While ceramics and glassware associated with the deceased have long been analysed typologically, the use of organic chemical and palaeogenetic analyses indicates what such receptacles held. Since the early 2000s, these studies have been conducted both individually and as part of major research programmes (e.g. Eerkens, 2005; Evershed, 2008; Heron *et al.*, 2013; Brettell *et al.*, 2014). For example, the MAGI (*Manger, Boire, Offrir pour l'Éternité en Gaule et Italie Préromaines*) programme, directed by Frère, Hugot and Lejars, concentrated on funerary offerings fashioned from natural by-product materials in the pre-Roman Celtic, Etruscan, Italic and Phoenician-Punic periods (5th–1st centuries BC) (Frère and Hugot, 2012). Organic residue analyses of more than a dozen perfume vases of the Classical and Hellenistic periods of the site of Apollonia in Cyrenaica, Libya, revealed a difference between the contents of ceramic and alabaster vases. The ceramic vases contained oily aromatic substances, probably of a cosmetic or medical kind, whereas the alabaster vases held material of plant and animal origin (Maffre *et al.*, 2013). Perfumes proper seem then to have been held in metal or alabaster vases, while ceramics were used for other compounds. The results of these analyses open up new prospects for the interpretation of deposits of tableware in graves, whatever the chronological period in question (Argant *et al.*, 2012).

Organic residue analysis can also provide evidence of the presence of resinous substances in burials and thus shed light on funerary practices. For example, molecular evidence for the use of resinous plant exudates in the Roman period illuminates the multiplicity of roles played by resinous substances in Roman funerary practices in acting to disguise the odour of decomposition, aiding temporary soft-tissue preservation and signifying the social status of the deceased (e.g. Devièse *et al.*, 2010; Brettell *et al.*, 2015).

Research into archaeological textiles in organic and mineralised forms developed from the 1960s onwards (Boyer *et al.*, 1987; Bender-Jorgensen, 1988; Alfaro *et al.*, 2011) and more occasionally in France (Carré *et al.*, 2018). As of the 1990s, the surge in the application of analytical techniques, including scanning electron microscopy (SEM), X-ray fluorescence (XRF), infrared and Raman spectroscopy, X-ray diffraction (XRD), in archaeology opened up new possibilities (e.g. Edwards and Chalmers, 2005; Pollard *et al.*, 2007; Weiner, 2010). Studies of associated remains within the grave of the Merovingian queen Aregund, discovered at Saint-Denis basilica in 1959, attest to this development. An initial study of textile samples was used to reconstruct the queen's clothing and finery (Fleury and France-Lanord, 1998). New analyses of organic residues and metal items (characterisation of coloured pigments of fabrics, metals and gems) in the 2000s led to a second, rather different reconstruction (Périn, 2015). This new study made it possible, in particular, to restore a very different veil, in yellow and red silk samit, probably of Byzantine origin (Rast-Eicher, 2010). This case provides a measure of the technological advances made in the space of a few decades and again shows how worthwhile it is to revise the study of older discoveries.

Today, the study of textile remains is still rare and patchy (Cardon and Feugère, 2000). They are often preserved in mineralised form, and many are destroyed without being examined, especially when metal objects adhering to them are restored. Fragments of fabric, leather and plants are often preserved in the oxidised gangue that surrounds objects that have been studied in the last 15 years or so (Médard and Moulhérat, 2008). Such studies are often limited to a technical approach aimed at characterising materials and weaving techniques. Consideration of the context in which textiles are discovered and their *in situ* observation remain rare and reserved for prestigious graves. For example, one of the burials in the mausoleum at Naintré (Vienne, France) dating from Late Antiquity contained the remains of a child aged about ten years at death. Observation of the well-preserved textiles enabled Desrosiers (2000) to suggest the body had been wrapped in three different fabrics, one of which was a gold-embroidered tunic.

More systematic consideration of these perishable remains in the context of field investigations would provide much additional information about funerary practices. Very promising initial results were obtained by the team formed around Carré and Rast-Eicher (Carré *et al.*, 2018), who developed a protocol for studying graves of the Early Middle Ages. Observation of remains and imprints around objects that were removed as lumps of earth, once recorded and photographed, attest to the presence of textiles, leather, furs or rarer items such as feathers. When combined with taphonomic analysis, such observations provide new insights into reconstructing clothing, associated remains and the position of the deceased in the grave.

Revelation of a greater variety of burial gestures/actions

The convergence of all these studies considerably re-invigorates the perception of burial gestures/ actions that, as a result, appear far more varied than before. In some instances, taphonomic analysis helps to distinguish what was in the grave from what was on the grave. This is the case for the Neolithic necropolis of Monéteau (Yonne, France), where the ceramic ware was deposited either directly on the grave cover or, more probably, on the ground surface. The recurrent shape of these ceramics, such as keeled bowls, led the excavators to suspect the bowls played an essential role in the funeral ceremony or in the course of commemorative events (Chambon and Augereau, 2009). For the Gallo-Roman period, it can sometimes be seen that objects were thrown onto the cover of the funerary container before the burial pit was covered over. On the site of La Grande Borne in Auvergne (France), numerous broken ceramic fragments were found in contact with the skeleton. Taphonomic analysis showed that the deceased had been buried in a coffin made of nailed planks and that the vessel had probably been thrown onto the lid before the grave was back-filled (Blaizot, 2018).

Today, careful taphonomic analysis also reveals that some dress accessories were laid out in the grave and not systematically worn by the deceased. For example, in the Early Middle Ages, belts (with wrought metal trimmings) were laid under the head or body of the deceased (Cartron, 2015). Further systematic observations and interpretation of these actions are still required, but they do change the perception of funerary practices.

Moreover, the case of colouring matter, mostly considered to be 'ochre', clearly illustrates that it is worth considering ephemeral remains in order to highlight preparatory treatments or actions performed during funerary ceremonies. For example, it was long thought that the presence of 'ochre' in early Neolithic graves in Italy and southern France was a reliable indicator of uniform funerary practices. The problem is that pigments were only considered in terms of their presence or absence in graves, whereas they occur in different forms (Zemour, 2013). They mostly occur as powder but in a variety of forms. At the Arene Candide (Liguria, Impressed Ware Culture) (Tiné, 1999), a large amount of colouring matter was crushed to fill the grave, whereas, at Grotta Patrizi (Lazio, Linear Pottery Culture), pigments might have been applied to the body during preparatory treatment (Grifoni Cremonesi and Radmilli, 2000–2001; Zemour, 2019). In an early–mid-Neolithic grave from La Balance-Ilot P (Avignon, Vaucluse, France), the pigment was used to stain shells, but at the time of burial, another pigment was sprinkled on the deceased (Zemour *et al.*, 2017). It is also found in the form of fragments as at the Impressa Arcaico (Archaic Impressed or Cardial Ware Culture) site of Torre Sabea (Puglia, Italy) (Radi, 2002), where two lumps of 'red ochre' were discovered in a small pit dug into the rock adjacent to the grave trench. Close examination of what is meant by the 'presence of ochre' in graves reveals a variety of colouring substances, forms, uses and functions, implying variation in burial gestures and practices (Figure 22.3). This variety could certainly be deciphered by more wide-spread physico-chemical characterisation of these pigments. The contribution of these analyses

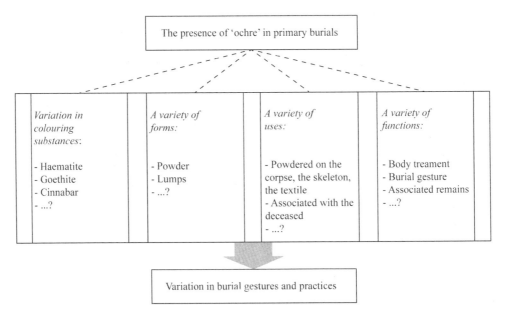

Figure 22.3 The various types, forms, uses and functions of pigments presented as 'ochre' in primary burials at the beginning of the Neolithic in the northwestern Mediterranean region (A. Zemour).

is particularly well illustrated by the physico-chemical characterisation of the multiple layers that once covered bodies and faces, and that filled four mummified human bodies and grave goods from the Chinchorro people of the far northern coast of Chile (Sepúlveda *et al.*, 2014). Scanning electron microscopy with energy-dispersive X-rays (SEM-EDX) and XRD pointed to the use of different types of iron, manganese and copper oxides. These were combined in different pigmented preparations for coating bodies and faces. Physico-chemical analyses thus revealed that 'the Chinchorro had a colour technology for mummifying their dead or to materialise bodies' (Sepúlveda *et al.*, 2014: 10). In Europe, it would be worthwhile to make this type of analysis more widespread, if not systematic, for all periods. The complementary nature of archaeological sciences and taphonomic analysis contribute so much to invigorating the interpretation of burials and, therefore to enhance understandings of social practices.

Associated remains and social practices: new perspectives

The interpretation of remains associated with the dead is an intricate matter on which much has been written. Such remains are perceived as identity markers in the broad sense of the term. It has become important to identify their role in funerary practices because such practices are thought of as social practices proper. Recently, attempts have been made to situate associated remains in funerary proceedings and, more broadly, within the mortuary process. Proximity to the body of the deceased and the nature of the artefacts are taken into account without seeking to set norms from these funerary gestures.

The place of associated remains within 'funerary time'

Among others, Pereira (2013) invited researchers to take up the challenge of reconstructing 'funerary time' ('*temps funéraire*') (Zemour, 2016). The grave and its contents are the outcomes of a set of sequences, processes and gestures, the timing of which is to be reconstructed. One of the

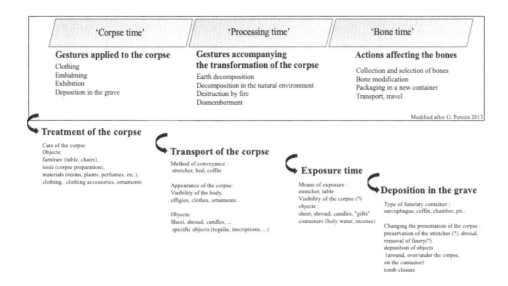

'Corpse time'	'Processing time'	'Bone time'
Gestures applied to the corpse Clothing Embalming Exhibition Deposition in the grave	**Gestures accompanying the transformation of the corpse** Earth decomposition Decomposition in the natural environment Destruction by fire Dismemberment	**Actions affecting the bones** Collection and selection of bones Bone modification Packaging in a new container Transport, travel

Modified after G. Pereira 2013

Treatment of the corpse

Care of the corpse
Objects:
furniture (table, chairs),
tools (corpse preparation),
materials (resins, plants, perfumes, etc.),
clothing, clothing accessories, ornaments

Transport of the corpse

Method of conveyance :
stretcher, bed, coffin

Appearance of the corpse:
Visibility of the body,
effigies, clothes, ornaments...

Objects:
Sheet, shroud, candles, ...
specific objects (regalia, inscriptions, ...)

Exposure time

Means of exposure :
stretcher, table
Visibility of the corpse (?)
objects :
sheet, shroud, candles, "gifts"
containers (holy water, incense)

Deposition in the grave

Type of funerary container :
sarcophagus, coffin, chamber, pit...

Changing the presentation of the corpse :
preservation of the stretcher (?), shroud,
removal of finery(?)
deposition of objects
(around, over/under the corpse,
on the container)
tomb closure

Figure 22.4 The details of the funerary processing of the body and its remains ('*temps funéraire*') (I. Cartron).

challenges is to try to situate the deposition of each of the associated remains within this process. In primary deposits, most objects are deposited between the time of corpse preparation and the time of burial. It is important to try to reconstruct the actions related to such deposits because they may correspond to different stages in the funerary rites (preparation of the body, public display, closing of the grave, and so on) (Figure 22.4). This observation must also be extended to the entire 'funerary time', especially where bones are manipulated or secondary deposits made (not discussed here). The relative importance assigned to any of these points in time provides a means of interpreting the implicit social meaning that can be perceived through the funerary rites. Allowance must be made, of course, for the fact that archaeological remains preserve only some of the gestures, meaning consideration of plausible scenarios for want of certainty about them.

For historic periods, for example, the first accessible stage is that from the beginning of the funerary ceremony, when the individual has become a corpse that is the subject of care, with a view to potential presentation to the group of which the individual was part. This 'final farewell' is a key moment of interaction between the deceased and what the group wishes to show. It crystallises emotions and symbolic gestures and provides insight into the identities and strategies of a community. The objects involved in the preparation of the body are set out, namely the various items of clothing (or coverings such as shrouds) and the adornments- in short, everything that is found nearest the body of the deceased. The body is often prepared for laying-out, where being in public view is a matter of importance: this is the substrate for interpretations of the social status of the deceased and the relationship with the body that is specific to each society. This raises questions about the visibility of certain parts of the body and the enhancement of them. For elite female graves in the Early Middle Ages, much of their finery was concentrated around the shoulders and head (necklaces, earrings, brooches, veils, pins) and some texts confirm that the dead were laid out with the face visible (Cartron and Castex, 2016).

While assemblages of adornments and dress accessories raise the issue of the social status of the deceased within the community, the status of each element should also be considered individually. Neither adornments nor dress accessories should be systematically perceived as possessions of the deceased (see above). They may have been chosen as being meaningful to the group, leading archaeologists to ponder the value of the objects and their significance for the creation of memory. These objects may have had various origins and may have been contributed at different times during the funerary ceremony. It is conceivable that objects might have been set beside the deceased when laid out and then buried with them in the grave. They may be objects that belonged to the deceased, or those of their kin, their community, and they may also have been gifts or part of commemorative rituals such as banquets. It is essential, therefore, to think about how the objects were set out in the grave (hard against the body, near it, on the lid of the container, in a funerary chamber, and before or after the grave was sealed (see above)).

The status and functions of associated remains

All associated remains discovered in a grave may be interpreted in their own right. Attention was long focussed on the function of each one, especially when they are artefacts. As a result of the many debates of the 1990s (cf. Gardin and Peebles, 1992; Cauvin, 1997), the need to consider symbolic functions has gradually been acknowledged, but the backlog in this area is substantial. The question arising is whether or not the symbolic or cultic sphere has a clearly identifiable repertoire and a space specific to it, or if such manifestations are to be found in domestic contexts as much as in funerary ones. Some studies conclude that there are no associated remains intended specifically for funerary purposes before the Iron Age (Bailly and Plisson, 2008), while others argue a uniquely funerary function was already apparent in earlier periods. This is the case, for instance, of the boar teeth found in graves of the Neolithic Cerny Culture (Sidéra, 1997: 502). In research on lithic artefacts unearthed in Neolithic graves in Bulgaria, (Gurova, 2008) has suggested that understanding and interpreting the dichotomy 'sacred versus profane and domestic' involves looking beyond such items as having just one function: 'They call for an in-depth, systematic and contextual approach showing the relationship between all material items in order to explore the semiological system to which they refer' (*'Elles exigent une approche approfondie, systématique et contextuelle montrant la relation entre tous les éléments du mobilier afin d'explorer le système sémiologique auquel elles se réfèrent'*) (Gurova, 2008: 133). Grinding stones, for example, are typically objects that connect economic and symbolic spheres of the *Impresso-Cardial* Early Neolithic societies. Grinding stones are found in domestic contexts, for crushing plant or mineral substances, as well as in symbolic contexts in the form of placed deposits. In funerary contexts, they may be found under the deceased's head or by their side. Grinding stones are sometimes fragmented and seemingly intentionally broken (Grifoni Cremonesi, 2006, 2007). In such instances, it might mean that the object had to have been altered for the transition from one sphere to another. Use-wear analyses are of great help in reconstructing the 'biography' of these objects by showing wear and re-use (e.g. Gibaja, 2002; Vanhaeren and D'Errico, 2003; Slimak and Plisson, 2008; Bonnardin, 2009; Rigaud, 2013).

For historic periods, the question of the variation in function or the multiple functions of one and the same object has only recently arisen. It is research into social anthropology that has opened up new intellectual fields with which archaeologists have not yet completely come to grips (Bailly and Plisson, 2008; Watteau, Perlès and Soulier, 2011). Since the 2000s, socio-cultural anthropologists have emphasised that each thing has a social life, a career while adopting the concept of 'object biography' used by Kopytoff (1986). Each object has a specific history that it is important to take into account. Its itinerary begins with stages related to its manufacture, but then the object 'passes through separate spheres of exchange where it alternates between the status of merchandise and the status of a unique object' (*'traverse des sphères d'échange distinctes où il se trouve balancé entre le statut de marchandise et celui d'objet singulier'*) (Bonnot, 2002: 5). Any attempt to establish the biography of an archaeological object amounts, then, to studying its uniqueness and its journey.

Novel interpretations are then possible with respect to the value and their influence on social memory of the objects unearthed in graves. For all periods, some objects show evidence of repair, wear and incompleteness. Where once these attributes were dismissed or overlooked, today, on the contrary, such characteristics are seen to have an importance for the creation of social memory (Cartron and Castex, 2011). This is particularly the case for items of finery, such as rings in the Early Middle Ages (Renou, 2018) and for Iron Age weapons (Bertaud, 2017). Interpreting the status of each associated item invariably reflects the status of the deceased and their multiple social *personas*.

Prestigious remains

Funerary practices have always provided privileged insights, used more or less successfully, with which to define the status of individuals and, in broader terms, the social organisation of past social groups. Generally, rather crude parallels are drawn between the simplicity and complexity of the grave and the wealth or poverty of the individual and the equal or unequal nature of the society. The idea of 'prestige goods' has often been discussed whatever the period in question. For some 15 years, this concept has been repeatedly challenged. For prehistoric periods, the notion is a fuzzy one, and it is unsatisfactory to base the estimation of wealth in the Neolithic on the number of objects (Chambon, 2006). The criteria defining 'prestige objects' are often haphazard and the only reliable features seem to be the exotic character of the materials used, the level of investment in their manufacture, and, above all, their inutility (Salanova, 1998). For the Occidental Middle Ages, other criteria contribute to the prestige of graves, such as their location near to or inside a church (Alduc-Le-Bagousse, 2009). The absence of valuable items may be driven by the humility of a good Christian. A saint or abbess, like Gertrude of Nivelles in the seventh century AD, who may have been buried with few associated remains yet still belonged to the social elite (Treffort, 1997).

In some periods, associated remains are indeed scarce. This is almost systematically interpreted as a sign of poverty of the buried individual or even reflects the egalitarian nature of the society. For example, for the Early Neolithic in the northwestern Mediterranean area, the scarcity or absence of associated remains has often been observed, to the extent that this is considered a criterion of uniform funerary practices (Zemour, 2013). The scarcity of non-perishable remains associated with the dead is beyond debate: 27% of individuals have such associated remains, 73% have none, or at least none that can be reliably identified as such (Zemour, 2013). Sometimes, few remains are deposited alongside the deceased or are worn by them. For example, the 'trench C' Impressa/dipinta bande rosse grave from Ripa Tetta (Puglia, Italy) (Tozzi, 2002) contained only an obsidian blade from Lipari, a location at some distance, on the opposite coast of the Italian peninsula from the grave-site. Several studies have described obsidian as a (raw) material with a fundamental role in farming and herding societies (Hallam, Warren and Renfrew, 1976; Radi and Bovenzi, 2007; Nicod *et al.*, 2019). Given the remoteness of the sources and the small quantities transported, the very presence of obsidian must be connected with social representation, in other words, with 'prestige' (Binder and Courtin, 1994: 311). This example indicates that it is not because associated remains are not abundant that they are worthless. Sometimes, the deceased seems to have been placed in the grave without any objects whatsoever. This is the case for a post-Cardial Ware grave at La Vésignié (Rhône Alpes, France) (Gilles *et al.*, 1989). The hyperflexion of the upper and lower limbs combined with other taphonomic evidence and the small size of the burial pit suggest the individual had been bound. The rock shelter of La Vésignié was clearly not a settlement site, and its location suggests it was remote from any such place. Bindings might have facilitated the transport of the body. Ultimately, the scarcity or absence of associated remains does not systematically attest to the absence of funerary gestures/actions or to the simplicity of the burial, as has often been argued. It is rather an indication of the variety and diversity of funerary actions and of burial context. Associated remains may appear 'wanting' but be of great value with regard to the symbolic system of the groups in question. The absence of associated remains may be just as much a cultural choice – a lack of offerings – as much as an indication of the material conditions of burial being incompatible with the action of offering (Zemour, 2013). All told, it is a contextual and a multi-scalar approach – considering the grave, the site and the region – that makes it possible to interpret the presence or absence of associated remains in social terms. For example, the growing scarcity of remains associated with the deceased at the end of the Early Middle Ages is related to several factors: economic (objects were bequeathed to the living rather than deposited with the deceased), religious (humbleness before God) and social (Cartron, 2018).

This discussion of the *persona* of the deceased cannot be complete without broaching the role played by associated remains in ascribing gender. Associated remains have for long been used when determining the sex of the deceased, especially when observations of skeletal remains prove inadequate, which has given rise to misinterpretations. Without going into detail on this subject, which deserves an article in its own right, it seems important to evoke the far-reaching renewal underway in this domain. In conjunction with the emergence of research on gender in the social sciences, attempts are now made to identify the 'gender' of associated remains, the biological sex of individuals and also to take account of other variables (such as age-at-death, social status, and so on). The point is 'to go beyond the use of the variables of chronological age and anatomical sex as units of analysis and to understand them archaeologically as a process (engendering). This term refers to the way men and women learn socially appropriate behaviour throughout the course of their lives' ('*dépasser l'utilisation des variables de l'âge chronologique et du sexe anatomique comme unités d'analyse et de les appréhender du point de vue archéologique en tant que processus (engendering). Ce terme fait référence à l'apprentissage du comportement socialement approprié pour les hommes et les femmes tout au long de leur vie*') (Belard, 2015). In this respect, the work by Duboscq (2017) seems exemplary, especially with regard to the methods employed. Based on a multi-disciplinary analysis of remains associated with the dead in Middle Neolithic graves in northeastern Spain, this study seeks to identify the position of women in this chrono-cultural context and to assess the classic hypothesis of a hierarchical society. By examining social structure by way of biological identity and gender, this study successfully documents the nature and the workings of inequalities in which gender, ultimately, does not seem to play a predominant part.

Conclusions and future prospects

Although not exhaustive, this overview highlights the potential of analyses relating to associated remains that have barely begun to be exploited, for example, the nature of these associations and their relationships with the deceased. This contribution shows that it is worthwhile making systematic use of a multi-disciplinary analytical protocol in excavation and, *a posteriori,* on pre-viously excavated assemblages. More specifically, it is necessary to really consider perishable or fleeting remains, pigments, charcoal, ash and pollen, for example, by combining the analysis of the position of skeletal remains with physico-chemical and botanical analyses of residues and sediments. This will make it more feasible to identify perishable furnishings associated with graves, such as rigid or flexible containers, winding cloths, coffins and couches.

It is essential to identify the nature and relative position of remains with respect to each other and to the skeleton in order to reconstruct as precisely as possible the funerary process and the status of each stage within this process and the part they played in the funerary ceremony. Investigating remains associated with the deceased therefore entails identifying what items were interred with the body of the deceased, what was involved in the funerary process, what was connected with the circumstances in which the funerary process unfolded, and what pertained to the ideology, or to the ideals of the ideology to be sustained (Zemour, 2013). Taphonomic analysis plays a major part in this type of enquiry, and the archaeological sciences are a valuable complement to it. Innovations such as 3D recording and modelling also serve as a major medium for taphonomic analysis, especially when it comes to better identifying the former presence of perishable items. It is, therefore, possible and desirable to make 3D modelling a tool for identifying burial gestures/actions and for as a means to aid taphonomic analysis (cf. Sachau-Carcel, Chapter 31, this volume). While it is often stated that those objects that remain at excavation are the only items that survived taphonomic processes, it seems that today, archaeothanatology provides a means of reconstructing a great many of the items that have since vanished.

Today, the interpretations of remains associated with the deceased have become more varied. The idea of 'multiple personas', which developed in the English-language literature, means each item can be assessed as a marker meant for a specific purpose. Accordingly, the social interpretation of the various remains associated with one and the same grave may make reference to many issues, gender, memory, beliefs and also the position of the deceased within the community. It is a matter of adjusting the focus to what is to be interpreted while making allowance for each socio-cultural context.

Acknowledgements

The text was translated from the French by Christopher Sutcliffe. Aurélie Zemour's participation in this chapter was financed by a grant from the French State under the auspices of the LabEx Sciences Archéologiques de Bordeaux (ANR-10-LABX-52).

References

Alduc-Le-Bagousse, A., ed. (2009). *Inhumations de prestige ou prestige des inhumations? Expression du pouvoir dans l'Au-delà (IV e–XV e siècles): actes de la table ronde cinquantenaire du Centre de Recherches Archéologiques et Historiques Anciennes et Médiévales (CRAHM), Université de Caen, 23–24 mars 2007.* Caen: Université de Caen.

Alfaro, C., Brun, J.-P., Borgard, P. and Pierobon Benoit, R. (2011). *Purpureae Vestes III. Textiles y tintes en la ciudad Antigua.* Valencia: Universitat de Valencia.

Argant J., Boucher, C., Frère, D., Garnier, N., Gillet, B., Hänni, C., Lacroix, S., Leroy-Langelin, E. and Louis, E., (2012). De la Fouille au Laboratoire: Analyses et Interprétations des Contenus de Céramiques et Verres Archéologiques. *Revue du Nord*, 17, pp. 479–504.

Bailly, M. and Plisson, H. (2008). La Valeur Fonctionnelle des Objets Sépulcraux. Actes de la Table Ronde d'Aix-en-Provence, 25–27 Octobre 2006, *Préhistoire Anthropologie Méditerranéennes*, 14, pp. 205–208.

Belard, C. (2015). La Notion de Genre ou Comment Problématiser l'Archéologie Funéraire. *Nouvelles de l'Archéologie, Archéologie du Genre*, 14, pp. 23–27.

Bender-Jorgensen, L. (1988). A Coptic Tapestry from the Frankish Boy's Grave from Cologne Cathedral. In: L. Bender-Jorgensen, B. Magnus E. and Munksgaard, eds., *Archaeological Textiles. Arkaeologiske Skrifter 2, North European Symposium for Archaeological Textiles, Copenhagen, 1–4 May 1984.* Copenhagen: Copenhagen University, pp. 126–132.

Bertaud, A. (2017). Iron Age weapons in Western Europe: from the biography of a weapon to the warrior's interactions during the last centuries BC. In: A. Gorgues, K. Rebay-Salisbury and R. B. Salisbury, eds., *Material Chains in Late Prehistoric Europe and the Mediterranean: Time, Space and Technologies of Production.* Bordeaux: Éditions Ausonius, pp. 183–194.

Binder, D. and Courtin, J. (1994). Un Point sur la Circulation de l'Obsidienne dans le Domaine Provençal. *Gallia Préhistoire*, 36, pp. 310–322.

Binford, L.R. (1971). Mortuary practices: their study and their potential. In: J.A. Brown, ed., *Approaches to the Social Dimensions of Mortuary Practices.* Washington: Society for American Archaeology, pp. 6–29.

Bizot, B. and Signoli, M., eds. (2009). *Rencontre autour des sépultures habillées. Actes de la rencontre de Carry-le-Rouet, 13–14 novembre 2008*. Gap: Éditions des Hautes Alpes.

Blaizot, F. (2018). Tradition and innovation. Burial during late Antiquity in eastern central Gaul. In: M.-D. Nenna, S. Hubert and W. Van Andringa, eds., *Constituer la Tombe, Honorer les Défunts en Méditerranée Antique*, Alexandria : Centre d'Études Alexandrines, pp. 487–542.

Böhner, K. (1978). Das Römisch-Germanische Zentralmuseum – eine vaterländische und gelehrte Gründung des 19 Jahrhunderts. *Jahrbuch des Römisch-Germanischen Zentralmuseums Mainz*, 25, pp. 1–48.

Bonnabel, L. and Carré, F., eds. (1996). *Rencontre autour du linceul*. Bulletin de Liaison du GAAFIF (Groupe d'Anthropologie et Archéologie Funéraire en Île de France), Reims: GAAFIF

Bonnardin, S. (2009). La Parure Funéraire au Néolithique Ancien dans les Bassins Parisien et Rhénan. Rubané, Hinkelstein et Villeneuve-Saint-Germain. *Société Préhistorique Française*, 48, pp. 301–312.

Bonnot, T. (2002). *La Vie des Objets*. Paris: Éditions de la Maison des Sciences de l'Homme.

Boyer, R., Arnaud, G., Fattori, Y. and Perrot-Vial, R. (1987). *Vie et mort à Marseille à la fin de l'Antiquité: inhumations habillées des Ve et VIe siècles et sarcophage reliquaire trouvés à l'Abbaye de Saint-Victor*. Marseille: Atelier du Patrimoine.

Brettell, R.C., Schotsmans, E.M.J., Walton Rogers, P., Reifarth, N., Redfern, R., Stern, B. and Heron, C.P. (2015). 'Choicest Unguents': Molecular Evidence for the Use of Resinous Plant Exudates in Late Roman Mortuary Rites in Britain. *Journal of Archaeological Science*, 53, pp. 639–648.

Brettell, R.C., Stern, B., Reifarth, N. and Heron, C. (2014). The 'Semblance of Immortality'? Resinous Materials and Mortuary Rites in Roman Britain. *Archaeometry*, 56, 3, pp. 444–459.

Brulet, R. (2016). Childéric (tombe de). In: B. Dumézil, ed., *Les Barbares*, Paris: Presses Universitaires de France (PUF), pp. 374–376.

Bui, T.M. and Girard, M. (2003). Pollens, Ultimes Indices de Pratiques Funéraires Évanouies. *Revue Archéologique de Picardie. Numéro spécial 21, Sens dessus dessous. la recherche du sens en préhistoire. recueil d'études offert à Jean Leclerc et Claude Masset*, pp. 127–137.

Cardon, D. and Feugère, M., eds. (2000). *Archéologie des Textiles, des Origines au ve Siècle*, Actes du Colloque de Lattes, Octobre 1999, Monographies Instrumentum, 14, Montagnac: Éditions Monique Mergoil.

Carré, F., Rast-Eicher, A., Bell, B. and Boisson, J. (2018). L'Étude des Matériaux Organiques dans les Tombes du Haut Moyen Âge (France, Suisse et Allemagne occidentale): Un Apport Majeur à la Connaissance des Pratiques Funéraires et du Vêtement. *Archéologie Médiévale*, 48, pp. 37–99.

Cartron, I. (2015). Variations autour d'un objet: la ceinture des femmes du haut Moyen Âge. In: L. Jégou, S. Joye, T. Lienhard and J. Schneider, eds., *Splendor Reginae. Passions, Genre et Famille, Mélanges en l'Honneur de Régine Le Jan*, Turnhout: Brepols, pp. 129–138.

Cartron, I. (2018). Ostentation ou humilité? Réflexions autour du vêtement du défunt et du dépôt d'objets dans les tombes au cours du haut Moyen Age. *Les Vivants et les Morts dans les Sociétés Médiévales, Actes du Colloque de la Sociéte des Historiens Médiévistes de l'Enseignement Supérieur Public (SHMESP), Jérusalem, mai 2017*, 48, Paris: Éditions de la Sorbonne, pp. 205–216.

Cartron, I. and Castex, D. (2011). La bague de la 'dame de Jau' (Aquitaine, Médoc): à propos de la mémoire familiale et du dépôt d'objets précieux dans les sépultures du haut Moyen Age. In: F. Watteau, C. Perles and P. Soulier, eds., *Profils d'Objets. Approches d'Anthropologues et d'Archéologues*, Paris: Maison René Ginouvès, 7, pp. 23–32.

Cartron, I. and Castex, D. (2016). L'archéologie face à la restitution des funérailles et à la mémoire de la tombe: à propos de quelques cas aquitains du haut Moyen Age. In: M. Lauwers and A. Zemour eds., *Qu'est-ce Qu'une Sépulture? Humanités et Systèmes Funéraires de la Préhistoire à nos Jours, Actes du Colloque des Rencontres d'Antibes*, Antibes: Éditions de l'Association pour la Promotion et la Diffusion des Connaissances Archéologiques (APDCA), pp. 399–412.

Cauvin, J. (1997). *Naissance des divinités, naissance de l'agriculture: la révolution des symboles au Néolithique*. Paris: Centre National de la Recherche Scientifique (CNRS).

Chambon, P. (2006). Des morts aux vivants: population et société au Néolithique. In: J. Guilaine, ed., *Séminaires du Collège de France, Populations Néolithiques et Environnements*. Paris: Érrance Collection des Hespérides, pp. 23–40.

Chambon, P. and Augereau, A. (2009). Le mobilier en contexte funéraire chasséen dans le Bassin parisien. In: D. Fabre, ed., *De Méditerranée et d'ailleurs … Mélanges Offerts à Jean Guilaine*. Toulouse: *Archives d'Écologie Préhistorique*, pp. 195–207.

Chambon, P. and Thévenet, C. (2016). Transporter et Installer le Corps dans sa Dernière Demeure: Les Premiers Contenants Mobiles du Néolithique Européen (Bassin Parisien et Plaine du Rhin supérieur, Ve millénaire). *Bulletins et Mémoires de la Société d'Anthropologie de Paris*, 28, pp. 24–31.

Clop, X. (2008). Céramique, fonctionnalité et dépôts funéraires. Quelques données, quelques réflexions. In: M. Bailly and H. Plisson, eds., *La Valeur Fonctionnelle des Objets Sépulcraux, Actes de la Table Ronde d'Aix-en-Provence, 25–27 Octobre 2006*, Préhistoire Anthropologie Méditerranéennes, 14, pp. 121–134.

Corbineau, R. (2014). *Pour une archéobotanique funéraire: enquêtes interdisciplinaires et analyses polliniques autour de la tombe et du corps mort (ère chrétienne, France – Italie)*, Unpublished Ph.D. Thesis, Université du Maine, France.

Corbineau, R. (2017). La mort au microscope: préambule pour les archéosciences funéraires. In: S. De Larminat, R. Corbineau, A. Corrochano, Y. Gleize and J. Soulat, eds., *Rencontre Autour de Nouvelles Approches de l'Archéologie Funéraire*. Reugny: Groupe d'Anthropologie et d'Archéologie Funéraire (*GAAF*), pp. 163–165.

Desrosiers, S. (2000). Textiles découverts dans deux tombes du Bas-Empire à Naintré (Vienne). In: D. Cardon and M. Feugère eds., *Archéologie des Textiles, des Origines au ve Siècle, Actes du Colloque de Lattes, Octobre 1999*, Montagnac: Éditions Monique Mergoil, Monographies Instrumentum, 14, pp. 195–207.

Devièse, T., Vanhove, C., Blanchard, P., Colombini, M.P., Regert, M. and Castex, D. (2010). Détermination et fonction des substances organiques et des matières minérales exploitées dans les rites funéraires de la catacombe des Saints Pierre-et-Marcellin à Rome (I–III siècle). In: I. Cartron, D. Castex, P. Georges, M. Vivas and M. Charageat, eds., *De Corps en Corps. Traitement et Devenir du Cadavre*, Pessac: Maison des Sciences de L'Homme d'Aquitaine, pp. 115–139.

Duboscq, S. (2017). *Caracterización de las relaciones sociales de las comunidades del Nor-este de la Península Ibérica entre la segunda mitad del V y la segunda mitad del IV milenio cal BC a partir del estudio de las prácticas funerarias*. Unpublished Ph.D. thesis, Universitat Autònoma de Barcelona.

Duday, H., Courtaud, P., Crubézy, E., Sellier, P. and Tillier, A.-M. (1990). L'anthropologie 'de terrain': reconnaissance et interprétation des gestes funéraires. *Bulletins et Mémoires de la Société d'Anthropologie de Paris*, 3–4, pp. 29–50.

Edwards, H.G.M. and Chalmers, J.M. (2005). *Raman spectroscopy in archaeology and art history*. Cambridge: The Royal Society of Chemistry.

Eerkens, J.W. (2005). GC-MS Analysis and Fatty Acid Ratios of Archaeological Potsherds from the Western Great Basin of North America. *Archaeometry*, 47, pp. 83–102.

Evershed, R.P. (2008). Organic Residue Analysis in Archaeology: The Archaeological Biomarker Revolution. *Archaeometry*, 50, pp. 895–924.

Fleury, M. and France-Lanord, A. (1998). *Les trésors mérovingiens de la Basilique de Saint-Denis*, Woippy: Gérard Klopp.

Frère, D. and Hugot, L., eds. (2012). *Les huiles parfumées en Méditerranée occidentale et en Gaule, VIIIe siècle av. VIIIe siècle apr. J.-C.* Rennes: Presses Universitaires de Rennes.

Gardin, J.-C. and Peebles, C.S. (1992). *Representations in archaeology*. Bloomington, IN: Indiana University Press.

Gibaja, F. (2002). *La función de los instrumentos líticos como medio de aproximación socioeconómica. Comunidades del V–IV milenio cal. BC en el noreste de la Península Ibérica*. Unpublished Ph.D. Thesis, Universitat Autònoma de Barcelona.

Gilles, R., Beaume, C., Gely, B. and Porte, J.-L. (1989). La sépulture de l'abri de la Vésignié à Saint-Marcel d'Ardèche. In: E. Mahieu, ed., *Anthropologie Préhistorique: Résultats et Tendances, Actes du Colloque de Sarrians, 2 au 4 Septembre 1989*. Sarrians: Études et Perspectives Archéologiques, pp. 27–36.

Gleize, Y. (2012). Des aménagements en bois dans les sarcophages? Réflexions sur deux exemples du haut Moyen Age. In: F. Carré and F. Henrion, eds., *Le Bois dans l'Architecture et l'Aménagement de la Tombe: Quelles Approches? Auxerre: Association Française d'Archéologie Mérovingienne*, pp. 335–339.

Grifoni Cremonesi, R. (2006). Sepolture e rituali funerari nel neolitico in italia. In: F. Martini ed., *La Cultura del Morire nelle Società Preistoriche e Protostoriche Italiane: Studio Interdisciplinare dei Dati e loro Trattamento Informatico dal Paleolitico all'età del Rame*. Firenze: Istituto Italiano di Preistoria e Protostoria, pp. 87–107.

Grifoni Cremonesi, R. (2007). Notes on Some Cultic Aspects of Italian Prehistory. *Documenta Praehistorica*, XXXIV, pp. 221–230.

Grifoni Cremonesi, R. and Radmilli, A. M. (2000–2001). La Grotta Patrizi al Sasso di Furbara (Cerveteri, Roma). *Bullettino di Paletnologia Italiana*, 91–92, pp. 63–120.

Gurova, M. (2008). Connotation fonctionnelle du mobilier funéraire en silex. Exemple de la Bulgarie. In: M. Bailly and H. Plisson, eds., *La Valeur Fonctionnelle des Objets Sépulcraux,*. Aix-en-Provence : Préhistoire Anthropologie Méditerranéennes (APPAM), 14, pp. 121–134.

Hallam, B., Warren, S. and Renfrew, C. (1976). Obsidian in the Western Mediterranean: Characterisation by Neutron Activation Analysis and Optical Emission Spectroscopy. *Proceedings of the Prehistoric Society*, 42, pp. 85–110.

Heron, C., Andernen, S., Fischer, A., Glykou, A., Hartz, S., Saul, H., Steele, V. and Craig, O. (2013). Illuminating the Late Mesolithic: Residue Analysis of 'Blubber' Lamps from Northern Europe. *Antiquity*, 87, pp. 178–188.

Kazanski, M. and Périn, P. (1988). Le Mobilier Funéraire de la Tombe de Childéric Ier. État de la Question et Perspectives. *Revue Archéologique de Picardie*, 3–4, pp. 13–38.

Knüsel, C.J. (2006). 'Of no more use to men than in ages before?': the Investiture Contest as a model for funerary interpretation. In: R. Gowland and C.J. Knüsel, eds., *Social Archaeology of Funerary Remains*. Oxford: Oxbow Books, pp. 209–223.

Kopytoff, A. (1986). The cultural biography of things: commoditization as process. In: A. Appadurai, ed., *The Social Life of Things: Commodities in Cultural Perspective*, Cambridge: Cambridge University Press, pp. 64–90.

Legendre, J.-P., Olivier, L., Schnitzler, D. and Lindenberg, D., eds. (2007). *L'Archéologie Nationale-Socialiste dans les Pays Occupés à l'Ouest du Reich, Actes de la Table-Ronde Internationale 'Blud und Boden' Tenue à Lyon dans le Cadre du xe Congrès de la 'European Association of Archaeologists (EAA)' les 8 et 9 Septembre 2004*, Gollion, CH: Infolio Éditions.

Leroi-Gourhan, A. (1968). Le Néanderthalien IV de Shanidar. *Bulletin de la Société Préhistorique Française. Comptes Rendus des Séances Mensuelles*, 65(3), pp. 79–83.

Maffre, J.-J., Frère, D., Garnier, N. and Dodinet, E. (2013). Vases à Parfum de la fin de l'Époque Classique Mis au Jour à Appolonia de Cyrénaïque: Les Analyses de Contenus. *Revue Archéologique*, 55, pp. 57–80.

Médard, F. and Moulhérat C. (2008). Les textiles mérovingiens: état des recherches et nouvelles perspectives. In: J. Guillaume and É. Peytremann, eds., *L'Austrasie. Sociétés, Économies, Territoires, Christianisation, Actes des XXVIe Journées Internationales d'Archéologie Mérovingienne, Nancy, 22–25 Septembre 2005*. Saint-Germain- en-Laye: Association Française d'Archéologie Mérovingienne, Nancy, pp. 123–132.

Nicod, P.Y., Perrin, T., Le Bourdonnec, F.X., Philibert, S., Oberlin, C. and Besse, M. (2019). First Obsidian in the Northern French Alps during the Early Neolithic. *Journal of Field Archaeology*, 44 (3), pp. 180–194.

O'Shea, J.M. (1984). *Mortuary variability: an archaeological investigation*. New York: Academic Press.

Pereira, G. (2013). Introduction. In: G. Pereira, ed., *Une Archéologie des Temps Funéraires? Hommage à Jean Leclerc, Les Dossiers de l'Archéologie*, 132, pp. 3–7.

Périn, P. (2015). Portrait Posthume d'une Reine Mérovingienne. Arégonde († c.580), Épouse de Clotaire Ier († 561) et Mère de Chilpéric Ier († 584). *Le Corti nell'alto Medioevo: Spoleto, 24–29 aprile 2014*, Spoleto: Fondazione Centro Italiano di Studi sull'Alto Medioevo, 62, pp. 1001–1048.

Pollard, M., Batt, C.M., Stern, B. and Young, S.M.M. (2007). *Analytical chemistry in archaeology*. Cambridge: Cambridge University Press.

Radi, G. (2002). Torre Sabea. M.A. Fugazzola Delpino, A. Pessina and V. Tiné, eds., *Le ceramiche impresse nel Neolitico Antico. Italia e Mediterraneo*, Roma: Istituto Poligrafico e Zecca dello Stato, pp. 651–658.

Radi, G. and Bovenzi, G. (2007). La circolazione dell'ossidiana nell'area Alto Tirrenica. In: C. Tozzi and M.C. Weiss, eds., *Préhistoire et Protohistoire de l'Aire Tyrrhénienne*. Ghezzano: Felici Editore: pp. 209–216.

Rast-Eicher, A. (2010). Garments for a queen. In: E. Andersson Strand, M. Gleba, U. Mannering, C. Munkholt and M. Ringgaard, eds., *North European Symposium for Archaeological Textiles X, 10e symposium North Europea Symposium for Archaeological Textiles, May 2008, Copenhagen*, Oxford: Oxbow Books, Series: Ancient Textiles, 5, pp. 208–210.

Renou, J. (2018). *Le pouvoir des anneaux: essais sur la parure digitale du haut Moyen Age. Approche archéologique des objets du sud-ouest de la Gaule*, Unpublished Ph.D. thesis, Université de Bordeaux-Montaigne.

Ricci, P., Mongelli, V., Vitiello, A., Campana, S., Sirignano, C., Rubino, M., Fornaciari, G. and Lubritto, C. (2012). The Privileged Burial of the Pava Pieve (Siena, 8th Century AD). *Rapid Communications in Mass Spectrometry*, 26, pp. 2393–2398.

Rigaud, S. (2013). Les Objets de Parure Associés au Dépôt Funéraire Mésolithique de Große Ofnet (Allemagne): Implications pour la Compréhension de l'Organisation Sociale des Dernières Sociétés Mésolithiques du Jura Souabe. *Anthropozoologica*, 48: pp. 207–230.

Salanova, L. (1998). Le Statut des Assemblages Campaniformes en Contexte Funéraire: La Notion de Bien de Prestige. *Bulletin de la Société Préhistorique Française*, 95(3), pp. 315–326.

Santinelli, E. (2014). Funérailles masculines, funérailles féminines: rituels communs et pratiques sexuées au haut Moyen Age. In: D. Boyer-Gardner and M. Vivas, eds., *Déplacer les Morts. Voyages, Funérailles, Manipulations, Exhumations et Réinhumations de Corps au Moyen Age*, Bordeaux: Thanat'Os, 2: pp. 13–36.

Schnapp, A. (2012). La Crise de l'Archéologie, de ses Lointaines Origines à Aujourd'hui. *Les Nouvelles de l'Archéologie*, 128, pp. 3–6.

Schotsmans, E.M.J., Toksoy-Köksal, F., Brettell, R.C., Bessou, M., Corbineau, R., Lingle, A.M., Castex, D., Knüsel, C.J., Wilson, A.S., Bouquin, D., Blanchard, P., Becker, K. and Chapoulie, R. (2019) 'Not All that is White is Lime' – White Substances from Archaeological Burial Contexts: Analyses and Interpretations. *Archaeometry*, 61, pp. 809–827.

Ségard, M. (2017). Le mausolée antique de Jaunay-Clan (Vienne): protocole d'étude de sépultures en milieu clos. In: S. De Larminat, R. Corbineau, A. Corrochano, Y. Gleize and J. Soulat, eds., *Rencontre autour de Nouvelles Approches de l'Archéologie Funéraire (GAAF 2014)*. Reugny: Publication du Groupe d'Anthropologie et d'Archéologie Funéraire (GAAF), 6, pp. 195–199.

Sepúlveda, M., Rousseliere, H., Van Elslande, E., Arriaza, B., Standen, V, Santoro, C.M. and Walter, P. (2014). Study of Color Pigments Associated to Archaic Chinchorro Mummies and Grave Goods in Northern Chile (7000–3500 B.P.). *Heritage Science*, 2, pp. 2–7.

Sidéra, I. (1997). Le mobilier en matières dures animales en milieu funéraire Cerny: symbolisme et socio-économie. In: C. Constantin, D. Mordant and D. Simonin, eds., *La Culture de Cerny. Nouvelle Économie, Nouvelle Société au Néolithique*, Actes du Colloque International (Nemours, 9–11 mai 1994), Nemours: Association pour la Promotion de la Recherche Archéologique en Ile-de-France (APRAIF), Mémoires du Musée de Préhistoire d'Ile-de-France, 6, pp. 499–513.

Slimak, L. and Plisson H. (2008). La sépulture paléolithique de l'enfant du Figuier (Ardèche, France), emboîtement d'une symbolique funéraire, In: M. Bailly and H. Plisson, eds., *La Valeur Fonctionnelle des Objets Sépulcraux*. Aix-en-Provence: Préhistoire Anthropologie Méditerranéennes (APPAM), 14, pp. 29–38.

Tiné, S. (1999). *Il Neolitico nella caverna delle Arene Candide (scavi 1972–1977)*. Collezione di monografie preistoriche ed archeologiche, 10, Bordighera, Genova, Istituto internazionale Studi Liguri; Istituto di Scienze Archeologiche.

Tozzi, C. (2002). Ripa Tetta. In: M.A. Fugazzola Delpino, A. Pessina and V. Tiné, eds., *Le Ceramiche Impresse nel Neolitico Antico: Italia e Mediterraneo*, Roma: Istituto Poligrafico e Zecca dello Stato, pp. 579–588.

Treffort, C. (1997). Sainte Gertrude de Nivelles. In: J.-P. Arrignon, B. Merdrignac and C. Treffort, eds., *Christianisme et Chrétientés en Occident et en Orient (Milieu VIIe–Milieu XIe Siècle)*, Paris: Ophrys, pp. 47–55.

Vanhaeren, M. and D'Errico. F. (2003). Le Mobilier Funéraire de la Dame de Saint-Germain-la-Rivière (Gironde) et l'Origine Paléolithique des Inégalités. *Paléo*, 15, pp. 195–238.

Watteau, F., Perlès, C. and Soulier, P. (2011). Profils d'objets. In: F. Watteau, ed., *Approches d'Anthropologues et d'Archéologues*. Paris: Maison René Ginouvès, pp. 307–316.

Weiner, S. (2010). *Microarchaeology. beyond the visible archaeological record*. Cambridge: Cambridge University Press.

Zemour, A. (2013). *Gestes, espaces et temps funéraires au début du Néolithique (6e millénaire et 1ère moitié du 5e millénaire cal. BC) en Italie et en France Méridionale. reconnaissance des témoins archéologiques de l'après-mort*. Unpublished Ph.D. thesis, Universities of Nice-Sophia Antipolis and Roma-La Sapienza.

Zemour, A. (2016). De l'anthropologie de terrain à l'archéologie de la mort: histoire, concepts et développements. In: M. Lauwers and A. Zemour eds., *Qu'est-ce Qu'une Sépulture? Humanités et Systèmes Funéraires de la Préhistoire à nos Jours, Actes du Colloque des Rencontres d'Antibes*. Antibes: Éditions de l'Association pour la Promotion et la Diffusion des Connaissances Archéologiques (APDCA), pp. 23–34.

Zemour, A. (2019). Trepanation and (Ritual?) Perimortem Actions in the Neolithic Period at Grotta Patrizi. *International Journal of Osteoarcheology*, 30(1), pp. 80–89.

Zemour, A., Binder D., Bonnardin S., D'Ovidio A.-M., Goude G., Gourichon L., Pradeau J.-V., Sorin-Mazouni, S., Bromblet, P., Buchet, L., Cotto, K.-Y. and Sénépart, I. (2017). Laboratory Excavation of a Neolithic Grave from Avignon-La Balance-Ilot P (France): Burial Practices and Garment Reconstruction. *Journal of Field Archaeology*, 42(1), pp. 54–68.

23

AN ARCHAEOTHANATOLOGICAL APPROACH TO THE IDENTIFICATION OF LATE ANGLO-SAXON BURIALS IN WOODEN CONTAINERS

Emma C. Green

DEPARTMENT OF ARCHAEOLOGY, UNIVERSITY OF SHEFFIELD, SHEFFIELD, UNITED KINGDOM

Introduction

Excavations of graves dating to the Late Anglo-Saxon period (9th–11th centuries AD) across England reveal variation in burials within and between cemeteries. In particular, a variety of rigid containers for the body were used: wooden coffins made of planks, tree trunk coffins, wooden chests, stone cists, stone sarcophagi and graves lined with materials such as stone, tiles and wood. This archaeological data has enabled revision of long-held assumptions that Christian burials were simple and uniform (cf. Hadley, 2001, 2002; Cherryson, 2005; Buckberry, 2007) and identified an increasing trend of containing the corpse at burial throughout the early medieval period (Thompson, 2002: 232–238). Researchers have argued that patterns exist in coffin provision, for example, between age groups and sexes (cf. Craig and Buckberry, 2010; Mahoney Swales, 2012). However, containers made of wood decompose completely in most burial environments, rendering them archaeologically invisible and confounding attempts to explore their character or provision. Thus, attempts to assess the full significance and prevalence of a key burial practice employed during the Late Anglo-Saxon period have been prevented by the rare and differential survival of wooden containers in the archaeological record.

This chapter uses a retrospective archaeothanatological approach to identify burials in wooden containers in late Anglo-Saxon cemeteries. In archaeothanatology detailed analysis and interpretation of the spatial positioning of skeletal remains in the grave helps to reconstruct features of the original burial which have long since disappeared from the archaeological record, including whether a body was buried in a container or in direct contact with the earth. Human bone has the potential to survive in environments where wooden objects may not, therefore surviving in graves in which wooden containers are no longer discernible through preserved wood or metalwork. Despite its clear potential to enhance understanding of burial practices involving containers, the archaeothanatological approach has seldom been applied to late Anglo-Saxon burials in England. This has resulted in a situation where potentially

DOI: 10.4324/9781351030625-27

valuable evidence for burial practices continues to be overlooked and patterns in the provision of containers incorrectly identified.

Burial in the Late Anglo-Saxon period

Burial practices of the 9th to 11th centuries AD are differentiated from non-Christian and transitional practices of the previous centuries by a more structured burial layout in graveyards associated with churches, an overall decline in grave good provision, an apparent increase in the use of burial containers, the use of elements to support the corpse such as stones placed around the head, evidence for shrouds/wrappings and the introduction of above-ground grave markers (Gilchrist, 2014: 381). In the archaeological record of the Late Anglo-Saxon period, there is no evidence for the universal adoption of any one homogeneous form of funerary practice. Indeed, differences exist in the frequency and types of grave variation between cemeteries and over time.

The identification of burial variations and the extent of their provision has proved vital for studies of the Late Anglo-Saxon period. If, as funerary archaeologists argue, the practices which created the funerary record are intentional, then this variation is not random and must have meaning (Chapman and Randsborg, 2009: 2). The archaeological record identifies repeated patterns of behaviour – practices and rituals encoded in the physical funerary features – that provide insight into the interpretive framework of the beliefs in which they were enacted (Nilsson Stutz, 2010: 36). Burials have the potential to provide both direct and indirect evidence about the individual for whom they were created, the people who created them and the social context within which they were created. Important social and cultural transitions of the Late Anglo-Saxon period have been illuminated by funerary studies, for example, the impact of Christianity and links between burial practices and social status (cf. Hadley, 2000; Thompson, 2002; Hadley and Buckberry, 2005; Craig and Buckberry, 2010; Hadley, 2010; Mahoney Swales, 2012).

Nevertheless, research concerning funerary practices of the Late Anglo-Saxon period is limited by the visibility of archaeological evidence (Reynolds, 2009: 35). This presents a fundamental problem for the interpretation of variation in the archaeological burial record. If the frequency of wooden containers cannot be determined, how accurately can their use be explored, and the true meaning of their deployment understood? It is apparent that previous studies which sought to characterise burial variation in late Anglo-Saxon graves and go on to interpret this within the wider context of religious belief, status and other aspects of individual and group identity have assumed too readily that the archaeologically recoverable residues of burial variation provide an unambiguous reflection of the original form of graves. The possibility of elaborations or containers formed of organic materials that have long decayed is acknowledged (Buckberry, 2004: 172; Cherryson, 2005: 118–121) but rarely adequately accounted for in interpretations. The consensus has been to label a burial as 'plain earth', that is, a grave cut into the earth into which the corpse is directly deposited without any form of container, grave lining or embellishment, such as grave goods (Buckberry, 2004: 172), unless it can be demonstrated to have been otherwise. In most situations, the identification of so-called plain-earth burials is based solely on the lack of direct archaeological evidence for any form of elaboration of the grave, or grave furniture placed in the grave, thus potentially erroneous in any but the best conditions of preservation. Assertions that the principal funerary practice for the Late Anglo-Saxon period is plain-earth burial (Buckberry, 2004: 22; Cherryson, 2005: 91) are thus founded on problematic and insecure evidence.

There are reasons to hypothesise that many more individuals were interred in containers than has been previously identified. Coffins and other burial containers are frequently identified based on the remains of metal fittings such as nails, clasps, hinges and plates. However, excavations in waterlogged conditions as at Swinegate, York (UK), and St. Peter's Church, Barton-upon-Humber,

Lincolnshire (UK) have demonstrated, through exceptional organic preservation, that many containers were constructed entirely from wood, with wooden dowels replacing metal nails. In most soil types, this sort of wooden container would decompose completely, leaving no direct archaeological residues. Thus, so-called 'plain-earth graves' might be interpreted in a significantly different way as graves originally containing solely organic containers that have since decayed. Excavation reports show that direct evidence of wooden containers is not found in all graves at a site and is potentially absent across the entirety of the site. At sites where all burials appear to have been of a plain-earth type, such as George Street, Aylesbury, Buckinghamshire (UK) (Allen and Dalwood, 1983) and Templecombe, Somerset (UK) (Newman, 1992), it is not clear if the practice of using containers was perhaps not employed at all, or if local funerary practices favoured organic components over their metal alternatives.

The archaeothanatological approach

An archaeothanatological approach offers a means of obtaining the information necessary to overcome some of the interpretative problems identified here. Archaeothanatology can be used as a tool for the reconstruction of the original burial deposition by observing the final spatial configuration of the skeletal remains and their depositional environment, focussing on decomposition and disarticulation of the corpse (cf. Duday *et al.*, 1990; Duday, 2009). The transformation of a once-fleshed corpse into bones is the result of numerous inter-related natural and anthropogenic post-mortem and post-depositional processes which have been acting upon the corpse since the time of death. As a result, the positions of the remains observed upon excavation are unlikely to be a direct representation of the placement of the body at the time of burial (Knüsel, 2014: 27). Gravity, a constant factor, acts on the skeletal remains once they have been freed by decomposition; however, the form of a burial and its immediate environment will either restrict natural movements or provide empty spaces that facilitate displacement (Duday, 2009) (Table 23.1). As a consequence, variations in skeletal positioning enable inferences about the characteristics of the original burial environment. Thus, by understanding the post-mortem processes acting on the body, characterising their effects and differentiating among them, archaeothanatology aims to reveal features of the grave, lost since initial interment, from their impact on the body.

Archaeothanatology requires the recording of detailed observations of the spatial relationships between skeletal elements but also features such as the grave cut, and *in situ* locations of objects within the grave. Ideally, archaeothanatology should begin in the field, but retrospective retrieval of information from photographs and excavation documentation is becoming increasingly accepted (Nilsson Stutz, 2006: 218). While there may be some limitations to assessment post-excavation, importantly, it facilitates collection of data from previously excavated sites that would otherwise be irretrievable.

An archaeothanatological approach to the study of burial containers

The successful application of archaeothanatology relies on a sound understanding of how bodily position is altered in different funerary situations. Thus, Duday (2009: 154) notes that it is important to study burials of known form and context to gather data to support interpretations where possible. Importantly for this study, a small number of late Anglo-Saxon cemeteries have produced graves in which both wooden containers and the skeletal remains of the corpse survive in varying states of completeness. A sample of 78 burials was selected from five sites in the United Kingdom (Table 23.2) at which the presence of a wooden container could be confirmed (Table 23.3). These burials were analysed using archaeothanatological principles to explore and characterise the impact of burial in a container on the interred corpse and the resulting skeletal

Table 23.1 Types of voids and their impact on the decomposing corpse

Types of void	Characteristics	Skeletal outcome
Original external void – empty space	A delimited space forming a barrier between the corpse and the surrounding sediment present at the time of burial results in delayed in-filling of sediment into areas of decomposed soft tissue.	Bones will move under gravity into the available space from positions of instability until they achieve a stable position. Bones will move outside of the original soft tissue volume of the corpse.
Secondary external void	A void which is not present at the time of burial but is subsequently created during or after decomposition outside the original soft tissue volume, which results from delayed in-filling of sediment into the newly created void.	Bones will move under gravity into the available space from positions of instability until they achieve a stable position. Bone(s) move outside the original soft tissue volume of the corpse.
Secondary internal void	A void which is not present at the time of burial but is created by the decomposing soft tissue of the corpse. This results from delayed in-filling of sediment into areas of decomposed soft tissue caused by a barrier in contact with the corpse (barriers include durable clothing, shrouds or winding cloths) or from burial in coarse-grained sediment or in a rigid container.	Bones will move under gravity within the areas formerly containing soft tissue. There is no clear displacement of bones outside the original soft tissue volume of the corpse.
No voids – filled space	There are no barriers present (e.g. no rigid container, cover, or shroud) such that the corpse is in direct contact with fine-grained sediment, which results in progressive in-filling of sediment into areas of decomposing soft tissue.	There is lack of displacement such that bones are maintained in approximate anatomical connection and position.

Table 23.2 The five cemeteries used to develop the archaeothanatology-based method in this study

Site (UK)	Publication reference	Total number of burials	Number of confirmed coffined burials (Based on criteria in Table 23.3)
St Oswald's Gloucester, Gloucestershire	Heighway and Bryant (1999)	160	16
St. Peter's Barton-upon-Humber, Lincolnshire	Waldron (2007) Rodwell and Atkins (2011)	453	8
Staple Gardens Winchester, Hampshire	Youngs, Clarke and Barry (1986) Gaimster, Margeson and Hurley (1990) Not fully published to date. Data held by Hampshire Cultural Trust	285	5
Swinegate York, North Yorkshire	Pearson (1989, 1990) Not fully published to date. Data held at York Archaeological Trust	100	24
Worcester Cathedral, Worcester, Worcestershire	Guy (2010) Not fully published to date. Data held at Worcester Cathedral	181	25

Table 23.3 Criteria for identifying confirmed wooden containers

Evidence type	Justification for use as evidence of a container
Preservation of wood representing a base and/or a lid and one or more sides	The presence of sides indicates the burial was not on a bier or provided with only a cover. A container is indicated.
Stains from decomposed wood representing a base and/or lid and one or more sides and voids in the grave fill	Staining identified as the remains of wood and voids left by decomposed wood that has not been in-filled by the surrounding sediment is considered to be adequate evidence that a wooden structure once existed. The evidence for sides indicates the burial was not on a bier or provided with only a cover.
Stains from decomposed wood representing a base and/or lid or sides, in conjunction with a minimum of two *in situ* nails or fittings positioned to indicate the sides/lid of the coffin	Combined evidence of staining and nails/fittings indicates that an enclosed structure once existed.
Nails/fittings located in *in situ* positions	The nails/fittings should be positioned identifying the outline of the container.

positioning found upon excavation. The aim of this preliminary stage of analysis was to identify patterning in the skeletal observations which could be attributed to decomposition in a late Anglo-Saxon wooden container as opposed to other forms of burial practices or taphonomic processes.

While the characteristics of bodily position following decomposition in a wooden container could be studied directly, the opportunity to analyse definitive plain-earth burials from the Late Anglo-Saxon period as comparators is problematic. There are few situations where plain-earth burials can be confirmed from direct archaeological evidence alone, with the possible exception of burials where the grave cut was exceptionally narrow with no capacity for the inclusion of a wooden container. However, to use burials that have been determined to be 'plain-earth' based only on the lack of direct evidence for the presence of a container would create a circular argument – there can be no independent evidence for the absence of burial containers.

While analysis of the data showed that no single specific configuration of skeletal elements was observed in all 78 burials, a number of repeated patterns were identified consistently in the majority (Table 23.4). These will be discussed in turn.

Table 23.4 Key patterns in skeletal positioning identified in the 78 confirmed container burials

	Skeletal position	Taphonomic explanation
1	External displacement of skeletal elements	Original voids, external to the body volume, present at the start of decomposition of the body
2	Internal displacement of skeletal elements	Voids developed by the decomposition of the soft tissue of the corpse
3	Displacement of elements outside the coffin structure	Voids developed external to the body volume during or sometime after decomposition of the body
4	Support of appendicular skeletal elements in positions of potential instability	An object exerted lateral support
5	Linear alignment of displaced skeletal elements	A barrier had been present
6	Support of skeletal elements in positions of potential instability that cannot relate to the sides of the coffin	Use of shrouds or clothing

Evidence for displacement into primary external voids

The depositional environment within a rigid container is one where there is a delimited space around the corpse separating it from the surrounding sediment. The evidence for decomposition in a void was convincing for all 78 burials (78/78, 100%); all burials displayed external displacement of skeletal elements outside the perceived original space occupied by the corpse ('the body volume') that could only have occurred if there had been unfilled space around the body during decomposition. Skeletal elements left in unstable (unsupported) positions, once freed from articulation by decomposition, would be susceptible to movement under the force of gravity into voids surrounding the corpse (cf. Duday and Guillon, 2006: 138). This was evident in the coffined burials by external displacement of one or more skeletal elements in all 78 burials, especially the *ossa coxae*, mandible and cranium, and the bones of the ankles and feet, all of which would be in unstable (unsupported) positions in a supine corpse (Figures 23.1 and 23.2). Indeed, in all burials, the external displacement of skeletal elements involved the posterior movement of bones – falling towards the base of the coffin – and in a lateral and/or inferior direction which appeared to have resulted predominantly under the force of gravity.

Posterior fall of clavicles, sternum (manubrium and *corpus sterni*) and ribs into a secondary internal void

Posterior fall of the *ulnae, radii* and hand bones into a secondary internal void

Posterior fall of the *ossa coxae* into an original external void

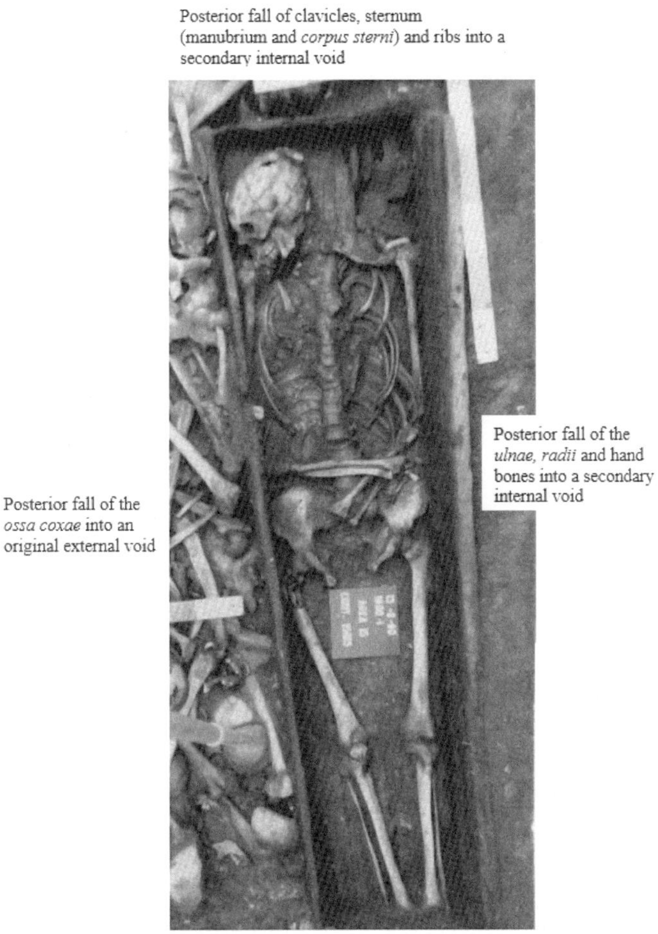

Figure 23.1 Burial displaying displacement of bones within original external and secondary internal voids (Skeleton 15015) (Reproduced with permission of York Archaeological Trust).

Evidence for compression of the upper body – verticalisation of the clavicles, superior and anterior rotation of the scapulae, medial rotation of the right humerus, narrowing of the thoracic volume

Support of elements in potential unstable positions – superior and anterior rotation of the right scapula, medial rotation of the right humerus, and the right *os coxae*

Posterior fall of the right ulna, radius and hand bones into secondary internal void

Posterior fall of clavicles, sternum (manubrium and *corpus sterni*) and ribs into secondary internal void. Ribs have not fallen completely to rest on base

Lateral and posterior fall of left radius into original external void

Posterior fall of left *os coxae* into secondary internal void

The tibiae, fibulae, ankle and foot bones display displacement above that expected under gravity alone

WCCH03 103

Linear alignment of bones (indicated by dotted lines) involving the right humerus, ulna, *os coxae*, patella, ankle and foot bones and on the left side the radius, carpal bone and metatarsals. Possible linear alignment of foot bones along the foot end – obscured by the north arrow

Figure 23.2   Burial displaying displacement into original external and secondary internal voids, including linear displacement of bones (Skeleton 103) (Photograph: C. Guy, Cathedral Archaeologist, Worchester Cathedral; Reproduced with permission of the Chapter of Worcester Cathedral).

In 31 burials (31/78, 40%), externally displaced bones presented linear alignments, indicating they had come to rest along the side(s) of the container (Figure 23.2). The fully intact coffins in the sample illustrated how the sides of the container can be affected by warping, clearly seen in the coffins at Swinegate and St Peter's and, as such, alignments of bones may not strictly appear to conform to a straight line. In 15 (15/31, 48%) of the burials with linear alignments of bones, the external displacement was more than could be attributed to movement under gravity and widespread throughout the coffin, as seen in Figure 23.2 by the displacement of the bones of the ankles and feet. It is unlikely that decomposition under the effect of gravity alone would result in this extent of movement, suggesting other taphonomic agents acting on the skeletal remains in a void. At both Swinegate and St Peter's, the wooden coffins had been preserved by water-logged sediment and evidence for the high-water content in the environment is clear from the images, where water partially fills the coffins at the time of excavation and displaces bones. It is plausible that fluctuation in the water table within the coffin void was responsible for the widely dispersed bones. However, at Worcester Cathedral, the environmental conditions were drier. The extensive movement involved the foot bones, skeletal elements whose joints are relatively labile. Alternative explanations for this extensive displacement could arise from the robust construction of the coffins that permitted the retention of the decomposition fluids in which the foot bones floated, or movement occurring during transportation of a coffined corpse where decomposition had already freed the foot bones from their articulations.

Evidence for displacement into internal secondary voids

Internal displacement, the movement of skeletal elements within the area formally occupied by the soft tissue of the corpse, was observed in all 78 burials (Figures 23.1 and 23.2). The bones which most frequently displayed internal displacement were the ribs, sternum (manubrium and/or *corpus sterni*), clavicles and sacrum. The bones of the forearms and hands also frequently displayed internal displacement in situations where they were inferred to have been originally positioned resting on the thorax/pelvis of the corpse. The bones displaying internal displacement appeared to present less variation than those externally displaced, though these also presented repeated patterns. In most burials, the bones appeared to have fallen posteriorly to rest on the container base. However, in two cases, in addition to a posterior fall, the bones had been displaced out of anatomical order around the thoracic region. Internal displacement results from the container acting as a solid barrier between the corpse and the soil, which impedes the surrounding sediment from progressively in-filling the spaces created by the decomposing soft tissue. This, in turn, allows for the creation of internal secondary voids into which bones could move under gravity. It can be concluded that evidence for internal displacement is not as informative as external displacement in determining the presence of a wooden container. Although important in excluding burial in direct contact with fine-grained sediment, internal displacement could occur in burials where the body is wrapped, clothed or covered as these would also act as a barrier to sediment, albeit not as durable. Or, if buried in soil comprising predominantly coarser grained, non-porous sediments, these movements can also be expected (Duday, 2006: 41).

Variation in the amount of displacement, the number of bones involved and the extent of movement will be influenced by differences in the durability, integrity and size of the container, and taphonomic processes such as environmental factors and human activity. Preserved wooden containers which maintain their integrity allow for the prolonged existence of voids. This increases the potential for bones to become displaced by taphonomic forces besides gravity (e.g. movement by water, putrefaction liquids or downslope movement of bones). Conversely, if the integrity of the container is compromised early in the decomposition sequence, allowing sediment to enter and fill voids while decomposition is still occurring, this will limit bone movement and fix them in place. The type of sediment will have an impact on both the speed of in-filling and container integrity. Fine-grained sediments may have the potential to infiltrate into the container through smaller fissures than would be accessible to coarser soils. Sediments high in clay are susceptible to shrinking and expansion, and this will have a physical effect on the container integrity (McGowan and Prangnell, 2015). The size of the container in relation to its occupant also affects skeletal displacement. If the container is larger, with more empty space, greater potential exists for external displacement, compared to a container in which the sides and ends are adjacent to the corpse. In the latter situation, external displacement may be limited and internal displacement dominant.

Evidence for displacement into external secondary voids

While external primary and secondary voids are both external to the original volume of the body, they need to be distinguished because they have different origins. External secondary voids are spaces that form around the corpse. These voids were not originally present but became accessible during or after decomposition. Evidence for external secondary voids is relevant to the identification of a container burial when the origin of the voids can be related to the decomposition of the container, and their presence thus provides evidence for the once existence of the container. In two burials (2/78, 3%), bones appeared displaced outside the limits originally imposed by the coffin. In both cases from Swinegate, the skeletal elements appeared displaced in a posterior direction following the decay/collapse of the base of the coffin beneath them.

Evidence for the support of bones in potentially unstable and unsupported positions

The decomposition of the supporting soft tissue results in instability of skeletal elements and, over time, bones should move under gravity to rest in more stable locations. Where bones are maintained in unstable positions on excavation, it can be concluded that something had been supporting them in that position (Duday, 2006: 41). Potential sources of this support can include the following: the grave fill being in direct contact with the corpse, a narrow or v-shaped grave cut, the presence of a perishable object such as a shroud, or the sides of a burial container. Bones were supported in potentially unstable positions in 64 burials (64/78, 82%), most frequently the *ossa coxae*, humeri and scapulae (Figure 23.2). It was clear that in most burials, the sides of the coffin provided support for appendicular skeletal elements. In three burials, it is possible that the support may have come from shrouding. In these burials, there appeared to be a small void present between the coffin side and the unsupported bone. Thus, as the coffin sides did not appear to be supporting the bones, this indicated a different source of support that had since decomposed.

The combination of displacement and support for skeletal elements in unstable positions was important in identifying container burials, as it was clear that frequently bones were supported in only approximate original positions, with disarticulation, internal, and external displacement also present. The support of bones in unstable positions also provides evidence for the location of the coffin sides and therefore provides strong evidence, akin to extensive displacement, for the dimensions of the container. However, in burials where there is limited evidence for the presence of a container, the source of this support must be interpreted via other means. Identification of a grave cut at a distance from the supported bones will exclude the possibility that support was provided by direct contact with the grave cut itself. This is fundamental to differentiating between sources of support for skeletal elements maintained in potentially unstable positions.

In some cases, without additional evidence provided by archaeological features such as the grave cut and/or inconclusive direct archaeological evidence (wood, metal work, voids, stains), the presence of a wooden container may remain a possibility rather than a certainty.

Evidence for compression of the upper body

A narrow container has the potential to compress and support the corpse in a constricted position. Evidence for bilateral compression, seen by one or more of a verticalised clavicles, anterior/ superior rotation of the scapulae, narrowing of the thoracic volume and medially rotated humeri, as seen in Figure 23.2, resulting from lateral pressure from the sides of the container, was recorded in 30 burials (30/51, 59%). For three burials from Swinegate, there appeared to have been a space between the coffin side and the supported lateral skeletal elements. In these cases, the corpse may have been shrouded within a coffin, and the lateral compression primarily the result of the shroud. In two burials, one from Swinegate and one from St Oswald's, bilateral compression was suggested by the narrowing of the thorax, but the scapulae and humeri did not display forward and medial rotation accordingly. The inference that could be drawn from the lack of medial rotation in the humeri was that the source of the compression had loosened before the shoulder joint had disarticulated, allowing the humeri access to a new void within the coffin. This could also present evidence for a shrouded corpse within a coffin, and a shroud would be expected to be less durable. Alternatively, a narrowing of the thorax has been discussed by Williams (2015: 96) as potential evidence for burial in clothing.

Developing a method for identifying wooden containers

This study provided evidence for a suite of skeletal indicators relating to decomposition in a container which can appear interchangeably. There was no one single diagnostic feature that could be attributed to burial in a wooden container, nor a set of characteristics identically replicated in all inhumed skeletons. This observation necessitated the development of a diagnostic method based on a flexible flowchart as opposed to a fixed set of criteria. In this method, observations of the *in situ* skeleton are made with reference to the statements in the flowchart, leading, by a process of elimination, to a conclusion about potential burial form. The progression through the flowchart is not necessarily meant to represent a hierarchy in which more important skeletal indicators take precedence. Rather, the starting point for the flowchart takes into consideration the apparent strength of the skeletal indicator for identifying decomposition in a rigid void, the frequency of the observations in the data set and if the observation required support from additional types of evidence. Working through the flowchart permits for the amalgamation of the skeletal evidence in a structured way (Figure 23.3 and Table 23.5).

Identification of previously unidentified wooden burial containers

The archaeothanatological method described in this study enabled the identification of containers in burials were limited, or no remains of the receptacles themselves survived. A sample of burials of this type was selected from three late Anglo-Saxon cemeteries for analysis: Worcester Cathedral, Worcester; Black Gate, Newcastle, Tyne and Wear; and Elstow Abbey, Bedfordshire (all UK). These three sites have burials where there is no evidence for wooden containers, but every reason to suspect that their use might have been more widespread than the preserved evidence suggests. The excavators of the three sites had previously inferred the presence of wooden containers in some graves from a variety of archaeological evidence, including rare fragments of preserved wood, soil stains, and metal fittings. These data suggest that 16% of the sampled burials

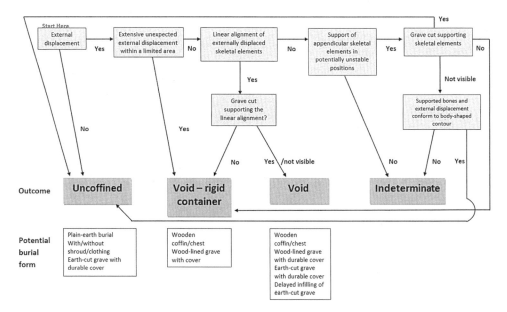

Figure 23.3 Flowchart for determining burial form in the absence of direct archaeological evidence for a burial container, based on late Anglo-Saxon burials.

were coffined (53/326). While some burials from Worcester Cathedral cemetery presented evidence for wooden containers in the form of preserved wood and were thus used in the development of the archaeothanatological method above, a separate group of interments from the same site were not so well-preserved and comprised burials for which there was inconclusive or no direct evidence for burial form (Table 23.6). At Black Gate cemetery, organic preservation was poor, with a limited amount of direct evidence for wooden containers in the form of fragmentary preserved wood and metal fittings, but the majority of graves have been labelled as plain-earth burials by default (Table 23.6). All of the late Anglo-Saxon burials at Elstow Abbey, with the exception of three, had been determined to be of plain-earth type due to a lack of direct archaeological evidence to the contrary (Table 23.6). The presence of a few soil stains indicates that organic preservation had been poor and, as such, containers constructed entirely from wood would not be expected to survive.

When applied to the three sites, the approach developed in this study indicates that 17% of burials (54/326) decomposed in a void identified as a rigid wooden container (Table 23.7). In these burials, as seen in the example in Figure 23.4, external and internal bone displacement was present. In 32 burials, skeletal elements formed a linear alignment (as seen in Figure 23.4) or were supported in potentially unstable positions at a distance from the grave cut leading to a void – rigid container outcome, whereas in two burials, the determining factor was a more extensive displacement of bones than expected under gravity alone. The presence of preserved wood fragments or soil stains, in combination with external displacement, leads to a void – rigid container outcome in 20 burials. A further 23% of burials (75/326) provided evidence strongly suggestive of decomposition in a void, but one that could not conclusively be determined to be a wooden container. In these, the extent of displacement could also have occurred in a grave supplied with only a durable cover or from a delay in the back-filling of the grave until after decomposition had occurred. Again, all burials displayed evidence for the displacement of bones into original external voids and secondary internal voids. In 30 burials, there was evidence for

Table 23.5 Explanation of the burial outcomes provided by the flowchart

Burial determination	Possible burial forms	Characteristic features
Void – rigid container	Wooden coffin/chest Wood-lined grave with cover	Skeletal evidence for decomposition in a void, formed by a long-lasting rigid barrier. Archaeological evidence either excludes the grave cut as a source of this barrier and/or provides evidence for the presence of a wooden structure in the grave that is not representative of a cover only. Presence of extensive unexpected skeletal displacement in a limited area excludes possibility of an earth-cut grave with no robust lining with only a durable cover. A grave with no form of durable lining would not be expected to maintain voids around the corpse for as long in comparison to one with a wooden lining or portable container.
Void	Wooden coffin/chest Wood-lined grave with cover Durable cover only in earth-cut grave with no form of robust lining Delayed backfilling of the grave	Skeletal evidence for decomposition in an original void. Archaeological evidence cannot determine the source of the barrier as there is insufficient direct archaeological evidence (wood, metal work) and no grave cut has been identified. Alternatively, there is archaeological evidence indicating the barrier cannot be a container – location of grave cut adjacent to skeletal elements and/or overall position of the corpse would not fit into a typical late Anglo-Saxon wooden container.
Indeterminate	Wooden coffin/chest Wood-lined grave with cover Durable cover only in earth-cut grave Durable loose shroud Durable clothing Delayed backfilling of the grave	Skeletal evidence indicates delayed in-filling, but the source of the barrier cannot be identified. There is limited evidence for external displacement and that recorded could have occurred within the confines of a body cavity maintained in the sediment enhanced by clothing/loose shroud, therefore decomposition in a filled space cannot be confidently excluded. A lack of archaeological evidence for the presence of a wooden container or durable cover.
Un-coffined	Plain-earth burial with/ without clothing/ shroud Durable cover only in earth-cut grave	Skeletal evidence for decomposition in a filled space – progressive or delayed in-filling present, limited amount of displacement observed (that which could be accounted for by secondary voids or those possible within clothing/shroud). Archaeological evidence indicating the barrier cannot be a container – location of grave cut adjacent to skeletal elements and/or overall position of the corpse would not fit into a typical late Anglo-Saxon wooden container.

either a linear alignment of bones or bones supported in unstable positions, but an absence of evidence for a grave cut meant that the cut could not be excluded as the source of the barrier (Figure 23.5). A void outcome was determined for 37 burials due to evidence for bone displacement beyond that attributed to movement under gravity. However, this was not considered to be sufficient to indicate a rigid, long-lasting void and therefore could not be solely ascribed to decomposition in a rigid container. For eight burials, a more limited amount of external bone displacement combined with preserved wood fragments indicated decomposition in a void. However, the location of the fragments could not eliminate the presence of a cover only.

In contrast, 32% of burials were conclusively determined not to have been supplied with a rigid container – an un-coffined outcome (105/326). The majority of these were concluded to be plain-earth burials, decomposing in a filled space with or without the presence of clothing or

Table 23.6 The three cemeteries assessed using the archaeothanatology-based method to identify wooden containers

Site	Publication	Adult burials suitable for analysis	Number of coffins identified by excavators	Evidence used by excavators to identify wooden containers
Worcester Cathedral, Worcester, Worcestershire	Guy (2010) Not fully published to date Data held at Worcester Cathedral	39	15	Fragments of preserved wood/ soil stains from decomposed wood
Black Gate, Newcastle, Tyne and Wear	Nolan (2010) Not fully published to date Data held by John Nolan	232	37	Corroded metal corner bracket (N=2) Corroded metal lock (N=2) Fragments of preserved wood/ traces of coffin (N=33)
Elstow Abbey, Elstow, Bedfordshire	Baker (1966, 1969, 1971) Not fully published to date Data held by David Baker	55	1	Soil stain from decomposed wood

shrouding (66/326, 20%). As illustrated in Figure 23.6, bone displacement is generally limited to movement into secondary internal voids, with no evidence for an original external void. Thus, this study has confirmed it is possible to generate positive evidence for the identification of plain-earth burials using skeletal positioning. In the other 39 burials, though there was evidence for decomposition in a void, the presence of a container was excluded due to the relationship of the corpse with another individual (N=2), the location of the grave cut or stone blocks in relationship to the skeletal elements (N=28) and the overall arrangement of the corpse (N=9). This left 28% of burials (92/326) for which the decompositional environment could not be confidently ascertained, meaning the presence of a wooden container could be neither confirmed nor excluded; in these burials, evidence for an original external void created by a barrier at a distance from the corpse was limited. Figure 23.7 illustrates a burial with bones displaced into secondary internal voids and limited movement of bones outside the original soft tissue volume of the corpse. The posterolateral decent of the *ossa coxae* could be equally attributed to movement within a soft barrier around the corpse as much as to a rigid container, especially as the upper limbs are parallel to the pelvis, thus creating additional soft tissue volume in this area. The displacement of the right-hand bones is potentially the only evidence for external space.

Table 23.7 Burial form determined using the archaeothanatology-based method for 326 late Anglo-Saxon burials

Cemetery	Void – rigid container	Void	Indeterminate	Un-coffined	Total
Worcester Cathedral	26 (67%)	1 (2.5%)	8 (20.5%)	4 (10%)	39 (100%)
Black Gate	26 (11%)	44 (19%)	67 (29%)	95 (41%)	232 (100%)
Elstow Abbey	2 (4%)	30 (54%)	17 (31%)	6 (11%)	55 (100%)
Total	54 (17%)	75 (23%)	92 (28%)	105 (32%)	326 (100%)

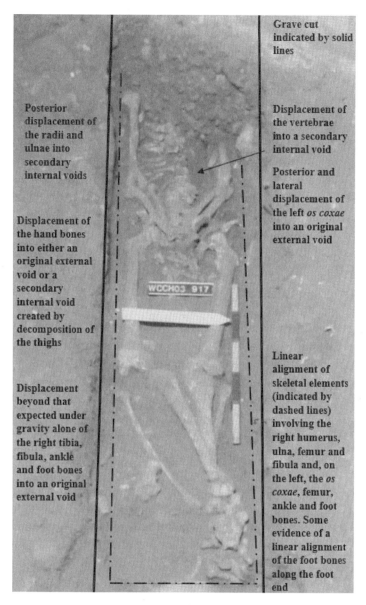

Grave cut indicated by solid lines

Posterior displacement of the radii and ulnae into secondary internal voids

Displacement of the hand bones into either an original external void or a secondary internal void created by decomposition of the thighs

Displacement beyond that expected under gravity alone of the right tibia, fibula, ankle and foot bones into an original external void

Displacement of the vertebrae into a secondary internal void

Posterior and lateral displacement of the left *os coxae* into an original external void

Linear alignment of skeletal elements (indicated by dashed lines) involving the right humerus, ulna, femur and fibula and, on the left, the *os coxae*, femur, ankle and foot bones. Some evidence of a linear alignment of the foot bones along the foot end

WCCH03 917

Figure 23.4 Example of a burial in a void – rigid container outcome (Skeleton 917) (Photograph: C. Guy, Cathedral Archaeologist, Worcester Cathedral; Reproduced with permission of the Chapter of Worcester Cathedral).

A total of 103 burials originally described as plain-earth graves were re-classified as a result of this study (103/326, 32%). Of these 103 burials, 24 were confidently identified as decomposing in a wooden container, while 66 were determined to have decomposed in an undetermined void and 13 in earth-cut graves beneath a durable cover. The approach applied in this study has corroborated prior determinations of the excavators, while identifying a number of previously unknown wooden containers and burials where decomposition took place in an uncharacterised void (Table 23.8). However, the results for Black Gate were more complex. This study identified

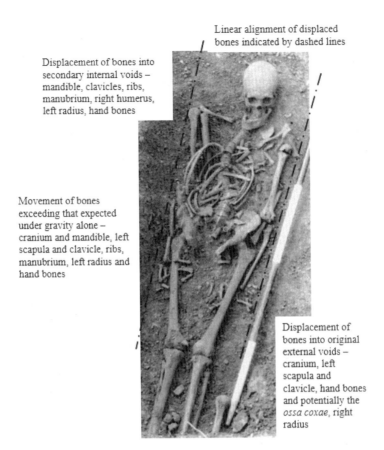

Linear alignment of displaced bones indicated by dashed lines

Displacement of bones into secondary internal voids – mandible, clavicles, ribs, manubrium, right humerus, left radius, hand bones

Movement of bones exceeding that expected under gravity alone – cranium and mandible, left scapula and clavicle, ribs, manubrium, left radius and hand bones

Displacement of bones into original external voids – cranium, left scapula and clavicle, hand bones and potentially the *ossa coxae*, right radius

Figure 23.5 Example of a burial with a void outcome from Elstow Abbey (Reproduced with permission of D. Baker).

12 previously unknown wooden containers and confirmed the prior conclusions of the excavators for the presence of a wooden container in three graves. For 19 burials in which the excavators had identified a container, the present study suggests the evidence used by the excavators, in combination with skeletal analysis, could not confirm the presence of a rigid container. These burials, therefore, were determined to have decomposed in an unidentified void. Furthermore, a single burial was determined by this study to be uncontained based on evidence for decomposition in a filled space, even though the excavators had concluded it had been coffined.

Discussion

This study has presented evidence to suggest that a considerable number of so-called plain-earth graves in late Anglo-Saxon cemeteries originally included a wooden burial container. The impact of improved identification of wooden containers varied between the three sites and was most marked at Elstow Abbey. Here, prior to this study, wooden containers had only been identified in one grave in the sample based on ephemeral evidence: soil stains left by decomposing wood on the base of the grave. The application of an archaeothanatological method revealed one burial with evidence for decomposition in a wooden container and 31 identified as buried in a void,

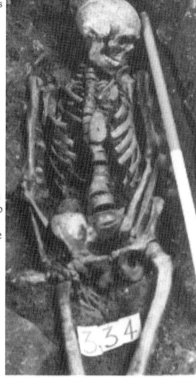

Displacement into secondary internal voids – mandible, ribs, manubrium and *corpus sterni*, vertebrae, sacrum, radii, left ulna, right hand bones

Support for - rotation of the scapulae, ribs, *ossa coxae*, right hand bones

No evidence for displacement into original external voids movement restricted to inside areas formally occupied by soft tissue

Figure 23.6 Example of a plain-earth burial, no container outcome (Image courtesy: Newcastle City Archaeological Unit, Newcastle City Council).

but not one that could be confidently deemed to be a wooden container. Of these 32 burials, 31 were re-classified from the original plain-earth determination of the excavators. This changes the interpretation of funerary practices at Elstow Abbey substantially. Instead of what appeared to be a fairly uniform burial custom with few containers, there is now evidence for a variety of different funerary practices. At both Black Gate and Worcester Cathedral, excavators had already inferred burial within wooden containers based on the survival of direct archaeological evidence. Nonetheless, the re-analysis presented here has revealed previously unknown wooden containers and provided support for cases where the direct archaeological evidence was less than conclusive. The evidence from Black Gate and Worcester Cathedral suggests that even where direct evidence has been found for wooden containers, it does not follow that this is a true reflection of the total number – the impact of differential preservation is varied and substantial. The significance of this study for late Anglo-Saxon funerary studies is that the current prevalence of burial in a wooden container must be seen as significant under-estimate, and broader conclusions drawn from these studies re-evaluated to account for a practice that was likely more common than plain-earth burial. As only 20% of the sample were confirmed to be plain-earth burials, this suggests that the majority of burials were elaborated in one way or another and therefore presents a challenge to the predominance of plain-earth burial in the late Anglo-Saxon period. Indeed, at Worcester Cathedral, the identification of a further 11 individuals buried in wooden containers increases

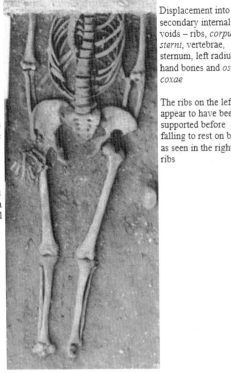

Displacement into secondary internal voids – ribs, *corpus sterni*, vertebrae, sternum, left radius, hand bones and *ossa coxae*

The ribs on the left appear to have been supported before falling to rest on base as seen in the right ribs

Displacement into original external voids –hand bones and potentially the *ossa coxae*

Possibly the movement of the hand bones relates to the creation of a secondary external void

Figure 23.7 Example of a burial with an indeterminate outcome from Elstow Abbey (Reproduced with permission of D. Baker).

the total from 15 (15/39, 38%) to 26 (26/39, 67%) and reveals that substantially more than half of all burials sampled at this site were provided with containers.

There are a number of discussion points that arise as a consequence of this study. Castex and Blaizot (2017: 282–284) consider the identification of the grave cut as vital for identifying a

Table 23.8 Comparison between previous coffin determinations by the excavators and the results of this study of decomposition in a void from all three cemeteries

Cemetery	Number of wooden containers previously identified by excavators	Number of burials with evidence for wooden containers identified in this study	Number of new wooden containers identified in this study	Number of burials with evidence for decomposition in an uncharacterised void identified in this study	Number of new burials identified in this study as decomposing in an uncharacterised void	Number of new burials with evidence for decomposition beneath a cover identified in this study
Worcester Cathedral	15 (38%)	26 (67%)	11	5 (13%)	5	2
Black Gate	37 (16%)	26 (11%)	12	44 (21%)	31	11
Elstow Abbey	1 (2%)	2 (4%)	1	30 (55%)	30	0
Total	53 (16%)	54 (17%)	24	79 (24%)	66	13

coffined burial. However, in all three sites, but especially at Elstow and Black Gate, grave cuts had proved elusive to the excavators. This does not mean they were necessarily absent, excavation methods and recording accuracy may have played a part. The inability to identify grave cuts resulted in burials being allocated either a void outcome, for those with clear evidence for decomposition in a void, or an indeterminate outcome, where burials exhibited limited external displacement of skeletal elements with bones supported in potentially unstable positions. However, without ascertaining the location of the grave cut, this could not be ruled out as a source of the barrier or support for the bones. Furthermore, a loss of three-dimensional data when using photographs resulted in a difficulty in assessing vertical displacement. This lack of depth perception in a photograph was compounded at all three sites by limited depth measurements for individual bones. At best, levels had been taken at the cranium, pelvis and feet. However, this data proved less than informative when attempting to assess specific movements of individual bones. The limited data on skeletal positioning and displacement on the vertical axis resulted in a situation where it was easier to identify horizontal movements as external displacement. This may have led to movements involving a vertical displacement being wrongly interpreted as internal rather than external. Although this interpretative ambiguity would have affected the study of all burials, it would have had the greatest impact on the interpretations of burials which did not have extensive external skeletal displacement, mainly those with an indeterminate outcome.

Conclusion

The approach developed in this study was able to identify a suite of features of skeletal positioning which characterises burial in a wooden container and enables the identification of burial containers in graves for which no independent archaeological evidence survived. Application of this method to three late Anglo-Saxon cemeteries successfully enabled a re-evaluation of the prevalence of containers and plain-earth burials, providing data to support the hypothesis that wooden containers were used more frequently than can be recognised from direct archaeological evidence alone (e.g. Buckberry, 2004: 172; Cherryson, 2005: 118–121; Mahoney Swales, 2012: 25–26, 33–34; Gilchrist, 2014: 385). Certainly, if this analysis had not taken place, a significant number of graves would have remained with an invalid, default determination of plain-earth burial. This study demonstrates the impact of a taphonomy-based assessment of the burial record, revealing the extent to which reliance on direct archaeological evidence for wooden containers presents a biased perception of late Anglo-Saxon funerary practices which changes the interpretation of funerary practices at Elstow Abbey substantially. More generally, the findings presented here establish the need for better incorporation of an archaeothanatological approach into funerary research in the UK, starting with a move to increase awareness of this approach amongst archaeologists in the field.

Acknowledgements

For allowing access to excavation archives, thanks extend to Christopher Guy (Worcester Cathedral), Christine McDonnell (York Archaeological Trust – Swinegate), David Baker (Elstow Abbey), David Rice (Gloucester City Museums – St Oswald's), Susan Harrison and the team at English Heritage (St Peter's), Helen Rees (Hampshire Cultural Trust – Staple Garden's) and John Nolan (Black Gate). For commenting on drafts of this paper, thanks go to Dr Elizabeth Craig-Atkins.

This research was funded by the White Rose College of Arts and Humanities Doctoral Training Programme and supervised by Dr Elizabeth Craig-Atkins.

References

Allen, D. and Dalwood, C.H. (1983). Iron Age Occupation, A Middle Saxon Cemetery and Twelfth to Nineteenth Century Urban Occupation: Excavation in George Street, Aylesbury, 1981. *Records of Buckinghamshire*, 25, pp. 1–60.

Baker, D. (1966). Excavations at Elstow Abbey, 1965–66: First Interim Report. *Bedfordshire Archaeology*, 3, pp. 22–30.

Baker, D. (1969). Excavations at Elstow Abbey, 1966–8: Second Interim Report. *Bedfordshire Archaeology*, 4, pp. 27–41.

Baker, D. (1971). Excavations at Elstow Abbey, 1968–70: Third Interim Report. *Bedfordshire Archaeological Journal*, 6, pp. 27–41.

Buckberry, J.L. (2004). *A social and anthropological analysis of Conversion period and later Anglo-Saxon cemeteries in Lincolnshire and Yorkshire*. Unpublished University of Sheffield PhD thesis.

Buckberry, J.L. (2007). On sacred ground: social identity and graveyard burial in Lincolnshire and Yorkshire, c.700–1100. In: S. Semple and H. Williams, eds., *Early Medieval Mortuary Practices. Anglo-Saxon Studies in Archaeology and History 14*. Oxford: Oxford University Committee for Archaeology, pp. 117–129.

Castex, D. and Blaizot, F. (2017). Reconstructing the original arrangement, organisation and architecture of burials in archaeology. In: E.M.J. Schotsmans, N. Márquez-Grant and S.L. Forbes, eds., *Taphonomy of Human Remains: Forensic Analysis of the Dead and the Depositional Environment*. Chichester: Wiley, pp. 277–296.

Chapman, R. and Randsborg, K. (2009). Approaches to the archaeology of death. In: R. Chapman, I. Kinnes, and K. Randsborg, eds., *Archaeology of Death*, Cambridge: Cambridge University Press, pp. 1–24.

Cherryson, A. K. (2005). *In the Shadow of the Church: Burial Practices in the Wessex Heartlands c. 600–1100 A.D.* Unpublished University of Sheffield PhD thesis.

Craig, E. and Buckberry, J.L. (2010). Investigating social status using evidence of biological status: a case study from Raunds Furnells. In: J.L Buckberry and A.K. Cherryson, eds. *Burial in Later Anglo-Saxon England c. 650–1100 A.D.* Oxford: Oxbow, pp. 128–42.

Duday, H. (2006). L'archéothanatologie ou l'archéologie de la mort (archaeothanatology or archaeology of death). Translated by C.J. Knüsel. In: R.L. Gowland, and C.J. Knüsel, *Social Archaeology of Funerary Remains*. Oxford: Oxbow Books, pp. 30–56.

Duday, H. (2009). *The archaeology of the dead: lectures in archaeothanatology*. Oxford: Oxbow Books.

Duday, H., Courtaud, P., Crubezy, É., Sellier, P. and Tillier, A. (1990). L'Anthropologie de terrain: reconnaissance et interprétation des gestes funéraires. *Bulletins et Mémoires de la Société d'anthropologie de Paris, Nouvelle Série*, 2(3–4), pp. 29–49.

Duday, H. and Guillon, M. (2006). Understanding the circumstances of decomposition when the body is skeletonized. In: A. Schmitt., E. Cunha, and J. Pinheiro, eds., *Forensic Anthropology and Medicine: Complementary Sciences from Recovery to Cause of Death*. Totowa: Humana Press Inc., pp. 117–157.

Gaimster, D.R.M., Margeson, S. and Hurley, M. (1990). Medieval Britain and Ireland in 1989. *Medieval Archaeology*, 34, pp. 162–252.

Gilchrist, R. (2014). Transforming medieval beliefs: the significance of bodily resurrection to medieval burials in medieval rituals. In: J.R. Brandt, M. Prusac, and H. Roland, eds., *Death and Changing Rituals. Function and Meaning in Ancient Funerary Practices*. Oxford: Oxbow Books, pp. 379–397.

Guy, C. (2010). An Anglo Saxon cemetery at Worcester Cathedral. In: J. Buckberry and A. Cherryson, eds., *Burial in Later Anglo Saxon England, c.650–1100AD*. Oxford: Oxbow Books Ltd. pp. 73–82.

Hadley, D.M. (2000). Burial practices in the Northern Danelaw, c. 650–1100. *Northern History*, 36, pp. 199–216.

Hadley, D.M. (2001). *Death in medieval England: an archaeology*. Stroud, Gloucestershire, UK: Tempus Publishing.

Hadley, D.M. (2002). Burial practices in northern England in the later Anglo-Saxon period. In: S. Lucy and A. Reynolds, eds., *Burial in Early Medieval England and Wales*. London: The Society for Medieval Archaeology, pp. 209–228.

Hadley, D.M. (2010). Burying the socially and physically distinctive in later Anglo-Saxon England. In: J. Buckberry and A. Cherryson, eds., *Burial in Later Anglo Saxon England, c.650–1100AD*. Oxford: Oxbow Books Ltd. pp. 103–116.

Hadley, D.M. and Buckberry, J.L. (2005). Caring for the dead in late Anglo-Saxon England. In: F. Tinti, ed., *Pastoral Care in Late Anglo-Saxon England*. Woodbridge: Boydell. pp. 121–147.

Heighway, C. and Bryant, R. (1999). *The golden minster: the Anglo-Saxon minster and later medieval priory of St Oswald at Gloucester*. Council for British Archaeology. Report 117. York: Council for British Archaeology.

Knüsel, C.J. (2014). Crouching in Fear: Terms of Engagement for Funerary Remains. *Journal of Social Archaeology*, 14(1), pp. 26–58.

Mahoney Swales, D.L. (2012). *Life and stress: a bio-cultural investigation into the later Anglo-Saxon population of the Black Gate Cemetery, Newcastle-Upon-Tyne*. Unpublished University of Sheffield PhD thesis.

McGowan, G. and Prangnell, J. (2015). A Method for Calculating Soil Pressure Overlying Human Burials. *Journal of Archaeological Science*, 53, 12–18.

Newman, C. (1992). A Late Saxon Cemetery at Templecombe. *Somerset Archaeology and Natural History the Proceedings of the Somerset Archaeology and Natural History Society for 1992*, 136, pp. 61–72.

Nilsson Stutz, L. (2006). Unwrapping the dead. Searching for evidence of wrappings in the mortuary practices at Zvejnieki. In L. Larsson and I. Zagorska, eds., *Back to the Origin: New Research on the Mesolithic-Neolithic Zvejnieki Cemetery and Environment in Northern Latvia*. Lund: Almqvist & Wiksell International, pp. 217–233.

Nilsson Stutz, L. (2010). The Way We Bury Our Dead. Reflections on Mortuary Ritual, Community and Identity at the Time of the Mesolithic-Neolithic transition. *Documenta Praehistorica*, 37, pp. 33–42.

Nolan, J. (2010). The Early Medieval Cemetery at the Castle, Newcastle-upon-Tyne. *Archaeologia Aeliana* 39, pp. 147–287.

Pearson, N.F. (1989). Swinegate Excavation. *Interim – The Archaeology of York*, 14, 4pp. 2–9.

Pearson, N.F. (1990). Swinegate Excavations. *Interim – The Archaeology of York*, 15, 1, pp. 2–10.

Reynolds, A. (2009). *Anglo-Saxon deviant burial customs*. Oxford: Oxford University Press.

Rodwell, W. and Atkins, C. (2011). *St Peter's, Barton-upon-Humber, Lincolnshire: a parish church and its community. Volume 1: History, Archaeology and Architecture*. Oxford: Oxbow Books.

Thompson, V. (2002). Constructing Salvation: A Homiletic and Penitential context for Late Anglo-Saxon Burial Practice. In: S. Lucy and A. Reynolds, eds., *Burial in Early Medieval England and Wales*. London: The Society for Medieval Archaeology, pp. 229–240.

Waldron, T. (2007). *St Peter's, Barton-upon-Humber, Lincolnshire: a parish church and its community. Volume 2: The Human Remains*. Oxford: Oxbow.

Williams, E. (2015). *Fresh cadaver to skeletal matter: text, practice and the Cluniac death-course*. Unpublished University of Southampton PhD thesis.

Youngs, S.M., Clarke, J. and Barry, T. (1986). Medieval Britain and Ireland in 1985. *Medieval Archaeology*, 30, pp. 114–198.

24

CERAMIC STUDIES IN FUNERARY CONTEXTS FROM ROMAN GAUL

Christine Bonnet

INSTITUT NATIONAL DE RECHERCHES ARCHÉOLOGIQUES PRÉVENTIVES (INRAP),
AUVERGNE-RHÔNE-ALPES, BRON, FRANCE

LABORATOIRE ARAR, ARCHÉOLOGIE AND ARCHÉOMÉTRIE, MAISON DE L'ORIENT ET DE LA
MÉDITERRANÉE, UMR 5138, LYON, FRANCE

Introduction

Between the end of the 1st century BC and the 5th century AD in Roman Gaul, the majority of artefacts collected from funerary contexts are ceramic vessels associated with either cremations or inhumations. The majority of these ceramics consisted of vessels used for eating and drinking during funerary banquets, while others were used as cinerary urns for cremated bones or as containers in pot burials for small children, most often amphorae. The abundance of vessels makes them the main evidence found within features. Owing to close collaboration between funerary archaeologists and ceramics specialists, they are also the main testaments to the various stages of funerary obsequies. The results presented here are the fruit of research developed since the mid-1980s in the central southeastern part of France (Blaizot, 2009). This contribution will focus on the data collected in the Lyon and the Rhône-Alps region with some recent additional material included from archaeological excavations of the Saône and the Rhône river valleys.

Whether they are assemblages of intact or complete but broken vessels, more or less incomplete vessels or a single sherd, it is very rare that a Roman funerary feature, in particular those related to the practice of cremation, be it a pyre, a secondary deposit, or a residual deposit, does not provide any evidence of ceramic vessels. In the Rhône-Alps region, during the Early Roman Empire, between 95% and 100% of the pyres and between 63% and 100% of the cremation deposits contained burnt ceramic vessels. Since the 1980s, it is these burnt vessels and the hundreds of associated sherds, most often found scattered in the pyres, which have encouraged ceramics specialists to develop working methods adapted to the arduous processing of this mass of data. Whilst French commercial archaeology was undergoing a period of great expansion, processing of large cremation assemblages in the Rhône valley, such as those from the site of Favorite in Lyon (Tranoy, 1995) and the Valladas site in Saint-Paul-Trois-Châteaux in the Drôme (Bel, 2002), witnessed a complete overhaul of both excavation methods of so-called 'field anthropology' (Duday *et al.*, 1990) and the recording methods for ceramics. The new archaeological excavation method was also a major step forward for ceramics specialist as, for the first time, the entire ceramic corpus was recorded down to the smallest sherd, and this without preconceived interpretation.

The history of recording methods and ceramics studies in a funerary context

In the 1960s and 1970s, the use of a number of methods to excavate graves left much room for personal initiative. The sampling of grave goods on an excavation was rarely exhaustive and depended largely on the excavator and the questions s/he intended to answer. The majority chose to record only the intact or at least the identifiable vessels and to ignore the question of broken or incomplete vessels and isolated sherds. There were some rare individuals who took care to record the maximum of information, even if their recording often remained incomplete and therefore difficult to use today (Allain, 1972; Perraud, 1974).

The difference between these two approaches became noticeable in the 1960s–1970s. In the first case, vessels were simply considered as static objects, food containers, deposited intact alongside the deceased in the manner of a *viaticum* (food for the journey to the afterlife). In the second case, the approach was finer, including essential questions such as the quantity of vessels, their functions and added new aspects in order to understand the way they had been handled during the funerary proceedings. In the latter, the precise recording of certain abnormalities, gaps, perforations and breakages, led the excavators to sense a more varied scenario involving actions carried out during the funerary cere-monies. These indications, which previously interested archaeologists, were already numerous during the excavations. The most common illustration is that of pyre ceramics which consisted of an appar-ently chaotic mass of vessels and more or less identifiable burnt sherds. It is important to mention that this complexity is not only reserved for cremation-related contexts. Against all preconceived notions, inhumations can also show complicated depositional patterns, even in the absence of burnt vessels.

Cremations and inhumations can consist of intact vessels, complete but broken vessels, well represented but incomplete vessels, and other, more or less incomplete and lone sherds. The complexity of observations during the excavation does not accord with the static postulate of the *viaticum* type. It is this more dynamic understanding, focussed on the question of funerary practices, which guided research of the following generation.

From the 1980s onwards, the new '*anthropologie de terrain*' combined not only the explosion in the number of commercial excavations of large Roman funerary complexes but also the work of historians, in particular Scheid (1984, 1998), provided renewed impetus in research. For archaeologists, the emphasis placed by Scheid (1984) on the importance of the funerary meal, through a re-reading of the few texts that refer to it, opened new perspectives on the role of the vessels found in various features. The *modus operandi* of the funerary meal was the sacrifice of a sow near the tomb for the goddess Ceres. While the deceased consumed his portion on the pyre, the family dined close by, at a table on which their portions were set (Figure 24.1). The purpose of this ritual meal was explicitly to separate the deceased from the living before burying the burnt remains.

From the pyre to the grave, the vessels became the main evidence of the different stages of the funerary ritual. Both Bel (1993) and Tranoy (1995), being responsible for large funerary excavations, adopted new methods of counting and studying ceramics which are much more capable of pro-viding answers to emerging questions in a variety of situations. All vessels and sherds, whatever the number preserved and recovered, were subjected to methodological and systematic documenting and cataloguing. Their percentage of representation was specified. And for the first time in the catalogues, burnt and unburnt vessels were clearly distinguished. The first, the burnt sherds, here-after called 'primary deposits', relate to the first stage of the rite, burning on the pyre. The unburnt vessels are called 'secondary deposits' because they mark the second stage, that of the burial of the remains. Another small revolution was the systematic recording of the scattered sherds discovered

Figure 24.1 Reconstruction of a funeral meal beside a pyre, Lugdunum Museum, Lyon, France (© Lugdunum; cf. Goudineau, 2009).

in upper fills or around the features that had rarely previously been taken into account. The results were exceptional, especially for the Gallo-Roman Valladas (Drôme, France) site, where Bel (1993) identified not only a very elaborate spatial organisation of the vessels in features but also an order for the deposition of the vessels that revealed a particularly detailed relative chronology. The question of vessel function and their functional associations with other objects was also clarified.

The ceramics specialist faced with the variety and complexity of Roman funerary practices

In light of these achievements, ceramics studies are now in a position to elucidate funerary treatments and to consider not only enriching existing research protocols but also to develop new research directions. The large amount of data accumulated from several decades of commercial excavation shows the diversity and complexity of Roman funerary practices. The challenge that the ceramics specialist now faces as part of a multi-disciplinary archaeothanatological research team relates to their full participation in contributing to understanding the variability of funerary practices. The inherent difficulties when studying vessels are due, on the one hand, to the mass of grave goods and the highly variable state of preservation that complicates recording and cataloguing of finds and, on the other hand, the diversity of features linked to cremations, which often constitute a real psychological barrier for the ceramics specialist.

Faced with these obstacles, recording methods were sometimes improvised or were as numerous as the many features investigated. For example, *bustum* (i.e. pyre) debris could be easily taken into account because of its better preservation, whilst the vessels from residual cremation deposits were only roughly counted because they were very fragmentary. However, with the realisation that the various features relating to cremation constitute different stages of the same ceremony and, therefore, to a single event, it seems logical to adopt the same recording method for all ceramic remains. In short, it is a question of being able to compare the results from one feature to another with a view to decoding the role that the vessels played during successive ritual sequences. Whilst the archaeological community generally acknowledges the complexity of studying grave goods in cremations, inhumation burials are often perceived as less challenging because vessels appear to be more clearly arranged. Here, again, excavations over the last forty years have brought to light many complex burials containing many sherds from broken and scattered as well as incomplete vessels, which require an adapted recording method. In view of all of these arguments, the decision to use a general approach with a single recording method for vessels in all types of funerary contexts, be they cremation or inhumation burials, including secondary features, such as ritual pits or on ancient surfaces, seemed entirely appropriate in an attempt to answer new questions.

A single ceramic recording method for all funerary contexts

As each vase and each sherd can provide important information, a systematic and exhaustive catalogue is now essential (Bonnet, 2016). The ceramics specialist receives the vessels and sherds grouped by squares or by spits. With the aim being to re-assemble the vessels whilst preserving the contextual origin of the sherds in order to analyse the dispersion of objects at the site, recording can become a very labourious exercise, especially in the case of a large pyre. Initially, the aim is to record the sherds by spits and squares in order to preserve the primary data whilst beginning to identify individual deposits. In a second stage, after the sherds have been marked and the vessels fitted back together, deposits are clearly identified. For each vase, the list of the original squares and spits is essential in order to understand their spatial distribution.

With regard to quantification methods, the aim is to obtain an exhaustive list of the vessels that played a role during the ceremony in whatever state of preservation they were at the time of discovery. The method of counting known as the 'real number of vessels' is the most often employed: the well-represented vessels are recorded, then each sherd, whether it is a rim, a handle, a bottom or a simple body sherd, which does not belong to a vase already counted, is added to the finds registers. Therefore, a single sherd, even if it is the only element of a vase accounted for, is tallied. Afterwards, the role of the vase can be discussed and, for example, the question of residual sherds can be raised, but designating residual presence beforehand would exclude the possibility of a *pars pro toto* hypothesis, the sherd, in this case, being the only remaining evidence of a vase that took part in the ceremony.

Once the vessels are identified, the actual ceramic study consisting of determining the family (fineware, coarseware, amphorae) and category (fabric) of the vase, as well as its type, is in no way different from the previously employed methods of analysis. On the other hand, what does differ from those methods is the extent of description of each vase, which in a funerary context is very detailed. All the details of the condition of the object, first the marks from the cremation fire, then the domestic use marks, the percentage of representativeness, missing parts, cuts, and perforations, are all recorded systematically. These observations make it possible to answer the various questions, developed below, which concern not only the choice of the vessels for the ceremonies but also the practices performed during these proceedings.

Situating the research

The supply of tableware for funeral ceremonies

To return to the heart of the subject, the funeral ceremony practices, it is important to identify the source of ceramic vessels used during the funerary sequence, be it for cremation or for inhumation. How did the family of the deceased obtain the vessels? Generally speaking, in Gaul, the majority of ceramics used during such ceremonies are products of the domestic use ceramics market. Objects deliberately manufactured for funerary use are extremely rare. Tableware, including fine ceramics and Samian ware are the most abundant during the Early Roman Imperial period, with common wares including jugs and everyday pots and platters well represented. The recycling of vessels already used in the domestic sphere is well recognised and attested, though, for example, from the evidence of wear on cooking pots and lead staples from repairs made to plates. The purchase of new vessels is known, however, from the accumulations of complete series of signed Samian ware made by the same potter and often forming a complete service. This would suggest that the entire assemblage was purchased on the same occasion. Cooking pots with no use wear or marks from exposure to fire are frequently observed and could have been purchased especially for the occasion, as they had never been used in the kitchen.

Faults, significant deformations, and hairline cracks from misfiring are regularly noted from among the new vessels bought specifically for the ceremony. Recent research undertaken in Lyon on the measurement of firing temperatures on a selection of cooking pots used as cremation urns (Thirion-Merle *et al.*, 2019) showed that the items with a fragile appearance and fine cracks were fired at a lower temperature than those used in the kitchen, therefore workshop rejects. Tranoy (1995) highlighted the use of a large majority of vessels of inferior quality amongst the Samian tableware during her research on the Favorite funerary complex in Lyon. At the end of the Augustan period, cheaply imitated Italic Samian vessels produced at the Lezoux workshop in central Gaul were often used; these were technologically less sophisticated than vessels from the Graufesenque workshop in southern Gaul dating also to the 1st century AD. Between 30 and 150 AD, the funerary complex from Favorite comprised from 83% to 98% of these less sophisticated Samian vessels from central Gaul, whereas the opposite proportion is generally found in residential contexts from Lyon.

Whether they were acquiring wasters or less technologically sophisticated vessels, the question of cost cannot be avoided. These 'reject' vessels may have been sold in shops alongside standard productions and chosen by families for their lower prices. It is difficult to demonstrate that these low-quality products were deliberately directed towards specifically oriented funerary outlets. Yet, it is tempting to imagine, at least for the major funerary complexes, stalls set up close by and selling all of the necessary items needed for these ceremonies, including cheap ceramics for one-off use. It seems that quantity was more important than the quality of the ceramic vessels involved in funerary practices. Recycled vessels may have passed their original lives as functional objects within the household of the deceased; this hypothesis is impossible to demonstrate, and the reasons, functional or sentimental, leading to the choice of the pots are equally as difficult to ascertain.

It is only through the rigorous identification of the ceramics and their use marks, repairs and deformations, that the supply mechanisms for tableware for funeral ceremonies can be appreciated. The families of the deceased either shopped for the occasion, purchasing standard quality wares, cheap inferior products, workshop rejects, or they recycled vessels that had already been used as domestic objects within their homes.

Functional associations

The function of the vessels is, of course, a key subject in order to understand their role during the ceremony. Most of the vessels, fine ceramics, common ceramics or amphorae, are for solid or liquid foods. Lamps, perfume burners and *balsamaria*, are present in smaller quantities. Unless solid foods are found in the vessels or chemical analyses are carried out on the residues absorbed by their fabrics, the question of the true function of the vessels and their contents is complex

(Bel, 2002, 2016). If certain forms are logically attributable to a certain function, for example, the jug and the beaker for liquids, the plate for solid foods, the use of other forms such as the cup, does not provide clear answers. In addition, the funerary context may cause the vessels to be diverted from their primary use, as indicated by the discovery of a Samian bowl containing eggs or a cup containing chicken bones, but this does not necessarily indicate ordinary use. It is, therefore, often possible to identify the function of vessels for liquids or solids without being able to identify the vessel contents. Moreover, according to the texts, the food of the funeral meal is specific and more symbolic than everyday food. The contents of vessels from the funerary context remain a vast question to explore and, over the last few years, the results of chemical analyses show that this could be the best way to progress on the subject.

The vessels for cremations: identification of vessels in 'primary' or 'secondary' contexts

Primary cremation deposits

The practices employed during cremation rituals can be divided into several stages: the first, burning on the pyre, is documented by burnt vessels called 'primary cremation deposits'. These are most often broken vessels and sherds found scattered in a pit. More rarely, a complete vase is burnt but intact. In Lyon and in the Rhône valley, primary cremation deposits date back to the Augustan period and last throughout the Early Roman Imperial period, in both pyres and in features containing cremation residues. These burnt vessels are numerous, but their quantity decreases with time: the average of 12 to 13 vessels found in Lyon in the time of Augustus falls to 4 or 5 vessels under the succeeding Flavians. In the Early Roman Empire, tableware, in particular Samian ceramics, constitute the majority of the vessels burnt on the pyre, often the common ceramic jug. What characterises most of the assemblages of vessels from pyres is the association of vessels designed for solid foods and liquids, which nevertheless appears to be very variable, of a regional or even local origin.

'Secondary cremation deposits' consist of secondary features that contain cremated remains or a simple pit containing these residues. Often present are the remains of burnt vessels that reflect the symbolic transfer from the pyre, although sometimes they might be reduced to only a few sherds. In the case of pits containing the cremated remains, the burnt vessels are only found in 'mixed deposits' into which a varying quantity of pyre residues have been transferred and not in the 'simple deposits' where the cremated remains are placed in a clean pit without residue.

Secondary cremation deposits

The vessels deposited within a secondary feature serving as a final resting place for the cremated remains are called 'secondary cremation deposits' as they characterise the second stage of the ceremony, the burial of the cremated remains. They are found in *busta*, in deposits associated with cremated remains and, in a few cases, they are deposited in a pit with residues from the pyre. Unburnt, they are clearly distinguishable from the burnt sherds collected from the pyre. Exceptionally, the Replat cremation complex from Aime in the Northern Alps (Savoie) contained pits with cremated remains and residue pits in which burnt vessels were carefully laid out in a secondary position. In this case, vessels burnt on the pyre were selected after the cremation to serve a secondary role.

The occurrence of secondary cremation deposits varies greatly throughout the region under study. They are more frequent in the Drôme than in Lyon and are always found in the Vaucluse.

In the Rhône-Alpes region as a whole, secondary deposits have up to seven vessels in the Drôme, and never more than three in Lyon. The number of vessels deposited tends to decrease after the middle of the 1st century AD. These vessels, which may be intact or more or less incomplete, were placed in a pit and generally accompanied the cremated remains. They consist of glass *balsamaria* and, more rarely, ceramic ones, sometimes lamps, but also liquid-related vessels, especially jugs. The systematic finds registers used since the 2000s have underlined the important role of jugs. In Lyon, the systematic presence of jugs as secondary deposits in Augusto-Tiberian complexes was noted. The re-recording of the primary deposits from features where the secondary deposit was jug-free showed that when one took into account even the smallest sherd, that jugs were, in fact, present on every occasion (Blaizot and Bonnet, 2007). The jug used for pouring or spraying liquids is an essential accessory to libation practices during sacrificial rites (Scheid, 1998). Further south, in the Drôme and Languedoc, secondary deposits of liquid-related vessels are present, but food vessels play a much more important role than they do in the Lyon area.

Cremation urns

Within the study area in the southeast of France, the most common vessels used as containers for cremated remains of the deceased are cooking pots (Bonnet *et al.*, 2016). Their shape makes a perfect container for the cremated remains, and they can be fitted with a lid. These everyday kitchen items were either purchased for the ceremony or recycled from domestic use. At sites from Lyon, some examples of cooking pots employed as cremation urns are workshop rejects, which were too fragile due to under-firing to have been used for culinary purposes. The arch-aeological evidence from sites in Lyon shows that during the first century AD the standard cremation vessel was a cooking pot with a fitted ceramic lid. During the second century AD, this choice changed, and the most frequently found vessels used as for cremations were jugs, but amphorae and occasionally pitchers were used as well. During the second century AD, cremation urns are mainly chosen from the liquid-related service in both cases. Most frequently, jugs are large vessels, but not systematically so. Sometimes, small jugs were used, which seems to be an impractical choice as the insertion of cremated remains through the narrow neck would not have been an easy task. The jugs would appear to have had several uses during the funerary process, from containing liquids poured for libations to containing bones in their final resting place. Later assemblages, from the third century AD, show a new preference for using a simple pot with a plate used as a lid.

Inhumation burial vessels

In the Rhône-Alpes region, inhumations that can be dated with certainty to the Early Roman Imperial period are rare and, amongst them, only 17% contain ceramic vessels. The most common occurrence in graves in Lyon is the deposit of a single vase, but in some earlier burials, multiple vase deposits have been identified. The reasons behind the drop in the number of vessels present in burials could be similar to those hypothesised for the secondary cremated deposits. It would seem that the ostentatious aspect no longer prevailed; even if further south, in Languedoc and Provence, the number of graves with vessels is more numerous at this time.

The Late Antique period furnishes the greatest amount of evidence but also evinces the most variation, sometimes within the same geographical region. Here, again, the Midi has sig-nificantly more graves containing vessels; they are 2.6 times more numerous than in the Lyon region. The number of vessels per grave is also higher, with an average of around 2.6, compared to 1.7 in Lyon. Even if the variability increases, the main trend is clear: between the 3rd and

Figure 24.2 Trio of vessels (jug, beaker and plate), Late Antique period, Savasse Les Terrasses, Drôme, Auvergne-Rhône-Alpes, France (Photograph: C. Bonnet; More information about the excavation: cf. Ronco, 2013).

the 5th centuries AD, the number of burials with vessels, and the number of vessels per feature, decreases to such a point that in the 5th century AD, the rare graves that contain ceramic deposits contain only one specimen.

As far as the function of the vessels is concerned, half of the Late Antique burials in Lyon containing vessels contain only a single vase and, most frequently, a liquid-related vessel (a jug, a beaker, or a pitcher). This phenomenon of employing a liquid-related vessel as the sole deposit is also the case in Rhône-Alps, Languedoc, and the region of central France as well as in Switzerland. In the fourth century AD, the middle Rhône valley, the south of the Drôme region and Languedoc provide interesting patterns, as reflected in the practice of depositing a pair of vessels at Le Verdier in Lunel (Hérault) (a liquid-associated vase and a solid-associated vessel) (Raynaud, 2011) or a trio of vessels (a jug, a beaker, and a plate) at Les Terrasses à Savasse (Drôme) (Ronco, 2013) (Figure 24.2).

The pot burial vessels

In the study region, amphorae used as 'coffins' for the burial of small children appear in the 4th and early 5th centuries AD. A recent synthesis of these coffin amphorae from Lyon lists about forty such containers, which is not a great number for a large city (Silvino and Bonnet, 2016). Most of these amphorae appear to have been chosen for their elongated shape (North African Keay 25 and African 3 or Lusitanian Almagro 51A/B and C amphorae). The Hispanic Dressel 23 globular amphora, impractical as a coffin, has been recorded once in Lyon.

Amphorae require preparation before placing a corpse within them. This usually consists of cutting the vase under the shoulder at the widest point, sliding the body into it, and closing the hole with the upper part of the amphora. In a few cases, the lower part of the vessel was sectioned above the foot, and the piece removed was deposited a short distance away within the same pit (Figure 24.3).

Figure 24.3 An amphora used as a coffin, Late Antique period, SP3141, 5th arrondissement, 1 Place Eugène Wernert, Lyon, France (Photograph: E. Ferber; More information about the excavation: cf. Ferber, 2018).

Manipulations of vessels: fire marks, cuts, breakage, perforations

Fire marks

Detailed observation of cremation vessels with marks left by fire makes it possible to identify two distinct scenarios. In the first case, once the burnt vessels had been refitted, the impact left by fire marks appears to be very different from one sherd to another, extremely burnt sherds fitting with sherds that had not been exposed to fire (Figure 24.4). In addition, straight breaks, splitting the vase into two or four parts, are associated with sinusoidal breaks that relate to vessels bursting in

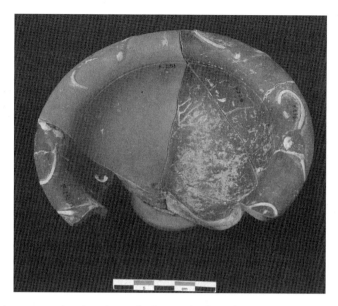

Figure 24.4 Primary cremation deposit, vase broken on the funeral pyre, burnt sherd fitting with unburnt sherd, Early Roman Imperial period, Aime Le Replat, Savoie Rhône-Alpes, France (Photograph: C. Bonnet; More information about the excavation: cf. Goudineau, 2009).

the fire. The explanation could be that the vessels were broken and thrown into the fire, some sherds falling into the flames, with others being spared either because they fell at the periphery or in an area of the pyre that had already cooled. Texts provide insight to permit interpretation of these characteristics as the intentional breaking of the vessels from the meal for the living was set on a table near the pyre. The vessels used for the funeral were considered to have been soiled by death, and none could return to be used in the domestic sphere. In the second scenario, which is less frequent, vessels can show homogeneous scorch marks. These vessels are interpreted as those placed alongside the deceased on the pyre.

Cuts and incisions

As mentioned earlier, the questions developed since the 2000s, thanks to the systematic finds registers and the precise description of the missing parts of vessels, make it possible to identify incisions. Incomplete unburnt vessels with cut marks and incisions can be found in the secondary cremation deposits, both in the pyre and in cremation burials. It is more difficult to interpret such marks in primary cremation deposits because they are most often broken and heavily burnt and their poor state of preservation does not permit reliable observations. In addition to an eventual intentional breakage and the burning on the fire, the primary cremation deposits had suffered breakage due to the interventions of the pyre attendant who stirred the body and the logs to achieve more complete combustion. However, in the Replat cremation complex from Aime, in the case described above, where primary cremation deposits were placed in a secondary structure, it was noted that the jugs were missing their upper parts, most often their necks and handles. These are the rare examples of vessels burnt on the pyre on which such marks can be observed and have significance for elucidating funerary practices. In the Rhône-Alps region, precise observations of missing parts in secondary cremation deposits are rare, except for a few jugs without necks and a beaker without a base in Aime. However, illustrations in excavation reports

Figure 24.5 Incomplete vessels, Late Antique period, Savasse Les Terrasses, Drôme, Auvergne-Rhône-Alpes, France (Photograph: C. Bonnet; More information about the excavation: cf. Ronco, 2013).

and publications regularly show jugs with missing upper parts. The recent discovery of several cremation complexes may provide an opportunity to explore this issue further in the future.

Observations are, therefore, most often based on the vessels from burials and, in particular, those from the Late Antique period, the corpus of which now includes several hundred examples. The cases described below from recent excavations and on-going studies show the possibilities of deciphering these actions. Among the 232 vessels collected from 95 burials of the large Savasse (Drôme) burial complex dating from the middle of the 4th century to the middle of the 5th century AD, only 28% of the vessels are complete, of which 7% are intact and 21% fragmented. Thus, 72% of the vessels are incomplete. Again, in the Drôme, in the contemporary funerary complex of Valence Les Boulevards (Ronco, 2011), only seven vessels out of 36 are complete. The fragments are very varied, from the simple small fragment of the rim called 'V-cut', to a larger part of the rim, or the handle, to all of the upper parts or a large portion of the vessel (Figure 24.5).

Even if archaeologists working in Northern Gaul were aware, early on, of these questions (Van Doorselaere, 1967), in Southern Gaul, the question of missing parts was rarely considered. It is only since the 1990s–2000s that these phenomena have been systematically addressed within the framework of the emerging questions with regard to funerary practices. The most visible phenomenon of many jugs is the absence of the upper part. Sometimes the whole of the neck, or the rim and the handle, or the handle alone are missing from secondary cremation deposits, for vessels from cremation burials and for jugs serving as receptacles for cremated remains. When the rim is preserved, the upper part of the vase can be altered in other ways, for example, by small missing parts on the rims of the vessels called 'V-cuts' (Figure 24.6). Jugs, open forms, cups and plates can all be altered in this way, whether or not they are fine ceramics, common ceramics, or glass. Missing parts of rims of jugs and small amphorae from Lyon were the subject of the first microscopic morphological analyses of cut marks by Vieugué (cf. Blaizot 2009: fig. 32). He showed that the V-gap on the rim of one of the vessels did not result from an accident as it had been deliberately filed. However, since then, microscopic morphological analyses have unfortunately not been repeated, but many objects carry very clear scars which do not seem compatible with accidental damage. The Late Antique funerary complex found at Savasse (Drôme) provided

Figure 24.6 'V-shaped cut' on a jug, Valence Boulevards, Drôme, Auvergne-Rhône-Alpes, France (Photograph: C. Bonnet; More information about the excavation: cf. Ronco, 2011).

some of the most interesting cut marks. They involve four cups of the same type, from four separate graves, the rims of which bear a very carefully executed rounded cut. Moreover, in one case, the sherd removed was also present in the grave but at some distance from the vase (Figure 24.7). Here, the meticulous incision, combined with the discovery of the 'missing' sherd in the grave, undeniably demonstrates the intentional motivation behind these phenomena.

Figure 24.7 Cut bowl with sherd, Late Antique period, Savasse Les Terrasses, Drôme, Auvergne-Rhône-Alpes, France (Photograph: C. Bonnet; More information about the excavation: cf. Ronco, 2013).

Figure 24.8 Cut jug, Late Antique period, Savasse Les Terrasses, Drôme, Auvergne-Rhône-Alpes, France (Photograph: C. Bonnet; More information about the excavation: cf. Ronco, 2013).

At the same site, another unusual incision was identified on the rim of a jug. A piece of the very high brim of the vessel has been carefully removed and a step created to avoid further accidental breakage of the rim (Figure 24.8). Whether it is the removal of the upper part of the jug, the small V-shaped gap in a rim or occasionally sophisticated incisions, the aim is clearly to mark the vase without breaking it and before depositing it in the grave. In the Early Roman Imperial period, these incisions are mainly found on the unburnt vessels of the dead, and mutilating them could help to distinguish them clearly from the dishes of the living. These actions could be conducted for the same reasons as inversion practices, as in placing vessels upside down.

Early texts do not mention anything about the transition from a two-stage ceremony, cremation, to a one-stage ceremony, inhumation burial. There is a certain continuity between the two systems through the deposit of the vessels for the meal of the dead and the mutilations of those used by the living, but Scheid (1984) also sees a reference to the commemoration meals fixing the dead in the 'image of an eternal banquet' that is no longer shared with the living.

Breakage

Ancient texts describe the destruction and discarding of containers used by the living during the funerary banquet on the burning pyre (Scheid, 1984: 131). It is to these completely intentional acts to which the many broken vessels and burnt and unburnt sherds are attributed. Jugs and amphorae are also found broken in pyre residues (Blaizot, 2009: fig. 115). They probably contained the liquids destined for libations that marked pyre closure and were broken once the process was completed. In six Late Antique burials from Forgettes at Quincieux (Rhône), Blaizot noted that vessels were scattered, and this sometimes occurred at two different stages before the deceased was placed in the coffin and after the closing of the lid (Blaizot and Motte, 2015). The breaking of the vessels in burials is similar to that which was practiced on the pyre in the Early Roman Imperial period, once the meal for the living had been consumed. Once again, it is a way of underlining the separation of the living from the dead (Blaizot, 2018).

Perforations

Another phenomenon, the perforation of the vessels is regularly noted. As mentioned above, the poor state of the primary cremation deposits limits the possibilities to observe possible holes in the vessels, but these are documented in the unburnt elements of secondary cremation deposits, in inhumation burial vessels and also on vessels containing cremated remains. In the secondary, unburnt, deposits, there are very few occurrences in Lyon, but a perforated jug was found in Voie de l'Océan, and even a small pierced metal bottle that was used during the pyre closure ritual in Sextant Rue du Commandant Charcot also in Lyon (Blaizot, 2009: fig. 116). Perforations are most commonly recorded on the cremation vessels and their covers. The handles of lids are either completely removed or pierced in their centres, and they are often placed upside down like a funnel. The cremation vessels- pots, jugs, and amphorae- are sometimes perforated. In one case in Lyon, the potter specifically manufactured the cremation receptacle with a hole in it. The perforations were intended to let liquids flow, libation practices being a major element of the Roman cult. Recent excavations at Porta Nocera in Pompeii have revealed numerous examples of cremation vessels and the upside-down perforated cover with a tube in it (Van Andringa, Duday and Lepetz, 2013). In Lyon in the 2000s, the same type of alteration was discovered in contexts dating from the 3rd century AD, thus dating from at least two centuries after the examples from Pompei (Figure 24.9). This device was intended to allow libation liquids to flow through the tube in the pierced cover from the surface of the cemetery onto the cremated bones within.

Conclusion

The methods for recording and studying ceramics from funerary contexts, in use since the 2000s, are based on an approach which considers that all contexts related to cremation and inhumation must be studied in the same way. In the case of cremations, several features mark the different

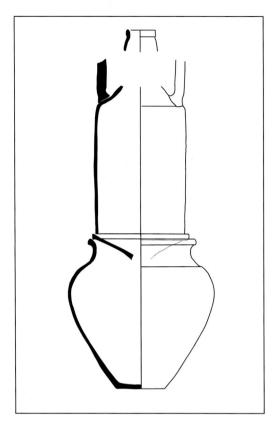

Figure 24.9 Drawing of an ossuary vase with a perforated cover and a tube made from an amphora, Early Roman Imperial period, 7th arrondissement, Rues Chevrier-Rochette, Lyon, France (Drawing: C. Bonnet; More information about the excavation: cf. Blaizot, 2009).

stages of the ceremony between the pyre and the final burial; in the case of inhumations, there is only one feature, but the questions remain the same. The comparison of assemblages between cremation vessels and inhumation burial vessels is the only way to observe how practices endure or change in Roman Gaul. In these instances, a particular approach has been put in place that not only consists in taking into account the smallest sherd but also in providing a precise description of the appearance of the vase from which it came and possible abnormalities in its construction. These systematic observations make it possible to decode the practices carried out during the funerary banquet. The breaking of vessels used for the meal of the living is undertaken on the pyre in the Early Roman Imperial period and around the burial in the Late Antique period. In the same way, the mutilation of the vessels containing the meal for the deceased is documented in cremation deposits and in inhumation burials. The final objective of these ritual practices is to gradually separate the dead from the living, first by breaking the vessels used during the banquet for the living and then by mutilating the vessels intended for the deceased in order to clearly distinguish them from one another.

Acknowledgement

A special thanks goes to Jemima Dunkley of Inrap (Institut National de Recherches Archéologiques Préventives), who helped with the translation of this chapter into English.

References

Allain, J. (1972). Secrets d'une Tombe Antique. *Archéologia*, 44, pp. 24–27.

Bel, V. (1993). Les Dépôts de Vases dans les Tombes: Les Données de l'Époque Romaine. *Revue Archéologique de l'Ouest*, Supplement number 6, pp. 279–283.

Bel, V. (2002). *Pratiques funéraires du Haut-Empire dans le midi de la Gaule, La nécropole gallo-romaine du Valladas à Saint-Paul-Trois-Châteaux (Drôme)*. Monographies d'Archéologie Méditerranéenne 11.

Bel, V., ed. (2016). Deux ensembles funéraires d'époque romaine, avenue Jean-Jaurès à Nîmes (Gard). Montpellier, 46th supplément à la Revue Archéologique de Narbonnaise.

Blaizot, F., ed., (2009). *Pratiques et espaces funéraires de la Gaule dans l'Antiquité*. Gallia 66/1, Paris: Centre National de la Recherche Scientifique (CNRS).

Blaizot, F. (2018), Tradition and innovation regarding burials during Late Antiquity in eastern central Gaul. In: M.-D. Nenna, S. Huber et W. Van Andringa, eds., *Constituer la Tombe, Honorer les Défunts en Méditerranée Antique, Études Alexandrines*. Alexandrie: Centre d'Etudes Alexandrines (CEAlex), 46, pp. 487–542.

Blaizot, F. and Bonnet, C. (2007). Traitements, modalités de dépôt et rôle des céramiques dans les structures funéraires gallo-romaines. In: L. Baray, P. Brun, A. Testard, eds., Actes du colloque interdisciplinaire de Sens des 12–14 juin 2003, *Pratiques funéraires et sociétés, Nouvelles approches en anthropologie sociale*. Dijon: Editions Universitaires de Dijon, pp. 209–228.

Blaizot, F. and Motte, S., ed., (2015). Quincieux, Rhône, Rhône-Alpes, Forgettes-A466, Liaison A6/A46. Auvergne-Rhône-Alpes. Rapport de fouille archéologique préventive, Institut national de recherches archéologiques préventives (Inrap), Service Régional de l'Archéologie de Rhône-Alpes, Lyon.

Bonnet, C. (2016). Le céramologue au service des problématiques funéraires: approche d'une méthode globale. La Société Française d'Étude de la Céramique Antique en Gaule (SFECAG), *Actes du Congrès d'Autun*, pp. 13–26.

Bonnet, C., Batigne Vallet, C., Brun, C. and Barreto, F. (2016). Les vases ossuaires en céramique à Lyon de la fin du Ier s. av. J.-C. au IIIe s. apr. J.-C. La Société Française d'Étude de la Céramique Antique en Gaule (SFECAG): Actes du Congrès d'Autun, pp. 175–202.

Duday, H., Courtaud, P., Crubezy, E., Sellier, P. and Tillier, A.-M. (1990). L'Anthropologie 'de Terrain': Reconnaissance et Interprétation des Gestes Funéraires. *Bulletin et Mémoires de la Société d'Anthropologie de Paris*, 2(3–4), pp. 29–50.

Ferber, E., ed., (2018). Lyon, Rhône, Rhône-Alpes, 1 Place Eugène Wernert. Rapport de fouille archéologique préventive, Institut national de recherches archéologiques préventives (Inrap), Service Régional de l'Archéologie de Rhône-Alpes, Lyon.

Goudineau, C., ed., (2009). Rites funéraires à Lugdunum. *Catalogue de l'exposition 'Post Mortem: Les rites funéraires à Lugdunum'*. Paris: Éditions Errance.

Perraud, R. (1974), Le bris rituel aux Ier et IIème siècles de notre ère, d'après les fouilles des Plantées à Briord (Ain), *Revue Archéologique de l'Est et du Centre-Est*, 25, pp. 7–16.

Raynaud, C. (2011). *Les nécropoles de Lunel-Viel (Hérault) de l'Antiquité au Moyen-Âge*. Revue Archéologique de Narbonnaise, supplement 40.

Ronco, C., ed., (2011). Valence, Drôme, Rhône-Alpes, Boulevards en centre ville Tranche 2. Drôme, Rapport de fouille archéologique préventive, Inrap, Service Régional de l'Archéologie de Rhône-Alpes, Lyon.

Ronco, C. ed. (2013). Les terrasses de Savasse 2, Drôme. Rapport de fouille archéologique préventive, Inrap, Service Régional de l'Archéologie de Rhône-Alpes, Lyon.

Scheid, J. (1984). Contraria, Facere: renversements et déplacements dans les rites funéraires. *Annali di dipartimento di studi del mondo classico e del mediterráneo antico*, Sezione di Archeologia e Storia Antica VI, Instituto Universitario Orientale, Naples, pp. 117–139.

Scheid, J. (1998). *La religion des Romains*. Paris: Armand Colin, Collection Cursus.

Silvino, T. and Bonnet, C. (2016) Le remploi des amphores comme cercueil durant l'Antiquité tardive: l'exemple de Lyon/Lugdunum. *Société Française d'Etudes de la Céramique Antique en Gaule (SFECAG)*, Actes du Congrès d'Autun, pp. 347–354.

Thirion-Merle, V., Batigne Vallet, C., Bonnet, C. and Bernet, A. (2019). *The use of dilatometry in determining the way of selecting ceramic wares for ossuary usage: the Lugdunum case during the Early Roman Empire*. European Meeting on Ancient Ceramics (EMAC), 6–9 September 2017, Bordeaux, pp. 97–106.

Tranoy, L. (1995). *Recherches sur les nécropoles antiques de Lyon. L'acquis des fouilles récentes de la Favorite et du Quai Arloing*. Unpublished Ph.D. thesis, Université Aix-Marseille I.

Van Andringa, W., Duday, H. and Lepetz, S. (2013). *Mourir à Pompéi: fouille d'un quartier funéraire de la nécropole romaine de Porta Nocera (2003–2007)*. Rome: Collection de l'École Française de Rome.

Van Doorselaere, A. (1967). *Les nécropoles d'époque romaine en Gaule Septentrionale*. Dissertationes Archaeologicae Gandenses 10, Bruges: De Tempel.

25

ANIMAL REMAINS IN BURIALS

Patrice Méniel

ARTEHIS, Archéologie, Terre, Histoire et Sociétés, UMR 6298,
CNRS-Université de Bourgogne, Dijon, France

Introduction

Archaeological analyses have the potential to reveal the role of animals in funerary practices of past societies. This aspect of the relationship between humans and animals, as glimpsed from the perspective of burials, benefits from favourable taphonomic conditions due to the care taken in the deposition of the remains and their rapid burial, which protects them from the action of scavengers and weathering. However, positive taphonomic conditions are not always sufficient to provide all of the answers to the questions raised by the animal remains present in burials. Indeed, practices are very diverse across the world and through time but can also vary between two contemporary burials in the same burial ground. This chapter presents some examples that highlight the role of collection methods, analysis, and interpretation of animal remains discovered in burials as it is impossible to propose an exhaustive inventory of all of these practices.

But even with these essentially methodological aspects, it is not possible to treat all cases, nor to take into account all preservation conditions encountered during archaeological excavations. The remains of animal products, for example, fat, meat, milk, which can be revealed by chemical analysis of residues in ceramics, are not treated here.

Recovery, documentation and recording

Animal remains in archaeological contexts are encountered in various ways, as complete articulated skeletons, articulated skeletal parts, isolated elements, or as fragments. In a funerary context, one often deals with calcined bones, the detail of study of which is heavily dependent on the degree of fragmentation, which means that results are rather less detailed than those obtained from the study of unburned bones (Figure 25.1).

All these remains, burned or not, large or small, must be carefully observed and kept in place before recording them on plans and/or photographing them. These steps are necessary to permit the reconstruction of the funerary practices that contributed to their deposition. In cases where there are several layers of remains, successive recording steps may be necessary and then combined to obtain an overall view of the deposit. However, what is deposited as a result of many funerary practices does not often lead to great accumulations, and it is often impossible to obtain a complete image of the whole of a funerary deposit without recording multiple layers.

Special attention should be paid to the burial fill, as not everything may be placed on the floor of the grave. Animal remains may be placed on tables, in chests, on shelves or on other organic grave furniture (Méniel, 2006). The decay of these materials, except in particular contexts

Figure 25.1   Animal deposits in Grave 55 of the Iron Age burial ground at Sajopetri (Hungary, 3rd century BC) (Photograph: P. Méniel).

(wet or dry environments), justifies paying particular attention to wall effects, alignments, angulations and empty zones. In the same spirit, attention must also be paid to the bones from the fill, which may have nothing to do with funerary practices, as well as burrows or nests of animals, such as moles, foxes, and badgers that can take advantage of the softer sediment of a burial dug into more compact soil. These animals can disturb the deposit and, for carnivores, may introduce additional bones into the burial context.

Recording of remains can be conducted in various ways depending on the means available during excavation, either through drawn plans or photographs made in the field, but also through the use of 3D photogrammetric reconstruction. The removal and numbering of bones must permit them to be located on the plan as well as their depth from the surface. Removal of bones can then be made individually, piece-by-piece or by anatomical groups, for example, especially when excavation time is limited. The presence of a faunal specialist during the excavation can make a substantial contribution. In addition, their presence during excavation can aid subsequent laboratory-based study. Therefore, it is beneficial that the archaeozoologist is invited to the excavation and not only confined to the laboratory study of bones after the excavation has been completed.

The study of unburned animal remains

Anatomical and species determinations of each fragment or anatomical group form the first steps of the study. These basic data can be supplemented by a certain amount of information, especially on age and sex. Stature and cranial measurements, as well as information from ancient DNA and isotopes, can also be obtained. This information permits the description of the constituents of the assemblage according to the elements present, their state of preservation and the number and species of animals involved. The methods of this study are detailed in a number of textbooks

(Chaplin, 1971; Lyman, 1994; Reitz and Wing, 1999; Chaix and Méniel, 2001). Even though they might consist of small quantities of fragmented bones, funerary deposits can reveal evidence of cutmarks, burning, and weathering. The study of cutmarks includes not only recording their presence on bones but also aids to determine the joints of meat obtained based on the position of the cutmarks on the bones and their position in the skeleton. It should be noted that animal carcasses can be disarticulated without leaving a mark on the bones, and only the location of isolated joints might testify to the butchery of these remains. Thus, the position of the bones and joints present as observed during excavation and recorded on field plans add further important information to the analysis of the remains.

Inventories of the remains make it possible to determine the number of individuals involved after identification of associated elements of single animals. Much attention is required at this stage, as several animals of the same age may be represented, leading to the identification of associations, such as a pair of hams, that can only be verified after careful examination. The impression that all quarters of pork come from a single individual, such as is sometimes concluded in the field, has often been questioned in burials of European Iron Age date.

Cremated animal bones

Fragmented, cracked, or deformed animal remains mixed with cremated human remains are often not easy to distinguish from one another. In some cases, a difference in visual appearance (colour or cracking) makes it possible to divide the remains of the cremation into two sets: those associated with the human remains and those of faunal inclusions. These distinctions may result from differences in the state of the remains when deposited on the pyre, whether fresh or dry bones, or cooked joints of meat, but methods are still in development to answer this question. The quantity and state of the cremated remains are decisive for the level of detail of the analysis, which could vary from a simple attestation that the remains of an animal are present to an inventory of lateralised elements, with age and sex determinations, and perhaps cutmarks.

In the case of bulk sampling of a calcined cluster such as may be found in an urn excavated in the laboratory, it is appropriate to apply the same protocol for numbering and location of the cremated human remains to those applied with the animal remains. This makes it possible to reconstruct the methods employed during the deposition of the remains and their collection from the pyre.

Apart from the degree of calcination and fragmentation of cremated remains, the impact of taphonomic damage can influence the extent of the reconstruction of funerary practices. The fact that a single pyre can be used several times can lead to the presence of bones from a previous cremation. Therefore the representativeness of each skeletal element must be defined from very challenging single fragments, to clusters where animals are represented by numerous bones that permit conjoining of fragments and articulations between elements to incomplete skeletons, such as those of poultry without feet or heads, or whole skeletons, such as those of small dogs. The question is clearly a much more delicate one when remains are heavily fragmented or when they consist of residual clusters: partial collection from the pyre or clusters removed following subsequent disturbances provides examples of the range of possible interpretations.

The question of indeterminate elements requires back and forth communication between faunal and human remains specialists because, as previously noted, it is important to distinguish at least a portion of the human remains from those of animals, making it possible to better indicate their relative frequency in the calcined cluster. In fact, apart from the differences in the extent of cancellous bone, identified remains are sometimes present, without satisfactorily explanation of whether or not they were fresh, dry, or cooked bones, as determined from differences in

appearance, colour, surface condition and/or porosity, which may also aid to distinguish the anatomically indeterminate parts of human remains from those of animals.

The nature of animal remains

First, bones deposited after the completion of funerary rites should be distinguished from those
that may have arrived accidentally or intrusively. Indeed, a burial dug into compact sediment is
a favourable place for the intrusion of burrowing animals, and disturbance of the soil can also
disturb bones scattered on the surface of the burial ground and incorporate them in the burial.
It is also necessary to consider bones collected from the pyre site from a previous cremation and
included in a subsequent burial.

The variety of animal remains discovered in burials can relate to a variety of circumstances.
They may be personal items of the deceased (a hunting trophy, jewellery, bone or wooden
utensil), hide (fur), pieces of meat or accompanying animals. The determination of the nature of
these various elements is based on their species-specific and anatomical origin and the evidence
of shaping, handling, working or cooking that they carry. The position in relation to the deceased
or, to a lesser extent, the cremated remains may help to clarify the nature of some of them.
Items of clothing or everyday equipment, ornaments, weapons or tools may be items of personal
adornment of the deceased, which may accompany the body in the grave without this implying
a ritual prescription or a specific funerary significance.

Another important category is animal parts that derive from food items. They may be pieces
of meat of species likely consumed by the group concerned. Some bones show cutmarks and are
sometimes marked with the effects of cooking such as localised burning of the ends of bones or
teeth. Indeed, the meat may have been cooked immediately before being deposited, but this is not
always easy to establish. Another question is whether or not the bones, especially when isolated,
were still (partly) covered with meat (soft tissue). These questions, which often remain unanswered,
pose limits for the reconstruction of funerary practices. Other food from animal origin can be
found in burials, including whole eggs or eggshells, for example. Remains of food of vegetable
origin are often included in burials and can be contained in ceramics, in addition to beverages,
such as mead, beer or wine, of which only typical containers may indicate their once presence.
The final category is that of the skeletons of small edible animals, poultry, in particular, deposited
in their entirety, or pets, a dog, for example, which may not have been a food animal at all.

Sacrifice, sharing and display of meat

The inventory of pieces of meat is usually marked by deficiencies with respect to what might have
been provided from animals sacrificed during funerary rites; indeed, it is not always obvious that
it is not meat eaten as part of normal diet that has been offered to the deceased. Apart from losses
due to taphonomy and excavation, it is usual for animals to be only partially represented. In the
case of cremation burials, even by adding joints to the pyre and being directly deposited with the
deceased on the pyre, the mammals consumed are often represented by only a small portion of
their bodies, such as less than a quarter in many burials in Iron Age northern Gaul (Méniel, 1998;
Metzler-Zens, Metzler and Méniel, 1999). The lacking parts, apart from the butchery waste, had
probably been consumed during funerary banquets, but the evidence of these is tenuous and even
in the burial grounds where animal remains are found in pits without human bones, it has not yet
been possible to establish a link with the parts of an animal deposited in a grave at the same site.

The treatment of small animals, especially poultry, is quite different because they are often
deposited complete, or simply prepared to be consumed after removal of the head and/or feet

Figure 25.2 Arrangement of pig remains in grave 1 at Lamadelaine (1st century BC, Luxembourg) (Photograph: P. Méniel).

and only the remains of these extremities may be found outside the graves. For large animals, beef cattle, in particular, it is quite the opposite. When they are represented by a single partial element, which is quite common in Iron Age Gaul, one must imagine either a very unequal distribution, the main part of the sacrificed animal being consumed at the banquet, or either the contribution of a piece from another origin, profane or ritual, the ox being a major sacrificial animal in many societies.

What may be only a few quarters of meat is sometimes carefully deposited to enhance its value. It is here that the study of the location of the remains justifies the accurate recording of their placement, which could be the result of taphonomic change, under the influence of decay, gravity, and the effects of in-filling soil, with animals or their parts possibly placed on grave furniture made of wood or other perishable materials. Thus it is sometimes possible to distinguish between deposits placed on a wooden structure within a grave chamber from those placed directly on the ground, depending on whether the decomposition of soft tissues occurred before or after the decomposition and collapse of the structures.

The most important offerings can be very clearly arranged and of varying elaborateness. Thus, at Lamadelaine in Luxembourg (1st century BC, Metzler-Zens, Metzler and Méniel, 1999), some parts of previously disarticulated pigs were collected in order to represent the image of an animal from only a few (5 of 14) pieces (Figure 25.2). In other cases, as in Sajopetri in Hungary (3rd century BC, Méniel, 2018), elements had been arranged symmetrically. But these variations in disposition appear only in several tens of burials within burial grounds, which demonstrate the diversity of practices found within the same population.

Spatial distributions and change through time

Like certain prestigious burials, such as chariot burials or those beneath tumuli, placed on a prominent point on the landscape, burials found in burial grounds are frequented for various periods of time in the majority of cases. This opens up two approaches to reveal the importance of animals in funerary practices: spatial and chronological. Without overlooking the state of burials, the degree of preservation of which can greatly affect bone deposits, in the case of especially cremation burial grounds, the absence of calcined bone may be due to its destruction, or because there are empty offering pits into which deposits were not made. Unless all skeletal material in the burials is well preserved, it is necessary to assess their degree of preservation as good, average, or poor (Metzler-Zens, Metzler and Méniel, 1999: 19).

One of the aims of this synthesis is to highlight a possible common practice, which is sometimes facilitated by the relative uniformity of animal bone deposits, but is usually quite delicate, especially when individualism seems to preside over the formation of funerary deposits, to the extent that it is impossible to discover two similar deposits in a cemetery. The causes of variability are multiple and at various scales, individual, family and community. The numbers are not always sufficient to compensate for the effects of these fluctuations and only major trends can be inferred, such as the list of species attested, possibly supplemented by a list of the element parts involved. It is thus possible, for example, in Iron Age northern Gaul, to see changes in the contribution of animals, with offerings often being quite limited in the fifth and fourth centuries BC but involving a fairly equal use of pork, beef and mutton. This is followed by an increase in the use of pork and the appearance of poultry in the third century BC, with the latter becoming very abundant in the Roman period. Game animals are always very rare. Dog remains are sometimes found in mixed assemblages in the 1st century BC, or as a pet, being very small adult dogs, included in cremations. However, these discoveries remain quite exceptional. There are many nuances and exceptions to such generalisations, but they make it possible to begin to identify general trends in the great variability of the individual deposits found within burial grounds.

Commemoration practices

The excavation of structures, pits, ditches and pyres located close to burials can reveal certain aspects of the treatments applied to animals, of which only a part is found in burials themselves. Apart from the pieces of meat shared during the ceremony itself, there is evidence of commemorative deposits, several examples of which were found around Gaulish burials in the region surrounding Trier, as at Clémency (Metzler *et al.,* 1991) or Gœblange (Metzler and Gaeng, 2009). These may be cremated remains of pork, accompanied by charcoal, sherds of amphorae and coins. These commemorative practices may be attested to span several decades near larger burials.

Another type of commemoration may affect animal bones deposited in graves. Some bones show signs of weathering due to surface exposure in burials, where most of the bones are otherwise perfectly preserved (Metzler-Zens, Metzler and Méniel, 1999). This is probably a consequence of the presence of libation conduits that are attested from time to time during protohistory and Antiquity. These conduits are intended to permit liquid offerings to the deceased that, in the process, leave some bones exposed to air, which is attested by their degree of erosion.

Atypical funerary practices

In addition to those found in burial grounds, deposits of associated human and animal remains are also found in various types of structures (pits, ditches, shafts, quarries) in a variety of contexts (near settlements, in sanctuaries, or in the surrounding areas of a site) (Figure 25.3) (Méniel, 2008, 2017). In the vast majority of cases, these associations of bodies or body parts (such as crania) involve simultaneous deaths, when some or all of the individuals were killed at the same time. Among the many possibilities, one can interpret these as victims of battles, epidemics, catastrophes or sacrifices, but these may also involve exceptional funerary practices. In the majority of cases,

Figure 25.3 A horse skeleton next to a human skeleton in a pit at Varennes-sur-Seine (Seine et Marne, 3rd century BC, France) (Photograph: P. Méniel).

whole bodies are found, although some individuals, both animal and human, may be only partially represented, often only by their crania or by post-cranial skeletons lacking the elements of the cephalic extremity.

The methods of excavation and analysis do not differ much from those used for more commonly encountered animal bones in burials. Particular attention should be paid to the question of the simultaneity of deposits since they must be distinguished from successive burials of a certain number of deceased individuals that occur due to natural causes. The contacts between the bones and the state of the articular connections are particularly important to this approach. Some very spectacular deposits result from the staging of a series of bodies, with either alignment in several rows within the whole of a ditched structure, for example, or in looser arrangements, with some individuals arranged quite haphazardly. A human male and a horse are very regularly associated, but there are also the whole series of deposits involving other animals, cattle, pigs and sheep for the most part.

One goal in the analysis of these assemblages is to determine the manner of death either by epidemic, violence-related trauma, or sacrifice, for example. Any signs of violence-related trauma or butchery cutmarks related to the recovery of the skin or tendons, in addition to the composition of the population sample (species, age-at-death, and sex), but also patterns in the dispositions of the animals, make it possible to interpret the circumstances that led to the creation of such deposits.

The horse and humans

Among the domestic animals, one, the horse, is distinguished by the special place it occupies in funerary practices of a great number of societies, as reflected in large burial grounds in China, in the Kurgans of central Asia, and in the chariot burials of Iron Age Europe, to name just a few examples. At these locations, and in many other areas, there are large and symbolic deposits, testaments to the various practices linking humans, often males, and horses.

Chariot burials, a common funerary practice during the European Iron Age, are highly variable. In many cases, especially in Champagne (France), horses are absent from the funerary chambers, but the inclusion of the chariot and harness indicates their symbolic connection to these burials (Desenne, Pommepuy and Demoule, 2009; Méniel, 2016). However, some remains are found in ditches surrounding burials and suggest the possibility of an exhibition of remains on the surface of the tumulus. Unfortunately, these encircling features are still too rarely excavated because they are poorly preserved due to having been disturbed in more recent centuries. In a few rare burials, horses are represented in their entirety, or partially by crania, but the most spectacular case known to date is the chariot burial beneath one of the tumuli from Sboryanovo (3rd century BC, Bulgaria), where two horses were buried standing upright and hitched to the chariot (Anastassov and Gergova, 2017). The arrangement required the construction of pits and trenches adapted to the anatomy of these two animals. The taphonomic alterations following the decomposition of the soft tissues of the body and the in-filling of the pits reveal modifications from settling of sediment and the maintenance of anatomical connections in evidence in the disposition of the two skeletons. The methods of excavation, and in particular those of the extremities of the limbs buried deeply in the narrow trenches, had to be adapted by using a succession of excavation levels, but overall, the procedures employed were not that different from those applied to animals lying on their flanks, which is the much more commonly occurring position.

Conclusion

The interpretation of animal remains encountered in burials, even if found in the fairly well-defined context of funerary practices, require a variety of approaches, thus making it difficult to establish an exhaustive list of all of them. As a consequence, it is necessary to consider different levels of interpretation; from the burial itself, through to the burial ground of which the burial is a part and to regional and chronological syntheses.

For the burial itself, there are many and diverse questions which depend on the nature of the practices and the deposits of which they are a part. They include:

- personal belongings, part of the deceased's once personal possessions, or as part of a funerary deposit
- the nature of the meat involved (species, age, sex, elements or parts of elements)
- whether or not the meat comes from a funerary sacrifice or was it already cut before deposition? Was it deposited raw or cooked? Was it included as part of a skin?
- the description of the means by which the deposit was made and the in-filling procedures of the feature
- the association with other grave inclusions (dishes, containers, kitchen utensils) and solid or liquid foods
- pet animals that were not eaten

For the burial ground, it is important:

- to record and map the deposits
- to note chronological change through time
- to identify recurring patterns in the composition of the animal deposits
- to assess individual variation in the assemblage, such as age, sex, and social standing

Finally, at the regional level:

- Ascertain the geographical and chronological limits of the practices by integrating areas without animals and the burials of corpses that diverge from more commonly encountered, traditional burial
- Monitor the changing animal deposits in burials through time
- Compare the status of animals in daily, funerary and sacrificial practices

This stratified approach, as imperfect as it may be, is meant to draw attention to the need to order the analysis from the particular to the general. Even if the context of these funerary deposits is among the best defined in the archaeological record, the great diversity of animal remains within a single burial ground at a given time is a common feature through time. Though difficult, it is necessary to synthesise these data and the practices they represent in order to elucidate the status of animals and their relationships with humans in the past.

References

Anastassov, J. and Gergova, D. (2017). Projet Shoryanovo, Bulgarie: Nécropoles et Territoire. *Archäologie der Schweiz*, 40 (3), pp. 44–45.

Chaix, L. and Méniel, P. (2001). *Archéozoologie. Les animaux et l'archéologie*. Paris: Errance.

Chaplin, R.E. (1971). *The study of animal bones from archaeological sites*. New York: Seminar Press.

Desenne, S., Pommepuy, C. and Demoule, J.-P., eds. (2009). *Bucy-Le-Long (Aisne). Une nécropole de La Tène ancienne (Ve–IVe siècle avant notre ère)*. Revue Archéologique de Picardie, 26, Bucy-Le-Long: Persee.

Lyman, R.L. (1994). *Vertebrate taphonomy*. Cambridge: Cambridge University Press.

Méniel, P. (1998). *Les animaux et l'histoire d'un village gaulois*. Reims: Mémoire de la Société Archéologique Champenoise, Le site protohistorique d'Acy-Romance (Ardennes), 3.

Méniel, P. (2006). Les Offrandes Animales de la Nécropole Celtique de Ludas-Varjù Dulo (Hongrie). *Acta Archaeologica Academiae Scientiarum Hungaricae*, 57, pp. 345–366.

Méniel, P. (2008). *Manuel d'archéozoologie funéraire et sacrificielle (Age du Fer)*. Gollion: Infolio.

Méniel, P. (2016). Le cheval à la Gorge-Meillet. In: L. Olivier, ed., *Autopsie d'une Tombe Gauloise. La Tombe à Char de la Gorge-Meillet à Somme-Tourbe (Marne)*. Saint-Germain-en-Laye: Cahiers du MAN (Musée d'archéologie nationale), 2, pp. 269–275.

Méniel, P. (2017). Les Dépôts Atypiques d'Animaux: Fouille, Étude et Interprétation. *Les Nouvelles de l'Archéologie*, 148, pp. 11–15.

Méniel, P. (2018). Les restes animaux des sépultures de Sajópetri. In: M. Szabó, Z. Czajlik et K. Tankó, eds., *La Nécropole Celtique à Sajópetri-Homoki-Szőlőskert*. Paris: L'Harmattan, pp. 273–319.

Metzler, J. and Gaeng, C. (2009). *Gæblange-Nospelt, une nécropole aristocratique trévire*. Luxembourg: Dossiers d'Archéologie du Musée National d'Histoire et d'Art, 13.

Metzler, J., Waringo, R., Bis, R. and Metzler-Zens, N. (1991). *Clémency et les tombes de l'aristocratie en Gaule belgique*. Luxembourg: Dossiers d'Archéologie du Musée National d'Histoire et d'Art, 1.

Metzler-Zens, N., Metzler, J. and Méniel, P. (1999). *Lamadelaine, une nécropole de l'oppidum du Titelberg*. Luxembourg: Dossiers d'archéologie du musée national d'histoire et d'art, 6.

Reitz, E.J. and Wing, E.S. (1999). *Zooarchaeology. Cambridge manuals in archaeology*. Cambridge: Cambridge University Press.

26

THE WALKING DEAD – LIFE AFTER DEATH

Archaeoentomological evidence in a Roman catacomb

(Saints Marcellinus and Peter, central area, 1st–3rd century AD)

Jean-Bernard Huchet

PACEA, De la Préhistoire à l'Actuel: Culture, Environnement et Anthropologie, UMR 5199, CNRS-Université de Bordeaux, Pessac, France

Muséum National d'Histoire Naturelle (National Museum of Natural History), Paris, France

Dominique Castex

PACEA, De la Préhistoire à l'Actuel: Culture, Environnement et Anthropologie, UMR 5199, CNRS-Université de Bordeaux, Pessac, France

Introduction

Among all the early Christian catacombs in Rome, the catacomb of Saints Marcellinus and Peter is an emblematic case. This is mainly due to its very well-preserved wall paintings and to the opportunity to access a remarkable example of a necropolis, a 'World of the Dead', that had gradually developed underground on a very large scale (approximately three hectares of surface area, and, about 4.5 km of underground networks on three levels containing between 20 000 and 25 000 graves).

Although generally limited to historians and archaeologists, the study of this catacomb has been opened up to more specifically anthropological investigations because of the discovery of unusual deposits of human remains in its central part that may reflect a mortality crisis. The unusual nature of these bone deposits, including associated remains, constitute a true laboratory for a variety of research interests. Due to the presence of many well-preserved insect remains, archaeoentomology finds itself in an especially privileged place for understanding these funerary deposits at a variety of interpretative levels.

DOI: 10.4324/9781351030625-30

The historical and bioarchaeological context

Located southeast of Rome on the ancient *Via Labicana*, this subterranean funerary complex served as a Christian cemetery from the last third of the 3rd century until the beginning of the 5th century AD (Giuliani and Guyon, 2011: 100, fig. 3). Originally used as a hydraulic network to supply water to small agricultural properties, but also to exploit pozzolana ash as a building material, this location was then exploited as a burial site by *fossores*, a term still in use today for those who specialise in what is now called funeral art, construction and decoration of graves (Giuliani and Guyon, 2011). The use of these new funerary spaces was a response to necessity, not only because of the growing population of Rome but also due to the humility practised by the first Christians, who sought increased simplicity in the treatment of the dead.

Although previously discovered in 1594 by Antonio Bosio, an Italian archaeologist of Maltese origin and the first systematic explorer of subterranean Rome, and despite numerous excavation campaigns through the 1970s (Guyon, 1987), this new funerary area was first discovered in 2004. It included the remains of a large number of individuals concentrated in several separate chambers (Figure 26.1). This central area appeared to be very much separated from the rest of the catacomb traditionally known for its galleries, the walls of which accommodated individual grave-niches, called *loculi*. New excavation campaigns were carried out between 2005 and 2010.

Archaeological analysis revealed a succession of several complex stratigraphic sequences comprised of skeletal remains in primary deposits. Within these sequences, specific observations of the relations between remains highlighted the simultaneity of these burials. These observations led to the conclusion that a mortality crisis had been responsible for their accumulation

Figure 26.1 Overall view of one of the tombs in the central sector of the catacomb (Photograph: D. Gliksman, Institut National de Recherches Archéologiques Préventives).

(Blanchard and Castex, 2007). 3D imaging reconstructions of the original space occupied by the cadavers demonstrated that funerary chambers had been re-used several times as a mass burial site in response to several successive mortality crises (Castex et al., 2014; Sachau-Carcel, 2014) (cf. Sachau-Carcel, Chapter 31, this volume). Complementary evidence consisting of artefacts, coins and radiocarbon determinations from bones, fabrics and grape seeds dates the use of these structures to quite a long timescale, between the late 1st century and early 3rd century AD, earlier than the first previously known funerary presence in the late 3rd century AD.

In spite of the poor preservation of the remains due to a very high relative humidity (95–100%), an anthropological study has been carried out on about 500 individuals of the total once buried in this area (Castex and Blanchard, 2011). Age and sex distributions show a predominance of young adults, a considerable deficit of immature individuals and a large majority of females (31%), but these characteristics do not in themselves permit the identification of a particular type of mortality crisis. However, in the absence of traumatic injuries related to violence, the hypothesis of a mortality crisis due to an epidemic seemed most probable. Some textual sources report the existence of major mortality crises in Rome during the Imperial Period and the burials discovered may be linked to the famous Antonine or Galenic 'plague', an epidemic that struck the Roman Empire at the end of the Antonine dynasty, during the reigns of Marcus Aurelius and Commodus, between 165 and 190 AD, which was most likely to have been an outbreak of smallpox (Gourevitch, 2013). Due to poor DNA preservation, biomolecular methods have not yet identified the pathogen(s) responsible for these multiple deaths, and thus an infectious disease from either a single cause or from a succession of epidemics of differing aetiologies cannot be excluded.

Funerary treatments of some of the dead highlight some original practices, especially the existence of linen shrouds, treated with gypsum plaster, tightly wrapping bodies (Figure 26.2), as well as the presence of rare and expensive materials such as gold threads, Baltic amber, sandarac resin and incense from Yemen. These artefacts might reflect a rather high social status of the deceased (Devièse et al., 2017). However, they could also be linked to the well-documented cosmopolitan character of the city of Rome and a funerary tradition specific to a particular group of individuals. The latter hypothesis is supported by the results of isotopic biogeochemical analysis ($\delta^{13}C$, $\delta^{15}N$, $\delta^{18}O$ and $^{87}Sr/^{86}Sr$) carried out on several types of remains (bone, dental enamel and hair). These analyses permitted the reconstruction of mobility patterns for some of the buried individuals that demonstrate several geographic origins, including Europe, Asia Minor, Africa and Arabia (Salesse, 2015).

All of this evidence converges on the hypothesis that the central area of the catacomb of Saints Marcellinus and Peter represents a primary focus for the understanding of the funerary treatment of mass deaths in the Roman Empire. However, several questions still remain and other types of analyses deserve to be explored. The arthropod remains showed excellent preservation and were directly observable on bones or in brain tissue (Figures 26.3a, 26.3d and 26.3f). Environmental monitoring in the catacomb showed consistent temperatures (between 16.6 °C and 17.6°C) and relative humidity (95–100%) with a lack of seasonal fluctuations (Schotsmans et al., 2019). The preservation of brain tissue, as well as hair, is rare, though not unique in high humidity burial environments (Serrulla, Etxeberría and Herrasti, 2017).

The presence of such remains provides an ideal opportunity for archaeoentomological investigation. This analysis provides a means to address funerary treatments of individuals, such as the exposure of bodies prior to burial, the circumstance(s) of death through the study of ectoparasitic insects that are vectors of epidemics, including fleas and lice, and to permit insight into the seasonality of deaths, a significant source of information when considering the potential simultaneity of deposits.

Figure 26.2 Plaster-coated individuals, with plaster halo around the head (Photograph: Archaeological missions 2005–2010).

In addition to the description and interpretation of these simultaneous deposits, it was questioned how these remains came to be placed in this area of the catacomb. In the close vicinity of the burial chambers, archaeological investigation revealed the presence of a vertical shaft connected to the outside of the structure, which may relate to the extraction of tufa that had been exploited when this area was a quarry. This shaft could have been used as an access point to the central chambers facilitating the deposition of corpses (see discussion section, below) (Ricciardi, Giuliani and Castex, 2018: 110, fig. 12).

Archaeoentomology: a brief history

Within the bioarchaeological disciplines, the study of insect remains from Quaternary sediments is a recent science that emerged in the second half of the 20th century (Osborne, 1969; Buckland, 1976; Coope, 1977, 1986, 1990). This discipline includes two distinct entities,

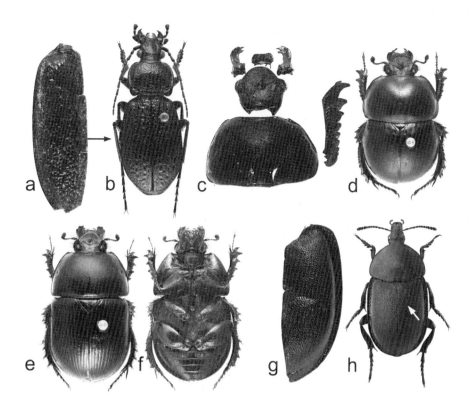

Figure 26.3 Insect remains from the X84 area of the catacomb and corresponding modern specimens: (a) *Carabus alysidotus* (Illiger), left elytron, (b) same species, modern specimen, (c) *Jekelius intermedius* (Costa), head, mandibles, labrum, thorax (pronotum) and right protibia, (d) same species, modern specimen, (e) *Geotrupes spiniger* (Marsham), modern specimen in dorsal view, (f) the same specimen in ventral view. (g) *Ablattaria laevigata* (Fabricius), right elytron, (h) same species, modern specimen (Photographs: J.-B. Huchet).

respectively designated under the term of 'palaeoentomology' and 'archaeoentomology'. Although both are based on the same principles and methods, the first relies on insect assemblages for palaeoclimatic and palaeoenvironmental reconstructions, while the second focusses on archaeological (anthropised) contexts. When preserved in archaeological contexts, entomofaunal assemblages are thus useful for both palaeoecological climatic and environmental inferences and ethnoarchaeological and anthropological inferences with regard to the practices and lifestyles of past societies (Coope, 1986; Ponel, 1993; Huchet, 2017). When insect remains are recovered from funerary contexts, their study is carried out in light of the principles and methods of forensic entomology. This approach is designated by the term 'funerary archaeoentomology' (Huchet, 1996, 2014; Vanin and Huchet, 2017). The investigations based on past thanatocoenoses appear as a relevant method to improve investigations of the treatment of the dead, taphonomic events, and, by extension, of the funerary practices of past societies (Huchet and Greenberg, 2010; Huchet, 2010a, 2014; Huchet *et al.*, 2013a, 2013b; Vanin, 2014; Giordani *et al.*, 2018, 2020).

Funerary archaeoentomology is based on the precepts of archaeothanatology, the 'archaeology of death' (Boulestin and Duday, 2005; Duday, 2005, 2009), in that it aims to reconstruct funerary gestures and practices from the funerary context, the analytical focus being more specifically centred on the skeleton, to retrodict decompositional changes in order to enable reconstruction of the original appearance of the remains upon deposition. Such practices require knowledge and understanding of the diagenetic processes and, more broadly, of taphonomy, including all physical and chemical interactions within a depositional setting. It is important to note, however, that the archaeoentomological approach differs from the forensic approach in the sense that it does not study dynamic (living) processes, the studied assemblage being inert, in the same way as the skeleton is within the grave. Thus, insects are part of the overall assemblage of the tomb, the 'fossilised history' of a past temporal fragment.

Investigations of subfossil entomological remains are reliant on the particularly resistant chemical component of the arthropod exoskeleton, namely the chitin, that permits these sclerotised ecofacts to survive in sediments for millennia. Due to the highly resistant nature of their exoskeletons, beetles (Coleoptera) have the propensity to preferentially preserve in archaeological assemblages. From their immense species diversity and ecological specialisations, beetles figure among the most important bio-indicators of environmental and climatic conditions. Other insects, mostly involved in forensic investigations, are true flies or Diptera. Contrary to beetles that preserve in their adult form (imago), fly remains recovered from archaeological contexts usually correspond to immature stages and only their highly sclerotised 'cocoon' called *puparia* (singular form: *puparium*) usually stand the test of time and preserve in sediments. True 'biological clocks', the necrophagous flies are among the main insects of forensic interest by making it possible to document both the pre-burial phase (i.e. highlighting the duration of exposure of a body) and the post-depositional phase, thus providing valuable insights into funerary practices, past environments and the seasonality of the deposits (Huchet and Greenberg, 2010; Huchet, 2010a, 2014, 2016a).

Finally, various other insect orders, including ectoparasitic forms such as Siphonaptera (fleas), Phthiraptera (head, body and pubic lice), and Hemiptera, Cimicidae (bedbugs), are likely to be preserved in archaeological contexts. These insects are of major interest in the knowledge of past sanitary conditions since they are frequently vectors of pathogenic organisms and permit the identification of possible zoonoses and/or epizootics of the past (Huchet *et al.*, 2013c; Otranto *et al.*, 2014; Huchet 2015, 2016a, 2016b).

It is worth noting that, to date, no archaeoentomological survey has been conducted on mass graves, making this contribution pioneering in this domain. A second novel aspect is that this catacomb, although of anthropogenic origin (tuff formerly exploited by humans), by its depth, darkness, constant hygrometry, and its 4.5 km long network of galleries, shares more similarities with a natural karst environment than with other burial sites belonging to the 'underground' domain, such as crypts and burial caves.

The catacomb entomofauna

The excellent preservation of arthropods, in contrast to skeletal remains, justified archaeoentomological investigation of this unique archaeological context. The main objectives of this research were to provide relevant information related to the environment of the catacomb during its use, to the funerary treatment of the dead, and to address the circumstance(s) of these multiple deaths. During successive excavation campaigns in the core of the catacomb between 2005 and 2010, numerous samples of bioarchaeological remains were collected from different places within the mass grave and their location precisely recorded. In the majority of cases, insect remains were directly associated with the bones since it was difficult to collect sediment samples related to the nature of the burial site excavated directly into the tuff. Because an epidemic nature of this assemblage was suspected, the initial analysis focussed on the potential recovery of haematophagous ectoparasite remains in association with the corpses, in particular human flea (*Pulex irritans*) or human body louse (*Pediculus humanus humanus*), both suspected to be primary vectors of epidemic diseases and, most notably, of the bacterium *Yersinia pestis* as the causative agent of plague (Dean *et al.*, 2018).

The presence of insect remains in archaeological funerary contexts results from two distinct phases of colonisation. The first phase, known as 'pre-depositional', mainly concerns necrophagous insects that colonise human corpses within a short period of time after death. This 'open-air' phase implies that the decaying corpse remains exposed on the surface for a period prior to burial. The second, 'post-depositional' phase occurs underground and includes specialised ecological groups that have a propensity to access and colonise buried remains. The characterisation of these two categories is of major interest in the *a posteriori* reconstruction of the grave and buried human taphocoenosis. In this respect, contrary to some misrepresentations, the presence of diptera puparia associated with human remains in an archaeological context does not necessarily imply that the individual remained exposed on the surface for a period prior to burial. As noted below, some taxa, including some Muscidae and Phoridae flies, are morphologically adapted to colonise corpses buried at depths of up to two metres (Bourel *et al.*, 2004; Martin-Vega, Gómez-Gómez and Baz, 2011; Huchet, 2013; Giordani *et al.,* 2018).

In most cases, human remains recovered from funerary archaeological contexts originate from exhumations and concern skeletonised individuals. In addition to the vicissitudes related to the *in situ* preservation of organic matter, the buried corpse community is incomparably less diversified than the surface entomofauna (Bourel *et al.*, 2004; Gunn and Bird, 2011). For these reasons, interpretations based on sub-fossil insect remains cannot equal the accuracy and predictability of modern forensic cases.

Despite a thorough analysis of bioarchaeological samples unearthed from the central sector of the mass burial, no ectoparasite remains were found. In all likelihood, this deficit is not linked to taphonomic processes, such as differential preservation bias, since numerous exoskeletal elements, which are less conducive to preservation, were identified within the archaeological samples and, moreover, because ectoparasite remains have a propensity for long-term survival in sediment (Rick *et al.*, 2002; Raoult *et al.*, 2006; Fornaciari *et al.*, 2009; Huchet, 2015, 2016a, 2016b). Although no flea or human lice were recovered, the initial analysis revealed four orders of arthropods, including Coleoptera, Diptera, Acarina and Pseudoscorpionida, represented by 11 families, 11 genera and 14 species within the catacomb deposits. Only the most representative and relevant taxa will be treated here. According to the biology of these representatives, some hypotheses related to palaeoenvironmental conditions as well as funerary practices are proposed.

Outside the catacomb: the natural environment

The samples from the catacomb produced several non-necrophilous species that provide a snapshot of the surrounding local environment during the period of catacomb use.

Carabidae (coleoptera)

Carabus (Archicarabus) alysidotus (Illiger, 1798) (Figure 26.3)

The ground beetle *Carabus alysidotus* (Carabidae), represented by a complete right elytron (Figures 26.3a and 26.3b), is particularly noteworthy. Very rare and localised, *C. alysidotus* is a north-western Mediterranean species representative of wetland ecosystems (marshy places, wet meadows, swamps) (Casale, Sturani and Vigna Taglianti, 1982). According to Magistretti (1965), this species is luticole (living, feeding, and breeding in muddy places), and highly hygrophilous. It often dives spontaneously under water, where it can remain submerged for up to 15 minutes (Sturani, 1962).

C. alysidotus is mainly active during winter and early spring (from the beginning of December to mid-March). It feeds upon earthworms, insects, gastropods; sometimes, it attacks and devours small snails breaking their shells (Casale, Sturani and Vigna Taglianti, 1982). Once very common, especially in the vicinity of Rome, the progressive anthropisation of marshland areas has meant that this species has become increasingly rare. Its mere presence, within the unique context of the catacomb, confirms that the site was originally built in a swampy area.

Geotrupidae (coleoptera)

The Geotrupidae (from Greek '*geos*' (earth) and '*trýpes*' (to bore)) are convex body scarab beetles that dig into the soil and fill the resulting burrows with cow dung, horse dung, dead leaves, or humus to provision their larvae. The Italian fauna includes 10 genera, 19 species and 7 subspecies of Geotrupidae (Ballerio *et al.*, 2010). Well-preserved remains of two distinct species were found associated with the skeletons.

Jekelius intermedius (Costa, 1839) (Figures 26.3c and 26.3d)

Contrary to most of the species belonging to this genus, more or less strictly coprophagous, *J. intermedius* is a polyphagous species (coprophagous, necrophagous, mycetophagous and saprophagous). This oligotrophic species (i.e. one surviving in environments with a low level of nutrients) mainly occurs in Mediterranean ecosystems (sandy coastal areas, open grazing areas, Mediterranean shrubland and mesophilic woods). Eco-ethological observations conducted by Crovetti et al. (1984) in the region of Pisa (Italy), showed that *J. intermedius* occurs in wetland forest biocoenoses, with sandy soil, where fallow deer (*Dama dama*), wild boar (*Sus scrofa*) and rabbit (*Oryctolagus cuniculus*) cohabitate. In such environments, the essential conditions required for the survival of the species are linked to the presence of deer and wild boar droppings. Within the genus, *J. intermedius* can be a sporadic scavenger, and it is likely that putrefactive odours emanating from the catacomb may have been attractive to this beetle. In the region of Latium, the period of annual activity of adults is relatively short (usually from mid-June to the first part of September). Like all other representatives of this genus, *J. intermedius* is apterous and only moves short distances. Its presence in the catacomb would suggest an access shaft relatively close to the burial chambers.

Geotrupes spiniger (Marsham, 1802) (Figures 26.3e and 26.3f)

G. spiniger is a dung beetle and figures among the most widespread members within the Geotrupidae. This species shows a preference for large vertebrate dung, such as that from horses and cattle, but also that of other species as well feeding on rotting fungi. Adults occur in cattle pasture, woodland, moorland and hillsides. Within the catacomb assemblages, the species was represented by a few exoskeleton fragments, notably elytron remains and abdominal segments that allow identification to the species level.

Silphidae (coleoptera)

The beetles belonging to this family are primarily necrophagous and feed on decaying organic matter and cadavers, but some genera include predacious species feeding upon other invertebrates, such as caterpillars and gastropods (land snails) (Portevin, 1926).

Ablattaria laevigata (Fabricius, 1775) (Figures 26.3g and 26.3h)

A. laevigata is a helicophagous species and mainly feeds upon terrestrial molluscs. This species is predaceous and feeds on live prey, as reflected in the elongated shape of its head, which is adapted to reach far into snail shells. It occurs in moderately covered or edge contexts in rural, ruderal and farming environments. Like the Geotrupidae and owing to its biology, it is probable that representatives of this species penetrated into the catacomb from a nearby access point or fell into an open pit. Since not all the above-mentioned species are scavengers, their presence in the catacombs, and also their way of access to the central area of the catacombs, raise a number of questions. Some hypotheses are proposed further on in the discussion.

Tenebrionidae (coleoptera)

Alphitobius diaperinus (Panzer, 1797)

Various species belonging to this genus infest stored foodstuffs, of which *A. diaperinus* appears as the most frequent and harmful. According to Delobel and Tran (1993), this species is native to the tropics of the Old World. Predatory, scavenger as well as mycophagous species, *A. diaperinus* is found in a large number of foodstuffs, both of animal and plant origin. This species occurs both in natural (caves, rodent nests) and anthropised environments (agricultural establishments, poultry houses) and feeds upon a large variety of biota, including fly larvae.

In the United Kingdom, *A. diaperinus*, appears in many archaeological contexts of Roman-period date, very likely introduced during the Roman conquest (Kenward, Hall and Jones, 1986; Kenward and Allison 1988, 1995). In Egypt, this species is also represented by numerous specimens at the ancient city of Akhenaten (1353 BC) (Panagiotakopulu, Buckland and Kemp, 2010) and at Amarna (Panagiotakopulu and Buckland 2009), where the authors suggest that it may have acted as a predator of fly larvae. It is very likely that this species colonised the catacomb for predation purposes.

The necrophagous entomofauna: the flies

Muscidae (diptera)

Hydrotaea capensis (Wiedemann, 1818) (Figures 26.4a and 26.4b)

The species belonging to the genus *Hydrotaea* Robineau-Desvoidy (dump flies) are frequently observed with buried corpses (Smith, 1986; Mégnin, 1894; Huchet, 1996; Bourel *et al.*, 2004) or corpses kept indoors, where pioneer flies (Calliphoridae) do not have access (Smith, 1986; Bourel *et al.*, 2004). Among the representatives of this genus, *H. capensis* is a highly synanthropic Old World species that widely dispersed through commerce and figures among the most frequent species encountered in funerary archaeological contexts. This fly is a typical representative of the post-depositional stage invaders since it colonises cadavers in an advanced stage of decay, frequently during the so-called 'ammoniac fermentation' stage (Turchetto and Vanin, 2004; Couri *et al.*, 2008), or even the drying stage when they are buried in empty spaces created by coffins and sarcophagi, for example, deposited in caves, or subterranean environments like crypts or catacombs (Huchet, 1996; Scharrer-Liska and Grassberger, 2005; Couri *et al.*, 2008; Vanin *et al.*, 2011; Vanin, 2016). This species was also reported in association with the remains of a First World War soldier buried in an underground tunnel (Huchet, 2013). According to a study conducted by

Figure 26.4 Insect remains from the X84 area of the catacomb and corresponding modern specimens:
(a) puparia of the dump fly *Hydrotaea capensis* (Wiedemann 1930) (white arrows) on a desiccated brain,
(b) puparium of *Hydrotaea capensis*, modern specimen, (c) *Necrobia rufipes* (De Geer), modern specimen,
(d) archaeoentomological specimen of the same species on a bone fragment, (e) numerous remains of
N. rufipes on a bone fragment, (f) close-up view of an archaeoentomological sample showing the very
high representation of *N. rufipes* among the bioarchaeological remains (Photographs: J.-B. Huchet).

Bourel and colleagues (2004), during autopsies of 22 exhumed cadavers at the Forensic Institute
of Lille (France), a large number of *H. capensis* puparia were recorded in association within 15
putrefied or desiccated corpses. Another close representative of the genus *Hydrotaea* (*H. aenescens*
(Wiedemann, 1830)) is reported from Mochica graves in Peru (Huchet and Greenberg, 2010).
A recent study related to the natural history and identification of the puparia of this most

relevant species of *Hydrotaea* from forensic and archaeological contexts was recently published by Giordani et al. (2018).

As a rule, all arthropods are poikilothermic (cold-blooded), and their growth is primarily temperature driven, with their rate of development increasing as the rearing temperature rises. Lefebvre and Pasquerault (2004a, 2004b), who studied the effect of temperature on the developmental rate of *H. capensis* (rearing temperature comprises between 17°C and 30°C) demonstrated that several other factors, such as variation of the photoperiod or relative humidity of substrate may also affect the duration of development. Based on temperatures of $17 \pm 1°C$, $24 \pm 1°C$ and $30 \pm 1°C$ the life cycle duration of *H. capensis* was evaluated to be 62. 21 and 12.5 days, respectively. Based on the average temperature of the catacomb (about 16°C), it can be estimated that completed development (from oviposition to adult) probably reached or exceeded two months. The persistence of a nutritious substrate (cadavers) as well as the recurrent supply of bodies allowed the development and maintenance of many generations of this dump fly within the catacomb.

H. capensis is undoubtedly the most frequent fly species within the catacomb and several hundred puparia, sometimes associated with mostly fragmented adult exoskeleton parts (heads, thorax), were recovered within the archaeoentomological assemblages. These swarming masses of maggots may explain the impressive number of the predatory beetle species *Necrobia rufipes* (De Geer, 1775) considered in the following section.

Calliphoridae

Calliphora sp. (cf. *vicina*)

In the particular context of the catacomb, it should be mentioned that the pioneer flies colonising corpses in the initial period following death (Calliphoridae, Sarcophagidae) proved to be significantly under-represented in entomofaunal assemblages in the central area of the catacomb. Analysis of the insect assemblages revealed only a small number (<10) of puparia remains that could be attributed to the flies of the genus *Calliphora* (cf. *vicina*) (Calliphoridae). The possible reasons for the under-representation of pioneer flies are discussed below.

The necrophagous entomofauna: the beetles

Dermestidae

Dermestes sp.

The genus *Dermestes* Linnaeus (Dermestidae), etymologically 'skin-eaters', includes nearly one hundred representatives worldwide. In nature, adults and their larvae are found mainly under carrion at different stages of *post-mortem* decomposition, with a predilection for corpses in an advanced stage of desiccation. In archaeological contexts, a small number of *Dermestes* species figure among the usual denizens of Egyptian mummies, including *D. frischii* Kugelann that was notably found during the autopsy on the mummy of Ramses II (Steffan, 1982; Huchet, 2010b, 2016a). *Dermestes* and *Necrobia* frequently occur simultaneously on the same body, when it releases volatile fatty acids and other caseic degradation products (Turchetto, Lafisca and Constantini, 2001). Remains of thorax (pronotum), elytrae and larval exuviae of *Dermestes* sp. were present in several samples originating from the central area of the catacomb.

Cleridae

Necrobia rufipes (De Geer, 1775) (Figures 26.4c, 26.4d, 26.4e and 26.4f)

This small, 3.5–7 mm long, metallic blue beetle belongs to the family Cleridae. This species colonises cadavers during the advanced stages of *post-mortem* decay. A 'classic' host of Egyptian mummies, this insect called the '*red-legged ham beetle*' was originally mentioned by the famous Egyptologist Jean-François J. Champollion-Figeac (1812): 'It was by examining the hands [of the mummy] attentively that we saw, in the interstice of the fingers, several dead beetles, pinkish-purple in all their brilliance …' ('*Ce fut en examinant les mains attentivement que nous aperçûmes, dans l'interstice des doigts, plusieurs coléoptères morts, de couleur rose-violet dans tout son éclat …*'). Perfectly preserved remains of this species were recently discovered in the visceral cavity of the mummy of the priest Namenkhet Amon (XXVth–XXVIth dynasty, 450–430 BC) (Huchet, 2010b). Today cosmopolitan, *N. rufipes* is sometimes used in forensic entomology to establish the Post-Mortem Interval (PMI) (Arnaldos *et al.,* 2004; Gennard, 2007). This beetle has greatly benefited from human movements to spread around the world. To demonstrate this phenomenon, recent investigations have repeatedly found this species in the visceral cavities of Egyptian mummies of the Late Period (1085 BC–333 AD) (Huchet, 2010b, 2016a), but also in Scythian tumuli in the Altai Mountains of Mongolia, inside a horse cranium on Easter Island and, more recently, associated with turtle carcasses on the very isolated Tromelin Island in the Indian Ocean (Huchet, personal observation).

The exact time when *Necrobia* had colonised the cadavers within the catacomb remains uncertain. Usually, *N. rufipes* is known to invade exposed cadavers at the beginning of the butyric fermentation stage, some 20 to 40 days after death according to Bornemissza (1957), and its activity continues until the dry decay stage several months after the death, when cadavers are drying out or almost dry. Byrd and Castner (2001) highlighted, however, that adults might sometimes be found on carrion in earlier stages of decomposition. Forensic experiments conducted on pig cadavers in South Africa confirmed that *N. rufipes* is present during active, advanced and dry stages of decay (Kelly, 2006). Total developmental time from egg to adult can last between 36 and 150 days, with development dependent on temperature, humidity, and the quality of available food (Kulshrestha and Satpathy, 2001).

The recurrent introduction of corpses into the burial chambers and consequently the putrefied smell emanating from the cadavers sustained a very numerous colony of *N. rufipes* within the catacomb as attested by the presence of several thousand specimens within all of the samples. Notable cases involved those found in a partially desiccated brain but also on many bone fragments. The many remnants of *N. rufipes* turned the bone fragments in an unexpected metallic blue colour (Figures 26.4e and 26.4f). *N. rufipes* is known to feed on the larvae of other beetle species and fly maggots. While searching for their preferred food source, they feed on high-protein content organic material and especially highly desiccated flesh. In all likelihood, the presence of the 'dump fly' *H. capensis* larvae attracted the predatory beetle *N. rufipes* that developed at the expense of this species and significantly proliferated within the catacomb.

Discussion

One of the main objectives of this study was to review evidence for ectoparasite vectors of pathogens; the results proved to be inconclusive. However, it is important to point out that the available samples were unearthed from the surface levels of some of the funerary chambers and not all of them were fully excavated, suggesting that further remains may be found later when excavations are resumed in these areas of the catacomb. Nevertheless, the entomofaunal assemblages collected to date do provide some initial elements of interpretation, both on the environmental context but also on certain aspects of the management of the dead during episodes of a mass mortality crisis. If, usually, the interpretations resulting from archaeoentomological study are based on the presence of some relevant species of forensic interest, the absence of some other taxa that were anticipated to be present but were not may be of similar significance in reconstructing past events. If it is assumed that the absence of some species is not due to differential preservation, the representativeness of fly puparia should be taken into consideration. A large quantity of puparia is a good indicator of accessibility to cadavers in the pre-burial and post-burial phases. Depending on the taxa and the burial mode, it may sometimes be possible to advance hypotheses about the time of the burial (seasonality), the possibility of pre-depositional exposure and the duration of this exposure. The absence of any traces of insects in an environment propitious to preservation can also be significant (extreme climatic conditions (cold) at the time of death, taphonomic incidences, rapid infilling of the body, etc.). Among the studied samples, the high representation of the necrophagous fly *H. capensis* demonstrates that corpses were heavily infested. This suggests a long period of bodies crawling with vermin in this subterranean context, animating otherwise lifeless human matter.

Within the two main orders – beetles and diptera – presence and absence of certain taxa make it possible to identify some features relating to the burial site and access to the corpses, as well as funerary management, including the state of decomposition of some individuals at the time of their burial in the catacomb. In the present case, the absence or very low representativeness of the pioneer flies Calliphoridae is of prime importance. Although *H. capensis* larvae can be facultative predators of larvae of other fly species (Skidmore, 1985), their absence would suggest that the bodies were very likely quickly processed and perhaps also quickly buried soon after death or buried during a cold period of the year, or both. However, 3D reconstruction of two distinct funerary chambers (Sachau-Carcel, 2014) demonstrated that the bodies were deposited in several temporal waves in a heterochronous way, suggesting that rapid burials could explain the absence of pioneer flies. The absence of these flies supports the hypothesis that simultaneous burial of the individuals took place in a very short period of time, as is generally the case during acute mortality events. An important point in the management of the deposits is provided by the archaeological analysis that strongly suggests the presence of a proximate access point (cf. plan of access shaft in gallery X53). This indicates the path used by the gravediggers to lower the bodies and arrange them in the different burial chambers. The occurrence of some epigeal[1] representative species such as *C. alysidotus, J. intermedius* or *G. spiniger,* clearly demonstrates the presence of an access shaft to this central area.

As clearly highlighted by Zurawski et al. (2009: 672): 'the fundamental question of whether or not any pioneer blowfly can fly in complete darkness has never been definitively answered in entomological literature.' However, in most experiments and cases studied, nocturnal oviposition on cadavers appears to be extremely unlikely to non-existent. One other factor, undoubtedly of equal importance as darkness, and, to our knowledge, with few or no experimental studies, is the distance or, in other words, the ability of pioneer flies such as Calliphoridae to fly several dozen meters in complete darkness and then oviposit in the dark.

Even with the suggested presence of a vertical shaft within the catacomb, its distance from the funerary chambers may have very likely constituted an ethological barrier that prevented fly

---

1 Organisms that live above the soil surface.

egg-laying upon fresh cadavers. If the presence of a proximate access point is accepted, then it was definitely located at a certain distance from the burial sites and the latter remained continuously in darkness. Acting as 'post-depositional' species and privileged hosts of this kind of subterranean context, the very high representation of the muscid fly *H. capensis* is not of great value because their presence only demonstrates that the cadavers decomposed within an empty space and were directly accessible, and only later covered with a substantial layer of sediment.

Finally, from an environmental point of view at the time of the use of the catacomb, it should be remembered that the underground funerary network of Saints Marcellinus and Peter, like all other Roman catacombs, was located far from the urban centre, in an agricultural landscape. This is attested by its re-use after it functioned originally as a hydraulic network intended for the irrigation of the land surface and used only opportunistically for the mass burial of corpses. The scarce literature on this topic (Guyon, 1987; Gioia and Volpe, 2004; Volpe, 2007) indicates that the catacomb was located in an agricultural area. These data are corroborated by the presence within the catacomb assemblages of coprophagous species, those more or less specialised in recycling large vertebrate dung (horse, cattle, etc.). However, the presence of the ground beetle *C. alysidotus* provides evidence that clearly indicates that the catacomb was originally located within a marshland environment.

Conclusion

Based on the presence of numerous insects recovered from the central area of the catacomb, this study provides original insights at different interpretative levels. Along with other bioarchaeological investigations carried out in this singularly interesting context, archaeoentomological analysis contributed, through different but complementary arguments, to discuss the funerary treatment given to individuals who died during one or more successive epidemic episodes during the first centuries of our era. The presence of specific taxa, as well as the absence of others, has reinforced the hypothesis of rapidly carried out burials leading to piles of corpses not covered with sediment in previously empty and dark underground cavities with access relatively close to the outside. In addition, this analysis permitted event-driven interpretations such as establishing the seasonality of the deaths, the hypothesis being that these deposits of corpses could have taken place during cold periods. This is a significant argument in the discussion on the simultaneity of the depositions and, probably short term, on the nature of the still unknown epidemic(s) responsible. These initial investigations in the environs of the catacomb have also provided a renewed image of a landscape of the Roman *suburbium* which, in addition to the archaeologically well-attested agricultural properties, was made up of areas of swamp, potential reservoirs for artisanal activities requiring large quantities of water, such as skin-working for example. Although the search for ectoparasitic insects that can act as vectors of epidemics has so far been unsuccessful, these results do emphasise the need for further investigation based on a well-documented sampling of such archaeological contexts.

By recording using a resolutely multi-proxy approach, the study of entomofaunal assemblages permits decipherment of some aspects of the interactions between past societies and their environments, the dynamics of the effects of anthropisation on biodiversity, the mechanisms of co-evolution between humans and their parasites and, via the 'funerary archaeoentomological approach', to obtain unprecedented information on past mortuary practices. Although still marginal and underdeveloped, archaeoentomology appears as an innovative heuristic approach that may contribute in a particularly efficient way to archaeological, bioarchaeological and archaeothanatological issues.

Acknowledgements

The authors acknowledge the contribution of several collaborating institutions that made this work possible, including the Centre National de la Recherche Scientifique (CNRS), École française de Rome, *Pontificia Commissione* di Archeologia Sacra (especially Raffaella Giuliani and Monica Ricciardi), the Institut national de recherches archéologiques préventives (Inrap, in particular Philippe Blanchard) and Maison des Sciences de l'Homme d'Aquitaine (MSHA). A special thanks to Frances Holden for translating this contribution from the original French. This contribution was written under the auspices of grant ANR-19-CE27-0012 from the French government.

References

Arnaldos, M.I., Sánchez, F., Álvarez, P. and García, M.D. (2004). A Forensic Entomology Case from the Southeastern Iberian Peninsula. *Anil Aggrawal`s Internet Journal of Forensic Medicine and Toxicology*, 5(1), pp. 22–25.

Ballerio, A., Rey, A., Uliana, M., Rastelli, M., Rastelli, S., Romano, M. and Colacurcio, L. (2010). *Coleotteri Scarabeoidei d'Italia*. Venice: Museo Civico Di Storia Naturale Carmagnola (To), *Progetto Biodiversità*, Comitato Parchi, Centro Studi Roma, Museo Di Storia Naturale; www.societaentomologicaitaliana. it/Coleotteri%20Scarabeoidea%20d'Italia%202014/index.htm. CD-Rom.

Blanchard, P. and Castex, D. (2007). A Mass Grave from the Catacomb of Saints Peter and Marcellinus in Rome, second-third century AD, *Antiquity*, 81, pp. 989–998.

Bornemissza, G.F. (1957). An Analysis of Arthropod Succession in Carrion and the Effect of Its Decomposition on the Soil Fauna, *Australian Journal of Zoology*, 5, pp. 1–12.

Boulestin, B. and Duday, H. (2005). Ethnologie et archéologie de la mort: de l'illusion des références à l'emploi d'un vocabulaire. In: C. Mordant and G. Depierre, eds., *Les Pratiques Funéraires à l'Âge du Bronze en France, Actes de la Table Ronde de Sens-en-Bourgogne (10–12 Juin 1998)*, Sens: Éditions du Comité des travaux historiques et scientifiques (CTHS), pp. 17–30.

Bourel, B., Tournel, G., Hédouin V. and Gosset, D. (2004). Entomofauna of Buried Bodies in Northern France. *International Journal of Legal Medicine*, 118, pp. 215–220.

Buckland, P.C. (1976). The use of insect remains in the interpretation of archaeological environments. In: D.A. Davidson and M.L. Shackley, eds., *Geoarchaeology. Earth Science and the Past*. London: Duckworth, pp. 369–396.

Byrd, J.H. and Castner, J.L. (2001). Insects of forensic importance. In: J.H. Byrd and J.L. Castner, eds., *Forensic Entomology, the Utility of Arthropods in Legal Investigations*. Boca Raton, Florida: CRC Press, pp. 43–79.

Casale, A., Sturani, M. and Vigna Taglianti, A. (1982). *Fauna d'Italia – Carabidae I – Introduzione, Paussinae, Carabinae*. Bologna: Edizione Calderini.

Castex, D. and Blanchard, P. (2011). Témoignages archéologiques d'une épidémie à la période Antique: Les inhumations du secteur central de la Catacombe des Saints Marcellin et Pierre (Rome, fin 1er – IIIe siècle. In: D. Castex, P. Courtaud, H. Duday, F. Le Mort and A.m. Tillier, eds., *Regroupement des Morts. Genèse et Diversité en Archéologie*, Pessac: Maison Ausonius et Maison des Sciences de l'Homme d'Aquitaine (MSHA) Editions, Collection Thanat'Os, pp. 281–292.

Castex, D., Kacki, S., Réveillas, H., Souquet-Leroy, I., Sachau-Carcel, G., Blaizot, F., Blanchard, P. and Duday H. (2014). Revealing Archaeological Features Linked to Mortality Increases. *Anthropologie (Brno)*, 52(3), pp. 299–318.

Champollion-Figeac, J.-J. (1812). Note sur une nouvelle espèce d'Insecte(s) [sic] du genre *Corynetes* de Fabricius, observée à Grenoble, ms. original, Grenoble, [décembre 1812] (ADI, Fonds Champollion, vol. 3, document number 296).

Coope, G.R. (1977). Quaternary Coleoptera as aids in the interpretation of environmental history. In: F.W., Shotton, (ed.), *British Quaternary Studies: Recent Advances*. Oxford: Oxford University Press, pp. 55–68.

Coope, G.R. (1986). Coleoptera analysis. In: B.E. Berglund, ed., *Handbook of Holocene Palaeoecology and Palaeohydrology*. New York: J. Wiley and Sons, pp. 703–713.

Coope, G.R. (1990). The invasion of Northern Europe during the Pleistocene by Mediterranean species of Coleoptera. In: F. di Castri, A.J. Hansen and M. Debussche, eds., *Biological Invasions in Europe and the Mediterranean Basin*. Dordrecht: Kluwer, pp. 203–215.

Couri, M.S., Souza, S.M., Cunha, A.M., Pinheiro, J. and Cunha, E. (2008). Diptera Brachycera Found Inside the Esophagus of a Mummified Adult Male from the Early XIX Century, Lisbon, Portugal. *Memórias do Instituto Oswaldo Cruz*, 103(2), pp. 211–213.

Crovetti, A., Raspi, A., Paparati, B., Santini, L. and Malfatti, P. (1984). Osservazioni Eco-Etologiche sul Coleottero Geotrupino *Thorectes intermedius* (Costa) (Coleoptera, Geotrupidae). VIII Contributo alla Conoscenza dei Coleotteri Scarabaeoidi. *Frustula Entomologica*, N.S 6(19), pp. 1–23.

Dean, K.R, Krauer, F., Walløe, L., Lingjærde, O.C., Bramanti, B., Stenseth, N.C. and Schmid B.V. (2018). Human Ectoparasites and the Spread of Plague in Europe during the Second Pandemic. *Proceedings of the National Academy of Sciences of the United States of America*, 115(6), pp. 1304–1309.

Delobel, A. and Tran, M. (1993). *Les Coléoptères des denrées alimentaires entreposées dans les régions chaudes*. Bondy, France: Orstom Editions.

Devièse, T., Ribechini, E., Castex, D., Stuart, B., Regert, M. and Colombini, M.-P. (2017). A Multi-analytical Approach Using FTIR, GC/MS and Py-GC/MS Revealed Early Evidence of Embalming Practices in Roman Catacombs. *Microchemical Journal*, 133, pp. 49–59.

Duday, H. (2005). L'archéothanatologie ou l'archéologie de la mort. In: O. Dutour, J.-J., Hublin and B., Vandermeersch, eds., *Objets et Méthodes en Paléoanthropologie*. Paris: Editions du Comité des travaux historiques et scientifiques (CTHS), pp.153–215.

Duday, H. (2009). *The archaeology of the dead: lectures in archaeothanatology*. Oxford: Oxbow Books.

Fornaciari, G., Giuffra, V., Silvia, M., Picchi Malayka, S. and Masetti, M. (2009). 'Royal' Pediculosis in Renaissance Italy: Lice in the Mummy of the King of Naples Ferdinand II of Aragon (1467–1496). *Memórias do Instituto Oswaldo Cruz*, 104, pp. 671–672.

Gennard, D.E. (2007). *Forensic entomology: an introduction*. Chichester, West Sussex: J. Wiley and Sons Ltd.

Gioia, P. and Volpe, R. (2004). *Centocelle I. Roma S.D.O. Le indagini archeologiche*, vol. 1, Soveria Mannelli: Rubbettino Editore.

Giordani, G., Erauw, C., Eeckhout, P.A., Owens, L.S. and Vanin, S. (2020). Patterns of Camelid Sacrifice at the Site of Pachacamac, Peruvian Central Coast, during the Late Intermediate Period (AD 1000–1470): Perspectives from Funerary Archaeoentomology. *Journal of Archaeological Science*, 114, 105065

Giordani, G., Tuccia, F., Floris, I. and Vanin, S. (2018). First Record of *Phormia regina* (Meigen, 1826) (Diptera: Calliphoridae) from Mummies at the Sant'Antonio Abate Cathedral of Castelsardo, Sardinia, Italy. *PeerJ*, 6, p. 4176.

Giuliani, R. and Guyon, J. (2011). La gestion du 'regroupement des morts' dans les cimetières communautaires de l'Antiquité: l'exemple des catacombes romaines, In: D. Castex, P. Courtaud, H. Duday, F. Le Mort and A.m. Tillier, eds., *Regroupement des Morts. Genèse et Diversité en Archéologie*, Pessac: Ausonius et Maison des Sciences de l'Homme d'Aquitaine (MSHA) Editions, Collection Thanat'Os, pp. 98–122.

Gourevitch, D. (2013). *Limos kai Loimos. A study of the Galenic Plague*, Paris: De Boccard, Collection Pathographie, 10.

Gunn, A. and Bird, J. (2011). The Ability of the Blowflies *Calliphora vomitoria* (Linnaeus), *Calliphora vicina* (Rob-Desvoidy) and *Lucilia sericata* (Meigen) (Diptera: Calliphoridae) and the Muscid Flies *Muscina stabulans* (Fallén) and *Muscina prolapsa* (Harris) (Diptera: Muscidae) to Colonise Buried Remains, *Forensic Science International*, 207, pp.198–204.

Guyon, J. (1987). *Le Cimetière 'aux deux lauriers'. Recherches sur les catacombes romaines*. Rome: Pontificio Istituto di Archeologia Christiana – Ecole Française de Rome.

Huchet, J.-B. (1996). L'Archéoentomologie Funéraire: Une Approche Originale dans l'Interprétation des Sépultures. *Bulletins et Mémoires de la Société d'Anthropologie de Paris*, 8 (3–4), pp. 289–302.

Huchet, J.-B. (2010a). Des insectes, des momies: l'apport de l'entomologie à l'étude des pratiques funéraires des sociétés anciennes. In: I. Cartron, D. Castex, P. Georges, M. Vivas and M. Charageat, eds., *De Corps en Corps, Traitement et Devenir du Cadavre*. Actes des séminaires de la Maison des Sciences de l'Homme d'Aquitaine 2007–2008, Pessac: Maison des Sciences de l'Homme d'Aquitaine (MSHA) Editions, pp. 33–55.

Huchet, J.-B. (2010b). Archaeoentomological Study of the Insect Remains Found within the Mummy of Namenkhet Amon, (San Lazzaro Armenian Monastery, Venice, Italy). *Advances in Egyptology*, 1, pp. 58–80.

Huchet, J.-B. (2013). L'archéo-entomologie: les insectes nécrophages associés aux soldats de Carspach. In: B. Schnitzler and M. Landolt eds., *A l'Est du Nouveau! Archéologie de la Grande Guerre en Alsace et en Lorraine*. Chapitre II. Les approches méthodologiques. Strasbourg: Musée de Strasbourg, pp. 109–110.

Huchet, J.-B. (2014). Insect Remains and their Traces: Relevant Fossil Witnesses in the Reconstruction of Past Funerary Practices. *Anthropologie (Brno)*, 52(3), pp. 329–346.

Huchet, J.-B. (2015). Ectoparasites de l'Homme: le regard de l'archéoentomologiste. In: F. Collard and E., Samama, eds., *Poux, Puces et Punaises, la Vermine de l'Homme, Découverte, Descriptions et Traitements. Antiquité, Moyen Âge, Temps Modernes*, Paris: L'Harmattan, pp. 45–60.

Huchet, J.-B. (2016a). Archéoentomologie et Archéoparasitologie d'une Momie Égyptienne. *Techné*, 44, pp. 79–83.

Huchet, J.-B. (2016b). L'Animal-Amphitryon: Archéologie de l'Ectoparasitisme. *Anthropozoologica*, 50, 1, pp. 55–65.

Huchet, J.-B. (2017). Insectes et archéologie. In: G. Bayle and S. Frère, eds., *L'Archéozoologie, entre homogénéisation des pratiques et innovations techniques. Les Nouvelles de l'Archéologie*, 148, pp. 40–44.

Huchet, J.-B. and Greenberg, B. (2010). Flies, Mochicas and Burial practices: A Case Study from Huaca de la Luna, Peru. *Journal of Archaeological Sciences*, 37(11), pp. 2846–2856.

Huchet, J.-B., Le Mort, F., Rabinovich, R., Blau, S., Coqueugniot, H. and Arensburg B. (2013a). Identification of Dermestid Pupal Chambers on Southern Levant Human Bones: Inference for Reconstruction of Middle Bronze Age Mortuary Practices. *Journal of Archaeological Sciences*, 40(10), pp. 3793–3803.

Huchet, J.-B., Pereira, G., Gomy, Y., Phillips, T.K., Alatorre-Bracamontes, C.E., Vásquez-Bolaños, M. and Mansilla J. (2013b). Archaeoentomological Study of a Pre-Columbian Funerary Bundle (Mortuary Cave of Candelaria, Coahuila, Mexico). *Annales de la Société Entomologique de France*, 49(3), pp. 277–290.

Huchet, J.-B., Callou, C., Lichtentberg, R. and Dunand, F. (2013c). The Dog Mummy, the Ticks and the Louse Fly: Archaeological Report of a Severe Ectoparasitosis in Ancient Egypt. *International Journal of Paleopathology*, 3(3), pp. 165–175.

Kelly, J.A. (2006). *The influence of clothing, wrapping and physical trauma on carcass decomposition and arthropod succession in central South Africa*. Unpublished Ph.D. thesis, Faculty of Natural and Agricultural Sciences Department of Zoology and Entomology, University of the Free State, South Africa.

Kenward, H., and Allison E.P. (1988). 'Insect Remains from the Roman Fort at Papcastle, Carlisle', *Ancient Monuments Laboratory Report* 145, Historic Buildings and Monuments Commission for England (English Heritage)

Kenward, H., and Allison E.P. (1995). 'Insect Remains from the Roman Fort at Papcastle, Cumbria', *Reports from the Environmental Archaeology Unit, 95/1*, York: York Archaeological Trust.

Kenward, H.K., Hall, A.R. and Jones, A.K.G. (1986). *Environmental evidence from a Roman well and Anglian pits in the Legionary Fortress. London: The Archaeology of York* 14(5), pp. 241–288.

Kulshrestha, P. and Satpathy, D.K. (2001). Use of beetles in forensic entomology. *Forensic Science International*, 120(1–2), pp. 15–17.

Lefebvre, F. and Pasquerault T. (2004a). Temperature-Dependent Development of *Ophyra aenescens* (Wiedemann, 1830) and *Ophyra capensis* (Wiedemann, 1818) (Diptera, Muscidae). *Forensic Science International*, 139(1), pp. 75–79.

Lefebvre, F. and Pasquerault T. (2004b). *Corrigendum* to 'Temperature-dependent development of *Ophyra aenescens* (Wiedemann, 1830) and *Ophyra capensis* (Wiedemann, 1818) (Diptera Muscidae) [139(1), pp. 75–79]', *Forensic Science International*, 146(1), p. 69.

Magistretti, M. (1965). *Coleoptera: Cicindelidae, Carabidae. Catalogo topografico*. Bologna: Fauna d'Italia, 8.

Martin-Vega, D. Gómez-Gómez, A. and Baz, A. (2011). The 'Coffin Fly' *Conicera tibialis* (Diptera: Phoridae) Breeding on Buried Human Remains after a Postmortem Interval of 18 years. *Journal of Forensic Sciences*, 56, pp. 1654–1656.

Mégnin, J.P. 1894. La Faune des cadavres: application de l'entomologie à la médecine légale. *L'Encyclopédie Scientifique des Aide-mémoire*. Paris: Masson et Cie.

Osborne, J. (1969). An Insect Fauna of Late Bronze Age Date from Wilsford, Wiltshire, *Journal of Animal Ecology*, 38, pp. 555–566.

Otranto, D., Huchet, J.-B., Giannelli, A., Callou, C. and Dantas-Torres, F. (2014). The Enigma of the Dog Mummy from Ancient Egypt and the Origin of 'Rhipicephalus sanguineus'. *Parasite Vector*, 7(2), pp. 1–6.

Panagiotakopulu, E. and Buckland P.C. (2009). Environment, Insects and the Archaeology of Egypt. In: S. Ikram and A. Dodson, eds., *Beyond the Horizon; Studies in Egyptian Art, Archaeology and History in Honour of Barry J. Kemp*. Cairo: Publications of the Supreme Council of Antiquities, pp. 347–360.

Panagiotakopulu, E., Buckland P. C. and Kemp B. (2010). Underneath Ranefer's Floors – Urban Environments on the Desert Edge. *Journal of Archaeological Science*, 37, pp. 474–481.

Ponel, P. (1993). Les Coléoptères du Quaternaire: Leur Rôle dans la Reconstruction des Paléoclimats et des Paléoécosystèmes. *Bulletin d'Ecologie*, 24(1), pp. 5–16.

Portevin, G. 1926. *Les grands nécrophages du globe. Silphini – Necrodini – Necrophorini. encyclopédie entomologique (Series A)*, 6, Paris: Lechevalier.

Raoult, D., Dutour, O., Houhamdi. L., Jankauskas, R., Fournier, P.E., Ardagna, Y., Drancourt, M., Signoli, M., Dang La, V., Macia, Y. and Aboudharam, G., (2006). Evidence for Louse-Transmitted Diseases in Soldiers of Napoleon's Grand Army in Vilnius. *Journal of Infectious Diseases*, 193, pp. 112–120.

Ricciardi, M., Giuliani, R. and Castex, D. (2018). Preesistenze di Natura Antropica in una delle Regioni Più Antiche delle Catacombe dei SS. Marcellino e Pietro a Roma, *Geologia dell'Ambiente*, Supplement 4, pp. 105–110.

Rick, F.M., Rocha, G.C., Dittmar, K., Coimbra, C.E., Reinhard, K., Bouchet, F., Ferreira L.F. and Araújo, A. (2002). Crab Louse Infestation in Pre-Columbian America. *Journal of Parasitology*, 88, pp. 1266–1267.

Sachau-Carcel, G. (2014). From Field Recording of Plural Burials to 3D Modelling. Evidence from the Catacomb of Sts. Peter and Marcellinus, Italy. *Anthropologie (Brno)*, 52 (3), pp. 285–297.

Salesse, K. (2015). *Archéo-biogéochimie isotopique, reconstitutions des régimes alimentaires et des schémas de mobilité, et interactions bioculturelles: Les sépultures plurielles de la catacombe des Sts Pierre-et-Marcellin (Rome, Ier-IIIe siècle après Jesus.-Christ),* Unpublished Ph.D. thesis, University of Bordeaux.

Scharrer-Liska, G. and Grassberger, M. (2005). Archäoentomologische Untersuchungen von Grab 34 des Awarischen Gräberfeldes von Frohsdorf, Niederösterreich. *Archäologisches Korrespondenzblatt*, 35(4), pp. 531–544.

Schotsmans, E.M.J., Toksoy-Köksal, F., Brettell, R.C., Bessou, M., Corbineau, R., Lingle, A.M., Castex, D., Knüsel, C.J., Wilson, A.S., Bouquin, D., Blanchard, P., Becker, K. and Chapoulie, R. (2019). 'Not all that is white is lime' – White substances from archaeological burial contexts: analyses and interpretations. *Archaeometry* 61, pp. 809–827.

Serrulla, F., Etxeberría, F. and Herrasti, L. (2017). Saponified brains of the Spanish Civil War. In: E.M.J. Shotsmans, N. Marquez-Grant, and S.L Forbes, eds., *Taphonomy of Human Remains. Forensic Analysis of the Dead and the Depositional Environment.* New York: Wiley, pp. 429–437.

Skidmore, P. (1985). *The biology of the Muscidae of the world.* Dordrecht, The Netherlands: Dr. W. Junk Publisher.

Smith, K.G.V. (1986). *A manual of forensic entomology.* London: The Trustees of the British Museum (Natural History).

Steffan, J.-R., (1982). L'Entomofaune de la Momie de Ramses II. *Annales de la Société Entomologique de France* 18(4), pp. 531–537.

Sturani, M. (1962). Osservazioni e Ricerche Biologiche sul Genere *Carabus* L. *Memorie della Societa entomologica italiana*, 41: pp. 85–203.

Turchetto, M., Lafisca, S. and Constantini, G. (2001). Post Mortem Interval (PMI) Determined by Study of Sarcophagous Biocoenses: Three Cases from the Province of Venice (Italy). *Forensic Science International,* 120, pp. 28–31.

Turchetto, M., and S. Vanin. 2004. Forensic evaluations on a crime case with monospecific necrophagous fly population infected by two parasitoid species. *Anil Aggrawal's Internet Journal of Forensic Medicine and Toxicology*, 5, pp. 12–18.

Vanin, S. (2014). Crime scene insects: una passeggiata tra l'entomologia forense e l'archeoentomologia funeraria. In: A. Andrella, D. Fondaroli, and G. Gruppioni, eds., *Dai 'Casi Freddi' ai 'Casi Caldi'. Le Indagini Storiche e Forensi tra Saperi Giuridici e Investigazioni Scientifiche*, Alphen aan den Rijn, Netherlands: Wolters Kluver Italia and Cedam, pp. 115–126.

Vanin, S. (2016). Archeoentomologia funeraria: risultati e prospettive dallo studio delle mummie di Roccapelago, In: F. Badiale, ed., *Roccapelago e le Sue Mummie: Studio Integrato della Vita di una Piccola Comunità dell'Appennino tra XVI e XVIII secolo.* Modena, Italy: Academy Editions, pp. 225–229.

Vanin, S., Gherardi, M., Bugelli, V. and Di Paolo, M. (2011). Insects Found on a Human Cadaver in Central Italy Including the Blowfly *Calliphora loewi* (Diptera, Calliphoridae), A New Species of Forensic Interest. *Forensic Science International*, 207, pp. 30–33.

Vanin, S. and Huchet, J.-B. (2017). Forensic Entomology and Funerary Archaeoentomology (chap. 14). In: E.M.J. Schotsmans, N. Márquez-Grant and S.L. Forbes, eds., *Taphonomy of Human Remains: Forensic Analysis of the Dead and the Depositional Environment.* New York: Wiley, pp. 167–186.

Volpe, R. (2007), *Centocelle II. Roma S.D.O. le indagini archeologiche*, vol. 2, Soveria Mannelli: Rubbettino Editore.

Zurawski, K.N., Benbow, M.E., Miller, J.R., and Merritt, R.W. (2009). Examination of Nocturnal Blow Fly (Diptera: Calliphoridae) Oviposition on Pig Carcasses in Mid-Michigan. *Journal of Medical Entomology*, 46(3), pp. 671–679.

PART IV

Applied sciences, experiments and legal considerations

FROM FLESH TO BONE

Building bridges between taphonomy, archaeothanatology and forensic science for a better understanding of mortuary practices

Eline M.J. Schotsmans

PACEA, De la Préhistoire à l'Actuel: Culture, Environnement et Anthropologie,
UMR 5199, CNRS-Université de Bordeaux, Pessac, France

Centre for Archaeological Science (CAS), University of Wollongong, Wollongong,
Australia

Patrice Georges-Zimmermann

Institut National de Recherches Archéologiques Préventives (Inrap),
Grand-Sud-Ouest, France

TRACES, Travaux et Recherches Archéologiques sur les Cultures, les Espaces et les
Sociétés, UMR 5608, CNRS-Université Toulouse Jean Jaurès, Toulouse, France

Maiken Ueland

Centre for Forensic Science, University of Technology Sydney, Sydney, Australia

Boyd B. Dent

Red Earth Geosciences, consultancy, Sydney, Australia

Introduction

Archaeothanatology goes beyond taphonomy and bones. It touches on cultural aspects, funerary practices and their socio-cultural interpretation (cf. Knüsel and Schotsmans, Introduction, this volume). In order to conduct an archaeothanatological analysis, taphonomy comes into play. The depositional environment, peri-mortem, post-mortem and post-depositional processes that affect preservation and degradation, should be assessed in order to discriminate human behaviour from natural processes (Schotsmans, Márquez-Grant and Forbes, 2017). Over the last 35 years, taphonomy has gained increased importance in several disciplines. As a result, the depositional environment received more attention because of the contextual information that it can provide. This was not the case in the past. Many remains, whether human remains, animal remains,

DOI: 10.4324/9781351030625-32

or, for example, stone tools, were (and still are) often studied without information about their depositional contexts. Although there is some overlap, in many countries the division between archaeology and anthropology is demonstrated by a separation between the field and the laboratory: the archaeologist excavates in the field, while the anthropologist studies skeletal remains in the laboratory. This goes against all principles of archaeothanatology. The importance of field analysis is, therefore, one of the foundations of archaeothanatology (Duday and Masset, 1987; Duday *et al.*, 1990; Duday, 2009). A thorough archaeothanatological analysis cannot be conducted without studying the depositional environment and understanding the process of decomposition. Many archaeo-anthropologists have never been confronted with a dead or decaying corpse. Without the understanding of decomposition and factors that influence decay, it becomes more difficult to analyse skeletal remains and interpret mortuary practices. If one does not know what decomposition does or can do to a corpse, incorrect interpretations might be made.

This chapter focusses on human decomposition and factors that influence decay from an archaeothanatological point of view. The examples are based on forensic and archaeo-anthropological experience of the authors, combined with repeated observations of human decomposition during actualistic experiments at the Australian Facility for Taphonomic Experimental Research (AFTER)[1] and modern cemetery research at Rookwood General Cemetery (RGC)[2] in Australia. Most examples in this chapter are based on observations of human remains during 'decomposition in a void', either deposited on the surface or in a coffin. In a few cases, reference is made to experiments with pigs. The authors are aware that the study of pig experiments is limited for archaeo-anthropological research and not directly comparable to those with humans (e.g. Dautartas *et al.*, 2018; Knobel *et al.*, 2019; Dawson, Barton and Wallman, 2020). Humans and pigs follow different decomposition rates. Humans undergo more differential decomposition (Knobel *et al.*, 2019), which is an important aspect to be considered in archaeothanatology (see section 'soft tissue preservation, delayed decay and differential decomposition' below). However, pig experiments increase sample size and the possibility of replication, so they should be seen as valuable complementary study material.

---

1 The Australian Facility for Taphonomic Experimental Research (AFTER) is dedicated to the study of human taphonomy. It is the only human decomposition facility in the Southern Hemisphere. AFTER is led by the University of Technology Sydney (UTS) in collaboration with partner universities, scientific organisations and law enforcement agencies. Donors are acquired through the UTS Body Donation Program overseen by the Surgical and Anatomical Science Facility (SASF) at UTS. Consent is provided by all donors to use their remains for the purposes of research at AFTER in accordance with the New South Wales Anatomy Act (1977).

2 Rookwood General Cemetery in Sydney, Australia, is the largest cemetery in the Southern Hemisphere. It occupies about 288 hectares and has been in continuous operation since 1867 with over 600 000 graves and the interred remains of over one million people. The original 200 acres (80.94 ha) purchased in 1862 has been expanded and altered in a number of well-documented stages. Current use is multi-faith with general burials, crematoria and memorialisation. Much of the site is heritage listed. The site is operationally administered by the Rookwood General Cemeteries Reserve Land Manager (RGC, responsible for about 2/3 of the area), the Catholic Metropolitan Cemeteries Trust, Rookwood Memorial Gardens & Crematorium and the Commonwealth War Graves. The Land Manager is responsible for about 1900 interments per annum and is currently undertaking a large and unique study of burial decomposition and related practices which affect operations. Eighty-one adult-sized pigs (as human analogues) have been buried in addition to 12 interments in an above-ground structure, under various experimental conditions emulating modern burials in order to investigate the difficulties encountered in cemetery practice in a heavy clay soil, in a temperate (hot summer) climate zone. This research has been designed by and is under the scientific control of one of the authors (BBD).

From flesh to bone: stages of decomposition from an archaeothanatological perspective

Decomposition refers to a variety of processes of degradation that commence as soon as an organism has died. It consists of complex processes whereby the soft tissues break down and eventually disintegrate, resulting in skeletonisation. The stages of decomposition have been repeatedly described in many forensic books and articles (e.g. Megyesi, Nawrocki and Haskell, 2005; Goff, 2010; Hamilton and Green, 2017; Wescott, 2018; Byard, 2020) with standard forensic descriptors such as 'fresh', 'active decay', 'advanced decay', 'skeletonisation', amongst many others. In literature focussed on archaeo-anthropology, these descriptors are often absent because the focus is on the skeleton. However, the influence the decomposition stages have on the final appearance of the skeletal remains is underestimated. In this section, the processes that occur in a body after death are discussed from an archaeothanatological perspective. For more details regarding immediate post-mortem changes, forensic pathology literature is recommended (e.g. Knight, 1996; DiMaio and DiMaio, 2001; Prahlow and Byard, 2012).

The fresh stage (0–48 h)

The three main changes that occur in the fresh stage of decomposition are *algor mortis*, *livor mortis* and *rigor mortis*. One of the first noticeable changes is a reduction in body temperature, called *algor mortis*. Heat that is present in life is lost to the external environment and equilibrates with the ambient temperature (Hamilton and Green, 2017; Byard, 2020). The process of hypostasis or *livor mortis*, refers to the dark, purple discolouration of the skin caused by the gravitational draining of blood to the lowest parts of the body. This can occur as soon as 0.5 hours after death and will be complete after about 16 hours (Byard, 2020). *Livor mortis* can be used to indicate the original position of the deceased after death. In other words, someone who died in a supine position should show *livor mortis* over the back. In forensic cases, *livor mortis* is used to identify if the body had been moved after death (Hamilton and Green, 2017; Byard, 2020).

The third process, and probably the most important one to consider in archaeothanatology, is *rigor mortis*. Post-mortem stiffening develops as the muscles become depleted of adenosine triphosphate (ATP) which results in actin and myosin microfilaments adhering to one another, causing muscles to stiffen (Hamilton and Green, 2017; Byard, 2020). The onset and development of *rigor mortis* are very variable. High ambient temperatures are associated with a more rapid onset. It also develops more rapidly in infants and in persons who died shortly after exercise because they may have depleted their stores of energy and ATP (Hamilton and Green, 2017; Byard, 2020). *Rigor mortis* is first observed in small muscle groups such as those in the fingers, the eyelids and in the muscles of the temporomandibular joint. This can occur as quickly as 20 minutes after death. For this reason, it is important to put the body in a desired position before *rigor mortis* commences. For example, to avoid being confronted with a slack-jawed staring face, the eyelids of the deceased should be closed immediately after death, and a jaw bandage or prop can be applied to keep the lower jaw from dropping open (Hamilton and Green, 2017). In countries where it was a custom to lay the deceased out for a wake or viewing, coins or stones were placed on the eyes to stop them from opening if *rigor* had begun to set in or to make sure they were closed before *rigor* started (Hamilton and Green, 2017). There is limited literature about this practice, but it must have been common as evidenced by the phrase 'stealing the pennies off a dead man's eyes' which is still used today when talking about someone cheap or stingy. Hertz (1928) refers to the widespread use of closing the eyes and other body openings with coins or beads. Crissman (1994), who wrote about changing burial practices in American mountain societies from the 1600s onwards, reports that the coins would remain on the eyelids for about a day until the position of the eye stabilised. The coin was subsequently taken off the face and buried within the coffin (Crissman, 1994: 31). This is different from the Greek and Roman custom of placing a coin in the mouth of the deceased to pay the ferryman for taking the soul from the world of the living to the world of the dead (Morris, 1992: 105). And different again from the Jewish custom of placing stones on the eyes so that the dead cannot report on what has happened on earth (cf. Blanchard, Chapter 19, this volume: Figure 19.10). One should also take into account that coins or pebbles can fall off the face during transportation of the coffin to the final resting place. From an archaeothanatological point of view, these examples might lead to the same or similar archaeological outcomes (equifinality): coins or pebbles in the coffin, near the eyes or around the cephalic extremity. It is then the responsibility of the archaeo-anthropologist to interpret the evidence for the practice or not, as the case may be. Therefore, it is necessary to determine the exact location of the coin in relation to the other elements in the grave. More information could be gained from observations of other burials at the same site by making comparisons to demonstrate that this particular action is repeated and, if possible, detailed in written sources. In other words, the presence of a coin in an ancient Greek grave does not necessarily make it an example of a Charon's obol.

Another example is the position of the hands and fingers. If the hand and fingers are not deliberately placed in a particular position, the hand will take a neutral position after death. This neutral position puts the least tension on the muscles and tendons. It includes the fingers being flexed with the thumb extended but relaxed (Figure 27.1a). In archaeology, phalanges can sometimes be found in a peculiar position. In the case of Figure 27.1b, the desiccated left index finger of a donor at AFTER shows an unusual extended position. Likewise, Duday (2009: 19–20) describes the 'Dame of Bonifacio' who was found in Corsica, France, with her right thumb, index finger and middle finger in an extended position, while the other two fingers were flexed. The question that arises with these peculiar examples is whether or not this position is a co-incidence, or intentional and thus part of a ritual action. It is the task of the archaeo-anthropologist to interpret these observations by verifying if the same position is repeated in other burials from the same chronological and cultural context that would then indicate a shared special gesture, or rather if the observation is an example of random movement during decomposition. The extended position of the index finger in Figure 27.1b appeared around 12 days due to heavy bloating.

Figure 27.1 The left hand of two different donors at the Australian Facility for Taphonomic Experimental Research (AFTER). A. After death, a hand normally takes this neutral, 'relaxed' position with flexed fingers and extended thumb. Photograph taken nine months after death; B. Left hand of another donor with the index finger in an unusual, extended position, five months after death (Photographs: E. Schotsmans).

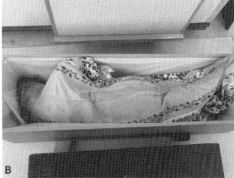

Figure 27.2 A. *Rigor mortis* makes body manipulation difficult; B. The rigidity of the limbs and torso of the pig corpse required considerable effort to properly settle the carcass in the coffin (Photographs: B. Dent).

The finger remained extended due to subsequent fixation by desiccation. The Bonifacio burial contained a coloured deposit that was deliberately added (Duday, 2009: 20), but if the position of the fingers was part of this ritual action or not remains an interpretation without immediate verification.

The rigidity of a corpse, in general, should be kept in mind when making archaeothanatological observations. Loosening of *rigor mortis* is temperature dependent. In cool and temperate climates, *rigor* starts to loosen between 24 and 48 hours after death but very often stiffness can still be detected a few days later (Madea, Krompecher and Knight, 1995; Hamilton and Green, 2017; Byard, 2020). In the RGC experiments, the handling of pigs that had been euthanised in the previous 4–6 hours was often very difficult due to *rigor mortis*. These research specimens were put in a coffin upon receipt following transport, but the disposition of the limbs and their general rigidity made this difficult and required considerable effort to properly settle the carcass in the coffin (Figure 27.2). Similarly, it is not always easy to turn the head into a certain direction after the neck muscles become fixed by *rigor mortis*. In other words, the head does not always stay in the position it is intended to be placed. This might be another reason why the direction of the face towards the *Qibla* in Muslim burials shows variation (cf. Gleize, Chapter 20, this volume). When the dead are buried in a flexed position, common in the Neolithic period, *rigor mortis* should also be taken into account when reflecting about the relative timing of burial. When *rigor mortis* is present, the manipulation of a corpse into a flexed position has proven very difficult. In forensic cases, when a corpse is found in an unusual flexed position, it is often assumed that this position was achieved in the first hours (1–4 h) after death, a stage called flaccidity (e.g. D'Souza *et al.*, 2011). In the Neolithic period, it is more likely that the deceased had been put in a flexed position immediately after death, or days later, after *rigor mortis* had passed. However, even when binding is used, it is unlikely to achieve hyperflexion with a fleshed corpse (for the interpretation of hyperflexion, see section 'soil and sediment' below).

Active and advanced decay

Autolysis and putrefaction

The processes of autolysis and putrefaction commence during the stage of early decomposition. Autolysis refers to the chemical breakdown of the cells and tissue by enzymes known as 'autodigestion' (Dent, Forbes and Stuart, 2004; Hamilton and Green, 2017; Byard, 2020).

Initiated by the mechanisms of autolysis, immunosuppression barriers no longer function, permitting micro-organisms to take over the body and use the tissues as a source of nutrients. This process of bacterial growth contributing to organ and soft tissue disintegration is called putrefaction (Dent, Forbes and Stuart, 2004; Hamilton and Green, 2017; Byard, 2020). The first visible sign of proliferation of bacteria during putrefaction is a green abdominal discolouration. The intervascular growth of bacteria and their dissemination throughout the body appears as a series of lines spreading from the abdomen to the extremities, called 'marbling' (Knight, 1996; Hamilton and Green, 2017; Byard, 2020). Aerobic organisms deplete the tissues of oxygen and, although their numbers are reduced as the available oxygen diminishes, they create favourable chemical conditions for anaerobic organisms. Anaerobic organisms are derived from the gastrointestinal tract but may also migrate from the soil into the remains during the later stages of decay (Evans, 1963; Dent, Forbes and Stuart, 2004) (more on oxygen in burials see section 'environmental variables' below).

As a result of putrefaction, a variety of gases form causing the abdomen and scrotum to become distended, known as the 'bloat stage' (Figure 27.3b). Gas and fluid accumulation is eventually purged from the rectum and other natural orifices accompanied by a strong odour (DiMaio and DiMaio, 2001: 30–34; Hamilton and Green, 2017). The skin begins to blister and skin slippage will be noticed, causing tattoos and old scars to be more clearly discernible (Hamilton and Green, 2017). At the same time as the external aspects of the body decay, similar processes occur internally (Hamilton and Green, 2017).

Corpse movement

From an archaeothanatological point of view in the context of decomposition in a void, it is important to take post-mortem corpse movement into account when trying to reconstruct the original position of the body. Figure 27.3a illustrates the concept for an unrestricted cadaver on the ground surface where the original placement of the deceased had both hands placed on the torso. Seventeen days later (Figure 27.3b), bloating caused both upper and lower limbs to move laterally. The right forearm and right knee of the deceased lifted anteriorly in standard anatomical position (superiorly towards the zenith with respect to a possible grave opening) due to the swelling and extension of the limb by putrefactive gases. This so-called 'putrefactive *rigor mortis*' should not be confused with genuine *rigor mortis* caused by the consumption of ATP (see above)

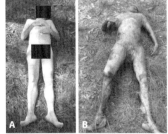

Figure 27.3 An example of post-mortem corpse movement during five time intervals. A. Original placement on Day 0 of an unrestricted cadaver with both hands placed on the torso; B. Seventeen days after deposition when bloating caused both upper and lower limbs to be moved laterally. The right forearm and right knee of the deceased lifted anteriorly (with respect to the standard anatomical position) due to the swelling and extension of the limb by putrefactive gases; C. Day 78; D. The skeletonised remains 1.5 years later; E. Four years after deposition (Photographs: M. Ueland and E. Schotsmans).

Figure 27.4 In-coffin, in-grave space can be extremely limited in all dimensions. A soldier buried for approximately 85 years in a metal coffin in Hildesheim, Germany (Image courtesy: M. Albrecht).

(Tsokos and Byard, 2012). The sequence in figures 27.3a to 27.3e shows that it becomes difficult to reconstruct the original position of the individual (Figure 27.3a) based on observations of the skeleton (Figure 27.3e). Figure 27.3 could represent decomposition in a void without restrictions at the sides. A coffin (to a very considerable extent) and a shroud would limit this movement spatially, including in the vertical dimension (Figure 27.4).

Movement caused by putrefactive gases produced during decomposition is commonly observed, as demonstrated in Figure 27.3, or by stretching and subsequent contracting of ligaments. For example, disarticulation and 're-articulation' was described during observations of donors at the Forensic Anthropology Research Facility (FARF) at Texas State University, San Marcos, Texas, USA, due to drying out of ligaments (Mickleburgh and Wescott, 2018) (for a discussion on disarticulation and 're-articulation' cf. Boulestin, Chapter 2, this volume). Wilson *et al.* (2020) quantified post-mortem movement by observing and filming one donor at AFTER over a 16-month period. They noted post-mortem movement in all limbs, with the most movement by the right radius, moving a total distance of 51.65 cm. Another finding was that the upper limbs produced more movement in early decomposition while the lower limbs appeared to be most active during advanced decomposition (Wilson *et al.*, 2020). Although this study was limited to

Figure 27.5 Rotating maggots moved the left tibia, fibula and proximal tibial epiphysis outside the space originally occupied by the pig carcass ('outside the pig's body volume') during the active stage of decomposition (Photograph: E. Schotsmans).

only a single subject, it is the first to confirm forensic observations of post-mortem movement in surface depositions.

An external cause of movement and an important factor during decomposition is the activity of insects. Maggot activity is often a primary driving force behind the removal of soft tissues (e.g. Dadour and Harvey, 2008; Vanin and Huchet, 2017; Dawson, Barton and Wallman, 2020; Wallman and Archer, 2020). Flies (Diptera) and beetles (Coleoptera) are the insects most frequently collected from corpses (cf. Huchet and Castex, Chapter 26, this volume). Not all species arrive at the corpse at the same time, hence the usefulness of successional studies in the calculation of the minimum post-mortem interval (mPMI) in forensic cases (Wallman and Archer, 2020). The longer a corpse is exposed before burial, the more chance of insect access (i.e. flies laying eggs) which, in turn, also has an influence on the decomposition rate (Bachmann and Simmons, 2010). Fly larvae rotate, alternating between the periphery and the centre of the aggregation, known as the 'maggot mass', for reasons of foraging behaviour, thermoregulation and to avoid hypoxic conditions (Rivers, Thompson and Brogan, 2011; Heaton, Moffatt and Simmons, 2018). If voids are present, the maggots can move small bones around. Figure 27.5 shows how a maggot mass of *Chrysomya* (Diptera: Calliphoridae) blow fly species expelled the left tibia, fibula and the proximal tibial epiphysis from a pig carcass during the active stage of decomposition (Further information on insects is discussed in section 'environmental variables' below). Similar observations were made in other human decomposition facilities (cf. Mickleburgh *et al.*, Chapter 28, this volume: figure 28.9).

Cadaver decomposition island

During active decay, decomposition fluids will be released from the body. The fluids contain nutrients, such as carbon, nitrogen, ammonium, nitrate, potassium and phosphorus (Szelecz *et al.*, 2018; Barton *et al.*, 2020). These fluids will leach several centimetres around the body and into the soil, providing localised changes in moisture, carbon and nutrients. As such, the decaying body produces a concentrated island surrounding the corpse, called a cadaver decomposition

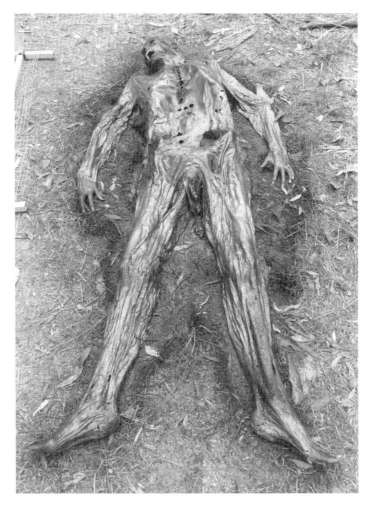

Figure 27.6 Example of a corpse with cadaver decomposition island (CDI) at the Australian Facility for Taphonomic Experimental Research (AFTER), 2.5 months after death. Decomposition fluids leach several centimetres around the body, providing localised changes in moisture, carbon and nutrients. This process also happens when a corpse is buried in a coffin (Photograph: E. Schotsmans).

island (CDI) (Figure 27.6). The bio-physicochemical characteristics of a CDI change over time, initially resulting in an alkaline environment, followed by an acidic environment. These changes can have a negative effect on surrounding vegetation, followed by a positive effect that eventually normalises (Carter and Tibbett, 2008). The CDI effects are also observed in surface vegetation of burials (Watson *et al.*, 2020). Various aspects of the nature of associated soil chemistry have been studied, including volatile fatty acids (VFAs), adipocere, salts and nutrients. The outcomes show general agreement but also differences based on the nature of the soils and the depositional environment, such as pH, temperature regime and other factors (e.g. Vass *et al.*, 1992; Cassar *et al.*, 2011; von der Lühe *et al.*, 2017).

When a body is buried directly in the soil, with or without a shroud, the decomposition fluids will leach into the burial environment. In the case of a coffin burial and depending on the porosity and material of the coffin, fluids might remain inside the coffin. It is unclear if this can cause body displacement. Most fluids are released during active decay when the deceased is still covered with soft tissue and bones are still articulated. Hence, gross bone displacement caused by decay fluids is considered to be minimal. In contrast, water percolation and the 'bucket effect' can certainly cause bone displacement in the skeletonisation stage (see section 'environmental variables' below).

The effect of decay fluids on the decay of a container is not well understood either. In the absence of groundwater (and plastic liners), body fluid would partially react with the coffin causing metal corrosion or possibly promoting anaerobic biodegradation of timber, stimulating resident fungi or chemically reacting with wood cellulose or hemicellulose. It also depends on whether or not the coffin has been filled with groundwater. The greater volume of percolated ground-water compared to the volume of body fluid in a coffin would mean that the hydrochemical in-coffin environment alters. However, the type of wood has a major influence on the outcomes. In Australia, some timbers such as turpentine or white cypress are very resistant to 'attack' of many kinds, while many timber varieties of the genus Eucalyptus strongly resist in-ground rot (see paragraph on coffin decay in section 'human behaviour' below).

Skeletonisation

Once the body has reached the skeletonisation stage, the bones begin to disarticulate if there is space available. One of the first questions that the archaeothanatologist tries to address is whether decomposition occurred in a void or in a filled space by observing displacements of skeletal elements outside the original space occupied by the body. However, it is important to keep in mind that the lack of bone displacement does not automatically mean that decomposition took place in a filled space (Duday, 2009: 32–40). In the past, one used to look at the evidence for a decayed container such as the presence of wood traces or nails. The absence of this evidence was often incorrectly interpreted as the absence of a container (cf. Green, Chapter 23, this volume). The analytical observations that distinguish between decomposition in a void or in a filled space are detailed in several papers (e.g. Duday and Guillon, 2006; Duday, 2009; Blaizot, 2014; Duday, Le Mort and Tillier, 2014; Castex and Blaizot, 2017). Hence, they are not repeated here. In the following section, head rotation and disarticulation sequences are discussed based on evidence gathered at AFTER.

Defining the original position of the head

When an individual is placed in a supine position, the head often rests on the occipital bone. The curved nature of the occipital makes this position unstable when muscles and ligaments degrade. As such, the cranium can turn on its lateral side or roll posteriorly. Observations of the cervical vertebrae enable the archaeothanatologist to determine if the head was originally placed in a lateral position or on the occipital bone (Duday, 2009: 18) (cf. Blaizot, Chapter 1, this volume). The range of motion of the cervical spine is up to 90 degrees of rotation to both sides (Swartz, Floyd and Cendoma, 2005). However, uniplanar movement of the neck does not produce movement between cervical vertebrae individually because interlocking unicate joints ensure that the cervical vertebrae of the neck function as a unit. The first cervical vertebra, the atlas, articulates with the articular facets of the occiput of the cranium, providing a 'cradle' for support of the head (Swartz, Floyd and Cendoma, 2005). Rotation and lateral flexion between the occiput and atlas are limited to 5 degrees due to the depth of the atlantal sockets, in which the occipital condyles rest (Cramer, 2014: table 5-5). This means that the atlas always follows the movement and rotation of the head. In other words, when the head rotates laterally, only the atlas follows its movement. So if C1 is in lateral view, and the other cervical vertebrae are in frontal view, then the head was

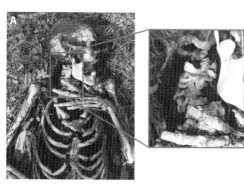

Figure 27.7 Defining the original position of the head based on observations of the cervical vertebrae. A. The first cervical vertebra, C1, is in lateral view, while the other cervical vertebrae are in frontal view. Because the atlas always follows the movement and rotation of the head, it can be concluded that the head of this individual was originally placed on its left lateral side (confirmed by the photographs from deposition day 0); B. All cervical vertebrae show a gradual inclination to one side, thus in lateral view, also including some of the first thoracic vertebrae. This suggests that the head had turned slowly and gradually to the right side during decomposition indicating that it was originally placed on the occiput, with the face of the deceased in anterior view (confirmed by photographs from deposition day 0) (Photographs: E. Schotsmans).

originally placed in a lateral position (Figure 27.7a). In contrast, when all cervical vertebrae show a gradual inclination to one side, thus in lateral view, potentially also including some first thoracic vertebrae, the head must have turned slowly and gradually to that side during decomposition indicating that the head was originally placed on the occiput, with the face of the deceased in anterior view (Figure 27.7b).

In archaeothanatology, the interpretation of a cranium rolling posteriorly caused by 'the rapid decay of a pillow' requires caution (e.g. Blaizot, 2017: 231–233). Observations of the authors at AFTER have shown that posterior rolling of the cranium is not necessarily caused by a pillow but related to small differences in the position of the head that are often defined by *rigor mortis* in combination with the development of the nuchal muscle attachments on the occipital. A slight hyper-extension of the neck might be enough to cause the cranium to rotate posteriorly. It is therefore important that the 'pillow hypothesis' is supported by contextual evidence and other analyses, such as botanical analysis for example (e.g. Deforce, van Hove and Willems, 2015; Jarosińska *et al.*, 2019) (cf. Cartron and Zemour, Chapter 22, this volume).

Relative sequences of disarticulation: labile and persistent joints?

It has long been known that decomposition varies and that there is no single sequence of disarticulation. However, to distinguish between primary and secondary burials Ambroise and Perlès (1975) suggested observing 'inter-locking' articulations (*articulations emboîtantes*) and 'non-inter-locking' articulations (*articulations non emboîtantes*). A similar distinction was made between 'labile' and 'persistent' joints (Duday *et al.*, 1990: 25–30; Duday, 2009). In archaeothanatology, a joint is classified as persistent when it is more resilient to disarticulation due to biomechanical constraints and major ligamentous and tendinous attachments. This category includes weight-bearing joints of the body, such as the tibio-femoral joints, for example. In contrast, labile joints are considered as unstable and less well-supported joints that break down more rapidly during decomposition. Details about which joints are classified as persistent or labile can be found in Duday (2009: 25–30) and are summarised in Knüsel (2014) and Knüsel and Robb (2016).

The labile/persistent differentiation is used to distinguish primary and secondary burials: 'to demonstrate the primary character of a burial, it is enough to demonstrate that connections are maintained in some joints, as long as these belong to the group of joints that break down more rapidly' (Duday, 2009: 27) and 'preservation of labile articulations is necessary to demonstrate a primary interment or deposit, [but] the opposite argument has no validity; the presence of dislocations [i.e. disarticulations] does not exclude the primary characteristic of the deposit. In other words, evident disorder in the organisation of the bones does not mean that they have been handled or moved after death' (Duday and Guillon, 2006: 128).

Based on the above, hypothetical 'paradoxical disarticulation' was proposed (Maureille and Sellier, 1996; Duday and Guillon, 2006; Sellier and Bendezu-Sarmiento, 2013) which refers to the reversed relationship between labile and persistent joints. In brief, if labile connections are maintained and persistent joints disarticulated, the individual may have been mummified prior to deposition (Maureille and Sellier, 1996; Sellier and Bendezu-Sarmiento, 2013).

There are several problems with the distinction between 'labile' and 'persistent' joints. First, the biomechanical function in life should not be linked to joint decomposition. In this context, an exception to the rule, noted by Duday, is important: the acetabulo-femoral joint or hip joint is considered a labile joint, despite most weight-bearing articulations being considered to be persistent (Duday, 2009: 27). Secondly, as acknowledged by Duday *et al.* (1990), the classification of labile and persistent joints is based on repeated archaeological observations of skeletons (the 'end' result). The relative sequence of disarticulation has never been validated by observing the decomposition of corpses from the moment of deposition onwards. In addition, there is no consensus among scholars. For example, the atlanto-occipital joint is classified as persistent by some scholars (Duday, 2009: 18; Knüsel, 2014; Knüsel and Robb, 2016) and labile by others (Micozzi, 1991). Thirdly, the validity of this classification in the context of differential decomposition (see section 'differential decomposition' below) has not been demonstrated when there are localised differences in preservation and decay. A final problem is the definition of the terms 'primary' and 'secondary' deposition both being based on the observation of articulations, an issue that has been raised by scholars in the past (Boulestin and Duday, 2005) (cf. Boulestin, Chapter 2, this volume; Knüsel, Gerdau-Radonić and Schotsmans, Chapter 34, this volume). In brief, classifying primary and secondary depositions based on articulations leads to confusion. Is a fully articulated skeleton always an indication of a primary deposition? For example, if a corpse is mummified and buried after a few years (Figure 27.8), it is technically a secondary deposition. Thousands of years later, when soft tissue has disappeared, archaeologists will be tempted to classify it as a primary deposition based on the skeleton being fully articulated.

In order to validate the above hypotheses of labile/persistent joints and paradoxical disarticulation, articulation sequences are currently being studied at AFTER. For the definition of articulation and disarticulation, the authors refer to Boulestin (Chapter 2, this volume). The AFTER field site consists of an open eucalypt woodland, defined as Cumberland Dry Sclerophyll Forest. The highest average daily temperature measured in summer is 43°C (January) and the lowest average daily temperature in winter is 7°C (July). On an annual basis, the temperatures fluctuate between 0°C and 47°C. There is rainfall during all months of the year with an average humidity of about 75%. The donors are protected from scavenging by cages. In general, most donors show an initial superficial desiccation on the uppermost side (cf. Schotsmans, Van de Voorde and Forbes, 2020) (see section 'soft tissue preservation' below) with skeletonisation attested after about a year. Table 27.1 shows the disarticulation sequence numbered from 1 to 10. The first five donors were placed in a supine position. The last three donors were intentionally mummified naturally (a) on a platform in a flexed side position (decubitus lateral) (donors 6 and 7) and (b) in a car (donor 8). The latter was moved out of the car after nine months to further decompose outdoors.

Figure 27.8 This individual was naturally mummified for 28 days at the Australian Facility for Taphonomic Experimental Research (AFTER) and subsequently moved to a burial as shown in this photograph. Thousands of years later, when soft tissues would have disappeared, archaeologists would classify this as a primary deposition based on the skeleton being fully articulated (Photograph: E. Schotsmans).

The results show that no relative order of disarticulation can be deduced, not even between individuals in the same position. In addition, 'labile' as well as 'persistent' joints seem to disarticulate over different time intervals, irrespective of their classification. Season of deposition does not appear to have an influence on the relative disarticulation sequence. At AFTER, the atlanto-occipital joint, C5-C6 and the sterno-clavicular joints are amongst the first to disarticulate. This contrasts with observations by Duday in Europe, where the atlanto-occipital joint is classified as persistent. Duday states that 'the atlas remains connected with the occipital for a long time' (Duday, 2009: 18) and that 'the temporo-mandibular joints usually decay before those of the cervical vertebrae' (Duday, 2009: 19).

Joint disarticulation is complex and influenced by many variables (see section 'factors influencing cadaver decomposition and bone displacement' below). Observations by the authors show that disarticulation mainly depends on slight differences in position. The two flexed donors placed on their left sides (left lateral decubitus position) disarticulated differently than the seated donor and the supine individuals. But even when comparing the supine donors, very small differences

Table 27.1 Disarticulation sequences of eight donors at the Australian Facility for Taphonomic Experimental Research (AFTER). The articulations that are not mentioned were still articulated at the time of the completion of this chapter. The order of disarticulation is numbered from 1 to 10, with the first disarticulation in dark grey and the second element to disarticulate in dotted light grey. The first column indicates the hypothetical classification of labile or persistent joints based on Dudzey (2009) and Knüsel and Robb (2016).

Hypothetical classification as labile or persistent joint		Donor 1	Donor 2	Donor 3	Donor 4	Donor 5	Donor 6	Donor 7	Donor 8
	Sex	F	M	M	M	M		F	F
	Age	88	57	74	82	84	8c	66	93
	Position	supine	supine	supine	supine	supine	flexed, left side	flexed, left side	seated
	Season of deposition	autumn	autumn	winter	spring	summer	summer	autumn	autumn
	Treatment	na	na	na	na	na	natural mummification	natural mummification	natural mummification in a car. Moved after 9 months to decompose outdoors
labile	Temporo-mandibular joint			2 (8m)					
labile	Hyoid			3 (9m)					
persistent	Atlanto-occipital	2 (1y4m)		1 (8m)			1 (8d)		2 (2y3m)
labile	C1-C2								1 (1y10m)
labile	C2-C3								1 (1y10m)
labile	C3-C4								3 (2y4m)
labile	C4-C5								3 (2y4m)
labile	C5-C6	1 (1y3m)				2 (10m)			4 (2y7m)
labile	Sternoclavicular joint (L)		1 (1y3m)	5 (1y1m)	1 (9m)	3 (1y)			2 (2y3in)
labile	Sternoclavicular joint (R)		1 (1y3m)	4 (10m)		3 (1y)			4 (2y7m)
persistent	Acromioclavicular joint (L)		2 (3y4m)	9 (1y4m)					4 (2y7m)
persistent	Acromioclavicular joint (R)								
labile	Manubriosternal (sternal angle) fibrocartilagenous joint								
labile	Costo-sternal joints (one or more) (R)			4 (10m)	3 (12m)	3 (1y)			5 (2y8m)
labile	Costo-sternal joints (one or more) (L)		3 (1y7m)						5 (2y8m)
labile	Costo-vertebral joints thoracic vertebr L+R	4 (1y5m)	2 (3y4m)	8 (1y3m)			2 (1t:d)	1 (1m)	
persistent	L2-L3	3 (1y4m)		4 (10m)					
persistent	Scapulo-humeral joint (R)			7 (1y2m)				3 (3m)	
persistent	Scapulo-humeral joint (L)			10 (1y5m)	4 (1y1m)	4 (1y1m)		2 (2m)	
persistent	Humero-radial joint (R)				3 (1y)				
persistent	Humero-ulnar joint (L)			10 (1y5m)	4 (1y2m)				
persistent	Humero-ulnar joint (R)			6 (1y2m)					
labile	Femoro-acetabular joint (R)								
labile	Femoro-acetabular joint (L)			10 (1y5m)					
persistent	Femoro-tibial joint (L)				4 (1y2m)	4 (1y1m)			
persistent	Femoro-tibial joint (R)								
labile	Patella (R)			9 (1y4m)			2 (9d)		4 (2y7m)
labile	Carpals (L)			9 (1y4m)	2 (11m)				4 (2y7m)
labile	Metacarpals (L)								4 (2y7m)
persistent	Talo-calcaneal (R)			11 (1y6m)	3 (12m)				
persistent	Talo-calcaneal (L)								4 (2y7m)
labile	Metatarsals (L)								
labile	Phalanges of feet (L+R)					1 (6m)			

Note: (y = year; m = months; d = days; L = left; R = right; C1–C6 = Cervical vertebrae 1 to 6; L2–L3 = Lumbar vertebrae 2 and 3).

in position appear to have an influence. The neck of donor 1 was slightly more extended due to *rigor mortis*, causing C5-C6 to disarticulate first. The examples show that it is important to note that 'supine' positions are never exactly the same and that *rigor mortis* plays an important role in fixing certain body parts into a position (see above). Additional factors that influence disarticulation are the presence of pathological conditions, such as Diffuse Idiopathic Skeletal Hyperostosis (DISH) and arthropathies, or acquired and congenital joint contractures, as in leprosy, tuberculosis and achondroplasia, for example.

Mickleburgh and colleagues (Chapter 28, this volume) made similar observations at the FARF in Texas (USA). A study of the disarticulation of 15 human cadavers for a period of six months did not match with the previously hypothesised labile-persistent joint classification. The order and timing of disarticulation were also different from those observed at AFTER. The results from both AFTER and FARF show that a strict differentiation between labile and persistent joints cannot be applied. This also means that the previously hypothesised 'paradoxical disarticulation' could not be confirmed. The three mummified individuals at AFTER (Table 27.1: donors 6, 7 and 8) showed several 'labile' articulations were amongst the first joints to disarticulate.

As with every case in archaeothanatology, contextual evidence is important, rather than blindly recording 'labile' and 'persistent' joints or looking at every individual articulation. An example is a case study of mummification described by Sellier and Bendezu-Sarmiento (2013) in the Marquesas Islands in the South Pacific. The authors observed 'paradoxical disarticulation' and concluded that the individual must have been a former mummy. Their arguments, however, were not solely based on labile/persistent analysis but also on the history of mummification in the Marquesas, including original texts by the first explorers and evidence for disarticulation by body part manipulation when moving the mummy to another location (hence disturbing certain 'persistent' joints like the sacro-iliac joint).

Factors influencing cadaver decomposition and bone displacement

Every deposition is unique due to a combination of intrinsic and extrinsic factors, a division that was originally described by Henderson (1987). Intrinsic factors depend on the nature of the body itself (sex, age-at-death, size, etc.), while extrinsic or 'external' factors consist of environmental variables, aspects from the depositional context, as well as aspects related to human behaviour (Figure 27.9). From an archaeological point of view, not all of the variables are important

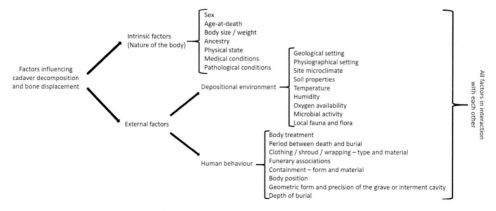

Figure 27.9 Schematic overview of factors influencing cadaver decomposition and bone displacement. This is by no means a complete list and care must be taken when considering these variables; they should not be regarded as comprising independent factors.

in the long term but it is important to be aware of them. All the variables are in interaction with each other and that means it is impossible to study them in isolation. The description below forms a theoretical base meant to describe the individual variables. It is by no means a complete list and care must be taken when considering these variables; they should not be regarded as comprising independent factors.

Environmental variables

Temperature is one of the most important variables that affects decomposition. An increase in temperature is associated with an accelerated rate of cadaver decomposition (e.g. Mann, Bass and Meadows, 1990; Megyesi, Nawrocki and Haskell, 2005), while cool or freezing temperatures have been shown to slow decomposition considerably (Meyer, Anderson and Carter, 2013; Cockle and Bell, 2017). This is mostly due to higher temperatures providing optimal conditions for the reproduction of bacteria, increased insect activity (Mann, Bass and Meadows, 1990; Campobasso, Di Vella and Introna, 2001; Megyesi, Nawrocki and Haskell, 2005) and increased speed of enzymatic and catalytic decomposition (Vass, 2011). In addition, the temperature in burials appears to be more uniform and stable than external temperature patterns (e.g. Wilson *et al.*, 2007; Schotsmans, Van de Voorde and Forbes, 2012). This was also observed by the authors during their experiments at AFTER and the RGC.

The amount of oxygen available is a critical factor in considerations of decomposition, as anaerobic microorganisms are less efficient than aerobic decomposers. Therefore, reduced oxygen conditions might slow the rate of decomposition (Dent, Forbes and Stuart, 2004; Fiedler, Schneckenberger and Graw, 2004; Vass, 2011). For example, in-grave conditions can rapidly alter from aerobic to anaerobic, this process being dependent on many factors including soil type, coffin type, potential breakdown of the coffin (e.g. collapse) during burial, the presence of moisture, waterlogging and grave backfill cavities. In numerical modelling of this aspect, Dent and colleagues (2004) concluded that for a typical grave modelled in sandy soils: 'that only about 150g – 200g (about 5 mole) of oxygen is available during a short timeframe for chemical decomposition (decay) processes and any direct respiration needs of micro-organisms'. The authors concluded that in-grave decomposition processes are mostly anaerobic after a very short period of time (Dent, Forbes and Stuart, 2004).

Another important factor that is associated with the rate of decomposition is humidity. This factor is correlated with increased insect activity (Mann, Bass and Meadows, 1990), as well as the introduction of moisture to the internal enzymatic decomposition process (Aufderheide, 2011; Vass, 2011). However, too much water can have a negative effect on decomposition, hence slowing the process. The RGC experiments investigated the 'bucket effect' as first expounded by Dent and Knight (1998). The disturbed nature of the soil means that the grave attracts and holds water. This phenomenon is attributed to the difference in permeability of grave infill material compared to that of the intact natural soil environment into which the graves have been cut. Rainfall or surface flow more quickly accesses the grave space than the normal infiltration in the surrounding areas, causing a groundwater mound (i.e. an enhanced ephemeral or permanent water table) (Figure 27.10). As a consequence, the coffin can also fill with water. As natural drainage or evapotranspiration takes place, the water levels can drop, only to be replaced sometime in the future by another event of rainfall and surface flow; some coffins do not empty for a very long time- that is, until influenced by coffin breakdown. Within a cemetery setting, this process appears to be differential (to the point of inconsistency between nearby graves), which has been measured at RGC. The effect is due to the nature of the immediate formation of the grave and variability in the backfilled soils (Figure 27.10). It is likely to be more dramatic in

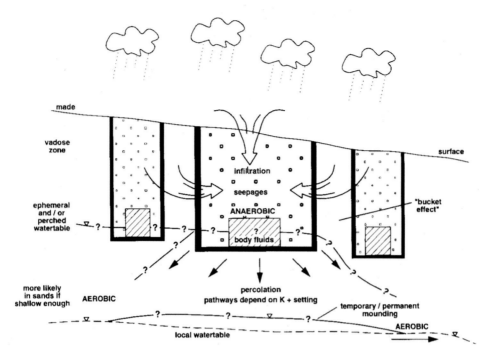

Figure 27.10 An overview of groundwater influences in and around a typical grave (after Dent, 2005).

clay-based formations compared to sandy materials. Typically, cemetery workers of large cemeteries report flooded graves in certain parts of the cemetery, indicating larger spatial and temporal
variability of this phenomenon. Figures 27.11a and 27.11b show how coffins can become filled
with groundwater, turning the coffin into a 'bucket', even in very dry conditions such as in South
Australia (Figure 27.11a).

Water is often mentioned in the archaeothanatological literature as a cause for the displacement
of skeletal remains when buried in a container (e.g. Blaizot, 2011: 48; Georges-Zimmermann
and Kacki, 2017: 76; Gleize, 2020). Based on experimental results, Gleize (2020) concluded that
bone displacement by water is limited to only the small bones and is very rare for larger bones.
However, in reality, the displacement of larger bones by flooding should not be underestimated.
Figure 27.12 shows a bear nest (bear hibernation hollow) in Grotte de Cussac, France, in which
an individual was deposited in a prone position between 35 000 and 25 000 years ago during
the Mid–Upper Palaeolithic (Kacki *et al.*, 2020). Disarticulation and re-arrangement of the bones
were likely caused by several flooding events, as evidenced by the layers of decantation clays
(Jaubert *et al.*, 2017: fig. 4). In studies on 'lift and deepen'[3] grave re-use processes, during the early
1990s at Centennial Park Cemetery in Adelaide (South Australia), similar bone displacements
were very often observed during exhumations which took place 60 to 100 years after burial.
The most likely cause was assumed to be the coffin filling and re-filling with groundwater, even
in very dry environmental conditions as in Adelaide (Hodgson, pers. comm.) (Figure 27.11).

---

3 A method for re-use of graves that involves the exhumation of human remains from an existing grave,
  deepening and enlarging the grave and re-interring the remains so that an expanded space is created for
  new interments.

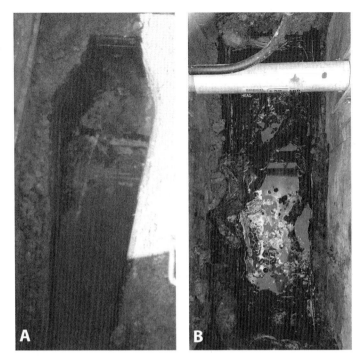

Figure 27.11 Coffins filled with groundwater. A. Centennial Park Cemetery, South Australia. Burial in very dry environmental conditions in heavy clay and sandy clay (about 618 mm/year average rainfall). The burial is estimated to be more than 60 years old (Image courtesy: G. Hodgson); B. Rookwood General Cemetery. The coffin was re-opened after three years of burial in a very wet environment (heavy clay soil, about 992 mm/year average rainfall) (Photograph: B. Dent).

Figure 27.12 A bear nest in *Grotte de Cussac* (Cussac Cave) with Gravettian human remains originally deposited in a prone position. Based on layers of decantation clay (cf. Jaubert *et al.,* 2017), it is likely that several flooding events caused the bones to disarticulate and become displaced (Photograph: N. Aujoulat, Centre National de Préhistoire, PCR Cussac, French Ministry of Culture).

Bone displacement in one waterlogged coffin can differ from bone displacement in another coffin. The causes are not always the same (e.g. fluctuating ground water, waterlogging due to the coffin being sealed, water being unable to freely or rapidly drain); the construction material of the coffin plays a role, the presence of a liner, the exact position of the burial on the site and external factors such as soil type (see section 'soil and sediment' below), and the number of times the event occurs. Archaeologists may not always realise that coffin flooding might occur several times a year. When multiplied by hundreds of years of burial (e.g. Fiedler *et al.*, 2009) and taking all the variables into account, it becomes difficult to link a particular pattern of bone displacement to a particular cause.

The depositional environment

Soil and sediment

Geologically, there is a difference between soil and sediment. Soil is considered the vertically weathered part of the surface of the Earth, with different zones in a developed soil profile called 'horizons'. This means that *in situ* soil represents residue from the original bedrock. Sediments are particles transported by water, wind or gravity called 'deposits'. In archaeological discourse, however, the words soil and sediments are often used interchangeably and refer to the 'dirt' surrounding the skeleton ('*sédiment*' in French). In a typical grave, the excavated feature is backfilled after the placement of the remains. The grave fill is not necessarily of local or immediate origin, and grave backfills may comprise secondary or imported materials for various practical or socio-cultural reasons. The volume of excavated material is always greater than that which can be replaced in the grave because the soil structure has been disrupted and the remains and/or coffin occupy space.

Buried bodies are influenced by the soil that surrounds them. Researchers used to think that the impact of soil type on decomposition was of minor importance within the first two years of burial (Mann, Bass and Meadows, 1990) or at the onset of advanced decay (Carter and Tibbett, 2008). However, experimental and cemetery research has shown that soil is important for understanding biodegradation and decomposition because soil properties, such as temperature, moisture, pH and nutrient availability for microbial communities have an important effect on decay (Dent, 2002; Dent, Forbes and Stuart, 2004; Wilson *et al.*, 2007).

The four major components of soil are minerals, organic matter, water and air. As described above, temperature, humidity/water and oxygen are important variables during decomposition. Soil particle size distribution has a direct effect on factors, such as drainage, temperature and soil oxygen content, as well as the ability of decomposition gases to percolate (White, 1997). A soil texture triangle helps to determine soil particle size and hence soil texture classification. The main classes are clay (less than 0.002 mm diameter), silt (between 0.002 and 0.06 mm diameter) and sand (between 0.06 and 2 mm diameter). Sand can be subdivided into fine sand, medium sand and coarse sand (White, 1997). Specific soil types are known to have specific decomposition dynamics. Clay is a fine-grained cohesive soil. Clay particles tend to stick together and inhibit movement. Clay has been associated with an inhibition of cadaver decomposition (e.g. Turner and Wiltshire, 1999; Fiedler, Schneckenberger and Graw, 2004) caused by the low rate of gas and moisture diffusion. The low rate at which oxygen is exchanged with CO_2 might not be sufficient to meet aerobic microbial decay and thus slows decomposition (Carter and Tibbett, 2008). This delay is also observed when a corpse is hermetically sealed in concrete (e.g. de Mendonça, 2017; Parham and Fleak, 2017; Schotsmans and Van de Voorde, 2017). In contrast, coarse-texture soils, such as sand, are associated with a high rate of gas diffusion and movement of moisture (Moldrup *et al.*, 1997), creating good decomposition conditions in a temperate environment. Moisture is important because not all sandy soils lead automatically to decomposition. In the desert, a sandy sediment might lead to natural mummification due to low humidity and high temperatures.

The presence of groundwater and the depth of the water table are also important, as explained in Figure 27.10. Where drainage is impeded or where there is a high water table, waterlogged soils have voids filled with water. The small amount of oxygen present will rapidly deplete through microbial activity and is only slowly replaced (Janaway, 1996). Directly related to site hydrology and depth of the water table is soil pH, which is determined by the activity of hydrogen ions (H$^+$). Very acidic (pH < 4) or very alkaline (pH > 10) depositional environments slow the decomposition because bacteria will not flourish in these conditions (Schotsmans *et al.*, 2014a), and intracellular chemical reactions and the catalytic ability of enzymes will also be affected (Vass, 2011). In turn, cadaver decomposition has an effect on soil pH and produces other localised changes in the depositional soil. It is generally accepted that a decomposing body initially results in an alkaline environment, followed by an acidic environment and eventually normalises (Carter and Tibbett, 2008). Providing localised changes in moisture, carbon and nutrients, the decaying body produces a concentrated island of fertility surrounding the corpse (see Cadaver Decomposition Island above) (Figure 27.6) (Carter and Tibbett, 2008; Barton *et al.*, 2020).

Dent (2002) provided a considered analysis of soil types for cemetery development and decomposition. Tables 27.2, 27.3 and 27.4 present a framework that is useful for considering both the development of new cemeteries and the investigation of older established ones. In the latter case, the tables provide clues to how soil properties may have influenced present-day findings. The soil classification uses the Unified Soil Classification System (USCS) developed by Casagrande (1948). This classification is originally based on engineering properties related to soil texture, which is explained above in Table 27.2. Considerations of decomposition and the broader chemical effects overlie this underlying paradigm. From an archaeo-anthropological point of view, Tables 27.2 and 27.3 act as an aid for the analysis and interpretation of bone movement and bone degradation.

With regard to the skeletonisation stage, examining site hydrology and pH can be useful for understanding bone degradation, particularly in instances where preservation is poor. When describing 'bone preservation', a distinction should be made between physical preservation and bone fragmentation. A bone can be well preserved but fragmented. In addition, the macroscopic physical appearance of bone does not say anything about its biomolecular integrity. For example, the outer appearance of cortical bone does not predict the degree of DNA preservation. DNA degradation processes are complex and much remains to be learnt about how and where DNA is preserved within the bone (Campos *et al.*, 2012; Ottoni, Bekaert and Decorte, 2017).

In general, bone preservation (of non-cremated individuals) is best in soils with a neutral or slightly alkaline pH and is worse in acidic conditions. When the pH drops below 7, the bone mineral rapidly dissolves (Gordon and Buikstra, 1981; Berna, Matthews and Weiner, 2004; Weiner, 2010: 110–111). For example, bone dissolution is accelerated in bone buried in sandy soils with a low water table, where flowing water creates an acidic pH (Gordon and Buikstra, 1981; Hedges and Millard, 1995; Hedges, 2002; Jans, 2005; Kibblewhite, Toth and Hermann, 2015). Empirical evidence is available on research relating to bone weathering where the influence of temperature, bone size and moisture have all been investigated. The work comprises both macro- and micro- examinations of bone structure and includes the examination of the removal of organic material, nitrogen and the deposition of crystals and other exchanges of elements in bone chemistry (e.g. Behrensmeyer, 1978; Badone and Farquhar, 1982; Von Endt and Ortner, 1984; Junod and Pokines, 2014).

Table 27.2 Properties and usage aspects of the Unified Soil Classification System (USCS) (after Dent, 2002). The scheme with further behaviour-related ideas was developed by Charman and Murray in 1993. USCS designation symbols: First symbol: G = gravel, S = sand, M = silt, C = clay; Second symbol: W = well graded, P = poorly graded, L = low plasticity, H = high plasticity, C = clayey

Typical description	USCS* symbol**	Permeability (1) when compacted	Shearing strength when compacted and saturated; piping resistance (4)	Compressibility when compacted and saturated; cracking resistance (5)	Workability as a construction material
Clayey gravels, poorly graded (2) gravel-sand mixtures	GC (3)	Pervious to semi-impervious to impervious	Good to fair 1	Very low 4	Good
Well-graded sands, gravelly sands, little or no fines	SW	Pervious	Excellent 3	Negligible –	Excellent
Poorly graded sands gravelly sands, little or no fines	SP	Pervious	Good 5	Very low –	Fair
Silty sands, poorly graded sand-silt mixtures	SM	Semi-impervious to impervious	Good 4	Low 3	Fair
Clayey sands, poorly graded sand-clay mixtures	SC	Impervious	Good to fair 2	Low 4	Good
Inorganic silts and very fine sands, silty or clayey fine sands with slight plasticity	ML	Semi-impervious to impervious	Fair 5	Medium 6	Fair
Inorganic clays of low to medium plasticity, gravelly clays, sandy clays, silty clays, lean clays	CL	Impervious	Fair 2	Medium 2 to 5	Good to fair
Inorganic clays of high plasticity, fat clays	CH (3)	Impervious	Poor 1	High 1	Poor

Notes: * The scheme was developed for using earthen materials for construction.

** Soils with dual symbols have a combination of properties of the two classes.

(1) Permeability refers here to the ease of transmission of water. This could be different in natural deposits where it varies with internal structure, texture and the presence of macropores.

(2) A poorly graded material shows an irregular (including constant) range of sizes throughout, such that all particles do not pack closely together.

(3) GC and CH (or MH – inorganic plastic silts) soils on their own are unsuitable, however, if part of soil with dual classification, they may well be acceptable.

(4) Value of 1 represents the highest resistance to piping in a non-tunnelling situation. Piping is the preferential removal of clays by water percolation leading to a loss of structure and a hole (a pipe) being created in a soil embankment.

(5) Value of 1 represents the highest resistance to differential settlement.

Even within a single archaeological site, localised differences can cause inter-burial variations in preservation. Figures 27.13a and 27.13b show two burials from the Bethel Chapel Crypt in Sunderland, UK. A skeleton was recovered from a vault at the northern side of the crypt with an alkaline pH of 8.6. The skeleton was very well preserved, while the wood of the coffin was completely degraded (Figure 27.13a). In contrast, the skeleton from a vault in the southern side of the crypt was crumbly, friable and badly preserved, while the wood of the coffin appeared well preserved. The pH of this vault appeared mildly acidic (pH 6.4) (Figure 27.13b). Organic material such as wood is known to preserve well in an acidic depositional environment, while bone does not preserve well in these circumstances (Janaway, 1996; Kibblewhite, Toth and Hermann, 2015). This example shows that differential decomposition can be caused by localised differences in soil pH.

Table 27.3 Soils unsuited to cemetery development based on soil properties and usage aspects of the Unified Soil Classification System (USCS) (Dent, 2002). USCS designation symbols: First symbol: G = gravel, S = sand, M = silt, C = clay; Second symbol: W = well graded, P = poorly graded, L = low plasticity, H = high plasticity, C = clayey

Soil description	USCS	Unsatisfactory aspects
Gravels – well or poorly graded, silty, gravel-sand mixtures with little or no fines	GW, GP, GM, GC	Drainage too rapid, excavation stability poor, permits free escape of gases, no or little attenuative properties
Organic silts and clays and organic silt-clays of low plasticity	OL or OH	Organic composition, workability and excavation problems, poor drainage
Inorganic silts or clays of medium to high plasticity, micaceous or diatomaceous fine sandy or silty soils	MH or CH	Poor drainage, ponding, swelling, workability, reduced gas circulation
Peat and other highly organic soils	PT	Workability, unsatisfactory drainage, wet, anaerobic, organic composition

Table 27.4 Soil suitability for interments (modified from Dent, 2002). CEC = Cation exchange capacity, meq = milliequivalents, mod = moderate. USCS designation symbols: First symbol: G = gravel, S = sand, M = silt, C = clay; Second symbol: W = well graded, P = poorly graded, L = low plasticity, H = high plasticity, C = clayey

USCS*	GC	SW	SP	SM	SC	ML	CL	CH
Encourages decomposition	Fair – good	Good	Good	Good	Fair – good	Some	No	No
Encourages drainage	Good	Good	Good	Fair	Fair	Slight	No	No
General Workability	Poor	Good to poor		Good	Good	Fair, check for mass movement	Fair, check for mass movement	Poor, check for mass movement
pH > 8 special precautions in karst	Decomposition fair	Fair – poor, enables soft tissue decomposition, preserves bone				Poor, retards decomposition		
pH 4–8	Good	Good	Good	Good	Good	Good	Good	Good
pH < 4	Generally poor, enables excess mobilisation of metals, significant loss of bone, variable negative effects on decomposition							
CEC < 40 meq/100 g	Poor	Good – fair				Poor, value is too low		
CEC > 40 meq/100 g	Good	Fair	Fair	Fair	Good – poor	Poor, does not aid decomposition, possible swelling problem		
encourages bacterial/viral Transmission (T) Survival (S)	High T Low S	High T	High T	Mod T Fair S	Low T Mod S	Low T High S	No T High S	No T High S

Note: * The scheme was developed for using earthen materials for construction.

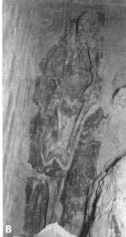

Figure 27.13 Two burials from the 19th-century Bethel Chapel Crypt in Sunderland, United Kingdom. A. A vault at the northern side of the crypt with alkaline soil (pH 8.6). The skeleton was very well preserved and solid, while the wood of the coffin was completely degraded, leaving only the metal coffin plate; B. Another vault at the southern side of the crypt indicated a mildly acidic pH (pH 6.4). The skeletal remains were crumbly, friable and badly preserved, while the coffin wood appeared very well preserved (Photographs: E. Schotsmans).

In addition to chemical degradation, bone disintegrates due to physical forces that include temperature fluctuation, frost action (freezing and thawing) and crystal growth. Examples of the latter are the formation of brushite and secondary gypsum, both shown to disintegrate archaeological bone (e.g. Schotsmans *et al.*, 2014b; Schotsmans *et al.*, 2019). The diagenetic mineral formation is complicated and dependent on the pH and element concentrations (Porta and Herrero, 1990; Herrero and Porta, 2000; Frost and Palmer, 2011).

From an archaeothanatological point of view, sediment is important with regard to progressive infilling of the original space occupied by the cadaver. In this context, sediment primarily refers to the grave backfill materials and secondarily to the movement of soils, weathered bedrock or sediment of the burial environment collapsing or being transported by water into voids. Should the grave space at some later stage be affected by further anthropological interference e.g. a carpark above a burial ground or building footings through gravesites, then some unknown influences may have to be accounted for. As Duday (Duday *et al.*, 1990; Duday, 2009) mentions, evidence for decomposition in a void is based on movement and displacements of bones outside the original space occupied by the body, called positive evidence. Evidence for decomposition in a filled space is far more difficult to attest because it is based on the lack of movement or displacement outside the 'body volume' (i.e. the original space occupied by the body). But a lack of movement or displacement can also happen in a void (Duday *et al.*, 1990; Duday, 2009; Castex and Blaizot, 2017) (cf. Blaizot, Chapter 1, this volume). In this case, the absence of bone displacement will not necessarily be a supporting argument attesting to decomposition in a container. Based on the literature, it is unclear if fine-grained sediment (e.g. clay) or course grained sediment (e.g. sand) is more responsible for progressive infilling of voids freed by the decay of soft tissue. For example, Duday (2009: 55) mentions 'fine powdery sands' as responsible for progressive infilling. Castex and Blaizot (2017: 281) speak of 'fine-grained loess soil' as being easy to crumble and fill empty spaces. In contrast, in this volume, Blaizot mentions that 'gravelly sediment' is more likely to cause progressive infilling (cf. Blaizot, Chapter 1, this volume), while Green mentions that 'fine-grained sediments may have the potential to infiltrate' (cf. Green, Chapter 23, this volume). Much depends on the context, geology and soil classification of the site. Duday (2009: 57) furnishes a more general answer by alluding to 'fluid' sediment, which again highlights the importance of humidity in relation to soils and sediments. In fact, 'soil consistency' is more important with relation to progressive infilling than the grain size itself, and of course, depending on the protection of a container. Soil consistency is the strength with which soil constituents are held together or the resistance of soils to deformation and rupture, in other words, its adhesive and cohesive properties. 'Stickiness' refers to the capacity of soil to adhere to other objects and plasticity is the degree which reworked soil can be deformed without rupturing (e.g. Andrade, Al-Qureshi and Hotza, 2011). For progressive infilling, one needs a non-sticky, non-plastic, loose soil. With clay often being stickier and of high plasticity, dry sand might be best for progressive infilling. However, very dry clay may also work. Moist clay, on the contrary, could form a 'temporary space' around the body that permits greater movement of bones than sandy soil that fills spaces gradually as decomposition advances (Duday *et al.*, 1990). In this case, decomposition in a filled space might be confused with decomposition in a void.

A question that often occurs when discussing delayed filling of a space freed by the decay of soft tissue is the closing of the inter-segmental angles of the body when the deceased is buried in a flexed position (Duday, 2009: 53–54). In other words, does the degree of flexion of the knee, hip and elbow change by gradual pressure exerted by the sediment? Is hyperflexion directly related to the corpse being bound? Or is hyperflexion an indication of mummification? An initial issue is the categorisation and definition of the words 'flexion', 'hyper-flexion', 'tight flexion', 'loose flexion', etc. Not all archaeo-anthropologists apply the same definitions. In addition, variation between individuals from one burial ground can simply be caused by different intrinsic factors and are not necessarily related to different mortuary practices. Experiments at AFTER have showed that it is very difficult for one person to tie a corpse with a rope into a flexed position because of its rigidity, even after dissipation of *rigor mortis*. Binding the dead in a flexed position requires skills and assistance of at least another person. In addition, manipulating the body also causes fluids to purge from orifices such as the anus or the mouth, which does not help the binding process. The experience of the authors (ES and MU) is that the degree of flexion depends on the nature of the corpse and the intensity of *rigor mortis*. Hyperflexion (angles of less than 30 degrees) cannot be achieved with a fleshed individual. The tight flexion in the mummified individual in Figure 27.8 was achieved by tightening the rope when the mummified donor was moved from one location to another. However, after many years of studying cemetery management and hydrogeology by one of the authors (BBD), it became clear that earth pressure exerts enormous forces creating disruption and change (also see coffin collapse in section 'human behaviour' below). Again, the pressure of the sediment depends on the nature of many factors such as burial fill, water fluxes, depth of the burial or external factors such as vibrations. In experiments with pigs at RGC, the pig limbs were tightly bound with unbleached cotton tape ('hog-tied') against the underbelly in order to assist with shroud wrapping and interment. During decomposition in plain or full earth burial, the bindings released and decayed, which made the pig limbs move towards their original anatomical position, even under the weight of the grave backfill. On-going experiments at AFTER will hopefully answer whether or not tight flexion can be caused by soil compaction, or if it is an indication of a particular pre-burial treatment such as mummification.

Faunal agents

If the remains are accessible to scavengers, decay will typically be accelerated due to soft tissue destruction and the consumption of flesh and bone (Mann, Bass and Meadows, 1990). All scavengers

Figure 27.14 The lateral side of the left arm of a donor at the Australian Facility for Taphonomic Experimental Research (AFTER). A. The maggot mass concentrated on the shoulder, probably around a break in the skin; B. This led to rapid skeletonisation of the left humerus, 12 days after death, while the rest of the body did not skeletonise further until a year post-mortem (Photographs: E. Schotsmans).

do not share the same scavenging behaviour or scatter patterns. Likewise, species-typical scavenging behaviours and scatter patterns can be affected by different scenarios. They are influenced by factors pertaining to the site of deposition (e.g. region, environment, weather, season), characteristics of human remains (e.g. carcass size, condition) and/or scavenger species (e.g. O'Brien *et al.*, 2010; Dabbs and Martin, 2013; Jeong *et al.*, 2016; O'Brien, Appleton and Forbes, 2017; Young, 2017; Steadman *et al.*, 2018; Wallman and Archer, 2020).

It is widely acknowledged that invertebrate activity plays an essential role in the degradation of remains. The opposite is also true: if a body is not exposed to insects, for example, due to being sealed in a container or tarpaulin, decomposition is likely to slow (Payne, King and Beinhart, 1968; Mann, Bass and Meadows, 1990; Vanin and Huchet, 2017). Maggots are responsible for a large majority of the loss of mass during decomposition. Insect activity can also cause differential decomposition and thus have an indirect influence on disarticulation (Figure 27.5). Figure 27.14 shows the lateral side of the left upper limb of a donor in AFTER. Although less common and without the presence of a wound, the maggot mass concentrated on the shoulder, leading to rapid skeletonisation of the left humerus twelve days after death, while the rest of the body did not further skeletonise until a year post-mortem. The survival of flies (Phoridae) in burials within a coffin has been a prominent aspect considered in the RGC experiments. Colonies of coffin flies of several generations have been found to be present to various extents in the majority of examined remains (62%, 28 out of 45 burials), from in-grave coffins re-opened at one-, two- and three-year intervals of burial. In one unusual event, unfamiliar to the present cemetery employees, the remains in a coffin in a dry environment contained active flies and maggots after one year of burial, there being an obvious opportunity for air renewal in that grave. The presence of flies is favoured in a dry grave environment by a 2:1 ratio compared to those in a moist or wet environment. Unless there is a constant source of oxygen, the fly colonies die out. At typical grave depth (1.5–2.1 m), the conditions become rapidly anaerobic. It is likely that oxygen in undisturbed, native soil pores and in the pores and cavities within grave backfill soils is consumed last as the propensity for biochemical reactions of decomposition is lower in those areas. The geological setting and soil types also have an influence on fly, other insect and micro-biota survival to variable extents. Pupal cases can also be found on the underside of coffin lids and on or within any fabric encapsulating the remains (Figure 27.15).

In the dry stages of decomposition, beetles continue to 'clean' the body (Vanin and Huchet, 2017; Dawson, Barton and Wallman, 2020; Wallman and Archer, 2020). They might even damage the bone, which, in turn, can be used to detect secondary mortuary practices (Huchet *et al.*, 2013).

In archaeological circumstances, it is often under-appreciated that the presence (or absence) of insect remains in graves can provide a range of environmental, ecological, taphonomical and sometimes even socio-cultural information linked with past burial practices (Huchet, 2014;

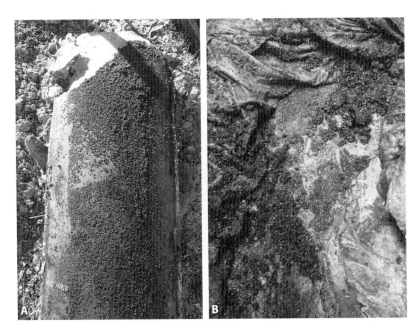

Figure 27.15 Re-opened graves at Rookwood General Cemetery show the presence of coffin fly pupal cases: A. at the underside of coffin lids; B. and on the outside of a burial shroud (Photographs: B. Dent).

Vanin and Huchet, 2017) (cf. Huchet and Castex, Chapter 26, this volume). These phenomena, however, require specific attention in the field, hence the importance of the archaeothanatological 'field' approach. It would not be the first time that insect remains were not recovered for the simple reason that no one was looking for them.

Additionally, the presence and concentrations of molluscs can also provide information about body decomposition and mortuary practices (André, 1987; Karali, 2008; Galvao *et al.*, 2015). During archaeological investigations of the Hellenistic Plinthine necropolis in Egypt, two graves were extremely rich in *Cecilioides acicula* (N=50) (O.F. Müller, 1774). *C. acicula* was found in the thoracic cavities of two skeletonised individuals, whereas these molluscs were absent in the other graves. In this case, the presence of *C. acicula* could be linked to the particular shrouds in which the deceased had been buried or, alternatively, related to the fact that the body had been mummified (Georges and Charlier, 2010). Excavation reports often mention the presence of molluscs without explanation. Skin folds in obese individuals can create pockets filled with air and liquid. These damp areas are known to attract molluscs. Similarly, during putrefaction, the lungs decay within the thoracic cavity, and the resulting space is gradually filled with putrefaction fluid that is particularly rich in nutrients. The abdominal cavity, as well as the interior part of the cranium, can play the same role in trapping the putrefaction fluid (Charlier *et al.*, 2008). The skeletal remains are often still covered with a layer of nutrients at the end of the putrefaction process, which is attractive for molluscs. It is, therefore, not uncommon to find molluscs in the close vicinity of buried skeletal remains (Georges and Charlier, 2010; Galvao *et al.*, 2015).

Human behaviour

People managing the dead decide how, where and when the deceased is deposited or buried, whether executed by relatives or a perpetrator of a crime (Figure 27.9). Treatment of the body, such as artificial mummification, embalming and the application of chemicals before and after death, has an influence on decay (e.g. Micozzi, 1991; Sledzik and Micozzi, 1997; Schotsmans and Van de Voorde, 2017). Metallic artefacts deposited around the decaying body can lead to localised conditions of toxicity which can decrease microbial activity, but even when a body is buried with extensive metal grave goods, there is usually insufficient metal to result in large-scale soft tissue preservation (Janaway, 1996). The manner of deposition plays an important role, whether buried or on the surface. The deeper a body is buried, or when it is covered with a large mass of earth (e.g. a tumulus), the longer decomposition takes as a result of lower temperatures, reduced oxygen and decreased insect and scavenger access. When a corpse is deposited on the surface or is buried in a shallow grave, it is more accessible to insects and scavengers and influenced by seasonal fluctuations (e.g. Janaway, 1996; Simmons, Adlam and Moffatt, 2010). This also means that the decay of tissues will be profoundly influenced by the period between death and burial (Boddington, Garland and Janaway, 1987; Dadour and Harvey, 2008). Several researchers have stated that a body bearing traumatic lesions decomposes faster than does a body without. This is mainly caused by the attraction of insects to open wounds (e.g. Mann, Bass and Meadows, 1990; Carter and Tibbett, 2008). Cross and Simmons (2010) contested this observation based on the results of a controlled experiment with a large sample size (N=34), which demonstrated that decomposition rates in bodies with penetrating trauma did not differ from those without trauma.

Furthermore, clothing and other coverings such as coffins or tarpaulins can partially negate the effect of the depositional environment and may delay the process of decay (e.g. Aturaliya and Lukasewycs, 1999; Card *et al.*, 2015). Airtight containers reduce the amount of oxygen and slow cadaver decomposition as anaerobic microorganisms are less efficient than their aerobic counterparts. However, coffins do not present a constant burial environment since they also breakdown gradually. This means that the initial protection from direct contact with burial sediments and their biotas, such as bacteria, fungi, plants and other organisms is not permanent (Pokines and Baker, 2013). It is evident that not every container decays in the same way. Much depends on the type of material from which the coffin is made, including woods of all kinds, stone and metals, mostly iron or forms of steel, but also copper and lead. There are only a limited number of studies on coffin decay (Puckle, 1926; Blanchette, 2000; Anson, 2004; Prangnell and McGowan, 2009; Pitt *et al.*, 2017). Puckle (1926) refers to the variable longevity of oak and elm in the United Kingdom. Nicol (cited in Anson 2004) mentions the use of cedar, oak and kauri species for coffins in South Australia. Blanchette (2000) provides an overview of wood degradation from several archaeological sites in Egypt, Turkey, the United States and the United Kingdom.

In archaeothanatology, slow wood deterioration is of less interest than coffin collapse and subsequent, sometimes considerable bone displacement. The power of coffin collapse cannot be underestimated. Modern cemetery studies have shown that collapsed coffin lids can push whole sets of remains against the coffin side and that coffin sides can collapse differentially (Figure 27.16). The same can happen by pressure from a side panel. The decay of the wood can be slow. This differential decay could result in several different forces affecting the bones, such that it becomes difficult to deduce the exact cause of bone displacement. Figure 27.17 shows human remains recovered at a medieval cemetery in France in an extremely constricted position (Georges-Zimmermann and Kacki, 2017). Traces of a container were visible together with the edges of the burial pit, both confirming that decomposition took place in a void. The individual was placed in a supine position with the skeletal elements still maintaining much of their original anatomical organisation. Constriction of the upper limbs and the verticalisation of the clavicles indicate that transverse compression had taken place at the level of the shoulders. The *ossa coxae* and femora also moved towards the mid-line of the body (Georges-Zimmermann and Kacki, 2017: 82). Initially,

Figure 27.16 After three years of burial in a standard grave of 1.8 m depth at Rookwood General Cemetery, the lid was found to be collapsed diagonally into the coffin dragging the plastic liner with it. The remains were compressed and displaced (Photograph: B. Dent).

it was thought that the container had been made from one piece of wood (*'sarcophage monoxyle'*). These coffins typically have a concave bottom, which can cause displacement of the bones towards the midline. However, after comparison to well-preserved *monoxylous* containers at the same site and the position of the skeletal remains they contained, the extreme constriction of the remains in Figure 27.17 could not be explained. It is possible that the skeleton was moved to the midline because of pressure from the side panels.

The subject

Personal characteristics of the deceased such as age-at-death, sex, body size (weight and stature), physique and medical conditions are considered to influence decomposition rates (Figure 27.9). However, the literature contains contradictions about the effects of personal characteristics on decomposition. Mant (1987) and Janaway (1996) state that thin bodies skeletonise more rapidly than heavier ones. On the contrary, Mann, Bass and Meadows (1990) observed that obese bodies lose body mass more quickly. Simmons, Adlam and Moffatt (2010) showed that body

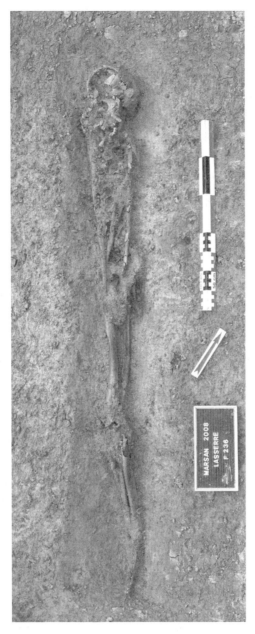

Figure 27.17   Human skeletal remains in an extremely constricted position recovered at the medieval cemetery of Marsan (Gers) in France (Photograph: P. Georges-Zimmerman).

size is a significant factor governing insect access to carcasses, with small carcasses decomposing faster than large carcasses. However, when insects were excluded, decomposition progressed at the same rate regardless of body size. Several other investigations of the effect of body size on the rate of decomposition were carried out on animal remains without a clear consensus about the results (e.g. Spicka *et al.*, 2011; Sutherland *et al.*, 2013), probably due to other variables at play that were not taken into account. After four years of experiments at AFTER, body size and weight also seem to be the main factors that influence decomposition, which has been attributed to the higher moisture content in the body.

Additionally, ante-mortem and peri-mortem medical conditions may accelerate decay caused by a high body temperature such as fever (Zhou and Byard, 2011). Other medical conditions, such as cancer treatment, can slow decomposition due to chemicals in the body that are less attractive to insects and which slow microbial growth as well (Schotsmans and Van de Voorde, 2017). This phenomenon has also been observed in surface depositions at AFTER by the authors.

Once the body is in a skeletal state, bone type and size also play a role. Von Endt and Ortner (1984) showed that small bones are not as well preserved as large bones. Waldron (1987) indicated that the large dense parts of the skeleton preserve best. Bello *et al.* (2006) studied the preservations state of bones from several osteological collections. They noted that the scapulae, sternum, vertebrae, sacrum, patellae, hand and foot bones were least well-represented in adults and sub-adults. Bones of males seemed better preserved than those of females. The authors highlight potential misleading interpretations of palaeodemographic profiles of past populations if preservation is not taken into account. They also state that the external factors play an important role (see above) and ultimately increase the differences in preservation based on intrinsic anatomical properties of the bones themselves (Bello *et al.*, 2006).

Soft tissue preservation, delayed decay and differential decomposition

Specific environments, such as dry, cold and bog environments, can lead to soft tissue preservation (e.g. Aufderheide, 2003; Piombino-Mascali, Gill-Frerking and Beckett, 2017; Schotsmans, Van de Voorde and Forbes, 2020). Whether desiccation occurs in a hot or cold environment, one of the most important aspects is the presence of an air current (Finaughty and Morris, 2019). Less often acknowledged is the fact that corpses still undergo all decomposition stages during situations of natural preservation. Decomposition does not suddenly stop; it is either slowed down or accelerated under the appropriate conditions. The remains continue to deteriorate from the inside outwards, with any kind of preservation often limited to only the outer layers of the body (Janaway *et al.*, 2009; Schotsmans *et al.*, 2014a; Schotsmans, Van de Voorde and Forbes 2020). The importance of airflow and the continuation of decay from the inside out was also observed in the mummified remains at AFTER (Figure 27.8). Any disruption of the stable environment of preserved remains increases the rate of taphonomic change. Preserved human remains, no matter how effective the natural forces were in the process of preservation, are all on their taphonomic journeys back to the elements (Piñar *et al.*, 2013).

In addition, minor differences in the local micro-environment might lead to major variation in preservation within the same body, referred to as differential decomposition. Even in temperate climates such as those of Belgium, France and the United Kingdom, differential decomposition is often observed due to a combination of decay, desiccation and/or adipocere formation (e.g. Orfila and Lesueur, 1831; Beaumont, 2007; Schotsmans *et al.*, 2011). This phenomenon is important for archaeothanatologists to consider. Differential decomposition can lead to the decay of one body part as seen in Figure 27.14 or to the preservation of specific body parts, such as the feet or the hands (Figures 27.1 and 27.18). Hands and feet can dry quickly, even in a mild climate, due to the small surface area to volume ratio. This phenomenon is an additional reason why relative sequences of decay or interpretations of paragraph 'paradoxical disarticulation' should be applied with caution (see above). Fossurier (2009) describes a burial from 7th-century France ('*Sépulture 18*'). The author interpreted a case of deposition in a constructed container based on bone movement outside the original body volume (the space occupied by the body) and linear alignment of skeletal elements. The foot bones were disarticulated and migrated towards the far end of the container. In contrast,

Figure 27.18 Right foot of a donor at the Australian Facility for Taphonomic Experimental Research (AFTER), deposited 5 months earlier in the winter time. While the individual was skeletonising, both hands and the right foot desiccated. After five months, the right foot started to skeletonise with a delay compared to the rest of the body. Also note the disarticulated talus (Photograph: E. Schotsmans).

the hand bones were in complete articulation (Fossurier 2009: figs. 8–9). There are indications of clothing through the presence of a belt. The maintained articulation of the hand bones is explained by the author through the presence of some sort of clothing with sleeves ('*une enveloppe souple à manches*') that kept the hand bones from migrating away. The author did not consider other possibilities such as localised mummification of the hands, for example, as seen in Figure 27.1. Differential decay and localised mummification are not unusual in burials, as observed during exhumations of modern cemetery graves up to 21 years after burial (Hodgson, pers. comm.), or as stated in reports of forensic exhumations in France (Orfila and Lesueur, 1831: 83, 167, 178, 348).

Adipocere can also cause differential preservation. Adipocere or 'grave wax' occurs through the alteration of subcutaneous fat of a corpse into a grey-white lipid mixture. Its formation is considered to result from bacterial action and occurs largely under anaerobic conditions wherein sufficient moisture is also present in the tissue (Stuart *et al.*, 2000; Takatori, 2001; Yan *et al.*, 2001; O'Brien and Kuehner, 2007; Forbes, 2008; Schoenen and Schoenen, 2013). With time, it becomes a hard, brittle shell which retards decomposition (Clark, Worrell and Pless, 1996; Fiedler and Graw, 2003). As long as the environment is stable, adipocere can persist for years, as attested by archaeological examples (e.g. Thali *et al.*, 2001; Fiedler *et al.*, 2009; O'Connor *et al.*, 2011; Prats-Muñoz *et al.*, 2013). Mechanisms of localised adipocere formation have to be mentioned in relation to the preservation of brain masses, also known as 'saponified brain'. Brain preservation is not unusual in mummified remains, where brain tissue persists together with other internal and external soft tissues that are not driven by adipocere formation (Aufderheide, 2003). Less known, but not uncommon, is the preservation of brain tissue in skeletonised remains from wet depositional environments (Tkocz, Bytzer and Bierring, 1979; Papageorgopoulou, Bianucci and Rühli, 2010; O'Connor *et al.*, 2011; Serrulla *et al.*, 2017) (cf. Huchet and Castex, Chapter 26, this volume). The preserved brains themselves do not attest directly to specific funerary practices, but they might reveal information about the circumstances surrounding death, the presence of pathological conditions, environmental factors and insect activity that may reveal aspects of body treatment (O'Connor *et al.*, 2011; Serrulla *et al.*, 2017) (cf. Huchet and Castex, Chapter 26, this volume).

Figure 27.19 An example of differential decay, called 'superficial desiccation', showing unequal decomposition between the uppermost side and the lowermost side of an individual deposited at the Australian Facility for Taphonomic Experimental Research (AFTER). The side of the body exposed to solar radiation becomes desiccated by air flow and sunlight. But when the body is turned over, it appears completely skeletonised. The human remains consist of only bones with a thin layer of desiccated skin on top (Photograph: M. Ueland).

Another example of differential decay is the unequal decomposition between the uppermost side and the lowermost side of an individual, called superficial desiccation (Schotsmans, Van de Voorde and Forbes, 2020, fig. 5.2). The side of the body that is exposed to solar radiation becomes desiccated due to air flow and sunlight. But when the body is turned over, it is completely skeletonised (Figure 27.19). The human remains seem to consist of only bones with a thin layer of desiccated skin on top.

Finally, differential decay is not only evident within a single body; it also occurs when multiple individuals are deposited together. It has, for example, been observed in mass graves with the same post-mortem and post-burial interval, as documented in forensic cases (Mant, 1987; Loe *et al.*, 2014; Barker *et al.*, 2017), within cemeteries (Orfila and Lesueur, 1831: 348) and in experimental contexts (Troutman, Moffatt and Simmons, 2014). Bodies at the edges of a mass grave tend to exhibit accelerated decomposition in comparison with bodies in the centre. This phenomenon is called the 'feather edge effect' (Mant, 1987; Barker *et al.*, 2017).

From observations to interpretations

An archaeothanatological analysis can be divided into three parts (cf. Boulestin, Chapter 2, this volume; also cf. Knüsel and Schotsmans, Introduction, this volume). First, observations are made (e.g. taphonomy, stratigraphy, spatial relations, etc.). Then, these observations are analysed and interpreted so that the original burial context and funerary/mortuary practices can be reconstructed. This is followed by another level of interpretation of the social behaviour of a particular society. Importantly, this whole reasoning process should be based on clear research questions ('*la problématique*' in French) and cannot be done randomly.

It has been mentioned previously that knowledge of human anatomy and human decomposition is important when making these observations (e.g. Duday, 2009: 16; Knüsel, 2014; Castex and Blaizot, 2017: 277) (cf. Blaizot, Chapter 1, this volume). But does a conventional biological anthropologist have enough knowledge of human decomposition? And what about the knowledge of environmental variables, differential decay and material degradation? This cannot be ascertained solely by excavating skeletons and looking only at the end-result of these processes. It is necessary to study decomposition from the start until the end of the process.

An extreme example of over-interpretation occurred in the description of a mummified child by Dunand and Lichtenberg (1998):'Mummy of a little girl frozen by pain, who probably died because of an appendicitis' (*'Momie d'une petite fille encore figée dans les douleurs de l'agonie, probablement morte d'appendicite'*) (Dunand and Lichtenberg, 1998: 220). The photograph shows a mummified girl. The diagnosis of appendicitis is made by observing the position of the right hand which rests in an unnatural flexed position on the abdomen. The girl's face is desiccated, emphasising her teeth by retraction of the skin. This is very common in desiccated remains and has nothing to do with pain. The supposed agony on the face and the cause of death by appendicitis are over-interpretations based on the lack of knowledge about the effects of the mummification processes on cadavers.

Hypotheses and interpretations should be treated with caution and validated. Therefore, it is important to gather data from burials of known form and context to support interpretations (Duday, 2009: 154). In addition, experimentation with human remains should be carried out. Over the past 35 years, post-mortem decay has been studied at decomposition facilities to support forensic investigations (Vidoli *et al.*, 2017). To date, these facilities have not often used for archaeothanatological research. To compensate for the time that human decomposition and material degradation takes, modern cemetery research is a valuable complement to experiments. However, interpretative limits will always remain in archaeo-anthropological research (Boulestin and Duday, 2005). The sub-discipline of ethnoarchaeology can provide alternative insights into different treatments and attitudes towards death and enable thought beyond culturally established patterns. Ethnographic parallels might serve as an example for the sociocultural interpretation of different mortuary treatments but there is never a direct analogy between the acts of a particular group and the remains of a given culture. In brief, in order to move from observations to interpretations, an interdisciplinary approach is necessary, including thorough method validation and contextualisation, based on good research questions.

Conclusion

This chapter shows that a broad knowledge base is fundamental in the field of archaeothanatology. Archaeo-anthropologists require knowledge about all stages of decomposition, factors that influence decay and bone movement, and about the degradation of different materials. This contribution highlights that human remains should be analysed in their broader depositional context. It also emphasises a critical use of terms and methods and the integration of interdisciplinary approaches such as forensic experiments and modern cemetery studies.

Scholars new to the discipline of archaeothanatology tend to apply archaeothanatological methods too rigidly, without critical reflection. A one-cause-to-one-interpretation was never intended by its founders (Boulestin and Duday, 2005). Over the years or millennia that a body has been buried, many variables are involved in bone displacement. Several causes might lead to the same end-result, known as equifinality. After all, the objective of archaeothanatology is not an exact reconstruction of every taphonomic event but a critical reflection with the goal being to learn something about societies and their chrono-cultural contexts. By observing and analysing the grave, its content, its site context and beyond, the archaeo-anthropologist should distinguish which phenomena have an anthropogenic cause and determine what that reveals about human behaviour. This interpretation should be based on multiple arguments. As Tiesler (2011) describes: 'Archaeothanatology is a mindset in scholarship which is anchored in a pro-active approach to conducting and thinking about funerary archaeology'. In other words, archaeothanatology makes us observe differently as well as think differently.

Acknowledgements

The authors would like to thank The Australian Facility for Taphonomic Research (AFTER) and all donors to the University of Technology Sydney Body Donation Program. Thanks to Jodie Ward, Shari Forbes, Mohammed Shareef, Vitor Taranto and Prisca Ng. We would like to thank James Wallman and Blake Dawson for permitting the use of images of their projects' donors and pig remains. We are also grateful to the students from the University of Technology Sydney (UTS) and from the University of Wollongong (UOW) for their assistance at AFTER.

We would also like to thank the Director of Research and Planning and his Team of the Rookwood General Cemetery Reserve Land Manager for permission to use data and discussion relating to the Rookwood General Cemetery (RGC) experiments presented here for its first external dissemination.

Many thanks to Geraldine Hodgson for sharing her images and useful information about cemetery management in South Australia.

The authors are grateful to the Belgian Police, French Police/Gendarmerie and Australian Federal Police for giving us the opportunity to work on forensic cases and thus enabling bridge-building between archaeothanatology and recent forensic cases.

Eline Schotsmans would like to thank Dominique Castex, Fanny Bocquentin and Bruno Boulestin for the interesting discussions, reflections and challenging conversations about French archaeothanatology. We are also grateful to Christopher Knüsel for the exchanges about archaeothanatology and useful comments on the manuscript.

Schotsmans' research is funded by the European Union's Horizon 2020 research and innovation programme (grant agreement 794891). Ueland's research is supported by a UTS Chancellor's Postdoctoral Fellowship. Ethics approval for work at AFTER was granted under the UTS Human Research Ethics Committee Program Approval number UTS HREC REF NO. ETH15-0029 and ETH18-2999.

Finally, the UOW and UTS-based authors acknowledge and pay respect to the Traditional Owners of the land on which their research facilities are built. They pay respects to Elders past, present and emerging and to Country itself.

References

Ambroise, D. and Perlès, C. (1975). Note sur l'Analyse Archéologique des Squelettes Humains. *Revue Archéologique du Centre de la France*, 14, pp. 49–61.

Andrade, F.A., Al-Qureshi, H.A. and Hotza, D. (2011). Measuring the Plasticity of Clays: A Review. *Applied Clay Science*, 51, pp. 1–7.

André, J. (1987). Contribution de la malacologie à l'étude des sépultures, un exemple: le dolmen des Peirières à Villedubert. In: H. Duday and C. Masset, eds., *Anthropologie Physique et Archéologie. Méthodes d'Étude des Sépultures*. Paris: Editions du CNRS, pp. 289–291.

Anson, T.J. (2004). *The Bioarchaeology of the St. Mary's Free Ground Burials: Reconstruction of Colonial South Australian Lifeways*. Unpublished Ph.D. Thesis, University of Adelaide, Australia.

Aturaliya, S.M.D. and Lukasewycs, A. (1999). Experimental Forensic Bioanthropological Aspects of Soft tissue Taphonomy: 1. Factors Influencing Postmortem Tissue Desiccation Rate. *Journal of Forensic Sciences*, 44, pp. 893–896.

Aufderheide, A.C. (2003). *The scientific study of mummies*. Cambridge: Cambridge University Press.

Aufderheide, A.C. (2011). Soft Tissue Taphonomy: A Paleopathology Perspective. *International Journal of Paleopathology*, 1, pp. 75–80.

Bachmann, J. and Simmons, T. (2010). The Influence of Preburial Insect Access on the Decomposition Rate. *Journal of Forensic Sciences*, 55, pp. 893–900.

Badone, E. and Farquhar, R. (1982). Application of Neutron Activation Analysis to the Study of Element Concentration and Exchange in Fossil Bones. *Journal of Radioanalytical and Nuclear Chemistry*, 69, pp. 291–311.

Barker, C., Alicehajic, E. and Naranjo Stantana, J. (2017). Post-mortem differential preservation and its utility in interpreting forensic and archaeological mass burials. In: E.M.J. Schotsmans, N. Márquez-Grant and S.L. Forbes, eds., *Taphonomy of Human Remains: Forensic Analysis of the Dead and the Depositional Environment*. Chichester: Wiley, pp. 251–276.

Barton, P.S., Reboldi, A., Dawson, B.M., Ueland, M., Strong, C. and Wallman, J.F. (2020). Soil Chemical Markers Distinguishing Human and Pig Decomposition Islands: A Preliminary Study. *Forensic Science, Medicine and Pathology*, 16, pp. 605–612.

Beaumont, G. (2007). Body on the Beach. A Case of Foot and Mouth? *Journal of Forensic and Legal Medicine*, 14, pp. 54–57.

Behrensmeyer, A.K. (1978). Taphonomic and Ecologic Information from Bone Weathering. *Paleobiology*, 4, pp. 150–162.

Bello, S.M., Thomann, A., Signoli, M., Dutour, O. and Andrews, P. (2006). Age and Sex Bias in the Reconstruction of Past Population Structures. *American Journal of Physical Anthropology*, 129, pp. 24–38.

Berna, F., Matthews, A. and Weiner, S. (2004). Solubilities of Bone Mineral from Archaeological Sites: The Recrystallization Window. *Journal of Archaeological Science*, 31, pp. 867–882.

Blaizot, F. (2011). *Les espaces funéraires de l'habitat groupé des Ruelles à Serris du VIIe au XIe s. (Seine et Marne, Île-de-France): taphonomie du squelette, modes d'inhumation, organisation et dynamique*. Unpublished Ph.D. Thesis, Université de Bordeaux 1, France.

Blaizot, F. (2014). From the Skeleton to the Funerary Architecture: A Logic of the Plausible. *Anthropologie: International Journal of the Science of Man*, 52(3), pp. 263–284.

Blaizot, F. (2017). *Les espaces funéraires de l'habitat groupé des Ruelles, à Serris (Seine et Marne) du VIIe au XIe s. Modes d'inhumation, organisation, gestion et dynamique*. Bordeaux: Maison des Sciences de l'Homme d'Aquitaine.

Blanchette, R.A. (2000). A Review of Microbial Deterioration Found in Archaeological Wood from Different Environments. *International Biodeterioration and Biodegradation*, 46, pp. 189–204.

Boddington, A., Garland, A.N. and Janaway, R.C. (1987). *Death, decay and reconstruction*. Manchester: Manchester University Press.

Boulestin, B. and Duday, H. (2005). Ethnologie et archéologie de la mort: de l'illusion des références à l'emploi d'un vocabulaire. In: C. Mordant and G. Depierre, eds., *Les Pratiques Funéraires à l'Âge du Bronze en France*. Paris: Éditions du Comité des Travaux Historiques et Scientifiques (CTHS) and Société Archéologique de Sens, pp. 17–31.

Byard, R.W. (2020). Estimation of time since death in the early postmortem period. In: J. Hayman and M. Oxenham, eds., *Estimation of the Time Since Death. Current Research and Future Trends*. London: Elsevier, pp. 11–28.

Campobasso, C.P., Di Vella, G. and Introna, F. (2001). Factors Affecting Decomposition and Diptera Colonization. *Forensic Science International*, 12, pp. 18–27.

Campos, P.F., Craig, O.E., Turner-Walker, G., Peacock, E., Willerslev, E. and Gilbert, M.T. (2012). DNA in Ancient Bone – Where Is It Located and How Should We Extract It. *Annals of Anatomy*, 194, pp. 7–16.

Card, A., Cross, P., Moffatt, C. and Simmons, T. (2015). The Effect of Clothing on the Rate of Decomposition and Diptera Colonization on *Sus scrofa* Carcasses. *Journal of Forensic Sciences*, 60, pp. 979–982.

Carter, D.O. and Tibbett, M. (2008). Cadaver decomposition and soil: processes. In: M. Tibbett and D.O. Carter, eds., *Soil Analysis in Forensic Taphonomy*. Boca Raton: CRC Press, pp. 29–52.

Casagrande, A. (1948). Classification and Identification of Soils. *Transactions of the American Society of Civil Engineers*, 113, pp. 901–930.

Cassar, J., Stuart, B.H., Dent, B.B., Notter, S.J., Forbes, S.L., O'Brien, C. and Dadour, I.R. (2011). A Study of Adipocere in Soil Collected from a Field Leaching Study. *Australian Journal of Forensic Sciences*, 43, pp. 3–11.

Castex, D. and Blaizot, F. (2017). Reconstructing the original arrangement, organisation and architecture of burials in archaeology. In: E.M.J. Schotsmans, N. Márquez-Grant and S.L. Forbes, eds., *Taphonomy of Human Remains. Forensic Analysis of the Dead and the Depositional Environment*. Chichester: Wiley, pp. 277–295.

Charlier, P., Georges, P., Bouchet, F., Huynh-Charlier, I., Carlier, R., Mazel, V., Richardin, P., Brun, L., Blondiaux, J. and Lorin de la Grandmaison, G. (2008). The Microscopic (Optical and SEM) Examination of Putrefaction Fluid Deposits (PFD). Potential Interest in Forensic Anthropology. *Virchows Archiv*, 453, pp. 377–386.

Clark, M.A., Worrell, M.B. and Pless, J.E. (1996). Postmortem changes in soft tissues. In: W.D. Haglund and M.S. Sorg, eds., *Forensic Taphonomy. The Postmortem Fate of Human Remains*. Boca Raton: CRC Press, pp. 151–164.

Cockle, D.L. and Bell, L.S. (2017). The Environmental Variables that Affect Human Decomposition in Terrestrially Exposed Contexts within Canada. *Science and Justice*, 57, pp. 107–117.

Cramer, G.D. (2014). The cervical region. In: D. Cramer and S.A. Darby, eds., *Clinical Anatomy of the Spine, Spinal Cord and ANS*. London: Elsevier, pp. 135–209.

Crissman, J.K. (1994). *Death and dying in Central Appalachia. Changing attitudes and practices*. Chicago: University of Illinois Press.

Cross, P. and Simmons, T. (2010). The Influence of Penetrative Trauma on the Rate of Decomposition. *Journal of Forensic Sciences*, 55, pp. 295–301.

Dabbs, G.R. and Martin, D.C. (2013). Geographic Variation in the Taphonomic Effect of Vulture Scavenging: The Case for Southern Illinois. *Journal of Forensic Sciences*, 58, pp. S20–25.

Dadour, I.R. and Harvey, M.L. (2008). The role of invertebrates in terrestrial decomposition: forensic applications. In: M. Tibbett and D.O. Carter, eds., *Soil Analysis in Forensic Taphonomy*. Boca Raton: CRC Press, pp. 109–122.

Dautartas, A., Kenyhercz, M.W., Vidoli, G.M., Jantz, L.M., Mundorff, A. and Steadman, D.W. (2018). Differential Decomposition among Pig, Rabbit and Human Remains. *Journal of Forensic Sciences*, 63, pp. 1673–1682.

Dawson, B.M., Barton, P.S. and Wallman, J.F. (2020). Contrasting Insect Activity and Decomposition of Pigs and Humans in an Australian Environment: A Preliminary Study. *Forensic Science International*, 316, 110515.

De Mendonça, M.C. (2017). Decomposition in an unusual environment: body sealed in concrete. In: E.M.J. Schotsmans, N. Márquez-Grant and S.L. Forbes, eds., *Taphonomy of Human Remains: Forensic Analysis of the Dead and the Depositional Environment*. Chichester: Wiley, pp. 452–453.

Deforce, K., van Hove, M.-L. and Willems, D. (2015). Analysis of Pollen and Intestinal Parasite Eggs from Medieval Graves from Nivelles, Belgium: Taphonomy of the Burial Ritual. *Journal of Archaeological Science: Reports*, 4, pp. 596–604.

Dent, B.B. (2002). *The hydrogeological context of cemetery operations and planning in Australia*. Unpublished Ph.D. Thesis, University of Technology Sydney, Australia.

Dent, B.B. (2005). Vulnerability and the unsaturated zone – the case for cemeteries. In: N.Z.H. Society, ed., Where Waters Meet, Proceedings of the NZHS-IAH-NZSSS 2005 Conference, 29 Nov.–1 Dec. 2005, Auckland, p. A13.

Dent, B.B., Forbes, S.L. and Stuart, B.H. (2004). Review of Human Decomposition Processes in Soil. *Environmental Geology*, 45, pp. 576–585.

Dent, B.B. and Knight, M.J. (1998). Cemeteries: a special kind of landfill. The context of their sustainable management. In: T.R. Weaver and C.R. Lawrence, eds., *Groundwater: Sustainable Solutions*. Melbourne: University of Melbourne, pp. 451–456.

DiMaio, V. and DiMaio, D. (2001). *Forensic pathology*. Boca Raton, FL: CRC Press.

D'Souza, D.H., Harish, S., Rajesh, M. and Kiran, J. (2011). Rigor Mortis in an Unusual Position: Forensic Considerations. *International Journal of Applied and Basic Medical Research*, 1(2), pp. 120–122.

Duday, H. (2009). *The archaeology of the death: lectures in archaeothanatology*. Oxford: Oxbow Books.

Duday, H., Courtaud, P., Crubezy, E., Sellier, P. and Tillier, A.-M. (1990). L'Anthropologie "de Terrain": Reconnaissance et Interpretation des Gestes Funeraires. *Bulletins et Mémoires de la Société d'Anthropologie de Paris*, 3–4, pp. 29–50.

Duday, H. and Guillon, M. (2006). Understanding the circumstances of decomposition when the body is skeletonised. In: A. Schmitt, E. Cunha and J. Pinheiro, eds., *Forensic Anthropology and Medicine: Complementary Sciences from Recovery to Cause of Death*. Totowa, NJ: Humana Press Inc., pp. 117–157.

Duday, H., Le Mort, F. and Tiller, A.-M. (2014). Archaeothanatology and Funeral Archaeology, Application to the Study of Primary Single Burials. *Anthropologie*, 52, pp. 235–246.

Duday, H. and Masset, C. (1987). *Anthropologie physique et archeologie: methodes d'étude des sépultures. Actes du colloque de Toulouse, 4. 5 et 6 novembre 1982*. Bordeaux: Centre National de la Recherche Scientifique.

Dunand, F. and Lichtenberg, R. (1998). *Les momies et la mort en Egypte*. Paris: Errance.

Evans, W.E.D. (1963). *The chemistry of death*. Springfield, IL: Charles C. Thomas.

Fiedler, S., Buegger, F., Klaubert, B., Zipp, K., Dohrmann, R., Witteyer, M., Zarei, M. and Graw, M. (2009). Adipocere withstands 1600 Years of Fluctuating Groundwater Levels in Soil. *Journal of Archaeological Science*, 36, pp. 1328–1333.

Fiedler, S. and Graw, M. (2003). Decomposition of Buried Corpses, with Special Reference to the Formation of Adipocere. *Naturwissenschaften*, 90, pp. 291–300.

Fiedler, S., Schneckenberger, K. and Graw, M. (2004). Characterization of Soils Containing Adipocere. *Archives of Environmental Contamination and Toxicology*, 47, pp. 561–568.

Finaughty, D.A. and Morris, A.G. (2019). Precocious Natural Mummification in a Temperate Climate (Western Cape, South Africa). *Forensic Science International*, 303, 109948.

Forbes, S.L. (2008). Decomposition chemistry in a burial. In: M. Tibbett and D.O. Carter, eds., *Soil Analysis in Forensic Taphonomy*. Boca Raton: CRC Press, pp. 203–224.

Fossurier, C. (2009). Le site de Chanteloup-en-Brie (Ile-de-France): études de cas et difficultés d'analyse taphonomique. In: B. Bizet and M. Signoli, eds., *Rencontre autour des Sépultures Habillees. Actes des Journées d'Étude Organisées par le Groupement d'Anthropologie et d'Archéologie Funéraire et le Service Régional de l'Archéologie de Provence-Alpes-Côte d'Azur*. Gap: Atelier, pp. 21–27.

Frost, R.L. and Palmer, S.J. (2011). Thermal Stability of the Cave Mineral Brushite CaHPO4.2H2O – Mechanism of Formation and Decomposition. *Thermochimica Acta*, 521, pp. 14–17.

Galvao, M.F., Pujol-Luz, J.R., Assis, V.D., Pujol-Luz, C., Almeida de Rosa, C.T., Simone, L.R.L., Nair Bao, S., Barros-Cordeiro, K.B., Pessoa, L. and Bissacot, G. (2015). Shells and Bones: A Forensic Medicine Study of the Association of Terrestrial Snail *Allopeas micra* with Buried Human Remains in Brazil. *Journal of Forensic Sciences*, 60, pp. 1369–1372.

Georges, P. and Charlier, P. (2010). Localisation Préférentielle de *Cecilioides acicula* (O.F. Müller, 1774) dans Deux Tombes Hellénistiques de Plinthine (Egypte). *MaLaCo*, 6, pp. 298–302.

Georges-Zimmermann, P. and Kacki, S. (2017). *Le cimetière médiéval de Marsan (Gers). Lecture archéothanatologique*. Paris: l'Harmattan.

Gleize, Y. (2020). Disturbance of early medieval graves in south-western Gaul: taphonomy, burial reopening and the reuse of graves. In: E. Aspöck, A. Klevnäs and N. Müller-Scheeßel, eds., *Grave Disturbances. The Archaeology of Post-Depositional Interactions with the Dead*. Oxford: Oxbow Books, pp. 115–135.

Goff, M.L. (2010). Early postmortem changes and stages of decomposition. In: J. Amendt, M.L. Goff, C.P. Campobasso and M. Grasserger, eds., *Current Concepts in Forensic Entomology*. Dordrecht: Springer, pp. 1–24.

Gordon, C.C. and Buikstra, J.E. (1981). Soil pH, Bone Preservation and Sampling Bias at Mortuary Sites. *American Antiquity*, 46, pp. 566–571.

Hamilton, S.J. and Green, M.A. (2017). Gross post-mortem changes in the human body. In: E.M.J. Schotsmans, N. Márquez-Grant and S.L. Forbes, eds., *Taphonomy of Human Remains: Forensic Analysis of the Dead and the Depositional Environment*. Chichester: Wiley, pp. 11–25.

Heaton, V., Moffatt, C. and Simmons, T. (2018). The Movement of Fly (Diptera) Larvae within a Feeding Aggregation. *The Canadian Entomologist*, 150, pp. 326–333.

Hedges, R.E.M. (2002). Bone Diagenesis: An Overview of Processes. *Archaeometry*, 44, pp. 319–328.

Hedges, R.E.M. and Millard, A.R. (1995). Bones and Groundwater: Towards the Modelling of Diagenetic Processes. *Journal of Archaeological Science*, 22, pp. 155–164.

Henderson, J. (1987). Factors determining the state of preservation of human remains. In: A. Boddington, A.N. Garland and R.C. Janaway, eds., *Death, Decay and Reconstruction*. Manchester: Manchester University Press, pp. 43–54.

Herrero, J. and Porta, J. (2000). The Terminology and the Concepts of Gypsum-Rich Soils. *Geoderma*, 96, pp. 47–61.

Hertz, R. (1928). *Mélanges de sociologie religieuse et folklore*. Paris: Les Presses Universitaires de France.

Huchet, J.-B. (2014). Insect Remains and Their Traces: Relevant Fossil Witnesses in the Reconstruction of Past Funerary Practices. *Anthropologie (Brno)*, 52, 329–346.

Huchet, J.-B., Le Mort, F., Rabinovich, R., Blau, S., Coqueugniot, H. and Arensburg, B. (2013). Identification of Dermestid Pupal Chambers on Southern Levant Human Bones: Inference for Reconstruction of Middle Bronze Age Mortuary Practices. *Journal of Archaeological Science*, 40, pp. 3793–3803.

Janaway, R.C. (1996). The decay of buried human remains and their associated materials. In: J. Hunter, C. Roberts and A. Martin, eds., *Studies in Crime. An Introduction to Forensic Archaeology*. London: Routledge, pp. 58–85.

Janaway, R.C., Wilson, A.S., Caprio Diaz, G. and Guillen, S. (2009). Taphonomic changes to the buried body in arid environments: an experimental case study in Peru. In: K. Ritz, L. Dawson and D. Miller, eds., *Criminal and Environmental Soil Forensics*. London: Springer, pp. 341–356.

Jans, M.M.E. (2005). *Histological characterisation of diagenetic alteration of archeological bone*. Amsterdam: Vrije Universiteit Amsterdam.

Jarosińska, M., Nowak, S., Noryśkiewicz, A.M. and Badura, M. (2019). Plant Identification and Significance in Funeral Traditions Exemplified by Pillow Filling from a Child Crypt Burial in Byszewo (18th/19th Centuries). *Analecta*, 14, pp. 187–197.

Jaubert, J., Genty, D., Valladas, H., Camus, H., Courtaud, P., Ferrier, C., Feruglio, V., Fourment, N., Konik, S., Villotte, S., Bourdier, C., Costamagno, S., Delluc, M., Goutas, N., Katnecker, E., Klaric, l., Langlais, M., Ledoux, l., Maksud, F., O'Farrell, M., Mallye, J.-B., Pierre, M., Pons-Branchu, E., Regnier, E. and Thery-Parisot, I. (2017). The Chronology of Human and Animal Presence in the Decorated and Sepulchral Cave of Cussac (France). *Quaternary International*, 432, pp. 5–24.

Jeong, Y., Meadows Jantz, L. and Smith, J. (2016). Investigation into Seasonal Scavenging Patterns of Raccoons on Human Decomposition. *Journal of Forensic Sciences*, 61, pp. 467–471.

Junod, C.A. and Pokines, J.T. (2014). Subaerial weathering. In: J. Pokines and S.A. Symes, eds., *Manual of Forensic Taphonomy*. Boca Raton: CRC Press, pp. 287–314.

Kacki, S., Trinkaus, E., Schotsmans, E.M.J., Courtaud, P., Dori, I., Dutailly, B., Guyomarc'h, P., Mora, P., Sparacello, V.S. and Villotte, S. (2020). Complex Mortuary Dynamics in the Upper Paleolithic of the Decorated Grotte de Cussac, France. *Proceedings of the National Academy of Sciences of the United States of America*, 117, pp. 14851–14856.

Karali, L. (2008). Les apports de la malacologie à la paléopathologie. In: P. Charlier, ed., *Ostéo-Archéologie et Techniques Médico-Légales, Tendances et Perspectives. Pour un Manuel Pratique de Paléopathologie Humaine*. Paris: De Boccard, pp. 77–79.

Kibblewhite, M., Toth, G. and Hermann, T. (2015). Predicting the Preservation of Cultural Artefacts and Buried Materials in Soil. *Science of the Total Environment*, 529, pp. 249–263.

Knight, B. (1996). *Forensic pathology*, New York: Arnold.

Knobel, Z., Ueland, M., Nizio, K.D., Patel, D. and Forbes, S.L. (2019). A Comparison of Human and Pig Decomposition Rates and Odour Profiles in an Australian Environment. *Australian Journal of Forensic Sciences*, 51, pp. 557–572.

Knüsel, C.J. (2014). Crouching in Fear: Terms of Engagement for Funerary Remains. *Journal of Social Archaeology*, 14, pp. 26–58.

Knüsel, C.J. and Robb, J.E. (2016). Funerary taphonomy: an overview of goals and methods. *Journal of Archaeological Science: Reports*, In: C.J. Knüsel and J.E Robb, eds., Special Issue on Funerary Taphonomy, 10, pp. 655–673.

Loe, L., Barker, C., Brady, K., Cox, M. and Webb, H. (2014). *'Remember Me to All': the archaeological recovery and identification of soldiers who fought and died in the battle of Fromelles 1916*. Oxford: Oxford Archaeology.

Madea, B., Krompecher, T. and Knight, B. (1995). Muscle and tissue changes after death. In: B. Knight, ed., *The Estimation of the Time Since Death in the Early Postmortem Period*. London: Arnold, pp. 138–220.

Mann, R.W., Bass, W.M. and Meadows, L. (1990). Time Since Death and Decomposition of the Human Body: Variables and Observations in Case and Experimental Field Studies. *Journal of Forensic Sciences*, 35, pp. 103–111.

Mant, A.K. (1987). Knowledge acquired from post-war excavations. In: A. Boddington, A.N. Garland and R.C. Janaway, eds., *Death, Decay and Reconstruction*. Manchester: Manchester University Press, pp. 65–80.

Maureille, B. and Sellier, P. (1996). Dislocation en Ordre Paradoxal, Momification et Décomposition: Observations et Hypothèses. *Bulletins et Mémoires de la Société d'Anthropologie de Paris*, 8, pp. 313–327.

Megyesi, M.S., Nawrocki, S.P. and Haskell, N.H. (2005). Using Accumulated Degree-Days to Estimate the Postmortem Interval from Decomposed Human Remains. *Journal of Forensic Sciences*, 50, pp. 618–626.

Meyer, J., Anderson, B. and Carter, D.O. (2013). Seasonal Variation of Carcass Decomposition and Grave Soil Chemistry in a Cold Climate. *Journal of Forensic Sciences*, 58, pp. 1175–1182.

Mickleburgh, H.L. and Wescott, D.J. (2018). Controlled Experimental Observations on Joint Disarticulation and Bone Displacement of a Human Body in an Open Pit: Implications for Funerary Archaeology. *Journal of Archaeological Science: Reports*, 20, pp. 158–167.

Micozzi, M.S. (1991). *Postmortem change in human and animal remains*. Springfield: Charles C. Thomas.

Moldrup, P., Olesen, T., Rolston, D.E. and Yamaguchi, T. (1997). Modeling Diffusion and Reaction in Soils: Predicting Gas and Ion Diffusivity in Undisturbed and Sieved Soils. *Soil Science Society of America Journal*, 162, pp. 632–640.

Morris, I. (1992). *Death-ritual and social structure in Classical Antiquity*. Cambridge: Cambridge University Press.

O'Brien, R.C., Appleton, A.J. and Forbes, S.L. (2017). Comparison of Taphonomic Effects due to the Necrophagic Activity of Geographically Disparate Scavenging Guilds. *Canadian Society of Forensic Science Journal*, 50, pp. 42–53.

O'Brien, R.C., Forbes, S.L., Meyer, J. and Dadour, I.R. (2010). Forensically Significant Scavenging Guilds in the Southwest of Western Australia. *Forensic Science International*, 198, pp. 85–91.

O'Brien, T.G. and Kuehner, A.C. (2007). Waxing Grave about Adipocere: Soft Tissue Change in an Aquatic Context. *Journal of Forensic Sciences*, 52, pp. 294–301.

O'Connor, S., Ali, E., Al-Sabah, S., Anwar, D., Bergström, E., Brown, K.A., Dorhling, K.M., Buckberry, J., Buckley, S., Collins, M., Denton, J., Edwards, H.G.M., Faria, E.C., Gardner, P., Gledhill, A., Heaton, K., Heron, C., Janaway, R.C., Keely, B.J., King, D., Masinton, A., Penkman, K., Petzold, A., Pickering, M.D., Rumsby, M., Schutkowski, H., Shackleton, K.A., Thomas, J., Thomas-Oates, J., Usai, M.-R, Wilson, A.S. and O'Connor, T. (2011). Exceptional Preservation of a Prehistoric Human Brain from Heslington, Yorkshire, UK. *Journal of Archaeological Science*, 38, pp. 1641–1654.

Orfila, M. and Lesueur, M.O. (1831). *Traité des exhumations juridiques*, vol. 1, Paris: Béchet Jaune.

Ottoni, C., Bekaert, B. and Decorte, R. (2017). DNA degradation: current knowledge and progress in DNA analysis. In: E.M.J. Schotsmans, N. Márquez-Grant and S. Forbes, eds., *Taphonomy of Human Remains: Forensic Analysis of the Dead and the Depositional Environment*. Chichester: Wiley, pp. 65–80.

Papageorgopoulou, C., Bianucci, R. and Rühli, F. (2010). Preservation of Cell Structures in a Medieval Infant Brain: A Paleohistological, Paleogenetic, Radiological and Physico-Chemical Study. *NeuroImage*, 50, pp. 893–901.

Parham, C. and Fleak, E. (2017). A case study from Los Angeles: baby in concrete. In: E.M.J. Schotsmans, N. Márquez-Grant and S.L. Forbes, eds., *Taphonomy of Human Remains: Forensic Analysis of the Dead and the Depositional Environment*. Chichester: Wiley, pp. 454–459.

Payne, J.A., King, E.W. and Beinhart, G. (1968). Arthropod Succession and Decomposition of Buried Pigs. *Nature*, 219, pp. 1180–1181.

Piñar, G., Piombino-Mascali, D., Maixner, F., Zink, A. and Sterflinger, K. (2013). Microbial Survey of the Mummies from the Capuchin Catacombs of Palermo, Italy: Biodeterioration Risk and Contamination of the Indoor Air. *FEMS Microbiology Ecology*, 86, pp. 341–356.

Piombino-Mascali, D., Gill-Frerking, H. and Beckett, R.G. (2017). The taphonomy of natural mummies. In: E.M.J. Schotsmans, N. Márquez-Grant and S.L. Forbes, eds., *Taphonomy of Human Remains: Forensic Analysis of the Dead and the Depositional Environment*. Chichester: Wiley, pp. 101–119.

Pitt, N., Casey, M., Lowe, A. and Stocks, R. (2017). The Old Sydney Burial Ground: The 2008 Archaeological Investigations. *Australasian Historical Archaeology*, 35, pp. 3–23.

Pokines, J.T. and Baker, J.E. (2013). Effects of burial environment on osseous remains. In: J. Pokines and S.A. Symes, eds., *Manual of Forensic Taphonomy*. Boca Raton: CRC Press, pp. 73–114.

Porta, J. and Herrero, J. (1990). Micromorphology and genesis of soils enriched with gypsum. In: L. A. Douglas, ed., *Soil Micro-Morphology: A Basic and Applied Science*. Amsterdam: Elsevier, pp. 321–339.

Prahlow, J.A. and Byard, R.W. (2012). *Atlas of forensic pathology*. New York, NY: Springer.

Prangnell, J. and McGowan, G. (2009). Soil Temperature Calculation for Burial Site Analysis. *Forensic Science International*, 191, pp. 104–109.

Prats-Muñoz, G., Galtés, I., Armentano, N., Cases, S., Fernández, P.L. and Malgosa, A. (2013). Human Soft Tissue Preservation in the Cova des Pas Site (Minorca Bronze Age). *Journal of Archaeological Science*, 40, pp. 4701–4710.

Puckle, B.S. (1926). *Funeral customs: their origin and development*. London: T. Werner Laurie Ltd.

Rivers, D.B., Thompson, C. and Brogan, R. (2011). Physiological Trade-Offs of Forming Maggot Masses by Necrophagous Flies on Vertebrate Carrion. *Bulletin of Entomological Research*, 101, pp. 599–611.

Schoenen, D. and Schoenen, H. (2013). Adipocere Formation – The Result of Insufficient Microbial Degradation. *Forensic Science International*, 226, pp. 301.e1–301.e6.

Schotsmans, E.M.J., Denton, J., Dekeirsschieter, J., Ivaneanu, T., Leentjes, S.C., Janaway, R.C. and Wilson, A.S. (2012). Effects of Hydrated Lime and Quicklime on the Decay of Buried Human Remains Using Pig Cadavers as Human Body Analogues. *Forensic Science International*, 217, pp. 50–59.

Schotsmans, E.M.J., Márquez-Grant, N. and Forbes, S.L. (2017). Introduction to taphonomy of human remains. In: E.M.J. Schotsmans, N. Márquez-Grant and S.L. Forbes, eds., *Taphonomy of Human Remains: Forensic Analysis of the Dead and the Depositional Environment*. Chichester: Wiley, pp. 1–7.

Schotsmans, E.M.J., Toksoy-Koksal, F., Brettell, R.C., Bessou, M., Cordbineau, R., Lingle, A.M., Bouquin, D., Blanchard, P., Becker, K., Castex, D., Knüsel, C.J., Wilson, A.S. and Chapoulie, R. (2019). 'Not All that is White Is Lime' – White Substances from Archaeological Burial Contexts: Analyses and Interpretations. *Archaeometry*, 61, pp. 809–827.

Schotsmans, E.M.J. and Van de Voorde, W. (2017). Concealing the crime: the effects of chemicals on human tissues. In: E.M.J. Schotsmans, N. Márquez-Grant and S.L Forbes, eds., *Taphonomy of Human Remains: Forensic Analysis of the Dead and the Depositional Environment*. Chichester: Wiley, pp. 335–351.

Schotsmans, E.M.J., Van de Voorde, W., de Winne, J. and Wilson, A.S. (2011). The Impact of Shallow Burial on Differential Decomposition of the Body: A Temperate Case Study. *Forensic Science International*, 206, pp. e43–e48.

Schotsmans, E.M.J., Van de Voorde, W. and Forbes, S.L. (2020). Time since death estimation in the advanced stages of decomposition. In: J. Hayman and M. Oxenham, eds., *Estimation of the Time Since Death. Current Research and Future Trends*. London: Elsevier Academic Press, pp. 81–102.

Schotsmans, E.M.J., Fletcher, J.N., Denton, J., Janaway, R.C. and Wilson, A.S. (2014a). Long-Term Effects of Hydrated Lime and Quicklime on the Decay of Human Remains Using Pig Cadavers as Human Body Analogues: Field Experiments. *Forensic Science International*, 238, pp. 141.e1–141.e13.

Schotsmans, E.M.J., Wilson, A.S., Brettell, R., Munshi, T. and Edwards, H.G.M. (2014b). Raman Spectroscopy as a Non-Destructive Screening Technique for Studying White Substances from Archaeological and Forensic Burial Contexts. *Journal of Raman Spectroscopy*, 45, pp. 1301–1308.

Sellier, P. and Bendezu-Sarmiento, J. (2013). Différer la Décomposition: le Temps Suspendu? Les Signes d'une Momification Préalable. *Les Nouvelles d'Archaeologie*, 132, pp. 30–36.

Serrulla, F., Etxeberría, F., Herrasti, L., Cascallana, J.L. and Del Olmo, J. (2017). Saponified brains of the Spanish Civil War. In: E.M.J. Schotsmans, N. Márquez-Grant and S.L. Forbes, eds., *Taphonomy of Human Remains. Forensic Analysis of the Dead and the Depositional Environment*. Chichester: Wiley, pp. 429–437.

Simmons, T., Adlam, R.E. and Moffatt, C. (2010). Debugging Decomposition Data – Comparative Taphonomic Studies and the Influence of Insects and Carcass Size on Decomposition Rate. *Journal of Forensic Sciences*, 55, pp. 8–13.

Sledzik, P.S. and Micozzi, M.S. (1997). Autopsied, embalmed and preserved human remains: distinguishing features in forensic and historic contexts. In: W.D. Haglund, and M.S. Sorg, eds., *Forensic Taphonomy. The Postmortem Fate of Human Remains*. Boca Raton, FL: CRC Press, pp. 483–497.

Spicka, A., Johnson, R., Bushing, J., Higley, L.G. and Carter, D.O. (2011). Carcass Mass Can Influence Rate of Decomposition and Release of Ninhydrin-Reactive Nitrogen into Gravesoil. *Forensic Science International*, 209, pp. 80–85.

Steadman, D.W., Dautartas, A., Kenyhercz, M.W., Meadows Jantz, L., Mundorff, A. and Vidoli, G.M. (2018). Differential Scavenging among Pig, Rabbit, and Human Subjects. *Journal of Forensic Sciences*, 63, pp. 1684–1691.

Stuart, B.H., Forbes, S.L., Dent, B.B. and Hodgson, G. (2000). Studies of Adipocere Using Diffuse Reflectance Infrared Spectroscopy. *Vibrational Spectroscopy*, 24, pp. 233–242.

Sutherland, A., Myburgh, J., Steyn, M. and Becker, P. (2013). The Effect of Body Size on the Rate of Decomposition in a Temperate Region of South Africa. *Forensic Science International*, 231, pp. 257–262.

Swartz, E.E., Floyd, R.T. and Cendoma, M. (2005). Cervical Spine Functional Anatomy and the Biomechanics of Injury due to Compressive Loading. *Journal of Athletic Training*, 40, pp. 155–161.

Szelecz, I., Koenig, I., Seppey, C., Le Bayon, R.-C. and Mitchell, E. (2018). Soil Chemistry Changes beneath Decomposing cadavers over a One-Year Period. *Forensic Science International*, 286, pp. 155–165.

Takatori, T. (2001). The Mechanism of Human Adipocere Formation. *Legal Medicine*, 3, pp. 193–204.

Thali, M.J., Lux, B., Lösch, S., Rösing, F.W., Hürlimann, J., Feer, P., Dirnhofer, R., Königsdorfer, U. and Zollinger, U. (2001). 'Brienzi' – The Blue Vivianite Man of Switzerland: Time Since Death Estimation of an Adipocere Body. *Forensic Science International*, 211, pp. 34–40.

Tiesler, V. (2011). Book review of 'The Archaeology of Dead: Lectures in Archaeothanatology'. *European Journal of Archaeology*, 14(3), pp. 491–494.

Tkocz, I., Bytzer, P. and Bierring, F. (1979). Preserved Brains in Medieval Skulls. *American Journal of Physical Anthropology*, 51, pp. 197–202.

Troutman, L., Moffatt, C. and Simmons, T. (2014). A Preliminary Examination of Differential Decomposition Patterns in Mass Graves. *Journal of Forensic Sciences*, 59, pp. 621–626.

Tsokos, M. and Byard, R.W. (2012). Putrefactive 'Rigor Mortis'. *Forensic Science, Medicine and Pathology*, 8, pp. 200–201.

Turner, B.D. and Wiltshire, P.E.J. (1999). Experimental Validation of Forensic Evidence: A Study of the Decomposition of Buried Pigs in a Heavy Clay Soil. *Forensic Science International*, 101, pp. 113–122.

Vanin, S. and Huchet, J.-B. (2017). Forensic entomology and funerary archaeoentomology. In: E.M.J. Schotsmans, N. Márquez-Grant and S.L. Forbes, eds., *Taphonomy of Human Remains: Forensic Analysis of the Dead and the Depositional Environment*. Chichester: Wiley, pp. 167–186.

Vass, A.A. (2011). The Elusive Universal Post-Mortem Interval Formula. *Forensic Science International*, 204, pp. 34–40.

Vass, A.A., Wolt, J.D., Foss, J.E., Ammons, J.T. and Bass, W.M. (1992). Time Since Death Determinations of Human Cadavers Using Soil Solution. *Journal of Forensic Sciences*, 37, pp. 1236–1253.

Vidoli, G.M., Steadman, D.W., Devlin, J.B. and Meadows Jantz, L. (2017). History and development of the first Anthropology Research Facility, Knoxville, Tennessee. In: E.M.J. Schotsmans, N. Márquez-Grant and S.L. Forbes, eds., *Taphonomy of Human Remains: Forensic Analysis of the Dead and the Depositional Environment*. Chichester: Wiley, pp. 463–475.

Von der Lühe, B., Fiedler, S., Mayes, R.W. and Dawson, L.A. (2017). Temporal Fatty Acid Profiles of Human Decomposition Fluids in Soil. *Organic Geochemistry*, 111, pp. 26–33.

Von Endt, D.W. and Ortner, D.J. (1984). Experimental Effects of Bone Size and Temperature of Bone Diagenesis. *Journal of Archaeological Science*, 11, pp. 247–253.

Waldron, T. (1987). The relative survival of the human skeleton: implications for palaeopathology. In: A. Boddington, A.N. Garland and R.C. Janaway, eds., *Death, Decay and Reconstruction*. Manchester: Manchester University Press, pp. 55–64.

Wallman, J.F. and Archer, M.S. (2020). The application of insects to the estimation of the time since death. In: J. Hayman and M. Oxenham, eds., *Estimation of the Time Since Death. Current Research and Future Trends*. London: Elsevier Academic Press, pp. 57–80.

Watson, C.J., Ueland, M., E.M.J., Schotsmans, Sterenberg, J., Forbes, S.L. and Blau, S. (2020). Detecting Grave Sites from Surface Anomalies: A Longitudinal Study in an Australian Woodland. *Journal of Forensic Sciences*, 66(2), pp. 479–490.

Weiner, S. (2010). *Microarchaeology. Beyond the visible archaeological record*. Cambridge: Cambridge University Press.

Wescott, D.J. (2018). Recent Advances in Forensic Anthropology: Decomposition Research. *Forensic Sciences Research*, 3, pp. 278–293.

White, R.E. (1997). *Principles and practice of soil science*. Oxford: Blackwell.

Wilson, A.S., Janaway, R.C., Holland, A. D., Dodson, H. I., Baran, E., Pollard, A.M. and Tobin, D J. (2007). Modelling the Buried Human Body Environment in Upland Climes Using Three Contrasting Field Sites. *Forensic Science International*, 169, pp. 6–18.

Wilson, A., Neilsen, P., Berry, R., Seckiner, D. and Mallett, X. (2020). Quantifying Human Post-Mortem Movement Resultant from Decomposition Processes. *Forensic Science International: Synergy*, 2, pp. 248–261.

Yan, F., McNally, R., Kontanis, E.J. and Sadik, O.A. (2001). Preliminary Quantitative Investigation of Postmortem Adipocere Formation. *Journal of Forensic Sciences*, 46, pp. 609–614.

Young, A. (2017). The effects of terrestrial mammalian scavenging and avian scavenging on the body. In: E.M.J., Schotsmans, N. Márquez-Grant and S.L. Forbes, eds., *Taphonomy of Human Remains. Forensic Analysis of the Dead and the Depositional Environment*. Chichester: Wiley, pp. 212–234.

Zhou, C. and Byard, R.W. (2011). Factors and Processes Causing Accelerated Decomposition in Human Cadavers. An Overview. *Journal of Forensic and Legal Medicine*, 38, pp. 111–115.

28

EXPLORING THE USE OF ACTUALISTIC FORENSIC TAPHONOMY IN THE STUDY OF (FORENSIC) ARCHAEOLOGICAL HUMAN BURIALS

An actualistic experimental research programme at the Forensic Anthropology Center at Texas State University (FACTS), San Marcos, Texas

Hayley L. Mickleburgh

DEPARTMENT OF CULTURAL SCIENCES, LINNAEUS UNIVERSITY, KALMAR, SWEDEN

FORENSIC ANTHROPOLOGY CENTER, DEPARTMENT OF ANTHROPOLOGY, TEXAS STATE UNIVERSITY, SAN MARCOS, UNITED STATES

Daniel J. Wescott

FORENSIC ANTHROPOLOGY CENTER, DEPARTMENT OF ANTHROPOLOGY, TEXAS STATE UNIVERSITY, SAN MARCOS, UNITED STATES

Sarah Gluschitz

DEPARTMENT OF ANATOMICAL SCIENCES, SCHOOL OF MEDICINE, ST. GEORGE'S UNIVERSITY, GRENADA, WEST INDIES

M. Victor Klinkenberg

FACULTY OF ARCHAEOLOGY, LEIDEN UNIVERSITY, LEIDEN, THE NETHERLANDS

Introduction

The recovery of buried human remains from both forensic and archaeological contexts involves careful excavation with the aim of securing as much evidence as possible pertaining to the circumstances surrounding the death and burial of the deceased individual(s). Understanding

DOI: 10.4324/9781351030625-33

the formation processes of human burials and distinguishing the effects of human modification of the remains and their surroundings from taphonomic processes is key to reconstructing the sequence of events leading up to death and burial. This requires careful consideration of the effects of taphonomic processes on the depositional environment and the remains.

The taphonomy of the grave and buried body has become an increasingly important area of research within mortuary and funerary archaeology. The French-developed field of archaeothanatology combines taphonomic principles with knowledge of anatomy and human decomposition to interpret the spatial configuration of bones in a deposit. Archaeothanatology has developed hypotheses of the relative sequence of joint disarticulation during decomposition and the spatial displacement of the bones in the burial environment to distinguish natural processes from funerary treatment. The anatomical relationships of the bones (articulated or disarticulated) and the direction and distance of bone displacement are carefully assessed and used to infer, among others, whether or not bones are in a primary or secondary position (Duday, 2009), distinguish collective burials (bodies accumulated over time) from multiple burials (simultaneous deposition of bodies) (Castex and Blaizot, 2017), reveal the presence of decayed body containers (Harris and Tayles, 2012; Ortiz, Chambon and Molist, 2013), determine body treatment and/or stage of decomposition upon burial (e.g. mummification; Maureille and Sellier, 1996), identify post-mortem and post-depositional manipulation of the body and grave (e.g. intentional removal of bodies/body parts) (e.g. Valentin *et al.*, 2010), and establish if burial occurred immediately after death or was delayed (Nelson, 1998).

The basis of archaeothanatological principles, understanding how taphonomic processes affect the preservation and spatial patterning of human remains, is a premise that is shared with the field of forensic taphonomy, a subfield of forensic anthropology. With regards to buried human remains, forensic anthropology and archaeothanatology have two important objectives in common: (1) distinguishing taphonomic alterations from human modification of the remains and their context, and (2) reconstructing the sequence and chronology of events surrounding death and deposition. Archaeothanatology has the potential to aid forensic investigation by helping to reconstruct the sequence of events that gave rise to a burial, helping determine the medico-legal significance of remains, assisting with identifying the *modus operandi* of perpetrators, and by providing highly detailed information on the manner and timing of treatment of the body. In medico-legal contexts involving clandestine burials (e.g. homicide cases) or mass graves, information on body treatment can be informative with regard to the methods and means of killing and burial, attempts to conceal or destroy evidence, and potentially as an aid to identify the perpetrator(s). Because of this capacity, some researchers have argued for the use of archaeothanatological methods in medico-legal contexts (Duday and Guillon, 2006; Castex and Blaizot, 2017). However, this use is impeded by the fact that its methods are currently not validated by data collected under controlled conditions (Mickleburgh, 2018; Schotsmans *et al.,* Chapter 27, this volume). For archaeothanatology to be used in medico-legal contexts, its methods must be tested. Systematic studies that control conditions to measure the effects of specific variables and use robust sample sizes are needed. Sizable samples and repetition/replication of experiments reduce the effects of chance variation on the results, making statistical inferences more reliable (Simmons, 2017; Mickleburgh, 2018; Mickleburgh and Wescott, 2018). The use of body analogues (e.g. pigs) in human disarticulation studies is not an option since studies of non-human disarticulation sequences indicate that they differ by species (Hill, 1980).

This chapter reviews some of the experimental forensic taphonomic research to improve the interpretation of human remains in both traditional and forensic archaeological contexts, and presents the findings of an innovative on-going research programme undertaking actualistic taphonomic experiments to improve and develop archaeothanatological methods. The research programme is the first systematic study of the joint disarticulation sequence and spatial patterning of human remains allowed to decompose under controlled conditions. The ultimate aim of the programme is to lay the foundations for an actualistic framework to further develop archaeothanatology for application in both traditional archaeological as well as medico-legal contexts. Furthermore, this chapter presents the method and research protocol of 3D documentation and analysis that was developed specifically to study the spatial relation and movement of human remains throughout the process of soft tissue decomposition and skeletal disarticulation. Finally, the important avenues for future development in this area of research are outlined.

The research programme of experimental forensic taphonomy for (forensic) archaeological applications

The on-going forensic taphonomy research programme at the Forensic Anthropology Center at Texas State University (FACTS) comprises a series of controlled actualistic taphonomic experiments developed to examine the effects of different variables on human decomposition, skeletal disarticulation and spatial patterning of bones within their depositional environment. This programme uses documented (i.e. with known demographic and health data) human bodies donated to FACTS in its experiments. FACTS receives whole body donations for scientific research purposes under the Texas Revised Uniform Anatomical Gift Act (National Conference of Commissioners on Uniform State Laws, 2009, Chapter 692A). Body donations are exclusively acquired through the expressed and documented willingness of the donors and/ or their legal next-of-kin. Body donations are made directly to FACTS, and donors and/or their next-of-kin are aware that donations are used for taphonomic studies. Demographic, health and other information are provided through a questionnaire completed by the donor or legal next-of-kin. The data are securely curated by FACTS. The body donation programme complies with all legal and ethical standards associated with the use of human remains for scientific research. Body donations are placed at the Forensic Anthropology Research Facility (FARF), an outdoor human decomposition research facility managed by FACTS and located in the Texas Hill Country, near San Marcos.

The programme focuses on replication of two distinct medico-legal/archaeological contexts: depositions of individuals and mass depositions. The programme examines fundamental taphonomic models used in archaeothanatology to reconstruct the original mode of deposition and ultimately aims to improve recognition of human and taphonomic alterations of a grave.

The programme uses an actualistic methodology. Actualism posits that contemporary knowledge can be applied to understand the past (uniformitarianism) and that there is a relationship between process and product. Actualistic studies have a long history in forensic anthropology, archaeology and palaeontology (Behrensmeyer and Kidwell, 1985; Lyman, 1994; Bass, 1997; Pobiner and Braun, 2005; Shirley, Wilson, and Meadows-Jantz, 2011; Wescott *et al.*, 2018). Actualistic studies can take different forms, but they often control for chosen observational parameters and examine the link between natural processes that permit deductive interpretation (Sorg and Haglund, 2002). Such studies replicate the taphonomic effects by reproducing hypothesised causal events in a relatively controlled situation. Since the programme studies the effects of different deposition types and stages of decomposition at placement on disarticulation and spatial bone patterning, variables known or thought to affect these processes, including body position, soil type, presence and type of clothing, and burial pit shape and dimensions, are controlled. Precautions are taken to ensure that these variables are the same for each experiment.

Archaeothanatological models

In this contribution, a distinction is made between sequences of joint disarticulation that have been defined based on post-hoc examination of a burial, as in traditional archaeothanatology (Duday, 2009), and observations of the actual process and sequence of disarticulation that are made during forensic taphonomic experiments on human decomposition.

Archaeothanatology makes use of a hypothesised sequence of joint disarticulation to distinguish natural from anthropogenic or bioturbation/scavenging processes (Duday, 2009). In the absence of actualistic taphonomic observations on the variables influencing the final bone position in the grave, this sequence is based on inferences resulting from repeated observation of patterns in the archaeological record and on the hypothetical understanding of joint durability based on their strength and type and amount of soft tissue in life. This model[1] distinguishes between 'labile' and 'persistent' joints. Labile joints are considered to be relatively unstable and disarticulate relatively soon after death and are therefore frequently found out of anatomical position, unless there is supporting burial soil. They include joints held together primarily by soft tissue attachments, such as the hyoid, temporo-mandibular, patellar, scapulo-thoracic, costo-sternal joints and the small bones of the hands and feet (Roksandic, 2002; Duday, 2009; Knüsel, 2014). The labile articulations, in particular, are used to assess if a burial is a primary or secondary one because, if these articulations are preserved, it is considered that burial occurred rapidly after death (Duday, 2009). Persistent joints are major weight-bearing joints with ligaments that are thought to resist disarticulation and frequently maintain their anatomical position. Notable exceptions to the labile/persistent distinction have been identified. The wrist is considered to be a strong joint in life due to the numerous ligaments connecting the carpal bones, but the ligaments are thought to decompose rapidly after death. The acetabulo-femoral (hip) joint was originally considered to be persistent due to its important weight-bearing function, but is now considered to be labile as the joint is maintained by thin capsular ligaments that can decay rapidly (Duday, 2009; Knüsel, 2014; Knüsel and Robb, 2016). In sum, the hypothetical sequence of joint disarticulation used in archaeothanatology is based on: 1) repeated post hoc observation of the anatomical relationships of bones in archaeological burials, and 2) the hypothesis that durability during decomposition is (partly) determined by the nature of soft tissue structures and biomechanical function. The use of post hoc observations of archaeological burials is problematic, however, since the precise variables that produced them are unknown. Appleby (2016) has argued that the hypothesised joint disarticulation order is problematic since the status of joint articulation is used to distinguish primary from secondary burials, but at the same time, the distinction between labile and persistent joints is based on repeated observations in burials interpreted as either primary or secondary. The hypothesis that the durability of joints during decomposition is related to their structure and biomechanical function in life is, as yet, not supported by actualistic taphonomic observations. The archaeologically observed exceptions discussed above (wrist and hip joints) furthermore indicate that the relation between joint strength and function in life and durability after death is not straightforward.

Another important model used in archaeothanatology concerns the relationship between spatial patterning of the bones and open spaces (voids) in the burial environment. Archaeothanatology uses the pattern of displacement of bones out of anatomical relationships to infer the type of 'burial architecture' (i.e. grave structure, body containers). Rotation and movement of bones are

---

1 That is, the framework of observations and ideas resulting in the hypothesised sequence of joint disarticulation and the proposed mechanisms of joint durability.

possible when there is open space within the depositional environment. Movement can occur due to gravity and normal decomposition processes if empty space is already present in the deposit, referred to as 'primary voids'. Primary open space can be present due to intentionally leaving the pit open throughout decomposition (Hofman *et al.*, 2012), or can be present within body containers such as coffins or woven baskets. 'Secondary voids' are created by the decomposition of soft tissues and structural elements such as wrappings or headrests (Duday, 2009). Bone displacement patterns are considered to differ depending on the type of open space: greater displacement is possible when primary open space is present around the body (Ambroise and Perlès, 1975; Duday *et al.*, 1990; Duday, 2009). The presence of primary open space is inferred based on the displacement of bones 'outside of the original body volume'. Any displacement within this space, it is reasoned, could result from the creation of secondary voids once the soft tissues of the body have decomposed. However, assessment of the position of the bones as within or outside of the original body volume is complicated due to the fact that the soft tissue volume can differ considerably between individuals of different size/corpulence.

In addition, the presence of both primary and secondary open spaces is related to soil type. As the soft tissues (and perishable burial architecture) decompose over time, they are replaced by soil. Two forms of filling are generally distinguished depending on soil type and are related to specific movements of the bones: (1) delayed filling, in which the decomposition of the soft tissues of, for example, the thorax and abdomen, creates a void in the deposit which is maintained for some time (Duday, 2009: 52–53), and (2) progressive filling, in which sediment continually fills newly formed voids ('hourglass effect') (Duday *et al.*, 1990; Duday, 2009: 54). Delayed filling is often associated with the 'flattening' of the ribcage and is also suggested to be the cause of 'hyper-flexed' burials, in which the skeleton of a body interred in flexed position takes on a very compact and hyper-flexed position due to the 'closing of the inter-segmental angles' of the joints as soft tissues decay (Duday, 2009: 53).

Some archaeological studies have suggested that the stage of decomposition of the body upon deposition can affect the order of disarticulation and displacement of bones. Burial in a mummified state is thought to lead to minimal bone displacement when compared to burial in a fresh stage of decomposition because the amount of soft tissue in a mummified body is much reduced and, therefore, will not create substantial secondary open space (Aoudia *et al.*, 2014). Based on this, it can be hypothesised that burial of bloated bodies (i.e. in active decomposition, bloat phase) will result in the creation of a greater volume of secondary open space and thus greater potential bone displacement. Researchers have also identified 'anomalous' disarticulation of the bones, where labile joints remain articulated and persistent joints appear disarticulated. This phenomenon is referred to as 'paradoxical disarticulation' (Maureille and Sellier, 1996; Sellier and Bendezu-Sarmiento, 2013; Knüsel and Robb, 2016) and has been suggested to be an indication of desiccation/mummification, which initially prevents disarticulation and bone movement, but can lead to paradoxical disarticulation if mummified remains are subsequently manipulated so that persistent joints become disarticulated, while labile joints are maintained (Maureille and Sellier, 1996; Sellier and Bendezu-Sarmiento, 2013).

The actualistic experiments at the forensic anthropology research facility (FARF)

The actualistic experiments at FARF were designed to collect a body of data suitable for statistical analysis, distinguishing the effects of specific variables and replication studies in other environments. An important objective of the experiments was to test the two fundamental taphonomic scenarios used in archaeothanatology: (1) the sequence of natural joint disarticulation and (2) the relation between spatial displacement of bones and primary and secondary voids in the burial environment. In addition, the programme examines the effects of the stage of decomposition of the body upon deposition on the disarticulation sequence and spatial patterning of the bones over time. Joint disarticulation and bone movement were documented in bodies placed in open and closed pits (i.e. buried), in different stages of decomposition and in individual deposits and mass graves. Variables that – based on archaeothanatological research – are thought to affect the final position of the bones in the deposit, such as soil type, the position of the body, and the shape and dimensions of the burial pit, were controlled in the experiments.

The following hypotheses were tested through the actualistic experiments:

1. The process of joint disarticulation of the human skeleton is predictable and ordered.

    a. The order of joint disarticulation during decomposition of the human body is determined by the properties of joint tissues and biomechanical function of the joint.
    b. The order of joint disarticulation differs depending on body position.

2. The spatial distribution of bones is different between decomposition in a void and a closed space (i.e. primary open space vs. secondary open space).
3. The spatial patterning of bones (i.e. amount and direction of displacement of the bones) differs depending on the original body position.
4. The spatial patterning of bones is different between bodies interred in an early stage of decomposition and bodies interred in the active decomposition (bloat) stage or mummified.
5. Bone displacement is different between mass graves and individual burials.

Environment

The terrain at FARF consists of shallow clay-rich soil overlying deposits of limestone with grassland punctuated by woodlands of primarily oak and cedar trees (Barnes *et al.*, 2000). The region has a semi-humid climate with hot summers and moderate winters. Bodies exposed to the sun and wind commonly desiccate/mummify. Annual precipitation is close to average for the United States but the region experiences droughts and flash flooding. The predominant vegetation consists of scrub bushes, ash juniper and Texas live oak trees. The soils in the Texas Hill Country are primarily shallow, stony and overlay Cretaceous limestone. At FARF, the two types of soils are (1) Rumple-Comfort Association, Ungulating (RUD) and (2) Comfort-Rock Outcrop Complex, Undulating (CrD). Both are characterised by relatively shallow, rocky, clay topsoils. Both soils are also relatively alkaline with high carbonate content and relatively low organic matter. Because of the high clay and rock content, the soils at FARF have relatively low permeability to air and water movement (Carson, 2000; Gillham, Young, and Long, 2003; Fancher *et al.*, 2017). As explained above, the type of soil in a grave is thought to affect bone movement by either preserving voids in the grave or not, depending on soil properties (i.e. texture, permeability and moisture carrying capacity). Based on the results of the programme thus far, the clay-rich soil at FARF ensures that secondary voids in the burial environment of shallow single graves are maintained long enough for the body to fully skeletonise within the void, leading to displacement of bones out of anatomical relation within the dimensions of the void (Mickleburgh, 2018; Mickleburgh and Wescott, 2018). The programme currently does not include actualistic study of the effects of different soil types, but to ensure that soil type is the same for each experiment, placements are done only in one area of FARF with RUD type soil. Furthermore, a basic analysis of soil properties was undertaken prior to each cadaver placement to ensure consistency of soil conditions.

Body donations

At the time of writing, 20 human body donations have been studied throughout the complete process of decomposition until skeletonisation and retrieval of the remains from the outdoor decomposition facility (described below). Continuation of the programme will expand the number of individual placements in primary voids as well as burials in both flexed and extended body positions. Furthermore, at least one mass deposition experiment will start in spring 2020. Six individuals were placed simultaneously in a fresh stage of decomposition in overlapping body positions and then covered with soil. Furthermore, photographic data is available from over 200 individuals from the past eight years previously recorded at FARF as a part of the FACTS longitudinal outdoor human decomposition study. These bodies were placed uniformly in an extended, supine position on the surface. Since these data were not collected with the aim to assess joint disarticulation and bone movement, they are used exclusively as an additional resource alongside the experiments in the programme, i.e. to assess potential differences related to seasonal weather, and age-at-death and health status of the body donors.

Methods

Prior to placement of the body donations, anthropometric variables, including stature, body weight, and chest, abdomen and thigh circumference were collected. Bodies that had been autopsied or had conditions that could affect normal decomposition and/or disarticulation were excluded from the programme. The use of obese donors (i.e. BMI > 30) is also avoided since obesity can potentially affect the rate of soft tissue decomposition (Zhou and Byard, 2011) and will likely affect bone movement within secondary voids. As a part of the 3D documentation and analysis methods developed for the programme, the mass grave cadavers were scanned using a full-body post-mortem CT scan, which provided highly precise anthropometric measurements as well as 3D models of the entire skeleton.

The dimensions and shape of placement pits were controlled and kept uniform. Individual burial pits for flexed bodies measure 65 cm by 95 cm wide and 70 cm deep. Mass grave pit(s) measure 200 cm by 200 cm wide and 120 cm deep. Cadavers placed in open pits are covered with a wire cage to prevent scavenging by large mammals and birds. While this can be an important taphonomic variable, it is beyond the scope of the current study to examine scavenging effects. Exposed (i.e. unburied) bodies were placed under the tree canopy to reduce solar and wind desiccation, which is common in open areas of FARF (Wescott et al., 2018). Clothing is known to affect decomposition rate, largely because of its restricting effects on insect access (Dautartas, 2009; Card et al., 2015). Clothing can also restrict bone movement, although the precise effects of different types of clothing and textiles on bone displacement are not well understood (Bouquin, Beauthier and Depierre, 2012). In order to restrict the number of variables affecting the spatial configuration of bones, all body donations studied to date have been unclothed.

The process of decomposition and disarticulation in an open pit and surface placements is documented on a daily basis using photography and a written form, providing disarticulation sequence data that is used to test hypotheses 1, 1a and 1b. The written form includes documentation of the stage of decomposition, joint disarticulation and taphonomic factors such as insect activity and weather conditions. Decomposition is quantified using the total body score (TBS) method following the guidelines in Megyesi and colleagues (2005) since this method is the most commonly used in forensic cases as well as for the collection of longitudinal decomposition data at most outdoor decomposition facilities worldwide. The joints are examined and recorded as articulated, expanded, or disarticulated each day for the duration of the study, or until all bones are in stable positions following Mickleburgh and Wescott (2018).

To determine if there is a correlation between disarticulation sequence and joint properties, the individual joints are classified according to their structure (i.e. synovial, fibrous or cartilaginous), functional classification (i.e. diarthrosis, synarthrosis or amphiarthrosis) and joint type (i.e. synovial, sutural, syndesmosis, symphyseal, gomphosis and synchondrosis) using Standring (2015). These categories are used in statistical analyses of the disarticulation sequence data in order to test the hypothesis that the order of joint disarticulation is determined by the structure or biomechanical function of the joint in life (hypothesis 1a).

Documentation of bone movement over time is achieved using a combination of 3D techniques to preserve, visualise and analyse spatial data. The research protocol used, described in detail above, is used to test hypotheses 2, 3, 4 and 5. In addition, time-lapse videos were recorded of both flexed body open pit placements throughout the first months of decomposition.

Body placement

Open pit placement: two individuals were placed in a fresh stage of decomposition in flexed positions in small, oval-shaped pits that remained open throughout the duration of the experiment to study the effects of a primary open void. The dimensions of the pits were approximately 65 cm by 95 cm and 70 cm deep. One of these two body donations was placed in an upright, seated position (for a full explanation of this experiment, see Mickleburgh and Wescott, 2018), and the other in a flexed supine position (Figure 28.1). Both body donations were recovered from FARF once skeletonisation was complete and bones had moved into stable positions (i.e. displacement had ceased; after approximately 7 months and 2 years, respectively).

Surface placement: Fifteen fresh stage body donations were placed in extended supine positions on the soil surface and observed from January to June 2018.

Burial: Two fresh stage body donations were placed in small, oval-shaped pits (65 cm by 95 cm and 70 cm deep) and were immediately covered with soil. One was placed in a seated position, the other in a flexed supine position. These placement modes permit examination of the effects of secondary voids and body position on bone displacement. A third body donation was allowed to mummify by solar and wind desiccation in a flexed body position by placing the body on a raised platform in an exposed area of FARF. The raised platform permitted maximum sun exposure and airflow around the body and consisted of coarse metal mesh to permit fly maggots to fall off the body but not crawl back up onto the body (insect activity is a major factor in soft tissue loss before desiccation occurs). Once the body donation was fully desiccated, it was buried in a flexed supine position in a small, oval-shaped pit (65 cm by 95 cm and 70 cm deep). All three burials were excavated after approximately two years.

3D documentation and analysis

Crucial to understanding the movement and patterning of bones is the recording of spatial information on the position and movement over time of the different body/skeletal elements. The documentation methods used in this study were designed to preserve spatial information and provide 3D data that can be used for both quantitative and qualitative analysis, visualisation and virtual animation (Mickleburgh, Klinkenberg and Gluschitz, 2018). The research protocol for spatial documentation and analysis of skeletal disarticulation and bone movement over time that was developed for the purposes of this research programme and used to date is presented here. Modifications to this research protocol for ongoing and future research have been made based on the initial research results, as well as on the specific research requirements of the mass grave context (see above).

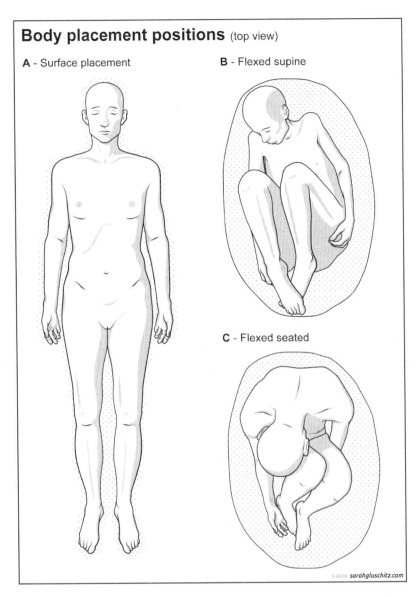

Figure 28.1 The body positions used for the individual body placements (©2020 sarahgluschitz.com).

Bone position over time was recorded using a combination of 3D techniques to preserve, visualise and analyse spatial data. Digital photography provided data for the production of 3D models using Structure from Motion (SfM) photogrammetry (Figure 28.2). Agisoft Photoscan software was used to produce 3D models from 2D digital images. These models permitted non-destructive and highly detailed (re-)analysis of taphonomic data and the sequence of disarticulation and movement of bones. A grid was established around the burial pits and surface donations, with fixed geo-markers. Open pit and surface placements were documented in this way at weekly intervals. Open-pit experiments were intended to examine the effects of 'primary voids' around the body during decomposition (as in cases where the body was left to decompose in an open

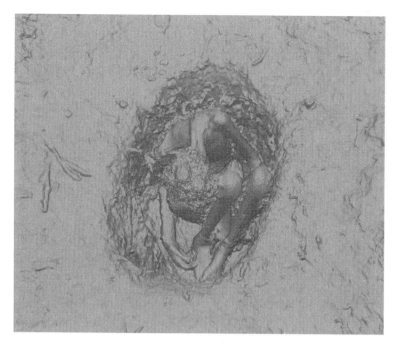

Figure 28.2   3D model of open pit with seated body placement.

pit or natural depression). Burials with soil were documented using SfM photogrammetry upon placement and during and after excavation to permit examination of the effects of filled space and 'secondary voids' around the body during decomposition.

The sequential 3D models (collected weekly or at placement and excavation of the body) were overlaid to assess spatial changes over time using distance and heat maps in open-source software packages such as Cloudcompare and Meshlab (Mickleburgh, Klinkenberg and Gluschitz, 2018). This method was found to be particularly effective in the later stages of decomposition, when the majority of the soft tissue had decomposed. Heat and distance maps provide both qualitative and quantitative information on bone movements and were found to support visualisation of the bone movement very well. However, particularly in earlier stages of decomposition, bone movement is obscured by changes in the soft tissue mass. Understanding bone movement and disarticulation early on in the decomposition process is very important to be able to test and substantiate archaeothanatological insights because the status of 'labile' joints is significant in archaeothanatological analysis.

In order to study bone movement throughout all stages of decomposition, a method of 3D reconstruction was developed that enables qualitative and quantitative analysis of the displacement of bones over time from the start of the experiment (i.e. when the body is still fully fleshed). At the end of each actualistic experiment, once the bones of each individual body donation have been cleaned and brought to the osteological lab, 3D models of each individual bone are produced using SfM photogrammetry. In collaboration with an anatomist, the 3D bone models are 're-fitted' into their anatomical position within the soft tissue volume of the body in the 3D models developed weekly during the experiment (Figure 28.3). This technique works well for individuals with normal to low BMI. This permits reconstruction of the position of the bones at weekly intervals throughout the experiment, visualising the position of the bones early on in the experiment when soft tissue is still present. The resulting weekly snapshots of the position

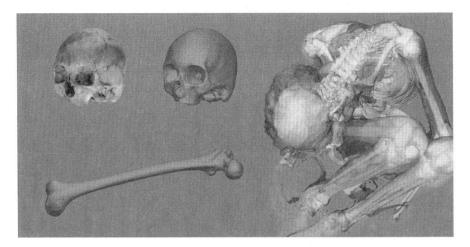

Figure 28.3 Left: 3D models of individual bones created with Structure from Motion (SfM); Right: 3D bone models 're-fitted' in a 3D model of the body with soft tissue.

of the bones of the body are suitable for comparative qualitative analysis. The models also allow for 3D animation of the process of bone movement for over time. Using Maxon Cinema 4D, a comprehensive 3D modelling, motion graphics and animation software studio, 3D animations of the process of disarticulation and bone movement were produced for visualisation, education and outreach purposes (Mickleburgh, Klinkenberg and Gluschitz, 2018).[2]

The 3D models created in this manner are also suitable for quantitative analysis of the distance and direction of movement of the bones over time. This is done using 3D GIS analysis. The 3D models are imported into ESRI ArcGIS, ArcScene 10.6 software. 3D polylines are created between pre-defined joint landmarks in order to map the distance between the points of articulation between contiguous bones in the 3D models as well as the same bones in sequential models. The relative displacement of the individual skeletal elements is calculated in distance, direction and rotation of bone displacement. These quantitative data permitted a comparison of displacement patterns between the different test cases (Figure 28.4). As a part of the ongoing actualistic experimental programme, consistent measurements across a large sample will be used to test whether 'signature' disarticulation patterns related to specific variables, such as body position, exist.

Results and discussion

Disarticulation sequence

Based on information derived from archaeological burials in temperate climates, it is thought that labile joints disarticulate within a few weeks while persistent joints are maintained for months or years (Duday *et al.*, 1990; Knüsel, 2014). The observations made in 15 body donations placed supine on the soil surface over a period of six months were therefore expected to provide particular insight into the disarticulation of the joints considered to be 'labile'. However, soft

---

2 Two short prototype examples of such 3D animations can be viewed online at: https://www.youtube.com/ watch?v= 70GX_NAttbM&feature=em-share_video_user and https://www.youtube.com/watch?time_ continue=13&v=4YcPZrNnPIc

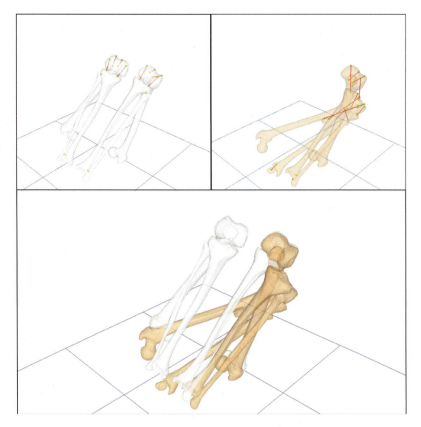

Figure 28.4 Top left: position of the lower limb bones on day 1 showing polylines in red; Top right: position of the lower limb bones after 219 days showing polylines in red; bottom: position of the lower limb bones on day 1 (white) and on day 219 (orange).

tissue decomposes more rapidly in Central Texas than in temperate climates (Suckling, 2011), and based on the first results of this research programme skeletal disarticulation appears to progress more quickly in this environment as well, so the results may also inform on disarticulations later in the sequence. The sequences of disarticulation observed in these individuals are visualised in Figure 28.5. Each line in the figure represents one body donation. If disarticulation sequences were similar over time, the lines would be expected to show a similar curve. It is clear from the figure that there is significant variation in the precise timing and sequence of joint disarticulations. Overall, the majority of body donations do show that the temporo-mandibular joints tend to disarticulate first or (in three bodies) as one of the first joints. This observation concurs with models based on archaeological burials. The overall observations and sequences do not appear to concur with the labile-persistent joint model (cf. Schotsmans *et al.*, Chapter 27, this volume).

Study of the two body donations placed in flexed body positions in open pits indicates that body position and architecture (i.e. the shape and dimensions of the pit) affect joint disarticulation due to the associated differences in pressure, gravity and support of the different body parts and bones during decomposition. The sequence of disarticulation observed in the flexed seated body donation (described in detail in Mickleburgh and Wescott, 2018) showed distinct differences from sequences described in the literature. Some joints considered to be labile, such as costo-sternal and left gleno-humeral joints, disarticulated relatively late in the sequence, while

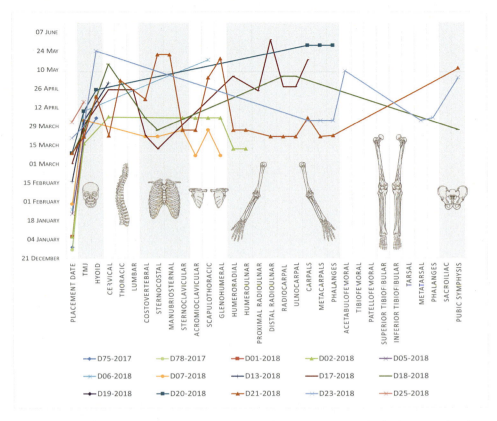

Figure 28.5 A simplified visualisation of the sequences of disarticulation in 15 body donations placed to decompose in a supine position on the soil surface. Shorter lines (i.e. with fewer points) represent body donations that showed fewer disarticulations during the period of observation.

other joints considered to be persistent (both superior tibio-fibular, right inferior tibio-fibular and atlanto-occipital joints) disarticulated relatively early in the sequence. In the case of the seated body donation, the effects of gravity and pressure related to the vertical body position appeared to be the main variable associated with the sequence of joint disarticulation. Relatively early disarticulation of the temporo-mandibular joint, predicted by the labile/persistent joint model, and also observed in the 15 supine surface donations, was not observed in this seated donation since the upright body position and movement (forward slumping) of the head and upper body throughout decomposition provided support for the joint, thus preventing disarticulation by the effects of gravity (Mickleburgh and Wescott, 2018). The late disarticulation of the costo-sternal joints can be explained both by the body position – the joints were supported in position on the pit floor after forward slumping of the thorax – as well as by age-related ossification of these joints, which maintained the articulations (Figure 28.6).

The sequence of disarticulation in the flexed supine body donation concurs more closely with the labile-persistent joint model, with the temporo-mandibular joint and the cervical vertebrae disarticulating early in the sequence. Nonetheless, this body donation also showed relatively early disarticulation of the right gleno-humeral and tibio-femoral joints (considered persistent). The supine position and open space around the body permitted closing of the inter-segmental angles between the flexed lower limbs as well as the distribution of the smaller bones of the hands and

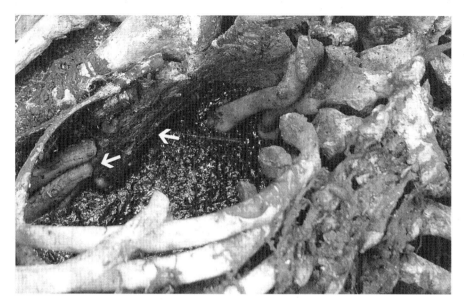

Figure 28.6 A portion of the upper thorax of body donation 1 showing the posterior aspect of the sternum (right arrow) and articulated left 5th–7th costo-sternal joints (left arrow) on day 51 of the experiment.

feet throughout the open pit. The latter was the result of the unstable position of these elements as well as two incidents of heavy rainfall during the experiment.

The fact that burial environment and body position are likely to affect the relative timing of joint disarticulation has been acknowledged previously (Duday *et al.*, 1990; Duday and Guillon, 2006; Duday, 2009). It has been pointed out that there is likely no 'single sequence' to speak of, but varying sequences depending on body position and burial environment (Peressinotto, 2007). Since the archaeological burials on which the model is based largely concern individuals in supine positions with primary voids around the body (i.e. coffin burials), caution must be applied when using it to interpret other burial modes. Despite this, the labile-persistent joint model has been widely applied in the field. The results of actualistic experimental research not only underscore the fact that body position is likely a very important variable affecting joint disarticulation, but also that sequences can be highly variable and complex, and are likely influenced by a number of other variables.

Other observations made during the course of the research thus far indicate that current knowledge and models derived from archaeological burials may not capture the entire process of skeletal disarticulation and account for all variables (Mickleburgh, 2018; Mickleburgh and Wescott, 2018). Some cases of 're-articulation' after initial disarticulation of joints were observed, a process that is not accounted for in the labile/persistent disarticulation model. In some joints, stretching of the connective soft tissues ('joint expansion') was observed for a number of days before disarticulation. Stretching was influenced by body position, gravity and moisture/ humidity in the depositional environment. Bones were no longer in anatomical relation and orientation but remained connected and supported in position by soft tissues. The lack of anatomically correct relationships between bones does not, therefore, always mean connective tissues were completely decomposed. These observations are significant because during excavation, the factors that determined the final position of the bones would not be discernible. The fact that disarticulation had taken place prior to re-articulation could not be established based on the final position of the bones, meaning that archaeological burials may not always accurately reflect the joint disarticulation sequence. Furthermore, archaeothanatology relies, among other things, on the 'unsupported' position of bones to determine the presence of primary/secondary voids in the grave, and/or to determine whether or not the body was wrapped or placed in a container. The fact that bones found out of anatomical order may be supported in position by soft connective tissues is not taken into account in the existing models of disarticulation.

Bone displacement

The relationship between bone displacement and voids was examined in five flexed body donations: two buried, two placed in open pits and one mummified prior to burial. Bones were observed to displace over greater distances when open space was present around the body from the start of the experiment, supporting the existing archaeothanatological model. As expected, based on archaeothanatological research, primary voids around the body facilitated displacement of some bones outside of the original soft tissue mass of the body. Immediate burial in soil resulted in secondary voids developing as a result of decomposition of the soft tissues. The clay-rich soils at FARF maintained secondary voids around the buried body donations for over two years, at which point the skeletonised remains were excavated. Upon excavation, clear impressions of the soft tissue mass of the body were observed in the soil (Figure 28.7). Body position was again

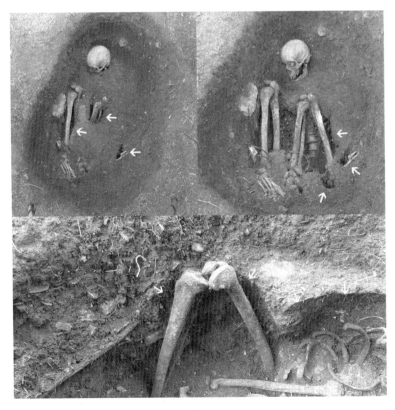

Figure 28.7 The secondary voids around the skeletonised remains of two buried body donations (delineation of the voids marked by arrows). Top left and right: supine flexed burial; bottom: upright, seated burial; the contours of the soft tissue body mass can be observed in the soil.

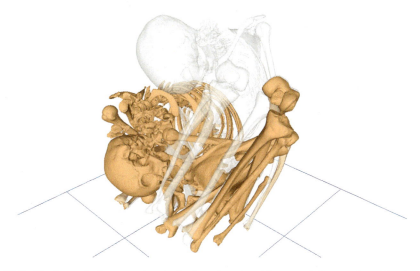

Figure 28.8 The bone displacement in a body donation placed in an upright, seated position in an open pit; white: position on day 1 of the experiment; orange: position on the final day (219) of the experiment.

observed to be an important factor in the spatial patterning of bones in both open and closed pit body placements. Differences were observed between supine flexed body positions and upright, seated body positions. The supine body position permitted less vertical bone displacement, and displacement was most prominent in the lower limbs and thorax (Figure 28.8).

Larger voids, particularly voids that allow a great degree of vertical displacement of bones due to gravity (both primary and secondary), result in greater distances of displacement of the bones than smaller voids or voids with smaller vertical dimensions. The dimensions of potential secondary voids are determined by both the soft tissue mass of the body as well as the body position. The amount of vertical bone displacement in the buried upright, seated body was very similar to the seated body placed in an open pit, due to the dimensions of the secondary void created by the vertical body position. Bones were able to move within a large secondary void that was maintained throughout skeletonisation. Buried bodies of emaciated individuals and desiccated bodies with a relatively small soft tissue mass show less displacement of the bones due to smaller secondary void development.

The role of insects

Insect activity is known to play a significant role in the loss of soft tissue during decomposition (Rodriguez and Bass, 1983; Simmons, Adlam and Moffatt, 2010). Observations made during this research highlight the fact that insects also play a role in the disarticulation and displacement of the small – and possibly also larger – bones of the body. While fly maggots focus primarily on the natural orifices and abdomen early in decomposition, their mechanical removal of soft tissues progresses rapidly throughout the body and can contribute to the loss of the tissues that maintain articulations between bones. Multiple instances of maggot activity associated with bone movement were observed in the 15 surface body donations, as well as in the two flexed open-pit body donations. Maggots attracted to the oral cavity were observed to cause post-mortem loss of single-rooted teeth from their sockets. Phalanges of the hands and feet of one donation, which were placed in a supported position on the bottom of the pit, became displaced by a large maggot mass (Mickleburgh and Wescott, 2018; Figure 28.9). In addition, in open pit placements, maggots attracted small animals such as birds and lizards, observed in time-lapse recordings, which may have contributed to the displacement of smaller bones.

The role of insects, including potential joint preference and seasonal variation in their activity, is not accounted for in current disarticulation sequences (cf. Schotsmans *et al.*, Chapter 27, this

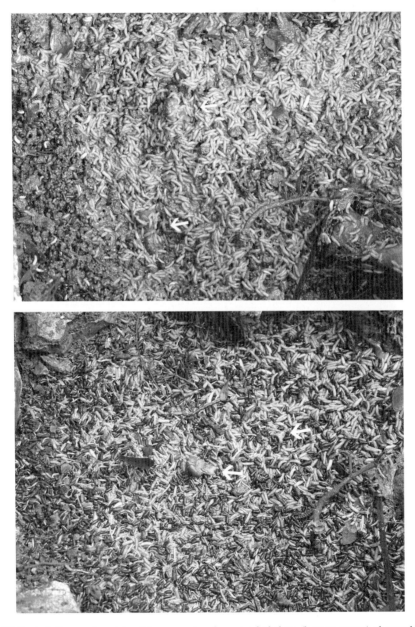

Figure 28.9 A. Left second metatarsal (top arrow) and proximal phalanx (bottom arrow) observed being displaced by maggot mass on day 14 of the experiment; B. left second metatarsal (left arrow) and a phalanx (right arrow) observed being displaced by maggot mass on day 16 of the experiment.

volume). Based on observations thus far in this research programme, it is unclear whether or not insects have a preference for particular joints of the body, such as those close to natural orifices and the abdomen, or for particular joints based on their structural, functional classification, or joint type.

Future avenues and further developments in this field of research

The initial results and outcomes of this research programme emphasise the fact that actualistic forensic taphonomy provides an exceptional and important opportunity to observe the entire process of decomposition, disarticulation and bone movement within a framework of clearly defined data collection protocols and controlled conditions. Observing the effects of different variables on the final outcome can help to identify taphonomic markers that can be used to distinguish between human actions and natural processes and to reconstruct the sequence of events from death to burial. Actualistic experiments provide information that cannot be derived from the archaeological record (cf. Schotsmans *et al.*, Chapter 27, this volume). For example, actualistic research could help resolve the question of whether or not particular joints are preferred by insects due to differences in accessibility or soft tissue mass and structure between joints. Experiments could likewise provide insights into the effects of different types of voids, clothing and coverings (this programme) or containers (cf. Alfsdotter, 2021) on disarticulation and bone movement. In order to develop and improve archaeothanatological methods and models, it is important to collect actualistic data from robust sample sizes that include control groups and to conduct replication studies studies in different environments (cf. Schotsmans *et al.*, 2017). Due to the fact that archaeothanatology relies on close observation and interpretation of the spatial distribution of bones within the burial environment, further development of both qualitative and quantitative analysis of actualistic spatial data represents an important area for continued research. The 3D GIS method developed in this research programme shows great potential, but for this method to generate the required data to assess if specific spatial patterns can be associated with specific variables, sample sizes must be increased.

Based on the results of the programme thus far, an important improvement of the 3D documentation and analysis protocol developed is the use of full-body post-mortem computed tomography (PMCT) to document the 3D soft tissue mass as well as the complete skeleton of human body donations at the start of the experiments. The method developed for this programme using retrospective positioning ('re-fitting') of the bones in the 3D models of the bodies during decomposition was found to be very cost-effective and successful in the analysis of individually placed bodies with normal or low BMI. However, greater corpulence poses a problem for re-fitting. In addition, this method is time-consuming because creating 3D models of each bone using SfM requires a large number of photographs and lengthy image processing, and is therefore not optimal for analysis of larger samples. Furthermore, for the mass grave experiment initiated in spring 2021, accurate retrospective positioning of the bones in the 3D models of the soft tissue mass is not feasible due to the close, commingled position of the bodies. The distinct taphonomic environment of a mass grave can lead to the displacement of bones over relatively large distances, in particular small bones which can fall into voids created by soft tissue decomposition (Sutherland, 2000; Tuller, Hofmeister and Daley, 2008; Duday, 2009; Cabo *et al.*, 2012). In order to accurately and precisely document the initial position of each individual bone within its soft tissue mass, all nine body donors in the mass grave experiment were fully CT scanned prior to placement.

Finally, it is important that the continued development of actualistic forensic taphonomic experiments for (forensic) archaeological contexts is rooted in an interdisciplinary approach.

While a major focus of the forensic taphonomy research programme described in this chapter is the collection of disarticulation and bone displacement data, the broader programme includes (among other studies) research on the effects of decomposition and diagenesis on the isotopic composition of different body tissues over time (Kootker *et al.*, 2020), research on the potential of using protein biomarkers for assessing the post-mortem interval and age-at death estimations (Mickleburgh *et al.*, 2021), and research on the use of the thanatomicrobiome for human identification and post-mortem interval estimation. Each of the human body donations are of immeasurable value to science and medico-legal investigation, and the interdisciplinary approach of the project is intended to achieve in the greatest possible scientific gain. The collection of a range of data on the same body donations means that data can be studied and interpreted within the context of a highly detailed set of taphonomic observations, as well as to address other lines of enquiry.

Acknowledgements

The authors would like to express their sincerest gratitude to the individuals who donated their bodies and their next of kin. Without them, this research would not have been possible. We also wish to thank the graduate students and our colleagues at the Forensic Anthropology Center at Texas State University, in particular Tim Gocha, J.P. Fancher, Sophia Mavroudas, Courtney Coffey Siegert, Lauren Meckel, Nandar Yukyi, Nicole Crowe, Chloe McDanald, Devora Gleiber, Cassie Skipper, Marilyn Isaacs, Hailey Duecker, Megan Veltri, Chaunesey Clemmons, Mindy Rogers, Briana New, Shelby Garza, and Kari Helgeson. Professor of Anatomy Dr. Jacques Spee (Maastricht University) is gratefully acknowledged for assisting with the anatomical 're-fitting' of digital bone replicas into digital replicas of bodies with soft tissue mass.

References

Alfsdotter, C. (2021). *The corporeality of death. Bioarchaeological, taphonomic, and forensic anthropological studies of human remains*. Kalmar: Linnaeus University Press.

Ambroise, D. and Perlès, G. (1975). Note sur l'Analyse Archéologique des Squelettes Humains. *Revue Archéologique du Centre de la France*, 14, pp. 49–61.

Aoudia, L., Bocquentin, F., Lubell, D. and Jackes, M. (2014). Dislocated Anatomical Blocks: A Complex Funerary Treatment from Capsian Context. *Anthropologie*, 52(3), pp. 319–328.

Appleby, J.E.P. (2016). Archaeothanatology in the English-speaking world: the belated spread and potential application of a methodologically rigorous approach to mortuary analysis. In: Ll. Lloveras and C. Rissech, eds., *What Bones Tell Us/El Que Ens Expliquen Els Ossos*. Barcelona: University of Barcelona, Seminari d'Estudis i Recerques Prehistòriques (SERP), pp. 13–24.

Barnes, P.W., Liang, S.-Y., Jessup, K.E., Ruiseco, L.E., Phillips, P.L. and Reagan, S.J. (2000). Soils, Topography and Vegetation of the Freeman Ranch. *Freeman Ranch Publication Series*, 1, p. 29.

Bass, W.M. (1997). Outdoor decomposition rates in Tennessee. In: W.D. Haglund and M.H. Sorg, eds., *Forensic Taphonomy: The Postmortem Fate of Human Remains*. Boca Raton: CRC Press, pp. 181–186.

Behrensmeyer, A.K. and Kidwell, S.M. (1985). Taphonomy's Contribution to Paleobiology. *Paleobiology*, 11, pp. 105–119.

Bouquin, D., Beauthier, J.-P. and Depierre, G. (2012). The dead do not dress: contribution of forensic anthropology experiments to burial practices analysis. 17th Conference on Cultural Heritage and New Technologies, November 2012, Vienne, Autriche. pp. 1–16.

Cabo, L.L., Dirkmaat, D.C., Adovasio, J.M. and Rozas, V.C. (2012). Archaeology, mass graves, and resolving commingling issues through spatial analysis. In: D.C. Dirkmaat, ed., *A Companion to Forensic Anthropology*. Chichester, UK: Wiley-Blackwell, pp. 175–196.

Card, A., Cross, P., Moffatt, C. and Simmons, T. (2015). The Effect of Clothing on the Rate of Decomposition and Diptera Colonization on *Sus scrofa* Carcasses. *Journal of Forensic Sciences*, 60(4), pp. 979–982.

Carson, D. (2000). *Soils of the Freeman Ranch, Hays County, Texas*. Freeman Ranch Publication Series, San Marcos: Southwest Texas State University Press, 4, pp. 1–11.

Castex, D. and Blaizot, F. (2017). Reconstructing the original arrangement, organisation and architecture of burials in archaeology. In: E.M.J. Schotsmans, N. Márquez-Grant and S.L. Forbes, eds., *Taphonomy of Human Remains: Forensic Analysis of the Dead and the Depositional Environment*. New York: John Wiley & Sons, pp. 277–295.

Dautartas, A.M. (2009). *The effect of various coverings on the rate of human decomposition*. Unpublished Master's Thesis, University of Tennessee, Knoxville.

Duday, H. (2009). *The archaeology of the dead: Lectures in archaeothanatology*. Oxford: Oxbow Books.

Duday, H., Courtaud, P., Crubezy, E., Sellier, P. and Tillier, A.-M. (1990). L'Anthropologie "de Terrain": Reconnaissance et Interpretation des Gestes Funeraires. *Bulletins et Mémoires de la Société d'Anthropologie de Paris*, 3–4, pp. 29–50.

Duday, H. and Guillon, M. (2006). Understanding the circumstances of decomposition when the body Is skeletonized. In: A. Schmitt, E. Cunha and J. Pinheiro, eds., *Forensic Anthropology and Medicine. Complementary Sciences from Recovery to Cause of Death*. Totowa: Humana Press, pp. 117–157.

Fancher, J.P., Aitkenhead-Peterson, J.A., Farris, T., Mix, K., Schwab, A.P., Wescott, D.J. and Hamilton, M.D. (2017). An Evaluation of Soil Chemistry in Human Cadaver Decomposition Islands: Potential for Estimating Postmortem Interval (PMI). *Forensic Science International*, 279, pp.130–139.

Gillham, D., Young, P. and Long, M. (2003). *Atlas of Freeman Ranch*. San Marcos: Department of Geography, Texas State University.

Harris, N.J. and Tayles N. (2012). Burial Containers – A Hidden Aspect of Mortuary Practices: Archaeothanatology at Ban Non Wat, Thailand. *Journal of Anthropological Archaeology*, 31(2), pp. 227–239.

Hill, A.P. (1980). Early postmortem damage to the remains of some contemporary East African mammals. In: A.K. Behrensmeyer and A.P. Hill, eds., *Fossils in the Making. Vertebrate Taphonomy and Paleoecology*. Chicago: University of Chicago Press, pp. 131–152.

Hofman, C.L., Hoogland, M.L.P., Mickleburgh, H.L., Laffoon, J.E., Weston, D.A. and Field, M.H. (2012). Life and Death at Precolumbian Lavoutte, Saint Lucia, Lesser Antilles. *Journal of Field Archaeology*, 37(3), pp. 209–225.

Kidwell, S.M. (1985). Palaeobiological and Sedimentological Implications of Fossil Concentrations. *Nature*, 318(6045), pp. 457–460.

Knüsel, C.J. (2014). Crouching in Fear: Terms of Engagement for Funerary Remains. *Journal of Social Archaeology*, 14(1), pp. 26–58.

Knüsel, C.J. and Robb, J. (2016). Funeral Taphonomy: An Overview of Goals and Methods. *Journal of Archaeological Science: Reports*, 10, pp. 655–673.

Kootker, L.M., Von Holstein, I.C.C., Broeders, J., Wescott, D.J., Davies, G.R. and Mickleburgh, H.L. (2020). The Effects of Decomposition and Environment on Antemortem H-Pb-Sr Isotope Compositions and Degradation of Human Scalp Hair: Actualistic Taphonomic Observations. *Forensic Science International*, 312, pp.1–10.

Lyman, R.L. (1994). *Vertebrate taphonomy*. Cambridge: Cambridge University Press.

Maureille, B. and Sellier, P. (1996). Dislocation en Ordre Paradoxal, Momification et Décomposition: Observations et Hypotheses. *Bulletins et Mémoires de la Société d'Anthropologie de Paris, Nouvelle Série*, 8(3–4), pp. 313–327.

Megyesi, M.S., Nawrocki, S.P. and Haskell, N.H. (2005). Using Accumulated Degree-Days to Estimate the Postmortem Interval from Decomposed Human Remains. *Journal of Forensic Science*, 50(3), pp. 618–626.

Mickleburgh, H.L. (2018). Actualistic experimental taphonomy of inhumation burial. In: P.M. Barone and W.J.M. Groen, eds., *Multidisciplinary Approaches to Forensic Archaeology*. Berlin: Springer Soil Forensics, Springer.

Mickleburgh, H.L., Klinkenberg, M.V. and Gluschitz, S. (2018). *Understanding human taphonomy through actualistic experiments and 3D modelling*. Presentation at TaphosNomos, Taphonomy Conference, November 2018. Preston, UK: University of Central Lancashire (UCLAN).

Mickleburgh, H.L., Schwalbe, E., Bonicelli, A., Mizukami, H., Sellitto, F., Starace, S., Wescott, D.J., Carter, D.O., and Procopio, N., (2021). The Human Bone Proteome Before and After Decomposition: Investigating the effects of Biological Variation and Taphonomic Alteration on Bone Protein Profiles and the Implications for Forensic Proteomics. *Journal of Proteome Research* 20(5): 2533–2546.

Mickleburgh, H.L. and Wescott, D.J. (2018). Controlled Experimental Observations on Joint Disarticulation and Bone Displacement of a Human Body: Implication for Funerary Taphonomy. *Journal of Archaeological Science: Reports*, 20, pp. 158–167.

Nelson, A.J. (1998). Wandering Bones: Archaeology, Forensic Science and Moche Burial Practices. *International Journal of Osteoarchaeology*, 8(3), pp. 192–212.

Ortiz, A, Chambon, P. and Molist, M. (2013). 'Funerary Bundles' in the PPNB at the Archaeological Site of Tell Halula (Middle Euphrates Valley, Syria): Analysis of the Taphonomic Dynamics of Seated Bodies. *Journal of Archaeological Science*, 40, pp. 4150–4161.

Peressinotto, D. (2007). *Chronologie de la dislocation articulaire du squelette axial et des ceintures au cours de la décomposition du cadavre. Apports à l'analyse des sépultures.* Unpublished Ph.D. thesis, University of Bordeaux, France.

Pobiner, B.L. and Braun, D.R. (2005). Applying Actualism: Considerations for Future Research. *Journal of Taphonomy*, 3, pp. 57–65.

Revised Uniform Anatomical Gift Act: https://statutes.capitol.texas.gov/Docs/HS/htm/HS.692A.htm (Last accessed 20 September 2021)

Rodriguez, W.C. and Bass, W.M. (1983). Insect Activity and Its Relationship to Decay Rates of Human Cadavers in East Tennessee. *Journal of Forensic Science*, 28(2), pp. 423–432.

Roksandic, M. (2002). Position of skeletal remains as a key to understanding mortuary behavior. In: W.D. Haglund and M.H. Sorg, eds., *Advances in Forensic Taphonomy: Method, Theory, and Archaeological Perspectives*. Boca Raton: CRC Press, pp. 99–117.

Schotsmans, E.M.J., Ueland, M., Luong, S., Prinsloo, L.C., Nizio, K., Wallman, J., Forbes, S.L. and Knüsel, C.J. (2017). Reconstructing the Mortuary chaîne opératoire in the Neolithic Near East: Conducting Actualistic Experiments for a Better Understanding of Burial Practices. *Abstracts of the 23rd Conference of the European Association of Archaeologists*, Maastricht, The Netherlands, p. 395.

Sellier, P. and Bendezu-Sarmiento, J. (2013). Différer la Décomposition: Le Temps Suspendu? Les Signes d'une Momification Préalable. *Les Nouvelles de l'Archéologie*, 132, pp. 30–36.

Shirley, N.R., Wilson, R.J. and Meadows-Jantz, L. (2011). Cadaver Use at the University of Tennessee's Anthropological Research Facility. *Clinical Anatomy*, 24, pp. 372–380.

Simmons, T. (2017). Post-mortem interval estimation: an overview of techniques. In: E.M.J. Schotsmans, N. Márquez-Grant and S.L. Forbes, eds., *Taphonomy of Human Remains: Forensic Analysis of the Dead and the Depositional Environment*. New York: Wiley, pp. 134–142.

Simmons, T., Adlam, R.E. and Moffatt, C., (2010). Debugging Decomposition Data – Comparative Taphonomic Studies and the Influence of Insects and Carcass Size on Decomposition Rate. *Journal of Forensic Science*, 55(1), pp. 8–13.

Sorg, M.H. and Haglund, W.D. (2002) Advancing forensic taphonomy: purpose, theory, and practice. In: M.H. Sorg and W.D. Haglund, eds., *Advances in Forensic Taphonomy: Method, Theory, and Archaeological Perspectives*. Boca Raton: CRC Press, pp. 3–30.

Standring, S. (2015). *Gray's anatomy: the anatomical basis of clinical practice*. Amsterdam: Elsevier.

Suckling, J.K. (2011). *A longitudinal study on the outdoor human decomposition sequence in Central Texas.* Unpublished MA Thesis, Texas State University, San Marcos, Texas.

Sutherland, T. (2000). Recording the grave. In: V. Fiorato, A. Boylston and C.J. Knüsel, eds., *Blood Red Roses: The Archaeology of a Mass Grave from Towton, AD 1461*. Oxford: Oxbow Books, pp. 36–44.

Tuller, H., Hofmeister, U. and Daley, S. (2008). Spatial analysis of mass grave mapping data to assist in the reassociation of disarticulated and commingled human remains. In: B.J. Adams and J.E. Byrd, eds., *Recovery, Analysis, and Identification of Commingled Human Remains*. Totowa, NJ: Humana Press, pp. 7–30.

Valentin, F., Bedford, S., Buckley, H.R. and Spriggs, M. (2010). Lapita Burial Practices: Evidence for Complex Body and Bone Treatment at the Teouma Cemetery, Vanuatu, Southwest Pacific. *Journal of Island & Coastal Archaeology*, 5(2), pp. 212–235.

Wescott, D.J., Wolfe-Steadman, D., Miller, N., Sauerwein, K, Clemmons, C.M., Gleiber, D.S., McDonald C.P., Meckel, L.A. and Bytheway, J.A. (2018). Validation of Total Body Score/Accumulated Degree-Day Model at Three Human Decomposition Facilities. *Forensic Anthropology*, 1(3), pp. 143–149.

Zhou, C. and Byard, R.W. (2011). Factors and Processes Causing Accelerated Decomposition in Human Cadavers – An Overview. *Journal of Forensic and Legal Medicine*, 18(1), pp. 6–9.

29

AN EXPERIMENTAL APPROACH TO THE INTERPRETATION OF PREHISTORIC CREMATION AND CREMATION BURIALS

Mogens B. Henriksen

ODENSE BYS MUSEER (ODENSE CITY MUSEUMS), ODENSE, DENMARK

Introduction

Approximately 25 000 prehistoric cremation burials have been recorded in Denmark, which indicates that cremation was practiced with varying intensity from the Mesolithic period until the end of the Viking period (*circa* 8 000 BC–*circa* AD 950). Cremation was particularly widespread towards the end of the Bronze Age (*circa* 1 000–500 BC) and in the Late Iron Age/Early Viking Age period, (*circa* AD 500–950) in Denmark as well as in the rest of Scandinavia.

Considering the large number of cremations, it is remarkable that only a few dozen well-documented pyre sites are known. For generations, this paradox was discussed by Danish archaeologists, as well as by archaeologists in other European countries where a similar discrepancy between the number of cremation burials and pyre sites had been noted. The consequence of the low number of well-documented pyre sites is that discussions of prehistoric cremation, its procedures, products and physical remains, in most cases, focused exclusively on finds from cremation burials. The conclusions from this research were frequently supplemented by contemporary observations from countries where cremation on open pyres is still practiced, or from osteological investigations of burnt bones from modern crematoria. However, until recently, data from systematic and well-documented cremation experiments were only included to a limited extent, preventing a more holistic discussion of the archaeological remains and of prehistoric cremation as a phenomenon.

This chapter presents parts of a study carried out between 1989 and 2016, where data from a large number of prehistoric cremation burials and a small number of pyre sites were used to define a number of research questions. These questions were then investigated by the application of systematic experiments, which were supplemented by data from similar experiments carried out by other researchers, as well as by data from ethnographic and ethnological sources, and forensic and pyrotechnical research.

DOI: 10.4324/9781351030625-34

Cremation graves – components and composition

Prehistoric cremation burials are characterised by great variation in their construction, the fill of the features, as well as the handling of the burnt bones and the grave goods. Differences in these characteristics have been used to divide cremations into a number of types, but this typology has generally been based on grave structural elements rather than on the processes responsible for the formation of the burials (Henriksen, 2009: 67ff; Harvig, Runge, and Lundø, 2014). In connection with the establishment of a cremation burial typology, limited interest has been shown to answer questions of whether the content of the features represent primary or secondary depositions – that is, whether the finds represent the remains of an *in situ* pyre, or whether they have been brought to the burial site from a separate pyre site. A key question in this context is whether the feature contains pyre debris or not.

To permit the archaeological material to shed light on these questions, it is essential that the excavations are recorded in detail, and that a precise and unambiguous terminology is applied. To clarify the formation processes responsible for a specific feature, it is also necessary to analyse variables in as many of the grave components as possible (Table 29.1). However, the main focus of the analysis should always be the central element of the grave, that is to say the remains of the deceased.

Most of the cremation burials from prehistoric cemeteries in Denmark represent secondary deposits, which were brought to the burial site after having been sorted at a pyre location. In most cases – and always in connection with graves devoid of pyre debris – the location of the pyre was separate from the grave. However, this observation does not provide information on the actual distance between the pyre and the grave. Frequently, the material selected at the pyre site was placed in a container (an urn) or a stone cist next to the remains of the pyre. In these cases, the pyre and the grave were located in the same place.

Prehistoric pyre sites

In situ cremations, cremations which were not manipulated after the pyre had burnt down, consist of a very small group of pyre sites. This group is generally dated to the Neolithic period and the earliest part of the Bronze Age in Southern Scandinavia, and includes cremated human remains and structural elements of timber and of stone. In these cases, it is hypothesised that the structure and location and not the deceased person may have been the focus of the event. All other pyre sites have been manipulated to some extent after the completion of the cremation, which affected the distribution and composition of the pyre debris. The archaeological material does not include any furnaces, but a small number of timber-built structures are known. Posts may have functioned as stabilising elements in connection with the construction of the pyre, or as elements in actual platforms on which the cremation took place; possible cremation platforms are known from the Roman Iron Age (AD 200–375). Only a very small number of pyre sites include paved areas or pits (Henriksen, 2016: 46ff).

Most of the well-documented pyre sites in Denmark have been dated to the Late Bronze Age or the Late Iron Age/Viking Age period, and in most cases, these features were discovered

Table 29.1 Variables associated with cremation burials

Elements in cremation graves	Analysis parameters
Burnt bones	Amount, size of fragments, location
Pyre debris	Amount, selection, location
Pyre goods	Selection, handling, location
Miscellaneous (e.g. fire-cracked stones, burnt clay)	Amount and location

underneath burial mounds, which protected the remains of the pyre sites against natural and cultural destruction processes. The small number of documented pyre sites from other periods were preserved by being sealed by aeolian sand, or as a result of the inclusion of structural posts that marked their location. These observations show that pyre sites that were constructed directly on top of the ground, not sealed immediately after use, were not preserved in the cultivated landscape. This is probably the main reason why the number of well-documented pyre sites is very low in Denmark, as well as across Europe in general.

The area of most well-documented pyre sites does not exceed that covered by an adult human being in a supine position. A small group of features exceed an area of *circa* 3 × 2 m, and they all seem to have been associated with unusual mound constructions and/or exclusive burial goods, indicating that the size of the pyre had a social dimension. The thickness of the layer of pyre debris is typically 2–5 cm, rarely more, and in most cases, the effect on the ground beneath the pyre was limited. Some *in situ* cremations represent the processing of several bodies at the same time, but in most cases, one person was cremated at a time, and the pyre site was used only once. Usually, the pyre debris contains only limited amounts of burnt bone and pyre goods, and the remains left at a pyre site are frequently so sparse that they may be missed entirely during an excavation, or misinterpreted.

What processes affected the cremated remains?

Burnt bones and burial goods from cremations and pyre debris are both characterised by notable physical effects. Frequently, pottery vessels would have fragmented into tiny slivers and spalls, and the recovered sherds only represent small parts of the original vessels. Larger iron objects tend to have buckled and/or they broke into small fragments. Similarly, the remaining burnt bones tend to represent only a small percentage of what would have been produced in the cremation of a complete individual (Henriksen, 2009: 104ff).

Generally, objects and bones from cremation burials and pyre sites show signs of extreme physical effects caused by the cremation process. In addition, the finds may have been exposed to handling before, during, as well as after the cremation. The remains were also exposed to natural destruction processes after deposition in the ground, and not least those associated with the archaeological investigations, during and after the excavation (Schiffer, 1987, 47ff; Henriksen, 2009: 35ff). As a result, when the archaeologist attempts to interpret the prehistoric cremation process on the basis of the contents of a cremation burial, it should be borne in mind that several processes had an influence on the material in question, and that it is difficult to assess the specific effects of those processes on the remains (Figure 29.1).

To permit the individual components from pyre sites and cremation burials to be used as part of the reconstruction of the procedures, products and physical remains of the cremation process, it is necessary to be able to isolate variables relating to intentional human activities from those relating to other physical actions. It is impossible to do this without detailed knowledge of the effects of the cremation process, and it is not possible to generate this knowledge entirely from the archaeological evidence alone. For this reason, data and observations from cremation experiments are an asset to cremation analyses and are the focus of this chapter.

The experimental approach

Over the last 150 years, more than 120 experiments have been carried out by different researchers to shed light on aspects of the prehistoric cremation process (Henriksen, 2016: 104ff). More than 40 of these experiments focused on the cremation of larger animals as part of a controlled programme, but detailed results have only been presented from a small number of these experiments

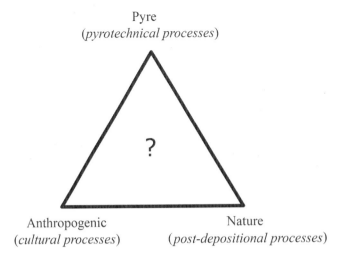

Pyre
(*pyrotechnical processes*)

?

Anthropogenic
(*cultural processes*)

Nature
(*post-depositional processes*)

Figure 29.1 The components of cremation burials and pyre sites are formed from a combination of three factors: the pyre, human activity and natural destruction processes.

presenting very similar results (Henriksen, 1991, 1993; Lambot, 1994; Becker *et al.*, 2006; Jonuks and Konsa, 2007; Marshall, 2011).

Several experiments were based on similar aims and objectives, and considerable resources have been spent on the repetition of the same kinds of experiments, simply because the individual researchers were unaware of the work of others, including the four experiments the author carried out during the period 1989–1992. The latter experiments have been labelled H1–H4 here and include excavation of three of the experimental pyre sites. In addition, a number of small-scale experiments were undertaken in 2013–2016, focusing on the cremation of 'green' and dry bones to shed light on how these different types of bones appeared after cremation, for example, if a pyre was extinguished by dousing it with water. Other small-scale experiments carried out by the author focused on producing material for subsequent crushing experiments, as well as for experiments to test how the remains reacted to exposure to acids and alkalines. The latter experiments were carried out to investigate the taphonomic aspects of deposition in an aggressive environment. Some results from experiments H1 and H4 have been published in Danish (Henriksen, 1991, 1993), whereas selected results from the four bigger experiments have been published in English (Henriksen, 2019). At present, a complete account of the project is only available in the form of the author's Ph.D. thesis in Danish (Henriksen, 2016).[1]

Experiments H1–H4: research questions, experimental set-up and initial observations

The four cremation experiments were organised with the aim to elucidate a number of specific problems regarding variables related to the construction of the pyre, the process of cremation, the products of the cremation, the sorting of material from the burnt-down pyre, as well

---

1 The author's supervisor was Senior Lecturer Henriette Lyngstrøm, Saxo-instituttet, Københavns Universitet in Denmark and the viva examiners were Senior Lecturer Liv Nilsson Stutz, Emory University (USA), Professor Frands Herschend, Uppsala University (Sweden) and Senior Lecturer Mikkel Sørensen, Saxo Instituttet, Københavns Universitet (Denmark).

Figure 29.2   Experiment H3, 27 minutes after ignition. Note the pig corpse on top of the pyre (Photograph: M. B. Henriksen, 21 October 1990).

as post-depositional effects on a buried pyre site (Figures 29.2 and 29.3). The main research problems are summarised in Table 29.2.

In this chapter, only the experiments and selected results in general will be presented, focusing on elements which may explain selected aspects of the archaeological material. The detailed experimental setup is summarised in Table 29.3.

In all four cases, wood from mixed deciduous trees was used as fuel, with adult pig carcasses *(Sus scrofa domesticus)* as substitutes for human bodies. Although human and pig skeletons differ in important ways, this animal was used as a research proxy because its size and mass correspond roughly to that of an adult human being. As the experiments aimed to clarify many other problems other than the osteological ones, the use of pigs was the best option.

The pyres were generally box-shaped, and in three cases (H2–H4), the pyre was placed over a pit. The archaeological literature suggests that pits were structural elements of the pyres, and that they would have had a chimney effect which would increase the effectiveness of the cremation

Figure 29.3 Experiment H4, 30 minutes after ignition. Note the pig limbs on the pyre (Photograph: M.B. Henriksen, 6 September 1992).

process (McKinley, 2000: 38ff.). In these three experiments, posts were hammered into the ground to stabilise the fuel. Three of the pig carcasses were placed within or on top of the pyre, whereas in experiment H2, the fuel was placed on top of the body (Table 29.3). The pits of three experiments varied in size ranging from 0.15 to 0.6 m depth (Table 29.3). The pig carcasses were accompanied by fragments of pottery, metal, and glass in order to test whether it would be possible to retrieve these pieces during sorting of the pyre debris, as well as to see how the cremation process affected them.

The four cremation experiments corroborated each other, and it was possible to characterise the development of the cremation process and the disintegration of the body in four phases. The *first phase* of the cremation process began with the igniting of the pyre and the beginning of the burning of it. It was observed that few flames developed while there was considerable smoke. When the fire took hold and spread to larger parts of the pyre stack, the temperature increased

Table 29.2 Thematic summary of the main research questions relating to experiments H1–H4

The construction of the pyre	The cremation	The feature	Post-cremation problems	Products
The construction of the pyre	The handling and position of the body	The effect of the pyre burning down naturally versus the effect of dousing the pyre with water	The sorting of material from the burnt-down pyre – invested time, complicated/ uncomplicated	Components from the burnt-down pyre – amount and nature
A pit underneath the pyre versus cremation on the surface	The course and duration of the cremation	The spatial distribution and nature of the pyre debris	The handling of grave goods and bones	Effects of the cremation on the soft tissues of the body and the skeleton
The effect of supporting posts	Smoke, sounds and smells during the process	Effects of the pyre on the surface of the ground	Formation processes relating to a buried pyre site	Effects of the cremation on accompanying equipment
Fuel – nature and amount	Complicated/ uncomplicated			

Table 29.3 Data from cremation experiments H1–H4

Experiment	Fuel	Size of pyre stack	Weight of pig	Location of corpse	Pit depth	Posts	Post cremation activity	Time between cremation and excavation
H1	*c.* 2 m³	2.0 × 1.5 × 1.2 m	*c.* 65 kg	Inside pyre stack	0	0	Sorting	1 day
H2	*c.* 1 m³	1.9 × 0.9 × 1.3 m	52 kg	Below pyre stack	0.15 m	6	Sorting, covering, excavation	23 years and 1 day
H3	*c.* 1 m³	1.2 × 1.2 × 1.2 m	63 kg	On pyre stack	0.2 m	4	Covering	Not excavated
H4	*c.* 3/4 – 1 m³	1.2 × 1.0 × 1.0 m	35 kg	Inside pyre stack	0.6 m	3	Covering, excavation	21 years and 9 months

significantly[2] but there was less smoke. The first phase had a duration of 10–15 minutes, with the corpse only affected to a limited degree.

During the *second phase* of the process, the entire stack became enveloped in fire, the flames were turbulent, and the temperatures were high, resulting in the production of much less smoke. The natural flow of the heat led the flames towards the top of the stack, with the highest temperatures were probably found at this point or immediately above the stack.

---

2 Temperatures were not measured electronically (as it was not an option in those days). Exact temperatures are not really relevant, as a successful combustion is a result of a combination of temperature, oxygen and time. Moreover, there is no 'average temperature' in an open fire as often stated in archaeological and osteological literature; the temperatures vary considerably from 'zone' to 'zone' in the pyre. In the top of the pyre (the absolute hot-spot), the temperature in an open, stable pyre will rise to more than 1 000°C when the fire is at its peak.

As the fuel was consumed, the pyre stack began to implode vertically and, if the construction became unstable, the corpse and the grave goods tended to slide out of the stack. It was therefore important to watch and maintain the pyre during this phase, when the supporting posts occasionally disintegrated.

If the corpse was placed at the top of the stack, it would be affected most heavily at the start of Phase 2, and the decomposition of the soft tissue would begin with scorching and charring, followed by crazing of the skin. During this phase, the thermal effects on the soft tissue cause the ligaments to contract, the limbs and extremities to flex, and the body takes on a pugilistic posture (cf. DiMaio and DiMaio, 2001). During this phase, peripheral bones were exposed, particularly at the extremities, and these bones were affected by the heat in such a way that they turned white and twisted along their long axes.

The *third phase* of the cremation process observed during the experiments began approximately one hour after the ignition of the pyre. During this phase, the fuel and the soft tissue of the corpse disintegrated almost completely. The supporting posts disintegrated and broke at the transition between Phase 2 and 3, or at the beginning of Phase 3. Only peripheral and possibly collapsed parts of the stack remained unaffected by the fire, whereas most of the wood was noticeably charred or had been turned into ash. The power of the flames decreased, and the fire reached a point of equilibrium. Particularly at the beginning of Phase 3, the pyre did not need to be watched, but towards the end of this phase, the remains of the fire had to be maintained and fuel needed to be added to permit the corpse to be cremated completely.

At the beginning of Phase 3, the entire surface of the corpse was charred, and the disintegration of the extremities was more or less completed. Following this, the disintegration of the torso accelerated, and the ribs, the spine and the pelvis became exposed. The disintegration of these parts only began when the peripheral bones had calcined completely, and when the fire had used much of its energy.

The *fourth phase* of the cremation process began approximately two hours after the ignition of the pyre, when the stack collapsed to form a heap of ash, embers and charred, but still burning wood fragments. If the fire did not receive additional energy in the form of fuel, it would have burned out when the organic material in the stack has been transformed into ash. New fuel had to be added no later than during Phase 4 to maintain a sufficiently high temperature around the remaining parts of the torso, thick layers of soft tissue and liquid-bearing intestines had not yet disintegrated. The deeper-lying bones, such as femora, humeri, pelvis and vertebrae, were only exposed during this phase, and subsequently disintegrated. As these body parts include the most robust bones of the body, such as the femur and *ossa coxae*, they are least likely to calcine completely. During Phase 4, watching the fire is therefore the most important part of the cremation process, and it is particularly important to maintain contact between the remaining body parts and the fuel, as the largest and most liquid-bearing parts of the body may otherwise turn into cremation slag (cf. Henderson, Janaway and Richards, 1987).

Towards the end of Phase 4, the pyre started to smoke slightly again due to the temperature stagnating when the fuel lost most of its energy. Furthermore, at this point, the pyre was starved of oxygen due to the accumulation of a thick ash layer at the base of the stack. Body parts and artefacts that were covered by this layer were less affected by the fire due to the insulating effects of the ash.

The course of the cremation process was more or less identical during the four experiments, but it was obvious that placing the corpse at the top of the stack, where the effects of the heat and the circulation of the oxygen were greatest, resulted in the most effective cremation of the body. During experiments H3 and H4, the stack was so high that the corpse was located 1.2 m and 0.6 m above the ground, respectively, which raised the centre of gravity substantially. In these

Figure 29.4 Experiment H4, excavation of the bottom of the second half of the pit, 21 years after the cremation experiment. Notice the dark grey and reddish zone of heat impact on the glacial sediments to the left – and the large number of large lumps of charcoal (Photograph: M.B. Henriksen, 6 July 2013).

cases, the supporting posts proved highly effective in preventing the stack from falling in, which would have resulted in incomplete cremation of the body. The posts disintegrated and broke *circa* 50–75 minutes after the ignition of the pyre – that is, at the transition between Phases 2 and 3 – but at this stage, the stack had collapsed to such an extent that they were no longer needed.

The different pit depths beneath stacks H2–H4 did not appear to influence the course of the cremation in any way, neither positively nor negatively. However, the 0.6 m-deep pit underneath stack H4 still contained burning embers 21 hours after the last addition of fuel, and it was therefore not possible to initiate the sorting of the pyre debris immediately after the cremation.

When the experimental pyres had burnt down, the cremation sites were documented and recorded. Experimental stack H1 was sorted, and so was H2. Afterwards, H2 was covered by soil and grass turf, and then excavated in 2013. This permitted recording of post-depositional formation processes of a sorted pyre site 23 years after the event. Stack H3 was covered with soil and grass turf without sorting, and at this point of time (2021), it has not yet been excavated. H4 was also covered by soil and grass turf, and the first half of the stack was excavated nine months after the cremation process, whereas the second half was excavated in 2013, 21 years after the process (Table 29.3; Figure 29.4).

The duration of the cremation process

Each cremation experiment was completed within 5–7.5 hours (Table 29.4). This corresponds to the time expenditure of comparative experiments from which detailed data have been published (Lambot, 1994; Becker *et al.*, 2006; Jonuks and Konsa, 2007; Graefe *et al.*, 2011; Marshall, 2011). It is difficult to calculate the duration of a cremation precisely, as the process involves a large number of variables. First and foremost, this is the case when the cremation is carried out in or on an open pyre (a pyre without a furnace construction), which in itself represents an

Table 29.4 Data relating to the physical remains and products of the experiments. As H3 was not excavated, there are no data concerning the burnt bones from this feature

Experiment	Duration of cremation	Extension of ash layer	Weight of burnt bones	Largest fragments	Ratio between weight of corpse and burnt bones
H1	7 h 30 m	3.0 × 2.0 m	0.995 kg	5 cm	6.53%
H2	7 h	1.9 × 1.7 m	0.720 kg	7 cm	7.22%
H3	5 h	1.95 × 1.55 m	–	–	–
H4	6 h 30 m	2.0 × 1.6 m	0.394 kg	7.5 cm	8.88%

uncontrolled situation. This is an important reason why it is not possible to uncritically apply ethnographic observations as direct parallels to prehistoric cremations.

Whereas it is easy to define the beginning of the process as the time when the stack is ignited, the end of the cremation process is a considerably more diffuse concept. The reason for this is that the duration of the cremation is defined not only by physical factors, such as the size of the pyre and the corpse, but also by subjective demands of those arranging and taking part in the cremation process. These demands may relate to the *purpose* of the cremation, as well as to the demands of the participants in terms of the *process* and its *products*. The archaeological evidence suggests that these demands varied across time as well as space. The definition of the duration of a cremation is therefore only relevant when discussing minimum time expenditure expected from an open pyre in terms of delivering products resembling the components recorded from prehistoric pyre sites and cremation burials. The observations from experiments H1–H4 show that the combustion of a body of the same size as an adult human in an open pyre would typically last 5 to 8 hours – depending on the physical factors – and usually requires 1–2 m^3 of wood.

The physical remains of the pyre

During the excavation of stack H1, it was observed that the heat had only affected the grass-covered surface below the pyre to a limited degree, and discolouration (reddening) of the soil was noted in only a few small lumps of clay. A thin grey-black crust was observed at the bottom of the 0.15 m-deep pit below stack H2, but the surface around the pit had not been affected. When the pit was re-excavated 21 years later, the crust had more or less been dissolved, and no discolouration of the soil was recorded. Stack H4 was constructed on top of a 0.6 m-deep pit, which had been dug into glacial sediments, and a clear crust had developed at the surface of the pit sides, as well as on top of the upcast around the pit. The crust was reddish (oxidised) towards the top of the pit and grey-black (reduced) towards the bottom of the feature. The crust was clearly visible during the excavation of both pit halves, also during the second half, as mentioned, excavated 21 years after the cremation (Figure 29.4). The marked heat effect of the pit sides corresponds to observations made in connection with the excavation of provincial Roman features of the *bustum* type, where the cremation took place on top of an open pit (Blaizot, 2009: 157).

It is therefore possible to conclude that the downwards heat effect of a pyre results in notable red burn marks, only if the pyre had been constructed on exposed subsoil, whereas a thin cover of humic soil or grass has an insulating effect and does not leave downward heat marks. A red crust was not observed in connection with the spatially and temporally widely distributed cremation pit graves from the Late Bronze Age and Early Iron Age. These graves have been incorrectly interpreted as the remains of a pyre construction containing primary deposits (Arcini, 2005; cf. Henriksen, 2019). Furthermore, in pit H4, it was noted that the lower fill consisted entirely of charcoal, *circa* 100 litres in total, and that burnt bones and burial goods were only present in a well-defined layer towards the top of the pit. This well-defined stratigraphy has also been recorded from cremations of *bustum* type, but never in cremation pit graves. This lack of evidence indicates that the latter pit graves never formed part of pyre sites, and thus cannot be considered as primary deposits.

In connection with the experiments H2, H3 and H4, it was observed that the supporting posts generally broke just above the ground surface. The excavations in 1993 and 2013 showed that the pointed bases of the posts were still *in situ* and that they had charred upper surfaces. When H2 was re-excavated 23 years later, two pointed post bases were recovered *in situ*, while four bases were missing and may have been removed by the activities of animals or humans passing across the site during the period between the first half excavation (1990) and the re-excavation (2013) – it was not even possible to identify the postholes from these posts.

Pyre products

The first half of H1 was excavated by trowel, whereas during the sorting of the second half of the pyre remains they were winnowed with a board to permit separation of the lighter fractions from the heavier elements of burnt bone, melted glass, and other remains. The latter approach proved highly effective. The fire of pyre H2 was extinguished with water to examine the possible thermal effects of this approach on bones and grave goods, but the method resulted in charcoal and ash sticking to them. It was subsequently concluded that the remains had to be sorted using a trowel. In connection with the re-excavation of the feature 23 years later, all the fills were processed by sieving and flotation. It was concluded that only a small number of very small pieces of bone had been missed during the initial excavation. These fragments were generally dark in colour and difficult to distinguish from the ash and charcoal. With regard to osteological material, 21.45 g of bone had been missed, or 3% of the total mass of bones, from the feature. The bone fragments from the re-excavation were smaller than 2 cm, with most being considerably smaller.

This experiment shows that it is possible to sort a pyre site in such a way that almost all bone fragments and fragments of grave goods can be recovered. This process appeared not to be complicated and did not exceed 1–2 hours. The excavation of a number of Late Bronze Age pyre sites in Denmark shows that a similar form of systematic sorting had taken place in the past (Thrane, 2004), whereas the excavation of Iron Age pyre sites indicated that artefacts as well as fragments of burnt bone had been missed (Henriksen, 2009: 82ff). Both forms of sorting processes represent deliberate methods of selection, but the presence of relatively large numbers of artefacts and bone fragments is not necessarily evidence that sorting did not take place.

In each of the four cremation experiments, the final ash layer covered an area approximately twice as large as the base of the pyre stack (Tables 29.3 and 29.4). The peripheral parts of this layer consisted predominantly of fine ash, whereas a thick ash layer with charcoal and burnt bones covered the central area immediately below the original stack. This suggests that the pyre stack collapsed vertically during the cremation in most cases. This suggestion is supported by the location of the grave goods in the burnt-out remains of the pyre; these objects were generally found almost directly below the point in the stack where they had been placed at the beginning of the cremation process. The various components of the corpse experienced similar movement within the stack, where particularly the vertebral column, ribs and larger bones, as well as those from the extremities (cf. hands and feet), although the latter were more likely to be displaced, were found in almost correct anatomical order in the ash. These bones are all characterised by having been exposed latest during the cremation, at a time when the mobile processes within the pyre had almost stopped (Figure 29.5).

Figure 29.5 Experiment H2 – the burnt-down pyre site with the torso of the skeleton in correct anatomical order. An intact pottery vessel is visible in the background (Photograph: M.B. Henriksen).

Experiments H1 and H2 created layers of pyre debris which were 0.12–0.15 m thick, but during the sorting process, the debris was scattered somewhat, and the thickness of these layers was reduced. At this stage, less than 10 litres of charcoal survived. During the cremation process, some wood slipped out of the stack, and if this fuel had not been pushed back into the flames, the amount of surviving charcoal might have been larger.

Burnt bones from experiments H1, H2 and H4 represent between 6.5% and 8.8% of the weight of the unburnt corpse (Table 29.4). The burnt bones from five other published cremation experiments (also based on the combustion of larger animals) represent between 3.8% and 5.0% of the corpse (Becker *et al.*, 2006; Jonuks and Konsa, 2007; Graefe *et al.*, 2011; Henriksen, 2016: fig. 59). It is difficult to determine whether or not the difference between the figures is due to more careful collection of burnt bones during the sorting of the debris produced by H1, H2 and H4, or whether the figures reflect variations in the intensity of the fire. Investigations of the relationship between the weight of a human corpse and the amount of surviving bone show that the cremation of an adult body usually results in the production of an amount of bone corresponding to *circa* 3.5% of body weight. The corresponding figure for children is *circa* 2.5% and for foetuses *circa* 1% (Warren and Maples, 1997). Although these investigations are based on the cremation of bodies in modern crematoria, the amount of surviving bone does not deviate significantly from the amount of bone produced by the cremation of larger animals in open pyres. It is also noteworthy that observations on cremation of children and foetuses in crematoria and cremation of small animals on open pyres show that even the skeletons of small children and animals do not disintegrate completely, although this is widely believed (Jæger and Johansen, 2014).

The burnt bones from all four experiments generally had a white appearance, although some incompletely calcined bones were coloured partially grey or black. These colours are described in the literature (e.g. Herrmann, 1972; Thompson *et al.*, 2017). In this experiment, the grey and black colours were particularly common for bones exposed during Phase 4 of the cremation process. These bones were crazed and twisted, and dental crowns had exploded, as is often seen in prehistoric cremation burials. The fragmentation ratio of the bones from the experiments also corresponded well with the figures from prehistoric features. Additionally, the bones seem to have been fragmented during the cremation process due to the heat of the pyre or from pyre collapse. Some bones may also have been fragmented when new fuel was added during the cremation process, or when the final layers of fuel and debris were manipulated to maintain contact between the corpse and the fuel. The experiments showed that it was neither necessary to clean (wash) the bones or crush them to create a product similar to the burnt bones from archaeological contexts. In addition, the bones may have been affected by post-depositional processes, such as the archaeological handling, which could have fragmented the bone material further (McKinley, 1994).

Reconstructed Iron Age pottery vessels and large potsherds were included in experiments H2–H4 to test how the cremation process affected ceramic material. Approximately 10 cm-high beakers formed part of experiments H2 and H3, and they sank vertically through the collapsing stack without being greatly affected. When the fire had burnt out, they were recovered intact from the ash layer. During experiments H2 and H3, larger sherds and vessels cracked at an early stage of the cremation process, and some conjoining parts were separated horizontally by as much as 0.9 m. Many recovered sherds were the size of a hand or larger despite the effects of the heat, the collapse of the stack, and the physical handling of the fire during the cremation. This size of sherd is rarely encountered in prehistoric cremation burials, where secondarily burnt pottery is usually only represented by tiny sherds. The small size of the sherds from archaeological contexts therefore probably reflects actions carried out between the sorting of the pyre debris and the deposition of the burnt material in the grave (Henriksen, 2009: 95ff).

During experiments, H2–H4 reconstructed Iron Age glass beads were also placed in the pyre stack. Most of them were recovered during the excavation of the features, and they included entirely unaffected pieces, broken and partially melted pieces, and amorphous glass lumps. This degree of variation was recorded within the individual experiments despite the fact that they had been deposited together as a necklace that had been placed around the neck of the experimental corpse. The variation reflects the physical dynamics of a pyre, not least during Phase 2, where the differential collapse of the stack results in some beads rolling out of the stack before they are affected by the fire, whereas others end up in layers of embers where they are deformed completely. This level of variation corresponds with the variation observed in prehistoric cremation burials (Henriksen, 2009: 135ff).

At the three systematically excavated experimental pyre sites (particularly H4), artefact categories were recovered which had not been placed deliberately in the pyre stack, such as fire-crazed flint and clay which had been burnt red. At pyre site H4, no less than 714 g of burnt flint and 60 g of burnt clay were recovered. Although objects belonging to both categories may occur at prehistoric pyre sites and in cremation burials, they are generally not recovered in amounts corresponding to those of H4. This probably reflects the fact that, in this case, the glacial deposits and their content of flint were exposed to the heat from the pyre.

From the experiments to archaeological evidence

The experiments show that at an unsorted and undisturbed pyre site, it should be possible to recover most of the cremated skeleton, and that the bones of the torso of the individual should be recovered in approximate anatomical order. The amount of burnt bone in prehistoric features is usually smaller than one would expect on the basis of the experiments, and it is suggested that this may largely be due to post-depositional processes. However, apart from mechanical effects and frost-thaw action, burnt bones tend to be quite resistant to degradation. To investigate this further, a laboratory experiment was carried out that included the exposure of calcined lamb bones to an aggressive chemical environment, such as an acid environment with a pH value of 2 and a basic environment with a pH value of 12. After eight months, there was no evidence of decomposition of the bone tissue, and there was also no loss of bone by weight either.[3] It is therefore unlikely that the frequently very low amount of burnt bone encountered in prehistoric cremation burials was produced exclusively by chemical and mechanical decomposition. It is more likely that the missing bones reflect the intentional behaviour of the participants in the process, as well as various post-depositional disturbances.

The experiments also showed that if pottery, bronze and glass objects were placed in the pyre, they should be recovered from the pyre debris in amounts roughly corresponding to the amount placed in the pyre. However, the physical form of the objects may have been altered considerably by the effects of the heat and other physical processes during the cremation. When these artefact categories are encountered at prehistoric pyre sites, and particularly at cremation burials, they are usually quite fragmented, and they appear to have been deposited following the *pars pro toto* principle. As shown by experiment H4, iron objects are usually very stable, and they tend not to become deformed by the heat. However, iron objects are also usually found as deformed (bent) pieces and commonly in the form of a fragment. These observations add to the evidence which suggests that cultural processes took place between the cremation process and the deposition of the remains in the grave. It seems these pieces were physically altered after the cremation.

The combination of observations and data from the current and other cremation experiments as well as archaeological evidence suggests that prehistoric pyre sites were sorted to a varying, but usually high, degree. It is also obvious that only some of the material removed from the pyre sites was deposited in the cremation burials. This is particularly obvious where a container or structure with burnt bones and possibly pyre goods was left at the pyre site after the cremation. In these cases, large parts, or most, of the material surviving the cremation was not deposited in the grave. This suggests that the content of the grave probably represents the deposition of an intentional selection of remains from a multi-phased sequence of selective actions (Table 29.5).

As the burnt bones and the burial goods are usually represented in prehistoric cremation burials in the form of a *pars pro toto* selection, they represent frequently, if not mostly, a form of symbolic deposition rather than an actual burial – if a burial is defined as the deposition of a complete or an almost complete cremated corpse. The archaeological evidence suggests that the

---

3 This experiment was called H13, and it was carried out at Odense City Museums in 2015–2016 (Henriksen, 2016).

Table 29.5 Cultural processes involved in the handling of burnt bones and grave goods in connection with prehistoric cremations

1	Selection of objects for pre-cremation rituals
2	Selection of objects for the pyre
3	Objects selected from the pyre debris
4	Handling of selected material (bent, broken, crushed)
5	Sorting of the handled material
6	Deposition of sorted material (3 and 5) in a burial
7	Deposition of sorted material (3 and 5) in other contexts – or re-circulation

material missing from pyre sites and cremation burials may have been deposited in a number of different contexts. There are examples of the deposition of material from one cremation in several different graves, deposition in middens and pits in cemeteries, and some finds from wetland contexts and domestic settlements are clearly identifiable as material from sorted pyre sites (Henriksen, 2016: 196). In addition, some material may have been deposited in contexts (e.g. water) characterised by poor preservation – or it may have been re-circulated.

Conclusion

Over a number of decades, research into burnt bones from prehistoric cremation burials focused almost entirely on the temperature of the pyre (e.g. Holck, 1997: table 26), which led to a number of erroneous conclusions regarding the construction of the pyre stack, as well as the procedures and interpretation of the cremation process (Henriksen, 2016: 123ff, 2019). However, it has become generally accepted that the character of the osteological material is a product of the *intensity* of the cremation, where not only temperature but also the duration of the cremation process and the supply of oxygen are important parameters (e.g. Duday, 2009: 150; Thompson, 2015: 5). Together, these three elements form the so-called 'fire triangle', but as this study has shown, the triangle in itself does not fully explain the appearance of the components of the prehistoric cremation burials. The model is missing the physical effects on the components caused by the collapse of the stack, the human handling during and after the cremation process, as well as post-depositional factors (Figure 29.6). This study shows that the demands and expectations of the participants in the cremation process also had a clear effect on the character, the composition, and the number of products deposited in the grave (Henriksen, 2016: 240f, 2019).

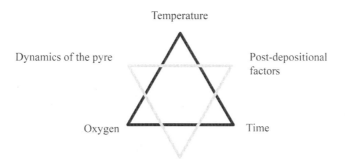

Requirements for the process and its products from the people carrying out the cremation

Figure 29.6 The evidence used by archaeologists and biological anthropologists to analyse prehistoric cremation rituals is a product of a number of physical and cultural factors.

In conjunction with other comparative research, experiments H1–H4 show that – given the right conditions and know-how – cremation of a human corpse in an open fire is not a *complicated* process. However, the many physical and cultural factors affecting the course of the cremation define the process as *complex*, and the people controlling the event are able to adjust the complexity as they wish. The sorting of the burnt-through pyre, and the location of the burnt bones and the burial goods amongst the pyre debris, was also uncomplicated and did not require much time. In summary, it was not necessary to involve any *technical* specialists to secure the successful completion of the cremation process, from stacking the pyre to the final deposition of the deceased.

The basic hypothesis of early research into prehistoric cremation customs was that the cremation process was simply a technical and clinical process, the purpose of which was to reduce and transform the corpse and its associated burial goods into products which could be deposited in a grave – exactly mirroring the activities of a modern crematorium. The multi-phased operational schemes of burial rituals, indicated by archaeological and experimental data, suggest that the processes associated with the burials may have been at least as important as the products relating to the pyre events. To permit the cremation and burial events to be completed at the right time and place, as prescribed by social and cultural conventions, it might have been necessary to involve ritual specialists. It was possible for these specialists to control and interpret the cremation and its associated activities, which constituted organised, multi-sensual events. As indicated by the experiments, these events affected not only the psychological sensory system but also the senses of sight, hearing, smell and touch, maybe even the sense of taste.

It must also be hypothesised that the processes may have involved much more than simply events at the cremation site. The actual cremation was only one event within the multi-phased operational scheme of the burial ceremony, of which little, or nothing, is known of the events taking place before the ignition of the pyre, and during and after extinguishing it. Or as put by Oestigaard (2013: 497), 'Cremation is not one, but many funeral practices'.

Acknowledgements

The author would like to thank Torben Bjarke Ballin for translating this contribution from the Danish.

References

Arcini, C. (2005). Pyre sites before our eyes. In: T. Artelius and F. Svanberg, eds., *Dealing with the Dead. Archaeological Perspectives on Prehistoric Scandinavian Burial Ritual. Riksantikvarieämbetets arkeologiska undersökningar, Skrifter 65*. Ödeshög: National Heritage Board, pp. 63–72.

Becker, M., Döhle, H-J., Hellmund, M., Leineweber, R. and Schafberg, R. (2006). Nach dem großen Brand. Verbrennung auf dem Scheiterhaufen – ein interdisziplinärer Ansatz. *Bericht der Römisch-Germanischen Kommission*. Band 86, pp. 61–195.

Blaizot, F. (2009). Rites et pratiques funéraires à Lvgdvnvm du 1er au IVe siècle. In: C. Goudineau, ed., *Rites Funéraires à Lvgdvnum*. Paris: Éditions Errance, pp. 155–185.

DiMaio, V.J. and DiMaio, D. (2001). *Forensic pathology* (Second Edition). Boca Raton: CRC Press.

Duday, H. (2009). *The archaeology of the dead. Lectures in archaeothanatology*. Oxford: Oxbow Books.

Graefe, J., Hugler, J., Pingel, C., Niven, L. and Orschiedt, J. (2011). Ein Scheiterhaufenexperiment aufgrund der Bauanleitung des Johann Ernst Clausen, Scharfrichter zu Lemgo. *Ethnographisch-Archäologische Zeitschrift*, 50, pp. 601–626.

Harvig, L., Runge, M.T. and Lundø, M.B. (2014). Typology and Function of Late Bronze Age and Early Iron Age Cremation Graves – A Micro-Regional Case Study. *Danish Journal of Archaeology*, 3, pp. 3–18.

Henderson, J., Janaway, R.C. and Richards, J.R. (1987). Cremation slag: a substance found in funerary urns. In: A. Boddington, A.N. Garland and R.C. Janaway, eds. *Death, Decay and Reconstruction. Approaches to Archaeology and Forensic Science*. Manchester: Manchester University Press, pp. 81–100.

Henriksen, M.B. (1991). Et forsøg med forhistorisk ligbrænding. Nogle kommentarer til undersøgelsen af brandgrave. In: B. Madsen, ed., *Eksperimentel Arkæologi. Studier i Teknologi og Kultur* nr. 1. Lejre: Historisk Arkæologisk Forsøgscenter, pp. 50–60.

Henriksen, M.B. (1993). Et ligbrændingsforsøg på Hollufgård – hvad kan det fortælle om jernalderens brandgrave? *Fynske Minder* 1993, pp. 99–116.

Henriksen, M.B. (2009). *Brudager Mark – en romertidsgravplads nær Gudme på Sydøstfyn.* Bind 1. Tekst. Fynske Jernaldergrave bd. 6,1. Fynske Studier 22. Odense: Odense Bys Museer.

Henriksen, M.B. (2016). *Bålets betydning: Ligbrænding i Danmarks oldtid belyst ved arkæologiske fund og ligbrændingseksperimenter.* Unpublished Ph.D. thesis, Saxo-instituttet, University of Copenhagen.

Henriksen, M.B. (2019). Experimental cremations – can they help us to understand prehistoric cremation graves? In: A. Cieslinski and B. Kontny, eds., *Interacting Barbarians, Contacts, Exchange and Migrations in the First Millennium AD. Neue Studien zur Sachsenforschung* 9. Warchau: Universität Warschau, pp. 289–296.

Herrmann, B. (1972). Zur Beurteilung von Kohlenstoffverfärbungen bei Leichenbränden. *Ausgrabungen und Funde. Nachrichtenblatt für Ur- und Frühgeschichte,* 176, pp. 275–277.

Holck, P. (1997). *A medical-anthropological study of an archaeological material on cremation burials.* Antropologiske Skrifter 1. 3rd revised edition. Oslo: Anatomisk Institutt – Universitetet i Oslo.

Jæger, J.H. and Johansen, V.L. (2014). The Cremation of Infants/Small Children: An Archaeological Experiment Concerning the Effects of Fire on Bone Weight. *Cadernos do Grupo Estudos em Evolução Humana (GEEvH),* 2(2), pp. 13–26.

Jonuks, T. and Konsa, M. (2007). The Revival of Prehistoric Burial Practices: Three Archaeological Experiments. *Folklore,* 37, pp. 91–110.

Lambot, B. (1994). Le bûcher expérimental d'Acy-Romance 11–12 Août 1989. In: Lambot, B., Friboulet, M. and Méniel, P., eds., *Le Site Protohistorique d'Acy-Romance (Ardennes) II. Les Necropoles dans Leur Contexte Régional.* Reims: Mémoires De La Société Archéologique Champénoise, 8, pp. 247–315.

Marshall, A. (2011). *Experimental archaeology: 1. Early Bronze Age cremation pyres.* British Archaeological Reports (British Series) 530. Oxford: Archaeopress.

McKinley, J.I. (1994). Bone Fragment Size in British Cremation Burials and Its Implications for Pyre Technology and Ritual. *Journal of Archaeological Science,* 21, pp. 339–342.

McKinley, J.I. (2000). Phoenix rising: aspects of cremation in Roman Britain. In: J. Pearce, M. Millett and M. Struck, eds., *Burial, Society and Context in the Roman World.* Oxford: Oxbow Books, pp. 38–44.

Oestigaard, T. (2013). Cremations in culture and cosmology. In: S. Tarlow and L. Nilsson Stutz, eds., *Handbook of the Archaeology of Death and Burial.* Oxford: Oxford University Press, pp. 497–509.

Schiffer, M.B. (1987). *Formation processes of the archaeological record.* Alberquerque: University of New Mexico Press.

Thompson, T. (2015). Fire and the body: fire and the people. In: T. Thompson, ed., *The Archaeology of Cremation: Burnt Human Remains in Funerary Studies.* Studies in Funerary Archaeology. Volume 8. Oxford: Oxbow Books, pp. 1–17.

Thompson, T.J.U., Gonçalves, D., Squires, K. and Ulguim, P. (2017). Thermal alteration to the body. In: Schotsmans E.M.J., Márquez-Grant N. and Forbes S., eds., *Taphonomy of Human Remains. Forensic Analysis of the Dead and the Depositional Environment.* Chichester: Wiley, pp. 318–334.

Thrane, H. (2004). *Fyns Yngre Broncealdergrave,* bind 1–2. Fynske Studier 20. Odense: Odense Bys Museer.

Warren, M.W. and Maples, W.R. (1997). The Anthropometry of Contemporary Commercial Cremation. *Journal of Forensic Sciences,* 42(3), pp. 417–423.

30

THE TAPHONOMIC AND ARCHAEOTHANATOLOGICAL POTENTIALS OF DIAGENETIC ALTERATIONS OF ARCHAEOLOGICAL BONE

Thomas J. Booth

NATURAL HISTORY MUSUEM, LONDON, UNITED KINGDOM

David Brönnimann

INTEGRATIVE PREHISTORY AND ARCHAEOLOGICAL SCIENCE (IPAS), UNIVERSITY OF BASEL, BASEL, SWITZERLAND

Richard Madgwick

ARCHAEOLOGY AND RELIGION, SCHOOL OF HISTORY, UNIVERSITY OF CARDIFF, CARDIFF, UNITED KINGDOM

Cordula Portmann

INTEGRATIVE PREHISTORY AND ARCHAEOLOGICAL SCIENCE (IPAS), UNIVERSITY OF BASEL, BASEL, SWITZERLAND

Introduction

Bone is a dynamic substrate in life (Lanyon and Rubin, 1984), after death (Hedges, 2002; Kendall *et al.*, 2018) and even after fossilisation (Saitta *et al.*, 2018). After an organism dies, the bone is transformed by a myriad of physical, chemical and biological processes (Hedges, 2002; Madgwick and Mulville, 2012; Madgwick, 2014; Villagran *et al.*, 2017; Kendall *et al.*, 2018). These transformations may take place during the decomposition of the body itself (Child, 1995; Bell, Skinner and Jones, 1996; White and Booth, 2014; Delannoy *et al.*, 2018), as a result of socio-cultural practices which interfere with processes of decomposition (Jans *et al.*, 2004; Nielsen-Marsh *et al.*, 2007; Madgwick, 2010; White and Booth, 2014) or transform the bone indelibly (e.g. cremation; Hanson and Cain, 2007; Lebon, *et al.*, 2010; Gonçalves, Thompson and Cunha, 2011; Squires *et al.*,

2011), as well as longer-term interactions between the bone and its depositional environment (Nielsen-Marsh and Hedges, 2000; Hedges, 2002; Reiche *et al.*, 2003; Smith *et al.*, 2007; Turner-Walker and Jans, 2008; Turner-Walker and Peacock, 2008). Strictly speaking, bone diagenesis refers to post-sedimentary taphonomic processes resulting in bone fossilisation or destruction. However, certain pre-sedimentary alterations of bone (i.e. heating) are often referred to as diagenetic, and the extent to which other transformations of bone defined as diagenetic occur pre- or post-deposition is poorly defined; therefore for convenience, all such physico-chemical changes described here are referred to a as diagenetic. Each of these processes transforms the microstructural and chemical properties of a bone in characteristic ways; therefore, ancient bone maintains an imprint of the diagenetic events to which it has been exposed, providing novel taphonomic information from bodies and bones and potential information about funerary practices.

Bone is composed of a mineral (hydroxyapatite) and protein phase, which are variably transformed by diagenetic processes. This can involve different mechanisms of degradation (i.e. biological and chemical) but also transformations of the bone through elemental exchange, infiltration by exogenous substances and autochthonous chemical reactions. The way in which these changes variably affect different aspects of the bone means that an array of analyses is required to properly quantify the whole spectrum of diagenetic change (Hedges *et al.*, 1995; Nielsen-Marsh and Hedges, 2000). These techniques can be broadly classified as histological analyses, involving visual inspection of internal microstructure (e.g. thin section light microscopy, scanning electron microscopy (SEM), micro-computed tomography (micro-CT)); those which measure organic degradation (e.g. collagen preservation using isotope ratio mass spectrometry (IRMS), accelerator mass spectrometry (AMS) or Raman Spectroscopy); those which measure alterations of the mineral phase (usually a measure of "crystallinity" defined by the Infrared Splitting Factor e.g. Fourier transform infrared (FTIR), x-ray diffraction (XRD)); and those which measure variability in chemical composition (e.g. Backscattered SEM (BSEM), Raman Spectroscopy) (Hedges *et al.*, 1995; Person *et al.*, 1995; Nielsen-Marsh and Hedges, 2000; Haynes *et al.*, 2002; Turner-Walker and Syversen, 2002; Ottoni *et al.*, 2009; Dal Sasso *et al.*, 2014, 2018; Booth, Redfern and Gowland, 2016). In addition, Mercury Intrusion Porosimetry (HgIP) quantifies porosity changes related to several forms of diagenesis (Nielsen-Marsh and Hedges 1999; Nielsen-Marsh *et al.*, 2007).

Diagenetic change is generally invisible macroscopically and diagenetic analyses often produce results that are contrary to macroscopic assessments of external bone preservation, meaning that it is a rich source of novel taphonomic data (Hedges, Millard and Pike, 1995; Hedges, 2002; Jans *et al.*, 2004). Synthesis of diagenetic and archaeothanatological approaches would provide novel applications to establishing the post-mortem fate of bones and bodies. This chapter will discuss various diagenetic changes affecting ancient bones and discuss how they can provide useful information regarding taphonomic events and funerary practices. The extent to which studies of bone diagenesis have engaged with traditional taphonomic analyses and archaeothanatological principles will be discussed to show the potential for how these methods might be synthesised in the future.

Microbial bioerosion

Degradation of internal bone microstructure by invasive microorganisms is one of the most prevalent forms of diagenesis observed in ancient bones (Turner-Walker *et al.*, 2002) (Figures 30.1–30.4). Microbes alter the bone microstructure in characteristic ways, producing distinctive tunnelling structures known as microfoci of destruction (MFD) (Hackett, 1981: 250). Hackett (1981: 250) defined four types of MFD: Wedl, linear longitudinal, lamellate and budded. Wedl tunnels differ

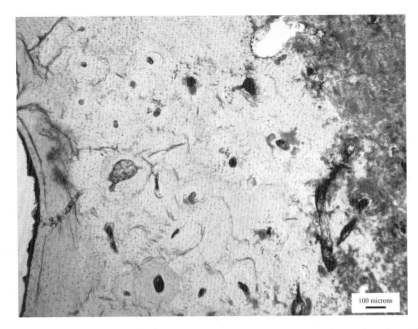

Figure 30.1 Transverse thin section of an archaeological human femoral bone focussed on the endosteal surface under normal light. The bone microstructure is generally well-preserved. Bacterial bioerosion can be observed encroaching on the right-hand side of the image.

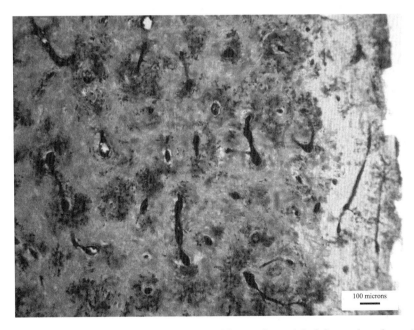

Figure 30.2 Transverse thin section of an archaeological human femoral shaft focussed on the periosteal surface under normal light. The microstructure has been extensively altered by bacterial bioerosion. Note the preservation of the periosteal fringe, dark inclusions present in natural porosities and orange-brown staining of the internal microstructure, probably indicating infiltration by iron oxides.

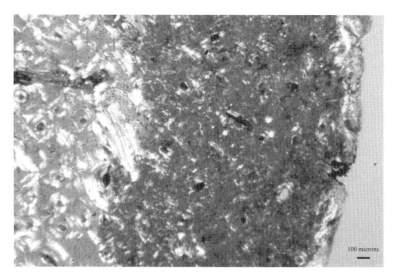

Figure 30.3 Transverse thin section of an archaeological adult femoral shaft focussed on the periosteal surface under cross-polarised light. Birefringence is present in areas of well-preserved bone on the periosteal surface and to the left of the image. Birefringence is reduced or absent in the bioeroded area.

from the other three forms in being smaller in diameter and travelling through the bone in a transverse rather than longitudinal orientation. Linear longitudinal, budded and lamellate tunnelling commonly occur together and are thought to have a similar aetiologies, and are therefore often referred to collectively as non–Wedl MFD. Several types of microbes have been identified as having colonised ancient bone, but the precise species responsible for MFD have not been

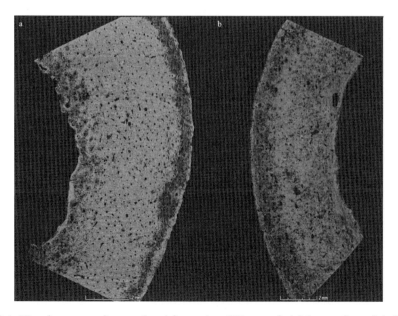

Figure 30.4 Virtual transverse slices produced from micro-CT scans of adult human femoral shafts. The bone in 4a shows minor bacterial bioerosion below the periosteal and endosteal surfaces. The bone in 4b has been bioeroded by bacteria more extensively, leaving islands of preserved bone.

determined directly (Hackett, 1981; Piepenbrink, 1986; Child, Gillard and Pollard, 1993; Grupe, Dreses-Werringloer and Parsche, 1993; Balzer *et al.*, 1997; Jackes *et al.*, 2001; Philips *et al.*, 2017). However, it is generally accepted based on the morphology of the microbial spongiform porosity, which constitutes non-Wedl MFD, that all three forms are produced by bacteria (Yoshino *et al.*, 1991; Grupe and Turban-Just, 1996; Jackes *et al.*, 2001; Turner-Walker and Syversen, 2002).

Bacterial tunnelling is the most common form of microbial alteration observed in archaeological human bones (Turner-Walker *et al.*, 2002). Anoxic or waterlogged environments inhibit osteolytic bacteria and have an overarching influence on bacterial bioerosion of bone, although this effect is variable depending on the extent to which these conditions fluctuate (Turner-Walker and Jans, 2008; Hollund *et al.*, 2011; Turner-Walker, 2012; Booth, 2016). Prolonged anoxic/waterlogged conditions at archaeological sites can often be recognised by thorough understandings of sedimentological, hydrological and geoarchaeological evidence, as well as microscopic signs of anoxic decomposition present in the bones themselves (e.g. autochthonous formation of framboidal pyrite) (Turner-Walker and Jans, 2008; Brönnimann *et al.*, 2018). The presence of bactericidal metals in the burial environment also appears to have a limiting effect on bacterial bioerosion of bone (Müller *et al.*, 2011; Mandl *et al.*, 2018).

Outside of anoxic/waterlogged conditions, studies of ancient human and faunal bone consistently find little relationship between burial environment (sediment type, pH value, etc.) and bacterial bioerosion (Jans *et al.*, 2004; Nielsen-Marsh *et al.*, 2007; Booth, 2016; Brönnimann *et al.*, 2018). In these cases, bacterial bioerosion relates to early taphonomic events that affect their exposure to soft tissue decomposition. Disarticulated faunal bone tends to show little or no bacterial bioerosion, whereas bone from articulated human and faunal bone shows high levels of bacterial attack (Jans *et al.*, 2004; Nielsen-Marsh *et al.*, 2007; Booth, 2016; Brönnimann *et al.*, 2018). This pattern has been explained by butchery practices having rapidly separated bone from decomposing soft tissue. Burial soon after death in an aerobic environment exposes the bone to maximal levels of bacterial soft tissue decomposition. Practices such as surface deposition exposure, where the majority of defleshing tends to occur as a result of insect and carnivore activity, would limit the extent to which bones are exposed to soft tissue decomposition (Fernández-Jalvo *et al.*, 2010; Vass, 2011; White and Booth, 2014). Predictable relationships between bone bioerosion and specific funerary practices have been recorded in European human bone assemblages (Booth, 2016). Real-time experiments looking at bioerosion in bone from pig cadavers recovered from a variety of depositional environments support an association between early taphonomic change and bacterial bioerosion of bone (White and Booth, 2014; Kontopoulos, Nystrom and White, 2016; Ross and Hale, 2018). These results have provoked on-going debates about how far osteolytic bacteria are enteric to an organism, and invade the bone during bodily putrefaction/decomposition, or are exogenous, and invade the bone from the soil post-skeletonisation (Booth, 2017; Kendall *et al.*, 2018). It is possible that both scenarios are true and bioerosive bacteria partly or mainly originate from the soil, but are still affected by early post-mortem treatment, for instance, if they are more attracted to bone surrounded by decomposing soft tissue or only become active in the presence of a decomposing corpse (Javan *et al.*, 2016; Zhou and Bian, 2018), hence the link with archaeothanatology.

Analysis of bacterial bioerosion of internal bone microstructures can be useful in the first instance for estimating the range of early taphonomic trajectories represented in a mortuary assemblage (Booth and Madgwick, 2016). Further experimental work is required to define precisely how specific funerary treatments may affect bacterial bioerosion (cf. Schotsmans *et al.*, Chapter 27, this volume). However, the predictable relationship between bacterial bioerosion and early taphonomic change suggests that models of soft tissue decomposition established in forensic anthropological studies can be used to guide interpretations of post-mortem treatment

(Booth, 2016). This approach would be particularly applicable to testing simple hypotheses of the extremes of expected variation in bacterial bioerosion, such as whether disarticulated assemblages of human bone were defleshed by excarnation or as a result of primary burial (cf. Booth and Madgwick, 2016).

Cyanobacterial attack in bone resembles Wedl tunnelling but is usually wider in diameter, less dendritic and exclusively located on peripheral surfaces. This is the predominant form of bioerosion seen in bones retrieved from aquatic contexts (Ascenzi and Silvestrini, 1984; Bell and Elkerton, 2008; Turner-Walker and Jans, 2008; Huisman *et al.*, 2017). Non-Wedl tunnelling is always absent from bone where the depositional history has been entirely aquatic. Cyanobacteria (blue-green algae) bore through the periosteal surface, usually in areas of bone exposed to sunlight (Bell and Elkerton, 2008). The presence of cyanobacterial attack in bones recovered from terrestrial environments would suggest that the bone or the body from which it originated had been deposited in an aquatic or highly moist environment. The presence of both cyanobacterial attack and non-Wedl MFD would indicate a complex taphonomic history involving initial terrestrial deposition followed by aquatic submersion or deposition in an environment with high humidity, either through changes in local conditions or re-deposition (Huisman *et al.*, 2017; Brönnimann *et al.*, 2018).

Wedl tunnels occur infrequently in ancient bones excavated from terrestrial contexts (Jans *et al.*, 2004; Brönnimann *et al.*, 2018). Wedl tunneling is not always confined to the peripheral periosteal surface. Wedl tunnels can appear translucent, dark or filled with bright materials in thin section (Figure 30.5). The correspondence between the shape and size of fungal hyphae and Wedl tunnelling, as well as the results of experimental work by Marchiafava, Bonucci and Ascenzi (1974) and Fernández-Jalvo *et al.* (2010) suggests that fungi are most likely responsible for Wedl MFD, although other researchers have questioned this association (Turner-Walker, 2012;

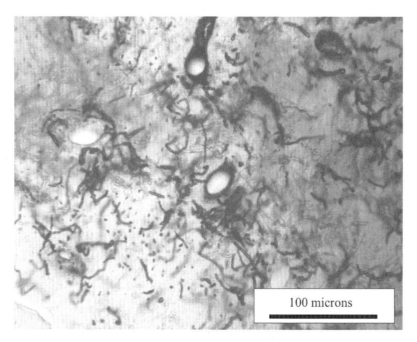

100 microns

Figure 30.5 A transverse thin section of an archaeological adult femoral mid-shaft under standard bright field light. The internal microstructure has been severely altered by Wedl tunnelling.

Kendall *et al.*, 2018). There are consistent patterns in the distribution of Wedl tunnelling among archaeological bones from terrestrial contexts. It is more commonly observed in butchered disarticulated animal bones and bones that had been deposited on ground surfaces (Jans *et al.*, 2004; Brönnimann *et al.*, 2018), which may be because disarticulated, partially fleshed, exposed and perhaps cooked bone provides an attractive substrate for the growth of airborne fungal spores. However, it may be the case that the lack of bacterial bioerosion in many disarticulated faunal bones means that Wedl tunnels are more visible. Real-time experiments with pig carcasses also identified Wedl tunnelling in bones from exposed cadavers (Kontopoulos, Nystrom and White, 2016). There is still ample uncertainty regarding the factors which promote Wedl MFD, but these patterns suggest that Wedl tunnels occur more often in bones that have remained unburied for a time (Brönnimann *et al.*, 2018), and may be indicative of excarnation (Jans *et al.*, 2004; Mandl *et al.*, 2018).

Inclusions and infiltrations

Mineral inclusions (substances found in natural bone porosities such as Haversian canals) are deposited from the external environment by percolating groundwater, or invasive microorganisms (Schultz, 1996; Turner-Walker and Jans, 2008; Hollund *et al.*, 2011; Hollund, Blank and Sjögren, 2018; Kendall *et al.*, 2018). Exogenous minerals can also infiltrate the broader microstructure and produce mineral staining. Inclusions and staining can form autochthonously as a result of bone decomposition under particular conditions. For instance, decomposition of organic matter by sulphate-reducing bacteria under anoxic conditions can produce framboidal pyrite inclusions (Turner-Walker and Jans, 2008; Hollund, Blank and Sjögren, 2018). A return to aerobic conditions can oxidise pyrite, releasing iron oxides and organic acids, which stain and demineralise the local bone microstructure. Humic acids released by decaying organic matter can produce dark staining in the bone microstructure (Figure 30.6). Such staining would indicate the high prevalence of decaying organic matter in the burial environment, as is often the case in occupation layers. In burials, this may be related to the type of soil but could also be indicative of organic grave goods/inclusions or wrappings (Lelong, 2014). Patterns of staining and inclusions that are not consistent with the *in situ* depositional environment can indicate variation in that environment over time or that bodies/bones had been re-deposited from a different environment (Parker Pearson *et al.*, 2005; Hollund, Blank and Sjögren, 2018).

Chemical and thermal alteration

Acidic dissolution produces characteristic changes of the internal microstructure, chemical properties and crystalline structure of bone (Hedges, 2002; Smith *et al.*, 2007; Turner-Walker and Peacock, 2008; Lebon *et al.*, 2010). Bone will usually not survive over archaeological timescales in contexts that are highly acidic but may persist in those that are slightly or episodically rendered so. Free-draining soils, such as sandy soils with a low water table, can also produce corrosive environments through episodic recharge upsetting the chemical equilibrium between the bone and the burial environment (Hedges, Millard and Pike, 1995; Hedges and Millard, 1995; Hedges, 2002; Reiche *et al.*, 2003). Localised demineralisation can occur as a result of fluctuating environments, caused, for instance, by the oxidation of framboidal pyrite (Turner-Walker and Jans, 2008; Hollund *et al.*, 2011). In neutral or alkaline environments that are unlikely to have ever been acidic, signs of acidic changes of bone can suggest that bodies or bones had originally been deposited in an acidic environment before being re-deposited in the contexts in which they were found (Parker Pearson *et al.*, 2005). Acidic dissolution of bone can be recognised in

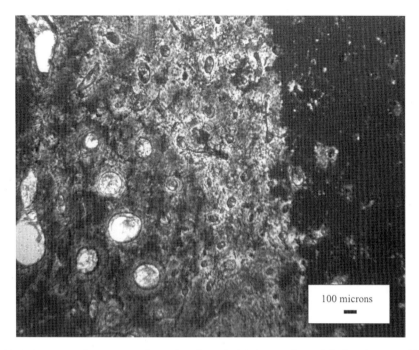

Figure 30.6 Transverse thin section of an archaeological adult human femoral shaft under normal light. Dark amorphous, hazy discolouration (generalised destruction) can be seen in the microstructure and associated with enlarged osteocyte lacunae, most likely as a result of penetration by humic acids. Staining is more intense on the right of the image where it has completely obscured microstructural features.

thin sections as enlarged canaliculi and osteocyte lacunae or as generalised destruction of the microstructure, usually involving a loss of lamellar structure and loss or enlargement of osteocyte lacunae (Turner-Walker and Jans, 2008; Turner-Walker and Peacock, 2008; Hollund *et al.*, 2011). Generalised destruction can be distinguished from bioerosion by its lack of structure and clinal distribution, appearing amorphous and hazy in bone thin sections. It most often originates from the bone surface or from Haversian canals. Acidic dissolution of the bone mineral can also be quantified directly using techniques such as FTIR, X-ray diffraction, X-ray scattering and Mercury Intrusion Porosimetry (Nielsen-Marsh and Hedges, 1999; Wess *et al.*, 2001; Parker Pearson *et al.*, 2005; Stathopoulou *et al.*, 2008; Dal Sasso *et al.*, 2018; Tjelldén *et al.*, 2018).

Accelerated collagen hydrolysis (ACH) involves collagen being leached from the bone without any alteration of the gross histological structure (Smith *et al.*, 2002; 2007; Delannoy *et al.*, 2018). However, this process usually causes extensive microfissuring and a loss of birefringence in histological thin sections, as well as altering the mineral phase (Smith *et al.*, 2002; Huisman *et al.*, 2017). It is most likely caused by factors that increase the rate of hydrolytic reactions, which break down the collagen molecule, such as increases in temperature (e.g. burnt bones), an abundance of percolating water or high alkalinity. Specific cases of ACH at the medieval site of Apigliano in southern Italy were explained by bones having been subject to shallow burial and experiencing rapid wetting and drying cycles (Smith *et al.*, 2002). Evidence for ACH in human bones can be indicative of extreme weathering caused by long-term exposure of the bone prior to burial (Booth and Madgwick 2016). As heat inevitably increases the rate of hydrolytic reactions, low-level heating such as cooking may also be responsible for ACH found in archaeological bone (Smith *et al.*, 2002). Clearly, a range of circumstances may trigger accelerated hydrolysis of bone collagen. Therefore, in cases where ACH is identified, discussion of the processes responsible would have to be circumspect and there would need to be careful consideration of the accompanying taphonomic, archaeological and historical evidence before a likely cause could be proposed.

Measurement of bone diagenesis can also be useful for identifying low-level heating, or defining the nature of cremation practices (Hanson and Cain, 2007; Gonçalves, Thompson and Cunha, 2011; Squires *et al.*, 2011). Cremation at different temperatures produces different colour and structural changes in the bone microstructure that can be identified through thin section light microscopy. High-temperature heating causes changes of the structure of the bone mineral that can be characterised through techniques such as FTIR (Gonçalves, Thompson and Cunha, 2011). Low-temperature heating can also produce bone colour and structural changes that are visible both macroscopically and in thin sections (Hanson and Cain, 2007; Squires *et al.*, 2011; Thompson *et al.*, 2017; Villagran *et al.*, 2017). However, these colour changes are sometimes difficult to distinguish from those produced by iron and manganese staining (Shahack-Gross, Bar-Yosef and Weiner, 1997). Heating degrades collagen, reducing birefringence in bone thin sections (Brönnimann *et al.*, 2018), although this can also be caused by environments promoting ACH (Smith *et al.*, 2002; Huisman *et al.*, 2017). Confirmation of low-level thermal alteration is possible through analysis by transmission electron microscopy (TEM) of collagen fibril degradation or structural changes to the mineral component through techniques such as FTIR (Koon, O'Connor and Collins, 2010; Gonçalves, Thompson and Cunha, 2011).

Histotaphonomy and archaeothanatology

The apparent relationship between bacterial bioerosion and early post-mortem treatment means that the assessment of bioerosion in human bones represents the aspect of bone diagenesis that is potentially most pertinent to archaeothanatology. Anoxic/waterlogged environments present a potential confounding factor and there is still some way to go before the variation in bone bioerosion is fully understood. There is currently a dependency on models of bodily decomposition in variable environments, which in themselves come with a certain level of uncertainty and may be unreliable from which to extrapolate (Vass, 2011). It is likely that the spectrum of bacterial attack associated with particular types of early post-mortem treatment will overlap, and are therefore reliable. Histotaphonomy is a valuable tool for the interpretation of burials that represent single deposit variations, such as fragmented remains, multi-stage manipulations, mummification and human–animal associations. Integration of the diagenetic and archaeothanatological data from a single individual may help refine interpretations on a probabilistic basis, particularly if all information presents a single solution. Most analyses of bone diagenesis that have investigated early post-mortem treatment have tended to focus on patterns among assemblages of bone, with only superficial reference to *post-hoc* archaeothanatological approaches. This section contains descriptions of the ways in which histological and traditional taphonomic analyses have been combined to investigate funerary practices in different time periods. It highlights how the proper integration of diagenetic and archaeothanatological approaches could significantly enhance interpretive power.

Neolithic period

Disarticulated bones representing the remains of at least three individuals were recovered from a modern gravel quarry at Watermead Park, Leicestershire, UK (Ripper, 2010). Individual 2 and Individual 3 produced radiocarbon determinations of 4280±45 bp (GrA-23586, 3010–2760 cal. BC) and 4290±45 bp (GrA-23588, 3020–2790 cal. BC), which placed them in the Late Neolithic. Individual 1 produced a radiocarbon determination of 2760±55 bp (OxA-6831, 1020–800 cal. BC), in the Late Bronze Age. The cervical vertebrae of Individual 1 showed cut marks on the posterior neural arch of the atlas vertebra, possibly indicating peri-mortem removal of the head through cutting of the surrounding neck musculature. The disarticulated and partial nature of all three individuals suggests that the *in situ* environment did not represent their primary depositional context. Mercury intrusion porosimetry (HgIP) analysis of three bones, a right femur associated with Individual 2; a right tibia, possibly belonging to Individual 1; and an unassigned clavicle found that none exhibited pore sizes corresponding with bacterial attack. This suggests that all bodies had been subjected to early post-mortem funerary practices involving the rapid loss of soft tissue, such as excarnation, defleshing or dismemberment, before some of their bones were re-deposited.

A study of variability in levels of bacterial bioerosion in archaeological human remains dating to the British Bronze Age (2450–700 BC) found that bacterial bioerosion was unusually absent or at low levels in a significant proportion of articulated skeletons from aerobic environments (Booth, Chamberlain and Parker Pearson, 2015; Booth, 2016). Histological analysis of bones from mummified bodies indicated that these are the only articulated remains outside of anoxic environments which consistently show low levels of bacterial bioerosion (Booth, Chamberlain and Parker Pearson, 2015). This is reasonable considering mummification processes alter processes of soft tissue decomposition (Aufderheide, 2003). This could suggest that a proportion of Bronze Age individuals from Britain had been mummified before being buried and could indicate that their preserved soft tissue had degraded in the burial environment. Analyses of bone diagenesis might provide a way of distinguishing bones from bodies that had previously been mummified. These observations could align with applications of archaeothanatology in using paradoxical patterns of skeletal disarticulation to infer similar interpretations of previous mummification (Maureille and Sellier, 1996). However, recent studies show that disarticulation patterns are not that straightforward to interpret and caution should be exercised with this kind of interpretation (cf. Mickleburgh *et al.*, Chapter 28, this volume; Schotsmans *et al.*, Chapter 27, this volume). The possibility of recognising mummification on a bone histological level is currently being studied on experimental remains at the Australian Facility for Taphonomic Experimental Research (AFTER) in Australia (Schotsmans *et al.*, 2017).

Bronze Age

Histological and *post-hoc* archaeothanatological techniques were integrated in a study of 22 Early Bronze Age human remains from the Franzhausen I cemetery in Austria, which has been dated to 2050–1700 BC (Mandl *et al.*, 2018). All of the skeletons were assumed to have been buried as whole bodies soon after death, although some were in variable states of articulation due to grave-robbing in antiquity. At least three skeletons were buried in highly flexed postures suggesting they had been tightly wrapped, and 15 showed additional archaeological and archaeothanatological evidence for coffin burial. Metal grave goods, some of which were likely to have been manufactured from copper or copper alloy, accompanied seventeen individuals. The majority of burials (18/22) showed extensive bacterial bioerosion, but bioerosion was entirely absent from four burials. The location and conditions of the site meant that it was unlikely that the burials had experienced prolonged periods of anoxic conditions or waterlogging. However, there was an association between an absence of bacterial bone bioerosion and intense macroscopic green/brown staining. Therefore, rather than these diagenetic signatures indicating intentional mummification, it was posited that impregnation of bodies and bones with bactericidal metals released from corroding grave goods, augmented by coffin burial, had impeded bacterial alteration of internal bone microstructures. Wedl tunnelling was observed in seven of the burials, and the authors considered that this may have been due to re-opening of graves in antiquity before bodies had fully decomposed. However, there was no association between Wedl tunnelling and osteological evidence for later disturbance, highlighting that the factors which influence the occurrence of Wedl tunnelling are not well resolved (Mandl *et al.*, 2018).

Iron Age

A cranium and mandible excavated from a waterlogged pit alongside wooden stakes and faunal bones at Heslington East, York, UK, showed evidence for strangulation and decapitation (O'Connor et al., 2011). The cranium, which was radiocarbon dated to 2469±34 bp (OxA-20677, 673–482 cal. BC), the Early Iron Age, contained the preserved, albeit much altered remains of the brain. Histological analysis of the cranium revealed that the microstructure was perfectly preserved, with no sign of bioerosion. Together, this evidence suggests that the head had been removed peri-mortem and quickly buried in the waterlogged pit before the soft tissue had fully decomposed.

A study of the early post-mortem treatment of Iron Age human remains recovered from the Danebury hillfort in Hampshire, UK, examined the relationship between diagenesis and the extent of skeletal articulation (Booth and Madgwick, 2016). Human bones were recovered in various stages of completeness and articulation from pits distributed throughout the Danebury settlement and have been radiocarbon dated to various points in the Iron Age (700 BC–43 AD; Cunliffe, Farrell and Dee, 2015). Disarticulated bones showed extensive bacterial bioerosion, whereas partially articulated and fully articulated skeletons showed intermediate levels of bacterial attack. A single bone, which was the only one to exhibit surface cortical modifications indicative of long-term exposure, showed only minor bacterial bioerosion and a substantial loss of birefringence indicative of ACH, consistent with excarnation.

The bacterial bioerosion present in the disarticulated human remains from Danebury represents what is normally found in articulated skeletons that were buried intact soon after death, suggesting they had come from primary burials that had been exhumed post-skeletonisation (Booth and Madgwick, 2016) or represent mass burials (Craig, Knüsel and Carr, 2005). The intermediate levels of bacterial bioerosion observed in the articulated and partially articulated bone were similar to those observed in ancient bones from sheltered environments such as caves and stone tombs (Booth, 2016). When combined with the contextual information from Danebury itself, this suggests that whole bodies had been placed in pits where they were rapidly buried by silting, or sheltered using textiles or skins. Some of these burials were then disturbed, manipulated and bones/body parts transported while they were decomposing.

Histological analysis of faunal samples from Danebury provides further examples of the utility of diagenetic analyses for investigating post-mortem histories and expand the scope beyond human remains to consider ritual treatment of other mammals. Twenty long bones from various domestic species were sampled for thin section analysis and analysed using methods outlined in Booth and Madgwick (2016). Bacterial bioerosion was assessed using the standard Oxford Histological Index (OHI) which translates the percentage of preserved microstructure into an ordinal score from 0 (extensive bacterial tunnelling) to 5 (little or no bacterial tunnelling; Hedges, Millard and Pike, 1995; Millard, 2001). The faunal samples had been recovered from pit features across the settlement in variable states of articulation and completeness, ranging from whole skeletons to discrete bones.

The majority of faunal bones show high to middling levels of bacterial bioerosion (OHI < 4) with only one bone, a sheep femur, showing no bacterial attack (OHI = 5, Table 30.1). There is some additional variation within low and middling OHI scores, but this is not associated with species, element, depositional context, or whether or not a skeleton was found in a deposit alongside human remains. The distribution of OHI scores in the faunal bones from Danebury is very similar to those recorded for the human bones from the same site (Booth and Madgwick, 2016 (Figure 30.7). This result is unusual and contrary to results from a range of European archaeological sites, although the majority of these bones are likely to have come from assemblages of butchery waste (Jans *et al.*, 2004; Nielsen-Marsh *et al.*, 2007; Brönnimann *et al.*, 2018; although see Mulville *et al.*, 2012). The single sheep femur from Danebury that was free from bacterial bioerosion showed colour changes and birefringence loss indicative of heat treatment, fitting the typical diagenetic profile for butchered faunal bone. The contextual information and patterns of articulation associated with most of the faunal samples from Danebury suggests that many do not reflect butchery waste but rather ritual deposits of faunal remains (Madgwick, 2008, 2010).

The histological results suggest that most of the faunal remains had been treated similarly or in ways which produced similar signatures of bacterial bioerosion. Taken at face value, the simplest explanation for patterns of bacterial bioerosion in the faunal bones from Danebury is that, like a subset of the human remains, they had been deposited in covered or rapidly silting pits before being disturbed and manipulated. This appeared to have occurred for humans and animals that were deposited in pit 923 (Craig, Knüsel and Carr, 2005). An alternative interpretation incorporating the broader results from the cortical bone modifications from British hillfort sites suggests that humans and faunal remains were treated differently but in ways which produced similar signatures of bacterial bioerosion (Madgwick, 2008). However, the assemblage of faunal bones studied histologically shows generally low levels of cortical weathering, with some exceptions, and it is possible that a subset of faunal remains was sampled which had been treated similarly to the human bones.

Evidence for complex treatment of the dead was also found at the Late Iron Age (150–80 BC) site of Basel-Gasfabrik in Switzerland. Two cemeteries located outside the settlement contained over 200 inhumations, but several articulated skeletons were recovered additionally from within the settlement itself, mostly from pits located within the settlement, as well as hundreds of isolated human bones (Pichler *et al.*, 2013). Twenty-five human bones from 20 individuals and 183 animal bone fragments were examined histotaphonomically (Brönnimann *et al.*, 2018). The human bones originated from cemetery inhumations, an articulated skeleton from a settlement pit and 15 single bones from different archaeological structures within the settlement. A new approach combining methods from osteoarchaeology and geoarchaeology was developed for the histotaphonomic investigation (Brönnimann *et al.*, 2018). Each individual bone was contextualised with regard to the sedimentation processes and the sediment type. This showed that the intensity of the Wedl tunnels depends mainly on the sedimentation process (exposure on a surface versus rapid burial in pits), while there is no relationship between bacterial attack (non-Wedl MFD) and sediment type or sedimentation process.

The combination of geoarchaeological and anthropological methods shows that different bioerosive phenomena have different causes. For this reason, an individual quantification of each bioerosive phenomenon using a 6-part scale based on the OHI was suggested (Brönnimann *et al.*, 2018) based on a Bacterial Attack Index (BAI), Wedl Tunnel Index (WTI) and a Cyanobacterial Attack Index (CAI), especially since the OHI documents the totality of the bioerosion.

Bone samples from the articulated human skeletons recovered from the cemeteries and settlement pits showed extensive bacterial tunnelling (BAI = 0), consistent with burial of intact bodies in aerobic soils soon after death. Thirteen of the 15 disarticulated single bones showed similar

Table 30.1 Results of histological analysis of the faunal assemblage from Danebury Iron Age hillfor:

Pit	Layer	Species	Element	Articulation	Cortical modification	Association	OHI	Non-Wedl MFD	Wedl MFD	Birefringence index	Inclusions/staining
321	5	Dog	R. Femur	Articulated	None	Animal	0	Present	Absent	0	None
321	1	Sheep	Tibia	Disarticulated	None	Animal	0	Present	Absent	0	None
366	6	Dog	Tibia	Articulated	None	Unknown	0	Present	Absent	0	None
697	3	Sheep	Tibia	Articulated	None	Animal	0	Present	Absent	0	None
802	5	Sheep	L. Femur	Unknown	None	Animal	5	Absent	Absent	0.5	Uniform orange discolouration
809	5	Pig	Humerus	Articulated	None	Animal	2	Present	Absent	0.5	None
809	5	Cattle	Tibia	Partially articulated	None	Animal	0	Present	Absent	0	None
923	6	Horse	Metatarsal	Partially articulated	None	Human	2	Present	Present	0.5	None
923	6	Pig	Humerus	Unknown	None	Human	3	Present	Present	0.5	None
923	3	Sheep	Femur	Disarticulated	None	Human	3	Present	Absent	0.5	None
935	6	Horse	Metapodial	Partially articulated	Weathering	Human	0	Present	Absent	0	Uniform orange discolouration
1078	7	Sheep	Femur	Disarticulated	None	Human	0	Present	Absent	0	None
1078	5	Horse	Radius	Disarticulated	Weathering	Human	0	Present	Present	0	None
1078	6	Dog	Radius	Disarticulated	Cut marks	Human	2	Present	Absent	0.5	None
1078	6	Cattle	Tibia	Disarticulated	Weathering	Human	1	Present	Absent	0.5	None
1299	1	Sheep	Tibia	Disarticulated	Carnivore gnawing	Animal	2	Present	Absent	0.5	None
2183	6	Pig	Femur	Disarticulated	None	Unknown	2	Present	Absent	0.5	None
2196	6	Cattle	Tibia	Partially Articulated	Weathering	Animal	3	Present	Present	0.5	None
2219	4	Cattle	Humerus	Partially Articulated	None	Unknown	2	Present	Absent	0.5	None
2199	6	Sheep	Radius	Partially Articulated	Weathering	Animal	0	Present	Absent	0	None

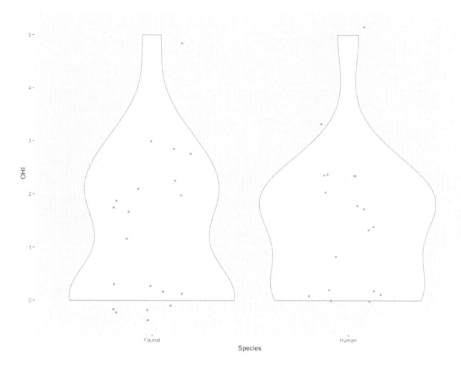

Figure 30.7 Scattered OHI scores and associated Kernal density estimates for faunal (left) and human remains (right) from Danebury Iron Age hillfort. Distributions for each category of remains are similarly focussed around low–intermediate scores.

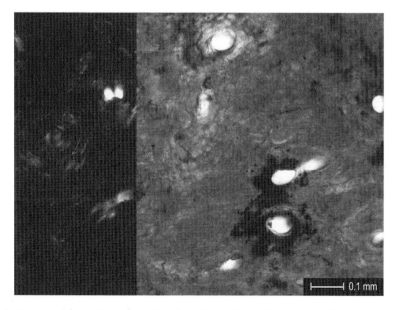

Figure 30.8 Transverse thin section of an archaeological adult human humerus shaft from an articulated skeleton excavated at the Basel-Gasfabrik burial site) under standard bright field light (right part of the image) and cross-polarised light (left part of the image). Note the complete destruction of bone microstructure caused by bacterial attack. The few intact areas show moderate collagen preservation in the left part of the image.

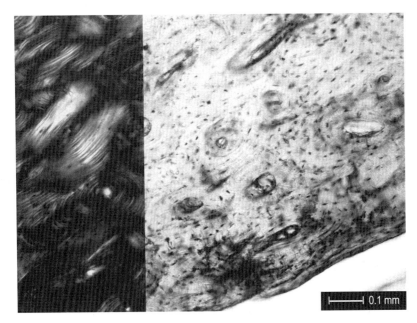

Figure 30.9 Transverse thin section of an isolated archaeological femoral shaft from an adult human from the Basel-Gasfabrik site under standard bright field light (right part of the image) and cross-polarised light (left part of the image). No bacterial attack but little Wedl tunnelling (surface) and some probable reddish iron oxide staining are visible. The collagen is very well preserved (left part of the image).

patterns of extensive bacterial bioerosion (Figure 30.8). It is postulated in these cases that bones had been exhumed from primary burials post-skeletonisation and re-interred in the settlement. However, two single bones relating to two separate individuals were free from bacterial attack (BAI = 5) and exhibited very good collagen preservation (Figure 30.9). For these two individuals, a different multi-stage post-mortem treatment, which may have involved defleshing or removal of extremities shortly after death can be inferred. Both of these bones originate from the same archaeological structure, although the meaning of this is difficult to assess given this structure was unique on the site. By contrast, faunal bone show significantly less bacterial attack than the human bones, underpinning the interpretation that they mainly formed parts of deposits from butchery waste.

In summary, for both Basel-Gasfabrik and Danebury a complex and, in some cases, multi-stage treatment of the dead can be hypothesised (Booth and Madgwick, 2016). There are striking parallels between both sites regarding the histotaphonomic signatures of isolated bones, but there are also clear differences among articulated skeletons. This comparison illustrates the value of histotaphonomic examinations in complementing interpretations from other disciplines.

Historical samples

Mollerup *et al.* (2016) combined thin-section light microscopy with taphonomic techniques to investigate the events leading up to the deposition of 2 335 disarticulated human remains representing at least 380 individuals in a bog at the site of Alken Enge in Denmark in the 1st century AD. Age-at-death and sex profiles, patterns of trauma and preservation of weaponry indicated that these individuals had died in battle. The bones showed extensive carnivore gnawing and patterns of disarticulation consistent with scavenging by domestic dogs and wolves. All of this evidence, when taken together, suggests that bodies were left to decompose on the battlefield before being collected and deposited in the bog. All sampled bones were free from bacterial bioerosion, similar to butchered archaeological faunal bones and consistent with the Alken Edge bodies having been rapidly defleshed as a result of subaerial exposure. The presence of framboidal pyrite inclusions supported patterns of articulation implying that bones had been deposited in the bog while some soft tissue remained. This evidence indicated that bodies had been left exposed on the battlefield for up to a year before they were deposited in the bog.

Scorrano et al. (2017) combined diagenetic analyses with traditional taphonomic assessment and historical records to investigate the treatment of the 14th-century Holy Roman Emperor Henry VII of Luxembourg. The disarticulated bones of Henry VII are kept in a wooden coffin in the Cathedral of Pisa in Italy. Henry VII had died away from Pisa, and historical records suggest that his body had been boiled then burnt to destroy soft tissue before the bones were transported to Pisa. Cranial fragments and a fragment of tibia from Henry VII were analysed using SEM, FTIR, XRD and collagen extracted to investigate whether they showed diagenetic changes consistent with these practices. The skeleton showed macroscopic signs of trauma consistent with peri-mortem beheading, as well as discolouration indicative of low-level burning. Results from FTIR and XRD analyses of bone mineral changes and SEM inspection of the external surfaces suggested that both the cranium and tibia had been subject to low-level heat treatment but that the tibia had been exposed to higher-temperature burning. This study did not involve histological assessment, but the low loss of collagen suggested that the bones were unlikely to have been extensively altered by bacteria, consistent with rapid post-mortem defleshing. The authors concluded that both the head and body had been boiled but that only the infra-cranial skeletal remains had been exposed to fire after the removal of remaining soft tissue.

Conclusion

This chapter seeks to provide a broad overview of the ways in which analyses of diagenesis can provide novel data to complement archaeothanatological approaches in elucidating some of the taphonomic events to which a skeleton was exposed over its entire depositional history, and specifically in the early post-mortem period. In providing a gauge of the extent to which a bone was exposed to decomposing soft tissue, analyses of bacterial bioerosion of bone microstructure can provide a particularly rich seam of data for investigating past post-mortem treatment. Few studies have integrated diagenetic analyses with traditional taphonomic techniques and archaeothanatology, but those that have demonstrated how the combination of these methods produces an interpretative potential that is greater than the sum of its parts. Together, these methods can produce richer, more detailed interpretations of past funerary treatment and practices. Effective combination of archaeo-anthropology with diagenetic analyses and with other disciplines, such as geoarchaeology, have great potential for future studies of funerary archaeology and thus the discipline of archaeology in general.

References

Ascenzi, A. and Silvestrini, G. (1984). Bone-boring Marine Micro-organisms: An Experimental Investigation. *Journal of Human Evolution*, 13(6), pp. 531–536.

Aufderheide, A.C. (2003). *The scientific study of mummies*. Cambridge: Cambridge University Press.

Balzer, A., Gleixner, G., Grupe, G., Schmidt, H.-L., Schramm, S., Turban-Just, S. (1997). *In Vitro* Decomposition of Bone Collagen by Soil Bacteria: The Implications for Stable Isotope Analysis in Archaeometry. *Archaeometry*, 39(2), pp. 415–429.

Bell, L.S. and Elkerton, A. (2008). Unique Marine Taphonomy in Human Skeletal Material Recovered from the Medieval Warship Mary Rose. *International Journal of Osteoarchaeology*, 18(5), pp. 523–535.

Bell, L.S., Skinner, M.F. and Jones, S.J. (1996). The Speed of Post Mortem Change to the Human Skeleton and Its Taphonomic Significance. *Forensic Science International*, 82(2), pp. 129–140.

Booth, T.J. (2016). An Investigation Into the Relationship between Funerary Treatment and Bacterial Bioerosion in European Archaeological Human Bone. *Archaeometry*, 58(3), pp. 484–499.

Booth, T., (2017). The rot sets in. In: D. Errickson and T. Thompson, eds., *Human Remains: Another Dimension*. Amsterdam: Academic Press, pp. 7–28.

Booth, T.J., Chamberlain, A.T. and Parker Pearson, M. (2015). Mummification in Bronze Age Britain. *Antiquity*, 89(347), pp. 1155–1173.

Booth, T.J. and Madgwick, R. (2016). New Evidence for Diverse Secondary Burial Practices in Iron Age Britain: A Histological Case Study. *Journal of Archaeological Science*, 67, pp. 14–24.

Booth, T.J., Redfern, R.C. and Gowland, R.L. (2016). Immaculate Conceptions: Micro-CT Analysis of Diagenesis in Romano-British Infant Skeletons. *Journal of Archaeological Science*, 74, pp. 124–134.

Brönnimann, D., Portmann, C., Pichler, S.L., Booth, T.J., Röder, B., Vach, W., Schibler, J. and Rentzel, P. (2018). Contextualising the Dead – Combining Geoarchaeology and Osteo-Anthropology in a New Multi-Focus Approach in Bone Histotaphonomy. *Journal of Archaeological Science*, 98, pp. 45–58.

Child, A.M. (1995). Microbial Taphonomy of Archaeological Bone. *Studies in Conservation*, 40(1), pp. 19–30.

Child, A.M., Gillard, R.D. and Pollard, A.M. (1993). Microbially-Induced Promotion of Amino Acid Racemization in Bone: Isolation of the Microorganisms and the Detection of Their Enzymes. *Journal of Archaeological Science*, 20(2), pp. 159–168.

Craig, C.R., Knüsel, C.J. and Carr, G.C. (2005). Fragmentation, mutilation and dismemberment: an interpretation of human remains on Iron Age sites. In: M. Parker-Pearson and I.J.N. Thorpe, eds., *Warfare, Violence, and Slavery*. British Archaeological Reports International Series 1374, Oxford: Archaeopress, pp. 165–180.

Cunliffe, B., Farrell, P. and Dee, M. (2015). A Happening at Danebury Hillfort – But When? *Oxford Journal of Archaeology*, 34(4), pp. 407–414.

Dal Sasso, G., Angelini, I., Maritan, L. and Artioli G. (2014). Bone Diagenesis at the Micro-Scale: Bone Alteration Patterns during Multiple Burial Phases at Al Khiday (Khartoum, Sudan) between the Early Holocene and the II Century AD. *Palaeogeography, Palaeoclimatology, Palaeoecology*, 416, pp. 30–42.

Dal Sasso, G., Angelini, I., Maritan, L. and Artioli G. (2018). Raman Hyperspectral Imaging as an Effective and Highly Informative Tool to Study the Diagenetic Alteration of Fossil Bones. *Talanta*, 179, pp. 167–176.

Delannoy, Y., Collard, T., Cannet, C., Mesli, V., Hedouin, V., Penel, G. and Ludes, B. (2018). Characterization of Bone Diagenesis by Histology in Forensic Contexts: A Human Taphonomic Study. *International Journal of Legal Medicine*, 132(1), pp. 219–227.

Fernández-Jalvo, Y., Andrews, P., Pesquero, D., Smith, C., Marín-Monfort, D., Sánchez, B., Geigl, E.-M. and Alonso, A. (2010). Early Bone Diagenesis in Temperate Environments. *Palaeogeography, Palaeoclimatology, Palaeoecology*, 288(1–4), pp. 62–81.

Gonçalves, D., Thompson, T.J.U. and Cunha, E. (2011). Implications of Heat-Induced Changes in Bone on the Interpretation of Funerary Behaviour and Practice. *Journal of Archaeological Science*, 38(6), pp. 1308–1313.

Grupe, G., Dreses-Werringloer, U. and Parsche, F. (1993). Initial stages of bone decomposition: causes and consequences. In: J.B. Lambert and G. Grupe, eds., *Prehistoric Human Bone: Archaeology at the Molecular Level*. Berlin: Springer, pp. 257–274.

Grupe, G. and Turban-Just, S. (1996). Serum Proteins in Archaeological Human Bone. *International Journal of Osteoarchaeology*, 6(3), pp. 300–308.

Hackett, C.J. (1981). Microscopical Focal Destruction (Tunnels) in Exhumed Human Bones. *Medicine, Science, and the Law*, 21(4), pp. 243–265.

Hanson, M. and Cain, C.R. (2007). Examining Histology to Identify Burned Bone. *Journal of Archaeological Science*, 34(11), pp. 1902–1913.

Haynes, S., Searle, J.B., Bretman, A. and Dobney, K. (2002). Bone Preservation and Ancient DNA: The Application of Screening Methods for Predicting DNA Survival. *Journal of Archaeological Science*, 29(6), pp. 585–592.

Hedges, R.E.M. (2002). Bone Diagenesis: An Overview of Processes. *Archaeometry*, 44(3), pp. 319–328.

Hedges, R.E.M. and Millard, A.R. (1995). Bones and Groundwater: Towards the Modelling of Diagenetic Processes. *Journal of Archaeological Science*, 22(2), pp. 155–164.

Hedges, R.E.M., Millard, A.R. and Pike, A.W.G. (1995). Measurements and Relationships of Diagenetic Alteration of Bone from Three Archaeological Sites. *Journal of Archaeological Science*, 22(2), pp. 201–209.

Hollund, H.I., Blank, M. and Sjögren, K.-G. (2018). Dead and Buried? Variation in Post-Mortem Histories Revealed through Histotaphonomic Characterisation of Human Bone from Megalithic Graves in Sweden. *PloS One*, 13(10), p. e0204662.

Hollund, H.I., Jans, M.M.E., Collins, M.J., Kars, H., Joosten, I. and Kars, S.M. (2011). What Happened Here? Bone Histology as a Tool in Decoding the Postmortem Histories of Archaeological Bone from Castricum, The Netherlands. *International Journal of Osteoarchaeology*, 22(5), pp. 537–548.

Huisman, H., Ismail-Meyer, K., Sageidet, B.M. and Joosten, I. (2017). Micromorphological Indicators for Degradation Processes in Archaeological Bone from Temperate European Wetland Sites. *Journal of Archaeological Science*, 85, pp. 13–29.

Jackes, M., Sherburne, R., Lubell, D., Barker, C. and Wayman, M. (2001). Destruction of Microstructure in Archaeological Bone: A Case Study from Portugal. *International Journal of Osteoarchaeology*, 11(6), pp. 415–432.

Jans, M.M.E., Nielsen-Marsh, C.M., Smith, C.I., Collins, M.J., Kars, H. (2004). Characterisation of Microbial Attack on Archaeological Bone. *Journal of Archaeological Science*, 31(1), pp. 87–95.

Javan, G.T., Finley, S.J., Can, I., Wilkinson, J.E., J Hanson, J.D. and Tarone, A.M. (2016). Human Thanatomicrobiome Succession and Time Since Death. *Scientific Reports*, 6, p. 29598.

Kendall, C., Eriksen, A.M.H., Kontopoulos, I., Collins, M.J. and Turner-Walker, G. (2018). Diagenesis of Archaeological Bone and Tooth. *Palaeogeography, Palaeoclimatology, Palaeoecology*, 491, pp. 21–37.

Kontopoulos, I., Nystrom, P. and White, L. (2016). Experimental Taphonomy: Post-Mortem Microstructural Modifications in *Sus scrofa domesticus* Bone. *Forensic Science International*, 266, pp. 320–328.

Koon, H.E.C., O'Connor, T.P. and Collins, M.J. (2010). Sorting the Butchered from the Boiled. *Journal of Archaeological Science*, 37(1), pp. 62–69.

Lanyon, L.E. and Rubin, C.T. (1984). Static vs Dynamic Loads as an Influence on Bone Remodelling. *Journal of Biomechanics*, 17(12), pp. 897–905.

Lebon, M., Reiche, I., Bahain, J.J., Chadefaux, C., Moigne A.-M., Fröhlich, F.F., Sémah, F., Schwarcz, H.P., and Falguères, C. (2010). New Parameters for the Characterization of Diagenetic Alterations and Heat-Induced Changes of Fossil Bone Mineral Using Fourier Transform Infrared Spectrometry. *Journal of Archaeological Science*, 37(9), pp. 2265–2276.

Lelong, O. (2014). Wrappings of Power: A Woman's Burial in Cattle Hide at Langwell Farm, Strath Oykel. *Proceedings of the Society of Antiquaries of Scotland*, 144, pp. 65–132.

Madgwick, R. (2008). Patterns in the modification of animal and human bones in Iron Age Wessex: revisiting the excarnation debate. In O. Davis, N. Sharples, and K. Waddington, eds., *Changing Perspectives on the First Millennium BC: Proceedings of the Iron Age Research Student Seminar 2006*. Oxford: Oxbow, pp. 99–118.

Madgwick, R. (2010). Bone modification and the conceptual relationship between humans and animals in Iron Age Wessex. In: J. Morris and M. Maltby, eds., *Integrating Social and Environmental Archaeologies: Reconsidering Deposition*. British Archaeological Reports (International Series) 2077. Oxford: Archaeopress, pp. 66–82.

Madgwick, R. (2014). What Makes Bones Shiny? Investigating Trampling as a Cause of Bone Abrasion. *Archaeological and Anthropological Sciences*, 6, pp. 163–173.

Madgwick, R. and Mulville, J. (2012). Investigating Variation in the Prevalence of Weathering in Faunal Assemblages in the United Kingdom: A Multivariate Statistical Approach. *International Journal of Osteoarchaeology*, 22, pp. 509–522.

Mandl, K., Novotny, F., Teschler-Nicola, M. and Weiss-Krejci, E. (2018). The Corpse in the Early Bronze Age. Results of Histotaphonomic and Archaeothanatological Investigations of Human Remains from the Cemetery of Franzhausen I, Lower Austria. *Archaeologia Austriaca*, 102, pp. 135–167.

Marchiafava, V., Bonucci, E. and Ascenzi, A. (1974). Fungal Osteoclasia: A Model of Dead Bone Resorption. *Calcified Tissue Research*, 14(3), pp. 195–210.

Maureille, B. and Sellier, P. (1996). Dislocation en Ordre Paradoxal, Momification et Décomposition: Observations et Hypothèses. *Bulletins et Mémoires de la Société d'Anthropologie de Paris*, 8(3), pp. 313–327.

Millard, A. (2001). The deterioration of bone. In: D. Brothwell and A.M. Pollard, eds., *Handbook of Archaeological Sciences*. Chichester, UK: John Wiley and Sons, pp. 637–647.

Mollerup, L, Tjellden, A.K.E., Hertz, E. and Holst, M.K. (2016). The Postmortem Exposure Interval of an Iron Age Human Bone Assemblage from Alken Enge, Denmark. *Journal of Archaeological Science: Reports*, 10, pp. 819–827.

Müller, K., Chadefaux, C., Thomas, N. and Reiche, I. (2011). Microbial Attack of Archaeological Bones Versus High Concentrations of Heavy Metals in the Burial Environment. A Case Study of Animal Bones from a Mediaeval Copper Workshop in Paris. *Palaeogeography, Palaeoclimatology, Palaeoecology*, 310(1–2), pp. 39–51.

Mulville, J., Madgwick, R., Powell, A., and Parker Pearson, M. (2012). Flesh on the bones: animal bodies in Atlantic roundhouses. In: A. Pluskowski, ed., *Animal Ritual Killing and Burial*. Oxford: Oxbow, pp. 205–219.

Nielsen-Marsh, C M. and Hedges, R.E.M. (1999). Bone Porosity and the Use of Mercury Intrusion Porosimetry in Bone Diagenesis Studies. *Archaeometry*, 41(1), pp. 165–174.

Nielsen-Marsh, C.M. and Hedges, R.E.M. (2000). Patterns of Diagenesis in Bone I: The Effects of Site Environments. *Journal of Archaeological Science*, 27(12), pp. 1139–1150.

Nielsen-Marsh, C.M., Smith, C.I., Jans, M.M.E., Nord, A., Kars, H., Collins, M.J. (2007). Bone Diagenesis in the European Holocene II: Taphonomic and Environmental Considerations. *Journal of Archaeological Science*, 34(9), pp. 1523–1531.

O'Connor, S., Ali, E., Al-Sabah, S., Anwar, D., Bergstroem, E., Brown, K.A., Buckberry, J., Buckley, S., Collins, M., Denton, J., Dorling, K.M., Dowle, A., Duffey, P., Edwards, H.G.M., Faria, E.C., Gardner, P., Gledhill, A., Heaton, K., Heron, C., Janaway, R., Keely, B.J., King, D., Masinton, A., Penkman, K., Petzold, A., Pickering, M.D., Rumsby, M., Schutkowski, H., Shackleton, K.A., Thomas, J., Thomas-Oates, J., Usai, M.-R., Wilson, A.S. and O'Connor, T. (2011). Exceptional Preservation of a Prehistoric Human Brain from Heslington, Yorkshire, UK. *Journal of Archaeological Science*, 38(7), pp. 1641–1654.

Ottoni, C., Koon, H.E., Collins, M.J., Penkman, K.E., Rickards, O. and Craig, O.E. (2009). Preservation of Ancient DNA in Thermally Damaged Archaeological Bone. *Die Naturwissenschaften*, 96(2), pp. 267–278.

Parker Pearson, M., Chamberlain, A., Craig, O., Marshall, P., Mulville, J., Smith, J., Chenery, C., Collins, M., Cook, G., Craig, G., Evans, J., Hiller, J., Montgomery, J., Schwenninger, J.-L., Taylor, G. and Wess, T. (2005). Evidence for Mummification in Bronze Age Britain. *Antiquity*, 79(305), pp. 529–546.

Person, A., Bocherens, H., Saliège, J.F., Paris, F., Zeitoun, V. and Gérard, M. (1995). Early Diagenetic Evolution of Bone Phosphate: An X-Ray Diffractometry Analysis. *Journal of Archaeological Science*, 22(2), pp. 211–221.

Philips, A., Stolarek I., Kuczkowska B., Juras A., Handschuh L., Piontek, J., Kozlowski, P., Figlerowicz, M. (2017). Comprehensive Analysis of Microorganisms Accompanying Human Archaeological Remains. *GigaScience*, 6(7), pp. 1–13.

Pichler, S.L., Rissanen, H., Spichtig, N., Röder, B., Schibler, J. and Alt, K.W. (2013). Die Regelmässigkeit des Irregulären: Menschliche Skelettreste vom spätlatènezeitlichen Fundplatz Basel-Gasfabrik. In: N. Müller-Scheessel, ed., '*Irregulär' Bestattungen in der Urgeschichte: Norm, Ritual, Strafe …?* Bonn: Dr. Rudolf Habelt GmbH, pp. 471–484.

Piepenbrink, H. (1986). Two Examples of Biogenous Dead Bone Decomposition and Their Consequences for Taphonomic Interpretation. *Journal of Archaeological Science*, 13(5), pp. 417–430.

Reiche, I., Favre-Quattropani, L., Vignaud, C., Bocherens, H., Charlet, L. and Menu, M. (2003). A Multi-Analytical Study of Bone Diagenesis: The Neolithic Site of Bercy (Paris, France). *Measurement Science and Technology*, 14(9), pp. 1608–1619.

Ripper, S. (2010). *Watermead County Park, Leicestershire: excavations of a late Neolithic burnt mound, human remains and a Saxon/bridge jetty in a watery context*. York: Archaeological Data Service [distributor]. https://doi.org/10.5284/1000126

Ross, A.H. and Hale, A.R. (2018). Decomposition of Juvenile-Sized Remains: A Macro- and Microscopic Perspective. *Forensic Sciences Research*, 54, pp. 1–10.

Saitta, E.T., Liang, R., Lau, C.Y., Brown, C.M., Longrich, N.R., Kaye, T.G., Novak, B.J., Salzberg, S. Donohoe, P., Dickinson, M., Vinther, J., Bull, I.D., Brooker, R.A., Martin, P., Abbott, G.D. Knowles, T.J.D., Penkman, K., Onstott, T.C. (2018). Life Inside A Dinosaur Bone: A Thriving Microbiome. bioRxiv, p.400176. Available at: https://www.biorxiv.org/content/early/2018/09/07/400176.abstract

Schotsmans, E.M.J., Ueland, M., Luong, S., Prinsloo, L.C., Nizio, K., Wallman, J., Forbes, S.L. and Knüsel, C.J. (2017). Reconstructing the Mortuary Chaîne Opératoire in the Neolithic Near East: Conducting Actualistic Experiments for a Better Understanding of Burial Practices. *Abstracts of the 23rd Conference of the European Association of Archaeologists*, Maastricht, The Netherlands, p. 395.

Schultz, M. (1996). Microscopic structure of bone. In: W.D. Haglund and M.H. Sorg, eds., *Forensic Taphonomy: The Postmortem Fate of Human Remains*. Boca Raton: CRC Press, pp. 187–198.

Scorrano, G., Mazzuca, C., Valentini, F., Scano, G., Buccolieri, A., Giancane, G., Manno, D., Valli, L., Mallegni, F., Serra, A. (2017). The Tale of Henry VII: A Multidisciplinary Approach to Determining the Post-Mortem Practice. *Archaeological and Anthropological Sciences*, 9(6), pp. 1215–1222.

Shahack-Gross, R., Bar-Yosef, O. and Weiner, S. (1997). Black-Coloured Bones in Hayonim Cave, Israel: Differentiating between Burning and Oxide Staining. *Journal of Archaeological Science*, 24(5), pp. 439–446.

Smith, C.I., Nielsen-Marsh, C.M., Jans, M.M., Arthur, P., Nord, A.G. and Collins, M.J. (2002). The Strange Case of Apigliano: Early "Fossilization" of Medieval Bone in Southern Italy. *Archaeometry*, 44(3), pp. 405–415.

Smith, C.I. Nielsen-March, C.M., Jans, M.M. and Collins, M.J. (2007). Bone Diagenesis in the European Holocene I: Patterns and Mechanisms. *Journal of Archaeological Science*, 34(9), pp. 1485–1493.

Squires, K.E, Thompson, T.J.U., Islam, M. and Chamberlain, A. (2011). The Application of Histomorphometry and Fourier Transform Infrared Spectroscopy to the Analysis of Early Anglo-Saxon Burned Bone. *Journal of Archaeological Science*, 38(9), pp. 2399–2409.

Stathopoulou, E.T., Psycharis, V., Chryssikos, G.D., Gionis, V. and Theodorou, G. (2008). Bone Diagenesis: New Data from Infrared Spectroscopy and X-Ray Diffraction. *Palaeogeography, Palaeoclimatology, Palaeoecology*, 266(3–4), pp. 168–174.

Thompson, T.J.U., Goncalves, D., Squires, K. and Ulguim, P. (2017). Thermal alteration to the body. In: E.M.J. Schotsmans, N. Márquez-Grant and S.L. Forbes, eds., *Taphonomy of Human Remains: Forensic Analysis of the Dead and the Depositional Environment*. Chichester: John Wiley & Sons Ltd., pp. 318–334.

Tjelldén, A.K.E., Kristiansen, S.M., Birkedal, H. and Jans, M.M.E. (2018). The Pattern of Human Bone Dissolution – A Histological Study of Iron Age Warriors from a Danish Wetland Site. *International Journal of Osteoarchaeology*, 28(4), pp. 407–418.

Turner-Walker, G. (2012). Early Bioerosion in Skeletal Tissues: Persistence through Deep Time. *Neues Jahrbuch für Geologie und Paläontologie – Abhandlungen*, 265(2), pp. 165–183.

Turner-Walker, G. and Jans, M. (2008). Reconstructing Taphonomic Histories Using Histological Analysis. *Palaeogeography, Palaeoclimatology, Palaeoecology*, 266(3–4), pp. 227–235.

Turner-Walker, G., Nielsen-Marsh, C.M., Syversen, U., Kars, H. and Collins, M.J. (2002). Sub-Micron Spongiform Porosity Is the Major Ultra-Structural Alteration Occurring in Archaeological Bone. *International Journal of Osteoarchaeology*, 12(6), pp. 407–414.

Turner-Walker, G. and Peacock, E.E. (2008). Preliminary Results of Bone Diagenesis in Scandinavian Bogs. *Palaeogeography, Palaeoclimatology, Palaeoecology*, 266(3–4), pp. 151–159.

Turner-Walker, G. and Syversen, U. (2002). Quantifying Histological Changes in Archaeological Bones Using BSE-SEM Image Analysis. *Archaeometry*, 44(3), pp. 461–468.

Vass, A.A. (2011). The Elusive Universal Post-Mortem Interval Formula. *Forensic Science International*, 204(1–3), pp. 34–40.

Villagran, X.S., Huisman, D.J., Mentzer, S.M. Miller, C.E. and Jans, M.M. (2017). Bone and their skeletal tissues. In: C. Nicosia and G. Stoops, eds., *Archaeological Soil and Sediment Micromorphology*. New York: John Wiley & Sons Ltd., pp. 9–38.

Wess, T.J., Drakopoulos, M., Snigirev, A., Wouters, J., Paris, O., Fratzl, P., Collins, M., Hiller, J. and Nielsen, K. (2001). The Use of Small-Angle X-Ray Diffraction Studies for the Analysis of Structural Features in Archaeological Samples. *Archaeometry*, 43(1), pp. 117–129.

White, L. and Booth, T.J. (2014). The Origin of Bacteria Responsible for Bioerosion to the Internal Bone Microstructure: Results from Experimentally-Deposited Pig Carcasses. *Forensic Science International*, 239, pp. 92–102.

Yoshino, M., Kimijima, T., Miyasaka, S., Sato, H. and Seta, S. (1991). Microscopical Study on Estimation of Time Since Death in Skeletal Remains. *Forensic Science International*, 49(2), pp. 143–158.

Zhou, W. and Bian, Y. (2018). Thanatomicrobiome Composition Profiling as a Tool for Forensic Investigation. *Forensic Sciences Research*, 3(2), pp. 105–110.

31

3D MODELS AS USEFUL TOOLS IN ARCHAEOTHANATOLOGY

Géraldine Sachau-Carcel

PACEA, De la Préhistoire à l'Actuel: Culture, Environnement et Anthropologie, UMR 5199, CNRS-Université de Bordeaux, Pessac, France

Introduction

Since the 1960s, various technological developments have changed research practices in all disciplines. These profound transformations are the consequences of the advent of computers and, above all, access to great computing power. Innovations and tools are rapidly being transferred from industry to the social sciences and humanities, and being adapted for use in archaeology and biological anthropology. The first symposium on quantitative methods in archaeology was the Computer Applications and Quantitative Methods in Archaeology (CAA) held in Birmingham, UK, in 1973 (Laflin, 2014). The development of computer tools has changed the recording of data in the field with the creation of databases to guide observations. This profoundly modified the analysis of archaeological sites by introducing multi-dimensional, quantitative and qualitative analysis of archaeological features (Djindjian and Vigneron, 1980). Similarly, the use of digital photography constitutes an important step for the discipline, with modification of not only excavation practices, recording and treatment of data, but also as an aid for framing of research questions. Indeed, digital photographs have made it possible to increase the number of field records but also offer the possibility of being aggregated, annotated or modified using specific software, thus contributing to the creation of new data. That way, they become a real research aid beyond the simple archive document. Digital photography enriches existing data, creates new data, and thus can contribute to the formulation of new research problems. Digital photographs can be both a working medium and a means of dissemination of an object or a site (Collet, 1996). This way, it becomes a real research aid, beyond the simple archive document. In addition, adding light colorimetry that modifies visualisation of statues and clarity of inscriptions also reveals details that permit new insights in a funerary context.

The early uses of 3D technology in archaeology came with private sponsorship, for example, the 3D visualisation of Thebes (Egypt) in 1987 by Vergnieux with the sponsorship of Electricité de France (EDF) (Golvin and Boccon-Gibod, 1990; Sullivan and Harrower, 2015). These early applications of 3D use permitted full integration of 3D tools in the research process through space and time for the disappeared remains. Of course, these 3D models do not stop at the production of an image. They participate in the research process by testing hypotheses formulated by archaeologists. Sponsorships contribute to research but also promote computer applications such as those offered by IBM (International Business Machines) for the creation of a 3D model of Cluny Abbey in 1992 (Père and Faucher, 2008). However, it was not until the 2000s that the archaeological community adopted 3D tools more generally.

3D methods and tools also developed in the fields of spatial analysis with GIS (e.g. Forte *et al.,* 2000 and the MayaArch3D project). Digital 3D modelling and data analysis have had a huge impact on the field of biological anthropology in recent decades as well. Computed Tomography (CT) scanners have contributed to the development of new research directions because these images can show both the interior and exterior architecture of an object. CT scanners can be extremely useful for non-destructive analyses of fossils and ancient remains for virtual autopsies of mummies, palaeopathological bone imaging (e.g. Ordureau and Lecuyot, 2009; Coqueugniot and Dutour, 2015) and virtual anthropology (Weber, 2014). Several symposia and specialist journals dedicated to the use of 3D tools in archaeology and biological anthropology have been held and published since the early 2000s providing an insight into major methodo-logical developments (e.g. Computer-Assisted Applications (CAA), International Society for Photogrammetry and Remote Sensing (ISPRS), Serving and Archiving Virtual Environments (SAVE), Virtual Retrospect). In addition, many symposia on funerary archaeology and bio-logical anthropology include sessions on the use of 3D tools in archaeo-anthropology (e.g. European Association of Archaeologists (EAA), British Association of Biological Anthropology and Osteoarchaeology (BABAO), Société d'Anthropologie de Paris (SAP), American Anthropological Association (AAA)). In 2014, a group of French laboratories pioneering the creation of 3D models established the TGIR (Très Grande Infrastructure de Recherche) Huma-Num (Humanités Numériques), a 3D consortium for Social and Historical Sciences (SHS) in order to meet a growing need for expertise on 3D practices in the social and historical sciences (cf. Consortium 3D). The purpose of this consortium was to define the field for the use of 3D in SHS in order to synthesise these practices by offering coordination at a national level with regularly published news about methods, vocabulary and about sharing, publishing, storing and preserving 3D data.

The use of 3D tools has enriched research processes, but it has also necessitated a reconsid-eration of data acquisition and processing. Indeed, the low-cost nature of the equipment has made it possible to consider the production of 3D models from the field phase and no longer only in the laboratory. The two main techniques used are photogrammetry and laser scanning. The choice of methods and 3D tools, whether in the field or in the laboratory, depends on the questions posed and the type of study subject.

3D tools can be used at different scales in biological anthropology and archaeo-anthropology: at the scale of the single bone (e.g. Zollikofer and Ponce de León, 2005; Coqueugniot *et al.*, 2014), the grave (e.g. Tchérémissinoff and Seguin, 2019; Jamestown Smithsonian 3D Digitization), or the site (e.g. Dutailly, Mora and Vergnieux, 2010; Wilhelmson and Dell'Unto, 2015). Data obtained from the analysis of 3D models complement the other data acquired and contribute to documenting the biology of an individual in addition to information on mortuary and cultural practices.

Modelling and 3D reconstruction offer new means to restore the original appearance of the grave and to better understand the populations of the past. The possibility to examine the bone internally and externally, to save an image of a grave at the time of its discovery and during its excavation, and the potential to recover perishable remains modify practices in archaeo-anthropology. The introduction of new, otherwise inaccessible data makes it possible to formulate new questions and thus open up new fields of research, whether on mortuary behaviour, the taphonomy of skeletal remains or funerary behaviour (e.g. Sachau-Carcel, 2014; cf. Mickleburgh *et al.,* Chapter 28, this volume). These advances have been established through the application of new recording methods and practices to aid the excavation of burials, as well as offering new forms of representation to enrich questions in bioarchaeology and archaeothanatology.

Recording the extant and restoring the past

In archaeology, 3D modelling for 3D reconstruction is used in two very different contexts: either to record existing remains or to restore perishable or poorly preserved remains. As with any tool or new method, 3D tools are first and foremost used based on the research design outlined for the study of the grave or site (Vergnieux, 2009). The use of reconstructions arises in the same way for funerary sites (Sachau-Carcel, Castex and Vergnieux, 2015). Recording of burials and skeletal remains can be performed directly on the site during the excavation or after the removal of the remains in the laboratory. Prior to excavation, the 3D tools chosen depend on the desired detail of the 3D model and the time allotted for its creation. When the excavation has already been completed, the choice of 3D tools will depend on the quality of the data collected and that of the field recording.

3D recording

In the case of 3D models generated during the excavation phase, the tools used for recording deposits depend on the timing of excavation accessibility, the weather and local field conditions. The application of 3D recording requires consideration of all facets of the excavation *before* fieldwork begins. The questions posed are fundamental elements to be considered, whether they concern the grave or the site, before any use of 3D tools commences (Sachau-Carcel and Castex, 2017). Indeed, the level of detail for recording depends, for the most part, on the research question(s) to be addressed. The study of each bone of each skeleton within a grave is different from the study of graves and their layout at the site. The research design permits adjustment of the required detail of recording and *de facto* the time necessary for recording in the field. The tools detailed here depend on the scale of the study and the time dedicated to recording.

First, in addition to the ease (or not) of accessibility for recording, it is necessary to determine the size and dimensions of the subject. Two major techniques can be used to acquire the surface of an object or archaeological feature: laser scanning and photogrammetry (Figure 31.1). These tools require very different types of technology, the choice of which depends on the type of excavation, the training of those using the tools, and the skills necessary for the treatment of data. The desired results are, however, the same with regard to the creation of 3D models.

Laser scanning

3D laser scanners come in many different types, for example, with or without contact, fixed arms or manual, palpable, triangulation, time-of-flight terrestrial and aerial (Pamart *et al.*, 2019). In archaeology and anthropology, the most commonly used laser scanner is without contact and associated with the time-of-flight methods, so the discussion here will be limited to these types of laser scanners. The operating principle of the laser scanner is based on the projection of a laser line on a surface. A detector measures the distance to the surface of the target object, calculating the time needed for the pulse of the laser beam to travel to the object and back again. Each point is geo-located by its X, Y and Z coordinates relative to the scanner and aggregated as part of a cloud of points by software provided by the laser scanner manufacturer. The precision of recording is defined before the acquisition of the surface and cannot be increased afterwards. The instrument permits acquiring surfaces of different scales, from a single grave to large excavated areas and can be deployed on site and manipulated by hand. The acquisition can be ground (terrestrial scanner) or air (with the scanner installed on an airplane, Aerial Laser Scanning (ALS) or Light Detection and Ranging LIDAR). The terrestrial time-of-flight laser scanner is most commonly used on

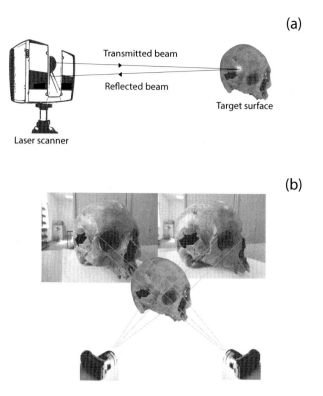

Figure 31.1 (a) Principles of a laser scanner, an example of 3D recording of a cranium (comparative anatomy collection of the Archéologie des Sociétés Méditerranéennes (ASM) Laboratory, UMR 5140, Montpellier); (b) the principles of photogrammetry, an example of 3D recording of a cranium (comparative anatomy collection of the ASM laboratory, UMR 5140, Montpellier) demonstrating the use of two images for the location of homologous points (Images: G. Sachau-Carcel).

archaeological sites (Howland, 2018). It provides a coloured and textured 3D surface model immediately after acquisition. The time of recording depends on the size and the complexity of the surface scanned and the desired precision or accuracy. Multiple scans may be necessary to achieve the desired results, but the acquisition of multiple scans can be a long and difficult process.

Models with structured light, also used in archaeology, offer great speed of acquisition but the luminous environment is an important factor because the laser line must be visible to obtain results. In many cases, electrical lighting is required to ensure good light levels, which can be a disadvantage to laser scanning in the field. This tool, therefore, requires a power supply as well. Laser scanner technology is relatively expensive and equipment costs include operator training, proprietary software licenses and hardware maintenance. Laser scanners also produce very heavy point clouds that need to be manipulated, recorded and stored, which in the end could pose a problem for the use and storage of data. Laser scanners can be used to record an archaeological site, an excavation area (Doneus and Neubauer, 2005), a building (De Luca, 2014) and even graves (Forte, Dell'Unto and Haddow, 2013). This technique is also used in the laboratory for the 3D acquisition of skeletal remains and graves lifted '*en bloc*' (block-lifted) (Zemour *et al.*, 2017; cf. Cartron and Zemour, Chapter 22, this volume). The laser scanner is also used for the recording, documentation and preservation of ancient monuments in the related fields of cultural heritage and for museographical purposes to save or reproduce existing objects (e.g. De Reu *et al.*, 2013).

Photogrammetry

Photogrammetry, also called image-based modelling, is based on the principle of overlap between two photographs. About 20 different types of software are available (e.g. Visual SFM, Metashape, Photomodeler and Colmap), most of which are freely available or require the purchase of a licence. All of these permit assembly of overlapping photographs. The method of data capture must necessarily adapt to the size and the shape of the object of interest. The photographs must have at least 30% in common.

The production of the 3D model takes place in several stages. The first step involves the recognition of key points between photographs, i.e. the recognition of homologous points in multiple photographs. The common point must be present on at least two photographs. An initial point cloud is generated and is called a sparse point-cloud. The second step is a significant increase in the number of points: dense clouds. The different points are then connected to form the mesh, the 3D surface. Once the mesh is built, a texture can be applied. Meshing and texture must be added to the point-cloud to obtain the 3D surface reconstruction of the object. These different steps can be carried out using the same software or in different software, which can be done either automatically or by manual adjustment of the settings. In most cases, if the photographs are not geo-referenced, the coordinates of the object and the scale need to be added. As with the laser scanner, image acquisition may require one or more acquisitions of the same object. Accuracy can be chosen for every step of the process of creation of the 3D model in photogrammetry. The quality of 3D models generated by photogrammetry depends on the quality of the photographs (cf. Historic England's *Photogrammetric applications for cultural heritage, guidance for good practice*). The light levels must be the same – and ideally without shadows – to achieve the best results. Photographs can simply be stored before being used and are much lighter than the point clouds generated by laser scanners. In addition, photographs are also used for other documents such as research reports.

After recording during the excavation, the point-cloud, mesh and texture of the 3D model are ready for study. The format may vary according to its use. The time necessary for the creation of 3D models varies according to the tools used, the selection of parameters and the extent of the subject (i.e. whole site or object). The technique is now also integrated into the recording protocol in the context of preventive or rescue excavation, regardless of the complexity of the grave (Tchérémissinoff and Seguin, 2019; Ducke *et al.*, 2011). The technology of photogrammetry can rival laser scanning when precisely and carefully used for the repeatability of measurements (e.g. Samsel and Sachau-Carcel, 2016; Sholts *et al.*, 2011). Three-dimensional tools have the advantage of being scalable and integrative. Photogrammetry is also associated with other types of tools such as GIS to create 3D databases, whether for the study of decorated caves (Dutailly, Chapoulie and Lacanette, 2020) or for 'virtual taphonomy' (Wilhelmson and Dell'Unto, 2015).

Computed microtomography scan

On a different scale, the recording of extant remains can also be carried out using 'tomographic' procedures. CT and micro-computed tomography are originally medical technologies usually used on living organisms and produce 2D and 3D images of an object. Images are based on X-ray technology, the rays are partly absorbed by the object that is penetrated, and the remaining X-rays are recorded by a detector behind the object (Weber, 2014). CT scans provide 2D images (slices) that are combined into a 3D image. This is a non-invasive diagnostic tool that permits examination of the digitised object externally and internally. Very soon after the introduction of CT in clinical trials conducted in the 1970s, CT was applied in studies of fossils, human remains and mummified remains (Jungers and Minns, 1979). The recent advances in micro-CT technology for high-resolution tomographic imaging make it possible to work on a microscopic level. The applications are diverse and concern many fields such as archaeology, archaeozoology, palaeoanthropology, biological anthropology and forensic science, including scans of dense and very dense objects such as bones, teeth, antlers, ivory, shells, stones and ceramics. Among the studies applying CT scan technology is that of 'Ötzi', a mummified body discovered in the Italian-Austrian Alps (Seidler, Bernhard and Teschler-Nicola, 1992). Other studies focus on single bones such as those of the cranium related to the evolution and modification of cranial shape (Zollikofer and Ponce de León, 2005). CT scans are also used in forensic anthropology to perform virtual autopsies of disaster victims (Uldin, 2017).

Applications in the field of palaeoanthropology concern the analysis of fossilised elements, the study of growth processes, means of locomotion and analysis of taphonomic bone damage that may bear witness to cultural practices (e.g. Rittemard *et al.*, 2019). CT scans thus make it possible to visualise and analyse internal anatomical structures, to virtually clean fossils of surrounding matrix, to reconstruct missing parts by symmetry, to combine anatomical elements borrowed from distinct individuals, and to correct post-mortem deformation (Dutailly *et al.*, 2008).

In bioarchaeological research, skeletal remains modelled by CT scan are used to document the state of health and trauma and to provide information on cultural practices, and they can also be used to study a burial, as in the case of cremations (André *et al.*, 2012; cf. Depierre, Chapter 4, this volume; Duday, Chapter 15, this volume) to study the inside of vases found in the grave (e.g. Inrap's analysis of Etruscan grave inclusions from Aleria-Lamajone in Haute-Corse, France) (https://www.inrap.fr/en/node/14328). The increasing use of this technology is reflected in the acquisition of CT and micro-CT scanners by museums, universities and research centres worldwide.

Comparison of techniques

Micro-CT and CT scan technologies make it possible to study internal and external structures without damaging the remains. This technology provides a complement to field investigations. For anthropological studies, 3D models of bones can be obtained by a CT scan, laser scan and photogrammetry and used for morphometric studies. In the field, these two techniques, scanning and photogrammetry, have the same precision – less than 1 mm – but the two processes are quite different and thus require different operating procedures and know-how (Howland, 2018). Photogrammetry is a more flexible recording tool than laser scans because it is more quickly set up in the field, only a camera being required. The laser scan offers the advantage of automated acquisition and also makes it possible in the case of LIDAR, for example, to by-pass vegetation.

Restoring the past?

The main applications of 3D recording are based on that of extant remains or, on the contrary, the reconstruction of no longer surviving remains (Vergnieux, 2009). The reconstruction protocol is particularly applicable for older excavations, and those where it was not feasible to set up an *in situ* 3D acquisition protocol. The software used for reconstruction in archaeology and archaeo-anthropology is freely available or purchased for modelling software offering advanced capabilities, such as geo-referencing of models, lighting and texture modelling, motion simulation and video production (e.g. Sketchfab, Blender, Meshlab, 3ds Max).

In the context of missing, no longer extant, or incomplete remains, several scenarios present themselves. If material remains have disappeared altogether and the aim is to restore an 'original image' of the remains, reconstruction of the disappeared remains complements written and iconographic source descriptions. Complete reconstruction of the object of study must also be based on comparisons, typologies and validation processes between different specialists according to the nature of the object to be reconstructed, whether ceramic vessel, grave, or temple, for example.

In the context of the partial destruction of archaeological remains, whether by excavation, anthropogenic or natural phenomena, as for the preserved material remains they can be acquired in 3D, regardless of the method, and augmented by the remains that have preserved. The archaeological, historical, epigraphic and iconographic information can be included in the 3D model. This way, it contributes to the appearance of the missing parts (Hermon, Nikodem and Perlingieri, 2006; Batino *et al.*, 2013).

3D modelling

Restoring the past is a deeply intellectual exercise. It requires in-depth reflection on the part of specialists as well as a collaborative, multi-disciplinary and ethically sensitive approach (Vergnieux, 2011). The difficulty lies in the manner of integration of hypothetical data, reconstructed from existing, tangible data, which was the topic of the *Virtual Retrospect Symposium* (2007) from which this chapter cites a number of contributions.

3D recording cannot be applied in all situations, but for older excavations, or those without 3D recording, a 3D model can be obtained by other means, provided that essential information from the excavation and, in the case of the burials, if all of the components of the grave are available (Sachau-Carcel, Vergnieux and Castex, 2015). The quality of documentation from old excavations can provide for the creation of a 3D model from the coordinates of each object from the original field documentation. Indeed, scaled 3D coordinates make it possible to place the 3D model back in its spatial location. However, the archaeological descriptions and any additional source permitting description and characterisation of the object of study is fundamental and depends on the extent of care taken in the field to collect the information.

Contributions and limits of 3D tools

The object of interest – in this case, a skeleton, burial or site – and surrounding area must be free from obstructions, without people, so it is not possible to continue the excavation during recording. The time allotted to recording must be correctly evaluated in order not to lose time or have extended periods of inactivity on site. This requirement is particularly problematic for rescue excavations. Accessibility to the object of interest can also present problems. It is necessary to be able to walk around the targeted context for photogrammetry or to focus on the point of interest, such as a cave, for laser scanning. The portability of the camera is a great advantage due to the ease of its use in enclosed or small spaces and without access to electricity. However, the levels of lighting can cause real problems for both, but the laser scanner fares better under variable lighting conditions. The techniques present advantages as well as limitations according to the characteristics of the excavation. It is necessary to adapt practices in accordance with budgetary constraints, available expertise and the type of research questions posed. It is important to consider recording at a specific point in time because it is impossible to start over after the completion of the excavation. The recording must be good from the first attempt, which is why it is necessary to define the object of interest and the precision required in the planning phase. While treatments can be re-done, the initial acquisition cannot. For this, the laser scan and taking photographs requires trained personnel. For photogrammetry, it is a question of taking good photographs but also of good preparation, such as respecting overlaps and angles, for example.

Regardless of the technique used, data acquisition requires investment in time and consideration. However, compared to conventional surveying and drawing techniques, 3D tools are faster and more accurate if used properly.

The basic advantage of these recording methods is the opportunity to view the object from all angles. Another important advantage is that depth, altitude and sections are all automatically generated from all angles. A drawing can be produced after the excavation and according to the most useful perspective. It is particularly interesting to have an overall view when a structure, like a building, or a grave was not expected to occur in the excavated area (e.g. Zanella *et al.*, 2016). Any 3D tool has the advantage of being non-invasive and manipulated simultaneously by different people in different places. It is reproducible and verifiable at any time, unlike the older methods of recording. The acquired objects can also be printed in 3D and distributed to the scientific community or the general public. Three-dimensional tools contribute to create a backup of the objects and ensure their durability and preservation over the long term. The resulting 3D models thus constitute a base for future examinations and studies and from novel research requiring simulations and reconstructions of the past.

Archaeothanatological applications

When they are well-produced, 3D models are a first-rate source for detailed research use in archaeothanatology. The advantages of 3D models are vast. These models offer the possibility to return to the deposit and its analysis and interpretation. At the same time, they constitute a working document, a means to archive results and to facilitate dissemination of them. The following examples illustrate the use of 3D models.

A complex burial context

An example of the use of a 3D model based only on the field documentation comes from two complex multiple burials of approximately 80 individuals found southeast of Rome in the catacomb of Saints Peter and Marcellinus[1], excavated in 2006 and 2008 (Castex and Blanchard, 2011; cf. Castex and Huchet, Chapter 18, this volume). The central sector of the catacomb consists of seven cavities, two of which have been exhaustively excavated. The latter contained between 76 and 80 individuals, some of whom were provided with individual burial goods. Early in the field phase, deposits separated by sedimentary levels could be identified. However, the organisation within each level of deposition and possible simultaneous deposits raised questions about the funerary use of the space. Therefore research on the use of 3D reconstruction of these burials was initiated at the end of the excavation. The goal of the reconstruction of these two burial deposits was to reveal the funerary practices through the analysis of these commingled individuals, which could not be resolved by other means (Sachau-Carcel, 2012). The reconstruction protocol created was essentially based on field documentation (photographs, field records and notes). Since the cavities were preserved, they could be acquired in 3D through the use of photogrammetry after completion of the excavation. Each constituent element of the central grave was restored in 3D, human remains, funerary inclusions and sedimentary levels. The 3D reconstruction made it possible to study each bone of each individual in order to work out the position of the deceased individual by individual. In contrast to traditional 2D documentation such as plans,

---

1 Variously called the catacomb of Saints Marcellinus and Peter.

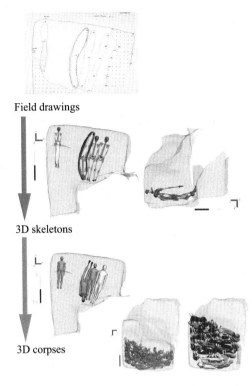

Field drawings

3D skeletons

3D corpses

Figure 31.2 The process of reconstruction of grave 18 from the catacomb of Saints Peter and Marcellinus, Rome (Italy). All of the individuals were reconstructed from the field drawings in the form of 3D skeletons of the bodies to help understand the layout of the deposits in the grave (Images: G. Sachau-Carcel).

the 3D model offered an immediate visualisation of the individual in space, from above and in profile. The model also permitted work on the overlaps between individuals and thus document simultaneous depositions of corpses. The reconstruction of the bodies was particularly innovative since it made it possible to visualise the bodies as deposited with soft tissue, including the space they occupied within the two studied cavities. The results showed that all the bodies could not have been deposited at the same time because the layers would have exceeded the height of the ceiling (Sachau-Carcel, 2012, 2019). This limitation made it possible to set chronological milestones by estimating the number of skeletal layers necessary to accommodate the deposition of new bodies (Figure 31.2).

The study made it possible to improve the understanding of the arrangement of the bodies by layer and to document the funerary use of each of the cavities studied. This would have been impossible using conventional tools as calculations of the altitude of each bone of each individual present in the layers would have been necessary, i.e. nearly 60 000 bones present in 43 different plans while relying only on photographs. Although the field notes, anthropological observations, plans and photographs were used as the basis for the 3D model, the 3D model made all of this quickly intelligible and permitted a detailed and precise analysis of each individual and of groups of individuals from all angles, which could then be re-contextualised in the burial space (Sachau-Carcel, 2014).

The reconstruction of complex burial deposits after their excavation was based on the innovative use of 3D models and provides an important contribution to older excavation reporting and publication. This protocol is fully transferable to all types of burials where the goal is to understand and display the organisation of the deposits, access to the grave, and treatment of the bodies in collective graves.

Cremation burials

Since 2014, Van Andringa, Creissen and Duday have directed the excavation of the Roman Cemetery of Porta Nocera in Pompeii (Italy) (cf. Duday, Chapter 15, this volume). This new excavation area permitted the implementation of a novel strategy for recording archaeological remains at the site. A specific strategy to create 3D models of the excavation was prepared in order to provide an exhaustive record of the site during excavation, which was greatly enhanced by the exceptional potential of the site and the time allotted to excavation that permitted testing of new methods. A photogrammetric recording protocol was established for all of the stratigraphic units excavated (Van Andringa, Creissen and Duday, 2014). All sediment units and artefacts were recorded. Photogrammetric acquisition took place throughout the time of excavation, sometimes for the entire excavated area and sometimes only for a part of it, as stratigraphic units were discovered. Each unit was recorded in 3D regardless of its location within the excavation area. Figure 31.3 shows the extent of excavation of the area between 2014 and 2015.

One of the many examples of the contribution of 3D models at this site concerns the discovery of cremation burial SP 301, found in the wall of a small enclosure in Zone A. A 3D protocol was applied to record the positioning of the glass urn in the wall and the position of the deposits within the urn, including their height. Not only did the models indicate the position of deposits in the wall, but they also aided the determination of the type of deposit, whether it had occurred in an empty or full-earth space, as well as the developmental sequence of the wall. The fragmentary nature of the urn made it impossible to retrieve the urn 'en bloc' through block-lifting, yet this was one of the only ways of knowing its precise location and position and its inclination within the wall. The location of each glass fragment had to be known in order to determine the precise position of the urn in the masonry. Systematic hand surveying of this type of material is particularly time-consuming. The photogrammetric survey of the urn in place with the cremated remains, and then after the dismantling of the wall, was, therefore, a more time-efficient and more accurate alternative solution to a manually drawn section.

The 3D recording protocol developed for the site excavation was adapted in order to record this cremation burial specifically. A separate 3D recording permitted the section to be documented. Two acquisitions were produced, one for the urn cremation and a second for the niche in the wall without the urned cremation in it. Photographs were taken with the field camera and each recording session took ten minutes. The wall and the urn were geo-located in order to locate them spatially and to scale them. Surface treatments were made immediately afterwards, a process which took thirty minutes. This means that the 3D model became available for study the same day it had been acquired in various formats, including a Portable Document Format (.pdf).

The creation of the 3D model of this cremation facilitated the interpretation of this burial. The 3D model made it possible to test the different possible perspectives and retain only the most informative ones. It permitted generation of multiple sections very quickly, whereas the implementation of recording of the sections in the field would have required leaving stratigraphic units in place, particularly at the foot of the enclosure wall. These sections permitted the urn to be portrayed as it had been inserted in the masonry (Figure 31.4). The visualisation of the cremation and the negative of the urn in the wall permitted definition of this position precisely. The height of the preserved deposit could be measured directly from the 3D model without the necessity of

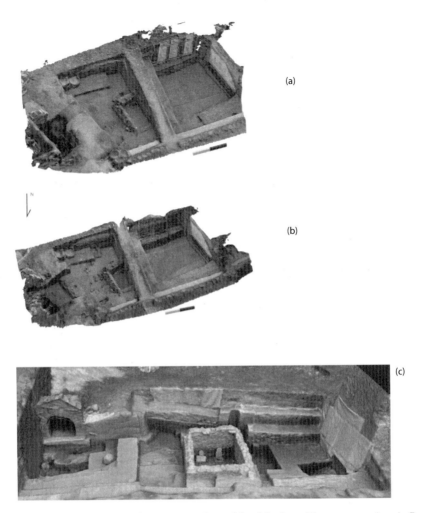

Figure 31.3 An extract from three photogrammetric models of the Porta Nocera excavations in Pompeii (Italy). All three images show the stratigraphic units excavated in two different steps in 2014 (upper image, a and b) and 2015 (lower image, c) (Images: G. Sachau-Carcel).

taking multiple height measurements to capture the oblique orientation of the urn and to compare this with disposition of the skeletal remains within it. The section produced from the 3D models permitted recording of the shape of the urn in place in the wall prior to fragmentation so that the type of the urn could be identified, despite its poor preservation. In summary, the 3D model was used to provide field documentation rapidly, saving time and constituting an archive document for future investigation of this archaeological feature and its burial.

3D recording of a cemetery

Systematic 3D recording of graves within a cemetery was undertaken at the Merovingian cemetery at Saint-Martin de Bruch in Lot et Garonne, France, directed by Castex and Cartron, in order to develop a more efficient and accurate protocol for 3D recording of graves, as well as

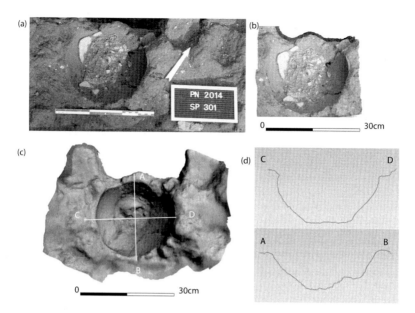

Figure 31.4 Burial SP301 of Porta Nocera (PN2014) exposed in the wall of mausoleum 26a, Pompei, superior view photograph during excavation. (a-b) superior view extracted from the 3D model; (c) extraction from the 3D model after total excavation of the urn with the section axes created afterwards from the model; (d) profile view of the two-section axes extracted from the 3D model (Images: G. Sachau-Carcel).

samples of entire cemeteries, in general (Cartron, Castex and Sachau-Carcel, 2013), and to be able to better exploit the information contained in a 3D model after excavation.

The cemetery consisted of a diverse variety of graves, including single and multiple burials, with various forms of architecture: from sarcophagi to solely earthen burials of both juveniles and adults. Their varied complexity and differential access influenced the type of protocol adopted. In addition, the excavation being a field school also impacted the protocol. Photogrammetry was chosen as the technique for 3D recording for two reasons: its less expensive material costs and the absence of a need to produce 3D models immediately. The photography for 3D recording was carried out systematically before the removal of the skeleton from the grave, and the creation of 3D models was made according to the demands imposed by each grave. Ten to fifteen minutes appeared to be enough recording time for each grave, whereas an accurate manual survey can take more than 1 hour depending on the complexity of the deposits, and more if the elevation of each bone is required, essential for archaeothanatological analysis. The complex removal of skeletons from the multiple burials required recording each step of the excavation of each layer. Photogrammetry permitted the development of a robust and flexible means to record the variable complexity of the burial according to the number of individuals, numerous superimpositions and altitude differences in the skeleton and grave furnishings present in each. From a technical point of view, the application of photogrammetry to complex burials provided the opportunity to establish the resolution needed to enhance 3D model quality as well as to determine the time required to do so. In practice, the material and the rules applied were quite simple, with a focus on producing good quality photographs. Because of its field school setting, a further aim was to involve each archaeological fieldworker in the process of creating a 3D model of a grave. It was necessary to identify and correct flaws in recording as the photogrammetric protocol had to be adjusted for each grave. The results obtained were satisfactory after field school students had undertaken two sessions of photograph acquisition. After corrections, the quality of the photographs enabled the generation of 3D models with an accuracy of less than a millimetre.

This project on a large sample consisting of twenty graves confirmed that 3D models offer greater opportunity for various observations, for taking measurements, recording levels and making taphonomic observations from both single and multiple burials. Interpretation of individual burials during the field phase appeared to be relatively straightforward. In these situations, the 3D model did not provide new insights but did simplify and speed recording. Additionally, 3D recording facilitated observations with greater accuracy. For more complex burials, however, whether single or multiple, 3D models proved to be essential when skeletal remains were commingled and obscured one another or when the bones were interlocked to obtain a more detailed understanding of the deposit. For example, in the case of sarcophagus 16 with four individuals, 3D models were used as the basis for the description of, especially, the super-imposed skeletal elements within the deposit (Figure 31.5). After the osteological study, the 3D models were further enhanced by the identification of different bones of each individual that offered novel opportunities to describe their position in three dimensions, including details not visible on the original photographs, but which become clearer in the 3D models due to the exhaustive

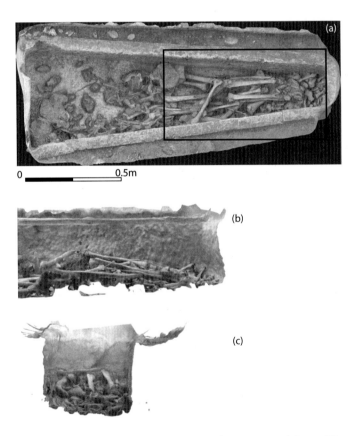

Figure 31.5 View of the superposition of deposits in a sarcophagus extracted from a 3D model of a grave from Bruch Merovingian cemetery (Lot et Garonne, France): (a) superior view; (b) lateral view through the wall of the sarcophagus and (c) a transverse view. The last two images permitted observation of the superposition of the limb bones (Images: G. Sachau-Carcel).

nature of the recording. Analysis of the photographs alone would not have permitted viewing of the information obtained at the level of clarity and resolution of a 3D model.

In this example, 3D models were not only a field recording method but also support for research. The multiple perspectives and the possibility to interrogate the images after completion of fieldwork influenced the quality of the results of the project. Through visualisation of the skeletal remains of the once corpse, the deposit, in general, was perceived differently because it was possible to appreciate changes in the overall deposit after deposition of each individual and re-arrangement of the grave. Three-dimensional models could thus be adjusted when necessary for individual graves in order to address the research questions posed. Such recording is never too time-consuming when it can serve for both archive photographs as well as 3D models. For this Merovingian cemetery site, the 3D recording of the burials also constituted a means to safeguard the discoveries against loss but also permitted re-positioning them in the stratigraphic relations within the sarcophagus and within site as a whole. In addition, it made it possible to reproduce archaeothanatological observations.

Extended applications

Another advantage of 3D models comes with the increased capacity to disseminate documents more quickly in order to achieve greater immediate impact. Once the 3D models are created, the applications are applicable for dissemination to both a specialised public as well as the general public. Three-dimensional models facilitate working virtually and physically through the 3D printing of fragile parts of fossilised remains and for otherwise inaccessible sites (e.g. Peignaux *et al.*, 2019).

Libraries of 3D models have been widely developed for both human or animal skeletons and individual bones. They are accessible online and come from facilities dedicated to the digitisation of models (i.e. California Academy of Sciences, eAnthropology of the University of Texas at Austin, Duke University and from research laboratories (i.e. Virtos, not available to the public) and museums (i.e. Smithsonian 3D Digitization), British Museum, the Musée d'Archéologie Nationale (National Archaeological Museum of France) and the Louvre) throughout the world. The Archeogrid website is the French national repository of 3D data and models produced in the Human and Social Sciences (cf. Archeogrid; Conservatoire National des Données 3D). Anyone can deposit 3D archives and promote their consultation by the entire research community. These digital collection libraries are also intended for teaching purposes and provide easy access to the remains needed for bone identification, such as that provided by 'Laetoli Production Vertebrates' or pathological identification of human bones, such as 'Digitised Diseases'.

However, while for academic institutions and research laboratories, the scientific protocols and the origin of remains are known, this is not the case for all on-line sites. The accuracy of the 3D models, the techniques and tools used in their preparation and the purpose of the 3D model libraries are not always available. It is thus not possible to see these as anything other than nice 3D models since it is impossible to appreciate how they were produced. Due to their intrinsic nature, 3D models are a formidable means by which to promote and disseminate research carried out in archaeology and archaeothanatology. Indeed, these working tools serve as a research resource that can be immediately made available to the general public. Three-dimensional vision system integrated virtual reality makes it possible to virtually visit a site (e.g. Athenaion of Poseidonia in Paestum in Italy and 3D archaeology at Çatalhöyuk, (Forte, Dell'Unto and Haddow, 2013)), a tomb (i.e. Pharaoh Ramesses VI tomb), Tomb of Queen Meresankh III, the Etruscan Regolini-Galassi tomb (Hupperetz *et al.*, 2012) or to visit virtual exhibitions enhanced with augmented reality (Pompeii in the Grand-Palais or Voyage virtuel de Palmyre à Mossoul in Institut du Monde Arabe.

Conclusion

The development of new recording techniques and the means to exploit this information modifies the practice of archaeothanatology in both the field and the laboratory. Three-dimensional tools offer a large range of possibilities to aid archaeo-anthropological studies as well as cognate areas of interest. Three-dimensional recording and processing is extremely useful when considering the range of its uses. A 3D model permits close examination of the skeletal remains and of the stratigraphic unit in which they are found, which is especially important when there are multiple skeletons, certainly if they are commingled and overlying one another. The advantages of 3D recording reside in its ability to aggregate additional information for use by archaeologists and biological anthropologists. A 3D model provides sections of high definition, coloured images that represent a faithful representation of both the grave structure and the skeletal remains. It also makes it possible to automate processes for the reconstruction of remains (Reuter *et al.*, 2011). The time allotted for 3D recording is less than needed for more traditional recording methods. This is a great advantage, but it is important to recognise that 3D records must be subjected to the same methods of interrogation and attention to detail as found in traditional recording methods. The capacity to obtain sections and feature information in post-excavation analysis is particularly attractive for use in preventive/salvage archaeology (cf. Guillon, Chapter 32, this volume). Although 3D recording is based on the same scientific approach, it constitutes a different and complementary recording method to traditional methods of observation and recording (Sachau-Carcel, 2014). Certainly, in cases where time is short, 3D methods are more efficient because they provide more information from one-step recording.

3D models have the capacity to enhance the study of graves because they permit visualisation from all perspectives, even those that are impossible to achieve in the field. The reconstruction of the original dimensions of the grave and the space occupied by the once corpse enhance the study of taphonomy. Comparisons between graves or sites are made easier as they are based on the same model of the remains, and they can thus more easily facilitate exchange between specialists. Three-dimensional models are thus easier to use in order to simulate the movement and displacement of bones and to test hypotheses in order to demonstrate the once presence of perishable funerary architecture.

3D models can be used to support and explain research questions as well as research results. The greatest contribution of archaeothanatological research is its capacity to reconstruct graves and their contents as they were at discovery and as they would have appeared to once living people. The facility to restore lost images of the past through a virtual image and through which researchers and the general public can more easily imagine the past. Finally, a further important benefit of 3D technology is the archiving of excavation records for longer-term storage. Regardless of the technique, 3D models can be used and re-used over and over. For photogrammetry, photographs can be treated with new software to achieve better resolution of key features. Photographs in this way also become raw material for re-use. The limit of these improvements, however, is the resolution of the original photographs. For laser-scanning the situation is different; the model of the instrument employed determines accuracy. However, the level of accuracy is always greater than that achievable by a human without it. Issues such as digital rights management, metadata structure, accurate representation of an object or a site, and also the preservation of such information remain impediments to research. Efforts are underway, and conversations are taking place regarding such concerns as 3D archaeology becomes a permanent fixture in the field. A major obstacle is the storage of 3D data and the size of the files. The server space required for the storage of photographs, CAD (Computer Assisted Design) images and 3D models can be problematic. Since the aim of storage is to permit consultation and exploitation of the files in the future, the choice of the format used and the resolution of images are very important topics for future discussion and consideration. Another question relates to how to set standards for the quality control of the 3D model. In other words, who is competent to decide if the accuracy/resolution is sufficient? This is a necessary conversation to have between the director of the excavation, the excavators, the specialists and collaborating institutions. Given that 3D recording and 3D models will become increasingly common in the future, it is essential that the person responsible is adequately trained in 3D recording to ensure the high quality of 3D models.

References

André, A., Coqueugniot, H., Desbarats, P. and Rottier, S. (2012). Apport de l'imagerie médicale et de la 3D à l'étude des crémations en contexte archéologiqique, *Proceedings of the 1837e Journées de la Société d'Anthropologie de Paris*, Poster presentation.

Batino, S., Callieri, M., Duranti, D., Dellepiane, M., Pingi, P., Siotto, E. and Scopigno, R. (2013). Virtual Reconstruction of an Etruscan tomb. In: W. Börner and S. Uhlirz, eds., *Proceedings of the 17th International Conference on Cultural Heritage and New Technologies, November 5-7, 2012,* Vienna: Museen der Stadt Wien, pp. (https://www.chnt.at/chnt-17-2012-proceedings/) (Last accessed 20 September 2021).

Cartron, I., Castex, D. and Sachau-Carcel, G. (2013). *Saint-Martin de Bruch (Lot-et-Garonne), habitat antique et nécropole du haut Moyen-Âge, Unpublished archaeological report,* Bordeaux.

Castex, D. and Blanchard, P. (2011). Le Secteur Central de la Catacombe des Saints Pierre-et-Marcellin (Rome, Ier-IIIe Siècle). Indices Archéologiques d'une Crise Brutale de Mortalité. *Mélanges de l'Ecole Française de Rome. Antiquité,* 123(1), pp. 274–280.

Collet, P. (1996). La Photographie et l'Archéologie: Des chemins inverses, *Bulletin de Correspondance Hellénique,* 120(1), pp. 325–344.

Coqueugniot, H. and Dutour, O. (2015). Apports de l'imagerie numérique 3D à l'étude de l'os ancien, normal et pathologique. In: J.-P. Brugal, M. Balasse, L. Reiche, E.M. Geigl and C. Oberlin, eds., *Messages d'Os. Archéométrie du Squelette Animal et Humain.* Paris: Éditions Archives Contemporaines, pp. 255–267.

Coqueugniot, H., Dutour, O., Arensburg, B., Duday, H., Vandermeersch, B. and Tillier, A.-m. (2014). Earliest Cranio-Encephalic Trauma from the Levantine Middle Palaeolithic: 3D Reappraisal of the Qafzeh 11 Skull, Consequences of Pediatric Brain Damage on Individual l-Life Condition and Social Care. *PLoS ONE,* 9(7), p. e102822.

De Luca, L. (2014). Methods, Formalisms and Tools for the Semantic-Based Surveying and Representation of Architectural Heritage. *Journal of Applied Geomatics,* 6, pp. 115–139.

De Reu, J., Plets, G., Verhoeven, G., De Smedt, P., Bats, M., Cherretté, B., De Maeyer, W., Deconynck, J., Herremans, D., Laloo, P., Van Meirvenne, M. and De Clercq, W. (2013). Towards a Three-Dimensional Cost-Effective Registration of the Archaeological Heritage. *Journal of Archaeological Science,* 40(2), pp. 1108–1121.

Djindjian, F. and Vigneron, E. (1980). L'Analyse des Données au Service de l'Archéologie Préhistorique. *Bulletins de la Société Préhistorique Française,* 27(6), pp. 177–180.

Doneus, M. and Neubauer, W. (2005). Laser scanners for 3D documentation of stratigraphic excavations. In: E.P. Baltsavias, A. Gruen, L. Van Gool and M. Pateraki, eds., *International Workshop on Recording, Modelling and Visualization of Cultural Heritage.* May 22–27, 2005. Ascona, Switzerland and Abingdon: Taylor & Francis, pp. 193–246.

Ducke, B., Score, D. and Reeves, J. (2011). Multiview 3D Reconstruction of the Archaeological Site at Weymouth for Image Series. *Computer Graphics,* 35 (2), pp. 375–382.

Dutailly, B., Chapoulie, R. and Lacanette, D. (2020). SIG 3D pour l'étude et la conservation en archéologie. In: F. Laroche, M. Chayani, X. Granier and C. Delevoie, eds., *Les rencontres du Consortium 3D Social and Human Sciences (SHS),* December 2019, Nantes: Université de Nantes, Faculté des Sciences et Techniques (FST), pp. 1–5.

Dutailly, B., Coquaugniot, H., Couture, C., Courtaud, P., Desbarats, P., Gueorguieva, S. and Synave R. (2008). Imagerie médicale et patrimoine anthropologique: vers un contrôle total de la chaîne des traitements dans l'analyse morphométrique tridimensionnelle. In: R. Vergnieux and C. Delevoie, eds., *Actes du Colloque Virtual Rétrospect 2007.* Bordeaux: Archéovision, Éditions Ausonius, pp. 45–51.

Dutailly, B., Mora, P. and Vergnieux, R. (2010). 3D reconstruction of archaeological sites using photogrammetry. In: A. Artusi, M. Joly, G. Lucet, D. Pitzalis and A. Ribes, eds., *Proceedings of VAST (Virtual Analytics and Science) 2010: The 11th International Symposium on Virtual Reality, Archaeology and Cultural Heritage.* Paris: The Eurographics Association.

Forte, M., Dell'Unto, N. and Haddow, S. (2013). Cyber Archaeology at Çatalhöyük, *Current World Archaeology*, 61, pp. 36–40.

Forte, M., Tilia, S., Bizzarro, A. and Tilia, A. (2000). 3D visual information and GIS technology for documentation of wall paintings in the 'M' sepulchre in the Vatican necropolis. In: W. Schmid, ed., *GraDoc: Documentation Systems in Mural Painting Conservation.* Rome: International Centre for the Study of the Preservation and Restoration of Cultural Property (ICCROM), pp. 221–238.

Golvin, J.-C. and Boccon-Gibod, H. (1990). Le Grand Temple d'Amon-Rê à Karnak, Reconstruit par l'Ordinateur. *Les Dossiers de l'Archéologie*, 153, pp. 8–19.

Hermon, S., Nikodem, J. and Perlingieri, C. (2006). Deconstructing the Virtual Reality (VR) – Data Transparency, Quantified Uncertainty and Reliability of 3D Models. *VAST 2006: The 7th International Symposium on Virtual Reality, Archaeology and Intelligent Cultural Heritage*, 6, pp. 1–7.

Howland, M.D. (2018). 3D recording in the field: style without substance. In: T. Levy and I. Jones, eds., *Cyber-Archaeology and Grand Narratives.* Berlin: Springer, pp. 21–33.

Hupperetz, W., Carlani, R., Pletinckx, D. and Pietroni, E. (2012). Etruscanning 3D Project. The 3D Reconstruction of the Regolini Galassi Tomb as a Research Tool and a New Approach in Storytelling. *Virtual Archaeology Review*, 3(7), pp. 92–96.

Jungers, W.L. and Minns, R.J. (1979). Computed Tomography and Biomechanical Analysis of Fossil Long Bones. *American Journal of Physical Anthropology*, 50, pp. 285–290.

Laflin, S. (2014). *Computer applications in archaeology 1973-1995.* Birmingham: University of Birmingham, Birmingham.

Ordureau, S. and Lecuyot G. (2009). Apport de l'imagerie médicale 3D à l'étude d'une momie du IVe s. av. J.-C. In: R. Vergnieux and C. Delevoie, eds., *Virtual Retrospect 2007.* Bordeaux: Archéovision 3, Éditions Ausonius, pp. 39–43.

Pamart, A., Albergel, V., Flammin, A., Morineau, C. and Paitier, H. (2019). Apport critique sur les matériels et logiciels 3D: Synthèse des outils et des technologies 3D. *Les Recommandations du Consortium 3D SHS, 2019.* (https://hal.archives-ouvertes.fr/hal-02159453) (Last accessed 20 September 2021).

Peignaux, C., Kacki, S., Guyomarc'h, P., Schotsmans, E.M.J. and Villotte, S. (2019). New Anthropological Data from Cussac Cave (Gravettian, Dordogne, France): *In Situ* and Virtual Analyses of Locus 3. *Comptes Rendus Palevol*, 18: pp. 455–464.

Père, C. and Faucher, S. (2008). Cluny: de la gestion de données à la réalité augmentée. In: R. Vergnieux and C. Delevoie, eds., *Virtual Retrospect 2007*, Bordeaux: Éditions Ausonius, pp. 61–67.

Reuter, P., Mellado, N., Granier, X., Hairy, I. and Vergnieux, R. (2011). Semi-Automatic 3D Acquisition and Reassembly of Cultural Heritage: The SeARCH Project. In: P. Kunz, ed., *European Research Consortium for Informatics and Mathematics (ERCIM) News. ICT (Information Communications Technology) for Cultural Heritage special issue*, 86, pp. 12–13.

Rittemard, C., Colombo, A., Desbarats, P., Dutailly, B., Dutour, O. and Coquaugniot, H. (2019). The Periosteum Dilemma in Bioarcheology: Normal Growth or Pathological Condition? 3D Discriminating Microscopic Approach. *Journal of Archaeological Science: Reports*, 24, pp. 236–243.

Sachau-Carcel, G. (2012). *Apport de la modélisation tridimensionnelle à la compréhension du fonctionnement des sépultures multiples. L'exemple du secteur central de la catacombe des Saints Pierre-et-Marcellin (Rome, Italie, Ier-milieu IIIe siècle après Jésus-Christ)*, Unpublished Ph.D. thesis, Université de Bordeaux 3 Montaigne.

Sachau-Carcel, G. (2014). From Field Recording of Plural Burials to 3d Modelling. Evidence from the Catacomb of Sts. Peter and Marcellinus, Italy. *Anthropologie (Brno)*, 52(3), pp. 285–297.

Sachau-Carcel, G. and Castex, D. (2017). Archéothanatologie et 3D : quels enjeux? In: S. de Larminat, R. Corbineau, A. Corrochano, Y. Gleize, J. Soulat, eds., *Rencontre autour de nouvelles approches de l'archéologie funéraire. Actes de la 6e Rencontre du Gaaf, Institut national d'histoire de l'art (Paris, 4–5 avril 2014)*, Reugny : Groupe d'anthropologie et d'archéologie funéraire, pp. 235–242.

Sachau-Carcel G. (2019). D'os en os, comprendre les sépultures complexes, vers un renouveau des outils? *Préhistoires Méditerranéennes*, http://journals.openedition.org/pm/1757 (Last accessed 29 October 2019).

Sachau-Carcel, G., Vergnieux, R. and Castex, D. (2015). Du terrain à la restitution tridimensionnelle: quels enregistrements de données pour quels résultats? In: R. Vergnieux and C. Delevoie, eds., *Actes du Colloque Virtual Rétrospect 2013*. Bordeaux: Archéovision, Éditions Ausonius, Bordeaux, pp. 165–171.

Samsel, M. and Sachau-Carcel, G. (2016). De l'os aux modèles tridimensionnels: réflexions autour de différentes méthodes d'acquisition de données craniométriques, *Proceedings of the 1841e Journées de la Société d'Anthropologie de Paris*, 27–29 Janvier 2016, poster presentation.

Seidler, H., Bernhard, W. and Teschler-Nicola M. (1992). Some Anthropological Aspects of the Prehistoric Tyrolean Ice Man. *Science*, 258, pp. 455–457.

Sholts, S.B., Walker, P.L., Kuzminsky, S.C., Miller, K.W. and Wärmländer, S.K. (2011). Identification of Group Affinity from Cross-sectional Contours of the Human Midfacial Skeleton Using Digital Morphometrics and 3D Laser Scanning Technology. *Journal of Forensic Sciences*, 56, pp. 333–338.

Sullivan, E. and Harrower, M. (2015). The future of spatial technologies in Egyptology. In: R. Jasnow and K.M. Cooney, eds., *Thebes: Egyptological Studies in Honor of Betsy M. Bryan*. Atlanta: Lockwood Press, pp. 447–460.

Tchérémissinoff, Y. and Seguin, M. (2019). Mise en place d'un protocole photogrammétrie et SIG dès la fouille préventive: la sépulture collective de Mas Rouge à Montpellier (Hérault), *Préhistoires Méditerranéennes*, http://journals.openedition.org/pm/1757 (Last accessed 24 April 2020).

Uldin, T. (2017). Virtual Anthropology – A Brief Review of the Literature and History of Computed Tomography. *Forensic Sciences Research*, 2(4), pp. 165–173.

Van Andringa, W., Creissen, T. and Duday, H. (2014). *Fouille de la nécropole romaine de la Porta Nocera: le secteur 26OS*, Rapport d'Opération 2014. Rome: École Française de Rome.

Vergnieux, R. (2009). Sauvegarder les données numériques 3D du patrimoine In: R. Vergnieux and C. Delevoie, eds., *Actes du Colloque Virtual Rétrospect 2007*. Bordeaux Archéovision 3, Bordeaux: Éditions Ausonius, pp. 181–184.

Vergnieux, R. (2011). Archaeological Research and 3D Models (Restitution, Validation and Simulation). *Virtual Archaeology Review*, 2(4), pp. 39–43.

Weber, G.W. (2014). Another Link between Archaeology and Anthropology: Virtual Anthropology. *Digital Applications in Archaeology and Cultural Heritage*. 1(1), pp. 3–11.

Wilhelmson, H. and Dell'Unto, N. (2015). Virtual Taphonomy: A New Method Integrating Excavation and Post-Processing in an Archaeological Context. *American Journal of Physical Anthropology*, 157(2), pp. 305–321.

Zanella, S., Cavassa, L., Laubry, N., Monteix, N., Chapelin, G., Coutelas, A., Delvigne Ryrko A., Errera, M., Gerardin, L., Lemaire, B., Macario, R., Ortis, F., Pelligrino, V. and Sachau-Carcel, G. (2016). Pompéi, *Porta Ercolano*: Organisation, Gestion et Transformations d'une Zone Suburbaine, *Chronique des Activités Archéologiques de l' École Française de Rome*, Les cités vésuviennes, online 08 Mars 2017.

Zemour, A., Binder, D., Bonnardin, S., D'Ovidio, A.-M., Goude, G., Gourichon, L., Pradeau, J.-V., Sorin-Mazouni, S., Bromblet, P., Buchet, L., Cotto, K.-Y. and Sénépart, I. (2017). Laboratory Excavation of a Neolithic Grave from Avignon–La Balance-Ilot P (France): Burial Practices and Garment Reconstruction. *Journal of Field Archaeology*, 42(1), 54–68.

Zollikofer, C.P. and Ponce De León, M. (2005). *Virtual reconstruction: a primer in computer-assisted paleontology and biomedicine*. New York: Wiley-Liss.

Websites

Archeogrid: https://www.archeogrid.fr/projects (Last accessed 3 May 2020).

Aleria-Lamajone Tomb: https://www.inrap.fr/nouvelles-decouvertes-sur-le-mobilier-etrusque-d-aleria-lamajone-haute-corse-14968 (Last accessed 5 May 2020).

Athenaion of Poseidonia: http://poseidonia.espaceweb.usherbrooke.ca/poseidonia/introduction/frame_general.htm (Last accessed 5 May 2020).

British Museum: https://sketchfab.com/britishmuseum (Last accessed 12 December 2018).

California Academy of Sciences: https://www.calacademy.org/skulls (Last accessed 4 April 2020).

Conservatoire National des Données 3D: https://3d.humanities.science (Last accessed 3 May 2020).

Consortium 3D pour les SHS: https://shs3d.hypotheses.org (Last accessed 4 April 2020).

Digitised Diseases: http://www.digitiseddiseases.org/alpha/ (Last accessed 3 May 2020).

Duke University: https://today.duke.edu/2016/02/virtualfossils (Last accessed 28 April 2020).

eAnthropology of the University of Texas at Austin: http://www.eanthro.org (Last accessed 28 April 2020).

Historic England, Photogrammetric Applications for Cultural Heritage, Guidance for Good Practice, Swindon, Historic England: https://historicengland.org.uk/images-books/publications/photogrammetric-applications-for-cultural-heritage/heag066-photogrammetric-applications-cultural-heritage/ (Last accessed 3 May 2020).

Institut National de Recherches en Archéologies Préventives (Inrap): https://www.inrap.fr/nouvelles-decouvertes-sur-le-mobilier-etrusque-d-aleria-lamajone-haute-corse-14968 (Last accessed 3 May 2020).

Jamestown Smithsonian 3D Digitization: https://3d.si.edu/collections/jamestown (Last accessed 23 July 2020).

Laetoli Production Vertebrates: https://laetoli-production.fr/en/works/12 (Last accessed 28 April 2020).

Louvre: https://cults3d.com/fr/mot-clefs/mus%C3%A9e%20du%20louvre (Last accessed 25 March 2022).

MayaArch3D project: https://mayaarch3d.org/en/ (Last accessed 25 March 2022).

National Archaeological Museum of France: https://musee-archeologienationale.fr/musee-collections/les-collections-en-3d

Pharaoh Ramesses VI tomb: http://thebanmappingproject.com/tombs/kv-09-rameses-v-and-rameses-vi (Last accessed 25 March 2022).

Pompeii in Grand-Palais: https://www.grandpalais.fr/en/node/51193 (Last accessed 15 June 2020).

Smithsonian 3D Digitization: https://3d.si.edu/(Last accessed 22 April 2020).

The National Archaeological Museum of France: https://musee-archeologienationale.fr/musee-collections/les-collections-en-3d (Last accessed 15 June 2020).

Tomb of Queen Meresankh III: https://my.matterport.com/show/?m=d42fuVA21To (Last accessed 15 June 2020).

Virtual Retrospect: https://archeovision.cnrs.fr/en/communication-2/editorial-collection/ (Last accessed 9 August 2020).

Voyage virtuel de Palmyre à Mossoul in Institut du Monde Arabe: https://www.imarabe.org/fr/expositions/cites-millenaires (Last accessed 15 June 2020).

32

USE OF ARCHAEOTHANATOLOGY IN PREVENTIVE (SALVAGE/RESCUE) ARCHAEOLOGY AND FIELD RESEARCH ARCHAEOLOGY

Mark Guillon

INSTITUT NATIONAL DE RECHERCHES ARCHÉOLOGIQUES PRÉVENTIVES (INRAP), ROUEN, FRANCE

PACEA DE LA PRÉHISTOIRE À L'ACTUEL: CULTURE, ENVIRONNEMENT ET ANTHROPOLOGIE, UMR 5199, CNRS-UNIVERSITÉ DE BORDEAUX, PESSAC, FRANCE

Introduction

This chapter provides an opportunity to take stock of the use of archaeothanatological principles in funerary archaeology and biological anthropology in the preventive or salvage/rescue context. Before discussing archaeothanatology, it is essential to outline the remit of preventive archaeology in the world and in France, and above all, to show how the specific characteristics of France have enabled the discipline to develop in the light of major national, thematic and chronological issues. In France, the development of preventive archaeology has led to the processing of very large quantities of data, but also to the implementation of innovative projects and the creation of a number of posts for anthropologists, all underpinned by an overriding need for tangible and intangible heritage safeguarding in an economic climate that puts great pressure on the scientific approach to archaeology.

Preventive archaeology took off in the 1980s, becoming more and more integrated into land-use planning projects. A pioneering seminar on archaeology and major development projects was held in Nice in 1987, under the aegis of the Council of Europe (1989). The attendees noted that while the 1970s marked the start of an increase in local and regional planning work in Europe, which caused a certain number of archaeological sites to be destroyed with general indifference, the 1980s saw a considerable increase in work and therefore destruction without excavation, finally raising awareness among communities of the need to safeguard the heritage that had been lost. The Valletta (Malta) Convention established in 1992 by the Council of Europe enabled many European countries to adopt the 'polluter-pays' principle. However, this principle has not been adopted by all, and where it has been adopted, there are variations in its application depending on the country or even the region. This is the case in Germany, for example, where funding

DOI: 10.4324/9781351030625-37

and operators are public or private, and where there are very different methods of negotiation between public authorities and developers in the 16 Länder (Kristiansen, 2009; Otten, 2010; Orschiedt, Wittwer-Backofen and Flohr, 2011). The consequence of this lack of uniformity has been non-systematic use of archaeological surveys and insufficient study budgets, especially in the western half of the country. Hungary is also in the difficult situation of over-all local management, as in Spain, with legislation which differs between its autonomous regions (Demoule, 2007: 12). Furthermore, Spain has few public archaeological agencies and makes massive use of private operators, who employ 2400 people, with the negative consequence of there being a disconnection between preventive archaeology and academic research (Marquez-Grant and Fibiger, 2011).[1] The same problem, to a lesser extent, has arisen in the UK in Wales and Scotland, but also in England, and has been well highlighted by Darvill *et al.* (2019) in a major survey over 10 years (1990–2010) since the implementation of PPG 16[2] with the consequence, among other things, that too many results have not been published. This lack of archaeological publications has been observed in many other countries, including Russia, Ireland, Spain, Portugal and the Flanders region in Belgium. Although the situation is fairly favourable in France, with, among other things, Inrap's (Institut National de Recherches Archéologiques Préventives, the acronym written '*Inrap*' in French) budgetary policy of publishing the results of preventive archaeology, there are still shortcomings in this area (Guillon, 2010).

All the countries of the Council of Europe have signed the Malta Convention (formally known as the European Convention on the Protection of the Archaeological Heritage), and while they all practice state control of preventive projects, the three main principles of the Convention are not always followed.[3] In addition, the integration of archaeological excavations into development projects has not been carried out everywhere at the same speed or in the same way. Some countries strongly favour the management of buried heritage at a national level, such as France, Greece and the Scandinavian countries, with the participation of local and regional authorities and access to private companies. In France, this opening up to private competition concerns excavations only. Archaeological surveys must be carried out by local authorities and Inrap, thus ensuring independent tendering calls for excavations carried out under the aegis of the State. In this context, Inrap, a national institute created in 2001, is an exception and world players in preventive archaeology welcome its existence.[4]

All components of archaeology have been impacted by this development, both in the field and in the laboratory. Archaeological knowledge of all periods has been disrupted by the influx of new data. Funerary archaeology has seen a huge increase in the excavation of necropolises and

---

1 In this respect, it should be pointed out that the vast majority of French archaeologists working in preventive archaeology are attached to universities, whether they are publicly employed (Inrap and other national bodies) or employees of private operators.

2 Planning Policy Guidance Note 16: Archaeology and Planning. There is no legislation for archaeology in the United Kingdom, hence the importance of this circular. This does not prevent a significant involvement of the British archaeological community in prevention, but under strong economic constraints.

3 Systematic planning of archaeology with land use planning; polluter = payer; all excavations must be followed by scientific feedback, benefiting the public and private developer as well as benefiting national and local authorities to ensure a return of results to the public.

4 Several symposia were held in the 2000s to take stock of the safeguarding of buried heritage threatened by development, notably in Lyon in 2002 (Archéologie et aménageurs: un partenariat pour demain', report published by Robert *et al.,* 2002), in 2007 in Vilnius (Bozoki-Ernyey, 2007) and Paris (Demoule, 2007), in 2010 in Leicester (Webley *et al.,* 2010) and in 2012 in Paris with the 'Rencontres nationales d'archéologie préventive', organised by the Ministry of Culture (L'archéologie préventive, une démarche responsable, 2012)'.

burials. But new constraints had to be faced in terms of time and sampling, especially in the field. The specific conditions of preventive archaeology imply obstacles which are the consequence of its place in this particular context that are directly linked to the constraints imposed by the site and the budget: partial excavations, short periods of site access, reduced teams, among them, but, that said, not all research excavations are exhaustive and not all of them have a huge budget, or an infinite timeframe- not to mention the exceptional discovery that so often occurs in the last days of fieldwork. The very nature of the funerary deposit, or of the lone deposit (cremation, isolated burial as opposed to large medieval cemeteries) has a great influence on whether or not a complete excavation is possible. But what is a complete sample? The complete funerary part? Or that part and that from the settlement? Or that of the settlement and activity areas if they are distinct?

It is, therefore, necessary to consider, on the one hand, the positive aspects of preventive intervention for retrieving archaeological remains and, more broadly, improving knowledge of ancient societies through access to buried heritage and, on the other hand, the negative aspects linked to constraints. These aspects are to be examined according to the length of the period of time considered: the short-term is that of the excavation report and the first published results, the medium-term is that of a possible monograph, and the long-term is that of the use of the results/ data by the scientific community- for synthesis, for example.

Preventive archaeology in France: a brief state of the art synopsis

The objectives of an excavation in a preventive context in France are established by the State services (Ministry of Culture) in the form of specifications based on the report of the results of an archaeological survey (Guillon, 2010). These specifications constitute the scientific part of the invitation to tender for the excavation. Inrap, which must meet all excavation requirements, and the other preventive archaeology organisations approved by the National Council for Archaeological Research (CNRA) who wish to respond to the call for tenders (local authority services and private companies among them) submit a scientific intervention proposal (PSI, '*projet scientifique d'intervention*' translated as 'Scientific Intervention Proposal' or SIP) accompanied by a budget proposal.

The PSI has the difficult task of responding to the recommendations of the State services in a spirit of scientific rigour and optimum results, but also in a context of constrained budgets and deadlines. While deadlines are often rigid with a narrow margin of manoeuvre imposed by the nature of the development and the property owner, the budget is an adjustable variable, with the number of researchers in the field and the extent of post-excavation analysis being the largest contributing factors. In the current context in France, public and private organisations are in competition and must find a balance between scientific choices and financial constraints in their proposals in order to convince the developer, as it is they who choose the organisation under the control of the Ministry of Culture services. Ideally, the PSI is drawn up with the future person in charge of the project and with the specialists approached, particularly the anthropologist, when the survey evaluation has shown that all or part of the site is a funerary context. Indeed, in order to obtain reliable data and field records that will lead to a solid study, the excavation of the graves and burial layers must be carried out with a minimum of delay; the presence of an anthropologist in the field, either as the person in charge or as a specialist (or both), is now an unavoidable requirement imposed by the state; it is even required that the person in charge of the project is an anthropologist if the site is predominantly funerary in nature. This last point has a negative side, especially during large operations: if the anthropologist is in charge of the site, he/she will not have not enough time to follow closely the excavation of the burial layers specifically; this often leads to the astonishing situation where a second anthropologist is needed, which is only possible in certain areas and when there are not too many competing funerary excavations. Even if it is sometimes difficult, it is acknowledged that the recruitment of anthropologists has been particularly intense for preventive archaeology in France over the last 25 years (with two periods of depression affecting all specialties, the late 1990s and the 2008 crisis accentuating an already difficult situation in the world of research), and this for all regions and all public and private organisations. The main contrast with neighbouring countries is that these are permanent positions and not time-limited contracts.

Funerary archaeology in a preventive context: field constraints and strategies

Since the 1970s, several phenomena have come together in archaeology to bring the grave, and especially its contents for which it was designed, the human remains, from a minor, if not to say neglected, position to the forefront, or at least of equal importance with the other archaeological remains. These phenomena are:

- The decline of archaeology focused on artefacts.
- The number of burials uncovered in preventive archaeology projects.
- Advances in human osteology.
- The emergence of funerary archaeology, with the goal of highlighting funerary practices through meticulous field and subsequent laboratory work.
- The development of research on the common people, both in archaeology and history, to the detriment of an archaeology of the elite.
- An increasingly regional and chronological understanding of the funerary behaviour of societies.
- A systemic approach addressing the links between the major components of society, for example demographic, economic, religious and health, among others, and at several scales of interest, including those of the grave, the cemetery, the village and the region (Guillon, 2020).

Things did not happen in every country in the same way and at the same time, but preventive archaeology was the triggering factor in many places. During the 1980s, it was no longer possible to leave thousands of graves to be destroyed or to accumulate thousands of skeletons in repositories without their archaeological context. In France, the strategy that applies to the excavation is therefore put in place in the PSI before the field phase begins. However, as the reliability of the preliminary evaluation survey is not guaranteed, and this is completely independent of the quality of the work, the occurrence of unforeseen events, such as the unexpected richness of a site, in the sense of scientific richness, cannot be excluded (Gallien and Guillon, 2007). It will therefore be necessary to anticipate this unforeseen event in the PSI by envisaging several scenarios up to the catastrophic scenario, such as 'we had foreseen 500 graves, and there are well over 1000!'.

Two examples from Normandy, both near Rouen in northern France, help to elucidate these scenarios. The first concerns a large necropolis of the Early Middle Ages in the village of Romilly-sur-Andelle (Eure region). The archaeological survey evaluation estimated the number of burials at 500. The excavation, carried out in 2007, uncovered 700 burials (Jouneau *et al.*, 2018) but found that there were the same number, or more, in the area that the team had not had time to excavate: a necropolis of at least 1,400 graves. The State decided to leave ('freeze') the unexcavated part and place it in an archaeological preserve, preventing the construction of one of the planned houses. This is still the situation to date. The second example concerns the site of Cléon (Seine-Maritime region), which, as foreseen in the survey report, provided evidence of a protohistoric complex with enclosures and Bronze Age burials. After a few weeks of excavation in 2016, and especially after exhaustive stripping of the excavation area (see below) of the site, a long oval structure of about 10 m turned out to be a funerary monument dating to the Late Neolithic, of which many other examples have been discovered in the region (Honoré, pers. comm.). The financial investment and the time needed to excavate this funerary monument alone could not be found, as the developer refused to participate, and the State could not bear the cost alone. Here, too, the burial site was placed in an archaeological preserve with a ban on any construction in the area. Another similar preserve was set aside in 1992 for a monumental funerary site dating to the end of the 3rd millennium BC in Val de Reuil (Eure region) (Billard, Guillon and Verron, 2010). The site consisted of a quarry for aggregate, which, after extraction, left a group of artificial lakes transformed into an ornithological preserve. The decision was taken by the State to isolate the Neolithic monument on an island in the middle of one of the lakes. A final example is that of a huge Integrated Development Zone ('Zone d'Aménagement Concerté', ZAC), planned just outside Caen (Calvados region), where surveys had revealed a vast Iron Age occupation with numerous burial sites. Faced with the cost of the archaeological intervention, the entire project, which included several dozen commercial organisations, was abandoned and the planned development re-located.

How does one assess the creation of these archaeological preserves and the abandonment of development projects? As far as abandonment of the project is concerned, the developers decide, either because they do not want to commit budgets, they consider the project too large or are put off by the delays imposed by the excavation. The first reason is the most frequent because, for major development projects, a schedule is established between excavation and the beginning of construction work. With regard to archaeological preserves, it should be recalled that they are always established by the State when it, alone, is not able to cover the additional cost of excavation of a site that is larger than planned. This is a good solution that makes it possible to avoid the need to excavate a site or part of a site in a hurry in order to reduce the sense of an 'archaeological mortgage' imposed by delays. However, the State services must take every precaution to ensure the sustainability of such a preserve and, to do so, it has two tools at its disposal: the archaeological map of France drawn up and updated by the Ministry of Culture and the theoretical obligation for all development projects involving the disturbance of the subsoil to be approved by the regional archaeology services. This obligation is theoretical because there are a very large number of applications to be investigated, and the regional services have undergone a sharp reduction in staff since the end of the 2000s following a policy of reducing the number of employees in the three civil service sectors: national, regional and health.

A preventive archaeological site is a 'one-shot' opportunity because the site and its remains that could not be removed will be destroyed by the development. In addition, in a preventive context even more than in a planned research context, archaeology destroys the subject of its study; on the one hand, the archaeologist himself takes samples (or destroys them in order to 'go down') and only the records will be able to furnish an account of the nature of the remains. On the other hand, the site will be destroyed after the excavation by the developer. It must be borne in mind that the planned development would have destroyed the site in any case.

The consequences are significant. Some structures, with their complex organisation – such as flint-knapping or pottery workshops, faunal assemblages, and, of particular interest here, burials, must be carefully treated during the field phase, with no possibility to turn back after removal. In the situation where the human skeleton has a known *a priori* organisation, its integrity is often disturbed in a grave, even if the skeleton is not completely disarticulated. For archaeothanatology in a preventive context, and in reference to the title of this chapter, one must consider two meanings of the term 'use': usage and utility or usefulness. These are: (1) Principles of Usage, which are operating principles of field anthropology; these principles can be adapted to constraints on the basis of methodological choices; and (2) Utility or Usefulness, an assessment of the contribution to the discipline. The quality of the results should not suffer from constraints; if the methods put in place following the strategic post-survey choices are good ones, only the quantity of data/results should be impacted, but not the quality.

A preliminary remark should be made at this stage. Not attempting to interpret before excavating is of great importance in a preventive context. The pressure that the team may feel can be a poor advisor in that the urgency of the situation may lead to an overly rapid interpretation of a site, or one of its components, particularly in the light of previous excavations. This is a risk that has two potential major flaws: the interpretation can be wrong, which is a qualitative aspect, and/or one deprives oneself of what can be important in a synthetic approach: the repetition of observations, thus affecting the quantitative aspect.

The question should be asked about whether or not there are specific research questions for excavations carried out in a preventive context. The answer is 'no' for the scientific aspects, but it is 'yes' for the methodological aspects. But it is not that simple. The question concerns the possibility of specific objectives for excavations being carried out in a preventive context. Ideally, for the same problem, the objectives should be the same, whatever the economic context of the project, with the exception of possible methodological or experimental objectives that may be envisaged in academic field research as in preventive contexts, for example, to improve techniques or to measure the loss of information during excavations that are too rapidly carried out (Guillon, 1990). It is then necessary to return to past projects in order to draw accumulated insights from this experience. From this point of view, preventive archaeology is an excellent tool, considering the enormous amount of data it provides to inspire reflection. Based on reviews of these archaeological endeavours, the funerary context is well placed to contribute to these attempts at synthesis, which are not without difficulties, however.

An important consideration when making excavation choices is that it will always be considered preferable to have a general view of the site than an accumulation of details. In funerary archaeology, this is a particularly sensitive issue since a funerary site is often made up of many smaller deposits (the individual grave being one of the best examples), and one will often be concerned to properly excavate these smaller deposits in order to gather enough information to interpret and understand the site as a whole. But understanding the organisation of a cemetery does not require the accumulation of the understanding of the organisation of individual graves; the whole cannot be reduced to the accumulation of its parts. This question is at the root of many technical-scientific conflicts. The quality of the training of team scientists comes into play in this thorny issue (training in its broad sense, which mixes academic knowledge and acquired experience). The question that arises is, therefore, whether or not the general view of the site should take precedence over the results of details, however interesting they may be.

Constraints linked to the excavation area

Constraints related to the excavation area (*'emprise de la fouille'*) are difficult to understand; the most difficult is often to estimate the share of remains in the unexcavated part of the site, which amounts to estimating the representativeness of the part excavated and studied (Guillon, 2004). This calculation comes to the heart of the difference between planned research excavations and preventive excavations: the first is aimed at excavating an entire site to address a previously defined problem; the second is primarily aimed at saving all or part of a site, the problem having been established on the basis of the nature and chronology of the remains brought to light at the time of the site survey.

Time constraints

Time constraints are (almost) always the consequence of budgetary limitations. In the competitive context of the excavation market (this expression is unfortunately not an oxymoron, and it grates on the ear), the budget proposal outlined in the PSI must comply with two major constraints: on the one hand, not to go below a minimum for which the study of the site is not scientifically possible (this minimum is hindered by subjectivity, depending as it does on the role of each of the protagonists involved in the project, the developer, the property owner, the archaeological organisation, and the State), and, on the other hand, to offer a bid that offers a chance to 'win' the contract in the face of competition. Therefore, the bidding exercise must cope with the notion of a financial threshold below which the excavation would be botched and the extent of information lost is unthinkable. There are several strategic possibilities to consider in compensating for a constrained period of excavation.

Sampling strategy

One part of the site should be excavated with all possible precision, while the remaining part of the site should be excavated in a faster manner. The question remains, though: which part to choose, according to which criteria, and why? Alternatively, one can choose to open only part of the area to be developed and sacrifice the rest. Another option is to carry out an exhaustive stripping of the upper-most parts of the site before making a decision, meaning this part will then be sacrificed and thus destroyed. Lastly, one could choose to conduct a quick and thorough search of the entire site, knowing that whatever the methodological choice, information will be lost. In this way, one can choose to excavate quickly to deal with the entire area to be developed, but this raises methodological questions about the choices to be made in order to move forward quickly, but how? What is being sacrificed? What steps should be accelerated? What information should be sacrificed?

In favouring the quantity of remains, the choice can be guided by the desire to collect as many archaeological remains as possible, and in this case, as many skeletons (or human bones in certain contexts with disarticulated remains) as possible. The objective would then be to carry out a biological study that is as complete as possible, bearing in mind that rapid removal of the bones should not damage them. However, such a choice can only be made if the context is perfectly known and the future study of the material takes precedence over the loss of archaeological information. Thus, the anthropological study of the human remains is the key to understanding the site.

In order to demonstrate the workings of such a decision, consider the example of a parish cemetery with a chapel that is attested in textual sources, historical documents or records. In the first case, the location of the chapel is unknown before the excavation, and thus exhaustive stripping is first necessary. In the second case, the location of the chapel is known before excavation, but where should excavation be concentrated? If, for example, the survey has shown that the area around the chapel is rich in graves of young children, the choice may be made to concentrate the excavation at this location to address the burials of individuals who died in the perinatal period. To take another example, if the survey showed that the burials in a sector far from the chapel are attributable to the earliest period of use of the cemetery and are rich in grave furnishings, as in Merovingian burials in an early medieval context, concentrated excavation exploring these phenomena, specifically, might be chosen. It should be noted here that the choice made might also depend on the region in which the excavation takes place, favouring less well-known occurrences in a given geographical area. The national programme of archaeological research that is regularly updated by the Ministry of Culture can also guide the choice. This programme is outlined in Paris by the Archaeology Department of the General Directorate of Heritage after consultation with the regional public services.

Impacts of constraints and adaptation strategies for the excavation of burial layers

Based on the options chosen, the excavation methods can be adapted. The practices and detail of the archaeothanatological approach may be adopted in part or in whole according to these choices, but it is also necessary to address the definition and selection of these practices based on the time needed to apply them and the loss of information that must be anticipated and accepted. It should be noted, however, that the nature and complexity of certain funerary layers make it almost impossible to conceive of speeding up the excavation phase, except by improving and perfecting the tools, such as adopting the use of hoovers/vacuum cleaners and photogrammetry, among other technological aids.

Although the methods used to excavate remains in a funerary environment are based on the same principles, regardless of the context of intervention, the field techniques have specific characteristics under preventive conditions. The specifics of the basis of different types of archaeological structures that yield human remains can be outlined and are considered in what follows.

Deposits containing a certain number of individuals

- The individual grave
- The individual cremation grave

Deposits with multiple layers

- Multiple burials
- Collective burials
- The pyre-sites
- The spreading of combustion residues

As unsatisfactory as this classification may be – because it is reductive – since some structures are not always attributable to a single depositional category, it will serve as a means by which to describe the constraints and difficulties that arise in a preventive context.

The individual grave

Many of the elements defining an individual grave are applicable to other types of burial sites and, therefore, will not be repeated here. Ideally, burial excavation should be carried out such that all remains are completely exposed (Duday *et al.*, 1990; Sellier, 1992; Duday and Guillon, 2006) because it is the location of the bones after soft tissue decomposition and their organisation in relation to that of the living individual that is the key to interpretation. Meticulous excavation followed by the identification and recording of all the skeletal elements *in situ* is absolutely fundamental.[5]

Furthermore, the dynamics of the filling of the grave-pit (immediate or delayed, rapid or progressive, anthropogenic or natural) can only be understood by observing the sedimentary layers (stratigraphic units) that characterise the fill (Duday, 2006; Duday and Guillon, 2006). Optimal excavation of the bones is based on two principal objectives: on the one hand, to expose as many bone elements and fragments as possible and, on the other hand, to leave them all (even the smallest and most fragile) in the exact location in which they were found, prior to recording them. All these field observations lend themselves to the interpretation of the grave (Sellier and Guillon, 2001), the identification of funerary gestures and the reconstruction of the grave furnishings, even if the architectural elements, such as coffins, planks, platforms, and wooden vaults, have disappeared.

The interpretative phase, after the implementation of these techniques and the field recording of the remains, is a dynamic process that aims to reconstruct the circumstances that led to the arrangement of the remains at discovery (Duday, 2006; cf. Boulestin, Chapter 2, this volume). This approach can therefore be applied to all types of contexts in which human bones are found. The same protocols can be applied to medico-legal murder and accident scenes since there is no chronological or geographical limit to their use; for both types of contexts, it is the technical constraints of the excavation that dictate methodological alterations (Duday, 2006; Duday and Guillon 2006).

Returning to the preventive context, if the structure of the graves and the arrangement of the bones are fairly repetitive, a method of rapid excavation and lifting can be implemented. It is sometimes possible to use this method when excavating large burial complexes (Guillon, 1990, 1997). The excavation phase being unavoidable, the quality of all documentation of the burials depends on the potential observations of and recording by means of good vertical and multiple perspective photographs of the grave and remains *in situ* (Guillon, 1990, 1997). Three-dimensional recording techniques may be of use in this endeavour (Sachau-Carcel, 2014; cf. Mickleburgh *et al.*, Chapter 28, this volume; Sachau-Carcel, Chapter 31, this volume).

If the urgency of the project causes the bones and grave furnishings to be removed too quickly and therefore only partially recorded, the taphonomic understanding of the burial context is difficult, if not impossible, and reconstruction of the architecture of the grave and the funerary actions/gestures will be weakened (Duday and Guillon, 2006). The relationship between the body of the deceased and funerary deposits might be difficult to establish if the excavation is not optimal, and it may even be impossible to establish the lay-out of the deposit associated with the deceased; for example, a vase placed between the feet does not have the same meaning as a vase placed on the coffin-lid, which has fallen or slipped between the feet when the lid decomposed and the underlying empty space was created. Moreover, if the skeleton is poorly

---

5 The identification of bone elements or fragments thereof must be done during removal and can be checked in the laboratory. The field documentation should therefore mention the identified bones (complete or fragmentary), whether they are left or right side (for paired bones), their inclination, orientation and the aspect that is upper-most (as seen from above), unless, of course, this information is clearly visible on the graphic or photographic documents. The elevation or depth dimension should be added. This information can be noted either on the plan or on record sheets, as recorded by various means (site level, laser level, water level, etc.) in a systematic manner (the reference level will be the same for all bone retrievals) and clear for anyone who may need to consult the documentation later (sometimes long after the excavation, at a time when it is no longer possible to question those who carried it out).

or incompletely excavated (i.e. freed of soil), the length of time needed to remove the bones without damaging them will be longer than when the excavation is more thorough, and this is all the more true when bone preservation is poor. Paradoxically, bone remains in poor condition will require more detailed excavation because of the necessity to collect as much information as possible in the field, and the removal is more delicate than when the bone is well preserved. As for the human remains and their biological study, an excavation, even a quick one, makes it possible to retrieve them in their entirety, taking the precaution of collecting the fill from areas containing small bones (hands, feet, coccyx). This can be difficult, however, and may limit the biological analysis, especially in cases of the graves of immature individuals and poor preservation of bones and/or furnishings.

For immature individuals, not being able to carry out an excavation with the optimal exposure of the remains is detrimental to both the study of the grave in which they are found and the biological study of them. Indeed, the location of the bones, and particularly the epiphyses, are a rich source of information, and rapid excavation and sampling may leave small pieces of bone in the field unless all the fill of the grave is removed. This is feasible for the grave of a small baby but less so for that of children over 10 years old. Recovering such remains involves a great deal of additional laboratory work for sieving, identification, lateralisation, and cataloguing, for which the financial and human resources are not always available. It should be added to these stipulations that excavating a grave of an individual who died in the perinatal period 'quickly' has the consequence of depriving oneself of taphonomic information, and consequently of understanding the mode of burial, research on this subject being particularly active (e.g. Portat *et al.*, 2016).

For poorly preserved bones, it is even more damaging to have to excavate quickly. Partial excavation will not allow the position of the bones and their relationships to be properly observed, and the field documentation will be poor, especially since photographs are not very informative in such a situation; lifting the remains under these conditions will further damage the bones, and laboratory biological analysis will be all the more incomplete.

Two examples will suffice to support these assessments. When the *ossa coxae* are in poor condition, the laboratory phase must be anticipated to avoid loss of information, especially as any reconstruction of them is likely to be very partial. It is, therefore, necessary to carry out as many field measurements as possible when the *ossa coxae* are still in place and at the time of sampling. This makes it possible to carry out a primary sex determination despite the poor preservation of the bones (Murail, Bruzek and Houët, 2000). Similarly, when the long bones of an immature individual appear to be degraded, it is more prudent to perform length measurements in the field (Guillon, 1993), which is often possible even when the required elements are in poor condition but are impossible to restore. It will then be possible to furnish an age-at-death assessment based on stature.

The fact that a cemetery is entirely made up of individual graves is no guarantee of simplicity; it can be very densely occupied, and this over a great depth, the latter not representing a chronological indicator, as some more recent graves may intersect and be deeper than older graves. This is referred to as a 'layered cemetery'. However, if the excavation is too rapid, chronological relationships between graves or parts of graves will be impossible to establish. The sediment of an intensely used cemetery is entirely anthropogenically altered and the boundaries of the pits may be difficult, if not impossible, to discern. In this case, it is the relative arrangement of the articulated bones that makes it possible to establish the succession of burial depositions, the excavation then being carried out from the most recent graves (theoretically the most complete and undisturbed) to the oldest (theoretically the most partial and disturbed).

The greatest care will have to be taken in the excavation of the grave-pit after the skeletal remains have been removed – for several reasons. Firstly, the relative chronology of the graves is often based on the reading of the excavation boundaries of features in the field. In a dense burial context, whether in plan, in depth, or both, the likelihood of a structure – a pit, coffin, or other container, or a skeleton being in place at the bottom or in the wall of the grave – is quite high. In addition, it is essential to record the profile of grave-pits in order to establish a typology of the burial features and to detect possible architecture, such as a bench/bank, cephalic niche, or faint traces of wood or of a sarcophagus. Profiles are very quick to record but can only be recorded if the pit excavation is accurate. Topographic tools save time (laser theodolite, three-dimensional recording by drone and photogrammetry), and in general preventive archaeological sites are well equipped in this type of instrumentation, but the cost of labour is a burden on the budget.

The individual cremation grave

For a detailed approach to cremation structures and bibliographical references, see the chapters by Depierre and Duday (cf. Depierre, Chapter 4, this volume; Duday, Chapter 15, this volume). For the purpose of this treatment, three frequently encountered types of single individual funerary deposits will be considered: a deposit in a vase, a deposit in a perishable container and a deposit made directly in the ground. In all three cases, those overseeing the cremation removed these deposits from the pyre. The case of an ashy deposit is the simplest type of context encountered during the field phase. There are two options in this case: the first consists of excavating the pit in which the ash was deposited, then removing the ashy deposit for subsequent excavation in the laboratory; the second, more difficult option, consists of completely dismantling the grave structure, including the pit, and, after the consolidation of the walls, lifting and transporting it to the laboratory for excavation. However, the second option is only possible when the grave-pit is small; it should be noted that the first option is always preferable as it permits a survey of the pit *in situ*, which guarantees accurate records for orientations, the general topography of the site and stratigraphic relationships.

In the case of a perishable container, if time constraints are important, it is better to excavate around the entire disposal pit if its dimensions permit it, or otherwise around the perishable container if the former is not possible. Unfortunately, the presence of a perishable container has little chance of being distinguished from a deposit in the ground (the third type of deposit), especially if the excavation is rapid. For both types of cremation, laboratory excavation is preferable. It should be kept in mind that a cremation deposit structure may be part of a more complex structure, such as a burial plot. The latter may be more or less well preserved and the excavation around the burial site will need to be performed with care. Alternatively, while individual cremation grave-pits rarely overlap, enclosures often do and thus provide a rich relative chronology. As for deposits with complex multiple deposits, these require the adoption of a different set of procedures.

The multiple burial

Recall that the indispensable steps mentioned for individual burials, above, also apply for burials containing more than a single individual. When a single grave structure contains the remains of several deceased individuals suspected to have been deposited at the same time, fine excavation is essential to demonstrate the contemporaneity of the depositions of bodies and to understand the organisation of the grave. Without being a multiple burial, a primary burial in which skeletal elements of other disarticulated skeletons are also found- in addition to the remains of the last deceased individual deposited – may contribute to the complexity of a funerary structure.

Furthermore, a complete skeleton associated with skeletal fragments may also be discovered. For the latter case, a careful excavation will be indispensable to establish the dynamics of the formation processes of the grave.

The field techniques being similar to those used for the excavation of collective graves are detailed with them below. There is, however, a difference between the two: for multiple burials, individualisation of those interred is systematic, whereas, for collective burials, the funerary and post-funerary gestures of successive interventions can make interpretations more difficult, requiring an excavation in multiple spits that do not focus on anatomical articulations (cf. Boulestin and Courtaud, Chapter 3, this volume; Castex and Kacki, Chapter 18, this volume; Schmitt, Chapter 12, this volume, and references therein).

Collective burial

A collective burial is distinguished from a multiple burial by the successive nature of the depositions in the same structure, burial vaults, caves, hypogea, among others (cf. Castex and Kacki, Chapter 18, this volume). Numerous excavations of sites through time from the Upper Palaeolithic to the modern period have revealed all possible stages in the preservation of the integrity of the bodies, ranging from the juxtaposition or superimposition of complete skeletons to the complete absence of articulations. An important question is whether or not the grave was a closed system in which no dry bones were added or removed or, conversely, an open system that remained in active use over a prolonged period of time. In the case of a closed system, all the bones in the grave (in articulation or not) belong to individuals deposited as fresh corpses, without any subsequent removal by human hands, the lacking elements being due to taphonomic events, including rodent burrowing, in-place decomposition, the collapse of funerary structures, and fluvial disturbance, among others. All these possibilities serve to emphasise the complex nature of such burials. The *modus operandi* of the deposits can be very difficult to define, but the analysis of the spatial distribution of the bones and movable remains (in the broadest sense) provides indispensable tools for interpreting the funerary and post-funerary history of such remains and their funerary context. Fine excavation is indispensable, as is the retrieval of remains with immediate cataloguing and xyz references, in addition to descriptions of the orientation of individual elements. The long-term use of a burial vault can cause considerable fragmentation of the remains, which makes the work of reconstruction even more delicate and requires highly accurate observations for the most reliable excavation recording and documentation. Although fine excavation is recommended, experiments conducted in a preventive context, particularly due to the urgency required near the end of projects in an attempt to speed up the retrieval phase, have lifted bones by quarters of a square metre (Billard, Guillon and Verron, 2010), after noting the absence of articulations. While this method did not interfere with the interpretation of bone or fragment displacements over distances greater than 1m in the vault, it did interfere with the fine observation of low amplitude displacements which are the basis of observations to identify bone storage and movements of remains at the time of deposition of a new body.

A great gain in quality has been achieved due to the application of GIS recording of multiple and collective burials. Recording, backed by a three-dimensional photogrammetric coverage, is a commonly used tool that saves time while ensuring greater precision and the possibility of returning to stored information (cf. Mickleburgh *et al.*, Chapter 28, this volume; Sachau-Carcel, Chapter 31, this volume). The graphic data and the associated database constitute a remarkable working tool. In the context of preventive excavations, the time saved compared to manual drawing is considerable, so much so that photogrammetric records are increasingly used for individual burials. The possibility of making camera recordings by hand, using a boom, or mounted on a drone provides great flexibility in use. Moreover, the positioning of individual burials within the archaeological site adds an undeniable advantage.

The pyre

After the cremation, the pyre can be left as it is; initially, a complete structure, it will be disturbed by natural elements (bad weather, animal interventions) that excavation will have difficulty reconstructing. If such structures are abandoned and then protected, they will be preserved in a complete state. If, however, parts of the cremation layer have been removed on one or more occasions before abandonment (see below on the spreading of combustion residues), there will be gaps which archaeological excavation and recording will try to identify and quantify, an exercise which is difficult but not impossible. Post-cremation disturbance without abandonment or protection from anthropogenic and natural disturbances represents the most complex case.

In all these cases, the archaeological analysis will have difficulty in reconstructing the fate of the pyre. The field method depends on the issues raised during the planning phase of the project, the latter taking into account both scientific and financial aspects. As with other types of funerary deposits, difficulties increase when the site is archaeologically denser than expected, and this problem is even greater when the funerary structures are not transportable and laboratory excavation is not possible.

The spreading of combustion residues

Combustion residues are a form of deposit from a hot or cold pyre taken as one or more samples over time. This sample can be spread on the ground or poured into an existing feature, such as a ditch or a pit dug for this purpose. The deposit is found in the ground, and it is thus not really a spread, the limits of the deposit not always being easy to establish, sometimes for taphonomic reasons. The same reasoning for the preservation of the remains presented above, for the pyre applies in this case as well, but the understanding of the phenomena and gestures is even subtler. In fact, in the absence of any specific feature, only a layer within a stratigraphic sequence is all that remains, even if excavated in plan. As a precaution, it is necessary to collect the entire cremation residue layer in order to be able to sort and study it in the laboratory. The possible rubefaction of the underlying sediment should not be overlooked, as it is an indication that the spreading of the material was carried out while the cinders were still hot, i.e. at the end of or shortly after the cremation. Considering this to be a burial layer, which is a discussion in its own right, the information sought is as follows: is the level homogeneous, was the spreading carried out once or several times, are burnt human remains present, is there a single individual, are pyre furnishings present, and if so, of what type, clothing or other offerings? Some of these questions can only be answered if field recovery is adequate, for example, by a vertical division of the spread, but other questions can be dealt with in the laboratory, such as estimates of the minimum number of individuals (MNI).

Archaeothanatology in a preventive context

After this overview of the most frequently uncovered types of funerary structures, what picture can be drawn of the specifics with regard to archaeothanatology in a preventive context? The two meanings proposed in the first part of this chapter should be reviewed: use and utility. Descriptive terms to use have been presented above and in several chapters of this book. The question of the usefulness of archaeothanatology no longer arises in many countries that have established preventive archaeology. In fact, the results of excavations over the last 40 years have been considerable and have added renewed vigour to many approaches, whether the interest is in mortuary gestures, chronology or site topography. Many research programmes address funerary questions, and these programmes often deal with problems set in time and space but which are linked to real social issues in prehistory, protohistory and history. The aim is to approach the behaviour of the living when confronted with death from a very broad cultural perspective, ranging from the individual funerary gesture, and therefore from a technical aspect of the treatment of the body to the more general perception of death in ancient societies.

Is the number of burial sites excavated a guarantee that all questions will be answered? Probably not, but it is a guarantee of a broader vision of funerary behaviour, from a geographical and chronological point of view. Preventive archaeology and major development projects, especially great linear works, such as those associated with motorway or railway line construction, cross entire regions and cumulative results of which provide a very large-scale picture of which the discipline had no idea of 50 years ago.

Research programmes in funerary archaeology have been made on the scale of natural topographic features, such as river basins and valleys, and political entities, such as provinces, kingdoms, duchies, bishoprics, have proffered remarkable results (cf., in particular, Demoule, 2004; Marx, Nura and Salas Rossenbach, 2017; the French publication 'Les Nouvelles de l'Archéologie' numbers 125, 132, 142 or 153). Moreover, the cross-referenced results offer the possibility of syntheses on very large scales, over many centuries, covering many regions and countries. The contribution of excavations linked to development work is therefore considerable. However, at no time should the difficulties linked to time constraints and forced sampling of sites (or parts of sites) excavated be overlooked. While it is not possible to address all of the problems introduced by these constraints, it is essential to think about two important and interrelated ones (Guillon, 2020):

- To what extent is it possible to compare results from different excavations?
- What is the extent of the loss of information caused by the constraints of prevention (speed, partial excavations, and sites left unexcavated)?

Conclusion

In most of the countries where preventive archaeology projects have been developed, there has been a considerable increase in the knowledge of ancient societies with an equally considerable contribution, especially in the field of funerary archaeology. Far from Europe, in Japan, knowledge of the Kofun period has increased significantly during the excavations linked to major works projects, even if it is regretful that human remains were not considered fully (Gilaizeau and Guillon, 2016). The archaeological information acquired in Colombia mainly concerns settlement and funerary sites; preventive work has advanced knowledge, but the country is faced with scandalous practices such as grave robbery and *guaquería* (looting) (Jaramillo and Oyuela, 1994; Jaramillo, 2007).

In Europe, a paradigm shift is taking place in Norway with respect to the inescapable detail of Viking heritage: apart from the important Iron Age discoveries made during excavations in the mountainous regions accompanying hydroelectric projects, the results of excavations carried out during road works in the western fjord region are crucial for the knowledge of Bronze Age burial mounds and Iron Age necropolises (Dommasnes, 2007). In Norway, it is precisely the impressive advances in the increased understanding of Viking burial practices that can be attributed to the advent and development of preventive archaeology.

These are just a few examples that could be multiplied many times over. In Western Europe as a whole, which has been the seat of considerable regional development with frequent interventions affecting the subsoil, all periods have benefited from the considerable influx of results from preventive archaeology, from the Upper Palaeolithic to the contemporary period, and funerary archaeology has benefited greatly from these results and impressions of mortuary practices has been overturned by new detail.

However, the picture is not idyllic; particularly in Europe, the Malta Convention has not resulted in sufficient general improvement and homogenisation of practices. To recall and emphasise two areas of concern: there are insufficient surveys in many countries and equally insufficient and very variable publication of data and the results of projects from one country to another. The latter concern is also fuelled by shortcomings and inadequacies in the management of archaeological material and perhaps especially in the management of archaeological documentation from excavations. In this respect, few countries have a satisfactory approach, and France is no exception, where the remains are piled up in huge repositories with fragile management structures and millions of unclassified and untreated excavation documents accumulating. The situation is improving, but much progress remains to be made in France as elsewhere. Only Japan seems to have taken the measure of the problem, with a remarkable level of treatment and management. The fact that there are more than 7 000 professional archaeologists (Demoule, 2007: 11) is not for nothing, and, on reflection, this is not an astronomical figure for a public archaeological service in a large, densely populated and wealthy country

It is important to point out that prevention has brought results to archaeothanatology at many levels. First of all, at the level of the grave, whatever its type; multiple observations and, above all, the detailed analysis of field data has led to great progress in the understanding of the phenomena that occur between the time of deposition and that of excavation. This highly technical work on the taphonomy of burials has shed light on many questions and has made it possible to highlight a multitude of unique, rare and frequent mortuary gestures. In many countries and for many preventive archaeological organisations, the more widespread use of detailed excavation of burial sites and the application of rigorous methods that, in turn, generate quality field documentation, even in sometimes difficult conditions, is to be welcomed. The application of these methods is an essential prerequisite if the discipline is to move beyond case studies, an exercise that is certainly rich in information and intellectual points of view, and a means to apprehend, on a large scale, human behaviour with respect to their dead.

Acknowledgement

The author thanks D. Honoré (Inrap Rouen, France) for the personal communication.

References

Billard, C., Guillon, M. and Verron G., eds. (2010). *Les sépultures collectives du Néolithique récent-final de Val de Reuil et Portejoie (Eure, France)*. Liège: Liège University Press, Études et Recherches Archéologiques de l'Université de Liège (ERAUL).

Bozoki-Ernyey, K. (2007). European preventive archaeology: papers of the European Partners against Corruption (EPAC) meeting 2004 Vilnius. Hungary and Council of Europe: National Office of Cultural Heritage.

Collective (2002). *Archéologie et Aménageurs. Un partenariat pour demain*. Roud Table, Lyon, unpublished.

Council of Europe (1989). *Archaeology and major works*. European colloquium, Nice 1987. Strasbourg: Architectural Heritage Reports and Studies No. 12.

Darvill, T., Barrass, K., Constant, V., Milner, E. and Russell, B. (2019). *Archaeology in the PPG 16 era: investigations in England 1990–2010*. Oxford: Oxbow Books.

Demoule, J.-P., ed. (2004). *La France archéologique. Vingt ans d'aménagement et de découvertes.* Paris: Hazan.

Demoule, J.-P., ed. (2007). *L'archéologie préventive dans le monde.* Paris: La Découverte.

Dommasnes, L.H. (2007). L'archéologie préventive en Norvège: entre gestion du patrimoine et recherche scientifique. In: J.-P. Demoule, ed., *L'Archéologie Préventive dans le Monde.* Paris: La Découverte, pp. 166–175.

Duday, H. (2006). Archaeothanatology or the archaeology of death. Translated by C.J. Knüsel. In: R. Gowland, and C.J. Knüsel, eds., *Social Archaeology of Funerary Remains.* Oxford: Oxbow Books.

Duday, H., Courtaud P., Crubézy E., Sellier P. and Tillier A.-m., eds. (1990). L'Anthropologie 'de Terrain': Reconnaissance et Interprétation des Gestes Funéraires. *Bulletins et Mémoires de la Société d'Anthropologie de Paris*, 2(3–4), pp. 29–50.

Duday, H. and Guillon, M. (2006). The role of the forensic specialist on death scene. Understanding the circumstances of deposition when the body is skeletonized. In: A. Schmitt, E. Cunha and J. Pinheiro, eds., *Forensic Anthropology and Forensic Medicine: Complementary Sciences From Recovery to Cause of Death.* Totowa, NJ: Humana Press, pp. 117–157.

Gallien, V. and Guillon, M. (2007). La pertinence du diagnostic des ensembles funéraires des périodes historiques. In: A. Augereau, H. Guy, A. Koelher, eds., *Le Diagnostic des Ensembles Funéraires.* Paris: Cahiers de l'Inrap pp. 88–103.

Gilaizeau, L. and Guillon, M. (2016). La perception de la sépulture aux périodes Yayoi et Kofun au Japon. Résultats et réflexions sur les investissements de ces sociétés dans leurs tombes et leurs nécropoles. In: M. Lauwers and A. Zemour, eds., *Qu'est-ce qu'une Sépulture? Humanités et Systèmes Funéraires de la Préhistoire à nos Jours.* Antibes: Association pour la Promotion et la Diffusion des Connaissances Archéologiques (APDCA), pp. 293–310.

Guillon, M. (1990). Fouiller, Dessiner et Démonter Plus de 1000 Tombes en 12 mois? L'Exemple du Cimetière Médiéval de Tournedos-sur-Seine. *Bulletins et Mémoires de la Société d'Anthropologie de Paris*, Nouvelle Série, 2(3–4), pp. 61–66.

Guillon, M. (1993). Fiabilité de l'Estimation, sur le Terrain, de l'Âge au Décès des Enfants. Application à une Série de Tournedos-Portejoie, *Bulletins et Mémoires de la Société d'Anthropologie de Paris*, Nouvelle Série, 5(1–2), pp. 237–244.

Guillon, M., (1997). *Anthropologie de terrain et paléodémographie: études méthodologiques sur les grands ensembles funéraires; applications au cimetière médiéval de Tournedos-Portejoie (Eure).* Unpublished doctoral thesis, University of Bordeaux I. https://tel.archives-ouvertes.fr/tel-01331196

Guillon, M. (2004). Représentativité des échantillons archéologiques lors de la fouille des gisements funéraires. In: L. Baray, ed., *Archéologie des Pratiques Funéraires, Approche Critique de la Fouille des Sépultures.* Glux-en-Glenne : Bibracte, pp. 93–112.

Guillon, M. (2010). Development-led archaeology in France. Practice and research, with particular reference to the Institut national de recherches archéologiques préventives (Inrap). In: L. Webley, M. Vander Linden, C. Haselgrove and R. Bradley, eds., *Development-led Archaeology in Europe.* Oxford and Oakville: Oxbow Books, pp. 165–172.

Guillon, M. (2020). *Approche systémique des grands ensembles funéraires.* Unpublished Habilitation à diriger des Recherches (HDR) thesis, University of Bordeaux.

Jaramillo, L.G. (2007). En quête du passé de la Colombie: chantiers de développement urbain, barrages et oléoducs. In: J.-P. Demoule, ed., *L'Archéologie Préventive dans le Monde.* Paris: La Découverte, pp. 258–270.

Jaramillo, L.G. and Oyuela, A. (1994). Colombia: a quantitative analysis. In: A. Oyuela, ed., *History of Latin American Archaeology.* Aldershot: Avebury, pp. 49–68.

Jouneau, D., Colleter, R., Gryspeirt N., Rolland, N. and Guillon, M., eds. (2018). *Romilly-sur-Andelle. Ruelle du Mont (Eure, France). Cimetière du haut Moyen Âge et prieuré médiéval*, archaeological report, Inrap.

Kristiansen, K. (2009). Contract Archaeology in Europe: An Experiment in Diversity. *World Archaeology*, 41, pp. 641–648.

Les Nouvelles de l'Archéologie: https://journals.openedition.org/nda/1968 (Last accessed 16/07/2020).

Marquez-Grant, N. and Fibiger, L., eds. (2011). *The Routledge handbook of archaeological human remains and legislation. An international guide to laws and practice in the excavation and treatment of archaeological human remains.* London: Routledge.

Marx, A., Nura, F. and Salas Rossenbach, K., eds. (2017). *Europeans and archaeology. A survey of the European perception of archaeology and archaeological Heritage.* Paris: NEARCH.

Murail, P., Bruzek, J. and Houët, F. (2000). Stability of the human pelvic sexual dimorphism pattern allows probabilistic sex diagnosis among Homo sapiens sapiens, *Abstracts of the 12th Congress of the European Anthropological Association*, Cambridge, England, 8–11 September, pp. 55–56.

L'archéologie préventive, une démarche responsable *(Preventive archaeology, a responsible approach)* (2012). Colloquium *Calenda*, 21 and 22 November 2012, https://calenda.org/228690 (Last accessed 20 September 2021)

Orschiedt, J., Wittwer-Backofen, U. and Flohr, S. (2011). Germany. In: N. Marquez-Grant and L. Fibiger, eds., *The Routledge Handbook of Archaeological Human Remains and Legislation. An International Guide to Laws and Practice in the Excavation and Treatment of Archaeological Human Remains*. London: Routledge, pp. 165–172.

Otten, T. (2010). Development-led archaeology in Germany: legal Framework. The example of North Rhine-Westphalia. In: L. Webley, M. Vander Linden, C. Haselgrove and R. Bradley, eds., *Development-led Archaeology in Europe*. Oxford and Oakville: Oxbow Books, pp. 100–107.

Portat, É., Detante, M., Bucquet-Macon, C. and Guillon, M., eds. (2016). *Rencontre Autour de la Mort des Tout-Petits: Mortalité Fœtale et Infantile*. Proceedings of the GAAF meeting in Saint-Germain-en-Laye on 3 and 4 December 2009. Corlet: Le Groupe d'Anthropologie et d'Archéologie Funéraire (GAAF).

Robert S., Vermeersch, D., Gaulthier, D. and Costa, L (2001). Archéologues et aménageurs, un partenariat pour demain: musée des Beaux-Arts de Lyon, 5-6 février 2001, *Les Nouvelles de l'archéologie*, 86, pp. 12–16.

Sachau-Carcel, G. (2014). From Field Recording of Plural Burials to 3D Modelling. *Evidence from the Catacomb of Sts. Peter and Marcellinus, Italy. Anthropologie, Special Issue: Methodological Approaches in Funerary Archaeology and Corpse Taphonomy*, 52(3), pp. 285–298.

Sellier, P. (1992). The contribution of paleoanthropology to the interpretation of a functional funerary structure. In: C. Jarrige, J.P. Gerry and R.H. Meadows, eds., *South Asian Archaeology 1989* Madison, WI: Prehistory Press (Monographs in World Archaeology), 14 pp. 253–266.

Sellier P. and Guillon M. (2001). Anthropologie et archéologie funéraire: méthodes pour l'étude de la préhistoire et l'histoire de la mort en Île-de-France. In: M. Tabeaud, ed., *La Mort en Île-de-France*. Paris: Publications de la Sorbonne, pp. 58–64.

Webley, L., Vander Linden, M., Haselgrove, C. and Bradley, R., eds. (2010). *Development-led archaeology in Europe*. Oxford and Oakville, CT: Oxbow Books.

33

MANAGING AND REBURYING ANCIENT HUMAN REMAINS IN FRANCE

From legal and ethical concerns to field practices

Gaëlle Clavandier

Centre Max Weber, Centre National de la Recherche Scientifique (CNRS), UMR 5283, University of Lyon, Université Jean Monnet (UJM), Saint-Etienne, Lyon, France

ADES, Anthropologie biologique, Droit, Éthique et Santé, Centre National de la Recherche Scientifique (CNRS), Etablissement Français du Sang (EFS), UMR 7268, Aix-Marseille Université, Marseille, France

Introduction

In the course of only a few decades, questions about the handling, study, conservation and potential exhibition of human remains have become more complex and have generated debates within the various professional communities involved. Archaeologists and anthropologists, along with museum curators, try to develop appropriate responses and adapt their working protocols. It should be noted that human remains consist of different types (i.e. complete bodies, fragments, embryos), in a great variety of forms or conditions (i.e. skeletal remains, with soft tissue, mummies), of which their identity may or may not be known, with some being very ancient, some being recent. This diversity poses its own problems for those whose work it is to oversee administrative matters involving these remains.

Handling, preserving, managing and exhibiting such collections, especially of human bones, have been the subject of debate for more than a decade (Cassman, Odergaard and Powell, 2006; Ardagna *et al.*, 2006; Cadot, 2009; Jenkins, 2011; *Technè*, 2016). This has led to a series of recommendations that have been incorporated into codes of ethics, including that of the International Council of Museums (ICOM). The latter now considers human remains as 'sensitive cultural material'. From an archaeological point of view, with regard to excavations, these same pre-occupations exist but tend to result in arrangements that are less normative than circumstantial, at least for the time being. The different types of situations involved, as well as the absence of exhibition of the remains, makes this activity less targeted by ethical questions than is the case for museums or collections. Nonetheless, regarding the handling of the recently dead (Weydert *et al.*, 2019), these questions are becoming more pressing. Protocols have been re-visited which could affect the handling of

DOI: 10.4324/9781351030625-38

all archaeological human remains. Any degree of closeness with the dead in question, be it temporal (e.g. recent deaths), or based on emotion and identity[1] (deaths that affect us), re-defines the practical framework. These human remains are no longer simply remains but rather a 'human body' connected to a human person. These reconfigurations are related to shifting sensibilities concerning dead bodies and to the transformation of the legal and ethical framework, as well as to scientific and technical advances. These new norms are impacting research protocols and are causing professional reference frameworks, including ethics, to change in France, as elsewhere.

Questions relating to the handling and the ultimate fate of human remains were occasionally asked in the past, during or after archaeological excavations, for example, but not with the objective of defining a general practical framework.

These questions have now taken on a new meaning because of increased protections for 'cadavers', and because new means of identifying bodies or at least obtaining some information about the individuals, such as age, sex, pathological conditions, make it possible to identify them. The materials in question thus no longer belong to the strict domain of reified things but rather become mortal remains that may contain traces of a person. Interventions on sites from World War I, as well as on the sites of hospital or municipal cemeteries that were active in the 19th and 20th centuries, were the precursors to this shift in the frame of reference because, at least in some cases, they enabled remains to be identified and given names and partial life stories, or even to be returned to their families or communities. Work on these sites in France and throughout Europe showed that it was no longer possible to avoid reflecting on the respect and, sometimes, the homage that these bodies deserve to be given in their handling and treatment. Starting with the decision to excavate, the recovery process employed and the conservation or the destruction of something that is no longer merely sensitive material, archaeologists and anthropologists now question and clarify their practices according to a reflective and normative process.

Reflections that were conceived in the context of interventions involving recent, complete and identifiable remains have become a leitmotif that is spreading through the field of funerary archaeology. Even at a great distance from the time of death and in cases where the remains no longer have a human form (because they are fragmentary or degraded) or for immature remains, special precautions must be considered. A whole set of arguments is being developed in order to adjust techniques and practices to accommodate the concerns of researchers, sponsors and the public. The hypothesis has been proposed that this double proximity (in time and in identity) can progressively lead to reconsideration of the meaning of these remains (recent or ancient, identified or unidentified, whole or fragmentary).

These practices may eventually become applicable to more 'ancient' archaeological sites and to all types of remains qualified as human. For example, though it contradicts what may be taken for granted, the excavation of a medieval cemetery, or even a modern one, could also raise questions of legitimacy in France, both on the opportuneness of the intervention and on the fate of the remains at the end of the excavation.

It seems very likely that these changes will gain a broader consideration. Maintaining an exclusively sensitive and dignified attitude towards the bodies of those who passed away recently or towards the communities to which they belonged[2] – could become the norm and could

---

1 Such as an ancestor or member of one's bloodline, or the forefathers of one's community.

2 The problem of restitution to indigenous communities is an aspect of this question that occupies a prominent place in the public mind. However, there is another dimension to be taken into account: that of 'belonging' to a religious community. This can also be a motive for returning remains and re-inhuming them in accordance with religious rituals.

extend to all human remains. The principles of decency, respect and dignity, the rights that apply to the deceased, could also come to apply to remains that are deemed to be 'intermediary' or 'liminal', which have not benefitted from this type of protection previously. Recommendations for inhuming all remains in cemeteries are becoming more insistent, especially for remains that have been clearly identified or are affiliated with a community (Blanchard and Salmona, 2018). However, it is important to consider another case: the removal of human remains that are positioned on the edges of an excavation, for which protocols are the least clearly established. In other words, what is to be done with human remains that are not included within the excavated area but are on its outer boundaries?

The categorising of human remains benefits from a certain degree of flexibility but also, at the same time, there is an on-going discussion about the possibility or even the necessity of applying the principle of human dignity to them. While much of the English-speaking literature focuses on the management of human remains in the English-speaking world, this chapter will examine how these recommendations can translate into practices in France. One of these, upon which this chapter will especially focus, consists in sending all remains to cemeteries.

An ambivalent status of human remains in France

An 'exceptional status' for ancient human remains?

There is no longer any gathering in the field of funerary archaeology, whether scholarly, institutional or for the general public, at which the issue of the status and the ultimate fate of so-called 'ancient' human remains or 'human vestiges' does not come up.[3] The transformations and controversies that they generate are very subtle, so that France has, until now, favoured the principle of the inalienability of public collections (Cornu *et al.*, 2012) and encouraged a strictly scientific approach to human remains uncovered during excavations.[4] From this point of view, the archaeological process, and also the status of collections for that matter, are relatively 'secure' in comparison with the situation in English-speaking countries,[5] where new ordinances are coming into effect in addition to heritage laws[6] and where their status is more variable than in France (Cassman, Odergaard and Powell, 2006; Jenkins, 2011; Cornu *et al.*, 2012).

Whatever the case may be, in most Western countries, the signs of a new kind of sensitivity, leading to repercussions affecting the management and scientific handling of collections, make it challenging to handle, preserve and exhibit human remains (Cadot, 2007: 10). This challenge is especially telling for museums, which have been re-thinking their practices and trying to adapt

---

3 *Vestiges humains* ['human vestiges/remnants'] is the term used by the French governmental advisory council on bioethics issues, called the Comité Consultatif National d'Éthique [CCNE, National Ethics Consulting Committee].

4 Funerary archaeology and archaeo-anthropology/human osteoarchaeology have earned their credentials and have become recognised fields within these disciplines.

5 In England, Wales and Northern Ireland, in 2004 (Scotland has its own legislation), the government added a clause to the *Human Tissue Act* (equivalent to French bioethical standards) that distinguishes between two categories of human remains: those that are more than 100 years old, and those that are less than 100 years old, the former of which can by law in cases of necessity and with adequate justification be exempted from the legislation governing more recent human tissue (cf. Cadot, 2007: 10–11). See: https://www.hta.gov.uk/policies/licensing-exemptions

6 These new ordinances were added to heritage laws, without discussion.

to this new configuration for approximately the last 15 years (*Tèchnè*, 2016). For the moment, archaeological excavation and research have been relatively spared thanks to the principally scientific character of these endeavours, whether planned or pre-emptive, but the question of the possible reactions of different publics to exhibits cannot be posed in the same terms as those for museums and is less directly pertinent. However, it is not impossible that the same type of difficulties and quandaries that museum curators face may soon confront archaeologists and anthropologists, and, consequently, the handling of human remains may become a real challenge for them as well.

This changing sensibility can be translated into legal texts and their applications. From a legal point of view, the status of human remains is still ambivalent. On the one hand, the French Penal Code (art. 225-17), as well as the Civil Code (art. 16-1), places no time limits on the protection of bodies or cadavers. It is important to recall that the respect due to the human body does not end with death and that the human body; its elements and its products cannot be covered under heritage laws (Civil Code). Damaging the integrity of cadavers and violating graves (including tombs and monuments dedicated to the dead) are punishable offences (Penal Code). This protection was strengthened by the law of 19 December 2008 stipulating that 'the remains of deceased persons, including the ashes of those who have been cremated, must be treated with respect, dignity and decency' (art. 11, integrated into article 16-1 of the Civil Code under art. 16-1-1). French law affords an 'overriding' character or special case for remains of the recently deceased and to those who handle them. This means that, on the one hand, human remains in public collections fall under the principle of inalienability. On the other hand, research on ancient human remains is not subject to the same rules as research on human bodies. In this case, 'human remains are not subject to any specific ordinance concerning their human origin. As cultural possessions, they benefit from the protection of the Heritage Code and are not treated in accordance with ordinances that relate to the human person'[7] (Bouteille-Brigant and Rouge-Maillart, 2014: 303–304). These human remains are thus not considered human bodies.

The ambivalence of the distinction between what is considered a human body as opposed to cultural material – even when the objects in question are qualified as sensitive by the authorities (Deontological Code of the ICOM) – persists due to a level of tolerance and to a certain way of interpreting the texts relative to the protection of bodies (including cadavers) that makes no distinction between the different kinds of human remains. This also continues because, according to the law, a cadaver (i.e. a person's mortal remains) is a thing, not a person, even if it may be qualified as a 'sacred' or 'extraordinary' thing to which the principle of human dignity could or should apply nonetheless (Labbée, 2012 [1990]; Popu, 2009; Cayol, 2011).

Human remains or bodies?

If human remains from archaeological excavations are an exception under French law, does this concern all of them? For now, the actors and institutions involved, along with the legal doctrine, grant them a particular status because of the interest they represent for science and for understanding heritage. However, 'recent human remains', those with reduced temporal proximity, draw attention and lead to reconsideration of the effects of interventions. They pose

---

7 '*Les restes humains ne font l'objet d'aucune disposition spécifique en ce qui concerne leur origine humaine. En tant que biens culturels, ils sont soumis à la protection que leur confère le Code du patrimoine et ne sont pas traités au titre des dispositions relatives à la personne humaine*', translated by Sarah Novak.

questions for the future handling or disposal of these bodies. They lead to an observation that 'though it is not easily formalised, there exists a line of demarcation between ancient and current. Thus, (…) the preservation of a testimony to history is legitimate when every possible link with human remains is broken'[8] (Le Coz, 2019). This is a position that implicitly favours a particular attentiveness to certain human remains as long as links with them are still effective, either because the identity of the remains can be determined or because the community of the deceased is involved. In both cases, such proximity means that the respect due to the deceased person must apply *a priori*.

Yet the division between ancient and recent is perhaps not as meaningful as it appears because, beyond the affinity dimension of these connections, the present time is witness to the dawn of a new value system in which remains represent not only a person but also that person's past humanity.

After a number of requests from cultural institutions and museums, but also from representatives of different associations and actors in civil society, in 2010, the French National Ethics Consultative Committee promulgated a government statement on the 'ethical problems posed by the use of cadavers with the objective of conservation or exhibition'.[9] Of course, this statement primarily concerns collections (including especially sensitive collections associated with a colonial context or, more recently, with collection methods that may be judged as dubious) and seeks to define a framework of good practice that can lead to the possible exhibition of these remains. At the same time, it lays out a broader model that integrates changing sensibilities and contemporary ethical issues into a context in which the entire category of human remains is reconsidered. To do this, it relies on the revision of bioethics laws, which now include respect for the identity and the body of the deceased person: 'Bioethics cannot be defined merely as the ethics of the living. It also involves defining what the living must forbid themselves to do to the bodies of the dead, to those remains that carry the memory of the deceased'.[10] It is interesting to observe that this statement mobilises two semantic systems, that of 'human remains' and that of 'the body, the cadaver, the deceased', the first emphasising the historical dimension and the capacity of the remains to bear witness to the past, the second emphasising their humanity, in so much as it refers to a human being and to humanity itself. Nonetheless, the line between these two systems is not hermetic because, 'although it is not without legitimacy, the historical argument – i.e. the need to preserve traces and vestiges of past times – deserves to be weighed against other values, such as respect for each civilisation and friendship between peoples'[11] (statement n°111, 14). Likewise, 'it seems that museum objects containing elements of human bodies should be treated with the respect as is due to once living persons. It is the present relationship with the past that is being questioned here. We must ask ourselves how we should deal with the remnants of those who departed long before the development of contemporary ethical principles and legal rules. The attitude towards

---

8 'Bien qu'elle ne soit pas aisément formalisable, il existe une ligne de démarcation entre l'ancien et l'actuel. Ainsi, (…) la préservation d'un témoignage de l'histoire est légitime lorsque tout lien possible avec les restes humains est rompu', translated by Sarah Novak.

9 Statement n°111, January 7, 2010.

10 Informational Report n°2235 of 'Révision des lois de bioéthique' ['Revision of bioethics laws'], Chapter 8, p. 423. 'la bioéthique ne saurait être définie comme étant seulement l'éthique du vivant. Elle implique aussi de définir ce que les vivants doivent s'interdire de faire avec les corps des morts, ces dépouilles qui portent la mémoire du défunt', translated by Sarah Novak.

11 'Sans être dépourvu de légitimité, l'argument historique – la nécessité de préserver des traces et des vestiges d'un passé révolu – vaut d'être mis en balance avec d'autres valeurs telles que le respect de chaque civilisation et de l'amitié entre les peuples', translated by Sarah Novak.

Māori heads must take into account the growing attachment to respecting the dignity of every human person, including after death'[12] (statement n°111, 11).

Even more directly, French legal experts are raising their voices to denounce the absence of any real status for ancient human remains as untenable in the current circumstances because the principle of the dignity of the human person should apply to all of them, without any restrictions, as soon as their humanity is established: 'While seeking the consent of the object of study would not be pertinent in matters involving ancient human remains, it would nonetheless be possible to take inspiration from solutions retained for recently deceased bodies in order to determine some of the principles that would govern a possible status for ancient human remains, conscious of the dignity of the human person, which would have to apply without distinction as soon as the humanity of the remains is confirmed (Bouteille-Brigant and Rouge-Maillard, 2014: 308).[13]

If in the view of these authors, scientific objectives remain legitimate, a regulatory body of the same type as the biomedical agency should nonetheless monitor them. In the same vein, for these authors, the preservation (whether provisional or 'perpetual') of these remains, or '*dépouilles*' [corpses, bodies],[14] cannot be automatically justified. And in cases where it is justified, it is still necessary to establish 'conditions for the preservation of remains that are compatible with their human dimension and in an appropriate location, respectful of the rituals and beliefs of the peoples who may potentially be concerned'[15] (Bouteille-Brigant and Rouge-Maillard, 2014: 309). Without a doubt, this is a minority perspective within the propositions that it aims to put into effect – propositions that move towards creating the new status of a lifeless person or dead or deceased person (Touzeil-Divina and Bouteille-Brigant, 2014: 419). In any event, the impulse to apply the principles of respect and dignity to these human remains, whatever they may be, is more and more commonly accepted within legal doctrine and outside of it.

Towards a new reign of sensitivity?

From a social point of view, the sensitivity of contemporaries regarding the handling and exhib-ition of human remains has incontestably changed; it is no longer anodyne to see mummies or foetuses presented in archaeological or anatomical collections. This sensitivity can sometimes be troubling in the view of the standards in force up to the present time, as it assimilates these remains with human persons towards whom one must have a respectful attitude; this respect manifests itself in the treatment reserved to 'bodies'. Memmi's (2014) work highlights the 'return

---

12 '*Les objets de musée impliquant des vestiges humains semblent donc devoir être traités avec le respect qui convient à des personnes ayant vécu. C'est notre rapport présent au passé qui se trouve ici questionné. Nous avons à nous poser la question de savoir comment nous rapporter aux vestiges de ceux qui ont disparu longtemps avant l'élaboration de nos principes éthiques et règles juridiques contemporaines. Le regard que nous portons sur les têtes māori doit tenir compte de notre attachement croissant au respect de la dignité de toute personne humaine, y compris après sa mort*', translated by Sarah Novak.

13 '*Si la recherche d'un consentement de l'objet d'étude ne serait, concernant les restes humains anciens, pas pertinente, il n'en reste pas moins qu'il semble possible de s'inspirer des solutions retenues à propos de la dépouille mortelle récente pour dégager quelques principes régissant un éventuel statut des restes humains anciens, soucieux de la dignité de la personne humaine qui doit s'appliquer indistinctement, dès lors que l'humanité des restes est confirmée*', translated by Sarah Novak.

14 The use of the term *dépouille* to define these human remains – '*lieux de conservation ou d'inhumation de la dépouille*' (Bouteille-Brigant and Rouge-Maillard, 2014: 309) – just like the possibility of mobilising the notion of the dignity of the human person on their behalf, supposes a transfer of meaning.

15 '*conditions de conservation des restes compatibles avec leur dimension humaine et dans un endroit adapté, respectueux des rites et croyances des peuples éventuellement concernés*', translated by Sarah Novak.

of the body', or at least an attempt to reincarnate the social definition of individuals, leading to the re-establishment of the body, whether living or dead. This new reign of sensitivity, which has come into being in large part thanks to the professionals who handle these human remains, re-introduces a degree of 'gravity' (Memmi, 2015: 141) and solemnity through the materiality of the body. It is clear, then, why this is not merely a matter of representation but also of real gestures and formal precautions.

This situation is certainly reinforced as soon as there are tangible signs marking the identity of the individual, either with a name or with belonging to a particular religion, community, or even political group, but it now seems to be moving towards becoming universal. Human remains, ancient and recent, are becoming increasingly embodied and, through this simple fact, are no longer being assimilated with objects, even if that is still their legal status. This concern for bodies translates into concern for the fate or disposal of these remains, whether or not they are of heritage interest. During archaeological excavations and after the resulting research is presented to the public, it is not unusual to address the following question: 'What will happen to the skeletons?'

The work of archaeologists and anthropologists does not take place 'above ground' and their prerogatives are all the more important because intermediary agents develop new regulations. Since legal texts in question allow for a certain degree of flexibility, arrangements are generally made at the level of 'delegated biopolitics',[16] notably by professionals (Memmi and Taïeb, 2009). Archaeologists, as well as anthropologists, are confronted with organisational constraints but also with the public scrutiny of their work. In addition, it must not be forgotten that they are also human beings, products of their own time, who are inevitably affected by the contemporary trend of questioning and reflecting upon the practices that they use. Their work often involves bones: recovering, cleaning, handling, curating and studying them. Each of these stages requires researchers to observe and handle human remains. Sometimes, this means that they must integrate certain curatorial pre-occupations into their practices that go far beyond scientific considerations.

Are we handling simple archaeological material, just like furniture or ceramics, or do we recognise the humanity of these remains and all the requirements and rules that this may imply? The answer can be found in the intervening space between the two. Although there is a relative consensus these days for considering these remains as sensitive material, precautions are now taken that did not exist in the recent past, or at least were not publicised – there is, however, no unambiguous model or concrete methodology defining the precise procedures to follow in preparation for the handling and the ultimate disposal of this type of material. Appropriate responses are worked out and decisions are made on a case-by-case basis. It is undeniable that

---

16 'Ce pouvoir contemporain sur la vie et la mort a donc (…) la particularité de ne pas être exclusivement un pouvoir d'État, rationalisateur et venant d'en haut. Il repose, par capillarité, sur une myriade d'agents sociaux qui, en vertu de la "biopolitique déléguée" contemporaine doivent en permanence inventer des relations avec le fœtus ou l'individu mort/à mourir/menacé de mort, prendre des décisions vitales le concernant, improviser avec son entourage, et construire progressivement et empiriquement un système de normes, de discours et de gestes utilisables dans ces situations particulières' (Memmi and Taïeb, 2009: 13). Translated by Sarah Novak: 'This contemporary power over life and death has thus (…) the particularity of not being exclusively a power of the State, rationalising and coming down from on high. It depends, by osmosis, on a myriad of social agents who, by virtue of contemporary "delegated biopolitics", must constantly invent relationships with the fetus or the individual who is dead/dying/threatened with death, make vital decisions about him/her, deal with his or her family and friends, and, progressively and empirically, construct a system of norms, discourses and gestures that would be usable in these particular situations' (Memmi and Taïeb, 2009: 13).

relationships tend to grow between researchers and their study objects in a societal and ethical context in which the handling of human remains is far from anodyne or self-evident.

Cemeteries: the place for the dead and for all human remains?

Towards generalised funerary protocols?

Concentrating on the materiality of remains and on their handling may seem to be missing the real issues as long as it is the legal and statutory dimension and the sensitive or even emotional dimension that dominate the debate. However, this perspective offers the definite advantage of concretely seizing upon the effects of these changing sensibilities by relying not on impressions but rather on tangible elements relative to this materiality (Hallam and Hockey, 2001; Hockey, Komaromy and Woodthorpe, 2010). The fate of dead bodies is an essential key for understanding the facts in question (Anstett, 2016). Whether ancient human remains enter into public collections or are reburied or destroyed, their ultimate treatment provides insight into the place of such remains and their social status (or the category in which they are situated). More broadly, such an approach makes it possible to document precisely the specifics of the contemporary relationship with death and with the dead and highlight notable transitions.

Placing the dead, every one of them, including fragments and embryos,[17] within the confines of cemeteries is an ideal to which a number of actors and institutions, including the French State, subscribe; this ideal is what Arnaud Esquerre (2011: 310) describes as the 'communauté morte-vivante' ('community of the living-dead'). It represents an attempt to 'immobilise the dead', or in other words, to set them within an immutable order. This fiction has the effect of grouping living human beings with cadavers, bones, fragments and ashes. This appears to be the principle governing the custodianship of human remains today. However, this is only a principle that orients decisions and practices; there is no question of effectively placing all human remains in cemeteries, which would be an impossible challenge because the dead would accumulate there as a legacy without any objective criteria for distinguishing between them, either in time or in space.

To understand the new ethos of the dead, one must consider the place and role of cemeteries in France since the 19th-century reforms (Bertrand and Carol, 2016). 'Municipal cemeteries' (which are secular and governed by national laws) have become the almost exclusive resting place for the dead, following a principle of equality and neutrality; this orientation is reinforced and confirmed by new laws concerning cremation.[18] Cemeteries are natural and legitimate places for receiving the dead – all the dead without exceptions. In addition, one might have the idea that the dignity of the human person can be extended to types of remains that, until now, were not covered by these regulations[19] because of their unique characteristics. The remains of foetuses, fragmentary remains and prehistoric osteological remains, because of their uncertain status and dissociation and distance from personhood, do not benefit from any special precautions based on their human origin. In this new normative environment, with some exceptions, when one considers the trajectory and, more precisely, the ultimate destination of human remains, it

---

17 Embryonic in the sense that the status of person (i.e. legal personhood) is not accorded to these beings because they were never born. Not in question here are the products of conception issuing from voluntary termination of pregnancy.

18 The scattering of ashes in natural areas is essentially tolerated (ordinance of March 13, 2007) subject to the will of the individual, according to the principle of the Funerary Freedom Law of 15 November 1887.

19 There is at least a debate surrounding this.

becomes normal (even in a number of new situations) for them to be placed and to reside in the cemetery, either buried in a private or common grave or deposited in an ossuary or in a space dedicated to the scattering of ashes.

Contextualised responses

These positions are definitely not only a matter of doctrine or of discourse: they are the specific subjects of transformations that are currently taking place in the field. It is clear that various parties, professionals being the first among them, are taking action in favour of decency, respect and dignity for the human remains that they handle, at least a certain number of them.

In the fields of archaeology and archaeothanatology, two cases especially stand out. It is no longer simply a question of thinking of 'human ancestors' but of establishing the closeness that joins present people with them, either by determining their lineage or ancestry or by re-assigning them to a community of belonging. From this point on, those who have become 'our dead' deserve dignified treatment. It is now well established that any human remains for which there is a relationship with the living or identity-based links – because they are recent, identified or identifiable – should be treated with respect because these are indeed dead beings, bodies and persons, not objects. From this point of view, the connections between these remains and ourselves create an emotional resonance that causes us to confer due respect on the cadaver, as if by mimicry.

In the field and, for that matter, from a more theoretical point of view as well, the line of demarcation between 'ancient' and 'contemporary' is difficult to determine because the temporal distinction is combined here with affinity and identities. For example, for princely or aristocratic lineages, affiliation can be established going back centuries, or even millennia, reconstituting a familial closeness that can be just as intimate as it is political. A sharp cut-off line may thus be created in the name of a social and symbolic hierarchy between human remains that are 'noble' and other 'non-noble' remains, for which memorial and biological affinity are more difficult to gather and verify or are simply absent. In another illustration of this, when closeness is expressed not through lineage but through belonging, temporal distance can become insignificant in the face of attachment to a given people or community. The difficulty is thus doubled because this attachment is based on multiple criteria: land, culture, bloodlines, sacredness, political engagement and/or identity, which can all re-define the contours of what is 'close' to living people by highlighting such connections. This 'proximity of belonging' has the peculiarity of refreshing or renewing relationships and links to the past through the living. In such a case, the issue of protection concerns both the deceased person and his or her community of belonging, to which one may defer (or perhaps not) in the course of the intervention on these human remains. Concretely, this may take the form of the restitution of collection pieces.[20] More discretely, after rescue archaeological excavation, skeletal remains may be handed over to a religious community to be interred in a cemetery (municipal or specifically denominational) following the rituals of the community in question, even though the potential scientific interest of studying the remains is still acknowledged.

Beyond this position predicated on reconsidering the status of certain human remains issuing from archaeological excavations or preserved in museum collections – in the name of

---

20 Examples from France include the restitution by the French State of the body of Saarjie Baartamn (called the 'Hottentot Venus') to South Africa in 2002 and the equally emblematic return of Māori remains (known as the Māori heads) to New Zealand in 2012.

identity[21] – the notion of respect transfers to remains with links with the present that are more tenuous or more ancient, in this case with their 'humanity' as a justification. Here, the debate shifts: it is no longer a question of degree (recent or identified human remains do benefit from a particular 'status'), but rather of *nature* (the condition of being human applies to all of these remains), under the cover of this question: 'are we not all, every one of us, representatives of the same Humanity?'[22] (Bouteille-Brigant and Rouge-Maillard, 2014: 308). In this case, the criteria of temporal closeness and of present connections with the remains become meaningless and meld into a single overriding principle, the human condition.

While, for the time being, there is no real controversy on this topic to be observed within the community of archaeologists and anthropologists, there nonetheless seem to be occasional indications that this second attitude could gain from being tested against practices and discourses. To the author's knowledge, this does not come into play when human remains from archaeological excavations enter into research contexts. In such cases, the scientific method prevails since it is perceived as ethically acceptable, with regard to both the recovery and handling, as well as in the curation and study of human remains. Even so, there is room for discussion. These debates, while they are not merely residual, have not yet had any notable influence on professional practices (aside, perhaps, from a few new precautions in practice and in writing), or at least have not yet brought into question their validity in France at least, if not elsewhere in the world.

The sensitive case of human remains situated in a liminal zone beyond the archaeological site

These new orientations are more directly perceivable when one looks at situations on the fringes of more usual archaeological work, notably when human remains do not fit directly into an established protocol. This situation arises from the fact that, by scientific choice but also due to financial or time constraints, excavation programmes can determine the limits of excavations (either ahead of time, at the moment of the initial assessment, or during the excavation, by re-evaluating the areas that should be studied, taking into account any newly exposed and unanticipated elements). In such cases, the urban works project may cover a larger area than the archaeological excavation, which means that further ground must be cleared. All the difficulty resides, then, in the fact that this liminal zone (outside the excavation area, but within the same site) does not make it possible to re-categorise these remains and to give them, for example, the status of 'ancient human remains'. They are not, properly speaking, sensitive archaeological material because they do not fall directly under the research protocol. Is this material simply detritus, then, or is it human remains – or human bodies worthy of respect, dignity and decency? Is the answer to this determined by their condition before being recovered, considering that in most of these cases, the human remains had been inhumed in a cemetery or a burial ground, or at least in graves?

In this precise case, delimiting the various prerogatives becomes more complex. Arrangements must be worked out between the developer, the local municipality, the representative of the State in charge of heritage conservation and the archaeologists authorised to carry out the excavation. *A priori*, human remains situated within the area of the excavation are subject to the Heritage Code and fall under the authority of archaeologists and anthropologists. What happens to those

---

21 Their own (identity through a name) or that of the group to which they belong (religious community, population of origin or people from whom they descend ...).
22 '*Ne sommes-nous pas, tous, des représentants de la même Humanité ?*', translated by Sarah Novak.

remains that are found beyond this zone is harder to predict. On the one hand, it might be argued that the handling and disposal of these remains should be subject to the law relating to the protection of the bodies and cadavers (Civil Code), as well as to recommendations relating to ancient human remains by ethics committees and codes of ethics. On the other hand, it is still possible to consider them as a type of material residue and treat them as such when they are not, or no longer, located in the area of excavation. In this circumstance, they would not benefit from the protection that would apply to remains within identified cemeteries.

The real question today is to work out a legitimate designation for these non-studied human remains, especially since these remains may be identical in every aspect to others that are present in excavated areas. What used to be euphemised as a 'deposit in a quarry' (a euphemism used by archaeologists in France to mean reburied *en masse* in a refuse area) becomes difficult to defend for the different professionals involved and can elicit unease or shame in cases where such practices are revealed by the media.[23] Depositing human remains, even ancient ones, in a garbage dump or on vacant land is now perceived as contrary to the proper order of public morality and human dignity. The norm seems to have shifted towards the interment of such remains by municipal funeral directors; how exactly this translates into reality still needs to be understood through a precise inventory of the latest excavation projects to date on French soil that meet all these criteria.

While these practices have existed for a long time – occasionally, human remains have been moved to cemeteries after an excavation – what is new here is the scale, the motive and the practical details of this type of intervention, in addition to the various steps[24] and discussions that it requires. These transfers to cemeteries, which in fact amount to funerals/burials in their own right, take place within a particular framework. They can:

- be carried out in compliance with article 16-1-1 of the Civil Code, which considers these materials as the remains of a deceased person;
- be handled by certified undertakers who oversee the recovery, the placing in reliquaries and the transportation of the 'bodies', followed by their burial or deposition within a monument;
- involve scores – in the hundreds at times – of individual sets of remains;
- lead to an expression of reverence during the interment, including speeches pronounced in the presence of officials, religious personalities or the professionals who worked on the site;
- provide memorials to the dead through the display of commemorative or informative plaques.

To some degree, the conjunction of these actions resembles the funerary process. The regulatory documents, as well as the professionals, practices and places involved, are all the same as those that are customarily invoked following the death of a person. In this context, how could one help but see bodies, funerals and graves, or at least 'almost bodies', 'almost funerals' and 'almost graves'? These remains, which would have been disqualified and abandoned to their condition as objects, or even as detritus, are thus rehabilitated. This rehabilitation unavoidably poses problems when confronted with the scientific approach used for the other remains and fragments present within the excavation zone. It is completely legitimate if one is reasoning from the principles

---

23 This situation can also be seen in cases of renovation or re-development of cemeteries or of work projects involving private and common gravesites: https://www.laprovence.com/article/edition-marseille/4953467/ossements-a-lair-libre-la-ville-se-defend-detre-dans-lillegalite.html https://www.laprovence.com/article/edition-marseille/4950375/au-cimetiere-des-vaudrans-des-ossements-et-des-capitons-de-cercueils-ont-ete-decouverts-sur-un

24 These new ordinances might also require a municipal decree or the opening of a public tendering system.

laid out by the Civil Code regarding deceased persons. Their classification as 'mortal remains' potentially turns them into bodies that enter or re-enter the space of the dead, and thus that of the living, making homage and reverence possible. However, the situation becomes less clear-cut when an attempt is made to take into account the two, three or even four 'paths'[25] that may be followed by these human remains, which sometimes come from the same site, belong to the same period of the past and are only separated by the area covered by the excavation but whose 'destinies' can vary considerably from one another. One can understand, therefore, why these are especially delicate subjects to bring up in the community of archaeologists and anthropologists, for there are some aspects of them that may offend the notions of science and heritage behind their work, and of course, these matters are largely beyond their control, especially because political and ethical issues can supersede the prerogatives of research and ethics that are specific to each profession. From this point of view, the notions of respect, decency and dignity take diverging paths, and it is hard to say whether determining appropriate solutions on a case-by-case basis may not be the most comfortable situation for all those involved.

Conclusion: a move towards the protection of human remains

The problem of the protection of ancient human remains is extremely complex due to their protean character, which, in a sociological context, requires focus on subjective criteria for analysis. One of these criteria concerns the future or the destination of these remains. There is a current trend favouring a funerary treatment for them, i.e. depositing them or interring them in cemeteries, when they are not of interest to museums or other archaeological repositories. This same tendency is also seen in cases of the restitution of an individual or of human-based material from a public collection to his or her community of origin[26] and also in rescue excavations involving the reburial of certain remains. In the cases mentioned above, remains entering the cemetery are classified as cadavers, which transforms them into 'bodies' and raises the question of the homage due to them. The first case (restitution) has not been addressed in this contribution; it has already been the subject of numerous publications and because it is already on the outer limits of the questions raised by this chapter, notably the issue of the inalienability of public collections. However, it does offer a point of comparison for considering the ultimate fate of these human remains (Roustan, 2014). It must be noted that one of the subjective criteria enabling this request to be granted is the assignation of these bodies to a funerary logic rather than a logic of heritage. In other words, there is favourable support for their restitution, or, more accurately, their repatriation, based on the principle that they will be interred[27] (or handled according to the rituals of their community), not that they will be exhibited in their community of origin.[28] They thus

---

25 If one considers public waste disposal and quarry sites as well as restitution to indigenous or religious communities.

26 An exceptional situation but nonetheless currently possible.

27 In the case of the return of the Māori heads to New Zealand, after these were placed in the Museum of New Zealand Te Papa Tongarewa, the fragments that had been identified (either by tattoos or by genetic analysis) were ritually buried or, in some cases, were deposited in a sacred space within the museum (Roustan, 2014: 195).

28 One of the principles that overrides the inalienability of collections, other than that countries of origin requesting the return of human remains must be those of 'current peoples', is that '*le vestige n'est pas destiné à être exposé ni conservé dans des réserves au sein du pays d'origine mais inhumé*' (Avis n°111, 13, CCNE)'. Translated by Sarah Novak: 'the remains are not destined to be exposed or kept in collections within the country of origin but rather inhumed'.

acquire the status of human remains and are considered, even in a fragmentary state, as persons (Mauss, 1991 [1950]).

This dynamic, which may appear completely anecdotal because it concerns only a small number of cases (rare on the scale of museum collections, infrequent on that of archaeological excavations) and occurs on the fringes of this field, would not cause a debate if this were not the case for other types of human remains in other instances in France and elsewhere in the world. These remains all have the peculiarity of being liminal for, at first glance at least, they do not directly involve a deceased person for whom a death certificate and a burial or cremation permit would be systematically delivered, and for whom a grave is not merely a principle but an obligation. It is this congruence between the pathways followed by isolated, disarticulated human remains such as fragmentary remains or very ancient remains, affecting widely varying populations and life histories and involving professionals from very different fields that draw the research interests of sociologists. Through what combination of circumstances, or through what new paradigm of unprecedented sensitivity, have these human remains been legitimately placed in or returned to the space within a cemetery – mostly starting in the 2000s – not as a place to store remains that one does not know what to do with, but as a legitimate resting place (Clavandier, 2017a and b; Charrier and Clavandier, 2018)? These gestures, which might be seen as relatively neutral and obvious, are nonetheless transforming the relationship with dead bodies and the status accorded to them, along with the professional practices of those who handle them.

This chapter has provided an overview of the key aspects of human remains management in France. The importance of questioning and understanding the origin of remains and collections is important in several disciplines. While these reflections are based on experience with archaeologically derived skeletons in France, many of these issues are universal and not limited to human remains.

Acknowledgements

This chapter is an edited and translated version from 'Inhumer les Restes Humains Anciens. Des Enjeux Juridiques et Éthiques, aux Pratiques sur le Terrain'. In: N. Weydert, S. Tzortzis, A. Richier, L. Lantéri and H. Guy, eds., *Rencontre autour de nos aïeux, la mort de plus en plus proche*, Actes de la 8ᵉ Rencontre du Groupement d'Anthropologie et d'Archéologie Funéraire (Gaaf) (25–27 mai 2016, Marseille), Reugny: Groupement d'anthropologie et d'archéologie funéraire. A special thanks goes to Sarah Novak for the translation of this contribution.

References

Anstett, E. (2016). Des Cadavres en Masse. Sociétés et Sciences Sociales Face à l'Impensé. *Techniques et Culture*, 60, pp. 126–143.

Ardagna, Y., Bizot, B., Boëtsch, G. and Delestre, X., eds. (2006). *Les collections ostéologiques humaines, gestion, valorisation, perspectives*. Aix-en-Provence: Bulletin Archéologique de Provence, 4.

Bertrand, R. and Carol, A. (2016). *Aux origines des cimetières contemporains. Les réformes funéraires dans l'Europe occidentale*. Aix-en-Provence: Presses Universitaires de Provence.

Blanchard, P. and Salmona, P. (2018). L'archéologie des communautés juives européennes. In: J.-P. Demoule, D. Garcia and A. Schnapp, eds., *Une Histoire des Civilisations*. Paris: La Découverte, pp. 446–451.

Bouteille-Brigant, M. and Rouge-Maillart, C. (2014). Recherche(s) et cadavre(s). In: M. Touzeil-Divina, M. Bouteille-Brigant and J.-F. Boudet, eds., *Traité des Nouveaux Droits de la Mort*. Le Mans: Lextenso – L'Epitoge, 2, pp. 289–309.

Cadot, L. (2007). Les restes humains: une gageure pour les musées? *La Lettre de l'OCIM (Office de Coopération et d'Information Muséales)*, 109, pp. 4–15.

Cadot, L. (2009). *En chair et en os: le cadavre au musée. valeurs, statuts et enjeux de la conservation des dépouilles humaines patrimonialisées*. Paris: Mémoires de recherche de l'Ecole du Louvre.

Cassman, V., Odergaard, N. and Powell, J. (2006). *Human remains: a guide for museums and academic institutions*. New York: AltaMira Press.

Cayol, A. (2011). Avant la Naissance et Après la Mort: l'Être Humain, une Chose Digne de Respect. *Cahiers de la Recherche sur les Droits Fondamentaux*, 9, pp. 117–126.

Charrier, P. and Clavandier, G. (2018). Aménagements autour du principe de sépulture. une tension entre des corps là et un au-delà des corps. In: P. Charrier, G. Clavandier, V. Gourdon, C. Rollet and N. Sage Pranchère, eds., *Morts Avant de Naître, Dead Before Being Born*. Tours: Presses Universitaires François Rabelais, pp. 273–292.

Clavandier, G. (2017a). *Principe de sépulture et statut de personne. Le sort des fœtus et mort-nés*. Habilitation à diriger la recherche (HDR) thesis, Université Lyon 2.

Clavandier, G. (2017b). Du corps comme support de la ritualité au fragment comme maintien de la personne. Étude des catastrophes contemporaines. In: V. García-Acosta and A. Musset, eds., *Dialogues et Discours Croisés: Les Catastrophes et l'Interdisciplinarité*. Louvain-La-Neuve: L'Harmattan.

Cornu, M., Fromageau, J., Poli, J.-F. and Taylor, A.-C. (2012). *L'Inaliénabilité des collections, performances et limites*. Paris: L'Harmattan.

Esquerre, A. (2011). *Les os, les cendres et l'Etat*. Paris: Fayard.

Hallam, E. and Hockey J. (2001). *Death, memory and material culture*. Oxford and New York: Berg.

Hockey, J., Komaromy, C. and Woodthorpe, K. (2010). *The matter of death: space, place and materiality*. Basingstoke: Palgrave Macmillan.

Jenkins, T. (2011). *Contesting human remains in museum collections: the crisis of cultural authority*. London: Routledge.

Labbée, X. (2012 [1990]). *La Condition juridique du corps humain avant la naissance et après la mort*. Lille: Presses Universitaires du Septentrion.

Le Coz, P. (2019). Respect du cadavre: jusqu'où et pourquoi? In: N. Weydert, S. Tzortzis, A. Richier, L. Lantéri and H. Guy, eds., *Rencontre autour de nos Aïeux, la Mort de Plus en Plus Proche, Actes de la 8e Rencontre du Groupement d'anthropologie et d'archéologie funéraire* (Gaaf) (25–27 mai 2016, Marseille). Reugny: Groupement d'Anthropologie et d'Archéologie Funéraire.

Mauss, M. (1991 [1950]). Une Catégorie de l'Esprit Humain: La Notion de Personne celle de 'Moi'. *Sociologie et Anthropologie*. Paris: Presses Universitaires de France (PUF), pp. 331–361.

Memmi, D. (2014). *La revanche de la chair. Essai sur les nouveaux supports de l'identité*. Paris: Seuil.

Memmi, D. (2015). Le Corps Mort dans l'Histoire des Sensibilités. *Communications*, 97, pp. 131–145.

Memmi, D. and Taïeb, E. (2009). Les Recompositions du 'Faire Mourir': Vers une Biopolitique d'Institution. *Sociétés Contemporaines*, 75, pp. 5–15.

Popu, H. (2009). *La dépouille mortelle, chose sacrée. À la redécouverte d'une catégorie juridique oubliée*. Paris: L'Harmattan.

Roustan, M. (2014). De l'Adieu aux Choses au Retour des Ancêtres. La Remise par la France des Têtes Māori à la Nouvelle-Zélande. *Socio-anthropologie*, 30, pp. 183–197.

Technè (2016). *Archives de l'humanité. Les restes humains patrimonialisés*. Paris: Centre de recherche et de restauration des musées de France, 44.

Touzeil-Divina, M. and Bouteille-Brigant, M. (2014). Du cadavre: autopsie d'un statut, In: M. Touzeil-Divina, M. Bouteille-Brigant and J.-F. Boudet, eds., *Traité des Nouveaux Droits de la Mort*. Le Mans: Lextenso – L'Epitoge, 2, pp. 403–429.

Weydert, N., Tzortzis, S., Richier, A., Lantéri, L. and Guy, H., eds. (2019). *Rencontre autour de nos Aïeux, la Mort de Plus en Plus Proche, Actes de la 8e Rencontre du Groupement d'Anthropologie et d'Archéologie Funéraire (Gaaf)* (25–27 mai 2016, Marseille), Reugny: Groupement d'Anthropologie et d'Archéologie Funéraire.

PART V

Lexicon of archaeothanatological terms

34

LEXICON OF TERMS USED IN ARCHAEOTHANATOLOGY

A work still in the process of becoming

Christopher J. Knüsel

PACEA, De la Préhistoire à l'Actuel: Culture, Environnement et Anthropologie, UMR 5199, CNRS-Université de Bordeaux, Pessac, France

Karina Gerdau-Radonić

Archimède, Maison Interuniversitaire des Sciences de l'Homme, UMR 7044, Université de Strasbourg, France

Centre for Archaeology and Anthropology, Bournemouth University, Poole, United Kingdom

Eline M.J. Schotsmans

PACEA, De la Préhistoire à l'Actuel: Culture, Environnement et Anthropologie, UMR 5199, CNRS-Université de Bordeaux, Pessac, France

Centre for Archaeological Science, University of Wollongong, Wollongong, Australia

Preamble: This lexicon is not intended to be exhaustive but as indicative of the relevant published sources available, as well as to aid with definitions of terms when reading contributions herein and elsewhere. Where appropriate and possible, sources in English and French have been included for further reading and research purposes. All translations have been performed by the authors of this lexicon and verified, if possible, with those previously suggested. Clearly, this lexicon owes a debt to French language scholarship, but it does not reproduce mere translations of terms. Rather, it tries to synthesise French and English-language scholarship and practice to advance understanding of how terms are used and why they have been selected.

Abandonment Burial: introduced originally by Villes (1987), '*sépulture de relégation*' in French, refers to the abandonment of a corpse or corpses for which no funerary rites were performed (cf. Boulestin and Baray, 2010; Le Roy and Rottier, Chapter 11, this volume; Schmitt, Chapter 6, this volume). In the absence of funerary rites, these are not formally interred but are in a **mortuary context** (cf. below). Alternatively, the archaeological context of some individuals may have evidence for funerary treatment but these are located away from the funerary area of the group (cf. Schmitt, Chapter 6, this volume). The phrase 'excluded in death' (i.e. buried in

 DOI: 10.4324/9781351030625-40

a manner not consistent with the norm for the majority of individuals) has also been used to describe such cases (Milella, Knüsel and Haddow, 2016), while 'excluded deposition' has been used when there is no evidence for a 'burial' in the sense of planned or intentional deposition following an established funerary tradition, thus the body of a deceased person lacking the more common funerary treatments and rituals of the group, including a shared location. This seems to be a special case of what has been referred to as '**irregular**' burial (Milella *et al.,* 2015), or previously as '**deviant**' burial (Murphy, 2008), or as '**atypical**' burial ('*sépulture atypique*' in French) (cf. below) (cf. Bocquentin *et al.,* 2010). At the present time, there is no disciplinary consensus, but the notion that all buried remains, and especially those lacking evidence for specific funerary treatments, are not necessarily intentional burials is a fundamental, shared concept. By the same token, individuals treated in a manner different from the majority of others in the same place or of the same date may have special social significance. Those treated in this way may be the remains of marginal or ostracised individuals, such as slaves, war captives, heretics, outcasts, transgressors, or perceived wrongdoers depending on the place, time and context.

Accompanying Dead: '*morts d'accompagnement*' in French, are identified as 'retainer burials' in English by Aufderheide and Rodríquez-Martín (1998: 43–44), but this designation has the connotation that the accompanying dead were sacrificed, which may not always have been the case. 'Retainer-burial' is used infrequently in recent English-language publications, perhaps due to problems in applying a term drawn from specific ethnographic and ethnohistoric sources. In Chapter 5, this volume, Boulestin defines the 'accompanying dead' as subordinate individuals who kill themselves or are killed on the occasion of the death of a person having a major public social role. In cases of hierarchical accompaniment, the grave displays elements of 'asymmetry' in mortuary treatment that can include fewer grave goods and grave inclusions, different treatment, including different skeletal dispositions and/or spatial separation in the grave, which indicate a status different from an individual having received more conventional treatment, like that found more commonly for the same place and/or period. The deaths of those individuals evincing a lack of the more common funerary treatment were precipitated by the death of the individual treated in the more commonplace manner and for whom the grave was prepared. In this case, these accompanying individuals could thus be considered as a type of grave inclusion.

In practice, accompanying dead form a type of '**plural**' deposition (more than a single individual in the same feature – cf. '**co-burial**' and '**plural**' **burial**) and possibly a multiple burial (interred simultaneously at one time as a primary deposition), such as the 'triplex burials' from Upper Palaeolithic Barma Grande (Italy) (Formicola, 1988) and Dolní Věstonice (Czech Republic) (Formicola, Pontrandolfi and Svoboda, 2001). The manner (i.e. the circumstances) of death remains an unanswered question in these examples, as in many others that indicate simultaneous deposition.

An example of the burial of one person containing several accompanying individuals comes in the form of the tombs of the 'Lords of Sipan' from the Lambayeque Valley, Peru, which consists of a clearly central figure and individuals placed around him (Alva and Donnan, 1993). In the absence of evidence for violent injury, the identification of these graves as relating to ritual killing is part of the interpretation of these contexts, but the remains often lack visible evidence of skeletal trauma, so strangulation, suffocation or poisoning may be implicated, or death due to acute disease leaving no skeletal trace. The term has been applied when several individuals in a disordered state and lacking grave goods/inclusions are found surrounding and separated from an identified 'central figure' in the same feature (cf. Lefranc and Chenal, 2019; Boulestin, Chapter 5, this volume).

Actualistic Studies (Actualism): experimental studies based on the proposition that contemporary knowledge and observations of physical processes, such as gravity; geological processes, such as flooding and erosion; and decomposition by bacterial and fungal decay, for example, which operate today, were also active in the past and can thus be applied as analogies for past events (i.e. uniformitarianism). When applied in archaeothanatology, taphonomic studies are predicated on the premise that there is a relationship between process and product, physical and chemical cause and effect, and thus the appearance and patterns of archaeological remains preserved in the archaeological record and the processes that created them (cf. Henriksen, Chapter 29, this volume; Mickleburgh *et al.*, Chapter 28, this volume; Schotsmans *et al.*, Chapter 27, this volume). Robust actualistic studies consist of replication of the experimental conditions so that **equifinality** (cf. below) and confounding variables can be controlled (cf. Simmons, 2017).

Anatomical (Re-)associations: observation of articulations is at the heart of archaeothanatological insights in order to associate remains of a single individual or of a single body segment. The means of re-associating remains can be divided into two main types:

> **First-Order Anatomical (Re-)associations/Connections:** in French: '*liaisons ostéologiques de premier ordre*' (Duday, 1987a: 53), also referred to, variously, as liaisons, connections, linkages, or links, which are *in situ* articulations of human remains observed upon excavation in the field indicating that skeletal remains are those of a single individual. These remains are thus described as 'in anatomical articulation', or as 'articulated remains', or as being found 'in articulation', the opposite of 'disarticulated' for remains that have lost their anatomical integrity. The second type of first-order linkage relates to fragments of the same element recovered during excavation, where it is obvious *in situ* that they fit together as demonstrated by the **re-fitting** or **conjoining** of fragments (cf. Duday, 2009: 123).

> **Second-Order Anatomical (Re-)associations/Connections**: in French: '*liaisons ostéologiques de second ordre*' (Duday, 1987a: 53), a laboratory-based protocol for re-associating bones of a single individual and/or fragments of a single skeletal element that was not or could not be recorded in the field because the remains were disarticulated and/or part of a commingled inhumation/deposition or cremated assemblage. Such linkages also apply to 'legacy' remains that were excavated in the past without sufficient extant records of their disposition. These second-order associations are of two kinds: one based on matching bilateral bone pairs (homologues), owing to similar robustness, size, maturational stage (cf. Gerdau-Radonić, 2007; Gerdau-Radonić and Makowski, 2011; Partiot *et al.*, 2020), appearance (such as dimensions and pathological lesions), and a more discriminating one based on snugly fitting articulations (a minority of articulations) shared between two or three elements based on articular congruity (Duday, 1987a; Villena i Mota, Duday and Houët, 1996; Villena i Mota, 2015). Articular congruity is based on close-fitting, contiguous articulations held tightly together in the living body due to close-fitting joints and complementary supporting structures, such as ligaments and tendons. 'Joint congruity' is used for articulations that are so closely fitting that even when bones become disarticulated and separated, they can still be joined with others from the same anatomical structure, like the humero-ulnar (elbow) joint, or some joints in the mid- and hind-foot (metatarsals and tarsals), for example (cf. Villena i Mota, Duday and Houët, 1996; Villena i Mota, 2015).

> The words 'matching' or 'pair-matching' are used for associating bilateral elements based on size or morphological similarity, including most recently internal bone trabecular distribution (e.g. Thibeault and Villotte, 2018) for the lower limbs. The lower limbs are not normally characterised by strong directional asymmetry resulting from the biomechanical effects of dominant limb preference that is present in the upper limbs, a phenomenon which hinders this sort of morphological matching because

the morphology of right and left elements does not differ due to habitual preferential limb use.

The term '**conjoining**' is used for re-fitting fragments to create more complete elements (cf. below).

Anthropologie de Terrain: a phrase which would literally translate as '**field anthropology**' in English, is the former name attributed to **archaeothanatology**, drawing its inspiration from the inclusion of trained archaeo-anthropologists/human bioarchaeologists in field excavation programmes/teams from the commencement of the project – not only after completion of the excavation – for skeletal analysis. This proviso is a reaction to the still not uncommon practice of sending skeletal remains to a researcher for analysis in the laboratory after they have been excavated, often with minimal field documentation, with the intention that the excavator will then make sense of the material in the final analysis. This division between excavation and analysis entails the loss of important observations that can only be made in the field during the process of excavation and with rigorous recording methods in place prior to commencing excavation (cf. Sachau-Carcel, Chapter 31, this volume). The separation of analysis of the remains from their archaeological context is detrimental to both.

Archaeo-anthropology: the transliteration of the French term '*archéo-anthropologie*', which can be seen as equivalent to human bioarchaeology (cf. Knüsel and Schotsmans, Introduction, this volume) and thus includes osteological studies of morphology, sex and age-at-death assessments, health and disease and taphonomy and, in combination with the burial context, interpretations they lend to understandings of past peoples, their social organisation and social structure. The term often applies to Holocene archaeological human remains to distinguish their study from those of earlier human ancestors as human palaeontology (cf. Knüsel and Maureille, 2018; Knüsel and Schotsmans, Introduction, this volume). Some researchers see archaeo-anthropology as equivalent to archaeothanatology, and, in this way, it has many synonyms and closely related terms, the subtle nuances of which tend to distinguish different research endeavours involving the dead and their depositional contexts.

Some scholars emphasise those biological aspects of the social identity of the deceased with a link to funerary behaviours, leaving aside the other biological aspects of the population sample. For example, Blaizot (2008: 27) identifies the goal of such studies as 'to define burial practices in a given period in order to appreciate their variability' ('*… définir les pratiques sépulcrales à une période donnée et d'en apprécier la variabilité*') and, more recently, Zemour (2016: 26) defines this pursuit as 'the quest for biological determinants linked to funerary practices' ('*la quête de déterminants biologiques liés aux pratiques funéraires*'). These objectives are not reflected in an overt way in human osteoarchaeology, with its abiding interest in osseous remains and the manner in which such studies are practiced or understood at present, but are part of '(human) **bioarchaeology**' (though funerary practices have been a less prominent aspect perhaps). These funerary practices are at the very core of **archaeothanatology**. Whatever term is used, the biological aspects of the deceased are the focus, and it is this orientation that archaeo-anthropology shares with **human bioarchaeology** and **archaeothanatology**.

Archaeology of Death: also referred to as the 'archaeology of death and burial' and sometimes used as synonymous with archaeothanatology among French scholars (Schmitt, 2017), this area of research interest combines burial archaeology, which 'uses archaeological sources from burial contexts to enrich [… our] understanding of the past', and the archaeology of death, which 'seeks to understand how people handled death and the dead' (Knüsel, 2016: 57, in discussion with Nilsson Stutz, 2016), or 'the meaning and expression of cultural reactions to death', as defined by Chapman and Randsborg (1981: 2). As noted in this volume, burial or funerary archaeology tends to focus on the features or on the objects found with the dead, but not on the dead themselves, which is the major distinction between burial archaeology and archaeothanatology/human bioarchaeology which focusses specifically on human remains of the dead and their context, as well as also addresses questions about funerary/mortuary practices and their social meaning in past societies (Knüsel and Schotsmans, Introduction, this volume).

Archaeothanatology: a transliteration from the French of '*archéothanatologie*', which derives its name from the compound word formed by 'archaeo' ('ancient') and 'thanatology' ('*thanatos*', the personification of death), which is the study of death and its practices in different chrono-cultural contexts, often invoking interest in the dead body ('the *raison d'être* of the grave and the central focus around which the funerary rites were organised') (Duday, 2006: 30) and, by extension, consciousness of the dead and of death (Pettitt, 2018). This term has superseded the term '*anthropologie de terrain*' ('**field anthropology**') and is sometimes seen as synonymous with '*archéo-anthropologie*' ('**archaeo-anthropology**') as well as, '*archéologie funéraire*' ('**funerary archaeology**'), but the key difference is that, unlike funerary archaeology, archaeothanatology focusses on the synthetic study of both the biological and sociological aspects of death in past societies (cf. Boulestin and Duday, 2005), generally, between the dead and the living and the living and death. While citing Boulestin (2012), Schmitt (Chapter 6, this volume) emphasises: 'Archaeothanatology … investigates funerary, post-funerary and non-funerary treatment of human remains. All of these treatments of dead bodies are therefore qualified as "**mortuary**", adding that all such remains characterised by "non-funerary treatment", the opposite of "funerary treatment", evinces disrespect for the body of the deceased'. As Leclerc (1990: 13) remarked, this endeavour requires '… the combination of the skills of a biological anthropologist and an archaeologist' ('… *la combinaison des compétences de l'anthropologue biologique et de l'archéologue*'). This type of training and the incorporation of biological anthropologists in field excavation was the inspiration for '*anthropologie de terrain*' ('**field anthropology**'), which is widely practiced in France and its overseas territories today (cf. Guillon, Chapter 32, this volume) and has increasing influence beyond these geographical limits. The major tenets of the subject are considered to include: (1) the taphonomic study of the cadaver, (2) the reconstruction of the original arrangement, organisation and architecture of burials and their content and context, and (3) the subsequent interpretation of funerary/mortuary practices in their chrono-cultural context to address social practices, in the past and, moreover, today (cf. Boulestin, Chapter 2, this volume).

In contrast to the original definition of Henri Duday, many researchers view archaeothanatology as a method, as a different way of analysing a burial and its human remains (cf. Bocquentin, Chapter 9, this volume). Many other practitioners, however, advance the notion that the subject is an all-encompassing approach – a paradigm – applied to the remains of the deceased and their contexts (cf. Knüsel and Schotsmans, Introduction, this volume).

Articulations: the anatomical term used to describe the joints between bones, referred to in French as '*connexion(s) anatomique(s)*' (literally '**anatomical connections**'). The state of articulation of both **persistent** and **labile joints** (cf. below) is used to indicate whether skeletal remains are in a primary or secondary depositional context. However, the use of these terms is contested (cf. Mickleburgh *et al.*, Chapter 28, this volume; Schotsmans *et al.*, Chapter 27, this volume) and, in the past, scholars have suggested other methods of classifying joints, such as 'inter-locking' articulations ('*articulations emboîtantes*') and 'non-inter-locking' articulations ('*articulations non emboîtantes*') (Ambroise and Perlès, 1975).

Associated Remains: a neutral term used to describe all objects found in the immediate vicinity of human remains, without presupposing how they might have been involved in funerary practices, as this involves interpretation and is thus separate from recording and description. These remains include **grave goods**, items of personal adornment worn by or as a part of the clothing of the deceased, and **grave inclusions**, items placed with the deceased by others at the time of or after interment. Melton *et al.* (2010) provide an example of the latter with absolute dating evidence for re-visitation of a grave and placement of branches over 250 years after initial use as a place of burial. The latter two, grave goods and grave inclusions, without distinguishing their different origins, have often been – and continue to be – used as the basis for the creation of chronologies for relative dating and subsequent **typo–chronologies**. Based on the analysis and interpretive arguments, the items may have diverse functions and symbolic associations or, on the contrary, none at all due to the mechanisms responsible for their deposition (cf. Cartron and Zemour, Chapter 22, this volume).

Bad Death: '*malemort*' in French, which is often associated with aberrant or **deviant burials** (cf. below) (cf. Blanchard, Chapter 19, this volume), a reflection of the status of the deceased in life or the manner of death, or both.

Bioarchaeology: a sub-disciplinary field of biological anthropology (North America) and/or archaeology (Europe) that aims to synthesise the biological study of the remains of the deceased within their archaeological context. Transliterated as '*bioarchéologie*' in French, the term was 'invented' at least twice, independently, in the United Kingdom in the early 1970s to represent the study of biota from archaeological sites and again, later, in North America to focus more specifically on the study of human remains in their archaeological context in order to address questions relating to the human condition and adaptation to natural and social environments, including especially health and well-being (Larsen, 1997; Knüsel, 2010). Since the original formulation included the study of all biota, the adjective 'human' often modifies the term more recently to distinguish it from its predecessor, and especially in the United Kingdom. In France, as in much of Europe and elsewhere, the original definition is used to indicate the study of biological remains retrieved from archaeological contexts, generally, with archaeothanatology occupying much the same disciplinary terrain covered by human bioarchaeology (Knüsel and Schotsmans, Introduction, this volume).

Buikstra (2006) aligns (human) bioarchaeological research interests along the following themes: (1) burial programmes and social organisation, (2) daily activities and division of labour, (3) palaeodemography, including estimates of population size and density, (4) population movement and genetic relationships and (5) diet and disease. In the initial formulation, Buikstra (1977) also included research methods related to field archaeology, including survey, determination of site density and site location for prospective excavation, as part of bioarchaeology. It is clear that archaeothanatology and bioarchaeology share much in their research orientations, even if differences in terminology and the place and stage of development of social theory differ, social theory being more expressly emphasised from the outset in bioarchaeology than it was early on in the development of archaeothanatology. More recently, however, more theoretically-guided studies have also begun to appear in the latter (for examples of the application of social analogies drawn from social anthropology/ethnology/sociology cf. Bocquentin, Chapter 9, this volume; Boulestin, Chapter 5, this volume; Schmitt, Chapter 6, this volume). Ultimately, both archaeothanatology and bioarchaeology of whatever stripe share the desire to synthesise and integrate the study of human remains with the study of their archaeological contexts in order to better address fundamental questions about human development in the past. It is the degree of the latter – about the context of human remains – which is much more explicitly emphasised in archaeothanatology and that distinguishes it from human bioarchaeology. Bioarchaeology is, at present, more closely integrated with biomolecular studies (isotopic, protein and aDNA analyses, among others), and this is a disciplinary trend that is rapidly expanding and integrated studies of these analyses with social aspects of the study of funerary remains are now more numerous and prominent (cf. Alt *et al.*, 2013; Deguilloux *et al.*, 2014; Gleize *et al.,* 2016; Beau *et al.*, 2017).

Biological Anthropology[1]: the bio-cultural and bio-social study of human diversity across geographic space and through time. The earlier 'physical anthropology', which has largely been superseded by biological anthropology, emphasised the study of human physical forms, where the context of those forms was of lesser importance. The two are sometimes equated today, but their methods and question universes are not identical. As an illustration, much of physical anthropology was directed at identifying the number of 'races' (today's 'geographic variants') that comprised human diversity in the past, 'race' being viewed as a basic analytical category, whereas biological anthropology is a much broader discipline that addresses the meaning of 'race' as an analytical category, as well as many other questions related to the human condition, past and present. Both archaeothanatology and human bioarchaeology developed within biological anthropology in order to better integrate human remains with archaeological field recovery, recording and analysis.

Bloc Craniofacial: a term used for the 'cranium' in French, thus without the mandible (cf. Boulestin, 2015).

Bundle Burial: '*paquet funéraire*' in French, which is a specific type of deposition in which the body is, variably, in a fresh, partially decomposed or mummified state, and is wrapped in one or several layers of textile or other material. In some instances, it can be considered a form of **delayed or postponed burial** (cf. below) if it can be demonstrated that the remains are in their final, though 'secondary', depositional context, often indicated by missing skeletal elements in an otherwise complete skeleton (cf. Herrmann and Meyer, 1993; Gerdau-Radonić, 2007; Aspöck, Gerdau-Radonić and Noterman, Chapter 16, this volume; Gerdau-Radonić *et al.*, Chapter 14, this volume).

Burial: '*sépulture*' in French, is (a) corpse(s)/cadaver(s)/remains intentionally placed/ deposited within a grave and covered with earth to form an inhumation or interment. In archaeothanatology, the presence of funerary treatment for the deceased is key to the identification of this archaeological feature and its associated remains.

However, the term 'burial' has been used variously and its meaning through time remains a subject of discussion. During a conference session on terminology in funerary archaeology, Smith (2015) noted that the word 'burial' has been used for a grave containing a corpse, for the buried corpse itself, the act of burying a corpse and the act of burying something else. Moreover, archaeologists often speak colloquially of 'burials' in reference to any human bone deposition, even when the bodies involved may not have been buried by human action (cf. Knüsel and Robb, 2016: 657). Andrews and Bello (2006: 15) correctly observe that how human remains are deposited is far more variable than the grave structures that often lend their names to depositional types. Some definitions of 'burial' ('*sépulture*') are close to the French phrase '*dépôt funéraire/ mortuaire*' (translated as **funerary/mortuary deposit**, cf. below), such as the following:

'... a burial is a context that contains the remains of one or several deceased individuals. It is construed as a definite and final deposition, and the remains were deposited during a ceremony honouring at least one of these deceased individuals through the treatment of his/her bodily remains' ('*une sépulture est un lieu où sont déposés les restes d'un ou de plusieurs défunts, ce dépôt étant conçu comme définitif et intervenant dans le cadre d'une cérémonie dont la finalité est d'honorer au moins un des défunts au travers de sa dépouille*') (Boulestin 2012: 37) (cf. Schmitt, Chapter 6, this volume).

---

1 In French, as in English, the word 'anthropologie'/'anthropology' can be used to refer to human remains and their analysis. This use was especially the case in the past, but the word still carries that connotation today in some circumstances.

'... a place where the remains of one or more deceased individuals have been deposited, and where there is enough archaeological evidence in this deposit to indicate the performance of a funerary deed/gesture (Leclerc and Tarrête, 1988: 1002), as well as the structure constructed on the occasion of this funerary gesture' (cited in Leclerc, 1990: 13) ('*une sépulture est un lieu où ont été déposés les restes d'un ou plusieurs défunts, et où il subsiste suffisamment d'indices pour que l'archéologie puisse déceler dans ce dépôt la volonté d'accomplir un geste funéraire; (...) structure constituée à l'occasion de ce geste funéraire* (Leclerc et Tarrête, 1988, cited in Leclerc, 1990: 13) (cf. Boulestin, Chapter 2, this volume; Maureille, Chapter 8, this volume).

The number of individuals contained in a burial feature can be indicated as being an **individual burial** ('*sépulture individuelle*' in French), which contains the remains of only a single individual, as opposed to the sometimes awkwardly translated '**plural burial**', correctly translated as '**multiple burial**' in English (cf. below) ('*sépulture plurielle*' in French), those that contain the remains of more than one individual. It is important to note here that a '**multiple burial**', although used in English publications without a notion of timing, *does not* translate directly as the French '*sépulture multiple*' (direct translation equating to '**multiple burial**'). The French phrase refers to timing as well as to the number of interred individuals, namely the *simultaneous* deposition of more than one individual. As such, the phrase is used according to its French meaning in many of the contributions to this volume (*contra* '**collective burial**', below).

Cemetery: as noted by Schmitt (Chapter 6, this volume), a historically specific and often exclusively faith-based 'funerary space' comprised of consecrated ground (cf. Blanchard, Chapter 19, this volume; Gleize, Chapter 20, this volume; Williams, Chapter 17, this volume, for Jewish, Islamic and Christian cemeteries, respectively), and from which individuals may be excluded due to transgression or malfeasance in life (as in excommunication in Christian canon law).

Cenotaph: a structure that imitates a grave or a tomb, but in which no remains are deposited and sometimes were never deposited. Such a construction often serves as a memorial to the dead of an event associated with mass mortality or missing persons.

Cephalic Extremity: a medically-derived term used to describe the cranium, mandible and, variously, the hyoid and cervical vertebrae and their associated soft tissues. This superior-most extremity of the axial skeleton is often the focus of manipulation of the corpse.

The use of this term permits differentiation between the 'head', which is a structure comprised of the cranium and mandible and associated soft tissues, as in the result of 'headhunting' that may also include various elements of the cervical region of the vertebral column, and upon which the cardinal orientation of complete skeletons is based. In the absence of the cranium and/or mandible – the elements of the head no longer being present – the remaining parts of the cephalic extremity (elements of the cervical region of the vertebral column) are relied upon for orientation in an otherwise incomplete or partial skeleton (cf. Bocquentin, Kodas and Ortiz, 2016; Haddow and Knüsel, 2017). In practice, it is often the latter, the remaining parts of the cephalic extremity and, specifically, the cervical vertebrae, that most faithfully indicate the once orientation of the body/corpse because they function in the living as a unit due to tightly inter-locking uncinate processes of the bodies and apophyseal articular processes of the vertebral arches. The orientation of the cervical vertebrae, then, indicates the original cardinal orientation of the cranium in an open space or void such as that created by a coffin because the cranium, as a spherical structure, tends to become displaced or roll upon decomposition of the associated soft tissue structures, when there is space around it, and especially when elevated on a support, such as a cushion or pillow stone. In this instance, upon exposure of the remains, the cranium will no longer be in its original position at the time of deposition of the deceased.

The cervical vertebrae can also be used to assess the orientation of individuals who have been decapitated, decapitation occurring through the cervical vertebrae in most instances, most commonly at the level of the second to fifth cervical vertebrae (Boylston *et al.*, 2000; Montgomery, Armit et al. 2011; Knüsel and Tucker, 2011; Tucker, 2014). The vertebrae located more superiorly to the transecting cut accompany the cranium, mandible, and, in some instances, the hyoid, which lies between the mandible anteriorly and the third cervical vertebra posteriorly these elements then forming parts of the detached cephalic extremity.

The orientation of the facial skeletal or viscerocranium/splanchnocranium is used to indicate 'facing' in a cardinal direction, as in Islamic burials where the cephalic extremity is oriented in a cardinal direction to face ('to look toward') Mecca (cf. Gleize, Chapter 20, this volume). The extent of rotation of the atlas on the axis indicates the original position of the facial skeleton, the position of the viscerocranium being dependent on the rotational movements afforded by these two vertebrae (cf. Schotsmans *et al.*, Chapter 27, this volume, for two examples of analyses of these structures for reconstruction of the original disposition of the cephalic extremity).

Cephalic Niche: an architectural recess carved into a stone sarcophagus or made in the soil that accommodates the cephalic extremity comprised of the cranium and mandible and sometimes some of the superior-most cervical vertebrae in skeletonised remains (cf. Blaizot, Chapter 1, this volume).

Co-burial: the remains of individuals found in the same feature, with no notion of depositional timing. This word is close to the meaning of the French '*sépulture plurielle*', literally '**plural burial**', thus multiple individuals deposited in the same feature, but a term that does not translate well into English (cf. '**plural burial**', '**multiple burial**' and '**collective burial**'). The term co-burial has been adopted for analytical purposes in studies of kinship patterns from burials in close proximity (cf. Yaka *et al.,* 2021).

Coffrage ou tombe en dalles de pierre: a '**tile-lined or stone-lined grave**', also called a '**stone-cist grave**', constructed from multiple flat stones, like paving stones, within the grave, as in Neolithic monumental multi-chamber graves (cf. Schmitt, 2015; Boulestin and Courtaud, Chapter 3, this volume; Schmitt, Chapter 12, this volume).

Collective Burial/Deposition: human bodies deposited successively or consecutively over time rather than in a single episode in the same grave, often inferred from variations in completeness of and articulation among remains of the deceased (cf. Gerdau-Radonić, 2007; Gerdau-Radonić and Makowski, 2011; Kacki, 2020; Boulestin and Courtaud, Chapter 3, this volume; Schmitt, Chapter 12, this volume). The definition has recently been re-visited (cf. Schmitt, Crevecoeur and Déderix, 2018; Schmitt and Déderix, 2019).

Commingled Remains: mixed deposits of disarticulated and often fragmented bones from multiple individuals; this mixing sometimes includes animal remains and/or artefacts. Commingling can result from funerary treatment (cf. Gerdau-Radonić, 2007) or caused by other phenomena (cf. Outram *et al.*, 2005; Gerdau-Radonić and Herrera, 2010; Adams and Byrd, 2015).

Compression Effect: '*effet de compression*' in French is synonymous with '*effets de contraintes*' ('**constraining effects**') which refer to bones that are found in close proximity due to the restriction of an anatomical segment by its close approximation to another object or skeletal element within the grave, or presence of some restrictive material, such as bindings (cf. Blaizot, 2008; Blaizot, Chapter 1, this volume; Castex and Kacki, Chapter 18, this volume; Tillier, Chapter 7, this volume).

Conjoining: also referred to as a type of '*liaison ostéologique*' in French, is the re-fitting of contiguous fragments from single skeletal elements; these are equivalent to conjoining parts of objects, such as ceramics, found in an archaeological context (cf. Bonnet, Chapter 24, this volume). The intent of conjoining exercises is to create more complete specimens for study and/ or display and, specifically in archaeothanatology, to associate features that contain parts of the same object or bone element.

Cranial Retrieval: *'prélèvement'*, in French meaning 'taking' or 'sampling' but equivalent in English to 'lifting' for the removal of remains from an archaeological context in the field, is the removal of the cranium alone. The retrieval of the cranium and mandible ('skull retrieval'), which may be in articulation at the tempo-mandibular joint or separated during decomposition of these connective tissue structures, and sometimes the still articulated atlas, is a variant of this treatment (cf. Bocquentin, Kodas and Ortiz, 2016; Haddow and Knüsel, 2017).

Cranium ('cranial', adjective; 'crania', plural): the principal element of the **cephalic extremity,** *cranium* meaning 'helmet' in Latin and referred to as the ***'bloc craniofacial'*** in French, the term refers to the splanchno- or viscero-, together with the neuro-cranium, the facial skeleton and cranial vault together, respectively, without the mandible. A variety of Latin terms, better described as 'Latinisms', including the *'calva'* (plural *'calvae'*), used for the cranium without the facial skeleton and cranial base, and the *'calvaria'* (plural *'calvariae'*), the cranium without the facial skeleton but retaining the cranial base, and the calotte, the superior part of the cranial vault, or the 'skull-cap', which is removed during autopsy/post-mortem investigations, all of which are parts of the 'brain box' (neurocranium), without the facial skeleton. The definition of these terms has become muddled among authors over long periods of use (as synthesised in Boulestin, 2015: 3, table 1).

The skull is *not* the equivalent of the cranium but is defined as both the cranium and mandible (cf. Aiello and Dean, 1990: 33). Use of 'skull', etymologically non-Latin and of uncertain linguistic history (possibly Scandinavian origin via Middle English) (*Webster's New International Dictionary of the English Language*, 1947) in professional descriptions is the source of much confusion and misunderstanding, often only resolved by recourse to images to ascertain the meaning in written descriptions employing the term.

To avoid confusion, it is best to refer to these structures by their element names (cf. Knüsel, 2014), cranium and mandible or *'mandibula'* (plural mandibles or *'mandibulae'*), to disentangle what has become a much-confused terminology (reviewed by Boulestin, 2015).

Because these parts of the cephalic extremity carry importance for social and personal identity, they are highly symbolic and the target of a considerable number of socio-cultural practices (mortuary as well as funerary practices among them), which are thus conflated and misconstrued – as much in French as in English- in the absence of use of clearly defined anatomical terms.

Cremation: the process of reducing the corpse to ash and bone fragments characteristic of cremated remains (cf. **'tended or managed cremation'**). In the Roman world, where cremation became the predominant funerary rite by the first century AD (Morris, 1992), a special cremation construction, the *ustrinum,* an area used repeatedly to cremate individuals in a public setting – and therefore of unrelated individuals – distinguishes this construction from the *bustum,* a pyre built inside a family funerary enclosure, for the use of possibly related individuals (Duday, Chapter 15, this volume). Cremated remains may be collected and placed within a receptacle, often an urn or other ceramic or organic vessel, designated as the *incinararium,* which was then buried, forming a secondary cremation burial, the remains having been cremated elsewhere. Both are distinct from the place of the burning of the corpse, the pyre (*'bûcher'* in French), upon which the corpse was burnt but might also be the place where some were also interred after cremation, forming a 'pyre-grave' (French: *'tombe bûcher'*), the latter designating both the place of cremation and where the remains were deposited in some instances in the past, thus primary cremation burials/graves. Cremated remains collected from the pyre and deposited in a grave are referred to as 'secondary cremation burials' because they had been moved from their initial funerary context (cf. Depierre, Chapter 4, this volume; Duday, Chapter 15, this volume; Henriksen, Chapter 29, this volume, for human remains; and Bonnet, Chapter 24, this volume, for cremated primary and secondary deposits of ceramics, this volume). Bocquentin *et al.* (2020) further distinguish primary cremation of a body/cadaver from secondary cremation of skeletal remains.

Decapitation: '*décapitation*' or '*décollation*', synonyms in French for beheading is a general term used for removal of the head when the soft tissue is still present, often with a heavy instrument by transection of the cervical vertebrae (cf. '**cephalic extremity**'). Decapitation can be performed as a form of execution/killing or as a part of a mortuary or funerary practice when the individual is already dead, as considered in the case of Neolithic Western Asia. These can be difficult to distinguish (cf. Testart, 2008: 42, 2012; Boulestin and Gambier, 2012; Bocquentin, Kodas and Ortiz, 2016; Haddow and Knüsel, 2017; Knüsel and Glencross, 2017).

Decomposition in a Filled Space (cf. '**full-earthen burial**'): when a corpse is placed in a filled space (i.e. one filled with earth), the surrounding soil prevents joint disarticulations and movement, thus preserving skeletal contiguity after soft tissue decomposition. This is the opposite of what occurs in decomposition in a void or space within a container (cf. '**decomposition in a void**'). Duday (1990; 2009) mentions that evidence for decomposition in a void is based on movement and displacements of bones outside the initial or original space occupied by the body, called positive evidence. Evidence for decomposition in a filled space is far more difficult to attest because it is based on the lack of movement or displacement outside the original space or volume occupied by the body, although movement or displacement can also occur due to internal and external secondary voids (cf. '**voids**') (cf. Duday *et al.*, 1990; Duday, 2009; Castex and Blaizot, 2017; Georges-Zimmermann and Kacki, 2017; Blaizot, Chapter 1, this volume; Gerdau-Radonić *et al.*, Chapter 14, this volume). For example, by observing that the elements of the torso (ribs) 'flattened' inferiorly, it is impossible to say if this happened during decomposition in a void or during decomposition in a filled space due to the creation of internal secondary voids (Duday *et al.*, 1990).

Decomposition in a Void (Open or Empty Space): an open or empty space ('*espace vide*' in French) is afforded by a coffin or other container for the body/corpse and permits a greater extent of joint disarticulation and movement of skeletal remains than is permitted in a **filled space** or **full-earthen burial**. Sometimes, the elements may fall outside of the original space occupied by the corpse (cf. '**outside the original volume of the body**'). Some of the skeletal dispositions associated with this type of decompositional space include the following: the pelvic girdle 'opens' completely or 'semi-opens' (disarticulates through the pubic symphysis and sacro-iliac joints), the mandible descends onto the torso, the patellae disarticulate and move out of anatomical position if the lower limbs are rotated laterally, for example (cf. variously, Duday *et al.*, 1990; Duday, 2006, 2009; Blaizot, Chapter 1, this volume; Green, Chapter 23, this volume; Mickleburgh *et al.*, Chapter 28, this volume; Rottier, Chapter 13, this volume; Schotsmans *et al.*, Chapter 27, this volume).

Delayed or Postponed Burial: '*sépulture d'attente*' or '*sépulture/inhumation différée*' in French, indicates a corpse that is left unburied for a time in a temporary location, exposed above ground, prior to interment (cf. Knüsel and Robb, 2016; Haddow *et al.*, 2020; Duday, Chapter 15, this volume; Schotsmans *et al.*, Chapter 27, this volume). Post-mortem treatments resulting in delayed burial occur cross-culturally, sometimes leading to desiccation, and have been documented for societies as disparate in time and space as ancient Egypt (Aufderheide, 2003; Papageorgopoulou *et al.*, 2015), Bronze Age Britain (Parker Pearson *et al.*, 2005), modern-day Papua New Guinea (Beckett, Lohmann and Bernstein, 2011; Beckett and Nelson, 2015) and medieval Europe (e.g. Weiss-Krejci, 2005; Knüsel *et al.*, 2010).

Deposit: '*dépôt*' in French, a neutral descriptive term, commonly used in archaeology and, when applied to human remains, anticipates that deposits of human remains may or may not be 'funerary' in nature, and thus there is no implicit intention involved in their presence in the archaeological record as part of funerary ritual (cf. Schmitt, Chapter 6, this volume) (cf. '**deposition**', below). The French word '*dépôt funéraire*', however, is always 'funerary' in nature. This can be a buried deposition or a deposition on the surface such as in caves (cf. Kacki *et al.*, 2020), and does not necessarily need to refer to human remains. An object from a funerary deposit can also be called a '*dépôt funéraire*' in French (also cf. '**burial**').

Deposition: also translates as '*dépôt*' ('deposit') in French, indicates any human remains or objects encountered in an archaeological context. A good generic term rather than 'burial', which has been used to indicate the grave, an archaeological feature, as well as an interred corpse and partial human skeletal remains and objects. A site of deposition could be on the ground surface, or as in a cut feature, an intentionally excavated grave or a pit, in which a body or bodies have been intentionally deposited. This term refers to the action of making an archaeological deposit (cf. '**deposit**'). The inspiration for both is to detach funerary intention from all instances of human remains found in an archaeological context, as burial/interment automatically intimates intentional behaviour. Even if remains are found in a cut feature, this does not immediately indicate funerary treatment, as the feature may already have existed and served another purpose or be a naturally occurring one used as a convenient depression to dispose of the dead. One of the effects of the supposition of intentionality for human remains deposits, even when accompanied by items of personal adornment or dress accessories, is that they represent intentional funerary treatment following established precepts of a funerary tradition based on repeated acts and archaeological patterning. They may also relate, though, to the deposition of clothed individuals who were killed as a result of the commission of illicit or unofficially sanctioned activity, conflict or catastrophe. The evidence for order or structured arrangement, reflective of care, is key in interpretation (cf. Boulestin, 2016; Boulestin, Chapter 5, this volume).

Deviant or Irregular Burials: the equivalent in French is '*sépulture atypique*' or '**atypical burial**' meaning funerary treatments that deviate from or are outside the norm ('*hors normes*' in French) for a particular archaeologically-defined group, place or time. This type of burial/deposition must be distinguished from the norm but also from those remains lacking funerary treatment in mortuary contexts, those without evidence of funerary treatments (cf. '**abandonment burial**'). However, the use of this term is contested (Boulestin, 2016).

Disarticulation: the process by which the bones of the skeleton become separated and lose the anatomical integrity that they possess when part of a complete skeleton held together and in place by soft tissue structures, ligaments and tendons. In French, this word is '*désarticulé*' (disarticulated) or '*disloqué*' ('dislocated', or 'out-of-place'), but in English, a dislocation refers more specifically to a type of injury in which elements, most often limb bones, come to be wholly (complete dislocation) or partly (partial dislocation) dislocated and thus out of normal anatomical alignment. Although 'dislocation' is both a French and English term spelled in the same way, in English, there is a distinction in its contextual meaning and use. In English, the verb 'displaced' ('*déplacé*' in French) or the noun 'displacement' ('*déplacement*' in French) best indicates the movement of remains in their place of deposition in a feature or layer (cf. Boulestin, Chapter 2, this volume), although it has to be mentioned that the French translations '*déplacé*' and '*déplacement*' denote that the elements are out of place by natural or other means.

Dispositif Funéraire and ***Appareil Funéraire***: French terms that cannot be translated by a single word in English. The closest translation previously used for both terms is 'burial arrangement, organisation and architecture' (Castex and Blaizot, 2017: 277). In practice, these terms refer to the nature and characteristics of a burial, from an architectural point of view, but also to the objects and all of the tangible elements that the burial contains, as well as how they relate spatially to each other and to the remains of the deceased. This translation captures the intent of these words, and implicit in their use is funerary treatment and funerary deposition. What they entail is more important because of the impact they make on recording and analysis, including the disposition, lay-out and organisation of the remains, individually and as associated objects; the nature of the grave feature; the form of the burial container; and additional grave furnishings/furniture, such as head supports or cushions, cushioned biers (the corpse lying on a mattress); or other objects used as part of the funerary treatment (cf. Blaizot, 2008). These characteristics define chrono-cultural traditions.

The French words '*dispositif*' and '*appareil*' should not be translated in this context as 'device' or 'apparatus', respectively. The use of the term '*dispositif*' or '*appareil*' here is similar to that of the phrase '*dispositif sanitaire*', which translates as 'sanitary or health measures', that is, actions/behaviours carried out within a particular context/situation that are dictated by beliefs and/or rules and regulations.

Disposition: refers to the mode of disposing of the dead once the original position of the body or its constituent elements within the grave and with respect to its furnishings and associated objects has been identified through taphonomic analysis (cf. Schmitt, Chapter 6, this volume).

Effects: researchers have defined terms to describe recurrent patterning in burials, '*effets*' in French. These are defined as follows (cf. 'compression effect', above):

> *Effet d'alignement* or *effet de délimitation linéaire*, in English translation '**alignment effect**' or '**delimitation effect**', is a phenomenon created by the rectilinear shape of the sides of the grave or an object, such as the sides of a coffin, that leaves skeletal elements or entire skeletons and other objects in a straight alignment by constraining or restricting their position in the grave during decomposition (cf. Blaizot, 2008: 20, fig. 10; Green, Chapter 23, this volume). This phenomenon should be distinguished from the '*effet d'appui*'/'*effet de butée*', below (cf. Duday, 2017: 226, footnote 31).

> *Effet d'appui or effet de butée* can be translated as '**support effect**' or '**stopper effect**', respectively, which describes a phenomenon that occurs when a skeletal element or other object, a stone, bone, ceramic vessel or fragment, or metal object, is maintained in an otherwise unstable position due to the presence of a supporting structure that stops it from falling (cf. Duday, 2017: 226, footnote 31).

> *Effet de gouffre* (Blaizot, 2014: 276, fig. 11), previously translated as 'dive effect' in Castex and Blaizot (2017: 10), the sense of this term is similar to recording of the placement and angle of an object in three-dimensional space. Thus one part or end of the bone or object lies at an angle (a 'dip angle' in geology), higher or lower, than the other end of the same bone or object, thus '**dip effect**' is the best translation.

> *Effet de gouttière*: '**gutter effect**', a displacement created by a v-shaped longitudinal dip ('*pendage*' in French) or hollow beneath the body into which skeletal elements or objects may fall or slide after decomposition of structural grave furnishings or architecture (Blaizot, 2017: 137).

> *Effet de paroi*: '**wall effect**', which is divided by Duday (2017) into an '*effet d'alignement*' (cf. above), when skeletal elements or objects are left in a linear arrangement (cf. Gerdau-Radonić, 2007; Gerdau-Radonić *et al.*, Chapter 14, this volume; Nilsson Stutz, Chapter 10, this volume), and an '*effet d'appui*'/'*effet de butée*' when bones or objects remain in a constricted or unstable position owing to the presence of a supporting structure (cf. Duday, 2017: 226, footnote 31) (cf. above).

> *Effet de planche*: '**flooring effect**', the movements of bones created by the decomposition of flooring constructed of perishable material beneath the body in a grave incorporating these funerary furnishings in its construction (for examples cf. Blaizot, 2008). This phenomenon, however, has never been validated, and Schotsmans *et al.*

(Chapter 27, this volume) argue that a unique and single cause of bone movement may not distinguishable after many years of burial.

Effet de Plaque: '**plate effect**', refers to bones from one anatomical region overlying bones of another anatomical region when in contact with one another (cf. Blaizot, 2008), as in geological plate tectonics for subductions, when one land mass slides beneath another. It refers to the displacement of a group of elements, such as hand or foot elements, during the collapse of an internal wooden funerary structure, or in the collapse of vertebrae in the same manner that can cause a 'shortening' (*'raccourcissement'* in French) of the vertebral column due to the inferior displacement of a series of vertebrae but not of the entire vertebral column. The appearance of 'shortening' can be created by the decomposition or movement of a series of boards or flat stone slabs beneath the body that supports it but with the position of bones depending on the amount of movement permitted by the spaces between contiguous boards and anatomical segments of the body. The decomposition of these funerary furnishings can be discerned by skeletal elements in anatomical connection at a certain distance from the remainder of the skeleton (cf. Blaizot, Chapter 1, this volume). However, as mentioned above, Schotsmans *et al.* (Chapter 27, this volume) argue that a single cause of bone movement may not distinguishable after years of burial.

Effet de sablier: '**hourglass effect**', refers to the gradual in-filling of voids in the grave by percolation of soil/sediment (*'colmatage progressif'* in French) (Duday, 2006).

Effet de terre: an '**earth effect**' is the effect exerted on the skeleton from the shape of the grave or floor of the feature (cf. Blaizot, Chapter 1, this volume).

Effet/loi de la pesanteur: '**effect or law of weight/gravity**', in French, is a uniformitarian concept based on the law of gravity that acts on the depositional environment, including within the grave, such that unstable or unsupported skeletal elements and objects fall to the bottom of the feature.

Equifinality: when different taphonomic phenomena create apparently similar patterns and a similar 'end result', hence rendering behavioural inferences drawn from them ambiguous. Attempts to resolve equifinality require actualistic study of human remains, the grave context and accompanying materials to replicate potential patterns. Resolving equifinality in depositions entails refutation of taphonomic causes that might lead to the same end result (cf. Schotsmans *et al.*, Chapter 27, this volume).

Excluded Deposition/Burial: an individual denied formal burial in the sense of a planned deposition following an established funerary tradition, but an '**abandonment**' (cf. above), a person excluded from funerary rites who is not, as a consequence, the recipient of **funerary actions or gestures** (*'gestes funéraires'*) (cf. Schmitt, Chapter 6, this volume).

Faits Archéologiques: a French phrase that refers to archaeological features. Duday (2017: 226–227, footnote 31) notes that 'it seems necessary to introduce a distinction in order to avoid any confusion between the typology of features observed and that of the processes which produced them' (*'il semble nécessaire d'introduire une distinction afin d'éviter toute confusion entre la typologie des faits observés et celle des processus qui les ont induits'*). The sense here is that of an archaeological observation of a feature humanly created or made that may have more than a single function, such as pits, for example, which can be distinguished based on close analysis of the processes employed in their formation and, moreover, their contents.

Fetal Position: *'position fœtale'* in French, is a term used to describe the position of a body or corpse involving flexion of a number of joints, including the feet at the ankles, as seen in foetuses *in utero*.

Fonctionnement: as in '*fonctionnement d'une sépulture collective néolithique*' in the title of Duday's (1987b) contribution, which translates literally as 'functioning of a Neolithic collective grave', but this is a poor translation that does not capture the intent behind the terms. This concept is best understood as the way in which the grave fulfils its function (containing the dead), including the creation and use of the feature as well as the treatment of the remains and items found within or in association with the feature throughout its entire 'use-life' (cf. Boulestin and Courtaud, Chapter 3, this volume).

Full-Earthen Burial: '*sépulture en pleine terre*' in French is a deposition where the corpse is placed directly in the ground, with or without other burial paraphernalia, and covered with earth before the skeleton disarticulates in advanced decomposition, in which internal and secondary voids can be in-filled by the enveloping soil. The soil acts to maintain articulations and prevents subsequent movement of elements from anatomical articulation (cf. '**decomposition in a filled space**') (cf. Duday, 1990, 2006; Duday *et al.*, 1990). Notwithstanding, some displacement can occur within the secondary internal and external voids created during the decomposition process (cf. '**secondary voids**').

Funerary Archaeoentomology: '*archéoentomologie funéraire*' in French, is the study of insect remains, mostly necrophagous, from archaeological mortuary contexts to reveal the state of the corpse at its initial deposition, the treatment of individuals, such as the exposure of bodies before burial, the circumstances of death, and to permit insight into the seasonality of deaths. Archaeoentomology, the study of archaeological insect remains, can also be a significant source of information for assessing the potential simultaneity of deposits (cf. Huchet, 1996; Vanin and Huchet, 2017; Huchet and Castex, Chapter 26, this volume).

Funerary Archaeology: part of archaeology concerned with funerary contexts, but which is often divided between those who start the interrogative process from the human remains, as in archaeothanatology, and those who concentrate on burial type, grave goods/inclusions, and distribution and spacing of burials and burial grounds. Both address time and spatial distributions, and there is also an emphasis on the social, cultural and spiritual dimensions of death (Boulestin and Duday 2005: 19). This type of division is that which **archaeothanatology** works to remedy or bridge and, although still observed, it is more and more accepted that this separation is not ideal and hinders insight (cf. Knüsel, 2016; Nilsson Stutz, 2016; Knüsel and Schotsmans, Introduction, this volume).

Funerary Complex: the sum of the funerary practices performed for the deceased at a given site. It implies organisation not only of the funerary ceremonies but also the physical management and placement of the body, the structure of the grave and the funerary space (cf. Duday, Chapter 15, this volume; Rottier, Chapter 13, this volume).

Funerary Gestures, Actions or Deeds: in French '*gestes funéraires*', a fundamental concept that applies to the whole of the treatments (to both **appareil funéraire** and **fonctionnement**, in French) of the corpse of the deceased. This concept relates to the precepts of the group for both practical/utilitarian purposes and ideological and cosmological perspectives that aid to identify the intentionality of depositions that contribute to their structure. The funerary gestures are the actions of those practicing a particular funerary rite – that is to say, the practices adopted during funerary obsequies.

Duday *et al.* (1990: 30) write: 'funerary gestures relate mainly to preparatory practices (prior to deposition), burial practices (structure of the grave, position of the corpse and funerary material) and post-burial practices (re-opening of the grave, handling of the remains, re-interment)' ('*les gestes funéraires se rapportent essentiellement aux pratiques préparatoires (antérieures au dépôt), aux pratiques sépulcrales (structure de la tombe, position du cadavre et du matériel funéraire) et aux pratiques post-sépulcrales (réouverture de la tombe, manipulation des restes, réinhumation)*').

Funerary actions/gestures/deeds must be demonstrated based on contextual evidence before ritual deposition of human remains can be accepted as such. Repetition of these actions/gestures defines funerary practices that, when repeated in succession, suggest rites linked to ceremonies and principles (beliefs, cosmologies) governing them. Duday (2005: 173) notes: 'to distinguish the significant elements from those which have only anecdotal value, it is advisable to search in the literature if the observations made for a particular burial can be found in several individuals from equivalent chronological and/or cultural contexts' ('*pour distinguer les éléments significatifs de ceux qui n'ont qu'une valeur anecdotique, il convient de rechercher dans la littérature si les observations effectuées sur une sépulture peuvent être retrouvées chez plusieurs sujets afférents à un contexte chronologique et/ou culturel équivalent*').

Funerary Practices: '*pratiques funéraires*' in French, are repeated actions/gestures/deeds that accompany the intentional deposition of the deceased. The repetition of these gestures in combination with contextual evidence defines them as practices in a given place and time. They are distinguished from **mortuary practices** (cf. below) which apply more broadly to the dead than do funerary practices.

Funerary Selection: '*recrutement*' (literally 'recruitment' in English) is a term used in French to indicate those individuals chosen or selected for funerary treatment and included in a burial or as part of a burial site, which can be based on age-at-death, sex, or other demographic, biological/ physiological or social characteristics of the deceased. When carried out to its full interpretative conclusion, recruitment may comprise an assessment/interpretation of the social identity of the individuals included in a feature. The English language equivalent refers to the (palaeo) demographic profile comprising the social identity, or what Binford (1972) referred to as the 'social *persona*', the composite social identities of the deceased, including age-at-death, sex, health status, etc. of deceased individuals who were selected or subjected to particular types of funerary treatments (cf. '**social identity**') (cf. Le Roy and Rottier, Chapter 11, this volume).

Funerary Sequences: sometimes referred as '*chaîne opératoire funéraire*' in French, the 'sequence of funerary actions' ('**gestes funéraires**') that contribute to funerary patterning (cf. Valentin *et al.*, 2014; Bocquentin, Chapter 9, this volume), which form steps in processing a corpse for both physical and spiritual intents, practices and beliefs, and which can be quite complex, involving many steps or stages (Sellier, 2016). To address questions of social organisation and social structure of past societies, it is necessary to develop textual descriptions from direct observations of buried individuals and graves to establish the funerary treatments and practices (cf. Duday, 2005, 2006) employed and their sequence in order to establish what may have often been variable, multi-stage funerary rituals (Valentin *et al.*, 2014, 2016) (cf. Bocquentin, Chapter 9, this volume; Bonnet, Chapter 24, this volume; Duday, Chapter 15, this volume; Schmitt, Chapter 12, this volume; Williams, Chapter 17, this volume).

Funerary Space: an area dedicated to the acting out of the funerary practices of burial/ deposition of the dead (cf. Schmitt, Chapter 6, this volume).

Funerary Taphonomy: (also cf. '**taphonomy**', below): the study of how taphonomic changes aid the interpretation of funerary practices (Knüsel and Robb, 2016). Although not intended to be, some (cf. contributions to the *Journal of Archaeological Science Reports* special issue 2016, edited by Knüsel and Robb) have used the term synonymously with archaeothanatology, while others see taphonomy as a set of processes acting after deposition of the corpse and its depositional environment. Both funerary taphonomy and archaeothanatology are related to funerary archaeology.

Duday, Le Mort and Tillier (2014: 236) define '**taphonomy**' the following way: 'The term "taphonomy" (from the Greek τάφοσ, burial and νόμος, law) is commonly used in archaeological literature. It usually refers to the modes of preservation – or alteration – of organic elements after burial, but sometimes also refers to the phases before burial (for example, cutmarks of butchery in archaeozoology) or to the objects transformed by humans (flint, ceramics, metals, etc.) or to archaeological sites. Funerary archaeology tends to give the term a meaning closer to its etymology: it refers to all the processes that affect human remains after their deposition, the preservation or non-preservation of every skeletal element and its arrangement in relation to others'.

While the two terms, archaeothanatology and funerary taphonomy, may variously be seen to include one another and thus be umbrella or encompassing terms for each other, the two are actually different but mutually beneficial approaches to attain a more detailed perspective on mortuary behaviour, which encompasses funerary behaviour. Taphonomy, which refers to the natural process of decay and decomposition, then, can be seen as a methodological tool to aid the archaeothanatological study – to reveal funerary practices (cf. Booth *et al.,* Chapter 30, this volume; Schotsmans *et al.,* Chapter 27, this volume).

Gathering: a term used to describe individuals deposited in close proximity, but which may not have been accorded funerary treatment. Individuals may be buried, 'gathered together' ('*rassemblées*' in French) or grouped ('*regroupés*' in French), in the same area, as in a medieval cemetery, for example, or grouped within a single feature or funerary space that may relate to social and/or biological relationships among the deceased (cf. Castex *et al.,* 2011; Schmitt and Déderix, 2018; Boulestin and Courtaud, Chapter 3, this volume). In English-language publications, a more commonly used term is '**co-burial**' for groups of the remains of individuals deposited in the same feature.

Grave: the cut feature in which a body or bodies had been intentionally deposited. This word is the equivalent of '*tombe*' in French and is *not* the equivalent of the buried individual, but both the remains of the dead and the feature are, confusingly, often referred to as a 'burial' in English. A grave feature must be identified as such from the evidence of an intentional deposition, planning and repetition, especially from the earliest times (cf. Maureille, Chapter 8, this volume).

Grave Associations: anything associated with the grave and the deposited individual, regardless of intent (in French '*mobilier associé*').

Grave Goods: part of '*mobilier funéraire*' in French, or movable items that accompany buried individuals. These are often comprised of dress items or '**items of personal adornment**' or '*parure*' in French (cf. below) that are intimately linked to the remains of the dead, such as shroud pins, or worn as dress accessories, in the hair, for example; repeated locations with respect to the skeletal remains indicate where these items had been worn as dress accessories. The latter may also include objects placed within clothing and in a bag or container worn by the deceased. The word 'grave good' connotes an intentional inclusion and is thus distinguished from '**grave associations**' (cf. above).

Grave Inclusions: items placed in the grave, which are usually not in direct contact with the remains of the deceased (i.e. worn) but form part of the funerary goods intended to accompany the body of the deceased. The French term '*mobilier funéraire*' (things that are mobile or movable) also includes these types of items. Sometimes in the past, and occasionally today, these may have been called 'grave offerings' ('*offrandes*' in French) in that they were not intended to be retrieved.

Head: the cranium, mandible and their associated soft tissues, which in French is '*tête*' (cf. Boulestin, 2015).

'Head-to-Tail' Burial Position: a translation of the French '*tête-bêche*' or '*position antipodale*', or head to tail (i.e. feet) orientation of individuals in a multiple burial context, thus inverted with respect to one another (for examples cf. Castex and Kacki, Chapter 18, this volume).

Items of Personal Adornment: '*parure*' in French, part of grave goods or '*mobilier funéraire*' (French 'movable objects'), refer to those items found 'on the body', respecting individual elements of the skeleton; the dead would have worn these items attached to clothing or they had been placed within the clothing and thus represent part of the funerary preparation of the body before interment. These items are distinguished from grave inclusions, which are placed items that are not intimately linked to the body of the deceased. In French '*parure du défunt*', jewellery or decorative items which the deceased was wearing are distinguished from '*objets de parure*' as part of grave inclusions that the deceased may not have been wearing but may have been worn in life. This dichotomy is based on the ability to distinguish items not associated with a particular part of the body/skeleton with dress accessories as identified in other grave contexts or in figurative artistic representations.

Labile Joints or Labile Articulations: joints that are considered to disarticulate more rapidly and thus earlier in the process of decomposition, such as those of the hands and feet, including the inter-phalangeal, metacarpo-phalangeal, carpo-metacarpal and inter-carpal joints and the distal inter-phalangeal joints of the feet. The joints between the cervical vertebrae, but not the atlanto-occipital joint, are also considered labile joints (Duday, 2017: 206). This hypothetical definition, based solely on repeated observation of archaeological remains, is today being questioned via experimental (i.e. actualistic) studies (Mickleburgh *et al.*, Chapter 28, this volume; Schotsmans *et al.*, Chapter 27, this volume). The absence of these elements, especially of the extremities, hands and feet, may indicate that the remains had been transported from elsewhere, thus indicating a secondary burial/deposition (Duday *et al.,* 1990; Duday, 2006, 2009). These labile articulations are defined based on comparisons with the state of articulation of persistent joints in archaeological skeletons (cf. '**articulations**' and '**persistent joints**').

Layered Cemetery: when more recent graves intersect and are, counter-intuitively, more deeply interred than older graves (cf. Guillon, Chapter 32, this volume).

Lift and Deepen: A method for re-use of graves that involves the exhumation of human remains from an existing grave, deepening and enlarging the grave and re-interring the remains so that additional space is created for new interments in over-crowded cemeteries (cf. Schotsmans *et al.*, Chapter 27, this volume).

Manipulation: intentional disturbance/handling of human remains.

Mass Grave: referred to, variously, as '*sépulture de crise*', '*sépulture de catastrophe*' or '*charnier*' in French, a type of grave formed by the deposition of a number of individuals simultaneously, or in very quick succession due to the 'handling of a large number of dead people accumulated within a very short time' (Meyer *et al.,* 2014) in a single episode (for instance, following a disaster, a massacre or epidemic). A mass grave is indicated by 'large' numbers of articulated individuals (although there is no consensus on the minimum number of individuals) placed tightly together, often in layers, in a single feature, and often in a disordered state (i.e. in various orientations), which departs from the norm in a given time and place. These individuals often bear a common pattern of traits related to the mode (i.e. the means by which death was caused, such as by blunt force trauma) and manner (i.e. the circumstances of death, as in homicide by armed violence, or disease, such as the Plague) (cf. Castex and Kacki, Chapter 18, this volume).

The 'organised grave group' is a variant of the mass grave in that a number of individuals are included, but they are more ordered/organised. However, organised grave groups still depart from the more commonly encountered type of burial deposition in any given sociocultural context (Skinner, York and Connor, 2002). These graves relate to suspended social mores in a period of crisis, but where there is an effort to create 'respectful' burials. This type of burial has been used during epidemics, in the aftermath of natural disasters, and when the dead killed as a result of a pogrom, genocide, or mass murder are recovered by friends or 'neutrals', rather than by foes (Komar, 2008). It is not only the number of individuals that is important in the definition of 'mass graves' (cf. Meyer *et al.*, 2014; Kissel and Kim, 2018), but the evidence for manner of death – by diseases such as Plague (those that leave no lesions due to the acute nature of the disease) or by violence-related trauma. These indicate the circumstances under which a number of individuals were deposited in the same feature. These features aid to distinguish catastrophic death assemblages resulting from a mass mortality event from attritional assemblages formed through the gradual accumulation of the dead over a period of time, as in a cemetery or burial ground (Margerison and Knüsel, 2002). Based on the defining characteristics provided in Knüsel (2005), up-dated here, for those contexts deriving from armed conflict, these are:

1. the presence of a body mass or masses, producing groups of skeletons, within a grave cut;
2. the presence of disorder in the orientation of the bodies/skeletons indicating an apparent disregard for the manner of deposition that is often outside the bounds of normative (i.e. more commonly encountered) practices for a particular time and place;
3. skeletal remains in anatomical connection/articulation (especially labile articulations/ connections) that relate to rapid burial;
4. skeletal remains of skeletonised bodies that are in contact with one another;
5. a common pattern of traits related to the manner, such as disease or violence-related injuries and, more rarely, cause of death;
6. often a lack of grave inclusions, but sometimes associated with items of personal adornment, among others, worn by or found on the deceased at the time of death.

Midden: French '*couches détritiques*', a refuse area for disused material that should not automatically carry the modern connotation of 'thrown out/unwanted/useless' (cf. Schmitt, Chapter 6, this volume), but may represent a chosen place for the burial of the deceased, such as shell middens, as found on the Pacific Northwest Coast of North America (Ames and Maschner, 1999: 89–90) and in Mesolithic Europe (Cunha, Cardoso and Umbelino, 2003).

Monoxylous Coffin: a coffin made from a single piece of wood, such as a hollowed-out log, a log-coffin (cf. Melton, Montgomery and Knüsel, 2013; Georges-Zimmermann and Kacki, 2017: 68–86, figs. 23–30; Blaizot, Chapter 1, this volume; Schotsmans *et al.*, Chapter 27, this volume).

Mortuary Practices/Mortuary Archaeology/Mortuary Behaviour: sometimes used in a reductionist sense as a synonym for funerary archaeology/funerary behaviour, especially in the English-language literature. The term '**mortuary behaviour**' is best employed for human remains found in an archaeological layer or feature, the origin of which does not only include evidence for the performance of funerary gestures/actions/deeds. All treatments of the bodies of the dead are therefore qualified as 'mortuary' (Boulestin, 2012), but those that reflect handling of the corpse in the funerary sphere define funerary behaviour. Such treatments must be demonstrated by analysing the archaeological context to ascertain if individuals share the more commonplace funerary treatments for a particular time and place. If they do not, then this may be indicative of mortuary but not funerary behaviour.

The embalmed body of Oliver Cromwell, decapitated post-mortem and then displayed – reflecting the fall from grace of the Lord Protector of England in death (Fitzgibbons, 2008) – is an example of a dead body treated in an unusual manner after death. The post-mortem decapitation was clearly not a funerary treatment but was a mortuary treatment performed on the body of the deceased.

Multiple Deposition: as defined by Knüsel and Robb (2016), the term 'deposition' ('*dépôt*' in French) is used to describe archaeological deposits of human remains to avoid the implicit sense of intentionality in the word 'burial' ('*sépulture*' or '*dépôt funéraire*' in French), thus entailing funerary behaviour. The adjective 'multiple' refers to the deposition of several bodies in the same place. In French, the use of '***dépôt multiple***' (literally 'multiple deposit') or '***sépulture multiple***' (literally 'multiple burial') refers to the deposition of several bodies in the same grave in a single event that distinguishes this type of deposition from a '*sépulture collective*', where individuals or parts of individuals are deposited over a period of time (cf. Castex *et al.*, 2014; Castex and Blaizot, 2017; Castex and Kacki, Chapter 18, this volume). In English-language sources, 'multiple' is a general term used to describe the remains of several individuals in the same feature, especially when first encountered in the field when the timing of deposition has not been demonstrated or remains unclear; this concept is rendered in French through the phrase '*sépulture plurielle*'. This has been awkwardly translated as '**plural burial**' (cf. below).

In English, there is no single term that describes the phenomenon of encountering more than a single individual in an archaeological feature as well as the relative timing of the depositions; the timing of these depositions are distinguished by using an adjective to distinguish those deposited *simultaneously* (i.e. 'all at once' or 'close in time') from those deposited successively or consecutively over a more extended period of time, sometimes a later burial disturbing one already present but in a minor way that suggests such disturbances were haphazard and unintentional. This use means that the timing and number are implicit in the terms currently in archaeothanatological use in French but not in English.

The sequencing of depositions requires both careful observation of skeletal element relationships upon excavation and detailed recording that permits checking of initial observations as the feature is excavated and the final stratigraphic relationships are defined (e.g. Castex and Blanchard, 2011; Sachau-Carcel, Chapter 31, this volume). Thus, this type of interpretation straddles excavation and post-excavation recording and analysis. The distinction between simultaneous ('***multiple***' in French) and successive depositions over a period of time ('***collective***' in French) is greatly dependent on whether or not there is physical contact between skeletal elements and, moreover, the state of preservation of the remains and whether or not articulated elements are identified.

If the remains are poorly preserved, articulations of joints and the contacts between skeletons can be greatly obscured, but an additional concern occurs in cases when deposition of bodies occurs in successive events over a period of time (e.g. Kacki *et al.*, 2014). In the latter case, the capacity of the grave, the number interred and its size (a volumetric measurement of the occupied space) of the deposited corpses, the spatial organisation of these deposits and aspects of their biological profiles are required to confirm the simultaneity of the burial deposit (cf. Gerdau-Radonić, 2007).

In essence and practically, these parameters also apply to mass graves, as for example, at late medieval Towton (West Yorkshire, UK), where multiple bodies of battle casualties were deposited as a series of 'dumps' (multiple consecutive or multiple successive depositions/deposits), perhaps wagon or cartloads, over a period of time in a 'cleaning up' operation of scattered corpses (cf. Sutherland, 2000).

Because '*sépulture plurielle*' ('plural burial' in French) is a term that does not fully equate to 'burials', i.e. the plural of burial in English, and 'plural burial' does not convey the same meaning in English, 'multiple deposition' has been adopted to compensate for this terminological problem (cf. Knüsel 2014; Knüsel and Robb 2016) (not to be confused with '***sépulture multiple***', cf. above and below). The important point with regard to the use of 'multiple deposition' (i.e. multiple burial) is to be explicit about the evidence used to interpret the sequence of deposition in order to distinguish burials of two or more individuals through a number of depositions over time ('***collective***' in French) from those that occurred simultaneously as a group at one time ('***multiple***' in French). There are occasions when this deposition occurs rapidly over a short time rendering the two phenomena indistinguishable. These would be the 'plural' burials described in French:

two or more individuals deposited in relatively rapid succession but without the tell-tale disturbance of individuals previously deposited in the grave.

To many francophone researchers, '*sépulture multiple*' indicates a number of corpses deposited at the same time; thus, this term has come to include timing of the deposit as well and is thus defined as several individuals or parts of individuals deposited simultaneously, 'at the same time'.

Necropolis: a 'burial ground' (literally 'city of the dead') that does not invoke the sanctity and the specifically codified norms of respect associated with the use of the word '**cemetery**' (cf. above), which is associated with more recent world religions. The term is thus often applied to burial grounds that pre-date the advent of burial grounds/sites associated with the more recent world religions.

Non-funerary Treatment: a phrase that indicates the absence of funerary gestures, deeds or actions, which are often indicated, but certainly not always, by the absence of accompanying objects (cf. '**grave goods**' and '**grave inclusions**') which could reflect a lack of funerary treatment. This concept is embedded in the definition of '**mortuary behaviour**' (cf. above). The abandonment of the corpse/deceased without a proper grave may represent one form of non-funerary treatment of the deceased. This lack of treatment may be linked to the ostracisation of socially undesirable individuals who may have evidence for funerary treatment but are also located away from the funerary area of the group (cf. Schmitt, Chapter 6, this volume).

Ossuary: '*ossuaire*' in French, referring to disarticulated remains intentionally gathered together in a container or building, and sometimes ordered by anatomical element, with the aim to store (and sometimes display) human skeletal material (cf. Bonnet, Chapter 24, figure 24.9, this volume).

Osteoarchaeology: the study of osseous remains (human and faunal) from archaeological contexts, with the adjective 'human' distinguishing human remains from those of other vertebrates and invertebrates that also contribute to archaeological analyses.

'**Outside the Original Volume of the Body**' is a translation of the French '*hors du volume initial du corps*' or '*à l'extérieur du volume originel du corps*' – a phrase meaning that skeletal elements have moved to a location outside the space originally occupied by the fleshed corpse upon deposition. This type of movement is more easily possible in a burial in a void, such as a coffin or other container, but can also be found in a full-earthen burial, i.e. a body deposited directly in the soil (i.e. without a container), if secondary voids form around the corpse due to subsequent decomposition of perishable materials (cf. '**voids**', below). Without voids, the skeletal remains are located 'within the original volume occupied by the body'. The word 'volume' when used in French ('*volume*') in a funerary context means 'space', as in three-dimensional space, a unit of measurement raised to a power of three, and it is 'original space' that is the most direct translation, as in the 'original space occupied by the corpse or body' (cf. Blaizot, Chapter 1, this volume; Green, Chapter 23, this volume; Mickleburgh *et al.*, Chapter 28, this volume; Schotsmans *et al.*, Chapter 27, this volume).

Paradoxical Disarticulation: '*dislocation en ordre paradoxal*' in French refers to a reverse pattern of disarticulation between **labile** and **persistent articulations**, with labile connections being maintained and persistent joints being disarticulated (Duday and Guillon, 2006). Paradoxical disarticulation is considered to be an indication of desiccation/mummification (Maureille and Sellier, 1996), but this hypothesis is currently being questioned and re-assessed (cf. Schotsmans *et al.*, 2017; Schotsmans *et al.*, Chapter 27, this volume). This phenomenon has been observed in seated burials, for example (Rottier, 2016).

Persistent Articulations or Persistent Joints: these are joints that, due to their weight-bearing role, require a large muscle mass and the support of large tendinous and capsular ligamentous attachments to maintain their functional integrity and contiguity (maintenance in articulation). As a consequence, they are hypothesised to be more resilient to decay/decomposition than their more labile counterparts and disarticulate more slowly. These include the major weight-bearing joints of the body, such as those at the knee, and tibio-femoral joints; as well as the atlanto-occipital joint, which remains in articulation longer than the other cervical vertebrae (Andrews and Bello, 2006; Duday, 2006); and those of the lumbar region of the vertebral column; those of the pelvic basin, the lumbosacral and sacro-iliac joints; and those of the ankle and tarsals. Exception to the rule, noted by Duday (2009: 27, is the acetabulo-femoral joint or hip joint, considered a labile joint, despite its weight-bearing function). The costotransverse joints of the rib cage seem to decompose more slowly (are longer persisting) than are the sterno-vertebral joints; this discrepancy in the relative speed of decomposition produces 'flattening' of the rib cage during decomposition (Duday, 2017: 218–219). Due to its strong, soft tissue support and complex morphology, the shoulder (gleno-humeral) and elbow (humero-ulnar) joints are also ones that are retained in articulation for a longer period of time. Because these are large joints, they are more easily recorded in an archaeological context. Unfortunately, because they persist for many months, if not years, the information they provide is not as informative as those of the **labile joints** (cf. '**labile joints**' and '**articulations**', above). The division and definition of persistent and labile joints are currently being questioned based on actualistic experiments (Mickleburgh *et al.*, Chapter 28, this volume; Schotsmans *et al.*, Chapter 27, this volume).

Pit Burial: a negative, i.e. dug, grave feature, sometimes translated as '*tombe en fosse*' in French.

Plank-built Coffin: '*coffrage*' in French, is a type of built structure within a grave that covers the excavated grave walls and floor, into which the deceased is placed, and may include a lid/cover that is found especially in early medieval Europe (cf. Blaizot, Chapter 1, this volume), but also in Chalcolithic/Bronze Age Europe (Parker Pearson, Sheridan and Needham, 2013). A '*coffrage*' may also be formed from roofing tiles in Roman-period graves.

'**Plural' Burial**: in French the term '*sépulture plurielle*' (literally translated as 'plural burial', a term that does not fully equate to the word 'burials', i.e. the plural of burial in English; also cf. '**multiple deposition**', above) has been used to mean a feature containing several individuals, but for which the relative chronology of the depositions cannot be determined. Schmitt and Déderix (2019: 103) define '*dépôt funéraire pluriel*' (literally 'plural funerary deposit') as 'all funerary structures containing more than one individual' ('*l'ensemble des structures funéraires contenant plus d'un individu*'). Its use is intended as a neutral term in which the notions of succession and simultaneity are absent. In current French use, this lack of evidence for the timing of depositions distinguishes the 'plural burial' from '**multiple**' (simultaneous) and '**collective**' (gradual accumulation) burials. The phrase 'plural burial' thus encompasses both of the latter terms and is especially used for deposits encountered in the field, prior to efforts to sequence the addition of bodies in a grave feature (cf. Boulestin and Courtaud, Chapter 3, this volume; Schmitt, Chapter 12, this volume). The addition of this term, but not the concept which emphasised the timing of depositions, clashes with the use of 'multiple burial' and 'mass burial' in most English sources to describe the same phenomenon, the burial of several individuals, the sequence not being specified (also cf. '**burial**' and '**multiple deposition**', above).

Ponderal Index: '*indice pondéral*' in French, is a proportional representation of the relative weight of parts of the skeleton to indicate the contribution of anatomically-defined areas, such as the skull (cranium and mandible), the axial skeleton, and the appendicular skeleton, the upper and lower limbs, and extremities, hands and feet, to the total weight of a complete skeleton, especially useful for comparing cremations and highly fragmented remains. This index, mostly used in French research, is used instead of, or in addition to fragment counts. The index is used in comparative analyses of cremated remains to quantify the anatomical part representation of the contents of cremation vessels/cremation deposits and the selection or exclusion – or loss – of certain skeletal elements or parts thereof, and to identify the inclusion and commingling/mixing of more than a single individual in a cremation deposit (cf. Depierre, Chapter 4, this volume; Duday, Chapter 15, this volume).

Post-funerary Treatment: funerary gestures or actions made after deposition of the deceased (cf. Schmitt Chapter 6, this volume). Placement of branches 250 years later on a previously interred receptacle at Gristhorpe in the Bronze Age of northern England (cf. Melton *et al.*, 2010) is an example of this type of treatment, as is the manipulation and re-assembly of skeletal remains (cf. Parker Pearson *et al.*, 2005).

Preventive Archaeology: a literal translation of the French *'archéologie preventive'*, which is now sometimes also found in English sources. The concept refers to archaeological excavation and study in response to modern planning and development. This type of responsive archaeological intervention is also called, variously, rescue, salvage, contract, commercial and developer-funded archaeology and is linked in North America to Cultural Resource Management (CRM) and, in the United Kingdom, has been referred to as Archaeological Resource Management or, more broadly, Cultural Heritage Management. In France, this type of archaeological endeavour is part of a national framework to protect cultural patrimony/cultural heritage and falls under the umbrella of the Ministry for Culture (*Ministère de la Culture*). In France and in French overseas territories, it is often the Institut National de Recherches Archéologiques Préventives (Inrap) that is engaged in archaeological excavation and research, as was its predecessor, the *Association pour les Fouilles Archéologiques Nationales* (AFAN), founded in 1973. However, privately run firms can also be authorised to undertake contractual archaeological excavations. The remit of all organisations engaged in this type of endeavour is to protect and preserve heritage, whether archaeological sites, buildings, traditional arts and crafts or performative arts (cf. Clavandier, Chapter 33, this volume; Guillon, Chapter 32, this volume).

Primary Deposit/Deposition or Primary Burial: *'dépôt ou sépulture primaire'*, in French a primary, undisturbed deposition, comprised of remains found in the initial or original – and final – place of deposition of the corpse. Often the primary nature of the deposition is inferred when bones are in anatomical articulation, affected only by the processes of decomposition *in situ*. There is thus an anatomical logic in the disposition of the remains. They are in anatomical articulation: 'the deposition of a cadaver or a portion of a cadaver while the elements of the skeleton still retain all of their anatomical relationships' (*'le dépôt d'un cadavre ou d'une portion de cadavre est réalisé alors que les éléments du squelette conservent encore la totalité de leurs relations anatomiques'*) (Boulestin and Duday, 2005: 26).

The terms primary and secondary deposition have been criticised (cf. Boulestin, Chapter 2, this volume; Schotsmans *et al.,* Chapter 27, volume). The presence of disarticulations, even if a substantial number, does not necessarily mean the deposition is not a primary one. In other words, the evident disorder in the organisation of the bones does not necessarily mean that they have been handled or moved after death (Duday and Guillon, 2006: 128). This means that disordered and disarticulated remains cannot be taken as *prima facie* evidence for the remains having been manipulated. Using current best practice, a primary burial is recognised in the field by the presence of a skeleton 'in a state of anatomical integrity' (Duday 2009: 14), or 'the deposition of a "fresh" cadaver in the place of final deposition, where the entire decomposition of the body had taken place' (*'l'apport d'un cadavre "frais" dans le lieu de dépôt définitif, où va donc s'opérer toute le décomposition du corps'*) (Duday, 2005: 165).

Primary Earthen Burials: in French *'sépulture primaire en pleine terre'*, depositions that accommodate the body of the deceased placed directly in the soil and covered with soil, with or without other material accompaniments, although the body may have been wrapped in material, such as a shroud, as attested by imagery and disposition of remains in the Late Medieval period, for example, as well as in other periods (cf. Nilsson Stutz, Chapter 10, this volume).

Prone: equivalent to a '**procubitus**' or '**ventral decubitus**' position (*'procubitus'* in French) which are Latin-derived terms (*'cubitus'* being the Latin for 'forearm' and *'cubitum'* for 'elbow') to describe a body placed on the chest and sometimes, though rarely, face down, the cephalic extremity more often being found rotated laterally to one side or the other, rather than with the facial skeletal oriented to the soil or base of a container. This position of the corpse/skeleton is the opposite of 'dorsal decubitus' (*'décubitus dorsal'* in French) or '**supine**' (cf. below).

'**Reduction(s)**' **of the Skeleton or of the Corpse**: *'réduction de corps'* in French, is the phrase employed to describe bones or skeletal parts that have been moved inside their primary deposit, and thus occupy less (a reduced) space in the grave or in a tomb, in order to provide room for the placement of additional depositions in a collective burial or a re-used grave (Blaizot, 1996). These remains thus show evidence of intentional re-organisation of the grave to accommodate a subsequent deposition (Duday, 2006: 47, 2009: 14, 72–73) (cf. Blanchard, Chapter 19, this volume; Rottier, Chapter 13, this volume).

Re-opened Grave: a secondary intervention into a grave undertaken to remove material from it, or to add material to it, including grave goods, grave inclusions, furnishings and/or human remains. These interventions leave remains of certain regions of the skeleton in a disordered state, often as indicated by an altered skeletal part representation (cf. Aspöck, Gerdau-Radonić and Noterman, Chapter 16, this volume).

Rite: the ceremonies and principles of an ideological framework that guide the performance of funerary/mortuary practices. Rites develop from the enactment of coded actions embedded in a collective (i.e. communal) ritual context where each actor has a more or less clearly defined role (cf. Bocquentin, Chapter 9, this volume). In French research, a distinction is made between funerary/mortuary practices and funerary/mortuary rites (for the difference between funerary and mortuary cf. '**funerary practices**' and '**mortuary practices**', above). While the first refers to repeated funerary actions (*'gestes funéraires'*) that define funerary practices, the second refers to the ceremonies, traditions and beliefs that guide in the execution of these practices. The reason behind this distinction made in archaeothanatology is based on the fact that one can only (partly) reconstruct funerary practices by looking at the archaeological record, which imposes an interpretative limitation. For the reconstruction of funerary rites one needs other sources, such as written sources, for example. It is, therefore, more difficult to reconstruct rites in prehistoric than in historic contexts. A concrete example of this distinction and that care should be exercised regarding its interpretation, is described in Schotsmans *et al.*, Chapter 27, this volume: The Greeks and Romans placed a coin in the mouth of the deceased (funerary practice) to pay the ferryman for taking the soul from the world of the living to the world of the dead (funerary rite). In other words, the first can be observed in a funerary context while the second is based on supplemental information from written sources.

Ritual: a series of repeated ceremonies performed in a prescribed order. The repeated nature of these ceremonies, when performed in the funerary realm, distinguishes intentional funerary practices from taphonomic changes, although the latter can sometimes mimic the archaeological patterns produced by rituals. The ceremonial rites that comprise ritual act to structure individual behaviour in societies. The rituals that accompany death are vitally important in order to transfer knowledge, rights, and privileges to successors and successive generations (cf. Mauss, 1990). Victor Turner (1972: 1100) writes: 'A ritual is a stereotyped sequence of activities, involving gestures, words and objects, performed in a sequestered place, and designed to influence preternatural entities or forces on behalf of the actors' goals and interests'. Rituals are thus performed because they are perceived to achieve, or help to ensure particular outcomes or responses.

Seated or Squatting Burial: *'sépulture en position assise ou accroupie'*, respectively in French, is an interment in which the vertebral column is vertically oriented with respect to the floor or bottom of the feature (i.e. with respect to the zenith) and in which the upright individual rests either on the ischia and/or on the feet in a plantigrade position, in a plantar-flexed or dorsiflexed position, unilaterally or bilaterally, with the lower limbs partially flexed, fully flexed or highly contracted. This position can be found in corpses that have been desiccated, bound, or those placed in a bundle ('***paquet funéraire***', in French) (cf. above), which is then positioned with the cephalic extremity uppermost in the grave (cf. Gerdau-Radonić, 2007, 2012; Rottier, 2016).

Secondary Deposition/Burial: the subsequent placement of human remains, often following intentional transfer from their primary location. These are partial or complete remains of the skeleton, often in a disarticulated or partially disarticulated state, sometimes with elements missing. Duday (2005: 195) describes these as '…"dry" bones in their final place of deposition' ('*apport d'os "secs" dans le lieu de dépôt définitif*'). In this, he makes an allusion to the processes of decomposition by which bones become defleshed in one location and then are deposited in a second location. Boulestin and Duday (2005: 27) define these as a '… secondary deposit of human remains carried out when the elements of the skeleton have partially or totally lost their anatomical relationships' ('*le dépôt secondaire est le dépôt de restes réalisé lorsque les éléments du squelette ont partiellement ou totalement perdu leurs relations anatomiques*').

The secondary nature of human remains is defined on the basis of their state of disarticulation, the selection of certain elements, re-inhumation and lack of small/fragile elements, such as those of the hands and feet (Blaizot, 1996; Duday 2009: 89–91). Nilsson Stutz (Chapter 10, this volume) refers to this type of deposition as 'a form of final deposition of the human remains after one or several previous depositions or treatments resulting in the partial or complete disarticulation of the skeleton', whereas Moutafi and Voutsaki (2016: 783, table 2) define '**secondary treatment**' as bones manipulated without the immediate need to inter another body in the grave or a tomb and define this concept as fully or partially disarticulated skeleton(s) transferred to a secondary location in or outside the original grave. This definition is similar, then, to the definition of 'primary loose' of Haddow *et al.* (2020), which indicates skeletons that have been disturbed but not subsequently re-organised by people in the past.

As mentioned above, the use of the terms primary and secondary depositions has been critiqued (cf. Boulestin, Chapter 2, this volume; Schotsmans *et al.*, Chapter 27, this volume). The presence of disarticulations, even if a substantial number, does not mean the remains have been handled or moved after death (Duday and Guillon, 2006: 128). The delayed deposition of a skeletally complete desiccated corpse (i.e. one retaining the terminal pedal and manual phalanges, for example) may result in a fully articulated individual that is not a primary deposition (cf. '**delayed burial**', above; Schotsmans *et al.*, Chapter 27, this volume).

Sediment: rock and mineral particles transported by water, wind or gravity, called 'deposits'. Geologically, there is a difference between soil and sediment (cf. '**soil**', below). However, in archaeological discourse, the words soil and sediments are often used interchangeably and refer to the 'dirt' surrounding the skeleton ('*sédiment*' in French) (cf. Schotsmans *et al.,* Chapter 27, this volume).

Skeletonisation: one of the last stages of decomposition when a corpse is reduced to its bone constituents.

Skull: a colloquial and thus non-standard anatomical term that indicates both the cranium and mandible (cf. Aiello and Dean, 1990: 33), but not the cranium alone, with which is erroneously used synonymously at times. This practice obscures element part representation and funerary practices as a consequence. It is best to use element names- thus 'cranium' and 'mandible'- and to avoid colloquial expressions that are not as restricted in their meaning (Knüsel, 2014). The term '***tête osseuse***' ('bony head') is used in French for the cranium and mandible together (cf. Boulestin, 2015) (also cf. '**head**' and '**cranium**').

Social Identity: self-defining characteristics accumulated through the life-course via interpersonal interactions that are represented by others at the death and burial of an individual. Interred objects and organisation of the remains and of the funerary space are 'indicators' but not direct reflections of the social identities in which the deceased partook in life. Binford (1971, 1972) referred to this as the 'social *persona*' of the deceased, which has been expanded today by the use of biochemical and biomolecular methods to reveal individual origins, kin relationships and dietary constituents that vary geographically and socio-culturally (e.g. Montgomery, Knüsel and Tucker, 2011) and genetic studies associated with specific funerary practices (e.g. Gleize *et al.*, 2016) (Also cf. Le Roy and Rottier, Chapter 11, this volume).

Soil: Soil is considered the vertically weathered part of the surface of the Earth, with different zones in a developed soil profile being called 'horizons'. This means that *in situ* soil represents the residual of the original bedrock. Geologically, there is a difference between soil and sediment (cf. '**sediment**'). However, in archaeological discourse, the words soil and sediment(s) are often used interchangeably and refer to the 'dirt' surrounding the skeleton or other deposited objects ('*sédiment*' in French) (cf. Schotsmans *et al.*, Chapter 27, this volume).

Supine: a position of the body equivalent to '**dorsal decubitus**' ('*décubitus*' in French), which is the Latin-derived term originally meaning 'reclining supported on the elbows', but used to mean 'lying on the back' more recently. This term is thus in opposition to the Latin terms 'procubitus' or 'ventral decubitus' meaning lying on the stomach, the ventral surface, or **prone** (cf. above). 'Supine' is the opposite of 'prone' in anatomical terms, in a way similar to supination and pronation of the forearm and hand.

Système Funéraire: a term that is similar to '**funerary programme**' in English, the steps in the care and handling of the deceased with ideological connections to social practices (cf. Bocquentin *et al.*, 2010; Lauwers and Zemour, 2016). Implicit in the use of these terms and concepts is to move from description to interpretation (cf. '**Rite**').

Taphonomy, -ic (adjectival form), (also cf. '**funerary taphonomy**'): in its original inception, processes related to the preservation or alteration of organic remains following burial, the transition from the biosphere to the lithosphere (cf. Lyman, 1994, 2010), thus an interdisciplinary study of what had happened to an organism between death and its recovery. Specifically, in the case of human remains, these processes are now increasingly understood to be active before, at deposition and in the post-depositional interval and, together, alter the archaeological record. Additional modifications due to storage conditions, destructive sampling and transportation may also be implicated in documenting the history of specific collections or assemblages. For the funerary archaeological record, these processes affect the human remains, the grave furnishings, the grave goods (items of personal adornment) and grave inclusions (placed items), as well as the grave and its constituent parts, often from interactions among them. **Taphonomic analysis** can be seen as a methodological tool to aid archaeothanatological study in order to reveal funerary practices (cf. Schotsmans, Márques-Grant and Forbes, 2017; Booth *et al.*, Chapter 30, this volume; Schotsmans *et al.*, Chapter 27, this volume).

Tended or Managed Cremation (also cf. '**cremation**' above): '**crémation conduite**' in French, a cremation that is tended by an '*ustor*', the Latin for attendant 'corpse burner' in order to ensure more thorough burning of the corpse and accompanying remains (cf. Depierre, Chapter 4, this volume; Duday, Chapter 15, this volume).

Tertiary Remains: isolated, scattered, disarticulated or partially articulated skeletal elements found outside a typical funerary or mortuary context that no longer clearly relate to a particular individual skeleton or set of human remains (cf. Haddow and Knüsel, 2017; Haddow *et al.*, 2020). Tertiary remains are, in fact, remains in a secondary context but described as 'tertiary' to indicate that they are isolated bones.

Tomb: '*tombeau*' in French, a built superstructure, as used by Schmitt (Chapter 12, this volume), into which complete or partial skeletons are placed. It may be constructed over or above the place of deposition of corpses, in the sense of a shrine that serves as a locus for honouring the memory of the dead (cf. Blaizot, 2016). This structure is *not* the equivalent of the English 'burial', with which it is sometimes translated from English into French, and *vice versa*, and used as synonymous. Individuals may be deposited in a tomb, an aboveground structure, sometimes constructed over a grave, which may thus be found beneath it. Tombs, as built superstructures, are not synonymous with burials, nor are they synonymous with graves in English use.

The French word '*tombeau*' should not be confused with the term '*tombe*' in French, which is a synonym of '*sépulture*', i.e. '**burial**' in English, rarely if ever used in scientific/archaeological French publications where the word '*sépulture*' or the phrase '*dépôt funéraire*' is preferred (cf. above).

Typo-chronology: '*typo-chronologie*' in French, refers to absolute and relative dating evidence of a burial and its associated remains which, when combined with all other burial observations, such as the arrangement, organisation and architecture, in combination with funerary practices, are used to establish a typo-chronology which groups chronological variations of burials and practices in archaeo-anthropology.

Unstable (position): when translating Duday's (2006) chapter in *Social Archaeology of Funerary Remains*, Knüsel translated the word '*déséquilibre*' as 'unstable', which captures the idea of 'unsupported (against gravity)', or 'prone to falling', or in a 'precarious' position. This is also the term used by Gerdau-Radonić (2012) to describe the precarious position of *ossa coxae*. In their translation of Duday's *Lectures* (2009), Cipriano and Pearce employed the term 'disequilibrium', and, although the two terms are clearly related, the main use in English for 'disequilibrium' is in finance, meaning 'not equal', which is not what is intended. So, 'unstable', 'unsupported', or 'unbalanced' is the sense in the context of skeletal elements in the grave, which entails that after decomposition of the soft tissue structures they could fall or be displaced if nothing (i.e. a support of some kind) stabilises them (cf. Gerdau-Radonić, 2007, 2012).

Verticalisation: a non-anatomical descriptive term applied to the position of the claviculae when oriented cranio-caudally rather than medio-laterally, as in standard anatomical position, as when the shoulders are elevated (i.e. as in shrugging). This is an extreme position not associated with everyday posture or movement, however, i.e. it is beyond the physiologically sustainable or comfortable norm of an elevated shoulder. It is thus often associated with binding, with shroud use, or with the shoulder abutting the wall of the grave, the side-wall of a narrow coffin or container or other restrictive structure (cf. Blaizot, 2008; Green, Chapter 23, this volume; Nilsson Stutz, Chapter 10, this volume).

Voids: empty spaces within the burial space between skeletal elements, individual skeletons, items in the burial and funerary structures in the grave, into which soil or sediment can percolate (French '*colmatage*', or in-filling) (Duday, 2006). These voids may be **primary voids** present at the time of burial or **secondary voids** due to subsequent decomposition of the soft tissues of the body and materials buried with it. These secondary voids can be divided into those that develop within (internally) the space once occupied by the corpse or that are external to the space once occupied by the corpse and are defined as follows:

> **Internal (Secondary) Spaces or Voids:** developed from a concept first defined by Duday and colleagues (1990), these spaces are located within the original space occupied by the corpse. After skeletonisation occurs, spaces form between segments of the body into which skeletal elements may move (cf. Green, Chapter 23, this volume) due to gravitational pull (cf. '**Gravity effect**' or '*effet/loi de la pesanteur*' in French). These result in changes in the disposition of elements, such as flattening of the rib cage and opening of the pubic symphysis. Skeletal elements may also descend, fall or

move into a newly created empty space after a delay of variable duration caused by the decomposition of soft tissues (cf. Méniel, Chapter 25, this volume; Schotsmans *et al.*, Chapter 27, this volume). One of the most common of these spaces or voids is created by decomposition of the viscera of the abdomen, elements of the wrist and hands often being found in proximity to the *ossa coxae* and sacrum upon excavation due to placing the wrists and hands on the pelvis when a corpse is prepared for burial and deposited.

External (Secondary) Spaces or Voids: spaces that form outside the original space occupied by the corpse. These voids appear as a consequence of the decomposition of objects or structures within the grave. Bone elements can be displaced into these spaces by the pull of gravity ('*effet/loi de la pesanteur*' in French) if they are in an unstable position once the ligaments and tendons and restraining clothing or wrappings have decomposed (cf. Duday, 2009: 46–52; Green, Chapter 23, this volume).

Acknowledgements

The authors thank Dominique Castex, Sacha Kacki and Bruno Boulestin for their advice and helpful discussions concerning this lexicon.

References

Adams, B.J. and Byrd, J.E., eds. (2015). *Recovery, analysis, and identification of commingled human remains.* Totowa: Humana Press.

Aiello, L.C. and Dean, M.C. (1990). *Human evolutionary anatomy.* London: Academic Press.

Alt, K.W., Benz, M., Müller, W., Berner, M.E., Schultz, M., Schmidt-Schultz, T.H., Knipper, C., Gebel, H.-G. K., Nissen, H.J. and Vach, W. (2013). Earliest Evidence for Social Endogamy in the 9,000-Year-Old-Population of Basta, Jordan. *PLoS ONE*, 8(6), p. e65649.

Alva, W. and Donnan, C.B. (1993). *Royal tombs of Sipán.* Los Angeles: Fowler Museum of Cultural History.

Ambroise, D. and Perlès, C. (1975). Note sur l'Analyse Archéologique des Squelettes Humains. *Revue Archéologique du Centre de la France*, 14(1-2), pp. 49–61.

Ames, K. and Maschner, H. (1999). *The peoples of the Northwest Coast.* London: Thames and Hudson.

Armit, I., Schulting, R., Knüsel, C.J. and Shepherd, I. (2011). Death, Decapitation, and Display? The Bronze and Iron Age Human Remains from the Sculptor's Cave, Covesea, North-East Scotland. *Proceedings of the Prehistoric Society*, 77, pp. 251–278.

Andrews, P. and S. Bello (2006). Pattern in human burial practice. In R. Gowland and C.J. Knüsel eds., *Social Archaeology of Funerary Remains*. Oxford: Oxbow, pp. 14–29.

Aufderheide, A. (2003). *The scientific study of mummies.* Cambridge, UK: Cambridge University Press.

Aufderheide, A.C. and Rodríguez-Martín, C. (1998). *The Cambridge encyclopaedia of human palaeopathology.* Cambridge: Cambridge University Press.

Beau, A., Rivollat, M., Réveillas, H., Pemonge, M.-H., Mendisco, F., Thomas, Y., Lefranc, P. and Deguilloux, M.F. (2017). Multi-Scale Ancient DNA Analyses Confirm the Western Origin of Michelsberg Farmers and Document Probable Practices of Human Sacrifice. *PLoS ONE*, 12(7), p. e0179742.

Beckett, R.G., Lohmann, U. and Bernstein, J. (2011). *A Field Report on the Mummification Practices of the Anga of Koke Village*, Central Highlands, Papua New Guinea. *Yearbook of Mummy Studies*, 1, pp. 11–17.

Beckett, R.G. and Nelson, A.J. (2015). Mummy Restoration Project among the Anga of Papua New Guinea. *The Anatomical Record*, 298, pp. 1013–1025.

Binford, L.R. (1971). Mortuary Practices: Their Study and Their Potential. *Approaches to the Social Dimensions of Mortuary Practices, Memoirs of the Society for American Archaeology*, 25, pp. 6–29.

Binford, L.R. (1972). Mortuary practices: their study and potential. In: L.R. Binford, ed., *An Archaeological Perspective.* New York: Seminar Press, pp. 108–243.

Blaizot, F. (1996). L'Apport des Méthodes de la Paléo-Anthropologie Funéraire à l'Interprétation des Os en Situation Secondaire dans les Nécropoles Historiques – Problèmes Relatifs au Traitement et à l'Interprétation des Amas d'Ossements. *Archéologie Médiévale*, 26, pp. 1–22.

Blaizot, F. (2008). Réflexions sur la Typologie des Tombes à Inhumation: Restitution des Dispositifs et Interprétations Chrono-Culturelles. *Archéologie Médiévale*, 38, pp. 1–30.

Blaizot, F. (2014). From the Skeleton to the Funerary Architecture: a Logic of the Plausible. *International Journal of the Science of Man*, *52*, pp. 263–284.

Blaizot, F. (2016). La sépulture comme un espace de construction des identités religieuses et sociales du 1er au Ve siècle de notre ère. In: M. Lauwers and A. Zemour, eds., *Qu'Est-Ce Qu'une Sépulture? Humanités et Systèmes Funéraires de la Préhistoire à Nos Jours.* Antibes: Éditions de l'Association pour la Promotion et la Diffusion des Connaissances Archéologiques (APDCA), pp. 215–233.

Blaizot, F. (2017). *Les espaces funéraires de l'habitat groupé des Ruelles, à Serris (Seine et Marne) du VIIe au XIe siècles: modes d'inhumation, organisation, gestion et dynamique.* Ausonius Éditions, Bordeaux: Maison des Sciences de l'Homme d'Aquitaine.0çà

Bocquentin, F., Anton, M., Berna, F., Rosen, A., Khalaily, H., Greenberg, H., Hart, T.C., Lernau, O., Kolska Horwitz, L. (2020). Emergence of Corpse Cremation during the Pre-Pottery Neolithic of the Southern Levant: A Multidisciplinary Study of a Pyre-pit Burial. *PLoS ONE*, 15(8), p. e0235386.

Bocquentin, F., Chambon, P., Le Goff, I., Leclerc, J., Pariat, J.-G., Pereira, G., Thevenet, C. and Valentin, F. (2010). De la Récurrence à la Norme: Interpréter les Pratiques Funéraires en Préhistoire. *Bulletins et Memoires de la Société d'Anthropologie de Paris*, 22, pp. 157–171.

Bocquentin, F., Kodas, E. and Ortiz, A. (2016). Headless but Still Eloquent! Acephalous Skeletons as Witnesses of Pre-pottery Neolithic North-South Connections and Disconnections, *Paléorient*, 42(2), pp. 33–52.

Boulestin, B. (2012). Champ de la Discipline: Concepts et Mise en Oeuvre. In: L. Bonnabel, ed., *Archéologie de la Mort en France*. Paris: La Découverte, pp. 24–39.

Boulestin, B. (2015). Conservation du Crâne et Terminologie: Pour en Finir avec Quelques Mots de Tête!/ Skull Conservation and Terminology: Time to Get Our Heads Together! *Bulletins et Mémoires de la Société d'Anthropologie de Paris*, 27 (1–2), pp. 16–25.

Boulestin, B. (2016). Norme funéraire: illusions et vérités. In: M. Lauwers and A. Zemour, eds., *Qu'est-ce qu'une Sépulture? Humanités et Systèmes Funéraires de la Préhistoire à Nos Jours.* Antibes: Éditions de l'Association pour la Promotion et la Diffusion des Connaissances Archéologiques (APDCA), pp. 363–377.

Boulestin, B. and Baray, L. (2010). Synthèses et perspectives. In: L. Baray and B. Boulestin, eds., *Morts Anormaux et Sépulture Bizarres. Les Dépôts Humains en Fosses Circulaires et en Silos du Néolithique à l'Âge du Fer.* Dijon: Éditions Universitaire de Dijon (EUD), pp. 227–232.

Boulestin, B. and Duday, H. (2005). Ethnologie et archéologie de la mort: de l'illusion des références à l'emploi d'un vocabulaire. In: C. Mordant and G. Depierre, eds., *Les Pratiques Funéraires à l'Âge du Bronze en France.* Actes de la table ronde de Sens-en-Bourgogne, (10–12 juin 1998). Paris: Éditions du Comité des Travaux Historiques et Scientifiques (CTHS), pp. 17–30.

Boulestin, B. and Duday, H. (2006). Ethnology and Archaeology of Death: From the Illusion of References to the Use of a Terminology. *Archaeologia Polona* 44, pp. 149–169.

Boulestin, B. and Gambier, D. (2012). Décapitation/decollation: une distinction justifiée? In: B. Boulestin and D. Gambier, eds., *Crânes Trophées, Crânes d'Ancêtres et autres Pratiques autour de la Tête: Problèmes d'Interprétation en Archéologie.* British Archaeological Reports (International Series), 2415. Oxford: Archaeopress, pp. 17–19.

Boylston, A., Knüsel, C.J., Roberts, C.A. and Dawson, M. (2000). Investigation of a Romano-British Rural Ritual in Bedford, England. *Journal of Archaeological Science*, 27, pp. 241–254.

Buikstra, J.E. (1977). Biocultural dimensions of archaeological study: a regional perspective. In: R.L. Blakely, ed., *Biocultural Adaptation in Prehistoric America.* Athens: The University of Georgia Press, pp. 67–84.

Buikstra, J.E. (2006). A historical introduction. In: J.E. Buikstra and L.A. Beck, eds., *Bioarchaeology: The Contextual Analysis of Human Remains.* Amsterdam: Academic Press, pp. 7–25.

Castex, D. and Blaizot, F. (2017). Reconstructing the original arrangement, organisation and architecture of burials in archaeology. In: E.M.J. Schotsmans, N. Márquez-Grant and S.L. Forbes, eds., *Taphonomy of Human Remains: Forensic Analysis of the Dead and the Depositional Environment.* Chichester: Wiley, pp. 277–295.

Castex, D. and Blanchard, P. (2011). Témoignages archéologiques de crise(s) épidémique(s): la catacombe des Saints Marcellin et Pierre (Rome, Fin Ier-IIe S.). In: D. Castex, P. Courtaud, H. Duday, F. Le Mort and A.M. Tillier, eds., *Regroupement Des Mort: Genèse Et Diversité Archéologique.* Bordeaux: MSHA Editions.

Castex, D., Courtaud, P., Duday, H., Le Mort, F. and Tillier, A.-M., eds. (2011). *Le regroupement des morts. Genèse et diversité archéologique.* Bordeaux: Maison des sciences de l'Homme d'Aquitaine et Ausonius.

Castex, D., Kacki, S., Réveillas, H., Souquet-Leroy, I., Sachau-Carcel, G., Blaizot, F., Blanchard, P. and Duday, H. (2014). Revealing Archaeological Features Linked to Mortality Increases. *Anthropologie: International Journal of the Science of Man*, II(3), pp. 299–318.

Chapman, R. and Randsborg, K. (1981). Approaches to the archaeology of death. In: R. Chapman, I. Kinnes and K. Randsborg, eds., *The Archaeology of Death*. Cambridge: Cambridge University Press, pp. 1–24.

Cunha, E., Cardoso, F. and Umbelino, C. (2003). Inferences about Mesolithic life style on the basis of anthropological data. The case of the Portuguese shell middens. In: L. Larsson, H. Kindgren, K. Knutsson, D. Loeffler and A. Åkerlund, eds., *Mesolithic on the Move: Papers Presented at the Sixth International Conference on the Mesolithic in Europe, Stockholm 2000*. Oxford: Oxbow Books, pp. 184–188.

Deguilloux, M.F., Pemonge, M.H., Mendisco, F., Thibon, D., Cartron, I. and Castex, D. (2014). Ancient DNA and Kinship Analysis of Human Remains Deposited in Merovingian Necropolis Sarcophagi (Jau-Dignac-et-Loirac, France, 7th–8th Century AD). *Journal of Archaeological Science*, 41, pp. 399–405.

Duday, H. (1987a). Contribution des observations ostéologiques à la chronologie interne des sépultures collectives. In: H. Duday and C. Masset, eds., *Anthropologie Physique et Archéologie, Méthodes d'Étude des Sépultures*, Actes du colloque de Toulouse, 4–6 novembre 1982. Paris: Centre National de la Recherche Scientifique (CNRS), pp. 51–59.

Duday, H. (1987b). Organisation et fonctionnement d'une sépulture collective néolithique. L'aven de la Boucle à Corconne (Gard). In: H. Duday and C. Masset, eds., *Anthropologie Physique et Archéologie: Méthodes d' Étude des Sépultures*. Paris: Centre National de la Recherche Scientifique (CNRS), pp. 89–104.

Duday, H. (1990). Observations Ostéologiques et Décomposition du Cadavre Sépulture Colmatée ou en Espace Vide. *Revue Archéologique du Centre de la France*, 29(2), pp. 193–196.

Duday, H. (2005). L'archéothanatologie ou l'archéologie de la mort. In: O. Dutour, J.-J. Hublin and B. Vandermeersch, eds., *Objets et Méthodes en Paléoanthropologie*. Paris: Comité des Travaux Historiques et Scientifiques (CTHS), pp. 153–215.

Duday, H. (2006). L'Archéothanatologie ou l'archéologie de la mort (Archaeothanatology or the archaeology of death). Translated by C.J. Knüsel. In: R.L. Gowland and C.J. Knüsel, eds., *Social Archaeology of Funerary Remains*. Oxford: Oxbow Books, pp. 30–56.

Duday, H. (2009). *Archaeology of the dead: lectures in archaeothanatology*. Translated by A.M. Cipriani and J. Pearce. Oxford: Oxbow Books.

Duday, H. (2017). Archéologie funéraire et taphonomie du cadavre. In: J.P. Brugal, ed., *TaphonomiS, Éditions des archives contemporaines*. Paris: Centre National de la Recherche Scientifique-Institut Écologie et Environnement)(CNRS-INEE), pp. 197–270.

Duday, H., Courtaud, P., Crubézy, E., Sellier, P. and Tillier, A.-M. (1990). L'Anthropologie de 'Terrain': Reconnaissance et Interprétation des Gestes Funéraires. *Bulletins et Memoires de la Société d'Anthropologie de Paris*, 2(3–4), pp. 26–49.

Duday, H. and Guillon, M. (2006). Understanding the circumstances of decomposition when the body is skeletonized. In: A. Schmitt, E. Cunha and J. Pinheiro, eds., *Forensic Anthropology and Medicine: Complementary Sciences From Recovery to Cause of Death*. Totowa, NJ: Humana Press, pp. 117–157.

Duday, H., Le Mort, F. and Tillier, A.-m. (2014). Archaeothanatology and Funeral Archaeology. Application to the Study of Primary Single Burials. *Anthropologie (Brno)*, LII(3), pp. 235–246.

Fitzgibbons, J. (2008). *Cromwell's head*. Richmond: The National Archives.

Formicola, V. (1988). The Triplex Burial of Barma Grande (Grimaldi, Italy). *Homo*, 39, pp. 130–143.

Formicola, V., Pontrandolfi, A. and Svoboda, J. (2001). The Upper Paleolithic Triple Burial of Dolní Věstonice: Pathology and Funerary Behavior. *American Journal of Physical Anthropology*, 115(4), pp. 372–379.

Georges-Zimmermann, P. and Kacki, S. (2017). *Le cimetière médiéval de Marsan (Gers). Lecture archéothanatologique*. Paris: l'Harmattan.

Gerdau-Radonić, K. (2007). *Les tombes collectives de Tablada de Lurin (Vallee de Lurin, Perou; Ier-IIIe s. ap. J.-C.)*. Unpublished Ph.D. thesis, Bordeaux: Université de Bordeaux 1.

Gerdau-Radonić, K. (2012). Archaeological insights into the disarticulation pattern of a human body in a sitting/squatting position. In: J. Buckberry and P. Mitchell, eds., *Proceedings of the Annual Conference of the British Association of Biological Anthropology and Osteoarchaeology* 12, pp. 151–160.

Gerdau-Radonić, K. and Herrera, A. (2010). Why Dig Looted Tombs? Two Examples and Some Answers from Keushu (Ancash Highlands, Peru). *Bulletins et Memoires de la Societe d'Anthropologie de Paris*, 22(3–4), pp. 145–156.

Gerdau-Radonić, K. and Makowski, K. (2011). Las sepulturas colectivas de Tablada de Lurín: una perspectiva desde la antropología biológica. In: L. Vetter, S. Tellez, R. Vega-Centeno, eds., *Arqueología Peruana: Homenaje a Mercedes Cárdenas*. Lima: Instituto Riva-Agüero, Pontificia Universidad Católica del Perú, pp. 145–176.

Gleize, Y., Mendisco, F., Pemonge, M.-H., Hubert, C., Groppi, A., Houix, B., Deguilloux, M.-F. and Breuil, J.-Y. (2016). Early Medieval Muslim Graves in France: First Archaeological, Anthropological and Palaeogenomic Evidence. *Plos One*, 11(2), p.e0148583.

Haddow, S.D. and Knüsel, C.J. (2017). Skull Retrieval and Secondary Burial Practices in the Neolithic Near East: Recent Insights from Çatalhöyük. *Turkey. Bioarchaeology International*, 1(1–2), pp. 52–71.

Haddow, S.D., Schotsmans, E.M.J., Milella, M., Pilloud, M.A., Tibbetts, B. and Knüsel, C.J. (2020). From parts to a whole? Exploring changes in funerary practices at Çatalhöyük. In: I. Hodder, ed., *Consciousness and Creativity at the Dawn of Settled Life*. Cambridge: Cambridge University Press, pp. 250–272.

Herrmann, B. and Meyer, R.-D. (1993). *Sudamerikanische mumien aus vorspanischer zeit: eine radiologische untersuchung*. Berlin: Museum für Völkerkunde.

Huchet, J.-B. (1996). L'Archéoentomologie Funéraire: Une Approche Originale dans l'Interprétation des Sépultures. *Bulletins et Mémoires de la Société d'Anthropologie de Paris*, 8(3–4), pp. 289–302.

Kacki, S. (2020). Black death: cultures in crisis. In: C. Smith, ed., *Encyclopedia of Global Archaeology*. Cham: Springer.

Kacki, S., Trinkaus, E., Schotsmans, E.M.J., Courtaud, P., Dori, I., Dutailly, B., Guyomarc'h, P., Mora, P., Sparacello, V.S. and Villotte, S. (2020) Complex mortuary dynamics in the Upper Paleolithic of the decorated Grotte de Cussac, France, *Proceedings of the National Academy of Sciences of the United States of America (PNAS)* 117 (26), pp. 14851–14856.

Kacki, S., Réveillas, H., Sachau-Carcel, G., Giuliani, R., Blanchard, P. and Castex, D. (2014). Réévaluation des Arguments de Simultanéité des Dépôts de Cadavres: L'Exemple des Sépultures Plurielles de la Catacombe des Saints Pierre-et-Marcellin (Rome)/Reappraising Evidence of Simultaneous Deposits of Cadavers: Example of the Mass Graves from the Catacomb of Saint Peter and Marcellinus (Rome). *Bulletins et Mémoires de la Société d'Anthropologie de Paris*, 26, pp. 88–97.

Kissel, M. and Kim, N.C. (2018). The Emergence of Human Warfare: Current Perspectives. *Yearbook of Physical Anthropology*, 168(S67), pp. 1–23.

Knüsel, C.J. (2005). The physical evidence of warfare- subtle stigmata? In M. Parker-Pearson and I.J.N. Thorpe, eds., *Warfare, Violence, and Slavery*. British Archaeological Reports (International Series), 1374. Oxford: Archaeopress, pp. 49–65.

Knüsel, C.J. (2010). Bioarchaeology: A Synthetic Approach/Bio-archéologie: Une Approche Synthétique. *Bulletins et Mémoires de la Société d'Anthropologie de Paris*, 22, pp. 62–73.

Knüsel, C.J. (2014). Crouching in Fear: Terms of Engagement for Funerary Remains. *Journal of Social Archaeology*, 14(1), pp. 26–58.

Knüsel, C.J. (2016). The Two Cultures: An Unfinished Synthesis. *Current Swedish Archaeology*, 24, pp. 57–64.

Knüsel, C.J., Batt, C.M., Cook, G., Montgomery, J., Müldner, G., Ogden, A.R., Palmer, C., Stern, B., Todd, J. and Wilson, A.S. (2010). The Identity of the St. Bees Lady, Cumbria: An Osteobiographical Approach, *Medieval Archaeology*, 54 (1), pp. 275–317.

Knüsel, C.J. and Glencross, B. (2017). Çatalhöyük, Archaeology, Violence. *Contagion: Journal of Violence, Mimesis, and Culture*, 23, pp. 23–36.

Knüsel, C.J. and Maureille, B. (2018). Archaeological approaches to human remains: France. In: B.O. Donnabhain and M.C. Lozada, eds., *Archaeological Human Remains: Legacies of Imperialism, Communism, and Colonialism*. New York: Springer, pp. 57–80.

Knüsel, C.J. and Robb, J.E. (2016). Funerary Taphonomy: An Overview of Goals and Methods. *Journal of Archaeological Science: Reports*. In C.J. Knüsel and J.E. Robb, eds., Special Issue on Funerary Taphonomy, 10, pp. 655–673.

Komar, D.A. (2008). Patterns of Mortuary Practice Associated with Genocide: Implications for Archaeological Research. *Current Anthropology*, 49(1), pp. 123–133.

Larsen, C.S. (1997). *Bioarchaeology: interpreting behavior from the human skeleton*. Cambridge: Cambridge University Press.

Lauwers, M. and Zemour, A. (2016). Introduction: des morts, de la sépulture et des sciences sociales. In: M. Lauwers and A. Zemour, eds., *Qu'est-ce Qu'une Sépulture? Humanités et Systèmes Funéraires de la Préhistoire à Nos Jours*. Antibes : Éditions de l'Association pour la Promotion et la Diffusion des Connaissances Archéologiques (APDCA), pp. 11–20.

Leclerc, J. (1990). La Notion de Sépulture. *Bulletins et Mémoires de la Société d'Anthropologie de Paris*, 2 (3–4), pp. 13–17.

Leclerc, J. and Tarrête, J. (1988). Sépulture. In: A. Leroi-Gourhan, ed., *Dictionnaire de la Préhistoire*. Paris: Presses Universitaires de France, pp. 1002–1003.

Lefranc, P. and Chenal, F. (2019). Deposits of Bodies in Circular Pits in the Neolithic Period (Mid-Fifth to the Mid-Fourth Millennium BC): Deposits, Waste, or Ritual Remnants? *Human Remains and Violence*, 5(1), pp. 18–32.

Lyman, R L. (1994). *Vertebrate taphonomy*. Cambridge: Cambridge University. Press.

Lyman, R.L. (2010). What Taphonomy Is, What It Isn't, and Why Taphonomists Should Care about the Difference. *Journal of Taphonomy*, 8(1), pp. 1–16.

Margerison, B.J. and Knüsel, C.J. (2002). A Comparison of Attritional and Catastrophic Cemeteries: The Palaeodemography of the Medieval Plague Cemetery at the Mint Site, London. *American Journal of Physical Anthropology*, 119(2), pp. 134–143.

Maureille, B. and Sellier, P. (1996). Dislocation en Ordre Paradoxal, Momification et Décomposition: Observations et Hypotheses. *Bulletins et Mémoires de la Société d'Anthropologie de Paris, Nouvelle Série*, 8(3–4), pp. 313–327.

Mauss, M. (1990). *The gift: the form and reason for exchange in archaic societies.* Translated by W.D. Halls. London: Routledge. (Original Title: *Essai sur le Don*, 1950).

Melton, N.D., Montgomery, J. and Knüsel, C.J., eds. (2013). *Gristhorpe man, a life and death in the Bronze Age.* Oxford: Oxbow Books.

Melton, N.D., Montgomery, J.M., Knüsel, C.J., Batt, C., Needham, S., Parker Pearson, M., Sheridan, A. with Heron, C., Horsley, T., Schmidt, A., Evans, A., Carter, E., Edwards, H., Hargreaves, M., Janaway, R., Lynnerup, N., O'Connor, S., Ogden, A., Taylor, T., Wastling, V. and Wilson, A. (2010). Gristhorpe Man: An Early Bronze Age Oak-Coffin Burial. *Antiquity*, 84(325), pp. 796–815.

Meyer, C., Lohr, C., Kürbis, O., Dresely, V., Haak, W., Adler, C.J., Gronenborn, D. and Alt, K.W. (2014). Mass graves of the LBK: patterns and peculiarities. In: A. Whittle and P. Bickle, eds., *Early Farmers: The View from Archaeology and Science*. Oxford: Proceedings of the British Academy 198, pp. 307–325.

Milella, M., Knüsel, C.J. and Haddow, S.D. (2016). A Neolithic Case of Fibrous Dysplasia from Çatalhöyük (Turkey). *International Journal of Paleopathology*, 15, pp. 10–18.

Milella, M., Mariotti, V., Belcastro, M.G. and Knüsel, C.J. (2015). Patterns of Irregular Burials in Western Europe (1st–5th Century A.D.). *PloS One*, 10(6), p. e0130616.

Montgomery, J.M., Knüsel, C.J. and Tucker, K.E. (2011). Identifying the origins of decapitated male skeletons from 3 Driffield Terrace, York, through isotope analysis: reflections of the cosmopolitan nature of Roman York in the time of Caracalla. In M. Bonogofsky, ed., *The Bioarchaeology of the Human Head: Decapitation, Decoration and Deformation*. Gainesville: University Press of Florida, pp. 141–178.

Morris, I. (1992). *Death-ritual and social structure in classical antiquity*. Cambridge: Cambridge University Press.

Moutafi, I. and Voutsaki S. (2016). Commingled Burials and Shifting Notions of the Self at the Onset of the Mycenaean Era (1700–1500 BC): The Case of the Ayios Vasilios North Cemetery, Laconia. *Journal of Archaeological Science: Reports*. In C.J. Knüsel and J.E. Robb, eds., Special Issue on Funerary Taphonomy, 10, pp. 780–790.

Murphy, E.M., ed. (2008). *Deviant burial in the archaeological record*. Oxford: Oxbow Books.

Nilsson Stutz, L. (2016). Building Bridges between Burial Archaeology and the Archaeology of Death: Where is the Archaeological Study of the Dead Going? *Current Swedish Archaeology*, 24, pp. 13–35.

Outram, A.K., Knüsel, C.J., Knight, S. and Harding, A.F. (2005). Understanding Complex Fragmented Assemblages of Human and Animal Remains: A Fully Integrated Approach. *Journal of Archaeological Science*, 32(12), pp. 1699–1710.

Papageorgopoulou, C., Shved, N., Wanek, J. and Rühli, F.J. (2015). Modeling Ancient Egyptian Mummification on Fresh Human Tissue: Macroscopic and Histological Aspects. *The Anatomical Record*, 298, pp. 974–987.

Parker Pearson, M., Chamberlain, A., Craig, O., Marshall, P., Mulville, J., Smith, H., Chenery, C., Collins, M., Cook, G., Craig, G., Evans, J., Hiller, J., Montgomery, J., Schwenninger, J.L., Taylor, G. and Wess, T. (2005). Evidence for Mummification in Bronze Age Britain. *Antiquity*, 79(305), pp. 529–546.

Parker Pearson, M., Sheridan, A. and Needham, S. (2013). Bronze Age tree-trunk coffin burials in Britain. In: N. Melton, J. Montgomery and C. Knüsel, eds., *Gristhorpe Man: A Life and Death in the Bronze Age*. Oxford: Oxbow Books, pp. 29–66.

Partiot, C., Trinkaus, E., Knüsel, C.J. and Villotte, S. (2020). The Cro-Magnon Babies: Morphology and Mortuary Implications of the Cro-Magnon Immature Remains. *Journal of Archaeological Science Reports*, 30, p. 102257.

Pettitt, P. (2018). Hominin Evolutionary Thanatology from the Mortuary to Funerary Realm: The Palaeoanthropological Bridge between Chemistry and Culture. *Philosophical Transactions of the Royal Society B*, 373, pp. 1–12.

Rottier, S. (2016). The Seated Dead: Evidence of Funerary Complexity from the Early Late Bronze Age, 14th–12th Centuries BCE in France. *Journal of Archaeological Science: Reports*. In C.J. Knüsel and J.E. Robb, eds., Special Issue on Funerary Taphonomy,10, pp. 810–818.

Schmitt, A. (2015). Pratiques Mortuaires en Fosse au Néolithique Moyen dans le Midi de la France: Caractérisations et Éclairages interprétatifs/Mortuary Practices in Pits during the Middle Neolithic in the South of France: Characteristics and Interpretative Indications. *L'Anthropologie*, 119, pp. 1–37.

Schmitt, A. (2017). Middle Neolithic Burials in Mediterranean France: Honouring or Rejecting the Dead? *West & East, 2*, pp. 63–82.

Schmitt, A. and Déderix, S. (2018). What defines a collective grave? Archaeological and ethnological perspectives on collective burial practices. In: A. Schmitt, S. Déderix and I. Crevecoeur, eds., *Gathered in Death. Archaeological and Ethnological Perspectives on Collective Burial and Social Organisation.* Louvain: Presses universitaires de Louvain, pp. 195–214.

Schmitt, A. and Déderix, S. (2019). Qu'est-ce qu'une sépulture collective ? Vers un changement de paradigme. *Bulletins et Mémoires de la Société d'Anthropologie de Paris*, 31(3–4), pp. 103–112.

Schmitt, A., Déderix, S. and Crevecoeur, I. eds. (2018). *Gathered in death. Archaeological and ethnological perspectives on collective burial and social organisation.* Louvain: Presses universitaires de Louvain.

Schotsmans, E.M.J., Márquez-Grant, N. and Forbes, S.L., eds. (2017). *Taphonomy of human remains. Forensic analysis of the dead and the depositional environment.* Chichester: Wiley.

Schotsmans, E.M.J., Ueland, M., Luong, S., Prinsloo, L.C., Nizio, K., Wallman, J., Forbes, S.L. and Knüsel, C.J. (2017). Reconstructing the Mortuary Chaîne Opératoire in the Neolithic Near East: Conducting Actualistic Experiments for a Better Understanding of Burial Practices. *Abstracts of the 23th Conference of the European Association of Archaeologists*, Maastricht, The Netherlands, p. 395.

Sellier, P. (2016). Différents Types de Sépulture ou Différentes Étapes d'une Même Séquence Funéraire? Un Exemple Démonstratif de Chaîne Opératoire Mortuaire chez les Anciens Marquisiens/Different Types of Burial or Different Steps in the Same Funerary Sequence? An illustrative Example of a Mortuary Chaîne Opératoire Found Among Ancient Marquesans, *Bulletins et Mémoires de la Société d'Anthropologie de Paris*, 28, pp. 45–52.

Simmons, T. (2017). Post-mortem interval estimation: an overview of techniques. In: E.M.J. Schotsmans, N. Márquez-Grant and S.L. Forbes, eds., *Taphonomy of Human Remains: Forensic Analysis of the Dead and the Depositional Environment.* Chichester: Wiley, pp. 135–142.

Skinner, M.F., York, H.P. and Connor, M.A. (2002). Postburial disturbance of graves in Bosnia-Herzegovina. In W.D. Haglund and M.H. Sorg, eds., *Advances in Forensic Taphonomy: Method, Theory, and Archaeological Perspectives.* Boca Raton: CRC Press, pp. 293–308.

Smith, M. (2016). Dead Certainties: the Need to Pin Down Ideas and Deflate Conflations in Funerary Archaeology. *Abstracts of the 21th Conference of the European Association of Archaeologists*, Glasgow, United Kingdom, p. 581.

Sutherland, T. (2000). Recording the grave. In V. Fiorato, A. Boylston and C.J. Knüsel, eds., *Blood Red Roses: The Archaeology of a Mass Grave from Towton, AD 1461.* Oxford: Oxbow Books, pp. 36–44.

Testart, A. (2008). Des Crânes et des Vautours ou la Guerre Oubliée. *Paléorient*, 34(1), pp. 35–58.

Testart, A. (2012). Pourquoi couper des têtes? In: B. Boulestin and D. Gambier, eds., *Crânes Trophées, Crânes d'Ancêtres et autres Pratiques autour de la Tête: Problèmes d'Interprétation en Archéologie.* British Archaeological Reports (International Series), 2415, Oxford: Archaeopress, pp. 29–33.

Thibeault, A. and Villotte, S. (2018). Disentangling Cro-Magnon: A Multiproxy Approach to Reassociate Lower Limb Skeletal Remains and to Determine the Biological Profiles of the Adult Individuals. *Journal of Archaeological Science: Reports*, 21, pp. 76–86.

Tucker, K. (2014). The osteology of decapitation burials in Roman Britain. A post-mortem burial rite? In: C.J. Knüsel and M.J. Smith, eds., *The Routledge Handbook of the Bioarchaeology of Human Conflict.* Abingdon: Routledge, pp. 213–236.

Turner, V. (1972). Symbols in African Ritual. *Science*, 179, pp. 1100–1105.

Valentin, F., Allièse, F., Bedford, S. and Spriggs, M. (2016). Réflexions sur la Transformation Anthropique du Cadavre: Le Cas des Sépultures Lapita de Teouma (Vanuatu) (Considerations on Anthropogenic Modifications of a Corpse: The Case of the Lapita Burials at Teouma (Vanuatu)). *Bulletins et Mémoires de la Société d'Anthropologie de Paris*, 28, 39–44.

Valentin, F., Rivoal, I., Thevenet, C. and Sellier. P., eds. (2014). *La Chaîne Opératoire Funéraire: Ethnologie et Archéologie de la Mort*. Paris: De Broccard.

Vanin, S. and Huchet, J.-B. (2017). Forensic entomology and funerary archaeoentomology. In: E.M.J. Schotsmans, N. Márquez-Grant and S.L. Forbes, eds., *Taphonomy of Human Remains: Forensic Analysis of the Dead and the Depositional Environment*. Chichester: Wiley, pp. 167–186.

Villena i Mota, N. (2015). *Hiérarchie et fiabilité des liaisons ostéologiques (par symmétrie et par contiguïté articulaire) dans l'étude des sépultures anciennes*. British Archaeological Reports (International Series) 2697. Oxford: Archaeopress.

Villena i Mota, N., Duday, H. and Houët, F. (1996). De la Fiabilité des Liaisons Ostéologiques. *Bulletins et Mémoires de la Société d'Anthropologie de Paris, n.s.*, 8(3–4), pp. 373–384.

Villes, A. (1987). Une hypothèse: les sépultures de relégation dans les fosses d'habitat protohistoriques en France septentrionale. In: H. Duday and C. Masset, eds., *Anthropologie Physique et Archéologie: Méthodes d'Études des Sépultures*. Paris: Centre National de la Recherche Scientifique (CNRS), pp. 167–174.

Webster's New International Dictionary of the English Language (1947). W.A. Neilson, T.A. Knott and P.W. Carhart, eds. Springfield: G. & C. Merriam Company Publishers.

Weiss-Krejci, E. (2005). Excarnation, evisceration, and exhumation in medieval and post-medieval Europe. In: G. Rakita, J. Buikstra, L. Beck and S. Williams, eds., *Interacting with the Dead. Perspectives on Mortuary Archaeology for the New Millennium*. Gainesville: University Press of Florida, pp. 155–172.

Yaka, R., Mapelli, I., Kaptan, D., Doğu, A., Chyleński, M., Erdal, O.D., Koptekin, D., Vural, K.B., Bayliss, A., Mazzucato, C., Fer, E., Çokoğlu, S.S., Kempe Lagerholm, V., Krzewińska, M., Karamurat, C., Gemici, H.C., Sevkar, A., Dağtaş, N.D., Kılınç, G.M., Adams, D., Munters, A.R., Sağlıcan, F., Milella, M., Schotsmans, E.M.J., Yurtman, E., Çetin, M., Yorulmaz, S., Altınışık, E., Ghalichi, A., Juras, A., Bilgin, C.C., Günther, T., Storå, J., Jakobsson, M., de Kleijn, M., Mustafaoğlu, G., Fairbairn, A., Pearson, J., Togan, İ., Kayacan, N., Marciniak, A., Larsen C.S., Hodder, I., Atakuman, C., Pilloud, M., Sürer, E., Gerritsen, F., Özbal, R., Baird, D., Erdal, Y.S., Duru, G., Özbaşaran, M., Haddow, S.D., Knüsel, C.J., Götherström, A., Özer, F. and Somel, M. (2021). Variable Kinship Patterns in Neolithic Anatolia Revealed by Ancient Genomes. *Current Biology*, 31, pp. 1–14.

Zemour, A. (2016). De l'anthropologie de terrain à l'archéologie de la mort: histoire, concepts et développements. In: M. Lauwers and A. Zemour, eds., *Qu'est-ce Qu'une Sépulture? Humanités et Systèmes Funéraires de la Préhistoire à Nos Jours*. Antibes: Éditions de l'Association pour la Promotion et la Diffusion des Connaissances Archéologiques (APDCA), pp. 23–34.

INDEX

Note: Page numbers appearing in **bold** indicate **tables**; page numbers in *Italics* indicate *figures*; FN stands for footnote.

movements of remains during the process of decomposition'), 33 ('tailored recording'), 37 ('recording of the pit in both plan and cross-section, if the contours are clearly defined, as well as taking depth measures to beneath the bones'), 47, 49, 69 ('recording cremated remains'), 70, 71, 74 ('requires recording during study that is more developed and flexible than that those of the tables of numbers and weights developed by Duday'), 164 ('to reconstruct the appearance of the original funerary space and identify post-depositional processes, archaeothanatology offers an unprecedented research avenue to address precisely the physical place occupied by the corpse and through it, the social role the dead played in the eyes of survivors after the completion of the funerary rituals'), 170 ('horizontal hand-stripping of layers of sediment, photographic coverage and systematic 3D recording of all elements'), 207, 208, 211 ('standard recording system of field anthropology was applied for human remains: each layer was photographed and a full inventory was made of all the bones within it'), 212, 215, 232 ('observation and recording of the relative position of each bone are essential during excavation to permit fundamental taphonomic analysis'), 240 ('extraordinary complexity of the burial positions observed could be addressed only through a long and necessarily highly descriptive recording of the human remains and the grave context'), 245 ('modern standards and approaches to the recording and interpretation of Iron Age burials *in situ* are relatively infrequent and often comprise only single examples when they occur'), 278 ('recording of information pertaining to the reopening was limited'), 305, 313 ('when skeletal recording in the field is confined to the more readily observable overall body orientation, placement (e.g. supine or prone), and limb positioning; the full potential of the osteoarchaeological record is therefore lost'), 314, 325 ('recording in the field should consider possible damage to skeletal elements including re-deposited remains that could have derived from such taphonomic events'), 421 ('the position and nature of every item in the grave at the time of discovery'), 431 ('3D recording and modelling also serve as a major medium for taphonomic analysis'), 438 ('detailed observations of the spatial relationships between skeletal elements but also features such as the grave cut, and *in situ* locations of objects within the grave'), 453 ('recording accuracy may have played a part'), 456, 515 ('contextual evidence is important, rather than blindly recording

'labile' and 'persistent' joints or looking at every individual articulation'), 549, 558 ('time-lapse recordings'), 571 ('recording of post-depositional formation processes of a sorted pyre site 23 years after the event'), 600 ('development of computer tools has changed the recording of data in the field with the creation of databases to guide observations'), 601–605 ('recording the extant and restoring the past'), 602 ('3D recording'), 603, *603* ('3D recording of a cranium'), 604, 605, 606–607 ('3D modelling'), 609 ('cremation burials'), 610–612 ('3D recording of a cemetery'), *610* ('photogrammetric models of the Porta Nocera excavations in Pompeii'), 611, *611*, 612, *612*, 613, 614, 615 ('3D recording and 3D models will become increasingly common in the future, it is essential that the person responsible is adequately trained in 3D recording'), 627 ('meticulous excavation followed by the identification and recording of all the skeletal elements *in situ* is absolutely fundamental'), 629, 630 ('recording, backed by a three-dimensional photogrammetric coverage, is a commonly used tool that saves time while ensuring greater precision and the possibility of returning to stored information'), 631, 656, 658, 659, 665, 672

Recycled, Recycling (Ceramics) 460, 462

'Reduction(s)' of the Skeleton or of the Corpse 35, 57, 167, 212–213, 217 ('successive "reductions" (remains disturbed and moved when others were deposited)', 286 ('reduced to make room for all the deceased'), 294 ('successive phases of deposition', *295*, 360 ('reductions of the remains from the re-use of a grave'), 402 ('gathered, disarticulated remains or collected and placed in ossuary pits'), 406, 407, 676 (lexicon)

Reflexive Archaeology 179

Regourdou 1 *141*, **142**, 146, 151, 152, 153

Relative Dating 72, 236, 658, 679

Reopened Grave(s) 277–305, **279**, *281*, *282*, *284*, 285 ('reopening pit'), 286 ('reopening pits'), 288 ('reopening pit'), *290* ('reopening pit'), 294 ('early medieval reopened graves in France'), *295*, *299* ('reopening pit'), 300–304 ('reopened graves in the Andes')

Respect (for the Dead) 115 ('some individuals placed in these refuse areas may have been treated with respect'), 144, 253, 259, 293, 304, 340 ('respectful handling of the dead'), 348, 414, 633, 637, 638–639 ('respect, dignity and decency'), 640 ('respect for the identity and the body of the deceased person'), 641, 641FN12, 641FN15, 644, 645 ('the notion of respect transfers to remains with links with the present that are more tenuous or more ancient, in this case with their 'humanity' as a justification'), 647, 670, 673